BUSINESS MATHEMATICS IN CANADA

TENTH EDITION

F. Ernest Jerome

Tracy Worswick

McGraw Hill

BUSINESS MATHEMATICS IN CANADA
Tenth Edition

ISBN-13: 978-1-26-006599-2
ISBN-10: 1-26-006599-5

1 2 3 4 5 6 7 8 9 0 M 23 22 21 20

Printed and bound in Canada.

Care has been taken to trace ownership of copyright material contained in this text; however, the publisher will welcome any information that enables them to rectify any reference or credit for subsequent editions.

Product Director: Rhondda McNabb
Portfolio Manager: Jade Fair
Senior Marketing Manager: Cathie Lefebvre
Content Developer: Peter Gleason
Photo/Permissions Editor: Photo Affairs, Inc.
Portfolio Associate: Tatiana Sevciuc
Senior Supervising Editor: Jessica Barnoski
Copy Editor: Kelli Howey
Plant Production Coordinator: Joelle McIntyre
Manufacturing Production Coordinator: Jason Stubner
Cover Design: Liz Harasymczuk
Cover Image: © anatoliy_glib/Shutterstock
Interior Design: Michelle Losier
Page Layout: Aptara®, Inc.
Printer: Marquis

About the Authors

F. Ernest Jerome received a B.Sc. degree in Honours Physics from McMaster University, where he was that university's first undergraduate to be a prize-winner in the annual Canadian Association of Physicists' Examination national competition. After earning a graduate degree in Oceanography at the University of British Columbia, he was appointed head of the Physics Department at Vancouver Island University (VIU) in Nanaimo, BC. Professor Jerome later obtained an MBA in finance from UBC, where he was awarded the Schulich Fellowship for Entrepreneurship. He subsequently taught courses in business mathematics, corporate finance,

personal financial planning, mutual funds, and securities analysis in VIU's Faculty of Business. He holds a Chartered Financial Planner designation, and received the 1987 Outstanding Achievement Award from the Canadian Institute of Financial Planning.

Tracy Worswick holds degrees in Mathematics from the University of Waterloo and Mathematics Education from the University of Western Ontario. Tracy's passion for teaching and desire to deliver quality mathematics education stems from over 35 years of experience teaching Mathematics, Statistics, Computer Science, Business, and Marketing Research courses in high schools and colleges in Ontario and Alberta. For the past 20 years, she has taught Mathematics and Statistics in Conestoga College's School of Business in Kitchener, Ontario.

Brief Contents

Contents

FIGURE	List of Figures

TABLE	**List of Tables**

SECTION	**Points of Interest**

CHAPTER	**List of Cases**

Preface

Most business administration programs in Canadian colleges include an introductory course in business mathematics or mathematics of finance. *Business Mathematics in Canada* is intended for use in such courses. The text's primary objective is to support the learning of mathematics (other than statistics) needed to succeed in fields such as accounting, finance, management, supply chain, operations management, insurance, marketing, personal financial planning, and business information systems.

This book may be adapted to either a one- or a two-semester course in business mathematics. It is suitable for courses that emphasize either an algebraic approach or a pre-programmed financial calculator approach to compound interest problems. (Optional spreadsheet templates provide a third alternative in many areas for students who have a basic familiarity with Microsoft Excel software.) Both algebraic solutions and financial calculator solutions are presented in most example problems for compound interest topics.

NEW IN THE TENTH EDITION

The tenth edition contains numerous changes reflecting input from faculty across the country, through reviews as well as invaluable suggestions from users of the ninth edition.

New and Updated Examples The worked examples now include **10** new problems with full solutions; another **50** examples have been updated to reflect current rates and prices.

New and Updated Exercises The Exercises contain **30** new problems, and another **100** problems have been updated to reflect current rates and prices.

Updated Tables and Charts The exposition, tables, and example problems incorporate the most recent data at the time of writing.

New Chapter 3 The topics of Percent and Percent Change have been broken out into their own chapter along with the applications Investment Returns from Stocks and Mutual Funds and (new in this edition) Market Share and Market Growth. Users now have the option of two different applications for percent and percent change and may choose to do one or both depending on time and program delivery.

New Tips and Traps The tenth edition features **3** new Tips and Traps: "Reverse BEDMAS" in Chapter 2, "There Are Two Sides to Every Formula" in Chapter 5, and "Dirty and Clean Bond Pricing" in Chapter 16. "Clues to the Type of Annuity" in Chapter 13 has been revised for more clarity.

New and Revised Figures The figures have been revised to incorporate the most recent data at the time of writing. New time line diagrams have been added in the annuities chapters.

Revised Cases and Points of Interest These features have been revised and refreshed to incorporate recent developments and time-sensitive data. The tenth edition features **11** new and revised Points of Interest: "Following the Ups and Downs of Gas Prices in Canada" and "The Process of Shrinkflation" in Chapter 3; "Any Free Lunches?" in Chapter 4; "Improving the Score on Your Credit Report" in Chapter 8; "The 'Magic' of Compound Interest" in Chapter 9; "Not in Your Best Interest" in Chapter 10; "Retirement Dreams Then and Now," "What Is Your Net Worth?" and "Should You Choose a Cash-Discount Incentive or Low-Interest-Rate Financing?" in Chapter 12; "Such a Deal!" in Chapter 14; and "No-Money-Down Mortgages Are No More" in Chapter 15.

PEDAGOGICAL FEATURES

Canadian Applications Throughout the exposition, Example problems, Exercise problems, and Points of Interest, the book presents a wide range of applications of mathematics in Canadian business and finance. Every effort has been made to reflect current practices. Real financial instruments and real economic data are frequently used.

Wide Selection of Problems Each section of a chapter is followed by a set of problems for applying and reinforcing the new material. The text contains over 2000 problems and concept questions. Questions are organized by "calculator-free," "basic," "intermediate," and "advanced." Considerable effort has been made to create problems that are instructive, practical, realistic, and interesting.

Graphs and Diagrams This text makes extensive use of graphs, diagrams, and interactive charts.

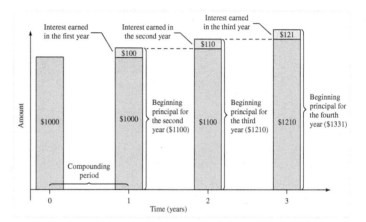

Solved Example Problems These examples provide detailed illustrations and applications of concepts in a step-by-step format.

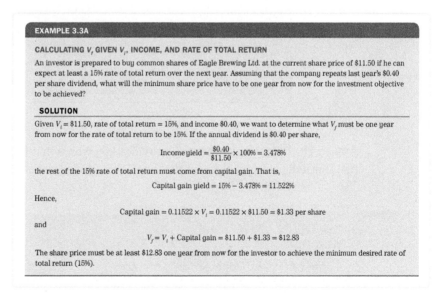

EXAMPLE 3.3A

CALCULATING V_f GIVEN V_i, INCOME, AND RATE OF TOTAL RETURN

An investor is prepared to buy common shares of Eagle Brewing Ltd. at the current share price of $11.50 if he can expect at least a 15% rate of total return over the next year. Assuming that the company repeats last year's $0.40 per share dividend, what will the minimum share price have to be one year from now for the investment objective to be achieved?

SOLUTION

Given V_i = $11.50, rate of total return = 15%, and income $0.40, we want to determine what V_f must be one year from now for the rate of total return to be 15%. If the annual dividend is $0.40 per share,

$$\text{Income yield} = \frac{\$0.40}{\$11.50} \times 100\% = 3.478\%$$

the rest of the 15% rate of total return must come from capital gain. That is,

$$\text{Capital gain yield} = 15\% - 3.478\% = 11.522\%$$

Hence,

$$\text{Capital gain} = 0.11522 \times V_i = 0.11522 \times \$11.50 = \$1.33 \text{ per share}$$

and

$$V_f = V_i + \text{Capital gain} = \$11.50 + \$1.33 = \$12.83$$

The share price must be at least $12.83 one year from now for the investor to achieve the minimum desired rate of total return (15%).

Tips and Traps Boxed elements inserted at appropriate points draw the student's attention to simplifications, pitfalls, shortcuts, calculator procedures, and common errors.

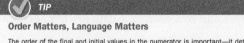

TIP

Order Matters, Language Matters

The order of the final and initial values in the numerator is important—it determines the sign of the percent change. If a quantity decreases in size, its percent change is negative.

To illustrate a point on language, consider the example of a company whose sales declined from $4 million in Year 1 to $3 million in Year 2. The percent change in sales is

$$\frac{\text{Year 2 sales} - \text{Year 1 sales}}{\text{Year 1 sales}} \times 100\% = \frac{\$3 \text{ million} - \$4 \text{ million}}{\$4 \text{ million}} \times 100\%$$
$$= \frac{-1}{4} \times 100\%$$
$$= -25\%$$

We can say either "the sales changed by −25%" or "the sales decreased by 25%" from Year 1 to Year 2. The direction of the change may be indicated either by an algebraic sign or by a descriptive word such as "rose," "fell," "increased," or "decreased." However, it would be incorrect and potentially confusing to say that "the sales decreased by −25%."

TRAP

Percent Changes Are Not Additive

As the preceding example demonstrates, the overall percent change for a series of intervals cannot be obtained simply by adding the percent changes for the individual intervals. The reason is that the initial value for the percent change calculation is different in each interval.

Point of Interest Boxes Most chapters contain two or three intriguing illustrations of the application or misapplication of mathematics to business and personal finance. See the Points of Interest list that follows the table of contents.

POINT OF INTEREST

The Price-to-Performance Ratio

People in the computer industry have recognized that the price-to-performance ratio comparison presented in advertisements can actually provide a reason *not* to purchase the advertised computer. Think about what, at a basic mathematical level, will make the price-to-performance ratio high. A large numerator (*high* price) and/or a small denominator (*low* performance) will make the ratio high. Therefore, a higher ratio represents a *lower* "bang for your buck."

The price-to-performance ratio can also be used to track changes in products over time. Computers in particular have a constantly fluctuating price-to-performance ratio. Over time the price of computers has dropped dramatically, making them more accessible to the average consumer while processing power has improved significantly.

App 4 That Each boxed feature provides key words that are searchable on a smart device to find free and paid apps relevant to the topic under discussion.

APP 4 THAT

Anyone interested in finance and saving money needs to have a good understanding of compound interest and its calculations. Search the App Store on your tablet, smartphone, or smart watch using the key words **COMPOUND INTEREST**.

You will find many free and paid apps that provide compound interest calculations for different compounding periods, floating rates of interest, and fluctuating balances. Some provide added features to calculate how long it will take to achieve your financial goals as well as provide adjustments in calculations for inflation.

Calculator Callout Boxes Many compound interest calculations can be performed using a calculator's financial functions. In the solutions for Example problems, we employ callout boxes: (1) to provide a clear visual indication of the algebraic computations that may be executed using the calculator's pre-programmed financial functions; and (2) to present the keystroke operations for employing the financial functions.

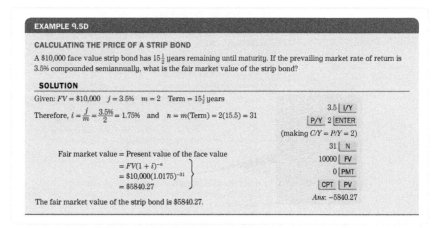

EXAMPLE 9.5D

CALCULATING THE PRICE OF A STRIP BOND

A \$10,000 face value strip bond has $15\frac{1}{2}$ years remaining until maturity. If the prevailing market rate of return is 3.5% compounded semiannually, what is the fair market value of the strip bond?

SOLUTION

Given: $FV = \$10,000$ $j = 3.5\%$ $m = 2$ Term $= 15\frac{1}{2}$ years

Therefore, $i = \frac{j}{m} = \frac{3.5\%}{2} = 1.75\%$ and $n = m(\text{Term}) = 2(15.5) = 31$

3.5 [I/Y]
[P/Y] 2 [ENTER]
(making $C/Y = P/Y = 2$)
31 [N]
10000 [FV]

Fair market value = Present value of the face value

$$= FV(1 + i)^{-n}$$
$$= \$10,000(1.0175)^{-31}$$
$$= \$5840.27$$

0 [PMT]
[CPT] [PV]

Ans: −5840.27

The fair market value of the strip bond is \$5840.27.

Highlighted Concepts Throughout the book, statements of key concepts are highlighted, signalling to students the importance of the concept or principle.

> **Valuation Principle**
> The fair market value of an investment is the sum of the present values of the cash flows expected from the investment. The discount rate used in the present-value calculations should be the prevailing market-determined rate of return on this type of investment.

Spreadsheet Templates Example problems and exercises indicated with a spreadsheet icon will direct students to an **optional** Microsoft Excel spreadsheet available on Connect. Each spreadsheet either demonstrates a solution of the example problem solved previously by algebraic or financial calculator methods or provides an alternative platform for solving the exercise problems. The spreadsheet is based on a pre-labelled and pre-formatted template.

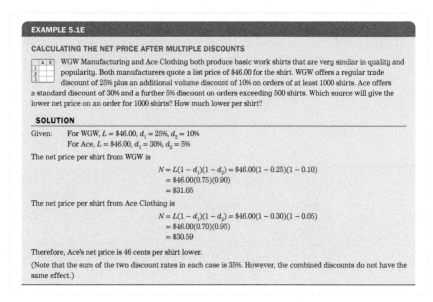

EXAMPLE 5.1E

CALCULATING THE NET PRICE AFTER MULTIPLE DISCOUNTS

WGW Manufacturing and Ace Clothing both produce basic work shirts that are very similar in quality and popularity. Both manufacturers quote a list price of \$46.00 for the shirt. WGW offers a regular trade discount of 25% plus an additional volume discount of 10% on orders of at least 1000 shirts. Ace offers a standard discount of 30% and a further 5% discount on orders exceeding 500 shirts. Which source will give the lower net price on an order for 1000 shirts? How much lower per shirt?

SOLUTION

Given: For WGW, $L = \$46.00$, $d_1 = 25\%$, $d_2 = 10\%$
For Ace, $L = \$46.00$, $d_1 = 30\%$, $d_2 = 5\%$

The net price per shirt from WGW is

$$N = L(1 - d_1)(1 - d_2) = \$46.00(1 - 0.25)(1 - 0.10)$$
$$= \$46.00(0.75)(0.90)$$
$$= \$31.05$$

The net price per shirt from Ace Clothing is

$$N = L(1 - d_1)(1 - d_2) = \$46.00(1 - 0.30)(1 - 0.05)$$
$$= \$46.00(0.70)(0.95)$$
$$= \$30.59$$

Therefore, Ace's net price is 46 cents per shirt lower.

(Note that the sum of the two discount rates in each case is 35%. However, the combined discounts do not have the same effect.)

Cases Some chapters include a case study in the end-of-chapter material. These cases usually call on concepts and skills from previous chapters as well as the current chapter.

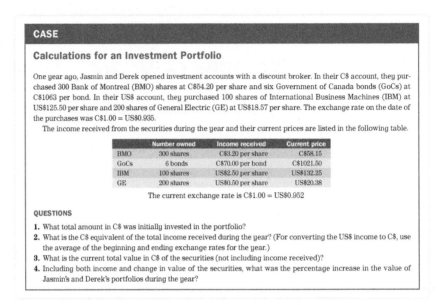

CASE

Calculations for an Investment Portfolio

One year ago, Jasmin and Derek opened investment accounts with a discount broker. In their C$ account, they purchased 300 Bank of Montreal (BMO) shares at C$54.20 per share and six Government of Canada bonds (GoCs) at C$1063 per bond. In their US$ account, they purchased 100 shares of International Business Machines (IBM) at US$125.50 per share and 200 shares of General Electric (GE) at US$18.57 per share. The exchange rate on the date of the purchases was C$1.00 = US$0.935.

The income received from the securities during the year and their current prices are listed in the following table.

	Number owned	Income received	Current price
BMO	300 shares	C$3.20 per share	C$58.15
GoCs	6 bonds	C$70.00 per bond	C$1021.50
IBM	100 shares	US$2.50 per share	US$132.25
GE	200 shares	US$0.50 per share	US$20.38

The current exchange rate is C$1.00 = US$0.952

QUESTIONS

1. What total amount in C$ was initially invested in the portfolio?
2. What is the C$ equivalent of the total income received during the year? (For converting the US$ income to C$, use the average of the beginning and ending exchange rates for the year.)
3. What is the current total value in C$ of the securities (not including income received)?
4. Including both income and change in value of the securities, what was the percentage increase in the value of Jasmin's and Derek's portfolios during the year?

Interactive Charts Through the online Connect platform, students can access interactive charts. Various Exercise problems (flagged by a "Connect" icon) invite the student to undertake an activity using an interactive chart. The student can change key variables and observe a graphic representation of the effect on the dependent variable (such as break-even point, present value, future value, market value, interest paid, amortization period, etc.).

End-of-Chapter Problems Each chapter ends with a comprehensive set of Review Problems covering the full range of topics and applications in the chapter.

Concept Questions Concept Questions are presented at the end of many sections. These questions exercise students' intuition and test their understanding of concepts and principles.

AWARD-WINNING TECHNOLOGY

McGraw-Hill Connect® is an award-winning digital teaching and learning solution that empowers students to achieve better outcomes and enables instructors to improve efficiency with course management. Within Connect, students have access to SmartBook®, McGraw-Hill's adaptive learning and reading resource. SmartBook prompts students with questions based on the material they are studying. By assessing individual answers, SmartBook learns what each student knows and identifies which topics they need to practice, giving each student a personalized learning experience and path to success.

Connect's key features also include analytics and reporting, simple assignment management, smart grading, the opportunity to post your own resources, and the Connect Instructor Library, a repository for additional resources to improve student engagement in and out of the classroom.

Instructor Resources for Business Mathematics in Canada, 10e

- Instructor Solutions Manual
- Test Bank
- Microsoft® PowerPoint® Presentations

ACKNOWLEDGMENTS

This tenth edition marks the 26th anniversary of Business Mathematics in Canada. I have been fortunate during my tenure teaching Business Mathematics to have used this text in my classroom since Ernie Jerome penned the second edition. I served as a reviewer for the fifth edition, the online content author for the sixth and seventh editions, and finally as the first author for the eighth, ninth, and tenth editions. I view this text as a living document and it has been my pleasure to witness how the book has evolved to reflect the continuing development of our courses, our students, and their learning environments.

A debt of gratitude is owed to the professors who participated in a review or worked on supplements for this edition. Their thoughtful comments and suggestions have contributed to the continued excellence of this text.

Our reviewers:

Steve Van Doormaal	*Conestoga College*
Rob Sorensen	*Camosun College*
Carol Leppinen	*Conestoga College*
Mariana Ionescu	*George Brown College*

I am further indebted to Jackie Shemko, who served as a Technical Reviewer and who has been instrumental in the preparation of supplemental resources for the book.

I wish to thank the staff at McGraw-Hill Ryerson for their ongoing support, professionalism, and guidance: Sara Braithwaite (Portfolio Manager), Jade Fair (Portfolio Manager), Peter Gleason (Content Developer), Jessica Barnoski (Supervising Editor), and all others involved in the development and production of this edition.

Thanks also go to all of the students who have passed through my classroom over the past two decades for providing their insights which have allowed me to see the courses and material through their eyes and to make this a better text.

Finally, I dedicate this book to my husband Mike for his love and encouragement and my children Leslie, John, Jeff, and Kasey for cheering me on as this tenth edition came to life.

Tracy Worswick

Effective. Efficient. Easy to Use.

McGraw-Hill Connect is an award-winning digital teaching and learning solution that empowers students to achieve better outcomes and enables instructors to improve course-management efficiency.

Personalized & Adaptive Learning

Connect's integrated SmartBook helps students study more efficiently, highlighting where in the text to focus and asking review questions to give each student a personalized learning experience and path to success.

High-Quality Course Material

Our trusted solutions are designed to help students actively engage in course content and develop critical higher-level thinking skills, while offering you the flexibility to tailor your course to meet your needs.

Analytics & Reporting

Monitor progress and improve focus with Connect's visual and actionable dashboards. Reporting features empower instructors and students with real-time performance analytics.

Seamless Integration

Link your Learning Management System with Connect for single sign-on and gradebook synchronization, with all-in-one ease for you and your students.

Impact of Connect on Pass Rates

72.5%

Without Connect

85.2%

With Connect

SMARTBOOK

NEW SmartBook 2.0 builds on our market-leading adaptive technology with enhanced capabilities and a streamlined interface that deliver a more usable, accessible and mobile learning experience for both students and instructors.

Available on mobile smart devices – with both online and offline access – the ReadAnywhere app lets students study anywhere, anytime.

SUPPORT AT EVERY STEP

McGraw-Hill ensures you are supported every step of the way. From course design and set up, to instructor training, LMS integration and ongoing support, your Digital Success Consultant is there to make your course as effective as possible.

Learn more about Connect at mheducation.ca

Chapter 1

Review and Applications of Basic Mathematics

CHAPTER OUTLINE

1.1 Order of Operations

1.2 Fractions, Decimals, and Percents

*1.3 Payroll

1.4 Simple and Weighted Averages

*1.5 Taxes

Appendix 1A: The Texas Instruments BA II PLUS Format Settings

(Sections and chapters preceded by an asterisk* may be omitted without loss of continuity.)

LEARNING OBJECTIVES

After completing this chapter, you will be able to:

LO1 Perform arithmetic operations in their proper order

LO2 Convert fractions to their percent and decimal equivalents

LO3 Maintain the proper number of digits in calculations

LO4 Perform calculations using fractions, decimals, and percents

LO5 Calculate the gross earnings of employees paid a salary, an hourly wage, or commissions

LO6 Calculate the simple average or weighted average (as appropriate) of a set of values

LO7 Perform basic calculations for the Goods and Services Tax, Harmonized Sales Tax, provincial sales tax, and real property tax

MATHEMATICS PLAYS A SIGNIFICANT ROLE in business. Clients and employers now expect higher education and outstanding performance from all levels of employees that includes a significant level of mathematics competency.

Even though most routine calculations in business are done electronically, the mathematics and statistics you study in your business program are more widely expected and more highly valued in business than ever before. As a successful business graduate you must know which information is relevant, which analyses or calculations should be performed, how to interpret the results, and how to explain the outcome in terms your clients and colleagues can understand.

Naturally, a college course in business mathematics or statistics will cover a broader range of topics (often in greater depth) than you might need for a particular industry. This broader education opens more career options to you and provides a stronger set of mathematical skills for your chosen career.

 TIP

How to Succeed in Business Mathematics

Since various Business Mathematics and Mathematics of Finance courses start at different points in the book, this Tip appears at the beginning of each of the first five chapters. Connect has a guide entitled "How to Succeed in Business Mathematics." Read its first two sections (A.1 and A.2) before you finish **Chapter 1**.

1.1 Order of Operations

LO1 When evaluating an expression such as

$$5 + 3^2 \times 2 - 4 \div 6$$

there is potential for confusion about the sequence of mathematical steps. Do we just perform the indicated operations in a strict left-to-right sequence called *chaining*, or is some other order intended? To eliminate any possible confusion, mathematicians have agreed on the algebraic operating system (AOS), which sets out the rules for the use of brackets and the order of mathematical operations. The rules are:

Rules for Order of Operations
1. Perform operations within brackets (in the order of Steps 2, 3, and 4 below).
2. Evaluate the powers.[1]
3. Perform multiplication and division in order from left to right.
4. Perform addition and subtraction in order from left to right.

 TIP

Remembering the Order of Operations: BEDMAS

To help remember AOS, the order of operations, you can use the acronym BEDMAS representing the sequence: **B**rackets, **E**xponents, **D**ivision and **M**ultiplication, **A**ddition and **S**ubtraction.

---

[1]   A power is a quantity such as 3^2 or 5^3 (which are shorthand methods for representing 3×3 and $5 \times 5 \times 5$, respectively). Section 2.2 includes a review of powers and exponents.

EXAMPLE 1.1A

EXERCISES ILLUSTRATING THE ORDER OF MATHEMATICAL OPERATIONS

a. $30 - 6 \div 3 + 5$ Do division before subtraction and addition.
$= 30 - 2 + 5$
$= 33$

b. $(30 - 6) \div 3 + 5$ Do operations within brackets first; then do division before addition.
$= 24 \div 3 + 5$
$= 8 + 5$
$= 13$

c. $\dfrac{30 - 6}{3 + 5} = \dfrac{24}{8} = 3$ Brackets are implied in the numerator and the denominator.

d. $72 \div (3 \times 2) - 6$ Do operations within brackets first; then do division before subtraction.
$= 72 \div 6 - 6$
$= 12 - 6$
$= 6$

e. $72 \div (3 \times 2^2) - 6$ Do operations within brackets (the power before the multiplication); then do division
$= 72 \div (3 \times 4) - 6$ before subtraction.
$= 72 \div 12 - 6$
$= 6 - 6$
$= 0$

f. $72 \div (3 \times 2)^2 - 6$ Do operations within brackets first, then the power, then divide, then subtract.
$= 72 \div 6^2 - 6$
$= 72 \div 36 - 6$
$= 2 - 6$
$= -4$

g. $4(2 - 5) - 4(5 - 2)$ Do operations within brackets first, then multiplication, then subtract.
$= 4(-3) - 4(3)$
$= -12 - 12$
$= -24$

EXERCISE 1.1

Answers to the odd-numbered problems are at the end of the book.

CALCULATOR-FREE PROBLEMS

Evaluate each of the following.

a. $10 + 10 \times 0$ **b.** $2 \times 2 + 4 - 8$

c. $(10 + 10) \times 0$ **d.** $2 \times (2 + 4) - 8$

e. $0 + 3 \times 3 - 3^2 + 10$ **f.** $12 - 2 \times 5 + 2^2 \times 0$

g. $0 + 3 \times 3 - (3^2 + 10)$ **h.** $(12 - 2) \times (5 + 2^2) \times 0$

i. $\dfrac{2^2 - 4}{(4 - 2)^2}$ **j.** $\dfrac{(2 - 4)^2}{5 - 2^2}$

BASIC PROBLEMS

Evaluate each of the following. In Problems 17–22, evaluate the answers accurate to the cent.

1. $20 - 4 \times 2 - 8$

2. $18 \div 3 + 6 \times 2$

3. $(20 - 4) \times 2 - 8$

4. $18 \div (3 + 6) \times 2$

5. $20 - (4 \times 2 - 8)$

6. $(18 \div 3 + 6) \times 2$

7. $54 - 36 \div 4 + 2^2$

8. $(5 + 3)^2 - 3^2 \div 9 + 3$

9. $(54 - 36) \div (4 + 2)^2$

10. $5 + (3^2 - 3)^2 \div (9 + 3)$

11. $\dfrac{8^2 - 4^2}{(4 - 2)^3}$

12. $\dfrac{(8 - 4)^2}{4 - 2^3}$

13. $3(6 + 4)^2 - 5(17 - 20)^2$

14. $(4 \times 3 - 2)^2 \div (4 - 3 \times 2^2)$

15. $[(20 + 8 \times 5) - 7 \times (-3)] \div 9$

16. $5[19 + (5^2 - 16)^2]^2$

17. $\$100\left(1 + 0.06 \times \dfrac{45}{365}\right)$

18. $\dfrac{\$200}{1 + 0.09 \times \frac{4}{12}}$

19. $\dfrac{\$500}{(1 + 0.05)^2}$

20. $\$1000(1 + 0.02)^3$

21. $\$100\left[\dfrac{(1 + 0.04)^2 - 1}{0.04}\right]$

22. $\$300\left[\dfrac{1 - \dfrac{1}{(1 + 0.03)^2}}{0.03}\right]$

1.2 | Fractions, Decimals, and Percents

Definitions

In the fraction $\frac{3}{4}$, the upper number (3) is called the **numerator** (or dividend) and the lower number (4) is the **denominator** (or divisor). In a **proper fraction**, the numerator is smaller than the denominator. An **improper fraction** has a numerator that is larger than the denominator. A **mixed number** contains a whole number plus a fraction. **Equivalent fractions** are fractions that are equal in value (even though their respective numerators and denominators differ). An equivalent fraction can be created by multiplying or dividing both the numerator and the denominator by the same number.

EXAMPLE 1.2A

EXAMPLES OF TYPES OF FRACTIONS

a. $\frac{6}{13}$ is a proper fraction.

b. $\frac{17}{13}$ is an improper fraction.

c. $2\frac{4}{13}$ is a mixed number.

d. $\frac{5}{13}, \frac{10}{26}, \frac{15}{39}$, and $\frac{20}{52}$ are equivalent fractions. Note that the second, third, and fourth fractions may be obtained by multiplying *both* the numerator and the denominator of the first fraction by 2, 3, and 4, respectively.

EXAMPLE 1.2B

CALCULATING AN EQUIVALENT FRACTION

Find the missing numbers that make the following three fractions equivalent.

$$\frac{7}{12} = \frac{56}{?} = \frac{?}{300}$$

SOLUTION

To create a fraction equivalent to $\frac{7}{12}$, *both* the numerator and the denominator must be multiplied by the same number. To obtain 56 in the numerator of the second equivalent fraction, 7 was multiplied by 8. Hence, the denominator must also be multiplied by 8. Therefore,

$$\frac{7}{12} = \frac{7 \times 8}{12 \times 8} = \frac{56}{96}$$

To obtain the denominator (300) in the third equivalent fraction, 12 was multiplied by $\frac{300}{12} = 25$.
   The numerator must also be multiplied by 25. Hence, the equivalent fraction is

$$\frac{7 \times 25}{12 \times 25} = \frac{175}{300}$$

In summary,

$$\frac{7}{12} = \frac{56}{96} = \frac{175}{300}$$

Decimal and Percent Equivalents

L02 In the fraction $\frac{3}{4}$, the denominator indicates the total number of parts or pieces and the numerator shows how many of the parts we are considering. In other words, $\frac{3}{4}$ is 3 of 4 parts.

The *decimal equivalent* value of a fraction is obtained by dividing the numerator by the denominator. The fraction $\frac{3}{4}$ then becomes the decimal equivalent 0.75, indicating 0.75 parts of one whole piece.

To express the fraction in *percent equivalent* form, multiply the decimal equivalent by 100 (shift the decimal point two places to the right) and add the % symbol indicating parts of 100. The fraction $\frac{3}{4}$ then becomes 75%, indicating 75 parts of 100 parts.

EXAMPLE 1.2C

FINDING THE DECIMAL AND PERCENT EQUIVALENTS OF FRACTIONS AND MIXED NUMBERS

Convert each of the following fractions and mixed numbers to its decimal equivalent and percent equivalent values.

a. $\frac{2}{5} = 0.4 = 40\%$ **b.** $\frac{5}{2} = 2.5 = 250\%$ **c.** $2\frac{3}{4} = 2.75 = 275\%$

d. $\frac{5}{8} = 0.625 = 62.5\%$ **e.** $1\frac{3}{16} = 1.1875 = 118.75\%$ **f.** $\frac{3}{1500} = 0.002 = 0.2\%$

 TIP

Adding or Subtracting Fractions

To add or subtract any but the simplest of fractions, the easiest approach is to first convert each fraction to its decimal equivalent value. Then add or subtract the decimal equivalents as required.

For example, $\frac{5}{12} + \frac{23}{365} = 0.41667 + 0.06301 = 0.4797$ to four-figure accuracy.

Rounding of Decimal and Percent Equivalents

L03 For some fractions, the decimal equivalent has an endless series of digits. Such a number is called a *nonterminating decimal*. In some cases a nonterminating decimal contains a repeating digit or a repeating group of digits. This particular type of nonterminating decimal is referred to as a *repeating decimal*. A shorthand notation for repeating decimals is to place a horizontal bar over the first occurrence of the repeating digit or group of digits. For example,

$$\frac{2}{9} = 0.222222 = 0.\overline{2} \qquad \text{and} \qquad 2\frac{4}{11} = 2.36363636 = 2.\overline{36}$$

When a nonterminating decimal or its percent equivalent is used in a calculation, the question arises: How many figures or digits should be retained? The following rules provide sufficient accuracy for the vast majority of our calculations.

Rules for Rounding Numbers
1. In intermediate results, keep one more figure than the number of figures required in the final result. (When counting figures for the purpose of rounding, do not count leading zeros used only to properly position the decimal point.)[2]
2. If the first digit dropped is 5 or greater, increase the last retained digit by 1.
3. If the first digit dropped is less than 5, leave the last retained digit unchanged.

Suppose, for example, the answer to a calculation is expected to be a few hundred dollars and you want the answer accurate to the cent. In other words, you require five-figure accuracy in your answer. To achieve this accuracy, the first rule says you should retain (at least) six figures in values used in the calculations. The rule also applies to intermediate results that you carry forward to subsequent calculations. The consequence of rounding can be stated in another way—if, for example, you use a number rounded to four figures in your calculations, you can expect only three-figure accuracy in your final answer.

EXAMPLE 1.2D

FRACTIONS HAVING REPEATING DECIMAL EQUIVALENTS

Convert each of the following fractions to its decimal equivalent value expressed in the repeating decimal notation.

a. $\dfrac{2}{3} = 0.6666\ldots = 0.\overline{6}$

b. $\dfrac{14}{9} = 1.555\ldots = 1.\overline{5}$

c. $6\dfrac{1}{12} = 6.08333\ldots = 6.08\overline{3}$

d. $3\dfrac{2}{11} = 3.181818\ldots = 3.\overline{18}$

e. $5\dfrac{2}{27} = 5.074074\ldots = 5.\overline{074}$

f. $\dfrac{5}{7} = 0.714285714285\ldots = 0.\overline{714285}$

---

[2] The following example illustrates the reasoning behind this instruction. A length of 6 mm is neither more nor less precise than a length of 0.006 m. (Recall that there are 1000 mm in 1 m.) The leading zeros in 0.006 m do not add precision to the measurement. They are inserted to properly position the decimal point. Both measurements have one-figure accuracy. Contrast this case with measurements of 1007 mm and 1.007 m. Here each zero comes from a decision about *what* the digit should be (rather than *where* the decimal point should be). These measurements both have four-figure accuracy. This rule applies to the total number of figures (other than leading zeros) in a value. It does not apply to the number of *decimal* places.

EXAMPLE 1.2E

CALCULATING AND ROUNDING THE DECIMAL EQUIVALENTS OF FRACTIONS

Convert each of the following fractions and mixed numbers to its decimal equivalent value rounded to four-figure accuracy.

a. $\frac{2}{3} = 0.6667$

b. $6\frac{1}{12} = 6.083$

c. $\frac{173}{11} = 15.73$

d. $\frac{2}{1071} = 0.001867$

e. $\frac{17,816}{3} = 5939$

TRAP

Common Rounding Errors

The following examples illustrate two of the most common rounding errors. Each example requires rounding to two decimal places or three-figure accuracy:

Example 1: $2.4449 = 2.445 = 2.45$ This is NOT correct.

For rounding to two decimal places, you only need to consider the third decimal place to apply Rule 3.
    Here, continuous rounding has been applied starting with the first digit that is 5 or larger. The correct answer is 2.44.

Example 2: $2.992 = 2.99 = 3.00$ This is NOT correct.

The value is originally rounded correctly using Rule 3 but then rounded again applying Rule 2.
    Round one time only to achieve the required number of significant digits. The correct answer is 2.99.

EXAMPLE 1.2F

DEMONSTRATING THE CONSEQUENCES OF TOO MUCH ROUNDING

Accurate to the cent, evaluate

$$\$140\left(1 + 0.11 \times \frac{113}{365}\right) + \$74\left(1 + 0.09 \times \frac{276}{365}\right)$$

SOLUTION

If you want five-figure accuracy in your answer, you cannot round to fewer than six figures *at any stage* of the calculations. The following table illustrates how too much rounding can result in an inaccurate answer.
    If we first evaluate the contents of the brackets before rounding, we obtain:

$$\$140(1.0340548) + \$74(1.0680548)$$

6-Figure Accuracy	5-Figure Accuracy	3-Figure Accuracy
$\$140(1.03405) + \$74(1.06805)$	$\$140(1.0341) + \$74(1.0681)$	$\$140(1.03) + \$74(1.07)$
$= \$144.767 + \$79.0357$	$= \$144.774 + \$79.0394$	$= \$144.20 + \$79.18$
$= \$223.8027$	$= \$223.8134$	$= \$223.38$
$= \$223.80$ (rounded to the cent)	$= \$223.81$ (rounded to the cent)	
Correct answer	$\$0.01$ larger than correct answer	$\$0.42$ smaller than correct answer

One more point is worth noting. Consider the first column, where you properly maintained six-figure accuracy. That is,

$$\$140(1.03405) + \$74(1.06805) = \$144.767 + \$79.0357$$

Suppose you round the two amounts on the right side to the nearest cent *before* you add them. The sum is then

$$\$144.77 + \$79.04 = \$223.81$$

which is $0.01 larger than the correct answer. The error arises because, just at the final addition, you failed to maintain six-figure accuracy (to ensure five-figure accuracy in the final answer).

 TIP

Optimal Use of Your Calculator

Whenever possible, use your calculator's memory registers to save intermediate results. This will save time and reduce keystroke errors during data re-entry. It also virtually eliminates the introduction of rounding errors, since most calculators internally retain two or three more figures than are shown in the display. **Example 1.2G** illustrates this approach.

EXAMPLE 1.2G

OPTIMAL USE OF YOUR CALCULATOR

We will again evaluate (accurate to the cent) the same expression as in **Example 1.2F**,

$$\$140\left(1 + 0.11 \times \frac{113}{365}\right) + \$74\left(1 + 0.09 \times \frac{276}{365}\right)$$

This time we will use our financial calculator in a way that (1) avoids manual re-entry of intermediate results, and (2) maintains maximum precision by avoiding rounding (other than rounding imposed by the inherent limitations of the calculator).

SOLUTION

We assume the Texas Instruments BA II PLUS calculator is set for a floating-decimal format and for the algebraic operating system (AOS) calculation method. (Refer to **Appendix 1A** for instructions on making these settings.) In the AOS mode, we can enter numbers, brackets, and operations in the same left-to-right sequence as they are written. The calculator performs the calculations according to the proper order of operations.

$$140 \boxed{\times} \boxed{(} \; 1 \boxed{+} \; 0.11 \boxed{\times} \; 113 \boxed{\div} \; 365 \boxed{)}$$
$$\boxed{+} \; 74 \boxed{\times} \boxed{(} \; 1 \boxed{+} \; 0.09 \boxed{\times} \; 276 \boxed{\div} \; 365 \boxed{)} \boxed{=} \; 223.80$$

The result is $223.80.

You see that it is possible to evaluate quite complex expressions without writing down intermediate results. However, if someone is going to read and readily understand your solution, you should present enough detail and intermediate results to reveal the steps in your solution.

 TIP

Using a Calculator's Power Function

Use the following sequence of keystrokes to evaluate 1.62^5 with the power function key $\boxed{y^x}$.

$$1.62 \boxed{y^x} \; 5 \boxed{=}$$

If the symbol y^x sits above a calculator key (rather than on it), the power function is the secondary function of the key. The keystroke sequence is then

$$1.62 \boxed{\text{2nd}} \boxed{y^x} \, 5 \, \boxed{=}$$

The answer to seven-figure accuracy is 11.15771.

Example 1.2H uses this feature.

Evaluating Complex Fractions

A **complex fraction** is a fraction containing one or more other fractions in its numerator or denominator. In simplifying complex fractions, particular attention should be paid to the correct order of mathematical operations as discussed in **Section 1.1**.

EXAMPLE 1.2H

EVALUATING COMPLEX FRACTIONS

Evaluate each of the following complex fractions accurate to the cent.

a. $\dfrac{\$425}{\left(1 + \frac{0.09}{12}\right)^{24}}$

b. $\dfrac{\$1265\left(1 + 0.115 \times \frac{87}{365}\right)}{1 + 0.125 \times \frac{43}{365}}$

c. $\dfrac{\$1}{1 + 0.025 \times \frac{5}{12}} + \dfrac{\$1}{1 + 0.04 \times \frac{2}{12}}$

SOLUTION

We assume the Texas Instruments BA II PLUS calculator is set for a floating-decimal format and for the algebraic operating system (AOS) calculation method. Refer to **Appendix 1A** for instructions on making these settings.

a. $425 \boxed{\div} \boxed{(} \, 1 \boxed{+} \, 0.09 \boxed{\div} \, 12 \boxed{)} \boxed{y^x} \, 24 \boxed{=} \; 355.23$

The result is $355.23.

b. One-step method where additional brackets must be used for the denominator:

$1265 \boxed{\times} \boxed{(} \, 1 \boxed{+} \, 0.115 \boxed{\times} \, 87 \boxed{\div} \, 365 \boxed{)}$

$\boxed{\div} \boxed{(} \, 1 \boxed{+} \, 0.125 \boxed{\times} \, 43 \boxed{\div} \, 365 \boxed{)} \boxed{=} \; 1280.81$

Two-step method using the calculator's memories to store intermediate answers:

$1265 \times (1 + 0.115 \times 87 \div 365) = 1299.674863$ STO 1
$1 + 0.125 \times 43 \div 365 = 1.014726027$ STO 2
RCL 1 $\div$ RCL 2 = $1280.81

The result is $1280.81

c. $1 + 0.025 \times 5 \div 12 = 1.0104166667$ 1/X (0.989690722) STO 1
$1 + 0.04 \times 2 \div 12 = 1.006666667$ 1/X (0.993377483) STO 2
RCL 1 + RCL 2 = $1.98

The result is $1.98.

Calculating Percent of a Number

L04 Calculating the percent of a number is one of the most common calculations in business. To find the percent of a number, convert the percent to its decimal equivalent by dividing the percent by 100 (shifting the decimal point two places to the left) and then multiplying by the number.

EXAMPLE 1.2I

a. What is 22% of $185?

b. What is $40\frac{1}{4}$% of $140.25?

c. How much is $0.08\overline{3}$% of $5000?

d. How much is 140% of $50?

SOLUTION

a. The question asks us to calculate a part (percent) of a given whole.

By converting 22% to its decimal equivalent we obtain

$$\frac{22}{100} \times \$185 = 0.22 \times \$185 = \$40.70$$

That is, 22% of $185 is $40.70.

b. $40\frac{1}{4}$% of $140.25 becomes

$$40.25\% \times \$140.25 = 0.4025 \times \$140.25 = \$56.45$$

That is, $40\frac{1}{4}$% of $140.25 is $56.45.

c. In converting $0.08\overline{3}$% to its decimal equivalent, we need to be careful to maintain the correct accuracy in calculations to have our answer accurate to the cent. Since 1% of $5000 is $50, then 0.1% of $5000 is only $5. Therefore, the answer will be a little less than $5. For the answer to be accurate to the cent, we seek three-figure accuracy.

$$0.08\overline{3}\% \times \$5000 = 0.0008333 \times \$5000 = \$4.17$$

Therefore, $4.17 is $0.08\overline{3}$% of $5000.

d. Here the percentage is greater than 100% so the answer will be larger than the original value of $50.

$$140\% \times \$50 = 1.40 \times \$50 = \$70$$

Therefore, 140% of $50 is $70.

 TRAP

Decimal Equivalent of Percentages Smaller Than 1%

When a percent is less than 1%, students sometimes forget to move the decimal two places to the left in order to obtain the decimal equivalent. For example, be clear on the distinction between 0.25% and 25%. The former is just $\frac{1}{4}$ of 1%—the latter is 25 *times* 1%. Their decimal equivalents are 0.0025 and 0.25, respectively. In terms of equivalent fractions, 0.25% equals $\frac{1}{400}$, but 25% equals $\frac{1}{4}$.

EXAMPLE 1.2J

A WORD PROBLEM REQUIRING THE USE OF PERCENTS

A battery manufacturer encloses a rebate coupon for 15% off in a package of two AAA batteries retailing for $6.29. What rebate does the coupon represent?

SOLUTION

In effect, the question is asking you to find 15% of the retail price.

$$Rebate = 0.15 \times \$6.29 = \$0.94$$

The manufacturer's 15% rebate on the batteries is equivalent to a cash rebate of $0.94.

CONCEPT QUESTIONS

1. If you want four-figure accuracy in your final result, what minimum number of figures must be retained in the values used in the calculations? **A)** 4 **B)** 5 **C)** 6

2. For a final result of approximately $7000 to be accurate to the cent, what minimum number of figures must be retained in the values used in the calculations? **A)** 6 **B)** 7 **C)** 8

3. If a final result of the order of $5 million is to be accurate to the nearest dollar, what minimum number of figures must be retained in the calculations? **A)** 6 **B)** 7 **C)** 8

4. If an interest rate (which could be greater than 10%) is to be calculated to the nearest 0.01%, what minimum number of digits must be retained in the numbers used to calculate the interest rate? **A)** 3 **B)** 4 **C)** 5

EXERCISE 1.2

Answers to the odd-numbered problems are at the end of the book.

CALCULATOR-FREE PROBLEMS

Express each of the following first as a decimal and then as a percent. Round your answers to two decimal places where rounding is needed.

a. $\dfrac{1}{10}$ b. $\dfrac{2}{5}$ c. $\dfrac{1}{4}$ d. $\dfrac{3}{4}$

e. $1\dfrac{1}{2}$ f. $2\dfrac{1}{3}$ g. $\dfrac{10}{5}$ h. $5\dfrac{2}{3}$

i. What is 25% of 80? j. What is 20% of 120?

k. Jeffrey puts 20% of every paycheque into a savings plan and 50% of the money in the savings plan is in a Tax-Free Savings Account (TFSA). If he earns $1000 every paycheque, how much money is he putting into the TFSA?

BASIC PROBLEMS

The following fractions and mixed numbers have terminating decimal equivalent forms. Express their decimal and percent equivalent forms to five-figure accuracy.

1. $\dfrac{7}{8}$ 2. $\dfrac{65}{104}$ 3. $\dfrac{47}{20}$ 4. $-\dfrac{9}{16}$

5. $\dfrac{-35}{25}$ 6. $1\dfrac{7}{25}$ 7. $\dfrac{25}{1000}$ 8. $\dfrac{1000}{25}$

9. $2\dfrac{2}{100}$ 10. $-1\dfrac{11}{32}$ 11. $\dfrac{37.5}{50}$ 12. $\dfrac{22.5}{-12}$

The following fractions and mixed numbers have repeating decimal equivalent forms. Express their decimal and percent equivalent forms in the repeating decimal notation. Show just the minimum number of decimal places needed to display the repeating digit or group of digits.

13. $\dfrac{5}{6}$ 14. $-\dfrac{8}{3}$ 15. $7\dfrac{7}{9}$ 16. $1\dfrac{1}{11}$

17. $\dfrac{10}{9}$ 18. $-\dfrac{4}{900}$ 19. $-\dfrac{7}{270}$ 20. $\dfrac{37}{27}$

Round each of the following to four-figure accuracy.

21. 11.3845 22. 9.6455 23. 0.5545454 24. 1000.49

25. 1.0023456 26. 0.030405 27. 40.09515 28. 0.0090909

Convert each of the following fractions and mixed numbers to its decimal equivalent and percent equivalent values, rounded to five figures.

29. $\frac{1}{6}$

30. $\frac{7}{6}$

31. $\frac{1}{60}$

32. $2\frac{5}{9}$

33. $\frac{250}{365}$

34. $\frac{15}{365}$

35. $\frac{0.11}{12}$

36. $\frac{0.095}{12}$

Evaluate each of the following, accurate to the nearest cent or two decimal places.

37. $\$92\left(1 + 0.095 \times \frac{112}{365}\right)$

38. $\$100\left(1 + 0.11 \times \frac{5}{12}\right)$

39. $\$454.76\left(1 - 0.105 \times \frac{11}{12}\right)$

40. $\frac{1}{(1 + 0.22)^3}$

41. $\$1447\left(1 + \frac{0.18}{2}\right)^3\left(1 + \frac{0.21}{3}\right)^2$

42. $\frac{\$790.84}{1 + 0.13 \times \frac{311}{365}}$

43. $\frac{\$3490}{1 + 0.125 \times \frac{91}{365}}$

44. $\frac{\$10,000}{1 - 0.10 \times \frac{182}{365}}$

45. $\$650\left(1 + \frac{0.105}{2}\right)^2$

46. $\$950.75\left(1 - \frac{0.095}{4}\right)^2$

47. $\frac{\$15,400}{\left(1 + \frac{0.13}{12}\right)^6}$

48. $\frac{\$550}{\left(1 + \frac{0.115}{2}\right)^4}$

49. What is $33\frac{1}{3}\%$ of $1527?

50. What is 2.75% of $2.75?

51. What amount is 250% of $25?

52. 0.025% of $200 is what amount?

53. How much is $\frac{1}{2}\%$ of $30?

54. A local hydro company uses smart meters to measure hydro consumption. Off-peak rates in the winter months apply from 7 p.m. to 7 a.m., mid-peak hours apply from 11 a.m. to 5 p.m., and on-peak hours apply from 7 a.m. to 11 a.m. and again from 5 p.m. to 7 p.m. What percentage of the total daily hours is attributed to off-peak, mid-peak, and on-peak rates?

55. Mike and Laurie are building a home and have budgeted 5.5% of the $458,000 construction cost for windows. If they purchase energy-efficient windows they can get a 12% rebate on the cost of the windows. What is the dollar value of the rebate on the windows?

56. Bethany and Irwin estimate their total cost for a vacation in Cuba to be $14,775. If 53% of this cost is for flights and accommodations and 42% is for meals, how much money will they be able to spend on entertainment?

57. In the month of July, a convenience store had total sales of $102,300 from its gas pumps and other in-store products. If the Harmonized Sales Tax (HST) is 13% of sales, how much HST was collected on the in-store products if these sales represent 36% of total sales?

58. In a basketball game, the Langara College Falcons scored $54.\overline{54}\%$ of 33 shots from the 2-point zone, $46.\overline{6}\%$ of 15 attempts from the 3-point distance, and 79.3% of 29 free throws (1 point each). How many points did the Falcons score?

INTERMEDIATE PROBLEMS

Evaluate each of the following, accurate to the nearest cent or two decimal places.

59. $\dfrac{\$6600\left(1 + 0.085 \times \frac{153}{365}\right)}{1 + 0.125 \times \frac{82}{365}}$

60. $\dfrac{\$780\left(1 + \frac{0.0825}{2}\right)^5}{\left(1 + \frac{0.10}{12}\right)^8}$

61. $\$1000\left[\dfrac{\left(1+\frac{0.09}{12}\right)^{7}-1}{\frac{0.09}{12}}\right]$

62. $\dfrac{\$350}{\frac{0.0975}{12}}\left[1-\dfrac{1}{\left(1+\frac{0.0975}{12}\right)^{5}}\right]$

63. $\dfrac{\$9500}{\frac{\left(1+\frac{0.075}{4}\right)^{5}-1}{\frac{0.075}{4}}}$

64. $\$45\dfrac{\left[1-\dfrac{1}{\left(1+\frac{0.0837}{2}\right)^{4}}\right]}{\frac{0.0837}{2}}+\dfrac{\$1000}{\left(1+\frac{0.0837}{2}\right)^{4}}$

65. The Calgary Flames hockey team announced that its season ticket sales represent 67.50% of the Scotiabank Saddledome's seating capacity of 19,289 seats. Rounded to the nearest 100, how many seats were not sold to season ticket holders?

66. The Royal Canadian Mint sells one-troy-ounce (31.16 g) platinum collector coins of 99.95% purity. How many milligrams of impurities are in a single coin?

67. Stan is a real estate salesperson. He receives 60% of the 4.8% commission that the real estate agency charges on sales. If his sales for the past year were $5,225,000, what was the dollar value of his commission?

68. The maximum amount an individual can contribute to her Registered Retirement Savings Plan (RRSP) for a year is set from time to time by the regulations of the Income Tax Act. For the year 2020, the maximum contribution is the lesser of $27,230 or 18% of the individual's "earned income" during 2019. What is the maximum RRSP amount that can be contributed in 2020 based on an income of $128,500 in 2019?

69. The label on a single-serving can of soup states that it contains 35% of an adult's daily sodium intake. If the maximum recommended sodium intake is 2300 mg, how many grams of sodium need to be consumed daily through other foods?

*1.3 Payroll

L05 An employee's **remuneration** may be based on an hourly wage, a salary, a piecework rate, or a rate of commission. In some cases, earnings are based on a combination of a commission with a wage or a salary. This section deals only with the calculation of *gross earnings*—the amount earned before any deductions.[3]

Salaries

Where employment tends to be predictable and steady, an employee typically receives a salary quoted in terms of a biweekly, monthly, or annual amount. A monthly salary is usually paid on a monthly or semimonthly basis.[4] An annual salary may be paid at monthly, semimonthly, biweekly, or weekly intervals. For monthly and semimonthly pay periods, the gross earnings per pay are calculated by dividing the annual salary by 12 and 24, respectively.

For purposes of this section, we assume there are exactly 52 weeks in a year. Therefore, we can divide an annual salary by 26 or by 52 to obtain the gross earnings per biweekly or weekly pay period, respectively.[5]

---

[3] Employers are required by law to withhold income tax and the employee's share of Canada Pension Plan contributions and employment insurance premiums. By agreement with the employees or their union, an employer may also deduct and remit various insurance premiums, union dues, and pension plan contributions.

[4] Provincial employment standards usually provide that, if requested by the employees, monthly salaries be paid no less frequently than semimonthly. Some employers satisfy the requirement by providing a midmonth advance of approximately half the monthly take-home pay.

[5] A 365-day year contains 52 weeks *plus* one day; a leap year contains 52 weeks *plus* two days. As an approximate average, one year in six will have 53 Fridays, the customary payday for weekly and biweekly payrolls. Accordingly, approximately one year in six will have 53 weekly paydays, and one year in 12 will have 27 biweekly paydays. Employers must take this into account when converting annual salaries to weekly or biweekly rates of pay.

If a salaried employee has a specified length of regular pay period and they are eligible for an overtime rate of pay, the usual hourly overtime rate is

$$1.5 \times \frac{Gross\ earnings\ for\ a\ regular\ pay\ period}{Hours\ in\ a\ regular\ pay\ period}$$

Because of the factor 1.5, this overtime rate is usually referred to as "time and a half."

EXAMPLE 1.3A

CALCULATING BIWEEKLY AND WEEKLY EARNINGS AND HOURLY OVERTIME RATE FROM AN ANNUAL SALARY

Benazir's annual salary is $45,000. Her regular workweek consists of four 10-hour workdays. She is eligible for overtime at "time and a half" on time worked in excess of 10 hours per day or 40 hours per week. Determine her gross earnings in a pay period if

a. she is paid semimonthly.

b. she is paid biweekly.

c. she works 6 hours of overtime in a biweekly pay period.

SOLUTION

a. Semimonthly gross pay $= \dfrac{\text{Annual salary}}{24} = \dfrac{\$45,000}{24} = \$1875.00$

b. Biweekly gross pay $= \dfrac{\text{Annual salary}}{26} = \dfrac{\$45,000}{26} = \$1730.77$

c. Regular hourly rate $= \dfrac{\text{Regular biweekly gross pay}}{\text{Regular hours in biweekly period}} = \dfrac{\$1730.77}{2 \times 4 \times 10} = \$21.635$

Overtime hourly rate = Overtime factor × Regular hourly rate = 1.5 × $21.635 = $32.453

Total gross earnings = Regular pay + Overtime pay = $1730.77 + 6 ($32.453) = $1925.49

Hourly Wages

In jobs where the amount of work available is irregular or unpredictable, or where overtime is a common occurrence, employees are typically paid an hourly wage. Usually, a collective agreement between the employer and employees sets the number of hours per day (typically 7.5 or 8) and hours per week (typically 37.5 or 40) beyond which higher overtime rates apply. If no such agreement exists, federal or provincial employment standards laws apply. The minimum and most common overtime rate is 1.5 times the regular hourly rate ("time and a half"). Some unions have negotiated more favourable overtime rates (such as "double time").

Each province recognizes certain holidays that, depending on the province, are called "statutory holidays," "public holidays," or "general holidays." New Year's Day, Good Friday, Canada Day, Labour Day, Thanksgiving Day, and Christmas Day are holidays common to all provinces. With a few exceptions, provincial employment standards require that employees receive their usual rate of pay for a statutory holiday *not* worked. If employees are required to work on a "stat" holiday, they must be paid an *additional premium* rate of 1.5 times their regular rate of pay.

You calculate the gross earnings for a pay period by adding overtime pay, "stat" holiday pay, and "stat" holiday premium pay to the regular pay. That is,

Regular hourly rate × Regular hours
+ Overtime hourly rate × Overtime hours
+ "Stat" holiday pay
+ "Stat" holiday premium hourly rate × "Stat" holiday hours worked
= Gross earnings

In calculations in this section, time worked on a "stat" holiday does *not* count toward the threshold for overtime hours in a week.[6]

Sometimes wages in production and manufacturing jobs are structured to create an incentive for higher productivity. A *piecework rate* is based on the unit of production, such as $1 per garment sewn, or $2 per typed page, or $15 per tonne of output.

$$\begin{pmatrix} \text{Piecework} \\ \text{earnings} \end{pmatrix} = \begin{pmatrix} \text{Number of} \\ \text{units produced} \end{pmatrix} \times \begin{pmatrix} \text{Piecework} \\ \text{rate} \end{pmatrix}$$

EXAMPLE 1.3B

CALCULATING THE GROSS EARNINGS OF AN HOURLY PAID EMPLOYEE

Steve is paid $36.60 an hour for his work on an assembly line. The regular workweek is 37.5 hours (five 7.5-hour shifts). In the most recent biweekly pay period (midnight Friday to midnight of the second following Friday), he worked full shifts from Monday to Friday of both weeks. The first Monday of the pay period was a statutory holiday. In addition, he worked 6 hours on each Saturday. Overtime is paid at 1.5 times the regular rate and the statutory holiday time premium is 1.5 times the regular rate. What was Steve's gross pay for the period?

SOLUTION

In addition to "stat" holiday pay for the first Monday, Steve will be paid a holiday premium rate of 1.5 times his regular rate for hours actually worked on that Monday. (These hours do not count toward the threshold of 37.5 hours per week for overtime eligibility.) Steve's hourly rate for overtime is 1.5 × $36.60 = $54.90.

The given information is summarized in the following table.

Week 1			Week 2		
Day	Hours	Rate of pay	Day	Hours	Rate of pay
Sat	6	Regular	Sat	6	Regular
Sun	0		Sun	0	
Mon	7.5	Holiday premium	Mon	7.5	Regular
Tues	7.5	Regular	Tues	7.5	Regular
Wed	7.5	Regular	Wed	7.5	Regular
Thur	7.5	Regular	Thur	7.5	Regular
Fri	7.5	Regular	Fri	7.5	1.5 hours regular; 6 hours overtime

The components of Steve's gross pay are:

Regular pay:	[6 + 4(7.5) + 6 + 4(7.5) + 1.5]$36.60 =	$2690.10
Overtime pay:	6($54.90) =	$ 329.40
Holiday pay:	7.5($36.60) =	$ 274.50
Holiday premium pay:	7.5($54.90) =	$ 411.75
Total:		$3705.75

Steve's gross pay for the two-week period was $3705.75.

---

[6] This is the basic standard established by Ontario's Employment Standards Act. As with many employment standards set by provincial legislation and regulations, unions typically negotiate more favourable remuneration and working conditions in their collective agreements.

EXAMPLE 1.3C

CALCULATING GROSS EARNINGS INCLUDING A PIECEWORK WAGE

An orchardist pays apple pickers $10 per hour plus $8 per 100 kg of apples picked. If a worker picks, on average, 180 kg of apples per hour for a 40-hour workweek, what are the worker's gross earnings for the week?

SOLUTION

$$\left(\begin{array}{c}\text{Gross}\\\text{earnings}\end{array}\right) = \left(\begin{array}{c}\text{Hourly}\\\text{rate}\end{array} \times \begin{array}{c}\text{Number}\\\text{of hours}\end{array}\right) + \left(\begin{array}{c}\text{Piecework}\\\text{rate}\end{array} \times \begin{array}{c}\text{Number of}\\\text{units}\end{array}\right)$$

$$= (\$10.00 \times 40) + \$8.00\left(\frac{180}{100} \times 40\right)$$

$$= \$400 + \$576$$

$$= \$976$$

The worker's gross earnings for the week are $976.

Commissions

For sales positions, it is standard practice to base at least a portion of the salesperson's remuneration on sales volume. If earnings are calculated strictly as a percent of sales, the salesperson is working on *straight commission*. A *graduated commission* structure pays progressively higher commission rates at higher levels of sales. A salesperson who receives a basic salary and a commission on sales is working on a *salary plus commission* basis. In some arrangements, the commission is paid only on sales exceeding a minimum level called the *quota*.

EXAMPLE 1.3D

CALCULATING GROSS EARNINGS BASED ON A SALARY PLUS COMMISSION

James manages a men's clothing store for a national chain. His monthly remuneration has three components: a $2500 base salary, plus 2% of the amount by which the store's total sales volume for the month exceeds $40,000, plus 8% of the amount by which his personal sales exceed $4000. Calculate his gross compensation for a month in which his sales totalled $9900 and other staff had sales amounting to $109,260.

SOLUTION

Base salary		$2500.00
Commission on total store's volume:	$0.02(\$109,260 + \$9900 - \$40,000)$	1583.20
Commission on personal sales:	$0.08(\$9900 - \$4000)$	472.00
Total compensation		$4555.20

James's gross earnings for the month are $4555.20.

EXAMPLE 1.3E

CALCULATING GROSS EARNINGS BASED ON A GRADUATED COMMISSION

Tanya sells mutual funds for Pacific Financial Services Ltd. On mutual fund sales, Pacific Financial Services charges a "front-end load" or gross commission rate of 6%. Tanya is paid on a graduated commission structure. She receives 40% of the gross commission on the first $100,000 worth of mutual funds she sells in a month, and 60% of the gross commission on all additional sales in the same month. What are her earnings for a month in which she sells $180,000 worth of mutual funds?

SOLUTION

Commission on first $100,000:	$0.40 \times 0.06 \times \$100,000$	$2400
Commission on next $80,000:	$0.60 \times 0.06 \times \$80,000$	2880
Total earnings		$5280

Tanya's earnings are $5280 from her total mutual funds sales of $180,000 in the month.

EXERCISE 1.3

Answers to the odd-numbered problems are at the end of the book.

BASIC PROBLEMS

In this Exercise, assume there are exactly 52 weeks in a year.

1. Aletta's annual salary of $58,800 is paid weekly. She is paid at time and a half for any over-time beyond her regular workweek of 35 hours. What is her gross pay for a week in which she works 39 hours?

2. Lucille receives an annual salary of $37,500 based on a 37.5-hour workweek. What are her gross earnings for a 2-week pay period in which she works 9 hours of overtime at 1.5 times her regular rate of pay?

3. Hasad is paid an annual salary of $54,600 based on a 40-hour workweek. What is his gross pay for a biweekly pay period if he works 43 hours in the first week and 46.5 hours in the second week? Overtime is paid at time and a half.

4. Ross's compensation is to be changed from an hourly rate of $31.50 for a 40-hour work-week to a salary paid semimonthly. What should he be paid semimonthly in order for his annual earnings to remain the same?

5. Allison's regular hourly rate of pay is $17.70. She is paid time and a half for all work on weekends and for any time over 7.5 hours on weekdays. Calculate her gross earnings for a week in which she works 4.5, 0, 7.5, 8.5, 6, 6, and 9 hours on Saturday to Friday, respectively.

6. Sam is paid $34.50 per hour as a power plant engineer. He is paid 1.5 times the regular rate for all time exceeding 8 hours in a day or 40 hours in a week. Statutory holidays worked are paid at double time (in addition to holiday pay). What are his gross earnings for a week in which he clocks 8, 9.5, 8, 8, 10, 0, and 8 hours on Saturday to Friday, respectively, where Monday is a statutory holiday?

7. Mary sews for a clothing manufacturer. She is paid $7.50 per hour plus a piecework rate that depends on the type of garment in production. The current production run is men's shirts, for which she is paid $3.00 for each unit exceeding her quota of 20 shirts in an 8-hour shift. What is her total pay for a regular workweek in which her output on successive days is 24, 26, 27, 28, and 30 shirts?

8. Herb packs fish in 500-g cans on a processing line. He is paid $8.25 per hour plus $0.18 per kilogram for production in excess of 500 kg in a 7.5-hour shift. How much will he earn per day if he packs 250 cans per hour?

9. Svetlana is an independent insurance broker placing various clients with any of several insurance companies. On homeowner insurance policies, each month she receives:
   - $20 for each renewal of an existing policy;
   - $35 for each policy placed with a new client; and
   - 5.5% of the annual premiums on all new and renewed policies written in the month.

In October, she placed 37 new client policies representing $14,375 in annual premiums and 126 policy renewals representing $47,880 in annual premiums. What amount did Svetlana earn in October?

10. Hillary sells cosmetics from her part-time home-based business. She receives a straight commission of 21% from her supplier. At the year-end, she also receives a 7% bonus on sales exceeding her annual quota of $100,000. What will her gross annual earnings be for a year in which her average monthly sales are $11,000?

11. Manfred is considering job offers of the same type of sales position from two retailers with similar product lines:
   - Supreme Audio & Video is offering a base salary of $2000 per month plus a 4% commission rate on sales.
   - Buy-Right Electronics will pay a base salary of $1500 per month plus commission rates of 3% on the first $25,000 of sales and 6% on additional sales in a month.

   Based on past experience in similar sales positions, Manfred is confident he can attain average monthly sales of $55,000. At this level of sales, what would be his average gross earnings per month from each retailer?

12. A shoe salesperson is paid the greater of $600 per week or 11% of sales.
   a. What are his earnings for a week in which sales are $5636?
   b. At what volume of sales per week will he start to earn more from the commission-based compensation?

13. Tom sells mutual funds on a graduated commission structure. He receives 3.3% on the first $50,000 of sales in a month, 4.4% on the next $50,000, and 5.5% on all further sales. What are his gross earnings for a month in which he sells $140,000 worth of mutual funds?

INTERMEDIATE PROBLEMS

14. Sharon is a manufacturer's representative selling office furniture directly to businesses. She receives a monthly salary of $2000 plus a 2.2% commission on sales exceeding her quota of $150,000 per month.
   a. What are her earnings for a month in which she has $227,000 in sales?
   b. If her average monthly sales are $235,000, what straight commission rate would generate the same average monthly earnings as her current basis of remuneration?

15. Julio is paid on a graduated commission scale of 5% on the first $20,000 of sales in a month, 7.5% on the next $20,000, and 10% on all additional sales.
   a. What is he paid for a month in which his sales are $54,880?
   b. What single commission rate on all sales would result in the same earnings for the month?

16. Karen works in a retail computer store. She receives a weekly base salary of $300 plus a commission of 3% of sales exceeding her quota of $20,000 per week. What are her sales for a week in which she earns $630.38?

17. Jason's gross pay for August is $3296.97 on sales totalling $151,342. If his base salary is $1500 per month, what is his rate of commission on sales exceeding his monthly quota of $100,000?

18. Daniella's gross monthly earnings are based on commission rates of 4% on the first $40,000 of sales, 5% on the next $50,000, and 6% on all additional sales for the month. What is her sales total for a month in which she earns $5350?

19. Trevor earns a base monthly salary of $2000 plus a commission of 3% on sales exceeding his monthly quota of $25,000. He receives a further 3% bonus on sales in excess of $50,000. What must his sales be in order to gross $4000 per month?

1.4 Simple and Weighted Averages

Simple Average

LO6 The type of average initially encountered in basic mathematics is called the simple average. To calculate the simple average, simply (of course) add the values for all items and then divide by the number of items. That is,

$$\text{Simple average} = \frac{\textit{Sum of the values}}{\textit{Total number of items}} \tag{1-1}$$

This average should be used in cases where each item has the *same* importance or each value occurs the *same* number of times.

Weighted Average

We will now consider a situation requiring a different approach to averaging. Suppose you operate a seasonal business that employs 10 people during the peak period of July, August, and September. Only 2 employees are retained during the rest of the year. Is the average number of people employed during the year $\frac{10+2}{2} = 6$? No—a simple average of "10" and "2" is not appropriate because these two employment levels lasted for different lengths of time. The value "2" should influence the average more than the value "10." More precisely, each employment value should influence the average in proportion to the length of time at the level of employment. Mathematicians have a rather odd way of expressing this sort of idea. In this case, they say: "Each employment level should be *weighted* by the time period for which it lasted." Consequently, we assign a *weighting factor* of 3 months to the value "10" and a weighting factor of 9 months to the value "2." Then the *weighted average* number of employees during the year is calculated as follows:

$$\frac{(3 \times 10) + (9 \times 2)}{3 + 9} = 4.0$$

In the numerator, each of the two employment values (10 and 2) is multiplied by its weighting factor (this counts 3 months when there were 10 employees and 9 months when there were 2 employees). The two products are then added. This sum is then divided by the sum of the weighting factors, which represents the employment levels for 12 months.

In general, *a weighted average should be calculated when the values being averaged have differing relative importance, or when some values occur more often than others.*

$$\text{Weighted average} = \frac{\textit{Sum of (Weighting factor} \times \textit{Value)}}{\textit{Sum of weighting factors}} \tag{1-2}$$

Formula (1-2)[7] implies three steps for calculating a weighted average:

1. First multiply each of the "values" by its "weighting factor." The weighting factors represent the relative importance of each value, or the number of times each value occurs.
2. Add all of the products calculated in Step 1.
3. Finally, divide the Step 2 result by the sum of the "weighting factors."

Weighted averages are frequently encountered in business. For example, the Toronto Stock Exchange's S&P/TSX Composite Index is based on a weighted average price of the shares of over 200 companies. Accountants sometimes use the weighted average price paid for goods to determine the overall value of a firm's inventory. Several more examples are presented in this section's Example problems and Exercise problems. When calculating weighted averages, you need to make careful decisions about which values should be averaged and which numbers should be used for the weighting factors. The flow chart in **Figure 1.1** suggests questions you should ask yourself before the "number crunching" begins.

---

[7] Note that if each of the "values" has the same importance, then each weighting factor is 1. The "weighted average" Formula (1-2) then reduces to the "simple average" Formula (1-1).

FIGURE 1.1	Approach for Problems on Averages

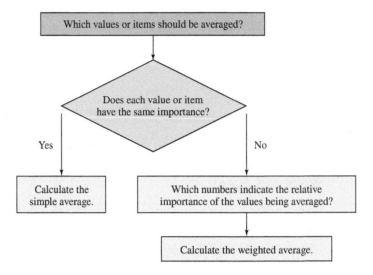

EXAMPLE 1.4A

CALCULATION OF SIMPLE AND WEIGHTED AVERAGES

Northern Transport has 86 drivers each earning $23.85 per hour, 14 clerical staff members each earning $18.50 per hour, and 8 mechanics each earning $35.50 per hour.

a. What is the simple average of the three hourly rates?

b. Calculate the weighted average hourly rate earned by the three categories of employees.

SOLUTION

a. Simple average $= \dfrac{\$23.85 + \$18.50 + \$35.50}{3} = \$25.95$

b. Each hourly rate should be assigned a weighting factor reflecting the relative importance of that rate. The greater the number of employees receiving a particular wage rate, the more importance should be given to that rate. It is natural, then, to use the number of employees receiving each hourly rate as the weighting factors.

$$\text{Weighted average} = \frac{(86 \times \$23.85) + (14 \times \$18.50) + (8 \times \$35.50)}{86 + 14 + 8}$$
$$= \frac{\$2051.10 + \$259.00 + \$284.00}{108}$$
$$= \$24.02$$

The weighted average is less than the simple average because a high proportion of the employees earn the two lower hourly rates.

EXAMPLE 1.4B

CALCULATING THE WEIGHTED AVERAGE RATE OF RETURN FOR AN INVESTMENT PORTFOLIO

One year ago, Mrs. Boyd divided her savings among four mutual funds as follows: 20% was invested in a bond fund, 15% in a money market fund, 40% in a Canadian equity fund, and 25% in a global equity fund. During the past year, the rates of return on the individual mutual funds were 10%, 4%, −2%, and 15%, respectively. What was the overall rate of return on her portfolio?

SOLUTION

A simple average of the four rates of return is not the appropriate calculation because Mrs. Boyd invested different amounts of money in each mutual fund. The −2% return on the Canadian equity fund should have twice the influence of the 10% return on the bond fund because she invested twice as much money in the equity fund as in the bond fund. Therefore, we should choose weighting factors that reflect the relative amount of money invested in each mutual fund.

Mutual fund	Rate of return (Value)	Fraction of money invested (Weighting factor)	(Weighting factor) × (Value)
Bond fund	10%	0.20	2.0%
Money market fund	4%	0.15	0.6%
Canadian equity fund	−2%	0.40	−0.8%
Global equity fund	15%	0.25	3.75%
Total:		1.00	5.55%

The weighted average rate of return on the portfolio was $\dfrac{5.55\%}{1.0} = 5.55\%$.

Mrs. Boyd's portfolio increased in value by 5.55%.

TIP

Determining the Weight Factor

In some questions it is not always clear which values are to be used as the weight factor, particularly when all values are measured in the same units as in **Example 1.4B**. Every word problem will ask a question indicating which of the values is to be averaged—the other value is then used as the weight factor.

EXAMPLE 1.4C

CALCULATING THE WEIGHTED AVERAGE OF A VARYING INVESTMENT IN A BUSINESS

As of January 1, Alan had already invested $63,000 in his business. On February 1 he invested another $5000. Alan withdrew $12,000 on June 1 and injected $3000 on November 1. What was his average cumulative investment in the business during the year? (Assume that all months have the same length, or weighting.)

SOLUTION

A common error made in this type of problem is to attempt, in some way, to average the amounts that are contributed to or withdrawn from the business. We should instead average the cumulative balance of the invested funds. The amounts contributed and withdrawn from time to time are used only to revise the cumulative investment. A weighted average should be calculated since the various amounts are invested for *differing* lengths of time. Each cumulative investment should be weighted by the number of months for which it lasted.

Period	Cumulative investment	Number of months
Jan. 1–Jan. 31	$63,000	1
Feb. 1–May 31	$63,000 + $5000 = $68,000	4
June 1–Oct. 31	$68,000 − $12,000 = $56,000	5
Nov. 1–Dec. 31	$56,000 + $3000 = $59,000	2

$$\text{Average investment} = \frac{(1 \times \$63,000) + (4 \times \$68,000) + (5 \times \$56,000) + (2 \times \$59,000)}{12}$$
$$= \$61,083.33$$

Alan's average cumulative investment in the business was $61,083.33.

EXAMPLE 1.4D

CALCULATING A WEIGHTED GRADE POINT AVERAGE

Most colleges compute a grade point average (GPA) as the measure of a student's overall academic achievement. To compute the GPA, each letter grade is first converted to a grade point value. Each course's grade point value is then weighted by the number of credits the course carries.

The first table gives City College's scale for converting letter grades to grade point values. The second table presents Louise's courses and grades. Calculate her GPA.

Letter grade	Grade point value
A	4.0
A–	3.7
B+	3.3
B	3.0
B–	2.7
C+	2.3
C	2.0
C–	1.7
D	1.0

Course	Credits	Grade
English 100	3	B+
Math 100	4	B
Business 100	2	A
Economics 120	3	B–
Accounting 100	4	C+
Marketing 140	2	A–
Computing 110	3	C
Total	21	

SOLUTION

The values to be averaged are the grade point scores Louise has achieved on her seven courses. However, these values are not given in a ready-to-use list. A new table should be constructed, showing the grade points earned on each course. (See the first three columns in the following table.)

A simple average of the grade point values is not appropriate because some courses carry more credits than others. A 4-credit course should count twice as much in the average as a 2-credit course. Therefore, each course's grade point score should be weighted by the number of credits that course carries (Column 4). The first step in the calculation of the weighted average is to multiply each grade point value (Column 3) by its weighting factor (Column 4). In the second step, the products in Column 5 are added.

Course	Grade	Grade points	Credits	Grade points × Credits
English 100	B+	3.3	3	9.9
Math 100	B	3.0	4	12.0
Business 100	A	4.0	2	8.0
Economics 120	B–	2.7	3	8.1
Accounting 100	C+	2.3	4	9.2
Marketing 140	A–	3.7	2	7.4
Computing 110	C	2.0	3	6.0
Total:			21	60.6

The third and last step is to divide the total in Column 5 by the total in Column 4. Hence,

$$\text{GPA} = \frac{60.6}{21} = 2.89$$

Louise's grade point average is 2.89.

EXAMPLE 1.4E

USING A WEIGHTED AVERAGE TO RANK RESPONSES IN A SURVEY

One hundred first-year students at a local college were surveyed to provide the college with feedback on their courses. They were asked to rate their level of satisfaction for their first-term courses on a scale of 1 to 5 where 1 = very dissatisfied and 5 = very satisfied. The following table shows the frequency of responses for each course.

Course	Very dissatisfied	Dissatisfied	Neutral	Satisfied	Very satisfied
Math100	0%	5%	22%	35%	38%
Comp100	11%	3%	27%	30%	29%
Econ100	2%	18%	40%	21%	19%
Mktg100	3%	21%	9%	29%	38%

Trying to evaluate the results using the percentages alone is difficult, so a weighted average rating is calculated using the 1 to 5 scale assigned to each level of satisfaction.

SOLUTION

For Math100, the weighted average rating is calculated as:

$$Average\ rating = \frac{(0 \times 1) + (5 \times 2) + (22 \times 3) + (35 \times 4) + (38 \times 5)}{100} = 4.06$$

The values being averaged are the 1 to 5 ratings and the weight factors are the percentages for each rating response. These weight factors sum to 100. Similarly, the weighted average ratings for the other level-one courses are:

$$Comp\ average\ rating = \frac{(11 \times 1) + (3 \times 2) + (27 \times 3) + (30 \times 4) + (29 \times 5)}{100} = 3.63$$

$$Econ\ average\ rating = \frac{(2 \times 1) + (18 \times 2) + (40 \times 3) + (21 \times 4) + (19 \times 5)}{100} = 3.37$$

$$Mktg\ average\ rating = \frac{(3 \times 1) + (21 \times 2) + (9 \times 3) + (29 \times 4) + (38 \times 5)}{100} = 3.78$$

The weighted average ratings for each course can then be used to compare the level of satisfaction for all the courses. The higher the weighted average rating, the more satisfied the students are with the course.

Course	Weighted average rating
Math100	4.06
Comp100	3.63
Econ100	3.37
Mktg100	3.78

Students are most satisfied with their Math100 course.

 CONCEPT QUESTIONS

1. In what circumstance should you calculate a weighted average instead of a simple average?
2. In what circumstance is the weighted average equal to the simple average?
3. How must you allocate your money among a number of investments so that your portfolio's overall rate of return will be the same as the simple average of the rates of return on individual investments?

Answers to the odd-numbered problems are at the end of the book.

BASIC PROBLEMS

1. A survey of 254 randomly chosen residences in a city revealed that 4 had four television sets, 22 had three TV sets, 83 had two TV sets, 140 had one TV set, and 5 had no TV set at all. Based on the survey, what would you estimate to be the average number of TV sets per household?

2. An investor accumulated 1800 shares of Microtel Corporation over a period of several months. She bought 1000 shares at $15.63, 500 shares at $19.00, and 300 shares at $21.75. What was her average cost per share? (*Note:* Investors who purchase shares in the same company or the same mutual fund at more than one price must eventually do this calculation. Tax rules require that the capital gain or loss on the sale of any of the shares be calculated using the weighted average price paid for all of the shares, rather than the particular price paid for the shares actually sold.)

3. A hockey goalie's goals against average (GAA) is the average number of goals scored against him per (complete) game. In his first 20 games in goal, O.U. Sieve had one shutout, two 1-goal games, three 2-goal games, four 3-goal games, seven 4-goal games, two 6-goal games, and one 10-goal disaster. Calculate his GAA.

4. Serge's graduated commission scale pays him 3% on his first $30,000 in sales, 4% on the next $20,000, and 6% on all additional sales in a month. What is his average commission rate on sales for a month totalling:
    a. $60,000?
    b. $100,000?

5. A baseball player's slugging percentage is the average number of hits a batter gets in all the "at bats" they have in their games played. This statistic differs from their batting average in that it is weighted based on the number of bases run for a single hit. Babe Ruth had 8399 "at bats" in his career where he had 714 home runs (4-base hits), 136 triples (3-base hits), 506 doubles (2-base hits), and 2873 singles (1-base hits). What was his slugging percentage?

6. Brianne spent the summer touring Canadian cities. She spent 4 nights in a hotel in Montreal at $158 a night, 2 nights in a Toronto hotel at $199 a night, 1 night in Niagara Falls for $239, 5 nights in Calgary at $130 a night, and 2 nights in Kamloops for $118 a night. What was the average cost of her hotel rooms for the entire trip?

7. The RBC Royal Bank offers an "add-on option" on fixed-rate mortgages. The option allows the customer to borrow additional funds partway through the term of the mortgage. The interest rate charged on the combined mortgage debt is the weighted average of the old rate on the former balance and the current competitive rate on new mortgage financing. Suppose Herschel and Julie had a mortgage balance of $37,500 at 8%, when they borrowed another $20,000 at 7%. What interest rate are they charged by the RBC Royal Bank on the new consolidated balance?

8. Margot's grades and course credits in her first semester at college are listed below.

Grade	C+	B–	B+	C–	B	C
Credits	5	3	4	2	3	4

    Using the table in **Example 1.4D** for converting letter grades to grade point values, calculate Margot's grade point average for the semester.

9. The distribution of scores obtained by 30 students on a quiz marked out of 10 is listed below.

Score	10	9	8	7	6	5	4	3	2	1
Number of students	2	6	9	7	3	2	0	1	0	0

What was the average score on the test?

10. Alihan's transcript shows the following academic record for four semesters of part-time college studies. Calculate his cumulative GPA at the end of his fourth semester.

Semester	Credits	GPA
1	6	3.5
2	9	3.0
3	12	2.75
4	7.5	3.2

11. The "age" of an account receivable is the length of time that it has been outstanding. At the end of October, a firm has $12,570 in receivables that are 30 days old, $6850 in receivables that are 60 days old, and $1325 in receivables that are 90 days old. What is the average age of its accounts receivable at the end of October?

12. One year ago, Sook-Yin allocated the funds in her portfolio among five securities in the proportions listed below. The rate of return on each security for the year is given in the third column of the table.

Security	Proportion invested (%)	Rate of return for the year (%)
Company A shares	15	14
Province B bonds	20	10
Company C shares	10	−13
Units in Fund D	35	12
Company E shares	20	27

Calculate the rate of return for the entire portfolio.

13. One of the methods permitted by Generally Accepted Accounting Principles (GAAP) for reporting the value of a firm's inventory is *weighted average inventory pricing*. The Boswell Corporation began its fiscal year with an inventory of 156 units valued at $10.55 per unit. During the year it made the purchases listed in the following table.

Date	Units purchased	Unit cost ($)
February 10	300	10.86
June 3	1000	10.47
August 23	500	10.97

At the end of the year, 239 units remained in inventory. Determine:
a. The weighted average cost of the units purchased during the year.
b. The weighted average cost of the beginning inventory and all units purchased during the year.
c. The value of the ending inventory based on the weighted average cost calculated in part (b).

14. Suppose a group of consumers spend 30% of their disposable income on food, 20% on clothing, and 50% on rent. If over the course of a year the price of food rises 10%, the price of clothing drops 5%, and rent rises 15%, what is the average price increase experienced by these consumers?

15. A restaurant owner sets her menu prices at a predetermined percentage of her input costs for food, ingredients, and beverages. The second column of the following table shows the prices as a percentage of these costs for various menu categories. The third column shows the breakdown of the restaurant's overall revenue from the four menu categories.
  a. On average, what are menu prices as a percentage of the basic input costs?
  b. Overall, what are the input costs as a percentage of revenue?

Menu category	Menu price as a percentage of costs	Percentage of sales revenue
Appetizers	300%	10%
Entrees	200%	50%
Desserts	225%	15%
Beverages	250%	25%

16. The balance on Nucorp's revolving loan began the month at $35,000. On the eighth of the month another $10,000 was borrowed. Nucorp was able to repay $20,000 on the 25th of the 31-day month. What was the average balance on the loan during the month? (Use each day's closing balance as the loan balance for the day.)

17. A seasonal manufacturing operation began the calendar year with 14 employees. During the year, employees were hired or laid off on various dates as shown in the following table.

Date	Employee changes
April 1	7 hired
May 1	8 hired
June 1	11 hired
September 1	6 laid off
October 1	14 laid off

What was the average number of employees on the payroll during the calendar year? (Assume that each month has the same length.)

18. Marcel must temporarily invest extra money in his retail business every fall to purchase additional inventory for the Christmas season. On September 1, he already had a total of $57,000 invested in his business. Subsequently, he invested or withdrew cash on various dates as shown.

Date	Additional investment or withdrawal
October 1	$15,000 investment
November 1	$27,000 investment
February 1	$23,000 withdrawal
March 1	$13,000 withdrawal
May 1	$6000 withdrawal

What was the average cumulative investment in the business during the period from September 1 to August 31? (Assume that each month has the same length.)

19. When a company calculates its earnings per common share for its financial statements, it uses the weighted average number of common shares outstanding during the year. Enertec Corp. began its fiscal year (January 1 to December 31) with 5 million common shares outstanding. Additional common shares were issued during the year as shown in the following table.

Date	Event	Additional shares issued
March 1	New public offering	1,000,000
June 1	Employees and officers exercise stock options	500,000
November 1	Convertible bonds exchanged for shares	750,000

What was the average number of common shares outstanding during the year? (Assume that each month has the same length.)

20. Lien, the proprietor of a grocery store, prepares her Deluxe Nut Combo Mix by mixing various ingredients she buys in bulk. The second column of the following table shows the amount of each ingredient Lien uses in making a batch of the combo mix. To set the retail price of the mix at 150% of her cost, Lien must determine her cost based on the average wholesale cost of the ingredients, which is shown in the third column.

Ingredient	Amount	Cost per kg
Peanuts	5 kg	$2.95
Cashews	2 kg	$9.50
Almonds	1 kg	$11.50
Sunflower seeds	500 g	$2.75
Raisins	400 g	$3.60
Smarties	300 g	$6.40

   a. What is Lien's average cost per 100 g of her Deluxe Nut Combo Mix?

   b. What is her retail price per 100 g?

21. The Rising Dough Bakery surveyed 100 customers to determine which of price, service, quality of goods, and promotions was the most important factor resulting in a recommendation to a friend or family member. Each factor was rated using a 4-point scale where 1 = not at all important and 4 = extremely important. Based on the results shown in the following table, what is the weighted average rating of the most important factor?

Factor	Not at all important	Somewhat important	Important	Extremely important
Price	19%	24%	28%	29%
Service	13%	30%	39%	18%
Quality	0%	43%	21%	36%
Promotions	11%	32%	45%	12%

*1.5 Taxes

LO7 A **tax rate** is the percentage of a price or taxable amount that must be paid in tax. The dollar amount of the tax payable is

$$\text{Tax payable} = \text{Tax rate} \times \text{Taxable amount}$$

This word equation is an application of finding the percent of a number as shown in **Section 1.2**.

Goods and Services Tax (GST); Harmonized Sales Tax (HST)

The Goods and Services Tax (GST) is a federal sales tax applied to the vast majority of goods and services. The tax is initially collected by the seller of a good or service from the purchaser. Consequently, a business *collects* the GST on the prices of goods and services it sells to customers, and it *pays* the GST on the prices of goods and services it buys from suppliers. As of January 1, 2018, the GST rate is 5%.

A business remits GST payments monthly or quarterly to the Canada Revenue Agency (CRA). The GST remittance is the amount by which the tax collected from sales exceeds the tax paid on purchases during the reporting period. In sales-tax jargon, the amount by which sales (the business's "outputs") exceeds purchases (the business's "inputs") is called the "value added." Consequently, the GST is a type of sales tax often described as a "value-added tax" because the GST rate is, in effect, applied to the

$$\text{Value added} = \text{Value of "outputs"} - \text{Value of "inputs"}$$

Then

$$\text{GST remittance} = 0.05 \times \text{Value added}$$

If, in a reporting period, the GST collected from sales happens to be less than the GST paid on purchases, the CRA will refund the difference to the business.

Five provinces (PEI, New Brunswick, Newfoundland and Labrador, Nova Scotia, and Ontario) have agreed with the federal government to blend their respective provincial sales tax with the GST in a single Harmonized Sales Tax (HST). The HST rates are given in Table 1.1. The HST is administered by the federal government through the CRA. Like the GST, the HST is a value-added tax.

TABLE 1.1 GST, HST, and PST Rates (as of January 1, 2018)*

Province	GST rate (%)	HST rate (%)	PST rate (%)	Total
Alberta	5	—	—	5
British Columbia	5	—	7	12
Manitoba	5	—	8	13
New Brunswick	—	15	—	15
Newfoundland and Labrador	—	15	—	15
Nova Scotia	—	15	—	15
Ontario	—	13	—	13
Prince Edward Island	—	15	—	15
Quebec	5	—	9.975	14.975
Saskatchewan	5	—	6	11

* Tax rates for all of Canada have remained the same since 2016. The last increase in HST was for Prince Edward Island on October 1, 2016, when PEI raised its HST 1%.

EXAMPLE 1.5A

CALCULATION OF THE GST OR THE HST PAYABLE BY A BUSINESS

Ace Appliance Repair files GST returns quarterly. During the first quarter of the year, Ace billed its customers $17,650 for labour, $4960 for parts, and then added the GST. In the same period, Ace paid $3250 to suppliers for parts, $1800 for rent, $673 for utilities, $594 for truck repairs, plus the GST on these goods and services.

a. What GST must be remitted by Ace (or refunded by the CRA) for the first quarter?

b. Repeat part (a) for the case where Ace also bought a new truck for $36,000 on the last day of the quarter.

c. Repeat part (a) for the case where Ace pays HST (at the rate of 13%) instead of GST.

SOLUTION

a. GST collected = 0.05($17,650 + $4960) = $1130.50
GST paid = 0.05($3250 + $1800 + $673 + $594) = $315.85
GST remittance payable = $1130.50 − $315.85 = $814.65

b. GST paid on the truck purchase = 0.05 × $36,000 = $1800.00

This GST credit exceeds the net GST calculated in part (a). Hence, Ace will qualify for a refund.

$$\text{GST refund receivable} = \$1800.00 - \text{Result in part (a)}$$
$$= \$1800.00 - \$814.65$$
$$= \$985.35$$

c. HST collected = 0.13($17,650 + $4960) = $2939.30
HST paid = 0.13($3250 + $1800 + $673 + $594) = $821.21
HST remittance payable = $2939.30 − $821.21 = $2118.09

Provincial Sales Tax (PST)

Manitoba, British Columbia, Quebec, and Saskatchewan charge a sales tax at the *retail* level. This tax typically applies to a somewhat narrower range of goods and services than the GST and HST. The provincial sales tax (PST) rates for these provinces are shown in Table 1.1. The tax rate is applied to the retail price. That is,

$$PST = \text{Sales tax rate} \times \text{Retail price}$$

EXAMPLE 1.5B

CALCULATING THE PST, GST, AND HST

Calculate the total sales taxes on a $100 item in

a. Manitoba

b. Quebec

c. Prince Edward Island

SOLUTION

a. $GST + PST = (0.05 + 0.08) \times \$100 = \$13.00$

b. $GST + PST = (0.05 + 0.09975) \times \$100 = \$14.98$

c. $HST = 0.15 \times \$100 = \$15.00$

Property Tax

Real estate property tax is not a sales tax, but rather an annual tax paid by the owners of real estate. Property taxes are paid to municipal and regional governments to cover costs of municipal services, public schools, policing, etc. Tax rates are set by municipal and regional governments, and by other agencies (such as school boards) authorized by the provincial government to levy property taxes. The taxable value (usually called the *assessed value*) of each property is set by a provincial agency. Assessed values are periodically revised to keep them in line with market values.

Property tax rates in most provinces east of Manitoba are quoted in terms of dollars of tax per $100 of assessed value. For example, if the rate for a municipality is $1.55 per $100 of assessed value, the property tax on a home assessed at $200,000 will be

$$\frac{\$1.55}{\$100} \times \$200,000 = \$3100$$

A tax rate of $1.55 per $100 of assessed value is equal to 1.55% of assessed value. Most municipalities in Ontario now specify property tax rates simply as a percentage of the assessed value.

Provinces west of Ontario quote property tax rates as mill rates. A **mill rate** indicates the amount of tax per $1000 of assessed value. For example, a mill rate of 13.732 means a tax of $13.732 per $1000 of assessed value. The percent equivalent of this mill rate is 1.3732%. If you choose to work with a mill rate rather than its percent equivalent, then

$$Property\ tax = \frac{Mill\ rate}{1000} \times Assessed\ value\ of\ the\ property$$

EXAMPLE 1.5C

CALCULATING THE PROPERTY TAX ON A RESIDENTIAL PROPERTY

A homeowner's tax notice lists the following mill rates for various local services and capital developments. If the assessed value of the property is \$164,500, calculate each tax levy and the current year's total property taxes.

Tax rate	Mill rate
Schools	6.7496
General city	7.8137
Water	0.8023
Sewer and sanitation	0.7468

SOLUTION

$$\text{School tax levy} = \frac{\text{School mill rate}}{1000} \times \text{Assessed value}$$

$$= \frac{6.7496}{1000} \times \$164,500$$

$$= \$1110.31$$

Similarly,

$$\text{General city levy} = \frac{7.8137}{1000} \times \$164,500 = \$1285.35$$

$$\text{Water levy} = \frac{0.8023}{1000} \times \$164,500 = \$131.98$$

$$\text{Sewer levy} = \frac{0.7468}{1000} \times \$164,500 = \$122.85$$

$$\text{Total property taxes} = \$1110.31 + \$1285.35 + \$131.98 + \$122.85$$

$$= \$2650.49$$

EXAMPLE 1.5D

CALCULATING A PROPERTY TAX RATE

The town council of Concord has approved a new capital levy component of the property tax to pay for a new recreation complex. The levy must raise \$400,000 in each of the next 10 years.

a. If the total assessed value of properties within Concord's jurisdiction is \$738 million, what tax rate (to five-figure accuracy) must be set for the capital levy? Determine the rate both as a mill rate and as dollars per \$100.

b. As a result of the capital levy, what additional tax will be paid each year by the owner of a property assessed at \$200,000?

SOLUTION

a. Let us first calculate the tax rate as a percentage.

$$\text{Capital levy tax rate} = \frac{\text{Required total tax}}{\text{Total assessed value}} \times 100\%$$

$$= \frac{\$400,000}{\$738,000,000} \times 100\%$$

$$= 0.054201\%$$

Therefore, the tax rate for the extra capital levy is \$0.054201 per \$100 of assessed value. This corresponds to \$0.54201 per \$1000 of assessed value. Hence, the mill rate is 0.54201.

b. With the tax levy quoted as $0.054201 per $100 of assessed value,

$$\text{Additional tax} = \frac{\$0.054201}{\$100} \times \$200{,}000 = \$108.40$$

With the tax levy quoted as 0.54201 mill,

$$\text{Additional tax} = \frac{0.54201}{\$1000} \times \$200{,}000 = \$108.40$$

EXERCISE 1.5

Answers to the odd-numbered problems are at the end of the book.

BASIC PROBLEMS

1. Johnston Distributing Inc. files quarterly GST returns. The purchases on which it paid the GST and the sales on which it collected the GST for the last four quarters were as follows:

Quarter	Purchases ($)	Sales ($)
1	596,476	751,841
2	967,679	627,374
3	823,268	1,231,916
4	829,804	994,622

   Calculate the GST remittance or refund due for each quarter.

2. Sawchuk's Home and Garden Centre in Toronto files monthly HST returns. The purchases on which it paid the HST and the sales on which it collected the HST for the last four months were as follows:

Month	Purchases ($)	Sales ($)
March	135,650	57,890
April	213,425	205,170
May	176,730	313,245
June	153,715	268,590

   Based on an HST rate of 13%, calculate the HST remittance or refund due for each month.

3. Calculate the total amount, including both GST and PST, that an individual will pay for a car priced at $39,500 in
   a. Alberta.
   b. Saskatchewan.
   c. Quebec.

4. How much more will a consumer pay for an item listed at $1000 (pretax) in Prince Edward Island than in Manitoba?

5. Angie's Flower Shop charges 13% HST on all purchases.
   a. How much HST will she report for a plant priced at $39.45?
   b. As of February 4, 2013, if a consumer pays cash and cannot give the exact change, the total amount of the transaction must be rounded up or down to the nearest five cents. How much change will be given if the above purchase is paid for with a $50 bill?

6. To attract shoppers, retailers occasionally advertise something like "Pay no HST!" Needless to say, neither the federal nor the provincial government is willing to forgo its sales tax. In this situation, the retailer must calculate and remit the HST as though the "ticket" price already includes these sales taxes. How much HST must a retailer in New Brunswick report on a $495 item that he sells on a "Pay no HST" basis? (*Hint:* What percentage is the HST of a HST-inclusive price?)

7. What are the taxes on a property assessed at $227,000 if the mill rate is 16.8629?

8. **a.** Express a property tax rate increase of 0.1 mill in terms of dollars per $100 of assessed value.

   b. If the mill rate increases by 0.1 mill, what is the dollar increase in property taxes on a $200,000 home?

9. The assessment on a farm consists of $143,000 for the house and $467,000 for the land and buildings. A mill rate of 15.0294 applies to residences, and a rate of 4.6423 applies to agricultural land and buildings. What are the total property taxes payable on the farm?

10. The assessed value on a property increased from $285,000 last year to $298,000 in the current year. Last year's property tax rate was $1.56324 per $100 of assessed value.

    a. What will be the change in the property tax from last year if the new tax rate is set at $1.52193 per $100?

    b. What would the new tax rate have to be for the dollar amount of the property taxes to be unchanged?

INTERMEDIATE PROBLEMS

11. The school board in a municipality will require an extra $2,430,000 for its operating budget next year. The current mill rate for the school tax component of property taxes is 7.1253.

    a. If the total of the assessed values of properties in the municipality remains at the current figure of $6.78 billion, what value must next year's school mill rate be set at?

    b. If the total of all assessed values rises by 5% over this year's aggregate assessment, what value must next year's school mill rate be set at?

12. The total assessed value of property in Brockton has risen by $97 million from last year's figure of $1.563 billion. The property tax rate last year for city services was $0.94181 per $100 of assessed value. If the city's budget has increased by $750,000, what tax rate should it set for the current year?

KEY TERMS

Complex fraction	Mill rate	Remuneration
Denominator	Mixed number	Tax rate
Equivalent fractions	Numerator	
Improper fraction	Proper fraction	

SUMMARY OF NOTATION AND KEY FORMULAS

FORMULA (1-1) $Simple\ average = \dfrac{Sum\ of\ the\ values}{Total\ number\ of\ items}$

FORMULA (1-2) $Weighted\ average = \dfrac{Sum\ of\ (Weighting\ factor \times Value)}{Sum\ of\ weighting\ factors}$

REVIEW PROBLEMS

Answers to the odd-numbered review problems are at the end of the book.

BASIC PROBLEMS

1. **LO1** Evaluate each of the following:

    a. $(2^3 - 3)^2 - 20 \div (2 + 2^3)$

    b. $4(2 \times 3^2 - 2^3)^2 \div (10 - 4 \times 5)$

    c. $\$213.85(1 - 0.095 \times \frac{5}{12})$

    d. $\dfrac{\$2315}{1 + 0.0825 \times \frac{77}{365}}$

    e. $\$325.75\left(1 + \dfrac{0.105}{4}\right)^2$

    f. $\dfrac{\$710}{\left(1 + \frac{0.0925}{2}\right)^3}$

    g. $\$885.75\left(1 + 0.0775 \times \dfrac{231}{365}\right) - \dfrac{\$476.50}{1 + 0.0775 \times \frac{49}{365}}$

    h. $\$859\left(1 + \dfrac{0.0825}{12}\right)^3 + \dfrac{\$682}{\left(1 + \frac{0.0825}{12}\right)^2}$

2. **LO1** Evaluate each of the following:

    a. $96 - (6 - 4^2) \times 7 - 2$

    b. $81 \div (5^2 - 16) - 4(2^3 - 13)$

    c. $\dfrac{\$827.69}{1 + 0.125 \times \frac{273}{365}} + \$531.49\left(1 + 0.125 \times \dfrac{41}{365}\right)$

    d. $\$550.45\left(1 + 0.0875 \times \dfrac{195}{365}\right) - \dfrac{\$376.29}{1 + 0.0875 \times \frac{99}{365}}$

    e. $\$1137\left(1 + \dfrac{0.0975}{12}\right)^2 + \dfrac{\$2643}{\left(1 + \frac{0.0975}{12}\right)^3}$

3. **LO4** What amount is 62% of $99?

4. **LO4** What amount is 80% of $156.25?

5. **LO4** $\frac{3}{4}$% of $133.\overline{33}$ is what amount?

6. **LO4** How many minutes is 12.5% of two hours?

7. **LO4** The profit forecast for the most recent fiscal quarter is $23,400. The actual profit is 90% of the forecast profit. What is the actual profit?

8. **LO4** Renalda sold Westel stock that she purchased at $2.20 per share one year ago for a 35% gain. At what price did she sell the stock?

9. **LO5** Luther is paid an annual salary of $56,600 based on a 37.5-hour workweek.
    a. What is his equivalent hourly wage? (Assume that a year has exactly 52 weeks.)
    b. What would be his total remuneration for a biweekly pay period of that year if he worked 4.5 hours of overtime at time and a half?

10. **LO5** Istvan earns an annual salary of $61,000 as an executive with a provincial utility. He is paid biweekly. During a strike, he worked 33 hours more than the regular 75 hours for a two-week pay period. What was his gross pay for that period if the company agreed to pay 1.5 times his equivalent hourly rate for overtime? (Assume that a year has exactly 52 weeks.)

11. **LO5** Sonja is paid $42.50 per hour as a veterinarian. She is paid $1\frac{1}{2}$ times the regular rate for all time exceeding $7\frac{1}{2}$ hours in a day or $37\frac{1}{2}$ hours per week. Work on a statutory holiday is paid at double time. What were her gross earnings for a week in which she worked 6, 0, 3, $7\frac{1}{2}$, 9, $7\frac{1}{2}$, and 8 hours on Saturday to Friday, respectively, and the Monday was a statutory holiday?

12. **LO5** Marion receives a monthly base salary of $1000. On the first $10,000 of sales above her monthly quota of $20,000, she is paid a commission of 8%. On any additional sales, the commission rate is 10%. What were her gross earnings for the month of August, in which she had sales amounting to $38,670?

13. **LO5** Lauren's gross pay for July was $3188.35 on net sales totalling $88,630. If her base salary is $1000 per month, what is her rate of commission on sales exceeding her monthly quota of $40,000?

14. **LO5** Havel signed a listing agreement with a real estate agent. The commission rate is 4% on the first $200,000 of the selling price, and 2.5% on the remainder.
    a. What commission will Havel pay if he sells his home for $289,000?
    b. What is the average commission rate on the selling price?

15. **LO6** "Souvenirs and Such" is a gift shop in Niagara Falls. Last year 22% of its revenue came from the sale of clothing, 18% from food items, 32% from novelty items, and the remainder from special services the shop provided for tourists. This past year the shop experienced a 5% increase in the sale of clothing, a 2% increase in the sale of food items, a 9% drop in novelty items, and a 2% drop in special services. What is the shop's average change in revenue for this year?

16. **LO6** Ms. Yong invested a total of $73,400 in three mutual funds as shown in the following table. The third column shows the change in value of each fund during the subsequent six months.

Mutual fund	Amount invested ($)	Change in value (%)
Canadian equity fund	16,800	−4.3
US equity fund	25,600	−1.1
Global equity fund	31,000	8.2

What was the percent change in value of Ms. Yong's overall mutual fund portfolio during the six-month holding period?

17. **LO6** One year ago Helga allocated the funds in her portfolio among five securities in the amounts listed in the following table. The rate of return on each security for the year is given in the third column of the table.

Security	Amount invested ($)	Rate of return for the year (%)
Company U shares	5000	30
Province V bonds	20,000	−3
Company W shares	8000	−15
Units in Fund X	25,000	13
Company Y shares	4500	45

Calculate the average rate of return for the entire portfolio.

INTERMEDIATE PROBLEMS

18. **LO6** Anthony began the year with $96,400 already invested in his Snow 'n Ice retail store. He withdrew $14,200 on March 1 and another $21,800 on April 1. On August 1, he invested $23,700, and on November 1, he contributed another $19,300. What was his average cumulative investment during the year? (Assume that each month has the same length.)

19. **LO6** The fiscal year for Pine Valley Skiing Ltd., the owner of a downhill skiing facility, ends on June 30. The company began the recently completed fiscal year with its summer maintenance crew of seven employees. During the fiscal year, employees were hired or laid off on various dates as shown.

Date	Employee changes
September 1	6 hired
November 1	18 hired
December 1	23 hired
March 1	11 laid off
April 1	20 laid off
May 1	16 laid off

What was the average number of employees working for Pine Valley during the fiscal year? (Assume that each month has the same length.)

APPENDIX 1A: THE TEXAS INSTRUMENTS BA II PLUS FORMAT SETTINGS

The calculator allows you to control some aspects of how values are displayed. This section explains how you gain access to and make changes to a list of format settings.

Immediately above the decimal key (in the bottom row of keys) you will find the word FORMAT. This position means that the "format" settings are the secondary function of the key. To access the list of settings, press the | 2nd | key followed by the decimal key. Hereafter, we will represent this keystroke sequence as | 2nd | Format |.

Press | 2nd | Format |. The calculator's display now shows:

DEC =	n

where n is one of the digits, 0 to 9. Before we discuss this particular display, you should know that the display is revealing just the first item in the following vertical list:

DEC =	n
DEG	
US	mm-dd-yyyy
US	1,000.
Chn	

You can move down the list using the scroll-down key | ↓ |. Scroll through the entire list by pressing | ↓ | four times. Return to the top of the list by pressing | ↑ | four times or by pressing | ↓ | one more time.

The first item in the list indicates the number, n, of decimal places that will be shown in your display. A setting of "9" gives you a floating-decimal display. This means you will see either the *actual* number of decimal places for a terminating decimal, or *nine* decimal places for a nonterminating decimal. (Both alternatives are subject to the limit of 10 digits in the display.) The floating-decimal display is the best general-purpose setting for us. If the current setting is not "9," change it to "9" by pressing

9 | ENTER |

Scroll down to the second item in the list (probably appearing as *DEG*). It does not concern us in business math. Scroll down to the third item. The factory setting is

US 12-31-1990

This means that the format for calendar dates is the American format of mm-dd-yyyy (rather than the European format of dd-mm-yyyy). Leave the calculator in the American format and scroll down to the fourth item. The factory setting is

US 1,000.

This means that the calculator is using the American and British convention of employing commas for separators in numbers (rather than the continental European convention of using dots).

Scroll down to the fifth and last item. In the display you will see either "*Chn*" or "*AOS.*" These are alternatives for how the calculator handles the sequence of mathematical operations you enter on the keypad. In the "*Chn*" (chain) calculation method, operations are performed in the sequence you enter them. That is, if you enter

$$5 \boxed{+} 4 \boxed{\times} 2 \boxed{=}$$

the calculator does the 5 + 4 addition before the multiplication, giving a result of 18. (Don't try it while you are still in the Format list.)

In the "*AOS*" (algebraic operating system) calculation method, the calculator performs operations according to the standard order of operations presented in **Section 1.1**. The same calculation then yields the result 13, because the calculator does the multiplication before the addition.

With either "*Chn*" or "*AOS*" in the display, you can switch to the other calculation method by pressing $\boxed{\text{2nd}}$ $\boxed{\text{SET}}$. By the $\boxed{\text{SET}}$ key, we mean the key having SET as its secondary function. The setting you choose is a matter of personal preference. In either case, you can use the calculator's bracket keys to provide further control over the order of calculations.

Now close and exit from the settings list by pressing $\boxed{\text{2nd}}$ $\boxed{\text{QUIT}}$. By the $\boxed{\text{QUIT}}$ key, we mean the key having QUIT as its secondary function. The settings you have made will remain (even after the calculator is turned off) until you change them.

Chapter 2
Review and Applications of Algebra

CHAPTER OUTLINE

2.1 Operations with Algebraic Expressions

2.2 Rules and Properties of Exponents

2.3 Solving Linear Equations

2.4 Manipulating Equations and Formulas

2.5 Solving Word Problems

LEARNING OBJECTIVES

After completing this chapter, you will be able to:

LO1 Simplify algebraic expressions by extracting common factors and applying rules of exponents

LO2 Solve a linear equation in one variable

LO3 Rearrange a formula or equation to isolate a particular variable

LO4 Solve "word problems" that lead to a linear equation in one unknown

ALGEBRA IS A BRANCH OF MATHEMATICS in which letters or symbols are used to represent various items (variables). Quantitative relationships (equations) can then be expressed in a concise manner. Algebra has rules and procedures for working with these equations. The rules enable us to calculate values of unknown variables and to derive new relationships among variables.

Algebra is vital for the application of mathematics to business. We (or our computers) make use of equations describing relationships among real-world variables. If your algebraic skills are rusty, you may need to spend more time doing exercises in the first four sections of the chapter than is allotted in your course schedule.

We begin by reviewing basic terminology, techniques for simplifying algebraic expressions, and procedures for solving linear equations. Our refurbished skills will then be employed in solving word problems.

 TIP

How to Succeed in Business Mathematics

Since various Business Mathematics and Mathematics of Finance courses start at different points in the book, this Tip appears at the beginning of each of the first five chapters. Connect has a guide entitled "How to Succeed in Business Mathematics." Read its first two sections (A.1 and A.2) as soon as possible.

If your course bypassed **Chapter 1** and you are using a Texas Instruments BA II PLUS calculator, refer to **Appendix 1A** for information about settings that affect the calculator's display and order of operations.

2.1 Operations with Algebraic Expressions

Definitions

Business problems that use standard calculations with different numbers for different situations use **algebraic expression** to provide a general solution. The algebraic expression uses letters or symbols as **variables** to represent the quantities that can vary in the solution to the problem.

We will use some simple examples from **Section 1.3** to illustrate some basic language of algebra.

Problem	Variables	Algebraic expression
Gross pay is $11.25 per *hour worked*	Let H represent the number of *hours worked*	Gross pay = $11.25 \times H$
Gross pay is $2500 a month plus 4% of *sales*	Let S represent monthly *sales*	Gross pay = $2500 + 0.04S$
A 5% bonus is awarded on all *sales* over $8000	Let S represent total *sales*	Bonus = $0.05(S - \$8000)$

To obtain a solution to any of the problems above, we simply substitute a specific value for the variable.

The components of an algebraic expression that are separated by addition or subtraction signs are called **terms**.

The expression $2x$, containing only one term, is called a **monomial**.

The expression $2x + 5$ is a **binomial**, containing two terms.

The expression $3x^2 + 2x + 5$ is a **trinomial** and has three terms.

The name **polynomial** may be used for any expression with more than one term.

Each term in an expression consists of one or more **factors** separated by multiplication or division signs. (Multiplication is implied by writing factors side by side with no multiplication symbol between them.) The numerical factor in a term is called the **numerical coefficient**, and the variable factors together are called the **literal coefficient**.

EXAMPLE 2.1A

IDENTIFYING THE TERMS, FACTORS, AND COEFFICIENTS IN A POLYNOMIAL[1]

$3x^2 + xy - 6y^2$ is a trinomial.

Term	Factors	Numerical coefficient	Literal coefficient
$3x^2$	$3, x, x$	3	x^2
xy	x, y	1	xy
$-6y^2$	$-6, y, y$	-6	y^2

Addition and Subtraction

L01 Sometimes an algebraic expression may be simplified by adding or subtracting certain terms before any values are substituted for the variables. Terms with the same *literal* coefficients are called **like terms**. Only like terms may be directly added or subtracted. Addition or subtraction of like terms is performed by adding or subtracting their numerical coefficients while keeping their common literal coefficient. For example, $2xy + 3xy = 5xy$. Adding or subtracting like terms is often referred to as *collecting* or *combining* like terms.

EXAMPLE 2.1B

SIMPLIFYING ALGEBRAIC EXPRESSIONS BY COMBINING LIKE TERMS

a. $3a - 4b - 7a + 9b$ $3a$ and $-7a$ are like terms; $-4b$ and $9b$ are like terms.

$= 3a - 7a - 4b + 9b$ Combine the numerical coefficients of like terms.

$= (3 - 7)a + (-4 + 9)b$

$= -4a + 5b$

b. $0.2x + 5x^2 + \frac{x}{4} - x + 3$ Convert numerical coefficients to their decimal equivalents.

$= 0.2x + 5x^2 + 0.25x - 1x + 3$ Then combine the like terms.

$= 5x^2 + (0.2 + 0.25 - 1)x + 3$

$= 5x^2 - 0.55x + 3$

c. $\frac{2x}{1.25} - \frac{4}{5} - 1\frac{3}{4}x$ Convert numerical coefficients to their decimal equivalents.

$= 1.6x - 0.8 - 1.75x$ Then combine the like terms.

$= (1.6 - 1.75)x - 0.8$

$= -0.15x - 0.8$

d. $\frac{3x}{1.0164} + 1.049x - x$ Evaluate the numerical coefficients.

$= 2.95159x + 1.049x - 1x$ Combine the like terms.

$= (2.95159 + 1.049 - 1)x$

$= 3.0006x$

e. $x\left(1 + 0.12 \times \frac{241}{365}\right) + \frac{2x}{1 + 0.12 \times \frac{81}{365}}$ Evaluate the numerical coefficients.

$= 1.07923x + \frac{2x}{1.02663}$ Combine the like terms.

$= (1.07923 + 1.94812)x$

$= 3.02735x$

---

[1] Exponents and powers are discussed in Section 2.2. For now, it is sufficient to recall that a^2 means $a \times a$, a^3 means $a \times a \times a$, and so on.

Multiplication and Division

Multiplication The product of a monomial and a polynomial is obtained by applying the **distributive property** of multiplication over addition. Every term in the polynomial is multiplied by the monomial. For example:

$$a(b + c) = ab + ac$$

To obtain the product of two polynomials, the distributive property requires the multiplication of *every term* of one polynomial by *every term* of the other polynomial. For example,

$$(a + b)(c + d + e) = a(c + d + e) + b(c + d + e)$$
$$= ac + ad + ae + bc + bd + be$$

After all possible pairs of terms are multiplied, like terms should be combined.

EXAMPLE 2.1C

MULTIPLICATION OF ALGEBRAIC EXPRESSIONS

Expand each of the following expressions by carrying out the indicated multiplication.

a. $-x(2x^2 - 3x - 1)$ Multiply each term in the trinomial by $(-x)$.
$= (-x)(2x^2) + (-x)(-3x) + (-x)(-1)$ The product of two negative quantities is positive.
$= -2x^3 + 3x^2 + x$

b. $3m(4m - 6n + 2)$ Multiply each term in the trinomial by $(3m)$.
$= 3m(4m) + 3m(-6n) + 3m(2)$ In each product, first multiply the numerical coefficients and
$= 12m^2 - 18mn + 6m$ then multiply the literal coefficients.

c. $2(3a - 2b) - (3b - 2a)$ Multiply each term in the first binomial by (2) and each term in
$= (2)(3a) + (2)(-2b) + (-1)(3b) + (-1)(-2a)$ the second binomial by (-1).
$= 6a - 4b - 3b + 2a$ Combine the like terms.
$= 8a - 7b$

d. $(7a - 2b)(3b - 2a)$ Multiply each term of the first binomial by the second binomial.
$= 7a(3b - 2a) - 2b(3b - 2a)$ Combine the like terms.
$= 21ab - 14a^2 - 6b^2 + 4ab$
$= 25ab - 14a^2 - 6b^2$

e. $(x - 2)(2x^2 - 3x - 4)$ Multiply each term of the binomial by the trinomial.
$= x(2x^2 - 3x - 4) - 2(2x^2 - 3x - 4)$ Combine the like terms.
$= 2x^3 - 3x^2 - 4x - 4x^2 + 6x + 8$
$= 2x^3 - 7x^2 + 2x + 8$

Division When dividing a polynomial by a monomial, *each term* of the polynomial must be divided by the monomial.

Although there are a few cases in this book where a monomial or a polynomial is divided by a polynomial, you will not be required to perform the division algebraically.

> ✓ **TIP**
>
> ### Dividing Out Common Factors
>
> When dividing out a common factor, remember that *every term* in the numerator and *every term* in the denominator must be divided by that common factor. This is sometimes called "cancelling" common factors. A common error made when dividing a polynomial by a monomial is to cancel one of the factors in the denominator with the same factor in just one of the terms in the numerator. The common factor must be divided out or cancelled in *every term* in the numerator.
>
> Suppose we want to simplify the expression $\dfrac{4x + 2}{2}$.
>
> The denominator 2 must be distributed to every term in the numerator. To illustrate this distribution we could rewrite the expression as:
>
> $$\frac{4x}{2} + \frac{2}{2}$$
>
> Simplifying each term gives us the correct simplified expression $2x + 1$.
>
> If you are ever in doubt, substitute a value for x into both the original and simplified expressions. If $x = 5$, then
>
> $$\frac{4(5) + 2}{2} = \frac{22}{2} = 11 \qquad \text{and} \qquad 2(5) + 1 = 10 + 1 = 11$$
>
> Since the values are the same, the simplification is correct.

EXAMPLE 2.1D

DIVISION BY A MONOMIAL

Simplify each of the following expressions.

a. $\dfrac{36x^2y}{60xy^2}$ Identify factors in the numerator and denominator.

$= \dfrac{3(12)(x)(x)(y)}{5(12)(x)(y)(y)}$ Divide out factors that appear in both the numerator and the denominator.

$= \dfrac{3x}{5y}$

b. $\dfrac{48a^2 - 32ab}{8a}$ Divide each term in the numerator by the denominator.

$= \dfrac{48(a)(a)}{8(a)} - \dfrac{32(a)(b)}{8(a)}$ Divide out factors that appear in both the numerator and the denominator.

$= 6a - 4b$

c. $\dfrac{225(1 + i)^4}{75(1 + i)^2}$ Identify factors that are common to both the numerator and the denominator.

$= \dfrac{3(75)(1 + i)^2 (1 + i)^2}{75(1 + i)^2}$ Divide out common factors.

$= 3(1 + i)^2$

Substitution

Substitution means assigning a numerical value to each of the algebraic symbols in an expression. Then evaluate the expression by carrying out all the indicated operations.

Referring back to our examples from **Section 1.3** it is possible to calculate a specific gross pay or bonus in each by substituting in a possible value for the variable.

Problem	Substitution for the variable	Solution
Gross pay is $11.25 per *hour worked*	Since H represents the number of hours worked let $H = 44$ hours	Gross pay $= \$11.25 \times H$ $= \$11.25 \times 44$ $= \$495.00$
Gross pay is $2500 a month plus 4% of *sales*	Since S represents monthly sales let $S = \$1900$	Gross pay $= \$2500 + 0.04S$ $= \$2500 + 0.04(\$1900)$ $= \$2500 + \$76.00$ $= \$2576.00$
A 5% bonus is awarded on all *sales* over $8000	Since S represents total sales let $S = \$12,000$	Bonus $= 0.05(S - \$8000)$ $= 0.05(\$12,000 - \$8000)$ $= 0.05(\$4000)$ $= \$200$

EXAMPLE 2.1E

EVALUATING ALGEBRAIC EXPRESSIONS AFTER SUBSTITUTING NUMERICAL VALUES FOR THE VARIABLES

Evaluate each of the following expressions for the given values of the variables.

a. $8p - 9q$ for $p = 2.5$, $q = -6$

b. $3x^2 - 7x - 4$ for $x = -3$

c. $P(1 + rt)$ for $P = \$100$, $r = 0.09$, $t = \frac{7}{12}$

d. $(1 + i)^m - 1$ for $i = 0.05$, $m = 2$

e. $\dfrac{S}{(1 + i)^n}$ for $S = \$1240$, $i = 0.025$, $n = 4$

f. $R\left[\dfrac{(1 + i)^n - 1}{i}\right]$ for $R = \$2000$, $i = 0.0225$, $n = 3$

SOLUTION

a. $8p - 9q = 8(2.5) - 9(-6)$ Replace p by 2.5 and q by -6.
$\quad\quad\quad\quad = 20 + 54$
$\quad\quad\quad\quad = 74$

b. $3x^2 - 7x - 4 = 3(-3)^2 - 7(-3) - 4$ Replace x by -3.
$\quad\quad\quad\quad\quad = 3(9) + 21 - 4$
$\quad\quad\quad\quad\quad = 27 + 17$
$\quad\quad\quad\quad\quad = 44$

c. $P(1 + rt) = \$100\left(1 + 0.09 \times \frac{7}{12}\right) = \$100(1 + 0.0525) = \$105.25$

d. $(1 + i)^m - 1 = (1 + 0.05)^2 - 1 = 1.05^2 - 1 = 1.1025 - 1 = 0.1025$

e. Particularly in later chapters, we will employ callout boxes to present a sequence of keystrokes that may be used on the Texas Instruments BA II PLUS financial calculator for an efficient computation. Here we present this style for the first time.

$$\frac{S}{(1 + i)^n} = \frac{\$1240}{(1 + 0.025)^4}$$

$$= \frac{\$1240}{1.025^4}$$

$$= \frac{\$1240}{1.103813}$$

$$= \$1123.38$$

1240 ÷

(1.025 y^x 4)

=

Ans: 1123.38

Note that we use a "curly" bracket called a *brace* to indicate the group of mathematical operations performed by the calculator. (You do not need to enter the brackets as indicated in the callout box if your BA II PLUS calculator is set in the AOS mode. See Appendix 1A regarding this and other FORMAT settings.)

f. $R\left[\dfrac{(1+i)^n - 1}{i}\right] = \$2000\left[\dfrac{(1 + 0.0225)^3 - 1}{0.0225}\right]$

$= \$2000\left(\dfrac{1.0225^3 - 1}{0.0225}\right)$

$= \$2000\left(\dfrac{1.0690301 - 1}{0.0225}\right)$

$= \$2000(3.068006)$

$= \$6136.01$

$(\quad 1.0225 \quad y^x \quad 3 \quad - \quad 1 \quad)$

$\div \quad 0.0225 \quad \times \quad 2000 \quad =$

Ans: 6136.01

EXERCISE 2.1

Answers to the odd-numbered problems are at the end of the book.

CALCULATOR-FREE PROBLEMS

Simplify each of the following and collect the like terms.

a. $(-p) + (-3p) + (4p)$

b. $5s - 2t - 2s - 4t$

c. $4x^2y - 3x^2y + (-5x^2y)$

d. $(5s - 2t) - (2s - 4t)$

e. $4x^2y + (-3x^2y) - (-5x^2y)$

f. $1 - (7e^2 - 5 + 3e - e^3)$

g. $(6x^2 - 3xy + 4y^2) - (8y^2 - 10xy - x^2)$

h. $(7m^3 - m - 6m^2 + 10) - (5m^3 - 9 + 3m - 2m^2)$

i. $2(7x - 3y) - 3(2x - 3y)$

j. $4(a^2 - 3a - 4) - 2(5a^2 - a - 6)$

k. $15x - [4 - 5x - 6]$

l. $6a - [3a - 2b - a]$

m. $15x - [4 - 2(5x - 6)]$

n. $6a - [3a - 2(2b - a)]$

Perform the multiplication or division indicated in each of the following expressions and collect the like terms.

o. $4a(3ab - 5a + 6b)$

p. $9k(4 - 8k + 7k^2)$

q. $-5xy(2x^2 - xy - 3y^2)$

r. $-(p^2 - 4pq - 5p)\left(\dfrac{2q}{p}\right)$

s. $(4r - 3t)(2t + 5r)$

t. $(3p^2 - 5p)(-4p + 2)$

u. $(4r - 3t) - (2t + 5r)$

v. $(3p^2 - 5p) + (-4p + 2)$

w. $3(a - 2)(4a + 1) - 5(2a + 3)(a - 7)$

x. $5(2x - y)(y + 3x) - 6x(x - 5y)$

y. $\dfrac{18x^2}{3x}$

z. $\dfrac{6a^2b}{-2ab^2}$

aa. $\dfrac{x^2y - xy^2}{xy}$

bb. $\dfrac{-4x + 10x^2 - 6x^3}{-0.5x}$

cc. $\dfrac{12x^3 - 24x^2 + 36x}{48x}$

dd. $\dfrac{32a^2b - 8ab + 14ab^2}{2ab}$

ee. $\dfrac{4a^2b^3 - 6a^3b^2}{2ab^2}$

ff. $\dfrac{120(1 + i)^2 + 180(1 + i)^3}{360(1 + i)}$

gg. $\dfrac{4a^2b^3 - 6ab^2 + 2ab^3}{2ab^3}$

hh. $\dfrac{12(1 + i) + 18(1 + i)^2}{36(1 + i)^2}$

BASIC PROBLEMS

Evaluate each of the following expressions for the given values of the variables. In Problems 1–11, calculate the result accurate to the nearest cent.

1. $3d^2 - 4d + \$15$ for $d = \$2.50$

2. $15g - 9h + \$3$ for $g = \$14$, $h = \$15$

3. $7x(4y - \$8)$ for $x = \$3.20$, $y = \$1.50$

4. $I \div Pr$ for $P = \$500$, $I = \$13.75$, $r = 0.11$

5. $\dfrac{I}{rt}$ for $r = 0.095$, $I = \$23.21$, $t = \dfrac{283}{365}$

6. $\dfrac{N}{1-d}$ for $N = \$89.10$, $d = 0.10$

7. $L(1 - d_1)(1 - d_2)(1 - d_3)$ for $L = \$490$, $d_1 = 0.125$, $d_2 = 0.15$, $d_3 = 0.05$

8. $P(1 + rt)$ for $P = \$770$, $r = 0.013$, $t = \dfrac{223}{365}$

9. $\dfrac{S}{1 + rt}$ for $S = \$2500$, $r = 0.085$, $t = \dfrac{123}{365}$

10. $\dfrac{S}{(1 + i)^n}$ for $S = \$850$, $i = 0.0075$, $n = 6$

11. $P(1 + i)^n$ for $P = \$1280$, $i = 0.025$, $n = 3$

INTERMEDIATE PROBLEMS

Simplify each of the following and collect the like terms. Maintain five-figure accuracy in Problems 12–19.

12. $\dfrac{x}{2} - x^2 + \dfrac{4}{5} - 0.2x^2 - \dfrac{4}{5}x + \dfrac{1}{2}$

13. $\dfrac{2x + 9}{4} - 1.2\,(x - 1)$

14. $\dfrac{2x}{1.045} - \dfrac{2.016x}{3} + \dfrac{x}{2}$

15. $\dfrac{8x}{0.5} + \dfrac{5.5x}{11} + 0.5(4.6x - 17)$

16. $y\left(1 - 0.125 \times \dfrac{213}{365}\right) + \dfrac{2y}{1 + 0.125 \times \frac{88}{365}}$

17. $\dfrac{P}{1 + 0.095 \times \frac{5}{12}} + 2P\left(1 + 0.095 \times \dfrac{171}{365}\right)$

18. $\dfrac{h}{(1 + 0.055)^2} - 3h(1 + 0.055)^3$

19. $k(1 + 0.04)^2 + \dfrac{2k}{(1 + 0.04)^2}$

Evaluate each of the following expressions for the given values of the variables. In Problems 21–24, calculate the result accurate to the nearest cent.

20. $(1 + i)^m - 1$ for $i = 0.0225$, $m = 4$

21. $R\left[\dfrac{(1 + i)^n - 1}{i}\right]$ for $R = \$550$, $i = 0.085$, $n = 3$

22. $R\left[\dfrac{(1 + i)^n - 1}{i}\right](1 + i)$ for $R = \$910$, $i = 0.1038129$, $n = 4$

23. $\dfrac{R}{i}\left[1 - \dfrac{1}{(1 + i)^n}\right]$ for $R = \$630$, $i = 0.115$, $n = 2$

24. $P(1 + rt_1) + \dfrac{S}{1 + rt_2}$ for $P = \$470$, $S = \$390$, $r = 0.075$, $t_1 = \dfrac{104}{365}$, $t_2 = \dfrac{73}{365}$

2.2 Rules and Properties of Exponents

The use of exponents allows us to write algebraic expressions containing repeated factors in a more concise form. If n is a positive integer, then a^n is defined by

$$a^n = a \times a \times a \times \ldots \times a \ (n \text{ factors})$$

In this notation, a is called the **base**, n is called the **exponent**, and a^n is read as "a to the n" or "a to the exponent n." The value obtained for a^n is referred to as "the nth power of a" or sometimes just as "the **power**." That is,

$$\text{Power} = \text{Base}^{\text{Exponent}}$$

For example, $4^3 = 4 \times 4 \times 4 = 64$. In this example, the base is 4, the exponent is 3, and the power is 64. The exponent tells us how many times the base is used as a factor. Note that the power is not the same thing as the exponent—the power is the product resulting from the multiplication. We will use powers extensively in later chapters for compound interest calculations.

EXAMPLE 2.2A

EVALUATING POWERS WITH POSITIVE INTEGRAL EXPONENTS

a. $3^4 = 3 \times 3 \times 3 \times 3 = 81$ The base is 3, the exponent is 4, and the power is 81. The fourth power of 3 is 81.

b. $0.1^4 = 0.1 \times 0.1 \times 0.1 \times 0.1 = 0.0001$

c. $\left(\frac{3}{4}\right)^3 = \left(\frac{3}{4}\right)\left(\frac{3}{4}\right)\left(\frac{3}{4}\right) = \frac{3 \times 3 \times 3}{4 \times 4 \times 4} = \frac{27}{64} = (0.75)(0.75)(0.75) = 0.421875$

d. $(1.035)^3 = 1.035 \times 1.035 \times 1.035 = 1.108718$

e. $(-2)^3 = (-2)(-2)(-2) = -8$ An odd power of a negative base is negative.

f. $(-0.9)^4 = (-0.9)(-0.9)(-0.9)(-0.9) = 0.6561$ An even power of a negative base is positive.

 TIP

The Immediate-Left Trick

Compare $(-2)^3$ and -2^3. In which situation is the negative sign part of the base?

We know that Power = Base^{Exponent}. The base is always to the immediate left of the exponent.

In **Example 2.2A** the powers $(-2)^3$ and $(-0.9)^4$ have a bracket to the immediate left of the exponent, meaning that the entire contents of the brackets, including the negative sign, is the base of the power. Without the brackets, the negative sign is NOT part of the base.

$$-0.9^4 \text{ also means } -1 \times 0.9^4 = -1 \times 0.9 \times 0.9 \times 0.9 \times 0.9 = -0.6561,$$
$$\text{whereas } (-0.9)^4 = (-0.9) \times (-0.9) \times (-0.9) \times (-0.9) = 0.6561$$

The same difference is true for powers such as $-\left(\frac{2}{3}\right)^3$ compared to $\left(-\frac{2}{3}\right)^3$ compared to $-\frac{2^3}{3}$.

The bases for these powers are $\frac{2}{3}$, $-\frac{2}{3}$, and 2, respectively.

A few mathematical operations involving powers occur so frequently that it is convenient to have a set of rules that provide shortcuts. The derivation of the following rules of exponents is straightforward and may be found in any introductory algebra text.

Rules of Exponents:

1. $a^m \times a^n = a^{m+n}$
2. $\dfrac{a^m}{a^n} = a^{m-n}$
3. $(a^m)^n = a^{m \times n}$
4. $(ab)^n = a^n b^n$
5. $\left(\dfrac{a}{b}\right)^n = \dfrac{a^n}{b^n}$

EXAMPLE 2.2B

USING THE RULES OF EXPONENTS TO SIMPLIFY ALGEBRAIC EXPRESSIONS

Simplify or evaluate the following expressions.

a. $3^2 \times 3^3 = 3^{2+3} = 3^5 = 243$ ⟶ Rule 1

b. $y^5 \times y^4 = y^{5+4} = y^9$ ⟶ Rule 1

c. $(1+i)^6 \times (1+i)^{11} = (1+i)^{6+11} = (1+i)^{17}$ ⟶ Rule 1

d. $\dfrac{1.01^8}{1.01^5} = 1.01^{8-5} = 1.01^3 = 1.030301$ ⟶ Rule 2

e. $\dfrac{(1+i)^{20}}{(1+i)^8} = (1+i)^{20-8} = (1+i)^{12}$ ⟶ Rule 2

f. $\dfrac{x^5 \times x^{14}}{x^9} = x^{5+14-9} = x^{10}$ ⟶ Rules 1 and 2

g. $(k^4)^5 = k^{4 \times 5} = k^{20}$ ⟶ Rule 3

h. $(3^2)^4 = 3^{2 \times 4} = 3^8 = 6561$ ⟶ Rule 3

i. $(5q)^3 = 5^3 q^3 = 125q^3$ ⟶ Rule 4

j. $\left(\dfrac{0.5}{x}\right)^2 = \dfrac{0.5^2}{x^2} = \dfrac{0.25}{x^2}$ ⟶ Rule 5

k. $\left(\dfrac{3x^6 y^3}{x^2 z^3}\right)^2 = \left(\dfrac{3x^4 y^3}{z^3}\right)^2$ ⟶ Rule 2

$\qquad = \dfrac{3^2 x^{4 \times 2} y^{3 \times 2}}{z^{3 \times 2}}$ ⟶ Rules 4 and 5

$\qquad = \dfrac{9x^8 y^6}{z^6}$

Zero, negative, and fractional exponents have the following rules in order to be consistent with the definition of a^n and the first three rules of exponents.

Rules of Zero, Negative, and Fractional Exponents:

6. $a^0 = 1$
7. $a^{-n} = \dfrac{1}{a^n}$ OR $\left(\dfrac{a}{b}\right)^{-n} = \left(\dfrac{b}{a}\right)^n$
8. $a^{1/n} = \sqrt[n]{a}$
9. $a^{m/n} = (\sqrt[n]{a})^m = \sqrt[n]{a^m}$

TIP

Using the Power Function Key with Negative Exponents

Press the "sign change" key, $+/-$, after you enter the exponent. For example, to evaluate 1.62^{-5}, the sequence of keystrokes is:

$$1.62 \boxed{y^x} \; 5 \boxed{+/-} \; \boxed{=}$$

The answer is 0.089624125.

TIP

Using the Power Function Key with Fractional Exponents

First calculate the decimal equivalent of the fraction and save it in the calculator's memory. Later, when you would normally enter the exponent manually, recall its value from the memory. For example, to evaluate $1.62^{1/6}$, the sequence of keystrokes is:

$$1 \boxed{\div} \; 6 \boxed{=} \boxed{STO} \; 1$$
$$1.62 \boxed{y^x} \boxed{RCL} \; 1 \boxed{=}$$

Alternatively, you can control the order of operations with brackets. A more efficient keystroke sequence is:

$$1.62 \boxed{y^x} \boxed{(} \; 1 \boxed{\div} \; 6 \boxed{)} \boxed{=}$$

The answer is 1.0837252.

EXAMPLE 2.2C

EVALUATING POWERS FOR ZERO, NEGATIVE, AND FRACTIONAL EXPONENTS

Simplify or evaluate the following. Obtain five-figure accuracy in the answers to parts (f) to (l).

a. $7.132^0 = 1$ Rule 6

b. $(0.001)^0 = 1$ Rule 6

c. $(0.001)^{-1} = \dfrac{1}{0.001} = 1000$ Rule 7

d. $(1 + i)^{-n} = \dfrac{1}{(1 + i)^n}$ Rule 7

e. $\left(\dfrac{x}{y}\right)^{-2} = \left(\dfrac{y}{x}\right)^2 = \dfrac{y^2}{x^2}$ Rules 7 and 5

f. $\left(-\dfrac{4}{5}\right)^{-2} = \left(-\dfrac{5}{4}\right)^2 = (-1.25)^2 = 1.5625$ Rule 7

g. $(1.0125)^{-5} = \left(\dfrac{1}{1.0125}\right)^5 = (0.987654)^5 = 0.93978$ Rule 7

$$1.0125 \boxed{y^x}$$
$$\boxed{(} \; 1 \boxed{\div} \; 5 \boxed{)} \boxed{=}$$

h. $(1.0125)^{1/5} = \sqrt[5]{1.0125} = (1.0125)^{0.2} = 1.0025$ Rule 8

Ans: 1.0025

i. $\left(\dfrac{3}{2}\right)^{3/2} = 1.5^{3/2} = \sqrt{1.5^3} = \sqrt{3.375} = 1.8371 = 1.5^{1.5} = 1.8371$ Rule 9

j. $\$321(1 + 0.025)^{-8} = \$321(0.820747) = \$263.46$ Rule 7

1.025 $\boxed{y^x}$ 8 $\boxed{+/-}$

$\boxed{\times}$ 321 $\boxed{=}$

Ans: 263.46

k. $(2.025)^{-(1/4)} = \left(\dfrac{1}{2.025}\right)^{\left(\frac{1}{4}\right)} = (0.493827)^{0.25} = 0.83829$ Rules 7 and 8

l. $\dfrac{1 - (1.025)^{-30}}{0.025} = \dfrac{1 - 0.476743}{0.025} = 20.930$ Assuming the "AOS" calculation setting (see Appendix 1A)   Rule 7

$\boxed{(}$ 1 $\boxed{-}$ 1.025 $\boxed{y^x}$ 30 $\boxed{+/-}$ $\boxed{)}$

$\boxed{\div}$ 0.025 $\boxed{=}$

Ans: 20.930

EXERCISE 2.2

Answers to the odd-numbered problems are at the end of the book.

CALCULATOR-FREE PROBLEMS

Simplify each of the following.

a. $a^2 \times a^3$ **b.** $(x^6)(x^{-4})$ **c.** $b^{10} \div b^6$

d. $h^7 \div h^{-4}$ **e.** $(1 + i)^4 \times (1 + i)^9$ **f.** $(1 + i) \times (1 + i)^n$

g. $(x^4)^7$ **h.** $(y^3)^3$ **i.** $(t^6)^{1/3}$

j. $(n^{0.5})^8$ **k.** $\dfrac{(x^5)(x^6)}{x^9}$ **l.** $\dfrac{(x^5)^6}{x^9}$

m. $[2(1 + i)]^2$ **n.** $\left(\dfrac{1 + i}{3i}\right)^3$ **o.** $\dfrac{4r^5t^6}{(2r^2t)^3}$

p. $\dfrac{(-r^3)(2r)^4}{(2r^{-2})^2}$

BASIC PROBLEMS

Evaluate each of the following expressions to six-figure accuracy.

1. $8^{4/3}$ **2.** $-27^{2/3}$ **3.** $7^{3/2}$

4. $5^{-3/4}$ **5.** $(0.001)^{-2}$ **6.** $0.893^{-1/2}$

7. $(1.0085)^5 (1.0085)^3$ **8.** $(1.005)^3 (1.005)^{-6}$ **9.** $\sqrt[3]{1.03}$

10. $\sqrt[6]{1.05}$

INTERMEDIATE PROBLEMS

Evaluate each of the following expressions to six-figure accuracy.

11. $(4^4)(3^{-3})\left(-\dfrac{3}{4}\right)^3$ **12.** $\left[\left(-\dfrac{3}{4}\right)^2\right]^{-2}$ **13.** $\left(\dfrac{2}{3}\right)^3 \left(-\dfrac{3}{2}\right)^2 \left(-\dfrac{3}{2}\right)^{-3}$

14. $\left(-\dfrac{2}{3}\right)^3 \div \left(\dfrac{3}{2}\right)^{-2}$ **15.** $\dfrac{1.03^{16} - 1}{0.03}$ **16.** $\dfrac{(1.008\overline{3})^{30} - 1}{0.008\overline{3}}$

17. $\dfrac{1 - 1.0225^{-20}}{0.0225}$ **18.** $\dfrac{1 - (1.00\overline{6})^{-32}}{0.00\overline{6}}$ **19.** $(1 + 0.0275)^{1/3}$

20. $(1 + 0.055)^{1/6} - 1$

2.3 Solving Linear Equations

Most of the applications and problems in this book will result in an equation containing a single variable or unknown. If this variable's exponent is 1, the equation is a **linear equation**. If the variable appears with an exponent other than 1, the equation is a **nonlinear equation**.

EXAMPLE 2.3A

EXAMPLES OF LINEAR AND NONLINEAR EQUATIONS

a. $3x - 7 = 5 - 9x$ is a linear equation.

b. $x^2 - x = 12$ is a nonlinear equation because x has an exponent different from 1 in one of the terms.

c. $\$150(1 + i)^4 = \$219.62$ is a nonlinear equation because of the presence of terms in i^4, i^3, and i^2 when $(1 + i)^4$ is expanded.

d. $2^x = 32$ is a nonlinear equation because x is in the exponent.

Solving a Linear Equation in One Unknown

L02 A **root** or solution of an equation is any numerical value of the variable that makes the two sides of the equation equal; it makes the equation true. For example, $x = 1$ is a root of $3x - 7 = 5 - 9x$ because both sides have the same value (-4) when you substitute $x = 1$.

A linear equation in one variable has only one root; a nonlinear equation may have more than one root. The process of determining the root or roots of the equation is called *solving the equation*. The procedure for solving a linear equation involves three steps:

1. Separate like terms, leaving terms containing the variable on one side of the equation and the remaining terms on the other side of the equation.
2. Combine the like terms on each side of the equation.
3. Obtain the root or solution by dividing both sides of the equation by the numerical coefficient of the variable.

After you calculate the root of an equation, you can verify that it is a root by substituting it in the original equation. The root is correct (and is said to *satisfy* the equation) if the resulting values of both sides of the equation are equal.

EXAMPLE 2.3B

SOLVING LINEAR EQUATIONS IN ONE UNKNOWN

Solve the following equations and verify the solutions.

a. $8x - 11 = 5x + 4$　　　　**b.** $0.5x - 0.75 + 7x = 3x + 1.5$　　　　**c.** $5(x - 4) + 2 = 2(x + 2) - 1$

SOLUTION

a.　　　$8x - 11 = 5x + 4$

$8x - 11 - \mathbf{5x} = 5x + 4 - \mathbf{5x}$　　Subtract $5x$ from both sides so that terms in x will be on the left side only.

$3x - 11 = 4$　　Simplify both sides by collecting like terms.

Note that moving $5x$ from the right side to the left side with a change of sign also produces this result. It is more efficient to use this shortcut (called *transposition*).

$3x - 11 + \mathbf{11} = 4 + \mathbf{11}$　　Add 11 to both sides so that numerical terms will be on the right side only.

$3x = 15$　　Simplify both sides.

Transposing the term "-11" with a change of sign from the left side to the right side produces this same result.

$$\frac{3x}{3} = \frac{15}{3}$$ Divide both sides by the numerical coefficient of x.

$$x = 5$$ Simplify both sides to solve for x.

Verification:

Left-hand side (LHS) $= 8x - 11$ Right-hand side (RHS) $= 5x + 4$

$= 8(5) - 11$ $= 5(5) + 4$

$= 29$ $= 29$

Since LHS = RHS, $x = 5$ is the root, or solution.

b. $0.5x - 0.75 + 7x = 3x + 1.5$ Transpose $3x$ to the LHS and -0.75 to the RHS, and change their signs.

$0.5x + 7x - \mathbf{3x} = 1.5 + \mathbf{0.75}$ Simplify both sides by collecting like terms.

$4.5x = 2.25$ Divide both sides by the coefficient of x.

$$x = \frac{2.25}{4.5}$$

$$x = 0.5$$

Verification:

LHS $= 0.5(0.5) - 0.75 + 7(0.5) = 0.25 - 0.75 + 3.5 = 3.0$

RHS $= 3(0.5) + 1.5 = 1.5 + 1.5 = 3.0$

Since LHS = RHS, $x = 0.5$ is the solution.

c. $5(x - 4) + 2 = 2(x + 2) - 1$

$5x - 20 + 2 = 2x + 4 - 1$ Expand each side using the distributive property of multiplication over addition.

$5x - 18 - \mathbf{2x} = 3$ Transpose $2x$ to the LHS and add the numerical terms to simplify.

$3x = 3 + \mathbf{18}$ Collect like terms on the LHS and transpose -18 to the RHS.

$$\frac{3x}{3} = \frac{21}{3}$$ Divide both sides by 3.

$$x = 7$$

Verification:

LHS $= 5(7 - 4) + 2 = 5(3) + 2 = 15 + 2 = 17$

RHS $= 2(7 + 2) - 1 = 2(9) - 1 = 18 - 1 = 17$

Since LHS = RHS, $x = 7$ is the solution.

EXAMPLE 2.3C

SOLVING LINEAR EQUATIONS HAVING FRACTIONAL COEFFICIENTS

Solve each of the following equations for x (accurate to two decimal places). Verify the solution.

a. $\frac{1}{4}x - \frac{2}{5} = \frac{1}{2}x + \frac{3}{10}$ **b.** $\dfrac{x}{1 + 0.11 \times \frac{75}{365}} + 2x\left(1 + 0.11 \times \frac{92}{365}\right) = \$1150.96$

SOLUTION

a. In this equation, the numerical coefficients are fractions; these coefficients should be changed to decimal form. Then carry on with the usual procedure for solving a linear equation.

$$\frac{1}{4}x - \frac{2}{5} = \frac{1}{2}x + \frac{3}{10}$$

$$0.25x - 0.4 = 0.5x + 0.3$$

$$0.25x - 0.5x = 0.3 + 0.4$$

$$-0.25x = 0.7$$

$$x = -\frac{0.7}{0.25}$$

$$x = -2.8$$

Verification:

$$\text{LHS} = \frac{1}{4}(-2.8) - \frac{2}{5} = 0.25(-2.8) - 0.4 = -1.1$$

$$\text{RHS} = \frac{1}{2}(-2.8) + \frac{3}{10} = 0.5(-2.8) + 0.3 = -1.1$$

Since LHS = RHS, $x = -1.1$ is the solution.

b. In this equation, the numerical coefficients are not simple numbers as in the previous examples. These coefficients should be reduced to a single number (which may not be an integer) by performing the indicated operations. Then carry on with the usual three-step procedure for solving a linear equation in one unknown.

$$\frac{x}{1 + 0.11 \times \frac{75}{365}} + 2x\left(1 + 0.11 \times \frac{92}{365}\right) = \$1150.96$$

$$\frac{1x}{1.0226027} + 2x(1.0277260) = \$1150.96$$

$$0.9778969x + 2.055452x = \$1150.96$$

$$3.033349x = \$1150.96$$

$$x = \frac{\$1150.96}{3.033349}$$

$$x = \$379.44$$

BA II PLUS Keystrokes
(when set for "*AOS*" calculations)

Step 1: Obtain the coefficient of x in the first term and save in memory.

1	+	0.11	×	75	÷	365

=	1/x	STO	1

Step 2: Obtain the coefficient of x in the second term.

2	×	(	1	+	0.11	×

92	÷	365	)	=

Step 3: Recall and add the first term's coefficient. Save this sum.

+	RCL	1	=	STO	2

Step 4: Divide the right side by this saved combined coefficient of x.

1150.96	÷	RCL	2	=

Ans: 379.44

Verification:

$$\text{LHS} = \frac{\$379.44}{1 + 0.11 \times \frac{75}{365}} + 2(\$379.44)\left(1 + 0.11 \times \frac{92}{365}\right)$$

$$= \frac{\$379.44}{1.0226027} + 2(\$379.44)(1.0277260)$$

$$= \$371.05 + \$779.92$$

$$= \$1150.97$$

$$= \text{RHS}$$

The \$0.01 difference between the LHS and the RHS arises from rounding the solution $x = \$379.4354$ to the nearest cent and then using the rounded value for the verification.

APP ❹ THAT

To find a quick way either to solve an equation or to gain further understanding on how to solve an equation in your homework problems, search the App Store on your tablet, smartphone, or smart watch using the key words **EQUATION SOLVER**.
   You will find many free and paid apps that generate step-by-step solutions to guide you through the solving process either by typing in the equation or by taking a photo of the equation to be solved.

EXERCISE 2.3

Answers to the odd-numbered problems are at the end of the book.

CALCULATOR-FREE PROBLEMS

Solve the following equations.

a. $2a - 9 = a + 1$

b. $5 + 3x = 20$

c. $6(y - 4) = 0$

d. $\frac{b}{3} - 1 = 5$

  e. $-7x - 10 = 11$ **f.** $4 = \dfrac{10 - m}{3}$

  g. $12 - 3x - 8 = -10x - 10$ **h.** $2(4x - 5) = x - 3$

  i. $\dfrac{x + 2}{x - 1} = 4$ **j.** $\dfrac{15p}{2} = 7p + 4$

BASIC PROBLEMS

Solve the following equations.

 1. $10a + 10 = 12 + 9a$

 2. $29 - 4y = 2y - 7$

 3. $0.5(x - 3) = 20$

 4. $\frac{1}{3}(x - 2) = 4$

 5. $y = 192 + 0.04y$

 6. $x - 0.025x = 341.25$

 7. $12x - 4(2x - 1) = 6(x + 1) - 3$

 8. $3y - 4 = 3(y + 6) - 2(y + 3)$

 9. $8 - 0.5(x + 3) = 0.25(x - 1)$

 10. $5(2 - c) = 10(2c - 4) - 6(3c + 1)$

 11. $3.1t + 145 = 10 + 7.6t$

 12. $1.25y - 20.5 = 0.5y - 11.5$

 13. $\dfrac{x + 2}{5} = x + 0.8$

 14. $\dfrac{3.5}{x - 1} = 2.5$

INTERMEDIATE PROBLEMS

Solve the following equations. The solutions to Problems 17–24 should be accurate to the cent.

 15. $\dfrac{10a}{2.2} + (2.2)^2 = 6 + a(2.2)^3$

 16. $21 - \dfrac{b}{1.45} = 5.5b - 9$

 17. $(1.065)^2 x - \dfrac{x}{1.065} = \$35$

 18. $12x - 4x(1.06)^4 = \$1800$

 19. $\dfrac{x}{1.1^2} + 2x(1.1)^3 = \$1000$

 20. $\dfrac{3x}{1.025^6} + x(1.025)^8 = \$2641.35$

 21. $\dfrac{2x}{1.03^7} + x + x(1.03)^{10} = \$1000 + \dfrac{\$2000}{1.03^4}$

 22. $x(1.05)^3 + \$1000 + \dfrac{x}{1.05^7} = \dfrac{\$5000}{1.05^2}$

 23. $x\left(1 + 0.095 \times \dfrac{84}{365}\right) + \dfrac{2x}{1 + 0.095 \times \frac{108}{365}} = \$1160.20$

 24. $\dfrac{x}{1 + 0.115 \times \frac{78}{365}} + 3x\left(1 + 0.115 \times \dfrac{121}{365}\right) = \$1000\left(1 + 0.115 \times \dfrac{43}{365}\right)$

2.4 Manipulating Equations and Formulas

An **equation** is a statement that one algebraic expression equals another algebraic expression. It represents a precise relationship among the variables and numbers. When the relationship described by an equation is a general one with broad application, we usually refer to the equation as a *formula*.

Most of the important formulas we will develop and use in this book are summarized at the end of each chapter and in the Summary of Key Formulas at the back of the book. Some of them are pre-programmed into your financial calculator.

Keep in mind that every one of these formulas is a shorthand description of a real-world relationship in business or finance. Some of the formulas are amazingly powerful.

L03 In a typical application, you will decide that a particular formula applies to the problem or situation at hand. From the given information you will be able to determine numerical values for all but one of the variables in the formula. If the remaining unknown variable is embedded in the right-hand side, you will have to manipulate (rearrange) the formula by a series of steps designed to isolate the unknown variable.

Let us use Formula (6-5) to describe two general approaches to manipulating formulas. There are several instances in our formulas where two letter symbols are used to represent a single variable. This is one such formula. At this point, it does not matter if you have absolutely no idea what the symbols NI, CM, X, and FC represent in the formula

$$NI = (CM)X - FC \qquad \text{(6-5)}$$

This formula has four variables: NI, CM, X, and FC. To be able to solve for any one of these, you need to know values for the other three variables.

Suppose you are given values for NI, CM, and FC and you must solve for X. You can choose to do either of the following:

- *First substitute* the numerical values for NI, CM, and FC, and *then manipulate (or rearrange)* the equation to solve for X; **or**
- *First rearrange* the formula to isolate X, and *then substitute* the numerical values for NI, CM, and FC.

Normally the first approach is easier because, after substitution, you can usually simplify the right-hand side to some degree. The second approach is more useful in situations when the rearrangement is going to be used over and over again.

Regardless of which approach you take for manipulating a formula or equation,[2] the same fundamental principle applies at every step:

Both sides of an equation must be treated in exactly the same way in order to maintain the equality.

For example,

- You can add the same number or variable to *both* sides;
- You can subtract the same number or variable from *both* sides;
- You can multiply *both* sides by the same number or variable;
- You can divide *both* sides by the same number or variable;
- You can raise *both* sides to the same exponent. This means, for example, that you can cube both sides (that is, raise both sides to the exponent "3"), or take the square root of both sides (that is, raise both sides to the exponent "$\frac{1}{2}$").

---

[2] When we substitute numerical values for some of the variables in a formula, we are applying a general formula to a particular situation. At this point, we usually start referring to the mathematical relationship simply as an equation because of its more limited applicability.

EXAMPLE 2.4A

DEMONSTRATING THE TWO APPROACHES FOR FORMULA MANIPULATION

In the formula $NI = (CM)X - FC$, suppose the values for NI, CM, and FC are given as $NI = \$3250$, $CM = \$75$, and $FC = \$8000$.

a. Calculate X by first substituting the given values into the formula and then rearranging the equation.

b. Calculate X by first rearranging the general formula to isolate X, and then substituting numerical values for NI, CM, and FC.

SOLUTION

a. Substitute the values $NI = \$3250$, $CM = \$75$, and $FC = \$8000$ into $NI = (CM)X - FC$, giving

$$\$3250 = \$75X - \$8000$$

To leave only the term containing X on the right-hand side, add $\$8000$ to *both* sides.

$$\$3250 + \$8000 = \$75X$$
$$\$11{,}250 = \$75X \qquad \text{Simplify the left-hand side.}$$

At the end, we want the term containing X by itself on the left-hand side. This can be accomplished by simply interchanging the left- and right-hand sides of the equation. It does not change the equality.

$$\$75X = \$11{,}250$$
$$X = \frac{\$11{,}250}{\$75} \qquad \text{Divide both sides by \$75 to leave } X \text{ with a coefficient of "1."}$$
$$X = \$150$$

b. We want an equivalent formula with X rather than NI on the left-hand side. Interchange the two sides of the formula $NI = (CM)X - FC$, giving

$$(CM)X - FC = NI$$
$$(CM)X = NI + FC \qquad \text{after adding } FC \text{ to both sides.}$$

Divide both sides by CM to leave X by itself on the left-hand side.

$$X = \frac{NI + FC}{CM}$$

Now substitute the values for NI, FC, and CM, giving

$$X = \frac{\$3250 + \$8000}{\$75}$$
$$X = \$150$$

 TIP

Reverse BEDMAS

In this section you have two options when using formulas to solve for an unknown variable.

If you first substitute values into a formula, use BEDMAS to remember the correct order of operations for solving the resulting equation.

If you choose to rearrange the formula first before substituting in the given values, use reverse BEDMAS, or SAMDEB, to determine the order in which you "move" the variables to isolate the one you are going to solve for in your rearrangement.

EXAMPLE 2.4B

DEMONSTRATING THE TWO APPROACHES FOR FORMULA MANIPULATION

Suppose the formula $S = P(1 + rt)$ applies to a situation for which $S = \$1040$, $P = \$1000$, and $t = 0.5$.

a. Calculate r by first substituting the given values into the formula and then rearranging the equation.

b. Calculate r by first rearranging the general formula to isolate r, and then substituting numerical values for S, P, and t.

SOLUTION

a. Substitute the values $S = \$1040$, $P = \$1000$, and $t = 0.5$ into $S = P(1 + rt)$, giving

$$\$1040 = \$1000[1 + r(0.5)]$$
$$\$1040 = \$1000(1 + 0.5r)$$
$$\$1040 = \$1000 + \$500r \qquad \text{after multiplying } both \text{ "1" and "0.5r" by "\$1000"}$$

To leave only the term containing r on the right side, subtract \$1000 from *both* sides.

$$\$1040 - \$1000 = \$1000 + \$500r - \$1000$$
$$\$40 = \$500r$$

At the end, we want r by itself on the left-hand side. You can simply interchange the left and right sides of an equation—it does not change the equality.

$$\$500r = \$40$$

Finally, divide *both* sides by "\$500" to make r's coefficient "1" instead of "\$500."

$$\frac{\$500r}{\$500} = \frac{\$40}{\$500}$$
$$r = 0.08$$

b. We want an equivalent formula with r rather than S isolated on the left side. Interchange the two sides of $S = P(1 + rt)$ to get r on the left side, giving

$$P(1 + rt) = S$$

Next multiply both "1" and "rt" by "P." These steps yield

$$P + Prt = S$$

To have only the term containing r remaining on the left side, subtract P from both sides.

$$P + Prt - P = S - P$$
$$Prt = S - P$$

Divide both sides by Pt to eliminate these variables from the left-hand side.

$$\frac{Prt}{Pt} = \frac{S - P}{Pt}$$

(You may draw a slash through the factors P and t in the numerator and denominator on the left-hand side to signify that these variables "cancel out." But note that you cannot "cancel" the Ps on the right-hand side because P does not appear in *both* terms of the numerator.)

$$r = \frac{S - P}{Pt}$$

Now substitute the values for S, P, and t, giving

$$r = \frac{\$1040 - \$1000}{\$1000 \times 0.5} = \frac{\$40}{\$500} = 0.08$$

TIP

A Shortcut

We obtained the intermediate outcome

$$Prt = S - P$$

in part (b) of **Example 2.4B** by subtracting P from *both* sides of $P + Prt = S$. The same outcome may be achieved by moving the term P with a *change of sign* to the other side of the equation.

Most people prefer the second approach, particularly in cases where they want to shift two or three terms at the same time. Hereafter, we will employ this shortcut (sometimes called *transposing a term*). Note that for a term like Prt, you cannot transpose just the factor P—all numerical and algebraic factors in a term may be transposed only as a complete "package."

EXAMPLE 2.4C

DEMONSTRATING THE TWO APPROACHES FOR FORMULA MANIPULATION

In a particular application of the formula $c = \dfrac{V_f - V_i}{V_i}$, the values for c and V_f are 0.15 and \$230, respectively.

a. Obtain V_i by first substituting the given values into the formula and then rearranging the equation.

b. Obtain V_i by first rearranging the general formula to isolate V_i, and then substituting numerical values for c and V_f.

SOLUTION

a. Substitute $c = 0.15$ and $V_f = \$230$ into

$$c = \frac{V_f - V_i}{V_i}$$

giving

$$0.15 = \frac{\$230 - V_i}{V_i}$$

Multiply both sides by V_i to get rid of the fraction on the right side.

$$0.15 V_i = \frac{\$230 - V_i}{V_i} \times V_i$$

$$0.15 V_i = \$230 - V_i$$

We want all terms containing V_i to be on the left side. Move the term V_i (with a change of sign) to the left side.

$$V_i + 0.15 V_i = \$230$$

Remember that V_i really means $1V_i$. Therefore, we can add the two terms on the left side, giving

$$1.15 V_i = \$230$$

Divide both sides by 1.15 to make V_i's coefficient "1."

$$\frac{1.15 V_i}{1.15} = \frac{\$230}{1.15}$$

$$V_i = \$200.00$$

b. We want an equivalent formula with V_i isolated on the left side. To clear the denominator on the right side, multiply both sides by V_i.

$$c\,(V_i) = \frac{V_f - V_i}{V_i} \times V_i$$

Now the right-hand side simplifies to

$$cV_i = V_f - V_i$$

Transpose V_i to the left side in order to collect all terms containing V_i on the left side.

$$V_i + cV_i = V_f$$

Now extract the common factor V_i on the left side.

$$V_i(1 + c) = V_f$$

The final step to isolate V_i is to divide both sides by $(1 + c)$. This will cancel the $(1 + c)$ factor on the left side, leaving

$$V_i = \frac{V_f}{1 + c}$$

If we now substitute $V_f = \$230$ and $c = 0.15$, we get

$$V_i = \frac{\$230}{1 + 0.15} = \frac{\$230}{1.15} = \$200.00$$

 TIP

Another Shortcut

We obtained the intermediate outcome

$$0.15V_i = \$230 - V_i$$

in part (a) of **Example 2.4C** by multiplying both sides of the equation

$$0.15 = \frac{\$230 - V_i}{V_i}$$

by V_i. The same outcome may be achieved by removing V_i from the denominator on the right side and multiplying it against the numerator on the left side of the equation.

Most people prefer this second approach (commonly called *cross-multiplication*), particularly when both sides of an equation are fractions. For example, to isolate x in the equation

$$\frac{a}{b} = \frac{c}{x}$$

you can first cross-multiply to obtain

$$ax = cb$$

Then divide both sides by a. This gives

$$x = \frac{cb}{a}$$

EXERCISE 2.4

Answers to the odd-numbered problems are at the end of the book.

BASIC PROBLEMS

1. Use Formula (7-1), $I = Prt$, to calculate P if $r = 0.05$, $I = \$6.25$, and $t = 0.25$.

2. Use Formula (14-1), $PV = \dfrac{PMT}{i}$, to calculate i if $PMT = \$900$ and $PV = \$150,000$. (There are several instances in our formulas where a two- or three-letter symbol is used for a variable. This is usually done to make the symbol more suggestive of the quantity it represents. For example, we use PMT to represent the amount of each payment in a series of regular payments. The symbol P has already been taken to represent another quantity that begins with "p.")

3. Use Formula (7-2), $S = P(1 + rt)$, to calculate P if $r = 0.004$, $S = \$3626$, and $t = 9$.

4. Use Formula (5-1), $N = L(1 - d)$, to calculate L if $N = \$891$ and $d = 0.10$.

5. Use Formula (5-1), $N = L(1 - d)$, to calculate d if $N = \$410.85$ and $L = \$498.00$.

6. Use Formula (7-2), $S = P(1 + rt)$, to calculate t if $r = 0.0025$, $S = \$5100$, and $P = \$5000$.

7. Formula (6-5), $NI = (CM)X - FC$, contains three two-letter symbols. Use it to calculate CM if $NI = \$15,000$, $X = 5000$, and $FC = \$60,000$.

8. Use Formula (6-5), $NI = (CM)X - FC$, to obtain X if $NI = -\$542.50$, $CM = \$13.50$, and $FC = \$18,970$.

9. Use Formula (5-2), $N = L(1 - d_1)(1 - d_2)(1 - d_3)$, to calculate L if $N = \$1468.80$, $d_1 = 0.20$, $d_2 = 0.15$, and $d_3 = 0.10$.

10. Use Formula (5-2), $N = L(1 - d_1)(1 - d_2)(1 - d_3)$, to calculate d_2 if $N = \$70.29$, $L = \$99.99$, $d_1 = 0.20$, and $d_3 = 0.05$.

11. Use the formula $FV = PV(1 + i_1)(1 + i_2)(1 + i_3)$ to determine i_1 if $PV = \$1000$, $FV = \$1094.83$, $i_2 = 0.03$, and $i_3 = 0.035$.

12. Use Formula (11-1), $FV = PMT\left[\dfrac{(1 + i)^n - 1}{i}\right]$, to obtain PMT if $FV = \$1508.54$, $n = 4$, and $i = 0.05$.

13. Use Formula (11-2), $PV = PMT\left[\dfrac{1 - (1 + i)^{-n}}{i}\right]$, to obtain PMT if $PV = \$6595.20$, $n = 20$, and $i = 0.06$.

14. Rearrange Formula (7-1), $I = Prt$, to isolate t on the left side.

15. Rearrange Formula (14-1), $PV = \dfrac{PMT}{i}$, to isolate i on the left side.

16. Rearrange Formula (5-1), $N = L(1 - d)$, to isolate d on the left side.

17. Rearrange Formula (6-5), $NI = (CM)X - FC$, to isolate CM on the left side.

18. Rearrange Formula (6-5), $NI = (CM)X - FC$, to isolate X on the left side.

19. Rearrange Formula (7-2), $S = P(1 + rt)$, to isolate r on the left side.

20. Rearrange Formula (7-2), $S = P(1 + rt)$, to isolate t on the left side.

21. Rearrange Formula (5-2), $N = L(1 - d_1)(1 - d_2)(1 - d_3)$, to isolate d_1 on the left side.

22. Rearrange Formula (5-2), $N = L(1 - d_1)(1 - d_2)(1 - d_3)$, to isolate d_3 on the left side.

23. Rearrange the formula $FV = PV(1 + i)^n$ to isolate PV on the left side.

INTERMEDIATE PROBLEMS

24. Use the formula $FV = PV(1 + i)^n$ to calculate i if $PV = \$2000$, $FV = \$9321.91$, and $n = 20$.

25. Use the formula $PV = FV(1 + i)^{-n}$ to calculate i if $PV = \$5167.20$, $FV = \$10,000$, and $n = 15$.

26. Rearrange the formula $FV = PV(1 + i)^n$ to isolate i on the left side.

2.5 | Solving Word Problems

LO4 In the preceding sections, we reviewed procedures for solving linear equations and working with formulas. With practice, solving linear equations becomes a mechanical procedure that follows a fairly routine series of steps. However, *practical* applications of mathematics rarely come as given equations that need only to be solved. Instead, a problem is presented to us in a more informal descriptive manner. We must deduce mathematical relationships from the given information and from our broader knowledge of general concepts and principles.

Constructing algebraic equations from given information cannot be reduced to mechanical steps (such as those previously listed for solving linear equations). We can, however, outline a *general approach* for solving word problems.

A General Approach for Solving Word Problems

Particularly if you are having difficulty with a word problem, use the following procedure to reduce the solution to small steps. Let us assume for now that there is only one unknown in the problem.

Step 1: *Read the entire problem* to gain a sense of the topic involved and what is being asked. For example, you might find that the problem involves a loan repayment and you are asked to determine the size of the monthly payment.

Step 2: Now take pencil and paper in hand. On a second reading, *extract and label the given data. Identify the unknown quantity and choose a symbol for it. Draw and label a diagram if appropriate.* There are standard symbols for many quantities. These should be used to label numerical values as they are extracted. Otherwise, use one or two words to identify each value. Choose a symbol to represent the unknown quantity. Diagrams are particularly useful in problems involving multiple payments over a period of time. Incorporate as much information as possible in the diagram.

Step 3: *Create a word equation* that relates what you know (the data) to what you want to know (the unknown quantity). The word equation may be based on a fundamental principle of broad application, or it may be a unique relationship stated or implied in the problem itself. An example of a word equation is

$$\text{Profit} = \text{Revenues} - \text{Expenses}$$

Step 4: *Convert the word equation to an algebraic equation.* Express the words and phrases in the word equation in terms of the unknown quantity's symbol and the numerical values extracted in Step 2.

Step 5: *Solve the equation.* Check that the answer is reasonable. Write a concluding statement that directly responds to the question asked.

Summary of the Steps for Solving Word Problems
1. Read the entire problem.
2. Extract and label the data. Identify the unknown quantity and specify its symbol. Draw and label a diagram if appropriate.
3. Create a word equation that relates the given data to the unknown quantity.
4. Convert the word equation to an algebraic equation.
5. Solve the equation.

To remember the steps, think of "REDWAS" representing **R**ead, **E**xtract and **D**raw, **W**ord equation, **A**lgebraic equation, and **S**olve.

  TIP

Overcoming That Old "I-Just-Can't-Seem-to-Get-Started" Feeling

Have you ever stared and stared at a word problem without getting anywhere? (If you have, you belong to a rather large club.) Think about how you have approached word problems in the past. Did you begin by trying to find a formula in which to substitute the given numbers? If so, you were really trying to do Steps 1, 2, 3, and 4 all at once! It's not surprising that you became stumped on problems of even moderate difficulty. Even if you happen to hit on the right formula and calculate the right answer, the "formula-browsing" approach is not an effective way to "do" mathematics. It omits Step 3, where you bring mathematical ideas and concepts to bear on a particular situation. For problems of any complexity, you should use our five-step ladder instead of trying to leap tall problems in a single bound.

The following examples illustrate the five-step approach for solving word problems.

EXAMPLE 2.5A

THE STEP-BY-STEP APPROACH TO SOLVING A WORD PROBLEM

a. Elsie wants to make $645 selling her pottery mugs at the local craft fair. The fee to rent a table is $75 and she plans on charging $12 for her mugs. How many mugs does she have to sell to reach her goal?

b. Elsie makes two sizes of mugs to sell. The number of large mugs she has is twice as many as the number of smaller mugs. If she charges $14 for the large mugs and $12 for the small mugs, what is the minimum number of each size she needs to sell to reach her goal?

SOLUTION

a. Step 1: Read the problem. (This step is assumed hereafter.)

Step 2: Extract and label the data. Identify the unknown and define its symbol.

$$\text{Goal (Profit)} = \$645 \quad \text{Price} = \$12 \text{ per mug} \quad \text{Rental fee (Expenses)} = \$75$$

Since the problem is asking for the number of mugs, we will let x represent the number of mugs.

Don't worry if you are not sure what to call values. A short description works just as well and can be refined in Step 3.

Step 3: Create a word equation that relates the given data to the unknown. This relation will often be described in the problem or you may have to use information you have learned in your course work. The given problem does not spell out the relationship between Elsie's goal and her price and costs, but we can generally state that:

$$\text{Elsie's goal} = \text{Money in} - \text{Money out}$$

In terms of this problem, we can refine this to:

$$\text{Profit} = \text{Revenue} - \text{Expenses}$$
$$\text{Profit} = (\text{Price} \times \text{Number of mugs sold}) - \text{Expenses}$$

Step 4: Convert the word equation to an algebraic equation, substituting in the known data.

$$\$645 = \$12x - \$75$$

Step 5: Solve the equation.

$$\$645 + \$75 = \$12x$$
$$\$720 = \$12x$$
$$x = 60$$

Elsie needs to sell 60 mugs to reach her goal of making $645.

Check: ($12 × 60 – $75 = $645)

b. Step 2: Goal (Profit) = $645   Price for small mug = $12 per mug

Price for large mug = $14 per mug   Rental fee (Expenses) = $75

We now have two quantities to solve for but we also know a relationship between the quantities.

$$\text{Number of large mugs} = 2 \times \text{Number of small mugs}$$

We will let x represent the number of small mugs.

That means $2x$ will represent the number of large mugs.

Step 3:   Profit = Revenue from small mugs + Revenue from large mugs – Expenses

Profit = (Price × Number of small mugs) + (Price × Number of large mugs) – Expenses

Step 4: $$\$645 = \$12x + \$14(2x) - \$75$$

Step 5:   Solve the equation. $$\$645 + \$75 = \$12x + \$14(2x)$$

$$\$720 = \$12x + \$28x$$

$$\$720 = \$40x$$

$$x = 18$$

Elsie needs to sell 18 of the small mugs and 36 (2×18) of the large mugs to reach her goal of making $645.

Check: ($\$12 \times 18 + \$14 \times 36 - \$75 = \$645$)

TIP

Avoid Fractions in Equations

You will avoid fractions in your equations, as seen in **Example 2.5A** part (b), if you let the variable x represent the smallest quantity in a relationship with two or more unknown quantities.

EXAMPLE 2.5B

A PROBLEM USING PERCENTS

A retailer reduced his prices by 15% for a fall sale. What was the regular price of an item on sale at $123.25?

SOLUTION

Step 2:   Extract and label the data. Identify the unknown and define its symbol.

Discount rate = 15%   Sale price = $123.25

Let P represent the regular price.

Step 3:   Create a word equation that relates the given data to the unknown quantity.

Sale price = Regular price – Price reduction

= Regular price – (Discount rate × Regular price)

Step 4:   Convert the word equation to an algebraic equation.

$$\$123.25 = P - 0.15P$$

Step 5:   Solve the equation.

$$\$123.25 = 0.85P$$

$$P = \frac{\$123.25}{0.85} = \$145.00$$

The original price of the item was $145.00.

Check: ($\$145 - 0.15 \times \$145 = \$145 - \$21.75 = \$123.25$)

EXAMPLE 2.5C

USING TABLES TO ORGANIZE INFORMATION IN A MIXTURES PROBLEM

Biko Confectionery intends to prepare and sell a Premier Nut Mix consisting of almonds and cashews. The manager obtains almonds at a wholesale cost of $10.38 per kilogram and cashews at a cost of $15.50 per kilogram. He wants to mix the nuts in a proportion that produces 12 kg of Premier Mix having an effective wholesale cost no greater than $12.30 per kilogram. What is the maximum weight of cashews that can be put in the mix?

SOLUTION

Step 2: The problem here is to determine the **weight** of cashews in a given mixture, so we will let C represent the weight of cashews in a 12-kg batch. Since the mixture contains only the two types of nuts, the remainder of the 12-kg mixture will be made up of almonds. This gives us $(12 - C)$ to represent the weight of the almonds.

This problem describes data for different **types of nuts** in a mixture and the **cost** of each type, so these will be our column headings for our table. Since we are looking for the **weight** of cashews used in the mixture, that will also need to be included in the table.

Type of nut	Cost per kg	Weight (kg)	Total cost
Cashews	$15.50	C	$15.50C$
Almonds	$10.38	$12 - C$	$10.38(12 - C)$
Premier Mix	$12.30 (maximum)	12	12.30×12

Step 3: The maximum cost of the mix will be reached when the maximum proportion of the more expensive component (cashews) is used.

Total cost of Premier Mix = Total cost of cashews + Total cost of almonds

where each total cost is the product of the number of kilograms and the cost per kilogram.

Step 4: $$\$12.30(12) = \$15.50C + \$10.38(12 - C)$$

Step 5: $$\$147.60 = \$15.50C + \$124.56 - \$10.38C$$
$$\$147.60 - \$124.56 = \$15.50C - \$10.38C$$
$$\$5.12C = \$23.04$$
$$C = 4.50 \text{ kg}$$

The maximum weight of cashews in the batch of Premier Nut Mix is 4.5 kg.

EXAMPLE 2.5D

USING TABLES TO ORGANIZE INFORMATION IN AN ALLOCATION PROBLEM

Digitech Inc. has a stock option incentive program for its employees. In any allocation of options, each of 8 senior managers receives twice as many options as each of 31 middle managers. Each middle manager receives 2.5 times as many options as each of 348 regular employees. The board of directors has just approved the issue of a total of 500,000 stock options. Rounded to the nearest whole number, how many options will each senior manager, middle manager, and regular employee receive?

SOLUTION

Step 2: The information presented in this problem talks about **types of managers**, **number** of each type of manager, and stock **options** for each type. These will become the headings for our table.

Since middle and senior managers receive more options than regular employees, we will let E represent the number of options each regular employee will receive. This will avoid the use of fractions in our solution.

Position	Number of individuals	Options per individual	Total options
Regular employee	348	E	$348E$
Middle manager	31	$2.5E$	$31(2.5E)$
Senior manager	8	$5E$	$8(5E)$

Total number of options = 500,000

Step 3:   Total number of options = (Number given to regular employees)
+ (Number given to middle managers)
+ (Number given to senior managers)

Step 4: $500{,}000 = 348E + 31(2.5E) + 8(5E)$

Step 5: $500{,}000 = 348E + 77.5E + 40E$

$= 465.5E$

$E = \dfrac{500{,}000}{465.5} = 1074.11$

Each regular employee will receive 1074 options, each middle manager will receive 2.5(1074.11) = 2685 options, and each senior manager will receive 5(1074.11) = 5371 options.

TIP

Look for the Bottom Line

A good strategy to use when you are overwhelmed with information in a word problem is to look for the "bottom line" question in the problem. In most cases this is the sentence with the question mark. This will give you direction in what the variable should represent and what type of relationship exists between the variables. Next, try to categorize what each sentence is talking about. These categories should be part of the relationship you need to solve the problem.

EXERCISE 2.5

Answers to the odd-numbered problems are at the end of the book.

CALCULATOR-FREE PROBLEMS

a. Four buses were chartered to take 177 business students on a field trip. If 9 students travelled by car and the rest filled the buses, how many students were in each bus?

b. A bookstore customer purchased a binder priced at $9.50 plus 4 pencils. The total cost of the order was $12.50 before taxes. How much did each pencil cost?

c. A computer salesperson earns $400 a week plus a 2% commission on all sales. If they earned $600 for the week, what was their level of sales?

d. Samuel won $2000 in a lottery and gave $200 to each of his siblings. If he was left with $600, how many brothers and sisters does Samuel have?

e. Josie used half of her weekly paycheque to pay her cell phone bill. To earn more money, she sold her skateboard on Kijiji for $50. How much was her paycheque if she was left with $170 for the week?

BASIC PROBLEMS

1. A Web site had $\frac{2}{7}$ more hits last month than in the same month of the preceding year. If there were 2655 hits last month, how many were there one year earlier?

2. The retail price of a pair of skis consists of the wholesale cost to the retailer plus the retailer's markup. If skis retailing for $712 are marked up by 60% of the wholesale cost, what is that wholesale cost?

3. The price tags in Angie's Flower Shop include the 13% Harmonized Sales Tax (HST). How much HST will she report for a plant sold at $39.55?

4. A stockbroker's commission on a transaction is 2.5% of the first $5000 of the transaction amount and 1.5% of the remainder. What was the amount of a transaction that generated a total commission of $227?

5. A caterer has the following price structure for banquets. The first 20 meals are charged the basic price per meal. The next 20 meals are discounted by $2 each and all additional meals are each reduced by $3. If the total cost for 73 meals comes to $1686, what is the basic price per meal?

6. Econocar offers two plans for one-week rentals of a compact car. A rate of $295 per week includes the first 1000 km. Extra distance costs 15 cents per kilometre. A weekly rate of $389 allows unlimited driving. Rounded to the nearest kilometre, beyond what driving distance is the unlimited driving plan cheaper?

7. Alicia pays 38% income tax on any additional earnings. She has an opportunity to work overtime at 1.5 times her base wage of $23.50 per hour. Rounded to the nearest quarter hour, how much overtime must she work to earn enough money (after tax) to buy a canoe that costs $2750 including sales taxes?

INTERMEDIATE PROBLEMS

8. Classic Homes has found from experience that there should be 40% as many two-bedroom homes as three-bedroom homes in a subdivision, and twice as many two-bedroom homes as four-bedroom homes. How many homes of each type should Classic build in a new 96-home subdivision?

9. Broadway Mazda usually spends half as much on radio advertising as on newspaper advertising, and 60% as much on television advertising as on radio advertising. If next year's total advertising budget is $160,000, how much (rounded to the nearest dollar) should be allocated to each form of advertising?

10. A city's commercial construction by-laws require five parking spaces for every 100 square metres of retail rental space in a shopping centre. Four percent of the parking spaces must be large spaces for the physically handicapped. Of the remainder, there must be 40% more regular-size spaces than "small-car" spaces. How many parking spaces of each type are required for a 27,500-square-metre shopping centre?

11. Erin has invested in both an equity mutual fund and a bond mutual fund. Her financial adviser told her that her overall portfolio rose in value by 1.1% last year. Erin noted in the newspaper that the equity fund lost 3.3% last year while the bond fund rose 7.7%. To the nearest 0.1%, what percentage of her portfolio was in the equity fund at the beginning of the year?

12. Steel is an alloy of iron and nickel. A steel recycling company has two piles of scrap steel. Pile A contains steel with 5.25% nickel content; Pile B contains steel with 2.84% nickel. The company has an order for 32.5 tonnes of steel containing 4.15% nickel. How much scrap steel should be taken from each pile for reprocessing?

13. The board of directors of Meditronics Inc. has designated 100,000 stock options for distribution to employees and management of the company. Each of three executives is to receive 2000 more options than each of eight scientists and engineers. Each scientist and engineer is to receive 50% more options than each of 14 technicians. Rounded to the nearest whole number, how many options will a person in each position receive?

14. Dash Canada offers two long-distance telephone plans. Plan X costs 6.5 cents per minute for calls between 8 a.m. and 6 p.m. weekdays (business hours) and 4.5 cents per minute at other times. Plan Y costs 5.3 cents per minute any time. Above what percentage of business-hour usage will Plan Y be cheaper?

15. Quality Grocer makes its own bulk "trail mix" by mixing raisins and peanuts. The whole-sale cost of raisins is $3.75 per kg and the cost of peanuts is $2.89 per kg. To the nearest 0.1 kg, what amounts of peanuts and raisins should be mixed to produce 50 kg of trail mix with an effective wholesale cost of $3.20 per kg?

16. A firm received a bill from its accountant for $3310, representing a combined total of 41 billable hours for both the Certified General Accountant (CGA) and her accounting technician for conducting the firm's audit. If the CGA charges her time at $120 per hour and the technician's time at $50 per hour, how many hours did each work on the audit?

17. Joan, Stella, and Sue have agreed to form a partnership. For the original capital investment of $32,760, Sue agrees to contribute 20% more than Joan, and Joan agrees to contribute 20% more than Stella. How much will each contribute?

18. The annual net income of the SGR partnership is to be distributed so that Sven receives 30% less than George, and Robert receives 25% more than George. If the past year's net income was $88,880, what amount should be allocated to each partner?

19. It takes 20 minutes of machine time to manufacture Product X and 30 minutes of machine time to manufacture Product Y. If the machine operated 47 hours last week to produce a combined total of 120 units of the two products, how many units of Y were manufactured?

20. The tickets for a hockey game cost $19.00 for the blue section and $25.50 for the red section. If 4460 tickets were sold for a total of $93,450, how many seats were sold in each section?

21. Mr. Parker structured his will so that each of his four children will receive half as much from the proceeds of his estate as his wife, and each of 13 grandchildren will receive one-third as much as each child. After his death, $759,000 remains after expenses and taxes for distribution among his heirs. How much will each child and grandchild receive?

22. To coordinate production in a three-stage manufacturing process, Stage B must be assigned 60% more workers than Stage A. Stage C requires three-quarters as many workers as Stage B. How should the site manager allocate 114 workers among the three stages?

23. Fred has centralized the purchasing and record-keeping functions for his three pharmacies in a single office. The annual costs of the office are allocated to the three stores. The Hillside store is charged $1000 less than twice the charge to the Barnett store. The Westside store is charged $2000 more than the Hillside store. What is the charge to the Westside store if the cost of operating the central office for a year is $27,600?

24. One hundred thousand dollars is to be distributed under a firm's profit-sharing plan. Each of three managers is to receive 20% more than each of 26 production workers. How much will each manager and production worker receive?

KEY TERMS

Algebraic expression	Like terms	Power
Base	Linear equation	Root
Binomial	Literal coefficient	Substitution
Distributive property	Monomial	Terms
Equation	Nonlinear equation	Trinomial
Exponent	Numerical coefficient	Variables
Factors	Polynomial	

REVIEW PROBLEMS

Answers to the odd-numbered review problems are at the end of the book.

BASIC PROBLEMS

1. **L01** Multiply and collect the like terms: $4(3a + 2b) - 5a(2 - b)$

2. **L01** Multiply and collect the like terms: $4(3a + 2b)(2b - a) - (2a - b)(a + 3b)$

3. **L01** Simplify and collect the like terms.

   a. $\dfrac{9y - 7}{3} - 2.3(y - 2)$

   b. $P\left(1 + 0.095 \times \dfrac{135}{365}\right) + \dfrac{2P}{1 + 0.095 \times \frac{75}{365}}$

4. **L01** Perform the indicated multiplication and division, and combine the like terms.

   a. $6(4y - 3)(2 - 3y) - 3(5 - y)(1 + 4y)$

   b. $\dfrac{5b - 4}{4} - \dfrac{25 - b}{1.25} + \dfrac{7}{8}b$

   c. $\dfrac{x}{1 + 0.085 \times \frac{63}{365}} + 2x\left(1 + 0.085 \times \dfrac{151}{365}\right)$

   d. $\dfrac{96nm^2 - 72n^2m^2}{48n^2m}$

5. **L01** Evaluate:

   $$P(1 + i)^n + \dfrac{S}{1 + rt}$$

   accurate to the cent for $P = \$2500$, $i = 0.1025$, $n = 2$, $S = \$1500$, $r = 0.09$, and $t\frac{93}{365}$.

6. **L01** Evaluate each of the following expressions for the given values of the variables. The answer should be accurate to the cent.

   a. $L(1 - d_1)(1 - d_2)(1 - d_3)$ for $L = \$340$, $d_1 = 0.15$, $d_2 = 0.08$, $d_3 = 0.05$

   b. $\dfrac{R}{i}\left[1 - \dfrac{1}{(1 + i)^n}\right]$ for $R = \$575$, $i = 0.085$, $n = 3$

7. **L01** Simplify:

   a. $\dfrac{(-3x^2)^3(2x^{-2})}{6x^5}$

   b. $\dfrac{(-2a^3)^{-2}(4b^4)^{3/2}}{(-2b^3)(0.5a)^3}$

8. **L01** Simplify:

   $\left(-\dfrac{2x^2}{3}\right)^{-2}\left(\dfrac{5^2}{6x^3}\right)\left(-\dfrac{15}{x^5}\right)^{-1}$

9. **LO1** Evaluate the following expressions to six-figure accuracy.

   a. $(1.0075)^{24}$

   b. $(1.05)^{1/6} - 1$

   c. $\dfrac{(1 + 0.0075)^{36} - 1}{0.0075}$

   d. $\dfrac{1 - (1 + 0.045)^{-12}}{0.045}$

10. **LO1** Evaluate the following expressions to six-figure accuracy.

    a. $\dfrac{(1.00\overline{6})^{240} - 1}{0.00\overline{6}}$

    b. $(1 + 0.025)^{1/3} - 1$

11. **LO2** Solve the following equations for x to five-figure accuracy.

    a. $\dfrac{2x}{1 + 0.13 \times \frac{92}{365}} + x\left(1 + 0.13 \times \dfrac{59}{365}\right) = \$831$

    b. $3x(1.03^5) + \dfrac{x}{1.03^3} + x = \dfrac{\$2500}{1.03^2}$

12. **LO2** Solve the following equations for x to five-figure accuracy and verify the solution.

    a. $\dfrac{x}{1.08^3} + \dfrac{x}{2}(1.08)^4 = \$850$

    b. $2x\left(1 + 0.085 \times \dfrac{77}{365}\right) + \dfrac{x}{1 + 0.085 \times \frac{132}{365}} = \$1565.70$

13. **LO3** Use Formula (5-2), $N = L(1 - d_1)(1 - d_2)(1 - d_3)$, to calculate d_2 if $N = \$324.30$, $L = \$498$, $d_1 = 0.20$, and $d_3 = 0.075$.

14. **LO3** Use the formula $V_f = V_i(1 + c_1)(1 + c_2)(1 + c_3)$ to determine c_2 if $V_f = \$586.64$, $V_i = \$500$, $c_1 = 0.17$, and $c_3 = 0.09$.

15. **LO3** Rearrange the formula $FV = PV(1 + i_1)(1 + i_2)$ to isolate i_1.

16. **LO3** Rearrange the formula $NI = (CM)X - FC$ to isolate CM.

INTERMEDIATE PROBLEMS

---

17. **LO4** Norman's Gourmet Tea wants to prepare a custom tea blend using a mixture of mint tea leaves that cost \$0.202 per gram and chamomile tea leaves that cost \$0.158 per gram. Norman's wants to prepare 2 kg of the mint-chamomile blend and price it at \$0.179 per gram. How many grams of mint tea leaves will be used in the blend?

18. **LO4** The annual net income of the Todd Bros. partnership is distributed so that Ken receives \$15,000 more than 80% of Hugh's share. How should a net income of \$98,430 be divided between the partners?

19. **LO4** The profits from a partnership are to be distributed so that Grace receives 20% more than Kajsa, and Mary Anne receives five-eighths as much as Grace. How much should each receive from a total distribution of \$36,000?

Chapter 3
Percent and Percent Change

CHAPTER OUTLINE

LEARNING OBJECTIVES

After completing this chapter, you will be able to:

LO1 Given any two of the three quantities percent rate, portion, and base, solve for the third

LO2 Solve problems involving percent change

LO3 Calculate the income yield, capital gain yield, and rate of total return on stocks and mutual funds

LO4 Combine rates of total return for successive holding periods

LO5 Calculate market share and market growth for a specific brand or market

PERCENTS ARE A VERY IMPORTANT PART of our everyday life and are used widely in business to quote the amount of interest charged on loans or the amount of interest paid for money invested. We have already seen percents used in the calculation of commission earned on sales in Section 1.3, and percents will continue to be used widely in future chapters where percent "of" a base value is used to express values for rates of discounting, profit and loss, simple interest, and compound interest.

Percent change is a simple way to show a degree of change over time and is used for many purposes in business and finance. It can be used with any quantity that is measured over time, and later in this chapter we will look at two specific applications where both percent and percent change are used—investment returns from stocks and mutual funds, as well as market share and market growth.

 TIP

How to Succeed in Business Mathematics

Since various Business Mathematics and Mathematics of Finance courses start at different points in the book, this Tip appears at the beginning of each of the first five chapters. Connect has a guide entitled "How to Succeed in Business Mathematics." Read its first two sections (A.1 and A.2) as soon as possible.

If your course bypassed Chapter 1 and you are using a Texas Instruments BA II PLUS calculator, refer to Appendix 1A for information about settings that affect the calculator's display and order of operations.

3.1 | The Basic Percentage Problem

In Section 1.2, we found a part or portion of a whole amount using percents. We will now look at a more general approach that can be used to compare a portion, or part of a quantity, to the whole amount. One measure of the relative size is the fraction

$$\frac{Portion}{Base}$$

where the term *base* is used to represent the whole or entire amount. The fraction is called the *rate*. That is,

THE BASIC PERCENTAGE FORMULA

$$Rate = \frac{Portion}{Base} \qquad\qquad (3\text{-}1)$$

This relation is used in a general way to compare a quantity (the *portion*) to some other standard or benchmark (the *base*).

In cases where the *portion* is smaller than the *base*, the *rate* will be less than 1 and the percent equivalent rate will be less than 100%.

In cases where the *portion* is larger than the *base*, the *rate* will be greater than 1 and the percent equivalent rate will be more than 100%.

LO1 Given any two of the three quantities *portion*, *base*, and *rate*, you can calculate the unknown quantity by using Formula (3-1). You can choose to do either of the following:

- *First substitute* the known values, and *then rearrange* the equation to solve for the unknown; **or**
- *First rearrange* the general formula to isolate the unknown quantity on the left side, and *then substitute* the values for the known quantities on the right side.

The first approach helps to keep your focus on a single fundamental relationship.

TIP

Distinguishing between the Base and the Portion

The key to solving percentage problems is to distinguish between the base and the portion. The base is always the standard or benchmark to which the portion is being compared.

Ask yourself the following questions to help distinguish between base and portion:

Is this quantity the entire amount that is available?

Is this the quantity I have?

If we look at the answers to these questions in the context of a test mark, say $\frac{35}{50}$, then:

The maximum number of marks available, 50, is the base.

The number of marks you achieved, 35, is the portion.

In the wording of problems such as "What percent is 35 *of* 50," the quantity following "*of*" is almost always the base.

EXAMPLE 3.1A

USING THE BASIC PERCENTAGE FORMULA

a. What is 35.25% of $215?

b. How much is $0.\overline{6}$% of $2000?

c. What percentage is 7.38 kg of 4.39 kg?

d. 250% of what amount is $10?

SOLUTION

a. The question asks us to calculate a part (portion) of a given whole (base). Substituting the known values into Formula (3-1)

$$Rate = \frac{Portion}{Base}$$

we obtain

$$0.3525 = \frac{Portion}{\$215}$$

Multiply both sides of the equation by $215 and then switch the left and right sides, giving

$$Portion = 0.3525 \times \$215 = \$75.79$$

That is, 35.25% of $215 is $75.79.

b. Again, the rate and base are given. As in part (a),

$$Portion = 0.00\overline{6} \times \$2000 = 0.0066666 \times \$2000 = \$13.33$$

In conclusion, $13.33 is $0.\overline{6}$ % of $2000.

c. We are given both the portion and the base for a comparison. Here, 7.38 kg is being compared to the reference amount (base) of 4.39 kg. The answer will be greater than 100% since the portion is larger than the base.

$$Rate = \frac{Portion}{Base} = \frac{7.38}{4.39} = 1.681 = 168.1\%$$

Thus, 7.38 kg is 168.1% of 4.39 kg.

d. Here, $10 is 250% of the unknown amount (base). Substituting the known values into

$$Rate = \frac{Portion}{Base}$$

we obtain

$$2.50 = \frac{\$10}{Base}$$

Hence,

$$2.50(Base) = \$10$$

and

$$Base = \frac{\$10}{2.50} = \$4.00$$

Therefore, 250% of $4.00 is $10.00.

EXAMPLE 3.1B

SOLVING FOR RATE GIVEN PORTION AND BASE

A battery manufacturer encloses a 50-cent rebate coupon in a package of two AAA batteries retailing for $4.29. What percent rebate does the coupon represent?

SOLUTION

In effect, the question is asking you to compare the rebate to the retail price. Therefore, the retail price is the base in the comparison.

$$Rate = \frac{Portion}{Base} = \frac{\$0.50}{\$4.29} = 0.117 = 11.7\%$$

The manufacturer's percent rebate on the batteries is 11.7%.

 TIP

Units of Portion and Base

The preceding example demonstrates that the portion and base must have the same units when calculating rate. (In other words, both quantities in **Example 3.1B** must be in dollars, or both must be in cents.)

EXAMPLE 3.1C

SOLVING FOR PORTION GIVEN RATE AND BASE

The number of students enrolled in a marketing program represents 18% of the total full-time enrolment in a business college that has 3750 full-time students. How many students are enrolled in other full-time programs at the college?

SOLUTION

We can use the rate of enrolment in a marketing program with the total enrolment in the college to find the portion of students in the college enrolled in marketing. That is,

$$Rate = \frac{Portion}{Base}$$

$$0.18 = \frac{Portion}{3750}$$

$$Portion = 0.18 \times 3750 = 675 \text{ students in the marketing program.}$$

Therefore, the number of students in other programs is

$$3750 - 675 = 3075 \text{ students.}$$

The business college has 3075 students enrolled in programs other than marketing.

EXAMPLE 3.1D

SOLVING FOR BASE GIVEN PORTION AND RATE

Juliette sold her 2009 Camry on Kijiji for 16% of what she originally paid for it. If she received $3200 for the car, what did she pay for it when she bought it new in 2009?

SOLUTION

The money she received from the sale of the car is a portion of what she originally paid. Therefore, we can find the base using

$$Rate = \frac{Portion}{Base}$$

$$0.16 = \frac{\$3200}{Base}$$

$$0.16 \times Base = \$3200$$

$$Base = \frac{\$3200}{0.16} = \$20,000$$

Juliette paid $20,000 for the car when she purchased it new.

 ### CONCEPT QUESTIONS

1. What is the percent rate if a quantity is four times the size of the base?
2. What is the percent rate if a quantity is $\frac{1}{1000}$ of the base?
3. If the percent rate is 1000%, what multiple is the portion of the base?
4. If the percent rate is 0.01%, what fraction is the portion of the base?

Answers to the odd-numbered problems are at the end of the book.

BASIC PROBLEMS

Calculate dollar amounts accurate to the cent and percent amounts to three-figure accuracy.

1. Calculate 1.75% of $350.

2. Calculate $6.\overline{6}$% of $666.66.

3. What percent is $1.50 of $11.50?

4. What percent is 88¢ of $44?

5. $45 is 60% of what amount?

6. $69 is 30% of what amount?

7. What amount is 233.3% of $75?

8. What amount is 0.075% of $1650?

9. $134 is what percent of $67?

10. $1.34 is what percent of $655?

11. 150% of $60 is what amount?

12. $0.58\overline{3}$% of $1500 is what amount?

13. $7\frac{1}{2}$% of what amount is $1.46?

14. $12\frac{3}{4}$% of what amount is $27.50?

15. What percent of $950 is $590?

16. What percent of $590 is $950?

17. 95% of what amount is $100?

18. $8\frac{1}{3}$% of what amount is $10?

19. 30 m is what percent of 3 km?

20. 500 g is what percent of 2.8 kg?

21. How much is $\frac{1}{2}$% of $10?

22. 0.75% of $100 is what amount?

23. $180 is 120% of what amount?

24. $559.35 is 113% of what amount?

25. $130\frac{1}{2}$% of $455 is what amount?

26. 0.0505% of $50,000 is what amount?

27. $281.25 is 225% of what amount?

28. 350% of what amount is $1000?

29. $10 is 0.5% of what amount?

30. $1.25 is $\frac{3}{4}$% of what amount?

31. Cecilia and Nathan estimate their total cost for a vacation in Australia to be $14,775.
    a. What percentage is this cost of their combined gross monthly income of $8775?
    b. If 72% of their gross monthly income is already consumed by rent, taxes, car payments, and other regular living expenses, what percentage is the trip's cost of their remaining annual disposable income?

32. In a one-month period, a convenience store had sales of $65,560 from its gas pumps and sales of $36,740 from other in-store products. What percent of total sales were from gasoline?

33. A 540-mL can of K-9 Diet dog food contains 28% protein, 15.5% fat, and 6% fibre.
    a. How many millilitres of other ingredients are there in the can?
    b. The recommended serving for a small dog is $\frac{5}{8}$ of a can. How many millilitres of protein are in one small-dog serving?

34. A provincial minister of education recently announced that his government's forecast expenditure of $2.68 billion on education next year represents 23.5% of the provincial budget. Rounded to the nearest million dollars, what is the province's total budget for the next year?

35. Unusually high snowfall during the past winter resulted in Brockton's costs for snow ploughing and removal to reach $320,200. This represents 127% of its budgeted cost. Rounded to the nearest $100, what amount did Brockton budget for snow clearance?

INTERMEDIATE PROBLEMS

36. If the royalty rate performing artists receive from songs downloaded from Apple iTunes is 5.7%, and a band received royalties from Apple of $99,736.41 for a year, how many song downloads at $0.99 each did the band have for that year?

37. Your regular workweek is 7.5 hours per day for five days. If you do not work on seven public holidays and you receive two weeks of vacation, what percentage of the total hours in a year are you actually at work? Assume that a year has exactly 52 weeks.

38. In the month of December, Bernie's Bargain Barn had sales of $9820 in their clothing department, $4025 in their shoe department, and $1830 in accessories. If 17% of the merchandise purchased from the clothing department was returned, 8% from the shoe department was returned, and 3% from accessories was returned, what percent of the total revenue for December were the returns if full refunds were given on all merchandise?

39. Ivory hand soap is advertised as being $99\frac{44}{100}$% pure. (It floats!) How many milligrams of impurities are in a 150-g bar of Ivory soap?

40. An online discount broker charges a transaction fee of $30 plus an additional 3 cents per share. A full-service broker charges a commission rate of 2.4% of the total dollar value of a stock transaction. Suppose you purchase 200 shares of the Bank of Nova Scotia at $55.40 per share. What percentage are the total fees charged by the online discount broker of the commission you would pay the full-service broker?

41. A full-service broker charges a commission rate of 2.2% of the total dollar value of a stock transaction. A discount broker charges a transaction fee of $25 plus an additional five cents per share. Suppose you purchase 800 shares of Talisman Energy at $21.75 per share. What percentage of the commission fee charged by the full-service broker would you save by using the discount broker?

42. A province's progressive income tax rates are structured as follows: 16% tax on the first $15,000 of taxable income, 26% on the next $20,000, 35% on the next $40,000, and 45% on any additional taxable income. What percentage is an individual's total income tax of his (taxable) income if his taxable income for a year is:
    a. $33,000?
    b. $66,000?
    c. $99,000?

43. In 2018, Canada's population was 36,954,000 and Japan's population was 127,185,000. Canada's land area is 9,093,500 square kilometres but Japan's area is only 377,835 square kilometres. To the nearest 0.01%, what percentage was Canada's population density (people per square kilometre) of Japan's population density in 2018?

44. A property sold for 250% of what the vendors originally paid for it. What was that original price if the recent selling price was $410,000?

45. The Calgary Flames hockey team announced that its season ticket sales of 13,500 represents 67.50% of the Scotiabank Saddledome's seating capacity. How many seats were not sold to season ticket holders?

46. Studies have shown that the average adult male requires 7.5 hours of sleep a night and females require 20 minutes more than males. If the average life expectancy in Canada is 82.7 years for women and 78 years for men, what percentage are the male waking hours of a female's waking hours for a lifetime?

47. Stan is a real estate salesperson. He receives 60% of the 4.8% commission that the real estate agency charges on sales. If his income for the past year was $150,480, what was the dollar value of his sales for the year?

48. A stockbroker is paid 45% of the commission her firm charges her clients. If she personally receives $134.55 on an $11,500 transaction, what is the firm's commission rate?

49. A mortality rate indicates the fraction of individuals in a population who are expected to die in the next year.
   a. If the mortality rate among 35-year-old males is 0.34%, what is the expected number of deaths per year among a province's total of 50,000 such males?
   b. If 35-year-old males constitute 0.83% of the overall population in a city of 1.45 million, how many deaths of such males are expected in that city in a year?

3.2 Percent Change

L02 When a quantity changes, the amount of the change is often expressed as a percentage of the initial value. That is,

$$\text{Percent change} = \frac{\text{Final value} - \text{Initial value}}{\text{Initial value}} \times 100\%$$

We can write a more compact formula if we define the following symbols:

$$V_i = \text{Initial (or beginning or original or old) value}$$
$$V_f = \text{Final (or ending or new) value}$$
$$c = \text{Percent change (or its decimal equivalent)}$$

Then

PERCENT CHANGE

$$c = \frac{V_f - V_i}{V_i} \times 100\%$$

(3-2)

Note that when a quantity doubles, the percent change is 100%. If a quantity triples, the percent change is 200%, and so on.

EXAMPLE 3.2A

CALCULATING THE PERCENT CHANGE

The minimum wage in Alberta in 2012 was $9.75 per hour. This increased to $15.00 per hour in 2018. What is the percent increase in the minimum wage in Alberta for this time period?

SOLUTION

From 2012 to 2018,

$$c = \frac{2018 \text{ wage} - 2012 \text{ wage}}{2012 \text{ wage}} \times 100\% = \frac{\$15.00 - \$9.75}{\$9.75} \times 100\%$$
$$= \frac{\$5.25}{\$9.75} \times 100\%$$
$$= 53.85\%$$

The minimum wage in Alberta increased by 53.85% from 2012 to 2018.

TIP

Order Matters, Language Matters

The order of the final and initial values in the numerator is important—it determines the sign of the percent change. If a quantity decreases in size, its percent change is negative.

To illustrate a point on language, consider the example of a company whose sales declined from $4 million in Year 1 to $3 million in Year 2. The percent change in sales is

$$\frac{\text{Year 2 sales} - \text{Year 1 sales}}{\text{Year 1 sales}} \times 100\% = \frac{\$3 \text{ million} - \$4 \text{ million}}{\$4 \text{ million}} \times 100\%$$

$$= \frac{-1}{4} \times 100\%$$

$$= -25\%$$

We can say either "the sales changed by −25%" or "the sales decreased by 25%" from Year 1 to Year 2. The direction of the change may be indicated either by an algebraic sign or by a descriptive word such as "rose," "fell," "increased," or "decreased." However, it would be incorrect and potentially confusing to say that "the sales decreased by −25%."

EXAMPLE 3.2B

CALCULATING THE PERCENT CHANGE

The share price of Klondike Resources rose from $2 on January 1, 2018 to $4 on December 31, 2018. It fell back to $2 by December 31, 2019. Calculate the percent change in share price during 2018, during 2019, and during the entire two-year period.

SOLUTION

For 2018,

$$c = \frac{\text{Dec. 31, 2018 price} - \text{Jan. 1, 2018 price}}{\text{Jan. 1, 2018 price}} \times 100\% = \frac{\$4 - \$2}{\$2} \times 100\% = 100\%$$

Similarly, for 2019,

$$c = \frac{\$2 - \$4}{\$4} \times 100\% = -50\%$$

For the entire two years,

$$c = \frac{\$2 - \$2}{\$2} \times 100\% = 0\%$$

The share price increased by 100% in 2018 and then decreased by 50% in 2019. For the entire two-year period, there was no net price change.

 TRAP

Percent Changes Are Not Additive

As the preceding example demonstrates, the overall percent change for a series of intervals cannot be obtained simply by adding the percent changes for the individual intervals. The reason is that the initial value for the percent change calculation is different in each interval.

POINT OF INTEREST

Following the Ups and Downs of Gas Prices in Canada

In February 2017, the average price for gasoline in Canada was 115.6¢ a litre. By May 2018, prices had jumped 17.5%. Then, in November of that year, prices were again down by the same 17.5%. However, at the pumps in November gas was selling for 112.0¢ a litre, not the 115.6¢ a litre it started at. How can that be?

If we look at the 17.5% increase in May 2018, 115.6¢ (1 + 17.5%) = 135.8¢ a litre.

The next increase is on the new changed value of 135.8¢ a litre.

So, in November 2018 the decreased price is 135.8¢ (1 − 17.5%) = 112.0¢ a litre.

The overall change from February 2017 to November 2018 is not 17.5% − 17.5% = 0%, but

$$\frac{112.0 - 115.5}{115.5} \times 100\% = -3.03\%$$

© Jupiterimages/Getty Images

The percent changes are not additive.

EXAMPLE 3.2C

CALCULATING THE PERCENT CHANGE IN A PERCENTAGE

A chartered bank raises the interest rate on its Visa card from 9% to 11%. What is the percent increase in the interest charges on a given balance?

SOLUTION

The interest charges increase proportionately with the rise in the interest rate. The interest rate change must be calculated in relative terms [using Formula (3-2)], not in absolute terms (11% − 9% = 2%). Therefore, the percent change in interest charges is

$$c = \frac{V_f - V_i}{V_i} \times 100\% = \frac{11\% - 9\%}{9\%} \times 100\% = \frac{2}{9} \times 100\% = 22.\overline{2}\%$$

The percent increase in the interest charges is 22.2%.

 POINT OF INTEREST

The Process of Shrinkflation

If you are an observant shopper, you will have noticed that the standard or regular package size of many consumer items (ice cream, pop, cookies, bacon, chips, etc.) changes from time to time for no apparent reason. For example, at one point or another during the past few years a chip bag has gone from 200 g to 180 g, and that tube of toothpaste has shrunk from 100 mL to 75 mL.

Food manufacturers are increasingly facing the challenge of rising costs. Using cheaper ingredients would be one way to manage this, but then businesses would be one bad review away from falling sales. Raising prices is the other option, but the food industry is keenly aware that price is a very important decision-making factor for consumers. So to keep prices low they simply reduce package sizes while keeping the price the same—or even increasing the price. This practice is so common that the term "shrinkflation" has been coined to describe it.

If the 200-g bag of chips is reduced to a 180-g size with no change in price, this results in an increase of over 10% in per unit pricing. For the toothpaste it is an increase of just over 33%. This type of calculation is presented in **Example 3.2D**.

© McGraw-Hill Education/Jill Braaten

Another part of the shrinkflation process is to get the new package size on the shelf so that it does not appear side by side with the older, larger packaging. Often, the originals will be cleared out at a greatly reduced price so that when the new package comes in with claims of "New Economy Size!" or "Contains One-Third More!" consumers will expect to pay more for the newer packaging. The former size is, of course, no longer available on store shelves for the consumer to compare the unit prices and note the increase.

EXAMPLE 3.2D

CALCULATING THE PERCENT CHANGE IN THE UNIT PRICE

a. Suppose the price of Colgate toothpaste drops from $1.19 to $0.98 when the tube size is reduced from 100 mL to 75 mL. Calculate the percent change in tube volume, tube price, and unit price.

b. If Colgate toothpaste had kept the price the same when the tube size was reduced from 100 mL to 75 mL, what would be the percent change in unit price?

SOLUTION

a. The percent change in the tube's volume is

$$c = \frac{V_f - V_i}{V_i} \times 100\% = \frac{75 \text{ mL} - 100 \text{ mL}}{100 \text{ mL}} \times 100\% = -25.00\%$$

The percent change in the tube's price is

$$c = \frac{\$0.98 - \$1.19}{\$1.19} \times 100\% = -17.65\%$$

The initial unit price is $\frac{\text{Price}}{\text{Volume}} = \frac{\$1.19}{100 \text{ mL}} = \$0.01190$ per mL, or 1.190¢ per mL.

The final unit price is $\frac{\$0.98}{75 \text{ mL}} = \$0.01307$ per mL, or 1.307¢ per mL.

The percent change in the unit price is

$$c = \frac{1.307 - 1.190}{1.190} \times 100\% = 9.83\%$$

b. Let the price for the original size and the reduced size be $1.00.

The unit price at the original size is then $\frac{1}{100}$ and the unit price at the new size is $\frac{1}{75}$.

The percent change in the unit price is

$$c = \frac{V_f - V_i}{V_i} \times 100\% = \frac{\frac{1}{75} - \frac{1}{100}}{\frac{1}{100}} \times 100\% = \frac{0.01\overline{3} - 0.01}{0.01} \times 100\% = 33.33\%$$

The percent change in the unit price is 33.33%.

Calculating V_i or V_f when c is known Sometimes the percent change and either the initial value or the final value are known. To calculate the remaining unknown, you can choose either of the two alternatives identified in **Section 2.4**. Either (i) *first substitute* the known values into Formula (3-2) and *then manipulate* the resulting equation to solve for the unknown; or (ii) *first rearrange* the general formula to isolate the desired variable and *then substitute* the known values. We will normally take the first approach because it usually requires fewer manipulations.

> ✓ **TIP**
>
> ## Signs Matter
>
> Whenever the percent change represents a decrease, a negative value must be substituted for c in Formula (3-2).

EXAMPLE 3.2E

CALCULATING V_i GIVEN V_f AND C

What amount when increased by 230% equals $495?

SOLUTION

We are given $c = 230\%$ and $V_f = \$495$. Note that the decimal equivalent of c is $c = 2.3$. Two solutions are presented. The first is based on Formula (3-2). The second is a more intuitive algebraic approach working from first principles.

Method 1:   Substituting in Formula (3-2),

$$230\% = \frac{\$495 - V_i}{V_i} \times 100\%$$

After dividing both sides by 100%, we have

$$2.3 = \frac{\$495 - V_i}{V_i}$$

Cross-multiply to obtain

$$2.3V_i = \$495 - V_i$$
$$2.3V_i + V_i = \$495$$
$$3.3V_i = \$495$$

Initial amount,

$$V_i = \frac{\$495}{3.3} = \$150$$

Method 2:   Creating and solving an algebraic equation.
Let x represent the initial amount. Express in mathematics the fact that the initial amount (x) increased by 230% (add $2.3x$) equals $495. That is,

$$x + 2.3x = \$495$$
$$3.3x = \$495$$
$$x = \frac{\$495}{3.3} = \$150$$

Therefore, $150 increased by 230% equals $495.

EXAMPLE 3.2F

CALCULATING V_f GIVEN V_i AND C

If $9550 is decreased by 0.75%, what amount remains?

SOLUTION

The initial amount is $9550, and we need to calculate the final amount after a decrease of 0.75% ($c = -0.0075$). As in the previous example, two solutions are presented.

Method 1:   Substituting in Formula (3-2),

$$-0.0075 = \frac{V_f - \$9550}{\$9550}$$

Cross-multiplying,

$$-0.0075(\$9550) = V_f - \$9550$$

After transposing terms to isolate V_f on the left side,

Final amount,

$$V_f = \$9550 - \$71.625 = \$9478.38$$

Method 2:   Formulating and solving an algebraic equation.

Let x represent the final amount. The initial amount ($9550) decreased by 0.75% of the initial amount (subtract $0.0075 \times \$9550$) equals the final amount (x). That is,

$$\$9550 - 0.0075 \times \$9550 = x$$
$$x = \$9550 - \$71.625 = \$9478.38$$

$9550 after a decrease of 0.75% leaves $9478.38.

EXAMPLE 3.2G

CALCULATING V_i GIVEN V_f AND C

For the fiscal year just completed, a company had sales of $157,500. This represents a 5% increase over the prior year. What were the sales in the prior year?[1]

SOLUTION

We are given the "final" sales and need to calculate the "initial" sales.

Method 1:   Substituting in Formula (3-2),

$$0.05 = \frac{\$157,500 - V_i}{V_i}$$

Cross-multiplying,

$$0.05V_i = \$157,500 - V_i$$
$$0.05V_i + V_i = \$157,500$$
$$1.05V_i = \$157,500$$

Prior year's sales,

$$V_i = \frac{\$157,500}{1.05} = \$150,000$$

Method 2:   Formulating and solving an algebraic equation.

Let x represent the prior year's sales. The most recent year's sales ($157,500) represent the prior year's sales (x) plus a 5% increase ($0.05x$). That is,

$$\$157,500 = x + 0.05x = 1.05x$$

Then

$$x = \frac{\$157,500}{1.05} = \$150,000$$

The sales in the prior year totalled $150,000.

---

[1]   It is tempting but incorrect to reason that the prior year's sales must be $100\% - 5\% = 95\%$ of $157,500 (which is $149,625). The 5% increase in sales means that

Most recent year's sales = 105% of (Prior year's sales)

rather than

Prior year's sales = 95% of (Most recent year's sales)

Reversing a percent difference Consider the following question: If x is 10% less than y, by what percentage is y greater than x? (The answer is *not* 10%.) To deal with this question we must first understand the interpretation of certain comparisons.

$$\text{"A is 40\% of B" means that } A = 0.40B$$

but

$$\text{"A is 40\% greater than B" means that } A = B + 0.40B = 1.40B$$

Note also that "A is 40% greater than B" has the same meaning as "A is 140% of B."

EXAMPLE 3.2H

REVERSING A PERCENT DIFFERENCE OF LESS THAN 100%

If x is 10% less than y, by what percentage is y greater than x?

SOLUTION

If x is 10% less than y, then

$$x = y - 0.10y = 0.90y$$

Hence, to find the reverse using Formula (3-2),

$$V_f = 1$$
$$V_i = 0.9$$
$$c = \frac{1 - 0.9}{0.9} \times 100$$
$$c = \frac{0.1}{0.9} \times 100$$
$$c = 11.1\%$$

Therefore, if x is 10% less than y, then y is 11.1% greater than x.

EXAMPLE 3.2I

REVERSING A PERCENT DIFFERENCE OF MORE THAN 100%

If a is 120% more than b, by what percentage is b less than a?

SOLUTION

If a is 120% more than b, then

$$a = b + 1.20b = 2.20b$$

Hence, using Formula (3-2),

$$V_i = 2.20$$
$$V_f = 1$$
$$c = \frac{1 - 2.20}{2.20} \times 100$$
$$c = \frac{-1.2}{2.2} \times 100$$
$$c = -54.\overline{54}\,\%$$

Therefore, if a is 120% more than b, then b is 54.5% less than a.

EXERCISE 3.2

Answers to the odd-numbered problems are at the end of the book.

CALCULATOR-FREE PROBLEMS

Calculate the missing value for Problems a–j.

Problem	Initial value	Final value	Percent change
a.	$100	$110	?
b.	$100	$90	?
c.	25 kg	75 kg	?
d.	50 kg	0 kg	?
e.	$200	?	−25
f.	80 g	?	50
g.	300 cm	?	200
h.	$400	?	−50
i.	?	$50	100
j.	?	$300	−50

BASIC PROBLEMS

In all problems, calculate dollar amounts accurate to the cent, and percent amounts accurate to the nearest 0.01%.

Calculate the missing value for Problems 1–12.

Problem	Initial value	Final value	Percent change
1.	$95	$100	?
2.	$100	$95	?
3.	35 kg	135 kg	?
4.	135 kg	35 kg	?
5.	0.11	0.13	?
6.	0.095	0.085	?
7.	$134.39	?	−12
8.	112 g	?	112
9.	26.3 cm	?	300
10.	0.043	?	−30
11.	?	$75	200
12.	?	$75	−50

13. $100 is what percent more than $90?

14. $100 is what percent less than $110?

15. What amount when increased by 25% equals $100?

16. What sum of money when increased by 7% equals $52.43?

17. $75 is 75% more than what amount?

18. How much is $56 after an increase of 65%?

19. $754.30 is what percent less than $759.00?

20. 77,787 is what percent more than 77,400?

21. How much is $75 after an increase of 75%?

22. $100 is 10% less than what amount?

23. What amount after a reduction of 20% equals $100?

24. What amount after a reduction of 25% equals $50?

25. What amount after a reduction of $16.\overline{6}\%$ equals $549?

26. How much is $900 after a decrease of 90%?

27. How much is $102 after a decrease of 2%?

28. How much is $102 after a decrease of 100%?

29. $750 is what percent more than $250?

30. $250 is what percent less than $750?

31. How much is $10,000 after an increase of $\frac{3}{4}\%$?

32. How much is $1045 after a decrease of 0.5%?

33. What amount when increased by 150% equals $575?

34. What amount after being increased by 210% equals $465?

35. How much is $150 after an increase of 150%?

36. The total cost of a coat (including HST of 13% on the retail price) is $281.37. What is the retail price of the coat?

37. On the purchase of a 4K HD Smart TV, the total cost to the customer (including 5% GST and 7% PST) came to $2797.76. How much GST and how much PST did the customer pay?

38. In 2018, Canada's population reached 36,950,000, a level that was 11.13% higher than 10 years earlier. Rounded to the nearest 10,000, what was the population figure for 2008?

39. Becker Tools sold 32,400 hammers at an average price of $15.10 in Year 1 and 27,450 hammers at an average price of $15.50 in Year 2. What was the percent change from Year 1 to Year 2 in:
   a. The number of hammers sold?
   b. The average selling price?
   c. The revenue from the sale of hammers?

40. An investor purchased shares of Digger Resources at a price of $0.55 per share. One year later, the shares traded at $1.55, but they fell back to $0.75 by the end of the second year after the date of purchase. Calculate the percent change in the share price:
   a. In the first year.
   b. In the second year.
   c. Over both years.

41. What was the percent change in unit price when the regular size of Lily soap bars dropped from 100 g to 90 g (with no change in the price per bar)?

42. After Island Farms increased the container size for its premium ice cream from 1.65 L to 2.2 L, the retail price increased from $5.49 to $7.98. What was the percent change in the unit price?

43. Fluffy laundry detergent reduced its regular size from 3.6 kg to 3 kg. The retail price dropped from $7.98 to $6.98. What was the percent change in the unit price?

44. The retail price of Paradise Island cheddar cheese dropped from $10.98 to $9.98 when the package size was reduced from 700 g to 600 g. What was the percent change in the unit price?

45. The Edmonton Real Estate Board reports that the average selling price of homes last month in the greater Edmonton area was $338,500, an increase of 8.7% over the past year. Rounded to the nearest $100, what was the average selling price one year ago?

46. Mountain Sports is advertising "30% off all ski equipment" in its Spring Clearance Sale. On ski boots marked down to $348.60, what is the regular price?

47. Last year, Canada's exports to the U.S. exceeded imports from the U.S. by 23%. By what percentage were the United States' exports to Canada less than its imports from Canada?

48. In one seven-month period Apple projects sales of 55.0 million iPhones. This outpaces the projected sales of Galaxy phones by 35%. What are the projected sales for the Galaxy phone for the same period (rounded to the nearest 10,000)?

49. In one three-month period, Apple sells 61.0 million iPhones. This represents a year-over-year increase of 40%. What were the sales for the iPhone for the same three-month period in the previous year (rounded to the nearest 10,000)?

50. Mutual Fund A charges an annual management fee of 2.38% of money under management. The corresponding management fee for Mutual Fund B is 1.65%. On the same invested amount, what percentage more fees will you pay to Fund A than to Fund B?

51. The number of daily active Snapchat users decreased from 191 million in March 2018 to 186 million users in September 2018. What is the resulting percent reduction in the number of daily active Snapchat users for this six-month period?

52. In June 2018, Facebook estimated it had 2,270,000,000 daily active users, up 9.6% from a year earlier. What was the absolute increase, year-over-year, in the number of daily active users (rounded to the nearest 10,000)?

53. The price of shares of Nadir Explorations Ltd. fell by 76% in the past year, to the current price of $0.45 per share. In dollars and cents, how much did the price of each share drop in the past year?

54. A piece of machinery has depreciated by 55% of its original purchase price during the past four years, to the current value of $24,300. What is the dollar amount of the total depreciation during the last four years?

55. General Paint and Cloverdale Paint normally offer the same prices. For its Spring Specials Sale, General Paint has marked down the price of outdoor latex paint by 30%. What percentage more will you pay if you buy paint at the regular price at Cloverdale?

56. Old Navy reported that its sales in November 2018 were up 19.7% from its sales in May 2018. What percentage were May sales of November sales?

57. If operating expenses are 40% of revenue, by what percentage does revenue exceed operating expenses?

58. A company has 50% less equity financing than debt financing. What percentage of the equity is the debt? What percentage more debt financing than equity financing does the company have?

INTERMEDIATE PROBLEMS

59. Elegance shampoo has a suggested retail price of $4.49 for its 500-mL bottle. The manufacturer of the shampoo wants to increase the unit retail price by 10% at the same time that it reduces the container size to 425 mL. What should be the suggested retail price of the smaller bottle?

60. The manufacturer of Caramalt chocolate bars wants to implement a 7.5% increase in the unit retail price along with a reduction in the bar size from 100 g to 80 g. If the current retail price of a 100-g bar is $1.15, what should be the price of an 80-g bar?

61. The share price of Goldfield Resources fell by $4 in Year 1 and then rose by $4 in Year 2. If the share price was $6 at the *end* of Year 1, what was the percent change in share price each year?

62. If the Canadian dollar is worth 6.5% less than the U.S. dollar, by what percentage does the U.S. dollar exceed the value of the Canadian dollar?

63. An owner listed a property for 140% more than she paid for it 12 years ago. After receiving no offers during the first three months of market exposure she dropped the list price by 10%, to $172,800. What was the original price that the owner paid for the property?

64. A car dealer normally lists new cars at 22% above cost. A demonstrator model was sold for $17,568 after a 10% reduction from the list price. What amount did the dealer pay for this car?

65. If the denominator of a fraction decreases by 20% and the numerator remains unchanged, by what percentage does the value of the fraction change?

66. The Hampton District school board decided to reduce the number of students per teacher next year by 15%. If the number of students does not change, by what percentage must the number of teachers be increased?

67. The Lightning laser printer prints 30% more pages per minute than the Reliable laser printer. What percentage less time than the Reliable will the Lightning require for long print jobs?

68. If the euro is worth 39% more than the Canadian dollar, how much less (in percentage terms) is the Canadian dollar worth than the euro?

69. A hospital can increase the dollar amount budgeted for nurses' overtime wages during the next year by only 3%. The nurses' union has just won a 5% hourly rate increase for the next year. By what percentage must the hospital cut the number of overtime hours in order to stay within budget?

*3.3 Application: Investment Returns from Stocks and Mutual Funds

LO3 There are two ways you can benefit from an investment. The first is by receiving **income**— money you receive without selling any part of the investment. Aside from any income it generates, an investment may grow in value. The increase in value of the investment is called the **capital gain**. The forms taken by the income and capital gain from various types of investments are presented in **Table 3.1**.

TABLE 3.1 Forms of Income and Capital Gain from Various Types of Investments		
Investment	**Income**	**Capital gain**
Stocks (or shares)	Dividends	Change in share price
Marketable bonds (**Chapter 16**)	Interest	Change in bond price
Mutual fund units	Distributions	Change in unit value
GICs (**Section 9.5**)	Interest	None (redeemable at purchase price)
Gold bullion	None	Change in market price of gold

A typical investment scenario is represented in **Figure 3.1**. The initial value (or beginning value) of the investment is V_i. In finance, the term **holding period** is used for the time interval over which we are calculating the income and capital gain. Income may be received from the investment at one or more points during the holding period. The final value of the investment at the end of the holding period is V_f. The capital gain is the increase in value, $V_f - V_i$. (If the value of an investment declines during the holding period, the capital gain will be negative, indicating a **capital loss**.) The sum of the income and capital gain from the investment is called the **total return**. In summary,

$$\text{Capital gain} = \text{Final value } (V_f) - \text{Initial value } (V_i)$$

$$\text{Total return} = \text{Income} + \text{Capital gain}$$

FIGURE 3.1 The Components of Investment Returns

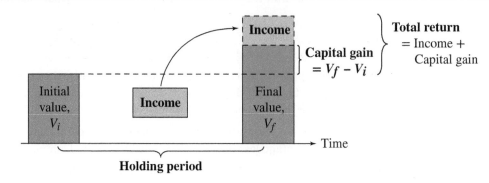

The distinction between the "income" and "capital gain" components of the "total return" is important for two reasons. One is that "income" represents actual cash inflow that can be used by the investor to cover living expenses. To convert the "capital gain" component into a usable cash inflow, the investor must first sell the investment. When the investment is sold, we say that "the capital gain is realized." (Up to that point it was an "unrealized capital gain," sometimes described in everyday language as a "paper gain.") The second reason for separating the "income" and "capital gain" components of "total return" is that capital gains are subject to a lower rate of income tax than investment income.

The income, capital gain, and total return amounts are all in terms of dollars. When discussing the performance of investments, investors prefer to express these amounts as a percentage of the initial value, V_i. Accordingly, we define investment yields and **rate of total return**:

INVESTMENT YIELDS AND RATE OF TOTAL RETURN

$$\textit{Income yield} = \frac{\textit{Income}}{V_i} \times 100\%$$

$$\textit{Capital gain yield} = \frac{\textit{Capital gain}}{V_i} \times 100\% = \frac{V_f - V_i}{V_i} \times 100\% \qquad \text{(3-3)}$$

$$\textit{Rate of total return} = \textit{Income yield} + \textit{Capital gain yield}$$

$$= \frac{\textit{Income} + \textit{Capital gain}}{V_i} \times 100\%$$

The calculation of **income yield** uses a version of Formula (3-1), the basic percent formula where income is the portion, V_i is the base, and the income yield is the rate of return from income.

The **capital gain yield** uses a version of Formula (3-2), the percent change formula. The rate of return from capital gain looks at the change in purchase price, $V_f - V_i$, as a percentage of the purchase price, V_i, of the investment.

 TIP

Watch for Key Words

The words "yield" and "rate" indicate amounts calculated as a percentage of the initial investment. Particular names may be used for specific types of income yield. For example, shareholders refer to a stock's "dividend yield," but bond investors speak of a bond's "current yield."

In everyday life, terms are sometimes used with less precision than in an academic environment. For example, "yield" may be dropped from "capital gain yield" when investors discuss capital gains.

EXAMPLE 3.3A

CALCULATING V_f GIVEN V_i, INCOME, AND RATE OF TOTAL RETURN

An investor is prepared to buy common shares of Eagle Brewing Ltd. at the current share price of $11.50 if he can expect at least a 15% rate of total return over the next year. Assuming that the company repeats last year's $0.40 per share dividend, what will the minimum share price have to be one year from now for the investment objective to be achieved?

SOLUTION

Given V_i = $11.50, rate of total return = 15%, and income $0.40, we want to determine what V_f must be one year from now for the rate of total return to be 15%. If the annual dividend is $0.40 per share,

$$\text{Income yield} = \frac{\$0.40}{\$11.50} \times 100\% = 3.478\%$$

the rest of the 15% rate of total return must come from capital gain. That is,

$$\text{Capital gain yield} = 15\% - 3.478\% = 11.522\%$$

Hence,

$$\text{Capital gain} = 0.11522 \times V_i = 0.11522 \times \$11.50 = \$1.33 \text{ per share}$$

and

$$V_f = V_i + \text{Capital gain} = \$11.50 + \$1.33 = \$12.83$$

The share price must be at least $12.83 one year from now for the investor to achieve the minimum desired rate of total return (15%).

Table 3.2 and Table 3.3 provide price and income data for selected stocks and mutual funds, respectively. These data are used in Example 3.3B and Exercise 3.3.

TABLE 3.2   Income and Price Data for Selected Stocks

Company name	Share price ($) at the end of:			Dividends ($) paid in:	
	2016	2017	2018	2017	2018
TD Bank	66.22	73.65	73.06	0.60	0.67
BCE Inc.	58.03	60.38	56.76	0.72	0.76
Suncor Energy	43.90	46.15	42.93	0.32	0.36
BlackBerry Ltd.	9.24	14.04	11.66	0.00	0.00
Canopy Growth Corp.	9.14	29.74	44.07	0.00	0.00

TABLE 3.3   Income and Price Data for Selected Mutual Funds

Name of mutual fund	Unit price ($) at the end of:			Distribution ($) in:	
	2016	2017	2018	2017	2018
AGF Canadian Dividend Fund	11.56	12.23	11.54	0.16	0.07
Mawer New Canada Fund	74.21	76.54	75.62	0.54	0.00
BMO Dividend Fund	63.69	70.23	68.44	0.40	0.30
Desjardins Dividend Growth Fund	19.50	19.85	19.03	0.16	0.10
Scotia Canadian Bond Fund	11.51	11.45	11.04	0.27	0.23

TIP

Excel Applications in Business Mathematics

Section 3.3 is the first point where, *as an optional approach*, we make Excel spreadsheets available in Connect to demonstrate functions in business mathematics. We assume that students already have a basic familiarity with Microsoft Excel™ software. In particular, students should be able to program a cell with a formula that performs calculations on data entered in other cells.

The Spreadsheet Templates presented in Connect are partially completed spreadsheet templates that demonstrate how to set up a spreadsheet to solve any of the Example problems that have the Spreadsheet Template icon shown above. Students may choose to use a similar Excel spreadsheet for solving some of the problems in that section's Exercise. Each Excel workbook consists of a page of instructions (click on the "Introduction" tab) and one or more templates (each on a separate worksheet).

To use a template, enter a problem's given information in the spreadsheet's pre-labelled and pre-formatted yellow "input" cells. Then program each blue and/or green "output" cell with the appropriate formula for the desired calculation. If a special built-in Excel function should be used, it is described on the workbook's Introduction page.

EXAMPLE 3.3B

CALCULATING INVESTMENT RETURNS FROM SECURITIES

 To the nearest 0.01%, calculate the income yield, capital gain yield, and rate of total return in each of 2017 and 2018 for Suncor Energy shares and for AGF Canadian Dividend Fund units. Use the data in Table 3.2 and Table 3.3.

SOLUTION

Security	Income yield $\left(\dfrac{\text{Income}}{V_i} \times 100\%\right)$	Capital gain yield $\left(\dfrac{V_f - V_i}{V_i} \times 100\%\right)$	Rate of total return (Income yield + Capital gain yield)
Suncor En. shares (2017)	$\dfrac{\$0.32}{\$43.90} \times 100\% = 0.73\%$	$\dfrac{\$46.15 - \$43.90}{\$43.90} \times 100\% = 5.13\%$	$0.73\% + 5.13\% = 5.86\%$
Suncor En. shares (2018)	$\dfrac{\$0.36}{\$46.15} \times 100\% = 0.78\%$	$\dfrac{\$42.93 - \$46.15}{\$46.15} \times 100\% = -6.98\%$	$0.78\% + (-6.98)\% = -6.20\%$
AGF Cdn. Div. (2017)	$\dfrac{\$0.16}{\$11.56} \times 100\% = 1.38\%$	$\dfrac{\$12.23 - \$11.56}{\$11.56} \times 100\% = 5.80\%$	$1.38\% + 5.80\% = 7.18\%$
AGF Cdn. Div. (2018)	$\dfrac{\$0.07}{\$12.23} \times 100\% = 0.57\%$	$\dfrac{\$11.54 - \$12.23}{\$12.23} \times 100\% = -5.64\%$	$0.57\% + (-5.64)\% = -5.07\%$

 POINT OF INTEREST

False Profits and Bull Marketing

The following tale reveals how little scrutiny is given to claims of investment performance. It also exposes our tendency to suspend critical analysis in the face of a good story.

In 1994 Hyperion published *The Beardstown Ladies' Common-Sense Investment Guide*. The book describes the homespun stock-picking methods of an investment club of 16 women living in Beardstown, Illinois (population 6000). We are told they range in age from 41 to 87. According to the book's introduction, "their hand-picked portfolio of fewer than 20 stocks earned an average annual return of 23.4%" over the preceding 10 years (1984–1993). This return was almost twice the rate of return earned by the benchmark Standard & Poor's 500 (S&P 500) portfolio, and more than twice the average annual return achieved by professional mutual fund managers! Naturally the story found great appeal among the general public—here was a group of savvy septuagenarians emerging from the Illinois cornfields to trounce Wall Street's overpaid MBAs. (The book also contained the ladies' favourite recipes, such as Ann's Kentucky Cream Cake and Helen's Springtime Pie.)

The Beardstown Ladies became celebrities almost overnight. The book was at the top of the *New York Times* bestseller list for three months and eventually sold over 800,000 copies in seven languages. The Beardstown Ladies were the subject of articles in scores of publications and appeared as guests on several television talk shows. Four more books followed in rapid succession. In early 1998, Shane Tritsch, a managing editor at *Chicago* magazine, started to write yet another warm fuzzy story about the lovable ladies from Beardstown. However, he was troubled by the following disclaimer, which appeared in the front material of the Beardstown Ladies' first book.

"Investment clubs commonly compute their annual 'return' by calculating the increase in their total club balance over a period of time. Since this increase includes the dues that the members pay regularly, this 'return' may be different from the return that might be calculated for a mutual fund or a bank. Since the regular contributions are an important part of the club philosophy, the Ladies' returns described in this book are based on this common calculation."

The "dues" refer to regular contributions of new money that most investment clubs require from each member. In the case of the Beardstown Ladies, each member contributed $25 per month right from the start in 1984. Anyone with a basic knowledge of investing should have an "Excuse me?" moment upon reading the disclaimer. It is preposterous to treat new injections of investment capital as part of the total return from a portfolio! Frankly, it is highly doubtful that this method of calculating returns is "commonly" used by investment clubs.

Tritsch wrote an article for the March 1998 issue of *Chicago* magazine exposing the flaw and challenging the claim of a 23.4% average annual return. The Beardstown Ladies allowed the international accounting firm Price Waterhouse to audit their records. Instead of the 23.4% average annual return, Price Waterhouse determined that the average annual rate of return was a modest 9.1%. This was far short of the publicized 23.4% return and well short of the 14.9% annual return on the unmanaged S&P 500 portfolio. The Beardstown Ladies and their publisher had built an empire based on a profoundly flawed calculation that went unchallenged by over 800,000 readers for four years!

The Beardstown Ladies are still around, using the same investing style that gave them their earlier fame. While most of the original members have now passed away, the current membership is 75% descendants of the original members. They continue to meet monthly and invest $25 every month. One thing that has changed is that they are no longer releasing the results of their investment audits.

Sources: The Beardstown Ladies' Investment Club, Leslie Whitaker, *The Beardstown Ladies Common-Sense Investment Guide: How We Beat the Stock Market—And How You Can Too*, Hyperion (Jan. 25, 1996); Noreen Rasbach, "20 Years On, Investing Ladies Haven't Changed Their Style," *The Globe and Mail*, March 1, 2010, updated August 23, 2012. © Copyright 2013 The Globe and Mail Inc.

L04 **Compounding rates of return** Suppose you read that a stock's price rose by 5% in Year 1, 10% in Year 2, and 20% in Year 3. Does this mean that the overall price increase for the three-year period was 5% + 10% + 20% = 35%? No—the understanding is that in Year 2 the price rose 10% from its value at the *end* of Year 1, and in Year 3 the price rose 20% from its value at the *end* of Year 2. In other words, the rates of return are cumulative for successive periods. This is also known as **compounding rates of return**.

Formula (3-2), the percent change formula, tells us that

$$c = \frac{V_f - V_i}{V_i} \times 100\%$$

where c in this example is also the rate of return from capital gain for an investment. We can rearrange this formula to solve for V_f where

$$V_f = V_i(1 + c)$$

Suppose you purchased stock for $10 a share and the rates of return from capital gain over a three-year period were 5%, 10%, and 20%, respectively. The stock price at the end of Year 1 would be calculated as

$$V_f = \$10(1 + 0.05) = \$10.50$$

The final stock price at the end of Year 1 is also the initial stock price for the beginning of Year 2. The stock price at the end of Year 2 would be

$$V_f = \$10.50(1 + 0.10) = \$11.55$$

The stock price at the end of Year 3 would then be

$$V_f = \$11.55(1 + 0.20) = \$13.86$$

For the successive three years, we can write this as:

$$V_f = \$10(1 + 0.05)(1 + 0.10)(1 + 0.20) = \$13.86$$

The formula for calculating a final value (V_f) using compounding rates of return for n periods is

$$V_f = V_i\,(1 + c_1)(1 + c_2)(1 + c_3) \ldots (1 + c_n) \qquad\qquad \textbf{(3-4)}$$

EXAMPLE 3.3C

COMPOUNDING RATES OF TOTAL RETURN ON AN INVESTMENT

The Waterloo-based firm BlackBerry sells stock (trading symbol BBRY) on the TSX. From 2013 to 2017, the rates of return from capital gain were −33.05%, 61.27%, 0.78%, −28.04%, and 51.95%, respectively.

a. If you had purchased $1000 in the stock at the beginning of 2013, what was your stock worth at the end of 2017?

b. What would have been the dollar amount of your capital gain in 2015?

SOLUTION

a. We can directly substitute the given values into Formula (3-4).

$$\begin{aligned}
V_f &= V_i(1 + c_1)(1 + c_2)(1 + c_3)(1 + c_4)(1 + c_5) \\
&= \$1000[1 + (-0.3305)]\,(1 + 0.6127)(1 + 0.0078)[1 + (-0.2804)](1 + 0.5195) \\
&= \$1000(0.6695)(1.6127)(1.0078)(0.7196)(1.5195) \\
&= \$1189.79
\end{aligned}$$

The stock is worth $1189.79 at the end of 2017.

b. In 2015 the rate of return from capital gain was 0.78%. The dollar amount of the return was

$$0.0078 \times (\text{Value of the investment at the end of 2015}) = 0.0078 \times \$1000(0.6695)(1.6127)$$
$$= \$8.42$$

The dollar amount of the return in 2015 was $8.42, or a capital gain of $8.42.

EXAMPLE 3.3D

COMPARING THE PERFORMANCE OF A MUTUAL FUND TO A BENCHMARK

The following table presents the rates of total return on the AGF Canadian Dividend mutual fund for each year from 2013 to 2017 inclusive. Corresponding figures are also given for the Toronto Stock Exchange's S&P/TSX Composite Total Return Index. (This index measures the performance of a portfolio of the common shares of over 200 of the largest Canadian companies trading on the Toronto Stock Exchange. The index is often used as the benchmark for evaluating the performance of other portfolios of Canadian stocks.)

What is the difference between the overall rate of total return on the mutual fund and on the benchmark portfolio represented by the S&P/TSX Index?

Fund name	Rate of total return (%)				
	2013	2014	2015	2016	2017
AGF Canadian Dividend Fund	18.60	11.75	3.37	11.52	7.57
S&P/TSX Composite Total Return Index	9.55	7.42	−11.09	17.51	6.03

SOLUTION

Suppose you invested an amount V_i in the AGF Canadian Dividend Fund at the beginning of 2013. By the end of 2017, the investment would have grown to

$$V_f = V_i(1 + c_1)(1 + c_2)(1 + c_3)(1 + c_4)(1 + c_5)$$
$$= V_i(1 + 0.1860)(1 + 0.1175)(1 + 0.0337)(1 + 0.1152)(1 + 0.0757)$$
$$= V_i(1.6435)$$

The final value is 1.6435 times the initial value or an increase of 64.4%. For the same initial investment in the portfolio represented by the S&P/TSX Composite Index,

$$V_f = V_i(1 + c_1)(1 + c_2)(1 + c_3)(1 + c_4)(1 + c_5)$$
$$= V_i(1 + 0.0955)(1 + 0.0742)(1 − 0.1109)(1 + 0.1751)(1 + 0.0603)$$
$$= V_i(1.3036)$$

The portfolio grew by 30.4%.

Therefore, the AGF Canadian Dividend mutual fund grew by

$$64.4\% − 30.4\% = 34.0\%$$

more than the S&P/TSX Index portfolio.

EXAMPLE 3.3E

CALCULATING ONE OF A SERIES OF PERCENT CHANGES

Hanako invested in a stock that doubled in the first year and rose another 50% in the second year. Now, at the end of the third year, Hanako is surprised to discover that the stock's price is up only 80% from her purchase price. By what percentage did the stock's price change in the third year?

SOLUTION

The stock's price is up 80% over the entire three-year period. Therefore,

$$V_f = 1.80V_i$$

In terms of the capital gain yield in individual years,

$$V_f = V_i(1 + c_1)(1 + c_2)(1 + c_3)$$
$$= V_i(1 + 1.00)(1 + 0.50)(1 + c_3)$$
$$= V_i(3.0)(1 + c_3)$$

For the same final value in both cases, we require

$$V_i(1.80) = V_i(3.0)(1 + c_3)$$
$$1.80 = 3.0(1 + c_3)$$
$$\frac{1.80}{3.0} = 1 + c_3$$
$$c_3 = 0.60 − 1 = −0.40 = −40\%$$

The stock's price declined 40% in Year 3.

POINT OF INTEREST

A 20% Gain Doesn't Offset a 20% Loss

Equal positive and negative rates of return in successive years have a curious lack of symmetry in their effects on the overall return from an investment. A 20% gain in Year 2 will not recoup a 20% loss in Year 1—you need a 25% gain to break even after a 20% loss!

Conversely, a 20% gain followed by a 20% loss also leaves you in a net loss position. A 20% loss will, in fact, erase an earlier 25% gain!

QUESTION 1

Show the calculation of the percent gains required to break even after losses of 50%, 60%, 80%, and 90%.

When a series of annual returns are given for an investment, you may be tempted to calculate the average of the annual returns to obtain a measure of the overall long-term performance of the investment. At best, this average is only an approximation of the investment's annual rate of growth. At worst, it can give a very misleading result. We can dramatically illustrate this point using the rather extreme example of a 100% gain followed by a 50% loss in successive years. The simple average of a 100% gain and a 50% loss is [100% + (−50%)]/2 = 25% per year. But if a $1000 investment doubles to $2000 (a 100% gain) and then loses half its value (a 50% loss), the investment will be right back at its beginning value of $1000. The actual two-year gain was 0%.

The average (25%) of the individual rates of return for the two years is meaningless!

You must therefore be very cautious about drawing conclusions based on a simple average of a series of annual rates of return. It will always *overstate* the actual performance. The more volatile the year-to-year rates of return, the greater will be the degree of overstatement.

QUESTION 2

Over a 10-year period, a mutual fund had rates of return of 37.9%, 34.5%, 200.3%, −27.9%, −43.8%, −48.9%, 16.2%, −5.2%, −4.2%, and 7.4%.

a. What was the average annual rate of return for the 10 years?

b. If a $1000 investment earned this average rate of return each and every year for 10 years, what was its final value?

c. If $1000 was invested in the fund at the beginning of the 10-year period, what was the actual value of the investment after 10 years?

 CONCEPT QUESTIONS

1. Can the income yield from an investment be negative? Explain or give an example.

2. Is it possible for the capital gain yield to exceed 100%? Explain or give an example.

3. Is it possible for a capital loss to be worse than −100%? Explain or give an example.

4. If a series of compound percent changes are all positive, is the overall percent increase larger or smaller than the sum of the individual percent changes? Justify your answer.

5. If a series of compound percent changes are all negative, is the overall percent decrease larger or smaller (in magnitude) than the sum of the individual percent changes? Justify your answer.

EXERCISE 3.3

Answers to the odd-numbered problems are at the end of the book.

 *Spreadsheet templates: The "Investment Returns" template provided in Connect found under the Student Resources for Chapter 3 may be used in Problems 1–12. The "Formula (9-4) Calculator" template in Connect under the Student Resources for Chapter 3 is helpful in answering Problems 23–32.*

BASIC PROBLEMS

Determine yields and rates of return to the nearest 0.01%. Calculate dollar amounts accurate to the cent.

1. A $100 investment purchased one year ago is now worth $110. It also earned $10 of income during the year. Determine the investment's:
   a. Income yield.   b. Capital gain yield.   c. Rate of total return.

2. A $100 investment purchased one year ago is now worth $90. It also generated $10 of income during the year. Determine the investment's:
   a. Income yield.   b. Capital gain yield.   c. Rate of total return.

3. Shares purchased one year ago for $8790 are now worth $15,390. During the year, the shares paid dividends totalling $280. Calculate the shares':
   a. Income yield.   b. Capital gain yield.   c. Rate of total return.

4. One year ago, $13,000 was invested in units of a mutual fund. The units paid a distribution of $260 during the year, but the mutual fund units are now worth only $11,400. What has been the:
   a. Income yield?   b. Capital gain yield?   c. Rate of total return?

5. Calculate the income yield, capital gain yield, and rate of total return in 2018 for BCE Inc. shares and Mawer New Canada Fund units. Use the data in Table 3.2 and Table 3.3.

6. Calculate the income yield, capital gain yield, and rate of total return in each of 2017 and 2018 for TD Bank shares and Desjardins Dividend Growth Fund units. Use the data in Table 3.2 and Table 3.3.

7. Calculate the income yield, capital gain yield, and rate of total return in each of 2017 and 2018 for BlackBerry shares and Scotia Canadian Bond Fund units. Use the data in Table 3.2 and Table 3.3.

8. One year ago, Art Vandelay bought Norwood Industries shares for $37 per share. Today they are worth $40 per share. During the year, Art received dividends of $0.60 per share. What was his income yield, capital gain yield, and rate of total return for the year?

9. Rose purchased units of the Trimark Fund one year ago at $24.10 per unit. Today they are valued at $25.50. On the intervening December 31, there was a distribution of $0.83 per unit. ("Distribution" is the term used by most mutual funds for income paid to unit holders.) Calculate Rose's income yield, capital gain yield, and rate of total return for the year.

10. The market value of Stephanie's bonds has declined from $1053.25 to $1021.75 per bond during the past year. In the meantime she has received two semiannual interest payments of $35 per bond. Calculate Stephanie's income yield, capital gain yield, and rate of total return for the year.

11. Vitaly's shares of Offshore Petroleum have dropped in value from $36.75 to $32.25 during the past year. The shares paid a $0.50 per share dividend six months ago. Calculate Vitaly's income yield, capital gain yield, and rate of total return for the year.

12. Jeff purchased some Target preferred shares on the Toronto Stock Exchange for $56.49. The shares pay a quarterly dividend of $0.30. Twelve months later the shares were trading at $65.75. What was Jeff's rate of total return for the year?

13. Adjusted for stock splits, the price of Microsoft shares rose 40.06%, 24.16%, 19.44%, and 12.00% in the years 2013 to 2016, respectively. In 2017, the share prices rose 37.66%.
   a. What was the overall five-year percent change in the price of Microsoft shares?
   b. If the share price at the end of 2017 was $85.54, what was the price at the beginning of 2013?

14. The federal government cut transfer payments to the provinces by a total of 20% over a five-year period. In the next budget speech, the Minister of Finance announced "the level of transfer payments will be restored to their former level by a 20% increase to be phased in over the next two years." Is this an accurate statement? Explain briefly.

15. The price of Bionex Inc. shares rose by 25% in each of two successive years. If they began the two-year period at $12 per share, what was the percent increase in price over the entire two years?

16. The price of Biomed Corp. shares also began the same two-year period (as in Problem 15) at $12, but fell 25% in each year. What was their overall percent decline in price?

17. What rate of return in the second year of an investment will wipe out a 50% gain in the first year?

18. What rate of return in the second year of an investment will nullify a 25% return on investment in the first year?

19. What rate of return in the second year of an investment is required to break even after a 50% loss in the first year?

20. What rate of return in the second year of an investment is required to break even after a rate of return of −20% in the first year?

21. After two consecutive years of 10% rates of return, what rate of return in the third year will produce a cumulative gain of 30%?

22. After two consecutive years of 10% losses, what rate of return in the third year will produce a cumulative loss of 30%?

23. The following table shows the rates of total return in successive years from 2013 to 2017 for Canopy Growth Corp. and for the benchmark Toronto Stock Exchange S&P/TSX Composite Index. By how much did this stock's overall percentage return exceed or fall short of the index's growth?

Fund name	Rate of total return (%)				
	2013	2014	2015	2016	2017
Canopy Growth Corp.	−90.00	8140.00	44.17	207.74	225.38
S&P/TSX Composite Total Return Index	9.55	7.42	−11.09	17.51	6.03

24. The following table shows the rates of total return in successive years from 2013 to 2017 for the BMO Dividend Fund and for the benchmark Toronto Stock Exchange S&P/TSX Composite Index. By how much did the dividend fund's overall percentage return exceed or fall short of the index's growth?

Fund name	Rate of total return (%)				
	2013	2014	2015	2016	2017
BMO Dividend Fund	17.92	13.54	−1.43	11.76	10.93
S&P/TSX Composite Total Return Index	9.55	7.42	−11.09	17.51	6.03

25. The following table shows the rates of total return in successive years from 2013 to 2017 for the Fidelity Canadian Asset Allocation Fund and for the benchmark Toronto Stock Exchange S&P/TSX Composite Index. By how much did the allocation fund's overall percentage return exceed or fall short of the index's growth?

Fund name	Rate of total return (%)				
	2013	2014	2015	2016	2017
Fidelity Canadian Asset Allocation Fund	9.78	9.53	−0.97	6.85	4.70
S&P/TSX Composite Total Return Index	9.55	7.42	−11.09	17.51	6.03

26. The following table shows the rates of total return in successive years from 2010 to 2014 for the PH&N Bond Fund and for the benchmark Toronto Stock Exchange S&P/TSX Composite Index. By how much did the bond fund's overall percentage return exceed or fall short of the index's growth?

Fund name	Rate of total return (%)				
	2013	2014	2015	2016	2017
PH&N Bond Fund	−1.26	8.66	3.24	1.85	2.04
S&P/TSX Composite Total Return Index	9.55	7.42	−11.09	17.51	6.03

INTERMEDIATE PROBLEMS

27. Assume that the Suncor Energy shares in Table 3.2 will pay a $0.40 per share dividend in 2019. What must the share price be at the end of 2019 for a total rate of return in 2019 of 10%?

28. Assume that the TD Bank shares in Table 3.2 will pay a $1.48 per share dividend in 2019. What must the share price be at the end of 2019 for a total rate of return in 2019 of 7%?

29. One year ago, Morgan invested $5000 to purchase 400 units of a mutual fund. He has just noted in the *Financial Post* that the fund's rate of return on investment for the year was 22% and that the current price of a unit is $13.75. What amount did the fund distribute as income per unit during the year?

30. The S&P/TSX Composite Index rose 3.4%, dropped 1.4%, and then rose 2.1% in three successive months. The index ended the three-month period at 9539.
    a. What was the index at the beginning of the three-month period?
    b. How many points did the index drop in the second month?

31. Victor cannot find the original record of his purchase four years ago of units of the Imperial Global Fund. The current statement from the fund shows that the total current value of the units is $47,567. From a mutual fund database, Victor found that the fund's rates of return for Years 1 to 4 have been 15.4%, 24.3%, 32.1%, and −3.3%, respectively.
    a. What was Victor's original investment in the fund?
    b. What was the dollar increase in the value of his investment in Year 3?

ADVANCED PROBLEM

32. *The Globe and Mail* Report on Business noted that shares of Compact Computers produced a 55% rate of total return in the past year. The shares paid a dividend of $0.72 per share during the year, and they currently trade at $37.50. What was the price of the shares one year ago?

*3.4 Application: Market Share and Market Growth

LO5 Businesses collect data, or metrics, to track and evaluate their performance. These metrics are often referred to as key performance indicators (KPIs). Two of these KPIs are market share and market growth.

Market share uses a variation of Formula (3-1), the basic percent formula, to look at sales volume for a specific product or brand relative to all sales for the industry the business competes in. A brand of smartphone, for example, may have a Canadian market share of 12%. That means that 12% of all smartphones sold in Canada are this particular brand. Market share can be measured in units sold, customers served, or as a dollar volume of sales.

Market growth uses a variation of Formula (3-2), the percent change formula, to quantify the growth of a specific brand or industry. The difference in sales volume from Year 1 to Year 2 is expressed as a percent of the sales volume in year one.

MARKET SHARE

$$Market\ share = \frac{Brand\ sales\ volume}{Total\ industry\ sales\ volume} \times 100\% \qquad (3\text{-}5)$$

MARKET GROWTH

$$Market\ growth = \frac{Year\ 2\ sales - Year\ 1\ sales}{Year\ 1\ sales} \times 100\% \qquad (3\text{-}6)$$

Market share and market growth work together to help businesses meet their goals and objectives. If, for example, a business has a low market share in an industry with high market growth it will be difficult (and costly) for them to increase or even maintain that market share. You will learn about market share and market growth in more depth in an introductory Marketing course.

EXAMPLE 3.4A

CALCULATE MARKET SHARE GIVEN BRAND SALES AND INDUSTRY SALES

Doritos tortilla chips had sales of $2.09B in 2017. The tortilla chip sector had total North American sales of $5.06B. What market share does Doritos hold in the tortilla chip sector in North America?

SOLUTION

Given brand sales of $2.09B and industry sales of $5.06B, we can use Formula (3-5) to find

$$Market\ share = \frac{\$2.09B}{\$5.06B} \times 100\% = 41.30\%$$

Doritos has a 41.3% market share of the North American tortilla chip market.

EXAMPLE 3.4B

CALCULATE BRAND SALES GIVEN MARKET SHARE AND INDUSTRY SALES

Honda's sales for November 2018 represent 8.34% of all sales of light vehicles in Canada for that month. If the sales volume of all light vehicles sold in Canada in November 2018 is $143,668,000, what is the dollar value of Honda sales for the same time period? Round your answer to the nearest $1000.

SOLUTION

Given the Honda brand market share is 8.34% and total industry sales are $143,668,000, we can use Formula (3-5) to calculate

$$0.0834 = \frac{Honda\ sales}{\$143,668,000}$$
$$Honda\ sales = 0.0834 \times \$143,668,000$$
$$= \$11,981,911.20$$

Honda sales for November 2018 were $11,982,000.

EXAMPLE 3.4C

CALCULATE THE SIZE OF A MARKET GIVEN MARKET SHARE AND BRAND SALES

A major Canadian cookie brand had 2018 sales of $94.56M, which represents 18% of the market. What is the sales volume for the cookie market Canada wide?

SOLUTION

We can calculate the size of the Canadian cookie market using Formula (3-5):

$$0.18 = \frac{\$94.56M}{\text{Industry sales}}$$

$$\text{Industry sales} = \frac{\$94.56M}{0.18}$$

$$= \$525.3M$$

The Canadian cookie market had 2018 sales of $525.3M.

EXAMPLE 3.4D

CALCULATE MARKET GROWTH GIVEN YEAR 1 AND YEAR 2 SALES

The athletic wear industry had sales for 2019 in Ontario of $141.2M, an increase from 2018 sales of $137.9M. What is the market growth from 2018 to 2019 for the athletic wear industry in Ontario?

SOLUTION

Given Year 1 sales = $137.9M and Year 2 sales = $141.2M, we can use Formula (3-6) to calculate

$$\text{Market growth} = \frac{\$141.2 - \$137.9}{\$137.9} \times 100\% = 2.39\%$$

The athletic wear industry experienced 2.39% market growth in Ontario from 2018 to 2019.

EXAMPLE 3.4E

COMPARING MARKET GROWTH FOR A BRAND TO THE INDUSTRY

The smart speaker market in North American had sales of $2.9M in 2017 and ballooned to sales of $9.0M in 2018. Amazon-brand smart speakers had an 80% share of this market in 2017. This plummeted to a 27.7% market share in 2018.

Compare the growth of the Amazon brand to the market growth of the smart speaker market from 2017 to 2018.

SOLUTION

Calculate the market growth for the smart speaker industry using Formula (3-6):

$$\text{Industry growth} = \frac{\$9.0 - \$2.9}{\$2.9} \times 100\% = 210.34\%$$

$$\text{2017 sales for Amazon} = 0.80 \times \$2.9M = \$2.32M$$

$$\text{2018 sales for Amazon} = 0.277 \times \$9.0M = \$2.493M$$

$$\text{Amazon market growth} = \frac{\$2.493 - \$2.32}{\$2.32} \times 100\% = 7.46\%$$

The Amazon brand had growth of 7.46% from 2018 to 2019 while the smart speaker industry saw growth of 210.34%.

EXERCISE 3.4

Answers to odd-numbered problems are at the end of the book.

BASIC PROBLEMS

1. Six different brands compete in the same Canadian market and their sales for 2018 and 2019 are shown in the following table. Calculate the market share for each brand for both 2018 and 2019.

	Brand	2018 sales in $M	2019 sales in $M
a.	Brand A	2.42	2.62
b.	Brand B	3.91	3.70
c.	Brand C	11.62	12.55
d.	Brand D	8.42	10.87
e.	Brand E	20.22	18.15
f.	Brand F	9.59	11.06

2. Fassbender Industries tracks the annual sales from each of its six divisions to help evaluate performance and plan budgeting for the following year. Calculate the market share (divisional share) for each division for both 2018 and 2019.

	Division	2018 sales in $M	2019 sales in $M
a.	Electrical	98.6	102.5
b.	Plumbing	76.2	79.4
c.	Paint	47.3	44.6
d.	Lumber	112.7	115.9
e.	Kitchen and Bath	126.6	138.4
f.	Lighting	86.6	84.2

3. Pepsi and Coke have been fighting for dominance in the soft drink industry for decades. In one year, Pepsi held 6.12% of the soft drink market and Coke held 11.95% of the market. If the market as a whole consumed 124.56B litres of soft drinks in the year, how many billions of litres of Coke and Pepsi were consumed?

4. Frito-Lay's two most popular brands of potato chips are Lays, with a 30.1% market share, and Ruffles, with a 10.4% market share. If sales in the potato chip market were $7.35B for the year, what were sales for Lays and Ruffles?

5. The home gym equipment industry in Canada had annual sales of $862.4M in 2019. Sales in the industry saw a slight decline of 2.5% in 2020. Sales for the top selling brands for the past two years are shown in the table below.
   a. Calculate the market share for each of the brands shown for 2019 and 2020.
   b. Calculate the market growth for each brand.
   c. What is the market growth for all other brands in the home gym equipment market?

	Brand	2019 sales in $M	2020 sales in $M
a.	Core Buster	103.49	102.61
b.	Life Fit	60.37	63.70
c.	Home Fit	43.12	42.55
d.	Torrent	155.23	160.87

6. Fassbender Industries tracks the annual sales from each of its six divisions to help evaluate performance and plan budgeting for the following year. Calculate the market growth (divisional growth) for each division.

	Division	2018 sales in $M	2019 sales in $M
a.	Electrical	98.6	102.5
b.	Plumbing	76.2	79.4
c.	Paint	47.3	44.6
d.	Lumber	112.7	115.9
e.	Kitchen and Bath	126.6	138.5
f.	Lighting	86.6	84.2

INTERMEDIATE PROBLEMS

7. BooBoo Banana Athletic Wear had sales of $146.27M in 2019, which represents a 3.6% market share. In 2020 their market share increased to 5.5% with sales of $239.11M. What is the market growth for the athletic wear industry?

8. Acme Ltd. had sales of $365M in 2019, which represents a 40% market share in the industry. In 2020 their market share decreased to 35% with sales of $309.82M. What is the market growth for the industry?

9. The top selling brand of cordless vacuums sold 14,000 units at $395 per unit in 2019. What is their market share if the cordless vacuum market had sales of $19.7M?

10. The two top selling brands in a specific market hold 24.5% and 18.6% market shares, respectively. If the top selling brand sold 242,650, how many units of the second top selling brand were sold during the year? Round your answer to the nearest whole number.

11. The smart speaker market in North America had sales of $2.9M in 2017 and ballooned to sales of $9.0M in 2018. Google-brand smart speakers had a 19.3% share of this market in 2017. This increased to a 36.2% market share in 2018. Compare the growth of the Google brand to the market growth of the smart speaker market from 2017 to 2018.

12. Industrial Supplies Warehouse tracks the performance of its sales team by looking at the sales share for the team and their annual sales growth. Calculate the missing values in the following table.

Salesperson	Yr 1 Sales	Yr 2 Sales	Yr 1 Share	Yr 2 Share	Growth
Adam	$200,000				5.00%
Beth		$147,000			−2.00%
Carl	$320,000	$332,800			
Dami		$126,000		12.0%	
Ephram	$230,000		23.0%		

KEY TERMS

Capital gain

Capital gain yield

Capital loss

Compounding rates of return

Holding period

Income

Income yield

Market growth

Market share

Rate of total return

Total return

SUMMARY OF NOTATION AND KEY FORMULAS

FORMULA (3-1) $Rate = \dfrac{Portion}{Base}$ Finding a percent

FORMULA (3-2) $c = \dfrac{V_f - V_i}{V_i} \times 100\%$ Finding the percent change in a quantity

V_i = Initial (or beginning or original or old) value
V_f = Final (or ending or new) value
c = Percent change (or its decimal equivalent)

FORMULA (3-3) $Income\ yield = \dfrac{Income}{V_i} \times 100\%$

$Capital\ gain\ yield = \dfrac{Capital\ gain}{V_i} \times 100\% = \dfrac{V_f - V_i}{V_i} \times 100\%$

         Finding investment yields and rate of total return

$Rate\ of\ total\ return = Income\ yield + Capital\ gain\ yield$

$= \dfrac{Income + Capital\ gain}{V_i} \times 100\%$

FORMULA (3-4) $V_f = V_i\,(1 + c_1)(1 + c_2)(1 + c_3) \ldots (1 + c_n)$ Finding final investment value after successive years of returns

FORMULA (3-5) $Market\ share = \dfrac{Brand\ sales\ volume}{Total\ industry\ sales\ volume} \times 100\%$

         Finding market share for one brand relative to the industry

FORMULA (3-6) $Market\ growth = \dfrac{Year\ 2\ sales - Year\ 1\ sales}{Year\ 1\ sales} \times 100\%$

         Finding the difference in annual sales volume for a brand or industry

REVIEW PROBLEMS

Answers to the odd-numbered review problems are at the end of the book.

BASIC PROBLEMS

1. **LO1** What percent of $6.39 is $16.39?
2. **LO1** 80% of what amount is $100?
3. **LO1** $\frac{3}{4}$% of what amount is $1.00?
4. **LO1** Fifteen minutes is what percentage of two hours?
5. **LO1** $150 is 200% of what amount?
6. **LO1** 450 grams is what percentage of 2 kg?
7. **LO1** How many dollars is 350% of 62¢?
8. **LO2** Solve each of the following:
   a. What amount is 17.5% more than $29.43?
   b. What amount reduced by 80% leaves $100?
   c. What amount reduced by 15% equals $100?
   d. What is $47.50 after an increase of 320%?
   e. What amount when decreased by 62% equals $213.56?
   f. What amount when increased by 125% equals $787.50?
   g. What amount is 30% less than $300?

9. **LO1** In a downtown Edmonton office building, 42% of its employees smoke. If 11% of the smokers join a stop-smoking group and the group has 17 members, how many employees are in the office building? Round your answer to the nearest whole person.

10. **LO2** Arctic sea ice has thinned in recent decades. In the mid 1960s the average thickness was 3.1 m. This dropped to an average thickness of 1.8 m in the mid 1990s. What was the percent reduction in ice thickness for this 30-year period?

11. **LO2** A Toyota Corolla could be purchased new in 1970 for $1686, while the more current 2019 model had a base price of $16,790. For this 49-year time period:
    a. What is the percent increase in the base price?
    b. If sales tax in 1970 was 5% and the current GST rate is 13%, what is the percent increase in the after-tax price?

12. **LO2** Yellowknife Mining sold 34,300 oz. of gold in Year 1 at an average price of $1160 per ounce. Production was down to 23,750 oz. in Year 2 because of a strike by the miners, but the average price obtained was $1280 per ounce. What was the percent change from Year 1 to Year 2 in:
    a. The amount of gold produced?
    b. The average selling price per ounce?
    c. The revenue from the sale of gold?

13. **LO2** Two years ago the shares of Diamond Strike Resources traded at a price of $3.40 per share. One year later the shares were at $11.50, but then they declined in value by 35% during the subsequent year. Calculate:
    a. The percent change in the share price during the first year.
    b. The current share price.

14. **LO2** Barry recently sold some stock after holding it for two years. The stock's price rose 150% during the first year, but fell 40% in the second year. At what price did he buy the stock if he sold it for $24 per share?

15. **LO2** Albion Distributors' revenues and expenses for the fiscal year just completed were $2,347,000 and $2,189,000, respectively.
    a. If in the current year revenues rise by 10% but expense increases are held to 5%, what will be the percent increase in profit?
    b. If, instead, revenues decline by 10% and expenses are reduced by 5%, what will be the percent change in profit?

16. **LO3** One year ago, Christos bought 1000 units of the Dominion Aggressive Growth Fund at $20.35 per unit. Today a unit's value is $19.10. During the year, the fund made a distribution of $0.40 per unit. On this investment, what is Christos's:
    a. Income yield?
    b. Capital gain yield?
    c. Total return in dollars?
    d. Rate of total return?

17. **LO4** A company's annual report states that its common shares had price gains of 23%, 10%, −15%, and 5% during the preceding four fiscal years. The share price stood at $30.50 after last year's 5% gain.
    a. What was the price of the shares at the beginning of the four-year period?
    b. How much (in dollars and cents) did the share price decline in the third year?

18. **LO4** A portfolio earned −13%, 18%, 5%, 24%, and −5% in five successive years. What was the portfolio's total rate of return for the five-year period?

19. **LO4** One of the more volatile mutual funds in recent years has been the AGF China Focus Fund. The fund's annual returns in successive years from 2007 to 2012 inclusive were 30.53%, −41.67%, 27.75%, 1.27%, −20.71%, and 17.0%, respectively. What was the fund's overall rate of return for the six years ended December 31, 2012?

20. **LO5** Home improvement stores in Ontario had sales of $12.8B in 2019, which represents 31.5% of the Canadian home improvement and building supplies industry.
    a. What were the total Canadian industry sales for 2019?
    b. What is the dollar value of industry sales Canada wide for 2020 if the industry is expecting growth of 2.6% in 2020?

21. **LO5** Bricks and Mortar Building Inc. has retail locations in five provinces.
    a. Calculate the market shares for each province for 2018 and 2019.
    b. Calculate the year-on-year market growth for each location.

Location	2018 sales in $M	2019 sales in $M
British Columbia	328.62	317.59
Alberta	388.54	397.52
Ontario	746.09	752.10
Quebec	558.27	548.77
Nova Scotia	98.66	97.15

INTERMEDIATE PROBLEMS

22. **LO1** Through a calculation on Canadian individual tax returns known as the Old Age Security (OAS) clawback, an individual receiving OAS benefits must repay an increasing portion of these benefits to the federal government as the individual's net income rises beyond a certain threshold. If the OAS clawback is 15% of net income exceeding $68,000, at what amount of net income must a taxpayer repay all $6300 of OAS benefits received in the year?

23. **LO3** Gabriel received $200 of income from an investment during the past year. This represents an income yield of 4%. If the capital gain yield for the year was 10%, what was the value of the investment (not including income) at the end of the year?

24. **LO3** An $8600 investment was worth only $7900 one year later. If the rate of total return for the year was −5%, how much income was received from the investment during the year?

Chapter 4
Ratios and Proportions

CHAPTER OUTLINE

LEARNING OBJECTIVES

After completing this chapter, you will be able to:

LO1 Set up and manipulate ratios

LO2 Set up and solve proportions

LO3 Use proportions to allocate or prorate an amount on a proportionate basis

LO4 Use quoted exchange rates to convert between currencies

LO5 Relate currency exchange rate movement to currency appreciation or depreciation

LO6 Interpret and use index numbers

RAW BUSINESS DATA CAN TAKE on greater meaning when comparisons are made between associated quantities. For example, a firm's profit for a year is an important figure in itself. However, profit relative to invested capital, profit relative to total sales, and current profit relative to last year's profit provide useful insights into the firm's profitability, efficiency, and profit growth. Ratios are widely used to make such comparisons. In accounting and finance, a primary technique for the detailed analysis and interpretation of financial statements is known as ratio analysis. Each financial statement ratio compares the size of one balance sheet or income statement figure to another. Each ratio provides an indication of a financial strength or weakness of the business. Ratios are routinely displayed in dashboards and used in funnel conversions to illustrate the efficiencies of online activities.

Ratios and proportions are also employed when resources, costs, profits, and so on must be allocated on a *pro rata*, or proportionate, basis. For example, a partnership's profits are commonly distributed among the partners in proportion to each partner's capital investment. Many quantities we encounter in economics and finance are ratios in disguise. Later in the chapter, we will discuss two examples—currency exchange rates and index numbers.

 TIP

How to Succeed in Business Mathematics

Since various Business Mathematics and Mathematics of Finance courses start at different points in the book, this Tip appears at the beginning of each of the first five chapters. Connect has a guide entitled "How to Succeed in Business Mathematics." If you have not done so already, carefully read its first two sections (A.1 and A.2) as soon as possible.

If your course bypassed **Chapter 1** and you are using a Texas Instruments BA II PLUS calculator, refer to **Appendix 1A** for information about settings that affect the calculator's display and order of operations.

4.1 | Ratios

L01 A **ratio** is a comparison, by division, of two or more quantities. Suppose that a store sells $2000 worth of Product X and $1500 worth of Product Y in a particular month. The ratio of the sales of Product X to the sales of Product Y may be expressed using any of the following notations:

- Using a colon, as in "2000 : 1500," which is read "2000 to 1500."
- As a common fraction, $\frac{2000}{1500}$.
- As the decimal equivalent of the common fraction, $1.3\overline{3}$.
- As the percent equivalent of the common fraction, $133\frac{1}{3}\%$.

In the first two forms, the components of the ratio separated by division are called the **terms of a ratio**.[1] Each of the terms in a ratio may be multiplied or divided by the same number to give an **equivalent ratio**. For example, both terms in the ratio 2000 : 1500 may be divided by 100 to give the equivalent ratio 20 : 15 or $\frac{20}{15}$.

Ratios may have as many terms as there are quantities being compared. If, in our example, the store sold $2500 worth of Product Z in the same month, the ratio of the sales of Products X, Y, and Z is 2000 : 1500 : 2500.

---

[1] It is unfortunate that the word *term* has two quite different uses in basic algebra. In **Chapter 2**, *term* referred to a component of an algebraic expression separated from other components by addition or subtraction signs. In this chapter, *term* refers to a component of a ratio set apart by division. The meaning of *term* must be inferred from the context in which it is used.

EXAMPLE 4.1A

EXPRESSING A RATIO USING DIFFERENT NOTATIONS

a. A hospital ward has 10 nurses caring for 60 patients. The ratio of nurses to patients can be expressed as:

$10:60$	Using the colon notation
$\frac{10}{60}$	As a common fraction
$0.1\overline{6}$	As a decimal equivalent
$16.\overline{6}\%$	As a percent equivalent

b. A survey of cars in a parking lot indicated that two-fifths of the cars were North American brands and one-quarter were Japanese brands. The ratio of North American to Japanese cars was:

$\frac{2}{5}:\frac{1}{4}$	Ratio with given terms in the colon notation
$0.4:0.25$	Using the colon notation with a decimal equivalent for each term
$\frac{0.4}{0.25}$	As a common fraction
160%	As a percent equivalent

Reducing a ratio to its lowest terms It is customary to express a ratio in its **lowest terms**; that is, as the equivalent ratio having the smallest integers possible for its terms. The relative size of the terms is then more apparent. Three cases require somewhat different procedures to reduce a ratio to its lowest terms.

1. If all terms in the given ratio are integers, divide every term by the common factors of all terms. For example, the terms in $2000:1500:2500$ have 100 and 5 as common factors. After dividing by 100 and 5 (or by their product, 500), the ratio becomes $4:3:5$. For an example, see **Example 4.1B**.
2. If one or more terms are decimal numbers, make all terms integers by moving the decimal point in *every* term to the right by the *same* number of places. Then reduce the ratio to its lowest terms as in the previous case. For an example, see part (b) of **Example 4.1C**.
3. If one or more terms contain a fraction, the terms should first be cleared of the fractions. Start by multiplying every term in the ratio by the denominator of any one of the fractions. Repeat this process using the denominator of any fraction that remains. When the ratio contains only integers, reduce the ratio to its lowest terms as in the first case. See part (c) of **Example 4.1C**.

EXAMPLE 4.1B

EXPRESSING A RATIO IN LOWEST TERMS

a. The costs of manufacturing an item are $150 for materials, $225 for labour, and $75 for overhead expenses. Express the ratio of labour cost to materials cost to overhead expenses in lowest terms.

$225:150:75$	Ratio with the given terms in the colon notation
$9:6:3$	Equivalent ratio (each term divided by 25)
$3:2:1$	Equivalent ratio with lowest terms (after division by 3)

b. A municipal development bylaw requires that a shopping centre provide four parking spots for each 100 m² of developed retail area. Express the ratio of parking spots to retail area in lowest terms:

$4:100$	Ratio with the given terms in the colon notation
$1:25$	Equivalent ratio with lowest terms (after division by 4)

Even though the two values in a ratio can have differing units (parking spaces and square metres in this case), the units are sometimes omitted when they are generally known from the context. In this case, one parking space is required for each 25 m² of retail area.

EXAMPLE 4.1C

REDUCING A RATIO TO ITS LOWEST TERMS

Reduce the following ratios to their lowest terms.

a. $105:63:84$

b. $1.2:1.68:0.72$

c. $\dfrac{3}{8}:\dfrac{5}{6}:\dfrac{1}{3}$

SOLUTION

a. $105:63:84$
   $= 35:21:28$ After dividing each term by 3.
   $= 5:3:4$ After dividing each term by 7.

b. $1.2:1.68:0.72$
   $= 120:168:72$ After multiplying each term by 100.
   $= 30:42:18$ After dividing each term by 4.
   $= 5:7:3$ After dividing each term by 6.

c. $\dfrac{3}{8}:\dfrac{5}{6}:\dfrac{1}{3} = \dfrac{9}{8}:\dfrac{5}{2}:1$ After multiplying each term by 3.

      $= \dfrac{18}{8}:\dfrac{10}{2}:2$ After multiplying each term by 2.

      $= 9:20:8$ After multiplying each term by 4.

 TIP

How Low Does It Go?

You can use the following checklist, in the order it appears below, to ensure you have a ratio in lowest terms.

A ratio is in lowest terms if it has:

1. No **fractions**
2. No **decimals**
3. No **common factors**

You should always re-check for common factors even if you have found one. If you have not used the highest common factor in the first division then the ratio still contains common factors. Repeat Step 3 until you have found all the factors. The product of all of the factors you have used will be the highest common factor.

Converting a ratio to an equivalent ratio whose smallest term is 1 The ratio $179:97:29$ is already in its lowest terms, but still contains rather large integers. In this situation, many people prefer to express the ratio as the equivalent ratio whose *smallest* term has the value 1. If we divide all terms by the smallest term, we obtain

$$\frac{179}{29}:\frac{97}{29}:\frac{29}{29} \text{ or } 6.17:3.34:1$$

where the terms have been rounded to three figures. The relative size of the terms is more apparent in $6.17:3.34:1$ than in $179:97:29$.

EXAMPLE 4.1D

DETERMINING AN EQUIVALENT RATIO HAVING 1 AS THE SMALLEST TERM

Convert each of the following ratios to an equivalent ratio having 1 as the smallest term. Round the resulting terms to three figures.

a. $117:79:167$

b. $1.05:8.1:2.2$

c. $\frac{18}{19}:1\frac{13}{14}$

SOLUTION

a. $117:79:167 = \frac{117}{79}:\frac{79}{79}:\frac{167}{79}$ After dividing each term by the smallest term, 79.

$= 1.48:1:2.11$

b. $1.05:8.1:2.2 = \frac{1.05}{1.05}:\frac{8.1}{1.05}:\frac{2.2}{1.05}$ After dividing each term by the smallest term, 1.05.

$= 1:7.71:2.10$

c. $\frac{18}{19}:1\frac{13}{14} = 0.947:1.929$ After converting the fractions to decimal equivalents.

$= \frac{0.947}{0.947}:\frac{1.929}{0.947}$ After dividing by the smaller term, 0.947.

$= 1:2.04$

APP ④ THAT

To gain an impression of how important and how widespread is the use of ratios in business and finance, search the App Store on your tablet, smartphone, or smart watch using the key words **FINANCIAL RATIOS**.

You will find many free and paid apps that define and calculate a variety of financial and business ratios. Some apps also provide data collection and analysis tools.

EXERCISE 4.1

Answers to the odd-numbered problems are at the end of the book.

CALCULATOR-FREE PROBLEMS

Express each of the following ratios in its lowest terms.

a. $5:75$ **b.** $20:4:36$ **c.** $0.2:0.8$

d. $0.2:2:0.02$ **e.** $\frac{1}{2}:\frac{1}{4}$ **f.** $\frac{1}{3}:\frac{1}{9}$

Express each of the following ratios as an equivalent ratio whose smallest term is 1.

g. $25:2.5$ **h.** $35:7:77$ **i.** $\frac{3}{2}:\frac{1}{4}$

Set up a ratio in each of Problems j and k and express the ratio in lowest terms.

j. A recipe for macaroni and cheese calls for 3 cups of macaroni and 1.5 cups of cheese for 6 servings. Write the ratio for servings to cheese to macaroni.

k. Lalita owns a 4-kg Chihuahua, a 28-kg Poodle, and a 48-kg German Shepherd. What is the ratio for the weights of the Poodle to the Chihuahua to the German Shepherd?

Express each of the following ratios in its lowest terms.

1. $12:64$

2. $56:21$

3. $45:15:30$

4. $26:130:65$

5. $0.08:0.12$

6. $2.5:3.5:3$

7. $0.84:1.4:1.96$

8. $11.7:7.8:3.9$

9. $0.24:0.39:0.15$

10. $0.091:0.021:0.042$

11. $\frac{1}{8}:\frac{3}{4}$

12. $\frac{4}{3}:\frac{3}{2}$

13. $\frac{3}{5}:\frac{6}{7}$

14. $\frac{11}{3}:\frac{11}{7}$

15. $1\frac{1}{4}:1\frac{2}{3}$

16. $2\frac{1}{2}:\frac{5}{8}$

17. $4\frac{1}{8}:2\frac{1}{5}$

18. $\frac{2}{3}:\frac{3}{4}:\frac{5}{6}$

19. $\frac{1}{15}:\frac{1}{5}:\frac{1}{10}$

20. $10\frac{1}{2}:7:4\frac{1}{5}$

Express each of the following ratios as an equivalent ratio whose smallest term is 1. Maintain three-figure accuracy.

21. $7.6:3$

22. $1.41:8.22$

23. $0.177:0.81$

24. $0.0131:0.0086$

25. $\frac{3}{7}:\frac{19}{17}$

26. $4\frac{3}{13}:\frac{27}{17}$

27. $77:23:41$

28. $11:38:27$

29. $3.5:5.4:8$

30. $0.47:0.15:0.26$

31. $\frac{5}{8}:\frac{17}{11}:\frac{6}{7}$

32. $5\frac{1}{2}:3\frac{3}{4}:8\frac{1}{3}$

Set up a ratio in each of Problems 33–40. If the ratio cannot be reduced to an equivalent ratio in terms of small integers, then express it as a ratio of decimal equivalents with the smallest term set at 1. Maintain three-figure accuracy.

33. An online business purchased 15,000 Google display ads that 1250 people clicked on, and 250 purchases were finalized as a result of the ads. What is the ratio of ads displayed to clicks to purchases?

34. An online catalogue business sent out 12,000 emails to previous customers in its database, of which 10,500 were successfully delivered and 750 were opened. What is the ratio of emails sent to emails delivered to emails opened?

35. Shaheed has budgeted 12% of his monthly spending to cell phone and internet, 22% to food, and 40% to rent and utilities. What is the ratio of his spending for cell phone and internet to food to rent and utilities?

36. Don, Bob, and Ron Maloney's partnership interests in Maloney Bros. Contracting are in the ratio of their capital contributions of $78,000, $52,000, and $65,000, respectively. What is the ratio of Bob's to Ron's to Don's partnership interest?

37. Victoria Developments has obtained $3.6 million of total capital from three sources. Preferred shareholders contributed $550,000 (preferred equity), common shareholders contributed $1.2 million (common equity), and the remainder was borrowed (debt). What is the firm's ratio of debt to preferred equity to common equity?

38. The cost to manufacture a fibreglass boat consists of $4480 for materials, $6330 for direct labour, and $2650 for overhead. Express the three cost components as a ratio.

39. A provincial government budget forecasts expenditures of $1.56 billion on education, $1.365 billion on health services, and $975 million on social services. Express the three budget items as a ratio.

40. The brine used in an industrial process is 12.5% salt by weight. What is the ratio (by weights) of salt to water in the brine?

41. The instructions for preparing the fuel mix for a two-cycle engine are to add 250 mL of oil to 5 L of gasoline. What is the ratio (by volumes) of gasoline to oil in the fuel mix?

42. Jenn spends 1 hour and 45 minutes a day playing online games. Her sister Amanda spends 3 hours and 30 minutes a day gaming online, and their brother Steve spends 6 hours and 15 minutes a day playing online games. Write the ratio for the number of hours Jenn, Amanda, and Steve play online games.

43. The bounce rate measures the percentage of visitors who leave a Web site after viewing only one page. If a Web page has a bounce rate of 62.5% what is the ratio of bounces to visitors?

4.2 | Proportions

LO2 In **Section 4.1** we introduced ratios using an example in which sales of Products X, Y, and Z in a month were $2000, $1500, and $2500, respectively. When we reduce this ratio to its lowest terms we have $4:3:5$. We will extend the same example to illustrate proportions. Mathematics has a special notation for a compact version of the statement "the ratio of the sales of X to the sales of Y is $4:3$." This notation is

$$\text{Sales of X}:\text{Sales of Y} = 4:3$$

If we let x represent "sales of Product X" and y represent "sales of Product Y," a still more compact statement is

$$x:y = 4:3$$

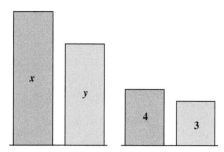

The diagram above illustrates what this equation is saying. It shows two columns having known heights "4" and "3," and two other columns of unknown heights "x" and "y." The equation provides the following additional information about columns "x" and "y"—they have the same relative height as the known columns. That is, although we do not know x or y individually, we do know that x is $33\frac{1}{3}\%$ larger than y because 4 is $33\frac{1}{3}\%$ larger than 3. With this extra information we recognize that, given a value for either x or y, we can then calculate the value of the other variable.

The equation "$x:y = 4:3$" is an example of a proportion. In general, a **proportion** is a statement of the equality of two ratios. The language we use to express this proportion is

"x is to y **as** 4 is to 3"

When using proportions to solve problems, first convert each ratio to its equivalent fraction. In the current example, we can rewrite the proportion as the equation

$$\frac{x}{y} = \frac{4}{3}$$

Given either x or y, you can solve for the other variable. For example, suppose that the sales of Product X in the next month are forecast to be $1800. What will be the sales of Product Y if the sales of the two products maintain the same ratio? You can answer this question by substituting $x = \$1800$ and solving for y:

$$\frac{\$1800}{y} = \frac{4}{3}$$

You can clear the equation of fractions by multiplying both sides by $3y$. This gives

$$\frac{\$1800}{y} \times 3y = \frac{4}{3} \times 3y$$

After simplifying each side, you obtain

$$\$1800 \times 3 = 4y$$

TIP

A One-Step Method for Clearing Fractions

To obtain

$$\$1800 \times 3 = 4y \text{ directly from } \frac{\$1800}{y} = \frac{4}{3}$$

you can use the single-step method of *cross-multiplication* to replace the method of clearing the fractions used above. Simply multiply each numerator by the denominator from the other side, as indicated below.

$$\frac{\$1800}{y} \diagdown \frac{4}{3}$$

It is also valid to perform just one of the two cross-multiplications. For example, to solve for w in

$$\frac{w}{\$1400} = \frac{7}{5}$$

just cross-multiply $\$1400$ by 7, giving

$$w = \frac{7 \times \$1400}{5} = \$1960$$

Returning to the calculation of y,

$$y = \frac{\$1800 \times 3}{4} = \$1350$$

The projected sales of Product Y in the next month are $1350.

EXAMPLE 4.2A

SOLVING A PROPORTION

a. $3:5 = 9:x$　　　　　　　　**b.** $2.5:y = 4:7$

SOLUTION

a.　$\dfrac{3}{5} = \dfrac{9}{x}$　　　　　Express each ratio as a fraction.

　　　$3x = 45$　　　　　Cross-multiply.

　　　$x = \dfrac{45}{3} = 15$　　　Divide both sides by the coefficient of x.

b.　$\dfrac{2.5}{y} = \dfrac{4}{7}$　　　　　Express each ratio as a fraction.

　　　$7(2.5) = 4y$　　　　Cross-multiply.

　　　$y = \dfrac{7(2.5)}{4} = 4.375$　　Divide both sides by the coefficient of y.

EXAMPLE 4.2B

SOLVING A WORD PROBLEM USING A PROPORTION

Betty and Lois have already invested $8960 and $6880, respectively, in their partnership. If Betty invests another $5000, what amount should Lois contribute to maintain their investments in the original ratio?

SOLUTION

Lois and Betty's additional investments must be in the same ratio as their initial investments. That is,

Lois's investment : Betty's investment = $6880 : $8960

Let Lois's additional investment be represented by x. Then

$$x : \$5000 = \$6880 : \$8960$$

Writing the ratios as fractions,

$$\frac{x}{\$5000} = \frac{\$6880}{\$8960}$$

Therefore,

$$x = \frac{\$6880 \times \$5000}{\$8960} = \$3839.29$$

Lois should contribute $3839.29 to maintain the same ratio of investment in the partnership.

Proportions with three variables From Section 4.1, the value of the ratio

Sales of X : Sales of Y : Sales of Z

was $4:3:5$ in the base month. That is,

$$x : y : z = 4:3:5$$

where x, y, and z represent the monthly sales of products X, Y, and Z, respectively. Read the proportion as follows:

"x is to y is to z **as** 4 is to 3 is to 5"

This proportion implies a separate proportion for each pair of terms. That is,

$$x : y = 4:3 \quad \text{and} \quad y : z = 3:5 \quad \text{and} \quad x : z = 4:5$$

We can construct the following three equations from them.

$$\frac{x}{y} = \frac{4}{3} \quad \text{and} \quad \frac{y}{z} = \frac{3}{5} \quad \text{and} \quad \frac{x}{z} = \frac{4}{5}$$

If we know just one of the three variables x, y, and z, these equations allow us to solve for the other two. Example 4.2C provides an illustration.

 TIP

Maintain Terms in a Consistent Order

When you extract a simple proportion from a more complex proportion, keep the proportion's terms in the same order on both sides of the simple proportion (and its corresponding equation). For example, if $a:5:7 = 4:3:c$, then you may write

$$a:5 = 4:3 \quad \text{or} \quad 5:a = 3:4 \quad \text{but } not \quad a:5 = 3:4.$$

Furthermore, you may write

$$\frac{a}{5} = \frac{4}{3} \quad \text{or} \quad \frac{5}{a} = \frac{3}{4} \quad \text{but } not \quad \frac{a}{5} = \frac{3}{4}$$

EXAMPLE 4.2C

SOLVING A PROPORTION HAVING TWO UNKNOWNS

Solve the following proportion for x and y.

$$2:5:3 = 7:x:y$$

SOLUTION

Based on the given proportion, we can construct two simpler proportions, each of which contains only one unknown.

$$2:5 = 7:x \quad \text{and} \quad 2:3 = 7:y$$

Then

$$\frac{2}{5} = \frac{7}{x} \quad \text{and} \quad \frac{2}{3} = \frac{7}{y}$$

After cross-multiplication, these equations become

$$2x = 35 \quad \text{and} \quad 2y = 21$$

Hence,

$$x = \frac{35}{2} = 17.5 \quad \text{and} \quad y = \frac{21}{2} = 10.5$$

 TRAP

Always Use Given Information

When solving a proportion with more than two terms it is possible to solve for the second unknown term using the solution for the first solved term. For **Example 4.2C**, where

$$2:5:3 = 7:x:y$$

we solved for $x = 17.5$ using $\frac{2}{5} = \frac{7}{x}$.

You could solve for y using $5:3 = x:y$.

Then $\frac{5}{3} = \frac{17.5}{y}$ using the solution for x calculated above.

The solution for y now depends on a correct solution for x. If x is incorrect, y will also be incorrect. Always use given information when solving complex proportions.

EXAMPLE 4.2D

SOLVING A PROBLEM USING A PROPORTION

A 560-bed hospital operates with 232 registered nurses and 185 other support staff. The hospital is about to open a new 86-bed wing. Assuming the same proportionate staffing levels, how many more nurses and support staff will need to be hired?

SOLUTION

Let n represent the number of additional nurses and s the number of additional staff. Then n and s must satisfy the proportion

$$\text{Beds:Nurses:Staff} = 560:232:185 = 86:n:s$$

Therefore,

$$\frac{560}{232} = \frac{86}{n} \qquad \text{and} \qquad \frac{560}{185} = \frac{86}{s}$$

$$560n = 86 \times 232 \qquad\qquad 560s = 86 \times 185$$

$$n = \frac{86 \times 232}{560} \qquad\qquad s = \frac{86 \times 185}{560}$$

$$= 35.6 \qquad\qquad\qquad = 28.4$$

Rounding the calculated values to the nearest integer, the hospital should hire 36 nurses and 28 support staff for the new wing.

EXAMPLE 4.2E

SOLVING A PROBLEM USING SUCCESSIVE PROPORTIONS

Trina spent 1/5 of her annual income on a vacation. Food and accommodations for the trip cost $4550, which represents 2/3 of her vacation budget. What is Trina's annual income?

SOLUTION

Let a represent Trina's annual income.

2/3 of 1/5 of her annual income is worth $4550:

$$\frac{2}{3} \times \frac{1}{5}a = \$4550$$

$$\frac{2a}{15} = \$4550$$

$$a = \frac{\$4550 \times 15}{2} = \$34{,}125$$

Trina's annual income is $34,125.

 POINT OF INTEREST

The Price-to-Performance Ratio

People in the computer industry have recognized that the price-to-performance ratio comparison presented in advertisements can actually provide a reason *not* to purchase the advertised computer. Think about what, at a basic mathematical level, will make the price-to-performance ratio high. A large numerator (*high* price) and/or a small denominator (*low* performance) will make the ratio high. Therefore, a higher ratio represents a *lower* "bang for your buck."

The price-to-performance ratio can also be used to track changes in products over time. Computers in particular have a constantly fluctuating price-to-performance ratio. Over time the price of computers has dropped dramatically, making them more accessible to the average consumer while processing power has improved significantly.

EXERCISE 4.2

Answers to the odd-numbered problems are at the end of the book.

CALCULATOR-FREE PROBLEMS

Solve the following proportions for the unknown quantities.

a. $7:2 = 21:x$

b. $3:z = 1.5:4$

c. $5:15:50 = 3:j:k$

d. $m:3 = \frac{1}{2}:\frac{1}{4}$

Solve the following problems using proportions.

e. A recipe for pasta sauce makes 6 servings with 3 cups of crushed tomatoes. How many cups of tomatoes would be needed to make 2 servings?

f. Mr. and Mrs. Bond pay their three children allowances that are proportional to their ages. If their children's ages are in the ratio $1:2:6$ how much should the youngest and oldest children get as an allowance if the middle child gets $5.00 a week?

BASIC PROBLEMS

Solve the following proportions for the unknown quantities (maintain three-figure accuracy in problems where rounding is needed).

1. $9:7 = 54:b$

2. $17:q = 119:91$

3. $88:17 = a:45$

4. $d:13.2 = 16:31$

5. $1.89:0.31 = 175:k$

6. $1.56:h = 56.2:31.7$

7. $0.043:y = 550:198$

8. $0.057:0.149 = z:0.05$

9. $m:\dfrac{3}{4} = \dfrac{1}{2}:\dfrac{9}{8}$

10. $\dfrac{10}{3}:\dfrac{12}{7} = \dfrac{5}{18}:r$

11. $6:7:5 = n:105:m$

12. $3:4:13 = x:y:6.5$

13. $625:f:500 = g:3:4$

14. $a:58:132 = 38:27:b$

15. $0.69:1.17:0.4 = r:s:6.5$

16. $8500:x:y = 1.\overline{3}:1:1.\overline{6}$

Solve the following problems using proportions.

17. The Borellis wish to purchase a larger house to accommodate their growing family. The current year's property tax on their home amounts to $3545 based on its assessed value of $328,000. The assessed value of a property they are seriously considering is $437,000. What property tax can the Borellis expect to pay on this home if property taxes are in the same ratio as assessed values?

18. The West Essex School Board employs 348 teachers for the 7412 students registered in the board's schools in the current year. The enrolment forecast for next year is 7780 students. Assuming the same student–teacher ratio for the next year, how many additional teaching positions must the board fill?

19. A high-definition movie lasting 1 hour and 45 minutes consumed 4.5 GB of memory on the hard drive of a personal video recorder (PVR). Rounded to the nearest minute, what is the maximum duration of high-definition recording that could be saved on the PVR's 80-GB hard drive?

20. Connie's neighbour sold 14.5 hectares of raw land for $128,000. If Connie were to sell her 23.25-hectare parcel at a proportionate price, to the nearest dollar, what amount would she receive?

21. Based on past experience, a manufacturing process requires 2.3 hours of direct labour for each $174 worth of raw materials processed. If the company is planning to consume $78,300 worth of raw materials, what total amount should it budget for labour at $31.50 per hour?

22. An international equity mutual fund includes American stocks, Japanese stocks, German stocks, and British stocks in the ratio $27:19:14:11$, respectively. If its current holdings of German stocks are valued at US$238 million, what are the values of its holdings in the securities of the other three countries?

23. The worldwide sales for Samsung, Apple, and Huawei smartphones in the first quarter of 2018 were in the ratio $21:14:11$. If Huawei had sales of 40.4 million units, what were the first-quarter sales for Apple and Samsung during the same time period?

24. A punch recipe calls for fruit juice, ginger ale, and vodka to be mixed in the ratio $6:2.5:1$. How much fruit juice and vodka should be mixed with a 2-L bottle of ginger ale?

25. A business consultant is analyzing the cost structure of two firms in the grocery business. On sales of $3.66 million, Thrifty's had wholesale costs of $2.15 million and overhead expenses of $1.13 million. If Economart had the same proportionate costs on its sales of $5.03 million, what would be its wholesale costs and overhead expenses?

26. A province's Ministry of Social Services has found that both the number of people needing social assistance and the province's total expenditures on social assistance are proportional to the rate of unemployment. Last August, when the provincial unemployment rate was 8.4%, the province provided assistance to 89,300 individuals at a total cost of $107.4 million. The forecast unemployment rate for next August is 7.9%. How many people can the province expect to need social assistance next August? What amount should the province budget for social assistance in August?

27. The Red Deer location of a national franchise has followers on Twitter, Facebook, and Instagram in the ratio of 14,500 : 22,300 : 8500. If this location is representative for the Alberta franchises, how many Twitter and Instagram followers should the Medicine Hat location expect if they have 17,200 Facebook followers? Round your answer to the nearest 100.

28. Statistics are kept for hockey goalies tracking their goals-against average (GAA), or the number of goals allowed in 60 minutes of play (not counting empty-net goals). If a goalie has a 1.35 GAA, how many goals would you expect them to allow in 150 minutes of play? Round your answer to the nearest whole number.

INTERMEDIATE PROBLEMS

29. Tom Nortons Donuts considers the Hamilton area to be its most mature, fully exploited market. The 59 outlets in the metropolitan area serve a population of 675,000 and generate annual sales of $66.67 million. The management of Tom Nortons views its Calgary market as underexploited. The 65 outlets generate annual sales of $63.05 million from a population of 1,075,000. If Tom Nortons had penetrated the Calgary market to the same degree and success as the Hamilton market, how many additional outlets would it have, and how much higher (rounded to the nearest $0.01 million) would its annual sales be?

30. The Ministry of Education reported that a certain province's average school district has 13,450 students in "K–12" programs, an annual budget of $87.4 million, and 635 full-time-equivalent teachers. The Middleton School District (MSD), with an annual budget of $69.1 million and 498 teachers, serves 10,320 students. What adjustments would have to be made to MSD's budget and staffing to have it in the same proportion to enrolment as the provincial average?

31. Shirley had a three-sevenths interest in a partnership. She sold three-fifths of her interest for $27,000.
    a. What is the implied value of the entire partnership?
    b. What is the implied value of Shirley's remaining partnership interest?

32. Regal Resources owns a 58% interest in a mineral claim. Yukon Explorations owns the remainder. If Regal sells one-fifth of its interest for $1.2 million, what is the implied value of Yukon's interest?

33. The statistics for a professional accounting program indicate that five-sevenths of those who enter the program complete Level 1. Two-ninths of the Level 1 completers do not finish Level 2. If 587 students completed Level 2 last year, how many (including this group of 587) began Level 1?

34. Executive Fashions sold four-sevenths of its inventory at cost in a bankruptcy sale. The remainder was sold at 45% of cost to liquidators for $6700.
    a. What was the original cost of the inventory that was sold to the liquidators?
    b. What were the proceeds from the bankruptcy sale?

4.3 Application: Allocation and Proration

L03 Many instances occur in business where an amount of money must be allocated among partners, departments, cost centres, and so on. If the allocation is not made equally then a procedure called **proration** must be used so that the allocation is made on a proportionate basis.

We will illustrate the formal approach to proration using the following example. Connor and Kristen invested $45,000 and $72,000, respectively, to start up CK Partners. The partnership's profit is to be allocated in proportion to their respective investments. In the first year, the profit was $58,500. What amounts should be allocated to Connor and Kristen?[2]

The situation is represented pictorially below. The profit of $58,500 must be split into two parts so that Connor's portion, C, relative to Kristen's portion, K, is the same as 45 relative to 72 ($45,000 relative to $72,000). In mathematics,

$$C:K = 45:72$$

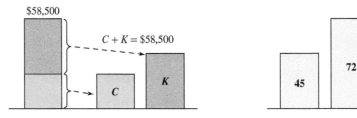

We can make the proportion more complete by adding a third term to represent the total amount to be allocated.

$$\left(\begin{matrix}\text{Connor's} \\ \text{portion}\end{matrix}\right) : \left(\begin{matrix}\text{Kristen's} \\ \text{portion}\end{matrix}\right) : \left(\begin{matrix}\text{Total profit} \\ \text{to be allocated}\end{matrix}\right) = 45 \text{ shares}:72 \text{ shares}:117 \text{ total shares}$$

$$C:K:\$58{,}500 = 45:72:117$$

Now we can determine C and K by solving two equations based on this proportion.

$$\frac{C}{\$58{,}500} = \frac{45}{117} \quad \text{and} \quad \frac{K}{\$58{,}500} = \frac{72}{117}$$

Using cross-multiplication, we obtain Connor's share as,

$$C = \frac{45 \times \$58{,}500}{117} = \$22{,}500$$

and Kristen's share as,

$$K = \frac{72 \times \$58{,}500}{117} = \$36{,}000$$

In general, if we have a proportion such as

$$x:y = a:b$$

then we can also write the proportion

$$x:y:(x + y) = a:b:(a + b)$$

and construct the equations

$$\frac{x}{y} = \frac{a}{b}, \frac{x}{x + y} = \frac{a}{a + b}, \quad \text{and} \quad \frac{y}{x + y} = \frac{b}{a + b}$$

Many more applications of proration are presented in the following examples and in the problems of **Exercise 4.3.**

---

[2] A more intuitive approach may occur to you for doing this profit allocation. But your intuition may fail you in situations that are more complex than this simple two-way split. The formal approach presented here will "pay dividends" when you encounter more complex scenarios.

EXAMPLE 4.3A

ALLOCATING PROFITS BASED ON THE AMOUNT INVESTED BY EACH OWNER

The partnership of Mr. X, Mr. Y, and Ms. Z has agreed to distribute profits in the same proportion as their respective capital investments in the partnership. How will the recent period's profit of $28,780 be allocated if Mr. X's capital account shows a balance of $34,000, Mr. Y's shows $49,000, and Ms. Z's shows $54,500?

SOLUTION

The ratio of a partner's share of the profit to the total profit will equal the ratio of that partner's capital investment to the total investment.

$$\text{Total investment} = \$34,000 + \$49,000 + \$54,500 = \$137,500$$

$$\frac{\text{Mr. X's share}}{\text{Total profit}} = \frac{\text{Mr. X's investment}}{\text{Total investment}}$$

$$\frac{\text{Mr. X's share}}{\$28,780} = \frac{\$34,000}{\$137,500}$$

$$\text{Mr. X's share} = \frac{\$34,000}{\$137,500} \times \$28,780 = \$7116.51$$

Similarly,

$$\text{Mr. Y's share} = \frac{\$49,000}{\$137,500} \times \$28,780 = \$10,256.15$$

Either of two approaches may now be employed to calculate Ms. Z's share. The longer approach has the advantage of providing a means of checking the answers. In it we calculate Ms. Z's share in the same manner as the other two shares:

$$\text{Ms. Z's share} = \frac{\$54,500}{\$137,500} \times \$28,780 = \$11,407.35$$

The allocations can be checked by verifying that their total, within rounding error, is $28,780:

$$\$7116.51 + \$10,256.15 + \$11,407.35 = \$28,780.01$$

The shorter method for calculating Ms. Z's share is to calculate the balance left from the $28,780 after Mr. X's and Mr. Y's shares have been paid out:

$$\text{Ms. Z's share} = \$28,780.00 - \$7116.51 - \$10,256.15$$
$$= \$11,407.34$$

However, with this method we do not have a means of checking the calculations since, in effect, we have forced Ms. Z's share to be the balance of the $28,780 (whether Mr. X's and Mr. Y's shares were calculated correctly or not).

EXAMPLE 4.3B

ALLOCATING A FIRM'S OVERHEAD COSTS

The Quebec plant of a manufacturing company produced 10,000 units of a product during the last fiscal quarter using 5000 hours of direct labour. In the same period, the Ontario plant produced 20,000 units using 9000 hours of direct labour. How will overhead costs of $49,000 for the period be allocated between the two plants if the allocation is based on:

a. Direct labour hours?

b. Units of output?

SOLUTION

a.

$$\frac{\text{Quebec's share}}{\text{Total overhead}} = \frac{\text{Quebec's labour hours}}{\text{Total labour hours}}$$

$$\frac{\text{Quebec's share}}{\$49,000} = \frac{5000}{5000 + 9000}$$

$$\text{Quebec's share} = \frac{5000}{14,000} \times \$49,000 = \$17,500.00$$

Similarly,

$$\text{Ontario's share} = \frac{9000}{14,000} \times \$49,000 = \$31,500.00$$

b.

$$\frac{\text{Quebec's share}}{\text{Total overhead}} = \frac{\text{Quebec's output}}{\text{Total output}}$$

$$\frac{\text{Quebec's share}}{\$49,000} = \frac{10,000}{10,000 + 20,000}$$

$$\text{Quebec's share} = \frac{10,000}{30,000} \times \$49,000 = \$16,333.33$$

Similarly,

$$\text{Ontario's share} = \frac{20,000}{30,000} \times \$49,000 = \$32,666.67$$

EXAMPLE 4.3C

PRORATING A REFUND BASED ON THE UNUSED TIME PERIOD

Franco paid $2116 for his automobile insurance coverage for the period July 1 to June 30. He sold his car and cancelled the insurance on March 8. The insurer's procedure is to calculate a refund prorated to the exact number of days remaining in the period of coverage. (March 8 is not included in the refundable days.) A $20 service charge is then deducted. What refund will Franco receive?

SOLUTION

The basis for calculating the refund (before the service charge) is:

$$\frac{\text{Refund}}{\text{Annual premium}} = \frac{\text{Number of remaining days of coverage}}{365 \text{ days}}$$

The "unused" days in the July 1 to June 30 period are the 23 days remaining in March plus all of April, May, and June. (See **Appendix 7A** for a method of determining the number of days in each month.) Hence,

$$\frac{\text{Refund}}{\$2116} = \frac{23 + 30 + 31 + 30}{365}$$

$$\text{Refund} = \frac{114 \times \$2116}{365}$$

$$= \$660.89$$

After deduction of the $20 service charge, the net refund will be $640.89.

EXAMPLE 4.3D

MAINTAINING PROPORTIONATE OWNERSHIP IN A BUYOUT

The ownership interests of the four partners in a marina are 20% for Pat, 30% for Quincy, 15% for Randolph, and 35% for Serge. The partners have agreed on an arrangement to buy out Pat for $100,000. Quincy, Randolph, and

Serge will divide the 20% interest and contribute to the $100,000 cost in proportions that leave them with the same relative ownership interests as they now possess.

a. What will their ownership interests be after the sale?

b. How much should each partner contribute toward the $100,000 purchase price?

SOLUTION

a. Before the sale, the ownership ratio for the three continuing partners is

$$\text{Quincy} : \text{Randolph} : \text{Serge} = \frac{30}{100} : \frac{15}{100} : \frac{35}{100} = 30 : 15 : 35$$

After the sale, 100% ownership is to be allocated to Quincy, Randolph, and Serge in the ratio $30 : 15 : 35$. Since

$$30 + 15 + 35 = 80$$

we can allocate the 100% ownership in the required ratio by assigning

$$\frac{30}{80} \times 100\% = 37.5\% \text{ to Quincy}$$

$$\frac{15}{80} \times 100\% = 18.75\% \text{ to Randolph}$$

$$\frac{35}{80} \times 100\% = 43.75\% \text{ to Serge}$$

After the sale of Pat's interest in the marina, Quincy, Randolph, and Serge will own 37.5%, 18.75%, and 43.75%, respectively, of the partnership.

b. The partners' allocation of the $100,000 purchase price should be in the same ratio as their ownership interests. Therefore,

$$\text{Quincy should contribute } 0.375 \times \$100,000 = \$37,500$$
$$\text{Randolph should contribute } 0.1875 \times \$100,000 = \$18,750$$
$$\text{Serge should contribute } 0.4375 \times \$100,000 = \$43,750$$

EXERCISE 4.3

Answers to the odd-numbered problems are at the end of the book.

CALCULATOR-FREE PROBLEMS

a. Shawn purchased a box of 1000 screws for a decking project that cost him $60.00 (before tax). When the project was completed he returned a part box of 400 screws. How much was the refund (without tax)?

b. Winnings from a lottery ticket are to be divided among four co-workers in the ratio $1:2:3:4$. If they collectively won $10,000, how much of the total winnings should each person receive?

c. Mr. and Mrs. Smith give their three children, Matt, Pat, and Stanley, weekly allowances in the ratio $1:3:6$. The total allowance for the three children is $90 a week. When Stanley got a full-time job, the Smiths decided to stop his allowance and divide it between Matt and Pat in proportions that leave them with the same relative allowances they had. How much will Matt and Pat now receive as allowances?

BASIC PROBLEMS

1. A three-year magazine subscription costing $136 may be cancelled at any time, and a prorated refund will be made for the remaining weekly issues. If Juanita cancels her subscription after receiving 17 issues in the second year, what refund should she get? Assume there are exactly 52 weeks in a year.

2. When real estate is sold, the year's property taxes are allocated to the vendor and the purchaser in proportion to the number of days that each party owns the property during the year. If the purchaser took possession of a property effective August 8 (of a 365-day year), how will the year's property taxes of $2849 be allocated to the vendor and purchaser?

3. On May 3, Mary Ann bought a two-year membership in a fitness club for $1260, on a special promotion. Cancellation is allowed at any time. A prorated refund will be paid, based upon the number of days remaining in the membership period. If she cancelled the membership on the following September 9, what refund should she receive? (Count both May 3 and September 9 as days used.)

4. If you use your car for both business and pleasure, the Canada Revenue Agency will usually allow you to report a portion of the costs of operating the vehicle as a business expense. This portion is determined by the ratio of the distance travelled on business to the total distance travelled in the year. Last year, Harjap spent a total of $11,348 on gasoline, oil, repairs and maintenance, and insurance. His travel log shows that he drove 14,488 km on business and 8329 km on personal use. What vehicle expense can Harjap report for the year?

5. If you operate a home-based business, the Canada Revenue Agency (CRA) will usually allow you to report certain "office-in-home" expenses. The portion of heat, insurance, electricity, property taxes, and mortgage interest that you may report must be (in the language of the CRA) "reasonable under the circumstances." Rose uses 2 of the 11 rooms in her home for her real estate appraisal business. The combined floor area of the 2 rooms is 36 square metres. The remainder of the house has an area of 147 square metres. Rose's total expenses in the home-related categories were $17,512 for the year. What amount will qualify as "office-in-home" expenses if the proration is based on:
   a. The number of rooms used for the business?
   b. The floor area devoted to business use?

6. The leases in multiple-unit commercial developments commonly permit the landlord to allocate to the tenants various common area and general costs such as property taxes, janitorial services, security services, and snow removal. These costs are usually prorated on the basis of the floor area leased to each tenant. Granny's Chicken, Toys'n Novelties, and Pine Tree Pharmacy are the three tenants in Pine Tree Square. They lease 172 square metres, 136 square metres, and 420 square metres, respectively. How should common costs totalling $9872 for the past year be allocated?

7. Andy, Candy, and Sandy agree to split the annual cost of $2739 for high-speed internet for the apartment they share. If the three roommates agree to allocate the cost of the service and their usage of the monthly download allowance in the ratio $3:8:5$, respectively:
   a. What is the cost per month for the service that each roommate is responsible for?
   b. How will the monthly usage allowance of 500 GB be distributed?

8. Mr. Bartlett's will specified that, upon liquidation of any asset, the proceeds be divided among his wife, his son, and his sister in the ratio of $7:5:3$.
   a. If the son received $9500 from the sale of securities, what amounts did Bartlett's wife and sister receive?
   b. What amount would the sister receive from the sale of the deceased's boat for $27,000?

9. Their partnership agreement requires Bella, Edward, and Jacob to provide capital "when and as required" by the partnership in the ratio $1:1.35:0.85$, respectively.
   a. The total initial capital requirement was $256,000. How much did each partner contribute?
   b. One year later, Jacob's share of an additional injection of capital was $16,320. What was Edward's share?

INTERMEDIATE PROBLEMS

10. Kevin, Lyle, and Marnie operate Food Country as a partnership. Their agreement provides that half of the profit in each calendar quarter be distributed in proportion to each partner's investment in the partnership, and that the other half be distributed in proportion to the total number of hours that each partner works in the business. The following table shows each partner's investment in the second column and the hours worked (during the most recent quarter) in the third column. How should the quarter's profit of $112,460 be allocated (rounded to the nearest dollar)?

Partner	Amount invested ($)	Hours worked
Kevin	130,000	210
Lyle	86,000	365
Marnie	29,000	632

11. The following table shows National Paper Products' capital investment in each of its three divisions, and the most recent year's gross sales for each division. The operating costs of the head office for the year were $839,000. These costs are allocated to the divisions before each division's profit is determined. How much (rounded to the nearest dollar) should be allocated to each division if the costs are prorated on the basis of:
    a. The capital investment in each division?
    b. The sales of each division?

Division	Investment ($)	Gross sales ($)
Industrial products	25,300,000	21,200,000
Fine paper	17,250,000	8,350,000
Containers and packaging	11,900,000	7,450,000

12. Statistics Canada reported the following sales of alcoholic beverages in Ontario and Quebec for the year 2017. (All figures are in $ billions.)

Province	Beer	Spirits	Wine
Ontario	$3.319	$2.060	$2.518
Quebec	$2.200	$0.727	$2.320

If Ontarians had allocated their total expenditures on alcoholic beverages in the same proportion as Quebecers,
    a. How much more would they have spent on wine?
    b. How would their expenditure on beer have differed?
    Round both answers to the nearest $0.001 billion.

13. Last year, Reliable Securities established a sales achievement bonus fund of $10,000 to be distributed at the year-end among its four-person mutual fund salesforce. The distribution is to be made in the same proportion as the amounts by which each person's sales exceed the basic quota of $500,000. How much will each salesperson receive from the fund if the sales figures for the year were $910,000 for Mr. A, $755,000 for Ms. B, $460,000 for Mr. C, and $615,000 for Ms. D?

14. Geological Consultants Ltd. is a private company with four shareholders: W, X, Y, and Z. The following table shows their respective shareholdings. X is retiring and has agreed to sell his shares to the other three shareholders for $175,000. The agreement calls for the 500 shares to be purchased and allocated among W, Y, and Z in the same ratio as their

present shareholdings. The shares are indivisible, and consequently the share allocation must be rounded to integer values.

Partner	Number of shares owned
W	300
X	500
Y	350
Z	400

    a. What implied value does the transaction place on the entire company?

    b. How many shares will W, Y, and Z each own after the buyout?

    c. What amount will W, Y, and Z each contribute toward the $175,000 purchase price? Prorate the $175,000 on the basis of the allocation of the shares in part (b).

ADVANCED PROBLEM

15. Canadian Can Co. operates a profit-sharing plan wherein half the annual profits are distributed to employees. By agreement, the amounts received by *individual* executives, supervisors, and production workers are to be in the ratio of $10:7:5$, respectively. During the last fiscal year, there were 4 executives, 8 supervisors, and 45 production personnel. What profit-sharing amount will each executive, supervisor, and production worker receive if the year's profit was $265,000?

4.4 | Application: Exchange Rates and Currency Conversion

LO4 International trade and tourism are growing components of commercial activity in Canada. Also, Canadians are increasingly investing in foreign securities. The vast majority of these transactions involve a conversion from Canadian dollars to a foreign currency, or vice versa. In this section, we will study the mathematics of currency conversion.

Suppose that

$$\$1.00 \text{ Canadian} = \$0.75 \text{ American}$$

In finance, this is usually written

$$C\$1.00 = US\$0.75$$

To get the C$ equivalent of US$1.00, divide both sides of the equation by 0.75, giving

$$C\$1.33333 = US\$1.00$$

The **exchange rate** between two currencies is defined as the amount of one currency required to purchase one unit of the other currency. Consequently, the exchange rate for a pair of currencies has two equivalent forms, depending on which currency is being purchased. For the C$ and US$, the exchange rate may be quoted as either

$$\frac{US\$0.75}{C\$1.00} \text{ or } \frac{C\$1.33333}{US\$1.00}$$

You should employ a formal approach for currency conversion in order to handle cases in which you do not have a feel for the relative values of two currencies.

EXAMPLE 4.4A

CURRENCY CONVERSION

Calculate the cost in C$ to purchase US$600 if C$1.00 = US$0.75.

SOLUTION

Using $\dfrac{US\$0.75}{C\$1.00}$, we can write the ratio

$$\frac{US\$600}{C\$x} = \frac{US\$0.75}{C\$1.00}$$

Cross-multiplication gives

$$C\$1.00 \times US\$600 = US\$0.75 \times C\$x$$

Then

$$C\$x = \frac{C\$1.00 \times US\$600}{US\$0.75} = C\$800.00$$

Therefore, it will cost C$800.00 to purchase US$600.

Financial institutions usually charge for their currency exchange services. Some charge a fee or a commission. However, a majority of them take the approach employed in retailing, in which inventory is bought at one price and then sold at a higher price. Similarly, these financial institutions buy a foreign currency at one price and sell it at a higher price. For example, a bank might pay you C$150 to buy the £100 you have left over after your trip to Great Britain. But a person immediately after you wanting to obtain £100 would have to pay something like C$160. The bank thereby makes a C$10 profit from the two transactions. Operationally, the bank uses a different exchange rate for buying a currency (the "buy rate") than for selling the same currency (the "sell rate").

While you are becoming familiar with currency exchange calculations, we will assume that a foreign currency may be bought or sold at the same exchange rate (perhaps with a commission involved). Later in this section, we will deal with situations involving differing buy and sell exchange rates.

EXAMPLE 4.4B

CURRENCY CONVERSION INCLUDING A COMMISSION

After spending a week in London, you are travelling on to France. Before departure from Gatwick Airport, you convert your remaining 87 British pounds (£) to euros (€) at the exchange rate £0.895 per € (that is, $\frac{£0.895}{€1.00}$). How many euros will you receive if the currency shop charges a 5% commission on transactions of this small size?

SOLUTION

Before any commission, equivalent currency amounts have a ratio equal to the exchange rate. Let €x represent the equivalent number of euros before deduction of the commission. Then,

$$\frac{£87.00}{€x} = \frac{£0.895}{€1.00}$$

Cross-multiplication gives

$$£87.00 \times 1.00 = £0.895 \times €x$$

Therefore,

$$€x = \frac{£87.00 \times €1.00}{£0.895} = €97.21$$

The commission charge is

$$0.05 \times €97.21 = €4.86$$

The net amount you will receive is €97.21 − €4.86 = €92.35

TIP

Is the Commission a Fee or a Charge?

Sometimes when you exchange currency you know how much you want to purchase of another currency and the amount it will cost is the unknown. In this case, the commission is a charge and is added to the cost of the purchase. Example: You wish to purchase 500 euros with C$. The commission is added to the C$ cost of the transaction.

When you know how much money you have to purchase another currency, the amount you will receive of the other currency is the unknown. In this case, the commission is a fee and is subtracted from the amount you will receive. Example: You wish to use C$500 to purchase euros. The commission is subtracted from the number of euros you receive for your C$500.

Currency exchange rates change constantly, which can make it challenging when you are travelling internationally and have to change currencies often. Search the App Store on your tablet, smartphone, or smart watch using the key words **CURRENCY CONVERSION**.

You will find many free and paid apps that use the most up-to-date exchange rates to quickly and easily convert from one currency to another. Some apps also provide discount and tip calculators and unit conversion tools.

Using exchange rate tables Each day, the financial pages of major Canadian daily newspapers present tables of currency exchange rates. Since most exchange rates change from hour to hour in foreign exchange markets, a table of exchange rates usually specifies the time on the preceding day when the quotations were obtained.

Exchange rates are normally presented in two formats. The less commonly traded currencies are listed in a table similar to Table 4.1. Exchange rates are reported in terms of "C$ per unit of foreign currency" and "US$ per unit of foreign currency." A few of them are presented in Table 4.1.

TABLE 4.1 Foreign Exchange Rates (2:00 p.m. ET, January 11, 2019)			
Country	**Currency**	**C$ per unit**	**US$ per unit**
Brazil	real	0.3582	0.2708
China	renminbi	0.1948	0.1472
Hong Kong	dollar	0.1688	0.1276
India	rupee	0.01879	0.01420
Indonesia	rupiah	0.00009	0.00007
Mexico	peso	0.06888	0.05206
New Zealand	dollar	0.8975	0.6783
Norway	krone	0.15614	0.11801
Russia	ruble	0.01976	0.01494
South Africa	rand	0.09533	0.07205
South Korea	won	0.00118	0.00089
Sweden	krona	0.14892	0.11255
Thailand	baht	0.04139	0.03128

Source: Oanda.com

The major currencies of international trade are usually presented in a currency cross-rate table such as Table 4.2. The figure in any cell of the table is the number of units of the currency in the *row* heading per unit of the currency in the *column* heading. For example, in the top row we see that it required C$1.32329 to purchase US$1.00, C$1.52586 to purchase €1.00, C$0.012238 to purchase ¥1.00, and so on. Expressed as ratios, these exchange rates are

$$\frac{C\$1.32329}{US\$1.00}, \frac{C\$1.52586}{€1.00}, \text{ and } \frac{C\$0.012238}{¥1.00}$$

TABLE 4.2 Currency Cross Rates (2:00 p.m. ET, January 11, 2019)							
	Per C$	**Per US$**	**Per €**	**Per ¥**	**Per £**	**Per Sw fr**	**Per A$**
Canadian dollar (C$)	•	1.32329	1.52586	0.012238	1.68925	1.35328	0.95043
U.S. dollar (US$)	0.75569	•	1.15307	0.009249	1.27654	1.02267	0.71823
Euro (€)	0.65537	0.86725	•	0.008021	1.10720	0.88697	0.62292
Japanese yen (¥)	81.71270	108.11980	124.67273	•	138.12155	110.61947	77.63975
British pound (£)	0.59198	0.78337	0.90318	0.00724	•	0.80122	0.56273
Swiss franc (Swfr)	0.73894	0.97783	1.12744	0.00904	1.24809	•	0.70245
Australian dollar (A$)	1.05216	1.39232	1.60535	0.01288	1.77704	1.42359	•

Source: Bank of Canada

Along the diagonal of the table (indicated by the dot icons), the obvious value 1.0000 has been omitted to avoid needless clutter. Note that each exchange rate below the diagonal is the reciprocal of its counterpart above the diagonal. For example,

$$US\$0.75569 \text{ per C\$} = US\$ \frac{1}{1.32329} \text{ per C\$}$$

and

$$£0.90318 \text{ per €} = £ \frac{1}{1.10720} \text{ per €}$$

Consequently, half of the values in the table are not really needed. It would be sufficient to have just the values above the diagonal or just the values below the diagonal.

EXAMPLE 4.4C

CURRENCY CONVERSION USING A CURRENCY CROSS-RATE TABLE

Using an exchange rate from Table 4.2, calculate the number of Swiss francs that C$650 could purchase at 2:00 p.m. ET on January 11, 2019.

SOLUTION

Let the number of Swiss francs be Swfr$y$. From Table 4.2, we can work with either

$$\frac{C\$1.35328}{Swfr1.00} \text{ or } \frac{Swfr0.73894}{C\$1.00}$$

If we choose the second version, then

$$\frac{Swfr y}{C\$650} = \frac{Swfr0.73894}{C\$1.00}$$

Multiplication of both sides by C$650 gives

$$Swfr y = \frac{Swfr0.73894}{C\$1.00} \times C\$650 = Swfr480.31$$

C$650 could purchase Swfr480.31 at 2:00 p.m. ET on January 11, 2019.

EXAMPLE 4.4D

TWO SUCCESSIVE CURRENCY CONVERSIONS

Suppose C$650 were first converted to U.S. dollars and then the U.S. dollars were converted to Swiss francs at the exchange rates in Table 4.2. Show that the same number of Swiss francs were purchased as in Example 4.4C. (Assume that no charges are imposed by the institutions providing the currency exchange services.)

SOLUTION

Let US$$b$ represent the number of U.S. dollars obtained from converting C$650. Then

$$\frac{US\$b}{C\$650} = \frac{US\$0.75569}{C\$1.00}$$

After multiplying both sides by C$650, we obtain

$$US\$b = \frac{US\$0.75569}{C\$1.00} \times C\$650 = US\$491.20$$

Converting the US$ to Swfr$y$, we have

$$\frac{Swfr y}{US\$491.20} = \frac{Swfr0.97783}{US\$1.00}$$

$$Swfr y = \frac{Swfr0.97783}{US\$1.00} \times US\$491.20 = Swfr480.31$$

We obtain the same answer as in Example 4.4C. We should expect agreement to four significant figures since the exchange rates are quoted to only five-figure accuracy.

Sell and buy rates for currency exchange The exchange rates quoted in Table 4.1 and Table 4.2 are known technically as mid-rates. A **mid-rate** is the exchange rate if there is no charge for providing the currency conversion service. But if you go to a bank to purchase a foreign currency, you will pay more (in terms of C$ per unit of foreign currency) than the mid-rate. The difference represents the bank's charge for providing this service. The bank calls this rate (at which it will *sell* you the foreign currency) the **sell rate**. When you return from a vacation with leftover foreign currency, the bank will *buy* the currency from you at its **buy rate**. This rate will be lower (in terms of C$ per unit of foreign currency) than the prevailing mid-rate. Again, the difference is the bank's charge for the service.

The percentage **spread** or difference between the sell and buy rates depends on many factors. Three important factors are:

- The overall volume of trading in the currency. For example, the percentage spread is smaller on the more heavily traded US$ than on the lower-volume British £.
- The form of the exchange transaction. For example, the spread is less on travellers cheques than on cash.
- The type of business handling the exchange. For example, the spread is smaller at domestic chartered banks than at airport currency exchange kiosks. As the following example and some of the Exercise problems will demonstrate, it is very costly for you to conduct currency exchange transactions at airport currency exchange businesses.

The convenience and security of credit cards, prepaid cash cards, and ATM/debit cards with the latest chip technology have drastically reduced travellers' need to carry foreign currency, and have made travellers cheques almost obsolete. But convenience has a price! Most travellers are unaware that the price of using these cards abroad carries fees that far exceed basic foreign currency exchange rates. When a foreign transaction is reported on a Canadian-dollar credit card's monthly statement, the full fee actually charged for the exchange-conversion service is not explicitly stated. Rather, it is embedded in the exchange rate applied to the transaction and is typically an additional 2.5% of the converted amount for both debit and credit transactions. While credit cards are convenient and secure, you will be hit with hefty fees (up to 4% of the amount of the transaction) if you use a credit card at an ATM to withdraw cash.

© JUPITERIMAGES/Thinkstock/ Alamy RF

Recently, merchants with a large volume of tourist business have been offering a service called *dynamic currency conversion*. Credit card purchases can be converted to the currency of the country where the card is issued at the point of sale. With this service, the purchaser can instantly see what they are paying for purchases in their home currency. Again, beware of the fees! This service is provided by a technology company that works for the merchant's bank. This adds another layer of fees (up to 3%) to the credit card company fees and your exchange fees charged by the bank that issued your credit card.

Using your ATM card at a bank machine that provides the Cirrus, Plus, or Star network services is a convenient way to get cash in a local currency abroad, but you could be charged up to three different fees for the service: the foreign exchange fee, a bank service charge, and an ATM network fee. These fees can add up to as much as 8% of the transaction amount. If you choose this method it is advisable to withdraw enough cash to last a few days as some of the fees are independent of the amount of the transaction.

As always, cash works well! You will be charged only the fee for the foreign exchange, but the tradeoff is that cash comes without all the security features of the more high-tech chip cards.

EXAMPLE 4.4E

CURRENCY CONVERSION AT SELL AND BUY RATES

The following table shows the buy and sell rates for US$ quoted by the RBC Royal Bank and a currency exchange kiosk at Vancouver International Airport on the same date that the mid-rate was C$1.3317 per US$. The kiosk also charges an additional flat fee of C$3.50 on every buy or sell transaction.

RBC Royal Bank		Currency exchange kiosk	
Buy rate	Sell rate	Buy rate	Sell rate
C$1.2826 / US$1	C$1.3621 / US$1	C$1.2597 / US$1	C$1.3699 / US$1

a. On a purchase of US$100, what was the percent transaction cost in each case? (The transaction cost includes the difference between the sell or buy rate and the mid-rate, plus any other fees charged.)

b. You returned from your trip with US$20. Assuming the exchange rates remained the same, what percent transaction cost would you have paid to convert US$20 back to C$ at the Royal Bank and at the airport kiosk?

SOLUTION

a. At the mid-rate, the purchase of US$100 (currency exchange selling to you) would have required

$$US\$100 \times \frac{C\$1.3317}{US\$1.00} = C\$133.17$$

Similarly, at the Royal Bank you would have paid C$136.21, and at the airport kiosk you would have paid C$136.99 + C$3.50 = C$140.49.

The percent transaction cost at the Royal Bank was

$$\frac{\text{C\$136.21} - \text{C\$133.17}}{\text{C\$133.17}} \times 100\% = 2.28\%$$

and the percent transaction cost at the kiosk was

$$\frac{\text{C\$140.49} - \text{C\$133.17}}{\text{C\$133.17}} \times 100\% = 5.50\%$$

b. At the mid-rate, the sale of US\$20 (currency exchange buying from you) would have yielded

$$\text{US\$20} \times \frac{\text{C\$1.3317}}{\text{US\$1.00}} = \text{C\$26.63}$$

At the Royal Bank you would have received

$$\text{US\$20} \times \frac{\text{C\$1.2826}}{\text{US\$1.00}} = \text{C\$25.65}$$

while at the airport kiosk you would have received

$$\text{US\$20} \times \frac{\text{C\$1.2597}}{\text{US\$1.00}} - \text{C\$3.50} = \text{C\$21.69}$$

The percent transaction cost at the Royal Bank was

$$\frac{\text{C\$26.63} - \text{C\$25.65}}{\text{C\$26.63}} \times 100\% = 3.68\%$$

and the percent transaction cost at the kiosk was

$$\frac{\text{C\$26.63} - \text{C\$21.69}}{\text{C\$26.63}} \times 100\% = 18.55\%$$

EXAMPLE 4.4F

COMPARING PRICES QUOTED IN TWO CURRENCIES

Gasoline sold for C\$1.249 per litre in Vancouver and US\$2.69 per gallon in Seattle on January 12, 2019. By what percentage (based on the Vancouver price) was gas cheaper in Seattle? Use the exchange rate in **Table 4.2**. (1 U.S. gal. = 3.785 L)

SOLUTION

You can get to the correct answer by more than one approach. Each approach will, effectively, require three steps. The three steps in our approach are: (1) calculate the price in Seattle of 1 L of gas, (2) convert the Step 1 result to C\$, and (3) calculate the percent difference between the Step 2 result and C\$1.089 per litre.

Step 1: Since 1 U.S. gal. = 3.785 L, the cost of 1 L in Seattle is

$$\frac{\text{US\$2.69}}{3.785} = \text{US\$0.71070}$$

Step 2: Let C\$$x$ represent the Seattle price expressed in C\$. Then

$$\frac{\text{C\$}x}{\text{US\$0.71070}} = \frac{\text{C\$1.32329}}{\text{US\$1.00}}$$

and

$$\text{C\$}x = \frac{\text{C\$1.32329} \times \text{US\$0.71070}}{\text{US\$1.00}} = \text{C\$0.9405 per litre}$$

Step 3: The percent difference from the price in Vancouver is:

$$\frac{\text{C\$0.9405} - \text{C\$1.249}}{\text{C\$1.249}} \times 100\% = -24.70\%$$

Gasoline was 24.7% cheaper in Seattle.

EXERCISE 4.4

Answers to the odd-numbered problems are at the end of the book.

BASIC PROBLEMS

For Problems 1–12, use the currency exchange rates in *Table 4.2* **(reproduced below) to calculate the equivalent amounts of currencies.**

TABLE 4.2   Currency Cross Rates (2:00 p.m. ET, January 11, 2019)

	Per C$	Per US$	Per €	Per ¥	Per £	Per Sw fr	Per A$
Canadian dollar (C$)	•	1.32329	1.52586	0.012238	1.68925	1.35328	0.95043
U.S. dollar (US$)	0.75569	•	1.15307	0.009249	1.27654	1.02267	0.71823
Euro (€)	0.65537	0.86725	•	0.008021	1.10720	0.88697	0.62292
Japanese yen (¥)	81.71270	108.11980	124.67273	•	138.12155	110.61947	77.63975
British pound (£)	0.59198	0.78337	0.90318	0.00724	•	0.80122	0.56273
Swiss franc (Swfr)	0.73894	0.97783	1.12744	0.00904	1.24809	•	0.70245
Australian dollar (A$)	1.05216	1.39232	1.60535	0.01288	1.77704	1.42359	•

Source: Bank of Canada

Problem	Given amount	Equivalent amount?
1.	US$1856	C$
2.	£123.50	€
3.	C$14,500	¥
4.	¥3,225,000	£
5.	€3251	C$
6.	£56,700	US$
7.	¥756,000	C$
8.	€159,500	US$
9.	C$94,350	£
10.	A$37,650	¥
11.	C$49,900	€
12.	£8950	¥

13. Calculate the desired exchange rate in the third column of the following table using the alternative version of the exchange rate given in the second column.

Part	Given exchange rate	Desired exchange rate
a.	Swedish krona 1.00 = C$0.14892	Swedish krona ? = C$1.00
b.	China renminbi 6.793 = US$1.00	US$? = China renminbi 1.00
c.	¥5.628 = Mexican peso 1.00	Mexican peso ? = ¥1.00
d.	C$1.00 = Indian rupee 53.22	C$? = Indian rupee 1.00

If the necessary exchange rates are not given in the following problems, use the exchange rates in *Table 4.2.*

14. How much will it cost in Canadian dollars to purchase 2000 pesos in Mexican currency at a bank that charges a 3.5% commission on the transaction? Use an exchange rate of C$1.00 = Mexican peso 12.28.

15. How much will it cost (in Canadian funds) to purchase £2000 worth of travellers cheques if the commission rate for this quantity of cheques is 0.5%?

16. Heinz returned from a holiday in Germany with €235. How much will he receive from his bank when he converts the currency back to Canadian dollars? The bank charges a 1.6% service charge for the transaction.

17. Keiko arrived in Oshawa to study English at Durham College. She used travellers cheques totalling ¥1,000,000 to open a Canadian-dollar bank account. What will her opening balance be if the bank charges 0.5% for the currency conversion?

18. Kevin lives in Calgary and wants to buy a 2016 Corvette. The best price he can find for a low-mileage model in Alberta is $59,000. (No GST would be payable on this private sale.) Through autotrader.com he tracked down a comparable car in California that he can purchase for US$34,500. To bring the car into Canada, he will have to pay 5% GST on the purchase price at Canada Customs. Additional costs will be C$287 for airfare to San Diego, US$350 in special transaction and documentation costs, and US$850 in travel and accommodation costs while driving the vehicle back to Calgary. How much will he save (in C$) by buying the Corvette in California?

19. In October of 2018, Marielle bought 1200 shares of Yakamura Trading Co. on the Tokyo Stock Exchange at a price of ¥1150 per share. The exchange rate at the time was ¥80.96 per C$. She sold the stock for ¥1310 per share in August of 2019 when the exchange rate was ¥81.13 per C$. In Canadian dollars, how much did Marielle gain or lose on the investment?

20. The following table presents the mid-rates, the Royal Bank's buy and sell rates, and ICE Currency Exchange's buy and sell rates (at their Vancouver International Airport operation) on January 12, 2019 for conversions between the Canadian dollar and three other major currencies.

| | Royal Bank | | ICE Currency Exchange | |
Mid-rate	Buy rate	Sell rate	Buy rate	Sell rate
C$1.3202 / US$1	C$1.2847 / US$1	C$1.3557 / US$1	C$1.2833 / US$1	C$1.3675 / US$1
C$1.7046 / £1	C$1.6657 / £1	C$1.7569 / £1	C$1.6368 / £1	C$1.7591 / £1
C$1.5211 / €1	C$1.4752 / €1	C$1.5696 / €1	C$1.4553 / €1	C$1.5772 / €1

   a. As a percentage of the mid-rate, calculate to the nearest 0.01% the percent spread (between buy and sell rates) on U.S.-dollar conversions for each of the Royal Bank and ICE.

   b. As a percentage of the mid-rate, calculate the percent buy–sell spread on British pound conversions for each of the Royal Bank and ICE.

   c. As a percentage of the mid-rate, calculate the percent buy–sell spread on euro conversions for each of the Royal Bank and ICE.

21. Based on the exchange rates in the table in Problem 20, how many more British pounds can you obtain with C$2000 at the Royal Bank than at ICE? On any currency exchange transaction, ICE applies a C$3.50 service charge.

22. Based on the exchange rates in the table in Problem 20, how many more euros can you obtain with C$1500 at the Royal Bank than at ICE? On any currency exchange transaction, ICE applies a C$3.50 service charge.

23. Based on the exchange rates in the table in Problem 20, how many fewer Canadian dollars will you receive if you convert US$165 at ICE instead of at the Royal Bank? On any currency exchange transaction, ICE applies a C$3.50 service charge.

24. Based on the exchange rates in the table in Problem 20, how many fewer Canadian dollars will you receive if you convert €96 at ICE instead of at the Royal Bank? On any currency exchange transaction, ICE applies a C$3.50 service charge.

INTERMEDIATE PROBLEMS

25. **a.** Based on the exchange rates in the table in Problem 20, to the nearest 0.01%, what was the percent transaction cost on your purchase of £250 from each of the Royal Bank and ICE? On any currency exchange transaction, ICE applies a C$3.50 service charge.
    b. You returned from your trip to Scotland with £16. Assuming the exchange rates remained the same, what percent transaction cost would you have paid to convert £16 back to C$ at the Royal Bank and at ICE?

26. **a.** Based on the exchange rates in the table in Problem 20, to the nearest 0.01%, what was the percent transaction cost on your purchase of €1100 from each of the Royal Bank and ICE? On any currency exchange transaction, ICE applies a C$3.50 service charge.
    b. You returned from your trip to Italy with €53. Assuming the exchange rates remained the same, what percent transaction cost would you have paid to convert €53 back to C$ at the Royal Bank and at ICE?

27. Using the exchange rates in Table 4.2, show that you will receive as many euros for C$1150 by first converting the dollars to pounds and then converting the pounds to euros as you would by converting the dollars directly to euros.

28. Using the exchange rates in Table 4.2, show that you will receive as many pounds for US$2560 by first converting the US$ to Australian $ and then converting the Australian $ to pounds as you would by converting the US$ directly to pounds.

29. A cross-border shopping trip reveals that milk sells for US$3.53 per one-gallon jug versus C$6.44 per four-litre jug in Canada. Calculate the percent difference between Canada and the United States in the exchange rate–adjusted price of milk. Use the Canadian price as the base in the comparison. (1 U.S. gal. = 3.785 L)

30. If pork chops cost US$3.99 per pound in the United States and C$10.49 per kilogram in Canada, in which country are the chops more expensive? How much more expensive are they in C$ per kg? (1 kg = 2.2 pounds)

31. Hamish and Grace MacDonald have been investigating the cost of a holiday in Britain. From their home in Welland, Ontario, it is equally inconvenient to fly out of Toronto or Buffalo, New York. On the internet, they have found that they can fly Buffalo–London return on American Airlines for US$2323 each, rent a hotel room in London for two people for one night at a cost of £149, and join Jolly Tours the next day for a two-week all-inclusive coach tour at a cost of £1950 per person. Alternatively, the MacDonalds can purchase an all-inclusive package (including a similar coach tour) from a local travel agent for C$7195 per person. Which alternative is cheaper? How much cheaper is it in C$ for two people?

32. ArcelorMittal Dofasco can buy iron ore pellets from Minnesota at US$133 per short ton (2000 pounds) or from Labrador at C$165 per metric tonne (1000 kg). Which source is more expensive? How much more expensive is it in C$ per metric tonne? (1 pound = 0.4536 kg)

33. The price of a 40-ounce bottle of rum at a U.S. border duty-free store was US$27.00. At the same time, the price of a 750-mL bottle of similar quality rum in an Ontario LCBO store was C$28.95. Using the Ontario price as the base, what is the percent saving (on the unit price) by buying rum at the duty-free store? (1 L = 35.2 fluid ounces)

*4.5 Application: Appreciation and Depreciation of Currencies

L05 If Currency A *appreciates* (or strengthens) relative to Currency B, it means that a unit of Currency A now buys *more* of Currency B. Consequently, the exchange rate expressed as

$$\frac{\text{Currency B}}{\text{Currency A}} \; increases$$

while the exchange rate in terms of

$$\frac{\text{Currency A}}{\text{Currency B}} \; decreases$$

Consider this example. Suppose the exchange rate between the US$ and the C$ changed from US$0.89 per C$ to US$0.90 per C$ over a period of one month. Which currency strengthened (appreciated) relative to the other during the month?

At the end of the month, a Canadian dollar purchased US$0.01 more than at the beginning of the month. Therefore, the Canadian dollar strengthened (appreciated) relative to the U.S. dollar. The flip side of the coin, so to speak, is that the U.S. dollar weakened (depreciated) relative to the Canadian dollar. In this circumstance, Canadians importing goods from the U.S. or travelling in the U.S. will benefit from the stronger "Canuck buck." It requires fewer C$ (than it did one month earlier) to purchase American goods and services. On the other hand, Americans importing goods from Canada or travelling in Canada require more US$ (than needed one month earlier) to pay prices denominated in C$.

EXAMPLE 4.5A

INTERPRETING CHANGES IN EXCHANGE RATES

The exchange rate between the Swiss franc and British pound changed from Swfr1.482 per £1.00 to Swfr1.378 per £1.00.

a. Which currency depreciated (weakened) relative to the other?

b. What were the beginning and ending exchange rates in terms of £ per Swfr?

SOLUTION

a. £1.00 purchased fewer Swfr after the change.

Therefore, the £ depreciated and the Swfr appreciated.

b. The two versions of an exchange rate are reciprocals of each other. Hence, the exchange rate went from

$$\pounds \frac{1}{1.482} \text{ per Swfr to } \pounds \frac{1}{1.378} \text{ per Swfr}$$

That is, from

$$\pounds 0.6748 \text{ per Swfr to } \pounds 0.7257 \text{ per Swfr.}$$

EXAMPLE 4.5B

CONSEQUENCES OF EXCHANGE RATE SHIFTS

Many commodities produced by Canadian resource extraction companies are priced in US$ in international markets. Suppose a Canadian producer sells newsprint for US$700 per tonne. What is the consequence for the C$ revenue per tonne if the exchange rate goes from US$0.75 per C$ to US$0.77 per C$?

SOLUTION

Let C$$x$ represent the C$ revenue per tonne. At the first exchange rate,

$$\frac{\text{US\$700}}{\text{C\$}x} = \frac{\text{US\$0.75}}{\text{C\$1.00}}$$

After rearranging to isolate C$$x$, we obtain

$$\text{C\$}x = \frac{\text{C\$1.00}}{\text{US\$0.75}} \times \text{US\$700} = \text{C\$933.33 per tonne}$$

Similarly, at the second exchange rate,

$$\text{C\$}x = \frac{\text{C\$1.00}}{\text{US\$0.77}} \times \text{US\$700} = \text{C\$909.09 per tonne}$$

The weakening of the US$ (strengthening of the C$) causes the producer's revenue to decrease by C$24.24 per tonne.

 POINT OF INTEREST

Any Free Lunches?

Using the exchange rates in **Table 4.2**, let's see if we make or lose money when we first convert C$1000 to US$, then convert the US$ to £, and finally convert the £ back to C$. Assume there are no service charges or commissions.

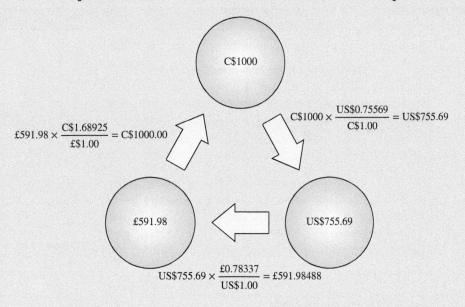

We end up with the *same* number of C$ with which we began (within the five-figure accuracy of the exchange rates). It turns out that you will get the same outcome if you take *any* currency through a full conversion cycle involving *any number* of other freely trading currencies! This seems amazing when you first become aware of it, particularly since most exchange rates change many times each day.

Let's try to understand why this outcome persists even as exchange rates fluctuate. Suppose we had ended up with C$1010 instead of C$1000 after the three conversions. In that event, we would have a risk-free moneymaking system—every time we put money through the cycle, we would end up with 1% more. If the end result had been C$990 instead of C$1000, then you need only reverse the conversion cycle (making it C$ → £ → US$ → C$) in order to gain 1% instead of lose 1%. Therefore, either hypothetical outcome would amount to the proverbial "free lunch."

There are many very bright people known as arbitrageurs, working for lots of very big financial institutions with very powerful computers continually looking for free lunches. Arbitrageurs can shift around huge sums of money that can turn a few tiny 0.1% morsels into a splendid meal!

Currency arbitrage involves the purchase of currencies that (in relative terms) are underpriced, and the simultaneous sale of overpriced currencies. The higher demand for underpriced currencies tends to cause them to appreciate, but the greater supply of overpriced currencies causes them to depreciate. Exchange rates shift until the arbitrage opportunity is eliminated. This results in the break-even outcome we obtained for the C$ → US$ → £ → C$ conversion cycle.

CONCEPT QUESTIONS

1. If the exchange rate in terms of units of currency N per unit of currency M decreases, which currency strengthened? Explain.

2. If the exchange rate in terms of units of currency P per unit of currency Q increases, which currency weakened? Explain.

3. If currency G weakens relative to currency H, will the exchange rate in terms of units of G per unit of H increase or decrease? Explain.

4. If currency R strengthens relative to currency S, will the exchange rate in terms of units of S per unit of R increase or decrease? Explain.

EXERCISE 4.5

Answers to the odd-numbered problems are at the end of the book.

*Table 4.2 **is provided below for convenient reference.***

TABLE 4.2   Currency Cross Rates (2:00 p.m. ET, January 11, 2019)

	Per C$	Per US$	Per €	Per ¥	Per £	Per Sw fr	Per A$
Canadian dollar (C$)	•	1.32329	1.52586	0.012238	1.68925	1.35328	0.95043
U.S. dollar (US$)	0.75569	•	1.15307	0.009249	1.27654	1.02267	0.71823
Euro (€)	0.65537	0.86725	•	0.008021	1.10720	0.88697	0.62292
Japanese yen (¥)	81.71270	108.11980	124.67273	•	138.12155	110.61947	77.63975
British pound (£)	0.59198	0.78337	0.90318	0.00724	•	0.80122	0.56273
Swiss franc (Swfr)	0.73894	0.97783	1.12744	0.00904	1.24809	•	0.70245
Australian dollar (A$)	1.05216	1.39232	1.60535	0.01288	1.77704	1.42359	•

Source: Bank of Canada

INTERMEDIATE PROBLEMS

1. If the number of £ per C$1.00 increases by 0.054 from the value in Table 4.2, which currency has depreciated and by what percentage?

2. If the number of C$ per ¥1.00 decreases by 0.00054 from the value in Table 4.2, which currency has appreciated and by what percentage?

3. If the C$ weakens by 0.5% relative to the € in Table 4.2, what will be the new values for € per C$1.00 and C$ per €1.00?

4. If the C$ strengthens by 1.2% relative to the US$ in Table 4.2, what will be the new values for US$ per C$1.00 and C$ per US$1.00?

5. If the C$ appreciates (from the value in Table 4.2) by C$0.0017 relative to the £, what will be the new value for £ per C$1.00?

6. If the C$ weakens (from the value in Table 4.2) by C$0.0033 relative to the US$, what will be the new value for US$ per C$1.00?

7. If the C$ strengthens by £0.0021 from the value in Table 4.2, what will be the new value of C$ per £1.00?

8. If the C$ weakens by €0.0211 from the value in Table 4.2, what will be the new value of C$ per €1.00?

9. If the C$ per US$ exchange rate decreases by C$0.005 from its value in Table 4.2, what will be the change in the US$ per C$ exchange rate?

10. If the US$ per £ exchange rate increases by US$0.006 from its value in Table 4.2, what will be the change in the £ per US$ exchange rate?

11. If the ¥ per A$ exchange rate increases by ¥1 from its value in Table 4.2, what will be the change in the A$ per ¥ exchange rate?

12. If the € per ¥ exchange rate decreases by €0.0007 from its value in Table 4.2, what will be the change in the ¥ per € exchange rate?

13. If the number of US$ per C$1.00 rises from 0.7588 to 0.7889, what will be the change in the C$ price to an importer of a US$1500 item?

14. If the number of ¥ per C$1.00 declines from 89.641 to 87.816, what will be the change in the C$ price to an importer of a ¥195,000 item?

15. If the number of £ per C$1.00 rises from 0.54182 to 0.55354, what will be the change in the C$ revenue from a foreign contract fixed at £23,000?

16. If the number of US$ per C$1.00 declines from 0.94168 to 0.92679, what will be the change in the C$ price per ounce of gold that a Canadian gold mine sells at the international price of US$975 per ounce?

*4.6 Application: Index Numbers

LO6 Index numbers are used to show change in a value as a percentage of a single base figure. For example, if sales of a product increased 25% this year and 125% next year then the corresponding index numbers would be 100 (using this year as the base year) and 125 for next year.

If you read the business section of a newspaper, you soon encounter index numbers such as the Consumer Price Index (CPI) and the Toronto Stock Exchange S&P/TSX Composite Index. The CPI is used to compare prices of goods and services purchased on different dates by a typical urban Canadian family. The S&P/TSX Composite Index is used to compare the general price levels on different dates of shares on the Toronto Stock Exchange.

We will use the Consumer Price Index (CPI) to illustrate the construction of an index. Statistics Canada tracks the prices of about 600 consumer goods and services (the CPI "basket"). The Consumer Price Index for a selected date is calculated from the following proportion:[3]

$$\frac{CPI}{100} = \frac{\text{Price of CPI basket on the selected date}}{\text{Price of CPI basket on the base date}}$$

---

[3] The price of the CPI "basket" is a weighted average price. The weighting factor for each item reflects the typical percentage of consumer expenditures on each item. The contents of the basket are updated every four years and the weights are updated every two years.

The *base date* Statistics Canada uses is June 2002. Multiplying both sides by 100 gives

$$\text{CPI} = \frac{\text{Price of CPI basket on the selected date}}{\text{Price of CPI basket on the base date}} \times 100$$

Because of rising price levels, CPI values are greater than 100 for any date since the base date. In November 2018, the CPI stood at 133.5. This means that prices were, on average, 33.5% higher than on the base date (in June 2002).

In general, an index number for a selected date is calculated from

$$\text{Index number} = \frac{\text{Price or value on the selected date}}{\text{Price or value on the base date}} \times \text{Base value}$$

The S&P/TSX Composite Index reflects the share prices of about 220 large companies trading on the Toronto Stock Exchange. The price ratio in the index is calculated in terms of the value of a portfolio of shares of all these companies.[4] A base value of 1000 was chosen for the base date in 1975. Hence,

$$\text{S\&P/TSX Composite Index} = \frac{\text{Value of portfolio on the selected date}}{\text{Value of portfolio on the base date}} \times 1000$$

On January 11, 2019, the S&P/TSX Composite Index stood at 14,939. Therefore, the value of the index portfolio on that date was 14.9 times the portfolio's value on the base date in 1975.

EXAMPLE 4.6A

CALCULATING AN INDEX NUMBER

Suppose the S&P/TSX portfolio cost $168,400 in 1975 (when the base value of the index was set at 1000). What value was quoted for the S&P/TSX Composite Index on a later date when the same portfolio had a value of $2,200,000?

SOLUTION

$$\text{S\&P/TSX Composite Index} = \frac{\text{Value of portfolio on the selected date}}{\text{Value of portfolio on the base date}} \times 1000$$

$$= \frac{\$2,200,000}{\$168,400} \times 1000$$

$$= 13,064.13$$

The index stood at 13,064.13 on the date the portfolio was worth $2,200,000.

APP ④ THAT

Stock prices change constantly through the day as stocks are bought and sold. Search the App Store on your tablet, smartphone, or smart watch using the key word **TSX**.

You will find many free and paid apps that provide up-to-date stock prices, real-time discussion boards, and numerous other tools to help build a portfolio, receive alerts, and perform calculations.

---

[4] The number of shares of each stock is chosen so that larger companies affect the portfolio and the index more than smaller companies. We need not be concerned here with the details.

EXAMPLE 4.6B

USING CPI DATA

The mid-year Consumer Price Index was 116.2 in 2010, 127.3 in 2015, and 133.6 in 2018.

a. What amount in mid-2010 had the same purchasing power as $1000 in mid-2015?

b. What was the overall percent inflation from mid-2010 to mid-2018?

c. Kay earned $65,000 in 2015. Approximately what amount did she have to earn in 2018 to keep pace with inflation?

SOLUTION

a. Amounts with the same purchasing power will be in the same ratio as the CPI on the respective dates. That is,

$$\frac{2010 \text{ amount}}{2015 \text{ amount}} = \frac{2010 \text{ CPI}}{2015 \text{ CPI}}$$

$$\frac{2010 \text{ amount}}{\$1000} = \frac{116.2}{127.3}$$

$$2010 \text{ amount} = 0.91280 \times \$1000 = \$912.80$$

b. The usual measure of inflation is the percent increase in the CPI. Hence,

$$\text{Percent inflation} = \frac{2018 \text{ CPI} - 2010 \text{ CPI}}{2010 \text{ CPI}} \times 100\% = \frac{133.6 - 116.2}{116.2} \times 100\% = 14.97\%$$

Mid-2018 consumer prices were, on average, 14.97% higher than mid-2010 prices.

c. To keep pace with inflation, salaries must be in the same ratio as the corresponding CPIs.

$$\frac{2018 \text{ salary}}{2015 \text{ salary}} = \frac{2018 \text{ CPI}}{2015 \text{ CPI}}$$

$$\frac{2018 \text{ salary}}{\$65,000} = \frac{133.6}{127.3} = 1.04949$$

$$2018 \text{ salary} = 1.04949 \times \$65,000 = \$68,216.85$$

Kay had to earn approximately $68,217 in 2018 to keep pace with inflation.

APP ❮4❯ THAT

Inflation affects every Canadian and impacts the purchasing power of their hard-earned dollars. Search the App Store on your tablet, smartphone, or smart watch using the key words **CONSUMER PRICE INDEX**.

You will find free apps that explain inflation, contain historical inflation data, and provide tools to demonstrate the effects of inflation on your purchasing power in Canada.

EXERCISE 4.6

Answers to the odd-numbered problems are at the end of the book.

BASIC PROBLEMS

Calculate the missing quantities in Problems 1–8 to four-figure accuracy.

Problem	Value on base date ($)	Base value	Current value ($)	Current index number
1.	3278	100	4961	?
2.	3278	1000	4961	?
3.	7532	100	?	119.5
4.	189.50	?	431.70	2278
5.	735	10	689	?
6.	8950	100	?	89.50
7.	?	1000	7729	2120
8.	451.10	?	398.60	441.8

9. The basket of goods and services included in the Consumer Price Index cost $21,350 on the base date. Eight years later, the same basket cost $26,090. What was the CPI on the later date?

10. A basket of goods and services representative of the CPI cost $2750 when the CPI stood at 118.3.
    a. What did the basket of goods cost 10 years earlier, when the CPI was at 93.1?
    b. What was the overall percent inflation experienced by consumers for the entire 10-year period?

11. In one year, the CPI increased from 106.3 to 108.9. How much money was required at the end of the year in order to have the same purchasing power as $1000 at the beginning?

12. A college student wishes to compare tuition fee increases during the period 2008 to 2018 to the general increase in the cost of living. Tuition increased from $355 per course in the 2008/09 academic year to $362 per course in the 2018/19 academic year. The CPI rose from 115.8 in mid-2008 to 134.3 in mid-2018. What would the tuition fee per course have been in the 2018/19 year if tuition increases had merely kept pace with inflation during the 10 years?

13. Statistics Canada calculates separate subindexes of the CPI for goods and for services. The goods index rose from 96.8 to 112.0 over a 10-year period. During the same period, the services index rose from 95.2 to 115.1.
    a. How much did representative goods, worth $1000 at the beginning, cost at the end of the 10-year period?
    b. How much did representative services, worth $1000 at the beginning, cost at the end of the 10-year period?
    c. What is the difference between the percent increase in the price level of services and the percent increase in the price level of goods during the decade?

INTERMEDIATE PROBLEMS

14. From the end of 1990 to the end of 2018, the S&P/TSX Composite Index rose from 3257 to 14,939. If you had invested $50,000 in a portfolio of the shares of the companies in the index at the end of 1990, what would the value of those shares have been at the end of 2018? (This calculation considers only the price appreciation of the original shares. It does not include additional growth in the portfolio's value resulting from the receipt and reinvestment of dividends.)

15. We want to compare the increase in value of the stock portfolio represented by the S&P/TSX Composite Index during the 28-year period described in Problem 14 to the general increase in prices of goods and services during the same period. The CPI rose from 79.8 at the end of 1990 to 133.5 at the end of 2018. Calculate the percent increase in the value of the portfolio and the percent increase in the general price level during the decade.

16. From the end of 1990 to the end of 2018, the Standard & Poor's 500 (S&P 500) U.S. stock index rose from 330.2 to 2506.9. If you had invested US$50,000 at the end of 1990 in a portfolio of the shares of the 500 companies in the index, what would the value (in US$) of those shares have been at the end of 2018? (This calculation considers only the price appreciation of the original shares. It does not include additional growth in the portfolio's value resulting from the receipt and reinvestment of dividends.)

17. The late 1970s and early 1980s were years of historically high rates of inflation in Canada. The CPI was at 70.8, 77.1, 84.5, 94.6, 105.4, and 114.1 at the beginning of 1978, 1979, 1980, 1981, 1982, and 1983, respectively. These price index numbers are quoted in terms of a base value of 100 in mid-1981.
    a. What amount was required at the beginning of 1983 in order to have the same purchasing power as $100 just five years earlier?
    b. What were the inflation rates for each of the years 1978 to 1982 inclusive?

KEY TERMS

Buy rate	Mid-rate	Sell rate (for a currency)
Equivalent ratio	Proportion	Spread
Exchange rate	Proration	Terms of a ratio
Lowest terms (of a ratio)	Ratio	

SUMMARY OF NOTATION AND KEY FORMULAS

$$\textit{Index number} = \frac{\textit{Price or value on the selected date}}{\textit{Price or value on the base date}} \times \textit{Base value}$$

REVIEW PROBLEMS

Answers to the odd-numbered review problems are at the end of the book.

BASIC PROBLEMS

1. **L01** Express each of the following ratios in its lowest terms.
   a. $0.18:0.60:0.45$
   b. $\frac{9}{8}:\frac{3}{4}:\frac{3}{2}$
   c. $\frac{1}{6}:\frac{1}{3}:\frac{1}{9}$
   d. $6\frac{1}{4}:5:8\frac{3}{4}$

2. **L02** Solve the following proportions for the unknown quantities.
   a. $t:26:10 = 24:39:s$
   b. $x:3600:y = 48:40:105$

3. **L02** Solve the following proportions to four-figure accuracy.
   a. $65:43 = 27.3:x$
   b. $1410:2330:870 = a:550:b$

4. **LO1** Mark, Ben, and Tanya own 4250, 2550, and 5950 shares, respectively, of MBT Inc. What is the ratio of their share holdings?

5. **LO1** Milan, Katka, and Shoshanna started their partnership with a total investment of $135,000 contributed in the ratio of $3:4:2$. If each partner contributes another $10,000, what will be the ratio of their total contributions?

6. **LO2** A test-marketing of a newly released Blu-ray disc in a representative Canadian city, with a population of 120,000, resulted in sales of 543 units in a three-month period. If the Blu-ray disc sells at the same rate in the rest of the country, where 21,000,000 Canadians have access to retail outlets, what three-month sales may be forecast for the disc?

7. **LO6** Three years ago, when the CPI was at 115.8, the members of a union were earning $22.25 per hour. Now, with the current CPI at 120.2, they are negotiating for a new hourly rate that will restore their former purchasing power. What hourly rate are they seeking?

8. **LO2** The new University Hospital is scheduled to have 436 beds. The ratio of nurses to beds to nurses' aides for staffing the hospital is $4:9:2$. How many nurses and aides will need to be hired?

9. **LO4** If Indonesian rupiah $1.00 = C\$0.0001121$, how many rupiah can be purchased with C$1500?

10. **LO2** For the last five years the sales of Departments D, E, and F have maintained a relatively stable ratio of $13:17:21$. Department E is forecasting sales of $478,000 for next year. Based on the past sales ratio, what sales would be expected for Departments D and F? Round to the nearest dollar.

11. **LO5** If C$1.00 rises from ¥87.94 to ¥89.78, what will be the change in the C$ price to an importer of a ¥2,965,000 car?

12. **LO2** A provincial government allocates 29% of its budget to education, 31% to health care, and 21% to social services. If the dollar amount budgeted for education is $13.7 billion, how much is budgeted for health care and for social services? Round to the nearest $0.01 billion.

13. **LO4** Before Mr. and Mrs. Percival left for Great Britain, they purchased British pounds at an exchange rate of C$1.5947 = £1.00. When they returned to Canada eight weeks later they converted their remaining £242 back to Canadian currency at the rate of C$1.632 = £1.00. How much did they gain or lose in Canadian dollars on the round-trip transaction involving the £242?

14. **LO3** How should common area costs totalling $28,575 be allocated among commercial tenants A, B, C, and D if the costs are prorated based on leased areas of 1260, 3800, 1550, and 2930 square feet, respectively?

15. **LO2** A profit-sharing bonus was divided among four employees—Ms. L, Mr. M, Ms. N, and Mr. P—in the ratio of $1.5:1:0.75:0.5$, respectively. If Ms. N received $2000, how much did each of the others receive?

16. **LO3** Wendy, Simone, and Leif share the costs of their coffee fund in the ratio $\frac{3}{2}:\frac{2}{3}:\frac{5}{3}$. How will costs of $50 be allocated among them?

17. **LO3** Mr. Nolan's will specifies that the proceeds from his estate be divided among his wife, son, and stepson in the ratio of $\frac{7}{5}:1:\frac{5}{7}$, respectively. Rounded to the nearest dollar, how much will each receive from the distribution of his $331,000 estate?

18. **LO6** The CPI stood at 96.4, 98.6, 101.2, 103.3, 105.7, and 108.9 on the same date in successive years.
    a. What was the inflation rate: (i) in the fourth one-year interval? (ii) in the fifth one-year interval?
    b. What amount was required at the end in order to have the same purchasing power as $100 five years earlier?

INTERMEDIATE PROBLEMS

19. **LO5** The exchange rate between the US$ and the C$ declines from US$1.3358 to US$1.3112 per C$. What will be the change in the C$ price to an importer of a US$2000 item?

20. **LO3** A partnership agreement provides that half of the annual profit be distributed in proportion to each partner's investment in the partnership, and that the other half be distributed in proportion to the total number of hours that each partner worked in the business during the year. How should the most recent year's profit of $84,780 be allocated if the amounts invested by Huey, Dewey, and Louie are $70,000, $30,000, and $45,000, and their hours of work for the year were 425, 1680, and 1440, respectively?

21. **LO4** A steel company in Hamilton can purchase Alberta coal at C$105 per metric tonne (1000 kg) or West Virginia coal at US$95 per ton (2000 lb) (1 kg = 2.205 lb). How much cheaper in C$ per metric tonne is the less expensive source if US$0.805 = C$1.00?

22. **LO5** The exchange rate between Currencies X and Y is currently Y0.05614 = X1.00. If X weakens by 1.5% relative to Y, what will be the new values for the exchange rates per unit of X and per unit of Y?

CASE

Calculations for an Investment Portfolio

One year ago, Jasmin and Derek opened investment accounts with a discount broker. In their C$ account, they purchased 300 Bank of Montreal (BMO) shares at C$54.20 per share and six Government of Canada bonds (GoCs) at C$1063 per bond. In their US$ account, they purchased 100 shares of International Business Machines (IBM) at US$125.50 per share and 200 shares of General Electric (GE) at US$18.57 per share. The exchange rate on the date of the purchases was C$1.00 = US$0.935.

The income received from the securities during the year and their current prices are listed in the following table.

	Number owned	Income received	Current price
BMO	300 shares	C$3.20 per share	C$58.15
GoCs	6 bonds	C$70.00 per bond	C$1021.50
IBM	100 shares	US$2.50 per share	US$132.25
GE	200 shares	US$0.50 per share	US$20.38

The current exchange rate is C$1.00 = US$0.952

QUESTIONS

1. What total amount in C$ was initially invested in the portfolio?
2. What is the C$ equivalent of the total income received during the year? (For converting the US$ income to C$, use the average of the beginning and ending exchange rates for the year.)
3. What is the current total value in C$ of the securities (not including income received)?
4. Including both income and change in value of the securities, what was the percentage increase in the value of Jasmin's and Derek's portfolios during the year?

Chapter 5
Mathematics of Merchandising

CHAPTER OUTLINE

5.1 Trade Discounts

5.2 Cash Discounts and Terms of Payment

5.3 Markup

5.4 Markdown

*5.5 Comprehensive Applications

5.2 Supplement: Other Notations for Terms of Payment (located online)

5.3 Supplement: Diagram Model for Markup Problems (located online)

LEARNING OBJECTIVES

After completing this chapter, you will be able to:

LO1 Calculate the net price of an item after single or multiple trade discounts

LO2 Calculate a single discount rate that is equivalent to a series of discounts

LO3 Understand the ordinary dating notation for the terms of payment of an invoice

LO4 Calculate the amount of the cash discount for which a payment qualifies

LO5 Solve merchandise pricing problems involving markup and markdown

MATHEMATICS TOUCHES ALMOST EVERY STAGE of product distribution and merchandising. Consider a retailer who buys goods from her suppliers, marks up the price, and sells the goods to her customers. The cost of the goods to the retailer is usually determined by deducting a "trade discount" from the supplier's "list price." The invoice she receives may offer a "cash discount" for prompt payment of the invoice. The amount of "markup" the retailer adds to the cost price must cover part of her overhead costs, and also generate a suitable profit. For a sale or special promotion, the retailer may offer a discount or "markdown" from the regular selling price.

In this chapter, we will learn the terminology and procedures for these calculations. We will also explore the mathematical relationships among pricing variables. This will help us understand how a change in one variable affects the other variables.

 TIP

How to Succeed in Business Mathematics

Since various Business Mathematics and Mathematics of Finance courses start at different points in the book, this Tip appears at the beginning of each of the first five chapters. Connect has a guide entitled "How to Succeed in Business Mathematics." Read its first two sections (A.1 and A.2) as soon as possible.

If your course bypassed **Chapter 1** and you are using a Texas Instruments BA II PLUS calculator, refer to **Appendix 1A** for information about settings that affect the calculator's display and order of operations.

5.1 | Trade Discounts

Goods move from a manufacturer to the ultimate consumer through the *distribution chain* or *merchandising chain*. In the chain illustrated by **Figure 5.1**, a product is first sold by a *manufacturer* to one or more *distributors*. The agreement between a manufacturer and a distributor usually gives the distributor the *exclusive* right to distribute the product in a fairly large geographic region, but prohibits the distributor from handling competing products. Typically, a distributor also has marketing responsibilities in the region. The distributor then resells the goods to a number of *wholesalers*. A wholesaler carries a wider range of products within a general category or theme. The majority of a wholesaler's product lines are complementary, but some will be competing. All are for resale to *retailers* within a smaller geographic area. Retailers sell mainly to the ultimate consumers of the goods.

FIGURE 5.1   The Distribution Chain

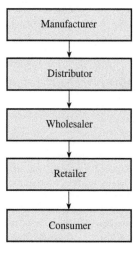

In many cases, one or more of the intermediate links may be absent. Large national retailers and *buying groups* of smaller retailers may have enough buying power to purchase directly from manufacturers.

L01 To understand how prices are usually established within the merchandising chain, imagine that you are a wholesaler buying from a distributor. The distributor is likely to have a catalogue of **list prices**. List prices are commonly chosen to approximate the ultimate retail selling price. (No doubt you have noticed terms such as "manufacturer's suggested retail price," "suggested list price," or "recommended selling price" on the packaging or in advertisements for certain products.) The distributor will offer you a percent discount from the list price[1] called the **trade discount** rate. The word "trade" signifies that the discount applies only to a transaction within the "trade"; that is, within the merchandising chain (but not including the consumer).

The resulting price after deducting the amount of the trade discount from the list price is called the **net price**. That is,

$$\text{Net price} = \text{List price} - \text{Amount of trade discount}$$
$$= \text{List price} - (\text{Rate of trade discount} \times \text{List price})$$

The following symbols will be used to convert the preceding word equation to an algebraic equation.

$$N = \text{Net price}$$
$$L = \text{List price}$$
$$d = \text{Rate of trade discount}$$

Replacing the quantities in the word equation by these symbols, we obtain

$$N = L - dL$$

Since L is a common factor on the right side, we can write the basic discounting formula[2] as

NET PRICE AFTER A DISCOUNT

$$N = L(1 - d) \tag{5-1}$$

EXAMPLE 5.1A

CALCULATING THE DISCOUNT AMOUNT AND NET PRICE

A wholesaler lists an item at $117 less 20%. What is the amount of the discount and the net price to a retailer?

SOLUTION

Given: $L = \$117$, $d = 0.20$

$$\text{Amount of discount} = dL = (0.20)(\$117) = \$23.40$$
$$\text{Net price} = \text{List price} - \text{Amount of discount}$$
$$= \$117 - \$23.40$$
$$= \$93.60$$

The discount was $23.40 and the retailer's net price was $93.60.

---

[1] The use of trade discounts in conjunction with fixed list prices makes it easier for the seller to set different prices for various categories of customers. For example, a manufacturer might offer one discount rate to a distributor in one part of the country, another discount rate to "big-box" retailers, and yet another rate to smaller buying groups. Every customer sees the same "up front" list price. Price flexibility is achieved in the setting of the trade discount rate.

[2] Formula (5-1) is really just an application of Formula (3-2) rearranged to isolate V_f; that is, $V_f = V_i(1 + c)$. The initial value, V_i, is the list price, L, and the final value, V_f, is the net price, N. To obtain the net price from the list price, we deduct the decimal equivalent of the discount rate, d, instead of adding the decimal equivalent of the percent increase, c.

EXAMPLE 5.1B

CALCULATING THE LIST PRICE

After a trade discount of 30%, a garage is able to purchase windshield wiper blades for a net price of $19.46. What is the list price of the blades?

SOLUTION

Given: $d = 0.30$, $N = \$19.46$

Substituting these values into Formula (5-1), we have

$$\$19.46 = L(1 - 0.30)$$

Solving for L, we obtain

$$L = \frac{\$19.46}{1 - 0.30} = \frac{\$19.46}{0.70} = \$27.80$$

The list price of the blades is $27.80.

EXAMPLE 5.1C

CALCULATING THE TRADE DISCOUNT RATE

A clothing store is able to purchase men's leather coats at a net price of $173.40 after a discount of $115.60. What rate of trade discount was obtained?

SOLUTION

Given: Net price = $173.40, Amount of discount = $115.60

The trade discount rate is

$$d = \frac{\text{Amount of discount}}{\text{List price}}$$

We must calculate the "List price" before we can obtain d.

$$\text{List price} = \text{Net price} + \text{Amount of discount}$$
$$= \$173.40 + \$115.60$$
$$= \$289.00$$

Hence,

$$d = \frac{\$115.60}{\$289.00} = 0.40$$

The trade discount rate is 40%.

EXAMPLE 5.1D

CALCULATING THE LIST PRICE AND NET PRICE

A 38% discount on paint is equivalent to a discount amount of $22.04. What are the list and net prices of the paint?

SOLUTION

Given: $d = 0.38$, Discount amount = $22.04

Expanding Formula (5-1), we have

$$N = L(1 - d)$$
$$N = L - Ld$$

where Ld represents the discount amount. Therefore,

$$\$22.04 = L(0.38)$$

Solving for L, we obtain

$$L = \frac{\$22.04}{0.38} = \$58.00$$

The list price of the paint is $58.00. The net price is then $58.00 − $22.04 = $35.96.

Multiple discounts (or series discounts) In the past, it was common for a seller/vendor in the merchandising chain to offer more than one discount. For example, in addition to the basic trade discount offered to all customers, the seller might also offer small discounts for large-volume purchases, for special promotions and cooperative advertising, and for early orders of seasonal items.

If a purchaser qualifies for more than one discount, the understanding is that the discounts should be compounded rather than added. This means that we use a formula[3] similar to Formula (5-1) but with a $(1 − d)$ factor for each discount. If there are three discounts, d_1, d_2, and d_3, then the net price is

NET PRICE AFTER THREE DISCOUNTS

$$N = L(1 − d_1)(1 − d_2)(1 − d_3) \qquad (5\text{-}2)$$

The granting of separate multiple discounts has been largely abandoned. It is now more typical for buyers and sellers to negotiate a single discount rate that can be adjusted over time as the business relationship evolves. Rather than offering a volume discount on individual orders, vendors increasingly pay a year-end discount (in the 2% to 5% range) dependent on a customer's total purchases during the year.

L02 **Single discount rate equivalent to multiple discounts** An **equivalent discount rate** is the single discount rate that gives the same net price as the combined effect of the multiple discounts. Suppose, for example, that the net amount after applying three discounts to a list price of $100 is $74. Then the dollar amount of the discount is $100 − $74 = $26, and the equivalent discount rate is

$$\frac{\$26}{\$100} \times 100\% = 26\%$$

This example suggests the most straightforward approach for calculating an equivalent discount rate. First, determine the net price after applying the given multiple discounts to a list price of $100. Then calculate the dollar amount of the discount—the percent equivalent discount rate is *numerically* equal to the amount of the discount. See **Example 5.1G**.

 TRAP

Do Not Add Series Discounts

The single rate that is equivalent to two or more discounts *cannot* be obtained by adding the individual discounts. The equivalent discount rate will always be smaller than the sum of the discounts. This happens because the second and third individual discounts are applied to amounts smaller than the list price, whereas the equivalent rate is applied to the full list price.

---

[3] Formula (5-2) is an application of Formula (3-4). The initial value V_i is the list price L, the final value V_f is the net price N, and the successive percent changes c_1, c_2, c_3 are represented by the discount rates d_1, d_2, and d_3.

Other applications Although Formula (5-1) was derived in the context of trade discounts, it may be used in any discount or "% off" calculation. Indeed, Formula (5-1) applies to any situation in which an amount (L) is reduced by d percent. Such applications include the calculation of the "sale" price after a percentage markdown, sales revenue net of commission, security prices after a percentage loss in value, and budget amounts after a percentage cut.

Similarly, Formula (5-2) may be employed in any situation where a beginning amount, L, undergoes a series of compound percent decreases. N represents the amount left after the decreases. For example, suppose a product's sales are forecast to decline from the past year's sales of $200,000 by 10%, 20%, and 15% in the next three successive years. Then sales in the third year are expected to be

$$N = \$200{,}000(1 - 0.10)(1 - 0.20)(1 - 0.15) = \$200{,}000(0.90)(0.80)(0.85) = \$122{,}400$$

Note that the three decreases result in an overall sales reduction of 38.8%. This is less than the sum (10% + 20% + 15% = 45%) of the three percentage decreases.

✓ TIP

Excel Applications in Business Mathematics

 If you have not covered **Section 3.3** in your course, go back and read the TIP box titled "Excel Applications in Business Mathematics" located in that section. It explains how Connect provides spreadsheet applications as an optional feature.

EXAMPLE 5.1E

CALCULATING THE NET PRICE AFTER MULTIPLE DISCOUNTS

 WGW Manufacturing and Ace Clothing both produce basic work shirts that are very similar in quality and popularity. Both manufacturers quote a list price of $46.00 for the shirt. WGW offers a regular trade discount of 25% plus an additional volume discount of 10% on orders of at least 1000 shirts. Ace offers a standard discount of 30% and a further 5% discount on orders exceeding 500 shirts. Which source will give the lower net price on an order for 1000 shirts? How much lower per shirt?

SOLUTION

Given: For WGW, $L = \$46.00$, $d_1 = 25\%$, $d_2 = 10\%$
For Ace, $L = \$46.00$, $d_1 = 30\%$, $d_2 = 5\%$

The net price per shirt from WGW is

$$\begin{aligned} N = L(1 - d_1)(1 - d_2) &= \$46.00(1 - 0.25)(1 - 0.10) \\ &= \$46.00(0.75)(0.90) \\ &= \$31.05 \end{aligned}$$

The net price per shirt from Ace Clothing is

$$\begin{aligned} N = L(1 - d_1)(1 - d_2) &= \$46.00(1 - 0.30)(1 - 0.05) \\ &= \$46.00(0.70)(0.95) \\ &= \$30.59 \end{aligned}$$

Therefore, Ace's net price is 46 cents per shirt lower.

(Note that the sum of the two discount rates in each case is 35%. However, the combined discounts do not have the same effect.)

EXAMPLE 5.1F

CALCULATING THE LIST PRICE AFTER MULTIPLE DISCOUNTS

Red Barn Lawn Services paid $449.28 for fertilizer after discounts of 10% and 4% were applied to their order. What was the list price of the fertilizer?

SOLUTION

The net price is equivalent to the list price after the two discounts are applied.

$$N = L(1 - d_1)(1 - d_2)$$
$$\$449.28 = L(1 - 0.10)(1 - 0.04)$$
$$\$449.28 = L(0.90)(0.96)$$
$$\$449.28 = L(0.864)$$

The list price for the fertilizer is:

$$L = \frac{\$449.28}{0.864} = \$520.00$$

The list price of the fertilizer is $520.00.

EXAMPLE 5.1G

CALCULATING AN EQUIVALENT DISCOUNT RATE

What single discount rate is equivalent to multiple discounts of 20% and 10%?

SOLUTION

Let us apply the two discounts to a beginning value of $100.

$$N = L(1 - d_1)(1 - d_2) = \$100(1 - 0.20)(1 - 0.10) = \$100(0.80)(0.90) = \$72.00$$

The amount of the discount is $100 − $72.00 = $28.00.

$$d = \frac{\$28.00}{\$100} \times 100\% = 28.0\%$$

Therefore, a single discount rate of 28.0% is equivalent to multiple discount rates of 20% and 10%.

EXAMPLE 5.1H

CALCULATING ONE OF A SERIES OF DISCOUNTS

A provincial government recently tabled a budget in which agricultural subsidies will be reduced by 10% in each of the next three years. Subsidies in the current fiscal year total $11,000,000. What will be the amount of the reduction in the third year?

SOLUTION

The third 10% reduction will apply to the amount left after the first two reductions. The subsidies paid in the second year will be

$$N = L(1 - d_1)(1 - d_2) = \$11,000,000(1 - 0.10)(1 - 0.10)$$
$$= \$11,000,000(0.90)(0.90)$$
$$= \$8,910,000$$

Reduction in the third year = $d_3 \times \$8,910,000 = 0.10(\$8,910,000) = \$891,000$.

EXAMPLE 5.1I

CALCULATING A DISCOUNT TO MATCH A NET PRICE

Atlas Movers has priced their basic moving package at $1850 less discounts of 15% and 8%. Two Guys and a Truck have priced their basic move at $1695 less a discount of 10%. What second discount must Two Guys and a Truck offer to match the net price of a move offered by Atlas Movers?

SOLUTION

Given: For Atlas Movers, $L = \$1850.00$, $d_1 = 15\%$, $d_2 = 8\%$
For Two Guys and a Truck, $L = \$1695.00$, $d_1 = 10\%$

The net price for a basic move with Atlas Movers is

$$N = L(1 - d_1)(1 - d_2) = \$1850.00(1 - 0.15)(1 - 0.08)$$
$$= \$1850.00(0.85)(0.92)$$
$$= \$1446.70$$

For Two Guys and a Truck to match the net price of $1446.70

$$\$1446.70 = \$1695.00(1 - 0.10)(1 - d_2)$$

The second discount will be

$$d_2 = 1 - \frac{\$1446.70}{\$1525.50} = 1 - 0.9483 = 0.0517$$

The second discount needed by Two Guys and a Truck to match the Atlas Movers net price is 5.17%.

EXERCISE 5.1

Answers to the odd-numbered problems are at the end of the book.

 ***Spreadsheet templates:*** *The solutions for all of the following problems can employ one of the three partially completed Excel templates. Use the template in Connect for "Series Discounts" found under the Student Resources for Chapter 5. Each worksheet includes instructions for completing its template.*

CALCULATOR-FREE PROBLEMS

Calculate the missing values in Problems a–j.

Problem	List price ($)	Discount rate (%)	Discount amount ($)	Net price ($)
a.	300.00	$33\frac{1}{3}$	?	?
b.	900.00	25	?	?
c.	200.00	?	?	150.00
d.	50.00	?	?	45.00
e.	?	20	20.00	?
f.	?	25	50.00	?
g.	?	?	5.00	95.00
h.	?	?	20.00	60.00
i.	?	50	?	120.00
j.	?	10	?	900.00

Calculate the missing values in Problems 1–14.

Problem	List price ($)	Discount rate (%)	Discount amount ($)	Net price ($)
1.	249.00	$33\frac{1}{3}$	?	?
2.	995.00	$16\frac{2}{3}$	?	?
3.	127.98	?	?	106.65
4.	49.95	?	?	34.97
5.	?	35	612.50	?
6.	?	40	7.99	?
7.	?	?	12.33	15.07
8.	?	?	258.75	891.25
9.	?	12.5	?	2849.00
10.	?	$16\frac{2}{3}$	?	413.05
11.	99.00	$30, 16\frac{2}{3}$	?	?
12.	595.00	$20, 12\frac{1}{2}, 8\frac{1}{3}$	?	?
13.	?	$25, 10, 7\frac{1}{2}$	?	93.03
14.	?	$20, 10, 8\frac{1}{3}$	?	989.00

15. The distributor of Nikita power tools is offering a trade discount of 38% to hardware stores. What will be the stores' cost to purchase a rotary saw listed at $135?

16. Best Buy Entertainment can obtain Panasonic MP3 players for $134 less a trade discount of 35%. A comparable Samsung model is available for $127 less a discount of 30%. Which MP3 player has the lower net cost? How much lower?

17. A 37.5% trade discount on a camera represents a discount of $223.14 from the suggested retail price. What is the net price to the buyer?

18. After a trade discount of 27.5%, a jeweller can obtain 0.50-carat (Empress Cut, F Colour) Canadian Polar Bear diamonds for $2138.75. What is the dollar amount of the trade discount?

19. The net price to a car dealer of a model with a manufacturer's list price of $34,900 is $28,687.80. What trade discount rate is the dealer being given?

20. Green Thumb Nursery sells spreading junipers to the gardening departments of local grocery and building supply stores. The net price per tree is $27.06 after a trade discount of $22.14. What rate of trade discount is the nursery giving to retailers?

21. Niagara Dairies gives convenience stores a trade discount of 24% on butter listed at $72.00 per case. What rate of discount will Silverwood Milk Products have to give on its list price of $74.50 per case to match Niagara's price to convenience stores?

22. A college bookstore buys back good-condition textbooks for 45% off the retail price of new books. What will a student receive for a book currently selling at $104.50 new?

23. The net proceeds to the vendor of a house after payment of a 5.5% real estate commission were $321,111. What price did the house sell for?

24. A merchant pays a 3.5% fee to the Bank of Montreal on all MasterCard sales.
    a. What amount will she pay on sales of $17,564 for a month?
    b. What were her gross sales for a month in which the bank charged total fees of $732.88?

25. Cynthia and Byron sell mutual funds for Syndicated Investors. Purchasers of mutual funds from agents of Syndicated Investors pay a front-end commission of 5.5%. The commission is paid on the total amount paid to Syndicated Investors, not on just the net amount actually invested in mutual funds.
    a. Mr. and Mrs. Stevens placed $5500 through Cynthia. What amount was actually invested in mutual funds after the commission was paid?
    b. If the net amount invested in mutual funds as a result of Byron's sale to Mrs. Stocker was $6426, what amount of commission was paid on the sale?

26. **a.** Mirabai's income tax rate on additional income is 42%. She has just received a wage increase of $1.25 per hour. What is her after-tax increase in hourly pay?

    b. Shira's tax rate on additional income is 47%. How much extra must he earn to keep an additional $1000 after tax?

27. The evening news reports that the S&P/TSX Composite Index dropped 1.7% on the day to close at 13,646 points. Rounded to the nearest integer, how many points did the index fall on the day?

28. At its current price of $0.80 per share, Golden Egg Resources stock is down 73% from its price one year ago. What was that price?

29. Office Outlet offers a standard 7% discount on all orders and a special 5.5% volume discount if the purchaser orders at least 1000 units. South District High School is placing an order for pens costing $1.69 each. How much money could they save by placing an order for 1000 pens instead of just ordering the 950 pens they need?

30. A manufacturer of snowmobiles sells through distributors in some regions of the country, through wholesalers in other regions, and directly to retailers in its home province. The manufacturer gives a 25% trade discount to retailers, an additional 10% discount to wholesalers, and a further 7.5% discount to distributors. What net price does the manufacturer receive from each buying level on a snowmobile listed at $9800?

31. Holiday Paws Kennel offers a standard 20% coupon discount, a 15% multi-pet discount, and a further 10% discount for boarding pets longer than 7 days. If their daily rate for boarding is $55 per pet, how much would it cost to board 2 cats for 8 days compared to 3 dogs for 5 days?

32. An invoice shows a net price of $176.72 after trade discounts of 30%, 10%, and 2% have been deducted.

    a. What was the list price of the goods?

    b. What single rate of trade discount would be equivalent to the discount series?

INTERMEDIATE PROBLEMS

33. **a.** In announcing its third-quarter results, Prime Manufacturing reported a decline in revenue of $26.43 million representing a 3.65% decrease from the second quarter. Rounded to the nearest $0.01 million, what is the third quarter's revenue?

    b. Prime also announced that, over the next six months, it will reduce its workforce by 4.5% to 8500 through attrition and retirement incentives. What will be the actual number of people leaving?

34. A retailer is offered a regular discount of 25%, a further discount of 7.5% if she places an order exceeding $10,000 (at list prices), and another 5% promotional allowance (discount) for participating in a joint promotion with the distributor.

    a. If the retailer is eligible for all three trade discounts, what will be the net price of an order totalling $11,500?

    b. What is the dollar amount of the saving from the quantity discount (assuming that she does not participate in the joint promotion)?

    c. What is the dollar amount of the promotional allowance?

35. A wholesaler lists an item for $48.75 less 20%. What additional "special promotion" discount must be offered to retailers to get the net price down to $36.66?

36. The representative for a European ski manufacturer offers Snow 'n Surf Sporting Goods a regular discount of 25%, a volume discount of 10% for an order of at least 100 pairs of skis, and an early booking discount of 5% for orders placed before July 1.

    a. If Snow 'n Surf is eligible for all three trade discounts on skis listed at a suggested retail price of $890, what is the net price per pair of skis?

    b. Assuming that Snow 'n Surf qualifies for the volume discount, what is the dollar amount of the early-order discount per pair of skis?

   c. The net price after all three trade discounts on a less expensive model of skis is \$410.40. What is the suggested retail price?

   d. What single trade discount rate would be equivalent to the three trade discounts?

37. In addition to the basic trade discount of 20%, an outboard engine manufacturer gives a boat dealer an additional discount of 12.5% for providing follow-up warranty service, and a 5% discount for cooperative advertising and boat-show promotions.

   a. After the basic trade discount, what further price reduction (in dollars) does the 12.5% discount represent on an engine with a list price of \$3000?

   b. After the first two discounts, what price reduction does the 5% discount give on the \$3000 engine?

38. Ever-rest sells its mattresses for \$960 less 25%. Posture-Perfect mattresses are listed at \$880 less 20% and 5%. What second trade discount would Ever-rest need to offer to match Posture-Perfect's net price?

5.2 Cash Discounts and Terms of Payment

Other than the final sale to the consumer, transactions within the merchandising chain commonly involve "trade credit." Under this arrangement, the vendor does not require payment for goods during a "credit period" that can range from a few days to a few weeks. No interest is charged during this interval. Following a transaction, the vendor sends the buyer an invoice, such as the sample shown in **Figure 5.2**. The invoice presents details of the "terms of payment," items purchased, unit prices, applicable trade discount rates, shipping cost, 15% Harmonized Sales Tax (HST), and the amount due.

FIGURE 5.2   A Sample Sales Invoice

ATLANTIC ATHLETIC WHOLESALE LTD.
177 Main Avenue
Halifax, Nova Scotia B3M 1B4

Sold to:
McGarrigle Sports
725 Kings Road
Sydney, N.S. B1S 1C2

Date: July 17, 2019
Terms: 2/10, n/30

Invoice No: 3498
Via: Beatty Trucking

Quantity	Product number	Description	Unit list price	Discount	Net amount
5	W-32	Universal Gymnasium	\$2300	30%	\$8050.00
150	S-4	Soccer balls	\$56.00	25%, 15%	5355.00
1000	H-8a	Hockey pucks	\$2.20	35%, 10%, 7%	1196.91

Invoice total:	\$14,601.91
Shipping charges:	546.00
HST:	2272.19
Total amount due:	\$17,420.10

1.5% per month on overdue accounts

Terms of Payment

An invoice normally provides information about any discount for prompt payment and the duration of credit extended to the customer. These **terms of payment** include:

- The length of the **credit period**. The credit period is the length of time for which trade credit is granted. The invoice amount is due at the end of the credit period. Normally, interest is not charged for the credit period. It is common practice to charge a penalty on overdue amounts.

The "1.5% per month" indicated on the sample invoice means that any portion of the invoice amount that goes overdue (anywhere from one day to one month) is liable for a 1.5% penalty. How strictly a vendor enforces the penalty is a judgment call.

- The **cash discount** rate offered (if any) and the length of the **discount period**. A cash discount is a deduction allowed for prompt payment[4] of the invoice amount (or any portion thereof). The time period within which a payment qualifies for the cash discount is called the discount period.
- The date on which both the credit period and the discount period begin.

L03 The most common system for presenting the terms of payment is known as **ordinary dating** or *invoice dating*. (Two other systems of dating are presented in Connect. In Chapter 5 of the Student Edition, find "Supplement to Section 5.2," which shows examples of EOM and ROG dating.) With ordinary dating, both the credit period and the discount period are measured from the invoice date (day "0"). For example, if an invoice dated July 3 has a 30-day credit period, then July 4 is counted as "Day 1," July 5 as "Day 2," and so on. August 2 will be "Day 30," the final day of the credit period. A payment received on August 2 falls within the credit period, but a payment received on August 3 is liable for the overdue-account penalty.

A shorthand notation is normally used on an invoice to present the terms of payment. **Figure 5.3** illustrates the ordinary dating notation in the particular case of a 2% cash discount offered during a 10-day discount period, and a 30-day credit period. The abbreviation "2/10, n/30" is read as "two ten, net thirty."

FIGURE 5.3   Interpreting the Terms of Payment in Ordinary Dating

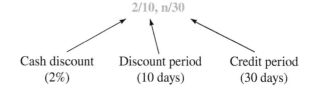

In **Figure 5.4** the invoice date, discount period, and credit period for the example 2/10, n/30 are plotted on a time axis. The 2% cash discount is credited on *either partial payments or full payment* made *on or before* the last day of the discount period. The balance is due by the end of the 30-day credit period.

FIGURE 5.4   Discount and Credit Periods for the Ordinary Dating Case 2/10, n/30

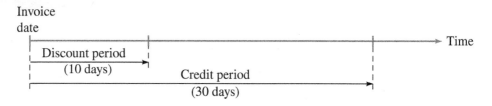

---

4   It is generally advisable for the purchaser to take advantage of a cash discount. Forgoing the discount is usually equivalent to paying a high interest rate for trade credit during the remainder of the credit period. Therefore, failure of a customer to take advantage of a cash discount provides an early warning signal that the customer may, at least temporarily, be in a weak financial condition. In recent years, there has been a trend away from offering cash discounts. Vendors find that many customers pay after the discount period but still deduct the cash discount from their remittance. Enforcement of the discount period cutoff gives rise to too many hassles with customers.

The following are common practices with ordinary dating (and with the two other notations described in the supplement to this section).

- If the last day of the discount period or the credit period falls on a non-business day, the period is extended to the next business day.
- If no cash discount is offered, only the "net" figure for the credit period is given (for example, n/15 or n/30).
- If a net figure for the credit period is not stated, it is understood that the credit period ends 20 days after the end of the discount period. For example, "2/10" by itself implies "2/10, n/30."

LO4 Formula (5-1), $N = L(1 - d)$, may be used to calculate the amount required to settle an invoice if the cash discount is taken. Substitute the invoice amount for L and the cash discount rate for d. The value calculated for N is the full payment that will settle the invoice within the discount period.

EXAMPLE 5.2A

INVOICE SETTLEMENT WITH ORDINARY DATING

An invoice for $1079.80 with terms 2/10, n/30 is dated November 25. What payment will settle the invoice if payment is made on:

a. December 1?　　　　**b.** December 5?　　　　**c.** December 7?

SOLUTION

a.,b. The last day of the discount period is the 10th day after the invoice date (November 25). November has 30 days. Therefore, payments made on or before December 5 are eligible for the 2% cash discount. The payment required to settle the invoice is:

$$N = L(1 - d) = \$1079.80(1 - 0.02) = \$1058.20$$

c. After December 5, the full amount must be paid to settle the invoice.
The payment required is $1079.80.

(Note that any payments made after the discount period ends can be thought of as having a 0% discount. The payment required is then calculated as $N = L(1 - 0\%)$ or $N = L$. It will become important in our discussion of partial payments to remember that all payments are *Net* amounts.)

A variation of the ordinary dating notation is "2/10, 1/30, n/60." In this case, a reduced cash discount of 1% is offered on payments made any time from the 11th to the 30th day after the invoice date. With this notation, only one of the discounts is applied to the payment based on the date payment is made.

EXAMPLE 5.2B

INVOICE SETTLEMENT WITH ORDINARY DATING AND MULTIPLE DISCOUNTS

An invoice dated March 12 for $5278.82 has terms 3/10, 1/30, n/60. What payment will settle the invoice if payment is made on:

a. March 20?　　　　**b.** March 31?　　　　**c.** April 13?

SOLUTION

a. The last day for the 3% discount is 10 days after the invoice date (March 12). March has 31 days. Therefore, payments made on or before March 22 are eligible for the 3% discount. The payment required to settle the invoice is:

$$N = L(1 - d) = \$5278.82(1 - 0.03) = \$5120.46$$

b. The second discount period begins March 23 (on the 11th day after the invoice date) and ends 20 days later on April 11. The payment required to settle the invoice on March 31 is:

$$N = L(1 - d) = \$5278.82(1 - 0.01) = \$5226.03$$

c. After April 11, the full amount must be paid to settle the invoice. The payment required is $5278.82.

Partial Payments

A **partial payment** is any payment smaller than the initial amount required to fully satisfy the invoice. Unless otherwise indicated on the invoice, partial payments made within the discount period are eligible for the cash discount. The basic discount Formula (5-1) may be used to calculate the amount credited to the customer's account. But you must be careful how you use it. See the following Trap box.

 TRAP

This One Catches a Majority of Students!

Suppose a vendor sends you an invoice for $1000 with the offer of a 2% cash discount. If you make a partial payment of $500 within the discount period, the vendor will credit your account for more than the $500 since you will also be credited with a cash discount. How much will that cash discount be? If your response is "2% of $500, which is $10," you have already fallen into the trap. The $500 payment is considered to have already been discounted. By finding 2% of $500, you are discounting a previously discounted value. You need to find the value of the $500 payment *before* it was discounted.

To understand the approach that should be taken, think about how you would calculate the amount you should pay if you intend to pay the invoice in full. You would begin with the basic discount Formula (5-1) and place the following interpretation on the variables:

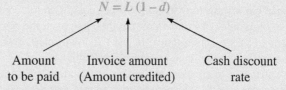

$$N = L\,(1 - d)$$

| Amount to be paid | Invoice amount (Amount credited) | Cash discount rate |

With a 2% discount on the invoice amount, $L = \$1000$, you need to pay only

$$N = \$1000(1 - 0.02) = \$980$$

The vendor will credit your account with the $980 payment plus a $20 cash discount. There are two points to note:

- The variable N represents the amount of the actual payment in a cash discount calculation.
- The cash discount is $d\%$ of the total amount credited (L), not $d\%$ of the actual payment (N). In a partial payment situation, we initially know N but not L. For a partial payment of $500 in the present case, we have

$$\$500 = L(1 - 0.02)$$

The amount credited will be

$$L = \frac{\$500}{0.98} = \$510.20$$

That is, the cash discount allowed on the $500 payment will be $10.20 (which is 2% of the $510.20 credited).

TIP

There Are Two Sides to Every Formula

When you use the formula for cash discounts, think about who "owns" each side of Formula (5-1).

Customer side	Business side
N	$= L(1 - d)$

The value for N, the full or partial payment, is determined by the customer. When you know the payment amount, you will be calculating actions on the side of the business—the amount credited to a customer account (L).

The values for L, the list amount, and d, the discount rate, are determined by the business. When you know both of these values you will be calculating the actions on the side of the customer—the amount of the payment sent to the business (N).

Keeping these two distinct and separate will help you avoid the Trap above.

 POINT OF INTEREST

The Cost of Not Taking a Discount

A business's ability to take advantage of a cash discount depends greatly on the cash flow of the business. If a business has free flowing cash, then it should always take advantage of any trade credit being offered. However, when cash is needed for other aspects of the business, paying invoices within the discount period may not be a priority. What does this really cost the business?

Consider a company with an invoice for $10,000 with terms 3/10, n/30. If they pay the invoice within the 10-day credit period they will have a discount of $300. If they cannot pay within the discount period it is worth looking at the cost of borrowing the $10,000. If this cost is less than the value of the discount then they are still ahead at the end of the 30-day period.

If we assume they can get a short-term loan for 5% per year, then the cost of borrowing $10,000 for 30 days using simple interest would be approximately $41 in interest. If they pay back the $10,000 principal at the end of the 30 days, then the business is still ahead $259. This example is just for one invoice. If we expand this type of savings across all of the invoices a business pays, then the savings are quite substantial.

Another way to look at this is to consider the option of investing the $10,000 to see if the interest earned would be at least equivalent to the value of the $300 discount. With today's current investment rates, say 2% per year, the simple interest earned on $10,000 in 30 days would be approximately $16, or 0.16%. This is quite a big difference from the 3% cash discount! In fact, to be equivalent, the $10,000 investment would have to earn a little over 36% per year to make up the cost of not taking advantage of the 3% discount.

EXAMPLE 5.2C

PARTIAL PAYMENTS WITH ORDINARY DATING

Roland Electric received an invoice for $3845 dated March 25 with terms 3/10, 1/20, n/60. Roland paid $1500 on April 4, $500 on April 12, and $500 on April 30. What balance was still owed after April 30?

SOLUTION

The 3% discount applies to any payment made on or before April 4 (March 25 + 10 days). The 1% discount applies to any payment made in the period April 5 to April 14, inclusive. Therefore, the $1500 payment qualifies for the 3%

discount, and the first $500 payment qualifies for the 1% discount. To determine the amount credited for each partial payment, solve for L in Formula (5-1). For the $1500 payment,

$$\$1500 = L(1 - 0.03) \text{ giving } L = \frac{\$1500}{0.97} = \$1546.39$$

For the first $500 payment,

$$\$500 = L(1 - 0.01) \text{ giving } L = \frac{\$500}{0.99} = \$505.05$$

The balance owed after April 30 was

$$\$3845 - (\$1546.39 + \$505.05 + \$500) = \$1293.56$$

EXAMPLE 5.2D

PARTIAL PAYMENTS TO REDUCE A BALANCE

Bartlett General Contractors received an invoice for $1872 dated October 17 with terms 2/15, 1/30, n/60. A payment of $1100 was made on November 1 and a second payment was made on November 10 that reduced the balance to $345.51. What was the amount of the second payment?

SOLUTION

The 2% discount applies to any payment made on or before November 1 (October 17 + 15 days). The 1% discount applies to any payment made in the period November 2 to November 16, inclusive. Therefore, the $1100 payment qualifies for the 2% discount, and the second unknown payment qualifies for the 1% discount. To determine the amount credited for each payment, solve for L in Formula (5-1). For the $1100 payment

$$\$1100 = L(1 - 0.02) \text{ giving } L = \frac{\$1100}{0.98} = \$1122.45$$

For the unknown payment, p

$$\$p = L(1 - 0.01) \text{ giving } L = \frac{\$p}{0.99}$$

The invoice amount can be expressed in terms of the two payments and the outstanding balance as

$$\$1872 = \$1122.45 + \frac{\$p}{0.99} + \$345.51$$

$$\frac{\$p}{0.99} = \$1872 - \$1122.45 - \$345.51$$

$$\$p = (0.99)\$404.04 = \$400.00$$

The amount of the payment on November 10 was $400.00.

EXERCISE 5.2

Answers to the odd-numbered problems are at the end of the book.

BASIC PROBLEMS

1. An invoice for $2365, dated September 25, has terms of payment 2/20, n/30. What amount on October 5 will pay the invoice in full?

2. The terms of payment on a $2365 invoice dated October 25 were $1\frac{1}{2}$/15, n/45. What amount will settle the invoice on November 10?

3. On June 29, Josef received an invoice for $815.49, dated June 27. If the terms of the invoice are 2/10, 1/20, n/60, what amount is required on July 7 to pay the invoice in full?

4. On March 26, Silke received an invoice in the amount of $5445, dated March 23, with terms 3/10, $1\frac{1}{2}$/20, n/60. What payment on April 13 will settle the invoice?

5. On May 25, Morris Hardware received an invoice from Precision Tools Inc. for $5076.64. The invoice was dated May 22 and offered terms of 2/10, 1/20, n/30. What payment will settle the invoice on:

   a. June 1? **b.** June 2? **c.** June 5?

6. White's Photography received an e-invoice from Fuji Canada dated February 27 of a leap year. The amount of the invoice is $2896.77, with terms $2\frac{1}{2}$/10, 1/30, n/60.

   a. What is the last date on which White's is eligible for the $2\frac{1}{2}$% discount?

   b. What amount will be required on that date to settle the invoice?

   c. Instead of the payment in part (b), what amount must be paid on March 29 to settle the invoice?

7. An invoice for $2365.00 has terms 2/10, n/30. The amount credited on a payment made within the discount period was $1365.00. What was the amount of the payment?

8. The terms of payment on an invoice for $2835.49 are 2/15, n/45. The balance owed after a payment within the discount period is $1135.49. What was the amount of the payment?

9. On June 3, Josh made a payment of $500 on an invoice for $1283.50, dated May 25. The terms of payment were 3/10, n/30. What amount was credited to Josh's account?

10. An invoice for $3868, dated June 26, had terms 2/10, 1/20, n/45. What amount was credited for:

    a. A payment of $1000 on July 5?

    b. A payment of $1000 on July 16?

    c. A payment of $1000 on August 10?

11. Contemporary Furnishings received an invoice on April 18 from Palliser Furniture. The invoice for $18,976.45 was dated April 16 with terms 2/15, 1/30, n/45.

    a. What is the balance after a payment of $10,000 on May 1?

    b. What additional payment on May 15 will settle the account?

12. Mayfair Distributors sent Bed 'n Bath an invoice dated December 23 for $5344.90 with terms 2/10, 1/20, n/30. The penalty on overdue accounts is $1\frac{1}{2}$% of the overdue balance.

    a. What is the balance after a payment of $3000 on January 3?

    b. What additional payment on January 30 will settle the account?

13. Payments of $1000 on January 5 and $800 on January 16 were made on a $2500 invoice dated December 27. The terms on the invoice were 4/10, 2/20, n/45. What was the balance owed after the second payment?

14. On March 25, Hannah received an invoice in the mail from Carpet Country for $4235. The invoiced was dated March 22 and had terms 3/15, $1\frac{1}{2}$/30, n/60. If she made payments of $1000 on each of April 2, April 9, and April 22, how much does Hannah still owe?

15. Ristorante Italiano made payments of $5000 on March 29 and $3000 on April 7 to General Restaurant Supplies on an invoice for $11,870. The invoice was dated March 21 and carried terms of $1\frac{1}{2}$/10, $\frac{1}{2}$/20, n/30.

    a. What is the balance after the second payment?

    b. On what date is the balance due?

16. Northern Outfitters' invoice to Rico's Menswear for $2463.80 was dated October 22 with terms 2/10, n/30. Late payments are charged a 1% penalty on the overdue balance. Rico made payments of $1000 on October 31 and $800 on November 20. What amount will pay off the balance on December 8?

17. A payment of $3000 on a $6000 invoice qualified for the larger cash discount in 3/10, 1/20, n/30. What additional payment 18 days after the invoice date will settle the invoice?

18. The Simcoe School Board has three invoices from Johnston Transport, all with terms 2/10, 1/20, n/60. Invoice 277, dated October 22, is for $14,200; Invoice 327, dated November 2, is for $8600; and Invoice 341, dated November 3, is for $11,500. What total payment to Johnston on November 12 will settle all three invoices?

19. What total amount must be paid on July 4 to settle invoices dated June 20 for $485, June 24 for $367, and June 30 for $722, all with terms $1\frac{1}{2}$/10, n/30?

INTERMEDIATE PROBLEMS

20. Jake received an invoice for $2500 with terms 5/10, 2/30, n/60. After one payment within the 10-day discount period, a second payment of $1057.37 within the 30-day discount period paid off the balance. What was the amount of the first payment?

21. Ballard Jewellers received an invoice dated August 22 from Safeguard Security Systems for $2856.57 with terms $2\frac{1}{2}$/10, 1/20, n/45. Ballard made payments of $900 on September 1, $850 on September 10, and $700 on September 30. What amount was still owed on October 1?

22. Peak Roofing sent Jensen Builders an invoice dated July 12 for $5400 with terms 3/10, $1\frac{1}{2}$/20, n/45. Jensen made a payment of $2000 on July 20, and a second payment on August 1 that reduced the balance owed to $1000. What was the size of the second payment?

23. On August 6, A&B Construction has three outstanding invoices payable to Excel Builder's Supply. Invoice 535, dated July 16, is for $3228.56; Invoice 598, dated July 24, is for $2945.31; and Invoice 678, dated August 3, is for $6217.69. All invoices have terms 4/10, 2/20, n/60. If A&B makes a $10,000 payment to Excel on August 6, what further payment on August 15 will settle the account? Note that Excel applies payments to the oldest invoices first.

ADVANCED PROBLEMS

24. Sutton Trucking made two equal payments, on June 25 and July 15, on an invoice for $6350 dated June 15 with terms 3/10, 1/30, n/60. The payments reduced the balance owed on the invoice to $1043.33. What was the amount of each payment?

25. An invoice for $2956.60, dated February 2, has terms 2/15, 1/30, n/90. What three equal payments on February 17, March 2, and May 2 will settle the account?

5.3 Markup

L05 The **markup** or **gross profit** is the amount added to the cost of an item to arrive at its selling price. Thus,

$$\text{Selling price} = \text{Cost} + \text{Markup}$$

The markup on each unit must be large enough to cover a portion of the overall operating expenses (such as wages, rent, and utilities) and also make a suitable contribution to the overall operating profit. Expressing this idea as a word equation,

$$\text{Markup} = \text{Overhead expenses per unit} + \text{Operating profit}^5 \text{ per unit}$$

---

[5] In accounting, the "operating profit" on a Statement of Earnings is the profit from normal business operations. Unusual revenues from the sale of capital assets or other nonrecurring events are not included. The "operating profit" in our discussion of markup corresponds to the operating profit from a Statement of Earnings, but calculated on a per unit basis.

Let us define the following symbols:

$$S = \text{Selling price (per unit)}$$
$$C = \text{Cost (per unit)}$$
$$M = \text{Markup (per unit)}$$
$$E = \text{Overhead or operating expenses (per unit)}$$
$$P = \text{Operating profit (per unit)}$$

The algebraic versions of the preceding word equations are

SELLING PRICE

$$S = C + M \tag{5-3}$$

MARKUP

$$M = E + P \tag{5-4}^6$$

If we replace M in Formula (5-3) by $E + P$, we obtain

SELLING PRICE

$$S = C + E + P \tag{5-5}$$

Figure 5.5 is a pictorial representation of these relationships. It shows that S may be viewed as being composed of C and M, or of C, E, and P. The boundary between E and P is shown as a dashed line because an *accurate* breakdown of M into its components may be done only at the *end* of an accounting period. Suppose, for example, that sales volume during a month is lower than normal. Then each unit's E must include a larger share of the fixed rent expense than it would in a month of higher sales. For a future operating period, a merchandiser can only estimate E based on his sales forecast and his experience in previous periods. (Managers prefer to think of each product line's E in terms of its percentage of C or its percentage of S.) The expected P based on an estimated E is also an approximation.

FIGURE 5.5　Markup Diagram

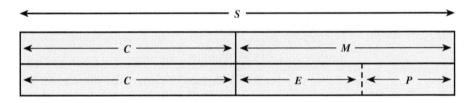

If a retailer is prepared to break even ($P = 0$) in order to clear out old stock, then the reduced price in a clearance sale needs to cover only the cost and the overhead expense. That is,

$$S(\text{break even}) = C + E \quad \text{and} \quad M(\text{break even}) = E$$

Merchandisers prefer to think of an item's markup in terms of its *percentage* of cost and its *percentage* of selling price. In the "real world," the terminology in this respect is inconsistent. We will use **rate of markup on cost**:

$$\textbf{\textit{Rate of markup on cost}} = \frac{M}{C} \times 100\% \tag{5-6}$$

and **rate of markup on selling price**:

$$\textbf{\textit{Rate of markup on selling price}}^7 = \frac{M}{S} \times 100\% \tag{5-7}$$

6　In applications of Formulas (5-3), (5-4), and (5-5) in this chapter, we will assume that E and P are constant over the range of sales being considered. In practice, economies of scale usually result in the operating expenses per unit decreasing as the sales volume rises.

7　Rate of markup on selling price is sometimes (especially in accounting terminology) called the gross profit margin.

When pricing merchandise, retailers usually first decide upon the rate of markup on cost for each product line. Then they calculate the corresponding dollar amount of the markup for each product and add it to the unit cost.

The accompanying table is a useful aid for setting up and solving markup problems. The middle column is for the components of the selling price S expressed in dollars. The third column is for the components of S expressed as percentages of S. Note that each column incorporates the Formulas (5-3), (5-4), and (5-5). Markup is the subtotal of E and P. Selling price is the sum of M and C, which also makes it the sum of E, P, and C.

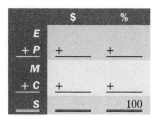

The first benefit from using the table is that it helps us organize the information given in the problem. Known dollar amounts should be entered in the "$" column. Given percentage values should be entered in the "%" column. The following table presents an example of how you translate information given in the problem to entries in the table when percentages are based on selling price.

	$	%	Given information
E	0.20S	20	The operating expenses are 20% of the selling price.
+P	+ 15	+	Estimated operating profit of $15 per unit.
M	0.42S	42	The rate of markup on selling price is 42%.
+C	+28.98	+	The retailer purchases the item for $28.98.
SP	1.00S	100	This is always true when percentages are based on selling price.

This next table presents an example of how you would translate information given in the problem to entries in the table when percentages are based on cost.

	$	%	Given information
E	5		Estimated operating expenses are $5 per unit
+P	+0.30C	+ 30	The operating profit is to be 30% of cost.
M	0.70C	70	The rate of markup on cost is 70%.
+C	+1.00C	+ 100	This is always true when percentages are based on cost.
SP	21.25		The retailer wants to set a selling price of $21.25 per unit.

In comparison to working directly with Formulas (5-3), (5-4), and (5-5), the main advantage of working with the table is that it is more apparent which quantity may be calculated next and how it may be calculated. Not only does the table build in the additive relationships of Formulas (5-3), (5-4), and (5-5), it also assists us in setting up proportions. The ratio of any two items from the "$" column is equal to the ratio of the corresponding two items from the "%" column.

As an alternative to the table model, Connect presents a different approach for solving problems in **Sections 5.3**, **5.4**, and **5.5**. In Chapter 5 of the Student Edition, find "Supplements to Sections 5.3, 5.4, and 5.5," which demonstrates the use of a markup diagram in alternative solutions for **Examples 5.3A, 5.3B, 5.3C, 5.3D, 5.3E, 5.4B, 5.5A, 5.5B,** and **5.5C.**

The Connection between the Net Price, *N*, and the Cost, *C*

In **Section 5.1**, we calculated the net price, *N*, after one or more trade discounts. In this section we use *C* to represent an item's (unit) cost. In most cases that we will encounter, *C* will equal the value of *N* calculated for one unit.

C will differ from *N* in two common situations. Since *cash discounts* for prompt payment are credited toward *N*, any cash discounts taken on the purchase of an item will make *C* less than *N*. Any *shipping charges* included in the invoice amount are added to the net price *after* trade discounts. Therefore, shipping charges on purchases will make *C* greater than *N*. Unless a cash discount or shipping charges apply in a problem, assume that the net price after trade discounts will also be the cost.

EXAMPLE 5.3A

CALCULATING THE MARKUP AND SELLING PRICE THAT WILL GIVE A DESIRED OPERATING PROFIT

Coastal Marine is importing a new line of inflatable boats at a unit cost of $1860. Coastal estimates that operating expenses per unit will be 30% of cost.

a. What should the markup and selling price be if Coastal Marine's desired operating profit per unit is 25% of cost?

b. What are Coastal Marine's rate of markup on cost and rate of markup on selling price for the inflatable boats?

SOLUTION

a. Although this problem may be simple enough for you to solve it without employing the table model, let's use the table to gain familiarity with it. After entering the given information, the table will appear as shown at right.

	$	%
E	0.30C	30
+P	+0.25C	+ 25
M		
+C	+ 1860	+
S		100

In the "$" column, we note that

$$M = 0.30C + 0.25C = 0.55C = 0.55(\$1860) = \$1023$$

After you calculate a value, enter it in the table. The table will then look like the second table.

	$	%
E	0.30C	30
+P	+0.25C	+ 25
M	1023	55
+C	+ 1860	+
S		100

It next becomes obvious that

$$S = \$1023 + \$1860 = \$2883$$

b. Enter the value for *S* in the table. Then

$$\text{Rate of markup on cost} = \frac{M}{C} \times 100\% = \frac{\$1023}{\$1860} \times 100\% = 55.0\%$$

[We could have immediately written this answer using the fact from part (a) that *M* = 0.55*C*.]

Finally,

$$\text{Rate of markup on selling price} = \frac{M}{S} \times 100\% = \frac{\$1023}{\$2883} \times 100\% = 35.5\%$$

 TIP

"Cost" Is Not the Selling Price

The term "cost" is used in merchandising word problems to describe the cost of an item to the business, not the cost to the consumer. The cost to the consumer is the selling price. To avoid confusing these two, always read word problems from the perspective of the business, not as a consumer.

EXAMPLE 5.3B

CALCULATING THE OPERATING PROFIT PER UNIT

Kabir is the proprietor of Fredericton Cycle. He wants to estimate the operating profit per unit on a new line of bicycles he may add to his inventory. His cost for each bicycle will be $385. Kabir does financial projections based on operating expenses of 35% of cost. If he matches the competition's retail price of $649 on these bicycles, what will be his operating profit per unit?

SOLUTION

Enter the given information in the table:

From the table, it is then apparent that

$$\$649 = \$385 + 0.35(\$385) + P$$

Therefore,

$$P = \$649 - \$385 - \$134.75 = \$129.25$$

Kabir's estimated operating profit will be $129.25 per bicycle.

	$	%
E	0.35C	35
+ P	+ ___	+ ___
M		
+ C	+ 385	+ 100
S	649	___

EXAMPLE 5.3C

CALCULATING THE SELLING PRICE THAT PRODUCES A DESIRED MARKUP ON SELLING PRICE

The cost of a gas barbecue to a retailer is $245. If the retailer wants a 30% rate of markup on selling price, determine the amount of the markup and the selling price.

SOLUTION

Construct a table and enter the given information. For this example expenses and profit are not known so they have not been included in the table. In the "%" column, it is immediately evident that C is 70% of S. (This value is also entered in the table.)

From the last two rows in the table, we can write the proportion

$$\frac{\$245}{70} = \frac{S}{100}$$

Hence,

$$S = \frac{\$245}{70} \times 100 = \$350.00$$

Then,

$$M = 0.30S = 0.30(\$350) = \$105.00$$

The selling price after a markup of $105 is $350.

	$	%
M	0.30S	30
+ C	+ 245	+ 70
S	___	100

 POINT OF INTEREST

Markup versus Margin

Rate of markup based on cost or *markup percentage* and rate of markup based on selling price or *gross profit margin* are often confused when talking about pricing. You may think that if an item is marked up by 30% then this translates to a 30% gross profit margin. Not so!

Markup looks at cost alone, while gross profit margin looks at the difference between the selling price and the profit. Since profit is calculated after expenses are tallied, the gross profit margin is a truer reflection of the bottom line.

In the calculations shown in **Example 5.3D**, the markup amount is independent of the cost in the calculation of the markup percentage. This means that the markup percentage can exceed 100%. However, when calculating the gross profit margin the markup is part of the selling price—so if the markup increases so does the selling price. This means that the gross profit margin can never exceed 100%.

Mathematically, markup is always larger than margin. The following chart illustrates this relationship for markup percentages between 10 and 2000 percent.

Markup percentage	10%	20%	25%	50%	75%	100%	200%	500%	2000%
Margin	9.09%	16.67%	20%	33.33%	42.86%	50%	66.67%	83.3%	95.25%

You would have to have a markup percentage of more than 1,000,000% to achieve a gross profit margin that is very close to 100%.

EXAMPLE 5.3D

USING RELATIONSHIPS AMONG PRICING VARIABLES

Cal-Tire retails its regular tires at $120 each and its high-performance tires at $175 each. Cal-Tire purchases the tires from the factory for $80 and $122, respectively. Overhead expenses are 20% of the selling price. For each line of tires, determine:

a. The amount of markup.

b. The rate of markup on cost.

c. The rate of markup on selling price.

d. The operating profit per tire.

SOLUTION

Enter the given information for each tire in separate tables. The quantities to be determined in parts (a), (c), and (d) are indicated in the tables below by the letters a, c, and d, respectively.

Regular tire

	$	%
E	0.20S	20
+ P	+ d +	
M	a	c
+ C	+ 80 +	
S	120	100

High-performance tire

	$	%
E	0.20S	20
+ P	+ d +	
M	a	c
+ C	+ 122 +	
S	175	100

An inspection of the tables reveals that M may be calculated immediately as the missing value needed in the lower section of the "$" column.

Regular tire:

a.
$$M + \$80 = \$120$$
$$M = \$120 - \$80 = \$40$$

The markup is $40.00.

High-performance tire:

$$M + \$122 = \$175$$
$$M = \$175 - \$122 = \$53$$

The markup is $53.00.

Enter these amounts in their respective tables.

b.
$$\text{Rate of markup on cost} = \frac{M}{C} \times 100\%$$
$$= \frac{\$40}{\$80} \times 100\%$$
$$= 50.00\%$$

$$\text{Rate of markup on cost} = \frac{M}{C} \times 100\%$$
$$= \frac{\$53}{\$122} \times 100\%$$
$$= 43.44\%$$

c.

$$\text{Rate of markup on selling price} = \frac{M}{S} \times 100\%$$

$$= \frac{\$40}{\$120} \times 100\%$$

$$= 33.33\%$$

$$\text{Rate of markup on selling price} = \frac{M}{S} \times 100\%$$

$$= \frac{\$53}{\$175} \times 100\%$$

$$= 30.29\%$$

d. As values are calculated, they should be entered in the appropriate cells of the tables. After part (c), the tables appear as follows:

Regular tire

	$	%
E	0.20S	20
+ P	+ d	+
M	40	33.33
+ C	+ 80	+
S	120	100

High-performance tire

	$	%
E	0.20S	20
+ P	+ d	+
M	53	30.29
+ C	+ 122	+
S	175	100

From the "%" column of the table on the left, it is evident that

$$P = (33.33\% - 20\%) \text{ of } S = 13.33\% \text{ of } S = 0.1333 \times \$120 = \$16.00$$

for the regular tire. Similarly, for the high-performance tire,

$$P = (30.29\% - 20\%) \text{ of } S = 10.29\% \text{ of } S = 0.1029 \times \$175 = \$18.01$$

EXAMPLE 5.3E

CALCULATING THE MARKUP AND SELLING PRICE THAT WILL GIVE A DESIRED OPERATING PROFIT

A sporting goods store sets the selling price of baseball gloves to include expected overhead expenses of 25% of the selling price and a desired profit of 20% of the selling price. Determine the selling price and the rate of markup on cost for a glove that costs the store $56.50.

SOLUTION

Construct a table and enter the given information. You may then add E and P to obtain values for M in both columns. Then the value for C in the "%" column is 55. The contents of the table at this stage are shown at right.

	$	%
E	0.25S	25
+ P	+ 0.20S	+ 20
M	0.45S	45
+ C	+ 56.50	+ 55
S		100

Using the C and S rows of the "$" and "%" columns, we can form a proportion to solve for S.

$$\frac{\$56.50}{55} = \frac{S}{100}$$

Hence,

$$S = \frac{\$56.50}{55} \times 100 = \$102.73$$

Then

$$\text{Rate of markup on cost} = \frac{M}{C} \times 100\% = \frac{0.45(\$102.73)}{\$56.50} \times 100\% = 81.82\%$$

After a markup of 81.82% on cost, the selling price of the glove is $102.73.

EXAMPLE 5.3F

THE RELATIONSHIP BETWEEN RATE OF MARKUP ON SELLING PRICE AND RATE OF MARKUP ON COST

a. If the rate of markup on selling price is 40%, what is the rate of markup on cost?

b. If the rate of markup on cost is 40%, what is the rate of markup on selling price?

SOLUTION

a. Construct a table and enter the rate of markup on selling price.

The value for C in the % column is 60. Using the M and C rows in the % column we can write the rate of markup on cost as:

	$	%
M	0.40S	40
+ C	+	+ 60
S		100

$$\frac{M}{C} \times 100\% = \frac{40}{60} \times 100\% = 66.67\%$$

In general, the rate of markup on cost $= \dfrac{\text{Rate of markup on selling price}}{1 - \text{Rate of markup on selling price}} \times 100\%$

b. Construct a table and enter the value of markup in the $ column as 40% of cost, or $0.40C$.

We can calculate the selling price as:

	$	%
M	0.40C	40
+ C	+ C	+ 100
S		140

$$S = 0.40C + C = 1.4C$$

This means that the selling price is 140% of the cost so the rate of markup on selling price is then

$$\frac{40}{140} \times 100\% = 28.57\%$$

In general, the rate of markup on selling price $= \dfrac{\text{Rate of markup on cost}}{1 + \text{Rate of markup on cost}} \times 100\%$.

CONCEPT QUESTIONS

1. For a given dollar amount of markup, which will be the larger number: the rate of markup on cost or the rate of markup on selling price? Explain.

2. Is it possible for the rate of markup on selling price to exceed 100%? Explain.

3. Is it possible for the rate of markup on cost to exceed 100%? Explain.

4. Under what unusual circumstance will the rate of markup on cost equal the rate of markup on selling price?

5. Does a retailer break even if an item is sold at the cost C?

EXERCISE 5.3

Answers to the odd-numbered problems are at the end of the book.

BASIC PROBLEMS

Calculate percentages to the nearest 0.1%.

1. An item that costs a store $152.50 is marked up by $47.45. Determine:
   a. The rate of markup on cost.
   b. The rate of markup on selling price.

2. A retailer obtains a product at a unit cost of $51.30 and sells it for $79.90. Determine:
   a. The rate of markup on cost.
   b. The rate of markup on selling price.

3. Omega Restaurant buys Shiraz wine at $16.95 per bottle, and sells it to customers at $34.95 per bottle. Calculate Omega's rate of markup on cost and rate of markup on selling price of the wine.

4. Loblaws purchases raisins at $85.75 per 25-kg box and then sells them in its bulk foods department for $0.59 per 100 g. What are Loblaws' rate of markup on cost and rate of markup on selling price of the raisins?

5. Unit operating expenses for an item costing $30 are estimated at 40% of cost, and the desired operating profit is 25% of cost. Determine:
   a. The selling price.
   b. The rate of markup on cost.
   c. The rate of markup on selling price.

6. A retailer prices her goods to cover operating expenses at 30% of cost and to generate a profit of 20% of cost. For an item she buys from her wholesaler at $49, determine:
   a. Its selling price.
   b. The rate of markup on cost.
   c. The rate of markup on selling price.

7. A merchant prices his inventory to allow for operating expenses at 30% of selling price and an operating profit of 20% of selling price. If an item is priced at $49.98, determine:
   a. The rate of markup on selling price.
   b. Its cost.
   c. The rate of markup on cost.

8. The price structure in a store is such that, for every $100 of sales, $40 is the cost of the goods sold and $45 goes to overhead costs. For an item with a wholesale cost of $119, determine:
   a. Its selling price.
   b. The rate of markup on cost.
   c. The rate of markup on selling price.
   d. The operating profit on the item.

9. A men's clothing store marks up suits by 75% of cost. This provides an operating profit of 15% of the selling price. If a suit's cost to the store is $132, determine:
   a. Its selling price.
   b. The rate of markup on selling price.
   c. The operating profit.

10. A grocery store prices fresh produce at twice its cost to the store. Determine:
    a. The rate of markup on cost.
    b. The rate of markup on selling price.

11. The markup on greeting cards in a drug store is 65% of the selling price. For a card priced at $4.95, determine:
    a. Its cost.
    b. The rate of markup on cost.

12. The markup on desserts in a restaurant is 70% of the menu price. The restaurant is adding key lime pie to its dessert list. The cost to the restaurant works out to $1.25 per slice. Determine:
    a. The menu price of a slice of pie.
    b. The rate of markup on cost.

13. Bath 'n Bedroom sets its prices to allow for overhead expenses that average 50% of unit cost and a normal profit of 30% of cost. For towel sets priced at $39.89, determine:
    a. The wholesale cost.
    b. The rate of markup on selling price.

14. The price of tools is set by a hardware store to cover operating expenses at 40% of cost, and to generate an operating profit of 25% of cost. What is the rate of markup on selling price for a rotary saw selling for $129?

15. Just Desserts buys cheesecakes from General Bakeries at $33.60 per cheesecake. It then cuts each cheesecake into 16 slices and sells them to customers at $6.50 per slice. Calculate the rate of markup on cost and the rate of markup on selling price.

16. The Annapolis Rotary Club sells hot dogs for $1.95 each at the annual Annapolis Fall Fair. The Rotary Club buys wieners at $3.95 per package of 10 wieners, and hot dog buns at $2.90 per dozen. It costs $78 for enough condiments for 1000 hot dogs. What are the Rotary Club's rate of markup on selling price and rate of markup on cost of the hot dogs?

17. Maritime Cellular purchases a Samsung smartphone model for $395 less trade discounts of 20% and 10%. Maritime's overhead expenses are $59 per unit.
    a. What should be the selling price to generate a profit of $40 per phone?
    b. What is the rate of markup on cost?
    c. What is the rate of markup on selling price?
    d. What would be the break-even selling price for the Annual Clear-Out Sale?

18. Damsels clothing store orders a line of jeans at a suggested retail price of $58 less trade discounts of 30% and 7%. The manager intends to sell the jeans at the suggested retail price. If overhead expenses are 25% of the selling price:
    a. What will be the operating profit on each pair of jeans?
    b. What is the rate of markup on cost?
    c. What is the rate of markup on selling price?
    d. What would be the break-even selling price for an inventory clearance sale?

19. The rate of markup on the cost of a toaster selling at $54.95 is 45%.
    a. What was the cost of the toaster to the retailer?
    b. What is the rate of markup on selling price?

20. Pet Mart purchased a litter of six puppies from a reputable breeder for $121 each. If the rate of markup on selling price is 45%:
    a. What is the selling price of each puppy?
    b. What is the rate of markup on cost?

INTERMEDIATE PROBLEMS

21. If the rate of markup on selling price of lettuce in a grocery store is 60%, what is the rate of markup on cost?

22. The rate of markup on the cost of fresh peaches in a grocery store is 125% because of the large losses from spoilage and bruising while the peaches are in storage and on display. What is the rate of markup on selling price?

23. Workers World buys rubber boots from the manufacturer for $15 per pair. The manager applies a 90% rate of markup on cost when pricing footwear. What is the operating profit per pair if overhead expenses work out on average to be 20% of the selling price?

24. A florist buys potted poinsettias from a nursery at $15 each, less series discounts of 40% and 10%. The florist prices her stock to allow for overhead of 55% of cost and an operating profit of 20% of the selling price. At what price should she sell the poinsettias?

25. Beaver Building Supply obtains 4-ft by 8-ft sheets of half-inch plywood from Macmillan Forest Products at $54 per sheet less discounts of 30% and 5%. The trade price is to be set to cover Beaver's overhead of 20% of the selling price and to provide an operating profit of 12% of the selling price. What should be the retail price per sheet?

26. Village Foods employs a 35% rate of markup on the cost of all dairy products. The store's overhead averages out to 20% of sales each month. What is the operating profit on a 4-L pail of ice cream for which the wholesale cost is $4.65?

27. Prestige Clothiers' regular prices for menswear are set to provide a 40% rate of markup on selling price. Overhead expenses are 30% of cost on average. What is the operating profit on a suit that sells for $495?

28. Digital Devices sets its retail prices on computers, monitors, and printers to generate a 30% rate of markup on selling price. Overhead expenses normally work out to be 30% of cost. What is the operating profit on a monitor that costs $345?

5.4 Markdown

L05 A **markdown** is a reduction in the selling price of an item. Retailers use markdowns for many reasons: to reduce excess inventory, to clear out damaged or discontinued items, or to increase sales volume during special "sale" events. Sometimes retailers will mark down a few popular items to the break-even point, or even below it, just to attract additional customers who they hope will also purchase other items. Grocery stores do this on a regular basis.

$$\text{Amount of markdown} = \text{Regular selling price} - \text{Reduced selling price}$$

Introducing the symbols

$$D = \text{Amount of markdown}$$
$$S = \text{(Regular) selling price}$$
$$S(\text{reduced}) = \text{Reduced selling price}[8] \text{ (or Sale price)}$$

the word equation becomes

$$D = S - S(\text{reduced})$$

The **rate of markdown** is the markdown calculated as a percentage of the regular selling price. That is,

$$\textbf{\textit{Rate of markdown}} = \frac{\textbf{\textit{D}}}{\textbf{\textit{S}}} \times \textbf{100\%} \tag{5-8}$$

If the regular selling price and rate of markdown are given, you can calculate the reduced selling price using the basic discounting formula $N = L(1 - d)$ restated as

$$S(\text{reduced}) = S(1 - \text{Rate of markdown})$$

---

[8] The term "reduced selling price" will be used consistently throughout the examples and exercises to make a clear distinction between "selling price" (the before-markdown price) and "sale price" (the after-markdown price).

EXAMPLE 5.4A

CALCULATING THE REDUCED SELLING PRICE

Toby's Cycle Shop advertises a 20% markdown on an Alpine mountain bike regularly priced at $445. Cycle City's regular selling price for the same model of bike is $429.

a. What is the reduced price at Toby's?

b. What rate of markdown would Cycle City have to offer to match Toby's reduced price?

SOLUTION

a. The reduced or marked-down price may be calculated using Formula (5-1) restated as

$$S(\text{reduced}) = S(1 - \text{Rate of markdown})$$
$$= \$445(1 - 0.20)$$
$$= \$356$$

The reduced price is $356.

b. In order to match Toby's reduced price, Cycle City must mark down its price by

$$D = S - S(\text{reduced}) = \$429 - \$356 = \$73$$

The necessary rate of markdown is

$$\frac{D}{S} \times 100\% = \frac{\$73}{\$429} \times 100\% = 17.0\%$$

A markdown of 17.0% will enable Cycle City to match Toby's reduced price.

EXAMPLE 5.4B

CALCULATING THE RATE OF MARKDOWN

An item costing $150 was marked up by 40% of the selling price. During the store's 10th anniversary sale, the selling price was reduced to $175. What was the regular selling price, and what was the rate of markdown during the sale?

SOLUTION

In the table at right, rows for E and P are omitted because these quantities are not involved in the problem. The information given in the statement of the problem has been entered.

In the C row of the "%" column, we see that 60% is the value. In other words, the unit cost is 60% of selling price. After entering 60% for C, it becomes apparent that we can solve for S by constructing a proportion using the C and S rows. That is,

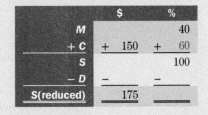

	$	%
M		40
+ C	+ 150	+ 60
S		100
− D	−	−
S(reduced)	175	

$$\frac{\$150}{60} = \frac{S}{100}$$

Hence,

$$S = \frac{\$150}{60} \times 100 = \$250$$

After entering $S = \$250$ in the "$" column, we readily see that

$$D = \$250 - \$175 = \$75$$

and

$$\text{Rate of markdown} = \frac{D}{S} \times 100\% = \frac{\$75}{\$250} \times 100\% = 30\%$$

The regular selling price was $250 and the rate of markdown was 30%.

EXAMPLE 5.4C

CALCULATING THE REGULAR AND REDUCED SELLING PRICES

K&M Clearance Centre sells premium coffee makers for 60% off the regular selling price, which represents a discount of $95.40. What are the regular and reduced selling prices?

SOLUTION

The reduced selling price can be calculated using the expanded version of Formula (5-1).

$$S(\text{reduced}) = S(1 - \text{Rate of markdown})$$
$$S(\text{reduced}) = S - S(\text{Rate of markdown})$$

where the dollar amount of the markdown (D) is calculated as

$$D = S(\text{Rate of markdown})$$
$$\$95.40 = S(0.60)$$
$$S = \frac{\$95.40}{0.60} = \$159.00$$

The regular selling price was $159.00, and the reduced selling price is $159.00 − $95.40 = $63.60.

This can be checked using

$$S(\text{reduced}) = S(1 - \text{Rate of markdown})$$
$$S(\text{reduced}) = \$159.00(1 - 0.60) = \$63.60$$

POINT OF INTEREST

Going for the Bait in Rebates

Some products offer a manufacturer's mail-in cash rebate. Typically, mail-in rebates are associated with higher-ticket items such as electronics, cameras, and software. But why not just give customers the price break at the checkout and save everybody the hassle?

Well, that's what manufacturers are (literally) banking on—it is a hassle for consumers to actually process mail-in rebates. To claim a typical rebate, the customer must gather several items (receipts, serial numbers, part of the package, etc.) and fill out tiny forms that provide too little space for the requested information. These must be sent off within a short period after the date of purchase in order to receive the rebate at some distant point in the future.

The reality is that the typical redemption rate for mail-in coupon programs is in the 1% to 5% range! Many people will buy a product because of the rebate, but few will actually claim the rebate. In the marketing world, this sort of behaviour is called "slippage," a rather understated description for this situation where consumers seem to gain little traction whatsoever.

CONCEPT QUESTIONS

1. Suppose an item that originally had a 40% rate of markup on cost is marked down 40%. Is its reduced selling price equal to C? Explain.

2. An item is marked down by the same percentage as the rate of markup on selling price. Will the reduced operating profit be positive, negative, or zero? Explain.

Answers to the odd-numbered problems are at the end of the book.

Calculate percentages to the nearest 0.1%

1. An item costing $185 was marked up by 50% of cost and subsequently marked down by $60 during a sale. Determine:
   a. The regular selling price.
   b. The rate of markdown.

2. An item was marked up from $58.50 to $95.00, then later marked down by 30% during a spring sale. Determine:
   a. The original rate of markup on selling price.
   b. The price during the spring sale.

3. An item was marked up from $24.99 to $49.98 before it was marked down to $24.99 and sold at cost. Determine:
   a. The rate of markup on cost.
   b. The rate of markdown.

4. The manager of a home and garden store buys patio furniture sets for $580 each and marks them up by 50% of cost. In late August, he clears out remaining inventory at a 30% markdown. Determine:
   a. The clearance price.
   b. The rate of markdown (from the regular price) to sell the floor display set at cost.

5. Calculate the reduced price if an item costing $19.25 is marked up by 35% of the selling price and then marked down by 25%.

6. Garden Centre purchases lawnmowers from a wholesaler for $249 and marks them up by 25% of selling price. At the end of the summer, a scratched floor-display mower's price is reduced to 10% above cost. What percentage price reduction should the price tag show?

7. Digital Devices plans to stop carrying the Casio FC-100 calculator. It normally marks up the calculator from the $71.50 wholesale cost to the regular selling price of $99.95.
   a. What is the normal rate of markup on selling price?
   b. What rate of markdown can be advertised if Digital Devices wishes to clear out the stock at the wholesale cost?

8. a. Merchant A operates on a rate of markup on cost of 45%. If she later marks the price of a few items down to their cost in order to attract additional customers to the store, what rate of markdown can she advertise?
   b. Merchant B operates on a 45% rate of markup on selling price. If he later marks the price of a few items down to their cost in order to attract additional customers to the store, what rate of markdown can he advertise?

9. Poles Apart obtains Nitro T1 snowboards at a cost of $345 and marks them up by 35% of the selling price. For its annual spring sale, Poles Apart marks down prices by 25%. What is the sale price of the Nitro T1 snowboards?

10. The sign on a rack of sport coats reads: "All prices already marked down 30%!" What is the regular selling price of a coat marked at:
    a. $100?
    b. $196.49?

11. Bargain Express advertises cookware sets at 40% off. Their ad claims, "You save $102." What are the regular and reduced selling prices for the cookware sets?

12. Calculate the reduced selling price on an item that is marked down 55%, an amount equivalent to a discount of $358.

13. Merchants C and D sell the same article at $69.95 and $64.95, respectively. They both advertise that they will match the price offered by any other store on any product that they stock.
    a. What discount rate must C give to match D's price marked down by 20% during a sale?
    b. What discount rate must D give to match C's price marked down by 20% during a sale?

14. Morgan's Department Store mailed out 15%-off coupons for its 20th Anniversary Sale. The coupons may be used for any products in the store. For items already on sale, the coupon applies to the sale price.
    a. What price would a coupon-holder pay for a bedspread (regular price $295) already on sale at 20% off?
    b. What single rate of markdown would have the same effect as the two price reductions?

INTERMEDIATE PROBLEMS

15. Workwear Station uses a markup on cost of 60% to establish its retail prices. This pricing rule builds in a profit of 25% of cost. What rate of markdown can Workwear Station offer and just break even on the reduced price?

16. A pharmacy marks up its springtime shipment of sunglasses to provide for overhead expenses of 40% of cost and a profit of 70% of cost. At the end of the summer, what rate of markdown can the pharmacy apply to the remaining inventory of sunglasses and still break even on sales at this level?

*5.5 Comprehensive Applications

L01 **L05** The problems in this section bring together elements from two or more sections of the chapter. Consequently, their solutions usually require several steps and have a higher degree of difficulty. The more complex the problem, the more benefits you will derive from using a diagram of the sort illustrated in the following examples.

The unit cost, C, and the operating (or overhead) expenses per unit, E, do not change when a retailer marks down the price. Therefore, the reduced operating profit, P(reduced), after a markdown is the difference between money in S(reduced) and money out (costs and expenses).

$$P(\text{reduced}) = S(\text{reduced}) - C - E$$

A merchant breaks even on a particular item when P(reduced) = 0; that is, when

$$S(\text{reduced}) = S(\text{break even}) = C + E.$$

EXAMPLE 5.5A

USING RELATIONSHIPS AMONG PRICING VARIABLES

Stereo World purchased Pioneer XL receivers at a discount of 45% from its supplier's suggested retail price of $480. Stereo World's normal rate of markup on selling price is 40%. The manager wants to clear out the remaining XL units because the manufacturer has discontinued the XL model. What rate of markdown can Stereo World offer and still break even on each unit? On average, operating expenses are 35% of cost.

SOLUTION

Construct a table that combines all of the information for markup and markdown as shown.

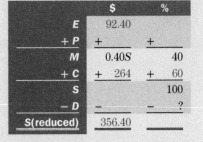

	$	%
E	92.40	
+P	+	+
M	0.40S	40
+C	+ 264	+ 60
S		100
−D	−	− ?
S(reduced)	356.40	

$$C = \$480(1 - 0.45) = \$264$$

Enter the given information in the table. You will immediately see that the value for C in the "%" column is 60. This value is also entered in the table. The question asks for the rate of markdown (which is the quantity at the location of "?" in the table).

$$E = 0.35C = 0.35(\$264) = \$92.40$$

If S(reduced) is a break-even price, then

$$S(\text{reduced}) = S(\text{break-even}) = \$264 + \$92.40$$

Therefore,

$$S(\text{reduced}) = \$356.40$$

Using the values for C and S in the "$" and "%" columns we can set up a proportion to solve for S.

$$\frac{\$264}{60} = \frac{S}{100}$$

The solution is

$$S = \frac{\$264}{60} \times 100 = \$440$$

After entering these values for S(reduced) and S in the table, you will quickly see how to calculate D in the "$" column. That is,

$$\$440 - D = \$356.40$$

Therefore,

$$D = \$440 - \$356.40 = \$83.60$$

and

$$\text{Rate of markdown} = \frac{D}{S} \times 100\% = \frac{\$83.60}{\$440} \times 100\% = 19.0\%$$

Stereo World can offer a markdown of 19.0% and still break even.

EXAMPLE 5.5B

USING RELATIONSHIPS AMONG PRICING VARIABLES

Standard Appliances obtains Frigid-Air refrigerators for $1460 less 30% and 5%. Standard's overhead works out to 18% of the regular selling price of $1495. A scratched demonstrator unit from their floor display was cleared out for $1195.

a. What is the regular rate of markup on cost?

b. What was the rate of markdown on the demonstrator unit?

c. What was the operating profit or loss on the demonstrator unit?

d. What rate of markup on cost was actually realized?

SOLUTION

Standard Appliances' cost for one refrigerator was

$$C = N = L(1 - d_1)(1 - d_2)$$
$$= \$1460(1 - 0.30)(1 - 0.05)$$
$$= \$970.90$$

	$	%
E	0.18S	18
+ P	+	+
M		
+ C	+ 970.90	+
S	1495.00	100
− D	−	− b
S(reduced)	1195.00	

Now construct a table, and enter all given values and the value calculated above for C. The solution for part (b) is indicated in the table.

a. The question asks for $\frac{M}{C} \times 100\%$. We can see in the "$" column how to obtain M.

$$M + \$970.90 = \$1495.00$$

Therefore,

$$M = \$1495 - \$970.90 = \$524.10$$

and

$$\text{Rate of markup on cost} = \frac{\$524.10}{\$970.90} \times 100\% = 54.0\%$$

The regular rate of markup on cost is 54.0%.

b. In the "$" column, we observe that

$$\$1495.00 - D = \$1195.00$$

Isolating D on the left side of the equation gives

$$D = \$1495.00 - \$1195.00 = \$300.00$$

Hence

$$\text{Rate of markdown} = \frac{D}{S} \times 100\% = \frac{\$300}{\$1495} \times 100\% = 20.1\%$$

The rate of markdown is 20.1%.

c. The values determined as of the end of part (b) are included in the table. This part asks for the value of the operating profit at the reduced price or P(reduced).

Therefore,

$$E = 0.18 \times \$1495 = \$269.10$$

and since

	$	%
E		18
+ P	+	+
M	524.10	
+ C	+ 970.90	+
S	1495.00	100
− D	− 300.00	− 20.1
S(reduced)	1195.00	79.9

$$P(\text{reduced}) = S(\text{reduced}) - C - E$$
$$P(\text{reduced}) = \$1195 - \$970.90 - \$269.10 = -\$45.00$$

The negative sign means that the store suffered a loss of $45.00 on the demonstrator unit.

d. The actual amount of markup at the reduced price was

$$M(\text{reduced}) = E + P(\text{reduced}) = \$269.10 + (-\$45.00) = \$224.10$$

The rate of markup on cost actually realized was

$$\frac{M(\text{reduced})}{C} \times 100\% = \frac{\$224.10}{\$970.90} \times 100\% = 23.1\%$$

Sales, sales, and more sales! Some merchants seem to have a sale of some sort going on almost all the time. A few "SALE!" signs around the premises help to induce curious shoppers to investigate potential bargains. Once in the store, the shopper may make other purchases. Some retailers initially price certain lines of merchandise at a level that provides "room" for a substantial planned markdown in a future sale event. Some merchandise may sell at the high "regular" price, but the merchant fully expects the bulk of the sales volume to occur at the reduced price.[9] In such cases, the merchant may regard the ultimate marked-down price as the primary selling price that provides the "normal" unit operating profit.

EXAMPLE 5.5C

USING RELATIONSHIPS AMONG PRICING VARIABLES

Fromme's Jewellers purchased sterling silver tea services for $960 each, less 35% and 15%. The "regular" selling price was set so that, in a "30% off" sale, overhead expenses represent 25% of the sale price and the operating profit is 15% of the sale price.

a. At what price will a tea service sell in a "30% off" sale?

b. What was the "regular" price before the markdown?

c. If the last set in inventory is cleared out at 50% off the regular price, what will the operating profit be on that set?

SOLUTION

Fromme's cost of a silver tea service was

$$C = N = L(1 - d_1)(1 - d_2)$$
$$= \$960(1 - 0.35)(1 - 0.15)$$
$$= \$530.40$$

	$	%
E	0.25S(reduced)	
+ P	+0.15S(reduced)	+
M		
+ C	+	530.40	+
S		100
− D	−	−	30
S(reduced)		70

a. From the relationship between S(reduced), C, E, and P, we notice that we can create an equation having S(reduced) as the only unknown.

Hence,

$$S(\text{reduced}) = \$530.40 + 0.25S(\text{reduced}) + 0.15S(\text{reduced})$$
$$S(\text{reduced}) - 0.40S(\text{reduced}) = \$530.40$$
$$S(\text{reduced}) = \frac{\$530.40}{0.60} = \$884.00$$

The price in a "30% off" sale will be $884.00.

b. We can enter 70 in the "%" column for S(reduced). Using S and S(reduced) in the "$" and "%" columns we can set up the proportion:

$$\frac{S}{\$884} = \frac{100}{70}$$

Hence,

$$S = \frac{\$884}{0.70} = \$1262.86$$

The "regular" price of the tea service was $1262.86.

---

9 Mattresses are an example of a product line for which the majority of sales occur at a significant markdown from the "regular" price. The following footnote appeared in a display advertisement placed in a Victoria newspaper by one of Vancouver Island's largest furniture stores: "The reference to our 'regular selling price' is to a price at which goods are regularly offered for sale in our store and is not a representation that this is the price at which most of a product is actually sold."

c. In this new scenario, $D = 0.50S$ *and* both S(reduced) and P(reduced) are unknown. C and E remain at

$$C = \$530.40 \quad \text{and} \quad E = 0.25(\$884) = \$221.00$$

Now

$$S(\text{reduced}) = S - D = S - 0.50S = 0.50S = 0.50(\$1262.86) = \$631.43$$

This is also evident from the table where you can see that S(reduced) is 50% of the selling price.

Then

$$P(\text{reduced}) = S(\text{reduced}) - C - E = \$631.43 - \$530.40 - \$221.00 = -\$119.97$$

Fromme's will lose $119.97 on the last tea set.

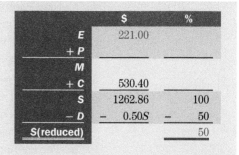

	$	%
E	221.00	
+ P		
M		
+ C	530.40	
S	1262.86	100
– D	– 0.50S	– 50
S(reduced)		50

★ POINT OF INTEREST

Misleading Price Representation

A few categories of consumer goods (expensive jewellery, for example) seem to be "ON SALE" so frequently or for so long that the consumer may wonder whether any significant volume of sales takes place at the "regular price."

Price representations usually fall under Section 74.01 of the federal Competition Act. In layperson's terms, the section states that any materially misleading representation as to the price at which a product is "ordinarily sold" is prohibited. The courts have interpreted "ordinary price" to include words and phrases (such as "Compare to…" or "X% off") used to imply that the comparison price is the price at which the product is ordinarily sold.

Section 74.01 states that the quoted or implied ordinary selling price should be one of the following:
- The price at which the product ordinarily sells in the market area.
- The advertiser's own regular selling price, clearly identified by such words as "our regular price."

The comparison price should be sufficiently recent to have relevance. The "ordinary price" implied or quoted for comparison should be one at which the product has had significant sales, not merely a price at which it was offered for sale. The volume needed in order to be regarded as "significant" depends on the product and the market. However, the volume should have been large enough to justify a consumer believing that the markdown represented a genuine bargain or true savings. On the other hand, if the price of a product had been raised for a few weeks during which very few sales took place, then the merchant should not state or imply that the inflated price was the regular or ordinary selling price. Furthermore, the use of a "Manufacturer's Suggested Retail Price" or "Suggested List Price" can constitute deceptive pricing if this price is not the product's ordinary selling price.

EXERCISE 5.5

Answers to the odd-numbered problems are at the end of the book.

BASIC PROBLEMS

Calculate percentages to the nearest 0.1%.

1. An item that cost $37.25 was marked up by 60% of cost. Later, the retail price was reduced to $41.72. If unit overhead expenses were 20% of cost, what was the unit operating profit at the reduced price?

2. A retailer marked up an item from its $7.92 cost to the regular selling price of $19.80. During the store's anniversary sale, the item was offered at 20% off. On a sale at this price, what was the (reduced) operating profit if unit overhead expenses were 70% of cost?

3. Elite Sports sells Kevlar-graphite shaft hockey sticks for $147 each. Elite's wholesale cost is $98. For a spring clearance sale, the prices are marked down by 20%. If overhead expenses are 15% of the regular selling price, what is the unit operating profit at the sale price?

4. Morgan Photography's markup on its antique picture frames is 35% of selling price. Its cost on the medium-size antique frame is $115.70. For portrait photos shot by Morgan's, this frame's price is reduced to $133.50. What is Morgan's operating profit or loss at this price if overhead expenses are 20% of the regular selling price?

5. Hi-Lites Inc. purchased a ceiling light fixture for $480 less 40% and 25%. The fixture was then marked up by 120% of cost. Overhead expenses are 55% of cost. In an anniversary sale, Hi-Lites offered the fixture at 40% off. Determine:
   a. The net cost of the fixture.
   b. The amount of the markup.
   c. The overhead expenses per fixture.
   d. The regular selling price.
   e. The sale price (reduced selling price).
   f. The rate of markup on cost at the sale price.
   g. The operating profit or loss at the sale price.

6. In February, Long Lake Nursery ordered lawn fertilizer at $18.60 less $33\frac{1}{3}$%, $12\frac{1}{2}$%, and 5% per 20-kg bag. The fertilizer is normally priced to provide a 55% rate of markup on selling price. Operating (overhead) expenses are 30% of cost. To clear out the remaining bags of fertilizer in July, they were marked down by 45%. Calculate:
   a. The net cost per bag.
   b. The operating expenses per bag.
   c. The regular selling price.
   d. The sale price (reduced selling price).
   e. The reduced markup at the sale price.
   f. The operating profit or loss at the sale price.
   g. The rate of markup on the sale price.

7. A retailer pays $81 to a wholesaler for an article. The retail price is set using a 40% rate of markup on selling price. To increase traffic to his store, the retailer marks the article down 20% during a sale. What is the sale price?

8. A bedroom suite costs Town & Country Furniture $5000 less 30% and 15%. The normal rate of markup on cost is 90%. The suite is marked down 30% in a mid-summer sale. What is the sale price?

9. Comfort Shoes' normal rate of markup on selling price is 45%. What rate of markdown can the store offer on a pair of shoes normally priced at $140 and still realize a 20% rate of markup on cost at the sale price?

10. Just Dresses sets its regular prices based on overhead expenses at 50% of cost and an operating profit of 40% of cost. What will be the operating profit (as a percent of cost) for dresses sold at a 20% discount?

INTERMEDIATE PROBLEMS

11. Water Sports Ltd. pays $360 less 25% for a backyard above-ground pool kit. Overhead expenses are $16\frac{2}{3}$% of the regular selling price, and the operating profit is 15% of the selling price.
    a. What is the maximum rate of markdown the store can offer and still break even?
    b. What is the profit or loss per unit if Water Sports clears out its remaining stock at 20% off in its Hot August Bargains Sale?

12. A lawn mower retails for $349. The dealer's overhead is 25% of cost, and normal operating profit is $16\frac{2}{3}$% of cost.
    a. What is the largest amount of markdown that will allow the dealer to break even?
    b. What rate of markdown will price the lawn mower at cost?

13. Rainbow Paints is discontinuing a line of paint that it purchased at $30 less 45% and 10% per 4-L pail. The store's overhead is 50% of cost, and normal operating profit is 30% of cost. If the manager of the store is prepared to accept a loss of one-quarter of the overhead expenses, what markdown rate can the store offer in order to clear out the paint?

14. United Furniture buys reclining rocking chairs at $550 less 40% and 10%. The price is marked up to allow for overhead of 50% of cost and profit of 35% of cost. The unit on display in the store acquired a stain. What rate of markdown from the regular price can the store offer on the display unit if it is to recover only half of the unit overhead costs?

15. Fashion Master purchased men's sweaters for $72 less 40% and 15%. The normal rate of markup on selling price is 40%, and overhead is 25% of the regular selling price. The sweaters were reduced to $45.90 for the store's Boxing Day Blowout.
    a. What was the rate of markdown for the sale?
    b. What was the profit or loss on each sweater at the sale price?
    c. At the sale price, what was the rate of markup on cost?

16. Mr. Vacuum obtains vacuum cleaners for $720 less $33\frac{1}{3}\%$ and 15%. A demonstration unit regularly priced at $750 was sold for $450. The shop's overhead is 22% of cost.
    a. What was the markdown rate on the vacuum cleaner?
    b. What was the profit or loss on the sale of the demonstrator?
    c. What rate of markup on cost was realized at the reduced price?

17. A discount furniture store bought a memory foam mattress at the wholesale price of $665. The "regular price" of the mattress is set so that, in a "20% off" sale, the rate of markup on selling price is 30%.
    a. What is the price of the mattress in a "20% off" sale?
    b. What is the "regular price" of the mattress?

18. A jewellery store purchased a diamond ring for $2500 less 40% and 5%. The store's average unit overhead expenses are 30% of cost. The "regular price" of the ring is established so that, if it is sold in a "20% off" sale, the unit operating profit at the reduced price will be 20% of cost.
    a. What is the reduced price of the ring in a "20% off" sale?
    b. What is the "regular price" of the ring?
    c. What is the operating profit if the ring happens to sell at the "regular price"?

19. Sonic Boom obtained a surround sound system for $2400 less 30% and 15%. The store's pricing is based on overhead expenses of 40% of cost. The "regular price" of the surround sound system is set so that, if it is sold in a "20% off" sale, the store's operating profit will be 25% of cost.
    a. What is the "regular price"?
    b. In a Midnight Madness Special, the system was sold at a "1/3 off" special price. What was the profit or loss at the special price?

ADVANCED PROBLEM

20. Furniture Warehouse bought upright freezers for $1800 less $33\frac{1}{3}\%$ and 5%. The store's overhead works out to 30% of cost. The freezers are initially priced so that a profit of $16\frac{2}{3}\%$ cost will be realized when a freezer is sold at a "15% off" price.
    a. What is the initial full rate of markup on cost?
    b. During its Scratch-and-Save Sale, customers qualify for an extra discount of either 5%, 7%, or 10%. This extra discount appears when the customer scratches a ticket at the time of a purchase. It is added to the basic 15% discount, making the combined discount 20%, 22%, or 25%, respectively. What is the store's profit or loss per freezer at each of these discounts?

KEY TERMS

Cash discount	Markdown	Rate of markup on cost
Credit period	Markup	Rate of markup on selling price
Discount period	Net price	Terms of payment
Equivalent discount rate	Ordinary dating	Trade discount
Gross profit	Partial payment	
List prices	Rate of markdown	

SUMMARY OF NOTATION AND KEY FORMULAS

L = List price

d = Rate of trade discount

N = Net price

In the broader context of calculating the final amount after a percentage reduction to a beginning amount:

L = Beginning amount

d = Decimal equivalent of percentage reduction

N = Final amount

The variables used in pricing and profit calculations are:

S = Selling price (per unit)

C = Cost (per unit)

M = Markup

E = Overhead or operating expenses (per unit)

P = Operating profit (per unit)

D = (Amount of) Markdown

S(reduced) = Reduced selling price (per unit)

P(reduced) = Reduced operating profit (per unit)

FORMULA (5-1) $N = L(1 - d)$ Finding the net amount or net price after applying a single rate of discount to the original amount or list price.

FORMULA (5-2) $N = L(1 - d_1)(1 - d_2)(1 - d_3)$ Finding the net price after a series of three compounding discount rates.

FORMULA (5-3) $S = C + M$ Selling price is the sum of the cost and the markup.

FORMULA (5-4) $M = E + P$ Markup is the sum of the overhead expenses and the operating profit.

FORMULA (5-5) $S = C + E + P$ Selling price is the sum of the cost plus overhead expenses plus operating profit.

FORMULA (5-6) $\textit{Rate of markup on cost} = \dfrac{M}{C} \times 100\%$

FORMULA (5-7) $\textit{Rate of markup on selling price} = \dfrac{M}{S} \times 100\%$

FORMULA (5-8) $\textit{Rate of markdown} = \dfrac{D}{S} \times 100\%$

REVIEW PROBLEMS

Answers to the odd-numbered review problems are at the end of the book.

BASIC PROBLEMS

Calculate percentages to the nearest 0.1%.

1. **L01** Specialty Builders Supply has two sources for the same power saw. Source A sells the saw at $196.00 less 20%, and Source B offers it at $186.60 less $16\frac{2}{3}$%. Which source is less expensive, and by how much?

2. **L01** A trade discount of 22.5% from the suggested selling price for a line of personal computers translates to a $337.05 discount. What net price will a retailer pay?

3. **L01** A 28% trade discount on a game console represents a discount of $136.92 from the suggested retail price. What is the net price to the buyer?

4. **L01** The net price of an item after a discount of 22% is $155.61. What is the amount of the discount?

5. **L01** Mr. and Mrs. Ogrodnik want to list their house at a price that will net them a minimum of $320,000 after a real estate commission of 5.5% of the selling price. Rounded to the nearest $100, what is the lowest offer they could accept on their home?

6. **L01** Chicken Little Farms gives convenience stores a trade discount of 25% on eggs listed at $43.00 per case. What trade discount will Sunnyside Farms have to give on its list price of $44.50 per case to match Chicken Little's price to convenience stores?

7. **L01** A merchant pays a 2.9% fee to the RBC Royal Bank on all Visa sales.
   a. What amount will he pay on sales of $28,476 for a month?
   b. What were his gross sales for a month in which the bank charged fees totalling $981.71?

8. **L01** At its current price of $1.10 per share, the price of Apex Resources stock is down 78% from its price one year ago. What was that price?

9. **L02** An invoice shows a net price of $199.16 after trade discounts of 22%, 7%, and 5% are deducted.
   a. What was the list price of the goods?
   b. What single trade discount would be equivalent to the discount series?

10. **L03** **L04** Custom Kitchens received an invoice dated November 17 from Idea Cabinets Ltd. for $7260 with terms 3/15, $1\frac{1}{2}$/30, n/60. If Custom Kitchens made a payment of $4000 on December 2, what further payment on December 16 will settle the account?

11. **L01** **L02** In addition to the regular trade discount of 25% and a volume purchase discount of $8\frac{1}{3}$% from the manufacturer, Appliance Warehouse is offered a further 5% discount for orders placed in January.
   a. What is the net price after all three trade discounts on refrigerators listed at $1195?
   b. What is the list price on an electric range whose net price works out to be $470.25?
   c. What single trade discount rate is equivalent to the three trade discounts?
   d. After the regular and volume discounts are both taken, what dollar amount of savings does the extra discount for January orders represent on a $1000 list price item?

12. **L04** A payment of $500 on an invoice for $887 reduced the balance owed to $378.09. What cash discount rate was allowed on the $500 payment?

13. **L01** In three successive years the price of the common shares of Bedrock Resources Ltd. fell 40%, 60%, and 70%, ending the third year at 50 cents.
   a. What was the share price at the beginning of the three-year skid?
   b. How much (in dollars and cents) did the share price drop in the second year?

14. **L01** The evening news reports that the S&P/TSX Index dropped 0.9% on the day to close at 13,123 points. How many points did the index fall?

15. **L05** If a grocery store's rate of markup on the selling price of tomatoes is 55%, what is the rate of markup on the cost of tomatoes?

16. **L03** **L04** Omega Restaurant received an invoice dated July 22 from Industrial Kitchen Equipment for $3691, with terms 2/10, 1/20, n/45. Omega made payments of $1100 on August 1, $900 on August 10, and $800 on August 31. What amount was still owed on September 1?

17. **L05** What is the cost of an item that sells for $87.49 if:
    a. The rate of markup on cost is 30%?
    b. The rate of markup on selling price is 30%?

18. **L03** **L04** What total amount must be paid on May 4 to settle invoices dated April 20 for $650, April 24 for $790, and April 30 for $465, all with terms $1\frac{1}{2}$/10, n/30?

19. **L05** Bosley's Pet Foods buys dog kibble for $19.50 per bag, less 40%. The store's overhead is $33\frac{1}{3}$% of the selling price, and the desired profit is 10% of the selling price.
    a. At what price per bag should the dog food be sold?
    b. At this price, what is the rate of markup on cost?
    c. What is the break-even price?

20. **L01** A uranium mining town reported population declines of 3.2%, 5.2%, and 4.7% for the three successive five-year periods 1985–89, 1990–94, and 1995–99. If the population at the end of 1999 was 9320:
    a. How many people lived in the town at the beginning of 1985?
    b. What was the population loss in each of the five-year periods?

INTERMEDIATE PROBLEMS

21. **L05** The Pro Shop at Sunny Lake Golf and Country Club prices its golf club sets to allow for overhead of $33\frac{1}{3}$% of cost and profit of 20% of cost.
    a. What is the regular selling price as a percentage of cost?
    b. What discount rate can the Pro Shop offer to club members if it will accept half of the normal profit on member purchases?

22. **L01** **L05** Central Ski and Cycle purchased ski boots for $360 per pair less $33\frac{1}{3}$% and 10%. The regular rate of markup on selling price of the boots is 40%. The store's overhead is 22% of the selling price. During a January clearance sale, the price was reduced to $270 per pair.
    a. What was the rate of markdown for the sale?
    b. What was the profit or loss on each pair of boots at the sale price?
    c. At the sale price, what was the rate of markup on cost?

23. **L01** **L05** Sunrise Building Supply obtains 4-ft by 8-ft sheets of wallboard from Canadian Gypsum at $30 per sheet less 30% and 10%. The price is to be set to cover Sunrise's overhead of 20% of the selling price and to provide an operating profit of 18% of the selling price. What should be the retail price per sheet?

24. **L01** **L05** Nelson Hardware ordered a shipment of gas barbecues at a suggested retail price of $459 less trade discounts of 25% and 10%. The manager intends to sell the barbecues at the suggested retail price. If overhead expenses are 20% of the selling price:
    a. What will be the unit operating profit?
    b. What is the rate of markup on cost?
    c. What is the rate of markup on selling price?
    d. What would be the break-even selling price for an inventory clearance sale?

25. **LO5** Ski 'n Cycle purchased Elan 200 skis for $492 per pair and priced them to give a 40% rate of markup on selling price. When this model was discontinued, the store marked down its remaining stock by 30%. What was the sale price after the markdown?

26. **LO5** A pharmacy marked up its sunscreen to provide for overhead expenses of 40% of cost and a profit of 45% of cost. At the end of the summer, what rate of markdown can the pharmacy apply to the remaining inventory of sunscreen and still break even on sales at the reduced price?

27. **LO5** A snow blower retails for $489. The dealer's overhead is 20% of cost, and normal operating profit is $16\frac{2}{3}\%$ of cost.
    a. What is the largest amount of markdown that will allow the dealer to break even?
    b. What rate of markdown will price the snow blower at cost?

Chapter 6
Applications of Linear Equations

CHAPTER OUTLINE

LEARNING OBJECTIVES

After completing this chapter, you will be able to:

LO1 Graph a linear equation in two variables

LO2 Express a linear equation in slope-intercept form

LO3 Solve two equations in two unknowns by a graphical method

LO4 Solve two equations in two unknowns by an algebraic method

LO5 Distinguish between fixed costs and variable costs

LO6 Perform cost-volume-profit analysis employing:
- The graphical approach
- The revenue and cost function approach
- The contribution margin approach

MANY QUANTITATIVE PROBLEMS ENCOUNTERED in business may be described or modelled by linear equations. They range from one- and two-variable problems of the kind included in this book to applications in production, transportation, scheduling, and distribution involving dozens of variables.

An important application of linear equations is forecasting a business's profit at various levels of sales. We will examine this application (known as cost-volume-profit analysis) in considerable detail.

6.1 Introduction to Graphical Techniques

The relationship between two variables may be presented in a variety of ways. Three common methods are:

- A table listing pairs of values for the two variables.
- An algebraic equation involving the two variables.
- A graph depicting the relationship between the two variables.

The graphical presentation is best for quickly giving an impression of the nature of the relationship between the two variables. It also allows a user to *quickly estimate* the value of one variable that corresponds to any selected value of the other variable.

An algebraic equation has the advantage of expressing the relationship with the greatest degree of precision. Graphical analysis is usually limited to three-figure precision.

Graphing a Linear Equation in Two Unknowns

L01 The notation used to indicate that a mathematical relationship exists between two variables, x and y, is

$$y = f(x)$$

which is read "y is a function of x." A pair of numerical values of the variables, customarily written in the order (x, y), is said to *satisfy* the equation if the two sides of the equation are equal after substitution of the values.

A single ordered pair of (x, y) values gives a point when plotted on graph paper. In the context of graphing, this ordered pair of values is called the *coordinates* of the point. A graph of the equation $y = f(x)$ is a plot of all ordered pairs of (x, y) values within a certain range that satisfy the equation. If the x-coordinate and the y-coordinate of *any* point on a plotted curve are substituted into the corresponding algebraic equation, both sides of the equation will have the same numerical value.

In practice, we obtain the graph of an equation through the following steps:

1. Construct a *table of values* consisting of ordered pairs of (x, y) values that satisfy the equation. Each ordered pair is obtained by assigning a value to one variable and then solving the resulting equation in one unknown for the other variable.
2. Construct and label the x-axis and the y-axis with appropriate scales to accommodate the range of values in the table.
3. Plot the (x, y) pairs from the table as the (x, y) coordinates of points on the graph.
4. Connect the plotted points with a straight line.

EXAMPLE 6.1A

GRAPHING A LINEAR EQUATION IN TWO VARIABLES

Graph the equation $2x - 3y = -6$ over the range $x = -6$ to $x = 6$.

SOLUTION

The first step listed above is to construct a table of values. Since the range over which the graph is to be plotted is specified in terms of x, it is natural to assign to x a series of values covering the range (such as $x = -6, -3, 0, 3, 6$). Since we will be repeatedly solving the equation for y, we should rearrange the equation so that y is isolated on one side.

Transposing $2x$ to the right side and dividing both sides by -3, we obtain

$$y = \tfrac{2}{3}x + 2$$

Now substitute a few values for x over the range $x = -6$ to $x = 6$:

$$x = -6: \qquad y = \tfrac{2}{3}(-6) + 2 = -2$$

$$x = -3: \qquad y = \tfrac{2}{3}(-3) + 2 = 0$$

$$x = 0: \qquad y = \tfrac{2}{3}(0) + 2 = 2$$

$$x = 3: \qquad y = \tfrac{2}{3}(3) + 2 = 4$$

$$x = 6: \qquad y = \tfrac{2}{3}(6) + 2 = 6$$

The table of values summarizing these (x, y) pairs is:

x:	−6	−3	0	3	6	← Assigned x values
y:	−2	0	2	4	6	← Calculated y values

The next step is to draw the two axes, with the x-axis including the range from -6 to $+6$ and the y-axis encompassing the range from -2 to $+6$. The five points can then be plotted and a straight line drawn to connect the points.

For this first example, the (x, y) pairs have been labelled.

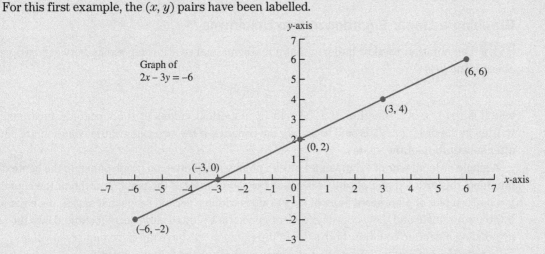

Graph of $2x - 3y = -6$

The general outcome for linear equations in two variables is that the plotted points will connect in a straight line. This is the reason they are called *linear* equations.

 TIP

Suggestions and Shortcuts

- To construct the graph of a *linear* equation, it is sufficient to have just two (x, y) pairs in the table of values. Plotting a third point provides a check of your calculations. If all three points do not lie on a straight line, then you have made an error in calculating the coordinates of the points or in plotting the points.
- Start the scales on both the x-axis and the y-axis at zero with the ordered pair $(0, 0)$, then number the scales using equal increments. The x-axis and y-axis can use different increments.
- For the best precision in constructing the graph of a linear equation, the two points used should be near the ends of the range over which the graph is to be drawn.

- The easiest (x, y) pairs to determine come from assigning the value 0 to x and then assigning the value 0 to y.
- If x has a fractional coefficient, assign values to x that are a multiple of the coefficient's denominator. This makes the calculations easier and is likely to yield "nicer" values to plot for y. In the preceding example, we used values for x that were multiples of 3.

EXAMPLE 6.1B

GRAPHING A LINEAR EQUATION IN TWO VARIABLES

Graph the equation $3y - 150x = 24{,}000$ over the range $x = 0$ to $x = 200$.

SOLUTION

The first step is to rearrange the equation to isolate y on the left side of the equation. This will make it easier to construct the table of values.

Transposing $-150x$ to the right-hand side gives:

$$3y = 150x + 24{,}000$$

Divide both sides by 3:

$$y = 50x + 8000$$

Construct a table of values for the range of x:

$$x = 0: \qquad y = 50(0) + 8000 = 8000$$
$$x = 100: \qquad y = 50(100) + 8000 = 13{,}000$$
$$x = 200: \qquad y = 50(200) + 8000 = 18{,}000$$

x:	0	100	200
y:	8000	13,000	18,000

Construct and label the axes. Then plot the points.

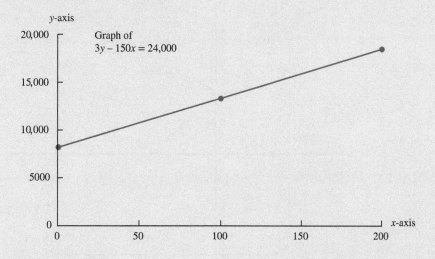

Note that in this example the x-axis and y-axis show all positive values. Only one quadrant is shown since the range of values for x are all positive.

The Slope-Intercept Form of a Linear Equation

L02 In **Examples 6.1A** and **6.1B** we rearranged the given linear equations so as to isolate y on the left side. Accordingly,

$$2x - 3y = -6 \qquad \text{was expressed as} \qquad y = \frac{2}{3}x + 2$$

$$\text{and} \quad 3y - 150x = 24{,}000 \qquad \text{was expressed as} \qquad y = 50x + 8000$$

We did this to simplify the calculations for creating tables of values to plot. A further benefit of expressing a linear equation in this form is that we can predict two important characteristics of the equation's straight-line graph.

First note that when $x = 0$, the first equation gives $y = 2$ and the second gives $y = 8000$. As you can see if you look back to their graphs, these are the values for y where the straight lines cross the y-axis. We call such a value the **y-intercept** of a straight line.

The second property we can predict is a measure of the steepness of the line. To understand this, consider the following table of values for $y = 50x + 8000$ over the range $x = 0$ to $x = 4$.

x:	0	1	2	3	4
y:	8000	8050	8100	8150	8200

Note that every time x increases by 1, y increases by 50 because 50 is the coefficient of x in the rearranged equation. The change in the y-coordinate per unit change in the x-coordinate is called the **slope** of the straight line. The steeper the line, the greater will be the value of the slope.

It is a general result that, if you express a linear equation in the form

$$y = mx + b$$

where m and b represent constants, then

$$\text{slope} = m \quad \text{and} \quad y\text{-intercept} = b$$

Consequently, it is referred to as the *slope-intercept form* of the equation of a straight line.

This knowledge enables us to write an equation corresponding to a given straight-line graph. Consider the linear relationship that is displayed in the following diagram. The y-intercept is clearly $b = 4$. To obtain the slope, first select any two points lying near opposite ends of the straight line. We have chosen the points $(-2, 8)$ and $(5, -6)$.

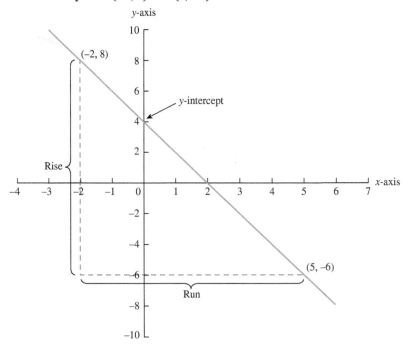

In general,

$$\text{Slope, } m = \frac{\text{Rise}}{\text{Run}} = \frac{\text{Vertical distance between the points}}{\text{Horizontal distance between the points}} = \frac{y_2 - y_1}{x_2 - x_1}$$

where (x_1, y_1) and (x_2, y_2) represent the coordinates of the two points. In this case,

$$m = \frac{(-6) - (8)}{(5) - (-2)} = \frac{-14}{7} = -2$$

Any line that slopes downward to the right has a negative slope. A line sloping upward to the right has a positive slope.

The final step is to substitute the values for m and b in the general form $y = mx + b$. The equation of the straight line in the graph is

$$y = -2x + 4$$

Graphical Method for Solving Two Equations in Two Unknowns

L03 Let us plot on the same set of axes both of the following linear equations over the range $x = -4$ to $x = 4$.

$$x - 2y = -2 \quad \text{①}$$
$$x + y = 4 \quad \text{②}$$

For each equation, we will first obtain the coordinates of the two points at opposite ends of the graphing range. Rearranging both equations to isolate y on the left side, we obtain:

$$y = \frac{1}{2}x + 1 \quad \text{①}$$

$$y = -x + 4 \quad \text{②}$$

For each equation, calculate the y-coordinates when $x = -4$ and $x = 4$.

$$y = \frac{1}{2}x + 1 \quad \text{①} \qquad\qquad\qquad y = -x + 4 \quad \text{②}$$

x:	−4	4
y:	−1	3

x:	−4	4
y:	8	0

Plot the two points for each equation and connect them by a straight line. The resulting graph is presented below. The coordinates of any point on a line satisfy that line's equation. But there is only one point that satisfies *both* equations because there is only one point that lies on both lines—the intersection point. In the present case, $(x, y) = (2, 2)$ is the *solution* to equations ① and ②.

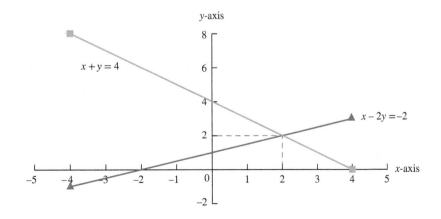

You can solve any two linear equations in two unknowns by this approach. However, when the coefficients in the equations are not small integers or simple fractions, this method can be time-consuming and "messy." The solution is limited to three-figure accuracy (at best) because of the imprecision of plotting points and reading the coordinates of the intersection point.

Graphical Method for Solving Two Equations in Two Unknowns Using Intercepts

L03 Notice in the graph above that the line $x - 2y = -2$ crosses the x-axis at -2 and the y-axis at 1. Similarly, the line $x + y = 4$ crosses the x-axis at 4 and the y-axis at 4. These points are the *x-intercept* and *y-intercept*.

You can draw a reasonably accurate graph for these two lines using just the intercepts for each equation.

Since each line has a y-value of zero at the point where the line crosses the x-axis, we can find the x-intercept by substituting the value $y = 0$ into each equation.

For the line $x - 2y = -2$, the x-intercept is calculated as:

$$x - 2(0) = -2$$
$$x = -2$$

For the line $x + y = 4$, the x-intercept is calculated as:

$$x + (0) = 4$$
$$x = 4$$

The ordered pairs representing the x-intercepts for the two lines are $(-2, 0)$ and $(4, 0)$, respectively.

Similarly, you can find the y-intercepts by substituting $x = 0$ into each equation.

$$(0) - 2y = -2 \qquad (0) + y = 4$$
$$-2y = -2 \qquad\quad y = 4$$
$$y = 1$$

The ordered pairs defining the y-intercepts for the two lines are $(0, 1)$ and $(0, 4)$, respectively. The y-intercepts can also be seen as the b value in the $y = mx + b$ forms of the equations.

EXERCISE 6.1

Answers to the odd-numbered problems are at the end of the book.

BASIC PROBLEMS

Graph each of the equations in Problems 1–7.

1. $-2x + y = 0$ over the range $x = -3$ to $x = 6$

2. $-2x + y = 4$ over the range $x = -3$ to $x = 6$

3. $2x + y = 4$ over the range $x = -3$ to $x = 6$

4. $y = 4$ over the range $x = -3$ to $x = 6$

5. $3x - 4y + 12 = 0$ over the range $x = -8$ to $x = 12$

6. $y = 60x + 6000$ over the range $x = 0$ to $x = 50$

7. $y = 4.5x + 5000$ over the range $x = 0$ to $x = 6000$

8. Determine the slope and y-intercept of each of the following equations.
   - **a.** $2x = 3y + 4$
   - **b.** $8 - 3x = 2y$
   - **c.** $8x - 2y - 3 = 0$
   - **d.** $6x = 9y$

9. Determine the slope and b-intercept of each of the following equations.
    a. $2b + 3 = 5a$
    b. $3a - 4b = 12$
    c. $0 = 2400 - 4a - 5b$
    d. $7a = -8b$

10. Determine the r-intercept and s-intercept of each of the following equations.
    a. $10r - 4s = 20$
    b. $3r + 4s - 12 = 0$
    c. $15 - 3r = 20s$
    d. $7r = 9s$

11. Determine the x-intercept and y-intercept of each of the following equations.
    a. $5x + 25y - 15 = 0$
    b. $0 = 63 - 7x + 21y$
    c. $13x = 35y$
    d. $11x + 110 = 22y$

12. A plumber charges a flat \$50 for a home service call plus \$10 per 15 minutes of labour. Write an equation for calculating the total charges, C, in terms of the hours of labour, H. If you were to plot a graph of C vs. H, what would be the slope and C-intercept of the line?

13. In his sales job, Ehud earns a base salary of \$1500 per month plus a commission of 5% on sales revenue. Write an equation for calculating his gross earnings, E, for a month in terms of his sales revenue, R. If you were to plot a graph of E vs. R, what would be the slope and E-intercept of the line?

14. The formula for converting from Celsius temperatures, C, to Fahrenheit temperatures, F, is $F = \frac{9}{5}C + 32$.
    a. If you were to plot a graph of F vs. C, what would be the slope and F-intercept of the line?
    b. The slope represents the change in F per unit change in C. Use the value of the slope to determine the increase in Fahrenheit temperature corresponding to a 10 Celsius-degree rise.
    c. Rearrange the given formula to obtain a formula for converting from Fahrenheit temperatures to Celsius temperatures. What would be the slope and C-intercept if C vs. F were plotted on a graph?

15. Randolph runs a home appliance repair business and charges a service call fee of \$85 plus \$15 per half hour for his labour. Write an equation for calculating the total charges, C, in terms of hours of labour, H. What would be the slope and C-intercept?

Use the graphical method to solve each of the following pairs of equations.

16. $x + y = 2$
     $x = 5$

17. $x - 3y = 3$
     $y = -2$

18. $6x = 3y$
     $4x - y = 1$

19. $x - 3y = 0$
     $x + 2y = -5$

20. $x + y = 4$
     $2x - y = 8$

21. $y - 3x = 11$
     $5x + 30 = 4y$

22. $4a - 3b = -3$
     $5a - b = 10$

23. $7p - 3q = 23$
     $-2p - 3q = 5$

6.2 Solving Two Equations in Two Unknowns

L04 A single linear equation in one unknown has only one solution. In contrast, a single linear equation in two variables has an *infinite* number of solutions. For example, the equation $y = x + 2$ has solutions $(x, y) = (0, 2), (1, 3), (2, 4)$, and so on.

If, however, *two* linear equations in two unknowns must be satisfied *at the same time*, there is *only one solution*. In other words, only one pair of values will satisfy *both* equations.

To find this solution, there are two common algebraic methods that can be used to combine the two equations in a way that will eliminate one variable, leaving a single linear equation in the other variable. They are:

- the substitution method
- the elimination method

The choice of method is largely dependent on the presentation of the system of equations.

EXAMPLE 6.2A

SOLVING TWO EQUATIONS USING THE SUBSTITUTION METHOD

Solve the following pair of equations. Check the solution.

$$y = 4x + 7 \quad \text{①}$$
$$3x + y = 14 \quad \text{②}$$

SOLUTION

The substitution method is a good choice in this example since the y variable in equation ① has the numerical coefficient of 1.

Equation ① is a statement of what y is equivalent to. Substitute this y equivalent into equation ② to eliminate y as follows:

$$3x + (4x + 7) = 14$$
$$7x + 7 = 14$$
$$7x = 14 - 7$$
$$7x = 7$$
$$x = 1$$

To solve for y, substitute $x = 1$ back into one of the original equations. We will use equation ①:

$$y = 4(1) + 7$$
$$y = 11$$

The solution is $x = 1$, $y = 11$.

Check:

Substitute $x = 1$ and $y = 11$ into equation ①:
LHS of ① $= 11$
RHS of ① $= 4(1) + 7 = 11$

Substitute $x = 1$ and $y = 11$ into equation ②:
LHS of ② $= 3(1) + 11 = 14$
RHS of ② $= 14$

EXAMPLE 6.2B

SOLVING TWO EQUATIONS USING THE ELIMINATION METHOD

Solve the following pair of equations. Check the solution.

$$2x - 3y = -6 \quad \text{①}$$
$$x + y = 2 \quad \text{②}$$

SOLUTION

This system of equations could be solved using the substitution method illustrated in **Example 6.2A** by first rearranging equation ② for either x or y.

Here, we notice that both equations are in the same form. We will use the elimination method to combine the two equations in a way that will eliminate one variable, leaving a single linear equation in one variable.

It is legitimate to add the respective sides of two equations, or to subtract the respective sides of two equations. However, to be able to eliminate one of the variables, either the x or y terms must have the same numerical coefficient.

If the numerical coefficient of x in equation ② is 2, then the subtraction ① − ② would produce an equation without a term in x. Furthermore, you can achieve this outcome if you multiply both sides of equation ② by 2 *before* the subtraction. Then the equations before subtraction are

$$
\begin{array}{r}
① \qquad 2x - 3y = -6 \\
② \times 2: \qquad 2x + 2y = 4 \\
\hline
\text{Subtraction gives:} \qquad -5y = -10
\end{array}
$$

$$y = \frac{-10}{-5} = 2$$

To solve for x, substitute $y = 2$ into either of the original equations. Substitution into equation ① gives

$$
\begin{aligned}
2x - 3(2) &= -6 \\
2x &= -6 + 6 \\
x &= 0
\end{aligned}
$$

The solution is $x = 0$, $y = 2$, or $(x, y) = (0, 2)$.

Check:

Substitute $x = 0$ and $y = 2$ into equation ①:
LHS of ① = $2(0) - 3(2) = -6$ = RHS of ①

Substitute $x = 0$ and $y = 2$ into equation ②:
LHS of ② = $(0) + 2 = 2$ = RHS of ②

 TIP

Treat Both Sides of an Equation in the Same Way

In **Example 6.2B**, remember to multiply *every term* on *both sides* of the equation by the chosen number. Choose to either add or subtract the resulting pair of equations depending on which will eliminate the desired variable.

EXAMPLE 6.2C

SOLVING TWO EQUATIONS HAVING INTEGER COEFFICIENTS

Solve the following pair of equations to three-figure accuracy. Check the solution.

$$
\begin{aligned}
7x - 5y &= 3 \qquad ① \\
5x + 2y &= 9 \qquad ②
\end{aligned}
$$

SOLUTION

To eliminate y, first make the numerical coefficients of y the same in both equations:

$$①\times 2: \qquad 14x - 10y = 6$$
$$②\times -5: \qquad -25x - 10y = -45$$

Subtracting the second equation from the first eliminates the variable y:

$$14x - (-25x) = 6 - (-45)$$
$$39x = 51$$
$$x = \frac{51}{39} = 1.308$$

Substitute this value for x into equation ② and solve for y:

$$5(1.308) + 2y = 9$$
$$2y = 9 - 6.540$$
$$y = 1.230$$

To three figures, the solution is $x = 1.31$, $y = 1.23$.

Check:

Substitute $x = 1.308$ and $y = 1.230$ into equation ①:

LHS of ① $= 7(1.308) - 5(1.230)$
$ = 3.006$
$ = $ RHS of ① to two figures.

This is one of a small minority of cases where four-figure accuracy in intermediate calculations does not give three-figure accuracy in the final result.

EXAMPLE 6.2D

SOLVING TWO EQUATIONS HAVING DECIMAL-FRACTION COEFFICIENTS

Solve the following pair of equations to three-figure accuracy. Check the solution.

$$1.9a + 3.8b = 85.5 \qquad ①$$
$$3.4a - 5.1b = -49.3 \qquad ②$$

SOLUTION

To eliminate a, make the coefficient of a the same in both equations.

$$① \times 3.4: \quad 6.46a + 12.92b = 290.7$$
$$② \times 1.9: \quad \underline{6.46a - 9.69b = -93.67}$$
$$\text{Subtract:} \qquad\qquad 22.61b = 384.37$$
$$b = 17.00$$

Substitute $b = 17.00$ into equation ①:

$$1.9a + 3.8(17.00) = 85.5$$
$$a = \frac{85.5 - 3.8(17.00)}{1.9}$$
$$= 11.00$$

To three figures, the solution is $a = 11.0$, $b = 17.0$.

Check:

Substitute $a = 11.0$ and $b = 17.0$ into equation ②:

$$\begin{aligned} \text{LHS of ②} &= 3.4(11.0) - 5.1(17.0) \\ &= 37.4 - 86.7 \\ &= -49.3 \\ &= \text{RHS of ②} \end{aligned}$$

EXAMPLE 6.2E

A WORD PROBLEM INVOLVING TWO EQUATIONS IN TWO UNKNOWNS

Whistling Mountain charges $72 for a day-pass for downhill skiing and $22.50 for a day-pass for cross-country skiing. If a day's total revenue from the sale of 760 passes was $43,434, how many of each type of pass were sold?

SOLUTION

Step 2: Cost of downhill pass = $72; Cost of cross-country pass = $22.50.

Total passes sold = 760; Total revenue = $43,434

Let d represent the number of downhill passes sold, and

Let c represent the number of cross-country passes sold.

Step 3:
$$\text{Total passes sold} = 760 \qquad ①$$

Step 4:
$$\text{Total revenue} = \$43{,}434 \qquad ②$$
$$d + c = 760 \qquad ①$$
$$72d + 22.5c = 43{,}434 \qquad ②$$

Step 5: Now eliminate c.

$$\begin{array}{rl}
① \times 22.5: & 22.5d + 22.5c = 17{,}100 \\
② \times 1: & \underline{72d + 22.5c = 43{,}434} \\
\text{Subtract:} & -49.5d = -26{,}334 \\
& d = 532
\end{array}$$

Substitute $d = 532$ into:

$$532 + c = 760$$
$$c = 760 - 532 = 228$$

On this particular day, 532 downhill skiing passes and 228 cross-country skiing passes were sold.

Check:

Substitute $d = 532$ and $c = 228$ into equation ②:

$$\begin{aligned} \text{LHS of ②} &= 72(532) + 22.5(228) \\ &= 38{,}304 + 5130 \\ &= 43{,}434 \\ &= \text{RHS of ②} \end{aligned}$$

EXAMPLE 6.2F

A WORD PROBLEM GIVING TWO EQUATIONS WITH LARGE COEFFICIENTS

Westwood Orchard received $3843.90 for its first shipment of 1530 kg of McIntosh apples and 945 kg of Delicious apples to the processing plant. Its second shipment, consisting of 2485 kg of McIntosh and 2370 kg of Delicious, resulted in a payment of $7395.70. What was Westwood Orchard paid per kilogram for each variety of apple?

SOLUTION

Shipment	McIntosh (kg)	Delicious (kg)	Total revenue ($)
1	1530	945	3843.90
2	2485	2370	7395.70

The details of each shipment are summarized in the table. Let M and D represent the price per kilogram that Westwood received for McIntosh and Delicious apples, respectively. The idea in words that provides the basis for constructing algebraic equations in terms of M and D is:

Revenue from McIntosh apples + Revenue from Delicious apples = Total revenue

Expressing this idea in algebraic terms for each shipment gives

$$1530M + 945D = \$3843.90 \quad ①$$
$$2485M + 2370D = \$7395.70 \quad ②$$

Since multiplication by the numerical coefficient of either M or D will result in large unwieldy numbers, divide each equation by its own coefficient of M. This will make the coefficient of M equal to 1 in both equations and permit the elimination of M by subtraction. We want a price per kilogram that is accurate to the cent. Since the orchardist will receive (at most) a few dollars per kilogram, we need three-figure accuracy in our final answer. Therefore, we must maintain four-figure accuracy if we round any intermediate results.

$$
\begin{array}{lll}
① \div 1530: & M + 0.6176D = & \$2.5124 \\
② \div 2485: & \underline{M + 0.9537D = \quad \$2.9761} \\
\text{Subtract:} & -0.3361D = -\$0.4637 \\
& D = \dfrac{\$0.4637}{0.3361} = \$1.380
\end{array}
$$

To solve for M with the least amount of work, substitute $D = \$1.380$ into one of the modified equations.

$$M = \$2.5124 - 0.6176 \times \$1.380 = \$1.660$$

Westwood Orchard receives \$1.38 per kilogram for Delicious apples and \$1.66 per kilogram for McIntosh apples.

Check:

Substitute $D = \$1.38$ and $M = \$1.66$ into equation ②:
LHS of ② = 2485(\$1.66) + 2370(\$1.38)
= \$4125.10 + \$3270.60
= \$7395.70

EXERCISE 6.2

Answers to the odd-numbered problems are at the end of the book.

BASIC PROBLEMS

Solve each of the following pairs of equations using either the substitution or elimination methods. Verify your solution in each case.

1. $3x - 2y = 6$
$\quad y = x - 1$

2. $4x + y = 5$
$\quad 2x - 3y = 13$

3. $x - y = 2$
$\quad 3x + 4y = 20$

4. $y - 3x = 11$
$\quad 5x + 30 = 4y$

5. $4a - 3b = -3$
$\quad 5a - b = 10$

6. $7p - 3q = 23$
$\quad -2p - 3q = 5$

7. $y = 2x$
$\quad 7x - y = 35$

8. $g - h = 17$
$\quad \frac{4}{3}g + \frac{3}{2}h = 0$

Solve each of the following pairs of equations to three-figure accuracy. Verify your solution in each case.

9.
$$d = 3c - 500$$
$$0.7c + 0.2d = 550$$

10. $0.03x + 0.05y = 51$
$$0.8x - 0.7y = 140$$

11.
$$2v + 6w = 1$$
$$-9w + 10v = 18$$

12.
$$2.5a + 2b = 11$$
$$8a + 3.5b = 13$$

13.
$$37x - 63y = 235$$
$$18x + 26y = 468$$

14. $68.9n - 38.5m = 57$
$$45.1n - 79.4m = -658$$

15. $0.33e + 1.67f = 292$
$$1.2e + 0.61f = 377$$

16.
$$318j - 451k = 7.22$$
$$-249j + 193k = -18.79$$

17. The annual dues for Southern Pines Golf Club are $2140 for regular members and $856 for student members. If the total revenue from the dues of 583 members for the past year was $942,028, how many members did the club have in each category?

18. The Hungry Heifer diner offers an all-you-can-eat buffet at $25.90 per adult and $17.90 per child. On a particular day, the diner had total buffet revenue of $6609.40 from 266 customers. How many of the customers were children?

19. Tina drove from Calgary to Vancouver, a distance of 1000 km, in 12.3 hours. She drove at 100 km/h on the "open road," but slowed to 50 km/h on urban and curving roads. What distance did she drive at each speed? (*Hint:* Travelling time at a particular speed is Time $= \frac{\text{Distance}}{\text{Speed}}$.)

20. Mr. and Mrs. Chudnowski paid $1050 to fly with their three children from Winnipeg to Regina. Mrs. Ramsey paid $610 for herself and two children on the same flight. What were the airfares per adult and per child?

21. Budget Truck Rentals offers short-term truck rentals consisting of an hourly rate plus a per-kilometre charge. Vratislav paid $54.45 for a two-hour rental during which he drove 47 km. Bryn paid $127.55 for five hours and 93 km driven. What rate did Budget charge per hour and per kilometre?

22. Buckerfields Garden Supply makes custom fertilizer by mixing appropriate combinations of bulk 6% nitrogen fertilizer with bulk 22% nitrogen fertilizer. How many kilograms of each type should be mixed to make 300 kg of 16% nitrogen fertilizer? (*Hint:* The weight of nitrogen in the mixture equals the total weight of nitrogen in the two components mixed together.)

23. Colby inherited a small savings-bond portfolio consisting of four $1000 face-value Canada Savings Bonds and six $1000 face-value Ontario Savings Bonds. In the first year, the portfolio earned $438 interest. At the end of the first year, Colby cashed in one of the Canada Savings Bonds and two of the Ontario Savings Bonds. In the following year, the remaining bonds earned $306 interest. What annual rate of interest did each type of bond earn?

24. Mr. LeClair and Ms. Bartoli own adjacent hobby farms. They have just received their property tax notices providing the following assessment and tax information:

Owner	Assessment on residence	Assessment on land and farm buildings	Total property tax
Mr. LeClair	$400,000	$300,000	$3870
Ms. Bartoli	$350,000	$380,000	$3774

The regional government applies one property tax rate to residences and a lower tax rate to land and farm buildings. What are these tax rates (expressed in percent to the nearest 0.01%)?

25. Product X requires 30 minutes of machining on a lathe, and Product Y requires 45 minutes of machining. If the lathe was operated for 60.5 hours last week for machining a combined total of 93 units of Products X and Y, how many units of each product were produced?

26. Marichka bought five litres of milk and four dozen eggs for $19.51. Lonnie purchased nine litres of milk and three dozen eggs for $22.98. What were the prices for a litre of milk and a dozen eggs?

27. Tiny-Tot School purchases the same amount of milk and orange juice each week. After price increases from $1.50 to $1.60 per litre of milk and from $1.30 to $1.37 per can of frozen orange juice, the weekly bill rose from $57.00 to $60.55. How many litres of milk and cans of orange juice are purchased every week?

28. In the first week of July, a beer and wine store sold 871 cases of beer and paid refunds on 637 cases of empty bottles, for a net revenue of $12,632.10. For the following week the net revenue was $13,331.70 from the sale of 932 cases and the return of 805 cases of empties. What refund did the store pay per case of empty bottles?

29. As a fundraiser, a local charity sold raffle tickets on a trip to Disney World at $2 each or three for $5. In all, 3884 tickets were sold for a total of $6925. How many people bought tickets at the three-for-$5 discount?

30. A convenience store sells canned soft drinks at $4.35 for a six-pack or 90 cents for a single can. If revenue from the sale of 225 cans of soft drinks on a weekend was $178.35, how many six-packs and how many single cans were sold?

31. A partnership in a public accounting practice has seven partners and 12 accounting technicians. Each partner draws the same salary, and each technician is paid the same salary. The partners calculate that if they give the technicians a raise of 8% and if they increase their own salaries by 5%, the gross annual salaries for all accounting personnel will rise from the current $1,629,000 to $1,734,750. What are the current annual salaries of a partner and an accounting technician?

ADVANCED PROBLEM

32. A manufacturing firm pays monthly salaries of $5100 to each production worker and $4200 to each assembly worker. As the economy drops into a recession, the firm decides to reduce its total monthly manufacturing payroll from $380,700 to $297,000 by laying off 20% of its production workers and 25% of its assembly workers. How many layoffs will there be from each of the assembly and production divisions?

6.3   Introduction to Cost-Volume-Profit Analysis

Fixed Costs and Variable Costs

L05 Many types of costs of an operating business can, with good approximation, be treated as being either fixed or variable. A strictly **fixed cost** does not change if sales increase or decrease. Examples include rent, management salaries, some forms of depreciation expense, and property taxes. **Variable costs** grow or decline in direct proportion to the volume of sales. This means that, if unit sales increase by 10%, total *variable* costs will increase by 10%. (Total *fixed* costs will not change in this example.) Variable costs typically include materials costs and direct labour costs in manufacturing, or the wholesale cost of goods in retailing.

The definitions of fixed costs and variable costs have important implications for the cost of producing an additional unit. To illustrate, consider a case where the number of units sold by a business doubles from one year to the next. By definition, *total fixed* costs do not change but *total variable* costs in the second year are double the total variable costs in the first year. Therefore, each *additional* unit produced in the second year adds *no* fixed costs, but each *additional* unit adds the *same* dollar amount of variable costs. We use the term **unit variable cost** for this cost of producing an additional unit. It can be calculated by dividing the total variable costs by the total units produced.

Some costs are neither strictly fixed nor purely variable. The compensation of sales personnel by a salary plus commission is an example of a *mixed cost* that has fixed and variable cost components. In such cases, the fixed and variable components may be separated and assigned to the respective fixed cost and variable cost categories.

In the following example, we describe a proposed business and analyze its costs. The following symbols will be used throughout the chapter.

$$S = \text{Selling price or revenue per unit}$$
$$VC = \text{Unit variable costs (or Variable costs per unit)}^{[1]}$$
$$FC = \text{(Total) fixed costs}$$

EXAMPLE 6.3A

CLASSIFYING COSTS

Chuck is considering the start-up of a furniture and equipment delivery service in his hometown. He can buy a used 15-foot cube truck (1600-kg payload capacity) for $32,000. He will need to hire a helper to assist with loading and unloading. After conferring with the operator of a similar service in another town of similar size, Chuck feels he can charge $60 per delivery and that each delivery will require an average round-trip driving distance of 25 km. He has estimated the following expenses:

Truck insurance and licence	$3000/year
Fuel	$100 every 400 km
Oil changes	$70 every 5000 km
Helper's wages	$2500/month
Chuck's wages	$3500/month
EI and CPP premiums	$300/month
Tires	$900 every 75,000 km
Cell phone	$75/month
Other truck repairs and maintenance	$1000 per 10,000 km
Business licence	$180/year
Depreciation*	$180 per 1000 km

* Chuck and his accountant estimate that the truck can be driven for another 150,000 km, after which it can be sold for $5000. The $27,000 decrease in value spread over 150,000 km represents a depreciation of $180 per 1000 km.

a. Classify the costs into two categories—fixed costs and variable costs.

b. Determine values for *FC*, the (total) monthly fixed costs, and *VC*, the variable costs per delivery.

SOLUTION

a. Fixed costs are those costs that remain the same, regardless of the number of deliveries per month. In the present case, costs expressed on a monthly or annual basis are fixed costs. Variable costs are costs that are proportional to the distance driven.

Fixed costs:	*Variable costs:*
Truck insurance and licence	Fuel
Helper's wages	Oil changes
Owner's wages	Tires
EI and CPP premiums	Other truck repairs and maintenance
Cell phone	Depreciation
Business licence	

---

[1] There are many instances in the book where we use two- or three-character symbols to represent a quantity. There are two main reasons for this. Sometimes it's because the multiple-character symbol is widely used in accounting and finance books. In other cases, the most obvious choice for a single-character symbol is used elsewhere in the book to represent another quantity. When writing the product of two symbols, we avoid potential confusion by placing one of the symbols within brackets. For example, we write the product of *VC* and *X* as (*VC*)*X* rather than as *VCX*.

b. *Fixed costs:*

Truck insurance and licence	= $3000/year =	$250/month
Helper's wages	=	$2500/month
Owner's wages	=	$3500/month
EI and CPP premiums	=	$300/month
Cell phone	=	$75/month
Business licence	= $180/year =	$15/month
	Total FC =	$6640/month

Let us first calculate the variable costs per km. Then we will multiply by 25 to obtain the variable costs per delivery.

Fuel = $100 every 400 km	$\Rightarrow$	$\frac{10,000\ ¢}{400\ km}$ = 25.0¢ per km
Oil changes = $70 every 5000 km	$\Rightarrow$	1.4¢ per km
Tires = $900 every 75,000 km	$\Rightarrow$	1.2¢ per km
Other R & M = $1000 per 10,000 km	$\Rightarrow$	10.0¢ per km
Depreciation = $180 per 1000 km	$\Rightarrow$	18.0¢ per km
		Variable costs = 55.6¢ per km

VC, the variable costs per delivery = 25(55.6¢) = 1390¢ = $13.90 per delivery.

Interpretation: Each delivery adds $13.90 to Chuck's costs. The remaining $46.10 of the $60 revenue from each delivery may be applied to the monthly fixed costs of $6640. Once the fixed costs are covered, $46.10 from each additional delivery provides Chuck with a profit on his $32,000 investment.

Cost-Volume-Profit (CVP) Analysis

L06 Imagine that you are doing a feasibility study for a new business. You wish to examine the profitability of the business at various levels of sales. Entrepreneurs and potential investors/lenders commonly begin by calculating the **break-even point**. This is the number of units of product that must be sold just to cover all costs. At this particular sales volume, there is neither a profit nor a loss. For the business proposal to merit further consideration, the volume of sales needed to break even should be attainable within a reasonable time frame.

The break-even point is one of the key outcomes from a cost-volume-profit analysis. **Cost-volume-profit analysis** is a technique for estimating a firm's operating *profit* at any sales *volume*, given the firm's fixed *costs* and unit variable *costs*. By "operating profit" (or "net income") we mean:

Total revenue – Operating expenses

At the break-even point, this difference is zero.

To begin a cost-volume-profit analysis, you must estimate FC, VC, and S (in a similar manner to **Example 6.3A**). Once you have values for FC, VC, and S, there are alternative methods for completing the cost-volume-profit analysis. We will present three approaches:

- The graphical approach, which provides a revealing "picture" of the cost-volume-profit relationships in business.
- The revenue and cost function approach, which uses an algebraic method to solve the system of revenue and cost function equations.
- The contribution margin approach, which efficiently and precisely provides insights to the economics of operating a business. This approach is the method most commonly used by managers and accountants for CVP analysis.

The following assumptions apply to all three methods:

- Each operating expense can be treated as either a fixed cost or a variable cost.
- The selling price per unit remains the same regardless of sales volume. (The analysis does not, therefore, accommodate volume discounts or price reductions during a sale or promotion.)
- Production volume equals sales volume. (Consequently, all expenses in an operating period are incurred for sales made in the same period.)

 POINT OF INTEREST

The Dragons Do the Math

Dragons' Den is a reality television program that airs in over 20 countries around the world. The show's contestants present their business ideas before a panel of potential investors with the hope of getting investment capital from wealthy entrepreneurs. In return, the contestants must sell a percentage of their business to the investors.

Typically, successful contestants' pitches contain the same basic elements: an innovative or unique selling idea, a confident presentation, a clear business strategy based on research, and a concrete financial plan. People on the show often pitch their "million-dollar business idea" even though they have never made a sale. In one episode, a confident entrepreneur reported sales of $300,000 and then admitted to an overall loss of $10,000. Contestants who know their numbers as they relate to gross margins, fixed and variable costs, market size, and break-even points are able to demonstrate the confidence needed to secure the funds they are seeking.

Behind the scenes, after each episode contestants' business plans still have to undergo the "due diligence" phase before the on-air promises become reality. Deals often fall apart once the numbers are crunched.

EXERCISE 6.3

Answers to the odd-numbered problems are at the end of the book.

BASIC PROBLEMS

1. Below is a list of costs. Classify each of them as variable, fixed, or mixed (a combination of variable and fixed components).
   a. Cost of raw materials used in producing a firm's products
   b. Property taxes
   c. Wages of sales staff paid on a salary plus commission basis
   d. Wages of hourly paid production-line workers
   e. Site licence for software
   f. Leasing costs for a delivery truck ($600 per month plus $0.40 per kilometre)
   g. Packaging materials for products
   h. Insurance

2. A company's sales revenue decreased by 15% from one operating period to the next. Assuming no change in the prices of its inputs and outputs, by what percentage did:
   a. Fixed costs change?
   b. Unit variable costs change?
   c. Total variable costs change?

3. Triax Corp. produced 50,000 gizmos at a total cost of $1,600,000 (including $400,000 of fixed costs) in the fiscal year just completed. If fixed costs and unit variable costs do not change next year, how much will it cost to produce 60,000 gizmos?

4. Dynacan Ltd. manufactured 10,000 units of product last year and identified the following manufacturing and overhead costs. (V denotes "variable cost" and F denotes "fixed cost.")

Materials used in manufacturing (V)	$50,400,000
Wages paid to production workers (V)	93,000,000
Wages paid to management and salaried employees (F)	22,200,000
Other materials and supplies (V)	16,000,000
Power to run plant equipment (V)	14,200,000
Other utilities (F)	19,200,000
Depreciation (straight line) on plant and equipment (F)	9,600,000
Property taxes (F)	5,000,000

If unit variable costs and fixed costs remain unchanged, calculate the total cost to produce 9700 units this year.

6.4 | Graphical Approach to CVP Analysis

L06 In this approach, we will graph a cost function and a revenue function on the same set of axes to determine their point of intersection or *break-even point* as illustrated in **Figure 6.1**. This chart, called a **break-even chart**, clearly illustrates the sales volume at which the business will break even.

FIGURE 6.1   Break-Even Chart

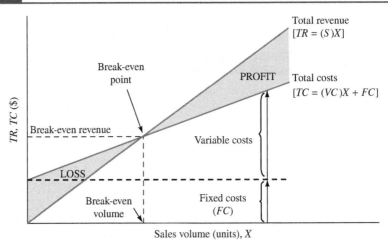

To generate this chart, first we need to develop general formulas for the total revenue and total cost equations for the sale of X units of a product. We will use the following symbols:

$$TR = \text{Total revenue (from the sale of } X \text{ units)}$$
$$TC = \text{Total cost (of the } X \text{ units sold)}$$

The total revenue from the sale of X units at a selling price of S per unit is simply

$$TR = (S)X$$

The total cost is the sum of the total variable costs plus the fixed costs. That is,

$$TC = (\text{Variable costs per unit} \times \text{Number of units sold}) + \text{Fixed costs}$$
$$TC = (VC)X + FC$$

The equation for TR is called the **revenue function** and the equation for TC is called the **cost function**.

In summary:

REVENUE FUNCTION

COST FUNCTION

$$TR = (S)X$$

$$TC = (VC)X + FC \qquad\qquad \textbf{(6-1)}$$

The intersection of the *TR* and *TC* lines is the only point at which total revenue equals total costs, and the firm breaks even. This intersection is therefore called the *break-even point*. The coordinates of the point give the sales volume and total revenue required for the firm to break even. At higher sales, the business will show a profit because the revenue line is above the total cost line. The profit equals the vertical separation of the lines. At any sales volume to the left of the break-even point, total costs exceed total revenue. The size of the loss is represented by the vertical distance between the two lines. At zero sales volume, there are no revenues or variable costs, but the business still incurs the fixed costs.

APP ④ THAT

All businesses need to have a clear understanding of the level of sales required to cover all costs and expenses. Search the App Store on your tablet, smartphone, or smart watch using the key words **BREAK EVEN POINT**.

You will find many free and paid apps that provide numerical as well as graphical details surrounding the concept of break even. Several apps also combine the break-even numbers with the markup and margins discussed in Chapter 5.

EXAMPLE 6.4A

GRAPHICAL CVP ANALYSIS OF THE BUSINESS DESCRIBED IN EXAMPLE 6.3A

We will use the data presented in Example 6.3A for Chuck's delivery service. We determined that

$$VC = \$13.90 \text{ per delivery and } FC = \$6640 \text{ per month}$$

The fixed costs included Chuck's personal wages and benefits in the amount of $3500/month. The revenue per delivery, *S*, was a flat $60.

a. What are the revenue and cost functions for this business?

b. Construct a break-even chart for the range 100 to 200 deliveries per month.

c. What is the break-even point in **(i)** deliveries per month? **(ii)** revenue per month?

d. Chuck can "get by" in the first year if he draws only $2500 per month on average instead of $3500. What average number of deliveries per month is needed to reach this minimum income requirement?

e. How much in wages and benefits is Chuck able to withdraw if he makes 174 deliveries in a month?

SOLUTION

a. Let *X* represent the number of deliveries per month. Using Formula (6-1), we obtain

Revenue function: $TR = (S)X = \$60X$
Cost function: $TC = (VC)X + FC = \$13.90X + \$6640$

b. Construct a table of values for both the revenue function and the cost function. The two end points of the range for *X* are good choices to plot.

X:	100	200
TR:	$6000	$12,000
TC:	$8030	$9420

Now plot both the *TR* and the *TC* lines.

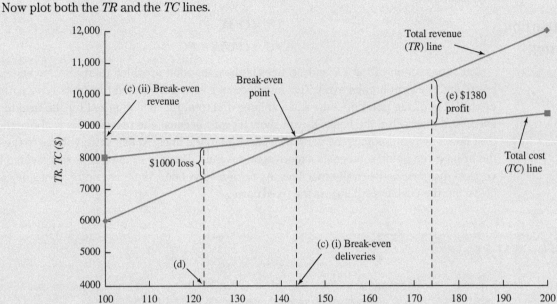

c. The break-even point is approximately **(i)** 144 deliveries per month and **(ii)** revenue of $8640 per month.

d. The point at which Chuck can draw only $2500 per month (instead of the $3500 per month already built into the *TC* function) is the point where a $1000 loss is indicated on the break-even chart. This occurs where the *TR* line is $1000 below the *TC* line; that is, at about 122 deliveries per month.

e. At 174 deliveries per month, the *TR* line is about $1380 per month above the *TC* line. Chuck can withdraw this $1380 profit in addition to the $3500 per month already included in the *TC* function. His total monthly withdrawal for wages and benefits would then be $4880.

Note: There are small differences between these answers and the answers obtained by other methods in Example 6.5A and Example 6.6A. These differences are due to the imprecise nature of the graphical approach.

EXAMPLE 6.4B

GRAPHICAL COST-VOLUME-PROFIT AND BREAK-EVEN ANALYSIS

The board of directors of a Tier 2 Junior A hockey team is preparing financial projections for the next season's operations. The team rents the city's 4000-seat arena for the entire season for $200,000 plus 25% of revenue from ticket sales. The city operates the food concessions at the games and pays the team one-third of the gross revenue.

The team will pay $200,000 for uniforms and equipment, $200,000 for travel costs, $100,000 for the coach's salary and benefits, $100,000 for housing subsidies for team members not living at home, and $40,000 for insurance. The average ticket price will be $16, and past experience shows that each fan spends an average of $6 on food and beverages at the games.

Use a break-even chart to answer the following questions.

a. What must the aggregate attendance for the 30 home games be for the team to just cover all of its costs for the season?

b. What will the profit or loss be if the attendance averages 75% of capacity?

c. The team has $280,000 in a contingency fund to absorb losses. What season attendance would just wipe out this fund?

SOLUTION

a. The total of the fixed costs is

$$FC = \$200{,}000 + \$200{,}000 + \$200{,}000 + \$100{,}000 + \$100{,}000 + \$40{,}000$$
$$= \$840{,}000$$

The unit variable cost is the 25% of the price of each ticket that the team must pay to the city as part of the rent.

$$VC = 0.25 \times \$16 = \$4 \text{ per ticket}$$

The cost function for the analysis is

$$TC = (VC)X + FC$$
$$= \$4X + \$840{,}000$$

Each ticket sold generates revenue for the team of $16 from the admission price and $2 from the team's share (one-third) of the concession revenue ($6 per fan). The revenue function is

$$TR = (\$16 + \$2)X$$
$$= \$18X$$

The cost and revenue functions should be plotted for the range from $X = 0$ to $X = 120{,}000$, which is full capacity (30×4000) for the season.

X:	0	120,000
TR:	$0	$2,160,000
TC:	$840,000	$1,320,000

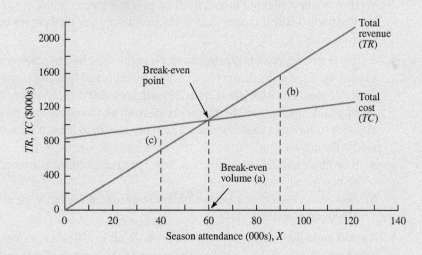

For the team to cover its costs, it must have the attendance figure at the break-even point.

Therefore, the team will just cover all its expenses if the total season attendance is 60,000.

b. The season attendance at 75% of capacity is

$$0.75 \times 120{,}000 = 90{,}000$$

At an attendance of 90,000, the *TR* line is $420,000 above the *TC* line.

The team will then have a profit of $420,000.

c. The answer will be the attendance at which the *TC* line is $280,000 above the *TR* line.

This separation occurs at an attendance of 40,000.

> ## EXERCISE 6.4

Answers to the odd-numbered problems are at the end of the book.

> ### BASIC PROBLEMS

Use the graphical approach to CVP analysis to solve the following problems.

1. CD Solutions Ltd. manufactures and replicates CDs for software and music recording companies. CD Solutions sells each disc for $2.50. The variable costs per disc are $1.00.
   a. To just break even, how many CDs must be sold per month if the fixed costs are $60,000 per month?
   b. What must sales be in order to have a profit of $7500 per month?

2. Clone Computers assembles and packages personal computer systems from brand-name components. Its Home Office PC System is assembled from components costing $1400 per system and sells for $2000. Labour costs for assembly are $100 per system. This product line's share of overhead costs is $10,000 per month.
   a. How many Home Office systems must be sold each month to break even on this product line?
   b. What will be the profit or loss for a month in which 15 Home Office systems are sold?

3. Huntsville Office Supplies (HOS) is evaluating the profitability of leasing a photocopier for its customers to use on a self-serve basis at 10¢ per copy. The copier may be leased for $300 per month plus 1.5¢ per copy on a full-service contract. HOS can purchase paper at $5 per 500-sheet ream. Toner costs $100 per bottle, which in normal use will last for 5000 pages. HOS is allowing for additional costs (including electricity) of 0.5¢ per copy.
   a. How many copies per month must be sold in order to break even?
   b. What will be the increase in monthly profit for each 1000 copies sold above the break-even point?

4. Jordan is developing a business plan for a residential building inspection service he wants to start up. Rent and utilities for an office would cost $1000 per month. The fixed costs for a vehicle would be $450 per month. He estimates that the variable office costs (word processing and supplies) will be $50 per inspection and variable vehicle costs will be $25 per inspection. Jordan would also spend $200 per month to lease a computer, and $350 per month for advertising.
   a. If he charges $275 per inspection, how many inspections per month are required before he can "pay himself"?
   b. How many inspections per month are required for Jordan to be able to draw a salary of $4000 per month?

5. A small manufacturing operation can produce up to 250 units per week of a product that it sells for $20 per unit. The variable cost per unit is $12, and the fixed costs per week are $1200.
   a. How many units must the firm sell per week to break even?
   b. Determine the firm's weekly profit or loss if it sells:
      (i)   120 units per week.
      (ii) 250 units per week.
   c. At what level of sales will the net income be $400 per week?

6. Valley Peat Ltd. sells peat moss for $10 per bag. Variable costs are $7.50 per bag and annual fixed costs are $100,000.
   a. How many bags of peat must be sold per year to break even?
   b. What will be the net income for a year in which 60,000 bags of peat are sold?
   c. How many bags must be sold for a net income of $25,000 in a year?
   d. What volume of sales would produce a loss of $50,000 in a year?

7. Reflex Manufacturing Corp. manufactures composters at a unit variable cost of $43. It sells them for $70 each. It can produce a maximum of 3200 composters per month. Annual fixed costs total $648,000.
   a. What is the break-even volume per month?
   b. What is the monthly net income at a volume of 2500 composters per month?
   c. What is the monthly net income if Reflex operates at 50% of capacity during a recession?

Use the interactive Break-Even Analysis Chart found in the "Interactive Charts" under the Student Resources for Chapter 6 to answer Problems 8–11.

8. Leaving other variables unchanged, what effect does increasing the value of *VC* have on:
   a. the fixed cost (*FC*) line?   b. the total cost (*TC*) line?
   c. the total revenue (*TR*) line?   d. the break-even point?

9. Leaving other variables unchanged, what effect does increasing the value of *S* have on:
   a. the fixed cost (*FC*) line?   b. the total cost (*TC*) line?
   c. the total revenue (*TR*) line?   d. the break-even point?

10. Leaving other variables unchanged, what effect does increasing the value of *FC* have on:
    a. the fixed cost (*FC*) line?   b. the total cost (*TC*) line?
    c. the total revenue (*TR*) line?   d. the break-even point?

11. Solve Problems 2, 3, and 4 earlier in this Exercise using the interactive chart and its accompanying report.

6.5 | Revenue and Cost Function Approach to CVP Analysis

L06 In this approach, we will develop the formula for net income based on the principal that it is the difference between money in (revenue) and money out (total costs) for the business. From that we will develop the formula for the break-even point based on the premise that a business has exactly covered all of its costs with its revenue at this point. In other words, its net income is zero.

In **Section 6.4** we defined

$$TR = (S)\,X$$
$$TC = (VC)\,X + FC$$

The net income (*NI*) from the sale of *X* units for a period is the total revenue minus the total cost. Hence,

$$NI = TR - TC$$
$$= (S)\,X - [(VC)\,X + FC]$$
$$= (S - VC)\,X - FC$$

Net income calculations use the formula:

NET INCOME FORMULA

$$NI = (S - VC)X - FC \qquad (6\text{-}2)$$

We can obtain the break-even volume in this approach by setting *NI* = 0 in Formula (6-2) for the special case where *X* = Break-even volume. That is,

$$0 = (S - VC)(\text{Break-even volume}) - FC$$

BREAK-EVEN FORMULA

$$\textbf{\textit{Break-even volume}} = \frac{FC}{S - VC} \qquad (6\text{-}3)$$

EXAMPLE 6.5A

CVP ANALYSIS (REVENUE AND COST FUNCTION APPROACH)

In Example 6.3A concerning Chuck's delivery service, we found that

$$VC = \$13.90 \text{ per delivery} \quad \text{and} \quad FC = \$6640 \text{ per month}$$

The fixed costs included Chuck's personal wages in the amount of $3500/month. The unit variable costs, VC, assumed an average round-trip driving distance of 25 km. The revenue per delivery, S, was a flat $60.

a. What is the break-even point in **(i)** deliveries per month? **(ii)** revenue per month?

b. Chuck can "get by" in the first year if he draws only $2500 per month on average instead of $3500. What average number of deliveries per month is needed to reach this minimum income requirement?

c. What personal wages can Chuck withdraw if he makes 174 deliveries in a month?

d. If the average distance per delivery turns out to be 30 km instead of 25 km, how many deliveries per month are needed to break even?

SOLUTION

Substituting the known quantities into Formulas (6-1) and (6-2) gives

$$TR = (S)X = \$60X$$
$$TC = (VC)X + FC = \$13.90X + \$6640$$
$$NI = (S - VC)X - FC = \$46.10X - \$6640$$

a. **(i)** Use Formula (6-3) to calculate the break-even volume.

$$\text{Break-even volume} = \frac{\$6640}{\$46.10} = 144.03 \Rightarrow 144 \text{ deliveries per month}$$

(ii) The break-even revenue (from 144 deliveries) is 144($60) = $8640.

b. Since monthly wages of $3500 are already included in $FC = \$6640$, a monthly draw of only $2500 reduces the fixed costs by $1000 to $5640. The break-even point is then lowered to

$$\frac{\$5640}{\$46.10} = 122.34$$

An average of 122.34 deliveries per month will provide Chuck with an income of $2500 per month.

c. In addition to the $3500/month already included in FC, Chuck can withdraw any available profit, NI. At $X = 174$ deliveries per month,

$$NI = \$46.10X - \$6640 = \$46.10(174) - \$6640 = \$1381.40$$

Therefore, Chuck can withdraw a total of

$$\$3500 + \$1381.40 = \$4881.40$$

d. Variable costs of $VC = \$13.90$ per delivery were based on an average distance of 25 km per delivery. This corresponds to variable costs of $\frac{\$13.90}{25} = \$0.556$ per km. At 30 km driving distance per delivery,

$$VC = 30(\$0.556) = \$16.68 \text{ per delivery}$$

Again solve for X when $NI = 0$.

$$NI = (S - VC)X - FC$$
$$0 = (\$60 - \$16.68)(\text{Break-even volume}) - \$6640$$

or

$$\text{Break-even volume} = \frac{\$6640}{\$43.32} = 153.28 \text{ deliveries per month}$$

An average of 153.28 deliveries per month are needed to break even.

EXAMPLE 6.5B

CVP ANALYSIS (REVENUE AND COST FUNCTION APPROACH)

A manufacturing company is studying the feasibility of producing a new product. A new production line could manufacture up to 800 units per month at a cost of $50 per unit. Fixed costs would be $22,400 per month. Variable selling and shipping costs are estimated to be $20 per unit. Market research indicates that a unit price of $110 would be competitive.

a. What is the break-even point as a percent of capacity?

b. What would be the net income at 90% of capacity?

c. What would unit sales have to be to attain a net income of $9000 per month?

d. In a serious recession sales might fall to 55% of capacity. What would be the resulting net income?

e. What dollar amount of sales would result in a loss of $2000 per month?

f. In the highest-cost scenario, fixed costs might be $25,000, production costs might be $55 per unit, and selling and shipping costs might be $22 per unit. What would the break-even point be in these circumstances?

SOLUTION

In the expected scenario, $S = \$110$, $VC = \$50 + \$20 = \$70$, and $FC = \$22,400$ per month. Hence,

$$TR = \$110X$$
$$TC = \$70X + \$22,400$$
$$NI = \$40X - \$22,400$$

a. At the break-even point, $NI = 0$. Hence

$$0 = \$40X - \$22,400$$

In this equation X represents the break-even volume. So,

$$\text{Break-even volume} = \frac{\$22,400}{\$40} = 560 \text{ units per month}$$

This represents

$$\frac{560}{800} \times 100\% = 70\% \text{ of capacity}$$

b. At 90% of capacity, production would be $0.9 \times 800 = 720$ units per month. Using the third equation,

$$NI = \$40(720) - \$22,400 = \$6400 \text{ per month}$$

c. Setting $NI = \$9000$ in the third equation, we obtain

$$\$9000 = \$40X - \$22,400$$

Unit sales would have to be $\qquad X = \dfrac{\$9000 + \$22,400}{\$40} = 785 \text{ per month}$

d. In the recession scenario, unit sales would be $0.55 \times 800 = 440$ per month. Then

$$NI = (\$40)440 - \$22,400 = -\$4800$$

The company would lose $4800 per month in the recession.

e. Substituting $NI = -\$2000$ per month in the third equation,

$$-\$2000 = \$40X - \$22,400$$

$$X = \frac{-\$2000 + \$22,400}{\$40} = 510 \text{ units per month}$$

The dollar amount of sales would be

$$TR = (\$110)X = (\$110)510 = \$56,100$$

f. In the highest-cost scenario, $FC = \$25,000$ per month and $VC = \$77$ per unit. The net income equation becomes

$$NI = (\$110 - \$77)X - \$25,000 = \$33X - \$25,000$$

At the break-even point, $NI = 0$.

$$0 = \$33(\text{Break-even volume}) - \$25,000$$

or

$$\text{Break-even volume} = \frac{\$25,000}{\$33} = 758 \text{ units per month}$$

The break-even point in this case would be 758 units per month (94.75% of capacity).

EXAMPLE 6.5C

CVP ANALYSIS WITH SALES VOLUME IN DOLLARS INSTEAD OF UNITS

Last year Marconi Printing had total revenue of $375,000 while operating at 75% of capacity. The total of its variable costs was $150,000. Fixed costs were $180,000.

a. What is Marconi's break-even point expressed:
   (i) in dollars of revenue?
   (ii) as a percent of capacity?

b. If the current S, VC, and FC are the same as last year, what net income can be expected from revenue of $450,000 in the current year?

c. If the variable costs were to increase to 50% of total unit sales while at the same time fixed costs decreased by 10%, how many dollars in revenue would be required to break even?

SOLUTION

In this situation, we let $S = \$1$ and then X represents the number of $1 units sold. The revenue function is simply

$$TR = \$1X$$

In the cost function, $TC = (VC)X + FC$, VC must be interpreted as the variable cost per $1 of revenue. In the present case,

$$VC = \frac{\text{Total variable cost}}{\text{Total unit sales}} = \frac{\$150,000}{375,000} = \$0.40$$

Then

$$TC = \$0.40X + \$180,000$$

and

$$NI = (\$1.00 - \$0.40)X - \$180,000 = \$0.60X - \$180,000$$

a. (i) Setting $NI = 0$ in the net income equation, we obtain

$$\text{Break-even point} = \frac{\$180,000}{\$0.60} = 300,000 \text{ units}$$

Since each unit is deemed to sell at $1, Marconi will break even on revenue of $300,000.

(ii) If revenue of $375,000 represents 75% of capacity, then

$$\text{Full capacity} = \frac{\$375,000}{0.75} = \$500,000 \text{ of revenue}$$

The break-even point of $300,000 of revenue represents

$$\frac{\$300,000}{\$500,000} \times 100\% = 60\% \text{ of capacity}$$

b. Substitute $X = 450,000$ in the net income equation.

$$NI = \$0.60(450,000) - \$180,000 = \$90,000$$

Revenue of $450,000 in the current year should produce a net income of $90,000.

c. If variable costs increase to 50% of total unit sales, then for every dollar in sales,

$$VC = \$0.50X$$

The new fixed costs are $FC = \$180,000 \, (1 - 0.10) = \$162,000$ and $TC = \$0.50X + \$162,000$.

Therefore,

$$\text{Break-even point} = \frac{\$162,000}{\$0.50} = 324,000 \text{ units}$$

Since each unit is deemed to sell at $1, Marconi will now break even on revenue of $324,000.

EXAMPLE 6.5D

CVP ANALYSIS USING AN INCOME STATEMENT

The following is an income statement for Corbinator Enterprises for the month of December 2019. The business operated at 80% of capacity for this period.

Income Statement for December 2019

Total revenue		$86,500
Total variable costs	$30,275	
Fixed costs	$31,850	
Total costs		$62,125
Net Income		$24,375

a. What is Corbinator's break-even point expressed

   (i) in dollars of revenue?

   (ii) as a percent of capacity?

b. What revenue is required to have a net income of $39,650 in January of 2020?

SOLUTION

As in **Example 6.5C**, we set the revenue function to:

$$TR = \$1X$$

In the cost function $TC = (VC)X + FC$, VC must be interpreted as the variable cost per $1 of revenue. In this example, we will use the values in the income statement for total variable costs and total revenue to establish the variable costs as:

$$VC = \frac{\text{Total variable cost}}{\text{Total unit sales}} = \frac{\$30,275}{86,500} = \$0.35$$

Then

$$TC = \$0.35X + \$31,850$$

and

$$NI = (\$1.00 - \$0.35)X - \$31,850 = \$0.65X - \$31,850$$

a. (i) Setting $NI = 0$ in the net income equation, we obtain

$$\text{Break-even point} = \frac{\$31,850}{\$0.65} = 49,000 \text{ units}$$

Since each unit is deemed to sell at $1, Corbinator will break even on revenue of $49,000.

  (ii) If revenue of \$86,500 represents 80% of capacity, then

$$\text{Full capacity} = \frac{\$86,500}{0.80} = \$108,125 \text{ of revenue}$$

The break-even point of \$49,000 of revenue represents

$$\frac{\$49,000}{\$108,125} \times 100\% = 45.32\% \text{ of capacity}$$

b. Substitute $NI = \$39,650$ in the net income equation.

$$\$39,650 = \$0.65(X) - \$31,850$$
$$\$0.65(X) = \$71,500$$
$$X = \$110,000$$

Revenue of \$110,000 in January of 2020 should produce a net income of \$39,650.

 TIP

Excel Applications in Business Mathematics

If you have not covered **Section 3.3** in your course, go back and read the TIP box titled "Excel Applications in Business Mathematics" located in that section. It explains how Connect provides spreadsheet applications as an *optional* feature.

Break-Even Worksheet on the Texas Instruments BA II PLUS With this worksheet, you can compute the value for any one of the five variables in the formula $NI = (S - VC)X - FC$ after entering values for the other four variables. **Appendix 6A** demonstrates the use of the Break-Even Worksheet.

EXERCISE 6.5

Answers to the odd-numbered problems are at the end of the book.

Spreadsheet templates: *Connect presents five partially completed Excel templates for CVP analysis. Go to the Student Edition of Connect and find "CVP Analysis" under the Student Resources for Chapter 6. After you program the output cell in each template, you can use the templates for solving Problems 1–14 and 19–26.*

Texas Instruments BA II PLUS Break-Even Worksheet: *We demonstrate the use of this worksheet in Appendix 6A. It provides another alternative for solving Problems 1–14 and 19–26.*

BASIC PROBLEMS

Problems 5–9 are repeated, with some variations from Problems 1–5, respectively, in Exercise 6.4. Problems 12 and 13 are expanded versions of Problems 6 and 7 in Exercise 6.4.

  1. Toys-4-U manufactures a toy that it sells for \$30 each. The variable cost per toy is \$10 and the fixed costs for this product line are \$100,000 per year. They estimate they can produce 8000 toys per production period.

    a. What is the break-even point in units?

    b. What is the break-even sales revenue?

    c. What is the break-even volume as a percent of capacity?

    d. What would their net income be if they sold 6200 toys?

    e. What level of output is required to have a net income of \$10,000?

2. Reliable Plastics makes containers that it sells for $2.55 each. Its fixed costs for this product are $2000 per month and the variable cost per unit is $1.30.
   a. What is the break-even point in units?
   b. What is the break-even sales revenue?

3. Ingrid processes and bottles jam in her home-based business. Her fixed costs are $250 per month and the variable cost per jar is $1.20. She sells the jam to local grocery stores for $3.20 each.
   a. How many jars must she sell per year to break even?
   b. What will be her profit if she sells 3000 jars in a year?
   c. How many jars must she sell per year to have a loss of no more than $1200?

4. ChildCare Industries manufactures infant car seats that it sells to retailers for $155 each. The costs to manufacture each additional seat are $65, and the monthly fixed costs are $18,000.
   a. How many seats must be sold per year to break even?
   b. What will ChildCare's loss be if it sells 2000 seats in a year?

5. CD Solutions Ltd. manufactures and replicates CDs for software and music recording companies. CD Solutions sells each disc for $2.50. The variable costs per disc are $1.00.
   a. To just break even, how many CDs must be sold per month if the fixed costs are $60,000 per month?
   b. What must sales be in order to have a profit of $7500 per month?
   c. What will their profit be if they have total revenue of $130,000 per month?
   d. How many CDs would have to be sold per month to break even if they increased their selling price to $3.50 each?

6. Clone Computers assembles and packages personal computer systems from brand-name components. Its Home Office PC system is assembled from components costing $1400 per system and sells for $2000. Labour costs for assembly are $100 per system. This product line's share of overhead costs is $10,000 per month.
   a. How many Home Office systems must be sold each month to break even on this product line?
   b. What will be the profit or loss for a month in which 15 Home Office systems are sold?

7. Huntsville Office Supplies (HOS) is evaluating the profitability of leasing a photocopier for its customers to use on a self-serve basis at 10¢ per copy. The copier may be leased for $300 per month plus 1.5¢ per copy on a full-service contract. HOS can purchase paper at $5 per 500-sheet ream. Toner costs $100 per bottle, which in normal use will last for 5000 pages. HOS is allowing for additional costs (including electricity) of 0.5¢ per copy.
   a. How many copies per month must be sold in order to break even?
   b. What will be the increase in monthly profit for each 1000 copies sold above the break-even point?

8. Jordan is developing a business plan for a residential building inspection service he may start. Rent and utilities for an office would cost $1000 per month. The fixed costs for a vehicle would be $450 per month. He estimates that the variable office costs (word processing and supplies) will be $50 per inspection and variable vehicle costs will be $25 per inspection. Jordan would also spend $200 per month to lease a computer, and $350 per month for advertising.
   a. If he charges $275 per inspection, how many inspections per month are required before he can "pay himself"?
   b. How many inspections per month are required for Jordan to be able to draw a salary of $4000 per month?

9. A small manufacturing operation can produce up to 250 units per week of a product that it sells for $20 per unit. The variable cost per unit is $12, and the fixed cost per week is $1200.
   a. How many units must the business sell per week to break even?
   b. Determine the firm's weekly profit or loss if it sells:
      (i) 120 units per week
      (ii) 250 units per week
   c. Determine the firm's weekly profit or loss if it has revenue of:
      (i) $4900 per week
      (ii) $1960 per week
   d. At what level of sales will the net income be $400 per week?

10. Alpha Corp. expects to operate at 80% of capacity next year. Its forecast operating budget is:

Sales revenue		$1,200,000
Fixed costs	$300,000	
Total variable costs	$800,000	
Total costs		$1,100,000
Net income		$100,000

   a. What is Alpha's break-even revenue?
   b. What would be Alpha's net income if it operates at full capacity? Round your answer to the nearest dollar.

11. Beta Inc. has based its budget forecast for next year on the assumption it will operate at 90% of capacity. The budget is:

Sales revenue		$18,000,000
Fixed costs	$10,000,000	
Total variable costs	$6,000,000	
Total costs		$16,000,000
Net income		$2,000,000

   a. At what percentage of capacity would Beta break even?
   b. What would be Beta's net income if it operates at 70% of capacity? Round your answer to the nearest dollar.

12. Valley Peat Ltd. sells peat moss for $10 per bag. Variable costs are $7.50 per bag and annual fixed costs are $100,000.
   a. How many bags of peat must be sold in a year to break even?
   b. What will be the net income for a year in which 60,000 bags of peat are sold?
   c. How many bags must be sold for a net income of $60,000 in a year?
   d. What annual sales in terms of bags and in terms of dollars would produce a loss of $10,000?
   e. How much do the break-even unit sales and break-even revenue increase per $1000 increase in annual fixed costs?

13. Reflex Manufacturing Corp. manufactures composters at a unit variable cost of $43. It sells them for $70 each. It can produce a maximum of 3200 composters per month. Annual fixed costs total $648,000.
   a. What is the break-even volume per month?
   b. What is the monthly net income at a volume of 2500 units per month?
   c. What is the monthly net income if Reflex operates at 50% of capacity during a recession?
   d. At what percent utilization would the annual net income be $226,800?
   e. If fixed and variable costs remain the same, how much do the monthly break-even unit sales change for a $1 increase in the selling price?

14. Bentley Plastics Ltd. has annual fixed costs of $450,000 and variable costs of $15 per unit. The selling price per unit is $25.
    a. What annual unit sales are required to break even?
    b. What annual revenue is required to break even?
    c. What will be the annual net income at annual sales of:
        (i) 50,000 units?
        (ii) $1,000,000?
    d. What minimum annual unit sales are required to limit the annual loss to $20,000?
    e. If the unit selling price and fixed costs remain the same, what are the changes in break-even unit sales and break-even revenue for a $1 increase in unit variable costs?

INTERMEDIATE PROBLEMS

15. The Woodstock plant of Goodstone Tires manufactures a single line of automobile tires. In its first fiscal quarter, the plant had total revenue of $4,500,000 and net income of $900,000 from the production and sale of 60,000 tires. In the subsequent quarter, the net income was $700,000 from the production and sale of 50,000 tires. Calculate the unit selling price, the total revenue in the second quarter, the variable costs per tire, and the total fixed costs per calendar quarter.

16. The Kelowna division of Windstream RVs builds the Wanderer model. The division had total revenue of $4,785,000 and a profit of $520,000 on the sale of 165 units in the first half of its financial year. Sales declined to 117 units in the second half of the year, resulting in a profit of only $136,000. Determine the selling price per unit, the total revenue in the second half, the unit variable costs, and the annual fixed costs.

17. In the past year, the Greenwood Corporation had sales of $1,200,000, fixed costs of $400,000, and total variable costs of $600,000.
    a. At what sales figure would Greenwood have broken even last year?
    b. If sales increase by 15% in the year ahead (but all prices remain the same), how much (in $) will the net income increase?
    c. If fixed costs are 10% lower in the year ahead (but sales and variable costs remain the same as last year), how much (in $) will the net income increase?
    d. If variable costs are 10% higher in the year ahead (but sales and fixed costs remain the same as last year), how much (in $) will the net income decrease?

18. The Morgan Company produces two products, G and H, with the following characteristics:

	Product G	Product H
Selling price per unit	$5	$6
Variable costs per unit	$3	$2
Forecast sales (units)	100,000	150,000

    Total fixed costs for the year are expected to be $700,000.
    a. What will be the net income if the forecast sales are realized?
    b. Determine the break-even volumes of the two products. Assume that the product mix (that is, the ratio of the unit sales for the two products) remains the same at the break-even point.
    c. If it turns out that Morgan sells twice as many units of H as of G, what will be the break-even volumes of the two products?

19. A college ski club is planning a weekend package for its members. The members will each be charged $270. For a group of 15 or more, the club can purchase a two-day downhill pass and two nights' accommodation for $220 per person. A 36-passenger capacity bus can be chartered for $1400.
    a. How many must sign up to break even?
    b. If the bus is filled, how much profit will the club make?
    c. If the student government agrees to cover any loss up to $400, what is the minimum number of participants required?

20. Genifax reported the following information for September:

Sales revenue	$180,000
Fixed manufacturing costs	22,000
Fixed marketing and overhead costs	14,000
Total variable costs	120,000
Unit price	9

    a. Determine the unit sales required to break even.

    b. What unit sales would generate a net income of $30,000?

    c. What unit sales would generate a profit of 20% of the sales revenue?

    d. What sales revenue is required to produce a profit of $20,000?

    e. If unit variable costs are reduced by 10% with no change in the fixed costs, what will be the unit sales to break even?

21. The social committee of a college's student government is planning the annual graduation dinner and dance. The preferred band can be signed for $1000 plus 10% of ticket revenues. A hall can be rented for $4400. Fire regulations limit the hall to 400 guests plus the band and caterers. A food caterer has quoted a price of $24 per person for the dinner.

    The committee thinks that the event will be a sellout if ticket prices are set at $46 per person. Some on the committee are in favour of less crowding at the dance and argue for a ticket price of $56. They estimate that 300 will attend at the higher price.

    a. Calculate the number of tickets that need to be sold at each price to break even.

    b. What will be the profit at the predicted sales for each ticket price?

22. This problem is designed to illustrate how the relative proportions of fixed and variable costs affect a firm's net income when the sales volume changes.

    Two hypothetical firms, Hi-Tech and Lo-Tech, manufacture and sell the same product at the same price of $50. Hi-Tech is highly mechanized with monthly fixed costs of $4000 and unit variable costs of $10. Lo-Tech is labour-intensive and can readily lay off or take on more workers as production requirements warrant. Lo-Tech's monthly fixed costs are $1000, and its unit variable costs are $40.

    a. Calculate the break-even volume for both firms.

    b. At each firm's break-even point, calculate the percentage of the firm's total costs that are fixed and the percentage that are variable.

    c. For a 10% increase in sales above the break-even point, calculate the dollar increase in each firm's net income. Explain the differing results.

    d. For a 10% decrease in sales below the break-even point, calculate the dollar decrease in each firm's net income. Explain the differing results.

    e. What is each firm's net income at sales of 150 units per month and each firm's loss at sales of 50 units per month?

23. In the year just ended, a small appliance manufacturer sold its griddle at the wholesale price of $37.50. The unit variable costs were $13.25, and the monthly fixed costs were $5600.

    a. If unit variable costs are expected to rise to $15.00 and fixed costs to $6000 per month for the next year, at what amount should the griddle be priced in order to have the same break-even volume as last year?

    b. What should be the griddle's price in order to have the same profit as last year on sales of 300 griddles per month in both years?

24. Mickey's Restaurant had a net income last year of $40,000 after fixed costs of $130,000 and total variable costs of $80,000.

    a. What was the restaurant's break-even point in sales dollars?

    b. If fixed costs in the current year rise to $140,000 and variable costs remain at the same percentage of sales as for last year, what will be the break-even point?

    c. What sales in the current year will result in a profit of $50,000?

25. A farmer is trying to decide whether to rent his neighbour's land to grow additional hay for sale to feedlots at $180 per delivered tonne. The land can be rented at $400 per hectare for the season. Cultivation and planting will cost $600 per hectare; spraying and fertilizer will cost $450 per hectare. It will cost $42 per tonne to cut, condition, and bale the hay, and $24 per tonne to transport it to the feedlots.
    a. How many tonnes per hectare must be produced to break even?
    b. How much is the break-even tonnage lowered if the selling price is $10 per tonne higher?
    c. What is the profit or loss at the $180 per tonne price if the crop yield is:
       (i) 15 tonnes per hectare?
       (ii) 10 tonnes per hectare?

26. A sporting goods manufacturer lost $400,000 on sales of $3 million in a year during the last recession. The production lines operated at only 60% of capacity during the year. Variable costs represent one-third of the sales dollars.
    a. At what percent of capacity must the firm operate in order to break even?
    b. What would its net income be at 80% of capacity?
    c. What dollar sales would generate a net income of $700,000?
    d. How much does each additional dollar of sales increase the net income?
    e. How much does every $1 increase in fixed costs raise the break-even sales?

6.6 Contribution Margin Approach to CVP Analysis

L06 Suppose we produce plastic toys that sell for $5 each ($S = \$5$), and the associated variable costs are $3 per toy ($VC = \$3$). This means that each additional toy we produce and sell adds $3 to our total costs.

In the contribution margin approach to CVP analysis, we take the following point of view. Think of the $5 from the sale of each toy as having two components: (1) the $3 needed to pay the variable costs of producing that particular toy, and (2) the remaining $2 available for other purposes.

For the early sales in a period, we put the $2 component toward the payment of fixed costs. Suppose our fixed costs are $1000 per month ($FC = \$1000$). Each toy contributes $2 toward paying fixed costs. These ideas are represented in the diagram below. The fixed costs will not be fully paid until we sell $1000/$2 = 500 toys in the month. This is our break-even point. If we fall 40 toys short of 500, we will have a loss of $2(40) = $80 for the month.

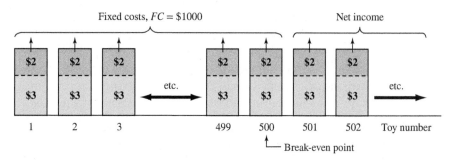

The 501st toy we sell in a month still costs an additional $VC = \$3$ to produce, but the extra $2 from its sale is "pure" profit. Each and every toy beyond the 500th contributes a full $2 to the net income or profit for the month. If we sell a total of 560 toys in a month, our net income will be $2(560 − 500) = $120.

Let us now generalize this discussion. We have talked about each toy *contributing* $2 first toward the payment of fixed costs and then, after we pass the break-even point, *contributing* $2 toward our net income. In accounting and marketing, this $2 component of the selling price is called the **contribution margin**. It is simply the difference between the selling price and the variable costs per unit. Introducing the symbol CM to represent contribution margin, we have,

CONTRIBUTION MARGIN

$$CM = S - VC \qquad\qquad (6\text{-}4)$$

As we readily deduced in the numerical example, the number of units that must be sold just to pay the fixed costs (and break even) is

$$\text{Unit sales at the break-even point} = \frac{FC}{CM}$$

The total contribution margin from the sale of X units will be $(CM)X$. The net income for a period will be the amount left over after we subtract the fixed costs from $(CM)X$. That is,

NET INCOME FORMULA

$$NI = (CM)X - FC \qquad\qquad (6\text{-}5)[2]$$

EXAMPLE 6.6A

CVP ANALYSIS USING THE CONTRIBUTION MARGIN APPROACH

In Example 6.3A concerning Chuck's delivery service, we found that

$$VC = \$13.90 \text{ per delivery} \quad \text{and} \quad FC = \$6640 \text{ per month}$$

The fixed costs included Chuck's personal wages in the amount of $3500/month. The unit variable costs, VC, assumed an average round-trip driving distance of 25 km. The revenue per delivery, S, was a flat $60.

a. Calculate and interpret the unit contribution margin (per delivery).

b. What is the break-even point in
   (i) deliveries per month?
   (ii) revenue per month?

c. Chuck can "get by" in the first year if he draws only $2500 per month on average instead of $3500. What average number of deliveries per month is needed to reach this minimum income requirement?

d. What personal wage can Chuck withdraw if he makes 174 deliveries in a month?

e. If the average distance per delivery turns out to be 30 km instead of 25 km, how many deliveries per month are needed to break even?

SOLUTION

a. The contribution margin per delivery is:

$$CM = S - VC = \$60.00 - \$13.90 = \$46.10$$

This means that, after covering variable costs (of $13.90), each delivery contributes $46.10 toward the payment of fixed costs. Once the cumulative total of unit contribution margins reaches the fixed costs for the month ($6640), each *additional* delivery will contribute $46.10 to the month's profit. (Chuck can withdraw this profit for personal use.)

b. (i) With each delivery contributing $46.10 toward fixed costs totalling $6640, the break-even point is

$$\frac{FC}{CM} = \frac{\$6640}{\$46.10} = 144.03 \Rightarrow 144 \text{ deliveries per month}$$

(ii) The break-even revenue (from 144 deliveries) is 144($60) = $8640.

---

[2] Note that if you substitute Formula (6-4) into Formula (6-5), you end up with the net income formula, $NI = (S - VC)X - FC$, that was derived in Section 6.4.

c. Since monthly wages and benefits of $3500 are already included in $FC = \$6640$, a monthly wage of only $2500 reduces the fixed costs by $1000 to $5640. The break-even point is then lowered to an average of

$$\frac{FC}{CM} = \frac{\$5640}{\$46.10} = 122.34 \text{ deliveries per month}$$

d. 174 deliveries in a month are $174 - 144 = 30$ deliveries more than the break-even point calculated in part (b). Of the $60 revenue from *each* of these extra deliveries, only $CM = \$46.10$ is available as profit that Chuck can withdraw for personal use. (The other $13.90 is required to pay the additional variable cost of each delivery.) Therefore, Chuck can withdraw a total of

$$\$3500 + 30(\$46.10) = \$4883.00 \text{ for that month}$$

e. Variable costs of $VC = \$13.90$ per delivery were based on an average distance of 25 km per delivery. This corresponds to variable costs of $\frac{\$13.90}{25} = \$0.556$ per km. At 30 km driving distance per delivery,

$$VC = 30(\$0.556) = \$16.68 \text{ per delivery}$$

The contribution margin becomes

$$CM = S - VC = \$60.00 - \$16.68 = \$43.32$$

and the break-even point becomes an average of

$$\frac{FC}{CM} = \frac{\$6640}{\$43.32} = 153.28 \text{ deliveries per month}$$

EXAMPLE 6.6B

CVP ANALYSIS USING THE CONTRIBUTION MARGIN APPROACH

A manufacturing company is studying the feasibility of producing a new product. A new production line could manufacture up to 800 units per month at a cost of $50 per unit. Fixed costs would be $22,400 per month. Variable selling and shipping costs are estimated to be $20 per unit. Market research indicates that a unit price of $110 would be competitive.

a. What is the break-even point as a percent of capacity?

b. What would be the net income at 90% of capacity?

c. What would unit sales have to be to attain a net income of $9000 per month?

d. In a serious recession sales might fall to 55% of capacity. What would be the resulting net income?

e. What dollar amount of sales would result in a loss of $2000 per month?

f. In the highest-cost scenario, fixed costs might be $25,000, production costs might be $55 per unit, and selling and shipping costs might be $22 per unit. What would the break-even point be in these circumstances?

SOLUTION

In the expected scenario, $S = \$110$, $VC = \$50 + \$20 = \$70$, and $FC = \$22,400$ per month.

Hence, $$CM = S - VC = \$110 - \$70 = \$40$$

a. The break-even volume is

$$\frac{FC}{CM} = \frac{\$22,400}{\$40} = 560 \text{ units per month}$$

This represents

$$\frac{560}{800} \times 100\% = 70\% \text{ of capacity}$$

b. At 90% of capacity, production would be $0.9 \times 800 = 720$ units per month. This is $720 - 560 = 160$ units above the break-even point. The contribution margin from these units goes entirely to net income. Therefore,

$$NI = 160(\$40) = \$6400 \text{ per month}$$

Note: This answer can also be obtained by substitution in Formula (6-5).

c. For a net income of $9000 per month, the number of units sold *in excess* of the break-even point would have to be

$$\frac{NI}{CM} = \frac{\$9000}{\$40} = 225$$

Total unit sales would have to be $560 + 225 = 785$ per month.

d. In the recession scenario, sales would be only $0.55 \times 800 = 440$ units per month. This number is $560 - 440 = 120$ units short of the break-even point, resulting in a loss of

$$120(CM) = 120(\$40) = \$4800 \text{ per month}$$

e. Each unit that the company falls short of the break-even point will contribute a loss of $CM = \$40$. For a loss of $2000 in a month, the company must fall

$$\frac{NI}{CM} = \frac{\$2000}{\$40} = 50 \text{ units}$$

short of the break-even point. Total unit sales would be $560 - 50 = 510$ units per month. The dollar amount of sales would be

$$510(S) = 510(\$110) = \$56,100 \text{ per month}$$

f. In the highest-cost scenario, $FC = \$25,000$ per month and $VC = \$77$ per unit.

Then

$$CM = \$110 - \$77 = \$33$$

and

$$\text{Break-even volume} = \frac{FC}{CM} = \frac{\$25,000}{\$33} = 757.6 \text{ units}$$

The break-even point in this scenario would be 757.6 units per month (94.70% of capacity).

EXAMPLE 6.6C

USING THE CONTRIBUTION MARGIN APPROACH TO CVP ANALYSIS

Alberta Oilseed Co. processes rapeseed to produce canola oil and rapeseed meal. The company can process up to 20,000 tonnes of rapeseed per year. The company pays growers $800 per tonne, and each tonne yields $2000 worth of oil and meal. Variable processing costs are $470 per tonne, and fixed processing costs are $3,400,000 per year at all production levels. Administrative overhead is $3,000,000 per year regardless of the volume of production. Marketing and transportation costs work out to $230 per tonne processed.

a. Determine the break-even volume in terms of:
   (i)   tonnes of rapeseed processed per year.
   (ii) percent capacity utilization.
   (iii) dollar amount of product sales for the year.

b. In order to attain a net income of $2,400,000 in a year,
   (i)   how many tonnes of rapeseed must be processed and sold in the year?
   (ii) what dollar value of oil and meal must be sold?

c. What is the maximum price that the company can pay per tonne of rapeseed and still break even on a volume of 16,000 tonnes per year?

SOLUTION

From the given information,

$$\text{Full capacity} = 20{,}000 \text{ tonnes per year}$$
$$VC = \$800 + \$470 + \$230 = \$1500 \text{ per tonne}$$
$$S = \$2000 \text{ per (input) tonne}$$
$$FC = \$3{,}400{,}000 + \$3{,}000{,}000 = \$6{,}400{,}000 \text{ per year}$$

Hence,

$$CM = S - VC = \$2000 - \$1500 = \$500 \text{ per tonne}$$

a. **(i)** Break-even volume $= \dfrac{FC}{CM} = \dfrac{\$6{,}400{,}000}{\$500} = 12{,}800$ tonnes per year

   (ii) 12,800 tonnes per year represent $\dfrac{12{,}800}{20{,}000} \times 100\% = 64\%$ of capacity

   (iii) Sales revenue at the break-even point is 12,800($2000) = $25,600,000

b. **(i)** Each tonne above the break-even point contributes $CM = \$500$ to the net income. A net income of $2,400,000 will require the sale of

$$\frac{\$2{,}400{,}000}{\$500} = 4800 \text{ tonnes more than the break-even point}$$

   Total sales must be 12,800 + 4800 = 17,600 tonnes in the year.

   (ii) The sales revenue required to generate a net income of $2,400,000 is 17,600($2000) = $35,200,000

c. In this scenario, S and FC are unchanged but VC is higher, raising the break-even point from 12,800 tonnes to 16,000 tonnes. Since

$$\text{Break-even volume} = \frac{FC}{CM}$$

then

$$CM = \frac{FC}{\text{Break-even volume}} = \frac{\$6{,}400{,}000}{16{,}000} = \$400 \text{ per tonne}$$

This is $100 per tonne less than the former CM. Therefore, the VC per tonne is $100 higher, representing the increase in the price paid to rapeseed growers. The maximum price that can be paid to growers and still break even at a volume of 16,000 tonnes is $800 + $100 = $900 per tonne.

Contribution Rate

The contribution margin expressed as a percentage of the unit selling price is called the **contribution rate**, CR. That is,

CONTRIBUTION RATE FORMULA

$$CR = \frac{CM}{S} \times 100\% \tag{6-6}$$

You can think of the contribution rate as the percentage of the unit selling price that is available first to pay fixed costs and then to produce a profit.

It is also possible to calculate the contribution rate from a firm's total revenue and total variable costs in an operating period. To see how this can be done, substitute $CM = S - VC$ in the numerator above, and then multiply both the numerator and the denominator by X, the total units sold. We obtain

$$CR = \frac{(S - VC)X}{(S)X} = \frac{(S)X - (VC)X}{(S)X} = \frac{\text{Total revenue} - \text{Total variable costs}}{\text{Total revenue}}$$

Hence, the contribution rate may also be viewed as the percentage of total revenue available first to pay fixed costs and then to generate a profit. When revenue and cost information is available on an aggregate rather than on a per-unit basis, this approach must be used to calculate the contribution rate. At the break-even point, revenue will exceed total variable costs by the fixed costs exactly. Therefore,

$$CR = \frac{FC}{\text{Break-even revenue}}$$

If you already know the values for FC and CR, rearrange this equation to obtain the break-even revenue. That is,

$$\text{Break-even revenue} = \frac{FC}{CR}$$

EXAMPLE 6.6D

CVP ANALYSIS WITH SALES VOLUME IN DOLLARS INSTEAD OF UNITS

Last year Marconi Printing had total revenue of $375,000 while operating at 75% of capacity. The total of its variable costs was $150,000. Fixed costs were $180,000.

a. What is Marconi's break-even point expressed:

(i) in dollars of revenue?

(ii) as a percent of capacity?

b. If the current S, VC, and FC are the same as last year, what net income can be expected from revenue of $450,000 in the current year?

SOLUTION

When no information is provided about the unit price and unit variable cost, cost-volume-profit analysis may still be undertaken. The further assumption required is that the firm sells a single product or, if more than one product, the product mix does not change from one period to the next.

Although we do not have sufficient information to calculate the unit contribution margin, we can calculate the total contribution margin and the contribution rate. That is,

$$CR = \frac{\text{Total revenue} - \text{Total variable costs}}{\text{Total revenue}} \times 100\%$$
$$= \frac{\$375,000 - \$150,000}{\$375,000} \times 100\%$$
$$= 60\%$$

The most useful interpretation of this figure is that 60 cents from every dollar of revenue is the amount available to pay fixed costs. Once fixed costs are covered for the period, 60 cents of each additional dollar of revenue "flows through to the bottom line" (that is, becomes net income or operating profit for the period).

a. (i) The break-even point will occur when

$$\text{Revenue} = \frac{FC}{CR} = \frac{\$180,000}{0.60} = \$300,000$$

(ii) If revenue of $375,000 represents 75% of capacity, then

$$\text{Full capacity} = \frac{\$375,000}{0.75} = \$500,000 \text{ of revenue}$$

The break-even point of $300,000 represents

$$\frac{\$300,000}{\$500,000} \times 100\% = 60\% \text{ of capacity}$$

b. The new revenue level of $450,000 is $150,000 beyond the break-even point. Since $CR = 60\%$, then 60 cents of each dollar beyond the break-even point becomes net income. Hence,

$$\text{Net income} = 0.60 \times \$150,000 = \$90,000$$

Revenue of $450,000 in the current year should produce a net income of $90,000.

CONCEPT QUESTIONS

1. What effect will each of the following have on a product's unit contribution margin? In each case, assume that all other variables remain unchanged.

   a. The business raises the selling price of the product.

   b. The prices of some raw materials used in manufacturing decrease.

   c. The local regional government increases the business's property tax.

   d. The company's president is given a raise.

   e. The production workers receive a raise in their hourly rate.

2. Once a business is operating beyond the break-even point, why doesn't each additional dollar of revenue add a dollar to net income?

3. What effect will each of the following have on a firm's break-even point? In each case, assume that all other variables remain unchanged.

   a. Fixed costs decrease.

   b. Variable costs increase.

   c. Sales volume increases.

   d. Unit selling price decreases.

   e. The contribution ratio increases.

EXERCISE 6.6

Problems 1–26 in Exercise 6.5 *may be solved using the contribution margin approach.*

27. **Interactive Contribution Margin Chart** Connect provides an interactive Contribution Margin Chart. This chart presents a pictorial display of the components of total cost and total revenue from a contribution margin point of view. In Chapter 6 under the Student Resources, you will find a link to the Contribution Margin Chart.

    To improve your intuitive understanding of the contribution margin approach to CVP analysis, use the chart to solve some of Problems 3–9 and 12–14 in Exercise 6.5.

KEY TERMS

Break-even chart	Cost function	Slope
Break-even point	Cost-volume-profit analysis	Unit variable cost
Contribution margin	Fixed cost	Variable costs
Contribution rate	Revenue function	y-intercept

SUMMARY OF NOTATION AND KEY FORMULAS

The following notation was introduced for cost-volume-profit analysis:

S = Selling price or revenue per unit

CR = Contribution rate

VC = Variable costs per unit

X = Total number of units sold in the period

FC = Fixed costs
NI = Net income (or operating profit) for the period
CM = Contribution margin per unit
TR = Total revenue for the period
TC = Total costs for the period

FORMULA (6-1)	$TR = (S)X$ $TC = (VC)X + FC$	Finding the total revenue and total costs from the sale of X units
FORMULA (6-2)	$NI = (S - VC)X - FC$	Finding the net income from the sale of X units
FORMULA (6-3)	$\textit{Break-even volume} = \dfrac{FC}{S - VC}$	Finding the break-even volume
FORMULA (6-4)	$CM = S - VC$	Finding the contribution margin
FORMULA (6-5)	$NI = (CM)X - FC$	Finding the net income from the sale of X units
FORMULA (6-6)	$CR = \dfrac{CM}{S} \times 100\%$	Finding the contribution rate

REVIEW PROBLEMS

Answers to the odd-numbered review problems are at the end of the book.

BASIC PROBLEMS

1. **L06** Memex Corp. manufactures memory expansion boards for microcomputers. The average selling price of its finished product is $180 per unit. The average variable cost per unit is $110. Memex incurs fixed costs of $1,260,000 per year.
   a. What is the break-even point in unit sales?
   b. What sales revenue must Memex achieve in order to break even?
   c. What will be the company's profit or loss at the following levels of sales for a year:
      (i)   20,000 units?
      (ii) 17,500 units?
   d. How many units must they sell to have a net profit of $315,000?
   e. What level of output would they have to sustain a loss of no more than $124,250?
   f. What would be the new break-even number of units if fixed costs were reduced by 10%?

2. **L06** The Armour Company had the following revenue and costs in the most recently completed fiscal year:

Total revenue	$10,000,000
Total fixed costs	$2,000,000
Total variable costs	$6,000,000
Total units produced and sold	1,000,000

   a. What is the unit sales volume at the break-even point?
   b. How many units must be produced and sold for the company to have a net income of $1,000,000 for the year?

3. **L06** Fisher Publishing Inc. is doing a financial feasibility analysis for a new book. Editing and preproduction costs are estimated at $45,000. The printing costs are a flat $7000 for setup plus $8.00 per book. The author's royalty is 8% of the publisher's selling price to bookstores. Advertising and promotion costs are budgeted at $8000.
   a. If the price to bookstores is set at $35, how many books must be sold to break even? Round the answer up to the nearest whole number.
   b. The marketing department is forecasting sales of 4800 books at the $35 price. What will be the net income from the project at this volume of sales?

c. The marketing department is also forecasting that, if the price is reduced by 10%, unit sales will be 15% higher. Which price should be selected? (Show calculations that support your recommendation.)

d. In a highest-cost scenario, fixed costs might be $5000 higher and the printing costs might be $9.00 per book. By how many books would the break-even volume be raised?

INTERMEDIATE PROBLEMS

---

4. **LO5** Durable Toys Inc. wants to calculate from recent production data the monthly fixed costs and unit variable costs on its Mountain Trike product line. In the most recent month, it produced 530 trikes at a total cost of $24,190. In the previous month, it produced 365 trikes at a total cost of $18,745. What are the fixed costs per month and the unit variable costs? *Hint:* Recall that

Total costs = Fixed costs + (Unit variable costs) × (Number of units produced)

5. **LO6** During an economic slowdown, an automobile plant lost $12,000,000 on the production and sale of 9000 cars. Total revenue for the year was $270,000,000. If the break-even volume for the plant is 10,000 cars per year, calculate:

a. The plant's total fixed costs for a year.

b. The net income if unit sales for the year had been equal to the five-year average of 12,000.

6. **LO6** Norwood Industries has annual fixed costs of $1.8 million. Unit variable costs are currently 55% of the unit selling price.

a. What annual revenue is required to break even?

b. What revenue would result in a loss of $100,000 in a year?

c. What annual revenue would produce a profit of $300,000?

d. Market research indicates that if prices are increased by 10%, total revenue will remain at the part (c) amount because the higher prices will be offset by reduced sales volume. Will the operating profit remain at $300,000? Present calculations to justify your answer.

7. **LO6** Cambridge Manufacturing is evaluating the introduction of a new product that would have a unit selling price of $100. The total annual fixed costs are estimated to be $200,000, and the unit variable costs are projected at $60. Forecast sales volume for the first year is 8000 units.

a. What sales volume (in units) is required to break even?

b. What volume is required to generate a net income of $100,000?

c. What would be the net income at the forecast sales volume?

d. At the forecast sales volume, what will be the change in the net income if fixed costs are:

(i) 5% higher than expected?

(ii) 10% lower than expected?

e. At the forecast sales volume, what will be the change in the net income if unit variable costs are:

(i) 10% higher than expected?

(ii) 5% lower than expected?

f. At the forecast sales volume, what will be the change in the net income if the unit selling price is:

(i) 5% higher?

(ii) 10% lower?

g. At the forecast sales volume, what will be the change in the net income if unit variable costs are 10% higher than expected and fixed costs are simultaneously 10% lower than expected?

8. **LO6** To raise funds for its community activities, a Lions Club chapter is negotiating with International Carnivals to bring its midway rides and games to town for a three-day opening. The event will be held on part of the parking lot of a local shopping centre, which is to receive 10% of the gross revenue. The Lions Club members will sell the ride and game tickets at the site. International Carnivals requires either $15,000 plus 30% of revenue or $10,000 plus 50% of revenue. The experience of other towns that have held the event is that customers spend an average of $10 per person on rides and games.
   a. What is the break-even attendance under each basis for remunerating International Carnivals?
   b. For each alternative, what will be the club's profit or loss if the attendance is:
      (i) 3000?
      (ii) 2200?
   c. How would you briefly explain the advantages and disadvantages of the two alternatives to a club member?

9. **LO6** The monthly fixed costs of operating a 30-unit motel are $28,000. The price per unit per night for next year is set at $110. Costs arising from rentals on a per-unit per-day basis are $12 for maid service, $6 for supplies and laundry, and $6 for heat and utilities.
   a. Based on a 30-day month, at what average occupancy rate will the motel break even?
   b. What will the motel's net income be at an occupancy rate of:
      (i) 40%?
      (ii) 30%?
   c. Should the owner reduce the price from $110 to $94 per unit per night if it will result in an increase in the average occupancy rate from 40% to 50%? Present calculations that justify your answer.

CASE

Estimating the Contribution Rate in a Multi-Product Business

Classifying individual costs as either purely fixed or purely variable can be problematic, especially when a firm produces more than one product. Rather than determining FC and VC by analyzing each cost, you can use an income statement approach for estimating a firm's FC and average contribution rate, CR.

We will use two familiar formulas to develop an equation that will enable us to estimate FC and CR from a business's income statements. Recall that

$$CR = \frac{CM}{S} \quad \text{①} \qquad \text{and} \qquad NI = (CM)X - FC \text{②}$$

From ①, $CM = CR \times S$. Substitute this product for CM in ②, giving

$$NI = (CR \times S)X - FC$$

But NI is the net income or "bottom line" of an income statement and the product $(S)X$ is the total revenue or "top line" of an income statement. Therefore,

$$\text{Net income} = CR \times (\text{Total revenue}) - FC$$

If the average CR for all products does not change significantly from one year to the next and the fixed costs remain constant, we can use the income statements for the two years to construct two equations in two unknowns (CR and FC).

Suppose the income statements for Miscellaneous Manufacturing Ltd. (MML) showed the following results for Years 1 and 2.

Year	Total revenue ($)	Net income ($)
1	750,000	105,000
2	825,000	127,500

QUESTIONS

1. What are MML's total annual fixed costs and contribution rate?
2. What total revenue does MML require to break even?
3. What will be next year's net income based on revenue forecast to be $875,000?

APPENDIX 6A: THE TEXAS INSTRUMENTS BA II PLUS BREAK-EVEN WORKSHEET

The BA II PLUS's Owner's Manual uses the term "worksheet" to refer to a list of settings and functions designed for a particular application. Usually, a worksheet is the second function of a key. For example, the letters **BRKEVN** appear above the ⬚ 6 ⬚ key. These letters indicate that the Break-Even Worksheet is the second function of this key. You can access it by pressing ⬚ 2nd ⬚ ⬚ 6 ⬚ in sequence (rather than at the same time). Hereafter, we will represent these keystrokes as ⬚ 2nd ⬚ ⬚ BRKEVN ⬚ The calculator's display then shows:

$$FC = \qquad\qquad n,nnn.nn$$

where the n's represent numerical digits. (Your display may show more or fewer digits.)

You should think of a worksheet as a single column of items that you can view one-at-a-time in the display. The Break-Even Worksheet's column consists of the following five items:

$FC =$	n,nnn.nn
$VC =$	nn.nn
$P =$	nn.nn
$PFT =$	nnn.nn
$Q =$	n,nnn

The calculator's display provides a "window" to the first item in the column. You can use the scroll keys ⬚ ↓ ⬚ and ⬚ ↑ ⬚ to move down or up the list. The five worksheet symbols are defined as follows. (Unfortunately, three of the five symbols differ from the symbols used in the book.)

$$FC = \text{(Total) fixed costs}$$
$$VC = \text{Variable costs per unit}$$
$$P = \text{Selling price per unit (S in the book)}$$
$$PFT = \text{Profit or Net income (NI in the book)}$$
$$Q = \text{Number of units sold (X in the book)}$$

The Break-Even Worksheet allows you to enter values for any four of these five variables and then compute the value of the remaining fifth variable. We will use the worksheet to solve Problem 5 from **Exercise 6.5**. But first close the worksheet by pressing ⬚ 2nd ⬚ ⬚ QUIT ⬚ . (By the ⬚ QUIT ⬚ key, we mean the key in the upper left corner of the keypad showing **QUIT** as its second function.)

EXAMPLE 6A.A

USING THE BREAK-EVEN WORKSHEET TO SOLVE PROBLEM 5 FROM EXERCISE 6.5

In terms of the book's notation, we are given $S = \$2.50$ and $VC = \$1.00$.

a. We want to determine the break-even volume if $FC = \$60,000$ per month.

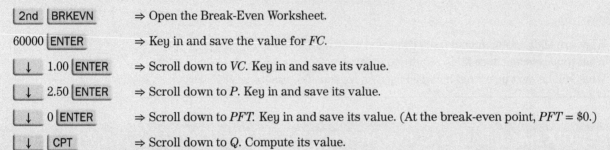

2nd BRKEVN	⇒ Open the Break-Even Worksheet.
60000 ENTER	⇒ Key in and save the value for FC.
↓ 1.00 ENTER	⇒ Scroll down to VC. Key in and save its value.
↓ 2.50 ENTER	⇒ Scroll down to P. Key in and save its value.
↓ 0 ENTER	⇒ Scroll down to PFT. Key in and save its value. (At the break-even point, $PFT = \$0$.)
↓ CPT	⇒ Scroll down to Q. Compute its value.

The answer that appears is 40,000. That is, 40,000 CDs per month must be sold to break even.

b. Now we want the number of units, X, that must be sold in order to have $NI = \$7500$ per month. If we do not clear the worksheet, the most recently entered and calculated values remain in memory. Therefore, we need only to change the value for "PFT" to \$7500 and then re-calculate "Q."

↑ 7500 ENTER	⇒ Scroll up to PFT. Key in and save its new value.
↓ CPT	⇒ Scroll back down to Q. Compute its new value.

The answer that appears is 45,000. That is, 45,000 CDs per month must be sold to generate a profit of \$7500 per month. (Press 2nd QUIT to close the worksheet.)

Chapter 7
Simple Interest

CHAPTER OUTLINE

7.1 Basic Concepts

7.2 Determining the Time Period (Term)

7.3 Maturity Value (Future Value) and Principal (Present Value)

7.4 Equivalent Payments

7.5 The Equivalent Value of a Payment Stream

*7.6 Loans: A Principle about Principal

*Appendix 7A: An Aid for Determining the Number of Days in Each Month

*Appendix 7B: The Texas Instruments BA II PLUS Date Worksheet

LEARNING OBJECTIVES

After completing this chapter, you will be able to:

LO1 Calculate interest, maturity value (future value), present value, rate, and time in a simple interest environment

LO2 Present details of the amount and timing of payments in a time diagram

LO3 Calculate the equivalent value on any date of a single payment or a stream of payments

EVERY DAY, MONEY IS BORROWED and loaned in millions of transactions. The transaction amounts range from a few dollars on credit-card purchases to multibillion-dollar refinancing of federal government debt.

Interest is the fee or rent that lenders charge for the use of their money. For many individuals and corporations, and for most provincial and federal governments, interest on debt is one of the largest expenditures in their annual budgets.

Clearly, debt plays a key role in our personal finances and our economic system. As a fundamental skill, you must be able to calculate interest on debt. But to be a truly effective participant in financial decision making, you must be able to analyze the broader effects that prevailing interest rates have on the value of personal investments and business assets. The remainder of the book is devoted to developing these skills and techniques.

In this chapter you will first learn how to calculate interest in the simple-interest system. We will then take the first step toward answering a central question in finance: "What is an investment worth?" This step involves the concept of "equivalent value." It is a far-reaching concept that will carry forward to the compound interest system in later chapters.

7.1 Basic Concepts

Borrowing and lending are two sides of the same transaction. The amount borrowed/loaned is called the **principal**. To the borrower, the principal is a *debt*; to the lender, the principal represents an *investment*.

The interest paid by the borrower is the lender's investment income. There are two systems[1] for calculating interest.

- **Simple interest** is used mainly for short-term loans and investments. (By "short-term," we mean durations of up to one year.) This chapter and **Chapter 8** cover the mathematics and applications of simple interest.
- *Compound* interest is used mainly for durations longer than one year. The mathematics and applications of compound interest are covered in **Chapter 9** and beyond.

The **rate of interest** is the amount of interest (expressed as a percentage of the principal) charged per period. Simple interest rates are usually calculated and quoted for a one-year period. Such a rate is often called a *per annum rate*. That is,

$$\text{Interest rate (per annum)} = \frac{\text{Annual interest}}{\text{Principal}} \times 100\%$$

Note: If a time interval (such as "per month") is not indicated for a quoted interest rate, assume the rate is an annual or per annum rate.

The rate of interest charged on a loan is the lender's rate of return on investment. (It seems more natural for us to take the borrower's point of view because we usually become borrowers before we become lenders.)

If you "go with your intuition," you will probably correctly calculate the amount of simple interest. For example, how much interest will $1000 earn in six months if it earns an 8% rate of interest? Your thinking probably goes as follows: "In one year, $1000 will earn $80 (8% of $1000). In six months ($\frac{1}{2}$ year), $1000 will earn only $40 ($\frac{1}{2}$ of $80)."

L01 Now write an equation for the preceding calculation, but in terms of the following symbols:

$$I = \text{Amount of interest paid or received}$$
$$P = \text{Principal amount of the loan or investment}$$
$$r = \text{Annual rate of simple interest}$$
$$t = \text{Time period (term), in years, of the loan or investment}$$

To obtain the $40 ($I$) amount, you multiplied $1000 ($P$) by 0.08 ($r$) and by $\frac{1}{2}$ year (t). In general,

AMOUNT OF SIMPLE INTEREST

$$I = Prt \qquad\qquad (7\text{-}1)$$

---

[1] We are *not* referring to two alternative methods for obtaining the same answer to an interest calculation. Rather, the two "systems" usually result in different amounts of interest being calculated.

TIP

Interest Rates in Algebraic Formulas

When substituting the numerical value for an interest rate into any equation or formula, you must use the decimal equivalent of the interest rate.

EXAMPLE 7.1A

CALCULATING THE AMOUNT OF INTEREST

What amount of interest will be charged on $6500 borrowed for five months at a simple interest rate of 6%?

SOLUTION

Given: $P = \$6500$, $t = \frac{5}{12}$ year, $r = 6\%$

Since no time period is given for the 6% rate, we understand that the rate is per year.

The amount of interest payable at the end of the loan period is

$$I = Prt = \$6500(0.06)\left(\tfrac{5}{12}\right) = \$162.50$$

EXAMPLE 7.1B

CALCULATING THE PRINCIPAL AMOUNT

If a three-month term deposit at a bank pays a simple interest rate of 1.5%, how much will have to be deposited to earn $100 of interest?

SOLUTION

Given: $t = \frac{3}{12}$ year, $r = 1.5\%$, $I = \$100$. Substitute these values into $I = Prt$.

$$\$100 = P(0.015)\left(\tfrac{3}{12}\right)$$
$$\$100 = 0.00375P$$

Solving for P,
$$P = \frac{\$100}{0.00375} = \$26{,}666.67$$

$26,666.67 must be placed in the three-month term deposit to earn $100 of interest.

EXAMPLE 7.1C

CALCULATING THE INTEREST RATE

Interest of $429.48 was charged on a loan of $9500 for seven months. What simple annual rate of interest was charged on the loan?

SOLUTION

Given: $I = \$429.48$, $P = \$9500$, and $t = \frac{7}{12}$ years. Substitute these values into $I = Prt$.

$$\$429.48 = \$9500(r)\tfrac{7}{12}$$
$$\$429.48 = \$5541.67r$$

Solving for r,
$$r = \frac{\$429.48}{\$5541.67} = 0.0775 = 7.75\%$$

An interest rate of 7.75% was charged on the loan.

EXAMPLE 7.1D

CALCULATING THE TIME PERIOD

The interest earned on a $6000 investment was $120. What was the term in months if the interest rate was 3%?

SOLUTION

Given: $P = \$6000$, $I = \$120$, and $r = 3\%$. Substitute these values into $I = Prt$.

$$\$120 = \$6000(0.03)t$$

Solving for t,

$$t = \frac{\$120}{\$6000(0.03)}$$

$$t = 0.66667 \text{ year} = 0.66667(12 \text{ months}) = 8 \text{ months}$$

The term of the investment was 8 months.

EXAMPLE 7.1E

USING MONTHS AS THE UNIT OF TIME

The simple interest rate being charged on a $5000 loan is three-quarters of 1% per month. If the principal and interest are to be paid in nine months, how much interest will be charged?

SOLUTION

Given: $P = \$5000$, term = 9 months, interest rate = 0.75% per month

We normally use Formula (7-1), with r representing the *annual* rate of interest and t representing the term in *years*. However, we can substitute the *monthly* interest rate for r if the term t is measured in *months*. We will present both approaches.

Method 1: With time expressed in years,

$$t = \tfrac{9}{12} = 0.75 \text{ year} \quad \text{and} \quad r = 12(0.75\%) = 9\% \text{ per year}$$
$$I = Prt = \$5000 \times 0.09 \times 0.75 = \$337.50$$

Method 2: With time expressed in months,

$$t = 9 \text{ months} \quad \text{and} \quad r = 0.75\% \text{ per month}$$
$$I = Prt = \$5000 \times 0.0075 \times 9 = \$337.50$$

The interest that will be charged on the loan is $337.50.

EXAMPLE 7.1F

REFINANCING A SIMPLE INTEREST LOAN

Lola borrowed $1500 at 6% simple interest for 9 months. At the end of 9 months, she could not repay the loan and decided to refinance the loan plus the accumulated interest for another 6 months at 7.5% simple interest. How much total interest was she charged?

SOLUTION

Given: $P = \$1500$, term = 9 months, interest rate = 6% per year
Substitute these values into $I = Prt$.

$$I = \$1500(0.06)\left(\tfrac{9}{12}\right)$$
$$I = \$67.50$$

For the next 6 months, $P = \$1500 + \$67.50 = \$1567.50$, term = 6 months, interest rate = 7.5% per year
Interest for the refinancing is

$$I = \$1567.50(0.075)\left(\tfrac{6}{12}\right)$$
$$I = \$58.78$$

The total interest that will be charged on the loan is $67.50 + $58.78 = $126.28.

EXERCISE 7.1

Answers to the odd-numbered problems are at the end of the book.

Spreadsheet template: *Connect presents a partially completed Excel template for a Simple-Interest Calculator. Go to the Student Edition of Connect and find "Simple-Interest Calculator" under the Student Resources for Chapter 7. After you program the output cells in the template, you can use it for solving any of the following problems.*

BASIC PROBLEMS

1. How much interest was paid on a $1500 loan for seven months at an annual interest rate of 4.5%?

2. Montel loaned $6800 to a friend for 13 months at an annual rate of 7.7% simple interest. How much interest did the borrower owe?

3. A $25,000 investment earned 0.25% per month simple interest for a three-month term. What total amount of interest was earned?

4. What was the term of a $4850 loan at 4.5% if the interest due at the end was $145.50?

5. The interest paid at the end of the term of a $9125 loan at 0.8% per month was $511.00. Calculate the term of the loan.

6. The interest paid on an 11-month loan at $10\frac{1}{4}$% was $328.85. What was the principal amount of the original loan?

7. What annual rate of interest was earned if a $15,000 investment for five months earned $546.88 in interest?

8. $890 interest was charged on $8900 borrowed on a simple interest basis for eight months. What was the interest rate per month on the loan?

9. How much interest will be earned on $5000 in five months if the interest rate is 5.5%?

10. An invoice states that interest will be charged on overdue accounts at the rate of $1\frac{1}{2}$% per month. What will the interest charges be on a $3760 billing that is three months overdue?

11. The interest owed on a loan after five months was $292.50. If the simple interest rate charged on the loan was 0.9% per month, what was the amount borrowed?

12. How much must be placed in a five-month term deposit earning 4.3% simple interest in order to earn $500 interest?

13. A five-month term deposit of $10,000 at Scotiabank earned $175 in interest. What annual rate of simple interest did the deposit earn?

14. Indira paid interest charges of $169.05 on a $4830 invoice that was two months overdue. What monthly rate of simple interest was she charged?

15. Morgan loaned $3100 to Rolf at a simple interest rate of 0.65% per month. What was the term of the loan if the total interest came to $221.65?

16. Asher cashed in a one-year term deposit after only five months had elapsed. In order to do so, he accepted an interest rate penalty—a reduction from the scheduled 5.5% rate of simple interest. If he was paid $145.83 interest on the $10,000 term deposit, what reduction was made in the per annum rate of simple interest?

INTERMEDIATE PROBLEM

17. Sumer put $10,000 in a three-month term deposit at TD Canada Trust, earning a simple interest rate of 2.2%. After the three months, she invested the entire amount of the principal and interest from the first term deposit in a new three-month term deposit earning the same rate of interest. How much interest did she earn on each term deposit? Why are the two interest amounts not equal?

18. Sergon has $5000 to invest for six months. The rates offered on three-month and six-month term deposits at his bank are 5.5% and 5.8%, respectively. He is trying to choose between the six-month term deposit and two consecutive three-month term deposits. What would the simple interest rate on three-month term deposits have to be, three months from now, for Sergon to end up in the same financial position with either alternative? Assume that he would place both the principal and the interest from the first three-month term deposit in the second three-month term deposit.

7.2 Determining the Time Period (Term)

Whenever possible, the time period t should be determined using the *exact* number of days in the term. If the only information you are given is that a loan is for a three-month term, the best you can do is to use $t = \frac{3}{12} = 0.25$ year. But if you know that the three-month loan was advanced on September 21, you should determine the exact number of days to the December 21 repayment date.

The most common practice among Canadian financial institutions is to count the starting date (September 21 in this case) *but not the ending date* (December 21). The reason for doing this is that they base their interest calculations on each day's *closing* balance on a loan or savings account. There is a non-zero balance on the day you receive a loan or make a deposit, but zero balance on the day you repay the loan in full or withdraw the deposit.

The numbers of days in each month are listed in **Table 7.1**. The three-month loan period from September 21 to December 21 includes 10 days in September (September 21 to 30, inclusive), 31 days in October, 30 days in November, and 20 days in December (December 1 to 20, inclusive), giving a total of 91 days. The value that should be used for t is $\frac{91}{365} = 0.24932$ year.

TABLE 7.1	The Number of Days in Each Month				
Month	Days	Month	Days	Month	Days
January	31	May	31	September	30
February	28 or 29	June	30	October	31
March	31	July	31	November	30
April	30	August	31	December	31

APP 4 THAT

Many business-related activities require knowing the exact number of days between two dates, the day of the week a particular date falls, and the dates for statutory holidays. Search the App Store on your tablet, smartphone, or smart watch using the key words **DAYS BETWEEN DATES**.

You will find many free and paid apps that provide date-related information for simple applications like calculating interest to more complex activities like project planning.

Figure 7.4 in **Appendix 7A** presents the "knuckle and valley" technique for determining which months have 31 days.

Instead of using **Table 7.1**, another method for calculating the number of days in a loan period employs **Table 7.2**. In **Table 7.2**, the days of the year are numbered serially. The number of days in the interval between any two dates in the same calendar year is simply the difference between the serial numbers for the dates. When the term of a loan or investment includes a year-end, the use of **Table 7.2** is somewhat tricky. **Example 7.2A** includes one such case.

TABLE 7.2 The Serial Numbers for Each Day of the Year

Day of Month	Jan	Feb	Mar	Apr	May	Jun	Jul	Aug	Sep	Oct	Nov	Dec	Day of Month
1	1	32	60	91	121	152	182	213	244	274	305	335	1
2	2	33	61	92	122	153	183	214	245	275	306	336	2
3	3	34	62	93	123	154	184	215	246	276	307	337	3
4	4	35	63	94	124	155	185	216	247	277	308	338	4
5	5	36	64	95	125	156	186	217	248	278	309	339	5
6	6	37	65	96	126	157	187	218	249	279	310	340	6
7	7	38	66	97	127	158	188	219	250	280	311	341	7
8	8	39	67	98	128	159	189	220	251	281	312	342	8
9	9	40	68	99	129	160	190	221	252	282	313	343	9
10	10	41	69	100	130	161	191	222	253	283	314	344	10
11	11	42	70	101	131	162	192	223	254	284	315	345	11
12	12	43	71	102	132	163	193	224	255	285	316	346	12
13	13	44	72	103	133	164	194	225	256	286	317	347	13
14	14	45	73	104	134	165	195	226	257	287	318	348	14
15	15	46	74	105	135	166	196	227	258	288	319	349	15
16	16	47	75	106	136	167	197	228	259	289	320	350	16
17	17	48	76	107	137	168	198	229	260	290	321	351	17
18	18	49	77	108	138	169	199	230	261	291	322	352	18
19	19	50	78	109	139	170	200	231	262	292	323	353	19
20	20	51	79	110	140	171	201	232	263	293	324	354	20
21	21	52	80	111	141	172	202	233	264	294	325	355	21
22	22	53	81	112	142	173	203	234	265	295	326	356	22
23	23	54	82	113	143	174	204	235	266	296	327	357	23
24	24	55	83	114	144	175	205	236	267	297	328	358	24
25	25	56	84	115	145	176	206	237	268	298	329	359	25
26	26	57	85	116	146	177	207	238	269	299	330	360	26
27	27	58	86	117	147	178	208	239	270	300	331	361	27
28	28	59	87	118	148	179	209	240	271	301	332	362	28
29	29	*	88	119	149	180	210	241	272	302	333	363	29
30	30		89	120	150	181	211	242	273	303	334	364	30
31	31		90		151		212	243		304		365	31

*For leap years, February 29 becomes day number 60 and the serial number for each subsequent day in the table must be increased by 1.

Some financial calculator models have a "Days" or "Date" function that provides a third approach for determining the number of days between two dates. Instructions for using the "DATE" worksheet of the Texas Instruments BA II PLUS are presented in **Appendix 7B**. This worksheet will be employed as Method 3 in **Example 7.2A**.

 POINT OF INTEREST

Which Years Are Leap Years?

A normal calendar year has 365 days, but every four years we add an extra day to compensate for the fact that Earth rotates just over 365 times in a year. Leap day, February 29, makes the calendar year 366 days long every four years. To know if any year is a leap year there are three criteria. You know it is a leap year if:
- The year CAN be evenly divided by 4 (e.g., 2016, 2020)
- The year CANNOT be evenly divided by 100, except if
  - The year CAN be divided by 400 (e.g., 2000, 2400)

February 2020						
SUN	MON	TUE	WED	THU	FRI	SAT
						1
2	3	4	5	6	7	8
9	10	11	12	13	14	15
16	17	18	19	20	21	22
23	24	25	26	27	28	29

© McGraw-Hill Education

EXAMPLE 7.2A

CALCULATING AND USING THE EXACT NUMBER OF DAYS

a. Calculate the term for each of the following loans.

b. Calculate the interest due on the repayment date for each loan.

	Loan principal ($)	Date advanced	Date repaid	Interest rate
(i)	3000	March 31, 2019	September 4, 2019	$7\frac{3}{4}\%$
(ii)	14,600	January 11, 2020	June 4, 2020	$9\frac{1}{4}\%$
(iii)	23,000	November 29, 2018	April 1, 2019	6.9%

SOLUTION

a. The term will be calculated by three methods:

Method 1:   Counting the number of days of each partial and full month within the interval (using **Table 7.1**).
Method 2:   Using the serial numbers of the beginning date and the ending date (from **Table 7.2**).
Method 3:   Using the "DATE" worksheet of the Texas Instruments BA II PLUS calculator.

Method 1:   (using **Table 7.1**)

(i)		(ii)		(iii)	
Month	**Days**	**Month**	**Days**	**Month**	**Days**
March	1	January	21	November	2
April	30	February	29	December	31
May	31	March	31	January	31
June	30	April	30	February	28
July	31	May	31	March	31
August	31	June	3	April	0
September	3				
Total	157	Total	145	Total	123

Method 2:   (using **Table 7.2**) Particularly when the term of the loan includes a year-end, it is helpful to draw a time line showing the dates on which the loan was advanced and repaid. Look up the serial numbers for these dates in **Table 7.2**, and write them on the time line.

(i)

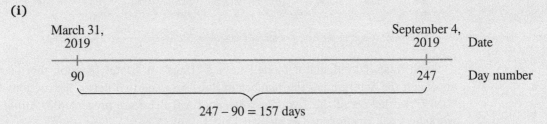

The term of the loan is 157 days.

(ii)   When a date falls after February 29 of a leap year, you must add one day to the serial number obtained from **Table 7.2**.

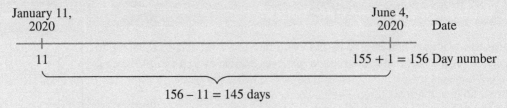

The term of the loan is 145 days.

(iii)

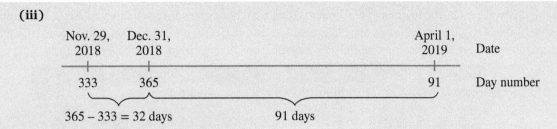

365 – 333 = 32 days   91 days

The term of the loan is 32 + 91 = 123 days.

Method 3:   Using the "DATE" worksheet of the Texas Instruments BA II PLUS calculator as described in **Appendix 7B**.

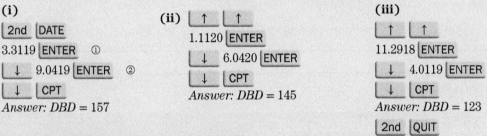

① This enters March 31, 2019 as the beginning of the interval.

② This enters September 4, 2019 as the end of the interval.

b. Each loan's term should be expressed as a fraction of a year when substituted in Formula (7-1).

(i) $I = Prt = \$3000(0.0775)\left(\dfrac{157}{365}\right) = \$100.01$

(ii) $I = Prt = \$14,600(0.0925)\left(\dfrac{145}{365}\right) = \$536.50$

When the term of a short-term loan or investment includes part of a leap year, there is no uniform practice across financial institutions for adjusting the length of the year in the denominator of t (*time*). The majority continue to use 365 days as the length of the year. In this book we will follow the majority and always use 365 days in the denominator. If a loan period includes February 29, as in this example, that extra day is counted in the numerator of t (*time*).

(iii) $I = Prt = \$23,000(0.069)\left(\dfrac{123}{365}\right) = \$534.80$

Variable or Floating Interest Rates

The interest rate on short-term loans is often linked to the "prime rate" charged by the chartered banks. The **prime rate of interest** is the banks' lowest lending rate—it is available only on the most secure loans. Less secure loans are charged anywhere from $\frac{1}{2}\%$ to 5% more than the prime rate. The chartered banks change the prime rate from time to time in response to interest rate movements in the financial markets. When a loan's interest rate is linked to the prime rate (for example, prime + 2%), it is described as a *variable* interest rate or a *floating* interest rate.

EXAMPLE 7.2B

FLOATING INTEREST RATES

Lajos borrowed $5000 on April 7 at prime + 1%. The prime rate was initially 3%. It increased to $3\frac{1}{4}\%$ effective May 23, and $3\frac{1}{2}\%$ effective July 13. What amount was required to repay the loan on August 2?

SOLUTION

The statement that the interest rate "increased to $3\frac{1}{4}\%$ effective May 23" means that interest was charged for May 23 (and subsequent days) at the new $3\frac{1}{4}\%$ rate. We need to break the overall loan period into intervals within which the interest rate is constant.

In the following table, the beginning and ending dates have been given for each interval. Since we count the first day but not the last day in an interval, May 23 is counted only in the second interval and July 13 is counted only in the third interval. This is consistent with the new interest rates taking effect on May 23 and July 13.

Interval	Number of days	Interest rate	Interest ($)
April 7 to May 23	24 + 22 = 46	3 + 1 = 4%	25.205 ①
May 23 to July 13	9 + 30 + 12 = 51	3.25 + 1 = 4.25%	29.692 ②
July 13 to August 2	19 + 1 = 20	3.5 + 1 = 4.5%	12.329
		Total:	67.23

① Interest $= Prt = \$5000(0.04)\frac{46}{365} = \$25.205$

② Interest $= Prt = \$5000(0.0425)\frac{51}{365} = \$29.692$

The amount required to repay the loan on August 2 was $5000 + $67.23 = $5067.23.

POINT OF INTEREST

Card Tricks: Taking More Interest

If you always pay your credit-card balance in full during the *grace period* (the time between the statement date and the payment due date), you pay no interest on retail purchases made on your credit card. The minimum grace period (set by government regulations) is 21 days. Approximately two-thirds of Canadians pay in full during the grace period. In effect, they receive an interest-free loan on each retail purchase from the date of purchase to the date on which the credit card's balance is paid.

The other one-third of Canadians, who make only partial payments each month, are usually aware of the interest rates charged by credit cards—9.4% to 14% on "low-rate" cards, 18% to 20% on "regular" cards. (Aren't we fortunate there are no "high-rate" cards?) But most people are unaware of the details of how these rates are applied—details that make credit-card debt more costly than consumers think.

Trick #1: The Vanishing Interest-Free Period—There are a couple scenarios under which the interest-free period will vanish.

Scenario A: After many months of paying your full balance before the due date, you pay only half the balance in a particular month. You might reasonably assume that no interest will be charged for the portion of your retail purchases covered by the partial payment. Wrong! In the following month's statement, you will be charged interest on all of the previous statement's purchases right from their purchase dates. Partial payments are not entitled to any interest-free period.

Scenario B: You have been making only partial payments for several months. You now have your financial act together and pay off the entire balance on the current October statement. You might reasonably expect that no interest charges will appear on your November statement for the purchases listed in the preceding October statement. Not necessarily so! Some credit card issuers require that the September statement *also* had to be paid in full for you not to be charged interest in the November statement for purchases appearing on the October statement. (You can obtain a vast amount of information about credit cards from the Web site of the Financial Consumer Agency of Canada: **www.fcac-acfc.gc.ca**. It describes two methods employed for determining interest-free status, and indicates the method used by each credit card.)

Trick #2: The Disappearing Grace Period—If you withdraw cash from your credit card account, you will be charged interest (at your credit card's high rate) for *every* day from the date of withdrawal to the date of repayment. In addition, you may be charged a service fee and an ABM fee. The grace period does not apply to a cash advance even if you pay your balance in full.

Trick #3: The Illusion of Convenience Cheques—The credit-card issuer will sometimes mail "convenience cheques" to you. If you use one to make a payment, the transaction is treated as a cash advance—no interest-free period, no grace period (and really no convenience!).

Trick #4: The Interest-Rate Switch—Many credit-card issuers offer a six-month low-interest-rate inducement for you to transfer your balance from another credit card. But if you are late on a single payment, the low rate is replaced by a much higher one.

Trick #5: Psychic Powers—Electronic messaging occurs at millisecond speed in cyberspace. You might reasonably expect that the processing of electronic payments is virtually instantaneous. This would allow you to make your online credit card payment on the due date or, just to be safe, on the preceding day. Some people who have done this later discovered late-payment finance charges on their subsequent statement. It turns out that the processing of online payments can be surprisingly slow. But that's the card issuer's problem, not yours—right? Wrong! The fine print of the typical Cardholder Agreement points out that "it is *your* responsibility to ensure that payments are received by us by each Payment Due Date." How are you supposed to know how long it will take—some sort of psychic power? One credit-card issuer cautions that it can take three to five days.

EXERCISE 7.2

Answers to the odd-numbered problems are at the end of the book.

A	B
1	
2	
3	

Spreadsheet template: *Connect presents a partially completed Excel template for a Days-Between-Dates Calculator. Go to the Student Edition of Connect and find "Days-Between-Dates Calculator" under the Student Resources for Chapter 7. After you program the output cell in the template, you can use it in the solutions for Problems 1–10, and 19–24.*

BASIC PROBLEMS

1. A $3800 loan at 7.5% was advanced on June 17, 2019. How much interest was due when the loan was repaid on October 1, 2019?

2. How much interest accrued from November 30, 2018, to March 4, 2019, on a $7350 loan at 7.5%?

3. An $85,000 investment earned a 3.9% rate of simple interest from December 1, 2019, to May 30, 2020. How much interest was earned?

4. $850 borrowed on January 7, 2019, was repaid with interest at an annual rate of 7% on July 1, 2019. What was the amount of interest?

5. The interest rate on $27,000 borrowed on October 16, 2020, was 5.7%. How much interest was owed on the April 15, 2021, repayment date?

6. A $14,400 loan taken out on May 21, 2018, was repaid with interest at $11\frac{1}{4}$% per annum on July 19, 2019. How much interest was paid?

7. If $40.52 interest accrued on a $1000 guaranteed investment certificate (GIC) from January 15, 2019, to July 7, 2019, what rate of simple interest did the GIC earn?

8. What was the principal amount of a loan at $9\frac{1}{2}$% if $67.78 of interest accrued from October 28, 2018, to April 14, 2019?

9. On June 26 Laura put $2750 into a term deposit until September 3, when she needs the money for tuition, books, and other expenses to return to college. For term deposits in the 60- to 89-day range, her credit union pays an interest rate of 3%. How much interest will she earn on the term deposit?

10. Raimo borrowed $750 from Chris on October 30 and agreed to repay the debt with simple interest at the rate of 12.3% on May 10. How much interest was owed on May 10? Assume that February has 28 days.

11. Joyce had $2149 in her daily interest savings account for the entire month of June. Her account was credited with interest of $2.65 on June 30 (for the exact number of days in June). What annual rate of simple interest did her balance earn?

12. Maia's chequing account was $329 overdrawn beginning on September 24. On October 9 she made a deposit that restored a credit balance. If she was charged overdraft interest of $2.50, what annual rate of simple interest was charged?

13. In addition to a $2163 refund of her income tax overpayment, the Canada Revenue Agency (CRA) paid Raisa $13.36 of interest on the overpayment. If the simple interest rate paid by the CRA was 5.5%, how many days' interest was paid?

14. Megan was charged $124.83 interest on her bank loan for the period September 18 to October 18. If the rate of interest on her loan was 8.25%, what was the outstanding principal balance on the loan during the period?

15. On June 26, 2019, $1000 was borrowed at an interest rate of 4.55%. On what date was the loan repaid if the amount of accrued interest was $11.47?

16. $1000 was invested on April 18, 2019, in a GIC earning 7.7% per annum. On its maturity date, the certificate paid $32.28 interest. On what date did it mature?

17. On what date was a $1000 loan granted if the interest accrued as of November 16, 2019, was $50.05? The interest rate on the loan was $7\frac{1}{4}$%.

18. The $1000 principal amount of a loan was repaid on March 13, 2019, along with accrued interest in the amount of $49.42. If the interest rate on the loan was 11%, on what date was the loan advanced?

19. Bruce borrowed $6000 from Darryl on November 23. When Bruce repaid the loan, Darryl charged $127.60 interest. If the rate of simple interest on the loan was $6\frac{3}{4}$%, on what date did Bruce repay the loan? Assume that February has 28 days.

20. Sharon's $9000 term deposit matured on March 16, 2019. Based on a simple interest rate of 3.75%, she received $110.96 in interest. On what date did she originally make the term deposit?

21. Mario borrowed $6000 on March 1 at a variable rate of interest. The interest rate began at 7.5%, increased to 8% effective April 17, and then fell by 0.25% effective June 30. How much interest will be owed on the August 1 repayment date?

22. Penny invested $4500 on October 28 at a floating rate of interest that initially stood at 6.3%. Effective December 2, the rate dropped by $\frac{1}{2}$%, and then it declined another $\frac{1}{4}$% effective February 27. What total amount of principal plus interest will Penny receive when the investment matures on March 15? Assume that the new year is a leap year.

23. How much will be required on February 1 to pay off a $3000 loan advanced on the previous September 30 if the variable interest rate began the interval at 4.7%, rose to 5.2% effective November 2, and then dropped back to 5% effective January 1?

24. The total accrued interest owed as of August 31 on a loan advanced the preceding June 3 was $169.66. If the variable interest rate started at $8\frac{3}{4}$%, rose to 9% effective July 1, and increased another $\frac{1}{2}$% effective July 31, what was the principal amount of the loan?

7.3 Maturity Value (Future Value) and Principal (Present Value)

LO1 When a loan or investment reaches the end of its term, we say it "matures." The last day of the term is called the **maturity date**. The **maturity value** (or **future value**) is the total of the original principal plus interest due on the maturity date. Using the symbol S to represent the maturity value (or future value), we have

$$S = P + I$$

Substituting $I = Prt$, we obtain

$$S = P + Prt$$

Extracting the common factor P yields:

MATURITY VALUE (FUTURE VALUE)

$$S = P(1 + rt) \tag{7-2}$$

EXAMPLE 7.3A

CALCULATING THE MATURITY VALUE

Celia invests $1500 by lending it to Adnan for eight months at an interest rate of $4\frac{1}{4}\%$. What is the maturity value of the loan?

SOLUTION

This problem reminds us that the borrower's debt is the lender's investment.

Given: $P = \$1500$, $t = \frac{8}{12}$ year, $r = 4.25\%$

The maturity value of the loan is:

$$S = (1 + rt)$$
$$= \$1500\left[1 + 0.0425\left(\tfrac{8}{12}\right)\right]$$
$$= \$1500(1.028333)$$
$$= \$1542.50$$

Note that this answer can be obtained just as easily by first calculating the interest due at maturity using $I = Prt$. Then simply add the principal to obtain the maturity value ($S = P + I$). The choice of method is a matter of personal preference.

The maturity value that Adnan must pay to Celia at the end of the eight months is $1542.50.

L01 The principal amount invested or (*present value*) can be determined by substituting in the values for S, r, and t in Formula (7-2) and solving for P. However, we will use a rearranged version of Formula (7-2) for the calculation of present value since it is used extensively in **Section 7.4**.

Using Formula (7-2)

$$S = P(1 + rt)$$

We rearrange to solve for P:

PRINCIPAL VALUE (PRESENT VALUE)
$$P = \frac{S}{1 + rt} \qquad (7\text{-}3)$$

EXAMPLE 7.3B

CALCULATING THE PRINCIPAL

What amount of money would have to be invested at $3\frac{3}{4}\%$ to grow to $10,000 after 291 days?

SOLUTION

Given: $r = 3.75\%$, $S = \$10,000$, $t = \frac{291}{365}$ years

Substitute the known values into Formula (7-3) and then solve for P.

$$P = \frac{S}{1 + rt}$$
$$P = \frac{\$10,000}{1 + 0.0375\left(\frac{291}{365}\right)} = \frac{\$10,000}{1.029897} = \$9709.71$$

The reasoning for showing seven figures in the value for $(1 + rt)$ is as follows. Common sense tells us that P will be less than $10,000 (the maturity value of the deposit). To obtain P accurate to the cent, we require six-figure accuracy in the final result. Therefore, we must maintain at least one more figure (for a total of seven figures) in intermediate results.

The required investment is $9709.71

TIP

Solving for "r" or "t"

If any three of the four variables S, P, r, and t are known, Formula (7-2) can be used to solve for the remaining variable. However, the manipulations required to solve for r or t are not trivial. In these cases it is usually simpler to first calculate $I = S - P$ and then solve $I = Prt$ for r or t. The following example illustrates the latter approach.

EXAMPLE 7.3C

CALCULATING THE INTEREST RATE

Liam put $9500 in a term deposit on May 22. It matured on September 4 at $9588.82. What interest rate did he earn on his term deposit?

SOLUTION

Given: $P = \$9500$; $S = \$9588.82$; the term runs from May 22 to September 4

Hence,

$$I = S - P = \$9588.82 - \$9500 = \$88.82$$

and, using **Table 7.2**,

$$t = 247 \text{ (September 4)} - 142 \text{ (May 22)} = 105 \text{ days}$$

The annual rate of simple interest is

$$r = \frac{I}{Pt} = \frac{\$88.82}{\$9500 \times \frac{105}{365}} = 0.03250 = 3.25\%$$

Liam earned an interest rate of 3.25% on his term deposit.

EXAMPLE 7.3D

REINVESTING SIMPLE INTEREST PROCEEDS

Kyle has a 90-day $5000 term deposit about to mature at the Bank of Nova Scotia. The interest rate on the term deposit is 3%. Since he does not need the money for at least another 90 days, Kyle instructs the bank to "roll over" the proceeds of the maturing term deposit into a new 90-day term deposit. The prevailing rate for 90-day deposits is now 2.75%. What will be the maturity value of the second term deposit?

SOLUTION

The maturity value of the first term deposit is

$$S = P(1 + rt) = \$5000\left(1 + 0.03 \times \frac{90}{365}\right) = \$5036.99$$

The entire maturity value of the maturing deposit becomes the beginning principal for the second term deposit. The maturity value of Kyle's second term deposit will be

$$S = P(1 + rt) = \$5036.99\left(1 + 0.0275 \times \frac{90}{365}\right) = \$5071.14$$

EXERCISE 7.3

Answers to the odd-numbered problems are at the end of the book.

A	B
1	
2	
3	

Spreadsheet templates: The solutions for all of the following problems can employ one or another of the four partially completed Excel templates. Use the template on Connect for "Simple Interest Calculator" found under the Student Resources for Chapter 7. The templates come with instructions for completing them.

BASIC PROBLEMS

1. What will be the maturity value after seven months of $2950 earning interest at the rate of $4\frac{1}{2}\%$?

2. $12,800 was invested in a 237-day term deposit earning $3\frac{3}{4}\%$. What was its maturity value?

3. What will be the maturity value in 15 months of a $4500 loan at a simple interest rate of 7.9%?

4. Cecile placed $17,000 in a 270-day term deposit earning 4.25%. How much will the bank pay Cecile on the maturity date?

5. What was the principal amount of a loan at $10\frac{1}{2}\%$, if total amount owed after 23 days was $785.16?

6. The maturity value of an investment earning 7.7% per annum for a 360-day term was $2291.01. What amount was originally invested?

7. The balance after 11 months, including interest, on a loan at 9.9% is $15,379.58. What are the principal and interest components of the balance?

8. $7348.25 was the amount required to pay off a loan after 14 months. If the loan was at $8\frac{1}{4}\%$ per annum simple interest, how much of the total was interest?

9. What was the interest rate on a $1750 loan, if the amount required to pay off the loan after five months was $1828.02?

10. A $2875.40 investment grew to $3000 after eight months. What annual rate of simple interest did it earn?

11. Marliss made a $780.82 purchase on her Visa card. Including 45 days' interest, the amount billed on her credit card was $798.63. What annual interest rate does her card charge?

12. The amount required to settle a $680 debt after 300 days was $730.30. What rate of interest was charged on the debt?

13. Janesh has savings of $9625.63. If he can invest this amount to earn 2.8%, how many days will it take for the investment to grow to $9,800?

14. The amount required to pay off a $3500 loan at 8.4% was $3646.60. What was the term (in days) of the loan?

15. A $7760 investment earning $6\frac{1}{4}\%$ matured at $8083.33. What was the term (in months) of the investment?

16. The interest rate on an $859.50 debt was $10\frac{1}{4}\%$. For how many months was the loan outstanding if it was settled with a payment of $907.22?

17. Judith received the proceeds from an inheritance on March 25. She wants to set aside enough on March 26 so that she will have $20,000 available on October 1 to purchase a car when the new models are introduced. If the current interest rate on 181- to 270-day term deposits is 3.75%, what amount should she place in the term deposit?

18. The bookkeeper for Durham's Garage is trying to allocate to principal and interest a payment that was made to settle a loan. The cheque stub has the note "$3701.56 for principal and 7 months' interest at 12.5%." What are the principal and interest components of the payment?

19. The annual $3600 membership fee at the Oak Meadows Golf Club is due at the beginning of the year. Instead of a single "lump" payment, a member can pay $1600 at the start of the year and defer the $2000 balance for five months by paying a $75 surcharge at the time of the second payment. Effectively, what annual rate of simple interest is Oak Meadows charging on the $2000 deferred payment?

20. The snow tires that you are planning to buy next October 1 at the regular price of $107.50 each are advertised at $89.95 in a spring clearance special that will end on the preceding March 25. What annual rate of simple interest will you earn if you "invest" in the new snow tires at the sale price on March 25 instead of waiting until October 1 to buy them at the regular price?

21. A&B Appliances sells a washer-dryer combination for $1535 cash. C&D Appliances offers the same combination for $1595 with no payments and no interest for six months. Therefore, you can pay $1535 now or invest the $1535 for six months and then pay $1595. What value would the annual rate of return have to exceed for the second alternative to be to your advantage?

22. How many days will it take $2500 to grow to $2614.47 at an annual rate of 8.75%?

INTERMEDIATE PROBLEMS

23. Karin borrowed $2000 at $10\frac{1}{4}\%$ on July 13. On what date would the amount owed first exceed $2100?

24. On what date did a corporation borrow $350,000 at 7.5% from its bank if the debt was settled by a payment of $356,041 on February 28?

25. Village Finance Co. advanced three loans to Kamiko—$2200 on June 23, $1800 on August 5, and $1300 on October 31. Simple interest at 7.25% was charged on all three loans, and all were repaid on December 31 when some bonds that she owned matured. What total amount was required to pay off the loans?

26. The cash balance in Amalia's account with her stockbroker earns interest on the daily balance at an annual rate of 4%. Accrued interest is credited to her account every six months—on June 30 and December 31. As a result of the purchase and sale of securities from time to time, the account's balance changed as follows:

Period	Balance
January 1 to March 3	$3347
March 4 to May 23	$8687
May 24 to June 16	$2568
June 17 to June 30	$5923

What interest was credited to Amalia's account on June 30? The brokerage firm includes interest for both January 1 and June 30 in the June 30 payment. Assume that February had 28 days.

27. Dominion Contracting invested surplus funds in term deposits. All were chosen to mature on April 1 when the firm intends to purchase a new grader.

Investment date	Amount invested	Interest rate	Maturity date
November 16	$74,000	6.3%	April 1
December 30	$66,000	5.9%	April 1
February 8	$92,000	5.1%	April 1

What total amount will be available from the maturing term deposits on April 1 (of a leap year)?

TIP

Now Hear This ...

The concepts that will be developed in **Sections 7.4** and **7.5** are fundamental to many other topics and applications in later chapters. If you invest extra effort at this stage to gain a thorough understanding of these concepts, it will pay substantial dividends later.

7.4 Equivalent Payments

Suppose you can choose to receive either $100 today or $105 one year from now. If you choose $100 today, you can invest it at 5% and receive $105 after one year. With either alternative, you *can* end up with $105 one year from now.

L03 This simple example illustrates the concept of *economically equivalent* payments (which we usually shorten to "equivalent payments") or the *time value of money*. Alternative payments that enable you to end up with the same dollar amount at a later date are called **equivalent payments**. Interest rates play a key role in determining equivalent payments. If the interest rate had been 6% instead of 5% in our example, you would require $106 one year from now as the amount equivalent to $100 today.

In the terminology of **Section 7.3**, the later equivalent payment ($105) is just the future value of the alternative payment ($100) after one year. That is,

$$S = P(1 + rt) = \$100(1 + 0.05 \times 1) = \$100(1.05) = \$105$$

In **Section 7.3**, Formulas (7-2) and (7-3) described the mathematical relationship between the principal (P) and the maturity value (S). It *also* represents the relationship between a **P**rior equivalent payment (P) and a **S**ubsequent equivalent payment (S). In this context, r represents the interest rate that invested funds can earn during the time interval, t, between the alternative payments. In our word problems, we use expressions such as "Money can earn x%" or "Money is worth x%" or "Money can be invested at x%" to specify this interest rate.

L01 The term **present value** is commonly used to refer to an economically equivalent amount at a *prior* date; **future value** is used for an equivalent amount at a *later* date.

EXAMPLE 7.4A

CALCULATING THE EQUIVALENT PAYMENT AT A LATER DATE

Herb is supposed to pay $1500 to Ranjit on September 20. Herb wishes to delay payment until December 1.

a. What amount should Herb expect to pay on December 1 if Ranjit can earn 2.25% on a low-risk investment?

b. Show why Ranjit should not care whether he receives the scheduled payment or the delayed payment.

SOLUTION

a. Herb is seeking a postponement of

$$11 + 31 + 30 = 72 \text{ days}$$

He should expect to pay an amount that is equivalent to $1500, 72 days later, allowing for a 2.25% rate of return. That is, he should expect to pay the future value of $1500, 72 days later.

September 20

December 1

$1500

72 days

Future value

Substituting $P = \$1500$, $t = \frac{72}{365}$, and $r = 2.25\%$ into Formula (7-2), the future value is

$$S = P(1 + rt) = \$1500\left[1 + 0.0225\left(\frac{72}{365}\right)\right] = \$1506.66$$

Herb should expect to pay $1506.66 on December 1 instead of $1500 on September 20.

b. Suppose that Herb makes the $1500 payment as scheduled on September 20. Since Ranjit can earn a 2.25% rate of return, by December 1 the $1500 will grow to

$$S = P(1 + rt) = \$1500\left[1 + 0.0225\left(\frac{72}{365}\right)\right] = \$1506.66$$

Ranjit should, therefore, be indifferent between receiving $1500 on September 20 or $1506.66 on December 1 because he can end up with $1506.66 on December 1 with either alternative.

EXAMPLE 7.4B

CALCULATING AN EQUIVALENT PAYMENT AT AN EARLIER DATE

What is the value of a payment to be received on March 12 if it is economically equivalent to a $1000 payment originally due on the subsequent July 6, if money is worth 6.8% per year?

SOLUTION

Since we want an equivalent payment at an earlier date, we should calculate the *present* value of $1000 on March 12.

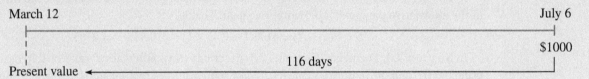

The number of days in the interval is

$$20 \text{ (for March)} + 30 + 31 + 30 + 5 \text{ (for July)} = 116$$

Substituting $S = \$1000$, $r = 6.8\%$, and $t = \frac{116}{365}$ into Formula (7-3), we obtain

$$P = \frac{S}{1 + rt} = \frac{\$1000}{1 + 0.068\left(\frac{116}{365}\right)} = \$978.85$$

$978.85 on March 12 is equivalent to $1000 on the subsequent July 6.

EXAMPLE 7.4C

CALCULATING A PRIOR EQUIVALENT PAYMENT

A furniture store advertises a dining table and chairs for $1495 with nothing down, no payments, and no interest for six months. What cash price should the store be willing to accept now if, on a six-month investment, it can earn a rate of return of

a. 4%?

b. 9%?

SOLUTION

The store faces the choice between the cash offer and $1495 to be received six months from now (if a customer takes the credit terms). The store should be willing to accept a cash amount that is today's equivalent of $1495. In other words, the store should accept the present value of $1495.

a. If money can earn 4%, $P = \dfrac{S}{1 + rt} = \dfrac{\$1495}{1 + 0.04\left(\frac{6}{12}\right)} = \dfrac{\$1495}{1.02} = \$1465.69$

The store should accept a cash offer of $1465.69.

b. If money can earn 9%, $P = \dfrac{\$1495}{1 + 0.09\left(\frac{6}{12}\right)} = \$1430.62$

The store should accept a cash offer of $1430.62.

Figure 7.1 presents a graph of equivalent values (present value and future value) of $100. Numerical values are indicated at two-month intervals before and after the scheduled payment date (zero on the time axis). We have chosen a simple interest rate of 12% because it is easy to work with 1% per month. The future value increases by $1 every month in a straight-line pattern. The present value decreases for longer time periods in advance of the scheduled payment. However, the rate of decrease is less than linear. This is evident from the widening gap between the present-value curve and the dashed straight line sloping downward to the left (at the rate of $1 per month) in the present value region.

FIGURE 7.1	Graph of Present Values and Future Values of $100

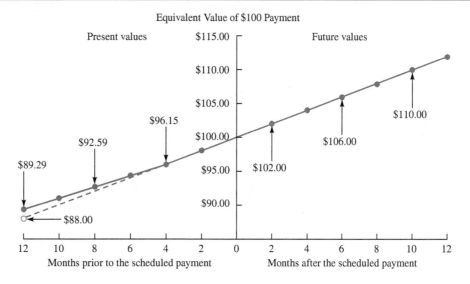

Comparing Payments

If money can earn 5.5%, is $65 today equivalent to $67 eight months from now?

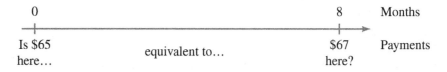

Trust your instincts. Two methods for answering this question may occur to you. One method is to calculate the future value of $65 after eight months and compare it to $67. The other approach is to calculate the present value of $67 eight months earlier and compare it to $65. If we do the latter, we obtain

$$P = \frac{S}{1 + rt} = \frac{\$67}{1 + 0.055 \times \frac{8}{12}} = \$64.63$$

Since the present value differs from $65, the two payments are not equivalent. Furthermore, $65 paid today is worth

$$\$65.00 - \$64.63 = \$0.37$$

more than $67 paid eight months from now.

Suppose you are asked to compare the economic values of three or four or more alternative payments. What should you do? In general, you can compare the economic values of any number of alternative payments by calculating their equivalent values all at the *same* date. (The date at which the equivalent values are calculated is often referred to as the **focal date**.) The alternative payments can then be ranked on the basis of their equivalent values.

EXAMPLE 7.4D

COMPARING THE ECONOMIC VALUES OF ALTERNATIVE PAYMENTS

Marcus can purchase an airplane ticket now on the airline's Early Bird Sale for $459, or he can wait and pay $479 in nine months. If he can earn a 3% rate of return on his money, which option should he choose?

SOLUTION

To compare today's economic values of the two alternatives, first calculate the present value of the regular price of $479.

$$P = \frac{S}{1 + rt} = \frac{\$479}{1 + 0.03\left(\frac{9}{12}\right)} = \$468.46$$

Marcus should choose the alternative having the *lower* economic value. That is, he should buy the ticket at the Early Bird price of $459. However, his true saving is not $479 − $459 = $20, but rather $468.46 − $459.00 = $9.46.

EXAMPLE 7.4E

FINDING THE RATE OF RETURN THAT MAKES TWO PAYMENTS EQUIVALENT

Extending the problem in **Example 7.4D**, what rate of return would Marcus have to earn in order to for there to be no difference between the two prices?

SOLUTION

There will be no difference between the two prices if $459 invested for nine months will grow to $479. In other words, he will be in the same financial position if $459 can earn $479 − $459 = $20 in nine months. The rate of return that would cause this to occur is

$$r = \frac{I}{Pt} = \frac{\$20}{\$459 \times \frac{9}{12}} = 5.8\%$$

If Marcus could earn a 5.8% rate of return, he could invest the $459 for nine months and it would mature at $479, providing exactly the right amount to buy the ticket.

(If Marcus could earn more than 5.8%, it would be to his advantage to invest the $459 now and buy the ticket nine months later.)

EXAMPLE 7.4F

COMPARING DIFFERENT PAYMENT OPTIONS

Fiona listed her car on Kijiji and has two offers both totalling $8000. Seth will pay her $2000 now and the balance in six months, while Joaquin will pay $3000 now and the balance in four months. If Fiona can earn 3.5% interest on a short-term investment:

a. What is the current economic value of the two offers?

b. Which offer should Fiona accept? How much more is the better offer worth in today's dollars?

SOLUTION

a. To compare the current economic value of the two offers, first calculate the present value of the payments to be made later in time.

The balance Seth owes is $6000 due in six months. The present value of the balance is:

$$P = \frac{S}{1 + rt} = \frac{\$6000}{1 + 0.035\left(\frac{6}{12}\right)} = \$5896.81$$

The balance Joaquin owes is $5000 due in four months. The present value of the balance is:

$$P = \frac{S}{1 + rt} = \frac{\$5000}{1 + 0.035\left(\frac{4}{12}\right)} = \$4942.34$$

The current economic value of Seth's offer is

$$\$2000 + \$5896.81 = \$7896.81$$

compared to the current economic value of Joaquin's offer of

$$\$3000 + \$4942.34 = \$7942.34$$

b. Fiona should accept Joaquin's offer as it is worth $7942.34 − $7896.81 = $45.53 more in current dollars.

EXAMPLE 7.4G

FINDING THE TIME BETWEEN TWO EQUIVALENT PAYMENTS

Aaron missed a payment of $2100 on a loan that had 6.5% interest. The lender now wants $2156.88 to make up for the missed payment. How many months was the payment late?

SOLUTION

The penalty for making the payment late is the difference between the original payment and the late payment. In effect, Aaron is being charged an additional $2156.88 − $2100.00 = $56.88 in interest for paying late.

$$t = \frac{I}{Pr} = \frac{\$56.88}{\$2100(0.065)} = 0.41670 \text{ years}$$

This represents 41.67% of a year or 0.41670 × 12 = 5.0 months.

Aaron was 5 months late in making the payment.

CONCEPT QUESTIONS

1. What is meant by "equivalent payments"?

2. Under what circumstance is $100 paid today equivalent to $110 paid one year from now?

3. How can you determine which of three payments on different dates has the largest economic value?

EXERCISE 7.4

Answers to the odd-numbered problems are at the end of the book.

BASIC PROBLEMS

1. Kathleen has a $560 loan payment due in five months. What amount of money should she be able to pay today if the interest on her loan is $3\frac{3}{4}\%$ per annum?

2. Caleb has a $1215 loan payment due today but he would like to defer the payment for seven months. How much is the equivalent payment seven months from today if he is being charged interest on the loan at $8\frac{1}{2}\%$ per annum?

3. What payment 174 days from now is equivalent to $5230 paid today? Assume that money is worth 5.25% per annum.

4. What amount should be accepted as equivalent 60 days before an obligation of $1480 is due if money can earn $6\frac{3}{4}\%$?

5. What amount paid on September 24 is equivalent to $1000 paid on the following December 1 if money can earn 5%?

6. What amount received on January 13 is equivalent to $1000 received on the preceding August 12 if money can earn 9.5%?

7. Rasheed wishes to postpone for 90 days the payment of $450 that he owes to Roxanne. If money now earns 2.75%, what amount can he reasonably expect to pay at the later date?

8. Avril owes Value Furniture $1600, which is scheduled to be paid on August 15. Avril has surplus funds on June 15 and will settle the debt early if Value Furniture will make an adjustment reflecting the current short-term interest rate of 7.25%. What amount should be acceptable to both parties?

9. Ruth-Ann has the option of paying $1936.53 today or $1975.00 100 days from today. What annual rate of return would money have to earn for the two options to be economically equivalent?

10. Cyril can purchase a trip to Aruba for an early booking price of $2370.00 now or wait 190 days and pay $2508.79. What annual rate of return would money have to earn for the two options to be economically equivalent?

11. A late payment of $850.26 was considered equivalent to the originally scheduled payment of $830.00, allowing for interest at 9.9%. How many days late was the payment?

12. What is the time interval (in months) separating equivalent payments of $3500.00 and $3439.80 if money is worth $5\frac{1}{4}\%$ per annum?

13. An early payment of $4574.73 was accepted instead of a scheduled payment of $4850.00, allowing for interest at the rate of $8\frac{3}{4}\%$. How many days early was the payment?

14. April missed a payment of $2740.00 on a loan with interest being charged at $4\frac{1}{2}\%$. The lender now wants $2755.20 as a late payment to settle up on the missed payment. How many days late was the payment?

15. If money can be invested at 0.6% per month, which has the greater economic value: $5230 on a specific date or $5500 exactly five months later? At what rate (per month) would the two amounts be economically equivalent?

16. Compare the economic values of $1480 today versus $1515 in 150 days. Assume money can earn 6.75%. At what rate would the two amounts be equivalent?

17. To settle a $570 invoice, Anna can pay $560 now or the full amount 60 days later. Which alternative should she choose if money can earn $10\frac{3}{4}\%$? What rate would money have to earn for Anna to be indifferent between the alternatives?

18. Jonas recently purchased a one-year membership at Gold's Gym. He can add a second year to the membership now for $1215, or wait 11 months and pay the regular single-year price of $1280. Which is the better economic alternative if money is worth 8.5%? At what discount rate would the alternatives be equivalent?

19. Nicholas can purchase the same furniture from Store A for $2495 cash or from Store B for $2560 with nothing down and no payments or interest for 8 months. Which option should Nicholas choose if he can pay for the furniture by cashing in Canada Savings Bonds currently earning 3.9% per annum?

20. A $5000 payment is scheduled for 120 days from now. If money can earn 7.25%, calculate the payment's equivalent value at each of nine different dates—today and every 30 days for the next 240 days.

21. A $3000 payment is scheduled for six months from now. If money is worth 6.75%, calculate the payment's equivalent values at two-month intervals beginning today and ending one year from now.

22. During its 50/50 Sale, Marpole Furniture will sell its merchandise for 50% down, with the balance payable in six months. No interest is charged for the first six months. What 100% cash price should Marpole accept on a $1845 chesterfield and chair set if Marpole can earn a 10.75% rate of return on its funds?

23. Mr. and Mrs. Chan have listed for sale a residential building lot they own in a nearby town. They are considering two offers. The offer from the Smiths is for $145,000 consisting of $45,000 down and the balance to be paid in six months. The offer from the Kims is for $149,000 consisting of $29,000 down and $120,000 payable in one year. The Chans can earn an interest rate of 4.5% on low-risk short-term investments.
    a. What is the current economic value to the Chans of each offer?
    b. Other things being equal, which offer should the Chans accept? How much more is the better offer worth (in terms of current economic value)?

INTERMEDIATE PROBLEMS

24. Westwood Homes is beginning work on its future College Park subdivision. Westwood is now pre-selling homes that will be ready for occupancy in nine months. Westwood is offering $5000 off the $295,000 selling price to anyone making an immediate $130,000 down payment (with the balance due in nine months). The alternative is a $5000 deposit with the $290,000 balance due in nine months. Mr. and Mrs. Symbaluk are trying to decide which option to choose. They currently earn 4.8% on low-risk short-term investments.
    a. What is the current economic cost of buying on the $130,000-down, $5000-off option?
    b. What is the current economic cost of buying on the $5000-deposit, full-price option?
    c. Which alternative should the Symbaluks choose? In current dollars, what is the economic advantage of the preferred alternative?

25. What interest rate must money earn for a payment of $1389 on August 20 to be equivalent to a payment of $1348 on the previous March 29?

7.5 The Equivalent Value of a Payment Stream

A **payment stream** is a series of two or more payments required by a single transaction or contract. To get their combined value, you must consider the economic value of the payments determined by when the payment is made. This property of money is often referred to as the **time value of money**. The simple addition of the payments ignores the time value of money and implies that a dollar on one date has the same economic value as a dollar on any other date. The time value of money tells us that the *economic* value of a dollar depends on when it is paid.

LO3 In **Section 7.4**, you learned how to calculate the equivalent value, on any date, of a *single* payment. A logical extension of this basic idea allows us to determine the equivalent value of a payment *stream*. We simply add the equivalent values (at the chosen focal date) of the individual payments. The following example illustrates the procedure.

Consider a payment stream consisting of three payments: $1000, $2000, and $3000, scheduled for March 1, May 1, and December 1 of the same year. Let us calculate the single payment on August 1 that is economically equivalent to the three scheduled payments. Suppose money can earn a simple interest rate of 8%.

LO2 For problems involving multiple payments, a **time diagram** is virtually essential to organize the data. It consists of a time axis or *time line* showing the dollar amounts and the dates of the payments. **Figure 7.2** shows the first steps in constructing a time diagram:

- Draw a straight line or time axis using the full width of your page
- Mark all of the dates identified in the problem on the time line with reasonably proportioned time intervals between the dates
- Mark the payment amounts on the time line at their originally scheduled payment dates
- Mark the rescheduled payment date or focal date on the time line

FIGURE 7.2   Entering Given Data on a Time Diagram

The solution idea for this problem is:

$$\begin{pmatrix} \text{The equivalent payment} \\ \text{on August 1} \end{pmatrix} = \begin{pmatrix} \text{The sum of the equivalent values on} \\ \text{August 1 of the individual payments} \end{pmatrix}$$

In **Figure 7.3**, the steps needed to carry out the solution are illustrated by:

- Drawing an arrow from each payment date to the August 1 focal date
- Writing the days in the time interval on each arrow
- Labelling the end of each arrow with either an S for future value or a P for present value for each equivalent value
- Indicate that the three equivalent values at the focal date need to be added

FIGURE 7.3   Showing the Solution Steps on a Time Diagram

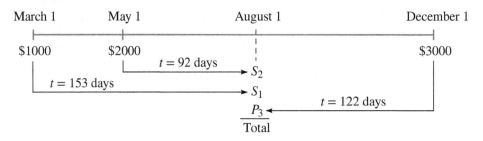

The written solution is now a matter of following the steps outlined in the diagram:

S_1 = Future value on August 1 of the $1000 payment

$$= \$1000\left(1 + 0.08 \times \frac{153}{365}\right)$$

$$= \$1033.53$$

S_2 = Future value on August 1 of the \$2000 payment

$$= \$2000\left(1 + 0.08 \times \frac{92}{365}\right)$$

$$= \$2040.33$$

P_3 = Present value on August 1 of the \$3000 payment

$$= \frac{\$3000}{1 + 0.08 \times \frac{122}{365}}$$

$$= \$2921.87$$

The equivalent value on August 1 of the payment stream is

$$S_1 + S_2 + P_3 = \$1033.53 + \$2040.33 + \$2921.87 = \$5995.73$$

The significance of this equivalent value is that a payment of \$5995.73 on August 1 is economically equivalent to the three scheduled payments. The recipient will be in the same economic position whether he accepts \$5995.73 on August 1 or he receives the three payments as scheduled.

 TRAP

Accidentally Compounding Simple Interest

You might think that the problem illustrated with **Figure 7.3** above could be solved by moving the March 1 payment to May 1, adding \$2000 and then moving this sum to the August 1 focal date. This does not work for simple interest.

If you move payments more than once in simple interest you are adding the interest to the payment before the focal date and thus compounding the interest when you move the payment again.

To avoid accidentally compounding the interest for simple interest loans or investments it is important to remember that:

1. Simple interest payments can be moved only once, individually to the focal date.
2. The only time simple interest payments can be added together is at the focal date.

EXAMPLE 7.5A

COMPARING THE ECONOMIC VALUE OF TWO PAYMENT STREAMS

Compare the economic values today of the following two payment streams if money can earn 6.5%: \$700 paid in four months plus \$300 paid in ten months, versus \$400 paid in six months plus \$600 paid in eight months.

SOLUTION

Construct a time line for each payment stream, indicating the scheduled payments and their equivalent values, P_1 to P_4, today. ("Today" has been labelled as time zero on the time line.) The stream with the larger total equivalent value today has the greater economic value.

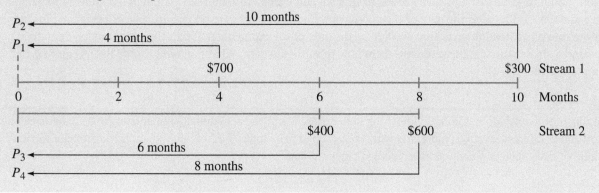

$$\text{Equivalent value of Stream 1} = P_1 + P_2$$

$$= \frac{\$700}{1 + 0.065\left(\frac{4}{12}\right)} + \frac{\$300}{1 + 0.065\left(\frac{10}{12}\right)}$$

$$= \$685.155 + \$284.585$$

$$= \$969.74$$

Note that we keep six figures in the second-to-last line in order to obtain five-figure accuracy in the final result.

$$\text{Equivalent value of Stream 2} = P_3 + P_4$$

$$= \frac{\$400}{1 + 0.065\left(\frac{6}{12}\right)} + \frac{\$600}{1 + 0.065\left(\frac{8}{12}\right)}$$

$$= \$387.409 + \$575.080$$

$$= \$962.49$$

Even though the sum of the nominal payments in each stream is $1000, the first stream's economic value today is $7.25 more than the second stream's value. This happens because, on average, the money in the first stream is received sooner (5.8 months for Stream 1 versus 7.2 months for Stream 2).

✓ TIP

Should I Calculate *S* or *P*?

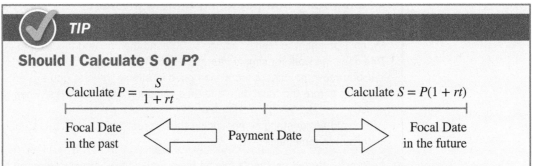

$$\text{Calculate } P = \frac{S}{1 + rt}$$

$$\text{Calculate } S = P(1 + rt)$$

Focal Date in the past ⬅ Payment Date ➡ Focal Date in the future

The time line diagram is essential in determining which calculation is appropriate for each payment in a payment stream. When payments are moved to a focal date in the future, the future value or maturity value Formula (7-2) is used to get an equivalent value that is higher than the original payment since interest will accumulate from the payment date to the future focal date.

When payments are moved to a focal date in the past, the present value or principal Formula (7-3) is used to get an equivalent value that is lower than the original payment. You can think of it as stripping interest out of the payment to find the principal that would grow into that payment for the period of time between the focal date and the payment date.

EXAMPLE 7.5B

CALCULATING A PAYMENT EQUIVALENT TO INTEREST-EARNING OBLIGATIONS

Four months ago Hassan borrowed $1000 from Sean and agreed to repay the loan in two payments to be made five and ten months after the date of the agreement. Each payment is to consist of $500 of principal plus interest at the rate of 9% in addition to that $500, from the date of the agreement. Today Hassan is asking Sean to accept instead a single payment three months from now to settle the debt. What payment should Sean require if money can now earn 7%?

SOLUTION

In this problem we do not initially know the dollar amounts of the scheduled payments because we do not know how much interest must be paid along with each $500 of principal. The first step, then, is to calculate the maturity value of each $500 payment on its scheduled payment date.

The maturity values are represented by S_1 and S_2 in the following time diagram. ("Now" has been labelled as time zero.)

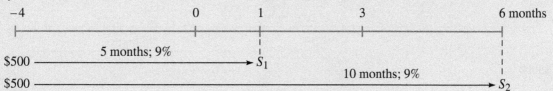

$$S_1 = \$500\left[1 + 0.09\left(\tfrac{5}{12}\right)\right] = \$518.75$$

$$S_2 = \$500\left[1 + 0.09\left(\tfrac{10}{12}\right)\right] = \$537.50$$

Now we can construct a time diagram presenting the scheduled payments and their equivalent values, S and P, on the date of the replacement payment.

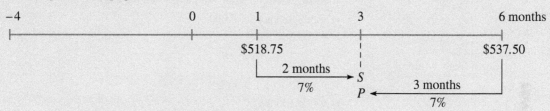

The *current* rate that money can earn, 7%, is used to calculate the equivalent values of the scheduled payments.

$$S = \text{Future value of \$518.75 on a date two months later}$$
$$= \$518.75\left[1 + 0.07\left(\tfrac{2}{12}\right)\right]$$
$$= \$524.802$$

$$P = \text{Present value of \$537.50 on a date three months earlier}$$
$$= \frac{\$537.50}{1 + 0.07\left(\tfrac{3}{12}\right)}$$
$$= \$528.256$$

The single equivalent payment is

$$S + P = \$524.802 + \$528.256 = \$1053.06$$

Sean should require a payment of $1053.06 on a date three months from now.

EXAMPLE 7.5C

CALCULATING AN UNKNOWN PAYMENT IN AN EQUIVALENT PAYMENT STREAM

Payments of $5000 due four months ago and $3000 due two months from now are to be replaced by a payment of $4000 today and a second payment in six months. What must the second payment be in order to make the replacement payment stream equivalent to the scheduled payment stream? Money in short-term investments can earn 5%. Use six months from now as the focal date.

SOLUTION

Each alternative payment stream is shown below on its own time line. We must determine the size of the payment x so that both payment streams have the same economic value six months from now. The equivalent values, at the focal date of the three known payments, are indicated by S_1, S_2, and S_3. The unknown payment, x, is already at the focal date.

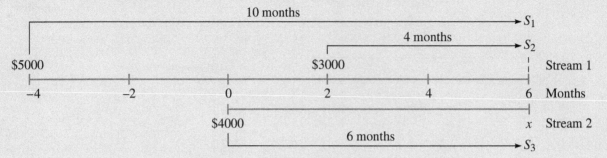

$$\text{Equivalent value of Stream 1} = S_1 + S_2$$
$$= \$5000\left(1 + 0.05 \times \tfrac{10}{12}\right) + \$3000\left(1 + 0.05 \times \tfrac{4}{12}\right)$$
$$= \$5208.333 + \$3050.000$$
$$= \$8258.333$$

$$\text{Equivalent value of Stream 2} = x + S_3$$
$$= x + \$4000\left(1 + 0.05 \times \tfrac{6}{12}\right)$$
$$= x + \$4100.0000$$

For the two streams to be economically equivalent, the sum of the value of Stream 2 on the focal date must be equivalent to the sum of the value of Stream 1 on the focal date, or:

$$x + \$4100.000 = \$8258.333$$

Hence,
$$x = \$4158.33$$

For the two streams to be equivalent, the second payment must be $4158.33.

CONCEPT QUESTIONS

1. What is meant by the "time value of money"?
2. We frequently hear a news item that goes something like: "Joe Superstar signed a five-year deal worth $25 million. Under the contract he will be paid $3 million, $4 million, $5 million, $6 million, and $7 million in successive years." In what respect is the statement incorrect? How should the value of the contract be calculated?
3. If the interest rate money can earn is revised upward, is today's economic value of a given stream of future payments higher or lower? Explain.

EXERCISE 7.5

Answers to the odd-numbered problems are at the end of the book.

BASIC PROBLEMS

1. Payments of $500 originally scheduled to be paid today and $300 originally scheduled to be paid three months from today are to be replaced with a single payment six months from today. Calculate the combined equivalent value of the two payments six months from today if money can earn $2\tfrac{1}{2}\%$.

2. A payment stream consists of $1000 payable now and $1500 payable five months from now. What is the equivalent value of the payment stream two months from now if money is worth 5.5%?

3. Payments of $900 due 30 days from now and $1000 due 210 days from now are to be replaced with a single equivalent payment 90 days from now. If money can be invested at 4%, what single payment made 90 days from now is equivalent to the payment stream?

4. What is the equivalent value, 30 days from now, of a payment stream comprised of $2500 due 70 days from now and $4000 due 200 days from now? Assume money can earn $6\frac{1}{4}$%.

5. A payment stream consists of three payments: $1000 due today, $1500 due 70 days from today, and $2000 due 210 days from today. What single payment, 60 days from today, is economically equivalent to the payment stream if money can be invested at a rate of 3.5%?

6. What single payment, made 45 days from now, is economically equivalent to the combination of three equal payments of $1750 each: one due 75 days ago, the second due today, and the third due 75 days from today? Money is worth 9.9% per annum.

7. Two payments of $2000 each are to be received 6 and 12 months from now. If money is worth 5%, what is the total equivalent value of the payments:
   a. Today?
   b. Six months from today?
   c. Explain why the answer in part (b) is larger.

8. Two payments of $3000 each are due in 50 and 100 days. What is their combined economic value today if money can earn:
   a. 9%?
   b. 11%?
   c. Explain why the answer in part (b) is smaller.

9. A payment of $850 scheduled to be paid today and a second payment of $1140 to be paid nine months from today are to be replaced by a single equivalent payment. What total payment made today would place the payee in the same financial position as the scheduled payments if money can earn $4\frac{1}{4}$%?

10. Payments of $1300 due five months ago and $1800 due three months from now are to be replaced by a single payment at a focal date one month from now. What is the size of the replacement payment that would be equivalent to the two scheduled payments if money can earn $4\frac{1}{2}$%?

11. If money earns 3.5%, calculate and compare the economic value today of the following payment streams:

    Stream 1: Payments of $900 due 150 days ago and $1400 due 80 days ago.

    Stream 2: Payments of $800 due in 30 days, $600 due in 75 days, and $1000 due in 125 days.

12. What is the economic value today of each of the following payment streams if money can earn 7.5%? (Note that the two streams have the same total nominal value.)
    a. $1000, $3000, and $2000 due in one, three, and five months, respectively.
    b. Two $3000 payments due two and four months from now.

INTERMEDIATE PROBLEMS

13. Eight months ago, Louise agreed to pay Thelma $750 and $950, 6 and 12 months, respectively, from the date of the agreement. With each payment, Louise agreed to pay interest on the respective principal amounts at the rate of 6.5% from the date of the agreement. Louise failed to make the first payment and now wishes to settle her obligations with a single payment four months from now. What payment should Thelma be willing to accept if money can earn 4.75%?

14. Ninety days ago Stella signed an agreement with Manon requiring her to make three payments of $400 plus interest 90, 150, and 210 days, respectively, from the date of the agreement. Each payment was to include interest on the $400 principal at the rate of 13.5% from the date of the agreement. Stella now wants Manon to renegotiate the agreement and accept a single payment 30 days from now, instead of the three scheduled payments. What payment should Manon require in the new agreement if money is worth 8.5%?

15. Payments of $2600, due 50 days ago, and $3100, due in 40 days, are to be replaced by payments of $3000 due today and the balance due in 30 days. What must the second payment be if the payee is to end up in an equivalent financial position? Money now earns 8.25%. Use 30 days from now as the focal date.

16. Three payments of $2000 each (originally due six months ago, today, and six months from now) have been renegotiated to two payments: $3000 due one month from now and a second payment due in four months. What must the second payment be for the replacement payments to be equivalent to the originally scheduled payments? Assume that money can earn an interest rate of 4%. Choose a focal date four months from now.

*7.6 | Loans: A Principle about Principal

LO3 In **Section 9.3**, we will develop (in the context of compound interest) an important relationship between the principal amount of a loan and the payments required to pay off the loan. The relationship applies to *all* compound interest loans and to *some* loans[2] at simple interest. **Section 9.3** is covered in virtually all business math courses but **Section 7.6** is commonly omitted. Therefore, we will simply state the relationship at this point and demonstrate its use.

A General Principle Concerning Loans

The original principal amount of a loan is equal to the sum of the present values of all the payments required to pay off a loan. The present-value calculation in effect strips the interest amount out of each payment leaving only the principal portion. The interest rate used for the present-value calculations is the interest rate charged on the loan.

EXAMPLE 7.6A

CALCULATING THE SIZE OF THE FINAL LOAN PAYMENT

A $5000 loan advanced on April 1 at a $6\frac{1}{2}$% interest rate requires payments of $1800 on each of June 1 and August 1, and a final payment on October 1. What must the final payment be to satisfy the loan in full?

---

[2] In general, a loan payment consists of a principal portion and an interest portion. Most loans are structured so that the interest portion of a payment is the accrued interest on the *entire* principal balance still outstanding. However, for the relationship presented in this section to apply precisely to a simple interest loan, the following condition must be met. The interest portion of a simple interest loan payment must be the accrued interest on *only the principal portion of that payment*. Accrued interest on other outstanding principal must be paid only when that principal is repaid. Instances of loans meeting this condition are rare.

SOLUTION

Let x represent the amount of the final payment. The payments and their equivalent (present) values, P_1, P_2, and P_3, are shown in the following time diagram.

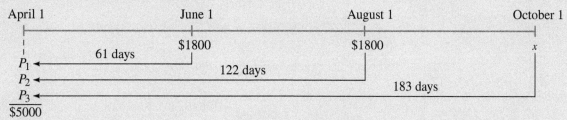

April 1   June 1   August 1   October 1

$1800 $1800 x

61 days

122 days

183 days

P_1, P_2, P_3

$5000

Since the original loan equals the combined present value of all of the payments, then

$$\$5000 = P_1 + P_2 + P_3$$

where

$$P_1 = \frac{\$1800}{1 + 0.065\left(\frac{61}{365}\right)} = \frac{\$1800}{1.0108630} = \$1780.657$$

$$P_2 = \frac{\$1800}{1 + 0.065\left(\frac{122}{365}\right)} = \frac{\$1800}{1.0217260} = \$1761.725$$

$$P_3 = \frac{x}{1 + 0.065\left(\frac{183}{365}\right)} = \frac{x}{1.0325890} = 0.9684395x$$

We maintain seven-figure precision in order to ensure six-figure accuracy in the final result.

Thus

$$\$5000 = \$1780.657 + \$1761.725 + 0.9684395x$$
$$\$1457.618 = 0.9684395x$$
$$x = \frac{\$1457.618}{0.9684395} = \$1505.12$$

The final payment on October 1 must be $1505.12.

EXAMPLE 7.6B

CALCULATING THE SIZE OF EQUAL LOAN PAYMENTS

A $4000 loan made at 7.75% is to be repaid in three equal payments, due 30, 90, and 150 days, respectively, after the date of the loan. Determine the size of the payments.

SOLUTION

Let the amount of each payment be represented by x. The payments and their equivalent (present) values are presented in the following time diagram.

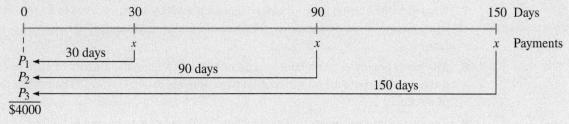

0   30   90   150   Days

         x x x Payments

30 days

90 days

150 days

P_1, P_2, P_3

$4000

The original loan is equal to the sum of the present values of all of the payments. Therefore,

$$\$4000 = P_1 + P_2 + P_3$$

where

$$P_1 = \frac{x}{1 + 0.0775\left(\frac{30}{365}\right)} = \frac{x}{1.0063699} = 0.9936704x$$

$$P_2 = \frac{x}{1 + 0.0775\left(\frac{90}{365}\right)} = \frac{x}{1.0191096} = 0.9812487x$$

$$P_3 = \frac{x}{1 + 0.0775\left(\frac{150}{365}\right)} = \frac{x}{1.0318493} = 0.9691338x$$

Thus,

$$\$4000 = 0.9936704x + 0.9812487x + 0.9691338x$$
$$= 2.9440529x$$
$$x = \frac{\$4000}{2.9440529} = \$1358.67$$

Each payment should be $1358.67.

EXERCISE 7.6

Answers to the odd-numbered problems are at the end of the book.

INTERMEDIATE PROBLEMS

1. A $3000 loan at 6% was made on March 1. Two payments of $1000 each were made on May 1 and June 1. What payment on July 1 will pay off the loan?

2. $5000 was borrowed at $9\frac{1}{2}$% on March 1. On April 1 and June 1, the borrower made payments of $2000 each. What payment was required on August 1 to pay off the loan's balance?

3. The interest rate on a $3000 loan advanced on March 1 was 5.2%. What must the first payment on April 13 be in order that two subsequent payments of $1100 on May 27 and $1100 on July 13 settle the loan?

4. A $3000 loan on March 1 was repaid by payments of $500 on March 31, $1000 on June 15, and a final payment on August 31. What was the third payment if the interest rate on the loan was $8\frac{1}{4}$%?

5. A $1000 loan at 5.5% was repaid by two equal payments made 30 days and 60 days after the date of the loan. Determine the amount of each payment.

6. Two equal payments, 50 days and 150 days after the date of the loan, paid off a $3000 loan at $10\frac{1}{4}$%. What was the amount of each payment?

7. What should be the amount of each payment if a $2500 loan at 3.5% is to be repaid by three equal payments due two months, four months, and seven months following the date of the loan?

8. $8000 was borrowed at an interest rate of $11\frac{1}{2}$%. Calculate the amount of each payment if the loan was paid off by three equal payments made 30, 90, and 150 days after the date of the loan.

9. The simple interest rate on a $5000 loan is 7%. The loan is to be repaid by four equal payments on dates 100, 150, 200, and 250 days from the date on which the loan was advanced. What is the amount of each payment?

10. A $7500 loan will be paid off by four equal payments to be made 2, 5, 9, and 12 months after the date of the loan. What is the amount of each payment if the interest rate on the loan is 9.9%?

11. Maurice borrowed $6000 from Heidi on April 23 and agreed to make payments of $2000 on June 1 and $2000 on August 1, and to pay the balance on October 1. If simple interest at the rate of 5% was charged on the loan, what is the amount of the third payment? Use April 23 as the focal date.

12. A loan of $10,000 is to be repaid by three payments of $2500 due in two, four, and six months, and a fourth payment due in eight months. What should be the size of the fourth payment if an interest rate of 11% is charged on the loan? Use today as the focal date.

13. A loan of $4000 at 6.25% is to be repaid by three equal payments due four, six, and eight months after the date on which the money was advanced. Calculate the amount of each payment. Use the loan date as the focal date.

14. Anthony borrowed $7500 on September 15 and agreed to repay the loan by three equal payments on the following November 10, December 30, and February 28. Calculate the payment size if the interest rate on the loan was $11\frac{3}{4}$%. Use September 15 as the focal date.

KEY TERMS

Equivalent payments	Maturity value	Rate of interest
Focal date	Payment stream	Simple interest
Future value	Present value	Time diagram
Interest	Prime rate of interest	Time value of money
Maturity date	Principal	

SUMMARY OF NOTATION AND KEY FORMULAS

P = Principal amount of the loan or investment; present value
r = Annual rate of simple interest
t = Time period (term), in years, of the loan or investment
I = Amount of interest paid or received
S = Maturity value of a loan or investment; future value

FORMULA (7-1)	$I = Prt$	Finding the amount of simple interest earned
FORMULA (7-2)	$S = P(1 + rt)$	Finding the maturity value or future value
FORMULA (7-3)	$P = \dfrac{S}{1 + rt}$	Finding the principal or present value

REVIEW PROBLEMS

Answers to the odd-numbered review problems are at the end of the book.

BASIC PROBLEMS

1. **LO1** What amount invested at $4\frac{1}{2}$% on November 19, 2019, had a maturity value of $10,000 on March 3, 2020?

2. **LO1** If $3702.40 earned $212.45 interest from September 17, 2018, to March 11, 2019, what rate of interest was earned?

3. **LO1** A loan of $3300 at $6\frac{1}{4}$% simple interest was made on March 27. On what date was it repaid if the interest cost was $138.44?

4. **LO1** Marta borrowed $1750 from Jasper on November 15, 2019, and agreed to repay the debt with simple interest at the rate of 7.4% on June 3, 2020. How much interest was owed on June 3?

5. **LO1** Petra has forgotten the rate of simple interest she earned on a 120-day term deposit at Scotiabank. At the end of the 120 days, she received interest of $327.95 on her $21,000 deposit. What rate of simple interest was her deposit earning?

6. **LO1** Jacques received the proceeds from an inheritance on March 15. He wants to set aside, in a term deposit on March 16, an amount sufficient to provide a $45,000 down payment for the purchase of a home on November 1. If the current interest rate on 181-day to 270-day deposits is $5\frac{3}{4}$%, what amount should he place in the term deposit?

7. **LO3** Sheldrick Contracting owes Western Equipment $60,000 payable on June 14. In late April, Sheldrick has surplus cash and wants to settle its debt to Western Equipment, if Western will agree to a fair reduction reflecting the current 3.6% interest rate that short-term funds can earn. What amount on April 29 should Sheldrick propose to pay to Western?

8. **LO3** Peter and Reesa can book their Horizon Holiday package at the early-booking price of $3900, or wait four months and pay the full price of $3995.
   a. Which option should they select if money can earn a 5.25% rate of return?
   b. At what interest rate would they be indifferent between the two prices?

9. **LO3** What amount on January 23 is equivalent to $1000 on the preceding August 18 if money can earn $6\frac{1}{2}$%?

10. **LO2 LO3** Three payments are scheduled as follows: $1200 is due today, $900 is due in five months, and $1500 is due in eight months. The three payments are to be replaced by a single equivalent payment due 10 months from now. What should the payment be if money is worth 5.9%? Use 10 months from now as the focal date.

11. **LO3** Two payments of $5000 each are to be received four and eight months from now.
    a. What is the combined equivalent value of the two payments today if money can earn 6%?
    b. If the rate of interest money can earn is 4%, what is the payments' combined equivalent value today?

12. **LO3** Thad is planning to buy a rototiller next spring at an expected price of $579. In the current sale flyer from Evergreen Lawn and Garden, the model he wants is advertised at $499.95 in a Fall Clearance Special.
    a. If money can earn 4%, what is the economic value on the preceding September 15 of the $579 that Thad will pay to purchase the rototiller next April 1? (Assume that February has 28 days.)
    b. What are his true economic savings if he purchases the rototiller at the sale price of $499.95 on September 15?
    c. What interest rate would money have to earn for Thad to be indifferent between buying the rototiller at $499.95 on September 15 or buying it for $579 on the subsequent April 1?

13. **LO1** Evelyn put $15,000 into a 90-day term deposit at Laurentian Bank that paid a simple interest rate of 3.2%. When the term deposit matured, she invested the entire amount of the principal and interest from the first term deposit into a new 90-day term deposit that paid the same rate of interest. What total amount of interest did she earn on both term deposits?

14. **LO1** Umberto borrowed $7500 from Delores on November 7, 2020. When Umberto repaid the loan, Delores charged him $190.02 interest. If the rate of simple interest on the loan was $6\frac{3}{4}$%, on what date did Umberto repay the loan?

15. **L03** Payments of $1000 scheduled to be paid five months ago and $7500 to be paid four months from now are to be replaced with a single payment two months from now. What payment two months from now is equivalent to the scheduled payments if money can earn $2\frac{1}{2}$%?

16. **L02** **L03** If money earns 7.5%, calculate and compare the economic value today of the following payment streams:

    Stream 1: Payments of $1800 made 150 days ago and $2800 made 90 days ago.

    Stream 2: Payments of $1600 due 30 days from now, $1200 due 75 days from now, and $2000 due 120 days from now.

INTERMEDIATE PROBLEMS

17. **L03** Mr. and Mrs. Parson are considering two offers to purchase their summer cottage. Offer A is for $200,000 consisting of an immediate $40,000 down payment with the $160,000 balance payable one year later. Offer B is for $196,500 made up of a $30,000 down payment and the $166,500 balance payable in six months.
    a. If money can earn 4%, what is the current economic value of each offer?
    b. Other things being equal, which offer should the Parsons accept? What is the economic advantage of the preferred offer over the other offer?
    c. If money can earn 6%, which offer should the Parsons accept? What is the economic advantage of the preferred offer?

18. **L03** A $9000 loan is to be repaid in three equal payments occurring 60, 180, and 300 days, respectively, after the date of the loan. Calculate the size of these payments if the interest rate on the loan is $7\frac{1}{4}$%. Use the loan date as the focal date.

19. **L02** **L03** Nine months ago, Muriel agreed to pay Aisha $1200 and $800 on dates 6 and 12 months, respectively, from the date of the agreement. With each payment Muriel agreed to pay interest at the rate of $8\frac{1}{2}$% from the date of the agreement. Muriel failed to make the first payment and now wishes to settle her obligations with a single payment four months from now. What payment should Aisha be willing to accept if money can earn $6\frac{3}{4}$%?

*APPENDIX 7A: AN AID FOR DETERMINING THE NUMBER OF DAYS IN EACH MONTH

Figure 7.4 presents a method for determining which months have 31 days. The knuckles and the spaces (or valleys) between them are assigned the names of the months as shown in the figure. Then each knuckle corresponds to a month with 31 days and each valley corresponds to a short month.

FIGURE 7.4   "Knuckle Months" Have 31 Days

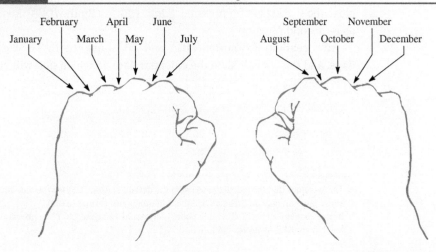

*APPENDIX 7B: THE TEXAS INSTRUMENTS BA II PLUS DATE WORKSHEET

The BA II PLUS's Owner's Manual uses the term "worksheet" to refer to a list of settings and functions designed for a particular application. Usually, a worksheet is the second function of a key. For example, the word **DATE** appears above the 1 key. You can access the **DATE** worksheet by pressing 2nd 1 in sequence (rather than at the same time). Hereafter, we will represent these keystrokes as 2nd DATE. The calculator's display then has the form:[3]

DT1 =	mm-dd-yyyy

The components of the display have the following meanings:

DT1 is the symbol used by the calculator for the *start* date (**DaTe 1**)
In place of "mm," you will see one or two digits representing the month.
In place of "dd," you will see two digits for the day of the month.
In place of "yyyy," you will see four digits for the year.

For example, the display

DT1 =	12-31-1990

means that the start date of the interval is December 31, 1990.

You should think of a worksheet as a single column of items that you can view one-at-a-time in the display. The DATE worksheet's column consists of the following four items:

DT1 =	mm-dd-yyyy
DT2 =	mm-dd-yyyy
DBD =	nnn
ACT	

The calculator's display provides a "window" to the first item in the column. You can use the scroll keys ↓ and ↑ to move down or up the list. *DT2* is the symbol used by the calculator for the *end* date (**DaTe 2**). *DBD* is the symbol for the number of **D**ays **B**etween **D**ates (that is, the number of days between *DT1* and *DT2*, counting the start date but not the end date). *ACT*[4] is short for **ACT**ual. This means that calculations are based on the *actual* number of days in each month. This is the *only* method used in Canada. Some calculations in the United States treat all months as having 30 days.

The DATE worksheet allows you to enter values for any two of the three quantities—*DT1*, *DT2*, and *DBD*—and then compute the value of the third quantity. (The calculator automatically makes adjustments for leap years.) **Examples 7B.A** and **7B.B** will demonstrate how to do this. But first close the worksheet by pressing 2nd QUIT. (By the QUIT key, we mean the key having **QUIT** as its second function.)

After reading **Examples 7B.A** and **7B.B**, use the DATE Worksheet to calculate your age in days, and then to calculate the calendar date on which you will be 20,000 days old.

---

[3] This assumes that the calculator is using the default setting (*US*) for the date format. In the calculator's "Format" worksheet, you can change to the alternative "dd-mm-yyyy" format (*EUR*).

[4] If your display shows "360" at this point, you should switch to "ACT" by pressing 2nd SET. By the SET key, we mean the key having **SET** as its second function.

EXAMPLE 7B.A

CALCULATING "DBD" GIVEN "DT1" AND "DT2"

Calculate the number of days in the interval November 8, 2020 to April 23, 2021.

SOLUTION

Here are the keystrokes with brief explanations.

2nd DATE	⇒ Open the DATE worksheet.
11.0820 ENTER	⇒ Key in and save the value for *DT1*. Date information is entered in the format *mm.ddyy* where *mm* is the one- or two-digit number for the month, *dd* is the *two*-digit number for the day of the month, and *yy* is the *last* two digits of the year. Pressing the ENTER key saves this new value for *DT1*.
↓	⇒ Scroll down to *DT2*.
4.2321 ENTER	⇒ Key in and save the value for *DT2*.
↓	⇒ Scroll down to *DBD*.
CPT	⇒ Compute the value of *DBD*, the number of days in the interval. The answer that appears is 166 days. The calculator will automatically handle leap years.
2nd QUIT	⇒ Close the worksheet.

EXAMPLE 7B.B

CALCULATING "DT1" GIVEN "DT2" AND "DBD"

Determine the date that is 257 days before June 23, 2019.

SOLUTION

2nd DATE	⇒ Open the DATE worksheet.
↓	⇒ Scroll down to *DT2*.
6.2319 ENTER	⇒ Key in and save the value for *DT2*.
↓	⇒ Scroll down to *DBD*.
257 ENTER	⇒ Key in and save the value for *DBD*.
↑ ↑	⇒ Scroll up to *DT1*.
CPT	⇒ Compute the value of *DT1*. The answer "*TUE* = 10-09-2018" appears in the display. Hence, the beginning date of the interval is Tuesday, October 9, 2018.
2nd QUIT	⇒ Close the worksheet.

Chapter 8
Applications of Simple Interest

CHAPTER OUTLINE

*8.1 Savings Accounts and Short-Term GICs

8.2 The Valuation Principle

8.3 Treasury Bills and Commercial Paper

8.4 Demand Loans

*8.5 Canada Student Loans

*Appendix 8A: Promissory Notes

LEARNING OBJECTIVES

After completing this chapter, you will be able to:

LO1 Calculate the interest paid on savings accounts and short-term guaranteed investment certificates

LO2 State the Valuation Principle and apply it to the calculation of the fair market value of an investment with known future cash flows

LO3 Calculate the market price and rate of return for Treasury bills and commercial paper

LO4 Describe typical terms, conditions, and repayment arrangements for revolving (demand) loans, fixed-payment (demand) loans, and Canada Student Loans

LO5 Prepare loan repayment schedules for revolving loans, fixed-payment loans, and Canada Student Loans

GUARANTEED INVESTMENT CERTIFICATES (GICS), TERM deposits, and Treasury bills are short-term, low-risk investments that are favoured by investors looking for ways to invest their money for a number of days or months with flexible options and no long-term commitment. The short-term market is a popular one, with the average size of Canadian money market mutual funds (that hold short-term investments) being similar to the average size of mutual funds that invest in stocks and bonds. When a "bear" market hits stocks, many investors move their money from stocks to these low-risk short-term investments.

In our discussion of short-term investments we will use the Valuation Principle to determine how much you should pay for an investment. We will look at the rules surrounding lines of credit and demand loans and specifically look at the interest calculations on student loans.

*8.1 Savings Accounts and Short-Term GICs

LO1 Banks, trust companies, and credit unions use $I = Prt$ for calculating the interest on a variety of savings accounts and short-term investment products. Most **savings accounts** offer daily interest, meaning the interest is calculated each day on the daily closing balance but the interest is not credited to your account until the last day of the month or the first day of the following month. Some savings accounts have a tiered scale of interest rates, with higher rates paid when the account's balance reaches certain higher levels. When the interest rates on savings accounts are *floating*, they are adjusted to follow the trend of short-term rates in the financial markets. Interest on a few savings and chequing accounts is calculated on only the *minimum monthly* balance and paid monthly or semiannually.

EXAMPLE 8.1A

SAVINGS ACCOUNT INTEREST BASED ON A FIXED INTEREST RATE

Veronica has a Premium Savings bank account that pays 2.5% interest. On June 1, the balance in her account was $2252.68. On June 7 she deposited $500; she deposited another $700 on June 18, and then withdrew $2400 on June 27. Calculate the interest she will receive for the month of June.

SOLUTION

The following table organizes the given information in preparation for the interest calculation:

Period	Number of days	Balance ($)
June 1–6	6	2252.68
June 7–17	11	2752.68
June 18–26	9	3452.68
June 27–30	4	1052.68

The interest earned for the period June 1 to 6 inclusive is

$$I(\text{June 1–6}) = Prt$$
$$= \$2252.68(0.025)\left(\tfrac{6}{365}\right) = \$0.926$$

Maintain four-figure precision for three-figure accuracy in the final answer.

Similarly,

$$I(\text{June 7–17}) = \$2752.68(0.025)\left(\tfrac{11}{365}\right) = \$2.074$$
$$I(\text{June 18–26}) = \$3452.68(0.025)\left(\tfrac{9}{365}\right) = \$2.128$$
$$I(\text{June 27–30}) = \$1052.68(0.025)\left(\tfrac{4}{365}\right) = \$0.288$$
$$\text{Total interest for June} = \$0.926 + \$2.074 + \$2.128 + \$0.288 = \$5.42$$

Veronica will earn $5.42 interest in June.

EXAMPLE 8.1B

SAVINGS ACCOUNT INTEREST BASED ON A TIERED INTEREST RATE

Mr. and Mrs. Hernandez have a Performance 55 bank account that pays a slightly higher rate to depositors aged 55 or older. Interest is calculated on the daily closing balance and received monthly as follows:

Portion of balance	Interest rate (%)
From 0 to $1000.00	1.5
From $1000.01 to $3000.00	1.75
Over $3000.00	2.0

On April 1, their balance was $1416.32. They withdrew $500 on April 9, deposited $1200 on April 15, and deposited another $1200 on April 29. Calculate the interest that they will receive for the month of April.

SOLUTION

The following table organizes the given information in preparation for the interest calculation:

Period	Number of days	Change	Balance ($)	Amount ($) subject to a rate of: 1.5%	1.75%	2.0%
April 1–8	8		1416.32	1000.00	416.32	—
April 9–14	6	− $500	916.32	916.32	—	—
April 15–28	14	+ $1200	2116.32	1000.00	1116.32	—
April 29–30	2	+ $1200	3316.32	1000.00	2000.00	316.32

The interest earned for the period April 1 to 8 inclusive is

$$
\begin{aligned}
I(\text{April } 1\text{–}8) &= P_1 r_1 t + P_2 r_2 t \\
&= (P_1 r_1 + P_2 r_2)t \\
&= [\$1000(0.015) + \$416.32(0.0175)]\left(\tfrac{8}{365}\right) \\
&= (\$15.00 + \$7.286)(0.02192) \\
&= \$0.489
\end{aligned}
$$

Similarly,

$$
I(\text{April } 9\text{–}14) = \$916.32(0.015)\left(\tfrac{6}{365}\right) = \$0.226
$$

$$
\begin{aligned}
I(\text{April } 15\text{–}28) &= [\$1000(0.015) + \$1116.32(0.0175)]\left(\tfrac{14}{365}\right) \\
&= (\$15.00 + \$19.54)(0.03836) \\
&= \$1.325
\end{aligned}
$$

$$
\begin{aligned}
I(\text{April } 29\text{–}30) &= [\$1000(0.015) + \$2000(0.0175) + \$316.32(0.02)]\left(\tfrac{2}{365}\right) \\
&= (\$15.00 + \$35.00 + \$6.33)(0.005479) \\
&= \$0.309
\end{aligned}
$$

$$
\text{Total interest for April} = \$0.489 + \$0.226 + \$1.325 + \$0.309 = \$2.349
$$

Mr. and Mrs. Hernandez will earn $2.35 interest in April.

Depositors can earn a higher interest rate if they are prepared to forgo access to their funds for at least 30 days. A **Certificate of Deposit** is a type of *locked-in* savings account with a fixed interest rate, usually higher than traditional savings accounts. Money held in a CD cannot be withdrawn until maturity, at which point the interest is paid.

Banks, trust companies, life insurance companies, and credit unions offer **Guaranteed Investment Certificates**, usually referred to as GICs. Typically, a GIC is issued by a mortgage-lending subsidiary of a financial institution, and is *unconditionally guaranteed* by the parent company.

The Canada Deposit Insurance Corporation also guarantees up to $100,000 per depositor on both CDs and GICs. Short-term GICs are issued with maturities of 30 to 364 days. (Long-term GICs, with maturities of one to seven years, will be discussed in Section 9.5.)

Most banks, trust companies, and credit unions offer both *non-redeemable* and *redeemable* versions of short-term GICs. Redeemable GICs may be redeemed or "cashed in" before the scheduled maturity date. Non-redeemable GICs do not permit you to recover your money before the maturity date except under extraordinary circumstances. (Some institutions use the term "cashable GIC" and others use "term deposit" instead of "redeemable GIC." At these institutions, any mention of a guaranteed investment certificate is understood to refer to the non-redeemable variety.)

Interest on short-term GICs is calculated on a simple-interest basis and is paid on the maturity date. Table 8.1 shows some sample interest rates available for GICs with varying terms and conditions.

TABLE 8.1	Sample GIC Rates and Terms (January 2019)		
Redeemable?	Registered?	Term	Simple Interest Rate
No	No	270 days	2.75%
No	No	180 days	2.50%
No	No	90 days	2.35%
No	Yes	180 days	0.70%
No	Yes	90 days	0.55%
Yes	No	270 days	0.15%
Yes	No	180 days	0.10%
Yes	No	90 days	0.05%

Source: Bank of Canada

The interest rates offered exhibit the following patterns, which are typical for all GICs:

- Higher rates are paid on non-redeemable GICs than on redeemable GICs.
- Higher rates are paid for longer terms (within the 30- to 364-day range).
- Higher rates are paid for non-registered GICs.
- Higher rates are paid on larger principal amounts.

EXAMPLE 8.1C

CALCULATION OF INTEREST ON SHORT-TERM GICS

Leslie wants to invest $15,000 in a 270-day GIC. She would like to be able to have the redemption privilege just in case she needs the funds before the GIC matures. How much interest (in dollars) must Leslie forgo in order to retain the redemption privilege? Use the rates shown in Table 8.1 for the redeemable and non-redeemable GICs.

SOLUTION

On a non-redeemable GIC, Leslie would earn

$$I = Prt = \$15{,}000(0.0275)\left(\tfrac{270}{365}\right) = \$305.14$$

On a redeemable GIC, she would earn

$$I = Prt = \$15{,}000(0.0015)\left(\tfrac{270}{365}\right) = \$16.64$$

Leslie must forgo $305.14 – $16.64 = $288.50 of interest earnings to retain the redemption privilege.

EXAMPLE 8.1D

CALCULATION OF MATURITY VALUE ON SHORT-TERM GICS

Brandt would like to invest $8000 for 180 days in a non-redeemable, non-registered GIC. Using the rates from Table 8.1:

a. What is the maturity value for a single 180-day investment?

b. What is the maturity value of the investment if Brandt invests in a 90-day GIC and then on maturity "rolls over" the combined principal and interest into a second 90-day GIC?

c. How much more (in dollars) is the maturity value of the better option?

SOLUTION

a. On the 180-day non-redeemable, non-registered GIC

$$S = P[1 + rt] = \$8000\left[1 + 0.0250\left(\tfrac{180}{365}\right)\right] = \$8098.63$$

b. On the first 90-day non-redeemable, non-registered GICs

$$S = P[1 + rt] = \$8000\left[1 + 0.0235\left(\tfrac{90}{365}\right)\right] = \$8046.36$$

The maturity value of the first 90-day GIC will become the principal for the second 90-day GIC:

$$S = \$8046.36\left[1 + 0.0235\left(\tfrac{90}{365}\right)\right] = \$8092.98$$

c. The single 180-day GIC is worth $8098.63 − $8092.98 = $5.65 more than the two 90-day GICs.

EXERCISE 8.1

Answers to the odd-numbered problems are at the end of the book.

BASIC PROBLEMS

1. **a.** What will be the maturity value of $15,000 placed in a 120-day term deposit paying an interest rate of 2.25%?

b. If, on the maturity date, the combined principal and interest are "rolled over" into a 90-day term deposit paying 2.15%, what amount will the depositor receive when the second term deposit matures?

2. The rates offered by a credit union for its non-redeemable 90- to 365-day GICs are shown in the following table:

Deposit Amount	Rate
$10,000 to $24,999	2.5%
$25,000 to $59,999	3.0%
$60,000 to $99,999	3.2%

Early redemption is permitted but will result in the rate being reduced to 1.75%. How much more interest will a 91-day $20,000 term deposit earn if it is held until maturity than if it is redeemed after 80 days?

3. Using the rate table from Question #2, how much more will an investor earn from a single $60,000, 270-day GIC than from two $30,000, 270-day GICs?

4. The rates offered by a bank on deposits between $10,000 and $24,999 are shown in the following table:

Term	Rate
180 to 269 days	3.15%
270 to 364 days	3.45%

How much more will an investor earn from a $10,000 investment in a 364-day GIC than from two consecutive 182-day GICs? (Assume that the interest rate on 180- to 269-day GICs will be the same on the renewal date as it is today. Remember that both the principal and the interest from the first 182-day GIC can be invested in the second 182-day GIC.)

5. Your local credit union offers the rates shown in the following table for short-term non-redeemable, non-registered GICs.

Term	Rate
90 to 179 days	2.65%
180 to 269 days	2.85%

How much more interest will an investor earn by placing $15,000 in a 180-day GIC than by purchasing two consecutive 90-day GICs? (Assume that interest rates do not change over the next 90 days. Remember that interest earned from the first 90-day GIC can be invested in the second 90-day GIC.)

6. Liam wants to deposit a $2300 bonus cheque into his high-rate savings account that pays interest of 3.15%. Interest is calculated on the daily closing balance and paid at the close of business on the last day of the month. If Liam's current balance is $9055 and he does not make any withdrawals, what interest will he earn on his savings account for the month of March by depositing the cheque on March 11?

7. Danica wants to deposit a cheque for $5000 into her premium-rate savings account that pays interest of 2.25%. Interest is calculated on the daily closing balance and paid at the close of business on the last day of the month. If Danica already has $12,500 in her savings account and does not make any withdrawals:
   a. How much interest would she earn for the month of June if she deposited the cheque on June 28?
   b. How much interest would she earn for the month of June if she deposited the cheque on July 1?

8. A Super Saver savings account pays interest of 2.15%. Interest is calculated on the daily closing balance and paid at the close of business on the last day of the month. How much interest will be lost for the month of May if $6000 is withdrawn from the account on May 3 and the opening balance on May 1 is $14,032?

9. A high-rate savings account pays interest of 3.05%. Interest is calculated on the daily closing balance and paid at the close of business on the last day of the month. A depositor had a $7255 opening balance on November 1, withdrew $520 on November 17, and deposited $915 on November 21. What interest will be credited to the account at the month's end?

10. A savings account pays interest of 1.5%. Interest is calculated on the daily closing balance and paid at the close of business on the last day of the month. A depositor had a $2239 opening balance on September 1, deposited $734 on September 7 and $327 on September 21, and withdrew $300 on September 10. What interest will be credited to the account at the month's end?

INTERMEDIATE PROBLEMS

11. Joan has savings of $12,000 on June 1. Since she may need some of the money during the next three months, she is considering two options at her bank. (1) An Investment Builder account earns a 2.25% rate of interest. The interest is calculated on the daily closing balance and paid on the first day of the following month. (2) A 90- to 179-day cashable term deposit earns a rate of 2.8%, paid at maturity. If interest rates do not change and Joan does not withdraw any of the funds, how much more will she earn from the term deposit option up to September 1? (Keep in mind that savings account interest paid on the first day of the month will itself earn interest during the subsequent month.)

12. Suppose that the current rates on 90- and 180-day GICs are 3.25% and 3.50%, respectively. An investor is weighing the alternatives of purchasing a 180-day GIC versus purchasing a 90-day GIC and then reinvesting its maturity value in a second 90-day GIC. What would the

interest rate on 90-day GICs have to be 90 days from now for the investor to end up in the same financial position with either alternative?

13. An Investment Savings account offered by a trust company calculates interest daily based on the daily closing balances as follows:

Interest rate (%)	Amount to which the rate applies
1.25%	First $1000 of daily closing balance
1.5%	Portion of the balance between $1000 and $3000
1.75%	Any balance in excess of $3000

What interest will be paid for the month of April if the opening balance was $2439, $950 was deposited on April 10, and $500 was withdrawn on April 23?

14. The Moneybuilder account offered by a chartered bank calculates interest daily based on the daily closing balance as follows:

Interest rate (%)	Amount to which the rate applies
0.00	Balance when it is below $1000
1.25	Entire balance when it is between $1000 and $3000
1.75	Portion of balance above $3000

The balance at the beginning of March was $1678. On March 5, $700 was withdrawn. Then $2500 was deposited on March 15, and $900 was withdrawn on March 23. What interest will be credited to the account for the month of March?

15. The Super Savings account offered by a trust company calculates interest daily based on the *lesser* of each day's opening or closing balance as follows:

Interest rate (%)	Amount to which the rate applies
0.50	Entire balance when it is between $0 and $2999.99
1.00	Entire balance when it is between $3000 and $4999.99
1.25	Entire balance when it is between $5000 and $9999.99
1.50	Entire balance when it is between $10,000 and $24,999.99
1.75	Entire balance when it is between $25,000 and $49,999.99
2.25	Entire balance when it is $50,000 or more

September's opening balance was $8572. The transactions in the account for the month were a $9500 deposit on September 6, a deposit of $8600 on September 14, and a withdrawal of $25,000 on September 23. What interest will be credited to the account at the end of September?

16. For principal amounts of $5000 to $49,999, a bank pays an interest rate of 2.95% on 180- to 269-day non-redeemable GICs, and 3.00% on 270- to 364-day non-redeemable GICs. Ranjit has $10,000 to invest for 364 days. Because he thinks interest rates will be higher six months from now, he is debating whether to choose a 182-day GIC now (and reinvest its maturity value in another 182-day GIC) or to choose a 364-day GIC today. What would the interest rate on 182-day GICs have to be on the reinvestment date for both alternatives to yield the same maturity value 364 days from now?

8.2 The Valuation Principle

LO2 Consider an investment that will deliver a single payment of $110 one year from today. What is the most you should pay to buy the investment if you require a minimum rate of return of 10%? (In other words, what is the current value of the investment to you?) After a little thought, you probably answer "$100" for the following reason. The $10 difference between the amount you pay ($100) and the amount you will receive ($110) represents a 10% rate of return on your $100 investment.

But how would you calculate the price to pay if the given numbers are not so "nice"? For example, what maximum price should you pay for an investment that will pay you $129 after

247 days, if you require a rate of return of 5.5%? Let us think about where the $100 came from in the first example. Note that $100 invested for one year at 10% will grow to $110. Since $110 is the *future* value of $100, then $100 is the *present* value of $110. That is,

$$P = \frac{S}{1 + rt} = \frac{\$110}{1 + 0.10 \times 1} = \$100$$

This demonstrates that the present-value calculation gives a price that "builds in" the required 10% rate of return. If your minimum required rate of return is only 8%, then you should be willing to pay up to

$$P = \frac{S}{1 + rt} = \frac{\$110}{1 + 0.08 \times 1} = \$101.85$$

The $8.15($110.00 − $101.85) you will earn during the next year provides a rate of return (on your $101.85 investment) of

$$\frac{\$8.15}{\$101.85} \times 100\% = 8.00\%$$

The lower the rate of return you are prepared to accept, the higher the price you can pay now for a given future payment.

In the language of finance, the process of calculating a payment's present value is often called **discounting a payment**. When you calculate the present value of a payment, you are effectively stripping the interest out of the payment to get a smaller number than the payment. The interest rate used in the present-value calculation is then called the **discount rate**.

To determine the price to pay for an investment that promises two or more future payments, we simply extend our basic idea. That is, first calculate the present value of each of the payments (using the required rate of return as the discount rate). Then add the present values.

For investments purchased privately, you have some flexibility to negotiate a *higher* rate of return by bargaining *down* the price. But for various types of investments available to the general public, the rates of return are determined by market forces of supply and demand. When an investment's price is established by competitive bidding among many buyers and sellers, we refer to the price as the **fair market value**. A particular fair market value corresponds to a specific rate of return from the investment. This rate of return is what we mean by the *market-determined rate of return*. For publicly traded investments, your only decision is whether or not to accept the prevailing price and the corresponding market-determined rate of return.

These ideas are so important and of such wide application in finance that they are formally embodied in the Valuation Principle.

Valuation Principle

The fair market value of an investment is the sum of the present values of the cash flows expected from the investment. The discount rate used in the present-value calculations should be the prevailing market-determined rate of return on this type of investment.

If the expected cash flows are received as forecast, the investor's actual rate of return on the amount invested will be precisely the discount rate used in the fair market value calculation.

EXAMPLE 8.2A

VALUATION OF A NON-INTEREST-BEARING OBLIGATION

An investment contract calls for a payment of $1000 five months from now and another payment, 10 months from now, of $1500.

a. What price will an investor be prepared to pay for the investment today if the required rate of return is 12%?

b. Demonstrate that the investor will realize a 12% rate of return on this price if the payments are received as expected.

SOLUTION

a. According to the Valuation Principle,

$$\text{Price} = \text{Present value of } \$1000 + \text{Present value of } \$1500$$
$$= \frac{\$1000}{1 + 0.12\left(\frac{5}{12}\right)} + \frac{\$1500}{1 + 0.12\left(\frac{10}{12}\right)}$$
$$= \$952.381 + \$1363.636$$
$$= \$2316.02$$

An investor requiring a 12% rate of return should be willing to pay $2316.02 today for the contract.

b. Think of the $952.38 and $1363.64 components of the $2316.02 price as separately buying the future cash flows of $1000 and $1500, respectively.

$952.38 invested for five months at 12% will grow to

$$S = P(1 + rt) = \$952.38\left[1 + 0.12\left(\tfrac{5}{12}\right)\right] = \$1000.00$$

Therefore, the $1000 payment received after five months recovers the $952.38 investment along with five months' interest on $952.38 at 12%.

Similarly, it can be shown that the $1500 payment received after 10 months pays back the $1363.64 component of the initial investment plus 10 months' interest on $1363.64 at 12%.

EXAMPLE 8.2B

VALUATION OF AN INTEREST-BEARING OBLIGATION

On March 1, Murray signed a contract to pay Anton or his designate $2000 plus interest at 8% on June 1, and $3000 plus interest at 8% on September 1. Anton sold the contract to Randy on May 1 at a price negotiated to provide Randy with a 10% rate of return. What price did Randy pay?

SOLUTION

According to the Valuation Principle, the price paid by Randy should be the present value on May 1 of the two scheduled payments discounted at 10%. Unlike Example 8.2A, we do not know at the outset the dollar amounts of the scheduled payments. As indicated in the following time diagram, we must first calculate the maturity value of each obligation using the contract's 8% interest rate. Then we can determine the present value of each scheduled payment using a discount rate of 10%. (The present-value calculations thereby build in a 10% rate of return to Randy.)

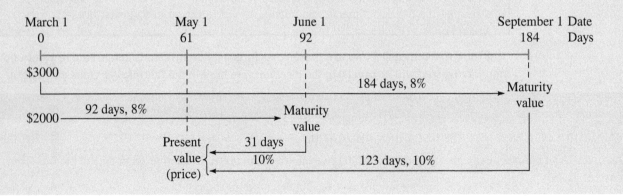

Payment due on June 1 = Maturity value of \$2000 = $\$2000\left[1 + 0.08\left(\frac{92}{365}\right)\right]$ = \$2040.33

Payment due on September 1 = Maturity value of \$3000 = $\$3000\left[1 + 0.08\left(\frac{184}{365}\right)\right]$ = \$3120.99

$$\text{Price} = \text{Present value of scheduled payments} = \frac{\$2040.33}{1 + 0.10\left(\frac{31}{365}\right)} + \frac{\$3120.99}{1 + 0.10\left(\frac{123}{365}\right)}$$

$$= \$2023.147 + \$3019.246$$
$$= \$5042.39$$

Randy paid \$5042.39 for the contract.

EXERCISE 8.2

Answers to the odd-numbered problems are at the end of the book.

BASIC PROBLEMS

1. An investment promises two payments of \$500, on dates three and six months from today. If the required rate of return on the investment is 4%:
   a. What is the value of the investment today?
   b. What will its value be in one month if the required rate of return remains at 4%?
   c. Give an explanation for the change in value as time passes.

2. An investment promises two payments of \$1000, on dates 60 and 90 days from today. What price will an investor pay today:
   a. If her required rate of return is 10%?
   b. If her required rate of return is 11%?
   c. Give an explanation for the lower price at the higher required return.

3. Certificate A pays \$1000 in four months and another \$1000 in eight months. Certificate B pays \$1000 in five months and another \$1000 in nine months. If the current rate of return required on this type of investment certificate is 5.75%, determine the current value of each of the certificates. Give an explanation for the lower value of B.

4. A contract requires payments of \$1500, \$2000, and \$1000 in 100, 150, and 200 days, respectively, from today. What is the value of the contract today if the payments are discounted to yield a 10.5% rate of return?

5. An agreement stipulates payments of \$4000, \$2500, and \$5000 in three, six, and nine months, respectively, from today. What is the highest price an investor will offer today to purchase the agreement if he requires a minimum rate of return of 3.25%?

INTERMEDIATE PROBLEMS

6. An assignable loan contract executed three months ago requires two payments to be paid five and ten months after the contract date. Each payment consists of a principal portion of \$1800 plus interest at 10% on \$1800 from the date of the contract. The payee is offering to sell the contract to a finance company in order to raise cash. If the finance company requires a return of 15%, what price will it be prepared to pay today for the contract?

7. Nadir bought a new home theatre system with 7.1 surround sound, 3D TV, and leather theatre seating for \$10,000 from Best Future Electronics on March 20. He paid \$2000 in cash and signed a conditional sale contract requiring a payment on July 1 of \$3000 plus interest on the \$3000 at a rate of 11%, and another payment on September 1 of \$5000 plus interest at 11% from the date of the sale. The vendor immediately sold the contract to a finance company, which discounted the payments at its required rate of return of 16%. What proceeds did Best Future receive from the sale of the contract?

8.3 Treasury Bills and Commercial Paper

LO3 **Treasury bills** (T-bills) are one of the safest investments available because you are directly investing in the Government of Canada. T-bills are paper contracts issued to lenders by the federal government and several provincial governments when they borrow money for terms of less than one year.

T-bills have all of the same benefits as Guaranteed Investment Certificates (GICs): they are easy to buy, they are secure, and they can be held inside a Registered Retirement Savings Plan (RRSP), Registered Retirement Income Fund (RRIF), and a Tax-Free Savings Account (TFSA). Since they are backed by the government, insurance protection is not needed.

The Government of Canada holds auctions every second Tuesday where it offers T-bills with maturities of 91, 182, and 364 days. The initial lenders (purchasers of the T-bills) are major investment dealers and chartered banks. In turn, these financial institutions sell most of the T-bills to their client-investors in face values of $5000, $25,000, $50,000, and $100,000.

In everyday loan transactions, we normally stipulate the principal amount and then calculate the payment or payments required to repay the principal plus interest. With T-bills, the arrangement is different. The denomination or **face value** of a T-bill is the full amount, *including interest*, payable at maturity of the T-bill. The purchase price (or amount loaned) will be less than the face value—the difference represents the interest[1] that will be earned on the loan. In investment language, T-bills are "issued at a discount to their face value."

How do you decide how much to pay (lend) for the right to receive a T-bill's face value on a known future date? This is the same type of question you were asked at the beginning of Section 8.2. You calculate the present value of the T-bill's face value, using your required rate of return as the discount rate.[2]

The purchaser of a T-bill is not required to hold it until it matures. There is an active market for the sale/purchase of T-bills that are partway through their terms. On any day, the price at which a T-bill may be bought or sold is the present value of its face value. The face value should be discounted at the *current* market-determined rate of return on T-bills over the *time remaining* until maturity. Typical market rates for a few maturities are listed in the financial pages of major newspapers each day. An example of T-bill quotations is presented in the middle column of Table 8.2.

TABLE 8.2 Treasury Bill and Commercial Paper Rates (January 30, 2019)		
Time remaining until maturity	Rate of return on Treasury bills (%)	Rate of return on commercial paper (%)
1 month	1.68	2.19
3 months	1.66	2.11
6 months	1.73	n/a
1 year	1.83	n/a

Source: Bank of Canada

---

[1] Rates of return (or yields) on T-bills and commercial paper for the most recent five business days are available on the Bank of Canada's Web site.

[2] For the initial auction of T-bills, participating financial institutions submit price bids just prior to the auction. The institutions use their own required rate of return as the discount rate when determining the present value of the face value. An institution arrives at its required rate of return based on prevailing short-term interest rates in financial markets, and on the expected demand for T-bills from its clients. The Bank of Canada accepts bids in order of decreasing prices until the government's borrowing requirements for the week are met. The *delivery date* for bids accepted on Tuesday is the subsequent Thursday. This means that the Bank of Canada must receive payment by Thursday, and the "clock" for the T-bills' terms starts on Thursday.

Some large corporations also borrow money for short periods by selling contracts called **commercial paper**. Commercial paper is essentially a corporation's version of T-bills. Common maturities are 30, 60, and 90 days (usually referred to as one-month, two-month, and three-month maturities). The minimum face value is usually $100,000. Like Treasury bills, commercial paper is priced at its discounted present value. The required rate of return (discount rate) on commercial paper is usually 0.4% to 0.8% higher than that on T-bills. (See Table 8.2.) The higher rate of return is required because of the small risk that the corporation might be unable to pay the face value on the due date.

EXAMPLE 8.3A

VALUATION OF A T-BILL ON ITS ISSUE DATE

Suppose the average rate of return or yield on 168-day Government of Canada Treasury bills sold at a Tuesday auction was 1.73%. At this yield, what price was paid for a T-bill with a face value of $100,000?

SOLUTION

$$\text{Price} = \text{Present value of } \$100,000 \text{ discounted at } 1.73\% \text{ for } 168 \text{ days}$$
$$= \frac{\$100,000}{1 + 0.0173\left(\frac{168}{365}\right)}$$
$$= \$99,210.02$$

To obtain a yield of 1.73%, $99,210.02 was paid for the 168-day, $100,000 face value T-bill.

EXAMPLE 8.3B

VALUATION OF A T-BILL

The institutional purchaser of the T-bill in Example 8.3A immediately sells it to a client at a higher price that represents a (lower) yield to the client of 1.71%. What profit did the institution make on the transaction?

SOLUTION

$$\text{Selling price to the client} = \frac{\$100,000}{1 + 0.0171\left(\frac{168}{365}\right)} = \$99,219.08$$
$$\text{Profit} = \text{Price charged to the client} - \text{Acquisition price}$$
$$= \$99,219.08 - \$99,210.02$$
$$= \$9.06$$

The institution's profit on the resale of the T-bill was $9.06.

EXAMPLE 8.3C

CALCULATION OF THE RATE OF RETURN ON A T-BILL SOLD BEFORE MATURITY

Suppose the client who purchased the 168-day, $100,000 T-bill in Example 8.3B for $99,219.08 sold the T-bill after 73 days in order to invest the proceeds elsewhere.

a. What price would she receive if the short-term interest rate for this maturity had risen to 1.76% by the date of sale?

b. What rate of return (per annum) did the client realize while holding the T-bill?

SOLUTION

a. Days remaining to maturity = $168 - 73 = 95$

Selling price = Present value of $100,000 discounted at 1.76% for 95 days

$$= \frac{\$100,000}{1 + 0.0176\left(\frac{95}{365}\right)}$$

$$= \$99,544.01$$

The client sold the T-bill for $99,544.01.

b. The client purchased an investment for $99,219.08 and sold it 73 days later for $99,544.01. We need to calculate the rate of return when $99,219.08 grows to $99,544.01 in 73 days. In effect, the initial investment of $99,219.08 earned interest amounting to

$$I = \$99,544.01 - \$99,219.08 = \$324.93$$

Formula (7-1) may now be used to obtain the corresponding rate of return.

$$r = \frac{I}{Pt} = \frac{\$324.93}{\$99,219.08\left(\frac{73}{365}\right)} = 0.0164 = 1.64\%$$

The client's rate of return during the 73-day holding period was 1.64%.

EXAMPLE 8.3D

CALCULATION OF THE RATE OF RETURN ON COMMERCIAL PAPER

Sixty-day commercial paper with face value $100,000 was issued by Suncor Inc. for $99,645. What rate of return will be realized if the paper is held until maturity?

SOLUTION

In effect, the interest earned on an investment of $99,645 for 60 days is

$$\$100,000 - \$99,645 = \$355$$

Using Formula (7-1) rearranged to solve for r, we have

$$r = \frac{I}{Pt} = \frac{\$355}{\$99,645\left(\frac{60}{365}\right)} = 0.0217 = 2.17\%$$

A 2.17% rate of return will be realized if the paper is held until it matures.

 CONCEPT QUESTIONS

1. Is the price of a 98-day $100,000 T-bill higher or lower than the price of a 168-day $100,000 T-bill? Why?

2. If short-term interest rates have increased during the past week, will investors pay more this week (than last week) for T-bills of the same term and face value? Explain.

3. If short-term interest rates do not change, what happens to a particular T-bill's fair market value as time passes?

EXERCISE 8.3

Answers to the odd-numbered problems are at the end of the book.

BASIC PROBLEMS

Calculate T-bill and commercial paper prices accurate to the nearest dollar and rates of return accurate to the nearest 0.001%.

1. Calculate the price of a $25,000, 91-day Province of British Columbia Treasury bill on its issue date if the current market rate of return is 1.672%.

2. Calculate the price on its issue date of $100,000 face value, 90-day commercial paper issued by GE Capital Canada if the prevailing market rate of return is 1.932%.

3. A money market mutual fund purchased $1 million face value of Honda Canada Finance Inc. 90-day commercial paper 28 days after its issue. What price was paid if the paper was discounted at 2.10%?

4. A $100,000, 91-day Province of Ontario Treasury bill was issued 37 days ago. What will be its purchase price today in order to yield the purchaser 1.55%?

5. Calculate and compare the issue-date prices of $100,000 face value commercial paper investments with 30-, 60-, and 90-day maturities, all priced to yield 1.5%.

6. Calculate and compare the market values of a $100,000 face value Government of Canada Treasury bill on dates that are 91 days, 61 days, 31 days, and one day before maturity. Assume that the rate of return required in the market stays constant at 3% over the lifetime of the T-bill.

7. Jake purchased a $100,000 182-day T-bill discounted to yield 1.85%. When he sold it 30 days later, yields had dropped to 1.79%. How much did Jake earn?

8. A $100,000, 90-day commercial paper certificate issued by Wells Fargo Financial Canada was sold on its issue date for $99,250. What rate of return will it yield to the buyer?

9. Debra paid $99,615 for a $100,000 T-bill with 30 days remaining until maturity. What (annual) rate of interest will she earn?

10. Over the past 35 years, the prevailing market yield or discount rate on 90-day T-bills has ranged from a low of 0.17% in February 2010 to a high of 20.82% in August 1981. (The period from 1979 to 1990 was a time of historically high inflation rates and interest rates.) How much more would you have paid for a $100,000 face value 90-day T-bill at the February 2010 discount rate than at the August 1981 discount rate?

INTERMEDIATE PROBLEMS

11. A 168-day, $100,000 T-bill was initially issued at a price that would yield the buyer 3.19%. If the yield required by the market remains at 3.19%, how many days before its maturity date will the T-bill's market price first exceed $99,000?

12. Lydia purchased a $100,000 150-day T-bill when the prevailing yield on T-bills was 4.5%. She sold the T-bill 60 days later when the prevailing yield was 4.2%. What interest rate did Lydia earn during the 60-day period?

13. A $100,000, 168-day Government of Canada Treasury bill was purchased on its date of issue to yield 2.1%.
    a. What price did the investor pay?
    b. Calculate the market value of the T-bill 85 days later if the rate of return then required by the market has:
       (i)   risen to 2.4%.
       (ii) remained at 2.1%.
       (iii) fallen to 1.8%.

    c. Calculate the rate of return actually realized by the investor if the T-bill is sold at each of the three prices calculated in part (b).

14. An investor purchased a 182-day, $25,000 Province of Alberta Treasury bill on its date of issue for $24,610 and sold it 60 days later for $24,750.

    a. What rate of return was implied in the original price?

    b. What rate of return did the market require on the sale date?

    c. What rate of return did the original investor actually realize during the 60-day holding period?

8.4 Demand Loans

Most businesses arrange demand loans or lines of credit to meet short-term financing requirements. Many individuals obtain personal lines of credit, set up on a demand basis, to meet their short-term borrowing needs.

Common Terms and Conditions

LO4 The name **demand loan** comes from the lender's right to demand full repayment of the loan at any time without notice. This rarely happens if the borrower fulfills the terms of the loan (unless the lender has reason to believe the borrower's financial condition is deteriorating). The borrower may repay any portion of the loan at any time without penalty.

    The interest rate charged on demand loans is usually "floating." This means that the rate is linked to the prime rate of interest in the banking system. Interest rates are then quoted as "prime plus" some additional amount. For example, if a small business is viewed by the lender as a moderate risk, the business might be charged a rate of prime plus 2% or prime plus 3%.

    Interest on a demand loan is paid on the same date each month. The most common approach is to calculate interest *from (and including)* the previous interest payment date *up to (but not including)* the current interest payment date. This procedure is consistent with the count-the-first-day-but-not-the-last-day rule for determining the length of the time interval in simple-interest calculations. The interest rate in effect each day is applied to each day's *closing* loan balance.

    Arrangements for repaying the loan principal are negotiated between the borrower and lender. Acceptable terms will depend upon the purpose of the loan, the nature of the security given, and the seasonality of the borrower's income. The two most common demand loan arrangements are:

- A revolving loan.
- A fixed-payment loan.

Revolving Loans

LO4 Revolving loans are preferred by businesses and individuals whose short-term borrowing requirements vary over the year. These loans give borrowers the flexibility to borrow additional funds at their discretion and to reduce their debt whenever extra funds are available. Most *lines of credit* and business *operating loans* are set up as revolving loans.[3]

---

[3] Visa and MasterCard accounts are in many respects similar to revolving lines of credit. Interest rates are usually fixed rather than floating. Interest (based on $I = Prt$ and the daily closing balance) is paid monthly. However, the calculations are complicated by special rules concerning waiver of interest when the balance is paid in full, different treatment for cash advances than for credit purchases, days of grace, etc. These rules make the interest calculations considerably more tedious (but not more mathematically instructive) than calculations for demand loans.

The borrower and the lending institution negotiate the terms and conditions of the loan—the credit limit, the security required, the interest rate, and so on. Subject to the credit limit and a few general guidelines, draws (or advances) of principal and repayments of principal are at the borrower's discretion.

For *fully secured* revolving loans, the minimum monthly payment may be only the accrued interest on the outstanding loan balance. In most other cases, the minimum monthly payment is something like "the greater of $100 or 3% of the *current* balance." The "current balance" in this context includes accrued interest. The lender usually requires that the borrower have a chequing account (sometimes called a *current account* for a business) with the lending institution. The required monthly payment is then automatically withdrawn from the chequing account on the interest payment date.

EXAMPLE 8.4A

CALCULATION OF INTEREST ON A REVOLVING LOAN

On March 20, Hank's Cycle Shop received an initial advance of $10,000 on its revolving demand loan. On the 15th of each month, interest is calculated (up to but not including the 15th) and deducted from Hank's bank account. The floating rate of interest started at 9.75% and dropped to 9.5% on April 5. On April 19, another $10,000 was drawn on the line of credit. What interest was charged to the bank account on April 15 and May 15?

SOLUTION

The one-month period ending on an interest payment date (April 15 and May 15) must be broken into intervals within which the balance on the loan *and* the interest rate are constant. In the following table, we should count the first day but not the last day in each interval. This will cause April 5 (the first day at the 9.5% interest rate) to be included in the second interval but not in the first interval.

Interval	Days	Principal ($)	Rate (%)	Amount of Interest
March 20–April 5	16	10,000	9.75	$10,000(0.0975)\left(\frac{16}{365}\right) = \$42.74$
April 5–April 15	10	10,000	9.5	$10,000(0.095)\left(\frac{10}{365}\right) = \underline{\ 26.03}$
				Interest charged on April 15: $\underline{\$68.77}$
April 15–April 19	4	10,000	9.5	$10,000(0.095)\left(\frac{4}{365}\right) = \$10.41$
April 19–May 15	26	20,000	9.5	$20,000(0.095)\left(\frac{26}{365}\right) = \underline{135.34}$
				Interest charged on May 15: $\underline{\$145.75}$

The interest charged to Hank's bank account on April 15 was $68.77 and on May 15 was $145.75.

L05 **Repayment schedule for a revolving loan** A **loan repayment schedule** is a table in which interest charges, loan draws and payments, and outstanding balances are recorded. The schedule helps us organize our calculations and properly allocate payments to interest and principal.

Figure 8.1 presents a format for a demand loan repayment schedule. You enter a row in the schedule when any of the following three events takes place:

- A principal amount is advanced or repaid.
- The interest rate changes.
- Interest (and possibly principal) is paid on an interest payment date.

| FIGURE 8.1 | Demand Loan Repayment Schedule |

(1)	(2)	(3)	(4)	(5)	(6)	(7)	(8)
Date	Number of days	Interest Rate	Interest	Accrued interest	Payment (Advance)	Principal portion	Balance

The columns in the table are used as follows. (Each item in the following list refers to the corresponding numbered column in **Figure 8.1**.)

1. In chronological order down column (1), enter the **dates** on which payments are made, the interest rate changes, or principal amounts are advanced to the borrower.
2. Enter into column (2) the **number of days** in the interval *ending* on each date in column (1). In any particular row, record the number of days from (and including) the *previous* row's date to (but not including) the date in the row *at hand*.
3. Enter into column (3) the **interest rate** that applies to each interval in column (2). When the date in column (1) is the date on which a new interest rate takes effect, the interest rate in column (3) is still the *previous rate*. The reason is that the days in column (2) are for the period *up to but not including* the date in column (1).
4. In column (4), enter the **interest** charge ($I = Prt$) for the number of days (t) in column (2) at the interest rate (r) in column (3) on the balance (P) from column (8) of the *preceding* line.
5. In column (5), enter the cumulative total of unpaid or **accrued interest** as of the current row's date. This amount is the interest just calculated in column (4) plus any previously accrued but unpaid interest [from column (5) in the *preceding* line].
6. In column (6), enter the amount of any **payment** (of principal and/or interest). A loan **advance** is enclosed in brackets to distinguish it from a loan payment.
7. On an interest payment date, the accrued interest in column (5) is deducted from the payment to obtain the **principal portion** of the payment. Put a single stroke through the accrued interest in column (5) as a reminder that it has been paid and should not be carried forward to the next period.

    If an *unscheduled* payment is entered in column (6), the entire amount is usually applied to principal. Enter it again in column (7). Similarly, the amount of any loan advance in column (6) should be duplicated in column (7).
8. The new loan **balance** is the previous line's balance *less* any principal repaid or *plus* any principal advanced [the amount in column (7)].

EXAMPLE 8.4B

REPAYMENT SCHEDULE FOR A REVOLVING OPERATING LOAN

The Bank of Montreal approved a $50,000 line of credit on a demand basis to Tanya's Wardrobes to finance the store's inventory. Interest at the rate of prime plus 2% is charged to Tanya's chequing account at the bank on the 23rd of each month. The initial advance was $25,000 on September 23, when the prime rate stood at 3.25%. There were further advances of $8000 on October 30 and $10,000 on November 15. Payments of $7000 and $14,000 were applied against the principal on December 15 and January 15, respectively. The prime rate rose to 3.75% effective December 5. What was the total interest paid on the loan for the period September 23 to January 23?

SOLUTION

A large amount of information is given in the statement of the problem. The best way to organize the data is to construct a repayment schedule using the format in Figure 8.1. In the date column, list in chronological order all of the dates on which a transaction or an event affecting the loan occurs. These are the dates of advances, payments of principal or interest, and interest rate changes. Next, enter the information that is given for each transaction or event. At this point the schedule has the following entries:

Date	Number of days	Interest rate (%)	Interest ($)	Accrued interest ($)	Payment (Advance) ($)	Principal portion ($)	Balance ($)
Sept 23	—	—	—	—	(25,000)	(25,000)	25,000
Oct 23		5.25				0	
Oct 30		5.25			(8000)	(8000)	
Nov 15		5.25			(10,000)	(10,000)	
Nov 23		5.25				0	
Dec 5		5.25				0	
Dec 15		5.75			7000	7000	
Dec 23		5.75				0	
Jan 15		5.75			14,000	14,000	
Jan 23		5.75				0	

Note that 5.25% (3.25% + 2%) has been entered on the December 5 line. Although the interest rate changes to 5.75% *effective* December 5, the "number of days" entry on this line will be the number of days from (and including) November 23 to (but not including) December 5. These 12 days are still charged interest at the 5.25% rate. The 5.75% rate will first apply to the December 5 to December 15 period, which is handled on the December 15 line.

The "number of days" column may be completed next. Then the calculations can proceed row by row to obtain the full schedule. The circled numbers (①, ②, etc.) in the following schedule refer to sample calculations listed after the schedule. Draw a stroke through an accrued interest figure when the interest is paid.

Date	Number of days	Interest rate (%)	Interest ($)	Accrued interest ($)	Payment (Advance) ($)	Principal portion ($)	Balance ($)
Sept 23	—	—	—	—	(25,000)	(25,000)	25,000
Oct 23	30	5.25	107.88①	~~107.88~~	107.88	0	25,000
Oct 30	7	5.25	25.17	25.17	(8000)	(8000)	33,000
Nov 15	16	5.25	75.95②	101.12③	(10,000)	(10,000)	43,000
Nov 23	8	5.25	49.48④	~~150.60⑤~~	150.60	0	43,000
Dec 5	12	5.25	74.22	74.22		0	43,000
Dec 15	10	5.75	67.74	141.96	7000	7000	36,000
Dec 23	8	5.75	45.37	~~187.33~~	187.33	0	36,000
Jan 15	23	5.75	130.44	130.44	14,000	14,000	22,000
Jan 23	8	5.75	27.73	~~158.17~~	158.17	0	22,000

① $I = Prt = \$25,000(0.0525)\left(\frac{30}{365}\right) = \$107.88$

② $I = \$33,000(0.0525)\left(\frac{16}{365}\right) = \$75.95$

③ Accrued interest $= \$25.17 + \$75.95 = \$101.12$

④ $I = \$43,000(0.0525)\left(\frac{8}{365}\right) = \$49.48$

⑤ Accrued interest $= \$101.12 + \$49.48 = \$150.60$

The total interest paid on the loan for the period September 23 to January 23 was

$$\$107.88 + \$150.60 + \$187.33 + \$158.17 = \$603.98$$

EXAMPLE 8.4C

REPAYMENT SCHEDULE FOR A REVOLVING PERSONAL LINE OF CREDIT

Warren Bitenko has a $20,000 personal line of credit with the RBC Royal Bank. The interest rate is prime + 1.5%. On the last day of each month, a payment equal to the greater of $100 or 3% of the current balance (including the current month's accrued interest) is deducted from his chequing account.

On July 6, he took his first advance of $2000. On August 15, he took another draw of $7500. The prime rate started at 3%, and rose to 3.25% on September 9. Prepare a loan repayment schedule up to and including September 30.

SOLUTION

Begin a schedule by entering, in chronological order, the dates of advances, interest rate changes, and payments. Information known about these events should also be entered. At this point, the schedule has the following entries and you are ready to begin the calculations.

Date	Number of days	Interest rate (%)	Interest ($)	Accrued interest ($)	Payment (Advance) ($)	Principal portion ($)	Balance ($)
July 6	—	4.5	—	—	(2000)	(2000)	2000
July 31		4.5					
Aug 15		4.5			(7500)	(7500)	
Aug 31		4.5					
Sept 9		4.5					
Sept 30		4.75					

Now proceed row by row to construct the loan schedule. The circled numbers (①, ②, etc.) in the following schedule refer to the sample calculations listed immediately after the schedule.

Date	Number of days	Interest rate (%)	Interest ($)	Accrued interest ($)	Payment (Advance) ($)	Principal portion ($)	Balance ($)
July 6	—	4.5	—	—	(2000.00)	(2000.00)	2000.00
July 31	25	4.5	6.16①	~~6.16~~	100.00②	93.84③	1906.16
Aug 15	15	4.5	3.53	3.53	(7500.00)	(7500.00)	9406.16
Aug 31	16	4.5	18.55	~~22.08~~	282.85④	260.77⑤	9145.39
Sept 9	9	4.5	10.15	10.15			9145.39
Sept 30	21	4.75	24.99	~~35.14~~	275.42	240.28	8905.11

① $I = Prt = \$2000(0.045)(\frac{25}{365}) = \$6.16$
② The payment is the greater of $100 or 0.03 × $2006.16 = $60.18. The larger amount is $100.
③ Principal repaid = $100 − $6.16 = $93.84
④ Required payment = 0.03 × Current balance = 0.03 × ($9406.16 + $22.08) = $282.85
⑤ Principal repaid = $282.85 − $22.08 = $260.77

Fixed-Payment Loans

L05 A fixed-payment loan requires *equal* monthly payments. The interest component of each payment is the interest that has accrued on the outstanding principal balance since the preceding payment. As the outstanding loan balance declines, each successive payment has a smaller interest component and a larger principal component.

EXAMPLE 8.4D

REPAYMENT SCHEDULE FOR A FIXED-PAYMENT LOAN

Bailey & Co. borrowed $4000 at prime plus 4.5% from its bank on May 29 to purchase a new computer system. The floating-rate demand loan requires fixed monthly payments of $800 on the first day of each month, beginning July 1. The prime rate was at 4.25% on May 29 and increased to 4.5% effective August 4. Construct a full repayment schedule showing details of the allocation of each payment to interest and principal.

SOLUTION

On a loan repayment schedule, enter the dates of payments and interest rate changes in chronological order. Information known about these events can also be entered. We can anticipate that a sixth payment (of less than $800) on December 1 will pay off the loan. At this point, the schedule has the following entries:

Date	Number of days	Interest rate (%)	Interest ($)	Accrued interest ($)	Payment (Advance) ($)	Principal portion ($)	Balance ($)
May 29	—	8.75	—	—	(4000)	(4000.00)	4000.00
July 1		8.75			800		
Aug 1		8.75			800		
Aug 4		8.75					
Sept 1		9			800		
Oct 1		9			800		
Nov 1		9			800		
Dec 1		9					

Proceed with the calculations row by row. The circled numbers (①, ②, etc.) in the following schedule refer to sample calculations listed after the schedule. Draw a stroke through an accrued interest figure when the interest has been paid.

Date	Number of days	Interest rate (%)	Interest ($)	Accrued interest ($)	Payment (Advance) ($)	Principal portion ($)	Balance ($)
May 29	—	8.75	—	—	(4000)	(4000.00)	4000.00
July 1	33	8.75	31.64①	~~31.64~~	800	768.36②	3231.64
Aug 1	31	8.75	24.02	~~24.02~~	800	775.98	2455.66
Aug 4	3	8.75	1.77	1.77			
Sept 1	28	9	16.95	~~18.72~~	800	781.28	1674.38
Oct 1	30	9	12.39	~~12.39~~	800	787.61	886.77
Nov 1	31	9	6.78	~~6.78~~	800	793.22	93.55
Dec 1	30	9	0.69	~~0.69~~	94.24 ③	93.55	0

① $I = Prt = \$4000(0.0875)\left(\frac{33}{365}\right) = \$31.64$
② Principal portion = $800 − $31.64 = $768.36
③ Final payment = $93.55 + $0.69 = $94.24

POINT OF INTEREST

Improving the Score on Your Credit Report

Personal debt is soaring as more and more people become bogged down in loans and credit card debt. The Canadian household debt-to-disposable-income ratio hit a record 178.5% at the end of 2018, meaning that the average Canadian owes $1.79 for every dollar of annual disposable income. Note that this average means some households owe more than this while others owe less.

In March of 2019 Equifax Canada reported that consumer delinquency rates continued to rise, and it would appear that this is becoming the norm for a lot of Canadian households.

As personal debt levels rise faster than income, personal credit reports and credit scores are increasingly important to the lenders providing consumer credit. Anyone who has ever borrowed money or applied for a credit card is likely to have a personal file with one or both of Canada's two main credit bureaus: Equifax Canada and TransUnion Canada. These are independent companies whose business is maintaining records on how every individual and business in Canada manages their debt.

Most businesses granting credit are members of one or both of these credit bureaus, and they supply the bureaus with information on how customers handle their credit. Any business thinking of granting credit to you, or providing you with a service that you will receive before you pay for it (such as telephone service or apartment rental) can obtain a comprehensive credit report on you from the credit bureau.

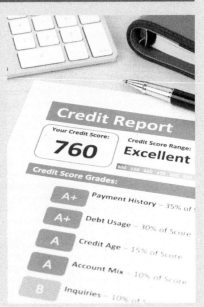

© Casper1774 Studio/Shutterstock

Your credit report contains information about every loan or credit card you've had in the previous six years, the credit limit on each account, how much you owe, whether you pay on time, and a list of authorized credit grantors that have accessed your file. Each account or loan has a *credit rating* notation. For example, revolving loans are rated from R1 (meaning that you have made payments "as agreed" or within 30 days of billing) to R9 (meaning your account has been classified as a "bad debt" or has been "placed for collection").

The credit bureau also assigns a single comprehensive *credit score* (often referred to as the FICO score or Beacon score). This score is based on a formula that takes into account several factors indicating creditworthiness. The score can range from 300 to 900—the higher the number the better. About 27% of the population have a score within the range 750 to 799. Statistically, only 2% of borrowers in this category will default on a debt within the next two years. Consequently, anyone with this score is very likely to get the loan or credit they are applying for.

You can (and probably should) periodically obtain a copy of your credit report. For a fee of $20 to $25, you can apply online to see your credit report. Alternatively, you can obtain one free credit report per year by a mail-in request. There are also numerous third-party services online that will provide you with your basic FICO score. These usually do not include a lot of additional in-depth information.

Generally, free credit scores are current to within a few days and use largely publicly available information. Paid credit scores are updated more frequently, use proprietary information, and offer additional services like credit analysis and fraud protection. It is also important to note that checking your credit score will not affect your credit.

If you are unhappy with your credit score, there are several things you can do to improve it.

- *Pay your debts on time.* This is the best way to improve your credit score.
- *Keep your credit card balances low.* Try not to run up the balances to your credit limit. It is recommended to keep balances below 70% of your credit limit.
- *Get a secured credit card.* Cardholders make an initial deposit equivalent to the credit limit on the card. There is no minimum credit requirement for these cards and payments on these cards get reported quickly to credit bureaus.

Source: "Statistics Canada Says Household Debt Grew Faster Than Income in Fourth-Quarter." CBC. https://www.cbc.ca/news/business/household-debt-income-1.5056159.

EXERCISE 8.4

Answers to the odd-numbered problems are at the end of the book.

Spreadsheet templates: *Connect presents two partially completed Excel templates for demand loan repayment schedules. Go to the Student Edition of Connect and find "Demand Loan Schedules" under the Student Resources for Chapter 8. You can use the Revolving Loan template for Problems 1–9 and the Fixed-Payment Loan template for Problems 10–14.*

INTERMEDIATE PROBLEMS

Revolving Demand Loans

1. Dr. Robillard obtained a $75,000 operating line of credit at prime plus 3%. Accrued interest up to but not including the last day of the month is deducted from his bank account on the last day of each month. On February 5 (of a leap year) he received the first draw of $15,000. He made a payment of $10,000 toward principal on March 15, but took another draw of $7000 on May 1. Prepare a loan repayment schedule showing the amount of interest charged to his bank account on the last days of February, March, April, and May. Assume that the prime rate remained at 5.5% through to the end of May.

2. Mr. Michaluk has a $50,000 personal (revolving) line of credit with the Canadian Imperial Bank of Commerce (CIBC). The loan is on a demand basis at a floating rate of prime plus 1.5%. On the 15th of each month, a payment equal to the greater of $100 or 3% of the combined principal and accrued interest is deducted from his chequing account. The principal balance after a payment on September 15 stood at $23,465.72. Prepare the loan repayment schedule from September 15 up to and including the payment on January 15. Assume that he makes the minimum payments and the prime rate remains at 5.25%.

3. McKenzie Wood Products negotiated a $200,000 revolving line of credit with the Bank of Montreal at prime plus 2%. On the 20th of each month, interest is calculated (up to but not including the 20th) and deducted from the company's chequing account. If the initial loan advance of $25,000 on July 3 was followed by a further advance of $30,000 on July 29, how much interest was charged on July 20 and August 20? The prime rate was at 3% on July 3 and fell to 2.75% on August 5.

4. On the June 12 interest payment date, the outstanding balance on Delta Nurseries' revolving loan was $65,000. The floating interest rate on the loan stood at 6.25% on June 12, but rose to 6.5% on July 3, and to 7% on July 29. If Delta made principal payments of $10,000 on June 30 and July 31, what were the interest charges to its bank account on July 12 and August 12? Present a repayment schedule supporting the calculations.

5. Scotiabank approved a $75,000 line of credit for Curved Comfort Furniture on the security of its accounts receivable. Curved Comfort drew down $30,000 on October 7, another $15,000 on November 24, and $20,000 on December 23. The bank debited interest at the rate of prime plus 3.5% from the business's bank account on the 15th of each month. The prime rate was 4.25% on October 7, and dropped by 0.25% on December 17. Present a loan repayment schedule showing details of transactions up to and including January 15.

6. Shoreline Yachts has a $1 million line of credit with the RBC Royal Bank, secured by its inventory of sailboats. Interest is charged at the floating (naturally!) rate of prime plus 2% on the 10th of each month. On February 10 (of a non–leap year), the loan balance stood at $770,000 and the prime rate at 6.5%. Shoreline took an additional $100,000 draw on March 1. Spring sales enabled Shoreline to make payments of $125,000 and $150,000 against the principal on March 30 and April 28. The prime rate rose by 0.5% on April 8. What total interest was Shoreline charged for the three months from February 10 to May 10? Present a repayment schedule showing how this interest figure was determined.

7. Hercules Sports obtained a $60,000 operating line of credit on March 26. Interest charges at the rate of prime plus 3.5% were deducted from its chequing account on the 18th of each month. Hercules took an initial draw of $30,000 on March 31, when the prime rate was 4%. Further advances of $10,000 and $15,000 were taken on April 28 and June 1. Payments of $5000 and $10,000 were applied against the principal on June 18 and July 3. The prime rate rose to 4.25% effective May 14. Present a repayment schedule showing details of transactions up to and including July 18.

8. Benjamin has a $20,000 personal line of credit at prime plus 2% with his credit union. His minimum end-of-month payment is the greater of $100 or 3% of the combined principal and accrued interest. After his payment on April 30, his balance was $3046.33. On May 23, he used his income tax refund to make a principal payment of $1000. On July 17, he took a $7000 advance to purchase a car. The prime rate began at 6%, rose 0.25% on June 25, and jumped another 0.25% on July 18. Prepare a loan repayment schedule showing details of payments on May 31, June 30, and July 31.

9. Bronwyn's $15,000 line of credit is at prime plus 2.5%. The minimum payment (the greater of $100 or 3% of the combined principal and accrued interest) is automatically deducted from her chequing account on the 15th of each month. After the payment on August 15, her balance was $3589.80. To reduce the loan faster, she makes an additional discretionary payment of $300 on the last day of each month. Each $300 payment is applied entirely to principal. Prepare a repayment schedule for the August 15 to November 15 period. The prime rate was at 6.25% on August 15 but dropped 0.25% effective October 11.

Fixed-Payment Demand Loans

10. A $5000 demand loan was advanced on June 3. Fixed monthly payments of $1000 were required on the first day of each month beginning July 1. Prepare the full repayment schedule for the loan. Assume that the interest rate remained at 8.75% for the life of the loan.

11. Giovando, Lindstrom & Co. obtained a $6000 demand loan at prime plus 1.5% on April 1 to purchase new office furniture. The company agreed to fixed monthly payments of $1000 on the first of each month, beginning May 1. Calculate the total interest charges over the life of the loan if the prime rate started at 2.75% on April 1, decreased to 2.5% effective June 7, and returned to 2.75% on August 27. Present a repayment schedule in support of your answer.

12. Donia borrowed $7000 from her credit union on a demand loan on July 20 to purchase a motorcycle. The terms of the loan require fixed monthly payments of $1400 on the first day of each month, beginning September 1. The floating rate on the loan is prime plus 3%. The prime rate started at 5.75%, but rose 0.5% on August 19, and another 0.25% effective November 2. Prepare a loan repayment schedule presenting the amount of each payment and the allocation of each payment to interest and principal.

13. Beth borrowed $5000 on demand from TD Canada Trust on February 23 for an RRSP (Registered Retirement Savings Plan) contribution. Because she used the loan proceeds to purchase the bank's mutual funds for her RRSP, she received a special interest rate of prime plus 0.5%. Beth was required to make fixed monthly payments of $1000 on the 15th of each month, beginning April 15. The prime rate was initially 4.75%, but it jumped to 5% effective June 15 and increased another 0.25% on July 31. (It was not a leap year.) Construct a repayment schedule showing the amount of each payment and the allocation of each payment to interest and principal.

14. Dr. Chan obtained a $15,000 demand loan at prime plus 1.5% on September 13 from the Bank of Montreal to purchase a new dental X-ray machine. Fixed payments of $700 will be deducted from the dentist's chequing account on the 20th of each month, beginning October 20. The prime rate was 7.5% at the outset, dropped to 7.25% on the subsequent November 26, and rose to 7.75% on January 29. Prepare a loan repayment schedule showing the details of the first five payments.

*8.5 Canada Student Loans

LO4 The first significant debt incurred by many who pursue postsecondary education is a student loan. All provincial and territorial governments offer student loan programs. The federal government also offers the Canada Student Loan Program. The governments of the Northwest Territories, Nunavut, and Quebec do not participate in the federal program. Currently, about 490,000 students (representing over half of postsecondary enrolment) borrow over $2.7 billion per year under the program.[4] Only the federal government's Canada Student Loans Program (CSLP) is discussed in this section.

No interest is charged on Canada Student Loans as long as you retain full-time student status (at least 60% of a full course load) under the CSLP. Six months after you cease to be a student, you must begin to make monthly loan payments. For example, if final examinations end on May 7 and you do not return to college the following September, the six-month grace period runs from June 1 to November 30. Interest accrues at the floating rate of prime $+2\frac{1}{2}\%$ during this six-month grace period. You may pay the accrued interest at the end of the grace period or have it *capitalized* (that is, converted to principal).[5]

Before the end of the grace period, you must make arrangements with the National Student Loans Service Centre to consolidate all Canada Student Loans into a single loan. The first payment on a consolidated loan is due one month after the end of the grace period. In the preceding example, the first payment is due December 31.

At the time of consolidation, you choose either a *floating* interest rate of prime plus $2\frac{1}{2}\%$ or a *fixed* rate equal to the prime rate (at the time of consolidation) plus 5%. The choice may not be changed later. You also choose the amount of the *fixed* monthly payment subject to a maximum term of 114 months.

LO5 The interest portion of each monthly payment is calculated using the daily-interest method with the exact number of days since the previous payment. A loan repayment schedule can be constructed using the same format as for demand loans in **Section 8.4**. (Canada Student Loans are not demand loans from the lender's point of view. However, the borrower may prepay additional principal at any time without penalty.)

POINT OF INTEREST

Repaying Student Loans Is a Must

After you graduate, do you have plans to travel or buy a new car or rent a better apartment? Such expenditures should be weighed against repaying your student loan. Paying off student loans is probably the most pressing financial matter facing a graduate, even ahead of as financially virtuous a move as starting a Registered Retirement Savings Plan.

If you are unable to manage your student debt, it could ruin your credit rating and make it difficult to get a mortgage or car loan in the future. Delinquent student loans are reported to credit bureaus and will affect your credit rating. On the other hand, smooth repayment of your student debts will help to establish you as a preferred borrower.

To partially offset the cost of interest on your student loan, there are federal and provincial tax credits you can claim on your personal tax return. The provincial tax credit varies somewhat from province to province, but the outcome is approximately this—for every $100 of interest you pay on a student loan, the amount of income tax you pay will be reduced by about $22.

---

[4] Source: www.canada.ca/en/employment-social-development/programs/canada-student-loans-grants/reports/cslp-statistical-2015-2016.html#h2.9

[5] Employment and Social Development Canada maintains a Web site for the Canada Student Loans Program (CSLP). Here, you can calculate the monthly payment you will face on your combined CSLs, not including any capitalized interest from the grace period.

If you are going to have difficulty making payments on your Canada Student Loan because you have a low-paying job or you are unable to find work for a few months, the federal student loan Repayment Assistance Program, introduced in August 2009, can provide help. Based upon the borrower's family income and family size, the program establishes the amount of an affordable monthly student-loan payment. The upper limit for an affordable monthly payment is 20% of family income; it could be as low as $0! If the affordable monthly payment is less than the prescribed monthly payment, the federal government will pay the interest on the student loan for up to five years. All of the borrower's payments will be applied directly to reducing the principal balance on the loan.

If the borrower's financial difficulties remain after the five years, the federal government may continue to cover the interest on the loan. In addition, the government may pay a portion of the monthly principal payment if the borrower's affordable monthly payment is insufficient to pay off the loan over the next 10 years.

For the first few years after leaving school, declaring personal bankruptcy is not an option for shedding student-loan debt. Seven years must pass for student loans to be discharged in personal bankruptcy. (In a case of undue hardship, a bankrupt individual may apply to the court for a discharge of student loans after five years.)

EXAMPLE 8.5A

CONSTRUCTING A REPAYMENT SCHEDULE FOR A CANADA STUDENT LOAN

Heidi had Canada Student Loans totalling $10,600 when she graduated from college. Her six-month grace period ended on November 30, and she chose to have the grace period's accrued interest converted to principal. Heidi selected the floating interest rate option (prime plus 2.5%) when the prime rate was at 3.6%. Monthly payments beginning December 31 were set at $150.

Prepare a loan repayment schedule up to and including the payment on the following March 31. The intervening February had 29 days. The prime rate increased from 3.6% to 3.85% effective August 3, and rose another 0.5% effective January 14.

SOLUTION

The period from June 1 to August 3 has $215 - 152 = 63$ days, and the period from August 3 to (and including) November 30 has $334 + 1 - 215 = 120$ days. The accrued interest at the end of the grace period was

$$I = Pr_1t_1 + Pr_2t_2$$
$$= \$10,600(0.061)(\tfrac{63}{365}) + \$10,600(0.0635)(\tfrac{120}{365})$$
$$= \$111.605 + \$221.293$$
$$= \$332.90$$

The consolidated loan balance at the end of November was

$$\$10,600.00 + \$332.90 = \$10,932.90$$

Date	Number of days	Interest rate (%)	Interest ($)	Accrued interest ($)	Payment (Advance) ($)	Principal portion ($)	Balance ($)
Dec 1	—	—	—	—	—	—	10,931.89
Dec 31	30	6.35	57.06①		150	92.94	10,838.95
Jan 14	14	6.35	26.40	26.40			
Jan 31	17	6.85	34.58	~~60.98~~	150	89.02	10,749.93
Feb 29	29	6.85	58.51	~~58.51~~	150	91.49	10,658.44
Mar 31	31	6.85	62.01	~~62.01~~	150	87.99	10,570.45

① $I = Prt = \$10,932.90(0.0635)(\tfrac{30}{365}) = \$57.06$

EXERCISE 8.5

Answers to the odd-numbered problems are at the end of the book.

*Spreadsheet templates: The Fixed-Payment Loan template provided for **Exercise 8.4** on Connect may be used for Canada Student Loan repayment schedules in Exercise 8.5. Go to the Student Edition of Connect and find "Demand Loan Schedules" found under the Student Resources for Chapter 8. Select the "Fixed-Payment Loan" worksheet.*

INTERMEDIATE PROBLEMS

1. Sarah's Canada Student Loans totalled $9400 by the time she graduated from Georgian College in May. She arranged to capitalize the interest on November 30 and to begin monthly payments of $135 on December 31. Sarah elected the floating rate interest option (prime plus 2.5%). The prime rate stood at 2.75% on June 1, dropped to 2.5% effective September 3, and then increased by 0.25% on January 17. Prepare a repayment schedule presenting details of the first three payments. February has 28 days.

2. Harjap completed his program at Nova Scotia Community College in December. On June 30, he paid all of the interest that had accrued (at prime plus 2.5%) on his $5800 Canada Student Loan during the six-month grace period. He selected the fixed-rate option (prime plus 5%) and agreed to make end-of-month payments of $95 beginning July 31. The prime rate was 8% at the beginning of the grace period and rose by 0.5% effective March 29. On August 13, the prime rate rose another 0.5%. The relevant February had 28 days.
   a. What amount of interest accrued during the grace period?
   b. Calculate the total interest paid in the first three regular payments, and the balance owed after the third payment.

3. Monica finished her program at New Brunswick Community College on June 3 with Canada Student Loans totalling $6800. She decided to capitalize the interest that accrued (at prime plus 2.5%) during the grace period. In addition to regular end-of-month payments of $200, she made an extra $500 lump payment on March 25 that was applied entirely to principal. The prime rate dropped from 6% to 5.75% effective September 22, and declined another 0.5% effective March 2. Calculate the balance owed on the floating rate option after the regular March 31 payment. The relevant February had 28 days.

4. Kari had Canada Student Loans totalling $3800 when she completed her program at Niagara College in December. She had enough savings at the end of June to pay the interest that had accrued during the six-month grace period. Kari made arrangements with the National Student Loans Service Centre to start end-of-month payments of $60 in July. She chose the fixed interest rate option (at prime plus 5%) when the prime rate was at 5.5%. Prepare a loan repayment schedule up to and including the September 30 payment.

5. Seth had accumulated Canada Student Loans totalling $5200 by the time he graduated from Mount Royal College in May. He arranged with the National Student Loans Service Centre to select the floating-rate option (at prime plus $2\frac{1}{2}$%), to capitalize the grace period's accrued interest, and to begin monthly payments of $110 on December 31. Prepare a loan repayment schedule up to and including the February 28 payment. The prime rate was initially at 3.25%. It dropped by 0.25% effective January 31. Seth made an additional principal payment of $300 on February 14.

KEY TERMS

Certificate of Deposit	Discounting a payment	Loan repayment schedule
Commercial paper	Face value	Savings accounts
Demand loan	Fair market value	Treasury bills
Discount rate	Guaranteed Investment Certificate	

SUMMARY OF NOTATION AND KEY FORMULAS

Valuation Principle
The fair market value of an investment is the sum of the present values of the cash flows expected from the investment. The discount rate used in the present-value calculations should be the prevailing market-determined rate of return on this type of investment.

REVIEW PROBLEMS

Answers to the odd-numbered review problems are at the end of the book.

BASIC PROBLEMS

1. **LO3** Calculate the price of a $50,000, 91-day Province of Nova Scotia Treasury bill on its issue date when the market rate of return was 1.273%.

2. **LO3** A $100,000, 182-day Province of New Brunswick Treasury bill was issued 66 days ago. What will it sell at today to yield the purchaser 4.48%?

3. **LO3** A $100,000, 90-day commercial paper certificate issued by Bell Canada Enterprises was sold on its issue date for $98,950. What annual rate of return (to the nearest 0.001%) will it yield to the buyer?

4. **LO1** A chartered bank offers a rate of 5.50% on investments of $25,000 to $59,999 and a rate of 5.75% on investments of $60,000 to $99,999 in 90- to 365-day GICs. How much more will an investor earn from a single $80,000, 180-day GIC than from two $40,000, 180-day GICs?

5. **LO1** An Investment Savings account offered by a trust company pays the following rates:

Portion of Balance	Interest Rate
Up to $1000	1.0%
Balance between $1000 and $3000	1.75%
Balance in excess of $3000	2.25%

   What interest will be paid for the month of January if the opening balance was $3678, $2800 was withdrawn on the 14th of the month, and $950 was deposited on the 25th of the month?

6. **LO2** An agreement stipulates payments of $4500, $3000, and $5500 in 4, 8, and 12 months, respectively, from today. What is the highest price an investor will offer today to purchase the agreement if he requires a minimum rate of return of 10.5%?

7. **LO1** Paul has $20,000 to invest for six months. For this amount, his bank pays 3.3% on a 90-day GIC and 3.5% on a 180-day GIC. If the interest rate on a 90-day GIC is the same three months from now, how much more interest will Paul earn by purchasing the 180-day GIC than by buying a 90-day GIC and then reinvesting its maturity value in a second 90-day GIC?

8. **LO1** Suppose that the current rates on 60- and 120-day GICs are 5.50% and 5.75%, respectively. An investor is weighing the alternatives of purchasing a 120-day GIC versus purchasing a 60-day GIC and then reinvesting its maturity value in a second 60-day GIC. What would the interest rate on 60-day GICs have to be 60 days from now for the investor to end up in the same financial position with either alternative?

INTERMEDIATE PROBLEMS

9. **LO3** A $100,000, 168-day Government of Canada Treasury bill was purchased on its date of issue to yield 1.97%.
   a. What price did the investor pay?
   b. Calculate the market value of the T-bill 85 days later if the annual rate of return then required by the market has:
   (i) risen to 2.0%.
   (ii) remained at 1.97%.
   (iii) fallen to 1.84%.
   c. Calculate the rate of return actually realized by the investor if the T-bill is sold at each of the three prices calculated in part (b).

10. **LO3** A $25,000, 91-day Province of Newfoundland Treasury bill was originally purchased at a price that would yield the investor a 5.438% rate of return if the T-bill is held until maturity. Thirty-four days later, the investor sold the T-bill through his broker for $24,775.
   a. What price did the original investor pay for the T-bill?
   b. What rate of return will the second investor realize if she holds the T-bill until maturity?
   c. What rate of return did the first investor realize during his holding period?

11. **LO2** A conditional sale contract requires two payments three and six months after the date of the contract. Each payment consists of $1900 principal plus interest at 12.5% on $1900 from the date of the contract. One month into the contract, what price would a finance company pay for the contract if it requires an 18% rate of return on its purchases?

12. **LO2** An assignable loan contract executed 3 months ago requires two payments of $3200 plus interest at 9% from the date of the contract, to be paid 4 and 8 months after the contract date. The payee is offering to sell the contract to a finance company in order to raise urgently needed cash. If the finance company requires a 16% rate of return, what price will it be prepared to pay today for the contract?

13. **LO5** Ruxandra's Canada Student Loans totalled $7200 by the time she finished Conestoga College in April. The accrued interest at prime plus 2.5% for the grace period was converted to principal on October 31. She chose the floating interest rate option and began monthly payments of $120 on November 30. The prime rate of interest was 5.5% on May 1, 5.25% effective July 9, and 5% effective December 13. Prepare a repayment schedule presenting details of the first three payments.

14. **LO5** George borrowed $4000 on demand from CIBC on January 28 for an RRSP contribution. Because he used the loan proceeds to purchase CIBC's mutual funds for his RRSP, the interest rate on the loan was set at the bank's prime rate. George agreed to make monthly payments of $600 (except for a smaller final payment) on the 21st of each month, beginning February 21. The prime rate was initially 6.75%, dropped to 6.5% effective May 15, and decreased another 0.25% on July 5. It was not a leap year. Construct a repayment schedule showing the amount of each payment and the allocation of each payment to interest and principal.

15. **LO5** Ms. Wadeson obtained a $15,000 demand loan from TD Canada Trust on May 23 to purchase a car. The interest rate on the loan was prime plus 2%. The loan required payments of $700 on the 15th of each month, beginning June 15. The prime rate was 4.5% at the outset, dropped to 4.25% on July 26, and then jumped by 0.5% on September 14. Prepare a loan repayment schedule showing the details of the first four payments.

16. **LO5** Mayfair Fashions has a $90,000 line of credit from the Bank of Montreal. Interest at prime plus 2% is deducted from Mayfair's chequing account on the 24th of each month. Mayfair initially drew down $40,000 on March 8 and another $15,000 on April 2. On June 5, $25,000 of principal was repaid. If the prime rate was 5.25% on March 8 and rose by 0.25% effective May 13, what were the first four interest deductions charged to the store's account?

17. **LO5** Duncan Developments Ltd. obtained a $120,000 line of credit from its bank to subdivide a parcel of land it owned into four residential lots and to install water, sewer, and underground electrical services. Amounts advanced from time to time are payable on demand to its bank. Interest at prime plus 4% on the daily principal balance is charged to the developer's bank account on the 26th of each month. The developer must apply at least $30,000 from the proceeds of the sale of each lot against the loan principal. Duncan drew down $50,000 on June 3, $40,000 on June 30, and $25,000 on July 17. Two lots quickly sold, and Duncan repaid $30,000 on July 31 and $35,000 on August 18. The initial prime rate of 5% changed to 5.25% effective July 5 and 5.5% effective July 26. Prepare a repayment schedule showing loan activity and interest charges up to and including the interest payment on August 26.

CASE

Debt Consolidation

Graham and Stacy are having difficulty stretching their salaries to pay their bills. Before their marriage three months ago, they purchased new furnishings for their apartment. Then they paid for their honeymoon with "plastic." Now the bills are all in. The following table lists their debts.

Debt	Balance ($)	Interest rate	Monthly payment Minimum	Monthly payment Fixed ($)
Car loan	6000	9.5%	—	300
Canada Student Loan	6800	Prime + 2.5%	—	100
Visa	4700	17.5%	5%	—
MasterCard	3900	15.9%	5%	—
American Express	3850	28.8%	4%	—
Canadian Tire	1250	28.8%	5%	—

The minimum monthly payment on each credit card is the indicated percentage of the *combined* principal balance plus accrued interest. The prime rate of interest is 6.5%.

With a view to consolidating their debts, Stacy and Graham have discussed their personal financial position with the Personal Banking Representative (PBR) at the bank close to their new apartment. The PBR is prepared to approve a $20,000 joint line of credit at prime plus 3% on the condition that $6000 be used immediately to pay off the car loan (obtained from another bank). The minimum monthly payment would be 3% of the combined principal balance plus accrued interest.

QUESTIONS

1. Assuming 30 days' interest on the indicated (principal) balances, what is the next minimum payment on each of the four credit cards?
2. If all the debt balances except the Canada Student Loan are consolidated in the new line of credit, what will be the first minimum payment? (Again assume a full 30 days' accrued interest on the principal for the fairest comparison with the "status quo.")
3. Based on the preceding results, what is the reduction in the first month's total debt service payments?
4. With respect to credit card debt only, what is the reduction in the first month's interest charges?
5. What (weighted) average interest rate are Graham and Stacy currently paying? What (weighted) average interest rate will they be paying after loan consolidation? (Include the Canada Student Loan in both calculations.)
6. Give two reasons why the PBR set the condition that Graham and Stacy use part of the line of credit to pay off the car loan.
7. Give two reasons why the PBR did not suggest a $27,000 line of credit and require that Graham and Stacy use the extra $7000 to pay off the Canada Student Loan.

*APPENDIX 8A: PROMISSORY NOTES

Concepts and Definitions

A promissory note is a written promise by one party to pay an amount of money to another party on a specific date, or on demand.

The required elements and the general rules of law that apply to promissory notes are set out in the federal Bills of Exchange Act. The basic information required in a promissory note is illustrated in **Figure 8.2**. A *demand* promissory note that might be used by a financial institution in connection with a demand loan is shown in **Figure 8.3**. The bracketed numbers in **Figures 8.2** and **8.3** refer to the following terms.

1. The **maker** of the note is the debtor promising the payment.
2. The **payee** is the creditor to whom the payment is to be made.
3. The **face value** is the principal amount of the debt.
4. The **issue date** is the date on which the note was written or "made" and the date from which interest, if any, is computed.
5. The term of the note is the length of the loan period. (A demand note is payable at any time the payee chooses.)
6. The Bills of Exchange Act provides that, unless otherwise specified,[6] an extra **three days of grace** are added at the end of a note's term to determine the note's legal due date. The maker is not in default until after the **legal due date**. No days of grace are allowed in the case of demand notes.
7. If interest is to be charged on the face value, the interest rate must be specified on the note. This makes it an interest-bearing promissory note. The days of grace are included in the interest period for calculating the maturity value (face value plus interest) of the note on the legal due date.[7] For terms of one year or less, it is understood that the simple interest method should be used. (The maturity value of a non-interest-bearing note is the same as its face value.)
8. The note can specify the location at which the maker is to make the payment to the payee's account.

FIGURE 8.2   Term Promissory Note

PROMISSORY NOTE

(3) $7200.00   *Edmonton, Alberta*   (4) *November 30, 2019*

(5) *Three months*   after date   *I*   promise to pay to the order of

(2) *Western Builders Supply Ltd.*

the sum of   *seventy-two hundred and*   – – – – – – – – – – – *00* /100 Dollars

at   (8) *RBC Royal Bank, Terminal Plaza Branch*

for value received, with interest at   (7) *12%*   per annum.

Due: (6) *March 3, 2020*   Signed: (1) *J. Anderson*

---

[6] To extinguish the normal three days of grace, "NO DAYS OF GRACE" should be indicated on the note by the payee.

[7] The Bills of Exchange Act provides that, whenever the last day of grace falls on a Saturday, Sunday, or legal holiday, the next following business day becomes the last day of grace. Technically, any extra calendar days added as a consequence of this provision should be included in the interest period. We will ignore this fine point of law to avoid the extra complication. The dollar amount involved (in relation to the maturity value otherwise calculated) is not material.

FIGURE 8.3	Demand Promissory Note

---

(3)

$5000.00   Hamilton, Ontario   April 30, 2019   (4)

ON DEMAND after date for value received, ___*I*___ promise to pay to the order of

(2) _____*Acme Distributing Ltd.*_____ at

(8) _____*the RBC Royal Bank of Canada, Limeridge Mall Branch*_____ the sum of

(3) ___*five thousand*___ – ___*00*___ /100 Dollars

(7) with interest thereon calculated and payable monthly at a rate equal to the RBC Royal Bank of Canada's prime interest rate per annum in effect from time to time plus __*2*_% per annum as well after as before maturity, default and judgment. At the date of this note, such prime interest rate is __*3*_% per annum.

Prime interest rate is the annual rate of interest announced from time to time by the RBC Royal Bank of Canada as a reference rate then in effect for determining interest rates on Canadian dollar commercial loans in Canada.

Signed: ___(1)___ *R. A. Matthews*

EXAMPLE 8A.A

DETERMINING THE LEGAL DUE DATE

Show how the due date of the promissory note in **Figure 8.2** is obtained.

SOLUTION

When the term of the note is specified in months, the end of the term is normally on the same numbered day in the expiry month as the date of issue. This particular instance is different, as there is no February 30. In such cases the last day of the expiry month is used as the end of the term. The legal due date is then three days later.

For the note in **Figure 8.2**, the term expires on February 28, 2020, and the legal due date is March 3, 2020.

EXAMPLE 8A.B

CALCULATING AN INTEREST-BEARING NOTE'S MATURITY VALUE

What is the maturity value of the note in **Figure 8.2**?

SOLUTION

Even though the term is specified in months, the interest is calculated to the exact number of days, including the three days of grace.

Month	Days of interest
November	1
December	31
January	31
February	28
March	2
	93

$$\text{Maturity value} = P(1 + rt)$$
$$= \$7200\left[1 + 0.12\left(\tfrac{93}{365}\right)\right]$$
$$= \$7420.14$$

The maturity value required to settle the note on March 3, 2020 is $7420.14.

EXAMPLE 8A.C

LEGAL DUE DATE AND MATURITY VALUE OF AN INTEREST-BEARING NOTE

What would be the legal due date of the promissory note in Figure 8.2 if the term were 120 days instead of three months? What would be the maturity value of the note?

SOLUTION

The legal due date will occur 123 days after the issue date.

Interval	Number of days of interest in the interval	Remaining days of interest in the term
Nov 30 and December	32	$123 - 32 = 91$
January	31	$91 - 31 = 60$
February	28	$60 - 28 = 32$
March	31	$32 - 31 = 1$
April 1 to April 2	1①	0

① We have counted the first day (Nov 30) of the term but not the last day (Apr 2).

The legal due date falls on April 2, 2020.

$$\text{Maturity value} = \$7200\left[1 + 0.12\left(\tfrac{123}{365}\right)\right] = \$7491.16$$

The maturity value on the legal due date is $7491.16.

Discounting Promissory Notes

Promissory notes are *negotiable*. This means that the payee can transfer ownership of the note by *endorsing* it—that is, by signing his name on the back of the note. The payee will do this if he sells the note to an investor at any time before the note's legal due date. The maker is then obliged to pay the maturity value to the holder of the endorsed note on its due date.

The usual reason for selling a note is that the payee needs cash before the due date of the note. The price received for the note is often referred to as the *proceeds* of the note. The general case is presented in Figure 8.4. The face value P of an interest-bearing note earns interest at the rate r_1 (specified in the note) for the time period t_1 until its legal due date. That maturity value will be

$$S = P(1 + r_1 t_1)$$

We want to calculate the value of the note on the date of sale, a time period t_2 prior to the due date.

FIGURE 8.4   Calculating the Proceeds of a Promissory Note

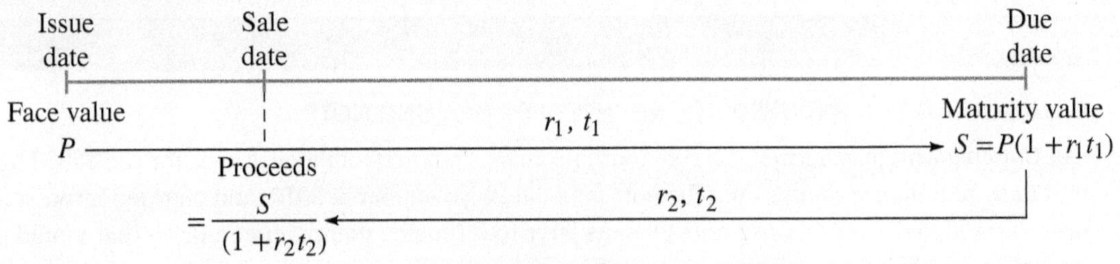

According to the Valuation Principle, the purchase price should be the present value of the maturity value discounted at the buyer's required rate of return. That is,

$$\text{Purchase price (Proceeds)} = \frac{S}{1 + r_2 t_2}$$

In summary, the calculation of the purchase price or proceeds of a promissory note is a two-step procedure.

1. Calculate the maturity value on the due date using the interest rate *specified in the note*. If the note does not bear interest, its maturity value is the same as its face value.
2. Calculate the present value, on the date of sale, of the maturity value using the discount rate agreed upon by the buyer and the seller.

EXAMPLE 8A.D

CALCULATING THE PROCEEDS OF A NON-INTEREST-BEARING NOTE

A 150-day non-interest-bearing note for $2500 was made on June 15. The note was sold on August 21 at a price reflecting a discount rate of 12.5%. What were the proceeds of the note?

SOLUTION

There are 153 days from the issue date until the legal due date. By August 21, $16 + 31 + 20 = 67$ of the days have passed and $153 - 67 = 86$ days remain.

This information and the solution approach are presented in the following time diagram.

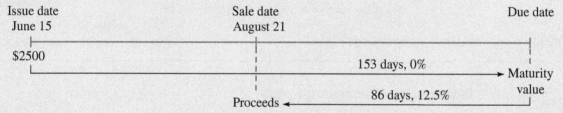

Since the face value does not earn interest, the maturity value will equal the face value of $2500.

The proceeds of the note will be the present value, 86 days earlier, of the maturity value discounted at the rate of 12.5%.

$$\text{Proceeds} = \frac{S}{1 + rt} = \frac{\$2500}{1 + 0.125\left(\frac{86}{365}\right)} = \$2428.48$$

Note: By paying this price, the extra

$$\$2500 - \$2428.48 = \$71.52$$

received on the note's legal due date provides a 12.5% rate of return for 86 days on the investment of $2428.48. To verify this, calculate

$$r = \frac{I}{Pt} = \frac{\$71.52}{\$2428.48\left(\frac{86}{365}\right)} = 0.125 = 12.5\%$$

EXAMPLE 8A.E

CALCULATING THE PROCEEDS OF AN INTEREST-BEARING NOTE

Old Country Antiques accepted a six-month promissory note from a customer for the $2850 balance owed on the purchase of a dining room suite. The note was dated November 8, 2019, and charged interest at 13%. The store's proprietor sold the promissory note 38 days later to a finance company at a price that would yield the finance company an 18% rate of return on its purchase price. What price did the finance company pay?

SOLUTION

The note's legal due date was May 11, 2020 (May 8 + 3 days). The total number of days from the issue date to the due date was

$$23 + 31 + 31 + 29 + 31 + 30 + 10 = 185 \text{ days}$$

When the note was sold, $185 - 38 = 147$ days remained until the due date. The given information and the steps in the solution can be presented in a time diagram.

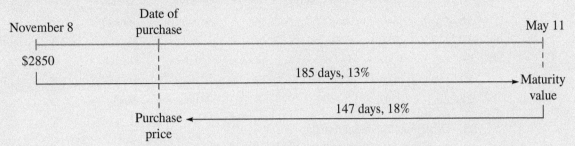

Maturity value of note $= \$2850\left[1 + 0.13\left(\frac{185}{365}\right)\right] = \$3037.79$

The price paid by the finance company was the present value, 147 days earlier, of the maturity value discounted at 18%.

$$\text{Price} = \frac{\$3037.79}{1 + 0.18\left(\frac{147}{365}\right)} = \$2832.46$$

The finance company paid $2832.46 for the promissory note.

EXERCISE 8A

Answers to the odd-numbered problems are at the end of the book.

Calculate the missing values for the promissory notes described in Problems 1–22.

Problem	Issue date	Term	Legal due date
1.	May 19	120 days	?
2.	June 30	90 days	?
3.	July 6	? days	Oct 17
4.	Nov 14	? days	Jan 31
5.	?	4 months	Feb 28
6.	?	9 months	Oct 3
7.	?	180 days	Sept 2
8.	?	60 days	March 1 (leap year)

Problem	Issue date	Face value ($)	Term	Interest rate (%)	Maturity value ($)
9.	April 30	1000	4 months	9.50	?
10.	Feb 15	3300	60 days	8.75	?
11.	July 3	?	90 days	10.20	2667.57
12.	Aug 31	?	3 months	7.50	7644.86
13.	Jan 22	6200	120 days	?	6388.04
14.	Nov 5	4350	75 days	?	4445.28
15.	Dec 31	5200	? days	11.00	5275.22
16.	March 30	9400	? days	9.90	9560.62

Problem	Face value ($)	Issue date	Interest rate (%)	Term	Date of sale	Discount rate (%)	Proceeds ($)
17.	1000	March 30	0	50 days	April 8	10	?
18.	6000	May 17	0	3 months	June 17	9	?
19.	2700	Sept 4	10	182 days	Dec 14	12	?
20.	3500	Oct 25	10	120 days	Dec 14	8	?
21.	9000	July 28	8	91 days	Sept 1	?	9075.40
22.	4000	Nov 30	8	75 days	Jan 1	?	4015.25

23. Determine the legal due date for:
    a. A five-month note dated September 29, 2019.
    b. A 150-day note issued September 29, 2019.

24. Determine the legal due date for:
    a. A four-month note dated April 30, 2019.
    b. A 120-day note issued April 30, 2019.

25. Calculate the maturity value of a 120-day, $1000 face value note dated November 30, 2020, and earning interest at 10.75%.

26. Calculate the maturity value of a $1000 face value, five-month note dated December 31, 2019, and bearing interest at 9.5%.

27. A 90-day non-interest-bearing note for $3300 is dated August 1. What would be a fair selling price of the note on September 1 if money can earn 7.75%?

28. A six-month non-interest-bearing note issued on September 30, 2019 for $3300 was discounted at 11.25% on December 1. What were the proceeds of the note?

29. A 100-day $750 note with interest at 12.5% was written on July 15. The maker approaches the payee on August 10 to propose an early settlement. What amount should the payee be willing to accept on August 10 if short-term investments can earn 8.25%?

30. The payee on a three-month $2700 note earning interest at 8% wishes to sell the note to raise some cash. What price should she be prepared to accept for the note (dated May 19) on June 5 in order to yield the purchaser an 11% rate of return?

31. A six-month note dated June 30 for $2900 bears interest at 13.5%. Determine the proceeds of the note if it is discounted at 9.75% on September 1.

32. An investor is prepared to buy short-term promissory notes at a price that will provide him with a return on investment of 12%. What amount would he pay on August 9 for a 120-day note dated July 18 for $4100 with interest at 10.25%?

Chapter 9

Compound Interest: Future Value and Present Value

CHAPTER OUTLINE

9.1 Basic Concepts

9.2 Future Value (or Maturity Value)

9.3 Present Value

9.4 Using Financial Calculators

9.5 Other Applications of Compounding

9.6 Equivalent Payment Streams

Appendix 9A: Instructions for Specific Models of Financial Calculators

LEARNING OBJECTIVES

After completing this chapter, you will be able to:

LO1 Calculate the future value and present value in compound interest applications, by both the algebraic method and the preprogrammed financial calculator method

LO2 Calculate the maturity value of compound interest Guaranteed Investment Certificates (GICs)

LO3 Calculate the price of strip bonds

LO4 Adapt the concepts and equations from compound interest to compound growth

LO5 Calculate the payment on any date that is equivalent to one or more payments on other dates

LO6 Calculate the economic value of a payment stream

EXAMPLES OF COMPOUND INTEREST ARE easy to find. If you obtain a loan to purchase a car, interest will be compounded monthly. The advertised interest rates on mortgage loans are semiannually compounded rates. Interest is always compounded in long-term financial planning. So if you wish to take control of your personal financial affairs or to be involved in the financial side of a business, you must thoroughly understand compound interest and its applications. The remainder of this book is devoted to the mathematics and applications of compound interest.

You will be able to hit the ground running! In **Chapters 7** and **8**, you learned the concepts of maturity value, time value of money, future value, and present value for the case of simple interest. These ideas transfer to compound interest. Now we just need to develop new mathematics for calculating future value and present value when interest is compounded. And there is good news in this regard! Most compound interest formulas are permanently programmed into financial calculators. After you become competent in the algebraic method for solving compound interest problems, your instructor may allow you to use a financial calculator to perform the computations. Before long, you will be impressed at the range of applications you can handle!

9.1 Basic Concepts

The *simple* interest method discussed in **Chapter 7** is restricted primarily to loans and investments having terms of less than one year. The *compound* interest method is employed in virtually all instances where the term exceeds one year. It is also used in some cases where the duration is less than one year.

In the **compound interest method**, interest is *periodically* calculated and *converted* to principal. "Converting interest to principal" means that the interest is added to the principal and is thereafter treated as principal. Consequently, interest earned in one period will itself earn interest in all subsequent periods. The time interval between successive interest conversion dates is called the **compounding period**. Suppose, for example, you invest $1000 at 10% compounded annually. "Compounded annually" means that "interest is compounded once per year." Therefore, the compounding period is one year. On each anniversary of the investment, interest will be calculated and converted to principal. The process is indicated in **Figure 9.1**. The original $1000 investment is represented by the column located at "0" on the time axis. During the first year, you will earn $100 interest (10% of $1000). At the end of the first year, this $100 will be converted to principal. The new principal ($1100) will earn $110 interest (10% of $1100) in the second year. Note that you earn $10 more interest in the second year than in the first year because you have $100 more principal invested at 10%. How much interest will be earned in the third year? Do you see the pattern developing? Each year you will earn more interest than in the preceding year—$100 in the first year, $110 in the second year, $121 in the third year, and so on. Consequently, the growth in value of the investment will accelerate as the years pass.

FIGURE 9.1   Converting Interest to Principal at the End of Each Compounding Period

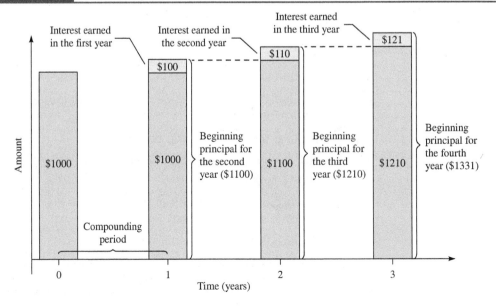

In contrast, if the $1000 earns 10% per annum *simple* interest, only the *original* principal will earn interest ($100) each year. A $1000 investment will grow by just $100 each year. After two years, your investment will be worth only $1200 (compared to $1210 with annual compounding).

In many circumstances, interest is compounded more frequently than once per year. The number of compounds per year is called the **compounding frequency**. The commonly used frequencies and their corresponding compounding periods[1] are listed in Table 9.1.

TABLE 9.1 Compounding Frequencies and Periods		
Compounding frequency	Number of compounds per year	Compounding period
Annually	1	1 year
Semiannually	2	6 months
Quarterly	4	3 months
Monthly	12	1 month

A compound interest rate is normally quoted with two components:

- A number for the annual interest rate; and
- Words stating the compounding frequency.

The two components together are called the **nominal interest rate**.[2] For example, an interest rate of 8% compounded semiannually means that half of the 8% nominal annual rate is earned and compounded each six-month compounding period. A rate of 9% compounded monthly means that 0.75% (one-twelfth of 9%) is earned and compounded each month. We use the term **periodic interest rate** for the interest rate per compounding period. In the two examples at hand, the periodic interest rates are 4% and 0.75%, respectively. In general,

$$\text{Periodic interest rate} = \frac{\text{Nominal interest rate}}{\text{Number of compoundings per year}}$$

If we define the following symbols:

$$j = \text{Nominal interest rate}$$
$$m = \text{Number of compoundings per year}$$
$$i = \text{Periodic interest rate}$$

The simple relationship between the periodic interest rate and the nominal interest rate is:

PERIODIC INTEREST RATE

$$i = \frac{j}{m} \tag{9-1}$$

TRAP

"*m*" for Quarterly Compounding

What is the value of *m* for quarterly compounding? Sometimes students incorrectly use $m = 3$ with quarterly compounding because $\frac{1}{4}$ year = 3 months. But *m* represents the number of compounds per year (4), not the length of the compounding period.

TIP

Give the Complete Description of an Interest Rate

Whenever you are asked to calculate or state a nominal interest rate, it is understood that you should include the compounding frequency in your response. For example, an answer of just "8%" is incomplete. Rather, you must state "8% compounded quarterly" if interest is compounded four times per year.

---

[1] Daily compounding interest exists but it is not a common practice. The CRA (Canada Revenue Agency) is the only organization that charges daily compounding interest on all outstanding balances.

[2] As you will soon understand, you cannot conclude that $100 invested for one year at 8% compounded semiannually will earn exactly $8.00 of interest. Therefore, we use the word "nominal," meaning "in name only," to describe the quoted rate.

EXAMPLE 9.1A

CALCULATING THE PERIODIC INTEREST RATE

Calculate the periodic interest rate corresponding to:

a. 10.5% compounded annually.

b. 9.75% compounded semiannually.

c. 9.0% compounded quarterly.

d. 9.5% compounded monthly.

SOLUTION

Employing Formula (9-1), we obtain:

a. $i = \frac{j}{m} = \frac{10.5\%}{1} = 10.5\%$ (per year)   **b.** $i = \frac{9.75\%}{2} = 4.875\%$ (per half year)

c. $i = \frac{9.0\%}{4} = 2.25\%$ (per quarter)   **d.** $i = \frac{9.5\%}{12} = 0.791\overline{6}\%$ (per month)

EXAMPLE 9.1B

CALCULATING THE COMPOUNDING FREQUENCY

For a nominal interest rate of 8.4%, what is the compounding frequency if the periodic interest rate is:

a. 4.2%?   **b.** 8.4%?

c. 2.1%?   **d.** 0.70%?

SOLUTION

The number of compounds or conversions in a year is given by the value of m in Formula (9-1).

Rearranging this formula to solve for m, we obtain $m = \frac{j}{i}$

a. $m = \frac{8.4\%}{4.2\%} = 2$, which corresponds to semiannual compounding.

b. $m = \frac{8.4\%}{8.4\%} = 1$, which corresponds to annual compounding.

c. $m = \frac{8.4\%}{2.1\%} = 4$, which corresponds to quarterly compounding.

d. $m = \frac{8.4\%}{0.7\%} = 12$, which corresponds to monthly compounding.

EXAMPLE 9.1C

CALCULATING THE NOMINAL INTEREST RATE

Determine the nominal rate of interest if:

a. The periodic rate is 1.75% per quarter.

b. The periodic rate is $0.8\overline{3}\%$ per month.

SOLUTION

Rearranging Formula (9-1) to solve for j, the nominal interest rate, we obtain $j = mi$.

a. $j = 4(1.75\%) = 7.0\%$ compounded quarterly

b. $j = 12(0.8\overline{3}\%) = 10.0\%$ compounded monthly

CONCEPT QUESTIONS

1. What does it mean to compound interest?
2. Explain the difference between "compounding period" and "compounding frequency."
3. Explain the difference between "nominal rate of interest" and "periodic rate of interest."

EXERCISE 9.1

Answers to the odd-numbered problems are at the end of the book.

BASIC PROBLEMS

1. Calculate the periodic rate of interest if the nominal interest rate is 6% compounded:
   a. monthly.   **b.** quarterly.   **c.** semiannually.

2. Determine the periodic interest rate for a nominal interest rate of 4.8% compounded:
   a. semiannually.   **b.** quarterly.   **c.** monthly.

3. What is the periodic rate of interest corresponding to:
   a. 5.4% compounded quarterly?   **b.** 5.4% compounded monthly?

4. Determine the periodic interest rate for a nominal interest rate of:
   a. 8% compounded semiannually.   **b.** 8% compounded monthly.

5. Calculate the nominal interest rate if the periodic rate is:
   a. 3.6% per half-year.   **b.** 1.8% per quarter.   **c.** 0.6% per month.

6. Determine the nominal rate of interest if the periodic rate is:
   a. 1.5% per month.   **b.** 1.5% per quarter.   **c.** 1.5% per half-year.

7. Determine the nominal interest rate if the periodic rate is:
   a. 1.25% per quarter.   **b.** $0.491\overline{6}\%$ per month.

8. What is the nominal rate of interest if the periodic rate is:
   a. $0.58\overline{3}\%$ per month?   **b.** 5.8% per year?

9. Calculate the compounding frequency for a nominal rate of 6.6% if the periodic rate of interest is:
   a. 1.65%.   **b.** 3.3%.   **c.** 0.55%.

10. For a nominal rate of 5.9%, determine the compounding frequency if the periodic interest rate is:
    a. 2.95%.   **b.** $0.491\overline{6}\%$.   **c.** 1.475%.

11. What is the compounding frequency for a nominal rate of 4.7% if the periodic interest rate is:
    a. 1.175%?   **b.** $0.391\overline{6}\%$?

12. For a nominal rate of 6.75%, determine the compounding frequency if the periodic interest rate is:
    a. 0.5625%.   **b.** 1.6875%.

9.2 | Future Value (or Maturity Value)

Calculating Future Value

L01 Remember from our study of simple interest in **Chapter 7** that the **maturity value** or **future value** is the combined principal and interest due at the maturity date of a loan or investment. We used $S = P(1 + rt)$ to calculate future value in the simple interest case. Now our task is to develop the corresponding formula for use with compound interest.

Consider an investment of $1000 earning interest at 5% compounding annually for 3 years.

Using the simple interest Formula (7-2), we can calculate the maturity value of the investment for one year (one compounding period in this case) then use the maturity value from each year as the principal for the maturity value calculation in the next year. This will compound the interest.

In year 1: $S = \$1000(1 + 0.05(1)) = \$1050$
In year 2: $S = \$1050(1 + 0.05(1)) = \$1102.50$
In year 3: $S = \$1102.50(1 + 0.05(1)) = \$1157.63$

Already, you can see a pattern in the calculations. If we write the three calculations above as one, we have

$$S = \$1000(1 + 0.05)(1 + 0.05)(1 + 0.05)$$

or $$S = \$1000(1 + 0.05)^3$$

From this simple example, we can see that we multiply the initial principal, P, by a factor of $(1 + i)$ for each compounding period. After n compounding periods the future value will be

$$S = P(1 + i)^n$$

Financial calculators, spreadsheet software, and the majority of finance resources employ the following symbols in compound interest functions:

FV = Future value (or maturity value)
PV = Principal amount of a loan or investment; Present value

FUTURE VALUE OR MATURITY VALUE (COMPOUND INTEREST)

Using this notation, the formula for compound interest becomes

$$FV = PV(1 + i)^n \qquad \text{(9-2)}$$

Usually, the term of a loan or investment is given in years, rather than as the total number of compounding periods, n. To calculate n, first determine m, the number of compounds per year, from the nominal interest rate. Then,

TOTAL NUMBER OF COMPOUNDING PERIODS

$$n = m \times (\textbf{Number of years in the term}) \qquad \text{(9-3)}$$

EXAMPLE 9.2A

CALCULATING THE MATURITY VALUE OF AN INVESTMENT

What will be the maturity value of $10,000 invested for five years at 3.75% compounded semiannually?

SOLUTION

Given: $PV = \$10,000$, Term of investment = 5 years, $j = 3.75\%$, $m = 2$

The interest rate per six-month compounding period is

$$i = \frac{j}{m} = \frac{3.75\%}{2} = 1.875\% \text{ (per half-year)}$$
$$n = m \times \text{Term (in years)} = 2(5) = 10$$

The maturity value will be

$$\begin{aligned} FV &= PV(1 + i)^n \\ &= \$10,000(1 + 0.01875)^{10} \\ &= \$10,000(1.2041379) \\ &= \$12,041.38 \end{aligned}$$

The investment will grow to $12,041.38 after five years.

EXAMPLE 9.2B

COMPARING TWO NOMINAL RATES OF INTEREST

Other things being equal, would an investor prefer an interest rate of 4.8% compounded monthly or 4.9% compounded annually for a two-year investment?

SOLUTION

The preferred rate will be the one that results in the higher maturity value. Pick an arbitrary initial investment, say $1000, and calculate the maturity value at each rate.

With
$$PV = \$1000, \ i = \frac{j}{m} = \frac{4.8\%}{12} = 0.4\%$$

and
$$n = m(\text{Term}) = 12(2) = 24,$$
$$FV = PV(1 + i)^n = \$1000(1.004)^{24} = \$1100.55$$

With
$$PV = \$1000, \ i = \frac{j}{m} = \frac{4.9\%}{1} = 4.9\%$$

and
$$n = m(\text{Term}) = 1(2) = 2,$$
$$FV = PV(1 + i)^n = \$1000(1.049)^2 = \$1100.40$$

The rate of 4.8% compounded monthly is slightly better. The higher compounding frequency more than offsets the lower nominal rate.

EXAMPLE 9.2C

CALCULATING THE MATURITY VALUE WHEN THE INTEREST RATE CHANGES

George invested $5000 at 4.25% compounded quarterly. After 18 months, the rate changed to 4.75% compounded semiannually. What amount will George have three years after the initial investment?

SOLUTION

For the first 18 months,
$$PV = \$5000, \ i = \frac{j}{m} = \frac{4.25\%}{4} = 1.0625\% \ (\text{per quarter}),$$
$$\text{and } n = m(\text{Term}) = 4(1.5) = 6$$

For the next 18 months,
$$i = \frac{j}{m} = \frac{4.75\%}{2} = 2.375\% \ (\text{per half-year})$$
$$\text{and } n = m(\text{Term}) = 2(1.5) = 3$$

Because of the interest rate change, the solution should be done in two steps, as indicated by the following diagram.

The future value, FV_1, after 18 months becomes the beginning "principal," PV_2, for the remainder of the three years.

Step 1: Calculate the future value after 18 months.
$$FV_1 = PV(1 + i)^n = \$5000(1.010625)^6 = \$5327.34$$

Step 2: Calculate the future value, FV_2, at the end of the three years (a further 18 months later).
$$FV_2 = PV_2(1 + i)^n = \$5327.34(1.02375)^3 = \$5716.00$$

George will have $5716.00 after three years.

EXAMPLE 9.2D

THE BALANCE OWED AFTER PAYMENTS ON A COMPOUND INTEREST LOAN

Fay borrowed $5000 at an interest rate of 3% compounded quarterly. On the first, second, and third anniversaries of the loan, she made payments of $1500. What payment made on the fourth anniversary will extinguish the debt?

SOLUTION

At each anniversary we will first calculate the amount owed (*FV*) and then deduct the payment. This difference becomes the principal balance (*PV*) at the beginning of the next year. The periodic interest rate is

$$i = \frac{j}{m} = \frac{3\%}{4} = 0.75\% \text{ (per quarter)}$$

The sequence of steps is indicated by the following time diagram.

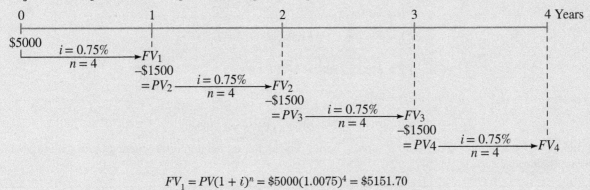

$$FV_1 = PV(1 + i)^n = \$5000(1.0075)^4 = \$5151.70$$
$$PV_2 = FV_1 - \$1500 = \$5151.70 - \$1500 = \$3651.70$$
$$FV_2 = PV_2(1 + i)^n = \$3651.70(1.0075)^4 = \$3762.49$$
$$PV_3 = FV_2 - \$1500 = \$3762.49 - \$1500 = \$2262.49$$
$$FV_3 = PV_3(1 + i)^n = \$2262.49(1.0075)^4 = \$2331.13$$
$$PV_4 = FV_3 - \$1500 = \$2331.13 - \$1500 = \$831.13$$
$$FV_4 = PV_4(1 + i)^n = \$831.13(1.0075)^4 = \$856.35$$

A payment of $856.35 on the fourth anniversary will pay off the debt.

Graphs of Future Value versus Time

A picture is worth a thousand words, but a graph can be worth more. The best way to develop our understanding of the effects of compounding and the roles of key variables is through the study of graphs.

The components of future value Let us investigate in greater detail the consequences of earning "interest on interest" through compounding. In **Figure 9.2**, we compare the growth of two investments:

- $100 invested at 10% compounded annually (the upper curve)
- $100 invested at 10% per annum simple interest (the inclined straight line)

For the compound interest investment,

$$FV = PV(1 + i)^n = \$100(1 + 0.10)^n = \$100(1.10)^n$$

The upper curve was obtained by plotting values of *FV* for *n* ranging from 0 to 10 compounding periods (years).

For the simple interest investment,

$$S = P(1 + rt) = \$100(1 + 0.10t)$$

FIGURE 9.2 The Components of the Future Value of $100

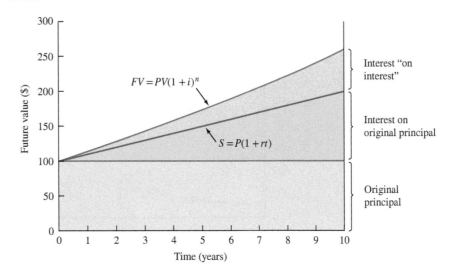

This gives an upward-sloping straight line when we plot values of S for t ranging from 0 to 10 years. In this case, the future value increases $10 per year because only the original principal of $100 earns 10% interest each year. At any point, the future value of the simple interest investment has *two* components:

1. The original principal ($100).
2. The interest earned on the original principal. In the graph, this component is the vertical distance from the horizontal line (at $100) to the sloping simple interest line.

Returning to the compound interest investment, we can think of its future value at any point as having *three* components: the same two listed above for the simple interest investment, plus

3. "Interest earned on interest"—actually interest earned on interest that was previously converted to principal. In the graph, this component is the vertical distance from the inclined simple interest line to the upper compound interest curve. Note that this component increases at an accelerating rate as time passes. Eventually, "interest on interest" will exceed the interest earned on the original principal! How long do you think this will take to happen for the case plotted in **Figure 9.2**?

The effect of the nominal interest rate on the future value Suppose Investment A earns 10% compounded annually, and Investment B earns 12% compounded annually. B's rate of return (12%) is one-fifth larger than A's (10%). You might think that if $100 is invested in each investment for, say, 25 years, the investment in B will grow one-fifth, or 20%, more than the investment in A. Wrong! Let's look into the outcome more carefully. It has very important implications for long-term financial planning.

In **Figure 9.3**, the future value of a $100 investment is plotted over a 25-year period for four *annually* compounded rates of interest.[3] The four rates are at 2% increments, and include the rates earned by Investments A (10%) and B (12%). We expect the separation of the curves to increase as time passes—that would happen without compounding. The most important observation you should make is the *disproportionate* effect each 2% increase in interest rate has on the long-term growth of the future value. Compare the future values after 25 years at the 10% and 12% rates. You can see that the future value at 12% compounded annually (Investment B) is about 1.5 times the future value at 10% compounded annually (Investment A). In comparison, the ratio of the two interest rates is only $\frac{12\%}{10\%} = 1.2$!

---

[3] An interactive version of **Figure 9.3**, "Find the Future Value of $100," is available on Connect.

| FIGURE 9.3 | Future Values of $100 at Various Compound Rates of Interest |

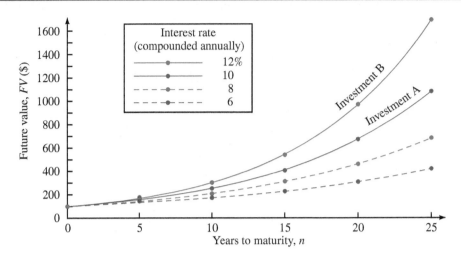

The contrast between long-term performances of A and B is more dramatic if we compare their *growth* instead of their future values. Over the full 25 years, B grows by

$$FV - PV = PV(1 + i)^n - PV$$
$$= \$100(1.12)^{25} - \$100$$
$$= \$1600.01$$

while A grows by

$$FV - PV = PV(1 + i)^n - PV$$
$$= \$100(1.10)^{25} - \$100$$
$$= \$983.47$$

In summary, B's growth is 1.63 times A's growth, even though the interest rate earned by B is only 1.2 times the rate earned by A. What a difference the extra 2% per year makes, especially over longer time periods! The implications for planning and managing your personal financial affairs include the following:

- You should begin an investment plan early in life in order to realize the dramatic effects of compounding beyond a 20-year time horizon.
- You should try to obtain the best available rate of return (at your acceptable level of risk). An extra 0.5% or 1% added to your annual rate of return has a disproportionate effect on investment growth, particularly in the long run.

The effect of the compounding frequency on the future value What difference will it make if we invest $100 at 12% compounded *monthly* instead of 12% compounded *annually*? In the first case, the $1 interest (1% of $100) earned in the first month gets converted to principal at the end of the month. We will then have $101 earning interest in the second month, and so on. With annual compounding, the $1 interest earned in the first month is not converted to principal. Just the original principal ($100) will earn interest in the second through to the twelfth month. Only then will the $12 interest earned during the year be converted to principal. Therefore, the original $100 will grow faster with monthly compounding.

The long-run effect of more frequent compounding is shown in **Figure 9.4**. As time passes, the higher compounding frequency produces a surprisingly large and ever-increasing difference between the future values. After 15 years, the future value with monthly compounding is about 10% larger than with annual compounding. Thereafter, the gap continues to widen in both dollar and percentage terms. After 20 years it is almost 13%, and after 25 years it is 16.4%.

FIGURE 9.4	Future Values of $100 at the Same Nominal Rate But Different Compounding Frequencies

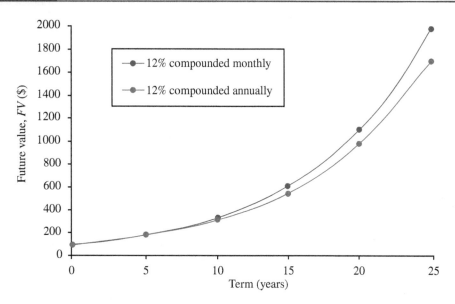

Where do you think the curves for semiannual and quarterly compounding would lie if they were included on the graph?

APP  THAT

Anyone interested in finance and saving money needs to have a good understanding of compound interest and its calculations. Search the App Store on your tablet, smartphone, or smart watch using the key words **COMPOUND INTEREST**.

You will find many free and paid apps that provide compound interest calculations for different compounding periods, floating rates of interest, and fluctuating balances. Some provide added features to calculate how long it will take to achieve your financial goals as well as provide adjustments in calculations for inflation.

L05 **Equivalent payments** Recall from Section 7.4 that **equivalent payments** are alternative payments that enable you to end up with the same dollar amount at a later date. The concepts we developed in Section 7.4 still apply when the time frame exceeds one year. The only change needed is to use the mathematics of *compound* interest when calculating a present value (an equivalent payment at an earlier date) or a future value (an equivalent payment at a later date). The rate of return employed in equivalent payment calculations should be the rate of return that can be earned from a low-risk investment. In real life, the prevailing rate of return[4] on Government of Canada bonds is the customary standard.

EXAMPLE 9.2E

CALCULATING THE PAYMENT AT A LATER DATE THAT IS EQUIVALENT TO TWO SCHEDULED PAYMENTS

A small claims court has ruled in favour of Mrs. Peacock. She claimed that Professor Plum defaulted on two payments of $1000 each. One payment was due 18 months ago, and the other 11 months ago. What is the appropriate amount for the court to order Plum to pay immediately if the court uses 6% compounded monthly for the interest rate money can earn?

---

[4] This rate of return can be found any day of the week in the financial pages of major newspapers. Government of Canada bonds are covered in detail in Chapter 16.

SOLUTION

The appropriate award is the combined future value of the two payments brought forward from their due dates to today. The periodic rate of interest is

$$i = \frac{j}{m} = \frac{6\%}{12} = 0.5\% \text{ (per month)}$$

The solution plan is presented in the following diagram.

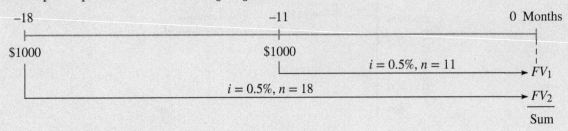

The amount today that is equivalent to the payment due 11 months ago is

$$FV_1 = PV(1 + i)^n = \$1000(1.005)^{11} = \$1056.396$$

Similarly,

$$FV_2 = \$1000(1.005)^{18} = \$1093.929$$

$$FV_1 + FV_2 = \$1056.396 + \$1093.929 = \$2150.33$$

The appropriate amount for Plum to pay is $2150.33.

 POINT OF INTEREST

The "Magic" of Compound Interest

"I don't know the names of the Seven Wonders of the World, but I do know the Eighth Wonder: Compound Interest."
— *Baron Rothschild*

There are thousands of books and articles on personal financial planning written with similar awe about the "miracle" or "magic" of compound interest. The authors make it appear that mysterious forces are involved.

Most people really do underestimate the long-term growth of compound interest investments. Also, they do not take seriously enough the advice to start saving and investing early in life. As we noted in **Figure 9.3**, compound growth accelerates rapidly beyond the 20-year horizon.

The reason why most people underestimate the long-term effects of compounding is that they tend to think in terms of proportional relationships. For example, most would estimate that an investment will earn about twice as much over 20 years as it will earn over 10 years at the same rate of return. Let's check your intuition in this regard.

© Pixtal/SuperStock

QUESTIONS

1. How do you think the growth of a $100 investment over 20 years compares to its growth over 10 years? Assume a return of 8% compounded annually. Will the former be twice as large? Two-and-a-half times as large? Make your best educated guess and then work out the actual ratio. Remember, we want the ratio for the *growth*, not the ratio for the *future value*.
2. Will the growth ratio be larger, smaller, or the same if we invest $1000 instead of $100 at the start? After making your choice, calculate the ratio.
3. Will the growth ratio be larger, smaller, or the same if the rate of return is 10% compounded annually instead of 8% compounded annually? After making your choice, calculate the ratio.

CONCEPT QUESTIONS

1. For a six-month investment, rank the following interest rates (number one being "most preferred"): 6% per annum simple interest, 6% compounded semiannually, 6% compounded quarterly. Explain your ranking.

2. Suppose it took x years for an investment to grow from $100 to $200 at a fixed compound rate of return. How many more years will it take to earn an additional

   a. $100?

   b. $200?

   c. $300?

   In each case, pick an answer from:

   (i) more than x years,

   (ii) fewer than x years,

   (iii) exactly x years.

3. Why is $100 received today worth more than $100 received at a future date?

EXERCISE 9.2

Answers to the odd-numbered problems are at the end of the book.

BASIC PROBLEMS

Note: In Section 9.4, you will learn how to use special functions on a financial calculator to solve compound interest problems. Exercise 9.4 suggests that you return to this Exercise to practise the financial calculator method.

1. What is the maturity value of $5000 invested at 3.0% compounded semiannually for seven years?

2. What is the future value of $8500 after $5\frac{1}{2}$ years if it earns 9.5% compounded quarterly?

3. To what amount would $12,100 grow after $3\frac{1}{4}$ years if it earned 2.5% compounded monthly?

4. What was a $4400 investment worth after $6\frac{3}{4}$ years if it earned 5.4% compounded monthly?

5. Assume that a $10,000 investment can earn 3% compounded quarterly. What will be its future value after:
   a. 15 years?   **b.** 20 years?
   c. 25 years?   **d.** 30 years?

6. How much will $10,000 be worth after 25 years if it earns:
   a. 6% compounded semiannually?   **b.** 7% compounded semiannually?
   c. 8% compounded semiannually?

7. To what amount will $10,000 grow after 25 years if it earns:
   a. 4% compounded annually?   **b.** 4% compounded semiannually?
   c. 4% compounded quarterly?   **d.** 4% compounded monthly?

8. $10,000 is invested at 7% compounded annually. Over the next 25 years, how much of the investment's increase in value represents:
   a. Earnings strictly on the original $10,000 principal?
   b. Earnings on reinvested earnings? (This amount reflects the cumulative effect of compounding.)

9. By calculating the maturity value of $100 invested for one year at each rate, determine which rate of return an investor would prefer.
   a. 3.0% compounded monthly
   b. 3.1% compounded quarterly
   c. 3.2% compounded semiannually
   d. 3.3% compounded annually

10. By calculating the maturity value of $100 invested for one year at each rate, determine which rate of return an investor would prefer.
    a. 12.0% compounded monthly
    b. 12.1% compounded quarterly
    c. 12.2% compounded semiannually
    d. 12.3% compounded annually

11. What is the maturity value of a $12,000 loan for 18 months at 7.2% compounded quarterly? How much interest is charged on the loan?

12. What total interest will be earned by $5000 invested at 5.4% compounded monthly for $3\frac{1}{2}$ years?

13. How much more will an investment of $10,000 be worth after 25 years if it earns 5% compounded annually instead of 4% compounded annually? Calculate the difference in dollars and as a percentage of the smaller maturity value.

14. How much more will an investment of $10,000 be worth after 25 years if it earns 6% compounded annually instead of 5% compounded annually? Calculate the difference in dollars and as a percentage of the smaller maturity value.

15. How much more will an investment of $10,000 earning 5% compounded annually be worth after 25 years than after 20 years? Calculate the difference in dollars and as a percentage of the smaller maturity value.

16. How much more will an investment of $10,000 earning 8% compounded annually be worth after 15 years than after 10 years? Calculate the difference in dollars and as a percentage of the smaller maturity value.

17. A $1000 investment is made today. Calculate its maturity values for the six combinations of terms and annually compounded rates of return in the following table.

	Term		
Rate of return (%)	20 years	25 years	30 years
8	?	?	?
10	?	?	?

18. Suppose an individual invests $1000 at the beginning of each year for the next 30 years. Thirty years from now, how much more will the first $1000 investment be worth than the 16th $1000 investment if both earn 8.5% compounded annually?

19. A $5000 payment due $1\frac{1}{2}$ years ago has not been paid. If money can earn 3.25% compounded annually, what amount paid $2\frac{1}{2}$ years from now would be the economic equivalent of the missed payment?

20. What amount three years from now is equivalent to $3000 due five months from now? Assume that money can earn 7.5% compounded monthly.

21. What amount today is equivalent to $10,000 four years ago, if money earned 5.5% compounded monthly over the last four years?

22. What amount two years from now will be equivalent to $2300 at a date $1\frac{1}{2}$ years ago, if money earns 6.25% compounded semiannually during the intervening time?

23. Payments of $1300 due today and $1800 due in $1\frac{3}{4}$ years are to be replaced by a single payment four years from now. What is the amount of that payment if money is worth 2% compounded quarterly?

24. Bjorn defaulted on payments of $2000 due three years ago and $1000 due $1\frac{1}{2}$ years ago. What would a fair settlement to the payee be $1\frac{1}{2}$ years from now, if the money could have been invested in low-risk government bonds to earn 4.2% compounded semiannually?

INTERMEDIATE PROBLEMS

25. Faisal borrowed $3000, $3500, and $4000 from his father on January 1 of three successive years at college. Faisal and his father agreed that interest would accumulate on each amount at the rate of 5% compounded semiannually. Faisal is to start repaying the loan one year after the $4000 loan. What consolidated amount will he owe at that time?

26. Interest rates were at historical highs in the early 1980s. In August of 1981, you could earn 17.5% compounded annually on a five-year term deposit with a Canadian bank. Since then, the interest rate offered on five-year term deposits dropped to a low of 2.25% compounded annually in February of 2019. On a $10,000 deposit for a term of five years, how much more would you have earned at the historical high interest rate than at the more recent low rate?

27. Mrs. Vanderberg has just deposited $5000 in each of three savings plans for her grandchildren. They will have access to the accumulated funds on their 19th birthdays. Their current ages are 12 years, 7 months (Donna); 10 years, 3 months (Tim); and 7 years, 11 months (Gary). If the plans earn 8% compounded monthly, what amount will each grandchild receive at age 19?

28. Nelson borrowed $5000 for $4\frac{1}{2}$ years. For the first $2\frac{1}{2}$ years, the interest rate on the loan was 8.4% compounded monthly. Then the rate became 7.5% compounded semiannually. What total amount was required to pay off the loan if no payments were made before the expiry of the $4\frac{1}{2}$-year term?

29. Alberto has just invested $60,000 in a five-year Guaranteed Investment Certificate (GIC) earning 6% compounded semiannually. When the GIC matures, he will reinvest its entire maturity value in a new five-year GIC. What will be the maturity value of the second GIC if it yields:
   a. The same rate as the current GIC?
   b. 7% compounded semiannually?
   c. 5% compounded semiannually?

30. An investment of $2500 earned interest at 4.5% compounded quarterly for $1\frac{1}{2}$ years, and then 4.0% compounded monthly for two years. How much interest did the investment earn in the $3\frac{1}{2}$ years?

31. A debt of $7000 accumulated interest at 9.5% compounded quarterly for 15 months, after which the rate changed to 8.5% compounded semiannually for the next six months. What was the total amount owed at the end of the entire 21-month period?

32. Megan borrowed $1900 three and a half years ago at 7% compounded semiannually. Two years ago she made a payment of $1000. What amount is required today to pay off the remaining principal and the accrued interest?

33. Duane borrowed $3000 from his grandmother five years ago. The interest on the loan was to be 5% compounded semiannually for the first three years, and 6% compounded monthly thereafter. If he made a $1000 payment $2\frac{1}{2}$ years ago, what is the amount now owed on the loan?

34. A loan of $4000 at 7.5% compounded monthly requires three payments of $1000 at 6, 12, and 18 months after the date of the loan, and a final payment of the full balance after two years. What is the amount of the final payment?

ADVANCED PROBLEMS

35. Dr. Sawicki obtained a variable-rate loan of $10,000. The lender required payment of at least $2000 each year. After nine months the doctor paid $2500, and another nine months later she paid $3000. What amount was owed on the loan after two years if the interest rate was 6.6% compounded monthly for the first year, and 7% compounded quarterly for the second year?

36. Access the interactive chart named "Future Value of $100" on Connect. In Chapter 9 under the Student Resources, you will find a link to the chart. Use the chart to help you answer these questions. What is the percentage increase in an investment's future value every five years if the investment earns:
    a. 7% compounded annually?
    b. 9% compounded annually?
    c. 11% compounded annually?

37. Access the interactive chart named "Future Value of $100" on Connect. In Chapter 9 under the Student Resources, you will find a link to the chart. Use the chart to help you answer:
    a. Problem 13.
    b. Problem 15.

38. Access the interactive chart named "Future Value of $100" on Connect. In Chapter 9 under the Student Resources, you will find a link to the chart. Use the chart to help you answer these questions. Over a 25-year period, how much more (expressed as a percentage) will an investment be worth if it earns:
    a. 6% compounded monthly instead of 6% compounded annually?
    b. 9% compounded monthly instead of 9% compounded annually?
    c. 12% compounded monthly instead of 12% compounded annually?

9.3 | Present Value

LO1 If money can earn 3% compounded annually, what amount would have to be invested *today* to grow to $1000 five years from now? This is an example of determining a payment's **present value**—an economically equivalent amount at an *earlier* date. In this instance, the present value is the (principal) amount you would have to invest at 3% compounded annually in order to end up with $1000 after five years. To calculate this initial investment, we need only rearrange

$$FV = PV(1 + i)^n$$

to isolate *PV*, and then substitute the values for *FV*, *i*, and *n*. Dividing both sides of the formula by $(1 + i)^n$ leaves *PV* by itself on the right side. We thereby obtain a second version of Formula (9-2):

$$PV = \frac{FV}{(1 + i)^n} = FV(1 + i)^{-n}$$

In summary, $PV = FV(1 + i)^{-n}$ applies to two types of problems:

- Calculating the initial investment needed to produce a particular maturity value, *FV*; and
- Calculating the present value of a scheduled payment, *FV*.

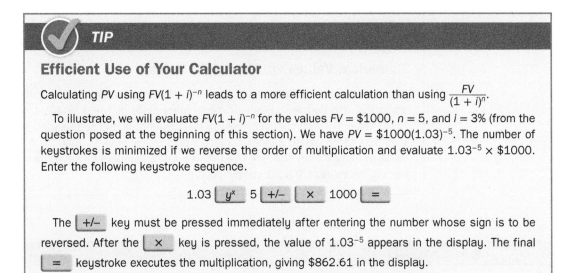

TIP

Efficient Use of Your Calculator

Calculating *PV* using $FV(1 + i)^{-n}$ leads to a more efficient calculation than using $\frac{FV}{(1 + i)^n}$.

To illustrate, we will evaluate $FV(1 + i)^{-n}$ for the values *FV* = $1000, *n* = 5, and *i* = 3% (from the question posed at the beginning of this section). We have $PV = \$1000(1.03)^{-5}$. The number of keystrokes is minimized if we reverse the order of multiplication and evaluate $1.03^{-5} \times \$1000$. Enter the following keystroke sequence.

$$1.03 \quad \boxed{y^x} \quad 5 \quad \boxed{+/-} \quad \boxed{\times} \quad 1000 \quad \boxed{=}$$

The $\boxed{+/-}$ key must be pressed immediately after entering the number whose sign is to be reversed. After the $\boxed{\times}$ key is pressed, the value of 1.03^{-5} appears in the display. The final $\boxed{=}$ keystroke executes the multiplication, giving $862.61 in the display.

The present value of a future payment will, of course, always be a smaller number than the payment. This is why the process of calculating a payment's present value is sometimes described as **discounting a payment**. The interest rate used in the present-value calculation is then referred to as the **discount rate**.

The longer the time period before a scheduled payment, the smaller the present value will be. **Figure 9.5** shows the pattern of decreasing present value for longer periods *before* the payment date. The decline is rapid in the first ten years, but steadily tapers off at longer periods. With a discount rate of 10% compounded annually, the present value seven years before the payment is about half the *numerical* value of the payment. Twenty-five years prior to the payment, the present value is less than one-tenth of the payment's size! In practical terms, payments that will be received more than 25 years in the future have little *economic* value today.

FIGURE 9.5 The Present Value of $1000 (Discounted at 10% Compounded Annually)

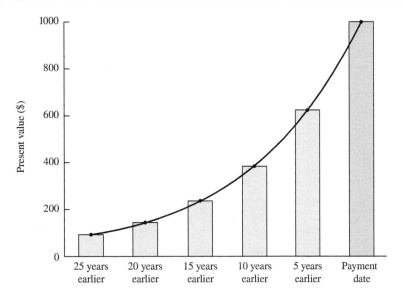

How would **Figure 9.5** change for a discount rate of 5% compounded annually? And how would it differ for a discount rate of 15% compounded annually?

TIP

Numerical Values vs. Economic Values

In terms of numerical values, a present value is smaller than the payment, and a future value is larger than the payment. However, these *numerically different* amounts all have the *same economic* value. For example, suppose a $100 payment is due one year from now, and money can earn 10% compounded annually. Today's present value is $100(1.10)^{-1} = \$90.91$. The future value two years from now is $110.00. The three amounts all have the same economic value, namely the value of $90.91 *current* dollars.

EXAMPLE 9.3A

THE INVESTMENT NEEDED TO REACH A PARTICULAR FUTURE VALUE

If an investment can earn 4% compounded monthly, what amount must you invest now in order to accumulate $10,000 after $3\frac{1}{2}$ years?

SOLUTION

Given: $j = 4\%$, $m = 12$, $FV = \$10,000$, and Term = 3.5 years

Then
$$i = \frac{j}{m} = \frac{4\%}{12} = 0.\overline{3}\% \text{ per month} \quad \text{and} \quad n = m(\text{Term}) = 12(3.5) = 42$$

Rearranging Formula (9-2) to solve for *PV*,
$$PV = FV(1 + i)^{-n} = \$10,000(1.00333333)^{-42} = \$8695.61$$

You must invest $8695.61 now in order to have $10,000 after $3\frac{1}{2}$ years.

 TIP

Efficient Use of Your Calculator

If you use any fewer than six 3s in the value for *i* in Example 9.3A, you will have some round-off error in the calculated value for *PV*. For the fewest keystrokes and maximum accuracy in your answer, avoid manual re-entry of calculated values. The most efficient sequence of keystrokes resulting in the highest accuracy of *PV* in Example 9.3A is

$$0.04 \boxed{\div} 12 \boxed{+} 1 \boxed{=} \boxed{y^x} 42 \boxed{+/-} \boxed{\times} 10000 \boxed{=}$$

When you employ the calculated value of *i* in this way, the calculator actually uses more than the seven 3s you see in the display (after pressing the first $\boxed{=}$ in the preceding sequence). The calculator maintains and uses two or three more figures than are shown in the display. In subsequent example problems, this procedure will be assumed but will not be shown.

EXAMPLE 9.3B

CALCULATING AN EQUIVALENT PAYMENT AT AN EARLIER DATE

Mr. and Mrs. Nguyen's property taxes of $3450 are due on July 1. What amount should the city accept if the taxes are paid eight months in advance and the city can earn 3.6% compounded monthly on surplus funds?

SOLUTION

The city should accept an amount that is equivalent to $3450, allowing for the rate of interest that the city can earn on its surplus funds. This equivalent amount is the present value of $3450, eight months earlier.

Given: $FV = \$3450$, $j = 3.6\%$ compounded monthly, $m = 12$, and $n = 8$

Then
$$i = \frac{j}{m} = \frac{3.6\%}{12} = 0.3\% \text{ (per month)}$$

and
$$\text{Present value, } PV = FV(1 + i)^{-n} = \$3450(1.003)^{-8} = \$3368.31$$

The city should be willing to accept $3368.31 on a date eight months before the scheduled due date.

EXAMPLE 9.3C

CALCULATING AN EQUIVALENT VALUE OF TWO PAYMENTS

Two payments of $10,000 each must be made one year and four years from now. If money can earn 3% compounded monthly, what single payment two years from now would be equivalent to the two scheduled payments?

SOLUTION

When more than one payment is involved in a problem, it is helpful to present the given information in a time diagram. Some of the calculations that need to be done may be indicated on the diagram. In this case, we can indicate the calculation of the equivalent values by constructing arrows from the scheduled payments to the date of the replacement payment. Then we write the relevant values for i ($\frac{3\%}{12} = 0.25\%$) and n on each arrow.

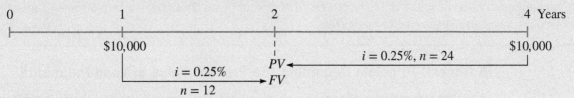

The single equivalent payment is equal to $PV + FV$.

$$\begin{aligned}
FV &= \text{Future value of } \$10,000, \text{ 12 months later} \\
&= \$10,000(1.0025)^{12} \\
&= \$10,304.160
\end{aligned}$$

$$\begin{aligned}
PV &= \text{Present value of } \$10,000, \text{ 24 months earlier} \\
&= \$10,000(1.0025)^{-24} \\
&= \$9418.351
\end{aligned}$$

The equivalent single payment is

$$\$10,304.160 + \$9418.351 = \$19,722.51$$

EXAMPLE 9.3D

DEMONSTRATING ECONOMIC EQUIVALENCE

Show why the recipient of the payments in **Example 9.3C** should be indifferent between receiving the scheduled payments and receiving the replacement payment.

SOLUTION

If the recipient ends up in the same economic position with either alternative, then he should not care which alternative is used.

We will calculate how much money the recipient will have four years from now with each alternative, assuming that any amounts received are invested at 3% compounded monthly.

The two alternatives are presented in the two following time diagrams.

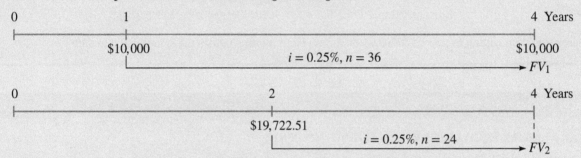

With the scheduled payments, the total amount that the recipient will have after four years is

$$FV_1 + \$10{,}000 = \$10{,}000(1.0025)^{36} + \$10{,}000$$
$$= \$10{,}940.51 + \$10{,}000$$
$$= \$20{,}940.51$$

With the single replacement payment, the recipient will have

$$FV_2 = \$19{,}722.51(1.0025)^{24} = \$20{,}940.51$$

With either alternative, the recipient will have $20,940.51 after four years. Therefore, the replacement payment is economically equivalent to the scheduled payments.

A General Principle Regarding the Present Value of Loan Payments

When the present value of a payment is calculated, the interest portion of the payment is, in effect, stripped from the payment amount leaving only the principal portion of that payment. When this is done for a series of loan payments their present values will always be equivalent to the amount of the original loan.

> **Present Value of Loan Payments**
> The sum of the present values of all of the payments required to pay off a loan is equal to the original principal of the loan. The discount rate for the present-value calculations is the rate of interest charged on the loan.

EXAMPLE 9.3E

CALCULATING THE ORIGINAL AMOUNT OF A LOAN

Three payments of $1500 each plus a different final payment of $856.35 were made on a loan at one-year intervals after the date of the loan. The interest rate on the loan was 3% compounded quarterly. What was the original amount of the loan?

SOLUTION

In **Example 9.2D**, three payments of $1500 each were made on a loan at one-year intervals after the date of the loan and the problem was to determine the additional payment needed to pay off the loan at the end of the fourth year. The answer was $856.35.

To solve this problem, we will calculate the sum of the present values of all four payments at the date on which the loan was granted using the interest rate on the loan as the discount rate. The calculation of each payment's present value is given in the following table.

Payment	Amount, FV	n	i	$PV = FV(1 + i)^{-n}$
First	$1500.00	4	0.75%	$PV_1 = \$1500(1.0075)^{-4} = \$1455.83$
Second	$1500.00	8	0.75%	$PV_2 = \$1500(1.0075)^{-8} = \$1412.96$
Third	$1500.00	12	0.75%	$PV_3 = \$1500(1.0075)^{-12} = \$1371.36$
Fourth	$856.35	16	0.75%	$PV_4 = \$856.35(1.0075)^{-16} = \$759.85$
				Total: $5000.00

The amount of the original loan is $5000.00.

EXAMPLE 9.3F

CALCULATING EQUAL PAYMENT AMOUNTS

A $3000 loan is to be repaid with three equal payments made three, six, and nine months, respectively, from the date of the loan. If interest on the loan is 6% compounded monthly, what is the amount of each payment?

SOLUTION

Applying the principal for the present value of loan payments:

Sum of the present values of the three payments = $3000

We will let x represent the payment amount shown in the time line diagram below:

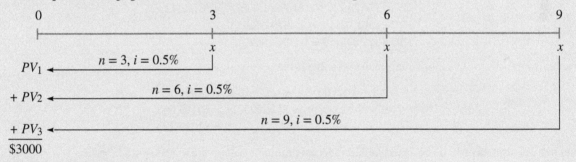

The present values of the three payments $PV_1 + PV_2 + PV_3 = \$3000$ ①

$$PV_1 = FV(1 + i)^{-n} = x(1.005)^{-3} = 0.985148759x$$
$$PV_2 = x(1.005)^{-6} = 0.970518078x$$
$$PV_3 = x(1.005)^{-9} = 0.95610468x$$

Now substitute these values into equation ① and solve for x.

$$0.985148759x + 0.970518078x + 0.95610468x = \$3000$$
$$2.911771517x = \$3000$$
$$x = \$1030.30$$

The amount of each of the three equal payments is $1030.30.

EXAMPLE 9.3G

CALCULATING TWO UNKNOWN LOAN PAYMENTS

Kramer borrowed $4000 from George at an interest rate of 7% compounded semiannually. The loan is to be repaid by three payments. The first payment, $1000, is due two years after the date of the loan. The second and third payments are due three and five years, respectively, after the initial loan. Calculate the amounts of the second and third payments if the second payment is to be twice the size of the third payment.

SOLUTION

Applying the fundamental principle developed in this section, we have

Sum of the present values of the three payments = $4000

The given data are presented on the following time line. If we let x represent the third payment, then the second payment must be $2x$. Notice how the idea expressed by the preceding word equation can (and should) be indicated on the diagram.

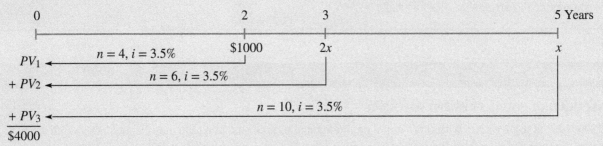

The second and third payments must be of sizes that will make

$$PV_1 + PV_2 + PV_3 = \$4000 \qquad ①$$

We can obtain a numerical value for PV_1, but the best we can do for PV_2 and PV_3 is to express them in terms of x. That is just fine—after we substitute these values into equation ①, we will be able to solve for x.

$$PV_1 = FV(1 + i)^{-n} = \$1000(1.035)^{-4} = \$871.442$$
$$PV_2 = 2x(1.035)^{-6} = 1.6270013x$$
$$PV_3 = x(1.035)^{-10} = 0.7089188x$$

Now substitute these values into equation ① and solve for x.

$$\$871.442 + 1.6270013x + 0.7089188x = \$4000$$
$$2.3359201x = \$3128.558$$
$$x = \$1339.326$$

Kramer's third payment will be $1339.33 and his second payment will be 2($1339.33) = $2678.66.

EXERCISE 9.3

Answers to the odd-numbered problems are at the end of the book.

BASIC PROBLEMS

Note: In Section 9.4, you will learn how to use special functions on a financial calculator to solve compound interest problems. Exercise 9.4 will invite you to return to this Exercise to practise the financial calculator method.

1. If money can be invested to earn 2.5% compounded annually, how much would have to be invested today to grow to $10,000 after:
   a. 10 years? **b.** 20 years? **c.** 30 years?

2. What amount would have to be invested today for the future value to be $10,000 after 20 years if the rate of return is:
   a. 5% compounded quarterly?
   b. 7% compounded quarterly?
   c. 9% compounded quarterly?

3. What amount invested today would grow to $10,000 after 25 years, if the investment earns:
   a. 4% compounded annually?
   b. 4% compounded semiannually?
   c. 4% compounded quarterly?
   d. 4% compounded monthly?

4. If money is worth 6% compounded annually, what amount today is equivalent to $10,000 paid:
   a. 12 years from now?
   b. 24 years from now?
   c. 36 years from now?

5. What is the present value of $10,000 discounted at 4.5% compounded annually over 10 years?

6. What principal amount will have a maturity value of $5437.52 after 27 months if it earns 8.5% compounded quarterly?

7. The maturity value of an investment after 42 months is $9704.61. What was the original investment, if it earned 3.5% compounded semiannually?

8. What amount today is economically equivalent to $8000 paid 18 months from now, if money is worth 5% compounded monthly?

9. If your client's objective is to have $10,000 in four years, how much should he invest today in a product earning 5.5% compounded annually?

10. Ross has just been notified that the combined principal and interest on an amount that he borrowed 27 months ago at 11% compounded quarterly is now $2297.78. How much of this amount is principal and how much is interest?

11. Your client has a choice of either receiving $5000 two years from now or receiving a lump payment today. If your client can earn 5.4% compounded semiannually, what amount received today is equivalent to $5000 in two years?

12. You owe $6000 payable three years from now. What alternative amount should your creditor be willing to accept today if she can earn 4.2% compounded monthly on a low-risk investment?

13. What amount $1\frac{1}{2}$ years from now is equivalent to $7000 due in 8 years if money can earn 6.2% compounded semiannually?

14. A payment of $1300 is scheduled for a date $3\frac{1}{2}$ years from now. What would be an equivalent payment nine months from now if money is worth 5.5% compounded quarterly?

15. What amount 15 months ago is equivalent to $2600 one and a half years from now? Assume money can earn 5.4% compounded monthly.

16. Mustafa can receive a $77 discount if he pays his property taxes early. Alternatively, he can pay the full amount of $2250 when payment is due in nine months. Which alternative is to his advantage if he can earn 6% compounded monthly on short-term investments? In current dollars, how much is the advantage?

17. What single amount, paid three years from now, would be economically equivalent to the combination of $1400 due today and $1800 due in five years if funds can be invested to earn 3% compounded quarterly?

18. Ramon wishes to replace payments of $900 due today and $500 due in 22 months by a single equivalent payment 18 months from now. If money is worth 5% compounded monthly, what should that payment be?

19. Mohinder has financial obligations of $1000 due in $3\frac{1}{2}$ years and $2000 due in $5\frac{1}{2}$ years. He wishes to settle the obligations sooner with a single payment one year from now. If money is worth 2.75% compounded semiannually, what amount should the payee be willing to accept?

20. What payment $2\frac{1}{4}$ years from now would be a fair substitute for the combination of $1500 due (but not paid) nine months ago and $2500 due in $4\frac{1}{2}$ years if money can earn 9% compounded quarterly?

21. What single payment six months from now would be economically equivalent to payments of $500 due (but not paid) four months ago and $800 due in 12 months? Assume money can earn 2.5% compounded monthly.

22. What single payment one year from now would be equivalent to $2500 due in three months, and another $2500 due in two years? Money is worth 7% compounded quarterly.

23. A scheduled payment stream consisted of three payments: $2100 due (but not paid) $1\frac{1}{2}$ years ago, $1300 due today, and $800 due in two years. What single payment six months from now would be economically equivalent to the payment stream? Money can earn 4.5% compounded monthly.

24. A debtor owing payments of $750 due today, $1000 due in 2 years, and $1250 due in 4 years requests a payout figure to settle all three obligations by means of a single economically equivalent payment 18 months from now. What is that amount if the payee can earn 9.5% compounded semiannually?

25. Alicia is considering two offers-to-purchase that she has received on a residential building lot she wishes to sell. One is a cash offer of $145,000. The other offer consists of three payments of $49,000—one now, one in six months, and one in twelve months. Which offer has the larger economic value if Alicia can earn 4.4% compounded quarterly on low-risk investments? How much more (in current dollars) is the better offer worth?

26. A bond pays $1000 interest at the end of every year for the next 30 years. What is the *current* economic value of each of the 15th and 30th payments if we discount the payments at:
    a. 5% compounded semiannually?
    b. 8% compounded semiannually?

INTERMEDIATE PROBLEMS

27. Pete Pylon has just signed a "four-year, $68-million deal" with the Ottawa Senators. The terms of the contract include a signing bonus of $4.8 million and salaries of $10 million, $17.2 million, $17.5 million, and $18.5 million in successive years of the contract. The news media always ignore the time value of money when they report the "value" of professional athletes' contracts. What is the economic value of Pete's contract on the date it was signed? Assume that the signing bonus was paid on that date, that the annual salaries will be paid in lump amounts $\frac{1}{2}$ year, $1\frac{1}{2}$ years, $2\frac{1}{2}$ years, and $3\frac{1}{2}$ years later, and that money is worth 5% compounded semiannually. Round the answer to the nearest $1000.

28. To motivate individuals to start saving at an early age, financial planners will sometimes present the results of the following type of calculation. How much must a 25-year-old individual invest five years from now to have the same maturity value at age 55 as an immediate investment of $1000? Assume that both investments earn 8% compounded annually.

29. Michelle has just received an inheritance from her grandfather's estate. She will be entering college in $3\frac{1}{2}$ years, and wants to immediately purchase three compound interest investment certificates having the following maturity values and dates: $4000 at the beginning of her first academic year, $5000 at the beginning of her second year, and $6000 at the beginning of her third year. She can obtain interest rates of 5% compounded semiannually for any terms between three and five years, and 5.6% compounded quarterly for terms between five and seven years. What principal amount should she invest in each certificate?

30. Daniel makes annual payments of $2000 to the former owner of a residential lot that he purchased a few years ago. At the time of the fourth-from-last payment, Daniel asks for a payout figure that would immediately settle the debt. What amount should the payee be willing to accept instead of the last three payments, if money can earn 8.5% compounded semiannually?

31. Commercial Finance Co. buys conditional sale contracts from furniture retailers at discounts that provide a 16.5% compounded monthly rate of return on the purchase price. What total price should Commercial Finance pay for the following three contracts: $950 due in four months, $780 due in six months, and $1270 due in five months?

32. Teresita has three financial obligations to the same person: $2700 due in 1 year, $1900 due in $1\frac{1}{2}$ years, and $1100 due in 3 years. She wishes to settle the obligations with a single payment in $2\frac{1}{4}$ years, when her inheritance will be released from her mother's estate. What amount should the creditor accept if money can earn 6% compounded quarterly?

33. A $15,000 loan at 5.5% compounded semiannually is advanced today. Two payments of $4000 are to be made one year and three years from now. The balance is to be paid in five years. What will the third payment be?

34. A $4000 loan at 10% compounded monthly is to be repaid by three equal payments due 5, 10, and 15 months from the date of the loan. What is the size of the payments?

35. A $10,000 loan at 4% compounded semiannually is to be repaid by three equal payments due $2\frac{1}{2}$, 4, and 7 years after the date of the loan. What is the size of each payment?

36. A $6000 loan at 9% compounded quarterly is to be settled by two payments. The first payment is due after nine months and the second payment, half the amount of the first payment, is due after $1\frac{1}{2}$ years. Determine the size of each payment.

37. A $7500 loan at 4% compounded monthly requires three payments at five-month intervals after the date of the loan. The second payment is to be twice the size of the first payment, and the third payment is to be double the amount of the second payment. Calculate the size of the second payment.

38. Three equal payments were made two, four, and six years after the date on which a $9000 loan was granted at 10% compounded quarterly. If the balance immediately after the third payment was $5169.81, what was the amount of each payment?

ADVANCED PROBLEMS

39. Repeat Problem 31 with the change that each contract accrues interest from today at the rate of 12% compounded monthly.

40. Repeat Problem 32 with the change that each obligation accrues interest at the rate of 9% compounded monthly from a date nine months ago when the obligations were incurred.

41. If the total interest earned on an investment at 8.2% compounded semiannually for $8\frac{1}{2}$ years was $1175.98, what was the original investment?

42. Peggy has never made any payments on a five-year-old loan from her mother at 6% compounded annually. The total interest owed is now $845.56. How much did she borrow from her mother?

9.4 Using Financial Calculators

LO1 The formulas for many compound interest calculations are permanently programmed into financial calculators. These calculators allow you to enter the numerical values for the variables into memory. Then you select the appropriate financial function to automatically perform the calculation.

Ideally, you should be able to solve compound interest problems using both the algebraic method and the financial functions on a calculator. The algebraic approach strengthens your mathematical skills and provides more flexibility for handling non-standard cases. It helps prepare you to create spreadsheets for specific applications. Financial calculators make routine calculations more efficient and reduce the likelihood of making arithmetic errors. Most of the example problems from this point onward will present both algebraic and financial calculator solutions.

Key Definitions and Calculator Operation

The financial calculator instructions and keystrokes shown in the main body of this book and in the Student's Solutions Manual are for the Texas Instruments BA II PLUS. General instructions for two other calculator models are provided in **Appendix 9A** and **Appendix 13A**.

APP 4 THAT

Most financial calculators have an app version available for laptops, tablets, smartphones, or smart watches. Search the App Store on your device using the key words **FINANCIAL CALCULATOR**.

There are apps available for the BA II PLUS and many other specific models that function exactly like the hand-held calculator. You will also find several apps that perform financial calculations using the same principles as the calculator functions.

The basic financial keys of the Texas Instruments BA II PLUS calculator are in the third row of its keyboard. The calculator's manual refers to them as the TVM (Time-Value-of-Money) keys. The definitions for these keys are as follows.

| N | represents the number of compounding periods, n
| I/Y | represents the nominal (annual) interest rate, j
| PV | represents the principal or present value, PV
| PMT | represents the periodic annuity payment (first used in **Chapter 11**)
| FV | represents the maturity value or future value, FV

Each of the five keys has two uses:

1. Saving in memory a numerical value for the variable.
2. Computing the value of the variable (based on previously saved values for all other variables).

As an example, let us compute the future value of $1000 invested at 3% compounded semiannually for 3 years. We must first enter values for | N |, | I/Y |, | PV |, and | PMT |. They may be entered in any order. To save $1000 in the memory, just enter the digits for 1000 and press | PV |. The display then shows[5]

$$PV = \qquad 1,000.$$

---

[5] The assumption here is that the calculator has previously been set for "floating-decimal format." See **Appendix 9A** for instructions on setting this format on the "Format worksheet."

Next enter values for the other variables in the same manner. (You do not need to clear your display between entries.) Note that the *nominal interest rate must be entered in percent form* (without the % symbol) rather than in its decimal equivalent form.

In summary, the keystrokes for entering these four known values are:

1000 PV   6 N   3 I/Y   0 PMT

The **TVM** function in the BA II PLUS is designed primarily to handle the compound interest annuity calculations presented beginning in Chapter 11. Since the compound interest calculations in this chapter and in Chapter 10 do not involve a series of regular payments, the payment amount (*PMT*) for all compound interest calculations will be set to $0 and the payment frequency (*P/Y*) will be set to match the compounding frequency (*C/Y*).

We have not yet entered any information about the compounding frequency. To key in and save the value for the number of compounds per year, you must first gain access to a particular list of internal settings. Note the *P/Y* symbol above the *I/Y* key. This indicates that the *P/Y* settings worksheet is the second function of the *I/Y* key. Therefore, to open this worksheet, press the key labelled "2nd" followed by the key labelled "*I/Y*." Hereafter, we will represent this keystroke combination by

2nd P/Y

After pressing these two keys, your calculator's display will show something like

P/Y =	12.

This display is actually a "window" to the first item in a list of just two items as shown.

P/Y =	12.
C/Y =	12.

You can scroll down to the second item by pressing the ↓ key. The definitions for these new symbols are:

P/Y   represents the number of annuity payments per year
C/Y   represents the number of compounds per year

Therefore, *C/Y* corresponds to the algebraic symbol m.

In the current example, we have semiannual compounding. Therefore, we need to set both *P/Y* and *C/Y* equal to 2. To do that, scroll back up to the *P/Y* line in the list. Then press

2 ENTER

The calculator display now shows

P/Y =	2.

Next, scroll down to *C/Y*. Observe that its value has automatically changed to 2. Entering a new value for *P/Y always* causes *C/Y* to change automatically to the same value. So for all problems in this chapter and Chapter 10, we need only set *P/Y* = m. That will produce the desired result of making[6] *C/Y* = *P/Y* = m.

Before we can compute the future value of the $1000, we must close the *P/Y* settings worksheet. Note that the second function of the key labelled CPT is **QUIT**. Pressing

2nd QUIT

---

[6] Later, in Chapter 11, *P/Y* and *C/Y* will have differing values in some annuity problems. We will deal with this matter when needed.

will close whatever worksheet is open. To execute the future-value calculation, press

The calculator will display

$$FV = \qquad\qquad -1,\!093.443264$$

Rounded to the nearest cent, the future value of the $1000 investment is $1093.44. The negative sign in the calculated *FV* indicates cash flow and will be discussed in the next subsection.

Let's summarize the complete sequence of keystrokes needed for the future-value calculation.

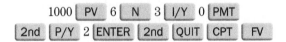

Efficient Use of Your Calculator

You can operate your calculator more efficiently if you take advantage of the following features.

1. After any computation, all internal settings and numbers saved in memory are retained until you change them or clear them. Therefore, you do not need to re-enter a variable's value if it is unchanged in a subsequent calculation.
2. Whenever you *accidentally* press one of the five financial keys, the number in the display at that moment will be saved as the value of that financial variable. At any time, you can check the value stored in a financial key's memory by pressing [RCL] followed by the key.
3. When you turn the calculator off, it still retains the internal settings and the values in memory. (When the calculator's battery becomes weak, this feature and other calculator operations are unreliable.)

Cash-Flow Sign Convention

Cash flow is a term frequently used in finance and accounting to refer to a cash payment. A cash inflow is a cash receipt; a cash outflow is a cash disbursement. A cash *inflow* should be saved in a financial calculator's memory as a *positive* value. A cash *outflow* should be entered as a *negative* number. These two simple rules have a rather overblown name in finance—the **cash-flow sign convention**.

> **Cash-Flow Sign Convention**
> Cash inflows (receipts) are positive.
> Cash outflows (disbursements) are negative.

Financial calculators, finance courses, finance resources, and the financial functions in spreadsheet software all employ the cash-flow convention.

To use the cash-flow sign convention, you must treat a compound interest problem as either an investment or a loan. The directions of the cash flows for these two cases are compared in the following table. When you invest money, you pay it (cash outflow) to some institution or individual. Later, you receive cash inflows from investment income and from the sale or redemption of the investment. In contrast, when you receive a loan, it is a cash inflow for you. The subsequent cash flows in the loan transaction are the loan payments (cash outflows).

Transaction	Initial cash flow	Subsequent cash flows
Investment	Outflow (negative)	Inflow (positive)
Loan	Inflow (positive)	Outflows (negative)

In our $1000 example above, the $1000 was entered as a positive value so the calculator interpreted it as a cash inflow or loan. The computed future value represents the single payment required to pay off the loan. Since this payment is a cash outflow, the calculator displayed it as a negative number. To properly employ the sign convention for the initial $1000 investment, we should have entered 1000 in $\boxed{\text{PV}}$ as a negative number. The calculator would then compute a positive future value—the cash inflow we will receive when the investment matures.

To illustrate the use of financial calculators, **Examples 9.3A**, **9.3C**, and **9.3G** will now be repeated as **Examples 9.4A**, **9.4B**, and **9.4C**, respectively.

EXAMPLE 9.4A

THE INVESTMENT NEEDED TO REACH A PARTICULAR FUTURE VALUE

What amount must you invest now at 4% compounded monthly to accumulate $10,000 after $3\frac{1}{2}$ years?

SOLUTION

Given: $j = 4\%$, $m = 12$, $FV = \$10,000$, and Term = 3.5 years

Then $\quad n = m \times \text{Term} = 12(3.5) = 42$

Enter the known variables and then compute the present value.

42 $\boxed{\text{N}}$ 4 $\boxed{\text{I/Y}}$ 0 $\boxed{\text{PMT}}$ 10000 $\boxed{\text{FV}}$

$\boxed{\text{2nd}}$ $\boxed{\text{P/Y}}$ 12 $\boxed{\text{ENTER}}$ $\boxed{\text{2nd}}$ $\boxed{\text{QUIT}}$ $\boxed{\text{CPT}}$ $\boxed{\text{PV}}$ *Answer:* −8,695.606596

Note that we entered the $10,000 as a positive value because it is the cash *inflow* you will receive 3.5 years from now.

The answer is negative because it represents the investment (cash outflow) that must be made today. Rounded to the cent, the initial investment required is $8695.61.

EXAMPLE 9.4B

CALCULATING AN EQUIVALENT VALUE OF TWO PAYMENTS

Two payments of $10,000 each must be made one year and four years from now. If money can earn 3% compounded monthly, what single payment two years from now would be equivalent to the two scheduled payments?

SOLUTION

Given: $j = 3\%$ compounded monthly, making $m = 12$ and $i = \dfrac{j}{m} = \dfrac{3\%}{12} = 0.25\%$

A time line diagram shows the solution strategy and required inputs for this problem. FV_1 represents the future value of the first scheduled payment and PV_2 represents the present value of the second payment.

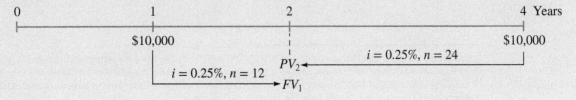

The single equivalent payment is $FV_1 + PV_2$. Before we start crunching numbers, let's exercise your intuition. Do you think the equivalent payment will be greater or smaller than $20,000? It is clear that FV_1 is greater than $10,000 and that PV_2 is less than $10,000. When the two amounts are added, will the sum be more than or less than $20,000? We can answer this question by comparing the time intervals through which we "shift" each of the $10,000 payments. The first payment will have one year's growth added, but the second payment will be discounted by two years' growth.[7] Therefore, PV_2 is farther below $10,000 than FV_1 is above $10,000. Hence, the equivalent payment will be less than $20,000. So if your equivalent payment turns out to be more than $20,000, you will know that your solution has an error. Returning to the calculations,

FV_1: 12 **N** 3 **I/Y** 10000 **PV** 0 **PMT**

2nd **P/Y** 12 **ENTER** **2nd** **QUIT** **CPT** **FV** *Answer:* −10,304.160

PV_2: Do not clear the values and settings currently in memory. Then you need enter only those values and settings that change.

24 **N** 10000 **FV** **CPT** **PV** *Answer:* −9,418.351

The equivalent payment two years from now is $10,304.160 + $9,418.351 = $19,722.51.

Note: An equivalent payment problem is neither a loan nor an investment situation. Loans and investments always involve at least one cash flow in each direction. In contrast, an equivalent payment is a payment that can *substitute for* one or more other payments. The substitute payment will flow in the *same* direction as the payment(s) it replaces. So how should you apply the cash-flow sign convention to equivalent payment calculations? Just enter the scheduled payments as positive numbers and ignore the opposite sign on the calculated equivalent value.

EXAMPLE 9.4C

CALCULATING TWO UNKNOWN LOAN PAYMENTS

Kramer borrowed $4000 from George at an interest rate of 7% compounded semiannually. The loan is to be repaid by three payments. The first payment, $1000, is due two years after the date of the loan. The second and third payments are due three and five years, respectively, after the initial loan. Calculate the amounts of the second and third payments if the second payment is to be twice the size of the third payment.

SOLUTION

Given: $j = 7\%$ compounded semiannually, making $m = 2$ and $i = \dfrac{j}{m} = \dfrac{7\%}{2} = 3.5\%$

Let x represent the third payment. Then the second payment must be $2x$. As indicated in the following diagram, PV_1, PV_2, and PV_3 represent the present values of the first, second, and third payments.

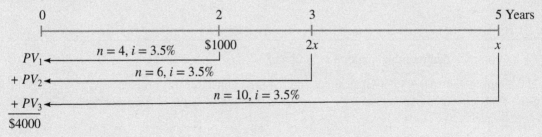

---

[7] You cannot conclude that the difference between $10,000 and FV_1 will be twice the difference between PV_2 and $10,000. To illustrate this sort of effect, consider that at 10% compounded annually, the future value of $100 one year later is $110 but the present value of $100 one year earlier is $90.91. We see that the increase ($10) when compounding ahead one year exceeds the decrease ($9.09) when discounting back one year.

Since the sum of the present values of all payments equals the original loan, then

$$PV_1 + PV_2 + PV_3 = \$4000 \qquad ①$$

PV_1: 4 [N] 7 [I/Y] 0 [PMT] 1000 [FV]

[2nd] [P/Y] 2 [ENTER] [2nd] [QUIT] [CPT] [PV] *Answer:* −871.442

At first, we may be stumped as to how to proceed for PV_2 and PV_3. Let's think about the third payment of x dollars. We can compute the present value of just $1 from the x dollars.

10 [N] 1 [FV] [CPT] [PV] *Answer:* −0.7089188

The present value of $1 paid five years from now is $0.7089188 (almost $0.71). Consider the following questions (Q) and their answers (A).

Q: What is the present value of $2?   A: It's about 2 × $0.71 = $1.42.

Q: What is the present value of $5?   A: It's about 5 × $0.71 = $3.55.

Q: What is the present value of x?   A: Extending the preceding pattern, the present value of x is about $x \times \$0.71 = \$0.71x$. Precisely, it is $PV_3 = \$0.7089188x$.

Similarly, calculate the present value of $1 from the second payment of $2x$ dollars. The only variable that changes from the previous calculation is [N].

6 [N] [CPT] [PV] *Answer:* −0.8135006

Hence, the present value of $2x$ is

$$PV_2 = 2x(\$0.8135006) = \$1.6270012x$$

Now substitute the values for PV_1, PV_2, and PV_3 into equation ① and solve for x.

$$\$871.442 + 1.6270012x + 0.7089188x = \$4000$$
$$2.3359200x = \$3128.558$$
$$x = \$1339.326$$

Kramer's third payment will be $1339.33 and his second payment will be 2($1339.33) = $2678.66.

EXERCISE 9.4

Solve the problems in Exercises 9.2 and 9.3 using the financial functions on a calculator.

Spreadsheet templates: *Two partially completed Excel templates for calculating present value and future value are provided on Connect. Go to the Student Edition of Connect and find "FV and PV of a Single Payment" under the Student Resources for Chapter 9. One or the other of these templates may be used in solving most of the problems in Exercise 9.2 and Exercise 9.3.*

9.5 Other Applications of Compounding

Compound Interest Investments

Guaranteed Investment Certificates (GICs) GICs may be purchased from banks, credit unions, life insurance companies, trust companies, and caisses populaires (mostly in Quebec). When you buy a GIC from a financial institution, you are in effect lending money to it or to one of its subsidiaries. The financial institution uses the funds raised from selling GICs to make loans—most commonly, mortgage loans. The interest rate charged on mortgage loans is typically 1.5% to 2% higher than the interest rate paid to GIC investors. The word "Guaranteed" in the name of this investment refers to the *unconditional guarantee* of principal and interest by the parent financial institution. In addition to this guarantee, there is usually some form of government-regulated deposit insurance.

Most GICs are purchased with maturities in the range of one to five years. Longer maturities (up to 10 years) are available, but are not covered by deposit insurance. Normally, you earn higher interest rates for longer maturities. Early redemption restrictions apply to many types of GICs. You must accept lower interest rates for more liberal redemption privileges. The following diagrams present typical alternatives for redemption privileges, the structure of interest rates, and for the payment of interest.

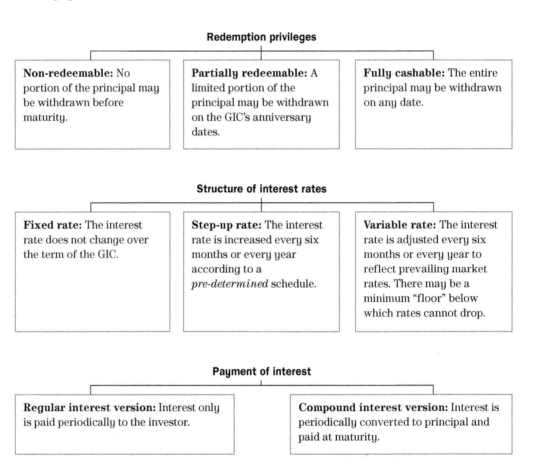

Redemption privileges

| **Non-redeemable:** No portion of the principal may be withdrawn before maturity. | **Partially redeemable:** A limited portion of the principal may be withdrawn on the GIC's anniversary dates. | **Fully cashable:** The entire principal may be withdrawn on any date. |

Structure of interest rates

| **Fixed rate:** The interest rate does not change over the term of the GIC. | **Step-up rate:** The interest rate is increased every six months or every year according to a *pre-determined* schedule. | **Variable rate:** The interest rate is adjusted every six months or every year to reflect prevailing market rates. There may be a minimum "floor" below which rates cannot drop. |

Payment of interest

| **Regular interest version:** Interest only is paid periodically to the investor. | **Compound interest version:** Interest is periodically converted to principal and paid at maturity. |

L02 The regular interest versions of GICs are not mathematically interesting since periodic interest is paid out to the investor instead of being converted to principal. For compound interest versions, there are two mathematically distinct cases.

1. If the interest rate is *fixed*, use $FV = PV(1 + i)^n$ to calculate the maturity value.
2. If the interest rate is either a *variable rate* or a *step-up rate*, the periodic rate i can differ for each compounding period. Then you must use a more general version of Formula (9-2) that allows for a different $(1 + i)$ factor for each compounding period. That is, use

FUTURE VALUE (VARIABLE AND STEP-UP INTEREST RATES)

$$FV = PV(1 + i_1)(1 + i_2)(1 + i_3) \ldots (1 + i_n) \tag{9-4}$$

EXAMPLE 9.5A

CALCULATING THE PAYMENT FROM A REGULAR-INTEREST GIC

What periodic payment does an investor receive from a $9000, four-year, monthly payment GIC earning a nominal rate of 2.25% payable monthly? (Only the accrued interest is paid each month.)

SOLUTION

The interest rate per payment interval is

$$i = \frac{j}{m} = \frac{2.25\%}{12} = 0.1875\%$$

The monthly payment is

$$PV \times i = \$9000 \times 0.001875 = \$16.88$$

EXAMPLE 9.5B

COMPARING GICS HAVING DIFFERENT NOMINAL RATES

Suppose a bank quotes nominal annual interest rates of 3.6% compounded annually, 3.58% compounded semiannually, and 3.54% compounded monthly on five-year compound interest GICs. Which rate should an investor choose?

SOLUTION

An investor should choose the rate that results in the highest maturity value. The given information may be arranged in a table.

j	m	$i = \frac{j}{m}$	n
3.6%	1	3.6%	5
3.58	2	1.79	10
3.54	12	0.295	60

Choose an amount, say $1000, to invest. Calculate the maturity values for the three alternatives.

$$\begin{aligned} FV = PV(1 + i)^n \\ = \$1000(1.036)^5 = \$1193.44 \qquad &\text{for } j = 3.6\% \text{ compounded annually} \\ = \$1000(1.0179)^{10} = \$1194.13 \qquad &\text{for } j = 3.58\% \text{ compounded semiannually} \\ = \$1000(1.00295)^{60} = \$1193.32 \qquad &\text{for } j = 3.54\% \text{ compounded monthly} \end{aligned}$$

Let's now calculate these same maturity values using our financial calculator. We will switch to a vertical format for presenting the keystrokes. The case $j = 3.6\%$ compounded annually is shown in Box 1. A good habit to develop for calculations in later chapters is to enter the interest rate information first. The first five lines (after the title) do this. The fourth line is just a reminder that, when we enter a new value for *P/Y*, it also changes *C/Y* to the same value. The sequence for entering the remaining values does not matter.

Box 1

$j = 3.6\%$ cmpd. annually

3.6 [I/Y]

[2nd] [P/Y]

1 [ENTER]

(making $C/Y = P/Y = 1$)

[2nd] [QUIT]

5 [N]

1000 [+/−] [PV]

0 [PMT]

[CPT] [FV]

Ans: 1193.44

Box 2

$j = 3.6\%$ cmpd. annually

3.6 [I/Y]

[P/Y] 1 [ENTER]

(making $C/Y = P/Y = 1$)

5 [N]

1000 [+/−] [PV]

0 [PMT]

[CPT] [FV]

Ans: 1193.44

Every time we need to change the value of P/Y or C/Y, we will have the same keystrokes 2nd P/Y to access these variables and the same keystrokes 2nd QUIT to return to the calculation. To avoid this repetition in our calculator solutions, we will shorten the display hereafter as shown in Box 2. It is left to you to supply the missing keystrokes.

The keystrokes for calculating the maturity values at the other two interest rates are displayed in Boxes 3 and 4. The calculator's memories retain the most recent values if you do not clear the TVM memories. Therefore, we show only those values that change from the preceding calculation.

Box 3	Box 4
$j = 3.58\%$ cmpd. semiann.	$j = 3.54\%$ cmpd. monthly
Same *PV, PMT*	Same *PV, PMT*
3.58 I/Y	3.54 I/Y
P/Y 2 ENTER	P/Y 12 ENTER
(making $C/Y = P/Y = 2$)	(making $C/Y = P/Y = 12$)
10 N	60 N
CPT FV	CPT FV
Ans: 1194.13	*Ans:* 1193.32

Answering the initial question, the investor should choose the GIC earning 3.58% compounded semiannually since it produces the highest maturity value.

EXAMPLE 9.5C

MATURITY VALUE OF A VARIABLE-RATE GIC

A chartered bank offers a five-year "Escalator Guaranteed Investment Certificate." In successive years it earns annual interest rates of 1.2%, 1.5%, 2%, 2.5%, and 4.3%, respectively, *compounded* at the end of each year. The bank also offers regular five-year GICs paying a fixed rate of 2.3% compounded annually. Calculate and compare the maturity values of $1000 invested in each type of GIC. (Note that 2.3% is the simple average of the five successive one-year rates paid on the Escalator GIC.)

SOLUTION

Using Formula (9-4), the maturity value of the Escalator GIC is

$$FV = \$1000(1.012)(1.015)(1.02)(1.025)(1.043) = \$1120.10$$

Using Formula (9-2), the maturity value of the regular GIC is

$$FV = \$1000(1.023)^5 = \$1120.41$$

The Escalator GIC will mature at $1120.10, but the regular GIC will mature at $1120.41 ($0.31 more). We can also conclude from this example that a series of compound interest rates does not produce the same future value as the *average* rate compounded over the same period.

 POINT OF INTEREST

RRSP vs. TFSA

For many years, the Registered Retirement Savings Plan or RRSP has been the cornerstone of long-term investing for retirement. Money invested within an RRSP is deductible from the contributor's taxable income, providing immediate tax savings. The tax is paid on an RRSP when the money is redeemed. In 2009, the Tax Free Savings Account or TFSA was born. Money held within a TFSA is after-tax earnings. There is no immediate tax savings, but money invested in a TFSA earns tax-free interest and is not taxed when it comes out. So the big question for Canadians is: *Will I save more by paying my taxes now instead of later?*

Consider the case of Darren and Cathy, who are both 30 years old and both earning salaries of $65,000 per year. Both intend to invest their $1000 year-end bonuses for their retirement. Being very conservative investors, both intend to build a portfolio of mutual funds and GICs. Darren intends to contribute his $1000 to an RRSP trust account, and invest the money within his RRSP. Cathy intends to hold her investments in a TFSA.

Let us compare the outcomes, 30 years later, of these alternative approaches for saving this year's $1000 bonuses. We will assume that their investments earn 6% compounded annually for the entire 30 years. Canadians with a $65,000 annual income are subject to a marginal income tax rate of close to 32%. (The figure varies somewhat from province to province.) This means that, if you earn an additional $100, you will pay $32 additional income tax and keep only $68 after tax. We will assume the 32% rate applies to Darren and Cathy for the next 30 years.

The following table summarizes their investments:

	Darren RRSP	Cathy TFSA
Bonus (before tax)	$1000	$1000
Taxes (@32%)	n/a	$320
Net investment	$1000	$680
Value after 30 years (@6%)	$5743.49	$3905.57
Tax payable on redemption (@32%)	$1837.92	$0
Net value of investment	$3905.57	$3905.57

The value of both investments after 30 years is identical! How can that be? We will give both Darren and Cathy credit for being smart investors. With Darren's RRSP, we will assume that he has not turned the $320 tax credit he received at the time of investment into a new golf club and, instead, invested it into his RRSP. Any benefits from the RRSP tax savings only exist if they are kept within the investment.

In Cathy's case, we will assume she has not raided her investment during the 30-year term for the down payment on her new car. TFSAs allow you to take money out at any time and then put it back at a future date. Even if Cathy did replace any money she withdrew, she would lose out on the interest for the time the money was removed from her investment.

Assuming both Darren and Cathy have great self-control when it comes to investing, the only circumstance in which the RRSP comes out ahead is if Darren's tax rate at redemption has dropped below 32%.

Valuation of Investments

With many types of investments, the owner can sell the investment to another investor. Such investments are said to be transferable.[8] The key question is: *What is the appropriate price at which the investment should be sold/purchased?* We encountered the same question in **Chapter 8** for investments earning simple interest. There we discussed the thinking behind the Valuation Principle (repeated here for ease of reference).

> **Valuation Principle**
> The fair market value of an investment is the sum of the present values of the expected cash flows. The discount rate used should be the prevailing market-determined rate of return on this type of investment.

For an investment with cash inflows extending beyond one year, the market-determined rate of return is almost always a compound rate of return. In this section, we will apply the Valuation Principle to two types of investments, strip bonds and long-term promissory notes.

L03 **Strip bonds** Many investors choose to hold **strip bonds**[9] in their RRSPs. You need to know only a few essential features of strip bonds in order to handle strip-bond calculations. If you

---

[8] Guaranteed Investment Certificates and Canada Savings Bonds are normally not transferable.

[9] Strip bonds are created when investment dealers (brokers) break up marketable bonds (**Chapter 16**) into simple components that investors can purchase. Normally, investment dealers do this only with some of the marketable bonds issued by federal and provincial governments.

buy a strip bond, you will receive a *single* payment (called the face value of the bond) on the bond's maturity date. The maturity date could be as much as 30 years in the future. You will receive no interest payments in the interim. Consider a $1000 face value strip bond that matures 18 years from now: its owner will receive a single payment of $1000 in 18 years. What is the appropriate price to pay for the bond today? Clearly, it will be substantially less than $1000. The difference between the $1000 you will receive at maturity and the price you pay today represents the earnings on your initial investment (the purchase price). The situation is similar to the pricing of T-bills in **Section 8.3.**

According to the Valuation Principle, the fair market price is the present value of the payment (of the face value) that will be received on the bond's maturity date. The discount rate you should use for "i" in $PV = FV(1 + i)^{-n}$ is the prevailing rate of return in financial markets for strip bonds of similar risk and maturity. **Table 9.2** presents quotes for a few strip bonds on January 18, 2019. The quoted "Prices" are per $100 of face value. The quoted "Yields" are understood in the financial world to be nominal rates with *semiannual* compounding.

TABLE 9.2 Strip Bond Price and Yield Quotations (January 18, 2019)

Issuer	Maturity Date	Price ($)	Yield (%)
Ontario	January 13, 2027	80.42	2.770
Saskatchewan	March 5, 2029	74.77	2.916
Government of Canada	December 1, 2033	72.67	2.172
Quebec	August 26, 2021	94.74	2.105
British Columbia	June 4, 2019	99.40	1.662

Source: "GIC & Bond Rates." RBC Direct Investing Inc. https://www.rbcdirectinvesting.com/pricing/gic-bond-rates.html.

Consider the Government of Canada strip bond maturing on December 1, 2033. The market-determined rate of return (yield) on this bond late in the afternoon of January 18, 2019 was 2.172% compounded semiannually. This yield can vary by a few hundredths of a percent from hour to hour as investors react to events and economic forces. The price of the bond is calculated as the *PV* of the future $100 payment discounted at 2.172% compounded semiannually.

Note: In example problems from this point onward, we will present financial calculator procedures in a callout box adjacent to the algebraic solution. A curly bracket will indicate the algebraic calculations that the calculator procedure can replace.

EXAMPLE 9.5D

CALCULATING THE PRICE OF A STRIP BOND

A $10,000 face value strip bond has $15\frac{1}{2}$ years remaining until maturity. If the prevailing market rate of return is 3.5% compounded semiannually, what is the fair market value of the strip bond?

SOLUTION

Given: $FV = \$10,000 \quad j = 3.5\% \quad m = 2 \quad \text{Term} = 15\frac{1}{2}$ years

Therefore, $i = \dfrac{j}{m} = \dfrac{3.5\%}{2} = 1.75\%$ and $n = m(\text{Term}) = 2(15.5) = 31$

$$\begin{aligned}
\text{Fair market value} &= \text{Present value of the face value} \\
&= FV(1 + i)^{-n} \\
&= \$10,000(1.0175)^{-31} \\
&= \$5840.27
\end{aligned}\left.\vphantom{\begin{aligned}&\\&\\&\\&\end{aligned}}\right\}$$

The fair market value of the strip bond is $5840.27.

3.5 I/Y
P/Y 2 ENTER
(making $C/Y = P/Y = 2$)
31 N
10000 FV
0 PMT
CPT PV
Ans: −5840.27

Long-term promissory notes A promissory note is a simple contract between a debtor and creditor setting out the amount of the debt (face value), the interest rate thereon, and the terms of repayment. A *long-term* promissory note is a note whose term is longer than one year. Such notes usually accrue compound interest on the face value.

The payee (creditor) on a promissory note may sell the note to an investor before maturity. The debtor is then obligated to make the remaining payments to the new owner of the note. To determine the note's selling/purchase price, we need to apply the Valuation Principle to the note's maturity value. The two steps are:

1. Determine the note's maturity value based on the contractual rate of interest on the note.
2. Discount (that is, calculate the present value of) the Step 1 result back to the date of sale/purchase. Since there is no "market" for private promissory notes, the seller and purchaser must negotiate the discount rate.

EXAMPLE 9.5E

CALCULATING THE SELLING PRICE OF A LONG-TERM PROMISSORY NOTE

A five-year promissory note with a face value of $3500, bearing interest at 11% compounded semiannually, was sold 21 months after its issue date to yield the buyer 10% compounded quarterly. What amount was paid for the note?

SOLUTION

We should find the maturity value of the note and then discount the maturity value (at the required yield) back to the date of the sale. These two steps are indicated on the following diagram.

Step 1: Given: $PV = \$3500$ $j = 11\%$ $m = 2$ Term = 5 years

Therefore, $i = \dfrac{j}{m} = \dfrac{11\%}{2} = 5.5\%$ and $n = m(\text{Term}) = 2(5) = 10$

$$\left.\begin{aligned}\text{Maturity value} &= PV(1 + i)^n \\ &= \$3500(1.055)^{10} \\ &= \$5978.51\end{aligned}\right\}$$

11 | I/Y
P/Y 2 | ENTER
(making $C/Y = P/Y = 2$)
10 | N
3500 | +/– | PV
0 | PMT
CPT | FV
Ans: 5978.51

Step 2: Given: $j = 10\%$ $m = 4$ and   Term = 5 years – 21 months = 3.25 years

Therefore, $i = \dfrac{j}{m} = \dfrac{10\%}{4} = 2.5\%$ and $n = m(\text{Term}) = 4(3.25) = 13$

$$\left.\begin{aligned}\text{Price paid} &= FV(1 + i)^{-n} \\ &= \$5978.51(1.025)^{-13} \\ &= \$4336.93\end{aligned}\right\}$$

Same *FV, PMT*
10 | I/Y
P/Y 4 | ENTER
(making $C/Y = P/Y = 4$)
13 | N
CPT | PV
Ans: –4336.93

The amount paid for the note was $4336.93.

Compound Growth

L04 The formula $FV = PV(1 + i)^n$ may be used in non-financial problems involving compound growth at a fixed periodic rate. Furthermore, you can use the financial functions of your calculator in such cases. Simply place the following interpretations on the variables.

Variable	General interpretation
PV	Beginning value, size, or quantity
FV	Ending value, size, or quantity
i	Fixed periodic rate of growth
n	Number of periods with growth rate i

If a quantity shrinks or contracts at a fixed periodic rate, it can be handled mathematically by treating it as *negative growth*. For example, suppose a firm's annual sales volume is projected to decline for the next four years by 5% per year from last year's level of 100,000 units. The expected sales volume in the fourth year may be obtained using $FV = PV(1 + i)^n$ with $n = 4$ and $i = (-5\%) = (-0.05)$. That is,

$$\text{Sales (in Year 4)} = 100{,}000[1 + (-0.05)]^4$$
$$= 100{,}000(0.95)^4$$
$$= 81{,}451 \text{ units}$$

In the financial calculator approach, you would save "–5" in the [I/Y] memory. The answer represents an overall decline of 18.55% in the annual volume of sales. Note that the overall decline is less than 20%, an answer you might be tempted to reach by simply adding the percentage changes.

Inflation and purchasing power A useful application of compound growth in financial planning is using forecast rates of inflation to estimate future prices and the purchasing power of money. As discussed in **Section 4.6**, the rate of inflation measures the annual percent change in the price level of goods and services. By compounding the forecast rate of inflation over a number of years, we can estimate the level of prices at the end of the period.

When prices rise, money loses its purchasing power—these are "two sides of the same (depreciating) coin." If price levels double, a given nominal amount of money will purchase only half as much. We then say that the money has half its former purchasing power. Similarly, if price levels triple, money retains only one-third of its former purchasing power. These examples demonstrate that price levels and purchasing power have an inverse relationship. That is,

$$\frac{\text{Ending purchasing power}}{\text{Beginning purchasing power}} = \frac{\text{Beginning price level}}{\text{Ending price level}}$$

If price levels rise 50% over a number of years, what will be the percent *loss* in purchasing power? This gets a little tricky—the answer is *not* 50%. If the ending price level is 50% higher than the beginning price level, the ratio of price levels (on the right side of the preceding proportion) is

$$\frac{100}{150} \text{ or } \frac{2}{3}$$

Therefore, money will *retain* $\frac{2}{3}$ of its purchasing power and *lose* the other $\frac{1}{3}$ or $33\frac{1}{3}\%$ of its purchasing power.

EXAMPLE 9.5F

THE LONG-TERM EFFECT OF INFLATION ON PURCHASING POWER

If the rate of inflation for the next 20 years is 2.5% per year, what annual income (rounded to the nearest $100) will be needed 20 years from now to have the same purchasing power as a $50,000 annual income today?

SOLUTION

The required income will be $50,000 compounded at 2.5% per year for 20 years.

Given: $PV = \$50,000$ $j = 2.5\%$ $m = 1$ Term = 20 years

Hence, $i = \dfrac{j}{m} = \dfrac{2.5\%}{1} = 2.5\%$ and $n = m(\text{Term}) = 1(20) = 20$

$$
\left.
\begin{aligned}
FV &= PV(1 + i)^n \\
&= \$50,000(1.025)^{20} \\
&= \$81,930.82
\end{aligned}
\right\}
$$

2.5 ⌊ I/Y

P/Y 1 ⌊ENTER

(making $C/Y = P/Y = 1$)

20 ⌊ N

50000 ⌊ PV

0 ⌊ PMT

⌊ CPT ⌊ FV

Ans: −81,930.82

After 20 years of 2.5% annual inflation, an annual income of $81,900 will be needed to have the same purchasing power as $50,000 today.

EXAMPLE 9.5G

COMPOUND ANNUAL DECREASE IN POPULATION

The population of a rural region is expected to fall by 2% per year for the next 10 years. If the region's current population is 100,000, what is the expected population 10 years from now?

SOLUTION

The 2% "negative growth" should be compounded for 10 years.

Given: $PV = 100,000$ $j = -2\%$ $m = 1$ Term = 10 years

Hence, $i = \dfrac{j}{m} = \dfrac{-2\%}{1} = -2\%$ and $n = m(\text{Term}) = 1(10) = 10$

$$
\left.
\begin{aligned}
FV &= PV(1 + i)^n \\
&= 100,000[1 + (-0.02)]^{10} \\
&= 100,000(0.98)^{10} \\
&= 81,707
\end{aligned}
\right\}
$$

2 ⌊ +/− ⌊ I/Y

P/Y 1 ⌊ENTER

(making $C/Y = P/Y = 1$)

10 ⌊ N

100000 ⌊ PV

0 ⌊ PMT

⌊ CPT ⌊ FV

Ans: −81,707

The region's population is expected to drop to about 81,707 during the next 10 years.

EXERCISE 9.5

Answers to the odd-numbered problems are at the end of the book.

   **Spreadsheet templates:** *A partially completed Excel template for calculating a future value using Formula (9-4) is provided on Connect. Go to the Student Edition of Connect and find "Formula (9-4) Calculator" under the Student Resources for Chapter 9. You can use this template in any problem in Exercise 9.5 that requires the use of Formula (9-4).*

BASIC PROBLEMS

1. Krista invested $18,000 in a three-year regular-interest GIC earning 4.2% payable semiannually. What is each semiannual interest payment?

2. Eric invested $22,000 in a five-year regular-interest GIC earning 4.5% payable monthly. What is each monthly interest payment?

3. Mr. Dickson purchased a seven-year, $30,000 compound interest GIC with funds in his RRSP. If the interest rate on the GIC is 2.25% compounded semiannually, what is the GIC's maturity value?

4. Mrs. Sandhu placed $11,500 in a four-year compound interest GIC earning 6.75% compounded monthly. What is the GIC's maturity value?

5. A trust company offers three-year compound interest GICs earning 4.8% compounded monthly or 4.9% compounded semiannually. Which rate should an investor choose?

6. If an investor has the choice between rates of 5.4% compounded quarterly and 5.5% compounded annually for a six-year GIC, which rate should she choose?

7. How, if at all, will the future value of $1000 invested in a three-year variable-rate GIC differ if it earns 2%, 3%, and 4% in successive years instead of 4%, 3%, and 2% in successive years?

8. Sun Life Financial offers a five-year compound interest GIC earning rates of 2.5%, 3%, 3.5%, 4.25%, and 5% in successive years. Manulife offers a similar GIC paying rates of 2.75%, 3.25%, 3.5%, 4%, and 4.25% in successive years. For a $10,000 investment, which GIC will have the greater maturity value after five years? How much greater?

9. Using the information given in Problem 8, calculate the interest earned in the second year from a $1000 investment in each GIC.

10. Using the information given in Problem 8, calculate the interest earned in the third year from a $10,000 investment in each GIC.

11. Calculate the maturity value of $2000 invested in a five-year compound interest GIC earning 2.1% compounded annually.

12. A compound interest GIC will earn 5% compounded annually for the first two years and 6% compounded annually for the last three years of its five-year term. What will be the maturity value of $3000 invested in this GIC?

13. $8000 is invested in a five-year compound interest GIC earning interest rates of 2%, 2.5%, 3%, 3.5%, and 5% in successive years. What amount will the investor receive at maturity?

14. Western Life's "Move-Up" compound interest GIC earns 4.125%, 4.25%, 4.5%, 4.875%, and 5% in successive years. What will be the maturity value of $7500 invested in this GIC?

15. The BMO Bank of Montreal advertised rates of 1.8%, 2.25%, 2.6%, 3%, and 3.25% for the five successive years of its five-year compound interest RateOptimizer GIC. At the same time, the bank was offering fixed-rate five-year compound interest GICs yielding 2.75% compounded annually. What total interest would be earned during the five-year term on a $5000 investment in each type of GIC?

16. On the same date that the CIBC advertised rates of 2%, 2.5%, 3%, 3.25%, and 7% in successive years of its five-year compound interest Escalating Rate GIC, it offered 2.75% compounded annually on its five-year fixed-rate GIC. How much more will a $10,000 investment be worth at maturity if the Escalating Rate GIC is chosen instead of the fixed-rate GIC?

17. Using the information given in Problem 16, calculate the interest earned in the fourth year from a $10,000 investment in each GIC.

18. Using the information given in Problem 16, how much would have to be initially invested in each GIC to have a maturity value of $20,000?

19. How much will you need 20 years from now to have the purchasing power of $100 today if the (compound annual) rate of inflation during the period is:

   a. 2%?   **b.** 3%?   **c.** 4%?

20. How much money was needed 15 years ago to have the purchasing power of $1000 today if the (compound annual) rate of inflation has been:
    a. 2%?   **b.** 4%?

21. If the inflation rate for the next 10 years is 3.5% per year, what hourly rate of pay in 10 years will be equivalent to $15/hour today?

22. Venezuela's political crisis during the late 2010s resulted in hyperinflation. By November of 2018, the annual inflation rate stood at 1,300,000%! Prices were doubling every 19 days on average. The government had to issue new currency that chopped five zeros off the denominations so people did not have to carry around so many bills.
    a. Consider a loaf of bread with a price of $4 at the beginning of the year. With an inflation rate of 1,300,000% per year, what would the loaf's price be at the end of the year in order to "keep pace" with inflation?
    b. In the scenario in part (a), what percentage of its purchasing power did a fixed nominal amount of currency lose at the end of the year?
    c. What monthly percent price increase would result in a 1,300,000% overall price increase during the year?

23. Mr. and Mrs. Rasuli would like to retire in 15 years at an annual income level that would be equivalent to $35,000 today. What is their retirement income goal if, in the meantime, the annual rate of inflation is:
    a. 2%?   **b.** 3%?   **c.** 5%?

24. According to the 2016 census Warman, Saskatchewan, was the fastest growing municipality in Canada, with a population of 11,020 in 2016. If the population grew 9.17% per year from 2011 to 2016, what was the population in 2011?

25. A $1000 face value strip bond has 22 years remaining until maturity. What is its price if the market rate of return on such bonds is 2.5% compounded semiannually?

26. What price should be paid for a $5000 face value strip bond with 19.5 years remaining to maturity if it is to yield the buyer 6.1% compounded semiannually?

27. Consider a $10,000 face value Government of Canada strip bond from the issue in **Table 9.2** that matures on December 1, 2033. Assume the yield does not change as years go by.
    a. What will be the bond's value on June 1, 2022?
    b. What will be the bond's value on June 1, 2026?
    c. Suppose you invest an amount equal to the answer from part (a) at 2.172% compounded semiannually for four years. What will its maturity value be?
    d. To three-figure accuracy, why do you get the same answers for parts (b) and (c)?

28. Consider a $5000 face value Province of Saskatchewan strip bond from the issue in **Table 9.2** that matures on March 5, 2029. If the yield does not change as years go by, what will be the bond's value on:
    a. March 5, 2019?   **b.** March 5, 2021?   **c.** March 5, 2023?

29. Mrs. Janzen wishes to purchase some 13-year-maturity strip bonds with the $12,830 in cash she now has in her RRSP. If these strip bonds are currently priced to yield 5.25% compounded semiannually, how many $1000 denomination bonds can she purchase?

30. If the current discount rate on 15-year strip bonds is 4.75% compounded semiannually, how many $1000 face value strips can be purchased with $10,000?

INTERMEDIATE PROBLEMS

31. For a given term of a compound interest GIC, the nominal interest rate with annual compounding is typically 0.125% higher than the rate with semiannual compounding and 0.25% higher than the rate with monthly compounding. Suppose that the rates for five-year GICs

are 5.00%, 4.875%, and 4.75% for annual, semiannual, and monthly compounding, respectively. How much more will an investor earn over five years on a $10,000 GIC at the most favourable rate than at the least favourable rate?

32. The late 1970s and early 1980s were years of historically high rates of inflation in Canada. For the years 1978, 1979, 1980, 1981, and 1982 the rates of inflation were 8.8%, 9.2%, 10.9%, 12.6%, and 10.0%, respectively.
    a. Suppose your hourly wage at the beginning of 1978 was $10 per hour. What wage did you need to earn at the end of 1982 just to keep pace with inflation?
    b. What percentage of its purchasing power did money lose over these five years?

33. A pharmaceutical company had sales of $28,600,000 in the year just completed. Sales are expected to decline by 4% per year for the next three years until new drugs, now under development, receive regulatory approval. Then sales should grow at 8% per year for the next four years. What are the expected sales for the final year of the seven-year period?

34. Wojtek purchased a $10,000 face value strip bond on a date when it had 14 years left until maturity. The purchase price was based on a market yield of 6.2% compounded semiannually. He sold the bond $4\frac{1}{2}$ years later when the market yield was 5.2% compounded semiannually. What was Wojtek's total gain on the investment?

35. A four-year $8000 promissory note bearing interest at 13.5% compounded monthly was discounted 21 months after issue to yield 12% compounded quarterly. What were the proceeds from the sale of the note?

36. An eight-year note for $3800 with interest at 11% compounded semiannually was sold after three years and three months to yield the buyer 14% compounded quarterly. What price did the buyer pay?

ADVANCED PROBLEMS

37. The contract for a $4000 loan at 9% compounded quarterly requires two payments. The first payment of $2000 is required two years after the date of the loan. (It is applied to the balance owed after conversion of interest to principal.) A second payment in the amount needed to pay off the loan is due one year later. What price would an investor pay for the contract six months after the date of the loan to earn 10% compounded semiannually on the purchase price?

38. A $5000 loan at 10% compounded annually is to be repaid by two payments three and five years from the date of the loan. The first payment of $3000 will be applied to the balance owed after conversion of interest to principal at the end of the first three years. What would an investor pay for the loan contract 20 months after the date of the loan if she requires a rate of return of 9% compounded monthly?

39. **Shopping for GICs** Go to Connect and find "RateSupermarket" under the Web links for Chapter 9 in the Student Edition. This Web page provides a comprehensive comparison of current rates available on GICs. How much more would you earn on $10,000 invested for five years at the highest available rate than at the lowest rate?

9.6 Equivalent Payment Streams

LO6 Sometimes a scheduled payment stream is replaced by another payment stream. This can happen, for example, in rescheduling payments on a loan. In this section we will learn how to make the new stream of payments economically equivalent to the stream it replaces. In this way, neither the payer nor the payee gains any financial advantage from the change.

The general principle we will develop is an extension of ideas from Sections 9.2 and 9.3. In those sections you learned how to obtain the equivalent value of a multiple-payment stream at a particular focal date. It was a two-step procedure:

1. Calculate the equivalent value of each payment at the focal date.
2. Add up the equivalent values to obtain the stream's equivalent value.

How, then, would you compare the economic values of two payment streams? Your intuition should be a good guide here. First calculate the equivalent value of each stream at the *same* focal date. Then compare the two equivalent values to rank them. For two payment streams to be economically equivalent, they must meet the following condition.

Criterion for the Equivalence of Two Payment Streams
A payment stream's equivalent value (at a focal date) is the sum of the equivalent values of all of its payments. Two payment streams are economically equivalent if they have the same equivalent value at the same focal date.

You must impose this requirement when designing a payment stream that is to be economically equivalent to a given payment stream. The criterion becomes the basis for an equation that enables us to solve for an unknown payment in the new stream.

 TIP

Choosing a Focal Date

Any interest conversion date may be chosen for the focal date in an equivalent-payment-stream problem. If two payment streams are equivalent at one conversion date, they will be equivalent at any other conversion date. Therefore, problems will generally not specify a particular focal date to be used in the solution. Calculations will usually be simplified if you locate the focal date at one of the unknown payments in the new stream. Then that payment's equivalent value on the focal date is simply its nominal value. But be careful to use the *same* focal date for *both* payment streams.

EXAMPLE 9.6A

CALCULATING AN UNKNOWN PAYMENT IN A TWO-PAYMENT REPLACEMENT STREAM

Payments of $2000 due one year from today and $1000 due five years from today are to be replaced by a $1500 payment due four years from today, and another payment due two years from today. The replacement stream must be economically equivalent to the scheduled stream. What is the unknown payment, if money can earn 7% compounded semiannually?

SOLUTION

The following diagram presents just the given information. Each payment stream has its own time line. The unknown payment is represented by x. We must calculate a value for x such that the two streams satisfy the Criterion for Equivalence.

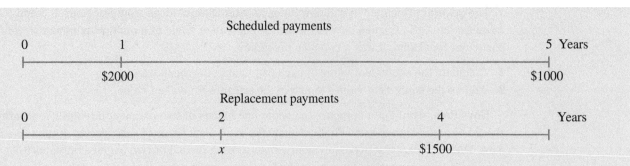

In the next diagram, the date of the unknown payment has been chosen as the focal date. Consequently, the unknown payment's equivalent value on the focal date is just x. The equivalent values of the other payments are represented by FV_1, PV_2, and PV_3.

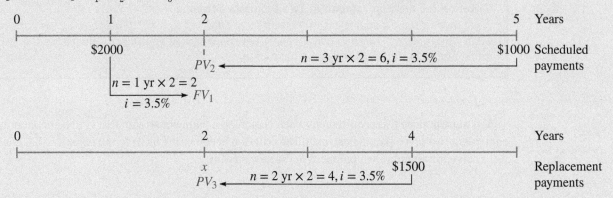

To satisfy the Criterion for Equivalence, the following must be true:

Sum of scheduled payments on the focal date = Sum of replacement payments on the focal date

or

$$FV_1 + PV_2 = x + PV_3 \qquad ①$$

The equivalent values of the individual payments are calculated in the usual way.

FV_1 = Future value of $2000, 1 year later

$\left. \begin{array}{l} = PV(1+i)^n \\ = \$2000(1.035)^2 \\ = \$2142.450 \end{array} \right\}$

7 I/Y

P/Y 2 ENTER

(making C/Y = P/Y = 2)

2 N

2000 PV

0 PMT

CPT FV

Ans: −2142.450

PV_2 = Present value of $1000, 3 years earlier

$\left. \begin{array}{l} = FV(1+i)^{-n} \\ = \$1000(1.035)^{-6} \\ = \$813.501 \end{array} \right\}$

Same I/Y, PMT, P/Y, C/Y

6 N

1000 FV

CPT PV

Ans: −813.501

$$PV_3 = \text{Present value of \$1500, 2 years earlier}$$
$$= \$1500(1.035)^{-4} \left.\begin{array}{c} \\ \\ \end{array}\right\}$$
$$= \$1307.163$$

Same *I/Y, PMT, P/Y, C/Y*

4 | N |
1500 | FV |
| CPT | PV |

Ans: −1307.163

Substituting these amounts into equation ①, we have

$$\$2142.450 + \$813.501 = x + \$1307.163$$
$$\$2955.951 - \$1307.163 = x$$
$$x = \$1648.79$$

The first payment in the replacement stream must be $1648.79.

EXAMPLE 9.6B

CALCULATING TWO PAYMENTS IN A THREE-PAYMENT REPLACEMENT STREAM

The original intention was to settle a financial obligation by two payments. The first payment of $1500 was due one year ago. The second payment of $2500 is due three years from now. The debtor missed the first payment, and now proposes three payments that will be economically equivalent to the two originally scheduled payments. The replacement payments are $1000 today, a second payment in $1\frac{1}{2}$ years, and a third payment (twice as large as the second) in three years. What should the second and third payments be if money can earn 8% compounded semiannually?

SOLUTION

Let the payment due in $1\frac{1}{2}$ years be x. The scheduled and replacement streams are presented in the following time diagrams. The date of the first unknown payment has been chosen as the focal date, and the symbols for equivalent values on the focal date are indicated.

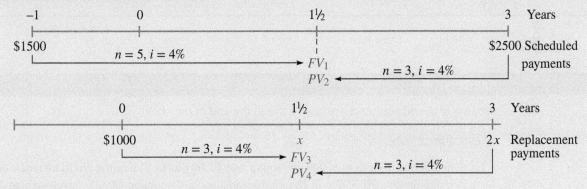

For equivalence of the two payment streams,

$$FV_1 + PV_2 = x + FV_3 + PV_4 \quad ①$$

$$FV_1 = \text{Future value of \$1500, } 2\tfrac{1}{2} \text{ years later}$$
$$= PV(1 + i)^n \left.\begin{array}{c} \\ \\ \\ \end{array}\right\}$$
$$= \$1500(1.04)^5$$
$$= \$1824.979$$

8 | I/Y |
| P/Y | 2 | ENTER |
(making *C/Y* = *P/Y* = 2)
5 | N |
1500 | PV |
0 | PMT |
| CPT | FV |

Ans: −1824.979

PV_2 = Present value of $2500, $1\frac{1}{2}$ years earlier

$\left. \begin{aligned} &= FV(1+i)^{-n} \\ &= \$2500(1.04)^{-3} \\ &= \$2222.491 \end{aligned} \right\}$

Same $I/Y, P/Y, C/Y, PMT$

3 | N

2500 | FV

CPT | PV

Ans: −2222.491

FV_3 = Future value of $1000, $1\frac{1}{2}$ years later

$\left. \begin{aligned} &= \$1000(1.04)^{3} \\ &= \$1124.864 \end{aligned} \right\}$

Same $N, I/Y, PMT, P/Y, C/Y$

1000 | PV

CPT | FV

Ans: −1124.846

PV_4 = Present value of $2x$, $1\frac{1}{2}$ years earlier

$\left. \begin{aligned} &= 2x(1.04)^{-3} \\ &= 1.777993x \end{aligned} \right\}$

Find the PV of $2

Same $N, I/Y, PMT, P/Y, C/Y$

2 | FV

CPT | PV

Ans: −1.777993

Substituting these values into equation ①, we obtain

$$\$1824.979 + \$2222.491 = x + \$1124.864 + 1.777993x$$
$$\$4047.470 = 2.777993x + \$1124.864$$
$$x = \frac{\$4047.470 - \$1124.864}{2.777993}$$
$$= \$1052.06$$

The payments should be $1052.06 in $1\frac{1}{2}$ years and $2104.12 in three years.

EXERCISE 9.6

Answers to the odd-numbered problems are at the end of the book.

BASIC PROBLEMS

1. Scheduled payments of $3000 due today and $2000 due in 15 months are to be replaced by two payments—$1500 due in 15 months and a second payment of undetermined size due in 24 months. What must the second payment be for the two streams to be economically equivalent? Assume that money can earn 3% compounded quarterly.

2. A two-payment stream consisting of $1750 due today and $2900 due in 18 months is to be replaced by an economically equivalent stream comprised of an undetermined payment due in 9 months and a payment of $3000 due in 19 months. Calculate the unknown replacement payment if money is worth 9% compounded monthly.

3. Patrice defaulted on payments of $1000 due one year ago and $1500 due six months ago. A small claims court judgment orders her to make three payments—$800 one month from now, $900 four months from now, and a third payment seven months from now. The third payment is to be determined so that the creditor will end up in the same economic position as if the original payments had been made on time. The court set the fair rate of return at 4.2% compounded monthly. What should the third payment be?

4. Marvin was supposed to make three payments of $2000 each—the first one year ago, the second one year from now, and the third three years from now. He missed the first payment and proposes to pay $3000 today and a second amount in two years. If money can earn 4.5% compounded semiannually, what must the second payment be to make the proposed payments equivalent to the scheduled payments?

INTERMEDIATE PROBLEMS

5. Payments of $850 due two years ago and $1760 due six months ago have not been made. The proposed alternative is two equal payments, three months and nine months from now, that will put the payee in an equivalent economic position allowing that money can earn 5.6% compounded quarterly. What is the amount of each of these payments?

6. Jorge is unable to make a $4500 payment due today. He proposes to settle the obligation by making three equal payments—one today, another in four months, and a third in nine months. What must each payment be to make the proposed payment stream equivalent to the scheduled payment if money can earn 7.2% compounded monthly?

7. The scheduled payment stream consists of $5000 due today and $10,000 due in five years. It is proposed to replace this stream by an economically equivalent stream comprised of three equal payments due one, three, and five years from now. Determine the size of each payment if money is worth 5% compounded annually.

8. Payments of $400 due eight months ago and $650 due three months ago were not made. Now the debtor is proposing to "make good" by two future payments that provide for a 7.5% compounded monthly rate of return to the creditor on the missed payments. The first payment will be made in two months. The second payment, *twice* as large as the first, will be made in seven months. Determine the amount of each payment.

9. Two payments of $2000 each are scheduled for six months from now and two years from now. They are to be rescheduled as follows: a payment one year from now and a second payment, *half* the size of the first payment, three years from now. What must the amount of each payment be for the replacement stream to be equivalent to the originally scheduled stream? Assume that money can earn 3.8% compounded semiannually.

10. The owner of a residential building lot has received two purchase offers. Mrs. A is offering a $20,000 down payment plus $40,000 payable in one year. Mr. B's offer is $15,000 down plus two $25,000 payments due one and two years from now. Which offer has the greater economic value if money can earn 9.5% compounded quarterly? How much more is it worth in current dollars?

11. During its January Sale, Furniture City is offering terms of 25% down with no further payments and no interest charges for six months, when the balance is due. Furniture City sells the conditional sale contracts from these credit sales to a finance company. The finance company discounts the contracts to yield 18% compounded monthly. What cash amount should Furniture City accept on a $1595 item in order to end up in the same financial position as if the item had been sold under the terms of the January Sale?

12. Henri has decided to purchase a $25,000 car. He can either liquidate some of his investments and pay cash, or accept the dealer's proposal that Henri pay $5000 down and $8000 at the end of each of the next three years.
    a. Which choice should Henri make if he can earn 7% compounded semiannually on his investments? In current dollars, what is the economic advantage of the preferred alternative?
    b. Which choice should Henri make if he can earn 11% compounded semiannually on his investments? In current dollars, what is the economic advantage of the preferred alternative?

(*Hint:* When choosing among alternative streams of cash *inflows*, we should select the one with the greatest economic value. When choosing among alternative streams of cash *outflows*, we should select the one with the least economic value.)

13. A lottery prize gives the winner a choice between (1) $10,000 now and another $10,000 in 5 years, or (2) four $6700 payments—now and in 5, 10, and 15 years.

    a. Which alternative should the winner choose if money can earn 3% compounded annually? In current dollars, what is the economic advantage of the preferred alternative?

    b. Which alternative should the winner choose if money can earn 4.5% compounded annually? In current dollars, what is the economic advantage of the preferred alternative?

14. CompuSystems was supposed to pay a manufacturer $19,000 on a date four months ago and another $14,000 on a date two months from now. Instead, CompuSystems is proposing to pay $10,000 today and the balance in five months, when it will receive payment on a major sale to the provincial government. What will the second payment be if the manufacturer requires 12% compounded monthly on overdue accounts?

15. Payments of $5000 due three years from today and $7000 due five years from today are to be replaced by two payments due $1\frac{1}{2}$ and four years from today. The first payment is to be half the amount of the second payment. What should the payments be if money can earn 3.5% compounded semiannually?

16. Two payments of $3000 each are due today and five years from today. The creditor has agreed to accept three equal payments due one, three, and five years from today. Assuming that money can earn 7.5% compounded monthly, what payments will the creditor accept?

17. Payments of $8000 due 15 months ago and $6000 due in six months are to be replaced by a payment of $4000 today, a second payment in nine months, and a third payment, three times as large as the second, in $1\frac{1}{2}$ years. What should the last two payments be if money is worth 6.4% compounded quarterly?

18. A $15,000 loan with interest being charged at 10% compounded quarterly was made $2\frac{1}{2}$ years ago and is due in two years. The debtor is proposing to settle the debt by a payment of $5000 today and a second payment in one year that will place the lender in an equivalent financial position, given that money can now earn only 6% compounded semiannually.

    a. What should be the amount of the second payment?

    b. Demonstrate that the lender will be in the same financial position two years from now with either repayment alternative.

ADVANCED PROBLEM

19. Three years ago, Andrea loaned $2000 to Heather. The principal with interest at 9% compounded semiannually is to be repaid four years from the date of the loan. Eighteen months ago, Heather borrowed another $1000 for $3\frac{1}{2}$ years at 8% compounded semiannually. Heather is now proposing to settle both debts with two equal payments to be made one and three years from now. What should the payments be if money now earns 6% compounded quarterly?

KEY TERMS

Cash flow

Cash-flow sign convention

Compound interest method

Compounding frequency

Compounding period

Discount rate

Discounting a payment

Equivalent payments

Future value

Maturity value

Nominal interest rate

Periodic interest rate

Present value

Strip bonds

SUMMARY OF NOTATION AND KEY FORMULAS

j = Nominal annual interest rate

m = Number of compoundings per year

i = Periodic rate of interest

PV = Principal amount of the loan or investment; Present value

FV = Maturity value of the loan or investment; Future value

n = Number of compounding periods

FORMULA (9-1) $\qquad i = \dfrac{j}{m}$ $\qquad$ Obtaining the periodic interest rate from the nominal annual rate

FORMULA (9-2) $\qquad \begin{cases} FV = PV(1 + i)^n & \text{Finding the maturity value or future value} \\ PV = FV(1 + i)^{-n} & \text{Finding the principal or present value} \end{cases}$

FORMULA (9-3) $\qquad n = m \times (\textbf{\textit{Number of years in the term}})$ $\qquad$ Finding the number of compounding periods

FORMULA (9-4) $\qquad FV = PV(1 + i_1)(1 + i_2)(1 + i_3) \dots (1 + i_n)$ $\qquad$ Finding the maturity value with compounding at a variable interest rate

---

Cash-Flow Sign Convention

Cash inflows (receipts) are positive.

Cash outflows (disbursements) are negative.

Present Value of Loan Payments

The sum of the present values of all of the payments required to pay off a loan is equal to the original principal of the loan. The discount rate for the present-value calculations is the rate of interest charged on the loan.

Criterion for the Equivalence of Two Payment Streams

A payment stream's equivalent value (at a focal date) is the sum of the equivalent values of all of its payments. Two payment streams are economically equivalent if they have the same equivalent value at the same focal date.

REVIEW PROBLEMS

Answers to the odd-numbered review problems are at the end of the book.

BASIC PROBLEMS

1. **LO5** What amount three years ago is equivalent to $4800 on a date $1\frac{1}{2}$ years from now if money earns 3% compounded semiannually during the intervening time?

2. **LO4** If the inflation rate for the next 10 years is 1.7% per year, what hourly rate of pay in 10 years will be equivalent to $15 per hour today?

3. **LO4** To satisfy more stringent restrictions on toxic waste discharge, a pulp mill will have to reduce toxic waste by 10% from the previous year's level every year for the next five years. What fraction is the target level of the current discharge level?

4. **LO2** If an investor has the choice between rates of 5.5% compounded semiannually and 5.6% compounded annually for a six-year GIC, which rate should be chosen?

5. **LO4** The population for the Region of Waterloo as recorded in the census of 2016 was 583,500. Estimates for population growth in the region are predicting increases of 1.85% per year for the next 15 years. What is the predicted population for the region in 2031? Round your answer to the nearest 1000 people.

6. **LO2** At the same time as compound interest Government Bonds were being sold with guaranteed minimum annual rates of 5.25%, 6%, and 6.75% in the first three years of their 10-year term, a trust company offered three-year Bond Beater GICs paying 5.75%, 6.5%, and 7.25% compounded annually in the three successive years. If the Government Bonds earn their minimum interest rates, how much more will $4000 earn over the three years if invested in the GIC?

7. **LO1** Jacques has just been notified that the combined principal and interest on an amount he borrowed 19 months ago at 8.4% compounded monthly is now $2297.78. How much of this amount is principal and how much is interest?

8. **LO1** Accurate Accounting obtained a private loan of $25,000 for five years. No payments were required, but the loan accrued interest at the rate of 9% compounded monthly for the first $2\frac{1}{2}$ years and then at 8.25% compounded semiannually for the remainder of the term. What total amount was required to pay off the loan after five years?

9. **LO2** A credit union's Rate Climber GIC pays rates of 2%, 2.5%, and 3% compounded semiannually in successive years of a three-year term.
   a. What will be the maturity value of $12,000 invested in this GIC?
   b. How much interest will be earned in the second year?

10. **LO3** What price should be paid for a $10,000 Government of Ontario strip bond with 17 years remaining to maturity if it is to yield the buyer 2.770% compounded semiannually?

11. **LO2** On the same date that the Alberta Treasury Branches were advertising rates of 2.25%, 3%, 3.75%, 4.5%, and 6.5% in successive years of their five-year compound interest Springboard GIC, they offered 3.5% compounded annually on their five-year fixed-rate compound interest GIC.
   a. What will be the maturity values of $10,000 invested in each GIC?
   b. How much interest will each GIC earn in the third year?

12. **LO5** Maynard Appliances is holding a "Fifty-Fifty Sale." Major appliances may be purchased for nothing down and no interest to pay if the customer pays 50% of the purchase price in six months and the remaining 50% in 12 months. Maynard then sells the conditional

sale contracts at a discount to Consumers Finance Co. What will the finance company pay Maynard for a conditional sale contract in the amount of $1085 if it requires a return of 14% compounded quarterly?

13. **LO6** Donnelly Excavating has received two offers on a used backhoe that Donnelly is advertising for sale. Offer 1 is for $10,000 down, $15,000 in 6 months, and $15,000 in 18 months. Offer 2 is for $8000 down, plus two $17,500 payments one and two years from now. What is the economic value today of each offer if money is worth 5.25% compounded semiannually? Which offer should be accepted?

14. **LO1** For the five-year period ended October 31, 2019, a Canadian Equity Income Fund had compound annual returns of 14.40% while a Canadian Dividend fund had returns of 4.31% compounding annually. How much more would an initial $1000 investment in the Canadian Equity Income Fund have earned over the five-year period compared to a $1000 investment in the Canadian Dividend fund?

15. **LO1** Isaac borrowed $3000 at 10.5% compounded quarterly $3\frac{1}{2}$ years ago. One year ago he made a payment of $1200. What amount will extinguish the loan today?

16. **LO1** For the five-year period ended October 31, 2019, a North American Resource Fund had a compound annual return of 7.99% compared to the average annual five-year returns of –0.337% for funds in the same category. How much more would an initial $1000 investment have earned over the five-year period in the North American Resource Fund compared to a $1000 investment fund earning the average rate of return?

17. **LO5** Todd agreed to pay Laurie two payments of $1500: one on May 1 and the second on October 1. Todd now wishes to settle the debt with one equivalent payment on August 1. If the money was borrowed at 4.25% compounded monthly, what single payment on August 1 will settle the debt?

18. **LO5** Payments of $2400 originally scheduled to be paid today, $1200 due 18 months from today, and $3000 due 33 months from today are to be replaced with a single payment due six months from now. Using 6% compounded quarterly as the rate of return money can earn, what payment six months from now would be equivalent to the three scheduled payments?

INTERMEDIATE PROBLEMS

19. **LO1** Jarmila borrowed $3000, $3500, and $4000 from her grandmother on December 1 in each of three successive years at college. They agreed that interest would accumulate at the rate of 4% compounded semiannually. Jarmila is to start repaying the loan on June 1 following the third loan. What consolidated amount will she owe at that time?

20. **LO1** A four-year $7000 promissory note bearing interest at 10.5% compounded monthly was discounted 18 months after issue to yield 9.5% compounded quarterly. What were the proceeds from the sale of the note?

21. **LO1** **LO4** For the 10 years ended December 31, 2018, the annually compounded rate of return on the portfolio of stocks represented by the S&P/TSX Composite Index was 7.9%. For the same period, the compound annual rate of inflation (as measured by the increase in the Consumer Price Index) was 1.65%.
    a. What was $1000 invested in the Index stock portfolio on December 31, 2008, worth 10 years later?
    b. What amount of money was needed on December 31, 2018, to have the same purchasing power as $1000 on December 31, 2008?
    c. For an investment in the Index stock portfolio, what was the percent increase in purchasing power of the original $1000?

22. `LO1` On February 1 of three successive years, Roger contributed $3000, $4000, and $3500, respectively, to his RRSP. The funds in his plan earned 9% compounded monthly for the first year, 8.5% compounded quarterly for the second year, and 7.75% compounded semiannually for the third year. What was the value of his RRSP three years after the first contribution?

23. `LO6` A loan contract called for a payment after two years of $1500 plus interest (on this $1500 only) at 8% compounded quarterly, and a second payment after four years of $2500 plus interest (on this $2500) at 8% compounded quarterly. What would you pay to purchase the contract 18 months after the contract date if you require a return of 10.5% compounded semiannually?

24. `LO1` Payments of $1800 and $2400 were made on a $10,000 variable-rate loan 18 and 30 months after the date of the loan. The interest rate was 11.5% compounded semiannually for the first two years and 10.74% compounded monthly thereafter. What amount was owed on the loan after three years?

25. `LO5` $6500 loan at 11.25% compounded monthly is to be repaid by three equal payments due 3, 6, and 12 months after the date of the loan. Calculate the size of each payment.

26. `LO5` `LO6` Payments of $2300 due 18 months ago and $3100 due in three years are to be replaced by an equivalent stream of payments consisting of $2000 today and two equal payments due two and four years from now. If money can earn 9.75% compounded semiannually, what should be the amount of each of these two payments?

27. `LO3` A $1000 face value strip bond has 19 years remaining until maturity. What is its price if the market rate of return on such bonds is 5.9% compounded semiannually? At this market rate of return, what will be the increase in the value of the strip bond during the fifth year of ownership?

28. `LO6` Two payments of $5000 are scheduled six months and three years from now. They are to be replaced by a payment of $3000 in two years, a second payment in 42 months, and a third payment, twice as large as the second, in five years. What should the last two payments be if money is worth 9% compounded semiannually?

29. `LO2` A five-year, compound interest GIC purchased for $1000 earns 4% compounded annually.
    a. How much interest will the GIC earn in the fifth year?
    b. If the rate of inflation during the five-year term is 2.2% per year, what will be the percent increase in the purchasing power of the invested funds over the entire five years?

30. `LO6` Three equal payments were made one, two, and three years after the date on which a $10,000 loan was granted at 10.5% compounded monthly. If the balance immediately after the third payment was $5326.94, what was the amount of each payment?

31. `LO1` If the total interest earned on an investment at 2.6% compounded monthly for $3\frac{1}{2}$ years was $618.55, what was the original investment?

ADVANCED PROBLEM

32. `LO1` `LO6` Four years ago John borrowed $3000 from Arlette. The principal with interest at 10% compounded semiannually is to be repaid six years from the date of the loan. Fifteen months ago, John borrowed another $1500 for $3\frac{1}{2}$ years at 9% compounded quarterly. John is now proposing to settle both debts with two equal payments to be made 2 and $3\frac{1}{2}$ years from now. What should the payments be if money now earns 8% compounded quarterly?

APPENDIX 9A: INSTRUCTIONS FOR SPECIFIC MODELS OF FINANCIAL CALCULATORS

SETTING THE CALCULATOR IN THE FINANCIAL MODE

Texas Instruments BA II PLUS	Sharp EL-738C	Hewlett Packard 10B
Calculator is "ready to go" for financial calculations.	Press MODE 0	Calculator is "ready to go" for financial calculations.

SETTING THE NUMBER OF DECIMAL PLACES DISPLAYED AT 9

Texas Instruments BA II PLUS	Sharp EL-738C	Hewlett Packard 10B
2nd Format 9 ENTER 2nd QUIT	SETUP 0 0 9	DISP 9

SETTING A FLOATING POINT DECIMAL[10]

Texas Instruments BA II PLUS	Sharp EL-738C	Hewlett Packard 10B
Set for 9 decimal places as in the preceding table.	SETUP 0 2	DISP •

CHECKING THE CONTENTS OF A FINANCIAL KEY'S MEMORY (USING THE PV KEY AS AN EXAMPLE)

Texas Instruments BA II PLUS	Sharp EL-738C	Hewlett Packard 10B
RCL PV	RCL PV	RCL PV

---

[10] With this setting, the calculator will show all of the digits but no trailing zeros for a terminating decimal. Non-terminating decimals will be displayed with 10 digits.

Chapter 10

Compound Interest: Further Topics and Applications

LEARNING OBJECTIVES

After completing this chapter, you will be able to:

LO1 Calculate the interest rate and term in compound interest applications

LO2 Given a nominal interest rate, calculate its effective interest rate

LO3 Given a nominal interest rate, calculate its equivalent interest rate at another compounding frequency

IN ALL OF THE COMPOUND INTEREST PROBLEMS in Chapter 9, the interest rate and the term of the loan or investment were known. With a little reflection, you can think of many situations requiring the calculation of an interest rate, or a rate of return, or a rate of growth. For example, if you invest $1000 in a mutual fund, what rate of return must it earn to grow to $5000 over a 15-year period? If a stock's price rose from $15.50 to $27.40 over the past five years, what has been its equivalent annual percent increase in price? What was the average annual rate of inflation for the last 10 years if the Consumer Price Index rose from 104.7 to 125.2?

In other circumstances, we want to know the time required for an amount to grow from a beginning value to a target value. How long, for example, will it take an investment to double if it earns 10% compounded annually? By the end of Section 10.2, you will be able to answer such questions.

Compound interest rates on loans and investments may be quoted with differing compounding frequencies. This gives rise to questions such as: "How do we compare 7.9% compounded semiannually to 8% compounded annually? What semiannually compounded rate is equivalent to 6% compounded monthly?" The techniques you will learn in Sections 10.3 and 10.4 will enable you to answer these questions. Later on, in Chapters 11 through 15, this ability will be used routinely in calculations involving annuities.

10.1 Calculating the Periodic Interest Rate, *i*

LO1 In cases where we know values for *PV*, *FV*, and *n*, the periodic and nominal rates of interest may be calculated.

Algebraic Method

Rearranging the basic equation $FV = PV(1 + i)^n$ to isolate *i* is more difficult than isolating *PV*. First divide both sides of the equation by *PV* and then interchange the two sides, giving

$$(1 + i)^n = \frac{FV}{PV}$$

Next take the *n*th root of both sides of the equation. This makes the left side simply $(1 + i)$, and we have

$$1 + i = \sqrt[n]{\frac{FV}{PV}}$$

PERIODIC RATE OF INTEREST

Therefore,[1]

$$i = \sqrt[n]{\frac{FV}{PV}} - 1 = \left(\frac{FV}{PV}\right)^{1/n} - 1 \qquad \text{(10-1)}$$

Financial Calculator Method

Enter values for the known variables—*PV*, *FV*, *n*, and *m*—into the appropriate memories. Then press [CPT] [I/Y] in sequence to compute *j*, the nominal annual rate of interest. If the value of *i* is required, calculate $i = \frac{j}{m}$.

 TRAP

Sign Convention Now Mandatory

When you enter values for both *FV* and *PV*, it is imperative that you employ the cash-flow sign convention. If you fail to use it, an error message will appear in your calculator's display. In all calculations of *I/Y*, *FV* and *PV* must have different signs.

---

[1] It was pointed out in Section 2.2 that the *n*th root of a quantity is equivalent to raising it to the exponent 1/*n*.

EXAMPLE 10.1A

CALCULATING THE PERIODIC AND NOMINAL RATES OF INTEREST

The maturity value of a three-year, $5000 compound interest GIC is $5788.13. To three-figure accuracy, calculate the nominal rate of interest paid on the GIC if interest is compounded:

a. Annually

b. Quarterly

SOLUTION

Given: $PV = \$5000$ and $FV = \$5788.13$

In part (a), $m = 1$, $n = m(\text{Term}) = 1(3) = 3$ compounding periods.

In part (b), $m = 4$, $n = m(\text{Term}) = 4(3) = 12$ compounding periods.

Formula (10-1) enables us to calculate the interest rate for one compounding period.

a. $$\begin{aligned} i &= \left(\frac{FV}{PV}\right)^{1/n} - 1 \\ &= \left(\frac{\$5788.13}{\$5000.00}\right)^{1/3} - 1 \\ &= (1.157626)^{0.\overline{3}} - 1 \\ &= 0.05000 \\ &= 5.000\% \end{aligned}$$	<div align="right"> $\boxed{\text{P/Y}}\ 1\ \boxed{\text{ENTER}}$ (making $C/Y = P/Y = 1$) $3\ \boxed{\text{N}}$ $5000\ \boxed{+/-}\ \boxed{\text{PV}}$ $0\ \boxed{\text{PMT}}$ $5788.13\ \boxed{\text{FV}}$ $\boxed{\text{CPT}}\ \boxed{\text{I/Y}}$ *Ans: 5.000* </div>

The nominal rate of interest on the GIC is $j = mi = 1(5.000\%) = 5.00\%$ compounded annually.

b. $$\begin{aligned} i &= \left(\frac{\$5788.13}{\$5000.00}\right)^{1/12} - 1 \\ &= (1.157626)^{0.08\overline{3}} - 1 \\ &= 0.01227 \\ &= 1.227\% \end{aligned}$$	<div align="right"> Same PV, PMT, FV $\boxed{\text{P/Y}}\ 4\ \boxed{\text{ENTER}}$ (making $C/Y = P/Y = 4$) $12\ \boxed{\text{N}}$ $\boxed{\text{CPT}}\ \boxed{\text{I/Y}}$ *Ans: 4.909* </div>

The nominal rate of interest on the GIC is $j = mi = 4(1.227\%) = 4.91\%$ compounded quarterly.

TIP

Don't Leave Out the Final Step

The calculation of i is usually not the last step in a problem. Formula (10-1) calculates the periodic interest rate and typically you are asked to determine either the nominal interest rate or the effective interest rate (to be discussed in **Section 10.3**). Do not forget to complete the extra step needed to directly answer the question.

EXAMPLE 10.1B

CALCULATING A SEMIANNUALLY COMPOUNDED RATE OF RETURN

Mr. Dunbar paid $10,000 for a $40,000 face value strip bond having $19\frac{1}{2}$ years remaining until maturity. (Recall that a strip bond is an investment that returns just one payment, the face value, at maturity.) What semiannually compounded rate of return will Mr. Dunbar earn on his investment?

SOLUTION

Given: $PV = \$10,000$ $FV = \$40,000$ Term $= 19\frac{1}{2}$ years $m = 2$

Then $n = m(\text{Term}) = 2(19.5) = 39$

$$
\begin{aligned}
i &= \left(\frac{FV}{PV}\right)^{1/n} - 1 \\
&= \left(\frac{\$40,000}{\$10,000}\right)^{1/39} - 1 \\
&= 4^{0.0256410} - 1 \\
&= 0.036185 \\
&= 3.6185\%
\end{aligned}
$$

| P/Y | 2 | ENTER |

(making $C/Y = P/Y = 2$)

39	N
10000 +/−	PV
0	PMT
40000	FV
CPT	I/Y

Ans: 7.237

$$j = mi = 2(3.6185\%) = 7.24\% \text{ compounded semiannually}$$

Mr. Dunbar will earn 7.24% compounded semiannually on his strip bond investment.

EXAMPLE 10.1C

CALCULATING AN ANNUALLY COMPOUNDED RATE OF RETURN THAT IS EQUIVALENT TO A SERIES OF INDIVIDUAL ANNUAL RETURNS

In the years 2016, 2017, and 2018, the Excel China Fund earned annual rates of return of 0.31%, 35.14%, and −12.41%, respectively. Calculate the fund's equivalent annually compounded rate of return for the three years. (This is the fixed annual rate of return that would produce the same overall growth.)

SOLUTION

The equivalent annually compounded rate of return for the three-year period cannot be obtained by simply averaging the three individual annual returns. Instead, we must use a two-step procedure:

Step 1:   Use $FV = PV(1 + i_1)(1 + i_2)(1 + i_3) \ldots (1 + i_n)$ to calculate how much an investment made on December 31, 2015, was worth on December 31, 2018.

Step 2:   Calculate the annually compounded rate of return that will produce the *same* growth in three years.

Step 1:   For the initial investment, choose a "nice, round" amount such as $100 or $1000.

$$
\begin{aligned}
FV &= PV(1 + i_{2016})(1 + i_{2017})(1 + i_{2018}) \\
&= \$1000(1 + 0.0031)(1 + 0.3514)(1 - 0.1241) \\
&= \$1187.36
\end{aligned}
$$

| P/Y | 1 | ENTER |

(making $C/Y = P/Y = 1$)

Step 2:

$$
\begin{aligned}
i &= \left(\frac{FV}{PV}\right)^{\frac{1}{n}} - 1 \\
&= \left(\frac{\$1187.36}{\$1000}\right)^{1/3} - 1 \\
&= 1.18736^{0.\overline{3}} - 1 \\
&= 0.058914 \\
&= 5.89\%
\end{aligned}
$$

3	N
1000 +/−	PV
0	PMT
$1187.36	FV
CPT	I/Y

Ans: 5.8914

$j = mi = 1(5.89\%) = 5.89\%$ compounded annually

The mutual fund's equivalent annually compounded rate of return for the three-year period ended December 31, 2018, was 5.89% compounded annually.

Postscript At the end of every month, the type of calculation in **Example 10.1C** is done for about 2000 mutual funds available in Canada. The equivalent compound annual rates of return are calculated for 3-year, 5-year, and 10-year periods terminating at the month-end. These returns are then published in monthly mutual fund supplements to major newspapers. They are also available on investment Web sites that specialize in mutual funds. (In fact, these equivalent rates of return are easier to find than the year-by-year returns on which they are based.) You may have noticed that mutual fund advertisements commonly quote mutual fund performance in terms of the 3-year, 5-year, and 10-year compound annual returns. Now you know how they are obtained and how to interpret them.

EXAMPLE 10.1D

CALCULATING AN INFLATION-ADJUSTED (REAL) RATE OF RETURN

Over a 10-year period, Brooke's investment in Suncor stock grew in value from $9480 to $17,580. During the same period, the Consumer Price Index (CPI) rose from 93.6 to 126.1. What was her *real* compound annual rate of return on the stock during the decade? (The real rate of return is the rate of return net of inflation. It represents the rate of increase in purchasing power.)

SOLUTION

With the CPI up from 93.6 to 126.1, Brooke needed $\frac{126.1}{93.6}$ times as many dollars at the end of the decade to purchase the same goods and services as at the beginning. The $9480 value of the stock at the beginning had to grow to

$$\$9480 \times \frac{126.1}{93.6} = \$12{,}772$$

just to maintain her purchasing power. In fact, it grew to $17,580. In terms of end-of-decade dollars, her purchasing power rose from $12,772 to $17,580. Hence, to obtain the real rate of return, use $PV = \$12{,}772$, $FV = \$17{,}580$, and $n = 10$.

$$
\left.
\begin{aligned}
i &= \left(\frac{FV}{PV}\right)^{1/n} - 1 \\[4pt]
&= \left(\frac{\$17580}{\$12772}\right)^{1/10} - 1 \\[4pt]
&= 1.37645^{0.1} - 1 \\[4pt]
&= 0.03247 \\[4pt]
&= 3.247\%
\end{aligned}
\right\}
$$

| P/Y | 1 | ENTER |

(making $C/Y = P/Y = 1$)

| 10 | N |

| 12772 | +/- | PV |

| 0 | PMT |

| 17580 | FV |

| CPT | I/Y |

Ans: 3.247

$j = mi = 1(3.247\%) = 3.25\%$ compounded annually

The real rate of return on the Suncor stock was 3.25% compounded annually.

Postscript Two points should be mentioned.

1. The same answer will be obtained if you choose to adjust for inflation by expressing $17,580 in terms of beginning-of-decade dollars.
2. An entirely different approach may have occurred to you. Suppose you separately calculate the rate of return on the stock, and the rate of inflation from the CPI data. (You would obtain 6.37% and 3.03% compounded annually, respectively.) You might think that:

$$
\begin{aligned}
\text{Real rate of return} &= \text{Actual rate of return} - \text{Rate of inflation} \\
&= 6.37\% - 3.03\% \\
&= 3.34\%
\end{aligned}
$$

This is a slightly larger value (by 0.09%) than the strictly correct answer we obtained in the "official solution." The reason for the small difference is quite subtle and technical—we will spare you the details. However, real rates of return are, more often than not, calculated this way. Since nominal rates of return and inflation rates are easily obtained from published data, this approximation is an easier approach and is good enough for most purposes.

CONCEPT QUESTIONS

1. If *FV* is less than *PV*, what can you predict about the value for *i*?

2. Is *FV* negative if you lose money on an investment?

3. Which scenario had the higher periodic rate of return: "$1 grew to $2" or "$3 grew to $5"? Both investments were for the same length of time at the same compounding frequency. Justify your choice.

EXERCISE 10.1

Answers to the odd-numbered problems are at the end of the book.

 **connect**

 **Spreadsheet template:** *A partially completed Excel template for calculating the periodic rate of return is provided on Connect. Go to the Student Edition of Connect and find "RATE Function" under the Student Resources for Chapter 10. The completed template may be used wherever you need to calculate i in Exercise 10.1.*

Calculate interest rates accurate to the nearest 0.01%.

BASIC PROBLEMS

1. No payments were made on a $3400 loan during its three-year term. What was the annually compounded nominal interest rate on the loan, if the amount owed at the end of the term was $4297.91?

2. What was the annually compounded nominal rate of growth if the future value of $1000 after 20 years was $4016.94?

3. An initial $1800 investment was worth $2299.16 after two years and nine months. What quarterly compounded nominal rate of return did the investment earn?

4. A strip bond that will mature $7\frac{1}{2}$ years from now at its $13,000 face value can be purchased today for $9042. What rate of return (compounded semiannually) will this strip bond provide to an investor?

5. The amount owed on a promissory note for $950 after two years and five months is $1165.79. What monthly compounded nominal rate of interest was charged on the debt?

6. Philippe contributed $4300 to an RRSP eight years and six months ago. The money was invested in a Canadian Equity mutual fund. The investment is now worth $10,440.32. Over the entire period, what annually compounded nominal rate of return has the investment delivered?

7. When he died in 1790, Benjamin Franklin left $4600 to the city of Boston, with the stipulation that the money and its earnings could not be used for 100 years. The bequest grew to $332,000 by 1890. What (equivalent) compound annual rate of return did the bequest earn during the 100-year period?

8. The Templeton Growth Fund has been around since 1954. If you had invested $10,000 in the fund when it was launched in 1954 it would have been worth $5.09 million 54 years later. What compound annual rate of return did the fund realize over this period?

9. Anders discovered an old pay statement from 11 years ago. His monthly salary at the time was $2550 versus his current salary of $4475 per month. At what (equivalent) compound annual rate has his salary grown during the period?

10. Mr. and Mrs. Markovich note that the condo they purchased 20 years ago for $70,000 is now appraised at $340,000. What was the (equivalent) annual rate of appreciation in the value of their condo during the 20-year period?

11. Jan and Chelsea purchased their home 15 years ago for $198,000 and it is now appraised at $430,000. What was the (equivalent) annual rate of appreciation in the value of their home during the 15-year period?

12. The maturity value of a $5000 four-year compound interest GIC was $6147.82. What quarterly compounded rate of interest did it earn?

13. Three years ago Mikhail invested $7000 in a three-year compound interest GIC. He has just received its maturity value of $7867.34. What was the monthly compounded rate of interest on the GIC?

14. **a.** The population of Canada grew from 24,343,000 in 1981 to 37,268,000 in 2019. What was the overall compound annual rate of growth in our population during the period?

    b. According to the Canadian Real Estate Association, the average selling price of Canadian homes rose from $67,000 in 1980 to $455,000 in 2018. What has been the overall compound annual appreciation of home prices?

15. The following table contains 1981 and 2018 population figures for five provinces. Calculate each province's equivalent compound annual rate of population change during the period.

Province	1981 Population	2018 Population
Alberta	2,237,700	4,330,206
British Columbia	2,744,500	5,016,322
Newfoundland and Labrador	567,700	525,073
Nova Scotia	847,400	964,693
Ontario	8,625,100	14,411,424

16. For an investment to double in value during a 10-year period,
    a. What annually compounded rate of return must it earn?
    b. What semiannually compounded rate of return must it earn?
    c. What monthly compounded rate of return must it earn?

17. For an investment to triple in value during a 15-year period,
    a. What annually compounded rate of return must it earn?
    b. What quarterly compounded rate of return must it earn?
    c. What monthly compounded rate of return must it earn?

18. What compound annual rate of return is required for an investment to double in:
    a. 12 years?   **b.** 10 years?   **c.** 8 years?   **d.** 6 years?

    For each case, multiply the annual rate of return (in %) by the time period (in years). Compare the four products. Does the comparison suggest a general rule of thumb?

19. Monty purchased a strip bond for his RRSP. He paid $3800 for a $5000 face value bond with three years remaining until maturity. What semiannually compounded rate of return will he realize over the three years?

20. If the number of workers in the auto industry in Canada declined by 32% from its peak at the end of 1999 to the beginning of 2011, what was the compound annual rate of attrition in the industry during this period?

21. The Canadian Consumer Price Index (based on a value of 100 in 1971) rose from 97.2 in 1970 to 210.6 in 1980. What was the (equivalent) annual rate of inflation in the decade of the 1970s?

22. The Consumer Price Index (based on a value of 100 in 1986) rose from 67.2 in 1980 to 119.5 in 1990. What was the (equivalent) annual rate of inflation in the decade of the 1980s?

23. The Consumer Price Index (based on a value of 100 in 1992) rose from 93.3 in 1990 to 113.5 in 2000. What was the (equivalent) annual rate of inflation in the decade of the 1990s?

24. The Consumer Price Index (based on a value of 100 in 2002) rose from 93.5 in 2000 to 115.1 in 2010. What was the (equivalent) annual rate of inflation in the first decade of the 2000s?

25. According to Statistics Canada, business students in an undergraduate program paid an average of $6838 in tuition fees for the 2018/2019 academic year compared to fees of $1464 for the 1990/1991 year. During the same period, the Consumer Price Index rose from 76.7 to 133.6.
    a. What would have been the average tuition fees for the 2018/2019 year if tuition fees had grown just at the rate of inflation since the 1990/1991 year?
    b. What was the (equivalent) compound annual rate of increase of tuition fees during the period?
    c. What was the (equivalent) compound annual rate of inflation during the period?

INTERMEDIATE PROBLEMS

26. Using the data given in Problems 21 and 22, calculate the annual rate of inflation for the 1970–1990 period. (*Note:* Simply averaging the two answers to Problems 21 and 22 will give only an approximation of the correct result.)

27. A five-year promissory note for $5700 plus interest at 6.75% compounded semiannually was sold 18 months before maturity for $6620. What monthly compounded nominal rate of return will the buyer realize on the investment?

28. A four-year promissory note for $3800 plus interest at 9.5% compounded semiannually was sold 18 months before maturity for $4481. What quarterly compounded nominal rate of return will the buyer realize on her investment?

29. A $6000, three-year promissory note bearing interest at 11% compounded semiannually was purchased 15 months into its term for $6854.12. What monthly compounded discount rate was used in pricing the note?

30. An investor's portfolio increased in value by 93% over a seven-year period in which the Consumer Price Index rose from 95.6 to 115.3. What was the compound annual real rate of return on the portfolio during the period?

31. An investment grew in value from $5630 to $8485 during a five-year period. The annual rate of inflation for the five years was 2.3%. What was the compound annual real rate of return during the five years?

32. An investment earned 6% compounded semiannually for two years and 8% compounded annually for the next three years. What was the equivalent annually compounded rate of return for the entire five-year period?

33. A portfolio earned annual rates of 20%, −20%, 0%, 20%, and −20% in five successive years. What was the portfolio's five-year equivalent annually compounded rate of return?

34. A portfolio earned annual rates of 20%, 15%, −10%, 25%, and −5% in five successive years. What was the portfolio's five-year equivalent annually compounded rate of return?

35. At the end of 2018, the RBC Canadian Dividend Fund was the largest equity mutual fund in Canada. The aggregate market value of its holdings at the end of 2018 was $18.8 billion. The fund's annual returns in successive years from 2009 to 2018 inclusive were 27.26%, 11.90%, −2.48%, 10.71%, 17.40%, 12.14%, −7.23%, 19.42%, 7.59%, and −8.60%, respectively. For the 3-year, 5-year, and 10-year periods ended December 31, 2018, what were the fund's equivalent annually compounded returns?

36. At the end of 2014, the Industrial Alliance (IA) Dividends Fund had the best 10-year compound annual return of any Canadian diversified equity mutual fund. During the 10-year period, this fund invested primarily in the shares of large Canadian companies. The fund's annual returns in successive years from 2005 to 2014 inclusive were 25.51%, 17.48%, 4.38%, −27.37%, 29.91%, 12.47%, −3.35%, 7.84%, 15.22%, and 9.54%, respectively. For 3-year, 5-year, and 10-year periods ended December 31, 2014, what were the fund's equivalent annually compounded returns?

37. BMO's Dividend Fund was launched in 1994 and had annual returns in successive years from 2009 to 2018 inclusive of 19.83%, 9.71%, −2.62%, 6.93%, 17.92%, 13.54%, −1.43%, 11.76%, 10.93% and –6.78%, respectively. For 3-year, 5-year, and 10-year periods ended December 31, 2018, what were the fund's equivalent annually compounded returns?

38. In June of 2006, AIC Limited published full-page advertisements focused on the fact that its AIC Advantage Mutual Fund was Canada's "Best Performing Canadian Equity Fund" over the 20 years ending May 31, 2006. The equivalent annual rate of return during the 20 years was 11.9% compared to 9.9% for the benchmark S&P/TSX Composite Total Return Index. But the advertisement failed to point out that during the second half of that 20-year period, the fund's 9.4% compounded annual return was actually less than the 10.2% growth rate for the S&P/TSX Composite Total Return Index. Furthermore, in the final five years of the 20-year period, the fund's 2.4% annual rate of return was far below the index's 9.5% annual growth. The Advantage Fund's five-year performance was even less than the *median* performance of all Canadian equity mutual funds. In short, AIC was still trying to capitalize on the initial 10 years of truly outstanding performance, even though the Advantage Fund's subsequent 10 years' performance was at best mediocre.

   a. What would $10,000 invested in the AIC Advantage Fund on May 31, 1986 have grown to after 20 years?
   b. What was this investment worth after the first 10 years?
   c. What compound annual rate of return did the AIC Advantage Fund earn during the first 10 years of the 20-year period?
   d. What was the overall percent increase in the value of an investment in the AIC Advantage Fund during: **(i)** The first 10 years? **(ii)** The second 10 years?

10.2 Calculating the Number of Compounding Periods, *n*

L01 If we know values for *PV*, *FV*, and *i*, we can calculate the number of compounding periods and the term of the loan or investment.

Algebraic Method

You can take either of two approaches.

1. If you are familiar with the rules of logarithms, you can substitute the values for *PV*, *FV*, and *i* into $FV = PV(1 + i)^n$ and then solve for *n*. Logarithms are briefly discussed in **Appendix 10B**.
2. If you are not comfortable manipulating logarithms, you can use Formula (10-2). It is, in fact, just a "dressed-up" version of $FV = PV(1 + i)^n$ in which *n* is already isolated for you. **Example 10B.B** derives the following formula for the number of compounding periods.

NUMBER OF COMPOUNDING PERIODS

$$n = \frac{\ln\left(\frac{FV}{PV}\right)}{\ln(1 + i)} \tag{10-2}$$

In **Example 10.2A**, we will demonstrate both algebraic methods. Thereafter, only the second approach will be used in the book.

Financial Calculator Method

Enter values for the four known variables—*PV*, *FV*, *i*, and *m*—into the appropriate memories. Then press CPT N in sequence to execute the calculation.

TIP

Don't Leave Out the Final Step

The calculation of *n* is usually not the last step in a problem. Formula (10-2) calculates the number of compounding periods and typically you are asked to determine the total time in years and months (rather than the number of compounding periods). Do not forget to complete the extra step necessary to directly answer the problem.

EXAMPLE 10.2A

CALCULATING THE NUMBER OF COMPOUNDING PERIODS

What is the term of a compound interest GIC if $4000 invested at 2.5% compounded annually earns interest totalling $525.63?

SOLUTION

Given: $PV = \$4000 \quad i = \frac{j}{m} = \frac{2.5\%}{1} = 2.5\%$ Total interest = $525.63

The maturity value of the GIC is

$$FV = PV + \text{Total interest} = \$4000 + \$525.63 = \$4525.63$$

Method 1: Use the basic formula $FV = PV(1 + i)^n$ to calculate the number of compounding periods required for $4000 to grow to $4525.63. Substitute the known values for *PV*, *FV*, and *i* giving

$$\$4525.63 = \$4000(1.025)^n$$

Therefore,

$$1.025^n = \frac{\$4525.63}{\$4000} = 1.131408$$

Now take logarithms of both sides. On the left side, use the rule that $\ln(a^n) = n(\ln a)$.

Therefore,

$$n(\ln 1.025) = \ln 1.131408$$

and

$$n = \frac{\ln 1.131408}{\ln 1.025} = \frac{0.123462}{0.0246926} = 5.000$$

Since each compounding period equals one year, the term of the GIC is five years.

Method 2: Substitute the known values into the derived Formula (10-2). The number of compounding periods required for $4000 to grow to $4525.63 is

$$
\begin{aligned}
n &= \frac{\ln\left(\frac{FV}{PV}\right)}{\ln(1 + i)} = \frac{\ln\left(\frac{\$4525.63}{\$4000}\right)}{\ln(1.025)} \\
&= \frac{\ln(1.131408)}{\ln(1.025)} \\
&= \frac{0.123462}{0.0246926} \\
&= 5.000
\end{aligned}
$$

2.5	I/Y
P/Y 1	ENTER
(making $C/Y = P/Y = 1$)	
4000 +/−	PV
0	PMT
4525.63	FV
CPT	N

Ans: 5.000

Since each compounding period equals one year, the term of the GIC is five years.

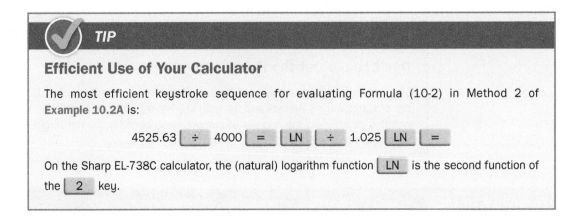

Non-integer Values for *n*

If Formula (10-2) or the financial calculator procedure gives a value for *n* that is not an integer, it means (as you would expect) that the term of the loan or investment includes a partial compounding period. In the final answer, we normally convert the fractional part of *n* to months, or to months and days (depending on the requested precision).

EXAMPLE 10.2B

CALCULATING AND INTERPRETING A NON-INTEGER *n*

Rounded to the nearest month, how long will it take a city's population to grow from 75,000 to 100,000 if the annual growth rate is 2%?

SOLUTION

In effect, we are given:

$$PV = 75,000 \quad FV = 100,000 \quad \text{and} \quad i = \frac{j}{m} = \frac{2\%}{1} = 2\% \text{ per year}$$

Using Formula (10-2) to calculate the required number of compounding periods, we obtain

$$\left.\begin{aligned}
n &= \frac{\ln\left(\frac{FV}{PV}\right)}{\ln(1+i)} \\
&= \frac{\ln\left(\frac{100,000}{75,000}\right)}{\ln(1.02)} \\
&= \frac{0.28768}{0.019803} \\
&= 14.527
\end{aligned}\right\}$$

$$\begin{aligned}
&2 \boxed{\text{I/Y}} \\
\boxed{\text{P/Y}} \ 1 \ &\boxed{\text{ENTER}} \\
(\text{making } C/Y &= P/Y = 1) \\
75000 \ \boxed{+/-} \ &\boxed{\text{PV}} \\
0 \ &\boxed{\text{PMT}} \\
100000 \ &\boxed{\text{FV}} \\
\boxed{\text{CPT}} \ &\boxed{\text{N}} \\
Ans: \ &14.527
\end{aligned}$$

It requires 14.527 compounding periods for the population to grow from 75,000 to 100,000. Since a compounding period equals one year,

$$14.527 \text{ compounding periods} = 14 \text{ years} + 0.527 \times 12 \text{ months}$$
$$= 14 \text{ years} + 6.32 \text{ months}$$

Rounded to the nearest month, it will take 14 years and 6 months for the city's population to reach 100,000.

EXAMPLE 10.2C

CALCULATING AN INVESTMENT'S DOUBLING TIME

How long will it take an investment to double in value if it earns:

a. 3% compounded annually?

b. 6% compounded annually?

Include accrued interest and round the answer to the nearest month.

SOLUTION

We require the maturity value of an investment to be twice the initial investment. Therefore, we can simply set $PV = \$1$ and $FV = \$2$.

In part (a), $i = \frac{j}{m} = \frac{3\%}{1} = 3\%$ per year. In part (b), $i = \frac{j}{m} = \frac{6\%}{1} = 6\%$ per year.

a. Substituting in Formula (10-2),

$$n = \frac{\ln\left(\frac{FV}{PV}\right)}{\ln(1 + i)}$$

$$= \frac{\ln(2)}{\ln(1.03)}$$

$$= 23.4498$$

| 3 | I/Y |
| P/Y | 1 ENTER |

(making $C/Y = P/Y = 1$)

1 +/−	PV
0	PMT
2	FV
CPT	N

Ans: 23.4498

The doubling time is

$$23.4498 \text{ years} = 23 \text{ years} + 0.4498 \times 12 \text{ months} = 23 \text{ years} = 5.397 \text{ months}$$

An investment earning 3% compounded annually will double in 23 years and 5 months (rounded to the nearest month).

b. Substituting in Formula (10-2),

$$n = \frac{\ln\left(\frac{FV}{PV}\right)}{\ln(1 + i)}$$

$$= \frac{\ln(2)}{\ln(1.06)}$$

$$= 11.896$$

Same *P/Y, C/Y*

Same *PV, PMT, FV*

| 6 | I/Y |
| CPT | N |

Ans: 11.896

The doubling time is

$$11.896 \text{ years} = 11 \text{ years} + 0.896 \times 12 \text{ months} = 11 \text{ years} + 10.75 \text{ months}$$

An investment earning 6% compounded annually will double in 11 years and 11 months (rounded to the nearest month).

POINT OF INTEREST
The Rule of 72

Investors have a rule of thumb to quickly *estimate* the number of years it will take an investment to double. Known as the **Rule of 72**, it says:

$$\text{Doubling time (in years)} \approx \frac{72}{\text{Percent annual rate of return}}$$

For example, an investment earning 10% compounded annually will double in approximately $\frac{72}{10} = 7.2$ years. This approximation is very good when annual interest rates are in the 5% to 15% range but the gap between the estimate and the actual value for doubling time grows as interest rates move outside of this range.

The following table illustrates how the Rule of 72 gets less precise for rates of return below 5% and above 15%.

Rate of return	1%	3%	5%	9%	15%	25%	50%
Rule of 72 estimate	72.0	24.0	14.4	8.0	4.8	2.9	1.4
Actual # of years	69.66	23.45	14.21	8.04	4.96	3.11	1.71

Valuing Strip Bonds and Other Single-Payment Investments

Most loans and investments are structured so that the full term equals an integer multiple of the compounding period. However, an existing loan or investment contract may be sold and transferred to a new investor on a date that does not coincide with an interest-conversion date. The time remaining until maturity includes a partial compounding interval which must be taken into account in the price calculation. Consequently, n is not an integer in such cases.

In Table 10.1, consider the Province of Saskatchewan strip bond maturing on March 5, 2029. Let us see how the market's required rate of return (2.715% in the Yield column) on February 15, 2019, determines the $76.43 market price quoted on that date. (Recall that bond prices are quoted in the media as the price per $100 of face value, and that yields are understood to be annual rates with semiannual compounding.)

TABLE 10.1 Strip Bond Price and Yield Quotations (February 15, 2019)

Issuer	Maturity Date	Price ($)	Yield (%)
Province of Quebec	August 15, 2022	93.41	1.976
Province of British Columbia	August 23, 2019	99.17	1.668
Province of Saskatchewan	March 5, 2029	76.43	2.715
Canada	December 1, 2033	73.86	2.071

Source: "GIC & Bond Rates." RBC Direct Investing Inc. https://www.rbcdirectinvesting.com/pricing/gic-bond-rates.html.

As indicated on the following time line, the quoted price should be the present value of the $100 face value discounted at 2.715% compounded semiannually all the way back from the maturity date (March 5, 2029) to February 15, 2019. For the present-value calculation, we need to know the number of compounding periods in this interval. In general, this number will not be an integer. Determine the integer and fractional components of the number separately. Working back from the maturity date, there are 10 years from March 5, 2029 back to March 5, 2019. Then there are an additional 18 days from March 5, 2019 back to February 15, 2019. In total, this is $10\frac{18}{365}$ or 10.0493 years (20.0986 compounding periods) from March 5, 2029 back to February 15, 2019.

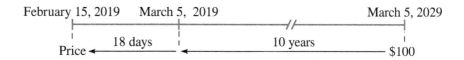

Therefore, $n = 20.0986$, $i = \frac{2.715\%}{2} = 1.3575\%$, and

$$\text{Price}, PV = FV(1 + i)^{-n} = \$100(1.013575)^{-20.0986} = \$76.26$$

This equals the quoted price to two-figure accuracy. (In general, a yield rounded to four figures guarantees only three-figure accuracy in the price.)

EXAMPLE 10.2D

CALCULATING THE TIME UNTIL MATURITY OF A STRIP BOND

A \$10,000 face value strip bond was purchased for \$4188.77. At this price, the bond provided the investor with a return of 5.938% compounded semiannually until the maturity date. To the nearest day, how long before the maturity date was the bond purchased? Assume that each half-year is exactly 182 days long.

SOLUTION

The purchase price of a strip bond equals the present value, on the date of purchase, of the bond's face value. The prevailing market rate of return should be used as the discount rate. In this example, \$4188.77 is the present value of \$10,000 discounted at 5.938% compounded semiannually. To determine the time interval used in the present-value calculation, we must first calculate the number of compounding periods. We are given:

$$PV = \$4188.77 \quad FV = \$10,000 \quad \text{and} \quad i = \frac{j}{m} = \frac{5.938\%}{2} = 2.969\%$$

Substituting in Formula (10-2),

$$
\left.\begin{aligned}
n &= \frac{\ln\left(\frac{FV}{PV}\right)}{\ln(1 + i)} \\[2mm]
&= \frac{\ln\left(\frac{\$10,000}{\$4188.77}\right)}{\ln(1.02969)} \\[2mm]
&= 29.74176
\end{aligned}\right\}
$$

5.938	I/Y
P/Y 2	ENTER

(making $C/Y = P/Y = 2$)

4188.77 +/-	PV
0	PMT
10000	FV
CPT	N

Ans: 29.74176

Since each compounding period is 0.5 year, the time remaining to maturity is

$$(0.50 \times 29) \text{ years} + (0.74176 \times 182) \text{ days} = 14.5 \text{ years} + 135.00 \text{ days}$$

Hence, the bond was purchased with 14 years, 6 months, and 135 days remaining until its maturity date.

EXAMPLE 10.2E

SOLVING FOR A NON-INTEGER _n_ IN A DISCOUNTING PROBLEM

A loan contract requires the payment of \$4000 plus interest two years after the contract's date of issue. The interest rate on the \$4000 face value is 9.6% compounded quarterly. Before the maturity date, the original lender sold the contract to an investor for \$4327.70. The sale price was based on a discount rate of 8.5% compounded semiannually from the date of sale. How many months before the maturity date did the sale take place?

SOLUTION

The selling price represents the present value (on the date of sale) of the loan's maturity value. In other words, $4327.70 was the present value of the maturity value, discounted at 8.5% compounded semiannually. Therefore, the solution requires two steps as indicated in the following time diagram.

1. Calculate the maturity value of the debt.

2. Determine the length of time over which the maturity value was discounted to give a present value of $4327.70.

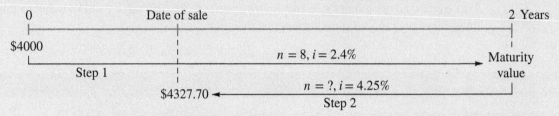

Step 1: For the maturity value calculation,

$$n = m(\text{Term}) = 4(2) = 8 \quad \text{and} \quad i = \frac{j}{m} = \frac{9.6\%}{4} = 2.4\%.$$

The maturity value of the contract is

$$FV = PV(1 + i)^n$$
$$= \$4000(1.024)^8$$
$$= \$4835.70$$

Step 2: For discounting the maturity value,

$$i = \frac{j}{m} = \frac{8.5\%}{2} = 4.25\%$$

The number of compounding periods between the date of sale and the maturity date is

$$n = \frac{\ln\left(\frac{FV}{PV}\right)}{\ln(1 + i)}$$
$$= \frac{\ln\left(\frac{\$4835.70}{\$4327.70}\right)}{\ln(1.0425)}$$
$$= 2.6666$$

Each compounding period is six months long.

Therefore, the date of sale was

$$2.6666 \times 6 \text{ months} = 16.00 \text{ months before the maturity date.}$$

Calculator steps:

9.6 I/Y
P/Y 4 ENTER
(making C/Y = P/Y = 4)
8 N
4000 +/− PV
0 PMT
CPT FV
Ans: 4835.70

Same PMT, FV
8.5 I/Y
P/Y 2 ENTER
(making C/Y = P/Y = 2)
4327.70 +/− PV
CPT N
Ans: 2.6666

 CONCEPT QUESTIONS

1. Under what circumstance does the value calculated for n equal the number of years in the term of the loan or investment?

2. Which investment scenario requires more time: "$1 growing to $2" or "$3 growing to $5"? Both investments earn the same rate of return. Justify your choice.

EXERCISE 10.2

Answers to the odd-numbered problems are at the end of the book.

Spreadsheet template: A partially completed Excel template for calculating the number of compounding periods is provided on Connect. Go to the Student Edition of Connect and find "NPER Function" under the Student Resources for Chapter 10. The completed template may be used wherever you need to calculate n in Exercise 10.2.

BASIC PROBLEMS

1. An $1100 investment earning 6.3% compounded annually grew to $4483.92. What was the term of the investment?

2. How long did it take $4625 earning 7.875% compounded annually to grow to $8481.61?

3. $5000 invested in a GIC earning 3.7% compounded semiannually matured at $5789.73. What was the term of the GIC?

4. The current balance on a loan is $3837.30. If the interest rate on the loan is 10% compounded monthly, how long ago was the $2870 loan made?

5. Marilyn was supposed to pay $1450 to Bernice on March 1. Some time later Marilyn paid Bernice an equivalent payment of $1528.01, allowing for a time value of money of 4.5% compounded monthly. When did Marilyn make the payment?

6. What is the remaining time until the maturity date of a $10,000 strip bond if it is purchased for $4011.33 to yield 6.4% compounded semiannually until maturity?

7. A number of years ago, your client invested $6000 at a rate of return of 9% compounded annually. If the investment is currently worth $10,968.25, for how long has she held the investment?

8. A few years ago Avtar invested $6000 in a compound interest GIC that earned 4.5% compounded semiannually. He recently received the maturity value of $7168.99. What was the term of the GIC?

9. Rounded to the nearest month, how long will it take a town's population to:
   a. Grow from 32,500 to 40,000 if the annual growth rate is 3%?
   b. Shrink from 40,000 to 32,500 if the annual rate of decline is 3%?

10. Rounded to the nearest month, how long will it take an investment to double if it earns:
   a. 8.4% compounded annually?
   b. 10.5% compounded semiannually?

11. Rounded to the nearest month, how long will it take an investment to triple if it earns:
   a. 9% compounded annually?
   b. 8% compounded quarterly?

12. Rounded to the nearest quarter year, how long will it take an investment to quadruple if it earns:
   a. 8% compounded annually?
   b. 9% compounded semiannually?

13. Rounded to the nearest month, how long before a scheduled payment of $10,000 would a payment of $5000 be an economically equivalent alternative? Assume money is worth 5% compounded annually.

14. How long before a future payment of $1000 would a payment of just $100 (only 10% of the nominal amount of the future payment) be an economically equivalent alternative? Round your answer to the nearest month. Assume money can earn 4.8% compounded semiannually.

15. Your client wants to invest a $250,000 inheritance and grow it to $325,000. Rounded to the nearest month, how long will this take if the investment earns 7% compounded annually?

16. Your client invests $10,000 today at a rate of return of 7.7% compounded quarterly. Rounded to the nearest month, how long will it take the investment to grow to $22,000?

INTERMEDIATE PROBLEMS

17. Rounded to the nearest month, how long will it take money to lose half of its purchasing power if the annual rate of inflation is:
    a. 2.5%?   **b.** 3.5%?

18. Rounded to the nearest month, how long will it take money to lose 25% of its purchasing power if the annual rate of inflation is:
    a. 2%?   **b.** 4%?

19. When discounted to yield 10.5% compounded monthly, a $2600 three-year promissory note bearing interest at 12.25% compounded annually was priced at $3283.57. How many months after the issue date did the discounting take place?

20. The proceeds from the sale of a $4500 five-year promissory note bearing interest at 9% compounded quarterly were $6055.62. How many months before its maturity date was the note sold if it was discounted to yield 10.5% compounded monthly?

21. A $4000 loan at 7.5% compounded monthly was settled by a single payment of $5000 including accrued interest. Rounded to the nearest day, how long after the initial loan was the $5000 payment made? For the purpose of determining the number of days in a partial month, assume that a full month has 30 days.

22. If money is worth 8% compounded quarterly, how long (to the nearest day) before a scheduled payment of $6000 will $5000 be an equivalent payment? For the purpose of determining the number of days in a partial calendar quarter, assume that a full quarter has 91 days.

23. Wilf paid $557.05 for a $1000 face value strip bond. At this price the investment will yield a return of 5.22% compounded semiannually. How long (to the nearest day) before its maturity date did Wilf purchase the bond? Assume that each half-year has exactly 182 days.

24. A $5000 face value strip bond may be purchased today for $1073.36 yielding the purchaser 7.27% compounded semiannually. How much time (to the nearest day) remains until the maturity date? Assume that each half-year has exactly 182 days.

25. $7500 was borrowed for a four-year term at 9% compounded quarterly. The terms of the loan allow prepayment of the loan based on discounting the loan's maturity value at 7% compounded quarterly. How long (to the nearest day) before the maturity date was the loan prepaid if the payout amount was $9380.24 including accrued interest? For the purpose of determining the number of days in a partial calendar quarter, assume that a full quarter has 91 days.

10.3 Effective Interest Rate

L02 The future value of $100 invested for one year at 10% compounded semiannually is $110.25. The future value of $100 invested for one year at 10.25% compounded annually is also $110.25. Therefore, an interest rate of 10% compounded semiannually has the *same effect* as a rate of 10.25% compounded annually. The **effective interest rate**, f, is defined as the *annually* compounded rate[2] that produces the *same* future value after one year as the given nominal rate. In the present example, 10% compounded semiannually has an effective rate[3] of 10.25%.

 TIP

Intuitive Approach for Calculating *f*

Note in the preceding example that the effective interest rate (10.25%) is numerically equal to the actual amount of interest ($10.25) that $100 will earn in one year at the given nominal rate. This is a general result for all nominal interest rates. We can use this idea for our financial calculator method for determining *f*. That is, we can calculate the future value of $100 after one year at the given nominal rate. Then we can just inspect the future value to see the amount of interest earned (and thereby identify the value of *f*).

We can readily derive a formula for *f*. Suppose you invest $100 for one year at the effective rate *f* (compounded annually) and another $100 for one year at the nominal rate $j = mi$. Their future values are calculated in parallel columns below.

The first $100 will undergo just one compounding of the effective rate *f*.	The second $100 will undergo *m* compoundings of the periodic rate *i*.
$FV = PV(1 + i)^n$	$FV = PV(1 + i)^n$
$= \$100(1 + f)^1$	$= \$100(1 + i)^m$

For *f* to be equivalent to the nominal rate *j*, these future values must be equal. That is,

$$\$100(1 + f) = \$100(1 + i)^m$$
$$1 + f = (1 + i)^m$$

EFFECTIVE INTEREST RATE

$$f = (1 + i)^m - 1 \qquad \textbf{(10-3)}$$

 TIP

Comparing Nominal Rates of Interest

To compare two nominal rates of interest, convert each to its effective interest rate. Then you can directly compare the effective rates, and thereby rank the given nominal rates.

---

[2] There is a natural preference in business for discussing interest rates on the basis of annual compounding. This is because an *annually* compounded rate of return represents the *actual* percentage increase in a year. For example, at a return of 9% compounded annually, you can immediately say that $100 will grow by 9% ($9) in the next year. But at a return of 9% compounded monthly, you cannot say how much $100 will grow in a year without a short calculation. In the second case, the *actual* percentage increase will be more than 9%.

[3] When an effective interest rate is quoted or calculated, the compounding frequency does not need to be specified. Everyone understands from the definition of effective interest rate that "effective" implies "annual compounding."

EXAMPLE 10.3A

CONVERTING A NOMINAL INTEREST RATE TO AN EFFECTIVE INTEREST RATE

What is the effective rate of interest corresponding to 10.5% compounded monthly?

SOLUTION

Given: $j = 10.5\%$ and $m = 12$

For the financial calculator solution, we will use the intuitive approach described in the first TIP above.

Then $i = \frac{j}{m} = \frac{10.5\%}{12} = 0.875\%$ per month and

$$
\left.\begin{array}{l}
f = (1 + i)^m - 1 \\
 = (1.00875)^{12} - 1 \\
 = 1.11020 - 1 \\
 = 0.11020 \\
 = 11.02\%
\end{array}\right\}
$$

10.5	I/Y
P/Y 12	ENTER
\multicolumn{2}{r}{(making $C/Y = P/Y = 12$)}
12	N
100 +/−	PV
0	PMT
CPT	FV
\multicolumn{2}{r}{*Ans:* 111.020}

The effective interest rate is 11.02% (compounded annually).

EXAMPLE 10.3B

COMPARING ALTERNATIVE NOMINAL INTEREST RATES

Which is the most attractive of the following interest rates offered on five-year GICs?

a. 5.70% compounded annually   **b.** 5.68% compounded semiannually

c. 5.66% compounded quarterly   **d.** 5.63% compounded monthly

SOLUTION

The preferred rate is the one having the highest effective rate. The algebraic calculations of the effective rates are presented in the table below.

	j	m	i	$f = (1 + i)^m - 1$
a.	5.70%	1	0.057	$f = j$ when $m = 1$; $f = 5.700\%$
b.	5.68%	2	0.0284	$f = (1.0284)^2 - 1 = 0.05761 = 5.761\%$
c.	5.66%	4	0.01415	$f = (1.01415)^4 - 1 = 0.05781 = 5.781\%$
d.	5.63%	12	0.004692	$f = (1.004692)^{12} - 1 = 0.05775 = 5.778\%$

In **Appendix 10A**, we describe and demonstrate the use of the Texas Instruments BA II PLUS's Interest Conversion Worksheet (ICONV). Let us now use this worksheet to calculate the effective interest rates in parts (b), (c), and (d).

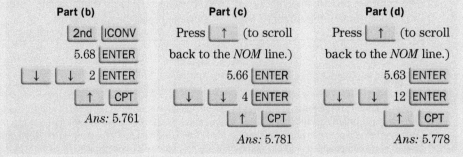

The most attractive rate is 5.66% compounded quarterly since it has the highest effective rate. For the alternative rates in this example, the ranking in terms of effective rates is in the reverse order of the nominal rates.

POINT OF INTEREST

Not in Your Best Interest

The Canada Revenue Agency (CRA) charges interest on overdue income tax, Canada Pension Plan contributions, and Employment Insurance premiums. The prescribed rate is adjusted by the CRA every three months based on changes in the Bank of Canada rate. For the first quarter of 2019, the prescribed nominal rate was 6%.

You now know that the compounding frequency matters. The more frequently a given nominal rate is compounded, the higher the effective rate of interest. Considering who is setting the rate in this case, you would probably guess that the prescribed rate is compounded monthly (the highest compounding frequency normally encountered in commerce). Not so! The CRA charges interest on overdue taxes at a prescribed rate that is compounded daily!

QUESTIONS

1. Calculate the effective rate of interest corresponding to 6% compounded daily.
2. How much more interest would accrue on a $1000 debt in a year at 6% compounded daily than at 6% compounded monthly?

EXAMPLE 10.3C

FINDING THE EFFECTIVE RATE GIVEN THE PRINCIPAL AND MATURITY VALUE

Calculate the effective rate of interest if $100 grew to $150 in $3\frac{1}{2}$ years with quarterly compounding.

SOLUTION

The problem can be solved by first finding the quarterly compounded nominal rate that produces the given maturity value. Then the corresponding effective rate may be calculated. But this two-step solution is unnecessarily long.

The essential question (which may be answered in one step) is: At what annually compounded rate will $100 grow to $150 after $3\frac{1}{2}$ years?

With $PV = \$100$, $FV = \$150$, $m = 1$, and $n = 3.5$, Formula (10-1) gives

$$
\left.
\begin{aligned}
i &= \left(\frac{FV}{PV}\right)^{1/n} - 1 \\
&= \left(\frac{\$150}{\$100}\right)^{1/3.5} - 1 \\
&= 1.5^{0.28571} - 1 \\
&= 0.12282
\end{aligned}
\right\}
$$

P/Y 1 ENTER	
(making $C/Y = P/Y = 1$)	
3.5 N	
100 +/− PV	
0 PMT	
150 FV	
CPT I/Y	

Ans: 12.28

Since $100 will grow to $150 in $3\frac{1}{2}$ years at 12.28% compounded annually, the effective interest rate is 12.28%.

 TIP

Clarification of Terminology

Be clear on the distinction between the descriptions "compounded semiannually" and "per half-year." The former refers to the compounding *frequency*. The latter refers to the compounding *period*. For example, if you hear or read "6% compounded semiannually," you are being given the *nominal rate* or the value for "*j*." Then $i = j/m = 6\%/2 = 3\%$ (per half-year). On the other hand, if an interest rate is described as "6% per half-year," you are being given the *periodic rate* or the value for "*i*" and the period to which it applies. Then $j = mi = 2i = 12\%$ compounded semiannually.

EXAMPLE 10.3D

CALCULATING THE EFFECTIVE INTEREST RATE ON A CREDIT CARD

A department store credit card quotes a rate of 1.75% per month on the unpaid balance. Calculate the effective rate of interest being charged.

SOLUTION

Since accrued interest is paid or converted to principal each month, we have monthly compounding with $i = 1.75\%$ per month, $m = 12$, and $j = mi = 12(1.75\%) = 21\%$ compounded monthly.

Therefore,

$$
\begin{aligned}
f &= (1 + i)^m - 1 \\
&= (1.0175)^{12} - 1 \\
&= 0.23144 \\
&= 23.14\%
\end{aligned}
$$

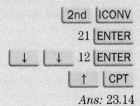

2nd |ICONV

21 ENTER

↓ ↓ 12 ENTER

↑ CPT

Ans: 23.14

The effective rate on the credit card is 23.14%.

EXAMPLE 10.3E

CONVERTING AN EFFECTIVE INTEREST RATE TO A NOMINAL INTEREST RATE

What monthly compounded (nominal) rate of interest has an effective rate of 10%?

SOLUTION

Given: $f = 10\%$ $m = 12$

Substitute these values into Formula (10-3) and solve for i.

$$
\begin{aligned}
f &= (1 + i)^m - 1 \\
0.10 &= (1 + i)^{12} - 1 \\
1.10 &= (1 + i)^{12}
\end{aligned}
$$

Now use the rule that

$$\text{If } x^m = a, \text{ then } x = a^{1/m}$$

Therefore,

$$
\begin{aligned}
1.1^{1/12} &= 1 + i \\
1 + i &= 1.1^{0.08\overline{3}} \\
i &= 1.007974 - 1 \\
&= 0.007974 \\
&= 0.7974\%
\end{aligned}
$$

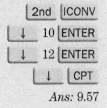

2nd |ICONV

↓ 10 ENTER

↓ 12 ENTER

↓ CPT

Ans: 9.57

Then $j = mi = 12(0.7974\%) = 9.57\%$ compounded monthly.

EXAMPLE 10.3F

CONVERTING AN INTEREST RATE FROM NOMINAL TO EFFECTIVE AND BACK TO NOMINAL

The department store mentioned in **Example 10.3D** has been charging 1.75% per month on its credit card. In response to lower prevailing interest rates, the Board of Directors has agreed to reduce the card's effective interest rate by 4%. To the nearest 0.01%, what will be the new periodic rate (per month)?

SOLUTION

To solve this problem, we must first calculate the effective rate corresponding to $i = 1.75\%$ per month. Then we must calculate the new monthly compounded rate whose effective rate is 4% lower.

Step 1: See the solution to **Example 10.3D** for this calculation. We obtained $f = 23.14\%$.

Step 2: The new effective rate must be 23.14% − 4% = 19.14%.

Substitute $f = 19.14\%$ and $m = 12$ into Formula (10-3).

$$\begin{aligned}
f &= (1 + i)^m - 1 \\
0.1914 &= (1 + i)^{12} - 1 \\
1.1914 &= (1 + i)^{12} \\
1 + i &= 1.1914^{1/12} \\
i &= 1.1914^{0.08\overline{3}} - 1 \\
&= 1.01470 - 1 \\
&= 0.01470 \\
&= 1.47\%
\end{aligned}$$

2nd │ICONV
↓   19.14 │ENTER
↓   12 │ENTER
↓   │CPT
Ans: 17.641

The new periodic rate will be

$$i = \frac{j}{m} = \frac{17.641\%}{12} = 1.47\%$$

The new periodic interest rate on the credit card will be 1.47% per month.

CONCEPT QUESTIONS

1. What is meant by the effective rate of interest?
2. Is the effective rate of interest ever numerically smaller than the nominal interest rate? Explain.
3. Is the effective rate of interest ever equal to the nominal interest rate? Explain.
4. A semiannually compounded nominal rate and a monthly compounded nominal rate have the same effective rate. Which has the larger nominal rate? Explain.

EXERCISE 10.3

Answers to the odd-numbered problems are at the end of the book.

Spreadsheet template: A partially completed Excel template for converting interest rates is provided on Connect. Go to the Student Edition of Connect and find "Interest Rate Conversion" under the Student Resources for Chapter 10. The completed template may be used throughout Exercise 10.3.

Calculate interest rates and growth rates accurate to the nearest 0.01%.

BASIC PROBLEMS

1. What is the effective interest rate corresponding to a nominal annual rate of:
   a. 6% compounded semiannually?
   b. 6% compounded quarterly?
   c. 6% compounded monthly?

2. What is the effective interest rate corresponding to a nominal annual rate of:
   a. 7.5% compounded semiannually?
   b. 7.5% compounded quarterly?
   c. 7.5% compounded monthly?

3. What is the effective interest rate corresponding to a nominal annual rate of:
   a. 9% compounded semiannually?
   b. 9% compounded quarterly?
   c. 9% compounded monthly?

4. What is the effective interest rate corresponding to a nominal annual rate of:
   a. 4% compounded monthly?
   b. 8% compounded monthly?
   c. 12% compounded monthly?

5. To have an effective rate of 5%, what must be the corresponding nominal interest rate with:
   a. Annual compounding?
   b. Semiannual compounding?
   c. Quarterly compounding?
   d. Monthly compounding?

6. For the effective rate to be 7%, what must be the corresponding nominal interest rate with:
   a. Annual compounding?
   b. Semiannual compounding?
   c. Quarterly compounding?
   d. Monthly compounding?

7. Which of the following nominal interest rates has the highest effective rate: 12% compounded annually, 11.9% compounded semiannually, 11.8% compounded quarterly, or 11.7% compounded monthly?

8. Which interest rate would you prefer to earn on a three-year GIC: 6% compounded monthly, 6.1% compounded quarterly, 6.2% compounded semiannually, or 6.3% compounded annually?

9. Which interest rate would you prefer to pay on a loan: 9% compounded monthly, 9.1% compounded quarterly, 9.2% compounded semiannually, or 9.3% compounded annually?

10. What is the effective rate of interest on a credit card that calculates interest at the rate of 1.8% per month?

11. If an invoice indicates that interest at the rate of 0.62% per month will be charged on overdue amounts, what effective rate of interest will be charged?

12. If the nominal rate of interest paid on a savings account is 2% compounded monthly, what is the effective rate of interest?

13. A company reports that its sales have grown 3% per quarter for the last eight fiscal quarters. What annual growth rate has the company been experiencing for the last two years?

14. If a $5000 investment grew to $6450 in 30 months of monthly compounding, what effective rate of return was the investment earning?

15. After 27 months of quarterly compounding, a $3000 debt had grown to $3810. What effective rate of interest was being charged on the debt?

16. Lisa is offered a loan from a bank at 7.2% compounded monthly. A credit union offers similar terms, but at a rate of 7.4% compounded semiannually. Which loan should she accept? Present calculations that support your answer.

17. Craig can buy a three-year compound interest GIC paying 4.6% compounded semiannually or 4.5% compounded monthly. Which option should he choose? Present calculations that support your answer.

18. Camille can obtain a residential mortgage loan from a bank at 6.5% compounded semiannually, or from an independent mortgage broker at 6.4% compounded monthly. Which source should she pick if other terms and conditions of the loan are the same? Present calculations that support your answer.

19. ABC Ltd. reports that its sales are growing at the rate of 1.3% per month. DEF Inc. reports sales increasing by 4% each quarter. What is each company's effective annual rate of sales growth?

20. Columbia Trust wants its annually, semiannually, and monthly compounded five-year GICs all to have an effective interest rate of 5.75%. What nominal annual rates should it quote for the three compounding options?

21. Belleville Credit Union has established interest rates on its three-year GICs so that the effective rate of interest is 7% on all three compounding options. What are the monthly, semiannually, and annually compounded rates?

INTERMEDIATE PROBLEMS

22. A department store chain currently charges 18% compounded monthly on its credit card. To what amount should it set the monthly compounded annual rate if it wants to add 2% to the effective interest rate?

23. An oil company wants to drop the effective rate of interest on its credit card by 3%. If it currently charges a periodic rate of 1.7% per month, at what amount should it set the periodic rate?

10.4 | Equivalent Interest Rates

The main purpose of this section is to prepare you for a routine calculation you will carry out for a broad category of annuities in **Chapters 11, 12, 13**, and **14**. The concept behind the calculation is developed here because it is an extension of ideas from **Section 10.3**.

L03 **Equivalent interest rates** are interest rates that produce the *same* future value after one year. For example, 8% compounded quarterly and 8.08% compounded semiannually are equivalent *nominal* interest rates. If you calculate the future value of $100 invested at either rate for one year, you will obtain $108.24. You can see that equivalent interest rates have *different numerical values* but produce the *same effect*.

If *nominal* rates are equivalent, so also are their respective *periodic* rates. From the preceding example, we can conclude that:

$$i = \frac{8\%}{4} = 2\% \text{ per quarter is equivalent to } i = \frac{8.08\%}{2} = 4.04\% \text{ per half-year}$$

They will both produce the same future value when compounded over a one-year term.

We want to be able to answer questions such as:

"What periodic rate per half-year is equivalent to 2.5% per quarter?"

To answer this and similar questions, we will derive a formula that answers the general question:

"What i_2 with a specified m_2 is equivalent to a given i_1 with a given m_1?"

For equivalence, $100 invested at each rate for one year must have the same future value. The two investments are shown in the following diagrams. Both future values are obtained using $FV = PV(1 + i)^n$.

0   1   years   0   1   years

$100 $\xrightarrow{\;n=m_1,\, i=i_1\;}$ $\$100(1+i_1)^{m_1}$ $100 $\xrightarrow{\;n=m_2,\, i=i_2\;}$ $\$100(1+i_2)^{m_2}$

We want to solve for the value of i_2 that makes the two future values equal. That is, solve for i_2 in

$$\$100(1+i_2)^{m_2} = \$100(1+i_1)^{m_1}$$
$$(1+i_2)^{m_2} = (1+i_1)^{m_1}$$

Divide both exponents by m_2, giving

$$1+i_2 = (1+i_1)^{m_1/m_2}$$

Hence,

EQUIVALENT PERIODIC RATE

$$i_2 = (1+i_1)^{m_1/m_2} - 1 \qquad\qquad (10\text{-}4)$$

To answer the question: "What periodic rate per half-year is equivalent to 2.5% per quarter?" substitute $m_2 = 2$, $i_1 = 2.5\% = 0.025$, and $m_1 = 4$ into Formula (10-4).

$$i_2 = (1+i_1)^{m_1/m_2} - 1 = (1.025)^{4/2} - 1 = 1.025^2 - 1 = 0.050625 = 5.0625\% \text{ per half-year}$$

EXAMPLE 10.4A

CALCULATION OF THREE EQUIVALENT INTEREST RATES

For a given interest rate of 10% compounded quarterly, what is the equivalent nominal rate of interest with:

a. Annual compounding?   **b.** Semiannual compounding?   **c.** Monthly compounding?

SOLUTION

The given rate is $j_1 = 10\%$ with $m_1 = 4$. Therefore, $i_1 = 2.5\%$ per quarter.

In the following columns, we substitute the given values for m_1, m_2, and i_1 into Formula (10-4).

a. $m_2 = 1$ **b.** $m_2 = 2$ **c.** $m_2 = 12$

$i_2 = (1.025)^{4/1} - 1$ $i_2 = (1.025)^{4/2} - 1$ $i_2 = (1.025)^{4/12} - 1$
$= 0.10381$ $= 0.050625$ $= 0.0082648$
$= 10.381\% \text{ per year}$ $= 5.0625\% \text{ per half-year}$ $= 0.82648\% \text{ per month}$

$j_2 = m_2 \times i_2$ $j_2 = m_2 \times i_2$ $j_2 = m_2 \times i_2$
$= 1 \times 10.381\%$ $= 2 \times 5.0625\%$ $= 12 \times 0.82648\%$
$= 10.381\% \text{ compounded}$ $= 10.125\% \text{ compounded}$ $= 9.918\% \text{ compounded}$
         annually   semiannually   monthly

To use the ICONV worksheet, first compute the effective rate corresponding to the given nominal interest rate. Then compute the requested nominal rates that are equivalent to this effective rate.

Part (a)

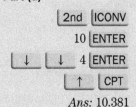

2nd ICONV
10 ENTER
↓ ↓ 4 ENTER
↑ CPT
    Ans: 10.381

Part (b)

Press ↓ (to scroll
down to the *C/Y* line.)
2 ENTER
↑ ↑ CPT
    Ans: 10.125

Part (c)

Press ↓ ↓
(to scroll down to the
C/Y line.)
12 ENTER
↑ ↑ CPT
    Ans: 9.918

a. $j = f = 10.381\%$ **b.** $j = 10.125\%$ **c.** $j = 9.918\%$
   compounded annually   compounded semiannually   compounded monthly

APP **4** THAT

Interest rates are a key factor when making investment and borrowing decisions. Search the App Store on your tablet, smartphone, or smart watch using the key words **INTEREST RATES**.

   You will find many free and paid apps that provide current rates for loans and investments, apps that will calculate compound interest rates, and still others that will convert interest rates between annual, semiannual, monthly, quarterly, weekly, and even daily compounding frequencies.

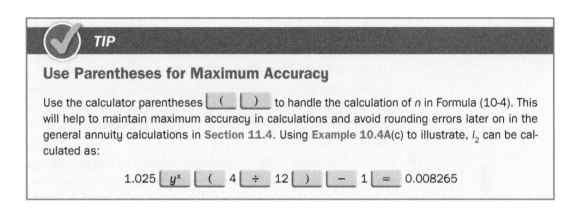

Use Parentheses for Maximum Accuracy

Use the calculator parentheses $(\quad)$ to handle the calculation of n in Formula (10-4). This will help to maintain maximum accuracy in calculations and avoid rounding errors later on in the general annuity calculations in **Section 11.4**. Using **Example 10.4A**(c) to illustrate, i_2 can be calculated as:

$$1.025 \boxed{y^x} \boxed{(} \ 4 \ \boxed{\div} \ 12 \ \boxed{)} \ \boxed{-} \ 1 \ \boxed{=} \ 0.008265$$

EXERCISE 10.4

Answers to the odd-numbered problems are at the end of the book.

BASIC PROBLEMS

Calculate interest rates accurate to the nearest 0.01%.

1. To be equivalent to 10% compounded annually, what must be the nominal rate with:
   a. Semiannual compounding?   **b.** Quarterly compounding?
   c. Monthly compounding?

2. To be equivalent to 10% compounded semiannually, what must be the nominal rate with:
   a. Annual compounding?   **b.** Quarterly compounding?
   c. Monthly compounding?

3. To be equivalent to 10% compounded quarterly, what must be the nominal rate with:
   a. Annual compounding?   **b.** Semiannual compounding?
   c. Monthly compounding?

4. To be equivalent to 10% compounded monthly, what must be the nominal rate with:
   a. Annual compounding?   **b.** Semiannual compounding?
   c. Quarterly compounding?

5. What annually compounded interest rate is equivalent to 6% compounded:
   a. Semiannually?   **b.** Quarterly?   **c.** Monthly?

6. What semiannually compounded rate is equivalent to 6% compounded:
   a. Annually?   **b.** Quarterly?   **c.** Monthly?

7. What quarterly compounded rate is equivalent to 6% compounded:
   a. Annually?   **b.** Semiannually?   **c.** Monthly?

8. What monthly compounded interest rate is equivalent to 6% compounded:
   a. Annually?   **b.** Semiannually?   **c.** Quarterly?

9. What semiannually compounded rate is equivalent to 4% compounded monthly?

10. What quarterly compounded rate is equivalent to 7.5% compounded semiannually?

11. What monthly compounded rate is equivalent to 6% compounded quarterly?

12. What semiannually compounded rate is equivalent to 8.5% compounded quarterly?

13. What quarterly compounded rate is equivalent to 10.5% compounded monthly?

14. For a three-year GIC investment, what nominal rate compounded monthly would put you in the same financial position as 5.5% compounded semiannually?

15. A trust company pays 2.5% compounded semiannually on its three-year GIC. For you to prefer an annually compounded GIC of the same maturity, what value must its nominal interest rate exceed?

16. You are offered a loan at a rate of 9% compounded monthly. Below what nominal rate of interest would you choose semiannual compounding instead?

17. Banks usually quote residential mortgage interest rates on the basis of semiannual compounding. An independent mortgage broker is quoting rates with monthly compounding. What rate would the broker have to give to match 3.45% compounded semiannually available from a bank?

18. A credit union pays 5.25% compounded annually on five-year compound interest GICs. It wants to set the rates on its semiannually and monthly compounded GICs of the same maturity so that investors will earn the same total interest. What should the rates be on the GICs with the higher compounding frequencies?

19. A bank offers a rate of 2.0% compounded semiannually on its four-year GIC. What monthly compounded rate should the bank offer on four-year GICs to make investors indifferent between the alternatives?

20. A life insurance company pays investors 5% compounded annually on its five-year GICs. For you to be indifferent as to which compounding option you choose, what would the nominal rates have to be on GICs with:
    a. Semiannual compounding?
    b. Quarterly compounding?
    c. Monthly compounding?

21. In your search for the best rate on a new-car loan, you note that various lenders quote rates with differing compounding frequencies. Your car dealer offers financing at 7.5% compounded monthly. For you to be indifferent as to which lending rate to choose, what would the nominal rate be on a loan from another lender with interest compounded
    a. Annually?
    b. Semiannually?
    c. Quarterly?

22. After completing your 2018 income tax return, you discover that you owe income tax. You can either pay the late payment penalty at 6% compounded daily for one year or borrow the money you need to pay your taxes. Below what semiannually compounded rate will the loan cost you less in interest?

23. Ted and Laurie need to borrow money to pay their annual golf membership dues or they will have to pay interest on the late dues at 9% compounded weekly. If they borrow money to pay the dues with a one-year payback period, at what quarterly compounded rate of interest will the loan cost them less in interest?

KEY TERMS

Effective interest rate   Equivalent interest rates   Rule of 72

SUMMARY OF NOTATION AND KEY FORMULAS

FORMULA (10-1) $i = \sqrt[n]{\dfrac{FV}{PV}} - 1 = \left(\dfrac{FV}{PV}\right)^{1/n} - 1$ Finding the periodic interest rate (or periodic rate of return)

FORMULA (10-2) $n = \dfrac{\ln\left(\dfrac{FV}{PV}\right)}{\ln(1 + i)}$ Finding the number of compounding periods

FORMULA (10-3) $f = (1 + i)^m - 1$ Finding the effective rate of interest (or effective rate of return)

FORMULA (10-4) $i_2 = (1 + i_1)^{m_1/m_2} - 1$ Finding an equivalent periodic interest rate

REVIEW PROBLEMS

Answers to the odd-numbered review problems are at the end of the book.

Calculate percentages accurate to the nearest 0.01%.

> ### BASIC PROBLEMS

1. **LO1** The home the Bensons purchased 13 years ago for $85,000 is now appraised at $215,000. What has been the annual rate of appreciation of the value of their home during the 13-year period?

2. **LO1** If the Consumer Price Index rose from 109.6 to 133.8 over an $8\frac{1}{2}$-year period, what was the equivalent compound annual inflation rate during the period?

3. **LO2** Which of the following rates would you prefer for a loan: 7.6% compounded quarterly, 7.5% compounded monthly, or 7.7% compounded semiannually?

4. **LO1** A $10,000 investment grew to $12,000 after 39 months of semiannual compounding. What effective rate of return did the investment earn?

5. **LO1** In 1859, 24 wild rabbits were released at Barwon Park in southern Victoria, Australia. By 1926, it was estimated that the rabbit population had grown to 400 million times this number. What is the effective compounded growth rate in the rabbit population?

6. **LO1** Maxine found an old pay statement from nine years ago. Her hourly wage at the time was $13.50 versus her current wage of $20.80 per hour. At what equivalent (compound) annual rate has her wage grown over the period?

7. **LO1** If a company's annual sales grew from $165,000 to $485,000 in a period of eight years, what has been the compound annual rate of growth of sales during the period?

8. **LO3** What monthly compounded nominal rate would put you in the same financial position as 5.5% compounded semiannually?

9. **LO3** You are offered a loan at a rate of 10.5% compounded monthly. Below what figure must a semiannually compounded nominal rate be to make it more attractive?

10. **LO3** A bank offers a rate of 5.3% compounded semiannually on its four-year GICs. What monthly and annually compounded rates should it quote in order to have the same effective interest rate at all three nominal rates?

11. **LO2** If an invoice indicates that interest at the rate of 1.2% per month will be charged on overdue amounts, what effective rate of interest will be charged?

12. **LO2** If the nominal rate of interest paid on a savings account is 3% compounded monthly, what is the effective rate of interest paid?

13. **LO2** If an interest rate of 6.9% compounded semiannually is charged on a car loan, what effective rate of interest should be disclosed to the borrower?

14. **LO1** If a $15,000 investment grew to $21,805 in $4\frac{1}{2}$ years of quarterly compounding, what effective rate of return was the investment earning?

15. **LO2** Camille can obtain a residential mortgage loan from a bank at 8.75% compounded semiannually or from an independent mortgage broker at 8.6% compounded monthly. Which source should she pick if other terms and conditions of the loan are the same? Present calculations that support your answer.

16. **LO3** A trust company pays 5.375% compounded annually on its five-year GICs. What semi-annually compounded interest rate would produce the same maturity value?

17. **LO3** Maritime Investments pays 4.625% compounded semiannually on its three-year GICs. What quarterly compounded rate of interest will produce the same maturity value?

18. **LO1** To the nearest month, how long will it take an investment to increase in value by 200% if it earns 7.5% compounded semiannually?

INTERMEDIATE PROBLEMS

19. **LO1** Rounded to the nearest month, how long will it take money to lose one-third of its purchasing power if the annual inflation rate is 3%?

20. **LO1** An investor paid $4271.17 to purchase a $10,000 face value strip bond for her RRSP. At this price the investment will provide a return of 6.47% compounded semiannually. How long (to the nearest day) after the date of purchase will the bond mature? Assume that each half-year is exactly 182 days long.

21. **LO1** An investor's portfolio increased in value by 53% over a five-year period while the Consumer Price Index rose from 121.6 to 135.3. What was the annually compounded real rate of return on the portfolio for the five years?

22. **LO1** Terry was supposed to pay $800 to Becky on March 1. At a later date, Terry paid Becky an equivalent payment in the amount of $895.67. If they provided for a time value of money of 8% compounded monthly, on what date did Terry make the payment?

23. **LO1** What is the time remaining until the maturity date of a $50,000 strip bond if it has just been purchased for $20,822.89 to yield 5.38% compounded semiannually until maturity?

24. **LO1** When discounted to yield 9.5% compounded quarterly, a $4500 four-year promissory note bearing interest at 11.5% compounded semiannually was priced at $5697.84. How long after the issue date did the discounting take place?

25. **LO1** The population of a mining town declined from 17,500 to 14,500 in a five-year period. If the population continues to decrease at the same compound annual rate, how long, to the nearest month, will it take for the population to drop by another 3000?

26. **LO1** To the nearest day, how long will it take a $20,000 investment to grow to $22,000 (including accrued interest) if it earns 7% compounded quarterly? Assume that a quarter-year has 91 days.

27. **L01** A company's sales dropped 10% per year for five years.
    a. What annual rate of sales growth for the subsequent five years would return the sales to the original level?
    b. To the nearest month, how long would it take for sales to return to the original level if they increased at 10% per year?

28. **L01** An investor's portfolio increased in value from $35,645 to $54,230 over a six-year period. At the same time, the Consumer Price Index rose by 26.5%. What was the portfolio's annually compounded real rate of return?

*APPENDIX 10A: THE TEXAS INSTRUMENTS BA II PLUS INTEREST CONVERSION WORKSHEET

Notice the letters **ICONV** above the [2] key. This means that the Interest Conversion Worksheet is the second function of the [2] key. You can access the worksheet by pressing [2nd] [2] in sequence. Hereafter, we will represent these keystrokes as [2nd] [ICONV]. The calculator's display then shows:

NOM =	n.nn

where the n's represent numerical digits. (Your display may show more or fewer digits.)

You should think of a worksheet as a single column of items that you can view one at a time in the display. The Interest Conversion Worksheet's column consists of the following three items:

NOM =	n.nn
EFF =	n.nn
C/Y =	n

The solid line around the first item indicates that the calculator's display currently provides a "window" to the first item in the column. You can use the scroll keys [↓] and [↑] to move down or up the list. The three worksheet symbols are defined as follows:

$$NOM = \text{Nominal annual interest rate, } j$$
$$EFF = \text{Effective interest rate, } f$$
$$C/Y = \text{Number of compoundings per year, } m$$

The Interest Conversion Worksheet allows you to enter values for any two of these three variables and then compute the value of the remaining third variable. Close the worksheet by pressing [2nd] [QUIT]. (By the [QUIT] key, we mean the key showing **QUIT** as its second function.)

Let us use the worksheet to answer **Example 10.3A**, which asks us to calculate the effective interest rate corresponding to 10.5% compounded monthly.

[2nd] [ICONV]	⇒ Open the Interest Conversion Worksheet.
10.5 [ENTER]	⇒ Key in and save the value for *NOM*.
[↓] [↓] 12 [ENTER]	⇒ Scroll down to *C/Y*. Key in and save its value.
[↑] [CPT]	⇒ Scroll back up to *EFF*. Compute its value.

The effective interest rate appearing in the display is 11.02%.

*APPENDIX 10B: LOGARITHMS

A strictly algebraic approach to the solution of certain compound interest problems involves the use of logarithms. However, if the financial functions of a calculator are employed, logarithms are not needed. Financial calculators all have a function labelled **ln** or **lnx**. This denotes the "natural logarithm" function where the base is the natural number e.

EXAMPLE 10B.A

CALCULATING NATURAL LOGARITHMS

a. $\ln 1 = 0$

b. $\ln 10 = 2.30259$

c. $\ln 1.1 = 0.09531$

d. $\ln 100 = 4.60517$

e. $\ln(1 + 0.01) = \ln 1.01 = 0.009950$

f. $\ln(1 + 0.06) = \ln 1.06 = 0.05827$

g. $\ln\left(\dfrac{\$5000}{\$2000}\right) = \ln 2.5 = 0.91629$

h. $\ln\left(\dfrac{\$3491.67}{\$1820.19}\right) = \ln 1.91830 = 0.65144$

Rules of Logarithms

The Rules of Logarithms show how the logarithm of a product, quotient, or power may be expanded in terms of the logarithms of the individual factors. Their derivation is straightforward and can be found in any algebra text that introduces logarithms.

Rules of Logarithms:
1. The Product Rule: $\ln(ab) = \ln a + \ln b$
2. The Quotient Rule: $\ln(a/b) = \ln a - \ln b$
3. The Power Rule: $\ln(a^k) = k(\ln a)$

EXAMPLE 10B.B

DERIVATION OF FORMULA (10-2)

Solve $FV = PV(1 + i)^n$ for n.

SOLUTION

First divide both sides of the equation by PV, then interchange the two sides, giving

$$(1 + i)^n = \frac{FV}{PV}$$

Next take logarithms of both sides. Use the Power Rule to expand $\ln(1 + i)^n$. We obtain

$$n \times \ln(1 + i) = \ln\left(\frac{FV}{PV}\right)$$

Finally, divide both sides by $\ln(1 + i)$ to yield

$$n = \frac{\ln\left(\dfrac{FV}{PV}\right)}{\ln(1 + i)}$$

Chapter 11

Ordinary Annuities: Future Value and Present Value

CHAPTER OUTLINE

11.1 Terminology

11.2 Future Value of an Ordinary Simple Annuity

11.3 Present Value of an Ordinary Simple Annuity

11.4 Future Value and Present Value of Ordinary General Annuities

LEARNING OBJECTIVES

After completing this chapter, you will be able to:

LO1 Define and distinguish between ordinary simple annuities and ordinary general annuities

LO2 Calculate the future value and present value of both ordinary simple annuities and ordinary general annuities

LO3 Calculate the fair market value of a cash flow stream that includes an annuity

LO4 Calculate the principal balance owed on a loan immediately after any payment

LO5 Calculate the interest rate per payment interval in a general annuity

A LARGE NUMBER OF PERSONAL and business transactions involve an annuity—a series of equal regular payments. Examples are loan payments, wages, pensions, rent, installment savings plans, insurance premiums, mortgage payments, leases, bond interest, and preferred share dividends. Annuities differ from regular compound interest loans and investments. In **Chapter 9** we saw that with regular compound interest, a single amount is invested or borrowed and all of the growth before maturity is due to compounding interest. With an annuity, money is continuously paid into the loan or investment at periodic intervals. These continuous infusions of cash will see investments grow faster due to the additional principal contributions, and loan balances reach zero at the end of their term due to regular loan payments. Many circumstances require the calculation of the future value or the present value of an annuity. For example, how much (future value) will you accumulate after 20 years if you invest $100 per month? What is the balance (present value) you owe on a loan that has 23 remaining monthly payments of $227?

In this chapter, you will learn the language of annuities and how to answer these questions. This chapter is also the foundation we will build upon throughout **Chapters 12** to **16**. If you master the content of **Chapter 11**, you will be in an excellent position to comfortably handle the later chapters.

11.1 Terminology

LO1 An **annuity** is a series of equal payments made at regular intervals. We will use the symbols

$$PMT = \text{Periodic payment in an annuity}$$

$$n = \text{Number of payments in the annuity}$$

In **Figure 11.1**, the n payments are shown on a time line. The time between successive payments is called the **payment interval**. The total time from the *beginning* of the first payment interval to the *end* of the last payment interval is the **term (of an annuity)**. Payments can be made either at the end or at the beginning of a payment interval. The frequency for payment intervals is typically annually, semiannually, quarterly, or monthly, and in some cases biweekly or even weekly. The compounding frequency of interest rates also follows this pattern.

FIGURE 11.1   Time Diagram for an *n*-Payment Ordinary Annuity

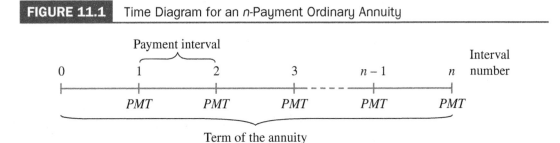

There are four categories of annuities, which are classified according to when payments are made and the compounding frequency of the interest for the annuity. **Table 11.1** summarizes the four categories. **Chapters 11** and **12** are concerned with **ordinary annuities**, in which payments are made at the *end* of each payment interval. Annuities are further classified as either simple or general, depending on whether the payment interval and compounding frequency are the same or different. **Chapter 13** will cover simple and general **annuities due**, in which payments are made at the *beginning* of each payment interval.

TABLE 11.1 Distinguishing Characteristics of Annuity Categories		
	Payment is made at the **END** of the payment interval	Payment is made at the **BEGINNING** of the payment interval
Payment frequency is **THE SAME** as compounding frequency	Ordinary Simple Annuity	Simple Annuity Due
Payment frequency is **NOT THE SAME** as compounding frequency	Ordinary General Annuity	General Annuity Due

To illustrate the use of these new terms, imagine you have obtained a personal loan to be repaid by 48 equal monthly payments. The *payment interval* is one month and the *term of the annuity* is 48 months, or four years. The first payment will be due one month after you receive the loan—that is, at the *end* of the first payment interval. If interest is being charged using monthly compounding, the payments form an **ordinary simple annuity**. If interest is being charged using any other compounding frequency, then the payments form an **ordinary general annuity**.

 TRAP

"Where Do We Begin?"

Don't confuse the *beginning of an annuity* with the "beginning of payments" or with the "date of the first payment." The beginning of an annuity means the beginning of the annuity's term or the beginning of the first payment interval. The beginning of an annuity occurs one payment interval *before* the first payment in an *ordinary annuity*.

Similarly, the *end of an annuity* refers to the "end of the annuity's term" or the "end of the last payment interval." It does coincide with the last payment in an ordinary annuity.

Let's use an example to illustrate how we attach specific dates to the start and end points of individual payment intervals. Suppose an ordinary annuity with monthly payments begins at 11:00 a.m. on November 1. The first payment interval ends one month later. Therefore, it ends at 11:00 a.m. on December 1, and the first payment is due at that point. The second payment interval begins at the same moment. Although both the end of the first payment interval and the beginning of the second interval fall on December 1, we do not end up "double counting" that day in the payment *intervals*. The first interval is from 11:00 a.m. November 1 to 11:00 a.m. December 1. The second interval is from 11:00 a.m. December 1 to 11:00 a.m. January 1, and so on. In the financial world, calculations of annuity payments and payments on *term* loans assume that all months have the same length.

 CONCEPT QUESTIONS

1. What distinguishes an ordinary simple annuity from an ordinary general annuity?
2. What is meant by the "term" of an annuity?
3. If you pay automobile insurance premiums by monthly pre-authorized chequing, do the payments form an ordinary annuity?
4. If an ordinary annuity with quarterly payments and a $5\frac{1}{2}$ year term began June 1, 2020, what are the dates of the first and last payments?

11.2 Future Value of an Ordinary Simple Annuity

L02 The **future value of an annuity** is the sum of the future values of all the payments (evaluated at the end of the last payment interval). We introduce the techniques for calculating an annuity's future value by considering a specific case.

Future Value Using the Algebraic Method

Figure 11.2 is a time diagram showing the investment of $1000 at the *end* of every six months for two years. Suppose the invested money earns 8% compounded semiannually. Since we have semiannual payments and semiannual compounding, the four $1000 payments form an ordinary *simple* annuity. The only way we can calculate the annuity's future value at this stage is to use $FV = PV(1 + i)^n$ to calculate the future value of each payment, one at a time. Then, as indicated in the time diagram, we add these future values to obtain the future value of the annuity.

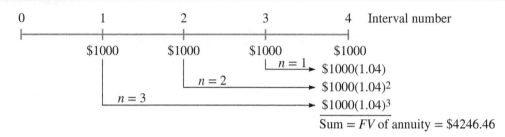

FIGURE 11.2 The Future Value of a Four-Payment Ordinary Simple Annuity

$$FV \text{ of annuity} = \$1000 + \$1000(1.04) + \$1000(1.04)^2 + \$1000(1.04)^3$$
$$= \$1000 + \$1040 + \$1081.60 + \$1124.864$$
$$= \$4246.46$$

The investments, including earnings, will amount to $4246.46 by the end of the annuity.

If an annuity consists of many payments, this "brute force" approach to the future-value calculation can become very time-consuming and laborious. Fortunately, there is a relatively compact formula for the future value of an ordinary simple annuity.

FUTURE VALUE OF AN ORDINARY SIMPLE ANNUITY

$$FV = PMT\left[\frac{(1 + i)^n - 1}{i}\right] \tag{11-1}$$

Let us now use Formula (11-1) to determine the future value of the annuity shown in **Figure 11.2**. We are given $PMT = \$1000$, $i = 4\% = 0.04$ per half-year, and $n = 4$. Substituting these values into Formula (11-1), we have

$$FV = \$1000\left[\frac{(1 + 0.04)^4 - 1}{0.04}\right] = \$1000\left(\frac{1.16985856 - 1}{0.04}\right) = \$4246.46$$

This is the same result obtained previously by the "brute force" approach.

> ⚠️ **TRAP**
>
> ### The Meaning of "*n*" Has Changed
>
> Formula (11-1) is derived from the compound interest formula $FV = PV(1 + i)^n$, where *n* represents the number of compounding periods. In Formula (11-1), *n* now represents the number of payments made over the term of the annuity. In the case of *simple annuities*, the compounding frequency matches the payment interval, so while *n* represents the number of payments it will also be equivalent to the number of compounding periods. You need to watch out for *general annuities* where the payment interval and compounding frequency differ. It will become very important to remember that *n* represents the number of payments.

Future Value Using the Financial Calculator Functions

Save the known values for n, j (the nominal annual interest rate), and *PMT* in the , I/Y , and PMT memories. Remember to use the cash-flow sign convention for the dollar amount entered in PMT . Except for the cases mentioned in the following TIP, zero should be entered in the PV memory. Open the *P/Y* worksheet and enter the number of payments per year. Remember that the calculator then *automatically* assigns the same value to *C/Y*, the number of compounds per year. (This automatic feature is a convenience with *simple* annuities where, by definition, *C/Y = P/Y*.) After quitting the *P/Y* worksheet, the keystrokes CPT FV instruct the calculator to compute the annuity's future value.

✓ **TIP**

Use of the *PV* Memory with Annuities

If you do not have zero in the PV memory when you perform a future-value calculation, the calculator interprets the amount in PV as an *additional single* cash flow occurring at the *beginning* of the annuity. At the CPT FV command, the calculator will compute the *combined* future value of the annuity and the future value of the amount in PV . This feature is useful in cases where, in a single calculation, we actually do want the combined future value of an annuity and a single beginning amount.

To calculate the future value of the annuity represented in **Figure 11.2**, the keystrokes are:

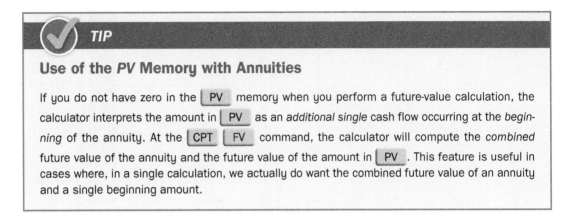

Answer: 4246.46

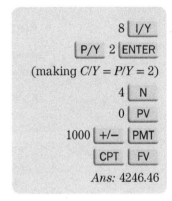

In Example problems, we will present the keystroke sequence in a callout box as shown at the right. For a reason that will become clear in **Section 11.4**, first we enter all of the information concerning the interest rate. To conserve space, we *represent* the actual keystroke sequence

2nd P/Y 2 ENTER 2nd QUIT

by the abbreviated sequence

P/Y 2 ENTER

You must supply the missing keystrokes.

Contribution of Each Payment to an Annuity's Future Value

When you use Formula (11-1) or a calculator's financial functions to calculate an annuity's future value, the amount each payment contributes to the future value is not apparent. **Figure 11.3** helps us see the pattern. Five $10 investments are represented by columns at one-year payment intervals along the time axis. Assuming the investments earn 10% compounded annually, each payment's contribution to the $61.05 future value is indicated at the right side of the diagram. It is no surprise that an early payment contributes more to future value than any subsequent payment. The interesting feature is that the difference between the contributions from successive payments does not stay the same. The first payment contributes $1.33 more than the second payment, the second payment contributes $1.21 more than the third payment, and so on. Putting it another way, each payment's contribution to future value increases in an *accelerating* manner as we look at earlier payments. This reinforces the point made in **Chapter 9** concerning the advantages of starting a savings plan as early in life as possible. Consider the following remarkable illustration of the relative effect of earlier versus later payments. Suppose you construct **Figure 11.3** to include

30 annual investments of $10.00. You would find that the first seven payments (in combination) contribute *more* to the future value than the remaining 23 payments (in combination)! Can you think of a way to verify this outcome?

Contribution of Each Payment to an Annuity's Future Value

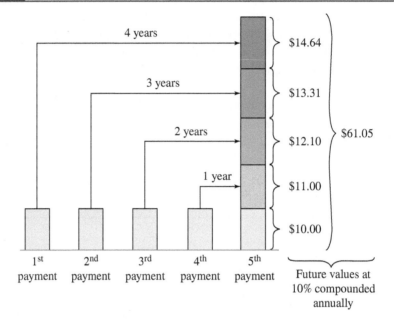

Applications of the Future Value of an Annuity

Most applications of the future-value calculation fall into two categories (with the first being much more common):

- Determining the total amount of principal plus interest that will be accumulated at the end of a series of equal regular investments.
- Determining the single payment at the end of an annuity that is economically equivalent to the annuity. The interest rate that should be used in this case is the rate of return that can be earned on a low-risk investment. (A suitable value is the rate of return currently available on Government of Canada bonds whose time remaining until maturity is similar to the term of the annuity.)

APP  THAT

Anyone interested in starting a savings plan or investing for future goals needs to be able to make informed investment decisions. Search the App Store on your tablet, smartphone, or smart watch using the key word **ANNUITY**.

You will find many free and paid apps that can provide projections for the future growth of your money, help set targets for regular contributions to an investment plan, and track the growth of your investments over time.

EXAMPLE 11.2A

THE FUTURE VALUE OF PERIODIC INVESTMENTS

Heinz has been contributing $300 at the end of each month for the past 15 months to a savings plan that earns 6% compounded monthly. What amount will he have one year from now if he continues with the plan?

SOLUTION

The total amount will be the future value of $n = 15 + 12 = 27$ contributions of $PMT = \$300$ each. Payments and compounding both occur at one-month intervals. Therefore, the payments form an ordinary simple annuity having $i = \frac{6\%}{12} = 0.5\%$ per month.

$$FV = PMT\left[\frac{(1+i)^n - 1}{i}\right]$$

$$= \$300\left[\frac{(1.005)^{27} - 1}{0.005}\right]$$

$$= \$300\left(\frac{1.14415185 - 1}{0.005}\right)$$

$$= \$8649.11$$

6 **I/Y**
P/Y 12 **ENTER**
(making $C/Y = P/Y = 12$)
27 **N**
0 **PV**
300 **+/−** **PMT**
CPT **FV**
Ans: 8649.11

One year from now, Heinz will have \$8649.11 in the plan.

EXAMPLE 11.2B

THE IMPACT OF TIME COMPARED TO INTEREST RATE

Paulette and Ruby each contributed \$100 a month in two different investments. Paulette made regular monthly contributions earning 5% compounded monthly for 20 years while Ruby found an investment that could earn 15% compounded monthly so she decided to contribute for only 10 years. Based on the future value of their two investment plans when they each mature, which has the greater impact on the future value of investments, length of time investing or interest rate?

SOLUTION

For Paulette, the value of her investment at maturity will be the future value of $n = 12 \times 20 = 240$ contributions of $PMT = \$100$ each. Payments and compounding both occur at one-month intervals. Therefore, the payments form an ordinary simple annuity having $i = \frac{5\%}{12} = 0.41\overline{6}\%$ per month.

$$FV = PMT\left[\frac{(1+i)^n - 1}{i}\right]$$

$$= \$100\left[\frac{(1.0041\overline{6})^{240} - 1}{0.0041\overline{6}}\right]$$

$$= \$100\left(\frac{2.712640286 - 1}{0.0041\overline{6}}\right)$$

$$= \$41,103.37$$

5 **I/Y**
P/Y 12 **ENTER**
(making $C/Y = P/Y = 12$)
240 **N**
0 **PV**
100 **+/−** **PMT**
CPT **FV**
Ans: 41,103.37

For Ruby, the value of her investment at maturity will be the future value of $n = 12 \times 10 = 120$ contributions of $PMT = \$100$ each. Payments and compounding both occur at one-month intervals. Therefore, the payments form an ordinary simple annuity having $i = \frac{15\%}{12} = 1.25\%$ per month.

$$FV = PMT\left[\frac{(1+i)^n - 1}{i}\right]$$

$$= \$100\left[\frac{(1.0125)^{120} - 1}{0.0125}\right]$$

$$= \$100\left(\frac{4.44021323 - 1}{0.0125}\right)$$

$$= \$27,521.71$$

15 **I/Y**
P/Y 12 **ENTER**
(making $C/Y = P/Y = 12$)
120 **N**
0 **PV**
100 **+/−** **PMT**
CPT **FV**
Ans: 27,521.71

Paulette's investment is worth \$41,103.37 − \$27,521.71 = \$13,581.66 more than Ruby's at maturity. The length of time investing has more of an impact on the future value of the investment than the interest rate.

EXAMPLE 11.2C

CALCULATING THE FUTURE VALUE WHEN THE RATE OF RETURN CHANGES DURING THE TERM OF THE ANNUITY

Calculate the future value of an ordinary annuity with payments of $600 every six months for 16 years. The rate of return will be 3.5% compounded semiannually for the first $5\frac{1}{2}$ years and 5% compounded semiannually for the subsequent $10\frac{1}{2}$ years.

SOLUTION

Because the compounding interval and the payment interval are both six months, we have an ordinary *simple* annuity with

$$i = \frac{j}{m} = \frac{3.5\%}{2} = 1.75\% \text{ and } n = 2(5.5) = 11 \text{ for the first } 5\frac{1}{2} \text{ years, and}$$

$$i = \frac{j}{m} = \frac{5\%}{2} = 2.5\% \text{ and } n = 2(10.5) = 21 \text{ for the subsequent } 10\frac{1}{2} \text{ years.}$$

Since the rate of return changes during the term of the annuity, we must consider the first $5\frac{1}{2}$ years separately from the subsequent $10\frac{1}{2}$ years. The algebraic solution has three steps, as indicated in the following time diagram.

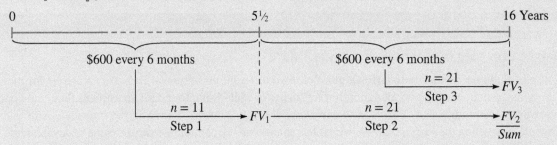

Step 1: Calculate the future value, FV_1, of the first 11 payments.

$$FV_1 = PMT\left[\frac{(1 + i)^n - 1}{i}\right]$$

$$= \$600\left[\frac{(1.0175)^{11} - 1}{0.0175}\right]$$

$$= \$600\left[\frac{1.210260 - 1}{0.0175}\right]$$

$$= \$7208.91$$

3.5 ⌊ I/Y

⌊ P/Y ⌋ 2 ⌊ENTER⌋

(making $C/Y = P/Y = 2$)

11 ⌊ N

0 ⌊ PV

600 ⌊ +/− ⌋ ⌊ PMT ⌋ *

⌊ CPT ⌋ ⌊ FV ⌋

Ans: 7208.91

* Invest the $600.

(Negative cash flow.)

Step 2: The value for FV_1 becomes a lump sum for the remaining term of the investment. It is no longer considered an annuity since payments have stopped at the original interest rate. Determine the future value, FV_2, of $7208.91 after an *additional* $10\frac{1}{2}$ years using Formula (9-2).

$$FV_2 = PV(1 + i)^n$$
$$= \$7208.91(1.025)^{21}$$
$$= \$12,107.95$$

Step 3: Calculate the future value, FV_3, of the last 21 annuity payments. Then add FV_2 and FV_3.

$$FV_3 = \$600\left[\frac{(1.025)^{21} - 1}{0.025}\right]$$

$$= \$600\left[\frac{1.679582 - 1}{0.025}\right]$$

$$= \$16,309.97$$

$$FV_2 + FV_3 = \$28,417.92$$

Same *PMT, P/Y, C/Y*

5 ⌊ I/Y

21 ⌊ N

7208.91 ⌊ +/− ⌋ ⌊ PV ⌋ †

⌊ CPT ⌋ ⌊ FV ⌋

Ans: 28,417.92

† Reinvest the $7208.91.

(Negative cash flow.)

The future value of the annuity is $28,417.92.

EXAMPLE 11.2D

CALCULATING THE FUTURE VALUE AFTER AN INTERRUPTION OF PAYMENTS

Mr. Cloutier, who just turned 43, has already accumulated $34,500 in his Registered Retirement Savings Plan. He makes monthly contributions of $300 to the plan and intends to do so until age 60. He plans to retire then and cease further contributions. The RRSP will be allowed to continue to accumulate earnings until he reaches age 65. If the RRSP earns 8% compounded monthly for the next 22 years, what amount will his RRSP contain when he reaches age 65?

SOLUTION

The amount in the RRSP will be the combined future value of the $34,500 already accumulated and future contributions. The number of additional $300 contributions that Mr. Cloutier will make to his RRSP is

$$n = m(\text{Years of contributions}) = 12(17) = 204$$

The periodic rate is $i = \frac{j}{m} = \frac{8\%}{12} = 0.\overline{6}\%$ per month. The following time diagram illustrates the three steps in the solution.

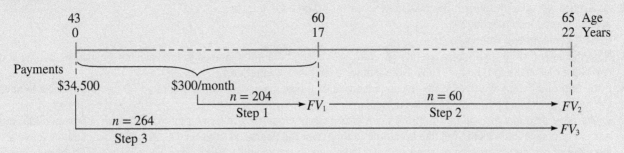

Step 1: Calculate FV_1, the future value at age 60 of the $300 per month annuity.

$$FV_1 = PMT\left[\frac{(1 + i)^n - 1}{i}\right]$$
$$= \$300\left[\frac{(1.00\overline{6})^{204} - 1}{0.00\overline{6}}\right]$$
$$= \$300\left[\frac{3.87864829 - 1}{0.00\overline{6}}\right]$$
$$= \$129{,}539.173$$

8	I/Y
P/Y 12	ENTER
(making $C/Y = P/Y = 12$)	
204	N
0	PV
300 +/−	PMT
CPT	FV

Ans: 129,539.17

Step 2: Calculate FV_2, the future value at age 65 of $129,539.17.

$$FV_2 = PV(1 + i)^n$$
$$= \$129{,}539.173(1.00\overline{6})^{60}$$
$$= \$192{,}993.381$$

Same *I/Y, P/Y, C/Y*

60	N
129539.17 +/−	PV
0	PMT
CPT	FV

Ans: 192,993.38

Step 3: Calculate FV_3, the future value at age 65 of the initial $34,500.

$$FV_3 = \$34{,}500(1.00\overline{6})^{264}$$
$$= \$199{,}361.269$$

The total amount in the RRSP when Mr. Cloutier reaches age 65 will be

$$FV_2 + FV_3 = \$192{,}993.38 + \$199{,}361.27 = \$392{,}354.65$$

Same *I/Y, P/Y, C/Y, PMT*

264	N
34500 +/−	FV
CPT	FV

Ans: 199,361.27

POINT OF INTEREST

Your Potential to Become a Millionaire!

One of the favourite themes of personal finance writers is to show you that, if you will only give up one or two of your wasteful habits and invest the money saved, you can become a millionaire. You can kick a filthy habit and become filthy rich! Attain better health and more wealth! Live longer and die richer!

Smoking is the primary target in these health-and-wealth scenarios. Suppose you give up a pack-a-day habit. At $14 per pack, that will save you about 30 × $14 = $420 per month.

QUESTIONS

1. If you invest the savings at the end of each month and earn 9% compounded monthly, how much (rounded to the nearest dollar) will you accumulate after:

   a. 20 years?   **b.** 30 years?   **c.** 40 years?

   9% compounded monthly is a realistic long-run rate of return. It is close to historical long-term rates of return achieved by diversified stock portfolios and equity mutual funds.

2. How much will your investment portfolio be worth after 40 years if it earns:

   a. 8% compounded monthly?

   b. 10% compounded monthly?

   Note the large difference an extra 1% rate of return over a long time frame makes to the value of a portfolio. But will you *feel* like a millionaire in Question 1(c)? (Note that we have ignored inflation.)

3. If the rate of inflation averages 2.4% compounded monthly, how many dollars will you need 40 years from now to have the same purchasing power as $1,000,000 today?

   We have also ignored the fact that the price of a pack of cigarettes will also rise in the future. Consequently, the amount you save each month will rise from time to time over the years. (In Chapter 14, we will show you how to handle the case of a steadily growing payment.) These increases in the monthly saving rate will largely offset (or even more than offset) the effect of inflation on the purchasing power of your investment portfolio. Consequently, the answers in Question 1 can be viewed as reasonable estimates of the purchasing power in today's dollars of your portfolio.

   If you are not a smoker, consider some other luxury you can forgo—a daily latte, two of the four beers you drink each weekend, lunches you buy (instead of getting out of bed five minutes earlier to pack a bag-lunch at half the cost), etc.

EXERCISE 11.2

Answers to the odd-numbered problems are at the end of the book.

Spreadsheet template: *A partially completed Excel template for calculating the future value of an ordinary simple annuity is provided on Connect. You can use this template for many of the problems in Exercise 11.2. Go to the Student Edition of Connect and find "FV of Ord. Simple Annuity" found under the Student Resources for Chapter 11.*

BASIC PROBLEMS

1. This problem demonstrates the dependence of an annuity's future value on the size of the periodic payment. Suppose a fixed amount will be invested at the end of each year and that the invested funds will earn 4% compounded annually. What will be the future value of the investments after 25 years if the periodic investment is:

   a. $1000 per year?   **b.** $2000 per year?   **c.** $3000 per year?

   Note that the future value of an annuity is proportional to the size of the periodic payment.

2. This problem demonstrates the dependence of the future value of an annuity on the number of payments. Suppose $1000 is invested at the end of each year. Assume the investments earn 10% compounded annually. Calculate the future value of the investments after each of the following numbers of payments:
   a. 5 **b.** 10 **c.** 15 **d.** 20 **e.** 25 **f.** 30

   Note that the future value increases proportionately *more* than n as n is increased.

3. This problem demonstrates the dependence of the future value of an annuity on the interest rate. Suppose $1000 is invested at the end of each year for 20 years. Calculate the future value if the investments earn an annually compounded rate of return of:
   a. 9% **b.** 10% **c.** 11% **d.** 12%

   Note that the future value increases proportionately *more* than the interest rate.

4. Calculate the future value after 25 years in each of the following scenarios:
   a. $6000 invested at end of each year earning 9% compounded annually.
   b. $3000 invested at end of each half-year earning 9% compounded semiannually.
   c. $1500 invested at end of each quarter earning 9% compounded quarterly.
   d. $500 invested at end of each month earning 9% compounded monthly.

   Note that the same total amount ($6000) is invested every year at nominally equal rates of return (9%). The combined beneficial effects of (i) smaller but earlier and more frequent payments, and (ii) more frequent compounding are quite significant.

5. Teddy plans on contributing $6,000 every year (the maximum allowable contribution in 2019) to his TFSA. What is the future value after 20 years if the funds earn 4.5% compounded annually?

6. $75 was invested at the end of every month for $2\frac{1}{2}$ years. Calculate the future value if the funds earned 8% compounded monthly.

7. Aaron contributed $2000 to his RRSP at the end of every half-year. What was the value of his RRSP after $12\frac{1}{2}$ years if the RRSP grew at 3.5% compounded semiannually?

8. Elga plans to invest $175 every month by purchasing units of a diversified equity mutual fund. If the fund generates an overall rate of return of 6% compounded monthly, what will her holdings be worth after $8\frac{1}{4}$ years?

9. Danica has purchased $700 worth of units in a Global Equity Fund every calendar quarter for the past 7 years and 9 months. On average, the fund has earned 9% compounded quarterly. What were Danica's holdings worth immediately after her last purchase?

10. What will be the future value after 6 years and 7 months of regular month-end investments of $435 earning 8.5% compounded monthly?

11. Assume that your client invests $1000 at the end of each of the next three years. The investments earn 4% compounded annually. What is the future value at the end of the three years?

12. Your client plans to invest $2000 at the end of each year. The rate of return on the investment is 7.5% compounded annually. What will be the value of the investment at the end of the 12 years?

13. Your client has systematically invested $1000 at the end of each half-year for the past 17 years. The invested funds have earned 6.4% compounded semiannually. What is the value of your client's investments today?

14. Marcus spends $60 per month on cigarettes. Suppose he quits smoking and invests the same amount at the end of each month for 20 years. If the invested money earns 7.5% compounded monthly, how much will Marcus accumulate after 20 years?

15. Pascal has just agreed with his financial planner to begin a voluntary accumulation plan. He will invest $500 at the end of every three months in a balanced mutual fund. How much will the plan be worth after 20 years if the mutual fund earns:

    a. 5% compounded quarterly?   **b.** 10% compounded quarterly?

16. Calculate and rank the equivalent values eight years from now of the following cash flow streams:

    (i) A single payment of $5000 today.
    (ii) An ordinary annuity starting today with eight annual payments of $910.
    (iii) An ordinary annuity starting in three years with five annual payments of $1675.

    Do the calculations and ranking for each of the following two cases:
    a. Money can earn 8% compounded annually for the next eight years.
    b. Money can earn 10% compounded annually for the next eight years.

17. Dave has saved $20,000 for a down payment on a home and plans to save another $5000 at the end of each year for the next five years. He expects to earn 2.25% compounded annually on his savings. How much will he have in five years' time?

*The strong dependence of an annuity's future value on **n** (as demonstrated in Example 11.2B) means that it is important to start a savings plan as early as possible in order to accumulate a substantial retirement fund. Problems 18 and 19 reinforce this point in different ways. Round your answers to the nearest dollar.*

18. How much more will you have in your RRSP at age 65 if you begin annual $1000 contributions to your plan on your 26th birthday instead of on your 27th birthday? Assume that the RRSP earns 8% compounded annually, and that the last contribution is on your 65th birthday.

19. How much more will you have in your RRSP 30 years from now if you start to contribute $1000 per year at the end of this year, instead of waiting five years to begin contributing $1000 at each year-end? Assume that the funds earn 8% compounded annually in the RRSP.

INTERMEDIATE PROBLEMS

20. Dakota intends to save for occasional major travel holidays by contributing $275 at the end of each month to an investment plan. At the end of every three years, she will withdraw $10,000 for a major trip abroad. If the plan earns 6% compounded monthly, what will be the plan's balance after seven years?

21. Amir started contributing $5500 to a TFSA at the end of every year beginning in 2017. In 2019, the maximum allowable annual contribution was increased to $6000 and Amir planned to continue to contribute the maximum amount at the end of every year for the next 15 years. How much will he have in his TFSA after 15 years of additional contributions if the maximum allowable annual contribution remains at $6000 and his average rate of return is 8% compounded annually?

22. Herb has made contributions of $2000 to his RRSP at the end of every six months for the past eight years. The plan has earned 9.5% compounded semiannually. He has just moved the funds to another plan that earns 8% compounded quarterly. He will now contribute $1500 at the end of every three months. What total amount will Herb have in the plan seven years from now?

23. Marika has already accumulated $18,000 in her RRSP. If she contributes $2000 at the end of every six months for the next 10 years, and $300 per month for the subsequent five years, what amount will she have in her plan at the end of the 15 years? Assume that her plan will earn 4% compounded semiannually for the first 10 years, and 4% compounded monthly for the next five years.

24. Rajeev's new financial plan calls for end-of-quarter contributions of $2000 to his RRSP. In addition, at each year-end, he intends to contribute another $5000 out of the annual bonus he receives from his employer. What will be the amount in his RRSP after four years if it earns 7% compounded quarterly?

25. Howard has been contributing $1200 every three months to an investment plan that has consistently earned 3% compounded quarterly. He did this for $4\frac{1}{2}$ years until he lost his job unexpectedly and had to stop contributing to the plan during the 9 months he was unemployed. Once he secured a new job, he re-started his contributions, increasing them to $1500 every three months. If the rate of return on his investment is now 4.5% compounded quarterly, how much can Howard expect to have in his investment plan after contributing for another 10 years in his new job?

26. Leona contributed $3000 to her RRSP on every birthday from age 21 to age 30 inclusive. She stopped employment to raise a family and made no further contributions. Her husband, John, started to make annual contributions of $3000 to his RRSP on his 31st birthday and plans to continue up to and including his 65th birthday. Assuming that both plans earn 8% compounded annually over the years, calculate and compare the amounts in their RRSPs at age 65.

27. An interactive Future Value Chart is available on Connect. In Chapter 11 of the Student Edition, find the "Future Value Chart" under the Student Resources.

    Any initial investment or accumulated amount should be entered in the box for "Starting amount." If you have a pure annuity problem, enter "0" in this box.

    Enter the amount of each annuity payment in the "Annuity payments" box and select the payment frequency in the drop-down list on the right.

    For terms up to 15 years, you will get a bar chart. The bar for each year represents the future value at the end of the year. If you move the cursor over a bar, the numerical amount of the future value will appear.

    For terms exceeding 15 years, the chart presents the future value as a continuous curve. You can view a table listing the interest earned each year and the future value at the end of each year by clicking on the "View Report" button.

    Use this chart to answer the following problems (rounded to the nearest dollar).
    a. Exercise 11.2, Problem 2
    b. Exercise 11.2, Problem 11
    c. Exercise 11.2, Problem 13
    d. Exercise 11.2, Problem 17

11.3 Present Value of an Ordinary Simple Annuity

L02 The **present value of an annuity** is the sum of the present values of all of the payments (evaluated at the beginning of the first payment interval). To illustrate the techniques for calculating an annuity's present value, we will consider a specific case.

Present Value Using the Algebraic Method

Figure 11.4 shows an ordinary annuity consisting of four semiannual payments of $1000. Suppose we want to find the present value of the annuity using a discount rate of 8% compounded semiannually. Since we have semiannual payments and semiannual compounding, the payments form an ordinary *simple* annuity. A "brute force" approach for determining the annuity's present value is shown in the diagram. In this approach, we calculate the present value of each payment using $PV = FV(1 + i)^{-n}$. Then we add the four present values to obtain the present value of the annuity.

FIGURE 11.4   The Present Value of a Four-Payment Ordinary Simple Annuity

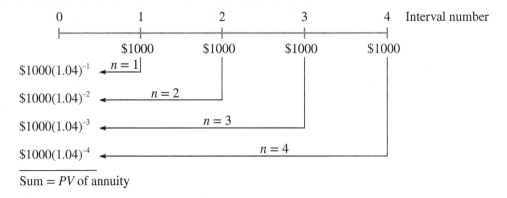

Sum = PV of annuity

The present value of the annuity is

$$PV = \$1000(1.04)^{-1} + \$1000(1.04)^{-2} + \$1000(1.04)^{-3} + \$1000(1.04)^{-4}$$
$$= \$961.54 + \$924.56 + \$889.00 + \$854.80$$
$$= \$3629.90$$

As in the case of the future-value calculation, there is a formula that makes the present-value calculation more efficient.

PRESENT VALUE OF AN ORDINARY SIMPLE ANNUITY

$$PV = PMT\left[\frac{1 - (1 + i)^{-n}}{i}\right] \qquad \textbf{(11-2)}$$

Substitute $PMT = \$1000$, $n = 4$, and $i = 0.04$ into Formula (11-2) to obtain the present value of the preceding four-payment annuity.

$$PV = \$1000\left[\frac{1 - (1 + 0.04)^{-4}}{0.04}\right]$$
$$= \$1000\left(\frac{1 - 0.8548042}{0.04}\right)$$
$$= \$3629.90$$

This is the same result we obtained previously by the "brute force" approach.

Present Value Using the Financial Calculator Functions

Save the known values for n, j (the nominal annual interest rate), and PMT in the ⬚ N , ⬚ I/Y , and ⬚ PMT memories. Remember to use the cash-flow sign convention for the dollar amount entered in ⬚ PMT . Except for the cases mentioned in the TIP preceding **Example 11.3C**, zero should be entered into the ⬚ FV memory. Open the P/Y worksheet and enter the number of payments per year. Remember that the calculator then *automatically* assigns the same value to C/Y, the number of compounds per year. (This automatic feature is a convenience with *simple* annuities where, by definition, $C/Y = P/Y$.) After quitting the P/Y worksheet, the keystrokes ⬚ CPT ⬚ PV instruct the calculator to compute the annuity's present value.

To calculate the present value of the annuity represented in **Figure 11.4**, the keystrokes are:

4 ⬚ N   8 ⬚ I/Y   1000 ⬚ PMT   0 ⬚ FV

⬚ 2nd ⬚ P/Y 2 ⬚ ENTER ⬚ 2nd ⬚ QUIT ⬚ CPT ⬚ PV   *Answer:* −3629.90

In Example problems, we will present the keystroke sequence in a callout box as shown at right. As we did for the future-value calculation in **Section 11.2**, we again *represent* the actual keystroke sequence

2nd P/Y 2 ENTER 2nd QUIT

by the abbreviated sequence

P/Y 2 ENTER

You must supply the missing keystrokes.

8 I/Y
P/Y 2 ENTER
(making $C/Y = P/Y = 2$)
4 N
0 FV
1000 PMT
CPT PV
Ans: −3629.90

Interpretation The present value ($3629.90) represents the initial investment required to generate the four $1000 payments. The computed value is negative because the initial investment is a cash outflow (negative) from the investor's point of view. The difference between the payments received and the initial investment is

$$4(\$1000) - \$3629.90 = \$370.10$$

This difference represents the earnings (at the rate of 8% compounded semiannually) on the balance that remains invested from time to time.

EXAMPLE 11.3A

THE PRESENT VALUE OF AN ORDINARY SIMPLE ANNUITY

Determine the present value of $500 paid at the end of each calendar quarter for $6\frac{1}{2}$ years. Use a discount rate of 6% compounded quarterly.

SOLUTION

Given: $PMT = \$500$, Term $= 6\frac{1}{2}$ years, $j = 6\%$ compounded quarterly

Therefore, $i = \frac{6\%}{4} = 1.5\%$ and $n = 4(6.5) = 26$

$$
\left.
\begin{aligned}
PV &= PMT\left[\frac{1 - (1 + i)^{-n}}{i}\right] \\
&= \$500\left(\frac{1 - (1.015)^{-26}}{0.015}\right) \\
&= \$500\left(\frac{1 - 0.67902052}{0.015}\right) \\
&= \$10{,}699.32
\end{aligned}
\right\}
$$

6 I/Y
P/Y 4 ENTER
(making $C/Y = P/Y = 4$)
26 N
500 PMT
0 FV
CPT PV
Ans: −10,699.32

Note that we keep eight-figure accuracy in 0.67902052 to get seven-figure accuracy in the answer.

The present value of the annuity is $10,699.32.

Contribution of Each Payment to an Annuity's Present Value

When you use Formula (11-2) or a calculator's financial functions to calculate an annuity's present value, the amount each payment contributes to the present value is not apparent. **Figure 11.5** helps us see the pattern. Five $10 payments are represented by columns at one-year intervals along the time axis. Using a discount rate of 10% compounded annually, each payment's contribution to the $37.91 present value is indicated at the left side of the diagram. Not surprisingly, each successive payment contributes a smaller amount to the present value. But notice that the *difference* between the contributions from two successive payments gets smaller as you look at later payments. For example, the second payment contributes $0.82 less than the first payment, the third payment contributes $0.76 less than the second payment, and so on. Eventually, distant payments contribute an insignificant amount to the present value. As an indication, suppose the annuity in **Figure 11.5** is extended to 30 years. The total present value is $94.27, to which the 30th payment contributes only $0.57 (0.6%). If a further 20 payments are added (in Years 31 to 50), they will add only a combined $4.88 or 5.2% to the present value.

FIGURE 11.5   Contribution of Each Payment to an Annuity's Present Value

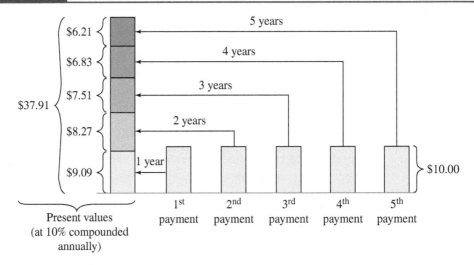

APP ④ THAT

It can be difficult to even begin to estimate how much money you would need to be able to support yourself in retirement. Search the App Store on your tablet, smartphone, or smart watch using the key words **INVESTMENT SIMULATOR**.

You will find many free and paid apps in the form of investment games and calculators as well as several magazine apps containing interactive features designed to guide you through the many different types of investments.

Applications of the Present Value of an Annuity

There are more applications of the present-value calculation than of the future-value calculation. Fundamentally, all present value applications are some form of *valuation*—placing a price tag on the "package" of annuity payments that are about to start. Three categories of applications are discussed in this section. A key issue in each category is how to choose the discount rate for the present-value calculation.

1. The market value of an annuity Clearly, the right to receive a series of future payments has value today. The *market* value of an annuity is the price at which it could be bought or sold among investors who are fully aware of investment alternatives. We look to the Valuation Principle (**Section 8.2**) for guidance in calculating the fair market value of any series of cash flows. It instructs us to calculate the present value of the cash flows, discounting them at the prevailing market rate of return (on investments of similar risk and duration). That is,

LO3

$$\left(\begin{array}{c}\text{Fair market value}\\\text{of an annuity}\end{array}\right) = \left(\begin{array}{c}\text{Present value of the annuity payments}\\\text{discounted at the } market \; rate \; of \; return\end{array}\right)$$

Current market rates offered by insurance companies to purchasers of annuities are periodically reported in the major financial newspapers. Market rates on annuities of various terms may also be obtained from annuity brokers.

The present-value calculation also allows you to estimate the amount you must accumulate by the time you retire in order to purchase, for example, a 25-year annuity paying $3000 per month. (You would have to make an assumption about the market rate of return at the date of the annuity purchase.)

The cash flows from some investments include an annuity component. For example, some types of bonds pay a fixed dollar amount of interest every six months until the face value of the bond is repaid at maturity. Some preferred shares pay fixed quarterly dividends until the "par value" of the share is repaid on the redemption date. These two types of investments may be bought or sold in the financial markets on any business day. Consequently, valuation at *prevailing market* rates of return is important on a day-by-day basis. The fair market value is the present value of *all* remaining payments. The annuity *component* can be valued separately and added to the present value of the *other* expected payments.

EXAMPLE 11.3B

CALCULATING THE PURCHASE PRICE OF AN ANNUITY

Suppose the funds used to purchase an annuity will earn 6% compounded monthly. What amount is needed to purchase an annuity paying $1000 at the end of each month for 20 years?

SOLUTION

The annuity is an ordinary simple annuity with $PMT = \$1000$ and $n = 12(20) = 240$ payments. The amount required to purchase the annuity is the present value of the payments discounted at $i = \frac{6\%}{12} = 0.5\%$ per month.

$$PV = PMT \left[\frac{1 - (1 + i)^{-n}}{i} \right]$$

$$= \$1000 \left(\frac{1 - (1.005)^{-240}}{0.005} \right)$$

$$= \$1000 \left(\frac{1 - 0.302096142}{0.005} \right)$$

$$= \$139{,}580.77$$

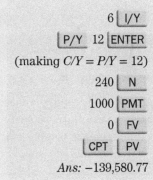

6 I/Y

P/Y 12 ENTER

(making $C/Y = P/Y = 12$)

240 N

1000 PMT

0 FV

CPT PV

Ans: −139,580.77

Note that we keep nine-figure accuracy in 0.302096142 to get eight-figure accuracy in the answer.

The purchase price of the annuity is $139,580.77.

 TIP

Use of the *FV* Memory with Annuities

If you do not have zero in the FV memory when you perform a present-value calculation, the calculator interprets the amount in FV as an *additional single* cash flow occurring at the end of the annuity. At the CPT PV command, the calculator will compute the *combined* present value of the annuity *and* the present value of the amount in FV . This feature is useful in cases where, in a single calculation, we actually do want the combined present value of an annuity and an additional payment coming at the end of the annuity.

EXAMPLE 11.3C

THE PRESENT VALUE OF AN ANNUITY AND A TERMINAL "LUMP" PAYMENT

A certain investment will pay you $50 at the end of every six months for 17 years. At the end of the 17 years, the investment will pay you an additional $1000 along with the last regular $50 payment. What is the fair market value of the investment if the prevailing rate of return on similar investments is 8.5% compounded semiannually?

SOLUTION

The fair market value of the investment is the present value of *all* of the payments discounted at the prevailing rate of return. The semiannual payments form an ordinary simple annuity having

$$PMT = \$50 \quad n = 2(17) = 34 \text{ payments} \quad i = \tfrac{8.5\%}{2} = 4.25\%$$

The combined present value of the annuity and the terminal lump payment is

Formula (11-2)   Formula (9-2)

$$PV = PMT\left[\frac{1 - (1 + i)^{-n}}{i}\right] + FV(1 + i)^{-n}$$

$$= \$50\left[\frac{1 - (1.0425)^{-34}}{0.0425}\right] + \$1000(1.0425)^{-34}$$

$$= \$50\left[\frac{1 - 0.24289235}{0.0425}\right] + \$1000(0.2428923)$$

$$= \$890.715 + \$242.892$$

$$= \$1133.61$$

8.5	I/Y
P/Y	2 ENTER
(making C/Y = P/Y = 2)	
34	N
50	PMT
1000	FV
CPT	PV

Ans: −1133.61

The fair market value of the investment is $1133.61.

EXAMPLE 11.3D

THE PRESENT VALUE OF TWO ANNUITIES IN SERIES

How much will it cost to purchase a two-level retirement annuity that will pay $2000 at the end of each month for the first 10 years, and $3000 per month for the next 15 years? Assume that the payments represent a rate of return to the annuitant (the person receiving the payments) of 7.5% compounded monthly.

SOLUTION

The purchase price will be the present value of all of the payments. Since we have month-end payments and monthly compounding, the payments form two ordinary simple annuities in sequence. The given information and a three-step solution strategy are presented in the time diagram.

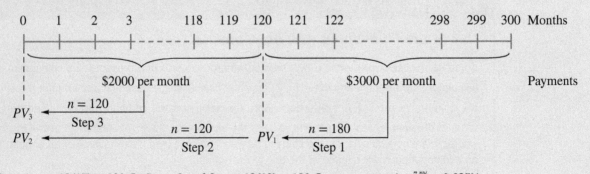

In Step 1, $n = 12(15) = 180$. In Steps 2 and 3, $n = 12(10) = 120$. In every step, $i = \tfrac{7.5\%}{12} = 0.625\%$.

Step 1: Calculate the present value, PV_1, of the $3000 annuity at its beginning.

$$PV_1 = PMT\left[\frac{1-(1+i)^{-n}}{i}\right]$$

$$= \$3000\left[\frac{1-1.00625^{-180}}{0.00625}\right]$$

$$= \$323,620.281$$

7.5 $\boxed{\text{I/Y}}$
$\boxed{\text{P/Y}}$ 12 $\boxed{\text{ENTER}}$
(making $C/Y = P/Y = 12$)
180 $\boxed{\text{N}}$
3000 $\boxed{\text{PMT}}$
0 $\boxed{\text{FV}}$
$\boxed{\text{CPT}}$ $\boxed{\text{PV}}$
Ans: −323,620.28

Step 2: Calculate the present value, PV_2, of the Step 1 result at time 0.

$$PV_2 = FV(1+i)^{-n}$$

$$= \$323,620.28(1.00625)^{-120}$$

$$= \$153,224.61$$

Step 3: Calculate the present value, PV_3, of the $2000 annuity at time 0.

$$PV_3 = \$2000\left[\frac{1-(1.00625)^{-120}}{0.00625}\right]$$

$$= \$168,489.485$$

Same *I/Y*, *P/Y*, *C/Y*
120 $\boxed{\text{N}}$
2000 $\boxed{\text{PMT}}$
323620.28 $\boxed{\text{FV}}$
$\boxed{\text{CPT}}$ $\boxed{\text{PV}}$
Ans: −321,714.10

The total present value will be

$$PV_2 + PV_3 = \$153,224.61 + \$168,489.49 = \$321,714.10$$

The purchase price of the two-level retirement annuity will be $321,714.10.

EXAMPLE 11.3E

PRICING AN ANNUITY TO PROVIDE A REQUIRED RATE OF RETURN

Crazy Ed's Furniture Mart is holding a "nothing-down-and-no-interest-to-pay" promotion on purchases exceeding $1000. Customers can pay six equal month-end payments with no interest charged. On such installment sales, the customer signs a conditional sale contract. Crazy Ed's immediately sells the conditional sale contract to Consumers Finance Company.[1] The finance company purchases the contract at a discounted price that builds in a rate of return (on its purchase price) of 15% compounded monthly. What will Consumers Finance pay for a $1200 contract (consisting of six payments of $200)?

SOLUTION

The six installment payments form an ordinary simple annuity. To build the required rate of return into the purchase price, the payments must be discounted at the required rate of return. So we need to calculate the present value of $n = 6$ payments of $PMT = \$200$, discounting at $i = \frac{15\%}{12} = 1.25\%$ per month.

$$PV = PMT\left[\frac{1-(1+i)^{-n}}{i}\right]$$

$$= \$200\left[\frac{1-(1+0.0125)^{-6}}{0.0125}\right]$$

$$= \$1149.20$$

15 $\boxed{\text{I/Y}}$
$\boxed{\text{P/Y}}$ 12 $\boxed{\text{ENTER}}$
(making $C/Y = P/Y = 12$)
6 $\boxed{\text{N}}$
200 $\boxed{\text{PMT}}$
0 $\boxed{\text{FV}}$
$\boxed{\text{CPT}}$ $\boxed{\text{PV}}$
Ans: −1149.20

The finance company will pay $1149.20 for the contract.

---

[1] It is common for furniture retailers to sell such conditional sale contracts to a finance company. The retailer gets immediate cash and avoids having to set up a credit department.

L04 **2. Loan balance and market value of a loan contract** In Section 9.3 we established the general principle that

> Original loan = $\begin{bmatrix} \text{Present value of } all \text{ payments (discounted} \\ \text{at the } contractual \ rate \ of \ interest \text{ on the loan)} \end{bmatrix}$

The original loan is also the initial balance on the loan. The balance at any later time is the present value of the *remaining* payments.

> Principal balance = $\begin{bmatrix} \text{Present value of the } remaining \text{ payments (discounted} \\ \text{at the } contractual \ rate \ of \ interest \text{ on the loan)} \end{bmatrix}$

Both principles apply to any pattern of loan payments. However, most loans require equal periodic payments.[2] In these cases, we use Formula (11-2) for the present-value calculation.

Most loan contracts permit the lender to sell the contract to another investor at any time during the term of the loan. The investor/buyer is then entitled to receive subsequent loan payments from the borrower. To determine a price for the loan contract, the buyer and seller first agree upon the rate of return the buyer should earn. (Current interest rates offered by financial institutions on *new* loans provide a reference point for negotiating the buyer's rate of return.) This rate of return is then "built in" or "locked in" by using it as the discount rate for calculating the present value of the remaining loan payments.

$$\text{Selling price of a loan contract} = \left(\begin{matrix} \text{Present value of the remaining payments} \\ \text{(discounted at the negotiated rate of return)} \end{matrix} \right)$$

EXAMPLE 11.3F

CALCULATING THE ORIGINAL LOAN AND A SUBSEQUENT BALANCE

The required monthly payment on a five-year loan bearing interest at 9% compounded monthly is $249.10.

a. What was the original principal amount of the loan?

b. What is the balance owed just after the 17th payment?

SOLUTION

The loan payments form an ordinary simple annuity having $PMT = \$249.10$, $n = 12(5) = 60$, and $i = \frac{9\%}{12} = 0.75\%$ per month.

Take borrower's viewpoint for the sign convention.

a. Original principal = Present value of all 60 payments

$$\text{Original principal} = PMT\left[\frac{1 - (1 + i)^{-n}}{i}\right]$$

$$= \$249.10\left(\frac{1 - 1.0075^{-60}}{0.0075}\right)$$

$$= \$249.10\left(\frac{1 - 0.63869970}{0.0075}\right)$$

$$= \$11,999.99$$

9 | I/Y

| P/Y 12 | ENTER

(making *C/Y* = *P/Y* = 12)

60 | N

249.10 | +/− | PMT

0 | FV

| CPT | PV

Ans: 11,999.99

---

[2] As a technical point, the last payment in so-called equal-payment loans usually differs slightly from the others. In Section 15.1 you will learn how to calculate the exact amount of the final payment. Until then, we will make the assumption that the final payment is the same as the others. When you assume the final payment equals the others in the present-value calculation for the "Original loan" or "Loan balance," your answer will have a small immaterial error. To obtain strictly correct present values, you must use the strictly correct value for the final payment.

b. Balance after 17 payments = Present value of the remaining 43 payments

$$\text{Balance} = \$249.10\left(\frac{1 - 1.0075^{-43}}{0.0075}\right)$$

$$= \$249.10\left(\frac{1 - 0.7252081}{0.0075}\right)$$

$$= \$9126.76$$

Same *I/Y, PMT, FV, P/Y, C/Y*

60 N

CPT PV

Ans: 9126.76

The original loan was $12,000 and the balance after 17 payments is $9126.76.

(Note that the calculated loan amount is only $11,999.99. This is attributed to the payment amount being rounded down by $0.0003.)

EXAMPLE 11.3G

CALCULATING THE SELLING PRICE OF A LOAN CONTRACT

Suppose the original lender in **Example 11.3F** wishes to sell the loan just after the 17th payment. What is the selling price if the negotiated rate of return to the buyer is to be:

a. 7.5% compounded monthly?

b. 9% compounded monthly (the same as the interest rate on the loan)?

c. 10.5% compounded monthly?

SOLUTION

In each case,

$$\text{Selling price} = \left(\begin{array}{c}\text{Present value of the remaining 43 payments} \\ \text{(discounted at the negotiated rate of return)}\end{array}\right)$$

Take buyer's viewpoint for the sign convention.

a. The periodic rate is $i = \frac{7.5\%}{12} = 0.625\%$

$$\text{Selling price} = PMT\left[\frac{1 - (1 + i)^{-n}}{i}\right]$$

$$= \$249.10\left(\frac{1 - 1.00625^{-43}}{0.00625}\right)$$

$$= \$9367.20$$

7.5 I/Y

P/Y 12 ENTER

(making *C/Y = P/Y* = 12)

43 N

249.10 PMT

0 FV

CPT PV

Ans: −9367.20

b. The periodic rate is $i = \frac{9\%}{12} = 0.75\%$

$$\text{Selling price} = \$249.10\left(\frac{1 - 1.0075^{-43}}{0.0075}\right)$$

$$= \$9126.76$$

Same *P/Y, C/Y, N, PMT, FV*

9 I/Y

CPT PV

Ans: −9126.76

c. The periodic rate is $i = \frac{10.5\%}{12} = 0.875\%$

$$\text{Selling price} = \$249.10\left(\frac{1 - 1.00875^{-43}}{0.00875}\right)$$

$$= \$8894.86$$

Same *P/Y, C/Y, N, PMT, FV*

10.5 I/Y

CPT PV

Ans: −8894.86

Postscript   Note that the answer in part (b) equals the actual loan balance (which we calculated in part (b) of **Example 11.3F**). The current **Example 11.3G** illustrates three scenarios summarized below.

Part	Rate of return vs. Interest rate on loan	Selling price vs. Balance on loan
a.	Rate of return < Interest rate on loan	Selling price > Balance on loan
b.	Rate of return = Interest rate on loan	Selling price = Balance on loan
c.	Rate of return > Interest rate on loan	Selling price < Balance on loan

Expressing the same relationships in another way,

- If the price you pay to purchase a loan is *equal* to the balance on the loan, the rate of return on your investment will be the *same* as the interest rate on the loan.
- Consequently, if you pay *more* than the loan balance, your rate of return will be *less* than the interest rate on the loan.
- Conversely, if you pay *less* than the loan balance, your rate of return will be *more* than the interest rate on the loan.

3. The economic value of an annuity   The *economic* value of a payment stream on a particular date (focal date) refers to a *single* amount that is an economic substitute for the payment stream. You will end up in the same financial position if you accept the economic value (on its focal date) instead of the scheduled payment stream.

The economic value of an annuity at the beginning of the annuity is just its present value. An appropriate value for the discount rate is the rate of return currently available on Government of Canada bonds (whose time until maturity is similar to the term of the annuity).

EXAMPLE 11.3H

COMPARING THE ECONOMIC VALUES OF TWO ANNUITIES

An eligible individual may elect to start collecting the Canada Pension Plan monthly retirement pension at any time between the ages of 60 and 65. The payments are then reduced by 0.6% for each month the pension is collected before age 65. For example, if the pension starts five years early, at age 60, the monthly payment will be decreased by $(5 \times 12 \text{ months}) \times (0.6\%) = 36\%$. The reduction is permanent, extending to payments after age 65 as well.

The average life expectancy of a woman aged 60 is another 25 years. If a retired woman aged 60 lives just the expected 25 years, compare the economic values at age 60 of the following two alternatives:

- Collect a 100% pension from age 65.
- Collect a 64% pension from age 60.

Assume that money is worth 6% compounded monthly.

SOLUTION

The economic value at age 60 of a stream of pension payments will be the present value of the payments discounted at $i = \frac{6\%}{12} = 0.5\%$ per month.

The *relative* economic values of the pension alternatives will not depend on whether a 100% pension represents $500, $1000, or $1500 per month. Let's work on the basis of $1000 per month. Then the woman can choose either a full pension after age 65 of $1000 per month or a reduced pension after age 60 of $640 per month. The alternative pension payments are illustrated in the following time diagrams. In the first diagram, PV_1 represents the present value at age 60 of the reduced pension payments.

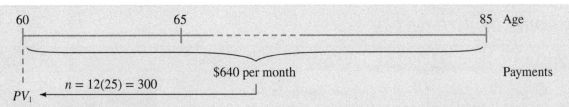

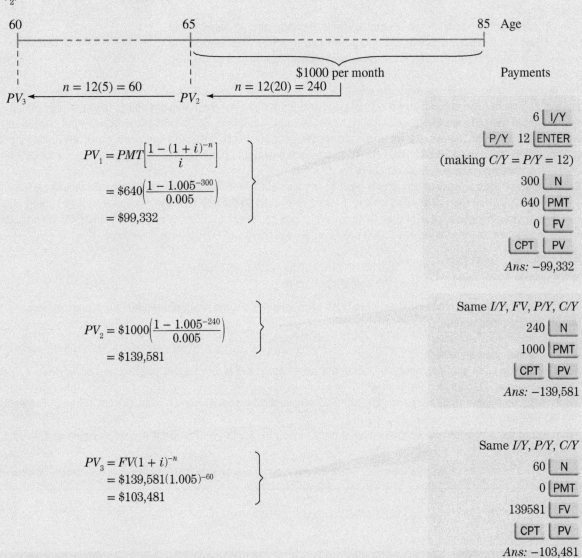

In the next diagram, PV_2 is the present value at age 65 of the full pension payments. PV_3 is the present value at age 60 of PV_2.

The economic value at age 60 of the early pension option is $99,332. The economic value, also at age 60, of the full pension option is $103,481.

Based on our assumptions for life expectancy and the time value of money, the early pension option is worth

$$\frac{\$99{,}332 - \$103{,}481}{\$103{,}481} \times 100\% = -4.01\%$$

less than the age 65 option. (We would see the same disadvantage of the early pension alternative for any dollar amount of the full 100% monthly pension.)

POINT OF INTEREST

"Got a Million Dollar Talent?"

In 2012, the City TV network debuted the Canadian version of the internationally popular "Got Talent" franchise. The programs, viewed in more than 60 countries since the introduction of the show in Britain in 2007, feature a wide variety of talented contestants who are voted on by the viewing audience to determine the ultimate winner.

© The Canadian Press/Nathan Denette

The top prize varies in each of the countries where the show airs. In Canada, the winner of Season 1 received $100,000 and a new car. In the United States, the *America's Got Talent* edition of the show tempts contestants with a $1,000,000 top prize.

The disparity in the two prizes is not as great as you might think. The $1,000,000 top prize is an annuity paid out over 40 years. The winner can either take 40 annual payments of $25,000 or they may choose to take the present value of the annuity. Should they choose the 40-year million dollar annuity, the annual $25,000 payments will have diminished buying power as time goes on. The average inflation rate for the past 40 years in Canada has been about 3% compounded annually. That would mean the $25,000 payment 40 years from now would purchase the equivalent of about $8,000 in today's dollars—and they would have to wait 40 years for it.

Should they choose to take the present value of the annuity, the taxable lump sum winnings would be far less than the million dollars. However, depending on the interest rate used to valuate the annuity and their investment choices for the next 40 years, the future value of their lump sum winnings could well exceed the original $1,000,000 annuity. Under the right circumstances, the Canadian $100,000 prize can exceed the $1,000,000 prize given time.

QUESTIONS

Assume that all payments are made at the end of each year.

1. On the day the $1 million prize is won, what is its economic value if the 40-year annuity is discounted using:
   a. 5% compounded annually?
   b. 7% compounded annually?
   c. 9% compounded annually?
2. For each of the lump sum payments in Question 1, what would the single payout prize money be worth in 40 years if it were invested at 7% compounded annually?
3. What is the equivalent value today of $25,000 paid 40 years from now if inflation averages 3% compounded annually for the 40 years?
4. What would the $100,000 *Canada's Got Talent* prize money be worth in 40 years if it were invested at 7% compounded annually?

Source: "Why the $1M 'AGT' Prize Is Not What It Seems." Shaw Media. http://globalnews.ca/news/713196/million-dollar-agt-prize-not-what-it-seems/.

 CONCEPT QUESTIONS

1. Suppose the discount rate used to calculate the present value of an annuity is increased (leaving n and *PMT* unchanged). Will the annuity's present value be (pick one): **(i)** larger or **(ii)** smaller than before? Give a reason for your choice.
2. Think of a 20-year annuity paying $2000 per month. If prevailing market rates decline over the next year, will the price to purchase a 20-year annuity increase or decrease? Explain.

EXERCISE 11.3

Answers to the odd-numbered problems are at the end of the book.

Spreadsheet template: *A partially completed Excel template for calculating the present value of an ordinary simple annuity is provided on Connect. You can use this template for many of the problems in Exercise 11.3. Go to the Student Edition of Connect and find "PV of Ord. Simple Annuity" found under the Student Resources for Chapter 11.*

BASIC PROBLEMS

1. This problem demonstrates the dependence of an annuity's present value on the size of the periodic payment. Calculate the present value of 25 end-of-year payments of:
   a. $1000　　　　　**b.** $2000　　　　　**c.** $3000

   Use a discount rate of 5% compounded annually. After completing the calculations, note that the present value is proportional to the size of the periodic payment.

2. This problem demonstrates the dependence of the present value of an annuity on the number of payments. Using 7% compounded annually as the discount rate, calculate the present value of an ordinary annuity paying $1000 per year for:
   a. 5 years.　　　**b.** 10 years.　　　**c.** 20 years.
   d. 30 years.　　　**e.** 100 years.　　　**f.** 1000 years.

   Observe that the present value increases with increasing n, but at a diminishing rate. In this case, the 970 payments from Year 30 to Year 1000 cause the present value to increase by just 15%.

3. This problem demonstrates the dependence of the present value of an annuity on the discount rate. For an ordinary annuity consisting of 20 annual payments of $1000, calculate the present value using an annually compounded discount rate of:
   a. 5%　　　　　　**b.** 10%
   c. 11%　　　　　　**d.** 15%

   Observe that the present value decreases as you increase the discount rate. However, the present value decreases proportionately *less* than the increase in the discount rate.

4. An ordinary annuity consists of quarterly payments of $100 for $5\frac{1}{2}$ years. What is the annuity's present value, discounting at 10% compounded quarterly?

5. Determine the present value of end-of-month payments of $75 continuing for $2\frac{1}{2}$ years. Use 8% compounded monthly as the discount rate.

6. How much will it cost to purchase an ordinary annuity delivering semiannual payments of $2000 for $12\frac{1}{2}$ years if the money used to purchase the annuity can earn 7.5% compounded semiannually?

7. A contract requires end-of-month payments of $175 for another $8\frac{1}{4}$ years. What would an investor pay to purchase this contract if she requires a rate of return of 3% compounded monthly?

8. A new loan at 9% compounded quarterly requires quarterly payments of $727.88 for seven years. Rounded to the nearest dollar, what amount was borrowed?

9. Semiannual payments of $1240 will pay off the balance owed on a loan in $9\frac{1}{2}$ years. If the interest rate on the loan is 5.9% compounded semiannually, what is the current balance on the loan?

10. The original lender wishes to sell a loan contract delivering month-end payments of $350 for another 11 years and 5 months. At what price would an investor be prepared to buy the contract in order to "build in" a rate of return of 8.75% compounded monthly?

11. Your client is scheduled to receive $2000 at the end of each year for the next 10 years. If money is currently worth 7% compounded annually, what is the present value of the annuity?

12. Determine the present value of payments of $100 at the end of each month for 20 years. Use a discount rate (interest rate) of 6% compounded monthly.

13. What is the present value of end-of-quarter payments of $2500 for seven years? Use a discount rate of 6% compounded quarterly.

14. Imperial Life Inc. is quoting a rate of return of 5.2% compounded quarterly on 15-year annuities. How much will you have to pay for a 15-year annuity that pays $5000 (at the end of) every three months?

15. The rate of return offered by Reliance Insurance Co. on its 20-year annuities is 4.8% compounded monthly. What amount is required to purchase a 20-year annuity with month-end payments of $1000?

16. Mr. and Mrs. Dafoe are doing some estimates of the amount of funds they will need in their RRSP to purchase an annuity paying $5000 at the end of each month. For each combination of term and monthly compounded interest rate in the following table, calculate the initial amount required to purchase the annuity.

	Interest rate	
Term of annuity	6%	7%
20 years	?	?
25 years	?	?

17. If money can earn 6% compounded monthly, how much more money is required to fund an ordinary annuity paying $200 per month for 30 years than to fund the same monthly payment for 20 years?

18. Isaac wishes to purchase a 25-year annuity providing monthly payments of $1000 for the first 15 years and $1500 for the remaining 10 years. An insurance company has quoted him a rate of return of 4.8% compounded monthly for such an annuity. How much will he pay for the annuity?

19. Harold and Patricia Abernathy made a loan to their son, Jason, to help him purchase his first car. To repay the loan, Jason made payments of $2000 at the end of each year for five years. If the interest rate on the loan was 5% compounded annually, what was the amount of the original loan?

20. Gabriela's monthly payments of $567.89 will pay off her mortgage loan in 7 years and 5 months. The interest rate on her mortgage is 6.6% compounded monthly. What is the current balance on the loan?

21. A 20-year loan requires semiannual payments of $1037.33 including interest at 6.8% compounded semiannually.
    a. What was the original amount of the loan?
    b. What is the loan's balance $8\frac{1}{2}$ years later (just after the scheduled payment)?

22. The monthly payments on a five-year loan at 7.5% compounded monthly are $200.38.
    a. What was the original amount of the loan?
    b. What is the balance after the 30th payment?

23. Kent sold his car to Carolyn for $2000 down and monthly payments of $295.88 for $3\frac{1}{2}$ years, including interest at 7.5% compounded monthly. What was the selling price of the car?

24. Manuel purchased a boat for $2000 down with the balance to be paid by 36 monthly payments of $224.58 including interest at 10% compounded monthly.
    a. What was the purchase price of the boat?
    b. What is the balance owed just after the ninth payment?

25. A conditional sale contract between Classic Furniture and the purchaser of a dining room set requires month-end payments of $250 for 15 months. Classic Furniture sold the contract to Household Finance Co. at a discount to yield 19.5% compounded monthly. What price did Household pay Classic Furniture?

26. Osgood Appliance Centre is advertising refrigerators for six monthly payments of $199, including a payment on the date of purchase. What cash price should Osgood accept if it would otherwise sell the conditional sale agreement to a finance company to yield 18% compounded monthly?

27. The Ottawa Senators fired their coach two years into his five-year contract, which paid him $90,000 at the end of each month. If the team owners buy out the remaining term of the coach's contract for its economic value at the time of firing, what will be the settlement amount? Assume that money can earn 7.5% compounded monthly.

28. The Montreal Canadiens have just announced the signing of Finnish hockey sensation Gunnar Skoroften to a 10-year contract at $3 million per year. The media are reporting the deal as being worth $30 million to the young Finn. Rounded to the dollar, what current economic value would you place on the contract if Skoroften will be paid $250,000 at each month-end, and money can earn 6% compounded monthly?

29. Your client has the following choices for an insurance benefit: She can receive $2000 at the end of each year for the next five years or one lump sum today. If the current interest rate is 4.5% compounded annually, what lump payment today is equivalent to the five payments?

30. You can purchase a residential building lot for $90,000 cash, or for $20,000 down and quarterly payments of $5000 for four years. The first payment would be due three months after the purchase date. If the money you would use for a cash purchase can earn 8% compounded quarterly during the next four years, which option should you choose? What is the economic advantage in current dollars of the preferred alternative?

31. You have received two offers on the used car you wish to sell. Mr. Lindberg is offering $9500 cash, and Mrs. Martel's offer is five semiannual payments of $2000, including one on the purchase date. Which offer has the greater economic value using a discount rate of 6% compounded semiannually? What is the economic advantage in current dollars of the preferred alternative?

INTERMEDIATE PROBLEMS

32. A Government of Canada bond will pay $50 at the end of every six months for the next 15 years, and an additional $1000 lump payment at the end of the 15 years. What is the appropriate price to pay if you require a rate of return of 6.5% compounded semiannually?

33. Pierre and Pat wish to structure the payments from a 20-year annuity so that the end-of-quarter payments increase by $500 every five years. Maritime Insurance Co. will pay 5% compounded quarterly on funds received to purchase such an annuity. How much must Pierre and Pat pay for an annuity in which the quarterly payments increase from $2000 to $2500 to $3000 to $3500 in successive five-year periods?

34. What is the maximum price you should pay for a contract guaranteeing month-end payments of $500 for the next 12 years if you require a rate of return of at least 8% compounded monthly for the first five years and at least 9% compounded monthly for the next seven years?

35. A mortgage broker offers to sell you a mortgage loan contract that will pay $800 at the end of each month for the next $3\frac{1}{2}$ years, at which time the principal balance of $45,572 is due and receivable. What is the highest price you should pay for the contract if you require a return of at least 7.5% compounded monthly?

36. A lottery offers the winner the choice between a $150,000 cash prize or month-end payments of $1000 for $12\frac{1}{2}$ years, increasing to $1500 per month for the next $12\frac{1}{2}$ years. Which alternative would you choose if money can earn 8.25% compounded monthly over the 25-year period?

37. For its No Interest for One Year sale, Flemming's Furniture advertises that customers pay only a 10% down payment. The balance may be paid by 12 equal monthly payments with no interest charges. Flemming's has an operating loan on which it pays interest at 8.4% compounded monthly. If Flemming's sells furniture in a cash transaction rather than on the 10%-down-and-no-interest promotion, Flemming's can use the extra cash proceeds to reduce the balance on its loan, and thereby save on interest costs. What percentage discount for cash could Flemming's give and still be no worse off than receiving the full price under the terms of the sale?

ADVANCED PROBLEMS

38. An individual qualifying for Canada Pension Plan benefits may elect to start collecting the CPP monthly retirement benefit at any time between the ages of 60 and 70. If the retirement benefit starts after age 65, the pension payments are increased (from the amount that would otherwise be paid at age 65) by 0.7% for each month after age 65. For example, if the retiree chooses to begin receiving the benefit after turning 68, the CPP payments will be increased by (36 months) × (0.7%) = 25.2%.

The average life expectancy of a man aged 65 is another 15 years. If a man aged 65 lives just the expected 15 years, compare the economic values at age 65 of the two alternatives of collecting a 100% pension from age 65 versus a 125.2% pension from age 68. Assume that money is worth 7.5% compounded monthly.

39. The British Columbia Teachers' Pension Plan allows a teacher to begin collecting a retirement pension before age 60, but the pension is reduced by 3% for each year the retiring teacher's age is under 60. For example, a teacher retiring at age 56 would receive 100% − 4(3%) = 88% of the monthly pension that she would receive at age 60 (with the same number of years of service). The reduction is permanent, extending to payments beyond age 60.

Suppose that a female teacher will live the average life expectancy of 28 additional years for a woman aged 55. Compare the economic values at age 55 of the two alternatives of collecting an 85% pension from age 55 versus collecting a 100% pension from age 60. Assume that money is worth 7.5% compounded monthly.

40. **Influence of Annuity Variables** Go to the Student Edition on Connect. Under the Student Resources for Chapter 11, you will find a link to the "Influence of Annuity Variables" chart. This interactive chart enables you to observe and compare the effects of changes in the variables *PMT*, *n*, and *i* on both the future value and present value of an annuity.

a. Enter *PMT* = $100 and *i* = 8% for both Annuity A and Annuity B. Set *n* = 20 for Annuity A and *n* = 40 for Annuity B. This means that B contains twice as many payments as A. In percentage terms, **(i)** How much larger is the present value of B than the present value of A? **(ii)** How much larger is the future value of B than the future value of A?

b. Enter *PMT* = $100 and *n* = 30 for both annuities. Set *i* = 8% for Annuity A and *i* = 9% for Annuity B. In relative terms, the interest rate for B is

$$\frac{9\% - 8\%}{8\%} \times 100 = 12.5\%$$

larger than the rate for A. In percentage terms,

(i) How much *smaller* is the present value of B than the present value of A?

(ii) How much *larger* is the future value of B than the future value of A?

11.4 Future Value and Present Value of Ordinary General Annuities

To this point, we have considered only ordinary *simple* annuities (in which the payment interval *equals* the compounding interval). We will now learn how to handle ordinary *general* annuities (in which the payment interval *differs from* the compounding interval). Actually, we have already covered all you need to know to calculate the future value and present value of an ordinary general annuity. We need only "link" two topics whose connection is not obvious.

Let us begin with Formula (11-1) for the future value of an ordinary simple annuity.

$$FV = PMT\left[\frac{(1+i)^n - 1}{i}\right] \tag{11-1}$$

L05 Keep in mind that this formula can be used *only* in cases where the compounding interval equals (or "matches") the payment interval. But if we can find a way to *transform* a general annuity into a simple annuity, then we can still use Formula (11-1).

Sometimes an insight comes more easily if we consider a specific numerical example. Suppose we wish to find the future value of an ordinary annuity consisting of 12 semiannual payments of $100 that earn 8% compounded quarterly. We are given:

$$PMT = \$100 \text{ every six months} \quad i = \tfrac{8\%}{4} = 2\% \text{ per quarter} \quad n = 12$$

Since the payment interval is six months but the compounding interval is three months, the payments form an ordinary *general* annuity. In order to use Formula (11-1), we need the periodic rate for six months (the payment interval) that is *equivalent* to the given periodic rate of 2% per quarter. This is precisely the type of calculation for which Formula (10-4) was derived in **Section 10.4**.

$$i_2 = (1 + i_1)^{m_1/m_2} - 1 \tag{10-4}$$

For the case at hand,

$$i_1 = \text{The } given \text{ periodic rate } (i = 2\%)$$
$$m_1 = \text{Number of compounds per year (4) at the } given \text{ interest rate}$$
$$m_2 = \text{Number of compounds per year at the } equivalent \text{ interest rate}$$
$$\text{[This will equal the number of payments per year (2).]}$$
$$i_2 = \text{Periodic interest rate for a payment interval}$$

In this case, the exponent m_1/m_2 in Formula (10-4) is

$$\frac{m_1}{m_2} = \frac{\text{Number of compoundings per year (at the given interest rate)}}{\text{Number of payments per year}} = \frac{4}{2} = 2$$

Substituting in Formula (10-4), the periodic rate per payment interval (six months) is

$$i_2 = (1 + i_1)^{m_1/m_2} - 1 = 1.02^{4/2} - 1 = 1.02^2 - 1 = 0.0404 = 4.04\%$$

Now substitute this value of i_2 for i in Formula (11-1).

$$FV = PMT\left[\frac{(1+i)^n - 1}{i}\right] = \$100\left[\frac{(1.0404)^{12} - 1}{0.0404}\right] = \$1506.03$$

The future value of the general annuity is $1506.03.

Let us streamline Formula (10-4) for use in general annuity problems. As noted in the preceding analysis,

$$i_1 = i \quad \text{and} \quad \frac{m_1}{m_2} = \frac{\text{Number of compoundings per year}}{\text{Number of payments per year}}$$

Since $\frac{m_1}{m_2}$ is a commonly occurring ratio in general annuities, we can simplify the appearance of Formula (10-4) if we define a new symbol:

NUMBER OF COMPOUNDINGS PER PAYMENT INTERVAL

$$c = \frac{\textit{Number of compoundings per year}}{\textit{Number of payments per year}} \qquad (11\text{-}3)$$

EQUIVALENT PERIODIC RATE FOR GENERAL ANNUITIES

Then we can write Formula (10-4) as

$$i_2 = (1 + i)^c - 1 \qquad (10\text{-}4c)$$

 TIP

The Logic Behind "c"

You do not have to commit the definition of c to memory. The logic behind the choice of the symbol "**c**" in Formula (11-3) reminds us that "compoundings per year" comes first (in the numerator). The financial functions on the BA II PLUS reinforce this idea. C/Y = the number of compoundings per year and P/Y = the number of payments per year can be expressed in the formula for c as:

$$c = \frac{C/Y}{P/Y}$$

L02 We have used the future-value calculation to introduce the mathematics of general annuities. The same approach works in all types of general annuity calculations. It is summarized below.

Approach for Solving a General Annuity Problem
Transform the general annuity problem into a simple annuity problem by:

1. Using $i_2 = (1 + i)^c - 1$ to calculate the equivalent periodic rate that matches the payment interval.
2. Using this equivalent periodic rate as the value for i in the appropriate simple annuity formula.

Using the Texas Instruments BA II PLUS for General Annuities Recall that, when you enter a value for P/Y, C/Y is automatically given the same value. This is appropriate for simple annuities. But for general annuities, after entering the value for P/Y you must scroll down to C/Y and enter its different value (this will not change P/Y). Then close the worksheet. The keystrokes for obtaining the future value of 12 semiannual payments of $100 earning 8% compounded quarterly are shown at right.

8	I/Y
P/Y 2	ENTER
C/Y 4	ENTER
12	N
0	PV
100 +/−	PMT
CPT	FV

Ans: 1506.03

TIP

Be Intentional about Identifying the Type of Annuity

A common error students make beyond this point in the course is to forget to make the necessary adjustments to calculations when the annuity is *not an ordinary simple annuity*. To avoid this omission, immediately after your initial reading of the question, you should note the type of annuity at hand. (By the time you are part way into Chapter 13, there will be *four* possible types.) If you intend to use your calculator's financial functions for the computation, you should also enter values for *I/Y*, *P/Y*, and *C/Y* at this early point. This is why we have been showing these values as being entered *first* in the callout boxes for the financial calculator solutions (even though we have been dealing only with ordinary simple annuities up to Section 11.4).

EXAMPLE 11.4A

CALCULATING THE EQUIVALENT PERIODIC INTEREST RATE

To five-figure accuracy, calculate the periodic interest rate that matches the payment interval for:

a. Semiannual payments earning 5% compounded annually.

b. Monthly payments discounted at 6% compounded quarterly.

SOLUTION

a. $i = \frac{5\%}{1} = 5\%$ per year and $c = \dfrac{1 \text{ compounding per year}}{2 \text{ payments per year}} = 0.5$

Thus,

$$i_2 = (1 + i)^c - 1 = 1.05^{0.5} - 1 = 0.024695 = 2.4695\% \text{ per half-year}$$

b. $i = \frac{6\%}{4} = 1.5\%$ per quarter and $c = \dfrac{4 \text{ compoundings per year}}{12 \text{ payments per year}} = 0.\overline{3}$

Thus,

$$i_2 = (1 + i)^c - 1 = 1.015^{0.\overline{3}} - 1 = 0.0049752 = 0.49752\% \text{ per month}$$

 TIP

Estimating i_2

You can easily *estimate* the value of i_2, the periodic rate for a payment interval. It is a good idea to do this to check the "reasonableness" of the value you calculate for i_2. In part (a), the interest rate for six months (the payment interval) will be *about* half the nominal annual rate of 5%; that is, $i_2 \approx 2.5\%$. (This number is only an approximation because it ignores compounding.) If Formula (10-4c) does not give you a value close to 2.5%, you have made an error in your calculations. To estimate i_2 in general, simply divide the given nominal rate by the number of payments per year.

TIP

Improving the Accuracy of Calculated Results

Sometimes the value for c is a *repeating* decimal. This happened in part (b) of the preceding example, where we obtained $c = 0.\overline{3}$. In such cases, use your calculator in a way that optimizes the accuracy of the value you obtain for i_2. For example, immediately after dividing 4 by 12 in the preceding part (b), save the quotient to memory. The calculator then retains at least two more digits than you see in the display. Later, when you need the exponent for the y^x function, recall the value for c from the memory.

Typically, the value you calculate for i_2 will be used in further calculations. Again, to optimize accuracy, i_2's value should be saved in memory immediately after you calculate it. The value in memory will have two or three more digits than you see in the display. Whenever i_2 is needed in a subsequent calculation, recall it from the memory. This procedure will improve both your efficiency in using the calculator and the accuracy of your results.

EXAMPLE 11.4B

CALCULATING THE FUTURE VALUE OF AN ORDINARY GENERAL ANNUITY

If $1000 is invested at the end of every year at 8% compounded semiannually, what will be the total value of the periodic investments after 25 years?

SOLUTION

Since the compounding period (six months) differs from the payment interval (one year), the regular investments form a general annuity having

$$PMT = \$1000 \quad n = 1(25) = 25 \quad \text{and } i = \tfrac{8\%}{2} = 4\%$$

The total value of the investments will be their combined future value.

Before we can calculate this future value, we must determine the periodic interest rate for the one-year payment interval. (It will be *about* 8%.) Since

$$c = \frac{2 \text{ compoundings per year}}{1 \text{ payment per year}} = 2$$

then

$$
\begin{aligned}
i_2 &= (1 + i)^c - 1 \\
&= 1.04^2 - 1 \\
&= 0.0816 \text{ per year}
\end{aligned}
$$

Substitute this value for i in Formula (11-1).

$$
\begin{aligned}
FV &= PMT\left[\frac{(1 + i)^n - 1}{i}\right] \\
&= \$1000\left(\frac{(1.0816)^{25} - 1}{0.0816}\right) \\
&= \$74,836.81
\end{aligned}
$$

8	I/Y
P/Y 1	ENTER
C/Y 2	ENTER
25	N
0	PV
1000 +/−	PMT
CPT	FV

Ans: 74,836.81

The total value after 25 years will be $74,836.81.

EXAMPLE 11.4C

CALCULATING THE FAIR MARKET VALUE OF A PREFERRED SHARE USING PRESENT VALUE

The preferred shares of Dominion Trust Co. will pay a $0.75 per share dividend at the end of every calendar quarter until they are redeemed (that is, bought back by Dominion Trust) $8\frac{1}{2}$ years from now. On the redemption date, a shareholder will receive the $40 par value of each share in addition to the last regular dividend. What is the fair market value of a share if preferred shares of similar risk are currently generating a total rate of return of 6.5% compounded semiannually?

SOLUTION

This is a valuation application of present value. The fair market value of a share will be the combined present value of the dividends and the $40 payment of the par value. The dividend stream constitutes an *ordinary general annuity* having

$$PMT = \$0.75 \quad n = 4(8.5) = 34 \quad \text{and } i = \tfrac{6.5\%}{2} = 3.25\%$$

Then

$$c = \frac{2 \text{ compoundings per year}}{4 \text{ payments per year}} = 0.5$$

and

$$i_2 = (1 + i)^c - 1 = 1.0325^{0.5} - 1 = 0.0161201 \text{ per quarter}$$

Fair market value = Present value of dividends + Present value of par value

$$= PMT\left[\frac{1 - (1 + i)^{-n}}{i}\right] + FV(1 + i)^{-n}$$

$$= \$0.75\left(\frac{1 - 1.0161201^{-34}}{0.0161201}\right) + \$40(1.0161201)^{-34}$$

$$= \$19.513 + \$23.224$$

$$= \$42.74$$

6.5	I/Y
P/Y 4	ENTER
C/Y 2	ENTER
34	N
0.75	PMT
40	FV
CPT	PV

Ans: −42.74

The fair market value of a preferred share is $42.74.

EXAMPLE 11.4D

CALCULATING THE FUTURE VALUE OF AN INVESTMENT WHEN THE INTEREST RATE CHANGES

Marina contributed $300 a month to an investment plan that paid 3% compounded semiannually for 7 years, then 4.5% compounded quarterly for another 8 years. What is the accumulated value of the investment after 15 years?

SOLUTION

Since the payment interval and the compounding frequency for the first 7 years and the subsequent 8 years differ, the regular investments form two general annuities.

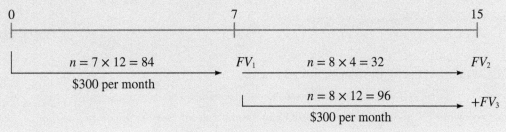

Step 1:   Calculate FV_1 for the first 7 years.

$$PMT = \$300 \quad n = 7(12) = 84 \text{ (number of payments)} \quad \text{and } i = \tfrac{3\%}{2} = 1.5\%$$

Then

$$c = \frac{2 \text{ compoundings per year}}{12 \text{ payments per year}} = 0.1\overline{6}$$

and

$$i_2 = (1 + i)^c - 1 = 1.015^{0.1\overline{6}} - 1 = 0.00248452 \text{ per month}$$

$$
\begin{aligned}
FV_1 &= PMT\left[\frac{(1 + i)^n - 1}{i}\right] \\
&= \$300\left(\frac{1.00248452^{84} - 1}{0.00248452}\right) \\
&= \$27,984.00
\end{aligned}
$$

3	I/Y
P/Y 12	ENTER
C/Y 2	ENTER
84	N
0	FV
300	PMT
0	PV
CPT	FV

Ans: −27,984.00

Step 2:   Calculate FV_2, the future value in 8 years for $27,984.00.

$$n = 8(4) = 32 \text{ (number of compounding periods) and}$$
$$i = \tfrac{4.5\%}{4} = 1.125\%\text{*}$$

$$
\begin{aligned}
FV_2 &= PV(1 + i)^n \\
&= \$27,984.00(1.01125)^{32} \\
&= \$40,029.75
\end{aligned}
$$

4.5	I/Y
P/Y 4	ENTER

(making $C/Y = P/Y = 4$)

32	N
0	PMT
27,984.00	FV
CPT	FV

Ans: −40,029.75

Step 3:   Calculate FV_3, the future value for the general annuity in the next 8 years.

$$PMT = \$300 \quad n = 8(12) = 96 \text{ (number of payments) and } i = \tfrac{4.5\%}{4} = 1.125\%$$

Then

$$c = \frac{4 \text{ compoundings per year}}{12 \text{ payments per year}} = 0.\overline{3}$$

and

$$i_2 = (1 + i)^c - 1 = 1.01125^{0.\overline{3}} - 1 = 0.003736025 \text{ per month}$$

$$
\begin{aligned}
FV_3 &= PMT\left[\frac{(1 + i)^n - 1}{i}\right] \\
&= \$300\left(\frac{1.003736025^{96} - 1}{0.003736025}\right) \\
&= \$34,564.93
\end{aligned}
$$

4.5	I/Y
P/Y 12	ENTER
C/Y 4	ENTER
96	N
300	PMT
0	PV **
CPT	FV

Ans: −34,564.93

The accumulated future value for the 15-year investment is:

$$FV_2 + FV_3 = \$40,029.75 + \$34,564.93 = \$74,594.68$$

* *You can also calculate* FV$_2$ *using* i $= 0.003736025$ *per month and 96 months of compounding.*

** *You can also calculate the sum of* FV$_2$ + FV$_3$ *by making* PV *$27,984 in this calculation.*

POINT OF INTEREST

The Alphabet Soup of Tax-Favoured Investing

To encourage people to save for retirement and their children's postsecondary education, the federal government has created programs under which investment contributions and/or the earnings thereon receive favourable income tax treatment. These programs usually have "Registered" in their name because every individual's plan is set up under a Declaration of Trust that is administered by a financial institution. The financial institution registers the "plan" with the Canada Revenue Agency (CRA), and reports to the CRA all contributions to and withdrawals from the plan.

The oldest (introduced in 1957) and best-known of these programs is the Registered Retirement Savings Plan (RRSP). Money invested within an RRSP is deductible from the contributor's taxable income providing immediate tax savings. The tax is paid on an RRSP when the money is redeemed.

In 1974, the Registered Education Savings Plan (RESP) was created to encourage parents and grandparents to save for their children's and grandchildren's postsecondary education. Unlike contributions to an RRSP, contributions to an RESP *may not* be deducted from the contributor's taxable income. Consequently, there is no initial tax "break" or tax "sheltering" of money contributed to an RESP. However, the federal government's Canada Education Savings Grant (CESG) provides a 20% "jump-start" for the growth of the RESP. For every $100 contributed per child per year to an RESP, the RESP receives a $20 grant (up to a maximum grant of $500 per child per year).

As with RRSPs, income and capital gains on investments held in an RESP are not taxed until they are withdrawn from the RESP. The income, capital gains, and CESG portions of RESP withdrawals must normally be paid to the beneficiary children for costs related to their postsecondary education. These portions (but not the portion representing original contributions) are subject to income tax *in the hands of the beneficiary/student*. However, a student normally qualifies for enough tax credits that he or she can receive at least $15,000 in a calendar year from employment income and RESP withdrawals before paying any income tax. In most cases, therefore, investment returns earned within RESPs are ultimately received tax-free by the beneficiary.

In 2007, the Registered Disability Savings Plan (RDSP) was introduced for Canadians with severe and prolonged disabilities and became available for purchase in 2008. These individuals, or the people who support them, can contribute up to $200,000 to the plan. Income and interest held within the plan are not subject to tax and contributions in the plan may be supplemented through grants and bonds. When payments are made from an RDSP, taxes are paid on the grant, bond, and investment income portions of the payment only.

In 2009, the Tax-Free Savings Account (TFSA) was added to the "alphabet soup." Any individual age 18 or older may contribute up to $6000 per year to a TFSA. Contributions are *not* deductible from taxable income. Investment returns within the plan are not subject to tax, and withdrawals of *both* contributions and earnings are not subject to income tax! Unused contribution "room" from one year can be carried forward and accumulated with new contribution room in subsequent years. For example, if you contributed nothing in 2017 and only $3000 in 2018, then in 2019 you may contribute

$$\$5500^3 \text{ (for 2017)} + \$2500 \text{ (for 2018)} + \$6000 \text{ (for 2019)} = \$14{,}000$$

(ignoring inflation adjustments to the annual maximum contribution).

On the withdrawal side, a TFSA is the most flexible of all the tax-favoured savings plans. If money is needed for an emergency or a major expenditure, funds may be withdrawn at any time *without* tax consequences. The amount withdrawn is added to the cumulative amount eligible for future contributions to the TFSA. The Point of Interest feature in **Section 9.5** compares the tax-reducing benefits of investing within RRSPs and TFSAs.

Source: "Savings and Pension Plans." Government of Canada. https://www.canada.ca/en/services/taxes/savings-and-pension-plans.html.

---

[3] The original maximum annual contribution was $5000 and increased to $5500 for 2013 and 2014. In 2015 the maximum annual contribution was increased to $10,000, but with the election of the federal Liberal government in late 2015, this amount was changed back to $5500 for 2016. The maximum contribution remained at $5500 for 2017 and 2018, then increased to $6000 for 2019.

EXERCISE 11.4

Answers to the odd-numbered problems are at the end of the book.

Spreadsheet template: *Partially completed Excel templates for calculating the future value and present value of an ordinary general annuity are provided on Connect. You can use these templates for many of the problems in Exercise 11.4. Go to the Student Edition of Connect to find "FV of Any Annuity" or "PV of Any Annuity" under the Student Resources for Chapter 11.*

BASIC PROBLEMS

1. The nominal interest rate associated with an ordinary general annuity is 3% compounded annually. Rounded to the nearest 0.001%, what is the corresponding periodic rate of interest that matches the payment interval for:
   a. Semiannual payments? b. Quarterly payments?
   c. Monthly payments?

2. The nominal interest rate associated with an ordinary general annuity is 7% compounded semiannually. Rounded to the nearest 0.001%, what is the corresponding periodic rate of interest that matches the payment interval for:
   a. Annual payments? b. Quarterly payments?
   c. Monthly payments?

3. The nominal interest rate associated with an ordinary general annuity is 4% compounded quarterly. Rounded to the nearest 0.001%, what is the corresponding periodic rate of interest that matches the payment interval for:
   a. Annual payments? b. Semiannual payments?
   c. Monthly payments?

4. The nominal interest rate associated with an ordinary general annuity is 8% compounded monthly. Rounded to the nearest 0.001%, what is the corresponding periodic rate of interest that matches the payment interval for:
   a. Annual payments? b. Semiannual payments?
   c. Quarterly payments?

5. This problem demonstrates the dependence of an annuity's future value on the compounding frequency. Suppose $1000 is invested at the end of each year for 25 years. Calculate the future value if the invested funds earn:
   a. 6% compounded annually. b. 6% compounded semiannually.
   c. 6% compounded quarterly. d. 6% compounded monthly.

6. This problem demonstrates the dependence of an annuity's present value on the compounding frequency. What minimum initial amount will sustain a 25-year annuity paying $1000 at the end of each year if the initial amount can be invested to earn:
   a. 6% compounded annually? b. 6% compounded semiannually?
   c. 6% compounded quarterly? d. 6% compounded monthly?

7. An ordinary annuity consists of quarterly payments of $400 for 11 years. Based on a nominal rate of 6.5% compounded annually, calculate the annuity's:
   a. Present value. b. Future value.

8. An annuity consists of end-of-month payments of $150 continuing for $6\frac{1}{2}$ years. Based on a nominal rate of 10% compounded quarterly, calculate the annuity's:
   a. Present value. b. Future value.

9. An ordinary annuity consists of semiannual payments of $2750 for a $3\frac{1}{2}$-year term. Using a nominal rate of 4% compounded monthly, calculate the annuity's:
   a. Present value.   **b.** Future value.

10. Payments of $1500 will be made at the end of every quarter for $13\frac{1}{2}$ years. Using a nominal rate of 7.5% compounded semiannually, calculate the annuity's:
    a. Present value.   **b.** Future value.

11. Payments of $3500 will be made at the end of every year for 17 years. Using a nominal rate of 5.25% compounded monthly, calculate the annuity's:
    a. Present value.   **b.** Future value.

12. An annuity consists of semiannual payments of $950 for a term of $8\frac{1}{2}$ years. Using a nominal rate of 9% compounded quarterly, calculate the ordinary annuity's:
    a. Present value.   **b.** Future value.

13. Lacey purchased a car with $1200 down and end-of-month payments of $352 for 4 years. What is the purchase price of the car if she has financed it at 7.55% compounded semiannually?

14. Mr. and Mrs. Krenz are contributing to an RESP they have set up for their children. What amount will they have in the RESP after eight years of contributing $500 at the end of every calendar quarter if the plan earns 6% compounded monthly? How much of the total amount is interest?

15. What is the future value eight years from now of each of the following cash flow streams if money can earn 4% compounded semiannually?
    a. A single payment of $5000 today.
    b. An ordinary annuity starting today with eight annual payments of $900.
    c. An ordinary annuity starting in three years with 20 quarterly payments of $400.

16. How much larger will the value of an RRSP be at the end of 25 years if the RRSP earns 9% compounded monthly instead of 9% compounded annually? In both cases a contribution of $1000 is made at the end of every three months.

17. What amount will be required to purchase a 20-year annuity paying $2500 at the end of each month if the annuity provides a return of 4.75% compounded annually?

18. An Agreement for Sale contract on a house requires payments of $4000 at the end of every six months. The contract has seven years to run. The payee wants to sell her interest in the contract. What will an investor pay in order to realize an annually compounded rate of return on the purchase price of:
    a. 8%?   **b.** 10%?

19. Kent sold his car to Carolyn for $2000 down and monthly payments of $259.50 for $3\frac{1}{2}$ years, including interest at 7.5% compounded annually. What was the selling price of the car?

20. LeVero's monthly payments of $567.89 will pay off his mortgage loan in 4 years and 7 months. The interest rate on his mortgage is 6.6% compounded semiannually. What is the current balance on the loan?

INTERMEDIATE PROBLEMS

21. Rebecca is trying to decide if she should make regular month-end $100 deposits to her TFSA or deposit $300 at the end of every three months instead. How much larger is the option with the higher future value after 20 years if both investments earn 4.25% compounded annually?

22. How much larger will the value of a TFSA be at the end of 25 years if the contributor makes month-end contributions of $300 instead of year-end contributions of $3600? In both cases the TFSA earns 8.5% compounded semiannually.

23. Mr. Eusanio contributed $1500 to his RRSP on March 1 and on September 1 of each year for 25 years. The funds earned 6% compounded monthly for the first 10 years and 7% compounded annually for the next 15 years. What was the value of his RRSP after his contribution on September 1 of the 25th year?

24. A savings plan requires end-of-month contributions of $100 for 25 years. What will be the future value of the plan if it earns 7% compounded quarterly for the first half of the annuity's term, and 8% compounded semiannually for the last half of the term?

25. Year-end contributions of $1000 will be made to a TFSA for 25 years. What will be the future value of the account if it earns $7\frac{1}{2}$% compounded monthly for the first 10 years and 8% compounded semiannually thereafter?

26. Monty expects to contribute $300 to his TFSA at the end of every month for the next 5 years. For the subsequent 10 years, he plans to contribute $2000 at the end of each calendar quarter. How much will be in his TFSA at the end of the 15 years if the funds earn 8% compounded semiannually?

27. Gloria has just made her ninth annual $2000 contribution to her RRSP. She now plans to make semiannual contributions of $2000. The first contribution will be made six months from now. How much will she have in her RRSP 15 years from now if the plan has earned and will continue to earn 8% compounded quarterly?

28. The Toronto Raptors announce the signing of one of their players to a "seven-year deal worth $43.2 million." The player will earn $400,000 at the end of each month for the first three years, and $600,000 at the end of each month for the subsequent four years. How do the Raptors get the $43.2 million figure? To the nearest $1000, what is the current economic value of the deal if money can earn 7% compounded annually?

29. Micheline wishes to purchase a 25-year annuity providing payments of $1000 per month for the first 15 years and $1500 per month for the remaining 10 years. Sovereign Insurance Co. has quoted her a rate of return of 5% compounded annually for such an annuity. How much will it cost Micheline to purchase the annuity from Sovereign?

30. Joshua wants to structure a 20-year annuity so that its end-of-quarter payments are $2000 for the first 10 years and $2500 for the next 10 years. Pacific Life Insurance Co. offers to sell this annuity with a 4.8% compounded monthly rate of return to the annuitant. What amount must Joshua pay to Pacific for the annuity?

ADVANCED PROBLEM

31. What will be the amount in an RRSP after 25 years if contributions of $3000 are made at each year-end for the first seven years and month-end contributions of $500 are made for the subsequent 18 years? Assume that the plan earns 8% compounded quarterly for the first 12 years, and 7% compounded semiannually for the subsequent 13 years.

KEY TERMS

Annuity	Ordinary annuities	Payment interval
Annuities due	Ordinary general annuity	Present value of an annuity
Future value of an annuity	Ordinary simple annuity	Term (of an annuity)

SUMMARY OF NOTATION AND KEY FORMULAS

PMT = Periodic payment in an annuity

n = Number of payments in the annuity

FV = Future value of an ordinary annuity

PV = Present value of an ordinary annuity

i = (Given) periodic interest rate

i_2 = Equivalent periodic interest rate (per payment interval for a general annuity)

$c = \dfrac{\text{Number of compoundings per year}}{\text{Number of payments per year}}$

FORMULA (11-1) $FV = PMT\left[\dfrac{(1 + i)^n - 1}{i}\right]$ Finding the future value of an ordinary simple annuity

FORMULA (11-2) $PV = PMT\left[\dfrac{1 - (1 + i)^{-n}}{i}\right]$ Finding the present value of an ordinary simple annuity

FORMULA (11-3) $c = \dfrac{\textit{Number of compoundings per year}}{\textit{Number of payments per year}}$ Finding the number of compoundings per payment interval

FORMULA (10-4c) $i_2 = (1 + i)^c - 1$ Finding the periodic interest rate that matches the payment interval in a general annuity

Original loan = $\left[\begin{array}{l}\text{Present value of } \textit{all} \text{ payments (discounted} \\ \text{at the } \textit{contractual rate of interest} \text{ on the loan)}\end{array}\right]$

Principal balance = $\left[\begin{array}{l}\text{Present value of the } \textit{remaining} \text{ payments (discounted} \\ \text{at the } \textit{contractual rate of interest} \text{ on the loan)}\end{array}\right]$

Approach for Solving a General Annuity Problem

Transform the general annuity problem into a simple annuity problem by:

1. Using $i_2 = (1 + i)^c - 1$ to calculate the equivalent periodic rate that matches the payment interval.
2. Using this equivalent periodic rate as the value for i in the appropriate simple annuity formula.

REVIEW PROBLEMS

Answers to the odd-numbered review problems are at the end of the book.

BASIC PROBLEMS

1. **LO2** Calculate the amounts that will be accumulated after 20 years if:
   a. $1000 is invested at the end of every six months at 5.5% compounded semiannually.
   b. $2000 is invested at the end of every year at 5.5% compounded annually.

2. **LO3** Louiselle purchased a motor home for $9000 down, with the balance to be paid by 60 monthly payments of $1176.40 including interest at 6% compounded monthly.
   a. What was the purchase price of the motor home?
   b. If the principal balance may be prepaid at any time, what is the payout amount two years after the purchase date (not including the scheduled payment on that date)?

3. **LO3** What price will a finance company pay for a conditional sale contract requiring 15 monthly payments of $180.50, if the company requires a rate of return of 21% compounded semiannually? The first payment is due one month from now.

4. **LO3** You can purchase a residential building lot for $60,000 cash, or for $10,000 down and month-end payments of $1000 for five years. If money is worth 7.5% compounded monthly, which option should you choose?

5. **LO2** A victim of a car accident won a judgment for wages lost over a two-year period that ended nine months before the date of the judgment. In addition, the court awarded interest at 3% compounded monthly on the lost wages from the date they would otherwise have been received to the date of the judgment. If the monthly salary was $5500, what was the total amount of the award (on the date of the judgment)?

6. **LO3** Dr. Wilson is buying a 50% ownership in a veterinary practice by end-of-month payments of $714.60, including interest at 7% compounded semiannually for 15 years. Rounded to the nearest dollar,
   a. What valuation was placed on the partnership at the beginning of the payments?
   b. What total amount of interest will she pay over the 15 years?

7. **LO2** What minimum amount of money earning 2.5% compounded semiannually will sustain withdrawals of $1000 at the end of every month for 12 years?

8. **LO4** A 15-year loan requires month-end payments of $587.33 including interest at 8.4% compounded monthly.
   a. What was the original amount of the loan?
   b. What is the balance on the loan after half of the payments have been made?

9. **LO2** Calculate the future value of an ordinary annuity consisting of monthly payments of $300 for five years. The rate of return was 9% compounded monthly for the first two years, and will be 7.5% compounded monthly for the last three years.

10. **LO2** How much larger will the value of an RRSP be at the end of 20 years if the contributor makes month-end contributions of $500, instead of year-end contributions of $6000? In both cases the RRSP earns 7.5% compounded semiannually.

11. **LO2** Dr. Krawchuk made deposits of $2000 to his RRSP at the end of each calendar quarter for six years. He then left general practice for specialist training and did not make further contributions for $2\frac{1}{2}$ years. What amount was in his RRSP at the end of this period, if the plan earned 10% compounded quarterly over the entire $8\frac{1}{2}$ years?

12. **LO3** A Province of Ontario bond has $14\frac{1}{2}$ years remaining until it matures. The bond pays $231.25 interest at the end of every six months. At maturity, the bond repays its $5000 face value in addition to the final interest payment. What is the fair market value of the bond, if similar provincial bonds are currently providing investors with a return of 7.8% compounded semiannually?

ADVANCED PROBLEMS

13. **LO2** A court-ordered award for family support calls for payments of $800 per month for five years, followed by payments of $1000 per month for 10 more years. If money is worth 6% compounded monthly, what is the economic value of the award one month before the first payment?

14. **LO2** Calculate the future value of investments of $800 at the end of each calendar quarter for seven years. The rate of return will be 10% compounded quarterly for the first 30 months and 9% compounded semiannually for the remainder of the annuity's term.

15. **LO2** Norma is planning a trip to India when she retires nine years from now and has calculated that she will need $30,000 in her savings to support her travels. If she contributes $800 to her savings at the end of every three months for the first four years of savings and $200 at the end of every month for the following five years, how close to her goal will she get if money can earn 3.5% compounding quarterly for the entire nine years?

16. **LO2** Charlene has made contributions of $3000 to her RRSP at the end of every half-year for the past seven years. The plan has earned 9% compounded semiannually. She has just moved the funds to another plan earning 7.5% compounded quarterly, and will now contribute $2000 at the end of every three months. What total amount will she have in the plan five years from now?

17. **LO2** What percentage more funds will you have in your RRSP 20 years from now if you make fixed contributions of $3000 at the end of every six months for the next 20 years, instead of waiting 10 years and making semiannual contributions that are twice as large for half as many years? Assume that the RRSP earns 8% compounded semiannually.

18. **LO3** A mortgage broker offers to sell you a mortgage loan contract delivering month-end payments of $900 for the next $2\frac{3}{4}$ years. At that point, the principal balance of $37,886 is due and payable. What should you pay for the contract, if you require a return of 7.2% compounded monthly?

19. **LO3** What is the appropriate price to pay for a contract guaranteeing payments of $1500 at the end of each quarter for the next 12 years? You require a rate of return of 6% compounded quarterly for the first five years, and 7% compounded quarterly for the next seven years.

20. **LO2** Suppose Evan contributes $2000 to his RRSP at the end of every quarter for the next 15 years, and then contributes $1000 at each month's end for the subsequent 10 years. How much will he have in his RRSP at the end of the 25 years? Assume that the RRSP earns 8% compounded semiannually.

Chapter 12

Ordinary Annuities: Periodic Payment, Number of Payments, and Interest Rate

CHAPTER OUTLINE

12.1 Calculating the Periodic Payment

12.2 Calculating the Number of Payments

12.3 Calculating the Interest Rate

Appendix 12A: Derivation of the Formula for *n* from the Formula for *FV* (located online)

Appendix 12B: The Trial-and-Error Method for Calculating the Interest Rate per Payment Interval (located online)

LEARNING OBJECTIVES

After completing this chapter, you will be able to:

LO1 Calculate the periodic payment in ordinary simple annuities and ordinary general annuities

LO2 Calculate the number of payments in ordinary simple annuities and ordinary general annuities

LO3 Calculate the interest rate in ordinary simple annuities and ordinary general annuities

IN CHAPTER 11, OUR DISCUSSION of ordinary annuities was restricted to applications of future-value and present-value calculations. But there are many circumstances in which one of the other variables must be determined. Consider the following questions:

- What is the monthly payment required to repay a $10,000 loan at 7% compounded monthly in four years?
- At a forecast rate of return, how long will it take to accumulate $500,000 in an RRSP if you contribute $300 per month?
- What rate of return is required for RRSP contributions of $400 per month to grow to $600,000 in 25 years?
- What interest rate are you being charged when you purchase equipment, furniture, insurance, memberships, magazine subscriptions, etc., on an installment plan instead of paying cash?

Clearly, the ability to answer such questions is important both in business and in your personal financial affairs. In this chapter, you will learn how to answer these questions if the payments form an ordinary annuity. (**Chapter 13** will examine cases in which the payments are at the beginning of each payment interval.)

12.1 Calculating the Periodic Payment

Some circumstances in which the periodic payment, *PMT*, must be calculated are:

- Determining the monthly payments on a loan.
- Determining the amount that must be saved on a regular basis to reach a savings goal.
- Determining the periodic payment from an annuity purchased with accumulated savings.

L01 In order to calculate *PMT*, you need to know the number of payments, n, and the periodic interest rate, i (or be able to readily determine them from the given information). In addition, you must know *either* the present value, *PV*, *or* the future value, *FV*, of the annuity.

Algebraic Method

The calculation of *PMT* may require up to four steps.

Step 1: If the payments form a *simple* annuity, go directly to Step 2.
        If the payments form a *general* annuity, use $i_2 = (1 + i)^c - 1$ to calculate the periodic interest rate that matches the payment interval. Use i_2 as the value for i in Step 2.

Step 2: If the annuity's *FV* is known, substitute values of *FV*, n, and i into
$$FV = PMT\left[\frac{(1 + i)^n - 1}{i}\right] \quad (11\text{-}1)$$

Step 2: If the annuity's *PV* is known, substitute values of *PV*, n, and i into
$$PV = PMT\left[\frac{1 - (1 + i)^{-n}}{i}\right] \quad (11\text{-}2)$$

Step 3: Calculate the quantity within the square brackets.

Step 4: Rearrange the equation to solve for *PMT*.

Financial Calculator Method (Texas Instruments BA II PLUS)

Enter the known values for $\boxed{\text{N}}$, $\boxed{\text{I/Y}}$, $\boxed{\text{PV}}$, $\boxed{\text{FV}}$, $\boxed{\text{P/Y}}$, and $\boxed{\text{C/Y}}$. Remember to use the cash-flow sign convention for amounts entered in $\boxed{\text{PV}}$ and $\boxed{\text{FV}}$. Then press $\boxed{\text{CPT}}$ $\boxed{\text{PMT}}$ to execute the computation.

EXAMPLE 12.1A

CALCULATING THE PERIODIC INVESTMENT NEEDED TO REACH A SAVINGS TARGET

Markham Auto Body wishes to accumulate a fund of $300,000 during the next 18 months in order to open at a second location. At the end of each month, a fixed amount will be invested in a money market savings account with an investment dealer. What should the monthly investment be in order to reach the savings objective? The planning assumption is that the account will earn 3.6% compounded monthly.

SOLUTION

The savings target of $300,000 represents the future value of the fixed *monthly* investments. Since earnings are compounded *monthly*, the *end-of-month* investments form an *ordinary simple* annuity. We are given:

Step 1: $FV = \$300,000$ $n = 18$ and $i = \frac{3.6\%}{12} = 0.3\%$ per month

Step 2:   Substitute the given values into Formula (11-1).

$$FV = PMT\left[\frac{(1 + i)^n - 1}{i}\right]$$

$$\$300,000 = PMT\left[\frac{1.003^{18} - 1}{0.003}\right]$$

Step 3: $\$300,000 = PMT(18.4664273)$

Step 4: $PMT = \dfrac{\$300,000}{18.4664273} = \$16,245.70$

3.6 | I/Y

P/Y 12 ENTER

(making $C/Y = P/Y = 12$)

18 | N

0 | PV

300000 | FV

CPT | PMT

Ans: −16,245.70

Markham Auto Body should make monthly investments of $16,245.70 in order to accumulate $300,000 after 18 months.

EXAMPLE 12.1B

CALCULATING THE PERIODIC LOAN PAYMENTS THAT FORM AN ORDINARY GENERAL ANNUITY

A $5000 loan requires payments at the end of each quarter for four years. If the interest rate on the loan is 9% compounded monthly, what is the size of each payment?

SOLUTION

The original loan equals the present value of all payments discounted at the loan's interest rate. Since interest is compounded *monthly* and payments are made at the *end* of each *quarter*, we have an *ordinary general* annuity with

$$PV = \$5000 \quad n = 4(4) = 16 \quad \text{and} \quad i = \frac{9\%}{12} = 0.75\% \text{ per month}$$

Step 1:   Then, $c = \dfrac{12 \text{ compoundings per year}}{4 \text{ payments per year}} = 3$

and $i_2 = (1 + i)^c - 1$
              $= (1.0075)^3 - 1$
              $= 0.02266917$ per quarter

Step 2:   Substitute the preceding values into Formula (11-2).

$$PV = PMT\left[\frac{1 - (1 + i)^{-n}}{i}\right]$$

$$\$5000 = PMT\left[\frac{1 - 1.02266917^{-16}}{0.02266917}\right]$$

Step 3: $\$5000 = PMT(13.29497)$

Step 4: $PMT = \dfrac{\$5000}{13.29497} = \$376.08$

9 | I/Y

P/Y 4 ENTER

C/Y 12 ENTER

16 | N

5000 | PV

0 | FV

CPT | PMT

Ans: −376.08

The size of each quarterly payment is $376.08.

EXAMPLE 12.1C

CALCULATING THE PERIODIC LOAN PAYMENT REQUIRED TO REACH A TARGET BALANCE

Simon owns a mobile welding business. Every three years, he trades in his old pickup truck and buys a new one. In each cycle, he finances the full purchase price with a loan structured so that the balance owed after three years will be the truck's anticipated trade-in value. Simon is about to purchase a new truck for $37,000, including taxes. The interest rate on the $37,000 loan will be 7.2% compounded monthly. What monthly payment will reduce the balance on the loan after three years to the expected trade-in value of $16,500?

SOLUTION

Again we will use the fundamental principle that

$$\text{Original principal} = \text{Present value of all payments}$$

This principle applies whether or not all payments are equal. (The $16,500 balance after three years can be viewed as the amount which, along with the last monthly payment, will pay off the loan.)

$$\$37,000 = \left(\begin{array}{c}\text{Present value of the}\\\text{loan payment annuity}\end{array}\right) + \left(\begin{array}{c}\text{Present value of}\\\text{the \$16,500 balance}\end{array}\right) \quad ①$$

Since we have *end-of-month* payments and *monthly* compounding, the payments form an *ordinary simple* annuity. For both the annuity and the terminal payment,

$$n = 12(3) = 36 \quad \text{and} \quad i = \tfrac{7.2\%}{12} = 0.6\%$$

Using Formulas (11-2) and (9-2) on the right side of equation ①, we obtain

$$PV = PMT\left[\frac{1 - (1 + i)^{-n}}{i}\right] + FV(1 + i)^{-n}$$

$$\$37,000 = PMT\left(\frac{1 - 1.006^{-36}}{0.006}\right) + \$16,500(1.006)^{-36}$$

$$\$37,000 = PMT(32.290749) + \$13,303.22$$

Solving for *PMT*,

$$32.290749(PMT) = \$37,000 - \$13,303.22 = \$23,696.78$$

$$PMT = \frac{\$23,696.78}{32.290749} = \$733.86$$

7.2 I/Y

P/Y 12 ENTER

(making C/Y = P/Y = 12)

36 N

37000 PV

16500 +/− FV

CPT PMT

Ans: −733.86

Monthly payments of $733.86 will reduce the balance to $16,500 after three years.

EXAMPLE 12.1D

CALCULATING THE PERIODIC INVESTMENT REQUIRED TO PURCHASE A SPECIFIED ANNUITY ON A FUTURE DATE

Douglas and Margaret Kuramoto want to retire in 15 years with enough funds in their RRSPs to purchase a 25-year annuity that will pay $5000 at the end of each month. They have already accumulated $125,000 in their RRSPs. In order to fulfill the plan, what RRSP contribution should they make at the end of each of the next 15 years? For the financial projections, they are assuming returns of 8% compounded annually on their RRSPs and 6% compounded monthly on the annuity purchased with their RRSP funds.

SOLUTION

The given information and the steps in the solution are presented in the time diagram.

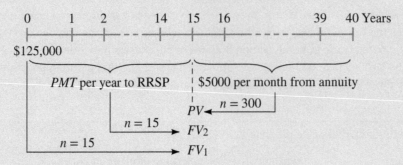

The total amount in the RRSPs 15 years from now will be the future value FV_1 of the $125,000 already in the RRSPs *plus* the future value FV_2 of 15 more annual contributions of size *PMT*. The amount needed to purchase the annuity paying $5000 per month will be the present value, *PV*, of the 12(25) = 300 payments discounted at $i = \frac{6\%}{12} = 0.5\%$. Each series of payments forms an ordinary simple annuity.

In order to have enough money in their RRSPs 15 years from now to purchase the desired annuity, the Kuramotos require

$$FV_1 + FV_2 = PV \quad ①$$

The amount that will be needed to purchase the annuity is

$$PV = PMT\left[\frac{1 - (1 + i)^{-n}}{i}\right]$$

$$= \$5000\left(\frac{1 - 1.005^{-300}}{0.005}\right)$$

$$= \$776,034.32$$

The future value of the $125,000 already saved is

$$FV_1 = PV(1 + i)^n$$
$$= \$125,000(1.08)^{15}$$
$$= \$396,521.14$$

The future value of the 15 annual contributions of *PMT* is

$$FV_2 = PMT\left[\frac{(1 + i)^n - 1}{i}\right]$$

$$= PMT\left(\frac{1.08^{15} - 1}{0.08}\right)$$

$$= 27.152114(PMT)$$

Substituting these values into equation ①, we obtain

$$\$396,521.14 + 27.152114(PMT) = \$776,034.32$$
$$27.152114(PMT) = \$379,513.18$$
$$PMT = \$13,977.30$$

The Kuramotos must make annual RRSP contributions of $13,977.30.

6 | I/Y |
| P/Y | 12 | ENTER |
(making $C/Y = P/Y = 12$)

300 | N |
5000 | PMT |
0 | FV |
| CPT | PV |
Ans: −776,034.32

8 | I/Y |
| P/Y | 1 | ENTER |
(making $C/Y = P/Y = 1$)

15 | N |
125000 | +/− | PV |
776034.32 | FV |
| CPT | PMT |
Ans: −13,977.30

TIP

Breaking Down the Pieces

In more complex questions, such as Example 12.1D, it helps to break down the problem into smaller pieces. First, identify all the individual cash flows and decide if they use regular compound interest calculations (these usually involve lump sum amounts) or if they form an annuity. If they are annuities, identify what type of annuity they are and what you are trying to calculate for each type. If you are unsure what you are trying to solve for, try approaching the problem by identifying what you know about each annuity. Lastly, work out the relationship between all of the cash flows to form the equation that will lead to the solution to the problem. As always, drawing a time line is an important step in the solution.

POINT OF INTEREST

Retirement Dreams Then and Now

Freedom 55 is quickly fading from the retirement dreams of Boomers and Gen Xers. The retirement plan of paying off the mortgage, accumulating one million dollars in investments, and living off your pension in a tropical paradise is not as realistic as it used to be.

For starters, people are living longer. The average life expectancy for Canadians in 2018 was 80 years for men and 84 years for women. This is an increase of about 6 years from 30 years ago and it is projected that by 2026, one in five Canadians will be 65 or older. (In 2001, this number was one in eight.) The impact on retirement savings means that your "nest egg" needs to sustain you longer.

The recession of 2008–2009 and the vicious "bear" market (which took the S&P/TSX Composite Index down from above 15,000 in June 2008 to below 7500 in March 2009) caused many middle-aged workers to postpone their planned retirement dates. Again in 2018, the market saw its worst performance since the 2008 recession losing 15%. The $1 million nest egg is no longer earning sufficient returns to sustain a longer retirement.

With interest on mortgages still at historically low rates, paying off the mortgage is no longer a priority before retirement. A typical payment on an average mortgage could be between $300 and $1500 a month (assuming 4%), depending on the amortization period. The old-school thinking of $1,000,000 to retire on assumes annual spending of $30,000 a year, investment returns of about 6.5%, and no debt. In today's scenario, mortgage payments alone could account for $18,000 of total annual spending. Since 1999, the number of Canadians aged 55 to 64 with a mortgage has increased from 34% to 46%.

Before you start banking on a big lottery win as your retirement income, there is some good news on the horizon. The best retirement plan is still to start saving when you are young and pay off debt. Many experts will tell you that it is safe to assume you can live off of 70% to 80% of your current salary and still maintain your current standard of living after retirement.

The following table shows how much you would have to save every year to have the equivalent of a $50,000 annual income (not counting your pension) measured in today's dollars (purchasing power at the starting age). The calculations are done assuming that you stop working at age 65 and live to age 90. A 5% return on investment and an inflation rate until retirement of 3% were used.

Starting at age	Savings required at age 65	Annual savings
20	$2,664,883	$16,687
35	$1,710,485	$25,745
50	$1,097,895	$50,879

QUESTIONS

1. For the starting-at-age-20 case, what income at age 65 will have the same purchasing power as $50,000 at age 20?
2. For the starting-at-age-20 case, show how the amounts for the "Savings required" and "Annual savings" are obtained.

Sources: "Life Expectancy in North America in 2018." Statista. https://www.statista.com/statistics/274513/life-expectancy-in-north-america/; "Canada's Economy and Household Debt: How Big Is the Problem?" Bank of Canada. https://www.bankofcanada.ca/2018/05/canada-economy-household-debt-how-big-the-problem/.

CONCEPT QUESTIONS

1. Suppose you choose to pay off a loan over 10 years instead of 5 years. The principal and interest rate are the same in both cases. Will the payment for the 10-year term be: **(i)** Half the payment for the 5-year term? **(ii)** More than half the payment? **(iii)** Less than half the payment? Give the reasoning for your choice.

2. You intend to accumulate $100,000 in 10 years instead of 20 years by making equal monthly investment contributions. Will the monthly contribution for a 10-year plan be: **(i)** Twice the monthly contribution for a 20-year plan? **(ii)** Less than twice the monthly contribution? **(iii)** More than twice the monthly contribution? Assume the same rate of return in both cases. Give the reasoning for your choice.

EXERCISE 12.1

Answers to the odd-numbered problems are at the end of the book.

Mc Graw Hill connect

Spreadsheet template: A partially completed Excel template for calculating the payment in an annuity is provided on Connect. You can use this template for many of the problems in Exercise 12.1. Go to the Student Edition of Connect and find "PMT for Any Annuity" found under the Student Resources for Chapter 12.

BASIC PROBLEMS

1. Calculate the amount that must be invested at the end of each year at 9% compounded annually in order to accumulate $500,000 after:
   a. 25 years.   **b.** 30 years.

   In each case, also determine what portion of the $500,000 represents earnings on the annual investments.

2. In order to accumulate $500,000 after 25 years, calculate the amounts that must be invested at the end of each year, if the invested funds earn:
   a. 6% compounded annually.   **b.** 7% compounded annually.
   c. 8% compounded annually.   **d.** 9% compounded annually.

   In each case, also calculate the total earnings.

3. A 20-year annuity is purchased for $400,000. What payment will it deliver at the end of each quarter, if the undistributed funds earn:
   a. 4% compounded quarterly?   **b.** 5% compounded quarterly?
   c. 6% compounded quarterly?   **d.** 7% compounded quarterly?

   In each case, also calculate the total earnings distributed over the life of the annuity.

4. The interest rate on a $100,000 loan is 7.5% compounded monthly. What must be the monthly payment for the loan to be repaid in:
   a. 5 years?   **b.** 10 years?
   c. 15 years?   **d.** 20 years?

   In each case, also calculate the total interest paid. (Note that a doubling of the term more than doubles the total interest paid over the life of the loan.)

5. Assume that the investments within an RRSP will earn 5% compounded annually. What monthly contribution must be made to the RRSP for it to grow to $750,000 in:
   a. 15 years?   **b.** 20 years?
   c. 25 years?   **d.** 30 years?

   In each case, also calculate the total earnings within the RRSP. (Note that the total earnings increase proportionately more than the duration of contributions.)

6. Marissa intends to make contributions to a TFSA such that the account will accumulate $150,000 after 20 years. What end-of-quarter contributions must be made if the TFSA earns 6% compounded:
   a. Annually?
   b. Semiannually?
   c. Quarterly?
   d. Monthly?

7. What monthly payment is required to pay off a $50,000 loan in seven years if the interest rate on the loan is 7.5% compounded:
   a. Annually?
   b. Semiannually?
   c. Quarterly?
   d. Monthly?

8. Norman financed the $2800 purchase price of his new washer and dryer with monthly payments at 6.4% compounded monthly made over two years. What will be the amount of each payment?

9. Kyle wants to save $15,000 so he can take a trip to Australia when he graduates from college three years from now. How much must he contribute to a savings plan at the end of every month if the plan earns 4% compounded monthly?

10. Claudette plans to retire this year. Currently she has $560,000 in accumulated capital. She wants to invest this capital to provide equal payments at the end of each year for 20 years, at which time the capital will be fully depleted. If her capital earns 7.5% compounded annually, what annual payment will Claudette receive?

11. Karen obtained a $20,000 loan at 4% compounded semiannually. What monthly payment will repay the loan in $7\frac{1}{2}$ years? How much interest will Karen pay over the life of the loan?

12. Brenda and Tom want to save $30,000 over the next four years for a down payment on a house. What amount must they regularly save from their month-end paycheques if their savings can earn 5.5% compounded semiannually?

13. Henry can buy a farm for $700,000 with terms of $100,000 down and the balance payable over 20 years by quarterly payments including interest at 8% compounded annually. What will be the size of the payments? How much interest will Henry pay over the life of the loan?

14. RBC Royal Bank approved a four-year $20,000 Royal Buy-Back Car Loan to Zaman at 7.5% compounded monthly. The monthly payments are to reduce the balance on the loan to the Royal Bank's guaranteed buy-back value of $7250. Calculate the monthly payment.

15. Ardith is scheduled to make a lump payment of $25,000, 11 months from now, to complete a real estate transaction. What end-of-month payments for the next 11 months should the vendor be willing to accept instead of the lump payment if he can invest the funds at 5.4% compounded monthly?

INTERMEDIATE PROBLEMS

16. In order to purchase another truck, Beatty Transport recently obtained a $50,000 loan for five years at 7.8% compounded semiannually.
    a. What are the monthly payments on the loan?
    b. What will be the loan's balance at the end of the second year?
    c. How much interest will Beatty pay in the first two years?

17. Mr. Bean wants to borrow $7500 for three years. The interest rate is 5.5% compounded monthly.
    a. What quarterly payments are required on the loan?
    b. What will be the balance owed on the loan at the start of the third year?

18. The interest rate on a $200,000 loan is 8% compounded quarterly.
    a. What payments at the end of every quarter will reduce the balance to $150,000 after $3\frac{1}{2}$ years?
    b. If the same payments continue, what will be the balance seven years after the date that the loan was received?
    c. How much interest will be paid during the first seven years?

19. As of Betty's 56th birthday, she has accumulated $195,000 in her RRSP. She has ceased contributions but will allow the RRSP to grow at an expected 5.4% compounded monthly until she reaches age 65. Then she will use the funds in the RRSP to purchase a 20-year annuity. What will her end-of-month annuity payments be if the money used to purchase the annuity earns 4.2% compounded monthly?

20. On the date of his granddaughter's birth, Mr. Parry deposited $5000 in a trust fund earning 6.2% compounded annually. After the granddaughter's 19th birthday, the trust account will make end-of-month payments to her for four years to assist with the costs of postsecondary education. If the trust account earns 4.8% compounded monthly during these four years, what will be the size of the monthly payments?

21. Elizabeth has been able to transfer a $25,000 retiring allowance into an RRSP. She plans to let the RRSP accumulate earnings at the rate of 5% compounded annually for 10 years, and then purchase a 15-year annuity making payments at the end of each quarter. What size of payment can she expect if the funds in the annuity earn 5.2% compounded quarterly?

22. Ken and Barbara have two children, aged three and six. At the end of every six months for the next $12\frac{1}{2}$ years, they wish to contribute equal amounts to an RESP. Six months after the last RESP contribution, the first of 12 semiannual withdrawals of $5000 will be made. If the RESP earns 8.5% compounded semiannually, what must be the size of their regular RESP contributions?

23. Four years from now, Tim and Justine plan to take a year's leave of absence from their jobs and travel through Asia, Europe, and Africa. They want to accumulate enough savings during the next four years so they can withdraw $3000 at each month-end for the entire year of leave. What amount must they pay into the fund at the end of every calendar quarter for the next four years to reach their goal? The planning assumptions are that their savings will earn 6% compounded quarterly for the next four years and 4.2% compounded monthly during the fifth year.

24. Beth and Nelson want to accumulate a combined total of $600,000 in their RRSPs by the time Beth reaches age 60, which will be 30 years from now. They plan to make equal contributions at the end of every six months for the next 25 years, and then no further contributions for the subsequent five years of semiretirement. For planning purposes, assume that their RRSPs will earn 7% compounded semiannually for the next 30 years.
    a. What should be their combined semiannual RRSP contributions?
    b. What monthly amount can they expect to receive if they use the $600,000 in their RRSPs 30 years from now to purchase a 25-year ordinary annuity? Assume that the funds used to purchase the annuity will earn 7.2% compounded monthly.

25. Dr. Collins wants the value of her RRSP 30 years from now to have the purchasing power of $500,000 in current dollars.
    a. Assuming an inflation rate of 2% per year, what nominal dollar amount should Dr. Collins have in her RRSP after 30 years?
    b. Assuming her RRSP will earn 8.5% compounded semiannually, what contributions should she make at the end of every three months to achieve the goal?

26. Harold, who just turned 27, wants to accumulate an amount in his RRSP at age 60 that will have the purchasing power of $300,000 in current dollars. What annual contributions on his 28th through 60th birthdays are required to meet this goal if the RRSP earns 8.5% compounded annually and the rate of inflation is 2.5% per year?

27. As of Brice's 54th birthday, he has accumulated $154,000 in his RRSP. What size of end-of-month payments in a 20-year annuity will these funds purchase at age 65 if he makes no further contributions? Assume that his RRSP and the investment in the annuity will earn 8.25% compounded monthly.

28. Leslie received a settlement when her employer declared her job redundant. Under special provisions of the Income Tax Act, she was eligible to place $22,000 of the settlement in an RRSP. Fifteen years from now, she intends to transfer the money from the RRSP to a Registered Retirement Income Fund (RRIF). Thereafter, Leslie will make equal withdrawals at the end of each quarter for 20 years. If both the RRSP and the RRIF earn 8.5% compounded quarterly, what will be the amount of each withdrawal?

29. A firm obtained a $3 million low-interest loan from a government agency to build a factory in an economically depressed region. The loan is to be repaid in semiannual payments over 15 years, and the first payment is due three years from today, when the firm's operations are expected to be well established.
   a. What will the payments be if the interest rate on the loan is 6% compounded semiannually?
   b. What is the nominal amount of interest that will be paid over the lifetime of the loan?

30. During a one-week promotion, Al's Appliance Warehouse is planning to offer terms of "nothing down and nothing to pay for four months" on major appliances priced above $500. Four months after the date of the sale, the first of eight equal monthly payments is due. If the customer is to pay interest at the rate of 12% compounded monthly on the outstanding balance from the date of sale, what will be the monthly payments on an automatic dishwasher priced at $995?

ADVANCED PROBLEMS

31. Jack Groman's financial plan is designed to accumulate sufficient funds in his RRSP over the next 28 years to purchase an annuity paying $6000 at the end of each month for 25 years. He will be able to contribute $7000 to his RRSP at the end of each year for the next 10 years. What year-end contribution must he make for the subsequent 18 years to achieve his objective? For these projections, assume that Jack's RRSP will earn 7.5% compounded annually, and that the annuity payments are based on a return of 7.5% compounded monthly.

32. Cynthia currently has $31,000 in her RRSP. She plans to contribute $5000 at the end of each year for the next 17 years, and then use the accumulated funds to purchase a 20-year annuity making month-end payments.
   a. If her RRSP earns 8.75% compounded annually for the next 17 years, and the fund from which the annuity is paid will earn 5.4% compounded monthly, what monthly payments will she receive?
   b. If the rate of inflation for the next 17 years is 2%, what will be the purchasing power (in today's dollars) of the monthly payments at the start of the annuity?

33. Mr. Parmar wants to retire in 20 years and purchase a 25-year annuity that will make equal payments at the end of every quarter. The first payment should have the purchasing power of $6000 in today's dollars. If he already has $54,000 in his RRSP, what contributions must he make at the end of every half-year for the next 20 years to achieve his retirement goal? Assume that the rate of inflation for the next 20 years will be 2.5%, the RRSP will earn 8% compounded semiannually, and the rate of return on the fund from which the annuity is paid will be 5.5% compounded quarterly.

34. **Using the "Cool Million" Chart** An interactive "Cool Million" chart on Connect enables you to visualize the growth of your retirement savings over several years. Another feature allows you to determine what changes you would need to make to your investment plan for you to attain nominal "millionaire" status on your 65th birthday.

    Go to the Student Edition on Connect. In Chapter 12, find "Cool Million."

    Enter data for an investment plan that will be reasonable for you after you gain full-time employment. Note that the "Expected rate of return" and the "Expected inflation rate" are both *annually* compounded rates. Click on the "Calculate" button to generate a new chart. The series of blue bars shows the growth of your investments. If you move your cursor over any bar, the numerical value (in $000s) will be displayed.

    The series of purple bars represents the inflation-adjusted value, or purchasing power, of the investments in terms of dollars at the very beginning—the "Your age" date.

    If you click on the "View Report" button, a window containing a bulleted list of three suggested changes will appear. *Any one* of these changes to your savings plan will enable you to accumulate (a nominal) $1,000,000 at your target retirement age. Adjust one or more items in your input data to arrive at a plan that represents your best chance of entering retirement as a millionaire. What will be the purchasing power of your nominal $1,000,000 in beginning dollars?

12.2 Calculating the Number of Payments

Circumstances in which the number of payments, n, must be calculated include:

- Determining the time required for periodic payments to pay off a loan.
- Determining the time required for a periodic savings plan to reach a savings target.
- Determining how long a single investment can sustain periodic withdrawals.

L02 In order to calculate the number of annuity payments, you need to know *PMT* and i (or be able to determine them from the given information). In addition, you must know either the *PV* or the *FV* of the annuity.

Suppose you substitute known values for *FV*, *PMT*, and i in Formula (11-1) for the future value of an annuity, or you substitute known values for *PV*, *PMT* and i in Formula (11-2), and then proceed to solve for n. The procedure is more complex than it was in **Section 12.1** for isolating *PMT*—it requires some familiarity with manipulating logarithms. For these reasons, we present the following versions of Formulas (11-1) and (11-2) rearranged to calculate n.

$$n = \frac{\ln\left(1 + \frac{i \times FV}{PMT}\right)}{\ln(1 + i)}$$
(11-1*n*)

$$n = -\frac{\ln\left(1 - \frac{i \times PV}{PMT}\right)}{\ln(1 + i)}$$
(11-2*n*)

Since these are merely new versions of Formulas (11-1) and (11-2), we will refer to them as (11-1*n*)[1] and (11-2*n*). If the payments form a general annuity, the periodic interest rate that matches the payment interval (that is, i_2) must be substituted for i. **Appendix 12A** shows the rearrangement of Formula (11-1) to get Formula (11-1*n*).

---

[1]   The derivation of Formula (11-1*n*) from Formula (11-1) is presented in Chapter 12 on Connect; see **Appendix 12A**.

TIP

Interpretation of "*n*" When It Is Not an Integer

The value obtained for *n* will not necessarily be an integer. To illustrate the interpretation of a non-integer value, suppose *n* = 21.3 in a particular case. This means that there are 22 payments, but the last payment is smaller than the others. Prevailing business practice is to allow a full payment interval for the final reduced payment. Even though the fractional part of *n* in this case is 0.3, it is only an approximation to say that the last payment is 30% of the size of the others. The method for calculating the exact size of the final payment will be presented in **Chapter 15**.

TIP

Obtaining the Term of an Annuity from the Value of "*n*"

A problem may ask for the *term* of the annuity rather than the number of payments. Let's consider a specific numerical example before addressing the general case. Suppose a question has asked you to determine the term of an annuity in which there are four payments per year. Suppose you obtained *n* = 34.5 payments. This means the annuity consists of 35 payments. (Remember the preceding TIP.) Since there are four payments per year, the annuity's term in years is

$$\frac{35 \text{ payments}}{4 \text{ payments per year}} = 8.75 \text{ years}.$$

In general,

$$\text{Term of annuity (in years)} = \frac{n(\text{rounded upward})}{\text{Number of payments per year}}$$

The common practice is to convert the fractional part of a year to months. Since

$$0.75 \text{ years} = 0.75(12 \text{ months}) = 9 \text{ months}$$

the term in our numerical example would normally be expressed as "8 years and 9 months."

EXAMPLE 12.2A

CALCULATING *n* GIVEN THE FUTURE VALUE OF AN ORDINARY GENERAL ANNUITY

One month from now, Maurice will make his first monthly contribution of $250 to a TFSA. Over the long run, he expects to earn 8% compounded annually. How long will it take for the contributions and accrued earnings to reach $100,000? (Round *n* to the next larger integer.)

SOLUTION

Since compounding occurs *annually* but the contributions are made *monthly*, the payments form a *general* annuity having

$$FV = \$100,000 \quad PMT = \$250 \quad \text{and} \quad i = \frac{8\%}{1} = 8\%$$

To obtain the periodic rate matching the monthly payment interval, first calculate

$$c = \frac{1 \text{ compounding per year}}{12 \text{ payments per year}} = 0.08\overline{3}$$

Then

$$i_2 = (1 + i)^c - 1 = 1.08^{0.08\overline{3}} - 1 = 0.00643403 \text{ per month}$$

Substitute these values into Formula (11-1*n*).

$$n = \frac{\ln\left(1 + \frac{i \times FV}{PMT}\right)}{\ln(1 + i)}$$

$$= \frac{\ln\left[1 + \frac{0.00643403\,(\$100{,}000)}{\$250}\right]}{\ln(1.00643403)}$$

$$= \frac{1.27358}{0.0064134}$$

$$= 198.58$$

8	I/Y
P/Y	12	ENTER
C/Y	1	ENTER
0	PV
250	+/−	PMT
100000	FV
CPT	N

Ans: 198.58

The annuity has 199 payments taking 199 months. We need to express the time required in years and months.

$$199 \text{ months} = \tfrac{199}{12} \text{ years} = 16.58\overline{3} \text{ years} = 16 \text{ years} + (0.58\overline{3} \times 12 \text{ months}) = 16 \text{ years, 7 months}$$

It will take 16 years and 7 months for Maurice to accumulate $100,000 in the TFSA.

EXAMPLE 12.2B

CALCULATING THE TIME REQUIRED TO PAY OFF A LOAN

Roy and Lynn are discussing the terms of a $28,000 home improvement loan with their bank's lending officer. The interest rate on the loan is 7.5% compounded monthly.

a. How long will it take to repay the loan if the monthly payments are $220?

b. How long will it take to repay the loan if they pay an extra $20 per month?

c. Calculate the approximate total nominal interest savings over the life of the loan as a result of making payments of $240 instead of $220 per month.

SOLUTION

The original loan equals the present value of all the payments. The payments form an ordinary simple annuity with $PV = \$28{,}000$ and $i = \frac{7.5\%}{12} = 0.625\%$. In part (a) $PMT = \$220$, and in part (b) $PMT = \$240$.

a. Substitute $PV = \$28{,}000$, $i = 0.625\%$, and $PMT = \$220$ into Formula (11-2n).

$$n = -\frac{\ln\left(1 - \frac{i \times PV}{PMT}\right)}{\ln(1 + i)}$$

$$= -\frac{\ln\left[1 - \frac{0.00625(\$28{,}000)}{\$220}\right]}{\ln(1.00625)}$$

$$= 254.71$$

| 7.5 | I/Y |
| P/Y | 12 | ENTER |
| (making C/Y = P/Y = 12) |
28000	PV
220	+/−	PMT
0	FV
CPT	N

Ans: 254.71

It will take 255 payments, requiring 255 months to pay off the loan.

$$255 \text{ months} = \tfrac{255}{12} \text{ years} = 21.25 \text{ years} = 21 \text{ years} + (0.25 \times 12) \text{ months}$$
$$= 21 \text{ years, 3 months}$$

Therefore, it will take 21 years and 3 months to pay off the loan.

b. Again, we can substitute $PV = \$28{,}000$, $i = 0.625\%$, and $PMT = \$240$ into Formula (11-2n). For those who prefer to work from first principles (and reduce the number of formulas with which they work), we will give one demonstration of calculating n from the basic PV Formula (11-2). Substituting the above values into Formula (11-2), we obtain

$$PV = PMT\left[\frac{1 - (1 + i)^{-n}}{i}\right]$$

$$\$28{,}000 = \$240\left[\frac{1 - 1.00625^{-n}}{0.00625}\right]$$

$$\frac{\$28{,}000}{\$240} \times 0.00625 = 1 - 1.00625^{-n}$$

$$0.7291\overline{6} = 1 - 1.00625^{-n}$$

Rearrange the equation to isolate 1.00625^{-n} on the left-hand side.

$$1.00625^{-n} = 1 - 0.7291\overline{6} = 0.2708\overline{3}$$

Taking logarithms of both sides,

$$-n\ln(1.00625) = \ln(0.2708\overline{3})$$

Hence,

$$n = -\frac{\ln(0.2708\overline{3})}{\ln(1.00625)} = -\frac{-1.30625}{0.00623055} = 209.65$$

> Same *I/Y, P/Y, C/Y*
> Same *PV, FV*
> 240 [+/−] [PMT]
> [CPT] [N]
> *Ans:* 209.65

It will take 210 months (17 years and 6 months) to pay off the loan.

c. With monthly payments of \$220, the total of all payments is approximately

$$254.71(\$220) \approx \$56{,}036$$

With monthly payments of \$240, the total of all payments is approximately

$$209.65(\$240) \approx \$50{,}316$$

Ignoring the time value of money, the saving of interest is *approximately*

$$\$56{,}036 - \$50{,}316 \approx \$5720$$

Postscript: By increasing their monthly payments by less than 10%, Roy and Lynn will pay off the loan in about 18% less time ($17\frac{1}{2}$ years instead of $21\frac{1}{4}$ years). Their total interest costs on the \$28,000 loan will be reduced by over 20% (from \$28,036 to \$22,316). This outcome is typical of long-term debt. It is one of the main reasons why financial planners encourage us to make even slightly larger payments on long-term debt. Note that the above calculations are only an approximation of the interest savings. In Chapter 15, we will look at calculating the exact values.

EXAMPLE 12.2C

CALCULATING THE TIME REQUIRED TO REACH A SAVINGS GOAL AND THE LENGTH OF TIME A FUND WILL SUSTAIN REGULAR WITHDRAWALS

a. Annual contributions of \$5000 will be made at every year-end to an RRSP. Rounding n upwards, how long will it take for the funds in the RRSP to grow to \$500,000 if they earn 7.5% compounded annually?

b. If the \$500,000 will be used to purchase an annuity earning 6% compounded quarterly and paying \$12,000 at the end of each quarter, how long after the purchase date will the annuity payments continue?

SOLUTION

In part (a), the future value of the contributions is to be \$500,000. The contributions form an ordinary simple annuity with $PMT = \$5000$ and $i = \frac{7.5\%}{1} = 7.5\%$.

In part (b), the accumulated \$500,000 becomes the present value of an ordinary simple annuity having $PMT = \$12{,}000$ and $i = \frac{6\%}{4} = 1.5\%$.

a. Substitute the known values into Formula (11-1n).

$$n = \frac{\ln\left(1 + \frac{i \times FV}{PMT}\right)}{\ln(1+i)}$$

$$= \frac{\ln\left[1 + \frac{0.075(\$500,000)}{\$5000}\right]}{\ln(1.075)}$$

$$= 29.59$$

7.5	I/Y
P/Y 1	ENTER

(making $C/Y = P/Y = 1$)

0	PV
5000 +/−	PMT
500000	FV
CPT	N

Ans: 29.59

Rounding n upward, it will take 30 years for the RRSP to accumulate $500,000.
(In this particular case, the interest earned during the 30th year will allow the RRSP to reach $500,000 before[2] the 30th contribution is actually made.)

b. Substitute the known values into Formula (11-2n).

$$n = -\frac{\ln\left(1 - \frac{i \times PV}{PMT}\right)}{\ln(1+i)}$$

$$= -\frac{\ln\left[1 - \frac{0.015(\$500,000)}{\$12,000}\right]}{\ln(1.015)}$$

$$= 65.88$$

6	I/Y
P/Y 4	ENTER

(making $C/Y = P/Y = 4$)

500000 +/−	PV
12000	PMT
0	FV
CPT	N

Ans: 65.88

There will be 66 quarterly payments, with the last payment being about 12% smaller than the others.
   Therefore, the annuity payments will run for

$$\frac{66 \text{ quarters}}{4 \text{ quarters per year}} = 16.5 \text{ years} = 16 \text{ years and 6 months}$$

---

[2] The calculation is actually telling us that the RRSP will reach $500,000 after 29.59135 years if a 30th payment of (essentially) 0.59135 × $5000 is paid into the plan after only 0.59135 of the 30th year. This is not what actually happens—no contribution will be made before the end of the 30th year. To calculate precisely when the RRSP will reach $500,000 (including accrued interest),
   • Calculate the amount in the RRSP after 29 contributions (years).
   • Use Formula (10-2) to calculate the fraction of a year required for the preceding amount to grow to $500,000 through the accrual of interest.

POINT OF INTEREST

What Is Your Net Worth?

How often do you admire your friend's new car, their frequent expensive vacations and all the new clothes and jewellery they seem to constantly be wearing? From the outside looking in, they appear wealthy. You might even say they were "rich." The truth of the matter is that the trappings of wealth are not a real indicator of true wealth. What you cannot see are all of the loans they are paying on and the bills that arrive at their door every month.

© Panther Media GmbH/Alamy

The true measure of personal wealth is your net worth. Net worth looks at the difference between the total value of what you own (your assets) and the total amount of what you owe (your liabilities). Your assets include all of your cash, the value of your investments, any money you have in a pension plan, real estate, cars, and anything else of value that you own. On the other side, your liabilities include all loans and mortgages, all of your credit card debts, and any outstanding student loans.

Your age plays a big part in your net worth. Typically when you are just starting out you are still paying off a student loan and have a car loan, a large mortgage, and wages that reflect the early years of employment. The simple truth is, you aren't earning enough money to overtake the value of your debts. All of this should improve with time provided that debts are paid off, some money is saved and invested, and spending is done responsibly.

In 2018, Casual Money Talk published a summary of the average net worth for single individuals broken down by age.

For all age groups, the majority of assets are attributed to owning property with the rest from investments like RRSPs and TFSAs. The flip side of this is that the main liability you will have is a mortgage, with the rest of your debt coming from loans and credit cards. Where you live also plays a major role in the net worth calculation. Real estate in a large city is more expensive, meaning you will most likely be carrying a larger mortgage than if you live in a smaller town. While salaries are typically higher in bigger centres, earning more money is often offset by the higher cost of living.

Average Net Worth of a Canadian			
Age Group	**Assets**	**Liabilities**	**Net Worth**
Under 35 years old	$158,952	$61,807	$97,145
35 to 44 years old	$169,524	$45,442	$124,082
45 to 54 years old	$282,980	$49,723	$233,257
55 to 64 years old	$534,095	$56,561	$477,534
65 years and older	$854,873	$24,823	$830,050

Sources: "Survey of Financial Security (SFS), Assets and Debts Held by Economic Family Type, by Age Group, Canada, Provinces and Selected Census Metropolitan Areas (CMAs) (x 1,000,000)." Statistics Canada. https://www150.statcan.gc.ca/t1/tbl1/en/tv.action?pid=1110001601, "How Does Your Net Worth Compare with the Average Canadian?" Casual Money Talk. http://casualmoneytalk.com/blog/2018/03/net-worth-compare-average-canadian/.

QUESTIONS

1. Calculate your net worth using the table at right.
2. For all of the items in the liabilities column, calculate how long it will take you to pay off each of these debts knowing what you currently owe on them (*PV*), your payment amount (*PMT*), and the rate of interest being charged on the debt (*I/Y*). Your net worth will increase by the amount of your liabilities in this time period.

ASSETS		LIABILITIES	
Value of Property	$____	Mortgage	$____
RRSPs, TFSAs, Pensions	$____	Lines of Credit	$____
Cash/Savings	$____	Unpaid Credit Cards	$____
Value of Cars	$____	Car Loan Balance	$____
Other Assets	$____	Other Loan Balances	$____
Total Assets	$____	Total Liabilities	$____

Net Worth = Total Assets − Total Liabilities = $_____

CONCEPT QUESTIONS

1. If you double the size of the monthly payment you make on a loan, will you pay it off in (pick one): **(i)** half the time? **(ii)** less than half the time? **(iii)** more than half the time? Give the reasoning for your choice.

2. If you contribute $250 per month to an RRSP instead of $500 per month, will the time required to reach a particular savings target be (pick one): **(i)** twice as long? **(ii)** less than twice as long? **(iii)** more than twice as long? Give the reasoning for your choice.

EXERCISE 12.2

Answers to the odd-numbered problems are at the end of the book.

Spreadsheet template: *A partially completed Excel template for calculating the number of payments in an annuity is provided on Connect. You can use this template for many of the problems in Exercise 12.2. Go to the Student Edition of Connect and find "NPER for Any Annuity" found under the Student Resources for Chapter 12.*

BASIC PROBLEMS

1. Semiannual payments of $3874.48 are made on a $50,000 loan at 6.5% compounded semian-nually. How long will it take to pay off the loan?

2. The future value of an annuity consisting of end-of-year investments of $1658.87 earning 5.2% compounded annually is $100,000. How many annual investments were made?

3. For $200,000, Jamal purchased an annuity that delivers end-of-quarter payments of $3341.74. If the undistributed funds earn 4.5% compounded quarterly, what is the term of the annuity?

4. If money in a new TFSA earns 8.25% compounded monthly, how long will it take for the plan to reach $30,000 in value based on end-of-month contributions of $209.59?

5. An endowment fund is set up with a donation of $100,000. If it earns 4% compounded monthly, for how long will it sustain end-of-month withdrawals of $1000? (Include the final smaller withdrawal.)

6. Rounding up the number of contributions to the next integer, how long will it take an RRSP to surpass $100,000 if it takes in end-of-quarter contributions of $3000 and earns 6% com-pounded quarterly?

7. For how long has William been making end-of-quarter contributions of $1200 to his RRSP if the RRSP has earned 4.75% compounded annually and is currently worth $74,385?

8. Monthly payments of $315.49 are required on a $20,000 loan at 5.5% compounded quarterly. What is the term of the loan?

9. How long will it take an RRSP to grow to $700,000 if it takes in month-end contributions of $1000 and it earns:
   a. 4% compounded monthly?　　　　**b.** 6% compounded monthly?
   c. 8% compounded monthly?　　　　**d.** 9% compounded monthly?

   Round up the number of contributions to the next integer.

10. How long will it take for monthly payments of $800 to repay a $100,000 loan if the interest rate on the loan is:
    a. 6% compounded monthly?　　　　**b.** 7% compounded monthly?
    c. 8% compounded monthly?　　　　**d.** 9% compounded monthly?

11. How long will it take for monthly payments of $740 to repay a $100,000 loan if the interest rate on the loan is:
    a. 7.5% compounded annually?　　　　**b.** 7.5% compounded semiannually?
    c. 7.5% compounded quarterly?　　　　**d.** 7.5% compounded monthly?

12. How long will it take an RESP to grow to $200,000 if the plan owner contributes $250 at the end of each month and the plan earns:
    a. 8% compounded monthly?
    b. 8% compounded quarterly?
    c. 8% compounded semiannually?
    d. 8% compounded annually?

    Round up the number of contributions to the next integer before calculating the total time.

13. Rounded to the next higher month, how long will it take end-of-month deposits of $500 to accumulate $100,000 in an investment account that earns 5.25% compounded monthly?

14. Silas is about to begin regular month-end contributions of $500 to a bond fund. The fund's long-term rate of return is expected to be 6% compounded semiannually. Rounded to the next higher month, how long will it take Silas to accumulate $300,000?

15. How long will $500,000, in an investment account that earns 3.25% compounded monthly, sustain month-end withdrawals of $3000?

16. Farah has $600,000 in her RRSP and wishes to retire. She is thinking of using the funds to purchase an annuity that earns 5% compounded annually and pays her $3500 at the end of each month. If she buys the annuity, for how long will she receive payments?

17. If $300,000 is used to purchase an annuity earning 7.5% compounded monthly and paying $2500 at the end of each month, what will be the term of the annuity?

18. a. How long will it take monthly payments of $400 to repay a $50,000 loan if the interest rate on the loan is 8% compounded semiannually?
    b. How much will the time to repay the loan be reduced if the payments are $40 per month larger?

19. How much longer will it take month-end RRSP contributions of $500 to accumulate $500,000 than month-end contributions of $550? Assume that the RRSP earns 7.5% compounded monthly. Round the time required in each case to the next higher month.

20. Suppose that you contribute $400 per month to your RRSP. Rounding up to the nearest month, how much longer will it take for the RRSP's value to reach $500,000 if it earns 7.5% compounded annually than if it earns 7.5% compounded monthly?

21. How much longer will it take to pay off a $100,000 loan with monthly payments of $1000 than with monthly payments of $1100? The interest rate on the loan is 10.5% compounded monthly.

22. How much longer will it take monthly payments of $1000 to pay off a $100,000 loan if the monthly compounded rate of interest on the loan is 10.5% instead of 9.75%?

23. What duration of annuity paying $5000 at the end of every quarter can be purchased with $200,000 if the invested funds earn 5.5% compounded semiannually?

24. Bonnie and Clyde want to take a six-month leave of absence from their jobs to travel extensively in South America. Rounded to the next higher month, how many months will it take them to save $40,000 for the leave if they make month-end contributions of $700 to their employer's salary deferral plan? The salary deferral plan earns 7.5% compounded semiannually.

25. Finest Furniture sells a television set priced at $1395 for $50 down and payments of $50 per month, including interest at 13.5% compounded monthly. How long after the date of purchase will the final payment be made?

INTERMEDIATE PROBLEMS

26. Rashid wants to use $500,000 from his RRSP to purchase an annuity that pays him $2000 at the end of each month for the first 10 years and $3000 per month thereafter. Global Insurance Co. will sell Rashid an annuity of this sort with a rate of return of 4.8% compounded monthly. For how long will the annuity run?

27. A 65-year-old male can purchase either of the following annuities from a life insurance company: a 25-year term annuity that will pay $307 at the end of each month or a life annuity that will pay $408 at the end of every month until the death of the annuitant. To what age must the man survive for the life annuity to have the greater economic value? Assume that money can earn 6% compounded monthly.

28. A 60-year-old woman can purchase either of the following annuities from a life insurance company: a 30-year term annuity that will pay $367 at the end of each month or a life annuity that will pay $405 at the end of every month until the death of the annuitant. To what age must the woman survive for the life annuity to have the greater economic value? Assume that money can earn 8% compounded monthly.

29. $10,000 was invested in a fund earning 7.5% compounded monthly. How many monthly withdrawals of $300 can be made if the first occurs $3\frac{1}{2}$ years after the date of the initial investment? Count the final smaller withdrawal.

30. Nancy borrowed $8000 from her grandfather to buy a car when she started college. The interest rate being charged is 4.5% compounded monthly. Nancy is to make the first $200 monthly payment on the loan three years after the date of the loan. How long after the date of the initial loan will she make the final payment?

31. Twelve years ago, Mr. Lawton rolled a $17,000 retiring allowance into an RRSP that subsequently earned 10% compounded semiannually. Three years ago he transferred the funds to an RRIF. Since then, he has been withdrawing $1000 at the end of each quarter. If the RRIF earns 8% compounded quarterly, how much longer can the withdrawals continue?

32. Novell Electronics recently bought a patent that will allow it to bring a new product to market in $2\frac{1}{2}$ years. Sales forecasts indicate that the product will increase the quarterly profits by $28,000. If the patent cost $150,000, how long after the date of the patent purchase will it take for the additional profits to repay the original investment along with a return on investment of 15% compounded quarterly? Assume that the additional profits are received at the end of each quarter.

33. Helen and Morley borrowed $20,000 from Helen's father to make a down payment on a house. The interest rate on the loan is 8% compounded annually, but no payments are required for two years. The first monthly payment of $300 is due on the second anniversary of the loan. How long after the date of the original loan will the last payment be made?

34. A property development company obtained a $2.5-million loan to construct a commercial building. The interest rate on the loan is 10% compounded semiannually. The lender granted a period of deferral, meaning that the first quarterly payment of $100,000 is not required until 21 months after the date of the loan. How long after the date of the original loan will the last payment be made?

35. Bernice is about to retire with $139,000 in her RRSP. She will make no further contributions to the plan, but will allow it to accumulate earnings for another six years. Then she will purchase an annuity providing payments of $5000 at the end of each quarter. Assume that the RRSP will earn 8.5% compounded annually and the funds invested in the annuity will earn 7.5% compounded monthly. How long after the purchase of the annuity will its payments continue?

ADVANCED PROBLEM

36. Harold's RRSP is already worth $56,000. Rounding n to the next higher integer, how long will it take the RRSP to reach $250,000 if additional contributions of $2000 are made at the end of every six months? Assume the RRSP earns 9.75% compounded monthly.

12.3 Calculating the Interest Rate

Circumstances in which you need to calculate the interest rate include:

- Determining the rate of return required for periodic savings to reach a goal in a particular length of time.
- Determining the rate of return earned on money used to purchase an annuity.
- Determining the interest rate implied by specified loan payments.
- Determining the interest rate being charged when an installment payment plan is offered as an alternative to a "cash" payment.
- Determining the interest rate built into the payments on a vehicle or equipment lease.

The interest rate most readily calculated is the periodic interest rate, i. To determine i, you must know the values for *PMT*, n, and either *FV* or *PV*.

L03 Problems requiring the calculation of i pose some special difficulties for an algebraic approach. Formulas (11-1) for *FV* and (11-2) for *PV* cannot be rearranged through algebraic manipulations to isolate i. Consequently, no formulas can be given for i (corresponding to those for n in **Section 12.2**).

Appendix 12B presents an approximation technique called the "trial-and-error method." The trial-and-error method is a systematic but time-consuming procedure for *improving an estimate* of an equation's solution. With each repetition, or *iteration*, of the procedure, the approximation gets closer to the correct solution. We illustrate the trial-and-error method in **Appendix 12B** by using it to solve **Example 12.3A** a second time.

In this section, we will show only the financial calculator method for the solutions to example problems. For the interest rate computation, the financial calculator also uses a repetitive iterative procedure when you press [CPT] [I/Y]. But the only evidence you may notice of this happening is that it takes the calculator slightly longer to compute [I/Y] than it takes to compute one of the other financial variables.

EXAMPLE 12.3A

FINDING THE RATE OF RETURN ON FUNDS USED TO PURCHASE AN ANNUITY

A life insurance company advertises that $50,000 will purchase a 20-year annuity paying $341.13 at the end of each month. What nominal rate of return and effective rate of return does the annuity investment earn?

SOLUTION

The purchase price of an annuity equals the present value of all payments. Hence, the rate of return on the $50,000 purchase price is the discount rate that makes the present value of the payments equal to $50,000. The payments form an ordinary annuity with

$$PV = \$50,000 \quad PMT = \$341.13 \quad m = 12$$
$$\text{and} \quad n = 12(20) = 240$$

Enter these values in your calculator as indicated in the first callout box.

P/Y 12 [ENTER]	Same N, PMT, PV, FV
(making C/Y = P/Y = 12)	
240 N	P/Y 12 [ENTER]
50000 [+/−] PV	C/Y 1 [ENTER]
341.13 PMT	[CPT] [I/Y]
0 FV	*Ans:* 5.536
[CPT] [I/Y]	
Ans: 5.400	

To find the equivalent effective rate of return, enter these values in your calculator as indicated in the second callout box.

The nominal rate of return we obtain is 5.40% compounded monthly.

Then $i = \frac{j}{m} = \frac{5.4\%}{12} = 0.450\%$ and the corresponding effective interest rate is 5.54%.

Algebraically, the effective rate is calculated as

$$f = (1 + i)^m - 1 = 1.00450^{12} - 1 = 0.05536 = 5.54\%$$

EXAMPLE 12.3B

CALCULATING THE RATE OF RETURN REQUIRED TO REACH A SAVINGS GOAL IN A SPECIFIED TIME PERIOD

What annually compounded rate of return must Rachel earn in her RRSP in order for month-end contributions of $500 to accumulate $600,000 after 25 years?

SOLUTION

The contributions form an ordinary annuity whose future value after 25 years is to be $600,000. That is,

$$FV = \$600{,}000 \quad PMT = \$500 \quad m = C/Y = 1 \quad P/Y = 12 \quad \text{and} \quad n = 12(25) = 300$$

Enter these values in your calculator as indicated in the box at right. The nominal rate of return we obtain is 9.82% compounded annually.

Rachel's RRSP must earn 9.82% compounded annually to reach her savings goal.

P/Y 12	ENTER
C/Y 1	ENTER
300	N
0	PV
500 +/−	PMT
600000	FV
CPT	I/Y

Ans: 9.823

EXAMPLE 12.3C

CALCULATING THE IMPLIED INTEREST RATE FOR AN INSTALLMENT PAYMENT OPTION

Rolling Meadows Golf and Country Club allows members to pay the annual membership fee by a single payment of $2400 or by payments of $220 at the end of each month. What effective rate of interest is paid by members who choose to pay by the month?

SOLUTION

Since payments are made at the end of the monthly payment period and we are calculating the effective (annually compounding) rate of interest, this payment plan forms a general annuity.

Again we use the fundamental principle that the original "loan" equals the present value of all payments. We need to calculate the discount rate that makes $2400 the present value of 12 end-of-month payments of $220. We have

$$PV = \$2400 \quad PMT = \$220 \quad P/Y = 12 \quad \text{and} \quad n = 12$$

Since we are asked for the effective rate, set $C/Y = m = 1$. Enter these values in your calculator as indicated in the box at right to obtain

$$I/Y = 19.53\% \text{ compounded annually}$$

Hence, members on the monthly payment plan are paying an effective rate of 19.53%.

P/Y 12	ENTER
C/Y 1	ENTER
12	N
2400	PV
220 +/−	PMT
0	FV
CPT	I/Y

Ans: 19.528

EXAMPLE 12.3D

CALCULATING THE INTEREST RATE EQUIVALENT OF A FORGONE CASH REBATE

An automobile manufacturer's advertisement announces: "1.8% factory financing over 48 months or $1000 cash back." Suppose a car buyer finances $15,000 of a car's purchase price at the low interest rate instead of paying a further $14,000 in cash (net of the $1000 cash-back rebate). If we include the forgone rebate as part of the cost of borrowing, what nominal rate of interest is the buyer paying?

SOLUTION

An additional front-end cost of the "cheap" 1.8% financing is the forgone $1000 rebate. To determine the true cost of the 1.8% financing, we will consider the following alternatives.

- Borrow $15,000 from the manufacturer at 1.8% (compounded monthly) for four years.
- Obtain a four-year loan for $14,000 elsewhere at the prevailing market interest rate. Use the $14,000 to complete a "full cash" purchase net of the $1000 rebate.

The alternatives are equivalent if the monthly loan payments are equal. Therefore, we will determine the interest rate in the second case that results in the same monthly payment as for the factory-financed loan. If we can find outside financing at a *lower* rate, we should borrow $14,000 from that source and choose the "$1000 cash-back" option.

Step 1: Calculate the monthly payment on a factory-financed $15,000 four-year loan. The payments form an ordinary annuity having

$$PV = \$15,000 \quad j = 1.8\% \quad m = 12 \quad n = 12(4) = 48$$

Enter these values in your calculator as indicated in the box at right to obtain $PMT = \$324.12$.

1.8	I/Y
P/Y 12	ENTER
(making $C/Y = P/Y = 12$)	
48	N
15000	PV
0	FV
CPT	PMT

Ans: −324.12

Step 2: Determine the interest rate on a four-year $14,000 loan that would result in the *same* monthly payment. For this loan,

$$PV = \$14,000 \quad PMT = \$324.12 \quad n = 48 \quad m = 12$$

Enter these values as indicated in the second box at right to obtain

$$j = 5.27\% \text{ compounded monthly}$$

Same P/Y, C/Y

Same N, PMT, FV

14000	PV
CPT	I/Y

Ans: 5.269

This result means that you will make the same monthly payment ($324.12) on either of the following loans:

- $15,000 for four years at 1.8% compounded monthly
- $14,000 for four years at 5.27% compounded monthly

Therefore, forgoing the cash rebate and financing at 1.8% compounded monthly has the same effect as external financing at 5.27% compounded monthly. (The buyer should arrange external financing if it can be obtained at any rate below 5.27% compounded monthly.)

POINT OF INTEREST

Should You Choose a Cash-Discount Incentive or Low-Interest-Rate Financing?

To promote vehicle sales, it is common for automobile manufacturers to offer the purchaser of a new vehicle the choice between:

- A discount (or incentive) on a "cash" purchase; or
- Financing at a lower interest rate than may be available from conventional lenders.

For example, in the spring of 2019 Toyota Canada offered buyers of a new 2019 Prius Prime (MSRP $32,990) the choice of a $2000 cash incentive (deducted from the MSRP) or financing at 0.99% APR on a 36-month loan. How do you decide which alternative to choose?

Your initial reaction may be that your personal financial condition will determine your choice. That is, if you have sufficient financial resources on hand, you will pay cash and take the discount. On the other hand, if you need financing, you will choose the below-market interest rate.

Let's think more carefully about the second scenario, and assume that you will need to finance $30,000 of the purchase price, including taxes. There is likely another option open to you. Instead of borrowing $30,000 at 0.99% APR through Toyota, you can approach a bank or credit union for a loan of only

$$\$30,000 - \$2000 = \$28,000$$

With the down payment you already have, this loan will give you enough to pay cash and qualify for the $2000 cash incentive. Now it is apparent that you must regard forgoing the $2000 incentive as an *additional* cost of the "cheap" 0.99% financing.

The following questions lead you through an analysis of the two financing alternatives. For the easiest comparison, let us assume the $28,000 bank loan has a three-year term.

QUESTIONS

1. What will the monthly payment be if you borrow $30,000 for 36 months through Toyota at 0.99% compounded monthly? (We will use monthly compounding for simplicity.)
2. If, by a remarkable coincidence, the monthly payment on the $28,000 bank loan is exactly the same amount, what interest rate is the bank charging?
3. What, then, should be your decision rule for whether to choose the bank loan and take the cash discount incentive, or to choose the 0.99% financing?
4. Now consider the other scenario, in which you have sufficient financial resources to pay cash without borrowing. Suppose you have investments that you could sell and use the proceeds to purchase the vehicle. Nevertheless, you may still choose to borrow at the below-market rate of 0.99% because your investments are generating a high rate of return. What should be your rule for deciding whether to liquidate investments or to use the Toyota financing to purchase the vehicle?

Source: Toyota. www.toyota.ca.

EXERCISE 12.3

Answers to the odd-numbered problems are at the end of the book.

Spreadsheet template: A partially completed Excel template for calculating the interest rates for an annuity is provided on Connect. You can use this template for many of the problems in Exercise 12.3. Go to the Student Edition of Connect and find "Rate for Any Annuity" under the Student Resources for Chapter 12.

Calculate all interest rates accurate to the nearest 0.01%.

BASIC PROBLEMS

1. An annuity purchased for $50,000 sustained quarterly withdrawals of $1941.01 for 7 years and 9 months. What nominal rate of return and effective rate of return were the retained funds earning?

2. The present value of an ordinary annuity of $500 per month for $8\frac{3}{4}$ years is $35,820. Calculate the nominal and effective values for the discount rate.

3. If RRSP contributions of $3030.02 at the end of every six months are projected to generate a plan worth $500,000 in 25 years, what nominal and effective rates of return were assumed in the forecast?

4. With end-of-month contributions of $251.33, a TFSA is expected to pass $100,000 in value after 15 years and 5 months. Determine the nominal and effective rates of return used in the projection.

5. Monty is checking potential outcomes for the growth of his RRSP. He plans to make contributions of $500 at the end of each month. What nominal rate of return must his RRSP earn for its future value after 25 years to be:

   a. $400,000?   **b.** $500,000?   **c.** $600,000?

   (Note that a modest increase in the rate of return over a long period produces substantially larger future values.)

6. Morgan has $500,000 accumulated in her RRSP and intends to use the amount to purchase a 20-year annuity. She is investigating the size of annuity payment she can expect to receive, depending on the rate of return earned by the undistributed funds. What nominal rate of return must the funds earn for the monthly payment to be:

   a. $3000?   **b.** $3500?   **c.** $4000?

7. If $100,000 will purchase a 20-year annuity paying $830 at the end of each month, what monthly compounded nominal rate and effective rate of interest will the invested funds earn?

8. If regular month-end deposits of $200 in an investment account amounted to $7727.62 after three years, what monthly compounded nominal rate and effective rate of interest were earned on the account?

9. After $10\frac{1}{2}$ years of contributions of $2000 at the end of every six months to an RRSP, the accumulated amount stood at $65,727.82. What semiannually compounded nominal rate of return and effective annual rate of return were earned by the funds in the RRSP?

10. What quarterly compounded nominal rate and effective rate of interest are being charged on a $5000 loan if quarterly payments of $302.07 will repay the loan in $5\frac{1}{2}$ years?

11. If TFSA contributions of $10,000 at the end of every year are projected to generate a plan worth $1,000,000 in 25 years, what effective rate of return was assumed in the forecast?

12. A finance company paid a furniture retailer $1050 for a conditional sale contract requiring 12 end-of-month payments of $100. What effective rate of return will the finance company realize on the purchase?

13. For $150,000, Continental Life Insurance Co. will sell a 20-year annuity paying $1200 at the end of each month. What effective rate of return does the annuitant earn?

14. In an insurance settlement for bodily injury, a court awarded Mr. Goodman $103,600 for two years' loss of wages of $4000 per month plus interest on the lost wages to the end of the two years. What effective rate of interest has the court allowed on the lost wages?

15. A major daily newspaper charges $260 (paid in advance) for an annual subscription, or $26 per month payable at the end of each month to the carrier. What is the effective interest rate being charged to the monthly payment subscribers?

INTERMEDIATE PROBLEMS

16. Vijay purchased a Province of Nova Scotia bond for $1050. The bond will pay $35 interest to Vijay at the end of every six months until it matures in seven years. On the maturity date the bond will pay back its $1000 face value (as well as the interest payment due on that date). What semiannually compounded rate of return will Vijay earn during the seven years?

17. Another type of sales promotion for vehicles is to advertise the choice between a "Cash Purchase Price" or "0% Purchase Financing." The tiny print at the bottom of a GM Canada full-page advertisement included the statement: "*The GMAC purchase finance rates are not available with and are not calculated on the 'Cash Purchase Price' shown. The difference between the price for the GMAC purchase finance offer and the 'Cash Purchase Price' offer is deemed under provincial laws to be a cost of financing.*" In other words, there are two prices for a vehicle—a lower price if you pay cash and a higher price if you want to take advantage of the "0% financing." An additional disconcerting aspect of this type of promotion is that the higher price for the 0% financing is usually not quoted in the advertisement. Rather, it must be negotiated with the dealer.

    Suppose the "Cash Purchase Price" of a car is $23,498, and the price that qualifies for full 0% financing (with 48 monthly payments) turns out to be $26,198. What effective interest rate will you be paying for the "0% financing"?

ADVANCED PROBLEMS

18. An advertisement for Hyundai cars offered "2.9% 12-month financing or $1000 cash back." A car buyer financed $17,000 at the low interest rate instead of paying $16,000 cash (after the $1000 rebate). What was the effective rate of interest on the loan if the forgone cash rebate was treated as part of the cost of financing? (The 2.9% interest rate was a monthly compounded nominal rate.)

19. A Ford advertisement offered "$1250 cash back or 1.9% factory financing over 48 months" to purchasers of new Ford vans. A customer financed $20,000 at the low interest rate instead of paying $18,750 cash (after the $1250 rebate). What was the effective rate of interest on the loan if the forgone cash rebate was treated as part of the cost of financing? (The 1.9% interest rate was a monthly compounded nominal rate.)

SUMMARY OF NOTATION AND KEY FORMULAS

FORMULA (11-1n) $$n = \frac{\ln\left(1 + \frac{i \times FV}{PMT}\right)}{\ln(1 + i)}$$ Finding the number of annuity payments given FV, PMT, and i

FORMULA (11-2n) $$n = -\frac{\ln\left(1 - \frac{i \times PV}{PMT}\right)}{\ln(1 + i)}$$ Finding the number of annuity payments given PV, PMT, and i

REVIEW PROBLEMS

Answers to the odd-numbered review problems are at the end of the book.

Calculate interest rates accurate to the nearest 0.01%.

BASIC PROBLEMS

1. **L01** Calculate the amount that must be invested at the end of every six months at 3.75% compounded semiannually in order to accumulate $500,000 after 20 years.

2. **L01** What monthly payment for 15 years will pay off a $50,000 loan at 8.25% compounded monthly?

3. **L03** For $100,000, Royal Life Insurance Co. will sell a 20-year annuity paying $802.76 at the end of each month. What monthly compounded nominal rate and effective rate of return does the annuitant earn on the invested funds?

4. **L02** If $400,000 accumulated in an RRSP is used to purchase an annuity earning 7.2% compounded monthly and paying $4500 at the end of each month, what will be the term of the annuity?

5. **L03** After contributing $2000 at the end of each quarter for $13\frac{3}{4}$ years, Foster has accumulated $205,064 in his RRSP. What effective rate of return was earned by the RRSP over the entire period?

6. **L03** What semiannually compounded rate and effective rate of interest are being charged on a $12,000 loan if semiannual payments of $1204.55 will repay the loan in seven years?

7. **L02** The interest rate on a $100,000 loan is 6% compounded monthly. How much longer will it take to pay off the loan with monthly payments of $1000 than with monthly payments of $1050?

8. **L03** If $100,000 will purchase a 20-year annuity paying $739 at each month's end, what monthly compounded nominal rate and effective rate of interest are earned by the funds?

9. **L02** An annuity purchased for $175,000 pays $4000 at the end of every quarter. How long will the payments continue if the funds earn 4% compounded semiannually?

10. **L03** A finance company paid a furniture retailer $1934 for a conditional sale contract requiring 12 end-of-month payments of $175. What effective rate of return does the finance company earn on the purchase?

11. **L01** Howardson Electric obtained a $90,000 loan at 6.75% compounded monthly. What size of semiannual payments will repay the loan in 10 years?

12. **L01** The interest rate on a $30,000 loan is 7.5% compounded monthly.
    a. What monthly payments are required to pay off the loan in eight years?
    b. What monthly payments would be required to reduce the balance to $10,000 after five years?

13. **L02** How much sooner will a $65,000 loan at 7.2% compounded monthly be paid off if the monthly payments are $625 instead of $600? What will be the approximate saving in (nominal) interest costs over the life of the loan?

14. **L03** $2000 will be contributed to an RRSP at the end of every six months for 20 years. What effective rate of return must the funds in the plan earn if it is to be worth $250,000 at the end of the 20 years?

15. **L01** What payments must be made at the end of each quarter to an RRSP earning 7.5% compounded annually so that its value $8\frac{1}{2}$ years from now will be $15,000?

INTERMEDIATE PROBLEMS

16. **L01** **L02** The McGowans are arranging a $90,000 mortgage loan from their bank. The interest rate on the loan will be 7.9% compounded semiannually.
    a. What will the monthly payments be if the loan has a 20-year term?
    b. If the McGowans choose to pay $800 per month, how long will it take to pay off the loan?

17. **L02** A series of $500 contributions were made at three-month intervals to a fund earning 3.5% compounded quarterly. The accumulated amount continued to earn 3.5% compounded quarterly for three years after the last contribution, ending the period at $10,770.82. How many $500 contributions were made?

18. **L02** Weston Holdings Ltd. loaned $3.5 million to a subsidiary to build a plant in Winnipeg. No payments are required for two years, to allow the operations of the plant to become well established. The first monthly payment of $40,000 is due two years after the date the loan was received. If the interest rate charged on the intercompany loan is 9% compounded monthly, how long (measured from the date of the first payment) will it take the subsidiary to pay off the loan?

19. **L01** Mr. Sandstrom's will directed that $20,000 be placed in each of two investment trusts for his grandchildren, Lena and Axel. On each grandchild's 18th birthday, he or she is to receive the first of a series of equal quarterly payments running for 15 years. Lena has just turned 13, and Axel's age is eight years, six months. If the funds earn 9.25% compounded semiannually, what size of payment will each grandchild receive?

20. **L01** The interest rate on a $100,000 loan is 7.5% compounded quarterly.
    a. What quarterly payments will reduce the balance to $75,000 after five years?
    b. If the same payments continue, what will be the balance 10 years after the date that the loan was received?

21. **L01** Mr. Braun wants the value of his RRSP 25 years from now to have the purchasing power of $400,000 in current dollars.
    a. Assuming an inflation rate of 2.5% per year, what nominal dollar amount should Mr. Braun have in his RRSP after 25 years?
    b. What contributions should he make at the end of every three months to achieve the goal if his RRSP earns 7.5% compounded semiannually?

22. a. **L02** How long will it take monthly payments of $600 to repay a $65,000 loan if the interest rate on the loan is 9.5% compounded semiannually?
    b. **L02** How much will the time to repay the loan be reduced if the payments are $50 more per month?

23. **L02** A 70-year-old man can purchase either of the following two annuities for the same price from a life insurance company. A 20-year-term annuity will pay $394 at the end of each month. A life annuity will pay $440 at the end of each month until the death of the annuitant. To what age must the man survive for the life annuity to have the greater economic value? Assume that money can earn 7.2% compounded monthly.

24. **L01** Noreen's RRSP is currently worth $125,000. She plans to contribute for 10 more years and then let the plan continue to grow through internal earnings for an additional five years. If the RRSP earns 8% compounded annually, how much must she contribute at the end of every six months during the 10-year period to have $500,000 in the RRSP 15 years from now?

25. **L02** $30,000 is placed in a fund earning 7% compounded quarterly. How many quarterly withdrawals of $2000 can be made if the first withdrawal occurs three years from today? Count the final withdrawal, which will be less than $2000.

26. **L02** Georgina is about to retire with $188,000 in her RRSP. She will make no further contributions to the plan, but will allow it to accumulate earnings for another five years. Then she will purchase an annuity providing payments of $6000 at the end of each quarter. What will be the annuity's term if the RRSP earns 8% compounded annually and the funds invested in the annuity earn 7.5% compounded monthly?

27. **L01** By the time he turns 60, Justin (just turned age 31) wants the amount in his RRSP to have the purchasing power of $250,000 in current dollars. What annual contributions on his 32nd through 60th birthdays inclusive are required to meet this goal if the RRSP earns 8% compounded annually and the rate of inflation is 2% per year?

ADVANCED PROBLEM

28. **L03** An advertisement for Ford trucks offered "2.9% financing (for 48 months) or $2000 cash back." A truck buyer financed $20,000 at the low interest rate instead of paying $18,000 cash (after the $2000 rebate). What was the effective rate of interest on the loan if the forgone cash rebate is treated as part of the cost of financing? (The 2.9% interest rate is a monthly compounded nominal rate.)

CASE

Should You Borrow to Make an RRSP Contribution?

Answering this question occupies dozens of financial commentaries as the March 1 RRSP contribution deadline approaches each year. Many financial institutions and mutual fund companies promote the idea of arranging an "RRSP loan" to obtain money for an RRSP contribution. They sometimes present a scenario giving the impression that borrowing to contribute to an RRSP is so advantageous it is virtually a "no-brainer." The conventional wisdom among financial planners seems to be that it is a good idea with two qualifications—the tax refund from the RRSP contribution should be applied to paying down the loan, and the loan should be paid off within a year. However, as often happens in financial analyses of even moderate complexity, the thinking is usually muddled and flawed.

In this case study, we will identify the key variable(s) for answering the question in the heading. We will discover that the decision (based strictly on financial considerations) turns on a single criterion. Here is the scenario. Suppose your marginal tax rate is 40%. Consequently, if you contribute $1000 to an RRSP, your taxable income will be reduced by $1000 and your income tax will be reduced by $400 (40% of $1000). To obtain the money for a $1000 RRSP contribution, you borrow $1000 at 6% compounded monthly and immediately use the $400 tax saving to reduce the loan balance to $600.

QUESTIONS

1. What is the monthly loan payment required to pay off the $600 balance in one year?
2. To what amount will the single $1000 contribution grow over the next 20 years if your RRSP earns 6% compounded monthly?

Virtually all analyses of the issue fail to mention a logical alternative to borrowing money for an RRSP contribution. If your budget permits monthly payments on an RRSP loan over the next year, then an alternative to borrowing for an immediate lump RRSP contribution is to use the same budget "room" to start monthly contributions to an RRSP. A subtle but key point will now be developed. In the loan scenario, you immediately applied the tax saving to reduce the loan balance. In effect, you needed to borrow only $600 to make a $1000 RRSP contribution. The $1000 contribution cost you only $600. Similarly, if you make a monthly RRSP contribution of $100, it will really cost you only $60 because of the $40 tax saving. In other words, your after-tax cost is only 60% of your monthly contribution.

Let's turn the last point around and answer this question: How much can you contribute to an RRSP if the after-tax cost to you is to be, say, $50? In this case, the $50 cost represents 60% of your contribution. Therefore, the contribution is $\frac{$50}{0.6} = 83.33.

QUESTIONS

3. What monthly RRSP contribution will have the same after-tax cost to you as the monthly loan payment calculated in Question 1?
4. Suppose you make these monthly RRSP contributions. What amount will you have in the RRSP just after the 12th contribution?
5. To what future value will the Question 4 amount grow over the subsequent 19 years?
6. The future values calculated in Questions 2 and 5 are the amounts in your RRSP 20 years from now under *two alternatives that have the same cost to you.* Comment on the outcome. What is your response to the question in the case's title when the interest rate on an RRSP loan is the same as the rate of return earned by your RRSP investments?
7. Suppose the RRSP earns 9% compounded monthly instead of 6% compounded monthly. Answer Questions 2, 4, and 5 again. Should you borrow for the RRSP contribution in this case?
8. What will be the nature of the outcome if the rate of return earned by the RRSP is *less* than the interest rate on the loan?
9. Summarize your findings as a general decision criterion. (Under what circumstance should you borrow to make an RRSP contribution?)

Chapter 13

Annuities Due

CHAPTER OUTLINE

LEARNING OBJECTIVES

After completing this chapter, you will be able to:

LO1 Calculate the future value and present value of annuities due

LO2 Calculate the payment size, number of payments, and interest rate for annuities due

IF YOU RENT RESIDENTIAL OR COMMERCIAL real estate, the typical lease contract requires payments at the beginning of each month. The leasing of vehicles, aircraft, office equipment, and computers is widespread—about one-quarter of new vehicles are leased rather than purchased. Lease payments are normally made at the beginning of each month or quarter. Insurance premiums must be paid at the beginning of each period of coverage. Membership dues are usually paid in advance. These are all examples of annuities due for which the payments occur at the beginning of each payment interval. Clearly, it is important that you understand the mathematics of annuities due. As you will soon learn, you can handle annuities due by making only a small change to the mathematics of ordinary annuities.

13.1 Future Value of an Annuity Due

In our early discussion of annuities in **Chapter 11**, we identified two *independent* criteria for classifying annuities in **Table 11.1**. Based on the *timing* of the payment within the payment interval, an annuity is classified as *either* an *ordinary* annuity *or* an annuity *due*. In **annuities due,**[1] the payments are made at the *beginning* of each payment interval. If the payment interval and the compounding frequency are the same, it is classified as a **simple annuity due** and if the payment interval and the compounding frequency differ then it is a **general annuity due**.

Figure 13.1 presents the time diagram for an annuity due consisting of *n* payments, each of size *PMT*. The serial number for each payment *interval* is placed above the tick mark at the *end* of the interval.

FIGURE 13.1   Time Diagram for an *n*-Payment Annuity Due

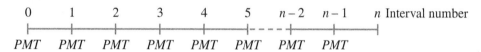

The future value of an annuity due is the sum of the future values of all of the payments (evaluated at the end of the annuity). We will use the symbol *FV*(due) for the future value of an annuity due. The symbols *PMT*, *n*, and *i* have the same meaning as for ordinary annuities.

 TRAP

What Is Meant by the End of an Annuity?

Don't confuse "the end of an annuity" with "the end of the payments" or "the date of the last payment." The end of an annuity means "the end of the annuity's *term*" or "the end of the last payment interval." It occurs one payment interval *after* the last payment in an annuity *due*.

Similarly, *the beginning of an annuity* refers to "the start of the annuity's term" or "the start of the first payment interval." It does coincide with the first payment in an annuity due.

Future Value Using the Algebraic Method

LO1 The formula for the future value of an annuity *due* may be quickly derived from the formula for the future value of an *ordinary* annuity.

---
[1] An annuity due is sometimes referred to as an annuity *in advance*. An ordinary annuity is then called an annuity *in arrears*.

FIGURE 13.2   *FV of Six Payments in an Ordinary Annuity*

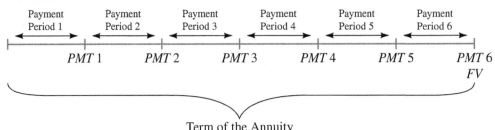

Consider an annuity with a term of 6 months, paid by 6 equal monthly payments. **Figure 13.2** illustrates the annuity with payments being made at the end of each of the 6 payment periods. This could be, for example, your paycheque for 6 months. The term of the annuity starts at the beginning of the first payment period, while the first payment is placed at the end of this first payment period. The cumulative *FV* of the annuity at the focal date coincides with the last payment, made at the end of the last payment period which is also the end of the term of the annuity. That last payment does not earn any interest during the last payment period.

In **Figure 13.3**, the payments are viewed as an annuity due. In this case, the payments might represent your rent for 6 months. The term of the annuity remains the same but now the first payment is made at the beginning of the first payment period and coincides with the beginning of the term of the annuity. The focal date for its future value, *FV*(due), is at the end of the term of the annuity (one payment interval after the last payment). Since this last payment is made at the beginning of the last payment period, it will now earn one more month's interest in that last payment period. The focal date for its future value, *FV*(due), is at the end of the term of the annuity (coincident with the last payment).

FIGURE 13.3   *FV(due) of Six Payments in an Annuity Due*

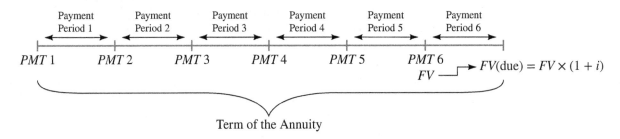

Each of these future values is economically equivalent to the *same* series of payments. The two future values are thus equivalent to each other, since the term of the annuity remains the same. Therefore, *FV*(due) equals the future value of *FV*, one payment interval later. That is,

$$FV(\text{due}) = FV \times (1 + i)$$

We see that the future value of an annuity due is simply $(1 + i)$ times the future value of an ordinary annuity. Substituting from Formula (11-1) for *FV*, we obtain

FUTURE VALUE OF A SIMPLE ANNUITY DUE

$$\boldsymbol{FV(\textbf{due}) = FV \times (1 + i)}$$
$$= PMT\left[\frac{(1 + i)^n - 1}{i}\right] \times (1 + i) \qquad \textbf{(13-1)}$$

If the payments form a general annuity due, use $i_2 = (1 + i)^c - 1$ to calculate the periodic interest rate that matches the payment interval. Then substitute this value for *i* in Formula (13-1).

Future Value Using the Financial Calculator Functions

Since FV(due) $= FV \times (1 + i)$, the approach that probably occurs to you is to compute the annuity's future value as though it were an *ordinary* annuity, and then multiply the result by $(1 + i)$. The financial calculator will do this multiplication automatically if it is first "informed" that the annuity is an annuity *due*. **Appendix 13A** provides instructions for setting various financial calculator models in the annuity due mode. In example problems, **BGN mode** indicates that the calculator should be set to the annuity due mode.

 TIP

Clues to the Type of Annuity

Information that helps you identify an annuity due may lie in subtle wording of a problem. Look for a key word or phrase that provides the clue. Some examples of wording that indicates an annuity due are:

- "Payments at the beginning of each ..."
- "Payments ... in advance"
- "First payment ... made today"
- "Payments ... starting now"

Examples of an annuity due include rental payments, lease payments, memberships, or any other kind of expense where the payment must be made BEFORE the goods or services are used.

EXAMPLE 13.1A

CALCULATING THE FUTURE VALUE OF A SIMPLE ANNUITY DUE

To the nearest dollar, how much will Stan accumulate in his RRSP by age 60 if he makes semiannual contributions of $2000 starting on his 27th birthday? Assume that the RRSP earns 8% compounded semiannually and that no contribution is made on his 60th birthday.

SOLUTION

The accumulated amount will be the future value of the contributions on Stan's 60th birthday. Viewed from the future value's focal date at his 60th birthday, the RRSP contributions are made at the *beginning* of every six months. Therefore, they form an annuity *due*. Since the payment interval equals the compounding interval, we have a *simple* annuity due with:

$$PMT = \$2000 \quad i = \tfrac{8\%}{2} = 4\% \quad \text{and} \quad n = 2(33) = 66 \text{ payments}$$

Substitute the preceding values into Formula (13-1)

$$
\begin{aligned}
FV(\text{due}) &= PMT\left[\frac{(1+i)^n - 1}{i}\right] \times (1 + i) \\
&= \$2000\left(\frac{1.04^{66} - 1}{0.04}\right) \times (1.04) \\
&= \$2000\left(\frac{13.310685 - 1}{0.04}\right)(1.04) \\
&= \$640{,}156
\end{aligned}
$$

BGN mode

8 ⌊ I/Y

⌊P/Y⌋ 2 ⌊ENTER⌋

(making $C/Y = P/Y = 2$)

66 ⌊ N

0 ⌊ PV

2000 ⌊+/−⌋ ⌊ PMT

⌊ CPT ⌋ ⌊ FV ⌋

Ans: 640,156

Stan will have $640,156 in his RRSP at age 60.

EXAMPLE 13.1B

CALCULATING THE FUTURE VALUE OF A GENERAL ANNUITY DUE

Repeat Example 13.1A with the change that the RRSP earns 8% compounded annually instead of 8% compounded semiannually.

SOLUTION

We now have a general annuity since the compounding interval (one year) differs from the payment interval (six months). The value we must use for i in the FV formula is the periodic rate for the six-month payment interval. (It will be about $\frac{8\%}{2} = 4\%$.) Substitute

$$i = \frac{8\%}{1} = 8\% \quad \text{and} \quad c = \frac{\text{Number of compoundings per year}}{\text{Number of payments per year}} = \frac{1}{2} = 0.5$$

into Formula (10-4c), giving

$$i_2 = (1 + i)^c - 1 = (1.08)^{0.5} - 1 = 0.039230485 \text{ per six months}$$

Use this value for i in Formula (13-1), giving

$$FV(\text{due}) = PMT \left[\frac{(1 + i)^n - 1}{i} \right] \times (1 + I)$$

$$= \$2000 \left(\frac{1.039230485^{66} - 1}{0.039230485} \right)(1.039230485)$$

$$= \$2000 \left(\frac{12.676050 - 1}{0.039230485} \right)(1.039230485)$$

$$= \$618,606$$

Stan will have $618,606 in his RRSP at age 60.

BGN mode

8 | I/Y

| P/Y 2 | ENTER
| C/Y 1 | ENTER

66 | N

0 | PV

2000 | +/− | PMT

| CPT | FV

Ans: 618,606

EXAMPLE 13.1C

COMPARING THE FUTURE VALUE OF A LONG-TERM ANNUITY VERSUS AN ANNUITY DUE

Ryan usually makes his annual contribution to his TFSA at the end of every calendar year. How much more will be in his TFSA after 25 years of $4000 contributions if he makes his contribution at the beginning of the year instead of at the end? Assume the investment can earn 6.5% compounded semiannually.

SOLUTION

Since the compounding interval and the payment intervals differ, the payments at the end of the year form an ordinary general annuity and the payments at the beginning of the year form a general annuity due.

The value we must use for i in the FV formula is the periodic rate for the one-year payment interval equivalent to $\frac{6.5\%}{2} = 3.25\%$.

Substitute

$$i = \frac{6.5\%}{2} = 3.25\% \quad \text{and} \quad c = \frac{\text{Number of compoundings per year}}{\text{Number of payments per year}} = \frac{2}{1} = 2$$

into Formula (10-4c), giving

$$i_2 = (1 + i)^c - 1 = (1.0325)^2 - 1 = 0.06605625 \text{ per year}$$

For the ordinary general annuity, use this value for i in Formula (11-1), giving

$$FV = PMT\left[\frac{(1+i)^n - 1}{i}\right]$$

$$= \$4000\left[\frac{(1 + 0.06605625)^{25} - 1}{0.06605625}\right]$$

$$= \$4000\left[\frac{4.948835482 - 1}{0.06605625}\right]$$

$$= \$239{,}119.57$$

If payments were made at the beginning of the year, then Ryan's contributions form a general annuity due:

$$FV(\text{due}) = PMT\left[\frac{(1+i)^n - 1}{i}\right](1+i)$$

$$= \$4000\left[\frac{(1 + 0.06605625)^{25} - 1}{0.06605625}\right](1.06605625)$$

$$= \$4000\left[\frac{4.948835482 - 1}{0.06605625}\right](1.06605625)$$

$$= \$254{,}914.91$$

Ryan will have $254,914.91 − $239,119.57 = $15,795.34 more after 25 years by making contributions at the beginning of the year instead of the end of the year.

EXAMPLE 13.1D

CALCULATING THE FUTURE VALUE OF AN ANNUITY DUE WHERE AN INTEREST RATE CHANGE OCCURS DURING THE TERM OF THE ANNUITY

Stephanie intends to contribute $2500 to her RRSP at the beginning of every six months, starting today. If the RRSP earns 8% compounded semiannually for the first seven years and 7% compounded semiannually thereafter, what amount will she have in the plan after 20 years?

SOLUTION

The amount in the plan will be the future value of the contributions.

Note: The wording of this question means that you are to determine the amount in the RRSP after *20 years of contributions*. There will be 40 contributions in 20 years. The 40th contribution will occur $19\frac{1}{2}$ years from now at the beginning of the 40th payment period. The 40 contributions form an annuity due when viewed from the future value's focal date 20 years from now.

The future value cannot be calculated in one step because the interest rate changes after seven years. The solution strategy is indicated in the following time diagram. Since the payment interval equals the compounding interval throughout, the payments form a simple annuity due in both segments of the 20 years.

Notice that *PMT* 14, the last payment made that earns 8% compounded semiannually, is paid at the beginning of the last payment interval for that annuity (at 6.5 years). *PMT* 15, the first payment made that earns 7% compounded semiannually, is paid at the beginning of the first payment interval for the next annuity (that starts at

7 years). Seven years on the time line diagram is both the end of the term for the first annuity and the beginning of the term for the second annuity.

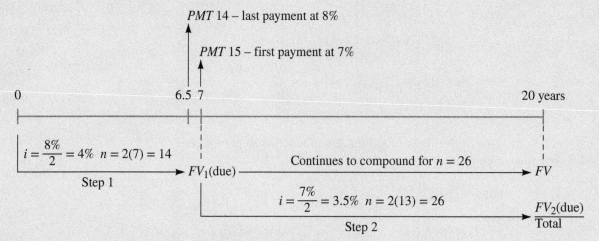

For the entire 20 years, payments are $2500 every six months.

The future value, after seven years, of the first 14 contributions will be

$$FV_1(\text{due}) = PMT\left[\frac{(1+i)^n - 1}{i}\right] \times (1+i)$$

$$= \$2500\left(\frac{1.04^{14} - 1}{0.04}\right) \times (1.04)$$

$$= \$2500(18.291911)(1.04)$$

$$= \$47,558.97$$

BGN mode

8 | I/Y |
| P/Y | 2 | ENTER |
(making $C/Y = P/Y = 2$)
14 | N |
0 | PV |
2500 | +/− | PMT |
| CPT | FV |

Ans: 47,558.97

When calculating the FV of $47,558.97, we will use $i = 3.5\%$ since this is the applicable rate for the remaining 13 years.

The future value of $47,558.97 an additional 13 years later will be

$$FV = PV(1 + i)^n = \$47,558.97(1.035)^{26} = \$116,327.27$$

The future value, 20 years from now, of the last 26 payments will be

$$FV_2(\text{due}) = \$2500\left[\frac{(1.035)^{26} - 1}{0.035}\right] \times (1.035)$$

$$= \$2500(41.3131017)(1.035)$$

$$= \$106,897.65$$

BGN mode

Same *PMT, P/Y, C/Y*

7 | I/Y |
26 | N |
47558.97 | +/− | PV |
| CPT | FV |

Ans: 223,224.92

The total amount in the RRSP after 20 years will be

$$FV + FV_2(\text{due}) = \$116,327.27 + \$106,897.65 = \$223,224.92$$

Stephanie will have $223,224.92 in her RRSP after 20 years.

POINT OF INTEREST

A Painful Truth and a Positive Spin

In 2011 *The Wealthy Barber Returns* by David Chilton was published by Financial Awareness Corp. Although it did not follow the same storyteller's format of the original *Wealthy Barber* published in 1989, it still offered the same common sense approach to personal financial planning as seen in the original book.

In Chapter 1, entitled "A Painful Truth and a Positive Spin," Chilton uses the following formula used in macroeconomics to explain how a small cutback in spending can dramatically increase your savings rate:

$$DY = C + S$$

where

DY = disposable income
C = consumption (spending)
S = savings

Using this formula, he demonstrates how C and S have to work together so that we can save for the future while still enjoying the present.

Let's say that you're currently saving four percent of your Disposable Income (DY). So from DY = C + S,

$$\$1.00 = \$0.96 + \$0.04$$

For every after-tax dollar you receive, you're also spending 96 cents and saving 4 cents.

Now some annoying financial advisor explains that based on your goals, pension details, age, etc., you'll have to raise your savings rate to at least 10 percent. "That's crazy!" you exclaim. "We can barely save the four percent—there's no way we can save two-and-a-half times as much. More than double our saving? Not happening!"

"You're right," the advisor concedes. "Let's forget the idea and focus on your spending. Instead of trying to raise your savings rate dramatically, a seemingly impossible goal, do you think you could start by cutting your spending rate by a mere 6.25 percent?"

"Yes, that seems much more reasonable," you allow.

Therefore, your new equation is:

$$\$1.00 = \$0.90 + \$0.10$$

How did I get that? Well, $0.90 is 6.25 percent less than $0.96.

Amazingly, you've raised your savings rate by 150 percent simply by cutting your spending by only 6.25 percent.

It's a money miracle!

QUESTIONS

1. Based on the increase in your savings rate from 4% to 10%, show how this represents a 150% increase in savings.
2. For an individual making $50,000 per year with a tax rate of 35%, how much would they have in an investment if they were to invest 4% of their after-tax income at the beginning of every month for the next 20 years? Assume an average rate of return of 6% compounding semiannually on their investment.
3. Repeat the calculation in #2 where the investment is 10% of their after-tax income. Use the same rate of return on the investment.
4. How much more will they have after 20 years by saving 10% instead of 4%? Is it 150% more?

Source: David Chilton, *The Wealthy Barber Returns*, 1st edition, 2011, Financial Awareness Corp.

CONCEPT QUESTIONS

1. Give three examples of an annuity due.

2. For the future value of an annuity due, where is the focal date located relative to the final payment?

3. Other things being equal, why is the future value of an annuity due larger than the future value of an ordinary annuity?

EXERCISE 13.1

Answers to the odd-numbered problems are at the end of the book.

 **Spreadsheet template:** *The partially completed Excel template developed in Section 11.4 for calculating the future value of any annuity may be used for many of the problems in Exercise 13.1. Go to the Student Edition and find "FV of Any Annuity" under the Student Resources for Chapter 11.*

BASIC PROBLEMS

1. Annual contributions of $1000 will be made to a TFSA for 25 years. The contributor expects investments within the plan to earn 7% compounded annually. What will the TFSA be worth after 25 years if the contributions are made:
   a. At the end of each year? b. At the beginning of each year?
   c. By what percentage does the answer to part (b) exceed the answer to part (a)?

2. Quarterly contributions of $1000 will be made to an RESP for 15 years. Assuming that the investments within the plan grow at 8% compounded quarterly, how much will the RESP be worth after 15 years if the contributions are made:
   a. At the end of each quarter? b. At the beginning of each quarter?
   c. By what percentage does the answer to part (b) exceed the answer to part (a)?

3. What is the future value of $100 invested at the beginning of every month for 25 years if the investments earn:
   a. 4% compounded monthly? b. 8% compounded monthly?

4. Svetlana intends to invest $1000 at the beginning of every six months. If the investments earn 7% compounded semiannually, what will her investments be worth (rounded to the nearest dollar) after:
   a. 25 years? b. 30 years?

5. Tanysha plans to invest $10,000 at the beginning of each year for the next 14 years. If her invested funds earn 5.1% compounded annually, what will be the total accumulated value of her investment after 14 years?

6. Phil has systematically contributed $3000 to his RRSP at the beginning of every three months for the past 17 years. If the RRSP has earned 8.8% compounded quarterly, what is the value of Phil's RRSP today?

7. Today Gus is making his first annual contribution of $2500 to a TFSA. How much will the plan be worth 16 years from now if it earns 5.25% compounded monthly?

8. Astrid has just opened an RESP for her children with her first quarterly deposit of $1700. What will the RESP be worth $11\frac{1}{2}$ years from now if the investments within the plan earn 7.5% compounded semiannually?

9. Salvatore will contribute $500 to a mutual fund at the beginning of each calendar quarter.
   a. What will be the value of his mutual fund after $6\frac{1}{2}$ years if the fund earns 7.6% compounded annually?
   b. How much of this amount represents investment earnings?

10. Monarch Distributing Ltd. plans to accumulate funds for the purchase of a larger warehouse seven years from now. If Monarch contributes $10,000 at the beginning of each month to an investment account earning 4.5% compounded semiannually, what amount (rounded to the nearest dollar) will Monarch accumulate by the end of the seven years?

11. If Hans contributes $1500 to his RRSP on February 1, 1998, and every six months thereafter up to and including February 1, 2025, what amount will he accumulate in the RRSP by August 1, 2025? Assume that the RRSP will earn 8.5% compounded semiannually. How much of the total will be earnings?

12. Many people make their annual RRSP contribution for a taxation year close to the end of the year. Financial advisers encourage clients to contribute as early in the year as possible. How much more will there be in an RRSP at the end of 25 years if annual contributions of $5000 are made at the beginning of each year instead of at the end? Assume that the RRSP will earn:
    a. 8% compounded annually.   **b.** 8% compounded monthly.

INTERMEDIATE PROBLEMS

13. For the past 25 years, Giorgio has contributed $2000 to his RRSP at the beginning of every six months. The plan earned 8% compounded annually for the first 11 years and 7% compounded semiannually for the subsequent 14 years. What is the value of his RRSP today?

14. Keiko has already accumulated $150,000 in her RRSP. She intends to continue to grow her RRSP by making contributions of $500 at the beginning of every month. How much will her RRSP be worth 15 years from now if the RRSP earns 8% compounded annually?

15. Johan recently received his annual performance bonus from his employer. He has set up an investment savings plan to which he will contribute $2000 each year from his bonus and $400 per month from his regular salary. Johan will make his initial contributions of $2000 and $400 today. Rounded to the nearest dollar,
    a. What will the plan be worth after 25 years if it earns 7.5% compounded monthly?
    b. How much did Johan's contributions earn during the 25 years?

16. What will be the amount in an RRSP after 25 years if contributions of $2000 are made at the beginning of each year for the first 10 years, and contributions of $4000 are made at the beginning of each year for the subsequent 15 years? Assume that the RRSP will earn 8% compounded quarterly.

17. Fay contributed $3000 per year to her RRSP on every birthday from age 21 to 30 inclusive. She then ceased employment to raise a family and made no further contributions. Her husband Fred contributed $3000 per year to his RRSP on every birthday from age 31 to 64 inclusive. Assuming that both plans earn 8% compounded annually over the years, calculate and compare the amounts in their RRSPs at age 65.

18. **Using the Future Value (Due) Chart** An interactive Future Value (Due) Chart is available on Connect. In Chapter 13 of the Student Edition, find "Future Value (Due) Chart." Use this chart to solve the following problems (rounded to the nearest dollar).
    a. Exercise 13.1, Problem 5   **b.** Exercise 13.1, Problem 7
    c. Exercise 13.1, Problem 9   **d.** Exercise 13.1, Problem 14

19. **Using the Cool Million (Due) Chart** This chart is the annuity due version of the (ordinary annuity) Cool Million chart described in Problem 34 of **Exercise 12.1**. Go to the Student Edition on Connect. In Chapter 13, find "Cool Million (Due)."

    Return to Problem 34 in **Exercise 12.1** to review the features of the chart. Use the same initial planning assumptions in both the Cool Million chart and the Cool Million (Due) chart. How much sooner will you become a millionaire if your regular savings are invested at the beginning of each month instead of at the end of each month?

13.2 Present Value of an Annuity Due

L01 The present value of an annuity due is the sum of the present values, at the beginning of the annuity, of all payments. Since payments occur at the *beginning* of each payment interval, the beginning of the annuity coincides with the first payment. We will use the symbol *PV*(due) for the present value of an annuity due.

Present Value Using the Algebraic Method

The formula for *PV*(due) may be derived from the formula for the present value of an ordinary annuity. The line of reasoning is the same as used in **Section 13.1** to derive the formula for *FV*(due). The outcome is that *PV*(due) is related to *PV* in the same way that *FV*(due) is related to *FV*. That is,

$$PV(\text{due}) = PV \times (1 + i)$$

Substituting from Formula (11-2) for *PV*, we obtain

PRESENT VALUE OF A SIMPLE ANNUITY DUE

$$PV(\text{due}) = PV \times (1 + i)$$
$$= PMT\left[\frac{1 - (1 + i)^{-n}}{i}\right] \times (1 + i) \qquad \textbf{(13-2)}$$

If the payments form a *general* annuity due, use $i_2 = (1 + i)^c - 1$ to calculate the periodic interest rate that matches the payment interval. Then substitute this value for *i* in Formula (13-2).

Present Value Using the Financial Calculator Functions

Set the calculator to the annuity due mode (so that "BGN" or "Begin" shows in the display). Then proceed as you would to compute the present value of an ordinary annuity.

EXAMPLE 13.2A

FINDING THE ECONOMIC VALUE OF A SIMPLE ANNUITY DUE

The BC Lottery Corporation runs the "Millionaire Life" lottery. The winner of the Grand Prize can choose either $1 million per year for 25 years or a single cash payment of $17 million. Which option should be chosen if the payments are made at the beginning of each year and, on low-risk investments, money can earn:

a. 3.2% compounded annually?

b. 3.8% compounded annually?

SOLUTION

The annuity option should be chosen if its economic value on the prize date exceeds $17,000,000. Its economic value is the present value of the 25 payments discounted at the rate of return money can earn. Since the first payment is received immediately and the payment interval (one year) equals the compounding interval (one year), the payments form a simple annuity due having

$$PMT = \$1,000,000 \quad \text{and} \quad n = 25$$

a. $j = 3.2\%$ compounded annually and $i = \frac{3.2\%}{1} = 3.2\%$ per year

Substituting in Formula (13-2), we obtain

$$PV(\text{due}) = PMT\left[\frac{1 - (1 + i)^{-n}}{i}\right] \times (1 + i)$$

$$= \$1,000,000\left(\frac{1 - 1.032^{-25}}{0.032}\right)(1.032)$$

$$= \$1,000,000\left(\frac{1 - 0.45499599}{0.032}\right)(1.032)$$

$$= \$17,576,379 \text{ (rounded to the nearest dollar)}$$

Select the 25-year annuity because its current economic value is $576,379 more than the lump payment.

b. $j = 3.8\%$ compounded annually and $i = \frac{3.8\%}{1} = 3.8\%$ per year

$$PV(\text{due}) = \$1,000,000\left(\frac{1 - 1.038^{-25}}{0.038}\right)(1.038)$$

$$= \$16,564,021 \text{ (to the nearest dollar)}$$

Select the single lump payment option because it is worth

$$\$17,000,000 - \$16,564,021 = \$435,979$$

more than the economic value of the annuity.

BGN mode

3.2 | I/Y

P/Y 1 ENTER

(making $C/Y = P/Y = 1$)

25 | N

1000000 | PMT

0 | FV

CPT | PV

Ans: −17,576,379

BGN mode

Same *P/Y, C/Y*

Same *N, PMT, FV*

3.8 | I/Y

CPT | PV

Ans: −16,564,021

Applications of the Present-Value Calculation

As with ordinary annuities, most applications of the present value of an annuity due involve some aspect of valuation. Since the payments on most leases form an annuity due, we are now able to address an additional valuation topic.

The book value of a lease When a business purchases equipment, its accountant records the acquisition of an asset (equipment). If the business instead leases the equipment, you might think the accountant would just record the monthly lease payments as they are made. However, there is an additional issue.

Most leases for a fixed term are "non-cancellable." This means that the lessee is required to continue the lease payments for the full term of the lease, even if the leased equipment is no longer needed. Generally Accepted Accounting Principles (GAAP) require this commitment to be recorded as a liability.[2]

This raises the question: "What amount should we use for this lease liability?" Should we simply add up all the payments for the entire term of the lease? No—that would place the same value on a dollar paid at the end of the lease as a dollar paid at the beginning. Instead, we should record the current economic value (present value) of the future lease payments. The follow-up question arises: "What discount rate should be used in the present-value calculation?"

To answer this second question, consider that the usual alternative to leasing equipment is purchasing the equipment using borrowed funds. For this reason, GAAP stipulates that the discount rate should be the interest rate the business would pay to finance the purchase of the equipment.[3]

---

[2] A leasehold asset is also recorded. The lease represents a long-term asset in the sense that the right to use the equipment will produce benefits over the term of the lease.

[3] This is consistent with a broader principle in accounting. The reported value of any long-term liability is the present value of future contractual payments discounted at the firm's borrowing rate (on the date the liability was incurred).

As time passes, the decreasing number of remaining payments represents a declining lease liability. In accordance with GAAP, the value of the lease liability is regularly reduced. At any point during the term of the lease, the present value of the *remaining* lease payments is known as the **book value of a lease** liability.

$$\begin{pmatrix} \text{Book value of a} \\ \text{long-term lease liability} \end{pmatrix} = \begin{pmatrix} \text{Present value of the remaining payments} \\ \text{(discounted at the interest rate on debt financing)} \end{pmatrix}$$

EXAMPLE 13.2B

THE BOOK VALUE OF A LEASE LIABILITY

National Engineering Services (NES) acquired a machine under a capital lease agreement. NES pays the lessor $2400 at the beginning of every three months for five years. If National can obtain five-year financing at 10% compounded quarterly,

a. What long-term lease liability will NES initially record?

b. What liability will be reported two years later?

SOLUTION

The initial liability (book value) is the present value of all of the lease payments. At any later date, the liability reported in the financial statements is the present value of the remaining payments. In both cases, the discount rate should be the interest rate at which the firm could have borrowed at the time of signing the lease. When viewed from the dates in either part (a) or part (b), the lease payments form a simple annuity due having $PMT = \$2400$ and $i = \frac{10\%}{4} = 2.5\%$.

a. $n = m(\text{Term}) = 4(5) = 20$ payments

The initial lease liability is

$$\left. \begin{aligned} PV(\text{due}) &= PMT\left[\frac{1-(1+i)^{-n}}{i}\right] \times (1+i) \\ &= \$2400\left(\frac{1-1.025^{-20}}{0.025}\right)(1.025) \\ &= \$38,349.34 \end{aligned} \right\}$$

BGN mode

10 I/Y
P/Y 4 ENTER
(making *C/Y* = *P/Y* = 4)
20 N
2400 +/− PMT
0 FV
CPT PV
Ans: 38,349.34

b. After two years, $n = 4(3) = 12$ payments remain.
The book value of the lease liability will be

$$\left. \begin{aligned} PV(\text{due}) &= \$2400\left(\frac{1-1.025^{-12}}{0.025}\right)(1.025) \\ &= \$25,234.10 \end{aligned} \right\}$$

BGN mode

Same *I/Y, P/Y, C/Y*
Same *PMT, FV*

12 N
CPT PV
Ans: 25,234.10

EXAMPLE 13.2C

PURCHASE OR LEASE A COMPUTER?

Best-Buy Computers advertises a gaming laptop computer for $1999.95. The same system may be leased for 24 months at $99 per month (at the beginning of each month). At the end of the lease, the system may be purchased for 10% of the retail price. Should you lease or purchase the computer if you can obtain a two-year loan at 7% compounded annually to purchase the computer?

SOLUTION

We cannot solve the problem by simply comparing the monthly loan payments to the monthly lease payments, for two reasons. Under the lease, you must pay an additional $200 two years from now to own the system. Also, lease payments are made at the beginning of each month but loan payments are made at the end of each month.

   We will compare the present values of the two alternatives. Since we are paying out money instead of receiving it, we should choose the alternative with the *lower* present value.

   From basic principles, we know that the present value of the loan payments, discounted at the interest rate on the loan, equals the initial loan ($1999.95). For a fair comparison, we should discount the lease payments (including the final payment to acquire ownership) using the same rate.

   Since the payment interval (one month) differs from the compounding interval (one year), the lease payments form a *general* annuity due having

$$PMT = \$99 \text{ per month} \quad n = 24 \quad \text{and} \quad i = \frac{7\%}{1} = 7\% \text{ per year}$$

First calculate the periodic interest rate for the one-month payment interval.

$$c = \frac{\text{Number of compoundings per year}}{\text{Number of payments per year}} = \frac{1}{12} = 0.08\overline{3}$$

$$i_2 = (1 + i)^c - 1 = 1.07^{0.08\overline{3}} - 1 = 0.005654145 \text{ per month}$$

Substitute this value for i in subsequent calculations.

The present value of the monthly lease payments is

$$PV(\text{due}) = PMT\left[\frac{1 - (1 + i)^{-n}}{i}\right] \times (1 + i)$$

$$= \$99\left[\frac{1 - 1.005654145^{-24}}{0.005654145}\right](1.005654145)$$

$$= \$2228.526$$

The present value of the end-of-lease purchase payment is

$$PV = FV(1 + i)^{-n} = \$200.00(1.005654145)^{-24} = \$174.688$$

The combined present value is $2228.526 + $174.688 = $2403.21.

The economic cost (in current dollars) of the lease is

$$\$2403.21 - \$1999.95 = \$403.26$$

more than the economic cost of purchasing the computer using borrowed funds. Therefore, the computer system should be purchased.

BGN mode

7 | I/Y |

| P/Y | 12 | ENTER |

| C/Y | 1 | ENTER |

24 | N |

99 | +/− | PMT |

200 | +/− | FV |

| CPT | PV |

Ans: $2403.21

POINT OF INTEREST

Rent to Own Real Estate

For some people, purchasing a home is out of reach. It could be for reasons of bad credit or not enough savings for the down payment. Rent to own could be the answer. In a rent-to-own deal, the seller leases the home with two contracts: one is the rental deal itself while the other sets out the terms for the lessee to eventually purchase the home.

In the purchase contract, a second monthly payment is calculated that will eventually form the down payment for the home in addition to an up-front down payment deposit of $5000 or more. The purchase price of the home will be negotiated at the time of signing the contract and the down payment can be as little as 5% of the purchase price. Typically, the purchase price is based on real estate values at the time the contract is made, but since real estate values are

© Thinkstock/Comstock Images/Getty Images

always changing it is not uncommon for the seller to build in a percent increase in the value of the property over the time of the contract.

At the end of the negotiated time to accumulate the necessary deposit, the potential buyer can walk away from the deal at any time. However, they will lose all of their deposit money and all additional payments made toward the down payment. The buyer also has to be able to qualify for a mortgage at the end of the contract. Since there are many risks to be considered, good legal advice is a key component for any rent-to-own purchase.

CONCEPT QUESTIONS

1. For the present value of an annuity due, where is the focal date located relative to the first payment?
2. Other things being equal, why is the present value of an annuity due larger than the present value of an ordinary annuity?
3. If the periodic interest rate for a payment interval is 3%, by what percentage will PV(due) exceed PV?
4. Other factors being equal, is the PV of an annuity due larger if the given nominal discount rate is compounded monthly instead of annually? Explain briefly.

EXERCISE 13.2

Answers to the odd-numbered problems are at the end of the book.

Spreadsheet template: *The partially completed Excel template developed in Section 11.4 for calculating the present value of an annuity may be used for many of the problems in Exercise 13.2. Go to the Student Edition and find "PV of Any Annuity" found under the Student Resources for Chapter 11.*

BASIC PROBLEMS

1. An annuity consists of quarterly payments of $950 for 8 years and 9 months. Discounting at 4% compounded quarterly, determine the present value of the annuity if the payments are made:
   a. At the end of each quarter.
   b. At the beginning of each quarter.
   c. By what percentage does the answer to part (b) exceed the answer to part (a)?

2. Using a discount rate of 6% compounded monthly, calculate the present value of monthly payments of $325 for $7\frac{1}{4}$ years if the payments are made:
   a. At the end of each month.
   b. At the beginning of each month.
   c. By what percentage does the answer to part (b) exceed the answer to part (a)?

3. What is the present value of an annuity due consisting of semiannual payments of $1000 for 25 years if money can earn:
   a. 4% compounded semiannually?
   b. 8% compounded semiannually?

4. Money can earn 6% compounded monthly. What is the present value of beginning-of-month payments of $100 if the payments continue for:
   a. 25 years?
   b. 30 years?

5. On the date of its financial statements, a company has $4\frac{1}{2}$ years remaining on the lease of a truck. The lease requires payments of $3000 at the beginning of every six months. What book value is reported for the lease liability if the company pays 5% compounded monthly on its medium-term debt?

6. If money can earn 5.25% compounded monthly, what is the value of an annuity consisting of annual payments of $2500 continuing for 16 years? The first payment will be received today.

7. Carmella purchased a refrigerator under a conditional sale contract that required 30 monthly payments of $60.26 with the first payment due on the purchase date. The interest rate on the outstanding balance was 18% compounded monthly.
   a. What was the purchase price of the refrigerator?
   b. How much interest did Carmella pay during the entire contract?

8. Rino has just purchased a five-year term life insurance policy. For his premium payments, Rino can choose either beginning-of-month payments of $38.50 or beginning-of-year payments of $455. In current dollars, how much will Rino save during the five years by choosing the lower-cost option? Assume that money can earn 4.8% compounded monthly.

9. Beaudoin Haulage has signed a five-year lease with GMAC on a new dump truck. Beaudoin intends to capitalize the lease and report it as a long-term liability. Lease payments of $2700 are made at the beginning of each month. To purchase the truck, Beaudoin would have had to borrow funds at 9% compounded monthly.
   a. What initial liability should Beaudoin report on its balance sheet?
   b. How much will the liability be reduced during the first year of the lease?

10. Under the headline "Local Theatre Project Receives $1 Million!" a newspaper article explained that the Theatre Project had just received the first of ten annual grants of $100,000 from the Hinton Foundation. What is the current economic value of all of the grants if money is worth 7.5% compounded monthly?

11. You have received two offers on the used car you wish to sell. Mr. Lindberg is offering $8500 cash, and Rosie Senario is offering five semiannual payments of $1900, including a payment on the purchase date. Whose offer has the greater economic value at a discount rate of 5% compounded semiannually? What is the economic advantage (in current dollars) of the preferred alternative?

12. Osgood Appliance Centre is advertising refrigerators for six monthly payments of $199, including a payment on the date of purchase. What cash price should Osgood accept if it would otherwise sell the conditional sale agreement to a finance company to yield 18% compounded monthly?

13. The life expectancy of the average 65-year-old Canadian male is about 16 additional years. Karsten wants to have sufficient funds in his RRIF at age 65 to be able to withdraw $40,000 at the beginning of each year for the expected survival period of 16 years. If his RRIF earns 4% compounded annually, what amount must he have in the RRIF at the time he turns 65?

14. A rental agreement requires the payment of $900 at the beginning of each month.
    a. What single payment at the beginning of the rental year should the landlord accept instead of 12 monthly payments if money is worth 6% compounded monthly?
    b. Show that the landlord will be equally well off at the end of the year under either payment arrangement if rental payments are invested at 6% compounded monthly.

15. What minimum amount of money earning 9% compounded semiannually will sustain withdrawals of $1200 at the beginning of every month for 15 years?

16. The lease contract for a computer workstation requires quarterly payments of $2100 at the beginning of every three-month period for five years. The lessee would otherwise have to pay an interest rate of 10% compounded quarterly to borrow funds to purchase the workstation.
    a. What amount will the lessee initially report in its financial statements as the long-term lease liability?
    b. What will the liability be at the end of the fourth year?

INTERMEDIATE PROBLEMS

17. Bram must choose between two alternatives for $1,000,000 of life insurance coverage for the next ten years. The premium quoted to him by Sun Life Insurance Co. is $51.75 per month. Atlantic Life will charge $44.25 per month for the first five years and $60.35 per month for the subsequent five years. In both cases, monthly premiums are payable at the beginning of each month. Which policy is "cheaper" if money can earn 4.8% compounded monthly? In current dollars, how much will Bram save by choosing the less costly policy?

18. What is the current economic value of an annuity due consisting of 22 quarterly payments of $700 if money is worth 6% compounded quarterly for the first three years, and 7% compounded quarterly thereafter?

19. Calculate and rank the economic values of the following cash flow streams:
    (i)   A single payment of $10,000 eight years from now.
    (ii) An annuity due starting today with eight annual payments of $850.
    (iii) An annuity due starting in eight years with eight annual payments of $1700.

    Do the calculations and ranking for each of two cases:
    a. Money can earn 5% compounded annually for the next 16 years.
    b. Money can earn 10% compounded annually for the next 16 years.

ADVANCED PROBLEMS

20. Two insurance companies gave the following quotations on premiums for essentially the same long-term disability insurance coverage for a 25-year-old. East Coast Insurance Co. quoted monthly premiums of $54.83 from ages 26 to 30 inclusive, and $78.17 from ages 31 to 64 inclusive. The monthly premiums from Provincial Insurance Co. are "flat" at $69.35 from ages 26 to 64 inclusive. All premiums are paid at the beginning of each month. The insurance broker recommended the Provincial coverage because the aggregate lifetime premiums up to the client's 65th birthday are $32,455.80 versus $35,183.16 for the East Coast policy. Is the choice that simple? (*Hint:* Calculate and compare the economic value on the client's 26th birthday of each policy's stream of premiums assuming money can earn 9% compounded monthly.)

21. The lease on the premises occupied by the accounting firm of Heath and Company will soon expire. The current landlord is offering to renew the lease for seven years at $2100 per month. The developers of a new building a block away from Heath's present offices are offering the first year of a seven-year lease rent-free. For the subsequent six years the rent would be $2500 per month. All rents are paid at the beginning of each month. Other things being equal, which lease should Heath accept if money is worth 7.5% compounded monthly?

13.3 Calculating the Periodic Payment, Number of Payments, and Interest Rate

L02 To calculate any one of these three quantities for an annuity due, follow the same procedure you would for an ordinary annuity, but with one change. You must use the annuity due formula that is the counterpart of the ordinary annuity formula. These counterparts are listed in the following table. Formulas (13-1n) and (13-2n) have not been presented before. They are versions of Formulas (13-1) and (13-2), respectively, rearranged to isolate n.

Ordinary annuity formula		Annuity due formula	
$FV = PMT\left[\dfrac{(1+i)^n - 1}{i}\right]$	(11-1)	$FV(\text{due}) = PMT\left[\dfrac{(1+i)^n - 1}{i}\right] \times (1+i)$	(13-1)
$PV = PMT\left[\dfrac{1 - (1+i)^{-n}}{i}\right]$	(11-2)	$PV(\text{due}) = PMT\left[\dfrac{1 - (1+i)^{-n}}{i}\right] \times (1+i)$	(13-2)
$n = \dfrac{\ln\!\left(1 + \dfrac{i \times FV}{PMT}\right)}{\ln(1+i)}$	(11-1n)	$n = \dfrac{\ln\!\left[1 + \dfrac{i \times FV(\text{due})}{PMT(1+i)}\right]}{\ln(1+i)}$	(13-1n)
$n = -\dfrac{\ln\!\left(1 - \dfrac{i \times PV}{PMT}\right)}{\ln(1+i)}$	(11-2n)	$n = -\dfrac{\ln\!\left[1 - \dfrac{i \times PV(\text{due})}{PMT(1+i)}\right]}{\ln(1+i)}$	(13-2n)

Calculating i algebraically requires the trial-and-error method described in **Appendix 12B**. We will use only the financial calculator method to solve for the interest rate in example problems.

The Mathematics of Vehicle Leasing

In recent years, just under 20% of new vehicles were leased. The main elements of a typical lease contract are as follows:

- The lessee makes fixed beginning-of-month payments for the term of the lease. The most common term is four years.
- The lessee is responsible for all vehicle operating costs (including insurance) during the term of the lease. In this respect, leasing does not differ from owning a vehicle.
- Most leases are "closed-end" or "walk away" leases. At the end of the term, the lessee can simply return the vehicle to the car dealer. Alternatively, at the option of the lessee, the vehicle may be purchased for a *predetermined* amount (called the **residual value**). The residual value represents the dealer's estimate of the market value of the vehicle at the end of the lease.

We will use a particular example to develop your understanding of the economics and mathematics of leasing. Suppose your down payment on a three-year lease is $3000. The car's purchase price is $30,000 and its residual value after three years is $15,000. We will now explain how the lease payment is calculated.

From the car dealer's point of view, the $27,000 "balance" is paid by 36 beginning-of-month payments plus a projected final payment of $15,000 after three years. This final payment will come either from you (if you exercise the purchase option) or from the sale of the vehicle at the end of the lease. Since the future selling price can only be estimated, the amount of the final payment is not known with certainty. The lease payments are calculated on the assumption that the final payment will be $15,000.

Except for the uncertainty in the amount of the final payment, the situation is similar to repaying a $27,000 loan by 36 beginning-of-month payments plus a final payment of $15,000 after three years. In that case, we know that the present value of all loan payments (discounted at the interest rate on the loan) is $27,000. Similarly, the present value of all lease payments and the residual value (discounted at the interest rate charged on the lease) is $27,000. In general,

$$\binom{\text{Purchase}}{\text{price}} - \binom{\text{Down}}{\text{payment}} = \binom{\text{Present value of}}{\text{the lease payments}} + \binom{\text{Present value of}}{\text{the residual value}}$$

The interest rate on a lease is applied as a monthly compounded rate. Therefore, the monthly lease payments form a simple annuity due.

There are six variables embedded in this mathematical relationship: the purchase price, the down payment, the residual value, the number of payments, the amount of the monthly payment, and the interest rate on the lease. If five of the variables are given, you can calculate the sixth. In the advertisements that car dealers place in newspapers, you may not find the values for all six variables. The most commonly omitted variable is the "residual value" (which may be called the "option to purchase at lease end"). If its value is given at all, it will be found among the details in the tiny print at the bottom of the advertisement.

APP  THAT

If you are looking to lease a new vehicle or are currently leasing a vehicle it is important to understand all of the factors that determine the ultimate long-term cost of the lease arrangement. Search the App Store on your tablet, smartphone, or smart watch using the key words **LEASE CALCULATOR**.

You will find many free and paid apps that will provide detailed analysis for many types of leases with calculations for monthly lease payments, residual value, and total lease cost. In the case of a car lease, there are several apps that also provide a mileage tracking feature and can log other lease costs such as maintenance and repairs.

EXAMPLE 13.3A

CALCULATING THE SIZE OF LEASE PAYMENTS

A lease that has $2\frac{1}{2}$ years to run is recorded on a company's books as a liability of $27,369. If the company's cost of borrowing was 6% compounded monthly when the lease was signed, what is the amount of the lease payment at the beginning of each month?

SOLUTION

The "book value" of the lease liability is the present value of the remaining lease payments. The discount rate employed should be the interest rate the company would have paid to borrow funds. The lease payments constitute a simple annuity due with

$$PV(\text{due}) = \$27{,}369 \quad n = 12(2.5) = 30 \quad \text{and} \quad i = \tfrac{6\%}{12} = 0.5\% \text{ per month}$$

Substitute the given values into Formula (13-2) and solve for *PMT*.

$$PV(\text{due}) = PMT\left[\frac{1 - (1+i)^{-n}}{i}\right] \times (1+i)$$

$$\$27{,}369 = PMT\left(\frac{1 - 1.005^{-30}}{0.005}\right)(1.005)$$

$$= PMT(27.79405)(1.005)$$

$$= PMT(27.93302)$$

$$PMT = \$979.81$$

The monthly lease payment is $979.81.

BGN mode

6 **I/Y**

P/Y 12 **ENTER**

(making *C/Y* = *P/Y* = 12)

30 **N**

27369 **PV**

0 **FV**

CPT **PMT**

Ans: −979.81

EXAMPLE 13.3B

CALCULATING THE *PMT* NEEDED TO ATTAIN A SAVINGS GOAL

Mr. Walters has already accumulated $104,000 in his Registered Retirement Savings Plan (RRSP). His goal is to build it to $250,000 with equal contributions at the beginning of each six-month period for the next seven years. If his RRSP earns 5.5% compounded semiannually, what must be the size of further contributions?

SOLUTION

The $250,000 target will be the combined future value of the $104,000 already in the RRSP and the simple annuity due formed by the next 14 payments. That is,

$$\$250,000 = \text{Future value of } \$104,000 + FV(\text{due}) \quad ①$$

with $n = 2(7) = 14$ and $i = \frac{5.5\%}{2} = 2.75\%$ per half-year.

The future value of the $104,000 will be

$$FV = PV(1 + i)^n = \$104,000(1.0275)^{14} = \$152,047.39$$

The future value of the 14 contributions will be

$$FV(\text{due}) = PMT\left[\frac{(1 + i)^n - 1}{i}\right](1 + I)$$

$$= PMT\left(\frac{1.0275^{14} - 1}{0.0275}\right)(1.0275)$$

$$= PMT(17.261781)$$

Substituting these amounts into equation ①, we obtain

$$\$250,000 = \$152,047.39 + PMT(17.261781)$$

$$PMT = \frac{\$250,000 - \$152,047.39}{17.261781} = \$5674.54$$

BGN mode

5.5 I/Y
P/Y 2 ENTER
(making C/Y = P/Y = 2)
14 N
104000 +/− PV
250000 FV
CPT PMT
Ans: −5674.54

Mr. Walters must make semiannual contributions of $5674.54 to reach the $250,000 target in seven years.

EXAMPLE 13.3C

CALCULATING THE PAYMENT ON A CAR LEASE

An automobile manufacturer is calculating the lease payments to charge on the SLX model, which has a selling price of $27,900. During a month-long promotion, the manufacturer will offer an interest rate of only 1.8% compounded monthly on a three-year lease. If the residual value is $14,500, what will be the lease payments, assuming a $2500 down payment?

SOLUTION

Earlier in this section, we developed the leasing equation:

$$\left(\begin{array}{c}\text{Purchase}\\\text{price}\end{array}\right) - \left(\begin{array}{c}\text{Down}\\\text{payment}\end{array}\right) = \left(\begin{array}{c}\text{Present value of}\\\text{the lease payments}\end{array}\right) + \left(\begin{array}{c}\text{Present value of}\\\text{the residual value}\end{array}\right)$$

For the SLX lease,

$$\$27,900 - \$2500 = \left(\begin{array}{c}\text{Present value of}\\\text{the lease payments}\end{array}\right) + \left(\begin{array}{c}\text{Present value}\\\text{of } \$14,500\end{array}\right) ①$$

The lease payments form a simple annuity due with $i = \frac{1.8\%}{12} = 0.15\%$ and $n = 36$.

The present value of the lease payments is

$$PV(\text{due}) = PMT\left[\frac{1 - (1 + i)^{-n}}{i}\right](1 + I)$$

$$= PMT\left[\frac{1 - 1.0015^{-36}}{0.0015}\right](1.0015)$$

$$= PMT(35.07224)$$

The present value of the $14,500 residual value is

$$PV = FV(1 + i)^{-n} = \$14,500(1.0015)^{-36} = \$13,738.32$$

Substitute these values into equation ① and solve for *PMT*.

$$\$25,400 = PMT(35.07224) + \$13,738.32$$

$$PMT = \frac{\$25,400 - \$13,738.32}{35.07224} = \$332.50$$

The beginning-of-month lease payment is $332.50.

BGN mode

1.8 │ I/Y
│ P/Y │ 12 │ ENTER
(making *C/Y = P/Y* = 12)
36 │ N
25400 │ +/− │ PV
14500 │ FV
│ CPT │ PMT
Ans: 332.50

EXAMPLE 13.3D

CALCULATING *n* GIVEN THE FUTURE VALUE OF A SIMPLE ANNUITY DUE

Rounding *n* upward to the next integer, how long will it take to accumulate $1,000,000 in an RRSP if the first quarterly contribution of $2000 is made today? Assume the RRSP earns 8% compounded quarterly.

SOLUTION

First, we need to find the number of contributions required for the future value to reach $1,000,000. Since the compounding interval equals the payment interval, the contributions form a simple annuity due having

$$PMT = \$2000 \quad i = \tfrac{8\%}{4} = 2\% \quad \text{and} \quad FV(\text{due}) = \$1,000,000$$

Substitute these values into Formula (13-1*n*).

$$n = \frac{\ln\left[1 + \dfrac{i \times FV(\text{due})}{PMT(1 + i)}\right]}{\ln(1 + i)}$$

$$= \frac{\ln\left[1 + \dfrac{0.02 \times \$1,000,000}{\$2000(1.02)}\right]}{\ln(1.02)}$$

$$= \frac{2.3799}{0.019803}$$

$$= 120.18$$

BGN mode

8 │ I/Y
│ P/Y │ 4 │ ENTER
(making *C/Y = P/Y* = 4)
0 │ PV
2000 │ +/− │ PMT
1000000 │ FV
│ CPT │ N
Ans: 120.18

The 121st contribution is required to reach $1,000,000. The time to the end of the 121st payment interval is

$$121 \text{ quarters} = \tfrac{121}{4} = 30.25 \text{ years} = 30 \text{ years and 3 months}$$

With *n* rounded to the next higher integer, it will take 30 years and 3 months to accumulate $1,000,000 in the RRSP. (Including accrued earnings, the $1,000,000 is actually reached quite early in the 121st interval.)

EXAMPLE 13.3E

CALCULATING *n* GIVEN THE PRESENT VALUE OF A GENERAL ANNUITY DUE

An investment fund is worth $210,000 and earns 9% compounded semiannually. If $2000 is withdrawn at the beginning of each month starting today, when will the fund become depleted?

SOLUTION

The initial amount in the account equals the present value of the future withdrawals. Since the first withdrawal occurs today, and the payment interval differs from the compounding interval, the withdrawals form a *general annuity due* having

$$PV\text{(due)} = \$210{,}000 \quad PMT = \$2000 \quad \text{and} \quad i = \tfrac{9\%}{2} = 4.5\%$$

The value we must use for i in Formula (13-2n) is the periodic rate for the one-month payment interval.

Substitute

$$c = \frac{\text{Number of compoundings per year}}{\text{Number of payments per year}} = \frac{2}{12} = 0.1\overline{6}$$

into

$$i_2 = (1 + i)^c - 1 = (1.045)^{0.1\overline{6}} - 1 = 0.00736312 \text{ per month}$$

Substitute the known values into Formula (13-2n).

$$n = -\frac{\ln\left[1 - \dfrac{i \times PV\text{(due)}}{PMT(1 + i)}\right]}{\ln(1 + i)}$$

$$= -\frac{\ln\left[1 - \dfrac{0.00736312(\$210{,}000)}{\$2000(1.00736312)}\right]}{\ln(1.00736312)}$$

$$= 198.85$$

BGN mode	
9	I/Y
P/Y 12	ENTER
C/Y 2	ENTER
210000 +/−	PV
2000	PMT
0	FV
CPT	N
Ans: 198.85	

The fund will permit 199 monthly withdrawals. The final withdrawal, smaller than $2000, will occur at the *beginning* of the 199th payment interval. But that will be 198 months from now.

So the fund will be depleted at the time of the 199th payment, which is 198 months or 16 years and 6 months from now.

EXAMPLE 13.3F

CALCULATING THE INTEREST RATE FOR AN ANNUITY DUE

Therese intends to contribute $3000 at the beginning of each six-month period to an RRSP. What rate of return must her RRSP earn in order to reach $350,000 after 25 years?

SOLUTION

The payments form an annuity due whose future value after 25 years is to be $350,000. That is,

$$FV\text{(due)} = \$350{,}000 \quad PMT = \$3000 \quad \text{and} \quad n = m(\text{Term}) = 2(25) = 50$$

If we set $P/Y = C/Y = 2$, we will obtain the semiannually compounded rate of return. Enter these values and compute I/Y.

BGN mode	
P/Y 2	ENTER
(making $C/Y = P/Y = 2$)	
50	N
0	PV
3000 +/−	PMT
350000	FV
CPT	I/Y
Ans: 6.03	

Therese's RRSP must earn 6.03% compounded semiannually.

EXAMPLE 13.3G

CALCULATING THE INTEREST RATE BUILT INTO AN INSTALLMENT PAYMENT OPTION

A $100,000 life insurance policy requires an annual premium of $420 or a monthly premium of $37. In either case, the premium is payable at the beginning of the period of coverage. What is the effective rate of interest policyholders pay when they choose the monthly payment plan?

SOLUTION

In effect, the insurance company lends the $420 annual premium to policyholders choosing the monthly payment option. These policyholders then repay the "loan" with 12 beginning-of-month payments of $37. Hence, $420 is the present value of the 12 payments that form an annuity due. We have

$$PV\text{(due)} = \$420 \quad PMT = \$37 \quad n = 12 \quad \text{and} \quad P/Y = 12$$

The effective interest rate is the same as the annually compounded rate ($C/Y = 1$). Enter these values and compute I/Y.

The effective interest rate on the monthly payment plan is 13.04%.

BGN mode	
P/Y 12	ENTER
C/Y 1	ENTER
12	N
420	PV
37 +/−	PMT
0	FV
CPT	I/Y

Ans: 13.04

EXAMPLE 13.3H

CALCULATING THE INTEREST RATE BUILT INTO LEASE PAYMENTS

A car dealer advertised the Hyundai Santa Fe GL AWD sport utility vehicle for sale at $33,610. The same vehicle could also be leased for five years at $379 per month, based on a $4310 down payment. At the end of the lease, the lessee could purchase the vehicle for $10,711. What monthly compounded interest rate was built into the lease?

SOLUTION

Mathematically, the problem is the same as calculating the interest rate charged on a loan where the balance is reduced from $29,300 (= $33,610 − $4310) to $10,711 by 60 beginning-of-month payments of $379. That is, $29,300 is the combined present value of 60 payments of $379 and a terminal payment of $10,711. In effect, we are given

$$PV\text{(due)} = \$29,300 \quad PMT = \$379 \quad n = 60 \quad \text{and} \quad FV = \$10,711$$

The interest rate built into the lease was 4.13% compounded monthly.

BGN mode	
P/Y 12	ENTER
(making $C/Y = P/Y = 12$)	
60	N
29300	PV
379 +/−	PMT
10711 +/−	FV
CPT	I/Y

Ans: 4.13

POINT OF INTEREST

"Rent-to-Own" or "Rent Too Onerous"?

Rent-to-own stores offer credit-challenged consumers yet another opportunity to dig themselves into a deeper financial hole. Furniture, appliances, and home electronics products may be rented under agreements that require weekly or monthly rent payments. The renter can terminate the rental agreement at any time without further cost. If the rental payments are made for a period specified in the agreement (18 months to four years, depending on the item rented), the renter takes ownership.

A study of rent-to-own consumers found that the primary reasons for consumers using rent-to-own stores were:

1. They want to obtain the goods right away rather than wait to accumulate savings.
2. They do not need to pass a credit check at rent-to-own stores.
3. They like the flexibility of returning the goods and cancelling the contract at any time.

Critics argue that rent-to-own stores charge exorbitant rental rates. Rent-to-own business operators respond that they incur high collection and default costs because of their high-risk clientele.

Some examples of *weekly* rental rates are: $13.66 for a Samsung 32-inch LCD HD TV; $13.66 for a Moffat full-size washer-dryer combo; and $10.93 for a JVC 60 GB Hard-Drive Camcorder. If the weekly rent is paid for 156 weeks, the renter takes ownership of the item. [The renter also pays HST (or GST plus PST) on the rental rates.]

QUESTIONS

1. In department and home entertainment stores, the Samsung 32-inch LCD HD TV mentioned above was priced in the neighbourhood of $650. Suppose we treat the rent-to-own transaction as a purchase-on-credit transaction wherein the $650 purchase price is paid off by beginning-of-week payments of $13.66 for 156 weeks. What are the imputed weekly compounded interest rate and effective interest rate? Assume there are exactly 52 weeks in a year. (Since the actual transaction is a rental transaction rather than a credit transaction, it is not subject to the Criminal Code's requirement that the effective rate of interest must not exceed 60%.)
2. The rent-to-own operation claimed in its advertising that the imputed interest rate (based on the $13.66 weekly rental rate and the retail value of the Samsung TV) was 29.9% compounded monthly. If this is correct, what retail value was used?
3. Suppose that the Samsung TV is purchased for $650 on a loan from a consumer-finance company that charges interest at 30% compounded monthly. What regular beginning-of-week payment would pay off the loan in three years?

CONCEPT QUESTIONS

1. An ordinary annuity and an annuity due have the same future value, n, and i. Which annuity has the larger payment? Give the reason for your answer.
2. An ordinary annuity and an annuity due have the same present value, n, and i. Which annuity has the smaller payment? Give the reason for your answer.
3. The term of the lease on a vehicle is about to expire. Answer parts (a) and (b) strictly on financial considerations.
   a. If the market value of the vehicle is less than the residual value, what should the lessee do?
   b. If the market value of the vehicle exceeds the residual value, what should the lessee do?
   c. In view of your answers to (a) and (b), will the interest rate on a lease contract tend to be higher or lower than the interest rate on a loan to purchase the same vehicle? Explain.

EXERCISE 13.3

Answers to the odd-numbered problems are at the end of the book.

Spreadsheet template: *The partially completed Excel templates introduced in Sections 12.1, 12.2, and 12.3 for calculating an annuity's PMT, n, and i, respectively, may be used in many of the problems in Exercise 13.3. Go to the Student Edition to find "PMT for Any Annuity" or "NPER for Any Annuity" or "Rate for Annuity" under the Student Resources for Chapter 12.*

BASIC PROBLEMS

Calculate nominal and effective interest rates accurate to the nearest 0.01%.

1. In order to accumulate $750,000 after 25 years, calculate the amounts that must be invested at the beginning of each year if the invested funds earn:
   a. 3% compounded annually.   **b.** 6% compounded annually.
   c. 8% compounded annually.   **d.** 9% compounded annually.

   Also calculate the total earnings in each case.

2. What beginning-of-month withdrawals can a $400,000 RRIF (Registered Retirement Income Fund) sustain for 20 years if the investments within the RRIF earn:
   a. 3% compounded monthly?   **b.** 4.5% compounded monthly?
   c. 6% compounded monthly?   **d.** 7.5% compounded monthly?

   Also calculate the total earnings distributed over the life of the annuity in each case.

3. How long will it take an RRSP to grow to $600,000 if it receives a contribution of $2500 at the beginning of each quarter and it earns:
   a. 3% compounded quarterly?   **b.** 6% compounded quarterly?
   c. 8% compounded quarterly?   **d.** 9% compounded quarterly?

4. For how long will a $100,000 fund sustain beginning-of-month withdrawals of $700 if the fund earns:
   a. 4% compounded monthly?   **b.** 5% compounded monthly?
   c. 6% compounded monthly?   **d.** 7% compounded monthly?

5. Ichiro is checking potential outcomes for the growth of his RRSP. He plans to make contributions of $500 at the beginning of each month. What nominal rate of return must his RRSP earn for its future value after 25 years to be:
   a. $400,000?   **b.** $500,000?   **c.** $600,000?

6. Gina has $500,000 accumulated in her RRSP and intends to use the amount to purchase a 20-year annuity. She is investigating the size of quarterly payment she can expect to receive, depending on the rate of return earned by the funds. What nominal rate of return must the funds earn for the beginning-of-quarter payment to be:
   a. $10,000?   **b.** $11,000?   **c.** $12,000?

7. Nitesh currently has accumulated capital of $560,000 and hopes to retire this year. He wants to receive an annuity payment at the beginning of each year for the next 20 years. If the capital can earn 6.5% compounded annually, what maximum annual payment can he receive and just deplete the capital after 20 years?

8. Liam purchases an annuity for $700,000 that provides beginning-of-month payments for 15 years. If the annuity earns 4.5% compounded monthly, what monthly payment will he receive?

9. Corbin wants to accumulate $1,000,000 over the next 25 years by investing the same amount at the beginning of each month. If he can expect a long-term rate of return of 8% compounded annually, how much must he invest each month?

10. To accumulate $200,000 after 20 years, what amount must be invested each year if the investment earns 9% compounded annually and the contributions are made:
    a. At the beginning of each year? **b.** At the end of each year?

11. What maximum annual withdrawals will a $200,000 fund earning 6% compounded annually sustain for 20 years if the withdrawals are made:
    a. At the beginning of each year? **b.** At the end of each year?

12. Triex Manufacturing wants to accumulate $500,000 for an expansion planned to begin in five years. If today Triex makes the first of equal quarterly payments into a fund earning 5.4% compounded monthly, what size should these payments be?

13. Felix has already accumulated $20,000 and plans to invest another $5000 at the beginning of each year for the next 15 years. He expects to earn a return of $7\frac{1}{4}$% compounded annually on his investments. What size monthly payments can be withdrawn from the matured investment beginning in the 16th year if it earns 4.5% compounded monthly for the next 15 years? Assume that the monthly payments will deplete the fund after 15 years.

14. An insurance company wishes to offer customers a monthly installment alternative to the annual premium plan. All premiums are payable at the beginning of the period of coverage. The monthly payment plan is to include an interest charge of 12% compounded monthly on the unpaid balance of the annual premium. What will be the monthly premium per $100 of annual premium?

15. Advance Leasing calculates the monthly payments on its three-year leases on the basis of recovering the capital cost of the leased equipment and earning a 13.5% compounded monthly rate of return on its capital investment. What will be the monthly lease payment on equipment that costs $8500?

16. Shane is about to have his 25th birthday. He has set a goal of retiring at age 55 with $700,000 in an RRSP. For planning purposes he is assuming that his RRSP will earn 8% compounded annually.
    a. What contribution on each birthday from age 25 to 54 inclusive will be required to accumulate the desired amount in his RRSP?
    b. If he waits five years before starting his RRSP, what contribution on each birthday from age 30 to 54 inclusive will be required to accumulate the target amount?

17. Wendy will soon turn 33. She wants to accumulate $500,000 in an RRSP by her 60th birthday. How much larger will her annual contributions have to be if they are made at the end of each year (from age 33 to age 59 inclusive) instead of at the beginning of each year? Assume that her RRSP will earn 9% compounded annually.

18. CompuLease leases computers and peripheral equipment to businesses. What lease payments must CompuLease charge at the beginning of each quarter of a five-year lease if it is to recover the $20,000 capital cost of a system and earn 12% compounded quarterly on its investment?

19. Island Water Taxi has decided to lease another boat for five years rather than finance the purchase of the boat at an interest rate of 7.5% compounded monthly. It has set up a long-term lease liability of $43,000. What is the lease payment at the beginning of each month?

20. The MSRP on a Nissan Maxima 3.5 SV is $38,625. The interest rate on a 48-month lease is 1.9% compounded monthly. What is the monthly lease payment, assuming a down payment of $5400 and a residual value of $11,990?

21. The $219.40 monthly payment on a 48-month lease of a Kia SOUL was based on a down payment of $1545, an interest rate of 3.9% compounded monthly, and a residual value of $6815. What is the full price (MSRP) for the car rounded to the nearest dollar?

22. With a down payment of $4850, the monthly payment on a four-year lease of a Ford F150 SuperCab (MSRP $27,629) is $369.27. The interest rate on the lease is 7.99% compounded monthly. What residual value was used in the calculation?

23. A Smart ForTwo cabriolet (MSRP $21,550) can be leased for $248 per month. This payment is based on an interest rate of 6.9% compounded monthly, a down payment of $1425, and a residual value of $14,794. What is the term of the lease?

24. What interest rate is being charged if the monthly payment on a 48-month lease of a Jaguar XF (MSRP $58,125) is $799? The required down payment is $2999 and the residual value is $24,059.

25. The MSRP for a BMW 528i is $58,499. The monthly payment on a 48-month lease at 1.9% compounded monthly is $697. The residual value at the end of the lease is $21,000. Rounded to the nearest dollar, what down payment was used in the lease calculation?

26. RentalTown advertised a computer system at a cash price of $1699 and at a rent-to-own rate of $129 at the beginning of each month for 24 months. What effective rate of interest is a customer paying to acquire the computer in a rent-to-own transaction?

27. Kim wants to save half of the $30,000 purchase price of a new car by making monthly deposits of $700, beginning today, into a T-bill savings account earning 4.2% compounded monthly. How long will it take him to reach his goal?

28. Central Personnel's accountant set up a long-term lease liability of $11,622.73 to recognize a new contract for the lease of office furniture. She used the firm's 10.5% monthly compounded cost of borrowing as the discount rate. If the lease payment at the beginning of each month is $295, what is the term of the lease?

29. The payments required on a contractual obligation are $500 per month. The contract was purchased for $13,372 just *before* a regular payment date. The purchaser determined this price based on his required rate of return of 9.75% compounded monthly. How many payments will he receive?

30. How much longer will a $100,000 fund earning 9% compounded monthly sustain beginning-of-month withdrawals of $900 than beginning-of-month withdrawals of $1000?

31. How many fewer deposits will it take to accumulate savings of $100,000 with beginning-of-month deposits of $220 than with beginning-of-month deposits of $200? The savings earn 5.4% compounded monthly.

32. If a furniture retailer offers a financing plan on a $1500 purchase requiring four equal quarterly payments of $400 including the first payment on the purchase date, what effective rate of interest is being charged on the unpaid balance?

33. An RRSP is now worth $223,000 after contributions of $2500 at the beginning of every six months for 16 years. What effective rate of return has the plan earned?

34. Pembroke Golf Club's initiation fee is $5500. It offers an installment payment alternative of $1000 down and $1000 at the end of each year for five years. What effective rate of interest is being charged on the installment plan?

35. If contributions of $1500 at the beginning of every three months resulted in an RRSP worth $327,685 after 20 years, what quarterly compounded nominal rate and effective rate of return did the RRSP earn?

36. As of the date of Victory Machine Shop's most recent financial statements, three years remained in the term of a capital lease reported as a long-term liability of $13,824. If the beginning-of-month lease payments are $450, what monthly compounded annual discount rate was used in valuing the lease?

37. If a furniture store offers to sell a refrigerator priced at $1195 on a conditional sale contract requiring 12 monthly payments of $110 (including a payment on the date of sale), what effective rate of interest is being charged to the customer?

38. For the past 13 years, Ms. Perrault has contributed $2000 at the beginning of every six months to a mutual fund. If the mutual fund statement at the end of the 13 years reports that her fund units are worth a total of $91,477, what has been the semiannually compounded nominal rate and the effective rate of return on her investments over the 13 years?

INTERMEDIATE PROBLEMS

39. Advantage Leasing Ltd. is in the business of purchasing equipment, which it then leases to other companies. Advantage calculates the payments on its five-year leases so that it recovers the original cost of the equipment plus a return on investment of 15% compounded quarterly over the term of the lease. What will be the required lease payments on a machine that cost $25,000 if the lease payments will be received:
   a. At the beginning of every month?
   b. At the beginning of each six-month period?

40. Mr. and Mrs. Friedrich have just opened an RESP for their daughter. They want the plan to pay $3000 at the beginning of each half-year for four years, starting nine years from now when their daughter will enter college or university. What semiannual contributions, including one today, must they make for the next nine years if the RESP earns 8.25% compounded semiannually?

41. Ambleside Golf Club's board of directors has set next year's membership fee at $1900, payable at the beginning of the year. The board has instructed its accountant to calculate beginning-of-quarter and beginning-of-month payment plans that provide a 6% semiannually compounded rate of return on the unpaid balance of the annual fee. What will be the amounts of the quarterly and monthly payments?

42. RRSP contributions of $5000 are made at the beginning of every six months. How many more contributions will it take to reach $750,000 if the RRSP earns 8% compounded semiannually than if it earns 10% compounded semiannually?

43. Mrs. McPherson wants to use $10,000 from her late husband's estate to assist her grandson when he enters college in seven years. Assume the $10,000 is invested immediately at 4% compounded monthly, and the grandson will make beginning-of-month withdrawals of $300 when he starts college. When will the final withdrawal occur?

44. If you contribute $1000 to an RRSP at the beginning of every three months for 25 years and then use the accumulated funds to purchase an annuity paying $3000 at the beginning of each month, what will be the term of the annuity? Assume that the RRSP earns 8.5% compounded quarterly, and the funds invested in the annuity earn 7.5% compounded monthly.

45. Quantum Research Ltd. has arranged debt financing from its parent company to complete the development of a new product. Quantum "draws down" $12,000 at the beginning of each month. If interest accumulates on the debt at 8.2% compounded quarterly, how long will it take to reach the credit limit of $1 million?

46. Jamshid borrowed $350 from his mother at the beginning of every month for $2\frac{1}{2}$ years while he attended Seneca College.
   a. If the interest rate on the accumulating debt was 6% compounded semiannually, what amount did he owe his mother at the end of the $2\frac{1}{2}$-year period?
   b. If he made the first monthly payment of $175 on the loan at the end of the first month following the $2\frac{1}{2}$-year period, how long after the date he entered college will he have the loan repaid?

47. The annual membership dues in the Rolling Meadows Golf and Country Club can be paid by four payments of $898.80 at the beginning of each calendar quarter, instead of by a single payment of $3428 at the beginning of the year. What effective rate of interest is the club charging the quarterly installment payers on the unpaid balance of their annual dues?

48. The Lifestyle Fitness and Exercise Centre charges annual membership fees of $600 (in advance) or six "easy" payments of $120 at the beginning of every two months. What effective interest rate is being charged on the installment plan?

49. A magazine offers a one-year subscription rate of $63.80 and a three-year subscription rate of $159.80, both payable at the start of the subscription period. Assuming that you intend to continue to subscribe for three years and that the one-year rate does not increase for the next two years, what rate of "return on investment" will be earned by paying for a three-year subscription now instead of three consecutive one-year subscriptions?

50. Continental Life Insurance Company of Canada offered $250,000 of term life insurance to a 40-year-old female nonsmoker for an annual premium of $447.50 (in advance) or for monthly premium payments (in advance) of $38.82 by preauthorized electronic debit. What effective rate of interest is charged to those who pay monthly?

51. The same disability insurance policy offers four alternative premium payment plans: an annual premium of $666.96, semiannual premiums of $341.32, quarterly premiums of $173.62, or monthly premiums of $58.85. In every case, the premiums are payable in advance. What effective rate of interest is the insurance company charging clients who pay their premiums:
    a. Semiannually?   **b.** Quarterly?   **c.** Monthly?

52. A $500,000 life insurance policy for a 26-year-old offers four alternative premium payment plans: an annual premium of $470.00, semiannual premiums of $241.50, quarterly premiums of $123.37, or monthly premiums of $42.30. In every case, the premiums are payable in advance. What effective rate of interest is the insurance company charging if the premium is paid:
    a. Semiannually?   **b.** Quarterly?   **c.** Monthly?

ADVANCED PROBLEMS

53. Mr. Ng contributed $1000 to an RRSP at the beginning of each calendar quarter for the past 20 years. The plan earned 10% compounded quarterly for the first 10 years and 12% compounded quarterly for the last 10 years. He is converting the RRSP to a Registered Retirement Income Fund (RRIF) and intends to withdraw equal amounts at the beginning of each month for 15 years. If the funds in the RRIF earn 8.25% compounded monthly, what maximum monthly amount can be withdrawn?

54. As a result of the closure of the mine at which he had been employed, Les Orr received a $27,000 severance settlement on his 53rd birthday. He rolled the severance pay into a new RRSP and then, at age 62, used the accumulated funds to purchase an annuity paying $491.31 at the beginning of each month. If the RRSP and the annuity earn 8.5% compounded annually, what is the term of the annuity?

55. Mr. van der Linden has just used the funds in his RRSP to purchase a 25-year annuity earning 8% compounded semiannually and paying $3509 at the beginning of each month. Mr. van der Linden made his last regular semiannual contribution of $2500 to his RRSP six months before purchasing the annuity. How long did he contribute to the RRSP if it earned 8% compounded annually?

*13.4 Comprehensive Annuity Problems

The example problems and exercises in each section of the text are usually chosen to illustrate the concepts and techniques introduced in that particular section. Each problem is an application primarily within the narrow scope of the section. However, when applications arise in business, the connections to the underlying concept and a solution idea usually require a combination of concepts and techniques.

The purpose of this section is to present some interesting, comprehensive, and challenging problems that may involve any type of annuity as well as individual payments. A problem's solution may call upon any topic in **Chapters 9** through **13**.

TIP

Identify the Type of Annuity at the Outset

Before doing any calculations for an annuity, you should write down the type of annuity involved. If you intend to use the financial calculator functions, set the calculator in the proper mode (ordinary or due) at this time. By doing these small steps at the outset, you are less likely to overlook them later when you become preoccupied with more profound aspects of the solution.

The flow chart in **Figure 13.4** presents a procedure for identifying the type of annuity and the relevant formulas.

FIGURE 13.4   Annuity Classification Flow Chart

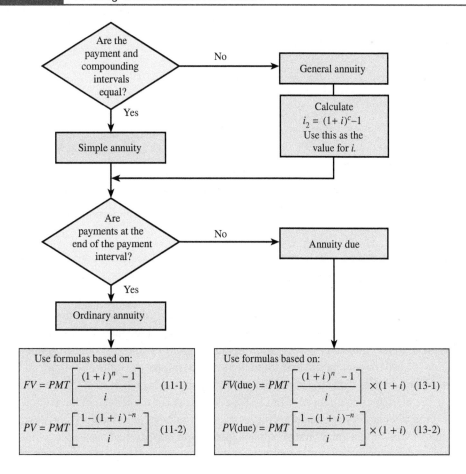

EXAMPLE 13.4A

REDUCING A LOAN'S TERM BY MAKING MORE FREQUENT, SMALLER PAYMENTS

Calculate the time required to pay off a $25,000 loan at 8.25% compounded monthly if the loan is repaid by:

a. Quarterly payments of $600.   **b.** Monthly payments of $200.   **c.** Semimonthly payments of $100.

d. In every case, a total of $600 is paid every three months. Explain why the time required to repay the loan short-ens as smaller payments are made more frequently.

SOLUTION

In every case, the present value of the payments is $25,000 and $i = \frac{8.25\%}{12} = 0.6875\%$. The payments form an ordinary *general* annuity in parts (a) and (c) where the payment interval differs from the compounding interval. In part (b), the payments form an ordinary *simple* annuity.

a. $c = \dfrac{\text{Number of compoundings per year}}{\text{Number of payments per year}} = \dfrac{12}{4} = 3$

$i_2 = (1 + i)^c - 1 = (1.006875)^3 - 1 = 0.020767122$ per quarter

Substitute this value and $PMT = \$600$ into Formula (11-2n).

$$n = -\frac{\ln\left[1 - \frac{i \times PV}{PMT}\right]}{\ln(1 + i)}$$

$$= -\frac{\ln\left(1 - \frac{0.020767122 \times \$25,000}{\$600}\right)}{\ln(1.020767122)}$$

$$= 97.53$$

8.25	I/Y
P/Y 4	ENTER
C/Y 12	ENTER
25000	PV
600 +/−	PMT
0	FV
CPT	N

Ans: 97.53

The loan will be paid off by 98 quarterly payments requiring $\frac{98}{4} = 24.5$ years, or 24 years and 6 months.

b. Substitute $i = 0.006875$ and $PMT = \$200$ into Formula (11-2n).

$$n = -\frac{\ln\left(1 - \frac{0.006875 \times \$25,000}{\$200}\right)}{\ln(1.006875)}$$

$$= 286.31$$

Same *I/Y, C/Y, PV, FV*

P/Y 12	ENTER
200 +/−	PMT
CPT	N

Ans: 286.31

The loan will be paid off by 287 monthly payments requiring $\frac{287}{12} = 23.92$ years, or 23 years and 11 months.

c. In a manner similar to part (a), we obtain $c = 0.5$, $i_2 = 0.003431612$, and $n = 569.58$.

Therefore, the loan will be paid off by 570 semimonthly payments requiring $\frac{570}{24} = 23.75$ years, or 23 years and 9 months.

d. It is apparent that the loan's term shortens as a given total annual amount is allocated to smaller, more frequent payments. This happens because the more frequent the payments, the earlier the principal balance is reduced. Subsequent interest charges are then lower.

Consider, for example, the cases of monthly and quarterly payments. The first $200 monthly payment will reduce the principal balance somewhat. The interest charged in the second month will be less than in the first month because it is calculated on the *reduced* principal. In contrast, the first quarterly payment must include interest on the *full* $25,000 for each of the first three months. Therefore, the interest component of the first quarterly $600 payment will be *greater* than the sum of the *interest* components of the first three $200 monthly payments. Accordingly, the *principal* component of the $600 payment will be *smaller* than the sum of the principal components of the first three $200 monthly payments. This same effect will repeat and compound every quarter. Therefore, monthly payments will reduce the principal balance faster (and pay off the loan sooner) than quarterly payments.

EXAMPLE 13.4B

A MULTIPLE-STEP PROBLEM IN PERSONAL FINANCIAL PLANNING

Victor and his financial adviser are checking whether Victor's savings plan will allow him to achieve his retirement goals. Victor wishes to retire in 30 years at age 58. His plan is to use some of the funds in his RRSP at age 58 to purchase a 10-year annuity paying $5000 at the end of each month. Then, at age 68, he intends to use the balance of the funds in his RRSP to purchase a 20-year annuity paying at least $7000 at each month's end.

   Victor anticipates that he will be able to contribute $5000 to his RRSP at the beginning of each of the next 15 years and $10,000 at the beginning of each of the subsequent 15 years. Can Victor achieve the desired retirement income if the RRSP earns 8% compounded semiannually and the funds used to purchase the annuities earn 7.5% compounded monthly?

SOLUTION

Victor's savings plan is presented in the following time diagram.

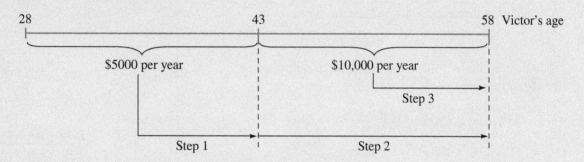

His desired retirement income stream is shown in the following time diagram.

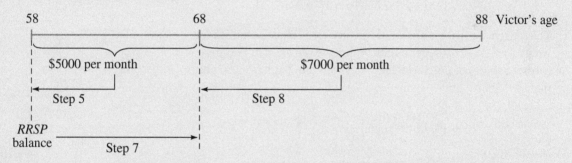

The key test to determine if Victor can achieve his objective for retirement income is whether there will be sufficient funds in his RRSP at age 68 to purchase a 20-year annuity paying $7000 at the end of each month. In general terms, our strategy for the solution is to:

- Calculate the expected amount in the RRSP at age 58. (Steps 1, 2, and 3 in the first diagram. Then for Step 4, add the results of Steps 2 and 3.)
- Determine the amount required to purchase the 10-year annuity. (Step 5 in the second diagram.) Then for Step 6, subtract the Step 5 result from the Step 4 result to obtain the "RRSP balance" after purchasing the annuity.
- Calculate the expected amount in the RRSP at age 68. (Step 7.)
- Calculate the amount required to purchase the 20-year annuity. (Step 8.) Then, in Step 9, compare the Step 8 amount to the Step 7 amount.

Step 1: Calculate the future value at age 43 of the RRSP contributions of $5000 per year. The contributions form a general annuity due for which

$$i = \frac{8\%}{2} = 4\%, \; n = m(\text{Term}) = 1(43 - 28) = 15, \text{ and}$$

$$c = \frac{\text{Number of compoundings per year}}{\text{Number of payments per year}} = \frac{2}{1} = 2$$

The periodic interest rate for a payment interval is

$$i_2 = (1 + i)^c - 1 = 1.04^2 - 1 = 0.0816 \text{ per year}$$

$$FV(\text{due}) = PMT\left[\frac{(1 + i)^n - 1}{i}\right](1 + i)$$

$$= \$5000\left(\frac{1.0816^{15} - 1}{0.0816}\right)(1.0816)$$

$$= \$148,680.07$$

Step 2: Calculate the future value at age 58 of the Step 1 result.

$$FV = PV(1 + i)^n = \$148,680.07(1.0816)^{15} = \$482,228.57$$

Step 3: Calculate the future value at age 58 of the 15 contributions of $10,000 per year.

$$FV(\text{due}) = \$10,000\left(\frac{1.0816^{15} - 1}{0.0816}\right) \times (1.0816)$$

$$= \$297,360.14$$

Step 4: Calculate the total amount in the RRSP at age 58.

$$\$482,228.57 + \$297,360.14 = \$779,588.71$$

Step 5: The retirement income annuities are ordinary simple annuities for which $i = \frac{7.5\%}{12} = 0.625\%$ per month. Calculate the amount required (present value) to purchase the 10-year annuity paying $5000 per month.

$$PV = PMT\left[\frac{1 - (1 + i)^{-n}}{i}\right]$$

$$= \$5000\left[\frac{1 - (1.00625)^{-120}}{0.00625}\right]$$

$$= \$421,223.71$$

Step 6: The RRSP balance at age 58 is the difference between the Step 4 result and the Step 5 result.

$$\text{Balance} = \$779,588.71 - \$421,223.71 = \$358,365.00$$

Step 7: Calculate the amount (future value) in the RRSP at age 68.
The balance from Step 6 grows at 8% compounded semiannually.

$$FV = \$358{,}365.00(1.04)^{20}$$
$$= \$785{,}221.85$$

8 I/Y

P/Y 2 ENTER

(making $C/Y = P/Y = 2$)

20 N

358365 +/− PV

0 PMT

CPT FV

Ans: 785,221.85

Step 8: Calculate the amount (present value) required to purchase the
20-year annuity earning 7.5% compounded monthly and paying
$7000 per month.

$$PV = \$7000\left[\frac{1 - (1.00625)^{-240}}{0.00625}\right]$$
$$= \$868{,}924.92$$

7.5 I/Y

P/Y 12 ENTER

(making $C/Y = P/Y = 12$)

240 N

7000 PMT

0 FV

Step 9: Compare the Step 7 and Step 8 results.

When Victor reaches age 68, the RRSP will not have enough funds to purchase the 20-year annuity paying $7000 per month. The projected shortage is about

CPT PV

Ans: −868,924.92

$$\$868{,}924.92 - \$785{,}221.85 = \$83{,}703.07$$

EXERCISE 13.4

Answers to the odd-numbered problems are at the end of the book.

INTERMEDIATE PROBLEMS

1. Monthly payments were originally calculated to repay a $20,000 loan at 7% compounded monthly over a 10-year period. After one year, the debtor took advantage of an option in the loan contract to increase the loan payments by 15%. How much sooner will the loan be paid off?

2. RentalTown advertised a television at a cash price of $599.99 and at a rent-to-own rate of $14.79 at the beginning of each week for 78 weeks. What effective rate of interest is a customer paying to acquire the television in a rent-to-own transaction? (Assume that a year has exactly 52 weeks.)

3. Sheila already has $67,000 in her RRSP. How much longer must she contribute $4000 at the end of every six months to accumulate a total of $500,000 if the RRSP earns 5% compounded quarterly? (Round the time required to the next higher month.)

4. What amount is required to purchase an annuity that pays $5000 at the end of each quarter for the first 10 years and then pays $2500 at the beginning of each month for the subsequent 10 years? The rate of return on the invested funds is 6% compounded quarterly.

5. Natalie's RRSP is currently worth $133,000. She plans to contribute for another seven years, and then let the plan continue to grow through internal earnings for an additional three years. If the RRSP earns 5.25% compounded annually, how much must she contribute at the end of every six months for the next seven years in order to have $350,000 in the RRSP 10 years from now?

6. Mr. Palmer wants to retire in 20 years and purchase a 25-year annuity that will make end-of-quarter payments. The payment size is to be the amount which, 20 years from now, has the purchasing power of $6000 today. If he already has $54,000 in his RRSP, what semiannual contributions must he make for the next 20 years to achieve his retirement goal? Assume that the annual rate of inflation for the next 20 years will be 2.5%, the RRSP will earn 8% compounded semiannually, and the rate of return on the fund from which the annuity is paid will be 5.6% compounded quarterly.

7. Interprovincial Distributors Ltd. is planning to open a distribution centre in Calgary in five years. It can purchase suitable land now for the distribution warehouse for $450,000. Annual taxes on the vacant land, payable at the end of each year, would be close to $9000. Rounded to the nearest dollar, what price would the property have to exceed five years from now to make it financially advantageous to purchase the property now instead of five years from now? Assume that Interprovincial can otherwise earn 12% compounded semiannually on its capital.

8. Canadian Pacific Class B preferred shares have just paid their quarterly $1.00 dividend and are trading on the Toronto Stock Exchange at $50. What will the price of the shares have to be three years from now for a current buyer of the shares to earn 7% compounded annually on his investment?

9. If Gayle contributes $1000 to her RRSP at the end of every quarter for the next 10 years and then contributes $1000 at each month's end for the subsequent 15 years, how much will she have in her RRSP at the end of the 25 years? Assume that the RRSP earns 8.5% compounded semiannually.

10. It will cost A-1 Courier $1300 to convert a van from gasoline to natural gas fuel. The remaining useful life of the van is estimated at five years. To financially justify the conversion, what must be the reduction in the monthly cost of fuel to repay the original investment along with a return on investment of 12% compounded monthly? Assume that the fuel will be purchased at the beginning of each month.

ADVANCED PROBLEMS

11. Conrad has two loans outstanding, which he can repay at any time. He has just made the 11th monthly payment on an $8500 loan at 10.5% compounded monthly for a three-year term. The 22nd monthly payment of $313.69 was also made today on the second loan, which has a five-year term and an interest rate of 9.5% compounded semiannually. Conrad is finding the total monthly payments too high, and interest rates on similar loans are now down to 8.25% compounded monthly. He wishes to reduce his monthly cash outflow by obtaining a debt consolidation loan just sufficient to pay off the balances on the two loans. What would his monthly payment be on a five-year term loan at the new rate?

12. Jeanette wishes to retire in 30 years at age 55 with retirement savings that have the purchasing power of $300,000 in today's dollars.
    a. If the rate of inflation for the next 30 years is 2% per year, how much must she accumulate in her RRSP?
    b. If she contributes $3000 at the end of each year for the next five years, how much must she contribute annually for the subsequent 25 years to reach her goal? Assume that her RRSP will earn 8% compounded annually.
    c. The amount in part (a) will be used to purchase a 30-year annuity. What will the month-end payments be if the funds earn 6% compounded monthly?

13. The average annual costs to support a child born today are estimated as follows:

Years 1–6	$12,000
Years 7–12	11,000
Years 13–17	10,000
Years 18–19	15,000

The costs in the early years include child care expenses or forgone earnings of the caregiving parent. Rounded to the nearest dollar:

a. What is the aggregate total cost (ignoring the time value of money) of raising a child to age 19?

b. What is the total economic value, at the date of birth of a child, of these future expenditures, if money can earn 6% compounded monthly? Assume that the annual costs are paid in equal end-of-month amounts.

c. What will be the economic value at age 19 of the past expenditures, assuming money can earn 6% compounded monthly?

14. To compensate for the effects of inflation during their retirement years, the Pelyks intend to purchase a combination of annuities that will provide the following pattern of month-end income:

Calendar years, inclusive	Income ($)
2025 to 2029	7500
2030 to 2034	9000
2035 to 2039	10,500
2040 to 2050	12,000

Rounded to the nearest dollar, how much will they need in their RRSPs when they retire at the beginning of 2025 to purchase the annuities, if the annuity payments are based on a rate of return of 6% compounded semiannually?

15. For its "Tenth Anniversary Salebration," Pioneer Furniture is offering terms of 10% down, no interest, and no payments for six months. The balance must then be paid in six equal payments, with the first payment due six months after the purchase date. The conditional sale contract calculates the monthly payments to include interest at the rate of 15% compounded monthly after the end of the interest-free period. Immediately after the sale of the furniture, Pioneer sells the contract to Afco Finance at a discount to yield Afco 18% compounded semiannually from the date of the sale. What cash payment will Pioneer receive from Afco on a piece of furniture sold for $2000?

16. Patrick contributes $1000 at the beginning of every quarter to his RRSP. In addition, he contributes another $2000 to the RRSP each year from his year-end bonus. If the RRSP earns 9.5% compounded semiannually, what will be the value of his RRSP after 23 years?

17. Reg is developing a financial plan that would enable him to retire 30 years from now at age 60. Upon reaching age 60, he will use some of the funds in his RRSP to purchase an eight-year annuity that pays $5000 at the end of each month. Then, at age 68, he will use the remaining funds to purchase a 20-year annuity paying $6000 at each month's end. What contributions must he make to an RRSP at the beginning of each quarter for 30 years to achieve his retirement goal, if the RRSP and the annuities earn 7.5% compounded monthly?

18. Cynthia currently has $55,000 in her RRSP. She plans to contribute $7000 at the end of each year for the next 17 years and then use the accumulated funds to purchase a 20-year annuity making end-of-month payments.

a. Assume that her RRSP earns 8.75% compounded annually for the next 17 years, and the fund from which the annuity is paid will earn 5.4% compounded monthly. What monthly payments will she receive?

b. If the average annual rate of inflation for the next 17 years is 2%, what will be the purchasing power in today's dollars of the monthly payments 17 years from now?

19. A major car manufacturer is developing a promotion offering new car buyers the choice between "below market" four-year financing at 1.9% compounded monthly or a cash rebate. On the purchase of a $35,000 car, what cash rebate would make a car buyer indifferent between the following alternatives?
    - Financing through the car dealer at the reduced interest rate.
    - Taking the cash rebate and obtaining bank financing at 6.6% compounded monthly for the net "cash" price.

20. The monthly payments on a $30,000 loan at 10.5% compounded monthly were calculated to repay the loan over a 10-year period. After 32 payments were made, the borrower became unemployed and, with the approval of the lender, missed the next three payments.
    a. What amount paid along with the regular payment at the end of the 36th month will put the loan repayment back on the original schedule?
    b. Instead of the "make-up" arrangement in part (a), suppose the regular loan payments (beginning with the payment at the end of the 36th month) are recalculated to put the loan back on its 10-year repayment track. What will be the new payments?

21. Martha's RRSP is currently worth $97,000. She plans to contribute $5000 at the beginning of every six months until she reaches age 58, 12 years from now. Then she intends to use half of the funds in the RRSP to purchase a 20-year annuity making month-end payments. Five years later she will use half of the funds then in her RRSP to purchase another 20-year annuity making month-end payments. Finally, at age 68, she will use all of the remaining funds to purchase a third 20-year annuity also making end-of-month payments. What will be her monthly income at age 65 and at age 70 if her RRSP and the annuities earn 7.5% compounded monthly?

KEY TERMS

Annuities due	General annuity due	Simple annuity due
Book value of a lease	Residual value	

SUMMARY OF NOTATION AND KEY FORMULAS

FV(due) = Future value of an n-payment annuity due

PV(due) = Present value of an n-payment annuity due

FORMULA (13-1) $\quad FV(\text{due}) = PMT\left[\dfrac{(1 + i)^n - 1}{i}\right] \times (1 + i) \qquad$ Finding the future value of an annuity due

FORMULA (13-2) $\quad PV(\text{due}) = PMT\left[\dfrac{1 - (1 + i)^{-n}}{i}\right] \times (1 + i) \qquad$ Finding the present value of an annuity due

FORMULA (13-1n) $\quad n = \dfrac{\ln\left[1 + \dfrac{i \times FV(\text{due})}{PMT(1 + i)}\right]}{\ln(1 + i)} \qquad$ Finding the number of payments, given FV(due)

FORMULA (13-2n) $\quad n = -\dfrac{\ln\left[1 - \dfrac{i \times PV(\text{due})}{PMT(1 + i)}\right]}{\ln(1 + i)} \qquad$ Finding the number of payments, given PV(due)

REVIEW PROBLEMS

Answers to the odd-numbered review problems are at the end of the book.

Calculate interest rates accurate to the nearest 0.01%.

BASIC PROBLEMS

1. **L01** Brunswick Trucking has signed a five-year lease with Ford Credit Canada Ltd. on a new truck. Lease payments of $1900 are made at the beginning of each month. To purchase the truck, Brunswick Trucking would have had to borrow funds at 6.25% compounded monthly.
   a. What initial liability should Brunswick report on its balance sheet?
   b. How much will the liability be reduced during the first year of the lease?

2. **L01** What minimum amount of money earning 7% compounded semiannually will sustain withdrawals of $1000 at the beginning of every month for 12 years?

3. **L02** What maximum annual withdrawals will a $300,000 fund earning 7.75% compounded annually sustain for 25 years if the withdrawals are made:
   a. At the beginning of each year?
   b. At the end of each year?

4. **L02** Regular investments made at the beginning of each quarter earn 6% compounded quarterly. How many more $1000 investments than $1100 investments will it take to accumulate $100,000?

5. **L02** An RRSP is now worth $316,000 after contributions of $3500 at the beginning of every six months for 17 years. What effective rate of return has the plan earned?

6. **L01** Calculate the amount that will be accumulated after 20 years if:
   a. $1000 is invested at the beginning of every six months at 8.5% compounded semiannually.
   b. $2000 is invested at the beginning of every year at 8.5% compounded annually.

7. **L01** A life insurance company quoted an annual premium of $387.50 (payable at the beginning of the year) for a $250,000 term insurance policy on a 35-year-old male nonsmoker. Alternatively, the insured can pay $33.71 at the beginning of each month by preauthorized electronic debit. Which payment plan would an applicant choose solely on the basis of money being worth 7.5% compounded monthly?

8. **L01** A seven-year capital lease of an executive jet requires semiannual payments of $200,000 at the beginning of each six-month period. The company can borrow funds for 5 to 10 years at 7.4% compounded semiannually.
   a. What long-term lease liability will the firm set up at the start of the term of the lease?
   b. What liability will remain halfway through the term of the lease?

9. **L02** Suppose that $5000 is contributed at the beginning of each year to an RRSP that earns 5% compounded annually.
   a. How many contributions will it take to accumulate the first $500,000?
   b. How many more contributions will it take for the RRSP to reach $1,000,000?

10. **L02** The membership dues at Shoreline Golf and Country Club are $2820 payable at the beginning of the year, or four payments of $736.56 payable at the beginning of each quarter. What effective rate of interest is the club charging members who pay their dues quarterly?

11. **L02** Excel Leasing calculates the payments on long-term equipment leases so that it earns a rate of return of 15% compounded quarterly on its investment in the equipment. What beginning-of-month payments will Excel charge on a four-year lease of a photocopier costing $7650? (Assume the photocopier has no residual value at the end of the lease.)

12. **L02** Apex Fabricating wants to accumulate $800,000 for an expansion expected to begin in four years. If today Apex makes the first of equal quarterly payments into a fund earning 6.75% compounded monthly, what should the size of these payments be?

13. **L02** How many more RRSP contributions of $300 at the beginning of every month are required to reach $200,000 if the funds earn 7.5% compounded monthly than if they earn 8.5% compounded monthly?

14. **L02** As of the date of Colony Farm's most recent financial statements, $3\frac{1}{2}$ years remained in the term of a lease reported as a long-term liability of $27,400. If the beginning-of-month lease payments are $750, what monthly compounded nominal discount rate was used in valuing the lease?

15. **L02** If a furniture store offers to sell a washer-dryer combination priced at $1395 on a conditional sale contract requiring 12 monthly payments of $125 (including a payment on the date of sale), what effective rate of interest is being charged?

16. **L02** Sovereign Life Insurance Company of Canada offers $250,000 of term life insurance to a 45-year-old male for an annual premium of $716 (in advance) or for monthly premium payments (in advance) of $62.50 by preauthorized electronic debit. What effective rate of interest is charged to those who pay monthly?

17. **L02** Fred is about to have his 27th birthday. He has set a goal of retiring at age 58 with $1,000,000 in his RRSP. For planning purposes, he is assuming that his RRSP will earn 8% compounded annually.
    a. What contributions on each birthday from age 27 to 57 inclusive will be required to accumulate the desired amount in his RRSP?
    b. If he waits five years before starting his RRSP, what contributions on each birthday from ages 32 to 57 inclusive will be required to reach the target?

INTERMEDIATE PROBLEMS

18. **L01** What is the initial economic value of an annuity due if it consists of 19 semiannual payments of $1500? Money is worth 5% compounded semiannually for the first five years, and 6% compounded semiannually thereafter.

19. **L01** What will be the amount in an RRSP after 30 years if contributions of $4000 are made at the beginning of each year for the first 10 years, and contributions of $6000 are made at the beginning of each year for the subsequent 20 years? Assume that the RRSP will earn 8.25% compounded annually.

20. **L01** Calculate the future value of an investment plan requiring contributions of $800 at the beginning of each calendar quarter for seven years. Assume that the rate of return will be 8% compounded quarterly for the first 30 months and 7% compounded semiannually for the remainder of the annuity's term.

21. **L02** Ms. Bowers wants to be able to purchase a 20-year annuity at age 62 that will pay her $3500 at the beginning of each month. She makes her first quarterly contribution to an RRSP on her 35th birthday and continues them up to but not including her 62nd birthday. What should be the amount of each contribution? Assume that her RRSP will earn 8% compounded quarterly and that the money used to purchase the annuity will earn 4.8% compounded monthly.

22. **LO2** Mr. and Mrs. Zolob contributed $50 on the first of each month to an RESP they set up for their grandson Jeff. By the time he entered Mohawk College, 14 years and 5 months of contributions had accumulated. The grandparents' contributions stopped, and Jeff started beginning-of-month withdrawals of $500. How long will these payments last if the RESP has earned and will continue to earn 8.25% compounded monthly?

23. **LO1** A rental agreement requires the payment of $1000 at the beginning of each month.
    a. What single payment at the beginning of the rental year should the landlord accept instead of 12 monthly payments if money is worth 8% compounded monthly?
    b. Show that the landlord will be equally well off at the end of the year under either payment arrangement if rental payments are invested at 8% compounded monthly.

24. **LO1** Mick contributed $5000 at the beginning of each year for 25 years to his RRSP. Assume that the RRSP earned 8% compounded annually. What percentage of the RRSP's value after 25 years comes from contributions made in the first five years?

25. **LO1** What amount is required to purchase an annuity that pays $4000 at the end of each quarter for the first five years and then pays $2500 at the beginning of each month for the subsequent 15 years? Assume that the annuity payments are based on a rate of return of 5.6% compounded quarterly.

26. **LO1** **LO2** Suppose that $5000 is contributed at the beginning of each year for 25 years to an RRSP that earns 10% compounded annually. By what percentage would annual contributions have to be increased in order to have the same future value after 25 years if the plan earns only 8% compounded annually?

27. **LO1** **LO2** Suppose you contribute $2500 to an RRSP at the beginning of every six months for 25 years, and then use the accumulated funds to purchase an annuity paying $2500 at the beginning of each month. How long after the start of the annuity will the last payment be made? Assume that the RRSP earns 8% compounded semiannually and the funds invested in the annuity earn 5.1% compounded monthly.

28. **LO2** Capital Leasing leases commercial kitchen equipment to restaurants, hotels, hospitals, and other institutions. Capital Leasing calculates the payments on its four-year leases so that it recovers the purchase price of the equipment plus a return on investment of 16% compounded annually over the term of the lease. What will be the required lease payments at the beginning of each quarter on equipment purchased by Capital for $57,000?

29. **LO2** New Look Fitness Centre offers a one-year membership for $500 in advance, or a three-month membership for $160 in advance. What effective rate of interest is an individual paying if she buys four consecutive three-month memberships instead of a one-year membership?

30. **LO2** A life insurance company is calculating the monthly premium that it will offer clients as an alternative to paying the full annual premium. With both alternatives, premiums are payable at the beginning of the period of coverage. If the monthly payment by preauthorized electronic debit is calculated to yield the insurance company 10% compounded semiannually on the unpaid balance of the annual premium, what should be the monthly premium per $100 of annual premium?

CASE

A "Lotto" Money

One of the largest lottery jackpots ever won was on March 27, 2019. The winning numbers for the $768,400,000 jackpot in America's biggest lottery game, Powerball, were on a single winning ticket sold in Wisconsin. The Powerball rules gave the winner a choice between receiving 30 graduated annual payments totalling $748.4 million (including one immediately) or an immediate lump payment of $477 million.

QUESTIONS

1. If each annual payment were an equivalent value of $24,946,667, what is the nominal sum of the 30 payments in the annuity due? Strictly speaking, is it legitimate for Powerball to report a $748.4 million jackpot? Explain your reasoning. (Many mega-prize lotteries employ a similar approach in their promotions.)
2. The Multi-State Lottery Association (MSLA) that administers Powerball determined the amount of the annual annuity payment as follows. First the MSLA determined that, from lottery ticket sales, it could pay $477 million as a single lump prize. The MSLA then obtained quotes in the financial markets on 30-year annual-payment annuities due that could be purchased with the $477 million. The best quote was $24.9467 million per year. Rounded to the nearest 0.01%, what was the rate of return on this annuity?
3. If the Powerball winners can earn 6% compounded annually on their personal investments, what was the initial economic value of the annuity to them? Which option should they have chosen in that case?
4. Until October 2002, the annuity due option for Powerball Jackpot winners was structured for 25 rather than 30 annual payments. What annual payment in a 25-year annuity due would the March 27, 2019 Powerball cash prize ($477 million) purchase? (Use the rate of return you calculated in Question 2.)
5. If the 25-year annuity option were still in place, what Powerball Jackpot prize would the MSLA have reported for the March 27, 2019 draw?
6. Why do you suppose the MSLA changed from a 25-year to a 30-year term for the annuity option?

APPENDIX 13A: SETTING YOUR CALCULATOR IN THE ANNUITY DUE MODE

This appendix illustrates the keystrokes needed to set your calculator for annuity due calculations.

Sharp EL-738	Texas Instruments BA II PLUS	Hewlett-Packard 10B
2nd F BGN "BGN" appears in the display when in this mode.	2nd BGN 2nd SET 2nd QUIT "BGN" appears in the display when in this mode.	BEG/END "BEGIN" appears in the display when in this mode.

When you repeat these keystrokes, your calculator will "toggle," or switch back, to the ordinary annuity mode (no indicator in the display). The calculator remains in the most recently selected mode, even after being turned off.

Chapter 14
Annuities: Special Situations

CHAPTER OUTLINE

14.1 Deferred Annuities

14.2 Perpetuities

*14.3 Constant-Growth Annuities

LEARNING OBJECTIVES

After completing this chapter, you will be able to:

LO1 Calculate the present value, payment, and period of deferral for a deferred annuity

LO2 Calculate the present value of a perpetuity and a deferred perpetuity

LO3 Calculate the present value and future value of an annuity whose payment size grows at a constant rate

THREE SPECIAL CASES OF ANNUITIES are examined in this chapter. The first is deferred annuities—annuities whose payments begin after a waiting period or period of deferral. Deferred annuities are common where retailers advertise "No Money Down, and No Payments for 1 Year!"

The second is perpetuities—annuities whose payments continue forever. For example, a college might receive a $200,000 gift or bequest to offer an annual scholarship in perpetuity. The mathematics of perpetuities turn out to be surprisingly simple.

The third special case is constant-growth annuities—annuities whose payments increase at a steady rate. We often make a "constant-growth assumption" in long-term financial planning. A growing annuity is usually a better approximation of our saving pattern than a constant payment annuity. As wages increase over time (even if only through inflation), most people are able to save more each year. Many pension plans index or link pension payments to the Consumer Price Index. The payments increase over time by the same percentage as the CPI. Again, a growing annuity is a good representation of this payment pattern.

14.1 Deferred Annuities

A **deferred annuity** may be viewed as an *ordinary* annuity that does not begin until a time interval (named the **period of deferral**) has passed. **Figure 14.1** shows a deferred *ordinary* annuity on a time line. In the figure, the deferral period ends at the same point in time where the term of the annuity begins.

Note that the first payment is at the end of the first payment period in the term of the annuity and the last payment coincides with the end of the term of the annuity. The period of deferral ends one payment interval *before* the first payment. Viewed from the *end* of the period of deferral, the payments form an ordinary annuity.

FIGURE 14.1   Time Diagram for a Deferred Ordinary Annuity

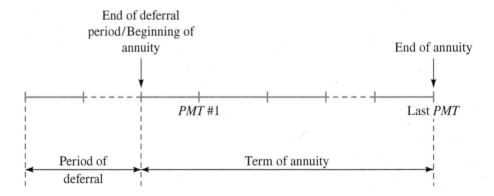

Figure 14.2 shows a deferred annuity due on a time line. In this figure, the point in time where the deferral period ends and the term of the annuity begins is also where the first payment is made in an annuity due—at the beginning of the first payment period in the annuity.

The future value of a deferred annuity or annuity due is the future value of all of the payments at the end of the last payment interval. Can you see what needs to be done to determine the future value? Looking back from the end of the final payment interval, the payments appear as they would for an ordinary annuity. So it is a simple matter of doing the same future value calculation you learned in **Section 11.2** for ordinary annuities.

FIGURE 14.2 Time Diagram for a Deferred Annuity Due

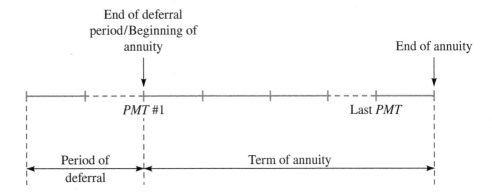

LO1 The present value of a deferred annuity is the present value of all of the payments at the *beginning* of the period of deferral. How can the present value be calculated, using ideas you have already learned? The two regions identified in **Figures 14.1** and **Figure 14.2** suggest a two-step procedure, indicated in **Figure 14.3**.

1. Calculate the present value, PV_1, of the payments at the *end* of the period of deferral—this is just the present value of an ordinary annuity or annuity due.
2. Calculate the present value, PV_2, of the Step 1 amount at the *beginning* of the period of deferral.

FIGURE 14.3 The Present Value of a Deferred Ordinary Annuity

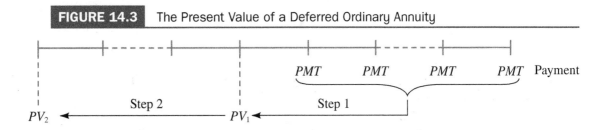

EXAMPLE 14.1A

CALCULATING THE PRESENT VALUE OF A DEFERRED ANNUITY

Mr. and Mrs. Templeton are setting up a fund to help finance their granddaughter's college education. They want her to be able to withdraw $3000 every three months for three years after she starts college. Her first withdrawal will be $5\frac{1}{2}$ years from now. If the fund can earn 7.2% compounded quarterly, what single amount contributed today will provide for the withdrawals?

SOLUTION

In this first example, we will present the solution as an *ordinary annuity* and also as a *simple annuity due*.

SOLUTION 1: ORDINARY ANNUITY

The money the Templetons invest now will have $5\frac{1}{2}$ years to grow before withdrawals start. Thereafter, further earnings of money still in the fund will help support the periodic withdrawals. The one-time "up front" contribution is the present value of the withdrawals.

The time diagram is presented as follows. Viewed from today, the withdrawals form a deferred annuity. In order to have an *ordinary annuity* following the period of deferral, the period of deferral must end three months before the first payment. This makes the period of deferral only $5\frac{1}{4}$ years.

$$d = \text{Equivalent number of payment intervals in the period of deferral}$$

Since payments and compounding both occur quarterly, we have a deferred *ordinary* annuity with

$$PMT = \$3000 \quad n = 4(3) = 12 \quad d = 4(5.25) = 21 \quad \text{and} \quad i = \frac{7.2\%}{4} = 1.8\%$$

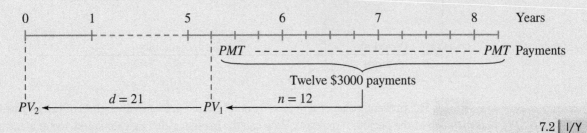

The present value of the payments $5\frac{1}{4}$ years from now is

$$
\left.
\begin{aligned}
PV_1 &= PMT\left[\frac{1-(1+i)^{-n}}{i}\right] \\
&= \$3000\left(\frac{1-1.018^{-12}}{0.018}\right) \\
&= \$32{,}119.23
\end{aligned}
\right\}
$$

7.2 ⌊I/Y
⌊P/Y⌋ 4 ⌊ENTER
(making *C/Y = P/Y* = 4)
12 ⌊ N
3000 ⌊PMT
0 ⌊ FV
⌊CPT⌋ ⌊PV
Ans: −32,119.23

The present value of the payments today is

$$
\left.
\begin{aligned}
PV_2 &= FV(1+i)^{-n} \\
&= \$32{,}119.23\,(1.018)^{-21} \\
&= \$22{,}083.19
\end{aligned}
\right\}
$$

Same *I/Y, P/Y, C/Y*
21 ⌊ N
0 ⌊PMT
32119.23 ⌊ FV
⌊CPT⌋ ⌊PV
Ans: −22,083.19

SOLUTION 2: SIMPLE ANNUITY DUE

The following time diagram shows the same situation viewed as a **deferred annuity due**. In order to have a simple *annuity due* following the period of deferral, the period of deferral must end on the same date as the payments begin. This makes the period of deferral $5\frac{1}{2}$ years.

Since payments and compounding both occur quarterly, we have a deferred *simple* annuity due with

$$PMT = \$3000 \quad n = 4(3) = 12 \quad d = 4(5.5) = 22 \quad \text{and} \quad i = \frac{7.2\%}{4} = 1.8\%$$

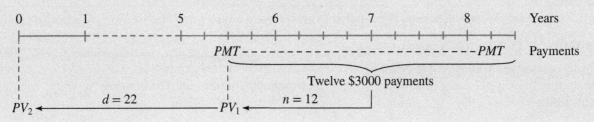

The present value of the payments $5\frac{1}{2}$ years from now is

$$
\begin{aligned}
PV_1 &= PMT\left[\frac{1-(1+i)^{-n}}{i}\right](1+i)\\[4pt]
&= \$3000\left[\frac{1-1.018^{-12}}{0.018}\right](1.018)\\[4pt]
&= \$32{,}697.38
\end{aligned}
$$

BGN mode

7.2 | I/Y

| P/Y 4 | ENTER

(making $C/Y = P/Y = 4$)

12 | N

3000 | PMT

0 | FV

| CPT | PV

Ans: −32,697.38

The present value of the payments today is

$$
\begin{aligned}
PV_2 &= \$32{,}697.38(1.018)^{-22}\\
&= \$22{,}083.19
\end{aligned}
$$

The Templetons can provide the desired financial support for their granddaughter by putting $22,083.19 into the fund today.

Same *I/Y, P/Y, C/Y*

22 | N

0 | PMT

32697.38 | FV

| CPT | PV

Ans: −22,083.19

✔ **TIP**

Equivalent Views of a Deferred Annuity

In many cases, it is not specifically indicated when the payments in an annuity begin following a "period of deferral." The length of the period of deferral may be chosen so that the first payment occurs one payment interval *after the end of* the period of deferral or may be chosen so the period of deferral ends at the same point in time as the first payment is made.

In Example 14.1A we demonstrated these alternative but equivalent viewpoints in the calculation of the present value of a deferred annuity. When viewed as a *deferred annuity due*, the deferral period stated in the question does not need to be altered in the calculation since payments begin on the same date the period of deferral ends, which is also the same date the term of the annuity due begins.

EXAMPLE 14.1B

CALCULATING THE PRESENT VALUE OF A DEFERRED GENERAL ANNUITY

Maureen has just had her 55th birthday and plans to retire from teaching at age 60. While reviewing Maureen's personal net worth statement, her financial adviser points out that she has overlooked a significant asset—the current economic value of her future pension. The adviser calculates that the 25 years of service Maureen has already accumulated entitle her to a pension of $3500 at each month's end starting at age 60.

Based on a 22-year life expectancy from age 60 and money worth 8% compounded semiannually, estimate, to the nearest dollar, the current economic value of Maureen's pension.

SOLUTION

The current economic value of the pension can be estimated by calculating the present value of the expected pension payments discounted at 8% compounded semiannually. With monthly payments and semiannual compounding, the pension (viewed from her 55th birthday) constitutes a *deferred* ordinary *general* annuity. The period of deferral is five years since the first payment will be made at the end of the month in which she turns 60. We are given

$$PMT = \$3500 \quad n = 12(22) = 264 \quad d = 12(5) = 60 \quad i = \tfrac{8\%}{2} = 4\%$$

The following diagram indicates the two main steps in the solution.

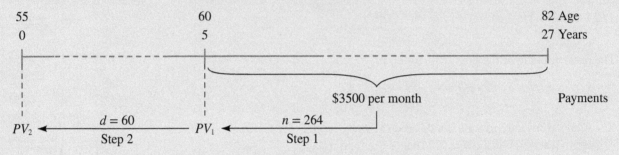

But first we must calculate the periodic rate that matches the one-month payment interval.

$$c = \frac{2 \text{ compoundings per year}}{12 \text{ payments per year}} = 0.1\overline{6}$$

Using Formula (10-4c),

$$i_2 = (1 + i)^c - 1 = 1.04^{0.1\overline{6}} - 1 = 0.006558197 \text{ per month}$$

Substitute this value for i in Formula (11-2) to obtain the present value of the pension at age 60.

$$\begin{aligned}
PV_1 &= PMT\left[\frac{1 - (1 + i)^{-n}}{i}\right] \\
&= \$3500\left[\frac{1 - (1.006558197)^{-264}}{0.006558197}\right] \\
&= \$438{,}662.91
\end{aligned}$$

Using Formula (9-2) in the form $PV = FV(1 + i)^{-n}$, the present value of $438,662.91 five years earlier is

$$\begin{aligned}
PV_2 &= \$438{,}662.91(1 + i_2)^{-d} \\
&= \$438{,}662.91(1.006558197)^{-60} \\
&= \$296{,}344.94
\end{aligned}$$

The current economic value of Maureen's pension is $296,345.

The significance of this number is that, if Maureen did not belong to the pension plan, she would need current savings of $296,345 in a personal RRSP earning 8% compounded semiannually in order to duplicate the future pension benefits to age 82.

8	I/Y
P/Y 12	ENTER
C/Y 2	ENTER
264	N
3500	PMT
0	FV
CPT	PV

Ans: −438,662.91

Same *I/Y, P/Y, C/Y*

60	N
0	PMT
438662.91	FV
CPT	PV

Ans: −296,344.94

EXAMPLE 14.1C

CALCULATING THE NUMBER OF PAYMENTS IN A DEFERRED ANNUITY

$10,000 is invested in a fund earning 4.25% compounded semiannually. Five years later, the first semiannual withdrawal of $1000 will be taken from the fund. After how many withdrawals will the fund be depleted? (The final payment that extinguishes the fund will be smaller than $1000. Include it in the count.)

SOLUTION

Viewed from the date of the investment, the withdrawals form a deferred simple annuity. The period of deferral is $4\frac{1}{2}$ years long since the withdrawals begin five years from the date of the investment and occur at the end of each semiannual period. We have

$$PMT = \$1000 \quad d = 2(4.5) = 9 \quad \text{and} \quad i = \tfrac{4.25\%}{2} = 2.125\%$$

In effect, the accumulated funds after 4.5 years purchase a "DIY" annuity. As indicated in the following diagram,

$$\left(\begin{matrix}\text{Future value of \$10,000}\\ \text{4.5 years from now}\end{matrix}\right) = \left(\begin{matrix}\text{Present value of the withdrawals}\\ \text{4.5 years from now}\end{matrix}\right)$$

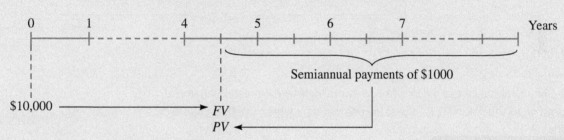

The future value of $10,000 after $4\frac{1}{2}$ years will be

$$\begin{aligned} FV &= PV(1 + i)^n \\ &= \$10,000(1.02125)^9 \\ &= \$12,083.39 \end{aligned}$$

4.25	I/Y
P/Y 2	ENTER
(making C/Y = P/Y = 2)	
9	N
10000 +/−	PV
0	PMT
CPT	FV
Ans: 12,083.39	

Now use Formula (11-2n) to obtain n.

$$\begin{aligned} n &= -\frac{\ln\!\left(1 - \dfrac{i \times PV}{PMT}\right)}{\ln(1 + i)} \\[2mm] &= -\frac{\ln\!\left(1 - \dfrac{0.02125 \times \$12{,}083.39}{\$1000}\right)}{\ln(1.02125)} \\[2mm] &= 14.11 \end{aligned}$$

Same *I/Y, P/Y, C/Y*	
12083.39 +/−	PV
1000	PMT
0	FV
CPT	N
Ans: 14.11	

The fund will be depleted after 15 withdrawals. (This counts 14 payments of $1000 plus a 15th smaller payment.)

EXAMPLE 14.1D

CALCULATING THE LENGTH OF THE DEFERRAL PERIOD

Mrs. Sevard purchased a deferred annuity from an insurance company for $10,971. The money used to purchase the annuity will earn 6% compounded quarterly. The annuity will provide 16 quarterly payments of $1000. If the first payment is to be received on October 1, 2021, when did Mrs. Sevard purchase the deferred annuity?

SOLUTION

The key idea on which we base the solution is that the purchase price is the present value, on the date of purchase, of all 16 annuity payments. The payments form a deferred simple annuity due with $PMT = \$1000$, $n = 16$, and $i = \frac{6\%}{4} = 1.5\%$. The data and solution steps are shown in the following diagram.

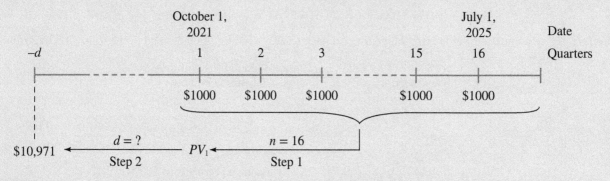

For the payments to be treated as a *simple annuity due*, the period of deferral must end on October 1, 2021 (at the same point in time where the first payment is made).

The present value of the payments on October 1, 2021 is

$$PV_1 = PMT\left[\frac{1 - (1 + i)^{-n}}{i}\right](1 + i)$$

$$= \$1000\left[\frac{1 - 1.015^{-16}}{0.015}\right](1.015)$$

$$= \$14,343.23$$

This amount is the future value, at the end of the period of deferral, of the $10,971 purchase price. We must now use Formula (10-2) to calculate the number of compounding periods required for $10,971 to grow to $14,343.23.

$$d = \frac{\ln\left(\frac{FV}{PV}\right)}{\ln(1 + i)}$$

$$= \frac{\ln\left(\frac{\$14,343.23}{\$10,971}\right)}{\ln(1.015)}$$

$$= 18.00$$

Therefore, the period of deferral is 18 calendar quarters (4 years, 6 months) up to October 1, 2021 when the first payment is made. That places the purchase date of the deferred annuity at April 1, 2017.

EXAMPLE 14.1E

CALCULATING THE PERIODIC PAYMENT IN A DEFERRED ANNUITY

Budget Appliances has a promotion on a washer-dryer combination selling for $1750. Buyers will pay "no money down and no payments for six months." The first of 12 equal monthly payments is required six months from the purchase date. What should the monthly payments be if Budget Appliances is to earn 15% compounded monthly on its account receivable during both the deferral period and the repayment period?

SOLUTION

Viewed from the date of the sale, we will consider the payments to form a deferred simple annuity—a 12-payment *ordinary simple annuity* following a five-month period of deferral. That is,

$$n = 12 \quad d = 5 \quad \text{and} \quad i = \tfrac{15\%}{12} = 1.25\%$$

In effect, Budget Appliances makes a $1750 loan to the customer on the date of the sale. As indicated on the following time line, the balance owed on the loan will increase to FV over the next five months as interest accrues. Then the 12 monthly payments will pay off this balance. Hence,

$$\begin{pmatrix}\text{Future value of \$1750} \\ \text{at the end of Month 5}\end{pmatrix} = \begin{pmatrix}\text{Present value of the payments} \\ \text{at the end of Month 5}\end{pmatrix}$$

The amount owed after five months will be

$$\begin{aligned}FV &= PV(1 + i)^n \\ &= \$1750(1.0125)^5 \\ &= \$1862.14\end{aligned}$$

15 ⌊ I/Y

⌊ P/Y ⌋ 12 ⌊ENTER

(making $C/Y = P/Y = 12$)

5 ⌊ N

1750 ⌊ +/− ⌋ ⌊ PV

0 ⌊PMT

⌊ CPT ⌋ ⌊ FV

Ans: 1862.14

This amount is the present value of the 12-payment ordinary simple annuity. Substituting in Formula (11-2),

$$PV = PMT\left[\frac{1 - (1 + i)^{-n}}{i}\right]$$

$$\$1862.14 = PMT\left[\frac{1 - (1.0125)^{-12}}{0.0125}\right]$$

$$\$1862.14 = PMT(11.07931)$$

Hence,

$$PMT = \frac{\$1862.14}{11.07931} = \$168.07$$

Same *I/Y, P/Y, C/Y*

12 ⌊ N

1862.14 ⌊ +/− ⌋ ⌊ PV

0 ⌊ FV

⌊ CPT ⌋ ⌊ PMT

Ans: 168.07

Monthly payments of $168.07 will provide Budget Appliances with a return of 15% compounded monthly on its account receivable.

POINT OF INTEREST

Card Tricks: The "No-Interest, No-Payments-for-a-Year" Trap

No interest and nothing to pay for a six-month or one-year period is a common type of promotion offered by furniture and appliance stores, and by department stores on the sale of furniture, major appliances, big-screen TVs, and so on. In most cases, you must put the purchase on the store's own credit card in order to qualify for the deferral of payment.

NO MONEY DOWN!
NO INTEREST!
NO PAYMENTS!

But here's the catch. If you don't pay the purchase price *before* the no-interest grace period ends, you are likely to be charged interest for the *entire* grace period at the credit card's full rate (typically 28.8%). Since this circumstance proves highly profitable for the retailer, you can't expect to receive a reminder from the retailer as you approach the end of your "interest-free" period.

Suppose you try to argue that "no interest" ought to mean "no interest payable for the grace period regardless of whether you pay during the grace period." You are then likely to be referred to the fine print in the purchase or credit card agreement where it indicates that interest actually accrues during the grace period, but this interest will be cancelled if you pay the principal within the grace period. So technically it's not an "interest-free" period, but rather a grace period during which the retailer will cancel or rebate the interest if the principal is paid on time.

QUESTIONS

On a $5000 purchase (including sales taxes) under a "no interest and nothing to pay for one year" promotion, how much interest will you be charged for the grace period if you are one day late on your payment of the principal? Use an interest rate of 28.8% compounded monthly.

 CONCEPT QUESTIONS

1. **a.** How long is the period of deferral if the first quarterly payment of a deferred ordinary annuity will be paid $3\frac{1}{2}$ years from today?

   b. How long is the deferral period if the first quarterly payment of a deferred annuity due will be paid $3\frac{1}{2}$ years from today?

2. For the same n, *PMT*, and i, is the present value of a deferred annuity larger or smaller than the present value of an ordinary annuity? Explain.

EXERCISE 14.1

Answers to the odd-numbered problems are at the end of the book.

BASIC PROBLEMS

1. The first of 10 semiannual payments of $2000 will be made $5\frac{1}{2}$ years from today. What is the present value of this deferred annuity using a discount rate of 7% compounded semiannually?

2. A life insurance company can invest funds to earn (after expenses) 8% compounded quarterly. A client wishes to purchase a five-year ordinary annuity that will commence $3\frac{1}{2}$ years from now. What will the insurance company charge for the annuity, if the quarterly payments are $750?

3. What minimum initial amount of money, invested to earn 4% compounded monthly, will support a monthly payout of $500 for $3\frac{1}{2}$ years if the first payment occurs 2 years and 10 months from now?

4. What amount of money invested now will provide monthly payments of $200 for five years, if the ordinary annuity is deferred for $3\frac{1}{2}$ years and the money earns 7.5% compounded monthly?

5. A deferred annuity consists of an ordinary annuity paying $2000 semiannually for a 10-year term after a 5-year period of deferral. Calculate the deferred annuity's present value using a discount rate of 4% compounded quarterly.

6. The first quarterly payment of $750 in a five-year annuity will be paid $3\frac{3}{4}$ years from now. Based on a discount rate of 8.25% compounded monthly, what is present value of the payments today?

7. A loan granted today will be repaid by payments of $500 per month running for $3\frac{1}{2}$ years. The first payment is due 2 years and 10 months from today. What amount was borrowed if the interest rate on the loan is 9% compounded quarterly?

8. Mr. Haddit plans to retire eight years from today. He projects that he will need $30,000 per year in his retirement, which he assumes will be for 15 years. The first payment will be nine years from today. To fund his retirement, Mr. Haddit will invest a lump amount today and later use it to sustain the 15 withdrawals. If his investment earns 6% compounded annually, how much must he invest today?

9. Marion's grandfather's will established a trust that will pay her $1500 every three months for 11 years. The first payment will be made six years from now, when she turns 19. If money is worth 6.5% compounded quarterly, what is today's economic value of the bequest?

10. Using an inheritance he recently received, Sam wants to purchase a deferred annuity that will pay $5000 every three months between age 60 (when he plans to retire) and age 65 (when his permanent pension will begin). The first payment is to be three months after he reaches 60, and the last is to be on his 65th birthday. If Sam's current age is 50 years and 6 months, and the invested funds will earn 6% compounded quarterly, what amount must he invest in the deferred annuity?

11. A deferred ordinary annuity is comprised of eight annual payments of $1500. What is the period of deferral if the present value of the payments, discounted at 7.9% compounded annually, is $6383.65?

12. For $30,000, Manny purchased a deferred ordinary annuity from an insurance company that will pay him quarterly payments of $1076.71 for $12\frac{1}{2}$ years. The payments are based upon the purchase amount earning 7% compounded quarterly. When will Manny receive the first payment?

13. Ronelda has accumulated $33,173.03 in her RRSP. If she makes no further contributions and her RRSP continues to earn 3.75% compounded monthly, for how long a period of deferral must she wait before her RRSP can sustain month-end withdrawals of $400 for 15 years?

14. A conditional sale contract requires the debtor to make six quarterly payments of $569, with the first payment due in six months. What amount will a finance company pay to purchase the contract on the date of sale if the finance company requires a rate of return of 16% compounded quarterly?

15. What price will a finance company pay to a merchant for a conditional sale contract that requires 15 monthly payments of $231 beginning in six months? The finance company requires a rate of return of 18% compounded monthly.

16. Noel has $300,000 with which to purchase an ordinary annuity delivering monthly payments for 20 years after a 10-year period of deferral. What monthly payment will he receive, if the undistributed funds earn 5% compounded semiannually?

INTERMEDIATE PROBLEMS

17. If money can earn 6.5% compounded annually for the next 20 years, which of the following annuities has the greater economic value today: $1000 paid at the end of each of the next 10 years, or 10 annual payments of $2000 with the first payment occurring 11 years from today?

18. Negotiations between Delco Manufacturing and the union representing its employees are at an impasse. The union is seeking a 4.5% wage increase. Delco's offer is 2%. The employees have passed a vote authorizing job action. Suppose the union succeeds in winning the 4.5% increase after a two-month strike. For an employee 10 years from retirement, will there be any economic gain? Compare the current economic values of (1) 10 years' end-of-month wages at the employer's offer (102% of last year's wages) vs. (2) wages including a 4.5% increase to the same time horizon but after a two-month strike. Assume money is worth 6% compounded monthly.

19. A $35,000 loan bearing interest at 5% compounded quarterly was repaid, after a period of deferral, by quarterly payments of $1573.83 over 12 years. What was the time interval between the date of the loan and the first payment?

20. A finance company paid a merchant $3975 for a conditional sale contract after discounting it to yield 18% compounded monthly. If the contract is for 20 monthly payments of $256.96 following a payment-free period, what is the time interval between the date of sale and the first payment?

21. A $10,000 investment will be allowed to grow at 4.5% compounded semiannually until it can support semiannual withdrawals of $1000 for 20 years. Rounded to the nearest month, how long before the first withdrawal must the investment be allowed to grow?

22. Mrs. Corriveau has just retired at age 58 with $160,360 in her RRSP. She plans to live off other savings for a few years and allow her RRSP to continue to grow on a tax-deferred basis until there is an amount sufficient to purchase a 25-year annuity paying $2000 at the end of each month. If her RRSP and the annuity each earn 7.5% compounded monthly, how much longer must she let her RRSP grow (before she buys the annuity)?

23. Mr. Donatelli moved from Toronto to Winnipeg to take a job promotion. After selling their Toronto home and buying a home in Winnipeg, the Donatellis have $85,000 in cash on hand. If the funds are used to purchase a deferred annuity from a life insurance company providing a rate of return of 5.5% compounded annually, what payments will they receive at the end of every six months for 20 years after a 9-year deferral period?

24. What amount must be invested today to provide for quarterly payments of $2500 at the end of every quarter for 15 years after a six-year deferral period? Assume that the funds will earn 5% compounded semiannually.

25. What is the current economic value of an inheritance that will pay $2000 to the beneficiary at the beginning of every three months for 20 years, starting when the beneficiary reaches 20 years of age, $4\frac{1}{2}$ years from now? Assume that money is worth 6% compounded monthly. (Round to the nearest dollar.)

26. To sell a farm that it had acquired in a foreclosure action, the RBC Royal Bank agreed to monthly payments of $2700 for 20 years, with the first payment due 15 months from the date of sale. If the purchaser paid 15% down and the interest rate on the balance is 9% compounded annually, what was the purchase price? (Round to the nearest $100.)

27. Sabrina borrowed $30,000 at an interest rate of 7% compounded quarterly. Monthly payments of $356.83 will commence after a period of deferral and will pay off the loan over the subsequent $12\frac{1}{2}$ years. What is the length of the period of deferral?

28. An investor purchased a deferred annuity contract for $4608.07, a price calculated to provide a rate of return on investment of 9.75% compounded monthly. The semiannual payments of $400, once started, continue for a term of 15 years. How long is the period of deferral?

29. For how long (before the beginning of the term of the annuity) must a $19,665 investment earning 3.5% compounded semiannually be allowed to grow before it can provide 60 quarterly withdrawals of $1000?

30. Duncan retired recently and plans to utilize other savings for a few years while his RRSP continues to grow on a tax-deferred basis. The RRSP is currently worth $142,470. How long will it be until the amount in the RRSP is large enough to purchase a 25-year annuity paying $1700 at the end of each month? Assume that the RRSP and the annuity will earn 8.75% compounded semiannually.

14.2 | Perpetuities

Suppose a $100,000 investment can earn 5% compounded annually. It will earn $5000 in the first year. If the $5000 is paid out from the investment account at the end of the year, the principal will remain at $100,000. As long as the investment continues to earn 5% compounded annually, $5000 can be paid out at the end of every year forever. The value of the investment (principal plus accrued interest) will rise steadily from $100,000 to $105,000 during any year, and then abruptly fall back to $100,000 when the $5000 is paid out on the last day of the year. Consequently, a graph of the investment's "Value" vs. "Time" has the saw-tooth pattern shown in **Figure 14.4**.

FIGURE 14.4	Value of $100,000 Investment That Pays Out Only Its Interest Earnings

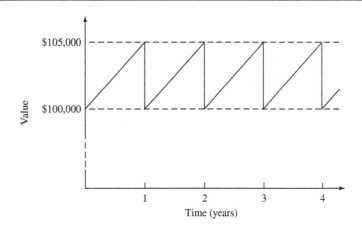

If more than $5000 is paid out at the end of each year, a portion of it will be principal. As the years go by, the principal balance will be eroded in an accelerating fashion because less and less interest is earned in each successive year. The trend is illustrated in **Figure 14.5**[1] where $6000 is paid each year. In conclusion, $5000 is the *maximum* amount that can be paid out at the end of every year *in perpetuity*.

---

[1] **Figures 14.4** and **14.5** were suggested by Oded Tal of Conestoga College.

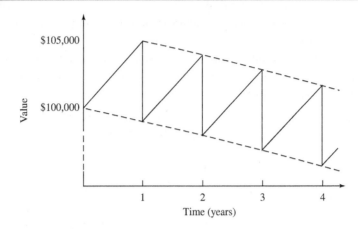

LO2 An annuity whose payments continue forever is called a **perpetuity**. **Figure 14.6** presents a time diagram for an **ordinary perpetuity** with payments of size *PMT* at the *end* of each payment interval. In a **perpetuity due**, the payments will occur at the *beginning* of each payment interval.

FIGURE 14.6   Time Diagram for the Payments of an Ordinary Perpetuity

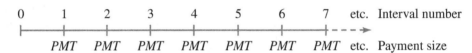

Let us use Formula (11-2) to calculate the present value of annual payments of $5000 in perpetuity, discounting at 5% compounded annually. (Do you have any hunch what the present value will be?) We have *PMT* = $5000 and $i = 5\% = 0.05$. But what value shall we use for *n*? To answer this question, recall that payments far in the future make a negligible contribution to present value. So let us just use $n = 1000$. (If you have any doubts about doing this, calculate the present value of the thousandth payment by itself.) We obtain

$$PV = PMT\left[\frac{1 - (1 + i)^{-n}}{i}\right] = \$5000\left[\frac{1 - (1.05)^{-1000}}{0.05}\right] = \$100,000$$

We could have anticipated this result from our knowledge that the present value of an annuity is the amount required to purchase the annuity. If money can earn 5% compounded annually, $100,000 can purchase a perpetuity paying

$$0.05 \times \$100,000 = \$5000$$

at the end of every year. Since "0.05" is the value of *i*, "$100,000" is the value of *PV*, and "$5000" is the value of *PMT*, the general relationship among these three variables for an ordinary perpetuity is

$$i(PV) = PMT$$

That is,

PRESENT VALUE OF AN ORDINARY PERPETUITY

$$PV = \frac{PMT}{i} \tag{14-1}$$

A perpetuity due may be viewed as the combination of a single immediate payment and an ordinary perpetuity. Therefore, the present value of a perpetuity due is just

$$PV(\text{due}) = PMT + PV = PMT + \frac{PMT}{i}$$

The future value of a perpetuity is an undefined quantity—since payments continue forever, the future value is infinite.

To this point, the perpetuity's payment interval has been equal to the compounding interval. If this is not the case, we are dealing with an ordinary *general* perpetuity or a *general* perpetuity due. Then we must make the same adjustment that we did for annuities. That is, we must use the formula $i_2 = (1 + i)^c - 1$ to calculate the periodic interest rate that matches the payment interval, and substitute this value of i_2 for i in the *PV* formula.

EXAMPLE 14.2A

CALCULATING THE ENDOWMENT AND RATE OF RETURN REQUIRED TO SUSTAIN AN ORDINARY PERPETUITY

A chartered bank is considering the establishment in perpetuity of a Visiting Professor Chair in Public Policy at a university. The ongoing cost will be $11,250 at the end of each month.

a. If money can earn 5.4% compounded monthly in perpetuity, what endowment is required to fund the position?

b. What monthly compounded nominal rate of return must an endowment of $2.25 million earn to fully fund the position?

SOLUTION

a. The payments form an ordinary simple perpetuity having

$$PMT = \$11{,}250 \quad \text{and} \quad i = \tfrac{5.4\%}{12} = 0.45\% \text{ per month.}$$

The required endowment is

$$PV = \frac{PMT}{i} = \frac{\$11{,}250}{0.0045} = \$2{,}500{,}000$$

b. With $PV = \$2{,}250{,}000$ and $PMT = \$11{,}250$ per month, the required interest rate per payment interval is

$$i = \frac{PMT}{PV} = \frac{\$11{,}250}{\$2{,}250{,}000} = 0.005 = 0.5\% \text{ per month}$$

The required nominal rate of return is

$$j = mi = 12(0.5\%) = 6\% \text{ compounded monthly}$$

EXAMPLE 14.2B

CALCULATING THE PRICE OF A PERPETUAL PREFERRED SHARE

Some preferred shares promise a fixed periodic dividend in perpetuity.

a. What is the fair market value of a perpetual preferred share just after payment of a quarterly $0.50 dividend? The market requires a dividend yield of 5% compounded annually on preferred shares of similar risk.

b. What will be an investor's annually compounded dividend yield if she is able to purchase these shares at $36.00 each?

SOLUTION

According to the Valuation Principle, the fair market value of a share is the present value of the expected dividend payments (discounted at the rate of return required in the financial market). Since a dividend has just been paid, the first dividend the purchaser will receive will be three months from now. Viewed from the purchase date, the dividend payments form an ordinary perpetuity. Since the payment interval is three months but the compounding interval is one year, the dividend payments form a general perpetuity.

a. Given: $PMT = \$0.50 \quad$ and $\quad i = \tfrac{5\%}{1} = 5\%$

We must first calculate the equivalent periodic rate for the three-month payment interval.

$$c = \frac{\text{Number of compoundings per year}}{\text{Number of payments per year}} = \frac{1}{4} = 0.25$$

Then

$$i_2 = (1 + i)^c - 1 = 1.05^{0.25} - 1 = 0.0122722 = 1.22722\% \text{ per quarter}$$

and

$$PV = \frac{PMT}{i_2} = \frac{\$0.50}{0.0122722} = \$40.74$$

Thus, the fair market value of a share is $40.74.

b. If the investor can purchase the shares at a lower price than the fair market value in part (a), her dividend yield will be greater than 5% compounded annually (because she will receive the same dividends from a smaller investment). The dividend yield per payment interval will be

$$i = \frac{PMT}{PV} = \frac{\$0.50}{\$36.00} = 0.013\overline{8} = 1.3\overline{8}\% \text{ per quarter}$$

The annually compounded nominal dividend yield is the same as the effective dividend yield. Using Formula (10-3)

$$f = (1 + i)^m - 1 = (1.013\overline{8})^4 - 1 = 0.0567 = 5.67\% \text{ compounded annually}$$

EXAMPLE 14.2C

CALCULATING THE INITIAL ENDOWMENT FOR A GENERAL PERPETUITY

What amount must be placed in a perpetual fund today if it earns 4.8% compounded semiannually, and the first monthly payment of $500 in perpetuity will be made:

a. One month from today?   **b.** One year from today?

SOLUTION

In both cases, the required initial amount is the present value of the payments. Since payments are made monthly but compounding takes place semiannually, the payments form a *general* perpetuity having

$$PMT = \$500 \text{ per month} \quad \text{and} \quad i = \tfrac{4.8\%}{2} = 2.4\% \text{ per six months}$$

We must calculate the equivalent periodic rate for the one-month payment interval.

$$c = \frac{\text{Number of compoundings per year}}{\text{Number of payments per year}} = \frac{2}{12} = 0.1\overline{6}$$

and

$$i_2 = (1 + i)^c - 1 = (1.024)^{0.1\overline{6}} - 1 = 0.003960577 = 0.3960577\% \text{ per month}$$

a. The required initial endowment is

$$PV = \frac{PMT}{i_2} = \frac{\$500}{0.003960577} = \$126,244.24$$

The initial amount required to fund the perpetuity is $126,244.24.

b. The perpetuity is shown on a time line in the following diagram. Viewed from a date 11 months from now, the payments form an ordinary perpetuity. Viewed from today, the payments form a deferred ordinary perpetuity with an 11-month period of deferral.

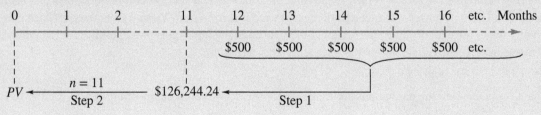

The calculation of today's present value of payments must be done in two steps. First determine the present value, 11 months from today, of the ordinary perpetuity. (This is the same as the $126,244.24 amount we calculated in part (a).) The amount that must be placed in the fund today is the present value of $126,244.24, 11 months earlier. Using Formula (9-2), this present value is

$$PV = FV(1 + i_2)^{-n} = \$126,244.24(1.003960577)^{-11} = \$120,872.73$$

The initial amount that must be placed in the perpetual fund is $120,872.73.

EXAMPLE 14.2D

CALCULATING THE PAYMENT IN A DEFERRED GENERAL PERPETUITY

Mrs. Paquette is setting up a trust fund with an initial contribution of $150,000. The funds are to be immediately invested, and the first semiannual payment of a perpetuity is to be made five years from now. The payments are to be used for the care of her son for the rest of his life, and then are to be paid to the Canadian Foundation for Multiple Sclerosis. If the funds in trust earn 5% compounded annually, what is the maximum payment the trust can make in perpetuity?

SOLUTION

The data and solution idea are shown in the following time diagram. Viewed from a focal date $4\frac{1}{2}$ years from now, the payments form an ordinary perpetuity. Since the payment interval (six months) does not equal the compounding interval (one year), the payments form a general perpetuity.

The future value of the $150,000 contribution after $4\frac{1}{2}$ years will be the amount (present value) sustaining the perpetuity. That is,

$$\begin{pmatrix} FV \text{ of } \$150,000 \\ 4.5 \text{ years from now} \end{pmatrix} = \begin{pmatrix} PV \text{ of the ordinary general} \\ \text{perpetuity, 4.5 years from now} \end{pmatrix}$$

Since

$$i = \tfrac{5\%}{1} = 5\% \quad \text{and} \quad c = \frac{\text{Number of compoundings per year}}{\text{Number of payments per year}} = \frac{1}{2} = 0.5$$

then

$$i_2 = (1 + i)^c - 1 = 1.05^{0.5} - 1 = 0.024695077 = 2.4695077\% \text{ per 6 months}$$

The future value of the $150,000 contribution in $4\frac{1}{2}$ years is:

$$FV = PV(1 + i_2)^n = \$150,000(1.024695077)^9 = \$186,828.49$$

The present value of the perpetuity in $4\frac{1}{2}$ years is:

$$PV = \frac{PMT}{i_2} = \frac{PMT}{0.024695077}$$

Since FV of the original contribution and PV of the perpetuity are both in $4\frac{1}{2}$ years (at exactly the same point on the time diagram), then

$$\$186,828.49 = \frac{PMT}{0.024695077}$$

Hence,

$$PMT = 0.024695077 \times \$186,828.49 = \$4613.74$$

The trust can make semiannual payments of $4613.74 in perpetuity.

CONCEPT QUESTIONS

1. A perpetuity and an annuity both have the same values for *PMT* and *i*. Which has the larger present value? Give a brief explanation.

2. If market interest rates rise, will it require a larger endowment to sustain a perpetuity with a particular payment size? Give a brief explanation.

3. Will the market value of a perpetual preferred share (paying a fixed periodic dividend) rise or fall if the rate of return (dividend yield) required by investors declines? Give a brief explanation.

EXERCISE 14.2

Answers to the odd-numbered problems are at the end of the book.

BASIC PROBLEMS

1. Mrs. O'Reilly donated $500,000 to Medicine Hat College for a perpetual scholarship fund for women in business studies. What amount can be awarded on each anniversary, if the scholarship fund earns $4\frac{1}{2}\%$ compounded annually?

2. What amount is required to fund a perpetuity that pays $10,000 at the beginning of each quarter? The funds can be invested to earn 5% compounded quarterly.

3. A perpetuity is to pay $10,000 at the end of every six months. How much less money is required to fund the perpetuity if the money can be invested to earn 5% compounded semi-annually instead of 4% compounded semiannually?

4. In 1752, the British government converted all of its outstanding bonds to perpetual bonds that paid a fixed interest rate. These bonds paid only the interest every three months—the principal amount of the debt would never be repaid. The perpetual bonds have come to be known as "Consols," and they trade in the British financial markets. The owner of a £1000 face-value (or denomination) Consol receives £6.25 every three months.
   a. What is the fixed interest rate (on the face value) paid by the Consols?
   b. If the prevailing long-term interest rate in the British financial markets is 4.5% compounded quarterly, what is the fair market value of a £1000 face-value Consol? (Assume that you will receive the first interest payment in three months.)

5. How much more money is required to fund an ordinary perpetuity than a 30-year ordinary annuity if both pay $5000 quarterly and money can earn 5% compounded quarterly?

6. Ranger Oil recently donated $750,000 to the Northern Alberta Institute of Technology (NAIT) to fund (in perpetuity) five annual bursaries for students in Petroleum Engineering Technology. If the first five bursaries are to be awarded immediately, what is the maximum amount of each bursary? Assume that the bursary fund earns 4.9% compounded semiannually.

7. An old agreement requires a town to pay $500 per year in perpetuity to the owner of a parcel of land for a water well dug on the property in the 1920s. The well is no longer used, and the town wants to buy out the contract, which has become an administrative nuisance. What amount (including the regular scheduled payment) should the landowner be willing to accept on the date of the next scheduled payment if long-term low-risk investments now earn 5.8% compounded annually?

8. The alumni association of Seneca College is initiating a one-year drive to raise money for a perpetual scholarship endowment fund. The goal is to offer ten scholarships per year, each worth $5000.

a. How large a fund is required to begin awarding the scholarships one year after the funds are in place if the funds can be invested to earn 5% compounded annually in perpetuity?

b. Suppose that, during its fundraising year, the alumni association finds an insurance company that will pay 5.5% compounded annually in perpetuity. How much less money does the association need to raise?

c. What dollar amount in scholarships can be awarded annually if the alumni association raises only $750,000? Use the interest rate from part (b).

9. A city sells plots in its cemetery for $1000 plus an amount calculated to provide for the cost of maintaining the grounds in perpetuity. This cost is figured at $25 per plot due at the end of each quarter. If the city can invest the funds to earn 4.8% compounded annually in perpetuity, what is the price of a plot?

10. A company's preferred shares pay a $2 dividend every six months in perpetuity. What is the fair market value of the shares just after payment of a dividend if the dividend yield required by the market on shares of similar risk is

    a. 4% compounded semiannually?   **b.** 5% compounded semiannually?

11. A company's perpetual preferred shares pay a semiannual dividend of $1.50. The next dividend will be paid tomorrow.

    a. At what price would the shares provide an investor with a 4.5% semiannually compounded rate of return? The investor will receive tomorrow's dividend.

    b. If the shares are trading at $70, what nominal rate of return will they provide to a purchaser?

12. Mr. O'Connor set up a trust account paying $500 per month in perpetuity to the local SPCA. These payments consume all of the interest earned monthly by the trust. Between what amounts does the balance in the trust account fluctuate if it earns 6% compounded monthly?

INTERMEDIATE PROBLEMS

13. What sum of money, invested today in a perpetual fund earning 5.5% compounded semiannually, will sustain quarterly perpetuity payments of $1000 if the first payment is made

    a. three months from today?   **b.** one year from today?

14. The common shares of Unicorp. are forecast to pay annual dividends of $2 at the end of each of the next five years, followed by dividends of $3 per year in perpetuity. What is the fair market value of the shares if the market requires an 8% annually compounded rate of return on shares having a similar degree of risk?

15. Mr. Chan has donated $1 million to a college to set up a perpetuity for the purchase of books and journals for a new library to be built and named in his honour. The donation will be invested and earnings will compound for three years, at which time the first of the quarterly perpetuity payments will be made. If the funds earn 6% compounded quarterly, what will be the size of the payments?

16. A wealthy benefactor has donated $1,000,000 to establish a perpetuity that will be used to support the operating costs of a local heritage museum scheduled to open in three years' time. If the funds earn 4.8% compounded monthly, what monthly payments, the first occurring three years from now, can the museum expect?

17. A legal dispute delayed for 18 months the disbursement of a $500,000 bequest designated to provide quarterly payments in perpetuity to a hospice. While under the jurisdiction of the court, the funds earned interest at the rate of 5% compounded semiannually. The hospice has just invested the $500,000 along with its earnings in a perpetual fund earning 5.2% compounded semiannually. What payments will the hospice receive beginning three months from now?

*14.3 Constant-Growth Annuities

In many situations in real life, regular payments that we make or receive do not remain constant. As a result of inflation and wage growth, we pay more for rent, memberships, insurance, etc., as the years go by. Usually we are able to increase our saving rate and RRSP contributions from time to time. Some pension plans (including the Canada Pension Plan, the Quebec Pension Plan, and the Old Age Security program) provide annual cost-of-living increases. Many businesses grow their revenue, profit, and dividends through real economic growth as well as through inflation.

For long-range financial projections and planning, it is natural to want to incorporate some sort of growth pattern in future payments. The constant-payment annuities we have been considering so far may not provide an adequate approximation of many patterns of increasing payments. In this section we consider the case of **constant-growth annuities**—annuities in which the payments change by the *same percentage* from one payment to the next. Let

$$g = \text{Rate of growth in payment size between successive payments}$$

For example, if each quarterly payment is 1.5% larger than the preceding payment, then $g = 1.5\% = 0.015$. In general, if we let PMT represent the amount of the *first* payment, then

$$\text{Second payment} = PMT + g \times PMT$$
$$= PMT(1 + g)$$
$$\text{Third payment} = (\text{Second payment}) + g \times (\text{Second payment})$$
$$= (\text{Second payment}) \times (1 + g)$$
$$= PMT(1 + g) \times (1 + g)$$
$$= PMT(1 + g)^2$$

You can now see the pattern. Each payment is a factor $(1 + g)$ larger than the preceding payment. In other words, the payment's growth rate, g, compounds every payment interval.

LO3 The formulas for the future value and the present value of a constant-growth ordinary simple annuity are:

FUTURE VALUE OF A CONSTANT-GROWTH ORDINARY ANNUITY

$$FV = PMT\left[\frac{(1 + i)^n - (1 + g)^n}{i - g}\right] \tag{14-2}^2$$

PRESENT VALUE OF A CONSTANT-GROWTH ORDINARY ANNUITY

$$PV = PMT\left[\frac{1 - (1 + g)^n(1 + i)^{-n}}{i - g}\right] \tag{14-3}$$

Note that these formulas have a structure somewhat similar to Formulas (11-1) and (11-2). If you substitute $g = 0$ (no growth in the size of payments) into Formulas (14-2) and (14-3), you will obtain Formulas (11-1) and (11-2). Hence, we can conclude that (11-1) and (11-2) are the "zero-growth case" of the more general Formulas (14-2) and (14-3).

Valuation of Common Shares

According to the Valuation Principle, the fair market value of common shares is the present value of all future dividends (discounted at the market's required rate of return). The further we look into the future, the more difficult it becomes to forecast the dividends. Because of this high degree of uncertainty, the rate of return at which investors discount the future dividends is appropriately high.

---

[2] Formulas (14-2) and (14-3) are not programmed into financial calculators. However, there is a way to trick your calculator into using its financial functions (designed for fixed-payment annuities) to calculate the future value or present value of a constant-growth annuity. It doesn't save much time, but if you find it satisfying to make a device do something for which it was not intended, here is what you do. Make the following "adjustments" to the values entered for *I/Y* and *PMT*.

FV Calculation: In the I/Y memory, enter the "adjusted" nominal annual rate: $m\left(\frac{1 + i}{1 + g} - 1\right) \times 100\%$. In the PMT memory, enter the "adjusted" payment: $PMT \times (1 + g)^{n-1}$.

PV Calculation: Use the same I/Y value as for the *FV* calculation above. In the PMT memory, enter the "adjusted" payment: $\frac{PMT}{1 + g}$.

One approach to stock valuation is to forecast separate dividend growth rates for the short run (three to five years during which forecasts are more reliable) and the long run (where the "crystal ball" becomes cloudy). For example, an analyst might forecast dividends growing at 15% per year for four years and 5% per year thereafter. During the first four years we have a growing annuity; thereafter we have a growing perpetuity. However, at the high discount rates employed in common stock valuation, dividends beyond 30 years contribute little to the present value of the dividend stream.

 POINT OF INTEREST

Such a Deal!

In the early 1990s, it was apparent that existing Canada Pension Plan (CPP) contribution levels could not sustain future benefits. In early 1998, the CPP was amended to phase in a dramatic increase in the required contribution rates. The new regulations took contribution rates from 5.85% of pensionable earnings in 1998 to 9.9% in 2003. (The rate was only 3.6% in 1966 when the CPP system began.) Pensionable earnings are basically annual employment or self-employment income falling between $3500 and an upper amount that is inflation-adjusted. In 2019, this upper limit was $57,400. Therefore, if your employment income in 2019 was more than $57,400, you and your employer each paid half of the maximum CPP contribution for 2019 of:

$$0.099 \times (\$57,400 - \$3500) = \$5336.10$$

The primary benefit that contributors expect to receive from the CPP is the retirement pension. This pension is indexed to the CPI. To be eligible for the maximum CPP pension, you must be age 65 and have made the maximum annual CPP contribution for 83% of the years since 1965 or age 18, whichever is the shorter period. In 2019, the maximum annual CPP retirement pension was $13,855.

In this Point of Interest, we will estimate the rate of return that CPP contributions must earn to deliver the expected pension. The assumptions are:
- Shona begins to make maximum CPP contributions ($5336.10) at age 25 in 2019.
- Thereafter, the rate of inflation (and, consequently, the annual increase in the CPP contribution and the retirement pension) will be 2.3%.
- Shona will retire and begin drawing the maximum retirement pension at age 65.
- Shona will live to age 86 (current life expectancy for a woman aged 65).
- CPP contributions and pension payments will be made at the end of each year.

If the pension is funded by Shona's contributions,

$$\begin{pmatrix} \text{Future value, at age 65,} \\ \text{of CPP contributions} \end{pmatrix} = \begin{pmatrix} \text{Present value, at age 65,} \\ \text{of pension payments} \end{pmatrix}$$

Since both the contributions and the pension payments grow at the constant rate of inflation, Formulas (14-2) and (14-3) must be used for these calculations.

QUESTIONS

1. What is the future value, at age 65, of Shona's CPP contributions if the rate of return they earn is:
   a. 3% compounded annually?   **b.** 4% compounded annually?
2. What will be the (indexed) CPP retirement pension in Shona's first year of retirement? (The maximum annual CPP retirement pension in 2019 was $13,855.)
3. What is the present value, at age 65, of Shona's pension payments if the discount rate is:
   a. 3% compounded annually?   **b.** 4% compounded annually?
4. Suppose Shona could take the amounts that she and her employer will contribute to the CPP and instead invest these amounts to provide for a do-it-yourself pension. What is your *estimate* of the minimum rate of return Shona's investments must earn to provide the same pension payments as we have projected for the CPP retirement pension?
5. Are you underwhelmed? (No explanation is required.)

Source: "Canada Pension Plan—How Much Could You Receive?" Government of Canada. www.canada.ca/en/services/benefits/publicpensions/cpp/cpp-benefit/amount.html.

APP ④ THAT

Life expectancy tables are based on overall population averages for each age group. Your life expectancy may differ from the overall average for your age group due to factors such as genetics, health, gender, and lifestyle. To see how personal factors affect your life expectancy, search the App Store on your tablet, smartphone, or smart watch using the key words **LIFE EXPECTANCY**.

You will find many free and paid apps that will calculate how long you will live based on the responses you give to questions concerning factors that affect your life expectancy. The age you can expect to reach is then calculated automatically. By changing your response to just one question, you can determine that factor's statistical effect on your life expectancy.

EXAMPLE 14.3A

FUTURE VALUE OF GROWING RRSP CONTRIBUTIONS

Monica intends to make RRSP contributions on February 28 of each year. She plans to contribute $3000 in the first year and increase the contribution by 3% every year thereafter.

a. Rounded to the nearest dollar, how much will she have in her RRSP at the time of her 30th contribution if the plan earns 8% compounded annually?

b. What will be the amount of her last contribution?

SOLUTION

a. The amount in the RRSP will be the future value of the 30 contributions. Viewed from the date of the 30th payment, the contributions form a constant-growth ordinary simple annuity having

$$PMT = \$3000 \qquad i = 8\% \qquad n = 30 \qquad \text{and} \qquad g = 3\%$$

Substitute these values into Formula (14-2).

$$FV = PMT\left[\frac{(1 + i)^n - (1 + g)^n}{i - g}\right]$$

$$= \$3000\left(\frac{1.08^{30} - 1.03^{30}}{0.08 - 0.03}\right)$$

$$= \$3000\left(\frac{10.0626569 - 2.4272625}{0.05}\right)$$

$$= \$458{,}124$$

Monica will have $458,124 in her RRSP at the time of her 30th contribution.

b. The final contribution will be the future value of $3000 after 29 compoundings at 3%.

$$\text{Final contribution} = \$3000(1.03)^{29} = \$7069.70$$

EXAMPLE 14.3B

AMOUNT REQUIRED TO PURCHASE AN INDEXED ANNUITY

If money accumulated in an RRSP is used to purchase a fixed payment annuity, the payments will steadily lose purchasing power due to inflation. For this reason, some retirees purchase indexed annuities in which the payments increase at a predetermined rate.

Rounded to the nearest dollar, how much will it cost to purchase a 20-year ordinary annuity making semiannual payments that grow at the rate of 2% compounded semiannually? The first payment is $10,000 and the funds used to purchase the annuity earn 6% compounded semiannually.

SOLUTION

The cost will be the present value of the payments.

The payments form a constant-growth ordinary simple annuity having

$$PMT = \$10,000 \quad i = \tfrac{6\%}{2} = 3\% \text{ per half-year} \quad n = 2\,(20) = 40 \quad \text{and} \quad g = \tfrac{2\%}{2} = 1\% \text{ per half-year}$$

Substitute these values into Formula (14-3).

$$PV = PMT\left[\frac{1 - (1 + g)^n(1 + i)^{-n}}{i - g}\right]$$

$$= \$10,000\left[\frac{1 - (1.01)^{40}(1.03)^{-40}}{0.03 - 0.01}\right] = \$271,789$$

The indexed annuity will cost $271,789.

EXAMPLE 14.3C

CALCULATING THE INITIAL PAYMENT IN A CONSTANT-GROWTH ANNUITY

Derek is 30 years old and intends to accumulate $1 million in his RRSP by age 60. He expects his income and annual RRSP contributions to keep pace with inflation, which he assumes will be 2.5% per year. Rounded to the nearest dollar, what will be his initial contribution one year from now if he assumes the RRSP will earn 8% compounded annually?

SOLUTION

$1 million is the future value of a constant-growth ordinary simple annuity having

$$FV = \$1,000,000 \quad i = 8\% \quad n = 30 \quad \text{and} \quad g = 2.5\%$$

Substitute these values into Formula (14-2).

$$FV = PMT\left[\frac{(1 + i)^n - (1 + g)^n}{i - g}\right]$$

$$\$1,000,000 = PMT\left(\frac{1.08^{30} - 1.025^{30}}{0.08 - 0.025}\right)$$

$$\$1,000,000 = PMT(144.820)$$

$$PMT = \frac{\$1,000,000}{144.820} = \$6905$$

Derek's initial contribution one year from now will be $6905.

EXERCISE 14.3

Answers to the odd-numbered problems are at the end of the book.

 **Spreadsheet template:** *A partially completed Excel template for calculating the future value and present value of a constant-growth annuity is provided in the Student Edition of Connect. You can use this template for many of the problems in Exercise 14.3. In Chapter 14 under the Student Resources, find "FV & PV of Constant-Growth Annuity."*

BASIC PROBLEMS

1. Suppose year-end contributions to an RRSP start at $3000 and increase by 2.5% per year thereafter. What amount will be in the RRSP after 25 years if the plan earns 9% compounded annually?

2. Chantal will make year-end contributions for 30 years to an RRSP earning 8% compounded annually.
    a. How much will she have after 30 years if the annual contribution is $2000?
    b. How much more will she have after 30 years if she increases the contributions by 2% every year?

3. Randall wants to accumulate $750,000 in his RRSP by the end of his 30-year working career. What should be his initial year-end contribution if he intends to increase the contribution by 3% every year and the RRSP earns 10% compounded annually?

4. How much will it cost to purchase a 20-year indexed annuity in which the end-of-quarter payments start at $5000 and grow by 0.5% every quarter? Assume that the money used to purchase the annuity earns 6% compounded quarterly.

5. Ed Monton is about to buy a 25-year annuity that will deliver end-of-month payments. The first payment will be $1000. How much more will it cost to index the annuity so that payments grow at the rate of 2.4% compounded monthly? Assume the money used to purchase the annuity earns 5.4% compounded monthly.

6. Vic Toria (age 65) is about to begin receiving a CPP retirement pension of $11,000 per year. This pension is indexed to the Consumer Price Index (CPI). Assume that the annual pension will be paid in a single year-end payment, the CPI will rise 3% per year, and money is worth 6% compounded annually. What is the current economic value of:
   a. 20 years of pension benefits?   **b.** 25 years of pension benefits?

INTERMEDIATE PROBLEMS

7. Petra Borough is about to retire from a government job with a pension that is indexed to the Consumer Price Index (CPI). She is 60 years old and has a life expectancy of 25 years. Estimate the current economic value of her pension, which will start at $20,000 per year. For the purpose of this estimation, assume that Petra will draw the pension for 25 years, the annual pension will be paid in a single year-end payment, the CPI will rise 2.5% per year, and money is worth 5% compounded annually. How much of the current economic value comes from indexing?

8. Cal Gary has accumulated $600,000 in her RRSP and is about to purchase a 25-year annuity from which she will receive month-end payments. The money used to purchase the annuity will earn 4.8% compounded monthly.
   a. What will be the monthly payment without indexing?
   b. What will be the initial payment if payments grow by 2.4% compounded monthly?
   c. How long will it be until the monthly payment from the indexed annuity exceeds the monthly payment from the constant-payment annuity?

9. Dean has already implemented the first stage of his financial plan. Over a 30-year period, he will continue to increase his annual year-end RRSP contributions by 3% per year. His initial contribution was $2000. At the end of the 30 years, he will transfer the funds to an RRIF and begin end-of-month withdrawals that will increase at the rate of 1.8% compounded monthly for 25 years. Assume that his RRSP will earn 9% compounded annually and his RRIF will earn 6% compounded monthly. What will be the size of his initial RRIF withdrawal?

10. Maritime Bank recently announced that its next semiannual dividend (to be paid six months from now) will be $1.00 per share. A stock analyst's best estimate for the growth in future dividends is 5% compounded semiannually.
    a. If you require a rate of return of 10% compounded semiannually on the stock, what maximum price should you be willing to pay per share? Ignore the present value of dividends beyond a 50-year time horizon.
    b. What price do you obtain if you do not ignore dividends beyond 50 years? (*Hint:* Use a large value, say 999, for n in the present-value calculation.)

11. The dividends on the common shares of Mosco Inc. are forecast to grow at 10% per year for the next five years. Thereafter, the best guess is that the annual dividend will grow at the same 3% annual rate as the nominal GNP. A $2.00 dividend for the past year was recently paid. Assume that the required rate of return is 9% compounded annually. What is the fair market value of the shares if we ignore all dividends beyond a 30-year time horizon?

12. **Using the Constant-Growth Annuity Chart** An interactive chart for the future value of a constant-growth annuity is available on Connect. In Chapter 14 of the Student Edition, find "Constant-Growth Annuity." The chart has data input boxes in which you can enter values for *PMT*, *j*, and *m* that are the same for each of two annuities. Then you can enter a different growth rate, *g*, for each annuity. The resulting bar chart shows the future values of both annuities at five-year intervals from 5 to 25 years. This display allows you to compare the effects of the growth rate on the future value of a constant-growth annuity.

   Use this chart to answer the following questions. Assume in every case that you make annual end-of-year contributions to an RRSP for 25 years. The RRSP earns 7.5% compounded annually. Compared to a "base case" of constant contributions of $3000, how much larger (in percentage terms) will the value of your RRSP be after 25 years if you increase the payments by:

   a. 1% per year?   **b.** 2% per year?   **c.** 4% per year?

KEY TERMS

Constant-growth annuities	Ordinary perpetuity	Perpetuity due
Deferred annuity	Period of deferral	
Deferred annuity due	Perpetuity	

SUMMARY OF NOTATION AND KEY FORMULAS

d = Equivalent number of payment intervals in the period of deferral

g = Rate of growth in payment size between successive payments

FORMULA (14-1) $PV = \dfrac{PMT}{i}$ Finding the present value of an ordinary perpetuity

FORMULA (14-2) $FV = PMT \left[\dfrac{(1 + i)^n - (1 + g)^n}{i - g} \right]$ Finding the future value of a constant-growth ordinary annuity

FORMULA (14-3) $PV = PMT \left[\dfrac{1 - (1 + g)^n (1 + i)^{-n}}{i - g} \right]$ Finding the present value of a constant-growth ordinary annuity

REVIEW PROBLEMS

Answers to the odd-numbered review problems are at the end of the book.

BASIC PROBLEMS

1. **LO1** What amount of money invested now will provide payments of $500 at the end of every month for five years following a four-year period of deferral? The money will earn 7.2% compounded monthly.

2. **LO1** What price will a finance company pay to a merchant for a conditional sale contract that requires 12 monthly payments of $249, with the first payment due six months from now? The finance company requires a return of 16.5% compounded monthly.

3. **LO2** If money can earn 6% compounded annually, what percentage more money is required to fund an ordinary perpetuity paying $1000 at the end of every year, than to fund an ordinary annuity paying $1000 per year for 25 years?

4.   **L02** A company's preferred shares pay a $1.25 dividend every three months in perpetuity. What is the fair market value of the shares just after payment of a dividend if the rate of return required by the market on shares of similar risk is:
   a. 5% compounded quarterly?   **b.** 6% compounded quarterly?

5.   **L02** Mr. Larsen's will directed that $200,000 be invested to establish a perpetuity making payments at the end of each month to his wife for as long as she lives and subsequently to the Canadian Heart Foundation. What will the payments be if the funds can be invested to earn 5.4% compounded monthly?

6.   **L02** Mrs. McTavish wants to establish an annual $5000 scholarship in memory of her husband. The first scholarship is to be awarded two years from now. If the funds can earn 6.25% compounded annually, what amount must Mrs. McTavish pay now to sustain the scholarship in perpetuity?

7.   **L03** How much will it cost to purchase a 15-year constant growth annuity paying $10,000 at the end of every year if it earns 5.5% compounded annually and is indexed to an inflation rate of 2% annually?

8.   **L03** Lola Fritola is planning for her retirement by making quarterly payments to an annuity with each payment increasing by 0.4% every quarter. Her first payment is $4500 and she plans to contribute for the next 10 years. How much will she have in her retirement savings if the money is invested to earn 4.2% compounded quarterly?

INTERMEDIATE PROBLEMS

9.   **L01** C&D Stereo sold a stereo system on a plan that required no down payment and nothing to pay until January 1 (four months away). Then the first of 12 monthly payments of $226.51 must be made. The payments were calculated to provide C&D Stereo with a return on the account receivable of 16.5% compounded monthly. What was the selling price of the stereo system?

10.   **L01** What is the current economic value of an inheritance that will pay $2500 to the beneficiary at the beginning of every three months for 20 years starting when the beneficiary reaches 21 years of age, $5\frac{1}{4}$ years from now? Assume that money can earn 6% compounded monthly.

11.   **L02** What minimum amount will have to be dedicated today to a fund earning 5.6% compounded quarterly, if the first quarterly payment of $2000 in perpetuity is to occur:
   a. Three months from now?   **b.** Five years from now?

12.   **L02** The common shares of Bancorp Ltd. are forecast to pay annual dividends of $3 at the end of each of the next five years, followed by dividends of $2 per year in perpetuity. What is the fair market value of the shares if the market requires a 10% annually compounded rate of return on shares having a similar degree of risk?

13.   **L02** How much more money is required to fund an ordinary perpetuity than a 25-year ordinary annuity, if the funds can earn 7% compounded quarterly, and both pay $500 monthly?

14.   **L02** Dr. Pollard donated $100,000 to the Canadian National Institute for the Blind. The money is to be used to make semiannual payments in perpetuity (after a period of deferral) to finance the recording of books-on-CD for the blind. The first perpetuity payment is to be made five years from the date of the donation. If the funds are invested at 5% compounded semiannually, what will be the size of the payments?

15.   **L02** What percentage more money is required to fund an ordinary perpetuity than to fund a 30-year ordinary annuity, if the funds can earn 5.8% compounded semiannually? The perpetuity and the annuity each pay $1000 semiannually.

16. **LO1** Fred asked two life insurance companies to give quotes on a 20-year deferred annuity (after a 5-year deferral period) that can be purchased for $100,000. Northwest Mutual quoted payments of $875 payable at the end of each month. Liberty Standard stated that all their annuity options provide a rate of return equal to 5.5% compounded annually. Which company should Fred choose?

ADVANCED PROBLEM

17. **LO1** A $30,000 loan bearing interest at 9% compounded monthly was repaid, after a period of deferral, by monthly payments of $425.10 for 10 years. What was the time interval between the date of the loan and the first payment?

CASE

Should You Choose to Start Receiving the CPP Retirement Pension at Age 60 Instead of Age 65?

Subject to certain restrictions, you may elect to start collecting the Canada Pension Plan (CPP) monthly retirement pension at any time after you reach age 60. The payments are then reduced by 0.6% for each month the pension is collected before age 65. For example, if the pension starts at age 60, the monthly payment will be decreased by

$$(5 \times 12 \text{ months}) \times (0.6\%) = 36\%$$

The reduction is permanent, extending to payments after age 65 as well.

In **Example 11.3H**, we compared the economic values of a pension starting at age 60 and a pension starting at age 65. At that point, we ignored an important feature of the CPP retirement pension. The payments are indexed to the cost of living—every January the payments are increased by the percent change in the CPI during a recent one-year period.

After studying constant-growth annuities, we can do a more rigorous analysis by incorporating an estimate of the rate of inflation in future years. Turn back the clock to consider Neil as he approaches age 60 at the end of 2018. The maximum CPP retirement pension at age 65 in the year 2019 is $13,855 per year. If Neil elects to start receiving the pension at age 60, it will be 0.64 × $13,855 = $8867.20 per year. In our analysis, we will assume the pension is received as a single payment at each year-end. The payments then form an ordinary annuity. Also assume a 2.3% annual rise in the CPI in the years ahead. The CPP will then increase by 2.3% per year.

QUESTIONS

1. Assuming that Neil lives another 21 years (the life expectancy of a 60-year-old male), what is the economic value (at the beginning of 2019) of the reduced pension if money can earn 6% compounded annually?
2. What will Neil's initial pension be if he waits until age 65 to start receiving it?
3. What is the economic value (at the beginning of 2019) of the full pension if Neil receives it for 16 years from age 65 to age 81? Again use 6% compounded annually for the discount rate.
4. Compare the economic values. Which choice should Neil make?
5. Repeat Questions 1, 3, and 4 assuming money can earn only 4.5% compounded annually.

Chapter 15
Loan Amortization: Mortgages

CHAPTER OUTLINE

15.1 Loan Amortization

15.2 Direct Calculation of the Interest and Principal Components of a Payment or Group of Payments

15.3 Mortgage Loans: Fundamentals

*15.4 Mortgage Loans: Additional Topics (located online)

*Appendix 15A: Instructions for the Texas Instruments BA II PLUS Amortization Worksheet

*Appendix 15B: Amortization Functions on the SHARP EL-738 Calculator

LEARNING OBJECTIVES
After completing this chapter, you will be able to:

LO1 Construct a loan's amortization schedule

LO2 Calculate the principal balance after any payment using both the prospective method and the retrospective method

LO3 Calculate the final loan payment when it differs from the others

LO4 Calculate the principal and interest components of any payment

LO5 Calculate mortgage payments for the initial loan and its renewals

LO6 Calculate mortgage loan balances and amortization periods to reflect prepayments of principal

LO7 Determine the maximum mortgage loan for which a borrower qualifies

LOAN AMORTIZATION IS THE PROCESS of repaying the original principal by equal periodic payments. Although all payments are the same size (the final payment may differ from the others), each one consists of a different combination of principal and interest. There are several applications in which we need to separate the principal and interest components of one or more payments. In **Sections 15.1** and **15.2**, you will learn the concepts needed to do these calculations.

The largest single amount most of us will ever borrow is a mortgage loan for the purchase of a home. In 2019, total residential mortgage debt in Canada was just over $1.44 trillion—about $46,000 for every person over the age of 19. This represented approximately 60% of total household debt (mortgage loans, personal loans, line-of-credit loans, and credit-card debt). Mortgage financing is also very common in the commercial sector. In fact, a higher proportion of commercial properties and residential rental properties have mortgage loans against them than do owner-occupied dwellings. Good management of mortgage debt is a key factor in growing your net worth.

15.1 Loan Amortization

A loan for a major purchase such as a vehicle, machinery, or real estate is usually set up as a term loan. In a **term loan**, the periodic payment and usually the interest rate are fixed for the term or duration of the loan. If the loan is for the purchase of a vehicle or equipment, the term of the loan is typically three to five years. The payments are calculated so that the loan will be fully repaid (or amortized) at the end of the term.

A loan obtained to finance the purchase of real estate is typically too large for the borrower to repay within five years. Payments are usually calculated to repay the loan over a longer time period (20, 25, or 30 years)[1] called the **amortization period**. But most lenders will agree to fix the interest rate for a maximum period of only five to ten years. Typically, loans secured by real estate (mortgage loans) are set up for a *term* of five or seven years, and an *amortization period* of 25 or 30 years. At the end of the loan's term, the principal balance becomes due. Lenders will normally renew the loan (for the amount of the loan balance) at a new market-based interest rate for another term. Usually, the loan payment is recalculated to maintain the loan on its original amortization path.

Amortization Schedules

LO1 A **loan amortization schedule** is a table that:

- Breaks down each payment into its interest and principal components, and
- Gives the principal balance outstanding after each payment.

Typical headings for the columns of an amortization schedule are presented in **Table 15.1**.

TABLE 15.1 Column Headings for an Amortization Schedule				
Payment number	Payment ($)	Interest portion ($)	Principal portion ($)	Principal balance ($)
0	—	—	—	Original loan
1				
etc.	etc.			

Each payment occupies a row in the schedule. The values entered in the last three columns are calculated as follows:

1. Calculate the "Interest portion" of the payment using

$$\text{Interest portion} = i \times \text{Principal balance after the previous payment}$$

where i is the periodic interest rate for one payment interval.

2. Calculate the "Principal portion" of the payment from

$$\text{Principal portion} = PMT - \text{Interest portion}$$

---

[1] On a mortgage with a down payment less than 20%, the maximum amortization period is 25 years.

3. Calculate the new "Principal balance" from

Principal balance = Previous principal balance − Principal portion

APP  THAT

Managing loans and mortgages effectively is essential to financial stability and knowing the details of loan payments can ensure timely repayment and help to identify potential interest savings. Search the App Store on your tablet, smartphone, or smart watch using the key words **LOAN CALCULATOR**.

You will find many free and paid apps that calculate loan payments and provide loan payment schedules (amortization tables) to help manage loans of all types.

EXAMPLE 15.1A

CONSTRUCTING A FULL AMORTIZATION SCHEDULE

Marpole Carpet Cleaning borrowed $7600 from Richmond Credit Union at 8% compounded quarterly. The loan is to be repaid by equal quarterly payments over a two-year term. Construct the amortization schedule for the loan.

SOLUTION

The loan payments form an ordinary simple annuity having

$$PV = \$7600 \quad n = 4(2) = 8 \quad \text{and} \quad i = \tfrac{8\%}{4} = 2\%$$

The payment amount must be calculated before beginning the amortization schedule. Substitute these values into Formula (11-2) and solve for *PMT*.

$$PV = PMT\left[\frac{1 - (1 + i)^{-n}}{i}\right]$$

$$\$7600 = PMT\left[\frac{1 - (1.02)^{-8}}{0.02}\right]$$

$$PMT = \frac{\$7600}{7.32548144}$$

$$= \$1037.474473$$

| 8 | I/Y |
| P/Y | 4 ENTER |

(making *C/Y* = *P/Y* = 4)

8	N
7600	PV
0	FV
CPT	PMT

Rounded to the nearest cent, Marpole's quarterly payment will be $1037.47. Now construct the amortization schedule.

Ans: −1037.474473

Payment number	Payment ($)	Interest portion ($)	Principal portion ($)	Principal balance ($)
0	—	—	—	7600.00
1	1037.47	152.00 ①	885.47 ②	6714.53 ③
2	1037.47	134.29	903.18	5811.35
3	1037.47	116.23	921.24	4890.11
4	1037.47	97.80	939.67	3950.44
5	1037.47	79.01	958.46	2991.98
6	1037.47	59.84	977.63	2014.35
7	1037.47	40.29	997.18	1017.17
8	1037.47	20.34	1017.13	0.04

① Step 1:   Interest portion = *i* × Previous balance
         = 0.02($7600) = $152.00

② Step 2:   Principal portion = *PMT* − Interest portion
         = $1037.47 − $152.00 = $885.47

③ Step 3:   Balance after payment = Previous balance − Principal portion
         = $7600.00 − $885.47 = $6714.53

The balance after two years does not turn out to be zero. We will now address this point.

The final payment in a loan amortization schedule In Example 15.1A, the loan balance at the end of the two-year term was not exactly zero (even though we calculated the payment so that it would pay off the loan after two years). The 4¢ balance is not a significant amount, but we should aim for utmost precision in financial calculations. Why didn't we get a zero balance? (Give this question some thought before reading on.)

When we make payments in everyday commerce, we do not deal in fractions of a cent. We acknowledged this fact in Example 15.1A when we rounded the loan payment to the nearest cent. But the mathematics tells us that the quarterly payment must be exactly $1037.474473 for eight payments to pay off the loan. Therefore, each payment was actually

$$\$1037.474473 - \$1037.47 = \$0.004473$$

(or 0.4473¢) too small. That shortfall will leave a balance after eight payments of *approximately*

$$8(\$0.004473) = \$0.03578$$

The *precise* balance will be the future value of the eight shortages. That is,

$$\text{Balance} = PMT\left[\frac{(1+i)^n - 1}{i}\right] = \$0.004473\left[\frac{(1.02)^8 - 1}{0.02}\right] = \$0.03839$$

which appears in the amortization table as $0.04 because all dollar amounts are rounded to the nearest cent.

In a case where the calculated payment is rounded *up* to the nearest cent, each actual payment includes a small *over*payment. The balance in the amortization schedule at the end of the loan's term will be a negative amount (equal to the future value of the individual overpayments). This negative balance represents a refund owed to the borrower.

In practice, lenders adjust the size of the *final* payment to make the final balance precisely zero. In Example 15.1A, the lender would increase the final payment to $1037.51, making the principal portion $1017.17 and the final balance $0.00.

In general, Steps 2 and 3 of the three-step procedure presented earlier in this section must be altered as follows for the *final* payment.

2. The principal portion of the *final* payment is simply the previous principal balance (in order to reduce the new balance to zero).
3. Calculate the final payment using

$$\text{Final payment} = \text{Interest portion} + \text{Principal portion}$$

Using the Texas Instruments BA II PLUS Amortization Worksheet This worksheet streamlines the calculation of the interest and principal components of a payment in the amortization schedule. Appendix 15A provides instruction on the use of the Amortization Worksheet. (Appendix 15B demonstrates the amortization functions on the Sharp EL-738 calculator.) We will employ the Amortization Worksheet in Example 15.1B.

EXAMPLE 15.1B

CONSTRUCTING A FULL AMORTIZATION SCHEDULE WHERE THE PAYMENTS FORM A GENERAL ANNUITY

Healey Fishing obtained a $40,000 loan for a major refit of a trawler. The loan contract requires seven equal annual payments including interest at 11.5% compounded semiannually. Construct the full amortization schedule for the loan. Calculate the total interest paid over the life of the loan.

SOLUTION

The loan payments form an ordinary *general* annuity in which

$$PV = \$40,000 \quad n = 7 \quad i = \tfrac{11.5\%}{2} = 5.75\% \quad \text{and} \quad c = \tfrac{2}{1} = 2$$

The periodic interest rate that matches the one-year payment interval is

$$i_2 = (1 + i)^c - 1 = 1.0575^2 - 1 = 0.11830625 \text{ per year}$$

Calculate the payment from

$$\$40,000 = \text{Present value of seven payments}$$

$$\$40,000 = PMT\left[\frac{1 - (1.11830625)^{-7}}{0.11830625}\right]$$

$$PMT = \frac{\$40,000}{4.5883725}$$

$$= \$8717.69$$

Now construct the amortization schedule.

11.5	I/Y
P/Y 1	ENTER
C/Y 2	ENTER
7	N
40000	PV
0	FV
CPT	PMT

Ans: −8717.688

Payment number	Payment ($)	Interest portion ($)	Principal portion ($)	Principal balance ($)
0	—	—	—	40,000.00
1	8717.69	4732.25	3985.44	36,014.56
2	8717.69	4260.75	4456.94	31,557.62
3	8717.69	3733.46 ①	4984.23 ②	26,573.39 ③
4	8717.69	3143.80	5573.89	20,999.50
5	8717.69	2484.37	6233.32	14,766.18
6	8717.69	1746.93	6970.76	7795.42
7	8717.67 ④	922.25	7795.42	0.00
Totals:	61,023.81	21,023.81	40,000.00	

① Interest portion = 0.11830625($31,557.62) = $3733.46
② Principal portion = $8717.69 − $3733.46 = $4984.23
③ Balance after payment = $31,557.62 − $4984.23 = $26,573.39
④ Last payment = $7795.42 + $922.25 = $8717.67

Same *I/Y, P/Y, C/Y, PV*

| 8717.69 | +/− | PMT |

2nd	AMORT
3	ENTER
3	ENTER
↓	*BAL* = 26,573.39
↓	*PRN* = −4984.23
↓	*INT* = −3733.46

Total interest paid = (Total of payments) − $40,000

$$= 6(\$8717.69) + \$8717.67 - \$40,000$$

$$= \$21,023.81$$

Precise Calculation of a Loan's Balance

LO2 In previous chapters we have calculated the balance owed after any payment by using the general principle that:

$$\text{Principal balance} = \left(\begin{array}{c}\text{Present value of the remaining payments} \\ \text{(discounted at the } contractual \text{ } rate \text{ } of \text{ } interest \text{ on the loan)}\end{array}\right)$$

This method, based on payments yet to come, is known as the **prospective method** for calculating a loan's balance. (The dictionary definition of "prospective" is "concerned with, or applying to, the future.")

We now know that the final payment on a term loan will usually differ from the other payments. Therefore, the prospective method for calculating a loan's balance will yield the precisely correct balance *only* if we *either*:

1. Use the *precisely correct* value of the final payment; *or*
2. Assume *all* the remaining payments are equal and use the *non-rounded* value for *n*, the number of remaining payments.

With either approach, the prospective method is less straightforward than it initially seemed. In the first approach, we must first determine the size of the final payment, and then calculate the combined present value of the final payment and the other remaining payments. (Later in this section, we will explain how to calculate the value of the final payment without working through the entire amortization schedule.) With the second approach, we must first determine the number of remaining payments, *n*, to several decimal places. Then we use this value for *n* in the present-value calculation. (We will demonstrate this approach in part (b) of **Example 15.1C**.)

To avoid these "messy" complications, it would be preferable to have an alternative method for calculating a loan's balance that does not depend on the final payment. We now turn our attention to such a method.

L02 **Retrospective method for loan balances** This name for our alternative method for calculating a loan's balance will make more sense after we develop the underlying concept. The loan balance immediately after any payment is the single amount that will replace all remaining payments. In **Figure 15.1**, the loan balance at the time of payment number *x* replaces the subsequent $n - x$ payments. Since

$$\text{Original loan} = \left(\begin{array}{c} \text{Present value of all payments} \\ \text{(discounted at the } \textit{contractual rate of interest} \text{ on the loan)} \end{array}\right)$$

then

$$\left(\begin{array}{c} \text{Original} \\ \text{loan} \end{array}\right) = \left(\begin{array}{c} \text{Present value of} \\ \text{the first } x \text{ payments} \end{array}\right) + \left(\begin{array}{c} \text{Present value of the balance} \\ \text{just after the } x\text{th payment} \end{array}\right)$$

This equation is really a statement that the original loan is economically equivalent to the combination of the first *x* payments and the balance after the *x*th payment. The implied focal date is the date of the original loan.

FIGURE 15.1   A Loan Is Equivalent to a Series of Payments and the Principal Balance After the Payments

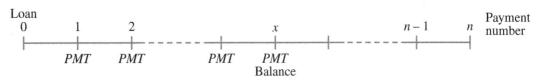

Let us now re-state this economic equivalence, but with the focal date at the *x*th payment as indicated in **Figure 15.2**.

$$\left(\begin{array}{c} \text{Future value of} \\ \text{the original loan} \end{array}\right) = \left(\begin{array}{c} \text{Future value of the} \\ \text{first } x \text{ payments} \end{array}\right) + \text{Balance after the } x\text{th payment}$$

FIGURE 15.2   Placing the Focal Date at the Balance Date

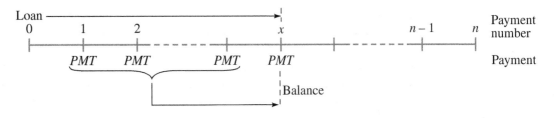

If we then rearrange this equation to isolate the "Balance after the xth payment," we have

$$\text{Balance after the } x\text{th payment} = \begin{pmatrix} \text{Future value of} \\ \text{the original loan} \end{pmatrix} - \begin{pmatrix} \text{Future value of the} \\ \text{first } x \text{ payments} \end{pmatrix}$$

or, if we think of the balance after the xth payment as the difference between what would be owed on the loan assuming no payments were made and the value of all the payments that were made, then,

$$\text{Balance} = \begin{pmatrix} \text{Future value of} \\ \text{the original loan} \end{pmatrix} - \begin{pmatrix} \text{Future value of the} \\ \text{payments already made} \end{pmatrix}$$

This method of calculating a loan's balance is based on the payments we see when *looking back* from a focal date coinciding with the balance. A dictionary definition of "retrospective" is "looking back on, or dealing with, the past." Now you see the reason for the name **retrospective method**. It is based on payments already made.

EXAMPLE 15.1C

COMPARISON OF PROSPECTIVE AND RETROSPECTIVE METHODS

A $57,000 mortgage loan at 6.9% compounded monthly requires monthly payments during its 20-year amortization period.

a. Calculate the monthly payment rounded to the nearest cent.

b. Calculate the balance after five years using both the retrospective method and the prospective method.

SOLUTION

The payments form an ordinary simple annuity having

$$PV = \$57,000 \quad i = \tfrac{6.9\%}{12} = 0.575\% \text{ per month} \quad \text{and} \quad n = 12(20) = 240$$

a. Substitute the given values into

$$PV = PMT\left[\frac{1 - (1 + i)^{-n}}{i}\right]$$

giving

$$\$57,000 = PMT\left[\frac{1 - (1.00575)^{-240}}{0.00575}\right]$$

Solving for PMT, we obtain $PMT = \$438.50545$, which we round to $438.51.

6.9 $\boxed{\text{I/Y}}$

$\boxed{\text{P/Y}}$ 12 $\boxed{\text{ENTER}}$

(making $C/Y = P/Y = 12$)

240 $\boxed{\text{N}}$

57000 $\boxed{\text{PV}}$

0 $\boxed{\text{FV}}$

$\boxed{\text{CPT}}$ $\boxed{\text{PMT}}$

Ans: −438.50545

b. Retrospective method:

$$\text{Balance} = \text{Future value of } \$57,000 - \text{Future value of first 60 payments}$$

Algebraic Approach:

Substitute $i = \tfrac{6.9\%}{12} = 0.575\%$, $PV = \$57,000$, $n = 60$, and $PMT = \$438.51$ into

$$\text{Balance} = PV(1 + i)^n - PMT\left[\frac{(1 + i)^n - 1}{i}\right]$$

$$= \$57,000(1.00575)^{60} - \$438.51\left[\frac{(1.00575)^{60} - 1}{0.00575}\right]$$

$$= \$80,403.940 - \$31,313.079 = \$49,090.86$$

The balance after five years is $49,090.86.

Financial Calculator Approach:

Recall that when you compute $\boxed{\text{FV}}$ on a financial calculator, you will obtain the future value of an initial single amount stored in $\boxed{\text{PV}}$ *plus* the future value of $\boxed{\text{N}}$ payments stored in $\boxed{\text{PMT}}$. In the retrospective method, you want the future value of the initial loan *minus* the future value of the payments already made. To accomplish this subtraction, simply enter the payment with a negative sign as in the box at the right.

Same *I/Y, P/Y, C/Y, PV*

60 $\boxed{\text{N}}$

438.51 $\boxed{+/-}$ $\boxed{\text{PMT}}$

$\boxed{\text{CPT}}$ $\boxed{\text{FV}}$

Ans: −49,090.86

This reasoning is consistent with our cash-flow sign convention. Our initial loan is a cash *inflow* (positive). The payments are cash *outflows* (negative). The computed future value (balance) is negative because it represents the single cash *outflow* still required to pay off the loan.

Prospective method:

After five years, 60 payments have been made and $12(20) - 60 = 180$ payments remain. However, the final payment will not be exactly \$438.51 because we rounded the calculated payment (\$438.50545) to the next higher cent. Using the rounded payment, let's calculate the non-integer number of payments for the entire loan. Substitute the given data into Formula (11-2n).

$$n = -\frac{\ln\left(1 - \frac{i \times PV}{PMT}\right)}{\ln(1 + i)}$$

$$= -\frac{\ln\left(1 - \frac{0.00575 \times \$57,000}{\$438.51}\right)}{\ln(1.00575)}$$

$$= -\frac{\ln(0.25258361)}{\ln(1.00575)}$$

$$= 239.9946411$$

Same *I/Y, P/Y, C/Y, PV,*
FV as in Part (a)

438.51 | +/− | PMT |

| CPT | N |

Ans: 239.9946411

To obtain the precisely correct balance after 60 payments using the prospective method, we must calculate the present value of the remaining

$$239.9946411 - 60 = 179.9946411 \text{ payments of } \$438.51$$

$$\text{Balance} = PMT\left[\frac{1 - (1 + i)^{-n}}{i}\right]$$

$$= \$438.51\left[\frac{1 - (1.00575)^{-179.9946411}}{0.00575}\right]$$

$$= \$49,090.86$$

Same *I/Y, P/Y, C/Y*
Same *PMT, FV*

179.9946411 | N |

| CPT | PV |

Ans: 49,090.86

This is the same answer as we obtained using the retrospective method. (If you had used $n = 180$ remaining payments, you would have obtained a balance of \$49,091.70, which is \$0.84 too high.) After comparing the prospective and retrospective methods, you are likely to conclude that the retrospective method is both shorter and less prone to user errors. For these reasons, hereafter we will usually employ the retrospective method to calculate a loan's balance.

Calculating the Final Payment

LO3 In the process of constructing the amortization charts in **Examples 15.1A** and **15.1B**, we noted that the final payment must cover the balance still owed after the second-to-last payment plus the interest on that balance for one payment interval. That is,

$$\left(\genfrac{}{}{0pt}{}{\text{Final}}{\text{payment}}\right) = \left(\genfrac{}{}{0pt}{}{\text{Balance after the}}{\text{second-to-last payment}}\right) + i \times \left(\genfrac{}{}{0pt}{}{\text{Balance after the}}{\text{second-to-last payment}}\right)$$

Since "$\left(\genfrac{}{}{0pt}{}{\text{Balance after the}}{\text{second-to-last payment}}\right)$" is a common factor on the right side, then

$$\boxed{\text{Final payment} = (1 + i) \times \left(\genfrac{}{}{0pt}{}{\text{Balance after the}}{\text{second-to-last payment}}\right)}$$

If the loan payments form a *general* annuity, replace i by i_2, the equivalent periodic rate that matches the payment interval. [Recall that $i_2 = (1 + i)^c - 1$.]

EXAMPLE 15.1D

CALCULATING A LOAN BALANCE AND THE FINAL PAYMENT

Meditech Laboratories borrowed $28,000 at 10% compounded quarterly to purchase new testing equipment. Payments of $1500 are made every three months.

a. Calculate the balance after the 10th payment.

b. Calculate the final payment.

SOLUTION

a. The loan payments form an ordinary simple annuity having

$$PV = \$28,000 \quad PMT = \$1500 \text{ (except for the last payment)} \quad \text{and} \quad i = \tfrac{10\%}{4} = 2.5\%$$

The loan in this example has been set up so that the regular payment is a nice "round," easily remembered number. In all likelihood, the final payment will differ substantially from $1500. Consequently, if we use the prospective method and assume all payments are the same, any loan balance we calculate will have a significant error. In contrast, if we use the retrospective method, we do not need to know either the final payment or the total number of payments.

$$\binom{\text{Balance after}}{10 \text{ payments}} = \binom{\text{Future value of \$28,000}}{\text{after 10 quarters}} - \binom{\text{Future value of the}}{10 \text{ payments already made}}$$

$$= PV(1+i)^n - PMT\left[\frac{(1+i)^n - 1}{i}\right]$$

$$= \$28,000(1.025)^{10} - \$1500\left[\frac{(1+0.025)^{10} - 1}{0.025}\right]$$

$$= \$35,842.367 - \$16,805.073$$

$$= \$19,037.29$$

10 I/Y

P/Y 4 ENTER

(making *C/Y = P/Y* = 4)

10 N

28000 PV

1500 +/− PMT

CPT FV

Ans: −19,037.29

b. To calculate the final payment, we need to know the balance after the second-to-last payment. But before we can calculate this balance, we must determine the total number of payments. In other words, this part requires three steps: (1) calculate the number of payments using Formula (11-2*n*), (2) calculate the balance after the second-to-last payment using the retrospective method, and (3) calculate the final payment.

$$n = -\frac{\ln\left(1 - \dfrac{i \times PV}{PMT}\right)}{\ln(1+i)}$$

$$= -\frac{\ln\left(1 - \dfrac{0.025 \times \$28,000}{\$1500}\right)}{\ln(1.025)}$$

$$= 25.457357$$

Same *I/Y, P/Y, C/Y*

Same *PV, PMT*

0 FV

CPT N

Ans: 25.457357

The loan requires 26 payments. The balance after 25 payments will be

$$\binom{\text{Balance after}}{25 \text{ payments}} = \$28,000(1.025)^{25} - \$1500\left[\frac{(1.025)^{25} - 1}{0.025}\right]$$

$$= \$51,910.435 - \$51,236.646$$

$$= \$673.79$$

Same *I/Y, P/Y, C/Y*

Same *PV, PMT*

25 N

CPT FV

Ans: −673.79

Final payment = (1 + *i*) × Balance after 25 payments

= 1.025 × $673.79

= $690.63

TRAP

An Incorrect Interpretation of the Fractional Part of "*n*"

In part (b) of Example 15.1D, it is natural to look at the value of $n = 25.457357$ and wonder if we can obtain the size of the last payment simply by multiplying *PMT* by the fractional part of *n*. Unfortunately, because of the nature of compound interest, this calculation will give only an approximate value for the amount of the last payment. In Example 15.1D the actual final payment was $690.63, whereas

$$(\text{Fractional part of } n) \times PMT = 0.457357 \times \$1500 = \$686.04$$

Notice that this amount is neither the final payment ($690.63) nor the principal component of the final payment ($673.79).

Partial Amortization Schedule

LO1 A particular circumstance may require only a portion of a loan's amortization schedule. Suppose, for example, you need amortization details for the monthly payments made in the fourth year of a five-year loan. The partial schedule needs to include only details of payments 37 to 48 inclusive. The key value you need to get started is the principal balance after the 36th payment. Once you have this value, you can use the same three-step routine that we outlined at the beginning of this section to obtain the interest portion, principal portion, and principal balance for each subsequent payment.

EXAMPLE 15.1E

A PARTIAL LOAN AMORTIZATION SCHEDULE

Kimberleigh obtained a loan from her bank for $11,000 at 10.5% compounded monthly to purchase a new car. The monthly payments were set at $250. Construct a partial amortization schedule showing details of the first two payments, Payments 27 and 28, and the last two payments. Calculate the total interest charges.

SOLUTION

The loan payments constitute an ordinary simple annuity in which

$$PV = \$11,000 \quad i = \frac{10.5\%}{12} = 0.875\% \quad \text{and} \quad PMT = \$250 \text{ (except for the final payment)}$$

Let us first determine how many payments will be required to pay off the loan. Using Formula (11-2n),

$$n = -\frac{\ln\left(1 - \frac{i \times PV}{PMT}\right)}{\ln(1 + i)}$$

$$= -\frac{\ln\left(1 - \frac{0.00875 \times \$11,000}{\$250}\right)}{\ln(1.00875)}$$

$$= 55.80$$

| 10.5 | I/Y |
| P/Y | 12 ENTER |

(making $C/Y = P/Y = 12$)

11000	PV
250 +/−	PMT
0	FV
CPT	N

Ans: 55.80

Therefore, 56 payments are needed to pay off the loan. The last two payments will be Payments 55 and 56.

Notes ①, ②, and ③ under the amortization schedule below present the calculations for obtaining the interest and principal components of the first payment, and the balance after the first payment. In the callout box to the right of the notes, we show how the same quantities may be computed using the amortization worksheet. Similar calculations should be repeated for the second payment.

For an algebraic approach with Payment 27, we first need to determine the balance after 26 payments. Using the retrospective method,

$$\begin{pmatrix} \text{Balance after} \\ \text{26 payments} \end{pmatrix} = \begin{pmatrix} \text{Future value of \$11,000} \\ \text{after 26 months} \end{pmatrix} - \begin{pmatrix} \text{Future value of the} \\ \text{26 payments already made} \end{pmatrix}$$

$$= \$11,000(1.00875)^{26} - \$250\left[\frac{(1.00875)^{26} - 1}{0.00875}\right]$$

$$= \$6533.07$$

Knowing this balance, we can now proceed as we did for Payments 1 and 2. (If you use the amortization worksheet, you do *not* need to first obtain the balance after Payment 26.)

For an algebraic approach with Payment 55, we first need to determine the balance after 54 payments. Using the retrospective method,

$$\begin{pmatrix} \text{Balance after} \\ \text{54 payments} \end{pmatrix} = \begin{pmatrix} \text{Future value of \$11,000} \\ \text{after 54 months} \end{pmatrix} - \begin{pmatrix} \text{Future value of the} \\ \text{54 payments already made} \end{pmatrix}$$

$$= \$11,000(1.00875)^{54} - \$250\left[\frac{(1.00875)^{54} - 1}{0.00875}\right]$$

$$= \$444.74$$

Now the calculations for the last two payments may be completed.

Payment number	Payment ($)	Interest portion ($)	Principal portion ($)	Principal balance ($)
0	—	—	—	11,000.00
1	250	96.25 ①	153.75 ②	10,846.25 ③
2	250	94.90	155.10	10,691.15
.	.	.	.	.
.	.	.	.	.
26	.	.	.	6533.07
27	250	57.16	192.84	6340.23
28	250	55.48	194.52	6145.71
.	.	.	.	.
.	.	.	.	.
54	.	.	.	444.74
55	250	3.89	246.11	198.63
56	200.37 ④	1.74	198.63	0.00
Total	13,950.37	2950.37 ⑤	11,000.00	

① Interest portion = $i \times$ Previous balance
    = 0.00875($11,000)
    = $96.25

② Principal portion = PMT − Interest portion
    = $250 − $96.25
    = $153.75

③ Balance after payment = Former balance − Principal portion
    = $11,000 − $153.75
    = $10,846.25

④ Last payment = Balance after 55 payments × (1 + i)
    = $198.63(1.00875)
    = $200.37

⑤ Total interest = Total of payments − Initial loan
    = 55($250) + $200.37 − $11,000
    = $2950.37

Same I/Y, P/Y, C/Y

Same PV, PMT

| 2nd | AMORT |

1 | ENTER

1 | ENTER

↓ $BAL = 10,846.25$

↓ $PRN = -153.75$

↓ $INT = -96.25$

POINT OF INTEREST

Just When You Thought You Had It All Figured Out ...

Jeff had been haggling with Joe, the car salesperson, for over an hour by the time they agreed on a price for the car Jeff wanted. As Joe started to write up the sale, he asked Jeff what portion of the purchase price he wished to finance. Jeff responded that he would pay cash. Joe gave him a look of disbelief. "Why pay cash? You will be better off putting your money in a GIC earning 5% and borrowing from us at 7.9% to finance the purchase of your car."

"Ya, right!" replied Jeff sarcastically.

"I'll show you," responded Joe. As Joe started to enter numbers into his computer, Jeff thought: "How can this guy make such a preposterous claim? It's a no-brainer!"

Joe's printer started to whir. "We'll have the analysis in a jiffy."

Jeff, a business graduate from the local college, was actually looking forward to seeing Joe humbled by the self-evident outcome. He leaned forward as Joe laid the printout on his desk.

Joe started to explain. "I chose $10,000 as the amount financed—just for the purpose of discussion. The monthly loan payment for three years would be $312.90. The total of your payments comes to $11,264.40. So the total interest you pay is $1264.40."

Joe continued: "Suppose that you purchase a three-year GIC with the $10,000 you are prepared to pay in a cash deal. After three years it will be worth $11,576.25. So the interest you earn is $1576.25. That's $311.85 more than the interest you pay on the loan! So there's the proof in cold hard numbers." Joe had that look of smug satisfaction as he leaned back in his leather-upholstered chair.

"There's gotta be a mistake," muttered Jeff. He reached for the printout with one hand and his financial calculator with the other. As he started to punch in the numbers, he thought: "Here's where my business math course will really pay off." Jeff first calculated the future value of the GIC at 5% compounded annually and confirmed Joe's number. "At least he got the simple part right," thought Jeff. He then assumed monthly compounding for the 7.9% rate and was surprised to get Joe's figure for the monthly payment. Jeff started to feel a little uneasy since this calculation seemed the most likely point where Joe would make an error. Jeff went on to verify the total interest charged and the interest differential. Joe's figures were correct to the penny.

Jeff stared at his calculator in disbelief. He kept asking himself: "How can it be that you earn more interest on a $10,000 GIC at only 5% compounded annually than you pay on a $10,000 loan at 7.9% compounded monthly?"

QUESTIONS

1. Answer Jeff's vexing question.
2. Prepare a rigorous analysis of the economic gain or loss (in current dollars) from financing $10,000 as proposed by Joe. Assume that money can earn 5% compounded annually.

EXERCISE 15.1

Answers to the odd-numbered problems are at the end of the book.

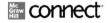 *Spreadsheet templates: Connect provides partially completed Excel templates for full and partial loan amortization schedules. You can use one or the other of these templates in all of the problems in Exercise 15.1. Go to the Student Edition of Connect and find "Loan Amortization Schedules" under the Student Resources for Chapter 15.*

All of the problems in this section are presented with two variations. Problems 1–4 and 9–14 give the duration of the loan, and problems 5–8 and 15–20 give the size of the regular loan payment instead.

BASIC PROBLEMS

1. Monica bought a $1250 4K Ultra HD TV for 20% down, with the balance to be paid with interest at 15% compounded monthly in six equal monthly payments. Construct the full amortization schedule for the debt. Calculate the total interest paid.

2. Dr. Alvano borrowed $8000 at 8% compounded quarterly to purchase a new X-ray machine for his clinic. The agreement requires quarterly payments during a two-year amortization period. Prepare the full amortization schedule for the loan. Calculate the total interest charges.

3. Gurwinder borrowed $2800 from his brother to purchase a 2005 Subaru Impreza. He agreed to repay the loan, with 2.5% interest compounding quarterly, in four quarterly payments. Construct the full amortization schedule for the loan. Calculate the total interest paid on the loan.

4. Falk Enterprises borrowed $8500 at 6.25% compounded semiannually to purchase a new forklift. The loan agreement stipulates regular semiannual payments be made over the next three years. Prepare the full amortization schedule for the loan. Calculate the total interest charges.

5. Monica bought a $1250 4K Ultra HD TV for 20% down and payments of $200 per month (except for a smaller final payment) including interest at 15% compounded monthly. Construct the full amortization schedule for the debt. Calculate the total interest paid.

6. Dr. Alvano borrowed $8000 at 8% compounded quarterly to purchase a new X-ray machine for his clinic. The agreement requires quarterly payments of $1000 (except for a smaller final payment). Prepare the full amortization schedule for the loan. Calculate the total interest charges.

7. Gurwinder borrowed $2800 from his brother to purchase a 2005 Subaru Impreza. He agreed to repay the loan, with 2.5% interest compounding quarterly, using quarterly payments of $600 (except for a smaller final payment) until the loan is paid in full. Construct the full amortization schedule for the loan. Calculate the total interest paid on the loan.

8. Falk Enterprises borrowed $8500 at 6.25% compounded semiannually to purchase a new forklift. The loan agreement stipulates regular semiannual payments of $1600 (except for a smaller final payment). Prepare the full amortization schedule for the loan. Calculate the total interest paid.

INTERMEDIATE PROBLEMS

9. Golden Dragon Restaurant obtained a $9000 loan at 9% compounded annually to replace some kitchen equipment. Prepare a complete amortization schedule if the loan is repaid by semiannual payments over a three-year term.

10. Valley Produce received $50,000 in vendor financing at 7.8% compounded semiannually for the purchase of harvesting machinery. The contract requires equal annual payments for seven years to repay the debt. Construct the amortization schedule for the debt. How much interest will be paid over the seven-year term?

11. Suppose that the loan in Problem 2 permits an additional prepayment of principal on any scheduled payment date. Prepare another amortization schedule that reflects a prepayment of $1500 with the third scheduled payment.

12. Suppose that the loan in Problem 10 permits an additional prepayment of principal on any scheduled payment date. Prepare another amortization schedule that reflects a prepayment of $10,000 with the second scheduled payment. How much interest is saved as a result of the prepayment?

13. Cloverdale Nurseries obtained a $60,000 loan at 7.5% compounded monthly to build an additional greenhouse. Monthly payments were calculated to amortize the loan over six years. Construct a partial amortization schedule showing details of the first two payments, Payments 43 and 44, and the last two payments.

14. Jean and Walter Pereira financed the addition of a swimming pool using a $24,000 home improvement loan from their bank. Monthly payments were based on an interest rate of 7.2% compounded semiannually and a five-year amortization. Construct a partial amortization schedule showing details of the first two payments, Payments 30 and 31, and the last two payments. What total interest will the Pereiras pay over the life of the loan?

15. Golden Dragon Restaurant obtained a $9000 loan at 9% compounded annually to replace some kitchen equipment. Prepare a complete amortization schedule if payments of $1800 (except for a smaller final payment) are made semiannually.

16. Valley Produce received $50,000 in vendor financing at 7.8% compounded semiannually for the purchase of harvesting machinery. The contract requires annual payments of $10,000 (except for a smaller final payment). Construct the complete amortization schedule for the debt. How much interest will be paid over the entire life of the loan?

17. Suppose that the loan in Problem 6 permits an additional prepayment of principal on any scheduled payment date. Prepare another amortization schedule that reflects a prepayment of $1000 with the third scheduled payment.

18. Suppose that the loan in Problem 16 permits an additional prepayment of principal on any scheduled payment date. Prepare another amortization schedule that reflects a prepayment of $10,000 with the second scheduled payment. How much interest is saved as a result of the prepayment?

19. Cloverdale Nurseries obtained a $60,000 loan at 7.5% compounded monthly to build an additional greenhouse. Construct a partial amortization schedule for payments of $1000 per month (except for a smaller final payment) showing details of the first two payments, Payments 56 and 57, and the last two payments.

20. Jean and Walter Pereira financed the addition of a swimming pool using a $24,000 home improvement loan from their bank. Monthly payments of $500 (except for a smaller final payment) include interest at 7.2% compounded semiannually. Construct a partial amortization schedule showing details of the first two payments, Payments 28 and 29, and the last two payments. What total interest will the Pereiras pay over the life of the loan?

21. **Using the Loan Amortization Chart** An interactive Loan Amortization Chart is provided on Connect. In Chapter 15 of the Student Edition, find "Amortizing Loan Calculator."

    The chart has data boxes in which you enter values for key variables. You can either enter the "Loan amount" and then calculate the monthly payment, or you can enter the "Monthly payment" and then calculate the initial amount of the loan. The chart will handle only loans having *monthly* payments and *monthly* compounding of interest. After entering new data, click on the "Calculate" button to generate a new chart.

    For loan terms of up to 30 months, the bar chart presents the balance *after* every payment. If you move the cursor over any bar in the chart, the balance (rounded to the nearest dollar) will be displayed. For terms of 31 to 120 months, there is a bar for every second or fourth *payment*. For terms of 121 months to 360 months, there is a bar for each *year* representing the *beginning* balance.

    Boxes below the data-entry area display the sum of the payments and the total interest paid over the life of the loan. If you click on the "View Report" button, a window will open showing the complete amortization schedule.

    Enter $10,000 for the "Loan amount" and 7.5% for the monthly compounded "Interest rate."

    a. Compare the profiles of the bar charts for loan terms of 30 months and 30 years. Approximately what percentage of the original principal is paid off midway through the term in each case?

    b. Prepare a table presenting the total interest paid over the life of the loan for terms of 5, 10, 15, 20, 25, and 30 years.

    c. Next, vary the "Term in months" to find the term for which the total interest paid over the life of the loan equals:
       (i) the original principal, and   (ii) 1.5 times the original principal.

22. **Use the Loan Amortization Chart** and its associated report to solve:
    a. Problem 1.   b. Problem 11.

15.2 Direct Calculation of the Interest and Principal Components of a Payment or Group of Payments

L04 Proper accounting procedures require a business to separate the principal and interest components of payments on amounts borrowed or loaned. Only the interest portion of a loan payment is an accounting expense for the borrower and an accounting revenue for the lender. *Individual* investors must also determine the interest portion of any loan payments they receive in order to report the interest income on their tax returns.

To calculate the total interest in a series of consecutive payments, you do not need to first construct a partial amortization table covering these payments, and then add the individual interest components. A similar statement applies to the total principal in a series of payments. In this section you will learn approaches that are more direct and more efficient.

You already know the basic concepts for calculating the interest and principal components of a *single* payment. That is,

> Interest component = i × Balance after the previous payment

Principal component = PMT − Interest component

Note that you can also obtain the principal component of a payment without first determining the interest component by using the idea:

> Principal component = $\left(\begin{array}{c}\text{Balance after the} \\ \text{previous payment}\end{array}\right) - \left(\begin{array}{c}\text{Balance after the} \\ \text{current payment}\end{array}\right)$

How can you extend the latter idea to obtain the total of the principal components in a group of consecutive payments? The combined effect of these principal components is to reduce the balance from its value just before the first of the payments, to the value just after the last payment in the series. That is,

$$\left(\begin{array}{c}\text{Total principal in a} \\ \text{series of payments}\end{array}\right) = \left(\begin{array}{c}\text{Balance before the} \\ \text{first of the payments}\end{array}\right) - \left(\begin{array}{c}\text{Balance after the} \\ \text{last of the payments}\end{array}\right)$$

Then

$$\left(\begin{array}{c}\text{Total interest in a} \\ \text{series of payments}\end{array}\right) = \left(\begin{array}{c}\text{Total of all the} \\ \text{payments in the series}\end{array}\right) - \left(\begin{array}{c}\text{Total principal in the} \\ \text{series of payments}\end{array}\right)$$

In our example problems, we will normally use the retrospective method for calculating loan balances.

EXAMPLE 15.2A

CALCULATING THE INTEREST AND PRINCIPAL COMPONENTS OF A SINGLE PAYMENT AND OF A GROUP OF CONSECUTIVE PAYMENTS

A $9500 personal loan at 7.5% compounded monthly is to be repaid over a four-year term by equal monthly payments.

a. Calculate the interest and principal components of the 29th payment.

b. How much interest will be paid in the second year of the loan?

SOLUTION

The loan payments form an ordinary simple annuity with

$$PV = \$9500 \quad n = 12(4) = 48 \quad \text{and} \quad i = \tfrac{7.5\%}{12} = 0.625\%$$

a. The size of the loan payments must be obtained before any balances can be calculated.

Solve for *PMT* in

$$PV = PMT\left[\frac{1 - (1 + i)^{-n}}{i}\right]$$

$$\$9500 = PMT\left[\frac{1 - (1.00625)^{-48}}{0.00625}\right]$$

$$= PMT(41.35837)$$

$$PMT = \frac{\$9500}{41.35837}$$

$$= \$229.6996$$

7.5	I/Y
P/Y 12	ENTER
(making $C/Y = P/Y = 12$)	
48	N
9500	PV
0	FV
CPT	PMT

Ans: -229.6996

Round the payment to $229.70.

We next want

$$\binom{\text{Interest component}}{\text{of Payment 29}} = i \times \binom{\text{Balance after}}{\text{28 payments}}$$

Using the retrospective method to calculate the balance after 28 payments,

$$\binom{\text{Balance after}}{\text{28 payments}} = \binom{\text{Future value of}}{\$9500 \text{ after 28 months}} - \binom{\text{Future value of the 28}}{\text{payments already made}}$$

$$= PV(1 + i)^n - PMT\left[\frac{(1 + i)^n - 1}{i}\right]$$

$$= \$9500(1.00625)^{28} - \$229.70\left[\frac{(1.00625)^{28} - 1}{0.00625}\right]$$

$$= \$11{,}310.678 - \$7004.844$$

$$= \$4305.83$$

Same *I/Y, C/Y, P/Y, PV*

28	N
229.70 +/−	PMT
CPT	FV

Ans: -4305.83

Hence,

$$\binom{\text{Interest component}}{\text{of Payment 29}} = 0.00625 \times \$4305.83 = \$26.91$$

and

$$\text{Principal component} = PMT - \text{Interest component}$$

$$= \$229.70 - \$26.91$$

$$= \$202.79$$

b. Total *interest* paid in Year 2 = 12(*PMT*) − Total *principal* paid in Year 2

where

$$\text{Total \textit{principal} paid in Year 2} = \text{Balance after Year 1} - \text{Balance after Year 2}$$

$$= \binom{\text{Balance after}}{\text{12 payments}} - \binom{\text{Balance after}}{\text{24 payments}}$$

Use the retrospective method to calculate both balances.

$$\binom{\text{Balance after}}{\text{12 payments}} = \binom{\text{Future value of}}{\$9500 \text{ after 12 months}} - \binom{\text{Future value of the 12}}{\text{payments already made}}$$

$$= \$9500(1.00625)^{12} - \$229.70\left[\frac{(1.00625)^{12} - 1}{0.00625}\right]$$

$$= \$7384.36$$

Same *I/Y, P/Y, C/Y*
Same *PV, PMT*

12	N
CPT	FV

Ans: -7384.36

$$\begin{pmatrix} \text{Balance after} \\ \text{24 payments} \end{pmatrix} = \begin{pmatrix} \text{Future value of} \\ \text{\$9500 after 24 months} \end{pmatrix} - \begin{pmatrix} \text{Future value of the 24} \\ \text{payments already made} \end{pmatrix}$$

$$= \$9500(1.00625)^{24} - \$229.70\left[\frac{(1.00625)^{24} - 1}{0.00625}\right]$$

$$= \$5104.47$$

Same *I/Y, P/Y, C/Y*
Same *PV, PMT*

24 | N |

| CPT | FV |

Ans: −5104.47

Therefore,

$$\text{Total principal paid in Year 2} = \$7384.36 - \$5104.47 = \$2279.89$$

and

$$\text{Total interest paid in Year 2} = 12(\$229.70) - \$2279.89 = \$476.51$$

Using the Texas Instruments BA II PLUS Amortization Worksheet This worksheet streamlines the calculation of the interest and principal components of a single payment, or of a group of consecutive payments. The worksheet will be employed for the financial calculator solutions in **Examples 15.2B** and **15.2C**.

EXAMPLE 15.2B

INTEREST AND PRINCIPAL COMPONENTS OF LOAN PAYMENTS THAT FORM A GENERAL ANNUITY

The monthly payments on a $10,000 loan at 7% compounded semiannually are $300. By how much will Payments 21 to 30 inclusive reduce the principal balance? What is the total interest in these payments?

SOLUTION

The loan payments form an ordinary *general* annuity having

$$PV = \$10{,}000, PMT = \$300 \text{ (except for the final payment)}, i = \tfrac{7\%}{2} = 3.5\%, \text{ and}$$

$$c = \frac{\text{Number of compoundings per year}}{\text{Number of payments per year}} = \frac{2}{12} = 0.1\overline{6}$$

We must use the periodic rate that matches the one-month payment interval.

$$i_2 = (1 + i)^c - 1 = 1.035^{0.1\overline{6}} - 1 = 0.0057500395$$

Reduction in principal = Balance after Payment 20 − Balance after Payment 30

Use the Retrospective Method to calculate both balances.

$$\begin{pmatrix} \text{Balance after} \\ \text{20 payments} \end{pmatrix} = \begin{pmatrix} \text{Future value of} \\ \text{\$10,000 after 20 months} \end{pmatrix} - \begin{pmatrix} \text{Future value of the 20} \\ \text{payments already made} \end{pmatrix}$$

$$= \$10{,}000(1.0057500395)^{20} - \$300\left[\frac{(1.0057500395)^{20} - 1}{0.0057500395}\right]$$

$$= \$4875.71$$

$$\begin{pmatrix} \text{Balance after} \\ \text{30 payments} \end{pmatrix} = \begin{pmatrix} \text{Future value of} \\ \text{\$10,000 after 30 months} \end{pmatrix} - \begin{pmatrix} \text{Future value of the 30} \\ \text{payments already made} \end{pmatrix}$$

$$= \$10{,}000(1.0057500395)^{30} - \$300\left[\frac{(1.0057500395)^{30} - 1}{0.0057500395}\right]$$

$$= \$2084.60$$

7 | I/Y |

| P/Y 12 | ENTER |

| C/Y 2 | ENTER |

10000 | PV |

300 | +/− | PMT |

| 2nd | AMORT |

21 | ENTER |

30 | ENTER |

↓   *BAL* =   2,084.60

↓   *PRN* = −2,791.11

↓   *INT* =   −208.89

Therefore,

$$\text{Reduction in principal} = \$4875.71 - \$2084.60 = \$2791.11$$

and

$$\text{Total interest paid} = 10(\$300.00) - \$2791.11 = \$208.89$$

Interest and Principal Components of Investment Annuity Payments

LO4 We normally think of the purchase of an annuity from a financial institution as an investment. The principal amount of the investment and the interest it earns generate the future stream of annuity payments. But the size and composition of the payments are no different if we take the following view of the transaction. In effect, the purchaser of the annuity "lends" the principal amount to the financial institution at the rate of interest earned by the annuity. The subsequent annuity payments repay the "loan." Therefore, we can use the concepts developed for loan payments to calculate an annuity's principal balance at any point, and to separate annuity payments into interest and principal components.

EXAMPLE 15.2C

CALCULATING THE INTEREST AND PRINCIPAL COMPONENTS OF PAYMENTS IN AN INVESTMENT ANNUITY

Joanna purchased a 20-year annuity with $100,000 accumulated in her RRSP. She receives equal payments at the end of every calendar quarter. The interest rate earned by the annuity is 5.6% compounded quarterly.

a. Calculate the interest component of the 15th payment.

b. Of the payments received in the 10th year, what dollar amount represents the recovery of principal from her initial investment of $100,000?

SOLUTION

a. We must first determine the size of the quarterly payment.

Substitute $PV = \$100,000$, $n = 20(4) = 80$, and $i = \frac{5.6\%}{4} = 1.4\%$ into Formula (11-2).

$$\$100,000 = PMT\left[\frac{1-(1.014)^{-80}}{0.014}\right]$$
$$= PMT(47.941138)$$
$$PMT = \$2085.8913$$

| 5.6 | I/Y |
| P/Y | 4 ENTER |

(making $C/Y = P/Y = 4$)

80	N
100000 +/−	PV
0	FV
CPT	PMT

Ans: 2,085.8913

Round *PMT* to $2085.89.

$$\left(\begin{array}{c}\text{Interest component}\\ \text{of Payment 15}\end{array}\right) = i \times \left(\begin{array}{c}\text{Balance after}\\ 14 \text{ payments}\end{array}\right)$$

Do not clear memories.

2085.89 PMT

Using the Retrospective Method,

$$\left(\begin{array}{c}\text{Balance after}\\ 14 \text{ payments}\end{array}\right) = \left(\begin{array}{c}\text{Future value of}\\ \$10{,}000 \text{ after } 14 \text{ quarters}\end{array}\right) - \left(\begin{array}{c}\text{Future value of the } 14\\ \text{payments already made}\end{array}\right)$$

$$= \$100{,}000(1.014)^{14} - \$2085.89\left[\frac{(1.014)^{14}-1}{0.014}\right]$$

$$= \$89{,}472.84$$

2nd AMORT

| 15 | ENTER |
| 15 | ENTER |

↓ $BAL = -88{,}639.57$
↓ $PRN = \quad 833.27$
↓ $INT = \quad 1{,}252.62$

Hence,

Interest component of Payment 15 $= 0.014 \times \$89{,}472.84 = \$1252.62$

b. Payments 37 to 40 inclusive will be received in the 10th year.

$$\binom{\text{Total principal in}}{\text{payments 37 to 40}} = \binom{\text{Balance after}}{\text{36 payments}} - \binom{\text{Balance after}}{\text{40 payments}}$$

where

$$\binom{\text{Balance after}}{\text{36 payments}} = \binom{\text{Future value of}}{\$100{,}000 \text{ after 36 quarters}} - \binom{\text{Future value of the 36}}{\text{payments already made}}$$

$$= \$100{,}000(1.014)^{36} - \$2085.89\left[\frac{(1.014)^{36} - 1}{0.014}\right]$$

$$= \$68{,}176.99$$

Similarly, the balance after 40 payments is $63,555.41. Therefore,

Principal received in Year 10 = $68,176.99 − $63,555.41 = $4621.58

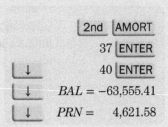

2nd	AMORT
37	ENTER
↓	40 ENTER
↓	$BAL = -63{,}555.41$
↓	$PRN = \;\;\; 4{,}621.58$

 CONCEPT QUESTIONS

1. Will a loan's balance midway through its amortization period be (pick one):
   (i) more than,
   (ii) less than, or
   (iii) equal to half of the original principal? Explain.

2. If the loan payments and interest rate remain unchanged, will it take longer to reduce a loan's balance from $20,000 to $10,000 than to reduce the balance from $10,000 to $0? Explain briefly.

3. The calculated monthly payment on a loan amortized over five years is rounded up by 0.2 cents to get to the nearest cent.
   a. Will the adjusted final payment be more than or less than the regular payment?
   b. Will the difference between the regular and the final payment be (pick one):
   (i) more than,
   (ii) less than, or
   (iii) equal to 0.2 cents × 60 = 12 cents? Explain.

4. The calculated monthly payment on a loan amortized over 10 years is rounded down by 0.3 cents to get to the nearest cent.
   a. Will the adjusted final payment be more than or less than the regular payment?
   b. Will the difference between the regular and the final payment be (pick one):
   (i) more than,
   (ii) less than, or
   (iii) equal to 0.3 cents × 120 = 36 cents? Explain.

EXERCISE 15.2

Answers to the odd-numbered problems are at the end of the book.

 ***Spreadsheet templates:*** *Connect provides a partially completed Excel template for calculating the principal and interest components of a single annuity payment or of a group of consecutive payments. You can use this template in many of the problems in Exercise 15.2. (You cannot use the template for a problem in which you are given the payment but not the number of payments.) Go to the Student Edition of Connect and find "CUMIPMT & CUMPRINC for Any Annuity" under the Student Resources for Chapter 15.*

In problems throughout this Exercise, round the calculated loan payments to the nearest cent before going on to calculate loan balances and/or interest and principal components.

BASIC PROBLEMS

1. A $40,000 loan at 6.6% compounded monthly will be repaid by monthly payments over ten years.
   a. Calculate the interest component of Payment 35.
   b. Calculate the principal component of Payment 63.
   c. Calculate the reduction of principal in Year 1.
   d. Calculate the reduction of principal in Year 10.

2. Monthly payments are required on a $45,000 loan at 6.0% compounded monthly. The loan has an amortization period of 15 years.
   a. Calculate the interest component of Payment 137.
   b. Calculate the principal component of Payment 76.
   c. Calculate the interest paid in Year 1.
   d. Calculate the interest paid in Year 14.

3. The interest rate on a $14,000 loan is 8.4% compounded semiannually. Semiannual payments will pay off the loan in seven years.
   a. Calculate the interest component of Payment 10.
   b. Calculate the principal component of Payment 3.
   c. Calculate the interest paid in Year 6.
   d. How much do Payments 3 to 6 inclusive reduce the principal balance?

4. A five-year loan of $25,000 at 7.2% compounded quarterly requires quarterly payments.
   a. Calculate the interest component of Payment 10.
   b. Calculate the principal component of Payment 13.
   c. Calculate the total interest in Payments 5 to 10 inclusive.
   d. Calculate the principal paid in Year 4.

5. A $125,000 loan at 6.0% compounded semiannually will be repaid by monthly payments over a 20-year amortization period.
   a. Calculate the interest component of Payment 188.
   b. Calculate the principal component of Payment 101.
   c. Calculate the reduction of principal in Year 1.
   d. Calculate the reduction of principal in Year 20.

6. Semiannual payments are required on an $80,000 loan at 8.0% compounded annually. The loan has an amortization period of 15 years.
   a. Calculate the interest component of Payment 5.
   b. Calculate the principal component of Payment 17.
   c. Calculate the interest paid in Year 1.
   d. Calculate the interest paid in Year 14.

7. The interest rate on a $50,000 loan is 7.6% compounded semiannually. Quarterly payments will pay off the loan in ten years.
   a. Calculate the interest component of Payment 8.
   b. Calculate the principal component of Payment 33.
   c. Calculate the total interest in Payments 21 to 30 inclusive.
   d. Calculate the reduction of principal in Year 3.

8. A five-year loan of $20,000 at 6.8% compounded quarterly requires monthly payments.
   a. Calculate the interest component of Payment 47.
   b. Calculate the principal component of Payment 21.
   c. Calculate the interest paid in Year 2.
   d. How much do Payments 40 to 45 inclusive reduce the principal balance?

9. The monthly payments on a $15,000 loan at 6.0% compounded monthly are $275.
   a. Calculate the interest component of Payment 13.
   b. Calculate the principal component of Payment 44.
   c. Calculate the final payment.

10. Quarterly payments of $3000 are required on an $80,000 loan at 8.0% compounded quarterly.
    a. Calculate the interest component of Payment 30.
    b. Calculate the principal component of Payment 9.
    c. Calculate the final payment.

11. The interest rate on a $100,000 loan is 7.2% compounded semiannually. The monthly payments on the loan are $700.
    a. Calculate the interest component of Payment 221.
    b. Calculate the principal component of Payment 156.
    c. Calculate the final payment.

12. A $30,000 loan at 6.7% compounded annually requires monthly payments of $450.
    a. Calculate the interest component of Payment 29.
    b. Calculate the principal component of Payment 65.
    c. Calculate the final payment.

13. A $37,000 loan at 8.2% compounded semiannually is to be repaid by equal semiannual payments over 10 years.
    a. What will be the principal component of the sixth payment?
    b. What will be the interest component of the 16th payment?
    c. How much will Payments 6 to 15 inclusive reduce the principal?
    d. How much interest will be paid in the third year?
    e. What will be the final payment?

14. A 10-year annuity providing a rate of return of 5.6% compounded quarterly was purchased for $25,000. The annuity makes payments at the end of each quarter.
    a. How much of the 25th payment is interest?
    b. What is the principal portion of the 13th payment?
    c. What is the total interest in Payments 11 to 20 inclusive?
    d. How much is the principal reduction in the second year?
    e. What is the final payment?

Problems 15 and 16 are variations of Problems 13 and 14, respectively. The size of the regular payment is given instead of the duration of the loan or investment annuity.

15. A $37,000 loan at 8.2% compounded semiannually is to be repaid by semiannual payments of $2500 (except for a smaller final payment).
    a. What will be the principal component of the 16th payment?
    b. What will be the interest portion of the sixth payment?
    c. How much will Payments 8 to 14 inclusive reduce the principal balance?
    d. How much interest will be paid in the fifth year?
    e. What will be the final payment?

16. An annuity providing a rate of return of 5.6% compounded quarterly was purchased for $27,000. The annuity pays $800 at the end of each quarter (except for a smaller final payment).
    a. How much of the 16th payment is interest?
    b. What is the principal portion of the 33rd payment?
    c. What is the total interest in Payments 20 to 25 inclusive?
    d. How much will the principal be reduced by payments in the sixth year?
    e. What will be the final payment?

INTERMEDIATE PROBLEMS

17. Guy borrowed $8000 at 7.8% compounded monthly and agreed to repay the loan in equal quarterly payments over four years.
    a. How much of the fifth payment will be interest?
    b. What will be the principal component of the 11th payment?
    c. How much interest will be paid by Payments 5 to 12 inclusive?
    d. How much will the principal be reduced in the second year?
    e. What will be the final payment?

18. A 25-year annuity was purchased with $225,000 that had accumulated in an RRSP. The annuity provides a semiannually compounded rate of return of 5.2% and makes equal month-end payments.
    a. What amount of principal will be included in Payment 206?
    b. What will be the interest portion of Payment 187?
    c. How much will Payments 50 to 100 inclusive reduce the principal balance?
    d. How much interest will be paid in the 14th year?
    e. What will be the final payment?

19. Guy borrowed $8000 at 7.8% compounded monthly and agreed to make quarterly payments of $500 (except for a smaller final payment).
    a. How much of the 11th payment will be interest?
    b. What will be the principal component of the sixth payment?
    c. How much interest will be paid by Payments 3 to 9, inclusive?
    d. How much will the principal be reduced in the third year?
    e. What will be the final payment?

20. An annuity paying $1400 at the end of each month (except for a smaller final payment) was purchased with $225,000 that had accumulated in an RRSP. The annuity provides a semiannually compounded rate of return of 5.2%.
    a. What amount of principal will be included in Payment 137?
    b. What will be the interest portion of Payment 204?
    c. How much will the principal be reduced by Payments 145 to 156 inclusive?
    d. How much interest will be paid in the 20th year?
    e. What will be the final payment?

21. Ms. Esperanto obtained a $40,000 home equity loan at 7.5% compounded monthly.
    a. What will she pay monthly if the amortization period is 15 years?
    b. How much of the payment made at the end of the fifth year will go toward principal and how much will go toward interest?
    c. What will be the balance on the loan after five years?
    d. How much interest did she pay during the fifth year?

22. Elkford Logging's bank will fix the interest rate on a $60,000 loan at 8.1% compounded monthly for the first four-year term of an eight-year amortization period. Monthly payments are required on the loan.
    a. If the prevailing interest rate on four-year loans at the beginning of the second term is 7.5% compounded monthly, what will be the monthly payments for the last four years?
    b. What will be the interest portion of the 23rd payment?
    c. Calculate the principal portion of the 53rd payment.

ADVANCED PROBLEMS

23. Christina has just borrowed $12,000 at 9% compounded semiannually. Since she expects to receive a $10,000 inheritance in two years when she turns 25, she has arranged with her credit union to make monthly payments that will reduce the principal balance to exactly $10,000 in two years.
    a. What monthly payments will she make?
    b. What will be the interest portion of the ninth payment?
    c. Determine the principal portion of the 16th payment.

24. Elkford Logging's bank will fix the interest rate on a $60,000 loan at 8.1% compounded monthly for the first four years. After four years, the interest rate will be fixed at the prevailing five-year rate. Monthly payments of $800 (except for a smaller final payment) are required on the loan.
    a. If the interest rate after four years is 7.5% compounded monthly, when will the loan be paid off?
    b. What will be the amount of the final payment?
    c. What is the interest portion of the 32nd payment?
    d. Calculate the principal portion of the 58th payment.

Mc Graw Hill connect

25. **Using the Loan Amortization Chart** In Chapter 15 of the Student Edition on Connect, find "Loan Amortization Chart." (The instructions for using the chart are provided in Problem 21 in Section 15.1.) Use this chart and its associated report to solve:
    a. Problem 21.
    b. Problem 22.

Mc Graw Hill connect

26. **Using the Composition of Loan Payments Chart** An interactive chart for investigating the composition of loan payments is provided on Connect. In Chapter 15 of the Student Edition, find "Composition of Loan Payments."

    The chart provides cells for entering the essential information about a loan (PV, j, m, PMT, and payments/year). You can then compare the composition (interest and principal components) of any two payments. Simply enter the serial numbers of the two payments and then click on the "Submit" button. Two bar diagrams provide a visual comparison of the interest and principal components. The actual numerical values are also displayed.

Consider a $120,000 mortgage loan at 6.5% compounded semiannually. Monthly payments of $800 will pay off the loan in 25 years and 4 months.

  a. How much more interest is paid by the 20th payment than the 220th payment?

  b. How long does it take before the interest component of a payment drops below 50%?

  c. Which payment number is closest to being comprised of:

     (i) 75% interest?

     (ii) 25% interest?

  d. Which payment number comes closest to having a mix of principal and interest that is the opposite of the first payment's mix?

  e. Which payment number comes closest to having double the principal component of the 5th payment?

  f. Which payment number comes closest to having half the interest component of the 10th payment?

15.3 Mortgage Loans: Fundamentals

Basic Concepts and Definitions

A mortgage loan is a loan secured by some *physical* property. Often the borrowed money is used to purchase the property. If the property securing the loan is not real estate, the mortgage is called a *chattel* mortgage. This section will deal only with mortgage loans secured by real property.

The **face value** of the mortgage is the original principal amount that the borrower promises to repay. In legal language, the borrower is called the **mortgagor** and the lender is called the **mortgagee**. The mortgage contract sets out the terms and conditions of the loan. It also specifies the lender's remedies should the borrower default on repayment of the loan. The key remedy is the ultimate power to foreclose on the property and cause it to be sold to recover the amounts owed. At the time a mortgage loan is granted, the lender registers the mortgage on the title of the property at the provincial government's land titles office. Anyone can search the title to determine potential claims against the property.

Even though a homeowner may already have a mortgage loan, the remaining equity in the home can sometimes be used as security for another mortgage loan. The second lender's claim will rank behind the existing claim of the first lender. If the borrower defaults on the first mortgage loan, the first lender's claim must be satisfied before any claim of the second lender. Because of this ranking of the claims, the existing mortgage is referred to as the *first mortgage* and the additional mortgage as the *second mortgage*. Since a second mortgage lender is exposed to greater risk, the interest rate on a second mortgage is significantly higher than the rate on a first mortgage. Loans advertised by financial institutions as "home equity loans" or "home improvement loans" will often be secured by a second mortgage.

The most common amortization period for a mortgage loan is 25 years. However, a lender will usually commit to a fixed interest rate for only a shorter period or term. The **term** of a mortgage loan is the length of time from the date on which the loan is advanced to the date on which the remaining principal balance is due and payable. Most institutional lenders offer terms of six months to seven years with the very rare occurrence of 25-year terms. At the expiry of the loan's term, the lender will normally renew the loan for another term, but at the prevailing market rate of interest on the date of renewal. The payments are adjusted so that the borrower continues with the original amortization period but at the new interest rate.

Calculating the Payment and Balance

L05 The federal Interest Act requires that the mortgage contract "contains a statement showing ... the rate of interest chargeable, calculated yearly or half-yearly, not in advance." In our terminology, the interest rate must be disclosed as the equivalent semiannually compounded nominal rate or the equivalent annually compounded rate.[2] The semiannually compounded rate has become the industry standard for disclosure in the mortgage contract. Mortgage interest rates advertised by most financial institutions are also semiannually compounded rates (even though the compounding frequency is not usually stated). Most mortgage loans are set up for monthly payments. With interest compounded semiannually, the monthly payments form an ordinary *general* annuity having

$$c = \frac{\text{Number of compoundings per year}}{\text{Number of payments per year}} = \frac{2}{12} = \frac{1}{6} = 0.1\overline{6}$$

The mortgage interest rates quoted by a minority of credit unions and a majority of independent mortgage brokers are monthly compounded rates. Monthly payments then form an ordinary *simple* annuity.

Most mortgage lenders will agree to semimonthly, biweekly, or weekly payments instead of monthly payments. For the *same dollar total* of mortgage payments in a year, you will pay off more principal if you spread the total over more frequent smaller payments than over less frequent larger payments. With more frequent smaller payments, money is (on average) paid sooner resulting in earlier reduction of principal and lower subsequent interest charges.

Usually the borrower chooses a standard amortization period of 15, 20, 25, or 30 years. The payments for the initial term are then calculated as though the interest rate is fixed for the *entire* amortization period. Occasionally, the borrower has a preference for a particular payment size. As long as the resulting amortization period is no more than 30 years,[3] most mortgage lenders will agree to such a proposal.

The principal balance on the mortgage loan after any payment may be calculated using either the prospective method or (preferably) the retrospective method. The balance at the end of a mortgage's term becomes, in effect, the beginning loan amount for the next term. The lender calculates a new payment size based on current interest rates and (normally) a continuation of the original amortization period. Part (b) of **Example 15.3A** demonstrates this procedure.

The principal and interest components of any mortgage payment may be calculated as described in **Section 15.2** for other term loans. Particularly when the amortization period is more than 20 years, the payments in the first few years are primarily interest. Consider a mortgage loan at 8.5% compounded semiannually with a 25-year amortization period. **Figure 15.3** shows how the interest and principal components of the fixed monthly payments change over the lifetime of the loan.

---

[2] The Interest Act makes the lender liable for a very severe penalty for failing to disclose the rate of interest as required by the Act. In that event, the Interest Act states that "no interest whatever shall be chargeable, payable, or recoverable, on any part of the principal money advanced." The borrower would be entitled to a refund of any interest already paid and consequently would have the loan on an interest-free basis.

[3] In July 2012, the government reduced the maximum amortization period on a mortgage to 25 years from 30 years in cases where the borrower has less than a 20% down payment. In cases where the down payment exceeds 20%, regulated mortgage lenders can offer amortization periods of up to 35 years. Unregulated private lenders may offer longer periods.

FIGURE 15.3   The Composition of Mortgage Payments During a 25-Year Amortization

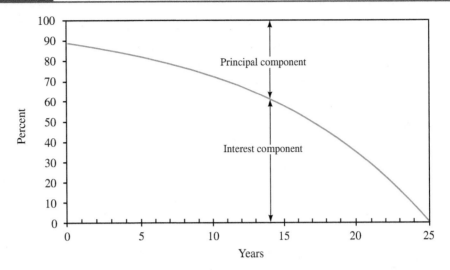

At any point in the 25-year amortization, the interest portion of a payment is the vertical distance below the curve. The principal portion of the payment is the remainder of the 100%; that is, the vertical distance above the curve. For example, the payment at the end of Year 14 is about 60% interest and 40% principal. During the first five years, more than 80% of every payment is interest. Consequently, the principal balance declines very slowly during the early years (as you will see in **Figure 15.4**).

FIGURE 15.4   A Mortgage's Declining Balance During a 25-Year Amortization

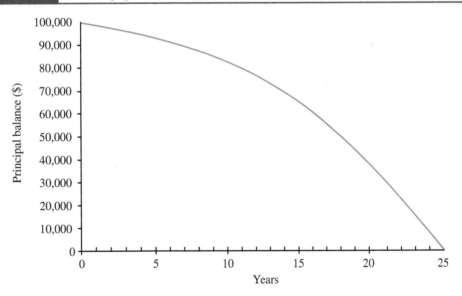

Figure 15.4 illustrates how the balance owed on a $100,000 mortgage loan at 8.5% compounded semiannually declines during its 25-year amortization period. As expected from the preceding discussion, the balance decreases slowly in the early years. It takes about one-quarter of the amortization period to pay off the first $10,000 (10% of the original loan). Almost *three-quarters* of the amortization period is required to reduce the balance to *one-half* of the original principal. The principal declines at an accelerating rate in later years as an ever-increasing portion of each payment is applied to the principal.

EXAMPLE 15.3A

CALCULATING THE PAYMENTS ON A MORTGAGE LOAN AT ITS BEGINNING AND AT RENEWAL

A $50,000 mortgage loan is written with a 20-year amortization period, a three-year term, and an interest rate of 4.5% compounded semiannually. Payments are made monthly. Calculate:

a. The balance at the end of the three-year term.

b. The size of the payments upon renewal for a five-year term at 4% compounded semiannually (with the loan maintaining its original 20-year amortization).

SOLUTION

a. Before the balance can be calculated, we must obtain the monthly payment. Use the amortization period rather than the term of the mortgage when calculating the payment. That is, calculate the monthly payment that will repay the loan in 20 years if the interest rate remains at 4.5% compounded semiannually. The mortgage payments constitute an ordinary general annuity having

$$PV = \$50,000 \quad n = 12\,(20) = 240 \quad i = \tfrac{4.5\%}{2} = 2.25\% \quad \text{and} \quad c = \tfrac{2}{12} = 0.1\overline{6}$$

The periodic interest rate that matches the one-month payment interval is

$$i_2 = (1 + i)^c - 1 = 1.0225^{0.1\overline{6}} - 1 = 0.00371532 \text{ per month}$$

Solve Formula (11-2) for *PMT*.

$$\$50,000 = PMT\left(\frac{1 - 1.00371532^{-240}}{0.00371532}\right)$$

$$\$50,000 = PMT(158.62814)$$

$$PMT = \$315.20$$

4.5	I/Y
P/Y 12	ENTER
C/Y 2	ENTER
240	N
50000	PV
0	FV
CPT	PMT

Ans: −315.203

Using the retrospective method, the balance after three years will be

$$\binom{\text{Balance after}}{36 \text{ payments}} = \binom{\text{Future value of }\$50,000}{\text{after 36 months}} - \binom{\text{Future value of the 36}}{\text{payments already made}}$$

$$= \$50,000(1.00371532)^{36} - \$315.20\left(\frac{1.00371532^{36} - 1}{0.00371532}\right)$$

$$= \$45,024.26$$

The balance after the initial three-year term will be $45,024.26.

Same *I/Y, PV, P/Y, C/Y*

36	N
315.20 +/−	PMT
CPT	FV

Ans: −45,024.26

b. The renewal is handled in the same way as a new mortgage whose original principal equals the balance from part (a), but with a 17-year amortization period and an interest rate of 4% compounded semiannually. That is,

$$PV = \$45,024.26 \quad n = 12(17) = 204 \quad i = \tfrac{4\%}{2} = 2\% \quad \text{and} \quad c = \tfrac{2}{12} = 0.1\overline{6}$$

The periodic interest rate that matches the one-month payment interval is

$$i_2 = (1 + i)^c - 1 = 1.02^{0.1\overline{6}} - 1 = 0.00330589$$

Solve Formula (11-2) for *PMT*.

$$\$45,024.26 = PMT\left(\frac{1 - 1.00330589^{-204}}{0.00330589}\right)$$

$$\$45,024.26 = PMT(148.21176)$$

$$PMT = \$303.78$$

Upon renewal of the mortgage at 4% compounded semiannually, the payments will drop to $303.78 per month.

Same *P/Y, C/Y*

4	I/Y
204	N
45024.26	PV
0	FV
CPT	PMT

Ans: −303.78

EXAMPLE 15.3B

CALCULATIONS WHERE THE MORTGAGE PAYMENT IS ROUNDED TO THE NEXT HIGHER $10

The monthly payments for the first five-year term of a $20,000 mortgage loan were based on a 10-year amortization and an interest rate of 7% compounded semiannually. The payments were rounded up to the next higher $10.

a. Calculate the size of the monthly payments.

b. What is the principal balance at the end of the five-year term?

c. If the interest rate at renewal is 6.6% compounded semiannually for a second five-year term, calculate the new monthly payments also rounded to the next higher $10.

d. Calculate the size of the final payment.

SOLUTION

a. The payments form an ordinary general annuity with

$$PV = \$20,000 \quad n = 12(10) = 120 \quad i = \tfrac{7\%}{2} = 3.5\% \quad \text{and} \quad c = \tfrac{2}{12} = 0.1\overline{6}$$

The periodic rate for the one-month payment interval is

$$i_2 = (1 + i)^c - 1 = 1.035^{0.1\overline{6}} - 1 = 0.00575003948 \text{ per month}$$

Solve Formula (11-2) for PMT.

$$\$20,000 = PMT\left[\frac{1 - 1.00575003948^{-120}}{0.00575003948}\right]$$

$$PMT = \$231.19$$

Rounded to the next higher $10, the monthly payment is $240.

7	I/Y
P/Y 12	ENTER
C/Y 2	ENTER
120	N
20000	PV
0	FV
CPT	PMT

Ans: −231.19

b. The balance after five years is

$$\begin{pmatrix}\text{Balance after} \\ \text{60 payments}\end{pmatrix} = \begin{pmatrix}\text{Future value of \$20,000} \\ \text{after 60 months}\end{pmatrix} - \begin{pmatrix}\text{Future value of the 60} \\ \text{payments already made}\end{pmatrix}$$

$$= \$20,000(1.00575003948)^{60} - \$240\left[\frac{1.00575003948^{60} - 1}{0.00575003948}\right]$$

$$= \$11,074.06$$

Same I/Y, PV, P/Y, C/Y

60	N
240 +/−	PMT
CPT	FV

Ans: −11,074.06

c. The balance from part (b) becomes the initial loan amount for the second five-year term. With

$$PV = \$11,074.06 \quad n = 60 \quad \text{and} \quad i = \tfrac{6.6\%}{2} = 3.3\%$$

we obtain

$$i_2 = (1 + i)^c - 1 = 1.033^{0.1\overline{6}} - 1 = 0.00542586532$$

and

$$\$11,074.06 = PMT\left[\frac{1 - 1.00542586532^{-60}}{0.00542586532}\right]$$

$$PMT = \$216.73$$

Rounded to the next higher $10, the monthly payment on renewal will be $220.

Same P/Y, C/Y

6.6	I/Y
60	N
11074.06	PV
0	FV
CPT	PMT

Ans: −216.73

d. Since the payment size has been rounded up, it may require fewer than 60 payments to pay off the debt, and the final payment will be less than $220. The number of payments is

$$n = -\frac{\ln\left(1 - \frac{i \times PV}{PMT}\right)}{\ln(1 + i)}$$

$$= -\frac{\ln\left(1 - \frac{0.00542586532 \times \$11,074.06}{\$220}\right)}{\ln(1.00542586532)}$$

$$= 58.95$$

Same *I/Y, PV, P/Y, C/Y*

220 [+/−] [PMT]

0 [FV]

[CPT] [N]

Ans: = 58.95

There will be 59 payments in the second term. The final payment will be the balance after 58 payments plus one month's interest. That is,

Final payment = Balance after 58 payments × (1 + *i*)

$$\binom{\text{Balance after}}{\text{58 payments}} = \binom{\text{Future value of \$11,074.06}}{\text{after 58 months}} - \binom{\text{Future value of the 58}}{\text{payments already made}}$$

$$= \$11,074.06(1.00542586532)^{58} - \$220\left[\frac{1.00542586532^{58} - 1}{0.00542586532}\right]$$

$$= \$208.04$$

Same *I/Y, P/Y, C/Y*

Same *PV, PMT*

58 [N]

[CPT] [FV]

Ans: −208.04

Hence,

Final payment = $208.04 × 1.00542586532 = $209.17

Qualifying for a Mortgage Loan

LO7 Mortgage lenders must determine whether a mortgage loan is adequately secured by the property, and whether the borrower has the financial capacity to make the mortgage payments. To do this, they calculate and set upper limits on three ratios:[4]

1. *Loan-to-value ratio* $= \dfrac{\text{Principal amount of the loan}}{\text{Lending value of the property}} \times 100\% \le 80\%$

The 80% *maximum* for this ratio means the borrower's *minimum* down payment is 20% of the "lending value." (The lending value is the lesser of the purchase price and the market value as determined by a certified appraiser.)

2. *Gross debt service ratio* (GDS ratio):

$$\text{GDS ratio} = \frac{\binom{\text{Total monthly payments for mortgage,}}{\text{condo fees, property taxes, and heat}}}{\text{Gross monthly income}} \times 100\% \le 39\%$$

The upper limit on this ratio means that the major costs of home ownership should not require more than 39% of the borrower's gross income.

---

[4] The indicated upper limits are typical for what are called "conventional first mortgages."

3. *Total debt service ratio* (TDS ratio):

$$\text{TDS ratio} = \frac{\left(\begin{array}{c}\text{Total monthly payments for mortgage,}\\ \text{property taxes, heat, and other debt}\end{array}\right)}{\text{Gross monthly income}} \times 100\% \leq 44\%$$

The upper limit on this ratio means that payments related to home ownership *and all other debt* should not require more than 44% of the borrower's gross income.

A borrower must qualify on *all three* ratios. The upper limits for the GDS and TDS ratios vary somewhat from one lender to another and can change depending on the borrower's credit score. Maximums of 35% for GDS and 42% for TDS are common where the borrower's credit score is below 680 and the borrower is considered to be a higher risk.

 POINT OF INTEREST

No-Money-Down Mortgages Are No More

The federal government plays an important role in setting and regulating the rules surrounding home ownership in Canada. The Canadian Mortgage and Housing Corporation (CMHC), formed in 1946, was established to help make home ownership a reality for World War II veterans returning home. CMHC offered new, low-cost housing with low mortgage rates, small down payments, and easy repayment terms. Today, the main function of CMHC is to provide insurance to Canadian mortgage lenders to protect them against mortgage defaults by borrowers who do not meet the minimum criteria for getting a conventional mortgage but still want to make their dream of owning a home a reality.

© Vstock LLC/Getty Images

There was a time in the mid 2000s when you could purchase a home with no money down and take 40 years to pay it off. Housing prices were on the rise and mortgage lending rates were low. Today, you need a minimum down payment of 5% of the purchase price and the maximum length of time to pay off your mortgage is only 25 years. So why do the mortgage rules seem to constantly change?

To understand why the government of Canada "tweaks" the mortgage rules every so often, consider what happened in the United States in the mid 2000s. Just like in Canada in the early 2000s, mortgage rates were dropping and there was high demand in the housing market in the United States. This increased demand led to a sharp increase in housing prices known as a "housing bubble." Lenders, viewing mortgages as safe investments with good collateral, wanted to get more people into homes so they started to extend mortgages to buyers with bad credit, no down payments, and no proof of income. These "subprime mortgages" had a high chance of default but the lenders were not too worried since they could foreclose on the property in the event the borrower failed to repay the mortgage. As expected, people did fail to repay their mortgages—and as the number of mortgage defaults rose, banks were foreclosing on an ever-increasing number of homes that they could not re-sell. As a result, housing prices dropped, the housing bubble burst, and even the people who were paying their mortgages found that the amount they owed on their mortgage soon exceeded the value of the property. Many homeowners simply walked away from their homes. The complex mortgage lending structure in the U.S. involved many players besides the initial lenders and the ripple effect of the housing market collapse led to the failure of 25 banks in the United States in 2008.

While Canadian mortgage rules were already tighter than those in the U.S., in that same year (2008) major changes started to happen for CMHC-insured mortgages in Canada. The no-money-down mortgage became obsolete, with all borrowers requiring a minimum 5% down payment. Any mortgage with a down payment of less than 20% requires insurance. The insurance premium is calculated as a percentage of the mortgage loan amount and varies depending on the size of the down payment. Currently, you would pay a 3.6% premium on your mortgaged amount with a 5% down payment. This premium amount is also subject to sales tax in Manitoba, Ontario, and Quebec.

The following table outlines some of the changes that occurred for CMHC-insured mortgages after 2006. For people looking to take advantage of the increased market value of their property, refinancing is available based on the market value of the property at the time of refinancing. The limits for this are shown in the fourth column of the table, and some of the other changes made that affect mortgages in Canada appear in the last column.

Year	Minimum Down Payment	Maximum Amortization Period	Limits for Refinancing	Other
2006	0%	40 years	95%	
2008	5%	35 years	90%	Minimum credit score 620
2010	5%	35 years	90%	All borrowers must meet standards for a five-year fixed rate mortgage
				Minimum 20% down needed for non–owner occupied properties
2011	5%	30 years	85%	CMHC no longer backs lines of credit secured by homes (home equity lines of credit)
2012	5%	25 years	80%	CMHC no longer backs mortgages for homes with a purchase price of $1M or more
2016	5%	25 years	80%	Homes priced at over $500,000 require a 15% down payment for the portion of the price between $500,000 and $999,999

In January 2018 the mortgage stress test rules came into effect for all Canadians, whether they are looking to qualify for a new mortgage or renew their mortgage. The stress test requires that anyone applying for a mortgage loan must qualify for the loan at either the Bank of Canada's five-year benchmark rate (5.34% as of April 2019) or the rate offered by their lender plus 2%—whichever is higher. The main goal of the stress test is to ensure that home buyers will be able to afford their mortgage even if interest rates increase on renewal.

QUESTIONS

1. Compare the down payment required in 2010 and 2016 for a property with a purchase price of:
   a. $250,000   **b.** $750,000
2. Calculate and compare the monthly payment for each of the properties in Question 1 given an interest rate of 5% compounded semiannually with the maximum amortization period for 2010 and 2016.

EXAMPLE 15.3C

DETERMINING THE MAXIMUM MORTGAGE LOAN FOR WHICH A BORROWER QUALIFIES

The Schusters have saved $65,000 for the down payment on a home. Their gross monthly income is $6300. They want to know the maximum conventional mortgage loan for which they can qualify in order to determine the highest price they can pay for a home. They have 18 payments of $600 per month remaining on their car loan. Their bank has upper limits of 32% for the GDS ratio and 40% for the TDS ratio.

a. Allowing for property taxes of $300 per month and heating costs of $225 per month, what maximum monthly mortgage payment do the GDS and TDS ratios permit?

b. What is the maximum mortgage loan for which the Schusters can qualify? (Use a 25-year amortization and an interest rate of 5.34% compounded semiannually for a five-year term. Round the answer to the nearest $100.)

c. Based on a $65,000 down payment and the maximum loan from part (b), what is the highest price they can pay for a home? Round the answer to the nearest $100.

SOLUTION

a. The GDS ratio allows

$$\frac{\left(\begin{array}{c}\text{Maximum mortgage payment}\\ +\text{ property taxes} + \text{heating cost}\end{array}\right)}{\text{Gross income}} = 0.32$$

That is,

$$\frac{\text{Maximum mortgage payment} + \$300 + \$255}{\$6300} = 0.32$$

Hence,

$$\text{Maximum mortgage payment} + \$300 + \$225 = 0.32(\$6300)$$
$$\text{Maximum mortgage payment} = 0.32(\$6300) - \$525$$
$$= \$1491$$

The TDS ratio allows

$$\frac{\left(\begin{array}{c}\text{Maximum payments on all debt} \\ + \text{ property taxes} + \text{heating cost}\end{array}\right)}{\text{Gross income}} = 0.40$$

Hence,

$$\text{Maximum mortgage payment} + \$300 + \$225 + \$600 = 0.40(\$6300)$$
$$\text{Maximum mortgage payment} = 0.40(\$6300) - \$1125$$
$$= \$1395$$

For the Schusters' situation, the TDS ratio is the more restrictive ratio. It limits the maximum mortgage payment to $1395 per month.

b. The TDS ratio restricts the Schusters to a maximum mortgage payment of $1395 per month. For a loan at 5.34% compounded semiannually with a 25-year amortization,

$$n = 12(25) = 300 \quad i = \tfrac{5.34\%}{2} = 2.67\% \quad c = 0.1\overline{6} \quad \text{and} \quad i_2 = 1.0267^{0.1\overline{6}} - 1 = 0.004401287$$

The maximum loan permitted by the TDS ratio is

$$PV = \text{Present value of 300 payments of } \$1395$$

$$= \$1395\left[\frac{1 - 1.004401287^{-300}}{0.004401287}\right]$$

$$= \$232,100 \text{ rounded to the nearest } \$100$$

c. Combining the maximum loan with the $65,000 down payment, the Schusters would have

$$\$232,100 + \$65,000 = \$297,100$$

available to purchase a home, subject to satisfying the criterion for a conventional mortgage. If they purchase a home for $297,100, the loan-to-value ratio[5] would be

$$\frac{\$232,100}{\$297,100} \times 100\% = 78.12\%$$

Since the ratio is less than 80%, the Schusters meet the loan-to-value criterion for a conventional mortgage.

Therefore, $297,100 is the maximum price they can pay for a home.

---

[5] Mortgage lenders usually base the loan-to-value ratio on the lesser of the purchase price or the market value placed on the property by an independent appraiser. In this example, the appraised value would have to be at least $232,100 ÷ 0.8 = $290,125 for the Schusters to qualify for a $232,100 mortgage loan. The Schusters also need to keep in mind that they will have significant legal, appraisal, survey, and registration costs in connection with the purchase of the home. A general rule of thumb is to allow 1.5% of the purchase price for these "closing costs."

POINT OF INTEREST

An Analysis of the Interest "Savings" from Choosing a Shorter Amortization Period

Many financial planners and commentators make a great ballyhoo about the large amount of interest that can be saved by choosing a shorter mortgage amortization period. Their typical analysis goes as follows. (We will use monthly compounding rather than semiannual compounding to simplify the math.)

Suppose you obtain a $100,000 mortgage loan at 5.2% compounded monthly. The following table compares 20- and 25-year amortizations.

Amortization period	Monthly payment ($)	Total of all payments ($)	Total interest ($)
25 years	596.30	178,890	78,890
20 years	671.05	161,052	61,052
Difference:	(74.75)	17,838	17,838

Source: CMHC

By choosing a 20-year amortization, you will have "interest savings" of $17,838. The "savings" result from eliminating payments of $596.30 per month during Years 21 to 25 by spending an extra $74.75 per month during Years 1 to 20. That is,

$$\text{Interest savings} = (5 \times 12 \times \$596.30) - (20 \times 12 \times \$74.75)$$
$$= \$17,838$$

It seems quite astounding—increasing the monthly mortgage payment by a little more than 12% reduces the total interest costs by over 22%! The usual conclusion is that reduction of your mortgage's amortization period should be one of your highest financial priorities because of the amazing "interest savings." In the present example, you will be "$17,838 ahead" by choosing the 20-year amortization.

Do you see any flaws in this conventional analysis? Is it complete? Does it violate any basic concept you have learned? (Clearly, the analysis must be problematic—otherwise, we would not be making an issue of it. But before reading on, cover up the remainder of the discussion and take five minutes to see if you can identify the error made by so many "experts.")

The main flaw in the analysis is that a basic concept in finance—the time value of money—has been ignored. Whenever you add nominal dollar amounts that are paid on different dates, you are ignoring the time value of money. The longer the time frame over which the payments are spread, the more serious the resulting error will be. In the preceding analysis, a dollar in Year 25 is treated as having the same value as a dollar in Year 1. In fact, individual dollars saved in Years 21 to 25 have, on average, significantly less economic value than extra dollars spent in Years 1 to 20.

Let us do a rigorous analysis to determine the amount of the economic advantage of the shorter amortization period.

QUESTIONS

1. For the first 20 years, the monthly payments on the 25-year amortization are $74.75 lower than the payments on the 20-year amortization loan. Suppose you invest this difference each month to earn the same rate of interest that you pay on either mortgage. How much will you accumulate after 20 years?
2. What will be the balance owed after 20 years on the 25-year mortgage? Compare this balance to the Question 1 result. Which mortgage alternative puts you in a better financial position 20 years from now? Where did all of the "interest savings" go?
3. How will the outcome differ if the rate of return on your investments is higher than the interest rate you pay on your mortgage?
4. Write a "decision rule" that your friends (who have not had the good fortune to take this course) can use to decide whether to select a longer or a shorter mortgage amortization period.

Postscript: We do not disagree with the advice that paying off your mortgage as fast as possible should be a high financial priority. We merely make the point that the usual analysis is flawed and overstated. Legitimate reasons for the advice are:
- When you use extra money to reduce the principal on your mortgage, you are certain of earning an after-tax rate of return equal to the interest rate on the mortgage. After you adjust returns from alternative investments for their risk and tax exposure, the mortgage "investment" is usually very attractive in comparison.

- Human nature is such that we are more readily motivated to accelerate mortgage repayment than to undertake some other investment plan.
- Reduction of household debt improves our ability to absorb financial shocks such as loss of income due to sickness or job loss.

Post-postscript: In the next section, you will learn about other possibilities for accelerating the repayment of a mortgage loan. Some books present calculations of the resulting "interest savings." We play down this fundamentally flawed perspective for the reasons discussed in this Point of Interest.

Common Prepayment Privileges and Penalties

LO6 Any payments other than the regular contractual payments on a mortgage loan are called **prepayments**. Unless they include a penalty, prepayments are applied entirely to the reduction of principal, since the regular payments already cover interest charges. A mortgage that places no restrictions or penalties on extra payments by the borrower is called an **open mortgage**. At the other extreme is a **closed mortgage**, which does not allow any prepayment without a penalty. A borrower must pay a higher interest rate on an open mortgage than on a closed mortgage having the same term—about 2% higher for a one-year-term open mortgage.

Between the two extremes just described are closed mortgages with prepayment options. These mortgages grant limited penalty-free prepayment privileges. The more common prepayment options are one or more of the following.

- **Individual (or Lump) Payments** Once each year the borrower can prepay without penalty up to 15% of the original amount of the mortgage loan. Mortgage "years" are measured from the date of the loan.
- **Increasing the Regular Payment** Once each year, the borrower can permanently increase the size of the regular payments. There is usually an upper limit (such as 15%) on the increase in any year.
- **"Double-Up"** On any payment date, the borrower can pay up to twice the regular monthly payment. Taken to the extreme, the borrower could double *every* payment.

If the mortgage contract allows more than one of these options, the borrower can take advantage of two or more simultaneously. However, unused privileges cannot be carried forward. For example, if you do not use a 15% lump prepayment privilege in the first year, you cannot carry it forward to enable you to prepay up to 30% in the second year.

Details of these prepayment privileges vary among lending institutions. For example, single prepayments may be permitted only once each year or several times (subject to the 10% or 15% annual limit).

Another increasingly common feature of mortgages is a "skip-a-payment" provision. This allows the borrower to miss one monthly payment each year. Whereas a prepayment will shorten the time required to ultimately pay off a mortgage, skipping a payment will lengthen the time.

It is not unusual for homeowners to sell their house partway through the term of a closed mortgage. If a mortgage has a *portability* clause, the balance owed may be transferred to the next property purchased by the borrower. Some mortgages are *assumable*. An assumable mortgage loan may be transferred to (or "assumed by") the purchaser of the property securing the mortgage *if* the purchaser satisfies the lender's GDS and TDS ratios. The most typical scenario, however, is for the vendor to "pay out" the balance owed on the mortgage. The mortgage contract provides for a financial penalty on any prepayment not specifically permitted by the contract. The most common prepayment penalty is the *greater* of:

- Three months' interest on the amount prepaid, or
- The lender's reduction in interest revenue from the prepaid amount (over the remainder of the mortgage's term).[6]

EXAMPLE 15.3D

THE CONSEQUENCES OF A 10% LUMP PREPAYMENT

The interest rate for the first five-year term of a $100,000 mortgage loan is 5.2% compounded semiannually. The mortgage requires monthly payments over a 25-year amortization period. The mortgage contract gives the borrower the right to prepay up to 15% of the original mortgage loan, once each year, without interest penalty. Suppose that, at the end of the second year of the mortgage, the borrower makes a prepayment of $10,000.

a. How much will the amortization period be shortened?

b. What will be the principal balance at the end of the five-year term?

SOLUTION

a. The $10,000 prepayment at the time of the 24th regular monthly payment will be applied entirely to reducing the principal. To answer part (a), we must take the following steps:

Step 1. Calculate the payments based on a 25-year amortization.

Step 2. Calculate the balance after 24 payments.

Step 3. Reduce this balance by $10,000.

Step 4. Calculate the number of monthly payments needed to pay off this new balance.

Step 5. Calculate the reduction in the original 25-year amortization period.

Step 1: The periodic rate for the one-month payment interval is

$$i_2 = (1 + i)^c - 1 = 1.026^{0.1\overline{6}} - 1 = 0.004287121 \text{ per month}$$

Solve Formula (11-2) for *PMT*.

$$\$100{,}000 = PMT\left[\frac{1 - 1.004287121^{-300}}{0.004287121}\right]$$

$$PMT = \$593.04$$

The monthly payment is $593.04.

5.2	I/Y
P/Y 12	ENTER
C/Y 2	ENTER
300	N
100000	PV
0	FV
CPT	PMT

Ans: −593.0425

Step 2: $\left(\begin{array}{c}\text{Balance after}\\\text{24 payments}\end{array}\right) = \left(\begin{array}{c}\text{Future value of }\$100{,}000\\\text{after 24 months}\end{array}\right) - \left(\begin{array}{c}\text{Future value of 24}\\\text{payments already made}\end{array}\right)$

$$= \$100{,}000(1.004287121)^{24} - \$593.04\left(\frac{1.004287121^{24} - 1}{0.004287121}\right)$$

$$= \$95{,}855.44$$

The balance after 24 payments is $95,855.44.

Step 3: The balance after the $10,000 prepayment is $85,855.44.

---

[6] The following is an extract from a mortgage contract describing this penalty: "The amount, if any, by which interest at the rate on this mortgage exceeds interest at the current reinvestment interest rate, calculated on the amount prepaid by you, for the remaining term of the mortgage. The 'current reinvestment interest rate' at the time of prepayment means the rate at which we would lend to you on the security of a similar mortgage of your property for a term starting on the date of prepayment and ending on the balance due date of the mortgage."

Step 4: Calculate the number of payments of $593.04 required to pay off the balance of $85,855.44.

$$n = -\frac{\ln\left(1 - \dfrac{i \times PV}{PMT}\right)}{\ln(1 + i)}$$

$$= -\frac{\ln\left(1 - \dfrac{0.004287121 \times \$85,855.44}{\$593.04}\right)}{\ln(1.004287121)}$$

$$= 226.58$$

After the $10,000 prepayment, 227 additional payments will pay off the loan.

Step 5: With the prepayment, a total of 24 + 227 = 251 monthly payments are required.

Therefore, the $10,000 prepayment reduces the amortization period by

300 − 251 = 49 months = 4 years and 1 month

b. Beginning with the balance of $85,855.44 after the $10,000 prepayment, calculate the new balance after another 36 payments.

$$\begin{pmatrix} \text{Balance after} \\ \text{36 payments} \end{pmatrix} = \begin{pmatrix} \text{Future value of \$85,855.44} \\ \text{after 36 months} \end{pmatrix} - \begin{pmatrix} \text{Future value of 36} \\ \text{payments already made} \end{pmatrix}$$

$$= \$85,855.44(1.004287121)^{36} - \$593.04\left(\frac{1.004287121^{36} - 1}{0.004287121}\right)$$

$$= \$77,118.41$$

The balance at the end of the five-year term will be $77,118.41.

EXAMPLE 15.3E

THE CONSEQUENCES OF A 10% INCREASE IN THE PAYMENT SIZE

Two and one-half years ago the Simpsons borrowed $90,000 secured by a mortgage against the home they purchased at the time. The monthly payments, based on an interest rate of 4.25% compounded semiannually for a five-year term, would amortize the debt over 25 years. The mortgage has a prepayment clause that allows the Simpsons to increase the monthly payments by up to 10% once in each year. Any increase is to be a permanent increase. If the Simpsons increase payments by 10% starting with the 31st payment:

a. How much will the amortization period be shortened?

b. What will be the principal balance at the end of the first five-year term?

SOLUTION

a. The following steps are required to answer the question.

Step 1. Calculate the original size of the payments.

Step 2. Calculate the balance after $2\frac{1}{2}$ years (30 payments).

Step 3. Calculate the size of the payments after a 10% increase.

Step 4. Calculate the number of the new larger payments needed to amortize the balance from Step 2.

Step 5. Calculate the reduction from the original 25-year amortization period.

Step 1: The periodic rate for the one-month payment interval is

$$i_2 = (1 + i)^c - 1 = -1.02125^{0.1\overline{6}} = 0.003510709 \text{ per month}$$

Solve Formula (11-2) for *PMT*.

$$\$90,000 = PMT\left[\frac{1 - 1.003510709^{-300}}{0.003510709}\right]$$

$$PMT = \$485.69$$

The monthly payment is $485.69.

4.25 | I/Y
P/Y 12 | ENTER
C/Y 2 | ENTER
300 | N
90000 | PV
0 | FV
CPT | PMT
Ans: −485.694

Step 2: $\begin{pmatrix}\text{Balance after} \\ \text{30 payments}\end{pmatrix} = \begin{pmatrix}\text{Future value of \$90,000} \\ \text{after 30 months}\end{pmatrix} - \begin{pmatrix}\text{Future value of 30} \\ \text{payments already made}\end{pmatrix}$

$$= \$90,000(1.003510709)^{30} - \$485.69\left[\frac{1.003510709^{30} - 1}{0.003510709}\right]$$

$$= \$84,640.32$$

The balance after 30 payments is $84,640.32.

Same *I/Y, PV, P/Y, C/Y*
30 | N
485.69 | +/− | PMT
CPT | FV
Ans: −84,640.32

Step 3: The higher payment is 1.1($485.69) = $534.26.

Step 4: Calculate the number of payments of $534.26 required to pay off the balance of $84,640.32.

$$n = -\frac{\ln\left(1 - \dfrac{i \times PV}{PMT}\right)}{\ln(1 + i)}$$

$$= -\frac{\ln\left(1 - \dfrac{0.003510709 \times \$84,640.32}{\$534.26}\right)}{\ln(1.003510709)}$$

$$= 231.80$$

232 additional payments are needed to pay off the loan.

Same *I/Y, P/Y, C/Y*
84640.32 | PV
534.26 | +/− | PMT
0 | FV
CPT | N
Ans: 231.797

Step 5: The total time to amortize the loan will be 30 + 232 = 262 months instead of the original 300 months.

Therefore, the amortization period will be shortened by

$$300 - 262 = 38 \text{ months, or 3 years and 2 months.}$$

b. By the end of the five-year term, the balance in Step 2 will be reduced by an additional 30 payments of $534.26.

$\begin{pmatrix}\text{Balance after} \\ \text{30 payments}\end{pmatrix} = \begin{pmatrix}\text{Future value of \$84,640.32} \\ \text{after 30 months}\end{pmatrix} - \begin{pmatrix}\text{Future value of 30} \\ \text{payments already made}\end{pmatrix}$

$$= \$84,640.32(1.003510709)^{30} - \$534.26\left(\frac{1.003510709^{30} - 1}{0.003510709}\right)$$

$$= \$77,152.69$$

The balance at the end of the five-year term will be $77,152.69.

Same *I/Y, P/Y, C/Y*
Same *PV, PMT*
30 | N
CPT | FV
Ans: −77,152.69

EXERCISE 15.3

Answers to the odd-numbered problems are at the end of the book.

BASIC PROBLEMS

1. A $100,000 mortgage loan at 5.2% compounded semiannually requires monthly payments based on a 25-year amortization. Assuming that the interest rate does not change for the entire 25 years, complete the following table.

Interval	Balance at the end of the interval ($)	Principal reduction during the interval ($)	Interest paid during the interval ($)
0 to 5 years			
5 to 10 years			
10 to 15 years			
15 to 20 years			
20 to 25 years			

2. The interest rate on a $100,000 mortgage loan is 7% compounded semiannually.
   a. Calculate the monthly payment for each of 15-year, 20-year, and 25-year amortizations.
   b. By what percentage must the monthly payment be increased for a 20-year amortization instead of a 25-year amortization?
   c. By what percentage must the monthly payment be increased for a 15-year amortization instead of a 25-year amortization?
   d. For each of the three amortization periods in part (a), calculate the total interest paid over the entire amortization period. Assume that the interest rate and payments do not change and the final payment equals the others.

3. A $100,000 mortgage loan has a 25-year amortization.
   a. Calculate the monthly payment at interest rates of 4%, 6%, and 8% compounded semiannually.
   b. By what percentage does the monthly payment on the 8% mortgage exceed the monthly payment on the 4% mortgage?
   c. Calculate the total interest paid over the entire 25-year amortization period at each of the three interest rates. (Assume the final payment equals the others.)

4. The Graftons can afford a maximum mortgage payment of $1000 per month. The current interest rate is 7.2% compounded semiannually. What is the maximum mortgage loan they can afford if the amortization period is:
   a. 15 years?   b. 20 years?   c. 25 years?

5. The Tarkanians can afford a maximum mortgage payment of $1000 per month. What is the maximum mortgage loan they can afford if the amortization period is 25 years and the interest rate is:
   a. 4.5% compounded semiannually?   b. 7.5% compounded semiannually?

6. A $100,000 mortgage loan at 7.6% compounded semiannually has a 25-year amortization period.
   a. Calculate the monthly payment.
   b. If the interest rate were 1% lower (that is, 6.6% compounded semiannually), what loan amount would result in the same monthly payment?

INTERMEDIATE PROBLEMS

7. The Switzers are nearing the end of the first five-year term of a $100,000 mortgage loan with a 25-year amortization. The interest rate has been 6.5% compounded semiannually for

the initial term. How much will their monthly payments decrease if the interest rate upon renewal is 3.5% compounded semiannually?

8. The Melnyks are nearing the end of the first three-year term of a $100,000 mortgage loan with a 20-year amortization. The interest rate has been 7.7% compounded semiannually for the initial term. How much will their monthly payments decrease if the interest rate upon renewal is 6.7% compounded semiannually?

9. The interest rate for the first three years of an $80,000 mortgage loan is 7.4% compounded semiannually. Monthly payments are calculated using a 25-year amortization.
   a. What will be the principal balance at the end of the three-year term?
   b. What will be the monthly payments if the loan is renewed at 4.8% compounded semiannually (and the original amortization period is continued)?

10. Five years ago, Ms. Halliday received a mortgage loan from the Scotiabank for $60,000 at 7.8% compounded semiannually for a five-year term. Monthly payments were based on a 25-year amortization. The bank is agreeable to renewing the loan for another five-year term at 6.8% compounded semiannually. Calculate the principal reduction that will occur in the second five-year term if:
   a. The payments are recalculated based on the new interest rate and a continuation of the original 25-year amortization.
   b. Ms. Halliday continues to make the same payments as she made for the first five years (resulting in a reduction of the amortization period).

11. A $40,000 mortgage loan charges interest at 6.6% compounded *monthly* for a four-year term. Monthly payments were calculated for a 15-year amortization and then rounded up to the next higher $10.
   a. What will be the principal balance at the end of the first term?
   b. What will be the monthly payments on renewal for a three-year term if they are calculated for an interest rate of 4.2% compounded monthly and an 11-year amortization period, but again rounded to the next higher $10?

12. Many mortgage lenders offer the flexibility of dividing a mortgage loan between a fixed interest rate portion and a variable interest rate portion. (A variable-rate mortgage is sometimes referred to as an adjustable-rate mortgage, abbreviated ARM.) The variable interest rate changes from time to time, following the trend of short-term interest rates in the capital markets. On average, quoted variable interest rates on mortgages are lower than quoted fixed rates for most terms. But at times variable rates can rise above (even substantially above) fixed rates, especially fixed rates that may have been "locked in" two or three years earlier.

   Suppose a $100,000 mortgage loan with a 25-year amortization is divided equally between a fixed-rate portion at 6.6% compounded semiannually and a variable-rate portion at 5.4% compounded monthly. (Quoted rates on variable-rate mortgages are normally monthly compounded rates.)
   a. What is the initial (combined) monthly payment?
   b. What will be the combined monthly payment if the variable rate jumps to 6.6% compounded monthly after two years?

13. The interest rate for the first five years of a $27,000 mortgage loan was 3.25% compounded semiannually. The monthly payments computed for a 10-year amortization were rounded to the next higher $10.
   a. Calculate the principal balance at the end of the first term.
   b. Upon renewal at 5.75% compounded semiannually, monthly payments were calculated for a five-year amortization and again rounded up to the next $10. What will be the amount of the last payment?

14. The Delgados have a gross monthly income of $6000. Monthly payments on personal loans total $500. Their bank limits the gross debt service ratio at 33% and the total debt service ratio at 42%.

    a. Rounded to the nearest $100, what is the maximum 25-year mortgage loan for which they can qualify on the basis of their income? Assume monthly heating costs of $200 and property taxes of $220 per month. Current mortgage rates are 6.8% compounded semiannually.

    b. Rounded to the nearest $100, what minimum down payment must they have to qualify for the maximum conventional mortgage (80% loan-to-value ratio) on a new home?

15. The Archibalds are eligible for CMHC mortgage loan insurance. Consequently, their limits are 95% for the loan-to-value ratio, 32% for the GDS ratio, and 40% for the TDS ratio.

    a. Rounded to the nearest $100, what is the maximum 25-year mortgage loan for which they can qualify if their gross monthly income is $5000 and their payments on personal debt amount to $600 per month? Assume monthly heating costs of $150 and property taxes of $200 per month. Current mortgage rates are 6.6% compounded semiannually.

    b. If they make the minimum down payment, what is the maximum price (rounded to the nearest $100) they can pay for a home? (Assume the purchase price equals the appraised value.)

16. Marge and Homer Sampson have saved $95,000 toward the purchase of their first home. Allowing $7000 for legal costs and moving expenses, they have $88,000 available for a down payment. Their bank uses 32% for the GDS ratio and 40% for the TDS ratio.

    a. Based only on a loan-to-value ratio of 80%, what is the maximum purchase price they can consider?

    b. After thorough investigation, the Sampsons made a $360,000 offer on a townhouse subject to arranging financing. Next they met with their banker. With an $88,000 down payment, the Sampsons will need a mortgage loan of $272,000. The current interest rate on a five-year term fixed-rate mortgage with a 25-year amortization is 5.4% compounded semiannually. The banker gathered data for calculating the Sampsons' GDS and TDS ratios. Annual property taxes will be $3000. Annual heating costs will be about $2400. The Sampsons make monthly payments of $800 on a car loan ($14,000 balance). Their gross monthly income is $7000. Calculate the GDS and TDS ratios for the Sampsons.

    c. Note that the Sampsons meet the GDS criterion ($\leq$32%) but exceed the TDS limit (40%). The item causing the problem is the $800 per month car payment. Suppose the Sampsons use $14,000 of their down payment savings to pay off the car loan. They will still have enough to make the minimum down payment ($0.2 \times \$360,000 = \$72,000$) but will have to increase the mortgage loan by $14,000 to $286,000. Re-calculate the GDS and TDS ratios. Do the Sampsons satisfy all three ratios by taking this approach?

17. The interest rate on a $100,000 mortgage loan is 4% compounded semiannually.

    a. What are the monthly payments for a 25-year amortization?

    b. Suppose that the borrower instead makes weekly payments equal to one-fourth of the monthly payment calculated in part (a). (In mortgage terminology, these are referred to as accelerated weekly payments.) When will the loan be paid off if the interest rate does not change? Assume there are exactly 52 weeks in a year.

18. A $200,000 mortgage at 6.6% compounded semiannually with a 25-year amortization requires monthly payments. The mortgage allows the borrower to prepay up to 10% of the original principal once each year. How much will the amortization period be shortened if, on the first anniversary of the mortgage, the borrower makes (in addition to the regular payment) a prepayment of:

    a. $10,000? **b.** $20,000?

19. A $200,000 mortgage at 6.6% compounded semiannually with a 20-year amortization requires monthly payments. The mortgage allows the borrower to prepay up to 10% of the original principal once each year. How much will the amortization period be shortened if, on the first anniversary of the mortgage, the borrower makes (in addition to the regular payment) a prepayment of:
    a. $10,000?   **b.** $20,000?

20. A $100,000 mortgage at 6.9% compounded semiannually with a 25-year amortization requires monthly payments. The mortgage entitles the borrower to increase the amount of the regular payment by up to 15% once each year. How much will the amortization period be shortened if, after the 12th payment, the payments are increased by:
    a. 7.5%?   **b.** 15%?

21. A $100,000 mortgage at 4.9% compounded semiannually with a 20-year amortization requires monthly payments. The mortgage allows the borrower to increase the amount of the regular payment by up to 10% once each year. How much will the amortization period be shortened if payments are increased by 10% after the 12th payment, and by another 10% after Payment 24?

22. A $100,000 mortgage at 6.2% compounded semiannually with a 25-year amortization requires monthly payments. The mortgage allows the borrower to "double up" on a payment once each year. How much will the amortization period be shortened if the borrower doubles the 10th payment?

23. A $100,000 mortgage at 6.8% compounded semiannually with a 20-year amortization requires monthly payments. The mortgage allows the borrower to "double up" on a payment once each year. How much will the amortization period be shortened if the borrower doubles the eighth payment?

24. A $100,000 mortgage at 6.75% compounded semiannually with a 20-year amortization requires monthly payments. The mortgage allows the borrower to miss a payment once each year. How much will the amortization period be lengthened if the borrower misses the ninth payment? (The interest that accrues during the ninth month is converted to principal at the end of the ninth month.)

25. A $100,000 mortgage at 4.3% compounded semiannually with a 25-year amortization requires monthly payments. The mortgage allows the borrower to miss a payment once each year. How much will the amortization period be lengthened if the borrower misses the 12th payment? (The interest that accrues during the 12th month is converted to principal at the end of the 12th month.)

26. A $100,000 mortgage at 7.1% compounded semiannually with a 20-year amortization requires monthly payments. How much will the amortization period be shortened if a $10,000 lump payment is made along with the 12th payment and payments are increased by 10% starting in the third year?

27. A $100,000 mortgage at 3.8% compounded semiannually with a 25-year amortization requires monthly payments. How much will the amortization period be shortened if payments are increased by 10% starting in the second year, and a $10,000 lump payment is made along with the 24th payment?

28. Monthly payments on a $150,000 mortgage are based on an interest rate of 6.6% compounded semiannually and a 20-year amortization. If a $5000 prepayment is made along with the 32nd payment:
    a. How much will the amortization period be shortened?
    b. What will be the principal balance after four years?

29. The interest rate for the first five years of a $120,000 mortgage is 4.15% compounded semi-annually. Monthly payments are based on a 25-year amortization. If a $5000 prepayment is made at the end of the second year:
    a. How much will the amortization period be shortened?
    b. What will be the principal balance at the end of the five-year term?

30. A $130,000 mortgage loan at 7.2% compounded *monthly* has a 25-year amortization.
    a. What prepayment at the end of the first year will reduce the time required to pay off the loan by one year? (Assume the final payment equals the others.)
    b. Instead of the prepayment in part (a), what prepayment at the end of the 10th year will reduce the time required to pay off the loan by one year?

31. After three years of the first five-year term at 6.3% compounded semiannually, Dean and Cindy decide to take advantage of the privilege of increasing the payments on their $200,000 mortgage loan by 10%. The monthly payments were originally calculated for a 30-year amortization.
    a. How much will the amortization period be shortened?
    b. What will be the principal balance at the end of the five-year term?

32. The MacLellans originally chose to make payments of $1600 per month on a $138,000 mortgage written at 7.4% compounded semiannually for the first five years. After three years they exercised their right under the mortgage contract to increase the payments by 10%.
    a. If the interest rate does not change, when will they extinguish the mortgage debt?
    b. What will be the principal balance at the end of the five-year term?

ADVANCED PROBLEMS

33. The monthly payments on the Wolskis' $266,000 mortgage were originally based on a 25-year amortization and an interest rate of 4.5% compounded semiannually for a five-year term. After two years, they elected to increase their monthly payments by $150, and at the end of the fourth year they made a $10,000 prepayment.
    a. How much have they shortened the amortization period?
    b. What was the principal balance at the end of the five-year term?

34. A marketing innovation is the "cash-back mortgage" wherein the lender gives the borrower an up-front bonus cash payment. For example, if you borrow $100,000 on a 3% cash-back mortgage loan, the lender will give you $3000 in addition to the $100,000 loan. You pay back only the $100,000 principal over the amortization period. The $3000 can be immediately applied as a prepayment to reduce the principal balance (to $97,000) or it can be used for any other purpose. You must keep your mortgage with the lender for at least five years.

    The cash-back mortgage seems like a good deal, but there is more you need to know about advertised mortgage interest rates. The rates you see posted in your local financial institution are just a starting point for negotiations. You can get $\frac{1}{4}$% knocked off just by asking for it. With some firm negotiating, you can probably get a $\frac{1}{2}$% reduction. If the institution really wants your business, you can get a $\frac{3}{4}$% or even 1% reduction. However, if you take advantage of some other promotion such as a cash-back offer, you will not get any rate discount. So the cash-back offer is not as good as it initially appears.

    Which of the following loans should a borrower choose?
    • A standard $100,000 mortgage loan at 6.5% compounded semiannually
    • A 3% cash-back mortgage loan for $100,000 at 7.25% compounded semiannually

    In both cases, the interest rate is for a five-year term and the payments are based on a 25-year amortization. For the cash-back mortgage, assume that the $3000 cash bonus is immediately applied to reduce the balance to $97,000. (Since the monthly payments are based on the $100,000 face value, the prepayment will shorten the time required to pay off the loan.) Assume money can earn 4.8% compounded monthly.

35. **Using the Mortgage Payoff Chart** To access this chart, go to the Student Edition of Connect. In Chapter 15, find "Mortgage Payoff Chart." Over the full amortization period, the chart plots graphs of both the mortgage balance and the cumulative interest paid. Note the "Definitions" section below the chart.

   You can select from a variety of accelerated payment and prepayment options. If you enter a non-zero "Prepayment amount," the chart presents additional graphs for the balance and cumulative interest under the prepayment plan. (Round prepayment amounts to the nearest dollar before entry.) These graphs enable you to see how much the prepayments reduce both the cumulative interest cost and the time required to pay off the loan. Use this chart (and its associated report) to answer the following problems from this Exercise. In parts (b) through (f), round the answer to the nearest 0.1 year. Also note that the reduction (referred to as "savings") in the total interest paid is over the life of the loan.

   a. Problem 1   **b.** Problem 17   **c.** Problem 19
   d. Problem 23   **e.** Problem 29   **f.** Problem 31

KEY TERMS

Amortization period	Mortgagee	Prospective method
Closed mortgage	Mortgagor	Retrospective method
Face value	Open mortgage	Term
Loan amortization schedule	Prepayments	Term loan

SUMMARY OF NOTATION AND KEY FORMULAS

In all but the last of the following equations, the relevant interest rate or discount rate is the loan's contractual rate of interest.

$$\text{Principal balance} = \left(\begin{array}{c}\text{Present value of the remaining payments}\\\text{discounted at the } \textit{contractual rate of interest} \text{ on the loan}\end{array}\right)$$

Prospective method for calculating a loan's balance.

$$\text{Original loan} = \left(\begin{array}{c}\text{Present value of all payments}\\\text{discounted at the } \textit{contractual rate of interest} \text{ on the loan}\end{array}\right)$$

We frequently use this concept to calculate the payment size or the amortization period.

$$\text{Balance} = \left(\begin{array}{c}\text{Future value of}\\\text{the original loan}\end{array}\right) - \left(\begin{array}{c}\text{Future value of the}\\\text{payments already made}\end{array}\right)$$

Retrospective method for calculating a loan's balance.

$$\text{Final payment} = (1 + i) \times \left(\begin{array}{c}\text{Balance after the}\\\text{second-to-last payment}\end{array}\right)$$

The final loan payment usually differs from the others.

$$\text{Interest component} = i \times \text{Balance after the previous payment}$$

$$\text{Principal component} = \left(\begin{array}{c}\text{Balance after the}\\\text{previous payment}\end{array}\right) - \left(\begin{array}{c}\text{Balance after the}\\\text{current payment}\end{array}\right)$$

The interest and principal components of a loan payment may be calculated from nearby balances.

REVIEW PROBLEMS

Answers to the odd-numbered review problems are at the end of the book.

BASIC PROBLEMS

1. **L01** Jessica bought a $1150 television set for 25% down and the balance to be paid with interest at 11.25% compounded monthly in six equal monthly payments. Construct the full amortization schedule for the debt. Calculate the total interest paid.

2. **L01** Givens, Hong, and Partners obtained a $7000 term loan at 8.5% compounded annually for new boardroom furniture. Prepare a complete amortization schedule in which the loan is repaid by equal semiannual payments over three years.

3. **L04** **L02** A $28,000 loan at 8% compounded quarterly is to be repaid by equal quarterly payments over a seven-year term.
   a. What will be the principal component of the sixth payment?
   b. What will be the interest portion of the 22nd payment?
   c. How much will the loan's balance be reduced by Payments 10 to 15 inclusive?
   d. How much interest will be paid in the second year?

4. **L04** **L02** A 20-year annuity was purchased with $180,000 that had accumulated in an RRSP. The annuity provides a semiannually compounded rate of return of 5% and makes equal month-end payments.
   a. What will be the principal portion of Payment 134?
   b. What will be the interest portion of Payment 210?
   c. How much will the annuity's balance be reduced by Payments 75 to 100 inclusive?
   d. How much interest will be paid in the sixth year?

5. **L01** Metro Construction received $60,000 in vendor financing at 10.5% compounded semiannually for the purchase of a loader. The contract requires semiannual payments of $10,000 until the debt is paid off. Construct the complete amortization schedule for the debt. How much total interest will be paid over the life of the loan?

6. **L01** Suppose that the loan in Problem 5 permits an additional prepayment of principal on any scheduled payment date. Prepare another amortization schedule that reflects a prepayment of $5000 with the third scheduled payment. How much interest is saved as a result of the prepayment?

7. **L04** **L02** **L03** An annuity providing a rate of return of 4.8% compounded monthly was purchased for $45,000. The annuity pays $400 at the end of each month.
   a. How much of Payment 37 will be interest?
   b. What will be the principal portion of Payment 92?
   c. How much interest will be paid by Payments 85 to 96 inclusive?
   d. How much principal will be repaid in the fifth year?
   e. What will be the amount of the final payment?

8. **L01** **L02** The interest rate on a $6400 loan is 10% compounded semiannually. If the loan is to be repaid by monthly payments over a four-year term, prepare a partial amortization schedule showing details of the first two payments, Payments 34 and 35, and the last two payments.

9. **LO3** **LO4** **LO2** A $255,000 amount from an RRSP is used to purchase an annuity paying $6000 at the end of each quarter. The annuity provides an annually compounded rate of return of 2.5%.
   a. What will be the amount of the final payment?
   b. What will be the interest portion of the 27th payment?
   c. What will be the principal portion of the 33rd payment?
   d. How much will the principal balance be reduced by Payments 14 to 20 inclusive?
   e. How much interest will be received in the sixth year?

INTERMEDIATE PROBLEMS

10. **LO5** **LO2** A mortgage contract for $45,000 written 10 years ago is just at the end of its second five-year term. The interest rates were 8% compounded semiannually for the first term and 7% compounded semiannually for the second term. If monthly payments throughout have been based on the original 25-year amortization, calculate the principal balance at the end of the second term assuming the amortization period of 20 years on renewal after the first five years.

11. **LO5** **LO6** The interest rate for the first three years of an $87,000 mortgage is 4.4% compounded semiannually. Monthly payments are based on a 20-year amortization. If a $4000 prepayment is made at the end of the 16th month:
    a. How much will the amortization period be shortened?
    b. What will be the principal balance at the end of the three-year term?

12. **LO1** **LO2** Niagara Haulage obtained an $80,000 loan at 7.2% compounded monthly to build a storage shed. Construct a partial amortization schedule for payments of $1000 per month showing details of the first two payments, Payments 41 and 42, and the last two payments.

13. **LO5** **LO2** The interest rate for the first five years of a $90,000 mortgage loan is 5.25% compounded semiannually. Monthly payments are calculated using a 20-year amortization.
    a. What will be the principal balance at the end of the five-year term?
    b. What will be the new payments if the loan is renewed at 6.5% compounded semiannually (and the original amortization period is continued)?

14. **LO5** A mortgage calls for monthly payments of $887.96 for 25 years. If the loan was for $135,000, calculate the semiannually compounded nominal rate of interest on the loan.

15. **LO5** A $25,000 home improvement (mortgage) loan charges interest at 6.6% compounded monthly for a three-year term. Monthly payments are based on a 10-year amortization and rounded up to the next $10. What will be the principal balance at the end of the first term?

16. **LO5** **LO6** The interest rate for the first five years of a $95,000 mortgage is 7.2% compounded semiannually. Monthly payments are based on a 25-year amortization. If a $3000 prepayment is made at the end of the third year:
    a. How much will the amortization period be shortened?
    b. What will be the principal balance at the end of the five-year term?

17. **LO5** **LO6** After two years of the first five-year term at 6.7% compounded semiannually, Dan and Laurel decide to take advantage of the privilege of increasing the payments on their $110,000 mortgage loan by 10%. The monthly payments were originally calculated for a 25-year amortization.
    a. How much will the amortization period be shortened?
    b. What will be the principal balance at the end of the five-year term?

*APPENDIX 15A: INSTRUCTIONS FOR THE TEXAS INSTRUMENTS BA II PLUS AMORTIZATION WORKSHEET

The Amortization Worksheet enables you to quickly obtain the interest and principal components of any loan payment, or to quickly obtain the total of the interest components and the total of the principal components in a group of consecutive payments.

Let us use an example to demonstrate the use of the Amortization Worksheet. A $10,000 loan at 6% compounded monthly is repaid by monthly payments over a five-year term. Suppose we want to determine the total interest and total principal in Payments 11 to 20, inclusive.

The basic information about the loan must be entered in the usual manner in the $\boxed{\text{N}}$, $\boxed{\text{FV}}$, $\boxed{\text{I/Y}}$, $\boxed{\text{PV}}$, $\boxed{\text{PMT}}$, $\boxed{\text{P/Y}}$, and $\boxed{\text{C/Y}}$ memories. In the present example, we do not know the value for $\boxed{\text{PMT}}$ at the outset. Therefore, we must first calculate it. Then we must re-enter the *rounded* value in the $\boxed{\text{PMT}}$ memory *before* accessing the Amortization Worksheet.

Find "AMORT" located above the $\boxed{\text{PV}}$ key. To access the Amortization Worksheet, press $\boxed{\text{2nd}}$ $\boxed{\text{AMORT}}$. Recall that a worksheet can be thought of as a column of items that you can view one at a time in the calculator's display. The "AMORT" worksheet's column contains the five items listed below. You see the top item when you first access the worksheet. Other items may be viewed using the scroll keys $\boxed{\downarrow}$ and $\boxed{\uparrow}$.

$P1 =$	nn
$P2 =$	nn
$BAL =$	n,nnn.nn
$PRN =$	n,nnn.nn
$INT =$	n,nnn.nn

$6\ \boxed{\text{I/Y}}$

$\boxed{\text{P/Y}}\ 12\ \boxed{\text{ENTER}}$

(making $C/Y = P/Y = 12$)

$60\ \boxed{\text{N}}$

$10000\ \boxed{\text{PV}}$

$0\ \boxed{\text{FV}}$

$\boxed{\text{CPT}}\ \boxed{\text{PMT}}$

Ans: -193.3280

$193.33\ \boxed{+/-}\ \boxed{\text{PMT}}$

P1 represents the serial number of the *first* payment in the group of consecutive payments. *P2* represents the serial number of the *last* payment in the group. *BAL* represents the principal balance *after* payment number *P2*. *PRN* and *INT* represent the total principal and total interest in payments *P1* to *P2 inclusive*. Where the letters nn and n,nnn.nn are indicated above, you will see numerical values in your display.

We want the total interest and total principal in Payments 11 to 20 inclusive. After accessing the worksheet,

Press		11	$\boxed{\text{ENTER}}$	to set $P1 = 11$
Press	$\boxed{\downarrow}$	20	$\boxed{\text{ENTER}}$	to scroll down and set $P2 = 20$
Press	$\boxed{\downarrow}$			to scroll down and view "$BAL = 6{,}993.06$"
Press	$\boxed{\downarrow}$			to scroll down and view "$PRN = -1{,}540.95$"
Press	$\boxed{\downarrow}$			to scroll down and view "$INT = -392.35$"
Press	$\boxed{\text{2nd}}$		$\boxed{\text{QUIT}}$	to exit from the worksheet

The balance after Payment 20 is $6993.06, the total principal in Payments 11 to 20 inclusive is $1540.95, and the total interest in the same group of payments is $392.35.

The computation took place at the moment you pressed the $\boxed{\downarrow}$ key after entering the value for *P2*. The calculator uses the retrospective method. Consequently, it ignores whatever value may be residing in the $\boxed{\text{FV}}$ memory.

If you want the interest and principal components of a *single* payment (and the balance after that payment), enter the payment's serial number for *both P1* and *P2*.

*APPENDIX 15B: AMORTIZATION FUNCTIONS ON THE SHARP EL-738 CALCULATOR

We will use the following example to demonstrate the use of the amortization functions on the Sharp EL-738 calculator. A $10,000 loan at 6% compounded monthly must be repaid by monthly payments over a five-year term. Suppose we want to determine: (a) the total interest and total principal in Payments 11 to 20 inclusive, and (b) the interest and principal components of Payment 15.

The basic information about the loan must be entered in the usual manner in the $\boxed{\text{I/Y}}$, $\boxed{\text{P/Y}}$, $\boxed{\text{C/Y}}$, $\boxed{\text{N}}$, $\boxed{\text{PV}}$, $\boxed{\text{PMT}}$, and $\boxed{\text{FV}}$ memories. Since the payment is not given in the current example, you must first calculate it. In this example, you obtain *PMT* = $193.3280. Then re-enter the value of *PMT rounded* to the nearest cent (and with the proper sign for the direction of the cash flow) in the $\boxed{\text{PMT}}$ memory.

a. Press $\boxed{\text{AMORT}}$ to access the amortization worksheet. The first line in the display reads "*AMRT P1 =*"

Press 11 $\boxed{\text{ENTER}}$ to set the first payment's serial number at *P1* = 11

Press $\boxed{\downarrow}$ 20 $\boxed{\text{ENTER}}$ to scroll down and set the second payment's serial number at *P2* = 20

Press $\boxed{\downarrow}$ to scroll down and view the balance after Payment 20: "*BALANCE* = 6993.06"

Press $\boxed{\downarrow}$ to scroll down and view the total principal in Payments 11 to 20: "Σ*PRINCIPAL* = −1540.95"

Press $\boxed{\downarrow}$ to scroll down and view the total interest in Payments 11 to 20: "Σ*INTEREST* = −392.35"

b. Scroll back to the initial "*AMRT P1 =*" line.

Press 15 $\boxed{\text{ENTER}}$ to set the first payment's serial number at *P1* = 15

Press $\boxed{\downarrow}$ 15 $\boxed{\text{ENTER}}$ to scroll down and also set the second payment's serial number at *P2* = 15

Press $\boxed{\downarrow}$ to scroll down and view the balance after Payment 15: "*BALANCE* = 7773.15"

Press $\boxed{\downarrow}$ to scroll down and view the principal component of Payment 15: "Σ*PRINCIPAL* = −153.70"

Press $\boxed{\downarrow}$ to scroll down and view the interest component of Payment 15: "Σ*INTEREST* = −39.63"

Press $\boxed{\text{ON/C}}$ when you are ready to exit from the worksheet.

Chapter 16
Bonds and Sinking Funds

CHAPTER OUTLINE

16.1 Basic Concepts and Definitions

16.2 Bond Price on an Interest Payment Date

16.3 Yield to Maturity on an Interest Payment Date

16.4 Bond Price on Any Date

*16.5 Sinking Funds

Appendix 16A: Instructions for the Texas Instruments BA II PLUS Bond Worksheet

LEARNING OBJECTIVES

After completing this chapter, you will be able to:

LO1 Calculate the market price of a bond on any date

LO2 Calculate the yield to maturity of a bond on an interest payment date

LO3 Calculate the payment for a sinking fund

LO4 Prepare a sinking fund schedule

THE PRIMARY MEANS BY WHICH our three levels of government and publicly listed corporations finance their long-term debt is by issuing the type of bonds described in this chapter. At the end of December 2018, $573B of Canada's $758 billion net federal debt was financed by these "marketable" bonds.

Even though you may never directly own marketable bonds, you will probably indirectly invest in them at some point in the future. Marketable bonds form a significant portion of many managed portfolios such as bond mutual funds, balanced mutual funds, and pension plans.

The purchaser of a bond is not "locked in" for the entire lifetime of the bond. There is an active, efficient bond market for the sale and purchase of bonds after their initial issue. In this chapter, you will learn how to calculate bond prices that are reported in the financial news.

16.1 Basic Concepts and Definitions

A bond is a certificate representing the borrower's debt obligation to the bond holder. The borrower is usually called the bond issuer. We will adopt the widespread practice of using the term *bond* loosely to refer to both true bonds and debentures. The technical distinction between a bond and a debenture is that a **bond** is secured by specific assets of the borrower, whereas a **debenture** is backed only by the general credit of the borrower. Therefore, Government of Canada "bonds" are, in fact, debentures since no particular assets secure them. The distinction is not important for the mathematics of bonds.

Unlike term loans, where each payment includes a principal portion that reduces the debt, bonds require that the borrower make periodic payments of interest only. Then, on the **maturity date** of the bond, the full principal amount is repaid along with the final interest payment. Bonds are issued with maturities ranging from 2 to 30 years.

The bond certificate sets out the main features of the loan contract. The following items are part of the information you need to calculate a bond's market price.

- The **issue date** is the date on which the loan was made and on which interest starts to accrue.
- The **face value** (or *denomination*) is the principal amount of the debt represented by the bond. The most common face values are $1000, $5000, and $25,000, although larger denominations are often issued to institutional investors. Normally, the issuer of a bond will redeem the bond on its maturity date at a **redemption price** equal to its face value. There are special circumstances under which a bond may be redeemed on or before its maturity date at a redemption price different from the face value. These circumstances are beyond the scope of coverage in this book. We assume that bonds will be redeemed on their maturity date for their face value.
- The **coupon rate**[1] is the contractual rate of interest paid on the face value of the bond. It is a *semiannually* compounded rate and is normally fixed for the life of the bond. The vast majority of bonds pay interest at six-month intervals, measured from the issue date.[2] Therefore, such interest payments form an ordinary *simple* annuity.

You should be clear on the distinction between *savings* bonds, and the *marketable* bonds discussed in this chapter. You can cash in a *savings* bond before its scheduled maturity date and receive the full face value plus accrued interest. *Marketable* bonds such as Government of Canada bonds do not have this open-redemption privilege. If you want to liquidate a marketable bond before it matures, you must sell it through an investment dealer who participates in the bond market. Let us now address the question of what determines the market value of a bond.

---

[1] This term originated many years ago when it was customary for the bond certificate to have interest coupons attached to its margin. At each interest payment date, the bond holder would clip off the matured coupon and present it at a bank to receive payment in cash. Most bonds are now registered in the owner's name, and interest payments are made by direct deposit to an investment account or by cheque sent through the mail.

[2] If a bond's maturity date is the last day of a month, both semiannual coupons are paid on the last days of the appropriate months. For example, a bond maturing on September 30 pays its March coupon on March 31 (rather than on March 30). A bond maturing on October 31 pays an April coupon on April 30. If a bond's maturity date is August 29 or 30, it pays a February coupon on February 28 (or February 29 in a leap year).

16.2 Bond Price on an Interest Payment Date

Most bonds pay interest semiannually, offer no early redemption privileges, and are redeemed for their face value at maturity. In this section we are concerned with pricing bonds that have these typical features. But before we begin discussing the mathematics of bond pricing, you should understand *why* bond prices change in the bond market.[3]

Dependence of Bond Price on Prevailing Interest Rates

On the date a bond is issued, its coupon rate must be a competitive rate of return. The bond issuer cannot expect a prudent investor to buy a new 6% coupon bond (for the full face value) if the investor can earn a 7% rate of return from other investments of similar risk.

Subsequent to the issue date, prevailing interest rates in the financial markets change (and the coupon rate offered on *subsequent new* bond issues must change accordingly). However, the coupon rate on a previously issued bond is *fixed* for the life of the bond. If its coupon rate *exceeds* the current competitive rate of return, investors will be willing to pay *more* than the face value to acquire the bond. If the bond's coupon rate is *less* than the current competitive rate of return, investors will not buy the bond unless its price is a suitable amount *below* face value.

To make our discussion more specific, consider the four hypothetical Government of Canada bonds listed in Table 16.1. The issue dates and initial terms have been chosen so that, as of today's date, every bond has five years remaining until maturity. Consequently, the four $1000 face value bonds represent identical investments except for differing coupon rates. The coupon rate on the *newly issued* Bond A is 6% compounded semiannually. Therefore, we can conclude that the prevailing competitive rate of return for five-year maturity bonds is also 6% compounded semiannually.

TABLE 16.1	Relative Prices of $1000 Face Value Bonds			
Bond	**Issue date**	**Initial term (years)**	**Coupon rate (%)**	**Bond price**
A	Today	5	6	$1000
B	5 years ago	10	7	More than $1000
C	10 years ago	15	6	$1000
D	15 years ago	20	5	Less than $1000

We will now develop the reasoning for the relative bond prices indicated in the last column. Bonds C and A both carry a 6% coupon and have five years remaining until maturity. Therefore, Bond C is identical to Bond A from this point onward. Its market value will always be the same as the market value of Bond A. Today that value is $1000. When a bond trades at its face value, it is said to trade "at par." Any bond will trade at par if its coupon rate equals the prevailing rate of return required in the bond market.

Bond B carries a coupon rate that is 1% above the current competitive rate. It will pay $70 interest per year ($35 every six months), whereas Bond A will pay only $60 per year. If you could buy Bond B for $1000, you would earn a 7% rate of return on your investment. Since the prevailing rate of return is only 6%, investors will prefer Bond B and bid its price above $1000. As the purchase price rises, the rate of return on the purchase price declines (because the future interest payments to the bond holder remain fixed, regardless of the amount paid for the bond).

---

[3] For the most part, bonds are not bought and sold at a particular physical location corresponding to the stock exchanges for common shares. The "bond market" consists of investment dealers who are linked by telecommunications networks and who act as intermediaries between bond buyers and sellers.

TRAP

Don't Overlook the Capital Gain or Loss Component of Total Return

You might think that Bond B's price will rise to the level at which the $70 interest received each year provides the required 6% rate of return. This price would be about $1167, since $\frac{\$70}{\$1167} \times$ 100% = 6.00%. But this line of reasoning misses part of the broader picture. Suppose you buy Bond B for $1167 and hold the bond until it matures. In addition to the final interest payment on the maturity date, you will be paid the $1000 face value, not the $1167 you paid for the bond. Therefore, you will suffer a $167 capital loss for the entire holding period. This reduces your annual rate of *total* return (Section 3.3) below the 6% we calculated for the income yield. For your rate of *total* return to be 6%, you can pay more than $1000 but not as much as $1167. Then the capital loss will be smaller and the income yield will exceed 6%. We will learn how to calculate the precise price point at which the extra income yield offsets the capital loss, leaving a 6% rate of total return.

Bond D pays only $50 interest per year ($25 every six months). Investors will not buy Bond D until its price falls to an appropriate level below $1000. If you buy a bond for *less* than its face value, you will realize a capital *gain* when the face value is received at maturity. The market value of Bond D is the price at which the interest payments, combined with the capital gain, provide a rate of *total* return equal to 6% compounded semiannually.

Summary The market value of Bond B is more than its face value because its coupon rate exceeds the required rate of return in the bond market. In other words, if the market rate *falls below* the coupon rate, the bond's price *rises above* its face value. The market value of Bond D is less than its face value because its coupon rate is less than the required rate of return in the bond market. In other words, if the market rate *rises above* the coupon rate, the bond's price *falls below* its face value. This inverse relation between market rate of return and market value is easily remembered using the "teeter-totter model" shown in **Figure 16.1**.

FIGURE 16.1   Effects of Interest Rate Changes on Bond Prices

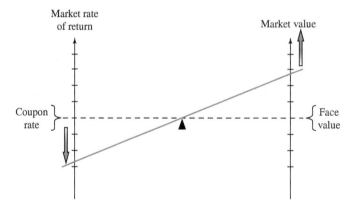

In the particular case shown in the diagram, the market rate of return has fallen below the bond's coupon rate. Pushing the market-rate-of-return end of the teeter-totter down below the coupon rate raises the market-value end above the bond's face value. (This is the Bond B case.) The more the market rate falls below the coupon rate, the higher the bond price will rise above the face value. If prevailing rates in the bond market start to rise (from the level depicted in the diagram), all bond prices will start to decline. But a particular bond's price will not fall below face value until the market's required rate of return rises above that bond's coupon rate.

Later in this section we will add another feature to the model that will make it particularly helpful.

Calculating a Bond's Price on an Interest Payment Date

L01 The pricing or valuation of bonds is yet another application where we use the Valuation Principle to determine an investment's fair market value. To apply the Valuation Principle to bonds, we need to:

1. Determine the amount and timing of future payments.
2. Determine the rate of return currently required in the bond market.
3. Calculate the present value of the future payments using this rate of return as the discount rate.

If we let

$$2b = \text{Coupon rate (compounded semiannually) and}$$
$$FV = \text{Face value of the bond}$$

then the interest rate for the six-month interest payment interval is b and the semiannual interest payment is:

$$b \times (\text{Face value}) = b \times FV$$

In this section we consider the special case where a bond is being sold on an interest payment date (with the interest payment going to the seller). **Figure 16.2** illustrates the future payments that a prospective purchaser/investor can expect to receive. There are n interest payments remaining until the bond matures. Each interest payment is $b(FV)$. At the time of the final interest payment, the face value FV will also be received. According to the Valuation Principle, the fair market value of the bond is the present value of these future payments discounted at the *prevailing rate of return* in the bond market. That is,

$$\left(\begin{matrix}\text{Fair market}\\\text{value of a bond}\end{matrix}\right) = \left(\begin{matrix}\text{Present value of the}\\\text{interest payments}\end{matrix}\right) + \left(\begin{matrix}\text{Present value of}\\\text{the face value}\end{matrix}\right)$$

FIGURE 16.2	Expected Payments from a Bond

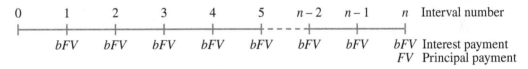

Since the interest payments form an ordinary annuity, we will use Formula (11-2) to obtain the present value of the interest payments. The present value of the face value can be calculated using $PV = FV(1 + i)^{-n}$. Hence, the combined present value is

BOND PRICE (ON AN INTEREST PAYMENT DATE)

$$\text{Bond price} = b(FV)\left[\frac{1 - (1 + i)^{-n}}{i}\right] + FV(1 + i)^{-n} \qquad \text{(16-1)}$$

where i is the prevailing six-month periodic rate of return in the bond market.

 TIP

Different Roles of Coupon Rate and Bond Market Rate of Return

The bond's coupon rate is used only to determine the size of the periodic interest payments. The prevailing rate of return in the bond market is used to discount the future payments when calculating the bond's price.

EXAMPLE 16.2A

CALCULATING THE PRICE OF A BOND ON AN INTEREST PAYMENT DATE

Calculate the market value of Bonds B, C, and D in Table 16.1 (reproduced below).

Bond	Issue date	Initial term (years)	Coupon rate (%)	Bond price
A	Today	5	6	$1000
B	5 years ago	10	7	More than $1000
C	10 years ago	15	6	$1000
D	15 years ago	20	5	Less than $1000

SOLUTION

Since the new issue of five-year bonds carries a 6% coupon rate, the current competitive rate of return on five-year bonds is 6% compounded semiannually. Therefore, we will use $i = \frac{6\%}{2} = 3\%$ to discount the remaining payments from Bonds B, C, and D.

For Bond B, $\quad\quad FV = \$1000, \quad n = 2(5) = 10, \quad b = \frac{7\%}{2} = 3.5\%, \quad b(FV) = 0.035(\$1000) = \$35$

Similarly, for Bond C, $\quad FV = \$1000, \quad n = 10, \quad\quad\quad b = 3\%, \quad\quad\quad b(FV) = \$30$

and for Bond D, $\quad\quad FV = \$1000, \quad n = 10, \quad\quad\quad b = 2.5\%, \quad\quad b(FV) = \$25$

$$\text{Price of Bond B} = b(FV)\left[\frac{1 - (1 + i)^{-n}}{i}\right] + FV(1 + i)^{-n}$$

$$= \$35\left(\frac{1 - 1.03^{-10}}{0.03}\right) + \$1000(1.03^{-10})$$

$$= \$298.56 + \$744.09$$

$$= \$1042.65$$

6 I/Y
P/Y 2 ENTER
(making $C/Y = P/Y = 2$)
10 N
35 PMT
1000 FV
CPT PV
Ans: −1042.65

$$\text{Price of Bond C} = \$30\left(\frac{1 - 1.03^{-10}}{0.03}\right) + \$1000(1.03^{-10})$$

$$= \$255.91 + \$744.09$$

$$= \$1000.00$$

Same *I/Y, P/Y, C/Y, N, FV*
30 PMT
CPT PV
Ans: −1000.00

$$\text{Price of Bond D} = \$25\left(\frac{1 - 1.03^{-10}}{0.03}\right) + \$1000(1.03^{-10})$$

$$= \$213.26 + \$744.09$$

$$= \$957.35$$

Same *I/Y, P/Y, C/Y, N, FV*
25 PMT
CPT PV
Ans: −957.35

The prices of Bonds B, C, and D are $1042.65, $1000, and $957.35, respectively.

These prices confirm the relative prices we deduced in the last column of Table 16.1.

Postscript Let us be clear on how the purchaser of Bond B will earn the market rate of return (6%) that the present-value calculation builds into the bond's price. The $70 annual interest by itself represents an *income yield* of

$$\frac{\$70}{\$1042.65} \times 100\% = 6.7\%$$

However, over the entire five years there will be a *capital loss* of $1042.65 − $1000 = $42.65. The capital loss per year is

$$\frac{\$42.65}{5} = \$8.53, \text{ representing a loss of } \frac{\$8.53}{\$1042.65} \times 100\% = 0.8\% \text{ per year}$$

$$\text{Rate of total return} = \text{Income yield} + \text{Capital loss yield} \approx 6.7\% + (-0.8\%) \approx 5.9\%$$

(The reason we do not get exactly 6% compounded semiannually is that our crude calculation ignores the timing of payments and the effect of semiannual compounding.)

EXAMPLE 16.2B

CALCULATING A BOND'S PRICE CHANGE RESULTING FROM A CHANGE IN THE PREVAILING INTEREST RATE

A $5000 face value bond has a coupon rate of 6.6% and a maturity date of March 1, 2035. Interest is paid semiannually. On September 1, 2019, the prevailing interest rate on long-term bonds abruptly rose from 6% to 6.2% compounded semiannually. What were the bond's prices before and after the interest rate change?

SOLUTION

Given: $FV = \$5000$, $b = \frac{6.6\%}{2} = 3.3\%$

September 1, 2019 was an interest payment date, after which $15\frac{1}{2}$ years remain until maturity of the bond ($n = 31$). The semiannual interest from the bond is

$$b(FV) = 0.033(\$5000) = \$165$$

On September 1, 2019, the prevailing periodic market rate rose from

$$i = \frac{6\%}{2} = 3\% \quad \text{to} \quad i = \frac{6.2\%}{2} = 3.1\%$$

$$\text{Bond price before rate increase} = b(FV)\left[\frac{1 - (1 + i)^{-n}}{i}\right] + FV(1 + i)^{-n}$$

$$= \$165\left(\frac{1 - 1.03^{-31}}{0.03}\right) + \$5000(1.03^{-31})$$

$$= \$3300.07 + \$1999.94$$

$$= \$5300.01$$

6	I/Y
P/Y	2 ENTER

(making $C/Y = P/Y = 2$)

31	N
165	PMT
5000	FV
CPT	PV

Ans: −5300.01

$$\text{Bond price after rate increase} = \$165\left(\frac{1 - 1.031^{-31}}{0.031}\right) + \$5000(1.031^{-31})$$

$$= \$3256.71 + \$1940.67$$

$$= \$5197.38$$

Same *P/Y, C/Y*

Same *N, PMT, FV*

6.2	I/Y
CPT	PV

Ans: −5197.38

The bond's price dropped from $5300.01 to $5197.38 as a result of the interest rate increase. [Although the bond's price remained above the face value (since $b > i$), the bond price decreased by $102.63.]

EXAMPLE 16.2C

CALCULATING THE CAPITAL GAIN FROM AN INVESTMENT IN BONDS

Mr. Manhas purchased 10 bonds, each with a face value of $1000 and paying a 6% coupon rate. On the purchase date, the bonds still had $9\frac{1}{2}$ years remaining until maturity, and the market rate of return for bonds of this maturity was 7% compounded semiannually. Two and one-half years later, when the interest rate had declined to 5.5% compounded semiannually, he sold the bonds. What was the capital gain (or loss) on the bond investment?

SOLUTION

$$\text{Capital gain} = 10(\text{Selling price per bond} - \text{Purchase price per bond})$$

For calculating the purchase price of each bond,

$$FV = \$1000 \quad b = \tfrac{6\%}{2} = 3\% \quad b(FV) = \$30 \quad n = 2(9.5) = 19 \quad \text{and} \quad i = \tfrac{7\%}{2} = 3.5\%$$

For calculating the selling price of each bond,

$$FV = \$1000 \quad b = 3\% \quad b(FV) = \$30 \quad n = 2(7) = 14 \quad \text{and} \quad i = \tfrac{5.5\%}{2} = 2.75\%$$

$$\text{Purchase price} = b(FV)\left[\frac{1 - (1 + i)^{-n}}{i}\right] + FV(1 + i)^{-n}$$

$$= \$30\left(\frac{1 - 1.035^{-19}}{0.035}\right) + \$1000(1.035^{-19})$$

$$= \$411.295 + \$520.156$$

$$= \$931.45$$

7 I/Y
P/Y 2 ENTER
(making $C/Y = P/Y = 2$)
19 N
30 PMT
1000 FV
CPT PV
Ans: −931.45

$$\text{Selling price} = \$30\left(\frac{1 - 1.0275^{-14}}{0.0275}\right) + \$1000(1.0275^{-14})$$

$$= \$344.730 + \$683.997$$

$$= \$1028.73$$

Same *P/Y, C/Y, PMT, FV*
14 N
5.5 I/Y
CPT PV
Ans: −1028.73

$$\text{Capital gain} = 10(\$1028.73 - \$931.45) = \$972.80$$

Bond Premium and Bond Discount

Figure 16.3 shows graphs of bond price versus the prevailing market rate of return for two 7% coupon, $1000 face value bonds. One bond has five years remaining until maturity, and the other has 10 years until maturity. For the reasons discussed earlier, the market values of both bonds are *below* their $1000 face value when the market rate of return *exceeds* the 7% coupon rate. In this circumstance, we say that each bond trades at a discount. The amount of the discount is

$$\textbf{Bond discount} = \text{Face value} - \text{Bond price when } i > b$$

FIGURE 16.3 Bond Price versus Market Rate of Return for Two Maturities of 7% Coupon Bonds

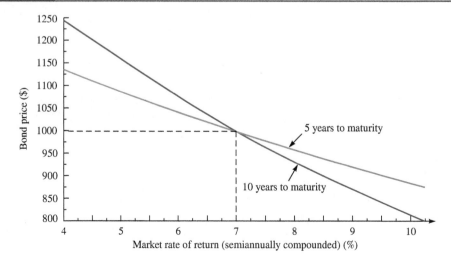

The discount is larger for the bond with the longer maturity.

Similarly, the market values of both bonds are *above* their face value when the market rate of return is *less* than the 7% coupon rate. In this circumstance, we say that each bond trades at a premium. The amount of the premium is

Bond premium = Bond price − Face value when $i < b$

The premium is larger for the bond with the longer maturity.

The dependence of the discount or premium on the time remaining until maturity can be added to our teeter-totter model as shown in **Figure 16.4**. Think of bonds with longer maturities as "sitting" farther out from the pivot point on the right arm of the teeter-totter. For a given interest rate movement of the left arm, bonds farther away from the pivot point will move through a larger vertical distance. That is, longer-term bonds will undergo a greater change in market value than shorter-term bonds.

FIGURE 16.4   Dependence of Bond Premium on Time to Maturity

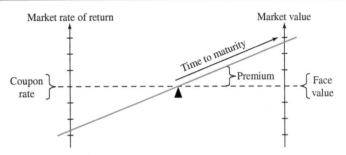

 CONCEPT QUESTIONS

1. Name four variables that affect a bond's price. Which ones, if any, have an inverse effect on the bond's price? That is, for which variables does a lower value of the variable result in a higher bond price?

2. Under what circumstance can you realize a capital gain on a bond investment?

3. Assuming that the bond issuer does not default on any payments, is it possible to lose money on a bond investment? Discuss briefly.

4. On a recent interest payment date, a bond's price exceeded its face value. If the prevailing market rate of return does not change thereafter, will the bond's premium be different on later interest payment dates? Explain.

5. If you are firmly convinced that prevailing interest rates will decline, how should you change the relative weighting of short-term and long-term bonds in your bond portfolio?

EXERCISE 16.2

Answers to the odd-numbered problems are at the end of the book.

 Spreadsheet template: *The Excel workbook "PV of Any Annuity" may be used for many of the problems in Exercise 16.2. Go to the Student Edition and find "PV of Any Annuity" under the Student Resources for Chapter 11.*

Note: Unless otherwise indicated, assume that:
- **Bond interest is paid semiannually.**
- **The bond was originally issued at its face value.**
- **Bonds are redeemed at their face value at maturity.**
- **Market rates of return are compounded semiannually.**

BASIC PROBLEMS

Calculate the purchase price of each of the $1000 face value bonds in Problems 1–8.

Problem	Issue date	Maturity date	Purchase date	Coupon rate (%)	Market rate (%)
1.	June 1, 2010	June 1, 2030	June 1, 2016	5.75	4.5
2.	June 15, 2005	June 15, 2030	Dec 15, 2011	5.0	6.0
3.	Dec 15, 1998	Dec 15. 2023	June 15, 2001	4.75	5.9
4.	Jan 1, 2007	Jan 1, 2027	July 1, 2015	7.3	3.8
5.	May 15, 2010	May 15, 2030	Nov 15, 2016	6.0	4.0
6.	Jan 31, 2009	Jan 31, 2039	July 31, 2011	5.1	6.0
7.	Mar 15, 2007	Mar 15, 2032	Sept 15, 2011	8.8	17.0
8.	Oct 31, 2002	Oct 31, 2027	Apr 30, 2019	16.0	5.7

9. Denis purchased a $10,000 face value Ontario Hydro Energy bond maturing in five years. The coupon rate was 6.5% payable semiannually. If the prevailing market rate at the time of purchase was 5.8% compounded semiannually, what price did Denis pay for the bond?

10. Bernard purchased a $50,000 bond carrying a 4.5% coupon rate when it had 8 years remaining until maturity. What price did he pay if the prevailing rate of return on the purchase date was 5.2% compounded semiannually?

11. A $1000, 6.5% coupon bond has $13\frac{1}{2}$ years remaining until maturity. Calculate the bond premium if the required return in the bond market is 5.5% compounded semiannually.

12. A $1000, 5.5% coupon bond has $8\frac{1}{2}$ years remaining until maturity. Calculate the bond discount if the required return in the bond market is 6.3% compounded semiannually.

13. A $5000, 5.75% coupon bond has 16 years remaining until maturity. Calculate the bond discount if the required return in the bond market is 6.5% compounded semiannually.

14. A $25,000, 6.25% coupon bond has $21\frac{1}{2}$ years remaining until maturity. Calculate the bond premium if the required return in the bond market is 5.2% compounded semiannually.

15. Eight years ago, Yan purchased a $20,000 face value, 6% coupon bond with 15 years remaining to maturity. The prevailing market rate of return at the time was 7.2% compounded semiannually; now it is 4.9% compounded semiannually. How much more or less is the bond worth today?

16. Bond A and Bond B both have a face value of $1000, each carries a 5% coupon, and both are currently priced at par in the bond market. Bond A matures in 2 years and Bond B matures in 10 years. If the prevailing required rate of return in the bond market suddenly drops to 4.7% compounded semiannually, how much will the market price of each bond change? What general rule does this outcome demonstrate?

17. Bond C and Bond D both have a face value of $1000, and each carries a 4.2% coupon. Bond C matures in 3 years and Bond B matures in 23 years. If the prevailing required rate of return in the bond market suddenly rises from the current 4.5% to 4.8% compounded semiannually, how much will the market price of each bond change? What general rule does this outcome demonstrate?

18. **Using the "Market Value of Bonds" Chart** Connect provides an interactive chart for comparing the response of the prices of two bonds to a given change in the bond market's required rate of return. In Chapter 16 of the Student Edition, find "Market Value of Bonds." Follow the instructions provided with this chart to solve:
    a. Problem 16.   b. Problem 17.

19. Bonds A, B, C, and D all have a face value of $1000 and carry a 7% coupon. The time remaining until maturity is 5, 10, 15, and 25 years for A, B, C, and D, respectively. Calculate their market prices if the rate of return required by the market on these bonds is 6% compounded semiannually. Summarize the observed pattern or trend in a brief statement.

20. Bonds E, F, G, and H all have a face value of $1000 and carry a 7% coupon. The time remaining until maturity is 5, 10, 15, and 25 years for E, F, G, and H, respectively. Calculate their market prices if the rate of return required by the market on these bonds is 8% compounded semiannually. Summarize the observed pattern or trend in a brief statement.

21. Bonds J, K, and L all have a face value of $1000 and all have 20 years remaining until maturity. Their respective coupon rates are 6%, 7%, and 8%. Calculate their market prices if the rate of return required by the market on these bonds is 5% compounded semiannually. Summarize the observed pattern or trend in a brief statement.

22. Bonds M, N, and Q all have a face value of $1000 and all have 20 years remaining until maturity. Their respective coupon rates are 7%, 6%, and 5%. Calculate their market prices if the rate of return required by the market on these bonds is 8% compounded semiannually. Summarize the observed pattern or trend in a brief statement.

INTERMEDIATE PROBLEMS

23. A $1000, 7% coupon bond has 15 years remaining until maturity. The rate of return required by the market on these bonds has recently been 7% (compounded semiannually). Calculate the price change if the required return abruptly:
    a. Rises to 8%.   b. Rises to 9%.
    c. Falls to 6%.   d. Falls to 5%.
    e. Is the price change caused by a 2% interest rate increase twice the price change caused by a 1% interest rate increase?
    f. Compare the magnitude of the price change caused by a 1% interest rate increase to the price change caused by a 1% interest rate decrease.

24. This problem investigates the sensitivity of the prices of bonds carrying differing coupon rates to interest rate changes. Bonds K and L both have a face value of $1000 and 15 years remaining until maturity. Their coupon rates are 6% and 8%, respectively. If the prevailing market rate decreases from 7.5% to 6.5% compounded semiannually, calculate the price change of each bond:
    a. In dollars.   b. As a percentage of the initial price.
    c. Are high-coupon or low-coupon bonds more sensitive to a given interest rate change? Justify your response using the results from part (b).

25. Three years after the issue of a $10,000, 6.5% coupon, 25-year bond, the rate of return required in the bond market on long-term bonds is 5.6% compounded semiannually.
    a. At what price would the bond sell?
    b. What capital gain or loss (expressed as a percentage of the original investment) would the owner realize by selling the bond at that price?

26. Four and one-half years ago Gavin purchased a $25,000 bond in a new Province of Ontario issue with a 20-year maturity and a 6.1% coupon. If the prevailing market rate is now 7.1% compounded semiannually:
   a. What would be the proceeds from the sale of Gavin's bond?
   b. What would be the capital gain or loss (expressed as a percentage of the original investment)?

27. Three years ago Quebec Hydro sold an issue of 20-year, 6.5% coupon bonds. Calculate an investor's percent capital gain for the entire three-year holding period if the current semi-annually compounded return required in the bond market is:
   a. 5.5%.   b. 6.5%   c. 7.5%.

28. Two and one-half years ago the Province of Saskatchewan sold an issue of 25-year, 6% coupon bonds. Calculate an investor's percent capital gain for the entire $2\frac{1}{2}$-year holding period if the current rate of return required in the bond market is:
   a. 6.5%.   b. 6%.   c. 5.5%.

ADVANCED PROBLEMS

29. During periods of declining interest rates, long-term bonds can provide investors with impressive capital gains. An extraordinary example occurred in the early 1980s. In September 1981, the bond market was pricing long-term bonds to provide a rate of return of 18.5% compounded semiannually. Suppose you had purchased 10% coupon bonds in September 1981 with 20 years remaining until maturity. Four and one-half years later (in March 1986) the bonds could have been sold at a prevailing market rate of 9.7% compounded semi-annually. What would have been your semiannually compounded rate of total return on the bonds during the $4\frac{1}{2}$-year period?

30. The downside of the long-term bond investment story occurs during periods of rising long-term interest rates, when bond prices fall. During the two years preceding September 1981, the market rate of return on long-term bonds rose from 11% to 18.5% compounded semi-annually. Suppose that in September 1979 you had purchased 10% coupon bonds with 22 years remaining until maturity, and then sold them in September 1981. What would have been your semiannually compounded rate of total return on the bonds during the two-year period?

16.3 Yield to Maturity on an Interest Payment Date

L02 Suppose you purchase a bond at the price given by Formula (16-1). If you intend to *keep the bond until it matures*, your future rate of return can be predicted with certainty. It is the market rate of return used on the purchase date to calculate the purchase price. In the language of bonds, this rate of return is called the **yield to maturity (YTM)**.[4] It is standard practice to quote the YTM as a semiannually compounded nominal rate. The yield to maturity is "locked in" by the price you pay for the bond—the higher the purchase price, the lower the bond's YTM.

If you purchase a bond at the price given by Formula (16-1) and intend to *sell it before it matures*, your future rate of return *cannot* be predicted with certainty. Your actual rate of return will depend on the ultimate selling price, which in turn will depend on the market rate of return on the date of sale. The prevailing market rate of return on a future date is not known in advance.

---

[4] The yield to maturity is sometimes called simply the "yield" or the "bond yield." For example, quotations of bond yields to maturity in newspapers' financial pages use just "yield" or "bond yield" to mean yield to maturity. However, "yield" is also used to refer to a bond's "current yield" (defined as the annual coupon interest as a percentage of the bond's market price). Therefore, use of the simple term "yield" to mean "yield to maturity" should be discouraged because of this ambiguity.

APP **4** THAT

If you are purchasing bonds, it is unlikely you are buying a newly issued bond and you will most likely pay an amount more or less than the bond's face value. This means that the actual rate of return on the bond will be different than the coupon rate. Search the App Store on your tablet, smartphone, or smart watch using the key words **BOND CALCULATOR**.

You will find many free and paid apps that will calculate your potential returns when investing in marketable bonds.

In **Section 16.2**, we learned how to answer the following question. Given the prevailing market rate of return (that is, given the yield to maturity required by the bond market), what is the market value of a bond? The other question a bond investor commonly faces is: What yield to maturity will a bond provide if it is purchased at its offered price?

To answer the second question, the mathematical task is to solve Formula (16-1) for i given the bond price. The (semiannually compounded) yield to maturity is then $2i$. The algebraic approach requires the trial-and-error method (**Appendix 12B**). In this method, you substitute estimates of i into the formula until you find an estimate that comes close to satisfying the formula. Since the financial calculator method for calculating the yield to maturity is more accurate and much more efficient, the algebraic method will be demonstrated in only one of the following examples.

EXAMPLE 16.3A

CALCULATING THE YIELD TO MATURITY OF A BOND

A $1000 face value Province of Manitoba bond bearing interest at 5.8% payable semiannually has 11 years remaining until maturity. What is the bond's yield to maturity (YTM) at its current market price of $972?

SOLUTION

This bond's yield to maturity is the discount rate that makes the combined present value of all remaining interest payments and the face value equal to the bond's market value. We are given:

$$FV = \$1000 \quad b = \frac{5.8\%}{2} = 2.9\% \quad b(FV) = \$29 \quad n = 22 \quad \text{and} \quad \text{bond price} = \$972$$

Substitute these values into

$$\text{Bond price} = b(FV)\left[\frac{1 - (1 + i)^{-n}}{i}\right] + FV(1 + i)^{-n}$$

The YTM is the value of $2i$, where i is the solution to

$$\$972 = \underbrace{\$29\left[\frac{1 - (1 + i)^{-22}}{i}\right]}_{\text{Term 1}} + \underbrace{\$1000(1 + i)^{-22}}_{\text{Term 2}}$$

| P/Y 2 ENTER |
| (making $C/Y = P/Y = 2$) |
| 22 N |
| 972 +/− PV |
| 29 PMT |
| 1000 FV |
| CPT I/Y |

Ans: 6.154

The bond's YTM is 6.154% compounded semiannually.

In the trial-and-error method, we try various values for i on the right-hand side (RHS) until we get a value for the RHS sufficiently close to $972. For an initial estimate, we can deduce that i will be greater than $b = 2.9\%$ because the bond price is less than its face value. Let us try $i = 3\%$. The results of the substitution are shown as Trial 1 in the table below.

With $i = 3\%$, the value of the RHS is $984.06. This is higher than the actual bond price of $972. For our second trial, we should choose a larger i because bond prices fall when market rates rise. Try $i = 3.1\%$ for Trial 2.

Trial number	Estimated i (%)	Term 1 ($)	Term 2 ($)	RHS ($)	Deviation from $972 (in $)
1	3.0	462.17	521.89	984.06	12.06
2	3.1	457.57	510.87	968.44	−3.56
3	3.07	458.95	514.15	973.10	1.10

Substitution of $i = 3.1\%$ gives RHS = \$968.44. After a couple of trials, we can use the "Deviation" values in the last column to make a more intelligent estimate for the third trial. In the present case, $i = 3.0\%$ makes the RHS too large and $i = 3.1\%$ makes the RHS too small. Therefore, the value of i that makes the RHS = \$972 is between $i = 3.0\%$ and $i = 3.1\%$. Furthermore, it is closer to 3.1% than to 3.0% because 3.1% produces a smaller deviation. Let us use $i = 3.07\%$ in Trial 3.

The Trial 3 deviation indicates that our estimate of $i = 3.07\%$ is a little too low because it makes RHS a little too large. By comparing the size of the deviations for Trials 2 and 3, we can see that the correct value of i to the nearest 0.01% is 3.08%.

The bond's YTM is $2i \approx 2(3.08\%) \approx 6.16\%$ compounded semiannually.

EXAMPLE 16.3B

CALCULATING THE YIELD TO MATURITY OF A HIGH-RISK OR "DEEP-DISCOUNT" BOND

A corporation's financial condition may deteriorate to the point where there is some doubt about its ability to make future interest payments on its bonds or to redeem the bonds at maturity. Investors are then unwilling to buy the bonds at a price based on market rates of return on bonds of healthy corporations. The price of bonds of the financially distressed corporation will fall to a level determined more by the perceived risk than by the prevailing market rates of return. It is still useful to calculate the YTM on such "deep-discount" bonds. The YTM represents the rate of return the bond purchaser will realize if (1) the corporation does manage to meet all scheduled payments on time, and (2) the bond is held until the maturity date.

Calculate the YTM on the \$1000, 9% coupon bonds of Beaucamp Corp., which are trading at \$500. The bonds have $7\frac{1}{2}$ years remaining until maturity.

SOLUTION

Given: $FV = \$1000$, $b = \frac{9\%}{2} = 4.5\%$, $b(FV) = \$45$, $n = 2(7.5) = 15$, and bond price = \$500

The YTM is the value of $2i$, where i is the solution to

$$\$500 = \$45\left[\frac{1-(1+i)^{-15}}{i}\right] + \$1000(1+i)^{-15}$$

The bond's YTM is $2i = 23.48\%$ compounded semiannually.

P/Y	2	ENTER

(making $C/Y = P/Y = 2$)

15	N

500	+/–	PV

45	PMT

1000	FV

CPT	I/Y

Ans: 23.48

EXERCISE 16.3

Answers to the odd-numbered problems are at the end of the book.

Spreadsheet template: *The partially completed Excel template introduced in Section 12.3 for calculating the interest rate in an annuity may be used for most of the problems in Exercise 16.3. To access the template, go to the Student Edition and find "Rate for Any Annuity" under the Student Resources for Chapter 12.*

Note: Unless otherwise indicated, assume that:
• *Bond interest is paid semiannually.*
• *The bond was originally issued at its face value.*
• *Bonds are redeemed at their face value at maturity.*
• *Market rates of return and yields to maturity are compounded semiannually.*

BASIC PROBLEMS

1. A bond with a face value of $1000 and 15 years remaining until maturity pays a coupon rate of 5%. Calculate its yield to maturity if it is priced at $900.

2. A bond with a face value of $1000 and 15 years remaining until maturity pays a coupon rate of 10%. Calculate its yield to maturity if it is priced at $1250.

3. Manuel bought a $100,000 bond with a 4% coupon for $92,300 when it had five years remaining to maturity. What was the prevailing market rate at the time Manuel purchased the bond?

4. Pina bought a 6% coupon, $20,000 face value corporate bond for $21,000 when it had 10 years remaining until maturity. What are her nominal and effective yields to maturity on the bond?

5. Bonds A and C both have a face value of $1000 and pay a coupon rate of 6.5%. They have 5 and 20 years, respectively, remaining until maturity. Calculate the yield to maturity of each bond if it is purchased for $950.

6. Bonds D and E both have a face value of $1000 and pay a coupon rate of 7%. They have 5 and 20 years, respectively, remaining until maturity. Calculate the yield to maturity of each bond if it is purchased for $1050.

INTERMEDIATE PROBLEMS

7. A $5000 Government of Canada bond carrying a 6% coupon is currently priced to yield 6% compounded semiannually until maturity. If the bond price abruptly rises by $100, what is the change in the yield to maturity if the bond has:
   a. 3 years remaining to maturity?   **b.** 15 years remaining to maturity?

8. A $10,000 Nova Chemicals Corp. bond carrying an 8% coupon is currently priced to yield 7% compounded semiannually until maturity. If the bond price abruptly falls by $250, what is the change in the yield to maturity if the bond has:
   a. 2 years remaining to maturity?   **b.** 12 years remaining to maturity?

9. In the spring of 1992 it became apparent that Olympia & York (O&Y) would have serious difficulty in servicing its debt. Because of this risk, investors were heavily discounting O&Y's bond issues. On April 30, 1992 an Olympia & York bond issue, paying an 11.25% coupon rate and maturing on October 31, 1998, traded at $761.50 (per $1000 of face value). (This was at a time when Government of Canada bonds with a similar coupon and maturity date were trading at a premium of about 10% above par.) If O&Y had managed to make the contractual payments on these bonds, what yield to maturity would investors who purchased those bonds on April 30, 1992 have realized? (P.S. They didn't!)

16.4 Bond Price on Any Date

In **Section 16.2**, we learned how to calculate a bond's price on an interest payment date. This limits us to valuing a particular bond on just the two days in a year when the interest payments are made. But bonds trade in the financial markets *every* business day. We need to develop the further steps required to calculate a bond's price on any date.

Calculating a Bond's Price on Any Date

L01 Regardless of the date of sale, a bond's market value will be the present value of the future payments discounted at the market's required rate of return. For a date of sale lying between interest payment dates, it appears that each payment must be discounted over a non-integral number of compounding intervals. We can, however, use our understanding of equivalent values to develop a simpler procedure. The present value of all payments on the date of sale may be obtained by the two steps indicated in **Figure 16.5**.

Step 1: Calculate the present value of the remaining payments on the *preceding* interest payment date. For the discount rate, use the market rate of return as of the date of sale.

Step 2: The bond price is the future value, on the date of sale, of the Step 1 result. Use $FV = PV(1 + i)^n$ with

$$i = \frac{\text{Market's required rate of return}}{2}$$

and

$$n = \frac{\text{Number of days since the preceding interest payment}}{\text{Total number of days in the full payment interval}}$$

FIGURE 16.5	Calculating a Bond's Price on Any Date

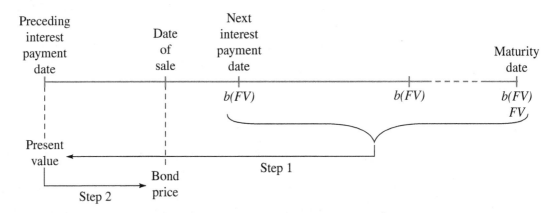

EXAMPLE 16.4A

PRICING A BOND BETWEEN INTEREST PAYMENT DATES

A $1000, 20-year, 6% coupon bond was issued on August 15, 2017. It was sold on November 3, 2019, to yield the purchaser 6.5% compounded semiannually until maturity. At what price did the bond sell?

SOLUTION

Given: $FV = \$1000$, $b = \frac{6\%}{2} = 3\%$, $b(FV) = \$30$, and $i = \frac{6.5\%}{2} = 3.25\%$

The two steps in the solution are indicated in the following diagram. First, determine the present value of the remaining payments at the most recent interest payment date (August 15, 2019). Then calculate the future value of this amount on the date of sale (November 3, 2019).

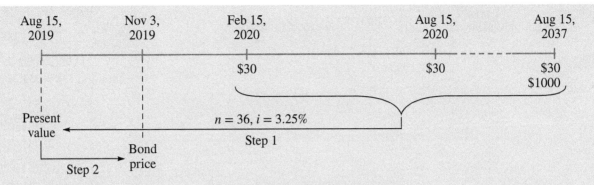

Step 1: Using Formula (16-1) with $n = 2(18) = 36$ interest payments of $30,

$$\text{Present value} = \$30\left(\frac{1 - 1.0325^{-36}}{0.0325}\right) + \$1000(1.0325^{-36})$$

$$= \$631.203 + \$316.197$$

$$= \$947.40$$

6.5	I/Y
P/Y 2	ENTER

(making $C/Y = P/Y = 2$)

36	N
30	PMT
1000	FV
CPT	PV

Ans: −947.40

Step 2: The interval from August 15 to November 3, 2019 is 80 days long. The total length of the interest payment interval from August 15, 2019 to February 15, 2020 is 184 days.

On the date of sale, the fraction of the payment interval that had elapsed was

$$n = \tfrac{80}{184} = 0.4347826$$

$$\text{Price (Nov. 3)} = PV(1 + i)^n$$

$$= \$947.40(1.0325)^{0.4347826}$$

$$= \$960.67$$

Same I/Y, P/Y, C/Y

0.4347826	N
947.40 +/−	PV
0	PMT
CPT	FV

Ans: 960.67

The bond sold for $960.67 on November 3, 2019. (It sold at a discount because the coupon rate was less than the market's required rate of return.)

EXAMPLE 16.4B

PRICING A BOND BETWEEN INTEREST PAYMENT DATES

On January 15, 2009, Westcoast Terminals Inc. issued 20-year bonds having a 7.6% coupon rate. At what price did $1000 face value bonds trade on April 10, 2019, if the required return was 6.2% compounded semiannually?

SOLUTION

Given: $FV = \$1000$, $b = \tfrac{7.6\%}{2} = 3.8\%$, $b(FV) = \$38$, and $i = \tfrac{6.2\%}{2} = 3.1\%$

Step 1: Calculate the present value of the remaining payments at the most recent interest payment date (January 15, 2019). At that point, $n = 2(10) = 20$ interest payments remain.

$$\text{Present value (Jan. 15)} = \$38\left(\frac{1 - 1.031^{-20}}{0.031}\right) + \$1000(1.031^{-20})$$
$$= \$560.152 + \$543.034$$
$$= \$1103.19$$

6.2 | I/Y

P/Y 2 ENTER

(making $C/Y = P/Y = 2$)

20 | N

38 | PMT

1000 | FV

CPT PV

Ans: −1103.19

Step 2: Calculate the future value on the date of sale (April 10, 2019) of the amount from Step 1. The interval from January 15 to April 10, 2019 is 85 days long. The total length of the interest payment interval from January 15 to July 15, 2019 is 181 days.

On the date of sale, the fraction of the payment interval that had elapsed was

$$n = \tfrac{85}{181} = 0.4696133$$

$$\text{Price (April 10)} = PV(1 + i)^n$$
$$= \$1103.19(1.031)^{0.4696133}$$
$$= \$1119.12$$

Same *I/Y, P/Y, C/Y*

0.4696133 | N

1103.19 | +/− | PV

0 | PMT

CPT FV

Ans: 1119.12

The bonds traded at $1119.12 on April 10, 2019. (They traded at a premium because the coupon rate was greater than the market's required rate of return.)

Quotation of Bond Prices

Even if prevailing interest rates do not change the price of a bond will change as time passes, for two reasons. First, the accrual of interest causes a bond's price to steadily rise after an interest payment. Then the price will abruptly fall by the amount $b \times FV$ on the day interest is paid. The result of this cycle repeating every six months is a "sawtooth" pattern for the graph of bond price versus time. **Figure 16.6** illustrates the pattern for the case of a bond selling at a premium. **Figure 16.7** presents the corresponding graph for a bond selling at a discount. The graphs show how the market value of a $1000 face value bond changes over the final six interest payment intervals before the maturity date (assuming that prevailing market rates of return do not change). Note that much of the bond price axis between $0 and $1000 has been omitted to reveal the details of bond price changes on a larger scale. Keep in mind that $b \times FV$ will be in the $20 to $50 range for coupon rates in the 4% to 10% range.

The second reason the bond's price will change is that the premium or discount will diminish over time. The premium on any date in **Figure 16.6** is the distance between the downward-sloping dashed line and the horizontal line at $1000. The discount on any date in **Figure 16.7** is the distance between the horizontal line at $1000 and the upward-sloping dashed line. The premium or discount decreases as time passes because the number of remaining payments decreases. It is the same reason that causes a long-term bond to sell at a larger premium or discount than a short-term bond (other variables being the same for both bonds). By the time a bond reaches its maturity date, any bond premium or discount has shrunk to zero.

FIGURE 16.6   Price Change over Time for a Bond Trading at a Premium

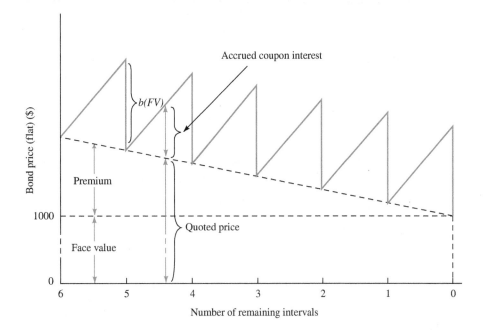

FIGURE 16.7   Price Change over Time for a Bond Trading at a Discount

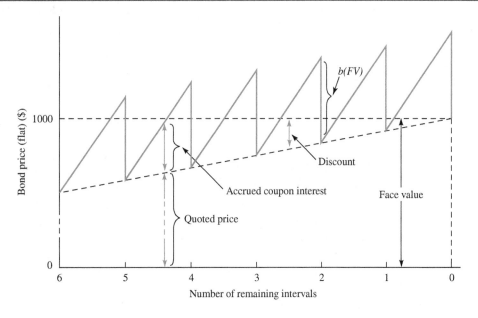

Flat price vs. quoted price   In bond terminology, the bond price we have been calculating (and plotting in **Figures 16.6** and **16.7**) is called the **flat price**. It is the *actual* amount paid by the purchaser and received by the seller (ignoring transaction charges). The flat price includes coupon interest that has accrued since the preceding interest payment date.

Before an investor can make meaningful comparisons among bond prices, the prices must be adjusted for their differing amounts of accrued coupon interest. As an extreme example, the flat prices of two otherwise identical bonds will differ by almost $b \times FV$ if one bond paid its coupon interest yesterday and the other bond will pay interest tomorrow. Accrued interest should be deducted from the flat prices of both bonds to obtain prices that may be fairly compared. For this reason, bond prices are quoted in the financial media and in the bond market with the accrued coupon interest already deducted from the flat price. That is,

Quoted price = Flat price − Accrued coupon interest

In **Figures 16.6** and **16.7**, the flat price on one particular date is broken down into its "accrued coupon interest" and "quoted price" components. The quoted price includes the premium or discount but does not include accrued coupon interest. When they purchase bonds, investors are aware that accrued coupon interest will be *added* to the quoted price, giving the flat price they will pay.

 TIP

Dirty and Clean Bond Pricing

Bond prices are often referred to as "dirty" versus "clean." These are simply alternate terms for the flat price versus the quoted price.

The "dirty" price (flat price) includes the interest that has accrued since the issue of the most recent coupon payment, while the "clean" price (quoted price) excludes this interest amount.

Table 16.2 lists some bond quotations at the close of the bond market on April 15, 2019. Since there can be several face value denominations in any bond issue, bond prices are quoted as a *percentage* of face value. The dollar price of any denomination can readily be calculated using this information. For example, the price of a $5000 face value bond quoted at 102.25(%) is

$$\$5000 \times 1.0225 = \$5112.50$$

Even though the bond yield (meaning yield to maturity) can be calculated from the other information in the table, it is nevertheless quoted in lists of this type because many bond investors are unable to perform the calculation.

TABLE 16.2   Bond Price Quotations (April 15, 2019)

Issuer	Coupon rate (%)	Maturity Date	Quoted price (%)	Bond yield (%)
Government of Canada	2.50	June 1, 2024	104.93	1.497
Province of New Brunswick	2.85	June 2, 2023	103.74	1.903
Province of Ontario	1.35	March 8, 2022	98.97	1.718
Province of British Columbia	3.70	December 18, 2020	103.36	1.652
Ontario Hydro	8.90	August 18, 2022	122.74	1.849

Source: "GIC & Bond Rates," RBC Direct Investing. www.rbcdirectinvesting.com/pricing/gic-bond-rates.html.

Calculating the accrued coupon interest We have mentioned that the buyer of a bond pays accrued coupon interest in addition to the quoted price. The prevailing practice is to calculate accrued coupon interest on a *simple interest* basis. Therefore,

$$\text{Accrued coupon interest} = Prt = (FV)bt$$

where t is the fraction of the payment interval (containing the date of sale) that has elapsed since the preceding interest payment. That is,

$$t = \frac{\text{Number of days since the preceding interest payment}}{\text{Total number of days in the full payment interval}}$$

EXAMPLE 16.4C

CALCULATING THE ACCRUED COUPON INTEREST AND QUOTED PRICE, GIVEN THE FLAT PRICE

In Example 16.4B, we calculated the (flat) price on April 10, 2019, of a $1000 face value, 7.6% coupon Westcoast Energy Inc. bond maturing January 15, 2029. The calculated price for a yield to maturity of 6.2% compounded semiannually was $1119.12.

a. How much of that price was interest that had accrued (in favour of the previous owner) since the preceding interest payment date?

b. What price did the financial media and securities brokers quote for these bonds on April 10, 2019?

SOLUTION

a. The period from the preceding interest payment on January 15, 2019 to the April 10, 2019 date of sale was 85 days long.

The number of days in the full payment interval (from January 15 to July 15) was 181.

The coupon interest that accrued over these 85 days was

$$I = Prt = (FV)bt = \$1000 \times 0.038 \times \tfrac{85}{181} = \$17.85$$

Hence, $17.85 of the $1119.12 flat price was accrued interest.

b. Brokers and financial media report the quoted price. (Bond investors understand that they must pay the accrued interest of $17.85 in addition to the quoted price.)

$$\begin{aligned} \text{Quoted price} &= \text{Flat price} - \text{Accrued interest} \\ &= \$1119.12 - \$17.85 \\ &= \$1101.27 \end{aligned}$$

Using the Texas Instruments BA II PLUS Bond Worksheet This worksheet enables you to compute either a bond's quoted price or its yield to maturity on any date. Appendix 16A provides instructions on the use of the Bond Worksheet. The worksheet will be used for the financial calculator solution in Example 16.4D.

EXAMPLE 16.4D

CALCULATING THE ACCRUED COUPON INTEREST AND QUOTED PRICE GIVEN THE YIELD TO MATURITY

For the Government of Canada bond listed in Table 16.2, show how the quoted price may be calculated from the other information provided in the table. What accrued interest (in addition to the quoted price) did an investor have to pay on April 15, 2019 to purchase a $10,000 denomination bond?

SOLUTION

From the table, we see that the Government of Canada bond matures on June 1, 2024. The bond market was pricing these bonds on April 15, 2019 to yield 1.497% (compounded semiannually) until maturity. We have

$$FV = \$10,000, \quad b = \tfrac{2.50\%}{2} = 1.25\%, \quad b(FV) = \$125.00, \quad i = \tfrac{1.497\%}{2} = 0.7485\%$$

The steps in the algebraic solution are:

Step 1: Calculate the present value of the remaining payments on the preceding interest payment date (December 1, 2018). After that date, $n = 2(5) + 1 = 11$ interest payments remain.

Step 2: Calculate the *flat* price on April 15, 2019 by calculating the future value of the Step 1 result with interest at 1.497% compounded semiannually.

Step 3: Calculate the coupon interest that accrues from December 1, 2018 to April 15, 2019.

Step 4: Deduct the accrued coupon interest from the flat price (Step 2 result) to get the *quoted* price.

If we use the Bond Worksheet on the Texas Instruments BA II PLUS calculator, we can directly obtain both the quoted price and the accrued interest.

Step 1: Present value (Dec. 1) $= \$125.00 \left(\dfrac{1 - 1.007485^{-11}}{0.007485} \right) + \$10,000(1.007485)^{-11}$

$= \$1315.20 + \$9212.46$

$= \$10,527.66$

Step 2: We need the fraction of the December 1 to June 1 payment interval that has elapsed as of April 15, 2019. There are 135 days from December 1, 2018 to April 15, 2019, and 182 days from December 1, 2018 to June 1, 2019. Therefore, the fraction of the payment interval that had elapsed was

$$n = \tfrac{135}{182} = 0.741758242$$

Flat price (January 13) $= \$10,527.66(1.007485^{0.741758242}) = \$10,586.05$

Step 3: Accrued coupon interest $= Prt$

$= (FV)bt$

$= \$10,000 \times 0.0125 \times \tfrac{135}{182}$

$= \$92.72$

Step 4: Quoted price = Flat price − Accrued interest

$= \$10,586.05 - \$92.72 = \$10,493.33$

The quoted price in **Table 16.2** is 104.93% of face value. Note that the yield we used in our calculations was quoted with only four-figure accuracy. Therefore, our calculated price can have a rounding error showing up in the third or fourth figure.

In addition to the quoted price, the purchaser of the $10,000 face value bond must pay accrued interest of $92.72. (In the Bond Worksheet approach, we obtained $AI = \$0.9272$ per $100 of face value. For a face value of $10,000, the accrued interest is $\tfrac{\$10,000}{\$100} \times 0.9272 = \$92.72$)

Calculator key sequence (right margin):

2nd BOND
4.1519 ENTER
↓ 2.5 ENTER
↓ 6.0124 ENTER
↓ 100 ENTER
↓ Set at "*ACT*"
↓ Set at "*2/Y*"
↓ 1.497 ENTER
↓ CPT
Ans: PRI = 104.93
↓ Ans: AI = 0.9272

EXERCISE 16.4

Answers to the odd-numbered problems are at the end of the book.

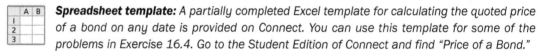

Spreadsheet template: *A partially completed Excel template for calculating the quoted price of a bond on any date is provided on Connect. You can use this template for some of the problems in Exercise 16.4. Go to the Student Edition of Connect and find "Price of a Bond."*

Note: Unless otherwise indicated, assume that:
- ***Bond interest is paid semiannually.***
- ***The bond was originally issued at its face value.***
- ***Bonds will be redeemed for their face value at maturity.***
- ***Market rates of return and yields to maturity are compounded semiannually.***

BASIC PROBLEMS

Calculate the purchase price (flat) of each of the $1000 face value bonds in Problems 1–8.

Problem	Issue date	Maturity date	Purchase date	Coupon rate (%)	Market rate (%)
1.	June 1, 2010	June 1, 2030	June 15, 2019	8.0	5.25
2.	March 15, 2002	March 15, 2027	Oct 5, 2008	5.5	6.0
3.	Jan 1, 2006	Jan 1, 2021	April 15, 2006	4.0	4.5
4.	Sept 20, 2008	Sept 20, 2028	June 1, 2011	5.0	5.8
5.	Aug 1, 2015	Aug 1, 2035	Dec 15, 2019	6.1	4.9
6.	July 1, 2012	July 1, 2032	April 9, 2013	4.3	5.5
7.	Dec 1, 2012	Dec 1, 2032	Mar 25, 2014	5.2	5.7
8.	April 1, 2013	April 1, 2037	June 20, 2015	5.4	6.1

INTERMEDIATE PROBLEMS

9. A $1000, 6.5% coupon bond issued by Bell Canada matures on October 15, 2039. What was its flat price on June 11, 2020 if its yield to maturity was 4.75% compounded semiannually?

10. A $1000, 6% coupon, 25-year Government of Canada bond was issued on June 1, 2015. At what flat price did it sell on April 27, 2019 if the market's required return was 4.6% compounded semiannually?

11. A $1000, 10% coupon bond issued by Ontario Hydro on July 15, 2011 matures on July 15, 2036. What was its flat price on June 1, 2020 when the required yield to maturity was 5.5% compounded semiannually?

12. A $1000, 6.75% coupon, 25-year Government of Canada bond was issued on March 15, 1971. At what flat price did it trade on July 4, 1981, when the market's required return was 17% compounded semiannually?

13. A $1000, 5.2% coupon, 20-year Province of Ontario bond was issued on March 15, 2019. Calculate its flat price on March 15, April 15, May 15, June 15, July 15, August 15, and September 15, 2020, if the yield to maturity on every date was 6% compounded semiannually.

14. A $1000, 7% coupon, 15-year Province of Saskatchewan bond was issued on May 20, 2017. Calculate its (flat) price on May 20, June 20, July 20, August 20, September 20, October 20, and November 20, 2019, if the yield to maturity on every date was 5.9% compounded semiannually.

Problems 15–19 require the calculation of quoted bond prices and accrued interest.

15. A $1000 face value, 7.6% coupon bond pays interest on May 15 and November 15. If its flat price on August 1 was $1065.50, at what price (expressed as a percentage of face value) would the issue have been reported in the financial pages?

16. A $5000 bond was sold for $4860 (flat) on September 17. If the bond pays $200 interest on June 1 and December 1 of each year, what price (expressed as a percentage of face value) would have been quoted for bonds of this issue on September 17?

17. If a broker quotes a price of 108.50 for a bond on October 23, what amount will a client pay per $1000 face value? The 7.2% coupon rate is payable on March 1 and September 1 of each year. The relevant February has 28 days.

18. Calculate the quoted price on April 15, 2006 of the bond described in Problem 3.

19. Calculate the quoted price on June 1, 2011 of the bond described in Problem 4.

Refer to Table 16.2, reproduced here for convenience, in answering Problems 20–23.

TABLE 16.2   Bond Price Quotations (April 15, 2019)

Issuer	Coupon rate (%)	Maturity Date	Quoted price (%)	Bond yield (%)
Government of Canada	2.50	June 1, 2024	104.93	1.497
Province of New Brunswick	2.85	June 2, 2023	103.74	1.903
Province of Ontario	1.35	March 8, 2022	98.97	1.718
Province of British Columbia	3.70	December 18, 2020	103.36	1.652
Ontario Hydro	8.90	August 18, 2022	122.74	1.849

Source: "GIC & Bond Rates," RBC Direct Investing. www.rbcdirectinvesting.com/pricing/gic-bond-rates.html.

20. Using the bond yield given in the final column of Table 16.2, verify the April 15, 2019, quoted price for the Province of New Brunswick 2.85% coupon bond maturing June 2, 2023.

21. Using the bond yield given in the final column of Table 16.2, verify the April 15, 2019, quoted price for the Province of Ontario 1.35% coupon bond maturing March 8, 2022.

22. Using the bond yield given in the final column of Table 16.2, verify the April 15, 2019, quoted price for the Province of British Columbia 3.70% coupon bond maturing December 18, 2020.

23. Using the bond price given in the second-to-last column of Table 16.2, verify the April 15, 2019, yield (to maturity) for the Ontario Hydro 8.90% coupon bond maturing August 18, 2020.

ADVANCED PROBLEMS

24. A $10,000, 14% coupon, 25-year bond issued on June 15, 2014, was purchased on March 20, 2017, to yield 9% to maturity, and then sold on April 20, 2020, to yield the purchaser 11.5% to maturity. What was the investor's capital gain or loss:
    a. In dollars?
    b. As a percentage of his original investment?

25. A $5000, 7% coupon, 20-year bond issued on January 21, 2015, was purchased on January 25, 2016, to yield 6.5% to maturity, and then sold on January 13, 2017, to yield the purchaser 5.2% to maturity. What was the investor's capital gain or loss:
    a. In dollars?
    b. As a percentage of her original investment?

*16.5 Sinking Funds

A **sinking fund** is an interest-earning account into which periodic deposits are made for the purpose of accumulating a required amount of money by a particular date. The accumulated funds are typically used for a capital expenditure or to retire the principal amount of a debt.

Sinking Fund for a Capital Expenditure

A sinking fund can be established by a business to accumulate funds for a future project, replacement of equipment, expansion of production facilities, or an acquisition.

L03 The simplest sinking fund arrangement requires *equal periodic* contributions. The payment size is calculated so that, at the expected rate of return, the *future value* of the payments on the target date equals the amount needed. We will deal only with cases where the interval between contributions equals the compounding interval. The payments then form a *simple* annuity. If the sinking fund payments are made at the *end* of each payment interval, you calculate their size by solving for *PMT* in:

$$FV = PMT\left[\frac{(1+i)^n - 1}{i}\right]$$

(11-1)

If the sinking fund payments are made at the *beginning* of each payment interval, solve for *PMT* in:

$$FV(\text{due}) = PMT\left[\frac{(1+i)^n - 1}{i}\right] \times (1+i)$$

(13-1)

L04 A table presenting details of the increase in the sinking fund each period is called a **sinking fund schedule**. The balance or accumulated amount in the sinking fund at the *end* of any interval is the future value of payments already made. The following relationships are used in constructing a sinking fund schedule.

$$\left(\begin{array}{c}\text{Balance at the end of}\\\text{any payment interval}\end{array}\right) = \left(\begin{array}{c}\text{Future value of the}\\\text{payments already made}\end{array}\right)$$

$$\left(\begin{array}{c}\text{Interest earned in}\\\text{any payment interval}\end{array}\right) = i \times \left(\begin{array}{c}\text{Amount in the sinking fund}\\\text{at the beginning of the interval}\end{array}\right)$$

TRAP

Interest Earned When Payments Form an Annuity Due

Be careful when using the preceding idea to calculate the interest earned during a payment interval of an annuity due. The interest-earning amount at the beginning of an interval is the previous interval's ending balance *plus* the new contribution at the beginning of the current interval.

$$\begin{pmatrix}\text{Increase in the sinking fund's balance}\\ \text{during any payment interval}\end{pmatrix} = PMT + \begin{pmatrix}\text{Interest earned}\\ \text{during the interval}\end{pmatrix}$$

This increase can be added to the balance from the end of the preceding interval to obtain the new balance. The format for a sinking fund schedule is presented in the following examples.

EXAMPLE 16.5A

PREPARATION OF A COMPLETE SINKING FUND SCHEDULE IN WHICH THE PAYMENTS FORM AN ORDINARY ANNUITY

Borland Engineering plans to undertake a $900,000 expansion six years from now. By that time, Borland wants to accumulate half of the cost of the expansion by making payments into a sinking fund at the end of each of the next six years. It is anticipated that the money in the sinking fund will earn 7% compounded annually.

a. What should be the size of the annual payments?

b. How much of the money in the sinking fund at the end of the six years will be interest earnings?

c. Prepare a sinking fund schedule. Verify the answer to part (b) by summing the "interest earned" column.

SOLUTION

a. The future value of the six sinking fund payments, invested at 7% compounded annually, must be $450,000. Substitute $FV = \$450,000$, $i = \frac{7\%}{1} = 7\%$, and $n = 1(6) = 6$ into Formula (11-1). Then solve for *PMT*.

$$FV = PMT\left[\frac{(1+i)^n - 1}{i}\right]$$

$$\$450,000 = PMT\left[\frac{(1.07)^6 - 1}{0.07}\right]$$

$$= PMT(7.1532907)$$

$$PMT = \$62,908.11$$

7 I/Y

P/Y 1 ENTER

(making *C/Y = P/Y* = 1)

6 N

0 PV

450000 FV

CPT PMT

Ans: −62,908.11

The annual sinking fund payment should be $62,908.11.

b. The total of the payments to the sinking fund will be

$$6 \times \$62,908.11 = \$377,448.66$$

The remainder of the $450,000 will be interest earned. That is,

$$\text{Interest earned} = \$450,000 - \$377,448.66 = \$72,551.34$$

c.

Payment interval number	Payment (at end) ($)	Interest earned ($)	Increase in the fund ($)	Balance in fund (end of interval) ($)
0	—	—	—	0
1	62,908.11	0	62,908.11	62,908.11
2	62,908.11	4403.57 ①	67,311.68 ②	130,219.79 ③
3	62,908.11	9115.39	72,023.50	202,243.29
4	62,908.11	14,157.03	77,065.14	279,308.43
5	62,908.11	19,551.59	82,459.70	361,768.13
6	62,908.11	25,323.77	88,231.88	450,000.01
	377,448.66	72,551.35 ④	450,000.01 ⑤	

① Interest earned = 0.07(Amount at the beginning of the interval) = 0.07($62,908.11) = $4403.57
② Increase in the fund = Interest earned + Payment = $4403.57 + $62,908.11 = $67,311.68
③ Balance = Previous balance + Increase in the fund = $62,908.11 + $67,311.68 = $130,219.79
④ Column total = $72,551.35 = Total interest earned (confirming the answer in part (b))
⑤ The total of the increases to the fund should equal the final total in the sinking fund.

EXAMPLE 16.5B

PREPARATION OF A COMPLETE SINKING FUND SCHEDULE IN WHICH THE PAYMENTS FORM AN ANNUITY DUE

Repeat Example 16.5A, with the change that the sinking fund payments are made at the beginning of each year.

SOLUTION

a. The future value of the six sinking fund payments, invested at 7% compounded annually, must be $450,000. Substitute $FV(\text{due}) = \$450,000$, $i = \frac{7\%}{1} = 7\%$, and $n = 1(6) = 6$ into Formula (13-1). Then solve for PMT.

$$FV(\text{due}) = PMT\left[\frac{(1+i)^n - 1}{i}\right] \times (1+i)$$

$$\$450,000 = PMT\left[\frac{(1.07)^6 - 1}{0.07}\right](1.07)$$

$$= PMT(7.6540211)$$

$$PMT = \$58,792.63$$

BGN mode

7 I/Y
P/Y 1 ENTER
(making $C/Y = P/Y = 1$)
6 N
0 PV
450000 FV
CPT PMT
Ans: −58,792.63

The annual sinking fund payment should be $58,792.63.

b. Interest earned = $450,000 − Total of payments
= $450,000 − (6 × $58,792.63)
= $97,244.22

c.

Payment interval number	Payment (at start) ($)	Interest earned ($)	Increase in the fund ($)	Balance in fund (end of interval) ($)
0	—	—	—	0
1	58,792.63	4115.48	62,908.11	62,908.11
2	58,792.63	8519.05 ①	67,311.68 ②	130,219.79 ③
3	58,792.63	13,230.87	72,023.50	202,243.29
4	58,792.63	18,272.51	77,065.14	279,308.43
5	58,792.63	23,667.07	82,459.70	361,768.13
6	58,792.63	29,439.25	88,231.88	450,000.01
	352,755.78	97,244.23	450,000.01	

① Interest earned = 0.07(Amount at the beginning of the interval) = 0.07(Balance at end of previous interval + PMT)
= 0.07($62,908.11 + $58,792.63) = $8519.05
② Increase in the fund = Interest earned + Payment = $8519.05 + $58,792.63 = $67,311.68
③ Balance = Previous balance + Increase in the fund = $62,908.11 + $67,311.68 = $130,219.79

EXAMPLE 16.5C

PREPARATION OF A PARTIAL SINKING FUND SCHEDULE

The board of directors of Borland Engineering decides that the firm's cash flows can be managed better if the sinking fund payments are made quarterly instead of annually (as in Example 16.5A). The goal is still to accumulate $450,000 after six years, but now with end-of-quarter payments. The sinking fund would earn 6.8% compounded quarterly. Construct a partial sinking fund schedule showing details of Payments 1, 2, 15, 16, 23, and 24.

SOLUTION

The first step is to calculate the size of the payments so that their future value will be $450,000. The payments form an ordinary simple annuity with $FV = \$450,000$, $n = 4(6) = 24$, and $i = \frac{6.8\%}{4} = 1.7\%$. Solve for PMT in

$$FV = PMT\left[\frac{(1+i)^n - 1}{i}\right]$$

$$\$450,000 = PMT\left[\frac{(1.017)^{24} - 1}{0.017}\right]$$

$$= PMT(29.332891)$$

$$PMT = \$15,341.14$$

6.8 **I/Y**

P/Y 4 **ENTER**

(making $C/Y = P/Y = 4$)

24 **N**

0 **PV**

450000 **FV**

CPT **PMT**

Ans: −15,341.14

In order to deal with Payments 15 and 16 in a sinking fund schedule, we need to determine the balance (future value) after 14 payments.

Future value after 14 payments $= \$15,341.14\left[\frac{(1.017)^{14} - 1}{0.017}\right]$

$$= \$240,200.61$$

Same *I/Y*, *P/Y*, *C/Y*, *PV*

14 **N**

15341.14 **+/−** **PMT**

CPT **FV**

Ans: 240,200.61

In order to deal with the last two payments (Payments 23 and 24), we need to calculate the balance after 22 payments.

Future value after 22 payments $= \$15,341.14\left[\frac{(1.017)^{22} - 1}{0.017}\right]$

$$= \$405,164.24$$

Same *I/Y*, *P/Y*, *C/Y*, *PV*, *PMT*

22 **N**

CPT **FV**

Ans: 405,164.24

Payment interval number	Payment (at end) ($)	Interest earned ($)	Increase in the fund ($)	Balance in fund (end of interval) ($)
0	—	—	—	0
1	15,341.14	0	15,341.14	15,341.14
2	15,341.14	260.80 ①	15,601.94 ②	30,943.08 ③
.	.	.	.	
14	.	.	.	240,200.61
15	15,341.14	4083.41	19,424.55	259,625.16
16	15,341.14	4413.63	19,754.77	279,379.93
.	.	.	.	.
22	.	.	.	405,164.24
23	15,341.14	6887.79	22,228.93	427,393.17
24	15,341.14	7265.68	22,606.82	449,999.99
	368,187.36 ④	81,812.63 ⑤	449,999.99	

① $0.017 \times \$15,341.14 = \$260.80$
② $\$260.80 + \$15,341.14 = \$15,601.94$
③ $\$15,601.94 + \$15,341.14 = \$30,943.08$
④ $24 \times \$15,341.14 = \$368,187.36$
⑤ $\$449,999.99 - \$368,187.36 = \$81,812.63$

Sinking Fund for Debt Retirement

Recall from the discussion of bonds earlier in this chapter that no principal is repaid to the bond investor before the maturity of the bond. In some circumstances, bond investors may have concerns about the ability of the borrower (bond issuer) to repay the full principal amount at a maturity date several years in the future. To ease this concern, many corporate, regional government, and municipal government bonds carry a sinking fund provision.[5] The purpose of the sinking fund is to provide for the repayment of all or a substantial portion of the principal amount of the bond issue.

A trust company is usually appointed as the trustee to administer the sinking fund. The bond issuer does not have access to the money in the sinking fund; the funds are accumulated for the express purpose of repaying the principal amount of the debt. There are two ways of setting up a sinking fund for a bond issue:

- The borrower makes periodic payments to the trustee. The trustee invests the funds in low-risk securities (such as federal government bonds and Treasury bills). On the maturity date of the bond issue, the accumulated funds are used to repay all or a substantial portion of the principal amount of the debt.
- The trustee uses the periodic payments received from the bond issuer to retire a portion of the bond issue each year. To do this in any particular year, the trustee chooses the cheaper of the following two alternatives:
  - **(i)** A specified percentage of the issue may be called and redeemed at a predetermined redemption price per bond.
  - **(ii)** If, however, the bonds can be purchased in the bond market for less than the redemption price, the trustee will buy enough bonds for the year's prescribed debt retirement.

The second sinking fund arrangement is more common. However, the first involves the more interesting mathematics, which we will discuss in the remainder of this section.

The simplest contribution arrangement requires *equal* regular payments to the sinking fund after the initial issue[6] of the bonds. The payment size is calculated so that

$$\begin{pmatrix} \text{Future value of the} \\ \text{sinking fund payments} \end{pmatrix} = \begin{pmatrix} \text{Principal amount of} \\ \text{the debt to be retired} \end{pmatrix}$$

A conservative compound rate of return is assumed for the sinking fund. We will consider only cases where contributions are made at the end of every six months and compounding occurs semiannually. In these cases, the sinking fund contributions form an ordinary simple annuity.

The sinking fund schedule for a debt retirement usually includes an additional column for the **book value of a debt**, defined as:

$$\begin{array}{c} \text{Book value} \\ \text{of the debt} \end{array} = \begin{array}{c} \text{Principal amount} \\ \text{of the debt} \end{array} - \begin{array}{c} \text{Balance in the} \\ \text{sinking fund} \end{array}$$

The book value of a debt can be interpreted as the balance that would still be owed on the debt if the money in the sinking fund were immediately applied to reduce the debt.

Keep in mind that, under a sinking fund arrangement for debt retirement, the borrower is making *two* series of payments, each one constituting an annuity. One is the sinking fund payments to the fund's trustee. The other is the interest payments to the lenders or bond holders. The combined total of a year's interest payments and a year's sinking fund payments is called the **annual cost of a debt**. It represents the total annual cash outflow arising from the debt obligation.

---

[5] Sinking funds are primarily associated with debentures rather than with true bonds because debentures are not secured by specific fixed assets of the borrower. A debt issue that has a sinking fund provision usually includes the words "sinking fund" in its full title.

[6] In cases where the sinking fund is structured to retire only a portion of the debt, there may be an initial five- or ten-year "contribution holiday" during which the issuer makes no sinking fund payments.

TIP

The Different Roles of the Coupon Rate and the Sinking Fund Rate of Return

Distinguish the roles of the two interest rates that are involved in sinking fund debt. The contractual rate of interest on the debt determines the regular interest expense paid by the borrower to the lender. The rate of return earned by the sinking fund determines the revenue earned by the sinking fund. Although the lender does not directly receive the earnings of the sinking fund, the lender still benefits from the interest earnings: they will eventually be used to repay the principal amount of the debt.

EXAMPLE 16.5D

CALCULATING THE SINKING FUND PAYMENT SIZE, ANNUAL COST OF DEBT, AND BOOK VALUE OF DEBT

Abacus Corp. raised $20 million from an issue of sinking fund bonds. The bonds have a 12-year term and a 9% coupon rate. The bond indenture requires Abacus to make equal semiannual contributions to a sinking fund to provide for the retirement of the full principal amount of the bond issue at its maturity.

a. If the sinking fund earns 6.5% compounded semiannually, what is the size of the semiannual sinking fund payments?

b. What is the annual cost of the debt?

c. What is the book value of the debt after six years?

SOLUTION

a. We want the future value of the sinking fund payments invested at 6.5% compounded semiannually for 12 years to be $20 million. The payments form an ordinary simple annuity having

$$FV = \$20,000,000 \quad i = \tfrac{6.5\%}{2} = 3.25\% \quad \text{and} \quad n = 2(12) = 24$$

Substitute into Formula (11-1) and solve for *PMT*.

$$FV = PMT\left[\frac{(1 + i)^n - 1}{i}\right]$$

$$\$20,000,000 = PMT\left[\frac{(1.0325)^{24} - 1}{0.0325}\right]$$

$$= PMT(35.525359)$$

$$PMT = \$562,978.13$$

6.5 I/Y
P/Y 2 ENTER
(making *C/Y* = *P/Y* = 2)
24 N
0 PV
20000000 FV
CPT PMT
Ans: −562,978.13

b. The annual cost of the debt is the total of the bond interest and sinking fund payments made in a year. The semiannual interest paid on the debt is

$$\tfrac{0.09}{2} \times \$20,000,000 = \$900,000$$

Hence,

$$\text{Annual cost of the debt} = 2(\$562,978.13 + \$900,000)$$

$$= \$2,925,956.26$$

c. The book value of the debt after six years is the principal amount of the debt less the amount in the sinking fund. The amount in the sinking fund is

$$FV = \$562{,}978.13\left[\frac{(1.0325)^{12} - 1}{0.0325}\right]$$

$$= \$8{,}104{,}230.90$$

Book value = $20,000,000 − $8,104,230.90 = $11,895,769.10

Same *I/Y, P/Y, C/Y, PV*

	12	N
562978.13	+/−	PMT
	CPT	FV

Ans: 8,104,230.90

EXAMPLE 16.5E

CONSTRUCTING A PARTIAL SINKING FUND SCHEDULE

In order to construct a secondary sewage treatment system, the town of Port Barlow has received approval to borrow $12 million through the provincial government's Municipal Finance Authority (MFA). The MFA is the central borrowing agency for financing the capital requirements of member municipalities and regional governments. It enters the capital markets to borrow the funds needed by its members. It also manages the collection of money from its members for both the payment of interest and the accumulation of sinking funds to retire the principal portion of each debt issue.

Bond coupon interest at the rate of 10% compounded semiannually is payable every six months. In addition, Port Barlow must make payments at the end of every six months into a sinking fund that will accumulate the full principal amount of the debt after 15 years. The sinking fund earns 8% compounded semiannually. Round sinking fund payments and interest earnings to the nearest dollar.

a. Calculate the combined interest and sinking fund payment that Port Barlow must send to the MFA every six months.

b. What will be the balance in the sinking fund halfway through the term of the debt?

c. How much will the balance in the sinking fund increase during the tenth year?

d. How much interest will the sinking fund earn in the first half of the seventh year?

e. Construct a partial sinking fund schedule showing details of the first two and the last two payments.

SOLUTION

a. The future value of the sinking fund payments after 15 years at 8% compounded semiannually must be $12,000,000. Substitute $FV = \$12{,}000{,}000$, $n = 2(15) = 30$, and $i = \frac{8\%}{2} = 4\%$ into Formula (11-1) and solve for *PMT*.

$$FV = PMT\left[\frac{(1+i)^n - 1}{i}\right]$$

$$\$12{,}000{,}000 = PMT\left[\frac{(1.04)^{30} - 1}{0.04}\right]$$

$$PMT = \$213{,}961$$

The semiannual interest payment is $12,000,000(0.05) = $600,000.

The combined semiannual payment is $213,961 + $600,000 = $813,961.

| | 8 | I/Y |
| P/Y | 2 | ENTER |

(making *C/Y = P/Y =* 2)

	30	N
	0	PV
12000000		FV
	CPT	PMT

Ans: −213,961

b. The amount in the sinking fund at any point will be the future value of the payments already contributed. After $7\frac{1}{2}$ years (15 payments), the sinking fund balance will be

$$FV = \$213{,}961\left[\frac{(1.04)^{15} - 1}{0.04}\right]$$

$$= \$4{,}284{,}267$$

Same *I/Y, P/Y, C/Y, PV*

	15	N
213961	+/−	PMT
	CPT	FV

Ans: 4,284,267

c. The increase in the balance during the tenth year

$$= \text{Balance after 10 years} - \text{Balance after 9 years}$$

$$= \$213{,}961\left[\frac{(1.04)^{20} - 1}{0.04}\right] - \$213{,}961\left[\frac{(1.04)^{18} - 1}{0.04}\right]$$

$$= \$6{,}371{,}347.5 - \$5{,}487{,}118.2$$

$$= \$884{,}229$$

Same *I/Y, P/Y, C/Y*
Same *PV, PMT*

18 [N]

[CPT] [FV]

Ans: 5,487,118

[STO] 1

20 [N]

[CPT] [FV]

Ans: 6,371,347

[−] [RCL] 1 [=]

Ans: 884,229

d. The interest earned in the first half of Year 7

$$= 0.04(\text{Amount in the fund at the end of Year 6})$$

$$= 0.04 \times \$213{,}961\left[\frac{(1.04)^{12} - 1}{0.04}\right]$$

$$= 0.04(\$3{,}214{,}936)$$

$$= \$128{,}597$$

Same *I/Y, P/Y, C/Y*
Same *PV, PMT*

12 [N]

[CPT] [FV]

Ans: 3,214,936

[×] 0.04 [=]

Ans: 128,597

e. Partial sinking fund schedule:

Payment interval number	Payment ($)	Interest earned ($)	Increase in the fund ($)	Balance in fund (end of interval) ($)	Book value of the debt ($)
0	—	—	—	0	12,000,000
1	213,961	0	213,961	213,961	11,786,039
2	213,961	8558 ①	222,519 ②	436,480 ③	11,563,520 ④
.	.	.	.	.	.
.	.	.	.	.	.
.	.	.	.	.	.
28				10,691,114 ⑤	1,308,886
29	213,961	427,645	641,606	11,332,720	667,280
30	213,961	453,309	667,270	11,999,990	10
	6,418,830	5,581,160	11,999,990		

① Interest earned = 0.04 (Amount at the beginning of the interval)
= 0.04 ($213,961)
= $8558

② Increase in the fund = Interest earned + Payment
= $8558 + $213,961
= $222,519

③ Balance = Previous balance + Increase in the fund
= $213,961 + $222,519
= $436,480

④ Book value = Debt principal − Sinking fund balance
= $12,000,000 − $436,480
= $11,563,520

⑤ Balance in the sinking fund = Future value of the first 28 payments
$$= \$213{,}961\left[\frac{(1.04)^{28} - 1}{0.04}\right]$$
$$= \$10{,}691{,}114$$

EXERCISE 16.5

Answers to the odd-numbered problems are at the end of the book.

	A	B
1		
2		
3		

Spreadsheet templates: Connect provides five partially completed Excel templates for various full and partial sinking fund schedules. You can use one or another of these templates in Problems 17–24 and 27–30 of Exercise 16.5. Go to the Student Edition on Connect and find "Sinking Fund Schedules."

BASIC PROBLEMS

For each of the sinking funds in Problems 1–8, calculate (rounded to the nearest dollar):
a. The size of the periodic sinking fund payment.
b. The balance in the sinking fund at the time indicated in the last column. (Round the sinking fund payment to the nearest dollar before calculating the balance.)

Problem	End-of-term amount of sinking fund ($ millions)	Term (years)	Sinking fund rate of return (%)	Payment and compounding interval	Payment at beginning or end of interval?	Calculate balance at the end of interval
1.	12	10	7	6 months	End	12
2.	7	10	3	6 months	End	6
3.	15	15	6.5	1 year	End	11
4.	8	10	7.5	1 month	End	65
5.	6	5	5.25	1 month	Beginning	27
6.	10	10	6.5	3 months	Beginning	28
7.	18	15	2.75	6 months	Beginning	19
8.	5	10	5.75	1 year	Beginning	8

INTERMEDIATE PROBLEMS

Each of the bond issues in Problems 9–16 has a sinking fund requirement for retiring the entire principal amount of the issue on its maturity date. The coupon rates and rates of return on the sinking fund investments are compounded semiannually. In each case calculate (to the nearest dollar):
a. The size of the sinking fund payment at the end of every six months.
b. The annual cost of the debt.
c. The book value of the debt at the end of the indicated interval. (Round the sinking fund payment to the nearest dollar before calculating the book value.)

Problem	Principal amount of bond issue ($ millions)	Term (years)	Sinking fund rate of return (%)	Coupon rate (%)	Calculate book value at the end of interval
9.	10	10	7	10	12
10.	8	5	6	8.5	6
11.	15	15	6.5	9	21
12.	12	10	7.5	10.5	15
13.	7	5	5.75	8	7
14.	9	10	6.5	9.25	18
15.	11	15	7.5	10.25	19
16.	10	10	7	9.75	11

For Problems 17–20, construct the complete sinking fund schedule. Calculate the total interest earned by adding up the "interest earned" column and by calculating the difference between the final balance in the fund and the total of the contributed payments. Round the sinking fund payments and periodic interest earnings to the nearest dollar.

Problem	End-of-term amount of sinking fund ($)	Term (years)	Sinking fund rate of return (%)	Payment and compounding interval	Payment at beginning or end of interval?
17.	800,000	3	7	6 months	End
18.	675,000	6	6	1 year	End
19.	1,000,000	5	6.75	1 year	Beginning
20.	550,000	4	5.75	6 months	Beginning

21. For the sinking fund described in Problem 2, prepare a partial sinking fund schedule showing details of Payments 1, 2, 11, 12, 19, and 20. Round the sinking fund payments and periodic interest earnings to the nearest dollar.

22. For the sinking fund described in Problem 5, prepare a partial sinking fund schedule showing details of Payments 1, 2, 39, 40, 59, and 60. Round the sinking fund payments and periodic interest earnings to the nearest dollar.

23. For the bond sinking fund described in Problem 9, prepare a partial sinking fund schedule (including the book value of the debt) showing details of the first two and the last two payments. Round the sinking fund payments and periodic interest earnings to the nearest dollar.

24. For the bond sinking fund described in Problem 10, prepare a partial sinking fund schedule (including the book value of the debt) showing details of the first two and the last two payments. Round the sinking fund payments and periodic interest earnings to the nearest dollar.

25. To provide for the automation of a production process in five years, Dominion Chemicals is starting a sinking fund to accumulate $600,000 by the end of the five years. Round the sinking fund payments and the periodic interest earnings to the nearest dollar.
   a. If the sinking fund earns 7.5% compounded monthly, what monthly payments starting today should be made to the fund?
   b. How much interest will be earned in the fourth year?
   c. In what month will the fund pass the halfway point?
   d. How much interest will be earned in the 35th month?

26. Repeat Problem 25, with the change that the sinking fund payments are to be made at the end of every month.

ADVANCED PROBLEMS

27. Thermo-Tech Systems recently sold a $20 million bond issue with a 20-year maturity and a coupon rate of 7% compounded semiannually. The bond indenture contract requires Thermo-Tech to make equal payments at the end of every six months into a sinking fund administered by National Trust. The sinking fund should accumulate the full $20 million required to redeem the bonds at their maturity. Round the sinking fund payments and periodic interest earnings to the nearest dollar.
   a. What must the size of the sinking fund payments be if the fund earns 4.5% compounded semiannually?
   b. How much interest will the fund earn in the sixth year?
   c. How much will the fund increase in the 27th payment interval?
   d. Construct a partial sinking fund schedule (including the book value of the debt) showing details of the first two and the last two payments, and the total of the interest earned.

28. The town of Mount Hope is financing a $4.5 million upgrade to its water system through the province's Municipal Finance Authority. The MFA obtained financing via a bond issue with interest at 7.5% per annum payable semiannually. Also, at the end of every six months, the town is to make equal payments into a sinking fund administered by the MFA so that the necessary funds will be available to repay the $4.5 million debt when it matures in 17 years. The sinking fund earns 4% compounded semiannually. Round the sinking fund payments and periodic interest earnings to the nearest dollar.
     a. Calculate the size of the sinking fund payments.
     b. How much will the fund increase in the 18th payment interval?
     c. How much interest will the fund earn in the 10th year?
     d. Construct a partial sinking fund schedule (including the book value of the debt) showing details of the ninth, tenth, and last two payments, and the total of the interest earned.

29. A sinking fund is to be set up to provide for the repayment of 80% of the principal amount of a $1 million debt in 10 years. Equal payments are to be made at the beginning of each quarter. The sinking fund will earn 7% compounded quarterly. Round the sinking fund payments and periodic interest earnings to the nearest dollar.
     a. Calculate the size of the sinking fund payments.
     b. Construct a partial sinking fund schedule (including the book value of the debt) showing details of the first two and the last two payments, and the total of the interest earned.

30. Repeat Problem 29, with the change that the sinking fund payments are to be made at the end of every quarter.

KEY TERMS

Annual cost of a debt	Debenture	Redemption price
Bond	Face value	Sinking fund
Bond discount	Flat price	Sinking fund schedule
Bond premium	Issue date	Yield to maturity (YTM)
Book value of a debt	Maturity date	
Coupon rate	Quoted price	

SUMMARY OF NOTATION AND KEY FORMULAS

In the context of bond pricing,

FV = Face value of the bond
b = Coupon rate per interest payment interval (normally six months)
i = The bond market's required rate of return per payment interval
n = Number of interest payments remaining until the maturity date

FORMULA (16-1) $\textbf{Bond price} = b(FV)\left[\dfrac{1-(1-i)^{-n}}{i}\right] + FV(1+i)^{-n}$ Finding the price of a bond on a coupon interest payment date

The following relationships were developed for sinking funds.

$$\begin{pmatrix}\text{Balance at the end of}\\\text{any payment interval}\end{pmatrix} = \begin{pmatrix}\text{Future value of the}\\\text{payments already made}\end{pmatrix}$$

$$\begin{pmatrix} \text{Interest earned in} \\ \text{any payment interval} \end{pmatrix} = i \times \begin{pmatrix} \text{Amount in the sinking fund} \\ \text{at the beginning of the interval} \end{pmatrix}$$

$$\begin{pmatrix} \text{Increase in the sinking fund's balance} \\ \text{during any payment interval} \end{pmatrix} = PMT + \begin{pmatrix} \text{Interest earned} \\ \text{during the interval} \end{pmatrix}$$

$$\begin{pmatrix} \text{Book value} \\ \text{of the debt} \end{pmatrix} = \begin{pmatrix} \text{Principal amount} \\ \text{of the debt} \end{pmatrix} - \begin{pmatrix} \text{Balance in the} \\ \text{sinking fund} \end{pmatrix}$$

REVIEW PROBLEMS

Answers to the odd-numbered review problems are at the end of the book.

BASIC PROBLEMS

1. **L01** A $1000, 7.5% coupon bond has $19\frac{1}{2}$ years remaining until maturity. Calculate the bond discount if the required return in the bond market is 8.6% compounded semiannually.

2. **L01** Four years after the issue of a $10,000, 9.5% coupon, 20-year bond, the rate of return required in the bond market on long-term bonds was 7.8% compounded semiannually.
   a. At what price did the bond then sell?
   b. What capital gain or loss (expressed in dollars) would the original owner have realized by selling the bond at that price?

3. **L01** Four and one-half years ago, Glenda purchased 15 $1000 bonds in a Province of New Brunswick issue carrying an 8.5% coupon and priced to yield 9.8% (compounded semiannually). The bonds then had 18 years remaining until maturity. The bond market now requires a yield to maturity on the bonds of 8.0% compounded semiannually. If Glenda sells the bonds today, what will be the dollar amount of her capital gain or loss?

4. **L01** A $1000 face value, 6.8% coupon, Province of Ontario bond with 18 years to run until maturity is currently priced to yield investors 6.5% compounded semiannually until maturity. How much lower would the bond's price have to be to make the yield to maturity 7% compounded semiannually?

5. **L01** Two and one-half years ago, Nova Scotia Power sold an issue of 25-year, 8% coupon bonds. If the current semiannually compounded return required in the bond market is 6.9%, calculate the percent capital gain or loss on the bonds over the entire $2\frac{1}{2}$-year holding period.

6. **L02** Calculate the yield to maturity on a $1000 face value bond purchased for $1034.50 if it carries a 7.9% coupon and has $8\frac{1}{2}$ years remaining until maturity.

INTERMEDIATE PROBLEMS

7. **L01** A New Brunswick Power bond issue carrying a 7.6% coupon matures on November 1, 2031. At what price did $1000 face value bonds trade on June 10, 2019, if the yield to maturity required by the bond market on that date was 5.9% compounded semiannually?

8. **L01** Calculate the quoted price on June 10, 2019, of the bond in Problem 7.

9. **L03 L04** The Cowichan Regional District borrowed $500,000 through the Provincial Finance Authority to purchase fire-fighting equipment. At the end of every six months, the regional district must make a sinking fund payment of a size calculated to accumulate $500,000 after seven years to repay the principal amount of the debt. The sinking fund earns 7% compounded semiannually. Construct a partial sinking fund schedule (including

the book value of the debt) showing details of the first two and the last two payments. Round the sinking fund payments and periodic interest earnings to the nearest dollar.

10. **LO2** A $1000, 9.5% coupon Government of Canada bond has 10 years remaining until its maturity. It is currently priced at 108.25 (percent of face value).
    a. What is the bond's yield to maturity?
    b. If the bond price abruptly rises by $25, what is the change in its yield to maturity?

11. **LO1** A $1000, 6.5% coupon, 20-year Government of Canada bond was issued on June 15, 2016. At what price did it trade on December 10, 2020, when the market's required return was 5.2% compounded semiannually?

12. **LO1** If a broker quotes a price of 111.25 for a bond on September 10, what amount will a client pay per $1000 face value? The 7% coupon rate is payable on May 15 and November 15 of each year.

13. **LO3** **LO4** Laurentian Airways is preparing for the replacement of one of its passenger jets in three years by making payments to a sinking fund at the beginning of every six months for the next three years. The fund can earn 6% compounded semiannually, and the capital required in three years is $750,000. Prepare a complete sinking fund schedule. Round the sinking fund payments and periodic interest earnings to the nearest dollar.

14. **LO3** **LO4** The municipality of Duncan has financed a sewage treatment plant by issuing $18 million worth of sinking fund debentures. The debentures have a 15-year term and pay a coupon rate of 9% compounded semiannually. Rounding the sinking fund payments, interest payments, and periodic interest earnings to the nearest dollar,
    a. What equal payments at the end of every six months will be necessary to accumulate $18 million after 15 years if the sinking fund can earn 6.25% compounded semiannually?
    b. What is the annual cost of the debt to Duncan taxpayers?
    c. Construct a partial sinking fund schedule (including the book value of the debt) showing details of the first three and the last three payments.

APPENDIX 16A: INSTRUCTIONS FOR THE TEXAS INSTRUMENTS BA II PLUS BOND WORKSHEET

This worksheet enables you to quickly compute either a bond's *quoted* price or its yield to maturity on any date.

Find "BOND" located above the [9] key. To access the Bond Worksheet, press [2nd] [BOND]. Recall that a worksheet can be thought of as a column of items that you can view one at a time in the calculator's display. The Bond Worksheet's column contains the nine items listed below. You see the top item when you first access the worksheet. You can view other items using the scroll keys [↓] and [↑]. (You may get an "Error 6" message if you scroll to the last item without first entering legitimate data for other variables.)

STD =	mm-dd-yyyy
CPN =	n.nn
RDT =	mm-dd-yyyy
RV =	nnn
ACT	
2/Y	
YLD =	n.nn
PRI =	nnn.nn
AI =	nnn.nn

STD   is the label for the date of the sale or purchase (sometimes called the *SettlemenT Date*). The formats for data entry and display are the same as for the Date Worksheet (**Appendix 7B**). That is, mm, dd, and yyyy represent the digits for the month, day, and year, respectively. To enter the date June 9, 2020, the keystrokes are

6.0920 | ENTER |

CPN   is the label for the *CouPoN* rate. To enter 5.75%, the keystrokes are

5.75 | ENTER |

RDT   is the label for the bond's maturity date (also known as the *Redemption DaTe*.) Enter this date in the same manner as for *STD*.

RV   is the label for the *Redemption Value*. Enter it as a percentage of face value. (In this chapter, we consider only the most common case where the redemption value equals the face value. For this case, set *RV* = 100.)

ACT   is a label meaning "*ACTual*." It means that the calculator will use the actual number of days in intervals. By repeatedly pressing | 2nd | | ENTER |, you can toggle between *ACT* and *360*, the two possible settings for this variable. For problems in this text, always use *ACT*.

2/Y   is a label meaning "two coupon payments per year." By repeatedly pressing | 2nd | | ENTER |, you can toggle between *2/Y* and *1/Y*, the two possible settings for this variable. For problems in this text, always use *2/Y*.

YLD   (standing for *YieLD*) and *PRI* (for *PRIce*) are the next two items. *You enter one of them and compute the other.* *YLD* must be entered as a semiannually compounded rate in percent equivalent form. The value for *PRI* is the *quoted* price entered as a percentage of face value. For example, a $5000 face value bond with a quoted price of $5210.50 would be entered as $104.21 \left(= \frac{\$5210.50}{\$5000} \times 100\% \right)$.

After entering the preceding values and settings, you compute the unknown *YLD* or *PRI* by scrolling to it and then pressing the | CPT | key. This also causes the computation of the last item in the list, *AI* (standing for *Accrued Interest*). The accrued interest is displayed as a percentage of face value. To obtain the flat price of the bond, add *AI* and *PRI*. If you use the worksheet to calculate a bond's price on an interest payment date (**Section 16.2** problems), *AI* will be zero.

Chapter 17

Business Investment Decisions

CHAPTER OUTLINE

LEARNING OBJECTIVES

After completing this chapter, you will be able to:

LO1 Calculate the net present value (*NPV*) of a capital investment and use the *NPV* to decide whether the investment should be made

LO2 Under conditions of capital rationing, choose the best combination of investments from a group of acceptable capital investment opportunities

LO3 Select the best investment from two or more mutually exclusive investments

LO4 Calculate the internal rate of return (*IRR*) of a capital investment and use the *IRR* to decide whether the investment should be made

LO5 Calculate the payback period of a capital investment

WHAT ANALYSIS SHOULD A BUSINESS undertake for investment decisions such as expanding production, adding another product line, or replacing existing plant or equipment?

In this chapter we will study techniques used by managers to make sound financial decisions on capital investments. We will study three criteria widely employed to guide business investment decisions. Two of them rest on a solid economic foundation. The third is flawed in some respects but, nevertheless, is frequently used in business—it is important that you understand its limitations.

Given the long-term nature of capital investments, any rigorous analysis must recognize the time value of money. Most of the concepts and mathematics you need to evaluate business investments have already been presented in previous chapters. What remains to be learned is the terminology and procedures for applying this knowledge to the analysis of potential business investments.

17.1 Comparing Business to Personal Investment Decisions

The fundamental principles that guide both personal and business investment decisions are the same. The Valuation Principle is as relevant to business investments as it is to personal investments. Use of the Valuation Principle to determine the fair market value of an investment requires three steps:

1. Identify or estimate the cash flows expected from the investment. If there are cash outflows as well as cash inflows in any particular period, estimate the period's

$$\text{Net cash flow} = \text{Cash inflows} - \text{Cash outflows}$$

2. Determine the rate of return appropriate for the type of investment.
3. Calculate the sum of the present values of the net cash flows estimated in Step 1, discounted at the rate of return determined in Step 2.

If cash flows are actually received as forecast in Step 1, an investor paying the amount calculated in Step 3 will realize the Step 2 rate of return. But a *higher* purchase price or *lower* (than forecast) cash flows will result in a rate of return that is *smaller* than the discount rate used in Step 2. On the other hand, a *lower* price or *higher* cash flows will result in a rate of return *greater* than the discount rate.

The *nature* of investments made by an *operating* business differs markedly from the nature of most personal investments. For the most part, personal investments fall into a limited number of categories such as Treasury bills, GICs, bonds, and stocks. With the exception of common stocks, there is a considerable degree of similarity among investments within each category. In addition, an individual investor can usually depend on competitive bidding in the financial markets to set fair prices for widely traded securities. In these cases, the investor may not explicitly use the Valuation Principle in selecting investments.

For investments in plant and equipment by a business, the way in which the asset will be used and the resulting pattern of cash flows tend to make each investment situation unique. Also, there are likely to be ongoing cash outflows as well as cash inflows associated with a business investment. These factors argue for a more comprehensive and rigorous approach in business to handle the great variety of investment possibilities.

Individual investors and business managers take different perspectives in determining the discount rate used with the Valuation Principle. An individual investor looks to the financial markets for benchmark rates of return on each category of investment. A business manager takes the view that a capital investment must be financed by some combination of debt and equity financing. Therefore, a business investment project must provide a rate of return *at least equal to* the return required by the providers of the financing. The weighted average rate of return required by a firm's providers of debt and equity financing is called the firm's **cost of capital**. *This cost of capital is the discount rate that should be used when applying the Valuation Principle* to a proposed capital investment project. The sum of the present values of the project's future (net) cash flows discounted at the firm's cost of capital represents the value of the project to the business. The business should not pay more than this value. The same project may be worth more or less to another business primarily because the project's future cash flows are likely to differ when operated by another business. It could also be the case that different firms would use differing discount rates because of differing costs of capital.

There are three possible outcomes of a comparison between the present value of future (net) cash flows and the initial capital investment required.

1. **Present value of the future cash flows = Initial investment** The cash flows will provide a rate of return (on the initial investment) exactly *equal* to the discount rate—the firm's cost of capital. The investment's net cash flows will be just enough to repay the invested capital along with the minimum required rate of return. This is, therefore, the *minimum condition* for acceptance of a capital investment project.

2. **Present value of the future cash flows < Initial investment** The project's net cash flows will not be enough to provide the suppliers of financing with their *full* minimum required rate of return (on top of the payback of their capital investment). Note that we are not necessarily saying that the project or the suppliers of capital lose money—we are saying only that the project will not provide the *full* rate of return embodied in the discount rate. In this case, the investment opportunity should be *rejected.*

3. **Present value of the future cash flows > Initial investment** The investment will earn a rate of return greater than the discount rate—more than the minimum needed to give the suppliers of capital their minimum required return (as well as their capital investment back). The project should be accepted.

The preceding discussion can be summarized in the following decision criterion:

Investment Decision Criterion
Undertake a business investment opportunity if the present value of the future net cash flows (discounted at the firm's cost of capital) is greater than or equal to the initial investment.

The Economic Value That an Investment Adds to a Firm

We have seen that the sources of investment capital receive their required rate of return (the cost of capital) when

$$\text{Present value of (net) cash flows} = \text{Initial investment}$$

In this circumstance, the economic value (present value) of the future cash flows is the same as the amount initially spent to buy the investment. Therefore, undertaking this investment does not change the firm's value. It follows that, in Case 3 of the preceding list, the difference

$$(\text{Present value of cash flows}) - (\text{Initial investment})$$

represents the *value immediately added* to the firm when it makes the initial investment.

That is,

$$\begin{pmatrix} \text{Value added} \\ \text{to the firm} \end{pmatrix} = \begin{pmatrix} \text{Present value of the} \\ \text{future net cash flows} \end{pmatrix} - \begin{pmatrix} \text{Initial} \\ \text{investment} \end{pmatrix}$$

The providers of debt financing have no claim on this added value. It belongs entirely to the firm's owners (the providers of equity capital).

The following example considers a business investment opportunity with typical features. Periodic cash flows are unequal and include a cash outflow subsequent to the initial investment. The investment, if undertaken, must be financed with borrowed funds.

Note: Since forecasts of future cash flows are imprecise, *all calculations in this chapter will be rounded to the nearest dollar.* Even this suggests a degree of precision that does not really exist in this sort of analysis. It does, however, permit you to verify the mathematical accuracy of your calculations.

EXAMPLE 17.1A

EVALUATING A BUSINESS INVESTMENT OPPORTUNITY

A low-risk, four-year investment promises to pay $3000, $6000, and $5000 at the end of the first, second, and fourth years, respectively. A cash injection of $1000 is required at the end of the third year. The investment may be purchased for $11,000, which would have to be borrowed at an interest rate of 5%. Use the Valuation Principle to determine whether the investment should be undertaken.

SOLUTION

The purchase price at which a 5% rate of return would be realized on the amount invested is the present value of the cash flows discounted at 5%.

$$\text{Price for a 5\% rate of return} = \frac{\$3000}{1.05} + \frac{\$6000}{1.05^2} + \frac{(-\$1000)}{1.05^3} + \frac{\$5000}{1.05^4}$$
$$= \$2857 + \$5442 - \$864 + \$4114$$
$$= \$11,549$$

The $11,000 price should be accepted. By paying a price that is *below* $11,549, the business will realize a rate of return on investment *greater* than the 5% cost of capital to finance the investment.

Interpretation: The $11,549 figure for the present value of the investment's cash flows represents the amount today that is *economically equivalent* to the cash flow stream from the investment. By paying $11,000 today for a payment stream that is worth $11,549 today, the firm's value is immediately increased by $549 (in current dollars).

EXAMPLE 17.1B

EVALUATING A BUSINESS INVESTMENT OPPORTUNITY

Repeat the problem in **Example 17.1A**, with the change that the interest rate on the loan to finance the investment is 8% instead of 5%.

SOLUTION

The purchase price at which an 8% rate of return would be realized on the amount invested is the present value of the cash flows discounted at 8%.

$$\text{Price for an 8\% rate of return} = \frac{\$3000}{1.08} + \frac{\$6000}{1.08^2} + \frac{(-\$1000)}{1.08^3} + \frac{\$5000}{1.08^4}$$
$$= \$2778 + \$5144 - \$794 + \$3675$$
$$= \$10,803$$

The $11,000 offering price should be rejected. Paying a price that is above $10,803 would result in a rate of return on investment that is less than the 8% cost of capital to finance the investment.

Cost Minimization

Suppose the replacement of a piece of machinery is essential to the operation of an entire production line. Either Machine A or Machine B will do the job equally well. In other words, the future benefits will be the same whether we obtain Machine A or Machine B. In such a case, the scope of the financial analysis can be narrowed to finding the lowest-cost alternative. This involves a comparison of the *current* economic values of the future cash *outflows* for each alternative. The best choice is the one having the *lower* present value of cash outflows.[1]

---

[1] If the alternatives do not have equal lifetimes, the analysis must go beyond a simple comparison of the present values of cash outflows for the respective lifetimes. The additional analysis needed will be presented in **Section 17.3**.

EXAMPLE 17.1C

EVALUATING LEASE VERSUS PURCHASE ALTERNATIVES

Laven and Co., Certified General Accountants, are considering whether to buy or lease a photocopy machine. A five-year lease requires payments of $450 at the beginning of every three months. The same machine can be purchased for $9000 and would have a trade-in value of $1800 after five years. If the accounting firm can borrow funds at 6% compounded quarterly, should it buy or lease a photocopy machine?

SOLUTION

The preferred alternative is the one having the lower present value of expenditures (net of any amounts recovered from resale, salvage, or trade-in).

As discussed in Section 13.2, leasing is usually regarded as an alternative to borrowing the funds to purchase the asset. Therefore, the appropriate discount rate to use in the present-value calculation is the firm's cost of borrowing. The lease payments form a simple annuity due, with

$$PMT = \$450 \quad n = 4(5) = 20 \quad \text{and} \quad i = \tfrac{6\%}{4} = 1.5\%$$

The present value of the lease payments is

$$
\left.
\begin{aligned}
PV(\text{lease}) &= PMT\left[\frac{1-(1+i)^{-n}}{i}\right]\times(1+i) \\
&= \$450\left(\frac{1-1.015^{-20}}{0.015}\right)(1.015) \\
&= \$7842
\end{aligned}
\right\}
$$

If the photocopy machine is purchased, there will be an initial expenditure of $9000 and an $1800 recovery from trading it in five years later. The present value of these payments is

$$
\left.
\begin{aligned}
PV(\text{purchase}) &= \$9000 - FV(1+i)^{-n} \\
&= \$9000 - \$1800(1.015)^{-20} \\
&= \$9000 - \$1336 \\
&= \$7664
\end{aligned}
\right\}
$$

Hence, purchase of the photocopy machine is the lower-cost alternative. The current economic value of the difference in net costs over the five-year lifetime is $7842 − $7664 = $178.

BGN mode

| 6 | I/Y |
| P/Y | 4 ENTER |

(making C/Y = P/Y = 4)

20	N
450 +/–	PMT
0	FV
CPT	PV

Ans: 7842

Same N, I/Y, P/Y, C/Y

0	PMT
1800	FV
CPT	PV

Ans: −1336

| + | 9000 | = |

Ans: 7664

EXERCISE 17.1

Answers to the odd-numbered problems are at the end of the book.

INTERMEDIATE PROBLEMS

Unless otherwise indicated in the following exercises, assume that the initial capital investment occurs at the beginning of the first year and subsequent cash flows occur at the end of each year.

1. Vencap Enterprises is evaluating an investment opportunity that can be purchased for $55,000. Further product development will require contributions of $30,000 in Year 1 and $10,000 in Year 2. Returns of $20,000, $60,000, and $40,000 are expected in the three following years.
   a. Use the Valuation Principle to determine whether Vencap should make the investment if its cost of capital is 6% (compounded annually).

b. By what amount will the current economic value of Vencap be increased or decreased if it proceeds with purchasing the investment for $55,000?

2. Repeat Problem 1 with the change that Vencap's cost of capital is 8%.

3. What price should Vencap offer for the investment opportunity described in Problem 1 if it requires a 9% return on investment?

4. The timber rights to a tract of forest can be purchased for $250,000. The harvesting agreement would allow 25% of the timber to be cut in each of the first, second, fourth, and fifth years. The purchaser of the timber rights would be required to replant, at its expense, the logged areas in Years 3 and 6. Arrowsmith Lumber calculates that its profit in each of the four cutting years would be $90,000 and that the cost of replanting the harvested areas in each of Years 3 and 6 would be $30,000.

   a. Should Arrowsmith Lumber buy the timber rights if its cost of capital is 5.5%?

   b. By what amount would the economic value of Arrowsmith Lumber be increased or decreased if it proceeded with purchasing the timber rights for $250,000?

5. Repeat Problem 4 with the change that Arrowsmith Lumber's cost of capital is 7%.

6. At what price would Arrowsmith Lumber be willing to purchase the timber rights described in Problem 4 if it requires a return on investment of 9%?

7. A machine can be leased for four years at $1000 per month payable at the beginning of each month. Alternatively, it can be purchased for $45,000 and sold for $5000 after four years. Should the machine be purchased or leased if the firm's cost of borrowing is:

   a. 6.6% compounded monthly? **b.** 9% compounded monthly?

8. A real estate salesperson can lease an automobile for five years at $500 per month payable at the beginning of each month, or purchase it for $32,000. She can obtain a loan at 3.75% compounded monthly to purchase the car. Should she lease or buy the car if:

   a. The trade-in value after five years is $5000?

   b. The trade-in value after five years is $8000?

9. A college can purchase a telephone system for $35,000 or lease a system for five years for a front-end charge of $3000 and regular payments of $1500 at the beginning of every quarter (including the first quarter). The system can be purchased at the end of the lease period for $3000.

   a. Should the college lease or buy the system if it can borrow funds at 5% compounded quarterly?

   b. What is the current economic value of the savings with the lower-cost option?

10. Rocky Mountain Bus Tours needs an additional bus for three years. It can lease a bus for $2100 payable at the beginning of each month, or it can buy a similar bus for $120,000, using financing at the rate of 7.5% compounded monthly. The bus's resale value after three years is expected to be $60,000.

    a. On strictly financial considerations, should the company lease or buy the bus?

    b. What is the financial advantage in current dollars of the preferred choice?

ADVANCED PROBLEM

11. Ralph Harder has been transferred to Regina for five years. He has found a one-bedroom condo that he can buy for $180,000 or rent for $1000 per month, payable at the beginning of each month. He estimates that the resale value of the condo in five years will be $200,000 net of the selling commission. If he buys the condo, the (month-end) condo fees will be $300. Should Mr. Harder rent or buy the condo if mortgage rates are:

    a. 7% compounded monthly? **b.** 6% compounded monthly?

17.2 The Net Present Value of an Investment

LO1 In this section, we will express the investment criterion and the concepts from **Section 17.1** in language customarily used for business investment analysis. Recall that

$$\begin{pmatrix} \text{Value added} \\ \text{to the firm} \end{pmatrix} = \begin{pmatrix} \text{Present value of the} \\ \text{future net cash flows} \end{pmatrix} - \begin{pmatrix} \text{Initial} \\ \text{investment} \end{pmatrix}$$

Since an operating period's "net cash flow" means[2]

$$\text{Cash inflows} - \text{Cash outflows}$$

we can expand the first quantity (in brackets on the right side) giving

$$\begin{pmatrix} \text{Value added} \\ \text{to the firm} \end{pmatrix} = \begin{pmatrix} \text{Present value of} \\ \text{future cash inflows} \end{pmatrix} - \begin{pmatrix} \text{Present value of} \\ \text{future cash outflows} \end{pmatrix} - \begin{pmatrix} \text{Initial} \\ \text{investment} \end{pmatrix}$$

If we include the "initial investment" among the cash *outflows*, the second and third terms may be combined to give

$$\begin{pmatrix} \text{Value added} \\ \text{to the firm} \end{pmatrix} = \begin{pmatrix} \text{Present value of} \\ \text{cash inflows} \end{pmatrix} - \begin{pmatrix} \text{Present value of} \\ \text{cash outflows} \end{pmatrix}$$

The right side can be viewed as the *net* amount by which the *present value* of cash inflows exceeds the *present value* of cash outflows. For this reason, the "value added to the firm" is customarily called the **net present value** (*NPV*) of an investment. That is,

$$NPV = \begin{pmatrix} \text{Present value of} \\ \text{cash inflows} \end{pmatrix} - \begin{pmatrix} \text{Present value of} \\ \text{cash outflows} \end{pmatrix}$$

The investment decision criterion developed in **Section 17.1** may be expressed more concisely in terms of the *NPV*.

NPV Investment Decision Criterion:

Accept the investment if *NPV* ≥ 0.
Reject the investment if *NPV* < 0.

The firm's cost of capital (for financing the investment) is used for the discount rate in the *NPV* calculation. To simplify the calculation of present values, the assumption is usually made that the cash inflows and outflows within each year occur at the *end* of the year.[3] The initial capital investment outlay is assumed to take place at the *beginning* of the first year.

Significance of an Investment's *NPV*

The *NPV* of an investment is the amount (in current dollars) by which the economic value of the cash inflows exceeds the economic value of the cash outflows. Therefore, the *NPV* represents the value added to the firm on the date the investment is made.

This added value belongs to the owners of the business and increases the market value of the owners' equity. A negative *NPV* does not necessarily mean that the investment will cause the firm to suffer an accounting loss. It does mean, however, that the project's cash flows are not sufficient to provide the suppliers of financing with their full minimum required rate of return. As a result, a negative *NPV* project would, if undertaken, reduce the market value of the firm's equity (by the amount of the *NPV*).

---

[2]   A rigorous analysis of capital investments requires the calculation of cash flows before interest charges but after income tax (including the tax savings from any capital cost allowance on a depreciable asset). You will learn these refinements if you take a course in managerial finance. In this chapter, we will use profit or operating profit to mean the net before-interest after-tax cash flow from the investment during an accounting period.

[3]   The errors introduced by ignoring the time value of money within each year are usually smaller than the uncertainties in forecasts of the amounts and the timing of the cash flows.

APP 4 THAT

Sound business investment decisions rely on accurate information that is often provided by the net present value (*NPV*) and the internal rate of return (*IRR*) discussed in Section 17.4. Search the App Store on your tablet, smartphone, or smart watch using the key word **NPV**.

You will find many free and paid apps that provide both the *NPV* and *IRR* for your business projects along with the ability to track and edit cash flows.

EXAMPLE 17.2A

USING THE *NPV* CRITERION TO EVALUATE A CAPITAL INVESTMENT

A firm is contemplating the purchase of a $12,000 machine that would reduce labour costs by $4000 in each of Years 1 and 2, and by $3000 in each of Years 3 and 4. The machine's salvage value at the end of Year 4 is $1000. Should the machine be purchased if the firm's cost of capital is 8% compounded annually?

SOLUTION

Profits would rise by $4000 in Years 1 and 2 and by $3000 in Years 3 and 4 as a result of purchasing the machine. These profit increases plus the salvage value in Year 4 are the net cash flows that the investment will generate.

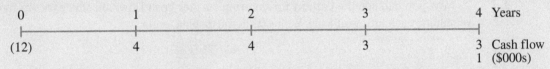

The firm should purchase the machine if the net present value of the net cash flows discounted at the 8% cost of capital is greater than zero.

$$NPV = \$4000(1.08)^{-1} + \$4000(1.08)^{-2} + \$3000(1.08)^{-3} + \$4000(1.08)^{-4} - \$12,000$$
$$= \$3704 + \$3429 + \$2381 + \$2940 - \$12,000$$
$$= \$454$$

Since the *NPV* > 0, the machine should be purchased. The savings will add $454 to the value of the firm (in addition to repaying the $12,000 capital cost and allowing for the 8% cost of capital).

Using the Texas Instruments BA II PLUS Cash Flow Worksheet This worksheet streamlines the calculation of net present values. We will first use a simple example to illustrate the use of the worksheet. Then we will employ it to solve Example 17.2A again.

The Cash Flow Worksheet employs the *primary* functions of *two* keys: CF and NPV. Consequently, you can access either key's list of items simply by pressing that key. Press CF, and then press 2nd CLRWORK to clear any data previously entered in the worksheet. Now we can be sure that, when you use the ↓ and ↑ scroll keys, you will see the items as they appear on the left in the diagram below. Later we will look at the items in the NPV key's list shown below.

CFo =	0.
C01 =	0.
F01 =	0.

I =	0.
NPV =	0.

Let's work out the *NPV* for an initial $1000 investment that will provide net cash inflows of $200, $300, $300, and $400 at the ends of Years 1, 2, 3, and 4, respectively. The cost of capital is 10%.

CFo represents the initial cash flow at time "0." With the *CFo* item in your display, enter

$$1000 \boxed{+/-} \boxed{\text{ENTER}}$$

Enter the $1000 initial investment with a negative sign because it is a cash *outflow*. *C01* represents the cash flow at the end of the first period. Scroll down to it and enter

$$200 \boxed{\text{ENTER}}$$

When you pressed the $\boxed{\text{ENTER}}$ key, two things happened away from your view. First, the value of *F01*, representing the number[4] of consecutive $200 cash flows, became "1." (This is the automatic default—a single cash flow of the amount entered for *C01*.) Second, two new items—*C02* and *F02*—were added at the bottom of the list. You can scroll down to see these changes.

The calculator is now ready to accept another cash flow. Our next cash flow is an inflow of $300. Move the *C02* item into your display. Since the subsequent cash flow is also $300, we can use the *F02* feature to enter both cash flows using the following sequence:

$$300 \boxed{\text{ENTER}} \boxed{\downarrow} 2 \boxed{\text{ENTER}}$$

These entries set *C02* = $300 and *F02* = 2 (and insert the new items *C03* and *F03* at the bottom of the list).

Now you can see the pattern for entering further cash flows. In this case we have just one remaining cash inflow of $400. With *C03* in the display, enter

$$400 \boxed{\text{ENTER}}$$

TRAP

Mismatched Numbering of Cash Flows

Note that *C03* = $400 is actually the cash flow at the end of the *fourth* interval because we previously told the calculator that two cash flows have the value *C02* = $300. When there are two or three groups of consecutive equal payments in a long string of cash flows, the mismatch between the interval or cash flow number on your time line and the calculator's cash flow number can become confusing and a source of error. The safe thing to do is write down the complete list of *C01, C02, C03,* … values with the corresponding *F01, F02, F03,* … values *before* entering them in the Cash Flow Worksheet.

Note the following points:
- The calculator will allow you to enter cash flows up to *C24*. (The value for each *Fnn* can be any integer up to 9999!)
- If any intermediate period's cash flow is "0," you must actually enter the value "0" even though it *appears* that "0" is the default value. It is only when you press the $\boxed{\text{ENTER}}$ key that the calculator creates a new *COn* item for the next cash flow.

Next enter the second list by pressing $\boxed{\text{NPV}}$. The two items in this list are:

I, representing the interest rate (per cash flow interval) we wish to use to discount the cash flows; and

NPV, representing the net present value.

---

[4] The manual for the BA II PLUS refers to *F01* as the "frequency" of the first cash flow. This is a very poor choice of name since "frequency" should refer to the number of events per unit of time. For example, we have often mentioned "compounding frequency" meaning "number of compoundings per year." The value we enter in F01 is not the number of cash flows per year, but rather the number of consecutive equally spaced cash flows each having the value in *C01*.

Now you can complete the computation of the *NPV* in our example. With the "*I*" item in the display, enter

10 ENTER   to set the discount rate at 10% per year

and then   ↓   CPT   to scroll down to *NPV* and execute the computation.

The answer *NPV* = −71.65 appears in the display. Since the investment has a *negative NPV*, its rate of return is *less* than the 10% cost of capital. To exit from the Cash Flow Worksheet, press 2nd QUIT.

Let's solve **Example 17.2A** using the Cash Flow Worksheet. Referring back to its time diagram, the cash flows at one-year intervals were:

Cash flows		Number of cash flows
CFo =	−$12,000	
C01 =	$4000	*F01* = 2
C02 =	$3000	*F02* = 1
C03 =	$4000	*F03* = 1

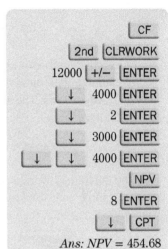

CF
2nd CLRWORK
12000 +/− ENTER
↓   4000 ENTER
↓   2 ENTER
↓   3000 ENTER
↓ ↓   4000 ENTER
NPV
8 ENTER
↓   CPT
Ans: NPV = 454.68

The $0.68 difference between the previous algebraic answer and the Cash Flow Worksheet's answer arises because we rounded to the nearest dollar only at the *final* step of the worksheet solution. In the algebraic calculation, the present value of each cash flow was rounded *before* the final addition.

Editing cash flows

1. To *change* an incorrect entry for a cash flow *or* the number of times it occurs, scroll to the value to be changed and enter the correct value.
2. To *delete* one of the periodic cash flows *and* the number of times it occurs, scroll to the cash flow and then press 2nd DEL. All subsequent cash flows will "bump up" one position in the list to fill in the gap. (If you wish only to change a cash flow's value to "0" and *not* have the gap filled in, enter "0" for the cash flow instead of deleting it.)
3. To *insert* an additional cash flow partway through a previously entered series, scroll to the position in the list where the additional cash flow is to be inserted. For example, if the cash flow is to be inserted *between* the existing *C03* and *C04*, you should scroll to *C04* and press 2nd INS. Then enter the value for the cash flow. The former *C04* and subsequent cash flows will "bump down" one position in the list.

EXAMPLE 17.2B

USING THE *NPV* CRITERION WHEN CASH FLOWS FORM ANNUITIES

Digitel Electronics' engineering and marketing departments have prepared forecasts for the development costs and operating profits of the next generation of their digital electrical meters. Development costs for each of the next three years will be $75,000. Manufacturing equipment costing $105,000 will be purchased near the end of Year 3. Annual profits for the normal five-year product life (Years 4 to 8 inclusive) are projected to be $80,000. The salvage value of the manufacturing equipment at the end of Year 8 is $20,000. Should Digitel proceed with the product development if its annually compounded cost of capital is:

a. 6%?

b. 7.5%?

SOLUTION

The cash flows are presented on a time line as follows. Our practice is to assume that each year's cash flows occur at the year's end unless otherwise indicated. Cash outflows (negative) are placed in parentheses. Digitel should proceed with the product development if the net present value of the cash flows, discounted at the cost of capital, is greater than or equal to zero.

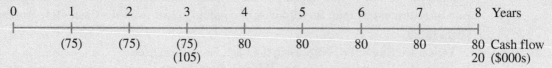

$$NPV = \text{Present value of cash inflows} - \text{Present value of cash outflows}$$

To reduce the number of algebraic calculations, do not break up annuities. In this problem there is an ordinary simple annuity with three $75,000 cash outflows, and a deferred (by three years) ordinary simple annuity with five $80,000 cash inflows. The single $105,000 outflow at three years and $20,000 inflow at eight years must be handled individually.

$$NPV = -\$75,000\left[\frac{1-(1+i)^{-3}}{i}\right] - \frac{\$105,000}{(1+i)^3} + \$80,000\left[\frac{1-(1+i)^{-5}}{i}\right] \times \frac{1}{(1+i)^3} + \frac{\$20,000}{(1+i)^8}$$

For the Cash Flow Worksheet, we need to combine the two cash flows that occur at three years and the two that take place at eight years. The table of data to be entered in the Cash Flow Worksheet is shown below.

Cash flows		Number of cash flows
CFo =	0	
C01 =	−$75,000	F01 = 2
C02 =	−$180,000	F02 = 1
C03 =	$80,000	F03 = 4
C04 =	$100,000	F04 = 1

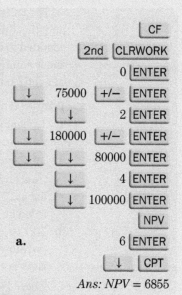

a. For $i = 6\%$,

$$NPV = -\$200,476 - \$88,160 + \$282,943 + \$12,548$$
$$= \$6855$$

Since $NPV > 0$, Digitel should proceed with the project. The interpretation of the NPV is that the current economic value of all the cash flows (after repaying the sources of financing) is $6855. This is also the increase in the firm's current market value as a result of investing in the product development project.

b. For $i = 7.5\%$,

$$NPV = -\$195,039 - \$84,521 + \$260,542 + \$11,214$$
$$= -\$7804$$

For $i = 7.5\%$, we obtain $NPV = -\$7804$. In this case the project will fall short (by $7804 in terms of current dollars) of repaying the financing along with the required 7.5% rate of return on investment. Digitel should not proceed in this case.

EXERCISE 17.2

Answers to the odd-numbered problems are at the end of the book.

Spreadsheet template: *A partially completed Excel template for calculating the net present value of an investment is provided on Connect. You can use this template with most of the problems in Exercise 17.2. Go to the Student Edition of Connect and under the Student Resources for Chapter 17 find "NPV & IRR Functions."*

INTERMEDIATE PROBLEMS

*Use the **NPV** investment criterion to answer the following problems. Unless otherwise indicated, assume that the initial capital investment occurs at the beginning of the first year and that subsequent cash flows occur at the end of each year. Show calculations that justify your decision.*

1. St. Lawrence Bus Lines is offered a contract for busing schoolchildren that will produce an annual profit of $70,000 for seven years. To fulfill the contract, St. Lawrence would have to buy three buses at a total cost of $433,000. At the end of the contract, the resale value of the buses is estimated to be $80,000. Should St. Lawrence Bus Lines sign the contract if its cost of capital is:

   a. 6%? **b.** 7%? **c.** 8%?

2. An automotive parts plant is scheduled to be closed in 10 years. Nevertheless, its engineering department thinks that some investments in computer-controlled equipment can be justified by the savings in labour and energy costs within that time frame. The engineering department is proposing the following four-phase capital investment program:

Phase	Initial investment	Annual savings
1	$80,000 now	$20,000 (end of Years 1–10)
2	$80,000 at start of Year 2	$17,000 (end of Years 2–10)
3	$80,000 at start of Year 3	$13,000 (end of Years 3–10)
4	$80,000 at start of Year 4	$15,000 (end of Years 4–10)

   The four phases are independent of one another. In other words, a decision not to proceed with an earlier phase does not affect the forecast savings from a later phase. The savings from any later phase are in addition to savings from earlier phases. There will be no significant residual value from any of the proposed investments. The firm's cost of capital is 8%. As the plant's financial analyst, what phases, if any, of the proposal would you accept?

3. The pro forma projections for growing a 20-hectare ginseng crop require the expenditure of $250,000 in the summer that the crop is planted, and an additional $50,000 in each of the next two summers to cultivate and fertilize the growing crop. After payment of the costs of harvesting the crop, the profit should be $200,000 in the third summer after planting, and $300,000 in the fourth summer. Allowing for a cost of capital of 9% compounded annually, what is the economic value of the project at the start of planting? (*Hint:* The project's economic value is its *NPV*.)

4. A proposed strip mine would require the investment of $3 million at the beginning of the first year and a further investment of $3 million at the end of the first year. Mining operations are expected to yield annual year-end profits of $1 million starting in Year 2. The ore body will sustain 10 years of mining operations. At the end of the last year of operations, the mining company would also have to spend $1 million on environmental restoration. Would the project provide the mining company with a rate of return exceeding its 10% cost of capital? (*Hint:* The project will provide a rate of return exceeding the cost of capital if it has a positive *NPV*.)

5. The development of a new product will require the expenditure of $150,000 at the beginning of each of the next three years. When the product reaches the market at the beginning of

Year 4, it is expected to increase the firm's annual year-end profit by $90,000 for seven years. Then the product line will be terminated, and $100,000 of the original expenditures should be recovered promptly. If the firm's cost of capital is 8.5%, should it proceed with the project?

6. The introduction of a new product will require an initial investment of $550,000. The annual profit expected from the new product is forecast to be $100,000 for Years 1 to 3, $70,000 for Years 4 to 6, and $50,000 for Years 7 to 12. Should the firm proceed with the investment if its required compound annual return is 6%?

ADVANCED PROBLEMS

7. Jasper Ski Corp. is studying the feasibility of installing a new chair lift to expand the capacity of its downhill-skiing operation. Site preparation would require the expenditure of $1,900,000 at the beginning of the first year. Construction would take place early in the second year at a cost of $5.8 million. The lift would have a useful life of 12 years and a residual value of $800,000. The increased capacity should generate increased annual profits of $600,000 at the end of Years 2 to 5 inclusive and $1 million in Years 6 to 13 inclusive. Should Jasper proceed with the project if it requires a return on investment of 7%?

8. A capital project would require an immediate investment of $150,000 and a further investment of $40,000 on a date four years from now. On the operating side, the project is expected to lose $30,000 in the first year and $10,000 in the second, to break even in the third year, and to turn annual profits of $70,000 in Years 4 to 7 and $40,000 in Years 8 to 10. The estimated residual value at the end of the tenth year is $50,000. Is the project acceptable if a return on investment of 10% is required?

9. To manufacture a new product, a company must immediately invest $375,000 in new equipment. At the end of Years 3 and 5, there will have to be a major overhaul of the equipment at a cost of $50,000 on each occasion. The new product is expected to increase annual operating profits by $75,000 in each of the first four years, and by $55,000 in each of the subsequent three years. The equipment will then be salvaged at the end of Year 7 to recover about $20,000. Should the product be manufactured if the company's cost of capital is 8% compounded annually?

10. A new machine that will lead to savings in labour costs of $16,000 per year can be purchased for $72,000. However, it will cost $1500 per year for the first four years and $2500 per year for the next four years to service and maintain it. In addition, its annual electrical power consumption will cost $1000. After a service life of eight years, the salvage value of the machine is expected to be $5000. Should the machine be acquired if the company requires a minimum return on investment of 7%?

11. Wildcat Drilling Contractors Inc. is considering the acquisition of a new deep-drilling rig at a cost of $14 million. With this added drilling capability, the company's net operating profits would increase by $2 million in the first year and grow by 10% per year over the seven-year service life of the rig. The salvage value of the rig after seven years would be about $2 million. Should Wildcat Drilling acquire the new drilling rig if its cost of capital is 8% compounded annually?

17.3 Comparing Investment Projects

Normally, a firm should accept every investment project that has a positive net present value. Any positive-*NPV* project produces a net economic benefit to the firm after the providers of financing have received their required returns. The *NPV* gives the magnitude of the economic benefit on the date of the initial capital expenditure.

There are two circumstances in which a business will not necessarily proceed with all of the positive-*NPV* investments available to it. In these situations, choosing one of the projects may exclude the selection of other positive-*NPV* projects. Some refinements to our selection criteria are needed to rank or select among projects that, in some sense, are competing alternatives.

Capital Rationing

L02 **Capital rationing** is the circumstance in which there is a limit on the total amount of capital funds that a firm may invest during a period. In this situation, the firm should *choose the group of projects that have the highest combined NPV* subject to the limitation on the total capital budget. By this choice, the increase in the firm's value is maximized.

EXAMPLE 17.3A

SELECTING CAPITAL PROJECTS SUBJECT TO A CAPITAL RATIONING CONSTRAINT

The strategic planning group at Hardy Toy Co. has identified the following positive-*NPV* projects, ranked in order of their *NPV*. All projects are independent—selection of any project neither requires nor precludes the selection of any other project.

Capital investment project	Initial capital investment ($)	Project *NPV* ($)
Expand production facilities	270,000	195,000
Open western distribution centre	250,000	155,000
Introduce Toy A	90,000	130,000
Buy out regional wood-toy maker	155,000	120,000
Introduce Game B	60,000	80,000
Purchase plastic moulding machine	54,000	70,000
Introduce Toy C	110,000	65,000
Introduce plastic recycling process	56,000	63,000
Replace old packaging machine	62,000	40,000
Introduce new doll	60,000	31,000

The board of directors has imposed a $600,000 capital expenditure limit for the next year. Which projects should the company undertake within the capital budget restriction?

SOLUTION

The company will want to choose the group of projects with the largest combined *NPV*, subject to the requirement that the total initial capital investment must not exceed $600,000. To obtain the biggest "bang per invested buck," it is helpful to calculate each project's *NPV* per dollar of initial investment. In the following table, the projects are ranked on the basis of this ratio (presented in the third column).

Project number	Capital investment project	NPV per invested dollar ($)	Initial capital investment ($)	Cumulative capital investment ($)
1	Introduce Toy A	1.44	90,000	90,000
2	Introduce Game B	1.33	60,000	150,000
3	Purchase plastic moulding machine	1.30	54,000	204,000
4	Introduce plastic recycling process	1.13	56,000	260,000
5	Buy out regional wood-toy maker	0.77	155,000	
6	Expand production facilities	0.72	270,000	
7	Replace old packaging machine	0.65	62,000	
8	Open western distribution centre	0.62	250,000	
9	Introduce Toy C	0.59	110,000	
10	Introduce new doll	0.52	60,000	

Until the capital budget constraint becomes a consideration, the projects with the highest *NPV* per invested dollar are automatically selected. The first four projects require a total investment of $260,000, leaving $340,000 available for others. If Project 5 is chosen next, Project 6 cannot be undertaken, because it would take the total investment beyond the $600,000 limit. But Projects 7 and 9 can still be included, along with 5, while remaining within the $600,000 limit. Therefore, one group of projects that must be considered is Projects 1, 2, 3, 4, 5, 7, and 9, for which

Required total capital investment = $587,000
Total net present value = $568,000

If we do not include Project 5, we can proceed with Project 6 and still have enough funds remaining in the $600,000 global budget to undertake Project 7 as well. This second combination (Projects 1, 2, 3, 4, 6, and 7) has

Required total capital investment = $592,000
Total net present value = $578,000

The second group should be selected since it adds $10,000 more economic value to Hardy Toy Co.

Mutually Exclusive Projects

L03 Alternative capital investments, any one of which will substantially satisfy the same need or purpose, are called **mutually exclusive projects**. For example, three different machines that fabricate the same product are mutually exclusive projects if any one of them will satisfy the firm's requirements. Only one will be selected, even if each one has a positive *NPV*.

If the mutually exclusive projects all have the *same* lifetime, a direct comparison may be made among the *NPV*s of the projects. The one with the largest positive *NPV* should be chosen because it provides the greatest economic benefit to the firm.

If projects have *unequal* lifetimes, it is *not* a simple matter of selecting the project with the largest lifetime *NPV*. A fair comparison requires a common time frame that might involve replacement cycles for one or more of the projects. However, we cannot arbitrarily pick the duration of the common time period because cash flows are unevenly distributed over each project's lifetime. Either of two methods—the *replacement chain method* or the *equivalent annual cash flow method*—may be used to deal with unequal investment lifetimes and uneven cash flows.

Replacement chain method The replacement chain approach repeats the replacement cycle of one or more of the mutually exclusive alternatives until *all* terminate on the *same* date. Then the *NPV*s of all cash flows within this common time horizon are calculated for each project. The one with the highest positive *NPV* should be selected.

EXAMPLE 17.3B

REPLACEMENT CHAIN METHOD WITH MUTUALLY EXCLUSIVE PROJECTS

A machine shop is trying to decide which of two types of metal lathe to purchase. The more versatile Japanese lathe costs $32,000, and will generate an annual profit of $16,000 for three years. Its trade-in value after three years will be about $10,000. The more durable German lathe costs $42,000, and will increase profits by $12,000 per year for six years. Its trade-in value at that point is estimated at $15,000. Based on an *NPV* calculation at a 10% cost of capital, which lathe should be purchased?

SOLUTION

We will first determine the lifetime *NPV* of a capital investment in each lathe.

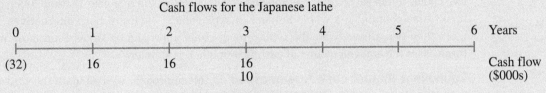

Cash flows for the Japanese lathe

0	1	2	3	4	5	6	Years
(32)	16	16	16 10				Cash flow ($000s)

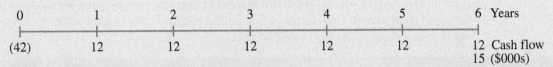

Cash flows for the German lathe

0	1	2	3	4	5	6	Years
(42)	12	12	12	12	12	12 15	Cash flow ($000s)

The *NPV* for the acquisition of the Japanese lathe is

$$NPV_J = PMT\left[\frac{1-(1+i)^{-n}}{i}\right] + FV(1+i)^{-n} - \$32,000$$

$$= \$16,000\left(\frac{1-(1.10)^{-3}}{0.10}\right) + \$10,000(1.10)^{-3} - \$32,000$$

$$= \$39,790 + \$7513 - \$32,000$$

$$= \$15,303$$

The *NPV* for the purchase of the German lathe is

$$NPV_G = \$12,000\left(\frac{1-(1.10)^{-6}}{0.10}\right) + \$15,000(1.10)^{-6} - \$42,000$$

$$= \$18,730$$

A comparison of the *NPV*s at this point would not necessarily lead to a valid conclusion (to purchase the higher-*NPV* German lathe). For a fair comparison, an adjustment must be made for the unequal service lives of the two lathes.

Since the machine shop is prepared to commit to the German lathe for six years, it is logical to infer that it is also prepared to have a Japanese lathe for six years. By including one replacement cycle of the Japanese lathe in the analysis, we obtain a common time frame of six years for both alternatives.

To reconsider the Japanese option, it is not necessary to begin again with a six-year time horizon. Remember the significance of the present value of a number of cash flows—it is the single amount that is equivalent, at the focal date, to all of the cash flows. Therefore, an investment's *NPV* is equivalent to all of the cash flows included in its calculation. The actual cash flows for six years with the Japanese lathe may be replaced by inflows of $15,303 at the beginning of each three-year service life (assuming no change in the purchase price). The following equivalent time diagram may be used for six years of operation with the Japanese lathe.

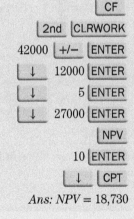

CF
2nd CLRWORK
32000 +/− ENTER
↓ 16000 ENTER
↓ 2 ENTER
↓ 26000 ENTER
NPV
10 ENTER
↓ CPT
Ans: NPV = 15,303

CF
2nd CLRWORK
42000 +/− ENTER
↓ 12000 ENTER
↓ 5 ENTER
↓ 27000 ENTER
NPV
10 ENTER
↓ CPT
Ans: NPV = 18,730

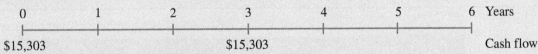

0	1	2	3	4	5	6	Years
$15,303			$15,303				Cash flow

The *NPV* for six years with the Japanese lathe is

$$NPV_J = \$15,303 + \$15,303(1.10)^{-3} = \$26,800$$

With the alternative investments transformed to a common time horizon, the Japanese lathe gives the higher *NPV*. Therefore, it should be selected.

The replacement chain method works well when the service life of one alternative is an integer multiple of the service life of a second alternative (as in **Example 17.3B**). But what if the service lives of two competing alternatives were five years and seven years? We would have to consider five cycles of the seven-year lifetime and seven cycles of the five-year lifetime to have a common time frame containing a whole number of replacement cycles of both alternatives. If there are more than two alternatives, the replacement chain approach becomes even more unwieldy. In these cases the equivalent annual cash flow method is simpler.

Equivalent annual cash flow method In this approach, we calculate the *constant annual cash flow* during each project's lifetime that has the same *NPV* as the *actual* cash flows. Since the equivalent annual flows also apply to any number of replacement cycles, we can directly compare the equivalent annual cash flows of competing projects. *The project with the largest positive equivalent annual cash flow should be selected.*

EXAMPLE 17.3C

EQUIVALENT ANNUAL CASH-FLOW METHOD WITH MUTUALLY EXCLUSIVE PROJECTS

Repeat **Example 17.3B** using the equivalent annual cash flow method.

SOLUTION

Recall that the *NPV* for one three-year investment cycle for the Japanese lathe was

$$NPV_J = \$15,303$$

and that the *NPV* for one six-year investment cycle for the German lathe was

$$NPV_G = \$18,730$$

For the Japanese lathe, the equivalent annual cash flow is the value of PMT_J satisfying Formula (11-2).

$$\$15,303 = PMT_J \left[\frac{1 - (1.10)^{-3}}{0.10} \right]$$

The solution is $PMT_J = \$6154$.

For the German lathe, the equivalent annual cash flow is the solution to

$$\$18,730 = PMT_G \left[\frac{1 - (1.10)^{-6}}{0.10} \right]$$

The solution is $PMT_G = \$4301$.

Since the Japanese lathe has the larger equivalent annual cash flow, it should be selected.

Note: The ratio of the two equivalent annual cash flows in this solution is

$$\frac{PMT_J}{PMT_G} = \frac{\$6154}{\$4301} = 1.431$$

The ratio of the *NPV*s of investments in the two lathes calculated in **Example 17.3B** for a common six-year time horizon is:

$$\frac{NPV_J \text{ for 6 years}}{NPV_G \text{ for 6 years}} = \frac{\$26,800}{\$18,730} = 1.431$$

The equality of the two ratios demonstrates the equivalence of the two methods.

 TIP

Unequal Lives Matter Only for Mutually Exclusive Projects

Remember that unequal lives do not have to be taken into account when *independent* projects are being selected under conditions of capital rationing. Unequal lives are a consideration only for *mutually exclusive* projects.

Cost minimization When mutually exclusive alternatives generate the same benefits or cash inflows, it is sufficient to focus on the cash outflows. We should select the lowest-cost alternative, recognizing the time value of money. When the time horizons of the competing alternatives are the same, the present values of the lifetime cash outflows may be directly compared. However, when the time horizons differ, calculate the *equivalent annual cash outflow* for each alternative. Select the alternative with the *smallest* equivalent annual cash outflow.

EXERCISE 17.3

Answers to the odd-numbered problems are at the end of the book.

INTERMEDIATE PROBLEMS

Problems 1, 2, and 3 require the selection of independent capital investments subject to a capital budget limitation.

1. A firm has identified the following four investment opportunities and calculated their net present values. If the firm's capital budget for this period is limited to $300,000, which projects should be selected?

Project	Initial investment ($)	NPV ($)
A	100,000	25,000
B	60,000	40,000
C	130,000	60,000
D	200,000	110,000

2. The investment committee of a company has identified the following seven projects with positive *NPV*s. If the board of directors has approved a $3 million capital budget for the current period, which projects should be selected?

Project	Initial investment ($)	NPV ($)
1	1,000,000	600,000
2	1,800,000	324,000
3	750,000	285,000
4	600,000	270,000
5	450,000	113,000
6	150,000	21,000
7	250,000	20,000

3. Mohawk Enterprises is considering the following investment opportunities.

Project	Initial investment ($)	Profit for year ($) Year 1	Year 2	Year 3	Year 4
A	30,000	12,000	9000	8000	20,000
B	36,000	6000	23,000	10,000	14,000
C	18,000	10,000	0	0	20,000
D	22,000	0	18,000	2500	11,000
E	28,000	26,000	0	0	17,000
F	20,000	6000	7000	10,000	11,000

If Mohawk's cost of capital is 8% and its capital budget is limited to $90,000, which projects should it choose?

Problems 4–11 require the selection of the best investment from two or more mutually exclusive alternatives.

4. A small regional airline has narrowed down the possible choices for its next passenger plane purchase to two alternatives. The Eagle model costs $600,000, and would have an estimated resale value of $100,000 after seven years. The Albatross model has a $750,000 price, and would have an estimated resale value of $300,000 after seven years. The annual operating profit from the Eagle would be $150,000. Because of its greater fuel efficiency and slightly larger seating capacity, the Albatross's annual profit would be $190,000. Which plane should the airline purchase if its cost of capital is 6.5%? In current dollars, what is the economic advantage of selecting the preferred alternative?

5. Carl Williams does custom wheat combining in southern Alberta. He will purchase either a new Massey or a new Deere combine to replace his old machine. The Massey combine costs $190,000, and the Deere combine costs $156,000. Their trade-in values after six years would be about $50,000 and $40,000, respectively. Because the Massey cuts an 18-foot swath versus the Deere's 15-foot swath, Carl estimates that his annual profit with the Massey will be 10% higher than the $70,000 he could make with the Deere. The Massey equipment dealer will provide 100% financing at 7% per annum, and the Deere dealer will approve 100% financing at 6% per annum. Which combine should Carl purchase? How much more, in current dollars, is the better alternative worth?

ADVANCED PROBLEMS

6. Machine A costs $40,000 and is forecast to generate an annual profit of $15,000 for four years. Machine B, priced at $60,000, will produce the same annual profits for eight years. The trade-in value of A after four years is expected to be $10,000, and the resale value of B after eight years is also estimated to be $10,000. If either machine satisfies the firm's requirements, which one should be selected? Use a required return of 8%.

7. A sawmill requires a new saw for cutting small-dimension logs. Model H, with a three-year service life, costs $119,000 and will generate an annual profit of $55,000. Model J, with a four-year service life, costs $160,000 and will return an annual profit of $58,000. Neither saw will have significant salvage value. If the mill's cost of capital is 5.5%, which model should be purchased?

8. A business is evaluating two mutually exclusive projects. Project A requires an immediate investment of $6000, plus another $8000 in three years. It would produce a profit of $6000 in the second year, $18,000 in the fourth year, and $12,000 in the seventh year. Project B requires an immediate investment of $5000, another $8000 in two years, and a further $5000 in four years. It would produce an annual profit of $5400 for seven years. Neither project would have any residual value after seven years. Which project should be selected if the required rate of return is 7%? What is the economic advantage, in current dollars, of the preferred project?

9. A company must choose between two investments. Investment C requires an immediate outlay of $50,000 and then, in two years, another investment of $30,000. Investment D requires annual investments of $25,000 at the beginning of each of the first four years. C would return annual profits of $16,000 for 10 years beginning with the first year. D's profits would not start until Year 4 but would be $35,000 in Years 4 to 10 inclusive. The residual values after 10 years are estimated to be $30,000 for C and $20,000 for D. Which investment should the company choose if its cost of capital is 9%? How much more is the preferred investment worth today?

10. A landscaping business will buy one of three rototillers. The initial cost, expected service life, and trade-in value (at the end of the service life) of each model are presented in the following table. The annual profit from rototilling services is $1400.

Model	Cost ($)	Service life (years)	Trade-in value ($)
A	2000	2	400
AA	2800	3	900
AAA	4200	6	1400

Which model should be purchased if the required return on investment is 8.5%?

11. An independent trucker is trying to decide whether to buy a 15-ton truck or a 25-ton truck. A 15-ton vehicle would cost $150,000; it would have a service life of seven years, and a trade-in value of about $30,000 at seven years of age. A 25-ton truck would cost $200,000, have a service life of six years, and be worth about $40,000 at six years of age. The estimated annual profit (after provision for a normal salary for the driver–owner) would be $35,000 for the smaller truck and $48,000 for the larger truck. Which truck should be purchased if the cost of financing a truck is 9% compounded annually? What is the average annual economic benefit of making the right decision?

Problems 12–15 require the selection of the lowest-cost alternative.

12. *Consumer Digest* recently reported that car batteries X, Y, and Z have average service lives of three, four, and six years, respectively. Grace found that the best retail prices for these batteries in her town are $95, $120, and $165. If money is worth 7% compounded annually, which battery has the lowest equivalent annual cost?

13. The provincial government's Ministry of Forest Resources requires a spotter plane for its fire service. The price of a Hawk is $240,000, and its annual operating costs will be $60,000. Given the heavy use it will receive, it will be sold for about $60,000 after five years and replaced. A more durable but less efficient Falcon, priced at $190,000, will cost $80,000 per year to operate, will last seven years, and will have a resale value of $80,000. If the provincial government pays an interest rate of 6.5% compounded annually on its mid-term debt, which plane has the lower equivalent annual cost?

14. Neil always trades in his car when it reaches five years of age because of the large amount of driving he does in his job. He is investigating whether there would be a financial advantage in buying a two-year-old car every three years instead of buying a new car every five years. His research indicates that, for the make of car he prefers, he could buy a two-year-old car for $18,000, whereas a new car of the same model sells for $30,000. In either case, the resale value of the five-year-old car would be $6000. Repairs and maintenance average $450 per year for the first two years of the car's life and $1500 per year for the next three. Which alternative has the lower equivalent annual cost if money is worth 7% compounded annually?

15. A construction company has identified two machines that will accomplish the same job. The Caterpillar model costs $160,000, and has a service life of eight years if it receives a $30,000 overhaul every two years. The International model costs $210,000, and should last 12 years with a $20,000 overhaul every three years. In either case, the overhaul scheduled for the year of disposition would not be performed, and the machine would be sold for about $20,000. If the company's cost of capital is 6%, which machine should be purchased?

17.4 Internal Rate of Return

L04 Business managers often prefer to discuss and compare investment opportunities in terms of an annual rate of return on investment. The net present-value calculation does not provide the rate of return on the invested funds.

Recall that the net cash flows from an investment project having an *NPV* of zero will be just sufficient to repay the project's financing, including a rate of return *equal* to the discount rate. Therefore, the rate of return on investment for a zero-*NPV* project equals the discount rate used in the *NPV* calculation. This special case suggests a technique for determining the rate of return on investment from any project. If we can find a discount rate that makes the *NPV* of the project's net cash flows equal to zero, then that discount rate is the project's rate of return on investment. In the context of business capital investments, this rate of return is often called the **internal rate of return** (*IRR*).

> **Internal Rate of Return (*IRR*):**
> An investment's *IRR* is the discount rate that makes the net present value of the investment equal to zero.

When the cash inflows from a capital investment form an annuity, you can use a financial calculator's basic financial functions to compute the interest rate that makes the annuity's present value equal to the initial capital investment. Some calculators have a special *IRR* function key that enables you to compute the *IRR* for a set of *unequal* periodic cash flows. The use of the *IRR* function on the Texas Instruments BA II PLUS calculator will be demonstrated in **Example 17.4A**.

A positive-*NPV* investment has an *IRR* greater than the cost of capital, whereas a negative-*NPV* investment has an *IRR* less than the cost of capital. The *NPV* investment decision criteria developed in **Section 17.2** may be restated in terms of the investment's *IRR*.

> **IRR Investment Decision Criteria:**
> Accept the investment if *IRR* ≥ Cost of capital.
> Reject the investment if *IRR* < Cost of capital.

As net cash flows are received from a project, the invested funds are gradually recovered. The *IRR* continues to be earned only on the *unrecovered* portion of the original investment. The recovered funds subsequently earn the rate of return for the next project in which they are reinvested.[5]

EXAMPLE 17.4A

USING THE TEXAS INSTRUMENTS BA II PLUS'S *IRR* FUNCTION

A project requires an immediate investment of $30,000 and an additional investment of $12,000 in one year. It will generate an annual profit of $8000 in Years 2 to 8, and have a residual value of $5000 at the end of the eighth year. Calculate the project's internal rate of return. Should the project be undertaken if the firm's cost of capital is 7%?

---

[5] An alternative definition of the *IRR* is "the discount rate that makes the present value of the future cash flows equal to the initial capital outlay." From this version of the definition, it is clearer that the *IRR* is a new name for a familiar concept. The returns on investment that we calculated for various investment instruments in previous chapters are the internal rates of return for those investments. For example, the yield to maturity on a bond (**Section 16.3**) could also be called the bond's *IRR*. It is merely prevailing business practice that dictates which term is used for the same quantity in different contexts.

SOLUTION

The cash flows are presented in the time diagram below.

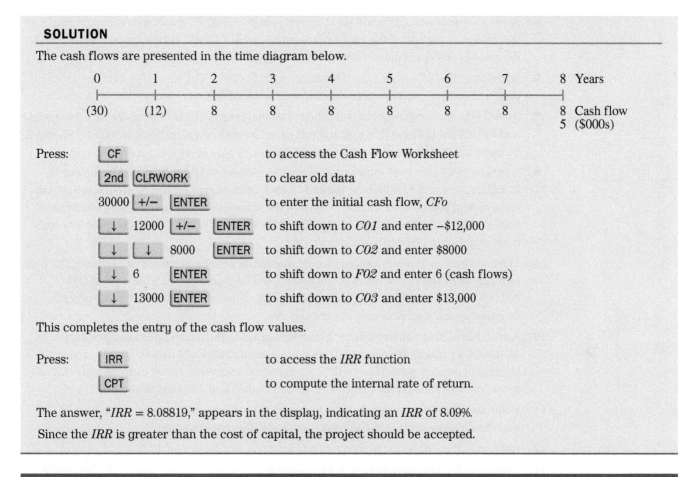

Press: CF   to access the Cash Flow Worksheet

        2nd CLRWORK   to clear old data

        30000 +/− ENTER   to enter the initial cash flow, *CFo*

        ↓ 12000 +/− ENTER   to shift down to *C01* and enter −$12,000

        ↓   ↓   8000 ENTER   to shift down to *C02* and enter $8000

        ↓   6   ENTER   to shift down to *F02* and enter 6 (cash flows)

        ↓   13000 ENTER   to shift down to *C03* and enter $13,000

This completes the entry of the cash flow values.

Press: IRR   to access the *IRR* function

        CPT   to compute the internal rate of return.

The answer, "*IRR* = 8.08819," appears in the display, indicating an *IRR* of 8.09%.

Since the *IRR* is greater than the cost of capital, the project should be accepted.

EXERCISE 17.4

Answers to the odd-numbered problems are at the end of the book.

Spreadsheet template: *A partially completed Excel template for calculating an investment's internal rate of return is provided on Connect. You can use this template with most of the problems in Exercise 17.4. Go to the Student Edition of Connect and find "NPV & IRR Functions" under the Student Resources for Chapter 17.*

Determine the IRR in the following problems to the nearest 0.1%.

BASIC PROBLEMS

1. A 10-year licence to distribute a product should increase the distributor's profit by $10,000 per year. If the licence can be acquired for $66,000, what is the investment's *IRR*?

2. Burger Master bought the food concession for a baseball stadium for five years at a price of $1.2 million. If the operating profit is $400,000 per year, what *IRR* will Burger Master realize on its investment?

INTERMEDIATE PROBLEMS

3. Calculate the *IRR* of each of the four stages of the cost-reduction proposal in Problem 2 of Exercise 17.2. Based on the *IRR* investment criterion, which stages should be approved at an 8% cost of capital?

4. A project requires an initial investment of $60,000. It will generate an annual profit of $12,000 for eight years and have a terminal value of $10,000. Calculate the project's *IRR*. Should it be accepted if the cost of capital is 15%?

5. An investment of $100,000 will yield annual profits of $12,000 for 10 years. The proceeds on disposition at the end of the 10 years are estimated at $15,000. On the basis of its *IRR* and a 6% cost of capital, should the investment be made?

6. Determine the *IRR* on the school bus contract in Problem 1 of Exercise 17.2. At which of the three costs of capital would the contract be financially acceptable?

7. An $80,000 capital investment will produce annual profits of $15,000 for the first five years and $10,000 for the next five years. It will have no residual value. What is its *IRR*? Should it be undertaken if the cost of capital is 8.5%?

8. A natural resource development and extraction project would require an investment of $1 million now and $1 million at the end of each of the next four years. Then it would generate annual profits of $2 million in each of the subsequent four years. There would be no residual value. What would be the *IRR* of the project? Would it be acceptable to a company requiring a 12% return on investment?

9. The introduction of a new product would require an initial investment of $120,000. The forecast profits in successive years of the anticipated four-year product life are $15,000, $60,000, $40,000, and $35,000. Determine the *IRR* of the investment. Should the product be introduced if the firm's cost of capital is 9%?

10. A venture requiring an immediate investment of $500,000 and an additional investment of $200,000 three years from now will generate annual profits of $150,000 for seven years starting in the first year. There will be no significant terminal value. Calculate the *IRR* of the investment. Should the investment be undertaken at a 13% cost of capital?

11. Determine the *IRR* on the strip mine proposal in Problem 4 of Exercise 17.2. Should the mine be developed, given the mining company's 10% cost of capital?

12. Determine the *IRR* on the ginseng crop in Problem 3 of Exercise 17.2.

13. Determine the *IRR* on the chairlift expansion in Problem 7 of Exercise 17.2. Should the expansion be undertaken, given Jasper Ski Corp.'s required return of 7%?

17.5 Comparing *NPV* and *IRR* Approaches

For independent projects, the *NPV* and *IRR* investment decision criteria lead to the same "accept" or "reject" conclusion.[6] If the *NPV* criterion is satisfied, the *IRR* criterion will also be met.

The *NPV* approach has the advantage that it also quantifies the magnitude of the economic benefit to the firm of undertaking a capital investment. The primary objective of the managers of a firm is to maximize the value of the firm. The *NPV* analysis relates directly to this objective, since it gives the amount that each potential investment will add to the firm's value. Nevertheless, studies of actual business practice reveal that more managers prefer to base business investment decisions on the *IRR* than on the *NPV*. This seems to reflect a traditional bias toward measures of profitability stated as percentage rates of return. Managers are also inclined to think in terms of the spread between the cost of capital and the (internal) rate of return on an investment.

L03 A flawed investment decision can result if the *IRR* is used to rank projects that are mutually exclusive, or to rank projects that are competing for a limited capital budget. In these cases, it can happen that the project with the larger *IRR* has the smaller *NPV*. The ranking should be based strictly on the projects' *NPV*s. Then you can be sure you are selecting the project that adds the most value to the firm.

---

[6] An exception sometimes occurs if there is more than one sign reversal among the periodic net cash flows. In such cases there can be more than one discount rate that makes the project's *NPV* equal to zero, and the *IRR* investment criteria will not necessarily apply. These cases will not be encountered in this text; they are considered in texts on managerial finance.

In summary, the *NPV* approach to evaluating and ranking capital investment opportunities always works. It also gives the amount by which the investment will increase the value of the firm. There are some situations, particularly the ranking of mutually exclusive investments, in which the *IRR* method can lead to a suboptimal decision.[7]

EXAMPLE 17.5A

RANKING MUTUALLY EXCLUSIVE PROJECTS

A company is considering two mutually exclusive projects. The initial investment required and the expected profits are presented in the following table. Neither project will have any residual value.

	Project A ($)	Project B ($)
Initial investment	50,000	130,000
Year 1 profit	20,000	50,000
Year 2 profit	20,000	50,000
Year 3 profit	20,000	50,000

a. Rank the projects on the basis of their *IRR*s.

b. Which project should be chosen if the company's cost of capital is 6.5%?

c. Which project should be chosen if the cost of capital is 5.5%?

SOLUTION

a. Each project's annual profits form a simple annuity. The *IRR* of Project A is the value of i satisfying

$$0 = \$20{,}000\left[\frac{1-(1+i)^{-3}}{i}\right] - \$50{,}000$$

Similarly, the *IRR* of Project B is the solution to

$$0 = \$50{,}000\left[\frac{1-(1+i)^{-3}}{i}\right] - \$130{,}000$$

When the periodic cash flows form an annuity, we can use the calculator's basic financial functions to solve for i.

Project A:

P/Y 1 ENTER
(making *C/Y* = *P/Y* = 1)
3 N
50000 +/− PV
20000 PMT
0 FV
CPT I/Y
Ans: 9.70

Project B:

Same *P/Y, C/Y, N, FV*
130000 +/− PV
50000 PMT
CPT I/Y
Ans: 7.51

The *IRR* of Project A is 9.70% compounded annually and of Project B is 7.51% compounded annually. On the basis of an *IRR* ranking, Project A should be selected over Project B.

---

[7] The fundamental reason for this limitation can be traced to a subtle point. Any valuation of cash flows based on a present-value calculation implicitly assumes that cash flows from the investment may be reinvested at the discount rate used in the present-value calculation. An *NPV* ranking of projects therefore assumes the same reinvestment rate (the cost of capital) for all projects. An *IRR* ranking of projects assumes a *different* reinvestment rate for each project—namely, each project's own internal rate of return. It is not a fair comparison to rank projects on the basis of a criterion that does not use the same reinvestment rate for all projects being compared. Therefore, an *IRR* ranking of projects may differ from an *NPV* ranking, and the latter should take precedence.

b. At a cost of capital of 6.5%,

$$NPV_A = \$20{,}000\left[\frac{1-(1.065)^{-3}}{0.065}\right] - \$50{,}000 = \$2970$$

$$NPV_B = \$50{,}000\left[\frac{1-(1.065)^{-3}}{0.065}\right] - \$130{,}000 = \$2424$$

Since $NPV_A > NPV_B$, Project A should be selected.

c. At a cost of capital of 5.5%,

$$NPV_A = \$20{,}000\left[\frac{1-(1.055)^{-3}}{0.055}\right] - \$50{,}000 = \$3959$$

$$NPV_B = \$50{,}000\left[\frac{1-(1.055)^{-3}}{0.055}\right] - \$130{,}000 = \$4897$$

Since $NPV_B > NPV_A$, Project B should be selected (even though $IRR_A > IRR_B$).

EXAMPLE 17.5B

RANKING MUTUALLY EXCLUSIVE PROJECTS

The initial investment and subsequent profits for two mutually exclusive, three-year projects are forecast as follows:

a. Rank the projects on the basis of their *IRR*s.

b. Rank the projects on the basis of their *NPV*s if the firm's cost of capital is 8.5%.

c. Rank the projects on the basis of their *NPV*s if the firm's cost of capital is 7%.

d. Which project should be selected if the cost of capital is 7%?

	Project S ($)	Project T ($)
Initial investment	100,000	100,000
Year 1 profit	80,000	20,000
Year 2 profit	20,000	20,000
Year 3 profit	20,000	90,000

SOLUTION

Let us first compute the *IRR*s and *NPV*s of both projects.

Project S:

		CF
	2nd	CLRWORK
100000	+/−	ENTER
↓	80000	ENTER
↓	20000	ENTER
↓	2	ENTER
		IRR
		CPT

Ans: IRR = 13.25

8.5	NPV
8.5	ENTER
↓	CPT

Ans: NPV = 6380

7	ENTER
↑	7 ENTER
↓	CPT

Ans: NPV = 8561

Project T:

		CF
	2nd	CLRWORK
100000	+/−	ENTER
↓	20000	ENTER
↓	2	ENTER
↓	90000	ENTER
		IRR
		CPT

Ans: IRR = 11.03

8.5	NPV
8.5	ENTER
↓	CPT

Ans: NPV = 5884

7	ENTER
↑	7 ENTER
↓	CPT

Ans: NPV = 9627

a. Project S has the larger *IRR* and, on that basis, ranks ahead of Project T.

b. At an 8.5% discount rate, Project S has the larger *NPV* and ranks ahead of Project T (as in the *IRR* ranking).

c. At a 7% discount rate, Project T has the larger *NPV* and ranks ahead of Project S. [From the results of parts (b) and (c), we note that an *NPV* ranking may depend on the cost of capital. A project's *IRR* is not affected by the cost of capital.]

d. At a 7% cost of capital, the *IRR* and *NPV* rankings do not agree—Project S has the greater *IRR* but the lesser *NPV*. We should let the *NPV* ranking take precedence and select the project that adds the greater value to the firm. Therefore, choose Project T.

EXERCISE 17.5

Answers to the odd-numbered problems are at the end of the book.

Spreadsheet template: *Partially completed Excel templates for calculating an investment's net present value and internal rate of return are provided on Connect. You can use these templates with some of the problems in Exercise 17.5. Go to the Student Edition on Connect and find "NPV & IRR Functions" under the Student Resources for Chapter 17.*

Calculate internal rates of return to the nearest 0.1%.

INTERMEDIATE PROBLEMS

1. Two mutually exclusive investments are available to a firm. Project C, requiring a capital investment of $200,000, will generate an annual profit of $43,000 for six years. Project D is expected to yield an annual profit of $30,000 for six years on an initial investment of $135,000.
   a. Calculate the internal rate of return on each project. Based upon their *IRR*s, which project should be selected?
   b. Which project should be selected if the firm's cost of capital is 7%?
   c. Which project should be selected if the firm's cost of capital is 5%?

2. Academic Publishing is trying to decide which of two books to publish. The larger book will cost $125,000 to publish and print. Sales are expected to produce an annual profit of $32,000 for five years. The smaller book will cost $76,000 to publish and print, and should generate an annual profit of $20,000 for five years.
   a. Calculate the internal rate of return on each book. On the basis of their *IRR*s, which book should be published?
   b. Which book should be published if the firm's cost of capital is 8%?
   c. Which book should be published if the firm's cost of capital is 6%?

3. Due to a restricted capital budget, a company can undertake only one of the following three-year projects. Both require an initial investment of $800,000 and will have no significant terminal value. Project X is anticipated to have annual profits of $400,000, $300,000, and $250,000 in successive years, whereas Project Y's only profit, $1.05 million, comes at the end of Year 3.
   a. Calculate the *IRR* of each project. On the basis of their *IRR*s, which project should be selected?
   b. Which project should be selected if the firm's cost of capital is 9%?
   c. Which project should be selected if the firm's cost of capital is 7%?

4. Two mutually exclusive projects each require an initial investment of $50,000 and should have a residual value of $10,000 after three years. The following table presents their forecast annual profits.

Year	Project 1 ($)	Project 2 ($)
1	10,000	30,000
2	20,000	20,000
3	30,000	8,000

   a. Calculate the *IRR* of each project. On the basis of their *IRR*s, which project should be selected?
   b. Which project should be selected if the firm's cost of capital is 8%?
   c. Which project should be selected if the firm's cost of capital is 6%?

5. A company is examining two mutually exclusive projects. Project X requires an immediate investment of $100,000 and produces no profit until Year 3. Then the annual profit is $40,000 for Years 3 to 5 inclusive. Project Y requires an investment of $50,000 now and another $50,000 in one year. It is expected to generate an annual profit of $30,000 in Years 2 to 5.
   a. Calculate the *IRR* of each project. On the basis of their *IRR*s, which project is preferred?
   b. Which project should be selected if the firm's cost of capital is 4%?
   c. Which project should be selected if the firm's cost of capital is 3%?

6. A company is evaluating two mutually exclusive projects. Both require an initial investment of $250,000 and have no appreciable disposal value. Their expected profits over their five-year lifetimes are as follows:

Year	Project Alpha ($)	Project Beta ($)
1	120,000	20,000
2	80,000	40,000
3	60,000	60,000
4	20,000	100,000
5	20,000	120,000

   The company's cost of capital is 7%. Calculate the *NPV* and *IRR* for each project. Which project should be chosen? Why?

17.6 The Payback Period

L05 Many smaller firms still use the payback period as a measure of the attractiveness of a capital investment. The **payback period** is the number of years it takes to recover an initial investment from the investment's future operating profits. For example, if an initial capital investment of $450,000 generates an annual profit of $100,000 for 10 years, it has a $4\frac{1}{2}$-year payback. A firm that uses this approach establishes a maximum payback period for an acceptable investment. Investment opportunities that have a payback period shorter than or equal to the maximum should be accepted.

The payback approach to investment selection has three serious shortcomings. The first is that the payback calculation ignores the time value of money—there is no discounting of the future cash flows. In the example above, $1 in Year 5 is treated as having the same value as $1 of the initial investment. A second flaw is that the payback calculation ignores the profits and residual value that would be received beyond the maximum payback period. The third weakness is that the maximum acceptable payback period is set by the firm in a rather arbitrary manner without rigorous economic justification. The payback method is included in our coverage of investment decision criteria not because it has any great merit, but only because it is still widely used.

EXAMPLE 17.6A

CALCULATION OF THE PAYBACK PERIOD: COMPARISON OF DECISIONS BASED ON PAYBACK VERSUS *NPV*

A firm is considering three independent projects. They all require the same initial investment of $110,000 and have no residual value after eight years. All three generate the same aggregate total of profits ($160,000), but the profits are distributed differently over the eight-year period, as presented in the following table.

	Annual profit		
Year	Project A ($)	Project B ($)	Project C ($)
1	25,000	20,000	0
2	25,000	20,000	0
3	25,000	20,000	45,000
4	25,000	20,000	45,000
5	15,000	20,000	15,000
6	15,000	20,000	15,000
7	15,000	20,000	20,000
8	15,000	20,000	20,000

a. Which projects should be accepted if the firm has a five-year payback requirement?

b. Which projects would be accepted on the *NPV* criterion if the firm's cost of capital is 9%?

SOLUTION

a. To be accepted on the payback criterion, a project must have cumulative profits after five years that equal or exceed the original capital investment ($110,000). The following table presents the cumulative profits from the three projects at the end of each year.

	Cumulative profits		
Year	Project A ($)	Project B ($)	Project C ($)
1	25,000	20,000	0
2	50,000	40,000	0
3	75,000	60,000	45,000
4	100,000	80,000	90,000
5	115,000	100,000	105,000
6	130,000	120,000	120,000
7	145,000	140,000	140,000
8	160,000	160,000	160,000

Assuming that the profits accumulate uniformly within each year, the payback periods are:

$$\text{Project A:} \qquad 4 + \frac{\$10,000}{\$15,000} = 4.7 \text{ years}$$

$$\text{Project B:} \qquad 5 + \frac{\$10,000}{\$20,000} = 5.5 \text{ years}$$

$$\text{Project C:} \qquad 5 + \frac{\$5,000}{\$15,000} = 5.3 \text{ years}$$

Project A will be accepted because it recovers the original investment within the five-year payback period. Projects B and C will be rejected on the same criterion.

b. The net present value of Project A is

$$NPV_A = \$25,000\left[\frac{1-(1.09)^{-4}}{0.09}\right] + \$15,000\left[\frac{1-(1.09)^{-4}}{0.09}\right](1.09)^{-4} - \$110,000$$
$$= \$80,993 + \$34,426 - \$110,000$$
$$= \$5419$$

The net present value of Project B is

$$NPV_B = \$20,000\left[\frac{1-(1.09)^{-8}}{0.09}\right] - \$110,000$$
$$= \$696$$

The net present value of Project C is

$$NPV_C = \frac{\$45,000}{1.09^3} + \frac{\$45,000}{1.09^4} + \frac{\$15,000}{1.09^5} + \frac{\$15,000}{1.09^6} + \frac{\$20,000}{1.09^7} + \frac{\$20,000}{1.09^8} - \$110,000$$
$$= \$34,748 + \$31,879 + \$9749 + \$8944 + \$10,941 + \$10,037 - \$110,000$$
$$= -\$3702$$

The following boxes present the procedures for obtaining the *NPV*s of the projects using the Cash Flow Worksheet.

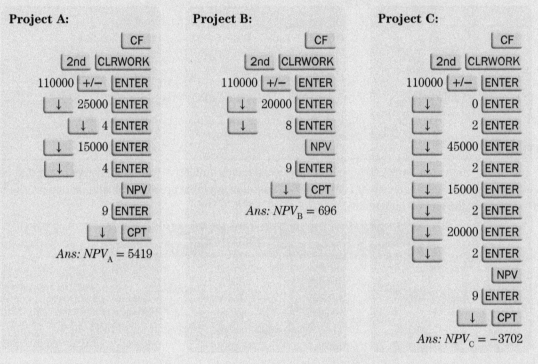

Project A:

CF
2nd CLRWORK
110000 +/− ENTER
↓ 25000 ENTER
↓ 4 ENTER
↓ 15000 ENTER
↓ 4 ENTER
NPV
9 ENTER
↓ CPT

Ans: NPV_A = 5419

Project B:

CF
2nd CLRWORK
110000 +/− ENTER
↓ 20000 ENTER
↓ 8 ENTER
NPV
9 ENTER
↓ CPT

Ans: NPV_B = 696

Project C:

CF
2nd CLRWORK
110000 +/− ENTER
↓ 0 ENTER
↓ 2 ENTER
↓ 45000 ENTER
↓ 2 ENTER
↓ 15000 ENTER
↓ 2 ENTER
↓ 20000 ENTER
↓ 2 ENTER
NPV
9 ENTER
↓ CPT

Ans: NPV_C = −3702

Since Projects A and B both have a positive *NPV*, they should be accepted. Project C, with a negative *NPV*, should be rejected.

Note: Since there is no fundamental economic rationale behind the payback period, we should not expect a high degree of consistency between investment decisions based on a payback period and decisions based on the *NPV* criterion. In this example Project B was accepted based on its *NPV* but was rejected because its payback period exceeded five years. A general statement that can be made is that the shorter a project's payback period, the more likely it is to have a positive *NPV*.

EXERCISE 17.6

Answers to the odd-numbered problems are at the end of the book.

BASIC PROBLEMS

1. The expected profits from a $52,000 investment are $8000 in Year 1, $12,000 in each of Years 2 to 5, and $6000 in each of Years 6 and 7.
   a. What is the investment's payback period?
   b. If the firm's required payback period is four years, will it make the investment?

2. A firm is considering the purchase of a $30,000 machine that would save labour costs of $5000 per year in the first three years and $6000 per year for the next four years. Will the firm purchase the machine if the payback requirement is:
   a. Five years?   b. Six years?

INTERMEDIATE PROBLEMS

3. Projects X and Y both require an initial investment of $100,000. Project X will generate an annual operating profit of $25,000 per year for six years. Project Y produces no profit in the first year, but will yield an annual profit of $25,000 for the seven subsequent years. Rank the projects based on their payback periods and on their NPVs (at an 8% cost of capital).

4. A capital investment requiring a single initial cash outflow is forecast to have an operating profit of $50,000 per year for five years. There is no salvage value at the end of the five years. If the investment has an IRR of 8%, calculate its payback period.

ADVANCED PROBLEM

5. Investment proposals A and B require initial investments of $45,000 and $35,000, respectively. Both have an economic life of four years with no residual value. Their expected profits are as follows:

Year	Proposal A ($)	Proposal B ($)
1	16,250	12,500
2	17,500	12,500
3	17,500	15,000
4	17,500	15,000

If the firm's cost of capital is 7%, rank the proposals based on their:
   a. NPVs.   b. IRRs.   c. Payback periods.

KEY TERMS

Capital rationing	Internal rate of return	Net present value
Cost of capital	Mutually exclusive projects	Payback period

SUMMARY OF NOTATION AND KEY FORMULAS

NPV = Net present value (of an investment)
IRR = Internal rate of return (on an investment)

$$NPV = \left(\begin{array}{c}\text{Present value of}\\\text{cash inflows}\end{array}\right) - \left(\begin{array}{c}\text{Present value of}\\\text{cash outflows}\end{array}\right)$$

NPV Investment Decision Criteria:
Accept the investment if $NPV \geq 0$.
Reject the investment if $NPV < 0$.

IRR Investment Decision Criteria:
Accept the investment if $IRR \geq$ Cost of capital.
Reject the investment if $IRR <$ Cost of capital.

REVIEW PROBLEMS

Answers to the odd-numbered review problems are at the end of the book.

BASIC PROBLEMS

1. **L05** The expected profits from an $80,000 investment are $15,000 in Year 1 and $20,000 in each of Years 2 to 7.
   a. What is the investment's payback period?
   b. If the firm's required payback period is four years, will it make the investment?
   c. If the firm's cost of capital is 8%, will it make the investment based on the *NPV* criterion?

2. **L04** A seven-year licence to distribute a product should increase the distributor's profit by $16,000 per year. If the licence can be acquired for $85,000, what is the investment's *IRR*?

INTERMEDIATE PROBLEMS

3. **L01** A proposed open-pit mine would require the investment of $3 million at the beginning of the first year and a further investment of $1 million at the end of the first year. Mining operations are expected to yield annual profits of $750,000, beginning in Year 2. The ore body will sustain eight years of ore extraction. At the beginning of the tenth year, the mining company must spend $1 million on cleanup and environmental restoration. Will the project provide the mining company with a rate of return exceeding its 5.5% cost of capital?

4. **L01** The development of a new product will require the expenditure of $175,000 at the beginning of each of the next two years. When the product reaches the market in Year 3, it is expected to increase the firm's annual profit by $50,000 for eight years. (Assume that the profit is received at the end of each year.) Then $75,000 of the original expenditures should be recoverable. If the firm's cost of capital is 8%, should it proceed with the project?

5. **L01** Rainbow Aviation needs an additional plane for five years. It can buy the plane for $360,000 using funds borrowed at 7.5% compounded monthly, and then sell the plane for an estimated $140,000 after five years. Alternatively, it can lease the plane for $5600 per month, payable at the beginning of each month. Which alternative should Rainbow Aviation choose? What is the financial advantage of the preferred alternative?

6. **L01** Huron Charters can purchase a sailboat for $100,000 down and a $60,000 payment due in one year. The boat would generate additional annual operating profits of $24,000 for the first five years and $15,000 for the next five years. New sails costing $16,000 would be required after five years. After ten years the boat would be replaced; its resale value would be about $60,000. Should Huron purchase the sailboat if its cost of capital is 6% compounded annually?

7. **L02** A company's board of directors has imposed an $800,000 limit on capital spending for the current year. Management has identified the following five projects with positive *NPV*s. Which projects should be chosen?

Project	Initial investment ($)	NPV ($)
A	200,000	63,000
B	400,000	100,000
C	350,000	90,000
D	250,000	75,000
E	100,000	20,000

8. **L03** A company is considering two mutually exclusive investment projects. Each requires an initial investment of $25,000. Project A will generate an annual profit of $6000 for eight

years and have a residual value of $5000. Project B's profits are more irregular: $15,000 in the first year, $19,000 in the fifth year, and $24,000 (including the residual value) in the eighth year. Which project should be chosen if the required return on investment is 8.5% compounded annually?

9. **LO1** A manufacturer's sales rep can lease an automobile for five years at $385 per month payable at the beginning of each month, or purchase it for $22,500. He can obtain a loan at 9% compounded monthly to purchase the car. Should he lease or buy the car if:
   a. The trade-in value after five years is $5000?
   b. The trade-in value after five years is $7000?

10. **LO2** The investment committee of a company has identified the following seven projects with positive *NPV*s. If the board of directors has approved a $4.5 million capital budget for the current period, which projects should be selected?

Project	Initial investment ($)	NPV ($)
1	1,125,000	428,000
2	2,700,000	486,000
3	675,000	170,000
4	375,000	30,000
5	1,500,000	900,000
6	225,000	32,000
7	900,000	405,000

11. **LO3** Machine X costs $50,000 and is forecast to generate an annual profit of $16,000 for five years. Machine Y, priced at $72,000, will produce the same annual profit for ten years. The trade-in value of X after five years is expected to be $10,000, and the resale value of Y after ten years is also thought to be $10,000. If either machine satisfies the firm's requirements, which one should be selected? Use a required return of 8%.

12. **LO3** A U-Print store requires a new photocopier. A Sonapanic copier with a four-year service life costs $35,000 and will generate an annual profit of $14,000. A higher-speed Xorex copier with a five-year service life costs $52,000 and will return an annual profit of $17,000. Neither copier will have significant salvage value. If U-Print's cost of capital is 6%, which model should be purchased?

13. **LO3** The provincial government's Ministry of Fisheries requires a new patrol boat. The price of a Songster is $90,000, and its annual operating costs will be $10,000. It will be sold for about $20,000 after five years, and replaced. A more durable and more efficient Boston Wailer, priced at $110,000, would cost $8000 per year to operate, last seven years, and have a resale value of $40,000. If the provincial government pays an interest rate of 6.5% compounded annually on its midterm debt, which boat has the lower equivalent annual cost?

14. **LO3** A potato farmer needs to buy a new harvester. Two types have performed satisfactorily in field trials. The SpudFinder costs $100,000 and should last for five years. The TaterTaker also costs $100,000 but requires an extra operator at $20,000 per season. This machine has a service life of seven years. The salvage value of either machine is insignificant. If the farmer requires a 7% return on investment, which harvester should she buy?

15. **LO5** A capital investment requiring one initial cash outflow is forecast to have the operating profits listed below. The investment has an *NPV* of $20,850, based on a required rate of return of 12%. Calculate the payback period of the investment.

Year	Operating profit ($)
1	74,000
2	84,000
3	96,000
4	70,000

16. **LO4** The introduction of a new product will require a $400,000 investment in demonstration models, promotion, and staff training. The new product will increase annual profits by $100,000 for the first four years and $50,000 for the next four years. There will be no significant recoverable amounts at the end of the eight years. The firm's cost of capital is 13%. Calculate the expected *IRR* on the proposed investment in the new product. Should the new product be introduced? Why?

17. **LO4** A $600,000 capital investment will produce annual profits of $90,000 for the first four years and $120,000 for the next four years. It will have no residual value. What is its *IRR*? Should the investment be undertaken if the cost of capital is 7%?

18. **LO4** An investment of $400,000 will yield annual profits of $55,000 for eight years. The proceeds on disposition of the investment at the end of the eight years are estimated at $125,000. On the basis of its *IRR* and a 9% cost of capital, should the investment be made?

ADVANCED PROBLEMS

19. **LO1** A new machine that will lead to savings in labour costs of $20,000 per year can be purchased for $80,000. However, it will cost $2000 per year for the first four years, and $3000 per year for the next four years to service and maintain the machine. In addition, its annual fuel consumption will cost $1500. After a service life of eight years, the salvage value of the machine is expected to be $10,000. Should the machine be acquired if the company requires a minimum annual rate of return on investment of 8%?

20. **LO3** **LO4** A company is examining two mutually exclusive projects. Project P requires an immediate investment of $300,000 and produces no profit until the fourth year. Then the expected annual profit is $120,000 for Years 4 to 7 inclusive. Project Q requires an investment of $260,000 now and is expected to generate an annual profit of $55,000 in Years 1 to 7. Neither project has any residual value after seven years.
    a. Calculate the *IRR* of each project. On the basis of their *IRR*s, which project is preferred?
    b. Which project should be selected if the firm's cost of capital is 10%?
    c. Which project should be selected if the firm's cost of capital is 6%?

21. **LO4** **LO3** The initial investment and expected profits from two mutually exclusive capital investments being considered by a firm are as follows:

	Investment A ($)	Investment B ($)
Initial investment	92,000	85,000
Year 1 profit	30,000	50,000
Year 2 profit	80,000	50,000

   a. Calculate the internal rate of return for each investment. Which one would be selected based on an *IRR* ranking?
   b. Which investment should be chosen if the firm's cost of capital is 10%?
   c. Which investment should be chosen if the firm's cost of capital is 7%?

22. **LO1** Jurgen Wiebe has been transferred to Winnipeg for five years. He has found an attractive house that he can buy for $360,000 or rent for $1850 per month, payable at the beginning of each month. He estimates that the resale value of the house in five years will be $390,000 net of the selling commission. If he buys the house, the average (end-of-month) costs for repairs, maintenance, and property taxes will be $1500. Should Mr. Wiebe rent or buy the house if the interest rate on five-year mortgage loans is 3.0% compounded monthly?

23. **LO3** A firm can manufacture the same product with either of two machines. Machine C requires an initial investment of $55,000 and would earn a profit of $30,000 per year for three years. It would then be replaced, because repairs would be required too frequently after three years. Its trade-in value would be $10,000. Machine D costs $90,000 and would have a service life of five years. The annual profit would be $5000 higher than Machine C's profit because of its lower repair and maintenance costs. Its recoverable value after five years would be about $20,000. Which machine should be purchased if the firm's cost of capital is 9%? What is the equivalent annual economic advantage of the preferred choice?

Answers to Odd-Numbered Problems

CHAPTER 1 Review and Applications of Basic Mathematics

Exercise 1.1

a. 10
c. 0
e. 10
g. −10
i. 0
1. 4
3. 24
5. 20
7. 49
9. 0.5
11. 6
13. 255
15. 9
17. $100.74
19. $453.51
21. $204.00

Concept Questions (Section 1.2)

1. You must retain at least one more figure than you require in the answer. To achieve four-figure accuracy in the answer, you must retain a minimum of five figures in the values used in the calculations. B)
3. We want seven-figure accuracy in the answer. Therefore, values used in the calculations must retain at least eight figures. C)

Exercise 1.2

a. $0.10 = 10\%$
c. $0.25 = 25\%$
e. $1.50 = 150\%$
g. $2.00 = 200\%$
i. 20
k. $100
1. $0.87500 = 87.500\%$
3. $2.3500 = 235.00\%$
5. $-1.4000 = -140.00\%$
7. $0.025000 = 2.5000\%$
9. $2.0200 = 202.00\%$
11. $0.75000 = 75.000\%$
13. $0.8\bar{3} = 83.\bar{3}\%$
15. $7.\bar{7} = 777.\bar{7}\%$

17. $1.\bar{1} = 111.\bar{1}\%$
19. $-0.02\overline{59} = -2.5\overline{92}\%$
21. 11.38
23. 0.5545
25. 1.002
27. 40.10
29. $0.16667 = 16.667\%$
31. $0.016667 = 1.6667\%$
33. $0.68493 = 68.493\%$
35. $0.0091667 = 0.91667\%$
37. $94.68
39. $410.99
41. $2145.44
43. $3384.52
45. $720.04
47. $14,435.88
49. $509.00
51. $62.50
53. $0.15
55. $3022.80
57. $4787.64
59. $6648.46
61. $7159.48
63. $1830.07
65. 6300
67. $150,480
69. 1.495 grams

Exercise 1.3

1. $1324.65
3. $2474.06
5. $796.50
7. $405.00
9. $7239.03
11. $4050
13. $6050.00
15. a. $3988.00
   b. 7.267%
17. 3.50%
19. $70,833.33

Concept Questions (Section 1.4)

1. You should calculate a weighted average when some of the values being averaged are more important or occur more frequently than other values.

3. If you invest the same amount of money in each investment, each rate of return has the same importance. The portfolio's rate of return will then equal the simple average of the individual rates of return.

Exercise 1.4

1. 1.53

3. 3.50

5. 85.12%

7. 7.65%

9. 7.53

11. 43.74 days

13. a. $10.67

    b. $10.66

    c. $2547.74

15. a. 226.25%

    b. 44.20%

17. 25.50

19. 6,250,000

21. Quality 2.93

Exercise 1.5

1.

Quarter	GST Remittance (Refund)
1	$7768.25
2	(17,015.25)
3	20,432.40
4	8240.90

3. a. $41,475.00

    b. $43,845.00

    c. $45,415.13

5. a. $5.13

    b. $5.40

7. $3827.88

9. $4317.16

11. a. 7.4837

    b. 7.1273

Review Problems

1. a. 23

    b. −40

    c. $205.39

    d. $2275.40

    e. $343.08

    f. $619.94

    g. $457.60

    h. $1549.56

3. $61.38

5. $1.00

7. $21,060.00

9. a. $29.03

    b. $2372.87

11. $2231.25

13. 4.50%

15. −1.98%

17. 7.96%

19. 26.1

CHAPTER 2 Review and Applications of Algebra

Exercise 2.1

a. 0

c. $-4x^2y$

e. $6x^2y$

g. $7x^2 + 7xy - 4y^2$

i. $8x + 3y$

k. $20x + 2$

m. $25x - 16$

o. $12a^2b - 20a^2 + 24ab$

q. $-10x^3y + 5x^2y^2 + 15xy^3$

s. $20r^2 - 7rt - 6t^2$

u. $-r - 5t$

w. $2a^2 + 34a + 99$

y. $6x$

aa. $x - y$

cc. $\dfrac{x^2 - 2x + 3}{4}$

ee. $2ab - 3a^2$

gg. $\dfrac{2ab - 3 + b}{b}$

1. $23.75

3. −$44.80

5. $315.11

7. $346.22

9. $2430.38

11. $1378.42

13. $-0.7x + 3.45$

15. $18.8x - 8.5$

17. $3.0509P$

19. $2.9307k$

21. $1794.22

23. $1071.77

Exercise 2.2

a. a^5

c. b^4

e. $(1 + i)^{13}$

g. x^{28}

i. t^2

k. x^2

m. $4(1 + i)^2$

o. $\dfrac{t^3}{2r}$

1. 16.0000

3. 18.5203

5. 1,000,000

7. 1.07006

9. 1.00990

11. −4.00000

13. −0.197531

15. 20.1569

17. 15.9637

19. 1.00908

Exercise 2.3

a. 10

c. 4

e. −3

g. −2

i. 2

1. 2

3. 43

5. 200

7. 0.5

9. 9

11. 30

13. −0.5

15. −0.19

17. $179.25

19. $286.66

21. $699.47

23. $391.01

Exercise 2.4

1. $500.00

3. $3500.00

5. 0.175

7. $15.00

9. $2400.00

11. 0.0270

13. $575.00

15. $i = \dfrac{PMT}{PV}$

17. $CM = \dfrac{NI + FC}{X}$

19. $r = \dfrac{(S - P)}{Pt}$

21. $d_1 = 1 - \dfrac{N}{L(1 - d_2)(1 - d_3)}$

23. $PV = FV(1 + i)^{-n}$

25. 0.045

Exercise 2.5

a. 42

c. $10,000

e. $240

1. 2065

3. $4.55

5. $25.00

7. $125\frac{3}{4}$ hours

9. Radio: $44,444
TV: $26,667
Newspaper: $88,889

11. 60.0%

13. Technician: 3082
Scientist and engineer: 4623
Executive: 6623

15. Peanuts: 32.0 kg
Raisins: 18.0 kg

17. Stella: $9000
Joan: $10,800
Sue: $12,960

19. 42 units of product Y

21. $73,451.62 per child
$24,483.87 per grandchild

23. $12,040

Review Problems

1. $2a + 5ab + 8b$

3. a. $0.7y + 2.2\overline{6}$
b. $2.996843P$

5. $4505.14

7. a. $-\dfrac{9}{x}$
b. $\dfrac{-8b^3}{a^9}$

9. a. 1.19641
b. 0.00816485
c. 41.1527
d. 9.11858

11. a. $280.97
b. $436.96

13. $0.120 = 12.0\%$

15. $i_1 = \dfrac{FV}{PV(1 + i_2)} - 1$

17. 954.55 grams

19. Kajsa = $12,203.39
Grace = $14,644.07
Mary Anne = $9152.54

CHAPTER 3 Percent and Percent Change

Concept Questions (Section 3.1)

1. If the *portion* is four times the size of the *base* then rate = 4/1 × 100 = 400%.

3. If the percent *rate* is 1000% and the *base* is 1 then the *portion* is 10 times the *base*.

Exercise 3.1

1. $6.13
3. 13.0%
5. $75.00
7. $174.98
9. 200%
11. $90.00
13. $19.47
15. 62.1%
17. $105.26
19. 1.00%
21. $0.05
23. $150.00
25. $593.78
27. $125.00
29. $2000.00
31. **a.** 168%
    b. 50.1%
33. **a.** 272.7 mL
    b. 94.5 mL
35. $252,100
37. 20.9%
39. 840 mg
41. 83.0%
43. 1.21%
45. 6500
47. $5,225,000
49. **a.** 170
    b. 41

Exercise 3.2

a. 10%
c. 200%
e. $150
g. 900 cm
i. $25
1. 5.26%
3. 285.71%
5. 18.18%
7. $118.26
9. 105.2 cm

11. $25.00
13. 11.11%
15. $80.00
17. $42.86
19. −0.62%
21. $131.25
23. $125.00
25. $658.80
27. $99.96
29. 200.00%
31. $10,075.00
33. $230.00
35. $375.00
37. GST: $124.90
    PST: $174.86
39. **a.** −15.28%
    b. 2.65%
    c. −13.03%
41. 11.11% increase
43. 4.96% increase
45. $311,400
47. 18.70% less
49. 43,570,000
51. 2.62% reduction
53. $1.43
55. 42.86% more
57. 150%
59. $4.20
61. −40.00%; 66.67%
63. $80,000
65. 25% increase
67. 23.08% less
69. 1.90%

Concept Questions (Section 3.3)

1. Yes. If the expenses associated with an investment exceed the income from the investment, then the net income and the income yield will be negative. For example, if you hold a piece of raw land as an investment, you will have no income from the property but you must pay property taxes each year. The net income and income yield are then negative.

3. Yes. Suppose, for example, you bought a $160,000 condominium as an investment property using $40,000 of your own money and $120,000 borrowed on a mortgage loan. Subsequently, the condo's market value fell to $100,000 because "leaky condo" problems were discovered in the building. At that

point, you have lost more than 100% of your initial $40,000 investment because the condo's market value is less than the amount owed on the mortgage loan. You must still repay the balance on the loan after the proceeds of the sale are applied to the loan.

5. The magnitude of the overall percent change is smaller than the sum. To illustrate, consider two successive 10% decreases from a beginning value of $1000. The first 10% decrease causes a $100 decrease to $900. The second 10% decrease acts on $900 rather than on the initial $1000. The dollar amount of the second reduction is only $90. The overall reduction is $190, which is only 19% (not 20%) of the original $1000.

Exercise 3.3

1. **a.** 10.00%
   b. 10.00%
   c. 20.00%
3. **a.** 3.19%
   b. 75.09%
   c. 78.27%
5. BCE Inc.   Mawer New Canada Fund
   a. 1.26%   **a.** 0.00%
   b. −6.00%   **b.** −1.20%
   c. −4.74%   **c.** −1.20%
7. BlackBerry 2017   BlackBerry 2018
   a. 0.00%   **a.** 0.00%
   b. 51.95%   **b.** −16.95%
   c. 51.95%   **c.** −16.95%
   Scotia Can. Bond   Scotia Can. Bond
     Fund 2017   Fund 2018
   a. 2.35%   **a.** 2.01%
   b. −0.52%   **b.** −3.58%
   c. 1.83%   **c.** −1.57%
9. Income yield: 3.44%
   Capital gain yield: 5.81%
   Rate of total return: 9.25%
11. Income yield: 1.36%
    Capital gain yield: −12.24%
    Rate of total return: −10.88%
13. **a.** 220.24%
    b. $26.71
15. 56.25%
17. −33.33%
19. 100% gain
21. 7.44% gain
23. Canopy Growth Corp. outperformed by 11,764.98%

25. Fidelity Canadian Asset Allocation Fund outperformed by 2.85%
27. $46.82
29. $1.50
31. **a.** $25,959.69
    b. $11,953.13

Exercise 3.4

1.

Brand	2018 Market Share	2019 Market Share
A	4.31%	4.44%
B	6.96%	6.28%
C	20.68%	21.29%
D	14.99%	18.44%
E	35.99%	30.79%
F	17.07%	18.76%

3. Coke = 14.89B litres
   Pepsi = 7.62B litres

5. **a.**

Brand	2019 Market Share	2020 Market Share
Core Buster	12.0%	12.20%
Life Fit	7.0%	7.58%
Home Fit	5.0%	5.06%
Torrent	18.0%	19.13%

b.

Brand	Market Growth
Core Buster	−0.85%
Life Fit	5.52%
Home Fit	−1.32%
Torrent	3.63%

c. −5.81%
7. 7.0% growth
9. 28.07%
11. 482.1% growth

Review Problems

1. 256.49%
3. $133.33
5. $75.00
7. $2.17
9. 368
11. **a.** 895.85%
    b. 971.72%
13. **a.** 238.24%
    b. $7.48
15. **a.** 79.27%
    b. −79.27%
17. **a.** $25.26
    b. $5.13

19. −8.62%

21. a.

Location	2018 Market Share	2019 Market Share
British Columbia	15.50%	15.03%
Alberta	18.33%	18.81%
Ontario	35.19%	35.59%
Quebec	26.33%	25.97%
Nova Scotia	4.65%	4.60%

b.

Location	Market Growth
British Columbia	−3.36%
Alberta	2.31%
Ontario	0.81%
Quebec	−1.70%
Nova Scotia	1.53%

23. $5500.00

CHAPTER 4 Ratios and Proportions

Exercise 4.1

a. 1 : 15
c. 1 : 4
e. 2 : 1
g. 10 : 1
i. 6 : 1
k. 7 : 1 : 12
1. 3 : 16
3. 3 : 1 : 2
5. 2 : 3
7. 3 : 5 : 7
9. 8 : 13 : 5
11. 1 : 6
13. 7 : 10
15. 3 : 4
17. 15 : 8
19. 2 : 6 : 3
21. 2.53 : 1
23. 1 : 4.58
25. 1 : 2.61
27. 3.35 : 1 : 1.78
29. 1 : 1.54 : 2.29
31. 1 : 2.47 : 1.37
33. 60 : 5 : 1
35. 6 : 11 : 20
37. 3.36 : 1 : 2.18
39. 8 : 7 : 5
41. 20 : 1
43. 5 : 8

Exercise 4.2

a. 6
c. $j = 9, k = 30$
e. 1
1. 42.0
3. 233
5. 28.7
7. 0.0155
9. $\frac{1}{3}$
11. $n = 90.0; m = 75.0$
13. $g = 5.00; f = 375$
15. $r = 11.2; s = 19.0$
17. $4723.06
19. 31 hours and 7 minutes
21. $32,602.50
23. Apple: 51.4 million units
　　Samsung: 77.1 million units
25. Wholesale costs: $2.95 million
　　Overhead expenses: $1.55 million
27. 11,200 Twitter; 6,600 Instagram
29. 29 outlets, $43.13 million
31. a. $105,000
　　b. $18,000
33. 1057

Exercise 4.3

a. $24
c. Matt: $22.50, Pat: $67.50
1. $75.85
3. $1035.62
5. a. $3184.00
　　b. $3444.98
7. a. Andy: $42.80 per month
　　　Candy: $114.13 per month
　　　Sandy: $71.33 per month
　　b. Andy: 93.75 GB; Candy: 250 GB; Sandy: 156.25 GB
9. a. Bella: $80,000
　　　Edward: $108,000
　　　Jacob: $68,000
　　b. $25,920
11. a. Industrial Products: $389,838
　　　Fine Paper: $265,799
　　　Containers & Packaging: $183,363
　　b. Industrial Products: $480,724
　　　Fine Paper: $189,342
　　　Containers & Packaging: $168,934
13. C: $0
　　A: $5256.41
　　B: $3269.23
　　D: $1474.36

15. Executive: $4127.73
Supervisor: $2889.41
Production worker: $2063.86

Exercise 4.4

1. C$2456.03
3. ¥1,184,834.15
5. C$4960.57
7. C$9251.93
9. £55,853.31
11. €32,702.96
13. **a.** Sw kr 6.715
    b. US$0.14721
    c. Mex peso 0.1777
    d. C$0.01879
15. C$3395.39
17. C$12,176.81
19. C$2330.86 gain
21. £3.41 more
23. C$3.74 less
25. **a.** 3.07% at Royal Bank
       4.02% at ICE
    b. 2.27% at Royal Bank
       16.80% at ICE
27. €753.68; €753.76
29. 23.35% more expensive in Canada.
31. Personally designed travel is C$1402.22 cheaper.
33. 18.55%

Concept Questions (Section 4.5)

1. If the number of units of currency N per unit of currency M decreases, it then requires *less* of currency N to purchase 1 unit of M. Therefore, currency N has strengthened.
3. If currency G weakens relative to currency H, it will require more of currency G to purchase 1 unit of H. Therefore, the exchange rate expressed as units of G per unit of H will increase.

Exercise 4.5

1. £ has depreciated −8.36%.
3. €0.65209 per C$1.00
C$1.5335 per €1.00
5. £0.5926
7. C$1.6833
9. increase of US$0.0029
11. decrease of A$0.00016
13. C$75.43 decrease
15. C$898.77 decrease

Exercise 4.6

1. 151.3
3. $9001
5. 9.374
7. $3646
9. 122.20
11. $1024.46
13. **a.** $1157.02
    b. $1209.03
    c. services rose 5.20% more than goods
15. Consumer prices increased: 67.29%
Portfolio increased: 358.67%
17. **a.** $161.16
    b. Inflation rate (1978): 8.90%
    Inflation rate (1979): 9.60%
    Inflation rate (1980): 11.95%
    Inflation rate (1981): 11.42%
    Inflation rate (1982): 8.25%

Review Problems

1. **a.** 6:20:15
    b. 3:2:4
    c. 3:6:2
    d. 5:4:7
3. **a.** 18.06
    b. $a = 332.8; b = 205.4$
5. 11:14:8
7. $23.10 per hour
9. rupiah 13,380,910
11. C$691.00 decrease
13. Gain of C$9.02
15. Ms. L: $4000
Mr. M: $2666.67
Mr. P: $1333.33
17. Mrs. Nolan: $148,798
Son: $106,284
Stepson: $75,917
19. C$28.09 increase
21. Alberta coal is C$25.11 cheaper per metric tonne.

CHAPTER 5 Mathematics of Merchandising

Exercise 5.1

a. $100; $200
c. $50; 25%
e. $100; $80
g. $100; 5%
i. $240; $120
1. $83.00; $166.00

3. $21.33; $16\frac{2}{3}$%
5. $1750.00; $1137.50
7. $27.40; 45.0%
9. $3256.00; $407.00
11. $57.75; $41.25
13. $149.00; $55.97
15. $83.70
17. $371.90
19. 17.8%
21. 26.55%
23. $339,800.00
25. a. $5197.50
    b. $374.00
27. 236 points
29. $7.86
31. $538.56; $561.00
33. a. $697.68 million
    b. 401 people
35. 6.00%
37. a. $300.00
    b. $105.00

Exercise 5.2

1. $2317.70
3. $799.18
5. a. $4975.11
   b. $5025.87
   c. $5025.87
7. $1337.70
9. $515.46
11. a. $8772.37
    b. $8684.65
13. $642.00
15. a. $3778.78
    b. April 20
17. $2878.15
19. $1557.67
21. $374.90
23. $2127.35
25. $975.61

Concept Questions (Section 5.3)

1. Both quantities have the same numerator, but the rate of markup on cost has the smaller denominator (since $C < S$). Therefore, the rate of markup on cost is larger than the rate of markup on selling price.

3. Yes. If an item is marked up (M) by more than the unit cost (C), then
   Rate of markup on cost $= \frac{M}{C} \times 100\% > 100\%$

5. No. At the break-even point, there is no profit. The selling price at the break-even point must cover E as well as C. If an item is sold at cost, the merchant will *lose E* per unit sold.

Exercise 5.3

1. a. 31.1%
   b. 23.7%
3. Rate of markup on cost: 106.2%
   Rate of markup on selling price: 51.5%
5. a. $49.50
   b. 65.0%
   c. 39.4%
7. a. 50.0%
   b. $24.99
   c. 100.0%
9. a. $231.00
   b. 42.9%
   c. $34.65
11. a. $1.73
    b. 185.7%
13. a. $22.16
    b. 44.4%
15. Rate of markup on cost: 209.5%
    Rate of markup on selling price: 67.7%
17. a. $383.40
    b. 34.8%
    c. 25.8%
    d. $343.40
19. a. $37.90
    b. 31.0%
21. 150.0%
23. $7.80
25. $52.81
27. $108.90

Concept Questions (Section 5.4)

1. No. The base for the rate of markup on cost is the unit cost C. The base for the markdown is the selling price, S. Since $C < S$, a 40% markup on cost represents a smaller dollar amount than a 40% markdown from the item's selling price. A 40% markup on cost followed by a 40% markdown will give a reduced selling price that is *less* than C.

Exercise 5.4

1. **a.** $277.50
   b. 21.6%
3. **a.** 100.0%
   b. 50.0%
5. $22.21
7. **a.** 28.5%
   b. 28.5%
9. $398.08
11. $255; $153
13. **a.** 25.7%
    b. 13.8%
15. 15.6%

Exercise 5.5

1. $2.98 loss
3. $2.45 loss
5. **a.** $216.00
   b. $259.20
   c. $118.80
   d. $475.20
   e. $285.12
   f. 32.0%
   g. $49.68 loss
7. $108.00
9. 34.0%
11. **a.** 15.0%
    b. $19.76 loss per unit
13. 23.6%
15. **a.** 25.0%
    b. $6.12 loss
    c. 25.0%
17. **a.** $950.00
    b. $1187.50
19. **a.** $2945.25
    b. $35.70 loss

Review Problems

1. Source B is $1.30 cheaper.
3. $352.08
5. $338,600
7. **a.** $825.80
   b. $33,852.07
9. **a.** $289.00
   b. 31.1%
11. **a.** $780.48
    b. $720.00
    c. 34.7%
    d. $34.38

13. **a.** $6.94
    b. $2.50
15. 122.2%
17. **a.** $67.30
    b. $61.24
19. **a.** $20.65
    b. 76.5%
    c. $18.59
21. **a.** 153.3% of cost
    b. 6.5%
23. $30.48
25. $574.00
27. **a.** $59.63
    b. 26.8%

CHAPTER 6 Applications of Linear Equations

Exercise 6.1

1. $\begin{vmatrix} x: \\ y: \end{vmatrix}$ $\begin{matrix} -3 & 0 & 6 \\ -6 & 0 & 12 \end{matrix}$

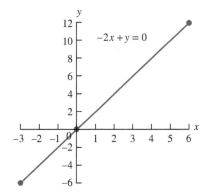

3. $\begin{vmatrix} x: \\ y: \end{vmatrix}$ $\begin{matrix} -3 & 0 & 6 \\ 10 & 4 & -8 \end{matrix}$

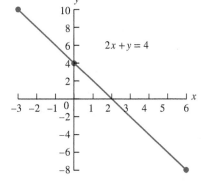

5. $\begin{vmatrix} x: \\ y: \end{vmatrix}$ $\begin{matrix} -8 & 0 & 12 \\ -3 & 3 & 12 \end{matrix}$

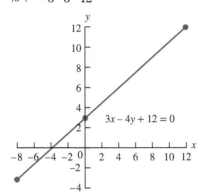

$3x - 4y + 12 = 0$

7. $\begin{vmatrix} x: \\ y: \end{vmatrix}$ $\begin{matrix} 0 & 3000 & 6000 \\ 5000 & 18{,}500 & 32{,}000 \end{matrix}$

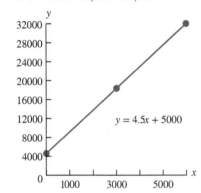

$y = 4.5x + 5000$

9. **a.** Slope: $\frac{5}{2}$

  b-intercept: $-\frac{3}{2}$

  b. Slope: $\frac{3}{4}$

  b-intercept: -3

  c. Slope: $-\frac{4}{5}$

  b-intercept: 480

  d. Slope: $-\frac{7}{8}$

  b-intercept: 0

11. **a.** y-intercept: $\frac{4}{5}$ **b.** y-intercept: -3

  x-intercept: 3 x-intercept: 9

  c. y-intercept: 0   **d.** y-intercept: 5

  x-intercept: 0 x-intercept: -10

13. $E = 0.05R + \$1500$

  Slope: 0.05

  E-intercept: $\$1500$

15. $C = \$85 + \$30H$

  Slope: $\$30$

  C-intercept: $\$85$

17. $x - 3y = 3$

$\begin{vmatrix} x: \\ y: \end{vmatrix}$ $\begin{matrix} -6 & 3 \\ -3 & 0 \end{matrix}$

$y = -2$ The solution is
                 $(x, y) = (-3, -2)$.

$\begin{vmatrix} x: \\ y: \end{vmatrix}$ $\begin{matrix} -6 & 3 \\ -2 & -2 \end{matrix}$

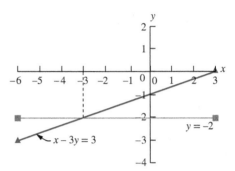

$x - 3y = 3$ $y = -2$

19. $x - 3y = 0$

$\begin{vmatrix} x: \\ y: \end{vmatrix}$ $\begin{matrix} -6 & 3 \\ -2 & 1 \end{matrix}$

$x + 2y = -5$ The solution is
                    $(x, y) = (-3, -1)$.

$\begin{vmatrix} x: \\ y: \end{vmatrix}$ $\begin{matrix} -6 & 3 \\ 0.5 & -4 \end{matrix}$

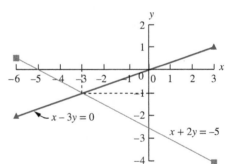

$x - 3y = 0$ $x + 2y = -5$

21. $y - 3x = 11$

$\begin{vmatrix} x: \\ y: \end{vmatrix}$ $\begin{matrix} -4 & 2 \\ -1 & 17 \end{matrix}$

$5x + 30 = 4y$ The solution is
                    $(x, y) = (-2, 5)$.

$\begin{vmatrix} x: \\ y: \end{vmatrix}$ $\begin{matrix} -4 & 2 \\ 2.5 & 10 \end{matrix}$

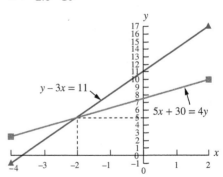

$y - 3x = 11$ $5x + 30 = 4y$

23. $7p - 3q = 23$

$\begin{vmatrix} p: \\ q: \end{vmatrix} \quad \begin{matrix} 0 & 6 \\ -7.67 & 6.33 \end{matrix}$

$-2p - 3q = 5$

The solution is $(p, q) = (2, -3)$.

$\begin{vmatrix} p: \\ q: \end{vmatrix} \quad \begin{matrix} 0 & 6 \\ -1.67 & -5.67 \end{matrix}$

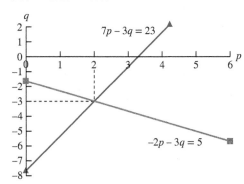

Exercise 6.2

1. $(4, 3)$

3. $(4, 2)$

5. $(3, 5)$

7. $(7, 14)$

9. $(500, 1000)$

11. $\left(\frac{3}{2}, -\frac{1}{3}\right)$

13. $(17.0, 6.24)$

15. $(251, 125)$

17. 238 student; 345 regular

19. 230 km at 50 km/hr; 770 km at 100 km/hr

21. $19.00 per hour; $0.35 per km

23. CSB: 4.2%; OSB: 4.5%

25. $x = 37, y = 56$

27. 25 L milk; 15 cans OJ

29. 843

31. partner = $117,000; technician = $67,500

Exercise 6.3

1. **a.** Variable cost   **b.** Fixed cost

  c. Mixed cost   **d.** Variable cost

  e. Fixed cost   **f.** Mixed cost

  g. Variable cost   **h.** Fixed cost

3. $1,840,000

Exercise 6.4

1. $TR = (S)X$

  $\quad = \$2.50X$

  $TC = (VC)X + FC$

  $\quad = \$1.00X + \$60,000$

$\begin{vmatrix} X: \\ TR: \\ TC: \end{vmatrix} \quad \begin{matrix} 20,000 & 60,000 \\ \$50,000 & \$150,000 \\ \$80,000 & \$120,000 \end{matrix}$

  a. 40,000 CDs/month

  b. 45,000 CDs/month

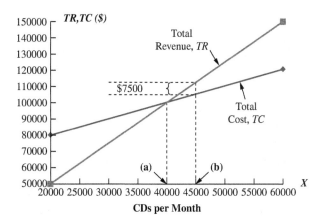

3. $TR = (S)X$

  $\quad = \$0.10X$

  $TC = (VC)X + FC$

  $\quad = \$0.05X + \$300$

$\begin{vmatrix} X: \\ TR: \\ TC: \end{vmatrix} \quad \begin{matrix} 4000 & 8000 \\ \$400 & \$8000 \\ \$500 & \$700 \end{matrix}$

  a. 6000 copies/month

  b. $50 per month

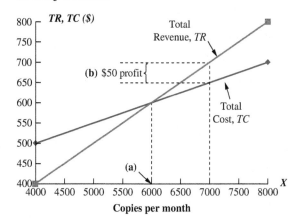

5. $TR = (S)X$
$\quad\quad = \$20X$
$\quad TC = (VC)X + FC$
$\quad\quad\quad = \$12X + \$1200$

X:	0	250
TR:	$0	$5000
TC:	$1200	$4200

a. 150 units/week
b. (i) $240 loss
$\quad$(ii) $800 profit
c. 200 units/week

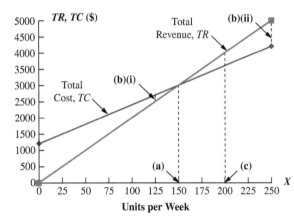

7. $TR = (S)X$
$\quad\quad = \$70X$
$\quad TC = (VC)X + FC$
$\quad\quad\quad = \$43X + \$54,000$

X:	1000	3200
TR:	$70,000	$224,000
TC:	$97,000	$191,600

a. 2000 composters per month
b. $13,500/month
c. $10,800/month loss

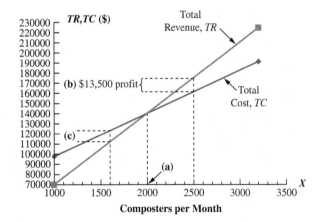

9. a. no effect
$\quad$**b.** no effect
$\quad$**c.** slope increases
$\quad$**d.** at lower volume

Exercise 6.5

1. a. 5000 toys per year
$\quad$**b.** $150,000 per year
$\quad$**c.** 62.5% of capacity
$\quad$**d.** $24,000 profit
$\quad$**e.** 5500 toys per year
3. a. 1500 jars per year
$\quad$**b.** $3000 per year
$\quad$**c.** 900 jars per year
5. a. 40,000 CDs per month
$\quad$**b.** 45,000 CDs per month
$\quad$**c.** $18,000 profit per month
$\quad$**d.** 24,000 CDs per month to break even
7. a. 6000 copies per month
$\quad$**b.** $50 per month
9. a. 150 units/week
$\quad$**b.** (i) $240 loss per week
$\quad\quad$(ii) $800 profit per week
$\quad$**c.** (i) $760 profit per week
$\quad\quad$(ii) $416 loss per week
$\quad$**d.** 200 units per week
11. a. 75% of capacity
$\quad$**b.** $666,667 loss
13. a. 2000 composters per month
$\quad$**b.** $13,500 per month
$\quad$**c.** $10,800 loss per month
$\quad$**d.** 84.4% of capacity
$\quad$**e.** Decrease by 71 composters per month
15. $S = \$75$ per tire
$\quad TR = \$3,750,000$ in Q2
$\quad VC = \$55$ per tire
$\quad FC = \$300,000$ per quarter
17. a. $800,000
$\quad$**b.** $90,000 increase
$\quad$**c.** $40,000 increase
$\quad$**d.** $60,000 decrease
19. a. 28 participants
$\quad$**b.** $400
$\quad$**c.** 20 participants
21. a. 311 tickets sold at $46.
$\quad\quad$205 tickets sold at $56.
$\quad$**b.** $1560 at $46
$\quad\quad$$2520 at $56
23. a. $40.97
$\quad$**b.** $40.58

25. a. 12.72 tonnes per hectare
   b. 1.03 tonnes per hectare.
   c. (i) $260 per hectare profit
      (ii) $310 per hectare loss

Concept Questions (Section 6.6)

1. a. Since $CM = S - VC$, CM will increase if S is increased.
   b. Raw materials are part of VC. VC will decrease if the cost of raw materials decreases. Therefore, CM will increase.
   c. The property tax is part of FC. There will be no change in CM.
   d. The salaries of executives are part of FC. There will be no change in CM.
   e. Wages of production workers are part of VC. VC will increase and CM will decrease.

3. a. The break-even volume will be lowered since fewer units need to be sold to cover the reduced fixed costs.
   b. If unit variable costs (VC) increase, the contribution margin ($CM = S - VC$) decreases and more units must be sold to cover the unchanged fixed costs. Therefore, the break-even point is higher.
   c. No change—the actual sales volume does not affect the break-even point.
   d. If S decreases, the contribution margin ($CM = S - VC$) decreases and more units must be sold to cover the unchanged fixed costs. Therefore, the break-even point is higher.
   e. If the contribution rate (or ratio) CR increases, a larger portion of each unit's selling price is available to pay fixed costs. Therefore, the break-even point is lower.

Exercise 6.6

1. a. 5000 toys per year
   b. $150,000 per year
   c. 62.5% of capacity
   d. $24,000 profit
   e. 5500 toys per year
3. a. 1500 jars per year
   b. $3000
   c. 900 jars per year
5. a. 40,000 CDs per month
   b. 45,000 CDs per month
   c. $18,000 profit per month
   d. 24,000 CDs per month to break even
7. a. 6000 copies per month
   b. $50 per month

9. a. 150 units per week
   b. (i) $240 loss per week
      (ii) $800 profit per week
   c. (i) $760 profit per week
      (ii) $416 loss per week
   d. 200 units per week
11. a. 75% of capacity
   b. $666,667 loss
13. a. 2000 composters per month
   b. $13,500 per month
   c. $10,800 loss per month
   d. 84.4% of capacity
   e. Decreases by 71 composters per month
15. $S = 75 per tire
   $TR = $3,750,000$ in Q2
   $FC = $300,000$ per quarter
   $VC = 55 per tire
17. a. $800,000
   b. $90,000 increase
   c. $40,000 increase
   d. $60,000 decrease
19. a. 28 participants
   b. $400
   c. 20 participants
21. a. 311 at $46
      205 at $56
   b. $1548.60 at $46
      $2508.00 at $56
23. a. $40.97
   b. $40.58
25. a. 12.72 tonnes per hectare
   b. 1.03 tonnes per hectare
   c. (i) $259.92 per hectare
      (ii) $310.08 loss per hectare

Review Problems

1. a. 18,000 units
   b. $3,240,000
   c. (i) $140,000 profit
      (ii) $35,000 loss
   d. 22,500 units
   e. 16,225 units
   f. 16,200 units
3. a. 2480 books
   b. $56,160
   c. Select the $35 price.
   d. 322 books
5. a. $120 million per year
   b. $24 million

7. a. 5000 units
  b. 7500 units
  c. $120,000
  d. (i) $10,000 lower
     (ii) $20,000 higher
  e. (i) $48,000 lower
     (ii) $24,000 higher
  f. (i) $40,000 higher
     (ii) $80,000 lower
  g. $28,000 lower
9. a. 36.2%
  b. (i) $2960/month
     (ii) loss of $4780 per month
  c. The owner should reduce the rental rate to $94 per unit per night since the net income will increase by $540 per month.

CHAPTER 7 Simple Interest

Exercise 7.1

  1. $39.38
  3. $187.50
  5. 7 months
  7. 8.75% per annum
  9. $114.58
 11. $6500.00
 13. 4.20% per annum
 15. 11 months
 17. Interest on the first term deposit: $55.00
     Interest on the second term deposit: $55.30

Exercise 7.2

  1. $82.77
  3. $1643.88
  5. $763.18
  7. 8.55%
  9. $15.60
 11. 1.50%
 13. 41 days
 15. September 26, 2019
 17. March 9, 2019
 19. March 18
 21. $196.03
 23. $3051.13

Exercise 7.3

  1. $3027.44
  3. $4944.38
  5. $780.00

  7. Principal component: $14,100.00
     Interest component: $1279.58
  9. 10.70%
 11. 18.50%
 13. 237 days
 15. 8 months
 17. $19,619.04
 19. 9.00%
 21. 7.82%
 23. January 8
 25. $5452.13
 27. $235,423.32

Concept Questions (Section 7.4)

  1. "Equivalent payments" are alternative payments (on different dates) that will put the recipient in the same economic position.
  3. Calculate the equivalent values of all three payments at the same focal date. The payment with the highest equivalent value on that focal date is the one with the largest economic value.

Exercise 7.4

  1. $551.38
  3. $5360.89
  5. $990.77
  7. $453.05
  9. 7.25%
 11. 90 days
 13. 251 days early
 15. $5500 payment; 1.03% per month
 17. Pay $560 now; 10.86%
 19. The two options are essentially equivalent.
 21. $2902.06 today
     $2933.99 in 2 months
     $2966.63 in 4 months
     $3000.00 in 6 months
     $3033.75 in 8 months
     $3067.50 in 10 months
     $3101.25 in 12 months
 23. a. Smith offer: $142,799.51
        Kim offer: $143,832.54
     b. The Kim offer is worth $1033.03 more.
 25. 7.71%

Concept Questions (Section 7.5)

  1. The economic value of a nominal amount of money depends on the date when it is paid. This property of money is called the time value of money.

3. Today's economic value is lower. This economic value is the lump amount today that is equivalent to the payment stream. In other words, the lump amount along with its interest earnings could pay the series of scheduled payments. (The last payment would reduce the remaining funds to zero.) When interest rates are higher, a smaller lump amount will be sufficient to generate the payment stream because more interest will be earned to help meet the payments.

Exercise 7.5

1. $808.13
3. $1892.94
5. $4475.96
7. a. $3855.98
   b. $3951.22
   c. The equivalent value of a specified payment stream will be greater at a later date than at an earlier date because of the time value of money.
9. $1954.78
11. Stream 1: $2323.68
   Stream 2: $2381.58
   Stream 2 payments have a $57.90 greater economic value.
13. $1804.52
15. $2719.68

Exercise 7.6

1. $1045.38
3. $839.18
5. $503.39
7. $843.84
9. $1291.81
11. $2082.60
13. $1374.91

Review Problems

1. $9872.20
3. November 27
5. 4.75%
7. $59,729.01
9. $1028.14
11. a. $9709.65
   b. $9804.34
13. $237.65
15. $8483.46
17. a. Offer A: $193,846.15
     Offer B: $193,235.29
   b. Accept Offer A: worth $610.86 more
   c. Accept Offer B: worth $707.09 more
19. $2173.14

CHAPTER 8 Applications of Simple Interest

Exercise 8.1

1. a. $15,110.96
   b. $15,191.07
3. $88.77
5. $14.16 more from the 180-day GIC
7. a. $24.04
   b. $23.12
9. $18.34
11. $16.51 more
13. $3.49
15. $18.12

Exercise 8.2

1. a. $985.25
   b. $988.49
   c. The closer the purchase date to the payments, the smaller the discount will be for a given time value of money.
3. a. $1944.28
   b. $1935.26
   c. The payments from B are received one month later. This makes their value today less than the value of the payments from A.
5. $11,308.81
7. $7854.11

Concept Questions (Section 8.3)

1. The price of the 98-day T-bill is higher because less time remains until the $100,000 face value is received. You do not need as large a difference between the face value and the purchase price to provide the required rate of return.
3. The fair market value will steadily rise, reaching the T-bill's face value on the maturity date.

Exercise 8.3

1. $24,896
3. $996,446
5. 30 days: $99,877
   60 days: $99,754
   90 days: $99,631
7. $174
9. 4.702%
11. 115 days
13. a. $99,043
   b. (i) $99,457
      (ii) $99,525
      (iii) $99,592
   c. (i) 1.795%
      (ii) 2.090%
      (iii) 2.380%

Exercise 8.4

1.

Date	Number of days	Interest rate	Interest	Accrued interest	Payment (Advance)	Principal portion	Balance
5-Feb	—	—	—	—	($15,000)	($15,000)	$15,000
29-Feb	24	8.50%	$83.84	~~$83.84~~	$83.84		15,000
15-Mar	15	8.50	52.40	52.40	10,000	10,000	5000
31-Mar	16	8.50	18.63	~~$71.03~~	71.03		5000
30-Apr	30	8.50	34.93	~~$34.93~~	34.93		5000
1-May	1	8.50	1.16	1.16	(7000)	(7000)	12,000
31-May	30	8.50	83.84	~~$85.00~~	85.00		12,000

The interest charged to Dr. Robillard's account was $83.84 on February 29, $71.03 on March 31, $34.93 on April 30, and $85.00 on May 31.

3.

Date	Number of days	Interest rate	Interest	Accrued interest	Payment (Advance)	Principal portion	Balance
3-Jul	—	—	—	—	($25,000)	($25,000)	$25,000
20-Jul	17	5.00%	$58.22	~~$58.22~~	$58.22		25,000
29-Jul	9	5.00	30.82	30.82	(30,000)	(30,000)	55,000
5-Aug	7	5.00	52.74	83.56			55,000
20-Aug	15	4.75	107.36	~~190.92~~	190.92		55,000

The amounts of interest charged on July 20 and August 20 were $58.22 and $190.92, respectively.

5.

Date	Number of days	Interest rate	Interest	Accrued interest	Payment (Advance)	Principal portion	Balance
7-Oct	—	—	—	—	($30,000)	($30,000)	$30,000
15-Oct	8	7.75%	$50.96	~~$50.96~~	$50.96		30,000
15-Nov	31	7.75	197.47	~~197.47~~	197.47		30,000
24-Nov	9	7.75	57.33	57.33	($15,000)	(15,000)	45,000
15-Dec	21	7.75	200.65	~~257.98~~	257.98		45,000
17-Dec	2	7.75	19.11	19.11			45,000
23-Dec	6	7.50	55.48	74.59	(20,000)	(20,000)	65,000
15-Jan	23	7.50	307.19	~~381.78~~	381.78		65,000

7.

Date	Number of days	Interest rate	Interest	Accrued interest	Payment (Advance)	Principal portion	Balance
31-Mar	—	—	—	—	($30,000.00)	($30,000)	$30,000
18-Apr	18	7.50%	$110.96	~~$110.96~~	110.96		30,000
28-Apr	10	7.50	61.64	61.64	(10,000.00)	(10,000)	40,000
14-May	16	7.50	131.51	193.15			40,000
18-May	4	7.75	33.97	~~227.12~~	227.12		40,000
1-Jun	14	7.75	118.90	118.90	(15,000.00)	(15,000)	55,000
18-Jun	17	7.75	198.53	~~317.43~~	5317.43	5000	50,000
3-Jul	15	7.75	159.25	159.25	10,000.00	10,000	40,000
18-Jul	15	7.75	127.40	~~286.65~~	286.65		40,000

9.

Date	Number of days	Interest rate	Interest	Accrued interest	Payment (Advance)	Principal portion	Balance
15-Aug	—	—	—	—	—	—	$3589.80
31-Aug	16	8.75%	$13.77	$13.77	$300.00	$300.00	3289.80
15-Sep	15	8.75	11.83	25.60	100.00	74.40	3215.40
30-Sep	15	8.75	11.56	11.56	300.00	300.00	2915.40
11-Oct	11	8.75	7.69	19.25			2915.40
15-Oct	4	8.50	2.72	21.97	100.00	78.03	2837.37
31-Oct	16	8.50	10.57	10.57	300.00	300.00	2537.37
15-Nov	15	8.50	8.86	19.43	100.00	80.57	2456.80

11.

Date	Number of days	Interest rate	Interest	Accrued interest	Payment (Advance)	Principal portion	Balance
1-Apr	—	—	—	—	—	—	$6000.00
1-May	30	4.25%	$20.96	$20.96	$1000.00	$979.04	5020.96
1-Jun	31	4.25	18.12	18.12	1000.00	981.88	4039.08
7-Jun	6	4.25	2.82	2.82			4039.08
1-Jul	24	4.00	10.62	13.44	1000.00	986.56	3052.52
1-Aug	31	4.00	10.37	10.37	1000.00	989.63	2062.89
27-Aug	26	4.00	5.88	5.88			2062.89
1-Sep	5	4.25	1.20	7.08	1000.00	992.92	1069.97
1-Oct	30	4.25	3.74	3.74	1000.00	996.26	73.71
1-Nov	31	4.25	0.27	0.27	73.98	73.71	0.00

Total of the interest charges = $73.98

13.

Date	Number of days	Interest rate	Interest	Accrued interest	Payment (Advance)	Principal portion	Balance
23-Feb	—	—	—	—	—	—	$5000.00
15-Apr	51	5.25%	$36.68	$36.68	$1000.00	$963.32	4036.68
15-May	30	5.25	17.42	17.42	1000.00	982.58	3054.10
15-Jun	31	5.25	13.62	13.62	1000.00	986.38	2067.72
15-Jul	30	5.50	9.35	9.35	1000.00	990.65	1077.07
31-Jul	16	5.50	2.60	2.60			1077.07
15-Aug	15	5.75	2.55	5.15	1000.00	994.85	82.22
15-Sep	31	5.75	0.40	0.40	82.62	82.22	0.00

Exercise 8.5

1. Grace period interest = $241.70

Date	Number of days	Interest rate	Interest	Accrued interest	Payment (Advance)	Principal portion	Balance
1-Dec	—	—	—	—	—	—	$9641.70
31-Dec	30	5.00%	$39.62	$39.62	$135.00	$95.38	9546.32
17-Jan	17	5.00	22.23	22.23		0.00	9546.32
31-Jan	14	5.25	19.22	41.45	135.00	93.55	9452.77
28-Feb	28	5.25	38.07	38.07	135.00	96.93	9355.84

3. Grace period interest = $286.67

Date	Number of days	Interest rate	Interest	Accrued interest	Payment (Advance)	Principal portion	Balance
1-Jan	—	—	—	—	—	—	$7086.67
31-Jan	30	8.25%	$48.05	~~$48.05~~	$200.00	$151.95	6934.72
28-Feb	28	8.25	43.89	~~43.89~~	200.00	156.11	6778.61
2-Mar	2	8.25	3.06	3.06			6778.61
25-Mar	23	7.75	33.10	36.16	500.00	500.00	6278.61
31-Mar	6	7.75	8.00	~~44.16~~	200.00	155.84	6122.77

5. Grace period interest = $149.91

Date	Number of days	Interest rate	Interest	Accrued interest	Payment (Advance)	Principal portion	Balance
1-Dec	—	—	—	—	—	—	$5349.91
31-Dec	30	5.75%	$25.28	~~$25.28~~	$110.00	$84.72	5265.19
31-Jan	31	5.75	25.71	~~25.71~~	110.00	84.29	5180.90
14-Feb	14	5.50	10.93	10.93	300.00	300.00	4880.90
28-Feb	14	5.50	10.30	~~21.23~~	110.00	88.77	4792.13

Review Problems

1. $49,841.81
3. 4.304%
5. $2.88
7. $18.41
9. a. $99,101.41   **b.** (i) $99,547.26   (ii) $99,554.03   (iii) $99,583.33
   c. (i) 1.932%   (ii) 1.961%   (iii) 2.088%
11. $3780.22
13. Grace period interest = $284.70

Date	Number of days	Interest rate	Interest	Accrued interest	Payment (Advance)	Principal portion	Balance
1-Nov	—	—	—	—	—	—	$7484.70
30-Nov	29	7.75%	$46.09	~~$46.09~~	$120.00	$73.91	7410.79
13-Dec	13	7.75	20.46	20.46			7410.79
31-Dec	18	7.50	27.41	~~47.87~~	120.00	72.13	7338.66
31-Jan	31	7.50	46.75	~~46.75~~	120.00	73.25	7265.41

15.

Date	Number of days	Interest rate	Interest	Accrued interest	Payment (Advance)	Principal portion	Balance
23-May	—	—	—	—	—	—	$15,000.00
15-Jun	23	6.50%	$61.44	~~$61.44~~	$700.00	$638.56	14,361.44
15-Jul	30	6.50	76.73	~~76.73~~	700.00	623.27	13,738.17
26-Jul	11	6.50	26.91	26.91			13,738.17
15-Aug	20	6.25	47.05	~~73.96~~	700.00	626.04	13,112.13
14-Sep	30	6.25	67.36	67.36			13,112.13
15-Sep	1	6.75	2.42	~~69.78~~	700.00	630.22	12,481.91

17.

Date	Number of days	Interest rate	Interest	Accrued interest	Payment (Advance)	Principal portion	Balance
3-Jun	—	—	—	—	($50,000)	($50,000)	$50,000
26-Jun	23	9.00%	$283.56	$283.56	283.56		50,000
30-Jun	4	9.00	49.32	49.32	(40,000)	(40,000)	90,000
5-Jul	5	9.00	110.96	160.28			90,000
17-Jul	12	9.25	273.70	433.98	(25,000)	(25,000)	115,000
26-Jul	9	9.25	262.29	696.27	696.27		115,000
31-Jul	5	9.50	149.66	149.66	30,000	30,000	85,000
18-Aug	18	9.50	398.22	547.88	35,000	35,000	50,000
26-Aug	8	9.50	104.11	651.99	651.99		50,000

Exercise 8A

1. September 19
3. 100 days
5. October 25
7. March 3
9. $1032.53
11. $2600.00
13. 9.00%
15. 45 days
17. $988.09
19. $2760.61
21. 7.50%
23. **a.** March 3, 2020
    b. February 29, 2020
25. $1036.23
27. $3257.12
29. $763.18
31. $3000.90

CHAPTER 9 Compound Interest: Future Value and Present Value

Concept Questions (Section 9.1)

1. We compound interest when we convert it to principal and calculate subsequent interest on both the principal and the converted interest.
3. The "periodic rate of interest" is the percent interest earned in a single compounding period. The "nominal rate of interest" is the *annual* interest rate you obtain if you *extend* the periodic interest rate to a full year. This extension is done by multiplying the periodic rate of interest by the number of compounding periods in a year.

Exercise 9.1

1. **a.** 0.5% per month   **b.** 1.5% per quarter
   c. 3.0% per half-year

3. **a.** 1.35% per quarter
   b. 0.45% per month
5. **a.** 7.2% compounded semiannually
   b. 7.2% compounded quarterly
   c. 7.2% compounded monthly
7. **a.** 5.00% compounded quarterly
   b. 5.90% compounded monthly
9. **a.** quarterly compounding
   b. semiannual compounding
   c. monthly compounding
11. **a.** 4 per year
    b. 12 per year

Concept Questions (Section 9.2)

1. The more frequent the compounding of the 6% nominal rate, the more interest will be earned by the investment. Therefore, 6% compounded quarterly is the preferred rate. (The other two rates both earn 3% interest in the 6-month term.)
   (1) 6% compounded quarterly;
   (2) 6% compounded semiannually and 6% simple interest (tied)
3. The fundamental reason is that money can be invested to earn interest. $100 received today can earn interest for a longer period than $100 received at a future date.

Exercise 9.2

1. $6158.78
3. $13,123.06
5. **a.** $15,656.81
   b. $18,180.44
   c. $21,110.84
   d. $24,513.57
7. **a.** $26,658.36
   b. $26,915.88
   c. $27,048.14
   d. $27,137.65

9. a. $103.04
  b. $103.14
  c. $103.23
  d. $103.30
      The investor would prefer 3.3% compounded annually.
11. Maturity value: $13,355.74
      Interest charged: $1355.74
13. $7205.19; 27.03%
15. $7330.57; 27.63%
17.

Interest Rate	20 years	25 years	30 years
8%	$4660.96	$6848.48	$10,062.66
10%	$6727.50	$10,834.71	$17,449.40

19. $5682.38
21. $12,454.51
23. $3290.63
25. $11,544.93
27. Donna: $8340.04
      Tim: $10,045.40
      Gary: $12,099.48
29. a. $108,366.67
  b. $113,743.60
  c. $103,219.59
31. $8206.23
33. $2766.14
35. $5617.79
37. a. 27.03%
  b. 27.63%

Exercise 9.3

1. a. $7811.98
  b. $6102.71
  c. $4767.43
3. a. $3751.17
  b. $3715.28
  c. $3697.11
  d. $3684.92
5. $6439.28
7. $8594.83
9. $8072.17
11. $4494.57
13. $4706.90
15. $2241.95
17. $3226.89
19. $2702.69
21. $1300.59
23. $4374.78
25. The $145,000 cash offer is worth $1158.46 more.
27. $61,559,000

29. $3365.06 in a $3\frac{1}{2}$-year certificate
      $4003.64 in a $4\frac{1}{2}$-year certificate
      $4418.92 in a $5\frac{1}{2}$-year certificate
31. $2804.31
33. $10,246.76
35. $3972.83
37. $2231.06
39. $2945.55
41. $1200.00

Exercise 9.5

1. $378.00
3. $35,086.56
5. 4.9% compounded semiannually
7. The future value will not differ.
9. 2%, 3%, 4% GIC: $30.60
      4%, 3%, 2% GIC: $31.20
11. $2219.01
13. $9362.26
15. RateOptimizer GIC: $678.79
      Fixed-rate GIC: $726.37
17. Escalating Rate GIC: $349.98
      Fixed-rate GIC: $298.32
19. a. $148.59
  b. $180.61
  c. $219.11
21. $21.16 per hour
23. a. $47,105.39
  b. $54,528.86
  c. $72,762.49
25. $578.92
27. a. $7800.22
  b. $8504.23
  c. $8504.23
  d. The strip bond's market value on any date
      impounds a rate of return equal to 2.172%
      compounded semiannually (csa) to the investor.
      The investor can earn this either in the bond or in
      another investment earning 2.172% csa.
29. 25
31. $88.01 more at 5.00% compounded annually
33. $34,425,064
35. $10,489.74
37. $4108.05

Exercise 9.6

1. $3696.13
3. $911.91
5. $1418.58
7. $4937.12

9. $2708.21 due in 1 year
   $1354.11 due in 3 years
11. $1492.77
13. **a.** Alternative (2) is worth $3139.29 more.
    b. Alternative (2) is worth $1828.25 more.
15. $3862.60 due in 1½ years
    $7725.20 due in 4 years
17. $2845.27 due in 9 months
    $8535.81 due in 1½ years
19. $2163.49

Review Problems

1. $4198.04
3. 59.05%
5. 768,000
7. Original principal: $2012.56
   Interest portion: $285.22
9. **a.** $12,928.44
   b. $307.94
11. **a.** Springboard GIC: $12,160.59
    Fixed-rate GIC: $11,876.86
    b. Springboard GIC: $394.94
    Fixed-rate GIC: $374.93
13. Offer 1: $38,494.48
    Offer 2: $40,393.23
    Accept Offer 2.
15. $2980.82
17. $3005.43
19. $11,106.47
21. **a.** $2139.02
    b. $1177.81
    c. 81.61%
23. $4327.07
25. $2311.51
27. Current price: $331.28
    Increase in value: $25.03
29. **a.** $46.79
    b. 9.12%
31. $6500.02

CHAPTER 10 Compound Interest: Further Topics and Applications

Concept Questions (Section 10.1)

1. If $FV < PV$, the quantity is decreasing in size as time passes. Therefore, the rate of growth is negative. That is, the value for i is negative.
3. Since the time interval is the same for both cases, the relative size of the periodic rates of return is indicated by the overall *percent* increase rather than the overall *dollar* increase. In the case "$1 grew to $2," the final value is twice the initial value (100% increase). In the case "$3 grew to $5," the final value is 1.667 times the initial value (66.7% increase). Therefore, the periodic rate of return was higher in the "$1 grew to $2" scenario.

Exercise 10.1

1. 8.13% compounded annually
3. 9.00% compounded quarterly
5. 8.50% compounded monthly
7. 4.37% compounded annually
9. 5.25% compounded annually
11. 5.31% compounded annually
13. 3.90% compounded monthly
15.

Province	Annual growth
Alberta	1.80%
British Columbia	1.64%
Newfoundland and Labrador	–0.21%
Nova Scotia	0.35%
Ontario	1.40%

17. **a.** 7.60% compounded annually
    b. 7.39% compounded quarterly
    c. 7.35% compounded monthly
19. 9.36% compounded semiannually
21. 8.04% compounded annually
23. 1.98% compounded annually
25. **a.** $2550.07
    b. 5.66% compounded annually
    c. 2.00% compounded annually
27. 12.22% compounded monthly
29. 10.80% compounded monthly
31. 6.11% compounded annually
33. –1.62% compounded annually
35. 5.50% compounded annually (3 yr.)
    4.09% compounded annually (5 yr.)
    8.23% compounded annually (10 yr.)
37. 4.94% compounded annually (3 yr.)
    5.28% compounded annually (5 yr.)
    7.64% compounded annually (10 yr.)

Concept Questions (Section 10.2)

1. In the case of annual compounding, the value calculated for n will equal the number of years in the term of the loan or investment.

Exercise 10.2

1. 23 years
3. 4 years
5. May 1 of the following year
7. 7.00 years
9. **a.** 7 years
   b. 6 years and 10 months
11. **a.** 12 years and 9 months
    b. 13 years and 10 months
13. 14 years and 2 months
15. 3 years and 11 months
17. **a.** 28 years and 1 month
    b. 20 years and 2 months
19. 23 months
21. 2 years, 11 months, and 24 days
23. 11 years and 129 days
25. 1 year, 9 months, and 57 days

Concept Questions (Section 10.3)

1. The effective rate of interest is the *equivalent annually compounded* rate.
3. Yes. The effective interest rate equals the nominal rate for annual compounding.

Exercise 10.3

1. **a.** 6.09%
   b. 6.14%
   c. 6.17%
3. **a.** 9.20%
   b. 9.31%
   c. 9.38%
5. **a.** 5% compounded annually
   b. 4.94% compounded semiannually
   c. 4.91% compounded quarterly
   d. 4.89% compounded monthly
7. 11.7% compounded monthly ($f = 12.35\%$)
9. 9.3% compounded annually ($f = 9.3\%$)
11. 7.70%
13. 12.55%
15. 11.21%
17. Choose the semiannually compounded GIC (0.06% higher effective rate).
19. ABC: 16.77%
    DEF: 16.99%
21. 6.78% compounded monthly
    6.88% compounded semiannually
    7.00% compounded annually
23. 1.49% per month

Exercise 10.4

1. **a.** 9.76% compounded semiannually
   b. 9.64% compounded quarterly
   c. 9.57% compounded monthly
3. **a.** 10.38% compounded annually
   b. 10.13% compounded semiannually
   c. 9.92% compounded monthly
5. **a.** 6.09% compounded annually
   b. 6.14% compounded annually
   c. 6.17% compounded annually
7. **a.** 5.87% compounded quarterly
   b. 5.96% compounded quarterly
   c. 6.03% compounded quarterly
9. 4.03% compounded semiannually
11. 5.97% compounded monthly
13. 10.59% compounded quarterly
15. 2.52% compounded annually
17. 3.43% compounded monthly
19. 1.99% compounded monthly
21. **a.** 7.76% compounded annually
    b. 7.62% compounded semiannually
    c. 7.55% compounded quarterly
23. 9.09% compounded quarterly

Review Problems

1. 7.40%
3. 7.5% compounded monthly
5. 28.17%
7. compound annual rate of 14.43%
9. 10.73% compounded semiannually
11. 15.39%
13. 7.02%
15. Take the bank mortgage (effective interest rate is 0.006% lower).
17. 4.60% compounded quarterly
19. 13 years and 9 months
21. 6.58%
23. 16 years and 6 months
25. 6 years and 2 months
27. **a.** 11.11%
    b. 5 years and 6 months

Exercise 10C

1. Simple rate = 3.00%
   Effective rate = 3.04%
3. Simple rate = 9.75%
   Effective rate = 10.20%
5. 8.72%
7. 4.67%

9. Simple rate = −9.33%
   Effective rate = −9.01%
11. Current (simple) yield = 5.06%
    Effective yield = 5.19%
13. 4.64%
15. **a.** 972.7%
    b. 227.5%

CHAPTER 11 Ordinary Annuities: Future Value and Present Value

Concept Questions (Section 11.1)

1. The two types of annuities are distinguished by comparing the payment interval to the compounding interval. If the payment interval *equals* the compounding interval, the annuity is a *simple* annuity. Otherwise, it is a general annuity.
3. No. Insurance premiums are paid at the beginning of the period of coverage. In the present case, the monthly payments will be made at the beginning of each month of coverage. To qualify as an ordinary annuity, the monthly payments would have to occur at the end of each month of coverage.

Exercise 11.2

1. **a.** $41,645.91
   b. $83,291.82
   c. $124,937.72
3. **a.** $51,160.12
   b. $57,275.00
   c. $64,202.83
   d. $72,052.44
5. $188,228.54
7. $62,054.92
9. $30,901.26
11. $3121.60
13. $59,942.63
15. **a.** $68,059.40
    b. $124,191.36
17. $48,504.15
19. $40,177
21. $199,202.30
23. $111,881.76
25. $112,100.43

Concept Questions (Section 11.3)

1. The annuity's present value will be (ii) smaller than before. The present value represents the amount which, invested at the discount rate, can generate the future payments. When money can earn a higher rate of return, *less* money needs to be invested *today* in order to generate the specified stream of future payments.

Exercise 11.3

1. **a.** $14,093.94
   b. $28,187.89
   c. $42,281.83
3. **a.** $12,462.21
   b. $8513.56
   c. $7963.33
   d. $6259.33
5. $2033.16
7. $15,330.60
9. $17,840.38
11. $14,047.16
13. $56,816.79
15. $154,093.30
17. $5442.17
19. $8658.95
21. **a.** $22,500.00
    b. $16,369.18
23. $12,899.99
25. $3304.30
27. $2,893,312.18
29. $8779.95
31. Mr. Lindberg's offer is worth $65.80 more.
33. $130,872.90
35. $64,550.64
37. 3.97% discount
39. The pension-at-age-55 option has a 31.9% higher economic value.

Exercise 11.4

1. **a.** 1.489% per half-year
   b. 0.742% per quarter
   c. 0.247% per month
3. **a.** 4.060% per year
   b. 2.010% per half-year
   c. 0.332% per month
5. **a.** $54,864.51
   b. $55,564.96
   c. $55,929.71
   d. $56,178.55
7. **a.** $12,598.41
   b. $25,186.12
9. **a.** $17,786.53
   b. $20,454.61

11. **a.** $38,367.94
    b. $93,482.61
13. $15,776.73
15. **a.** $6863.93
    b. $8304.63
    c. $8803.36
17. $390,165.12
19. $11,600.00
21. Monthly contributions are worth $129.59 more.
23. $188,316.36
25. $73,953.35
27. $195,703.17
29. $195,760.96
31. $313,490.72

Review Problems

1. **a.** $71,268.14
   b. $69,736.64
3. $2376.15
5. $138,953.22
7. $124,388.36
9. $21,901.45
11. $82,819.01
13. $108,158.40
15. $631.88
17. 59.56%
19. $50,239.95

CHAPTER 12 Ordinary Annuities: Periodic Payment, Number of Payments, and Interest Rate

Concept Questions (Section 12.1)

1. The payments will be (ii) *more* than half as large because you will pay more total interest if you pay off the loan over 10 years instead of 5 years. (The total of the principal components of the payments will be the same in both cases.)

Exercise 12.1

1. **a.** $5903.13; $352,421.75
   b. $3668.18; $389,954.60
3. **a.** $7287.54; $183,003.20
   b. $7938.61; $235,088.80
   c. $8619.33; $289,546.40
   d. $9328.37; $346,269.60
5. **a.** $2832.06; $240,229.20
   b. $1848.18; $306,436.80
   c. $1280.44; $365,868.00
   d. $919.82; $418,864.80

7. **a.** $760.86
   b. $764.09
   c. $765.77
   d. $766.91
9. $392.86
11. $257.28; $3155.20
13. $14,839.78; $587,182.40
15. $2222.05
17. **a.** $682.53
    b. $2638.38
19. $1952.59
21. $981.65
23. $1962.61
25. **a.** $905,680.79
    b. $1708.17
27. $3241.66
29. **a.** $177,435.91
    b. $2,323,077.30
31. $12,554.29
33. $2875.94

Concept Questions (Section 12.2)

1. You will pay off the loan in (ii) less than half the time. If payments are doubled, you will pay less interest over the life of the loan. Therefore, the total of the nominal payments (principal + interest) will be reduced and you will pay off the loan in less than half the time.

Exercise 12.2

1. 8 years and 6 months
3. 25 years
5. 10 years and 2 months
7. 11 years and 9 months
9. **a.** 30 years, 2 months
   b. 25 years, 2 months
   c. 21 years, 10 months
   d. 20 years, 6 months
11. **a.** 23 years, 6 months
    b. 24 years, 3 months
    c. 24 years, 8 months
    d. 24 years, 11 months
13. 12 years
15. 18 years and 6 months
17. 18 years and 7 months
19. 13 months
21. 4 years and 8 months
23. 14 years and 9 months
25. 2 years and 9 months

27. To at least the age of 79 years and 8 months
29. 51
31. 18 years and 9 months
33. 10 years and 11 months
35. 26 years

Exercise 12.3

1. 4.80% compounded quarterly; 4.89%
3. 8.50% compounded semiannually; 8.68%
5. **a.** 6.92% compounded monthly
   b. 8.31% compounded monthly
   c. 9.41% compounded monthly
7. 7.90% compounded monthly; 8.19%
9. 8.50% compounded semiannually; 8.68%
11. 10.11% compounded annually
13. 7.67%
15. 41.30%
17. 5.57%
19. 5.27%

Review Problems

1. $8504.56
3. 7.45% compounded monthly; 7.71%
5. 8.77%
7. 9 months longer
9. 14 years and 6 months
11. $6288.35
13. 1 year sooner; $3094
15. $322.29
17. 18.00
19. Lena: $946.39
    Axel: $1421.64
21. **a.** $741,577.64
    b. $2598.90
23. 86 years
25. 23 withdrawals
27. $4270.26

CHAPTER 13 Annuities Due

Concept Questions (Section 13.1)

1. Insurance premium payments, rent payments, lease payments, newspaper and magazine subscriptions, membership dues.
3. Each payment in an annuity due earns interest for *one more* payment interval than the corresponding payment in an ordinary annuity.

Exercise 13.1

1. **a.** $63,249.04
   b. $67,676.47
   c. 7.0%
3. **a.** $51,584.33
   b. $95,736.66
5. $207,416.86
7. $64,273.29
9. **a.** $16,803.44
   b. $3803.44
11. $326,252.08; $243,752.08
13. $280,678.01
15. **a.** $505,315
    b. $335,315
17. Fay: $642,566.44
    Fred: $513,950.41
    Fay will have $128,616.03 more in her RRSP.

Concept Questions (Section 13.2)

1. The focal date is at the beginning of the *first* payment interval. Since payments are at the *beginning* of each payment interval, the focal date coincides with the first payment.
3. Since $PV(\text{due}) = PV \times (1 + i)$, then $PV(\text{due})$ is $i\%$ larger than PV. In the particular case at hand, $PV(\text{due})$ will exceed PV by 3%.

Exercise 13.2

1. **a.** $27,938.15
   b. $28,217.53
   c. 1.0%
3. **a.** $32,052.08
   b. $22,341.47
5. $24,486.41
7. **a.** $1468.90
   b. $338.90
9. **a.** $131,043.62
   b. $21,730.97
11. Rosie Senario's offer is worth $547.75 more.
13. $484,735.50
15. $120,339.78
17. Bram will save $39.13 by choosing the Atlantic Life policy.
19. **a.** The $1700 annuity has the largest economic value and the $850 annuity has the lowest value.
    b. The $850 annuity now has the largest economic value and the $1700 annuity has the lowest value.
21. Heath should accept the lease on the new location since it represents a saving of $2754.54.

Concept Questions (Section 13.3)

1. If *PMT*, *n*, and *i* are the same for an ordinary annuity and an annuity due, the ordinary annuity will have the smaller *FV*. Therefore, if *FV*, *n*, and *i* are the same, the ordinary annuity has the larger *PMT*.
3. **a.** The lessee should not exercise the purchase option. If the lessee wishes to purchase the vehicle, an equivalent vehicle can be purchased at a lower price in the used-car market.
   b. The lessee should exercise the purchase option. If the lessee does not wish to own the vehicle, it can be sold for more than the residual value in the used-car market.
   c. If the lessee does the rational thing, the lessor loses

   Residual value – Market value

   in case *a*, but does not gain or capture the difference

   Market value – Residual value

   in case *b*. The lessor's exposure to this market value risk is one reason why the interest rate on a lease contract is normally higher than the interest rate on a loan to purchase the same vehicle.

Exercise 13.3

1. **a.** $19,971.75; $250,706.23
   b. $12,896.26; $427,593.50
   c. $9499.15; $512,521.25
   d. $8123.57; $546,910.75
3. **a.** 34 years, 6 months
   b. 25 years, 6 months
   c. 22 years
   d. 20 years, 9 months
5. **a.** 6.88% compounded monthly
   b. 8.27% compounded monthly
   c. 9.36% compounded monthly
7. $47,721.67
9. $1093.09
11. **a.** $16,449.92
    b. $17,436.91
13. $1482.54
15. $285.24
17. $401.90
19. $856.28
21. $17,145
23. 36 months
25. $6792

27. 1 year and 8 months
29. 30 payments
31. 14 fewer deposits
33. 11.54%
35. 8.80% compounded quarterly; 9.09%
37. 24.79%
39. **a.** $585.12
    b. $3405.38
41. $485.58 quarterly; $162.66 monthly
43. 3 years and 11 months
45. 5 years and 6 months
47. 13.74%
49. 21.26% compounded annually
51. **a.** 9.86%
    b. 11.52%
    c. 13.45%
53. $2919.74
55. 27 years

Exercise 13.4

1. 1 year and 6 months
3. 22 years
5. $6612.60
7. $863,467
9. $572,376.63
11. $335.88
13. **a.** $218,000
    b. $130,178
    c. $405,883
15. $1643.50
17. $1692.37
19. $3107.54
21. Monthly income at age 65: $3031.42
    Monthly income at age 70: $4885.46

Review Problems

1. **a.** $98,198.89
   b. $17,270.48
3. **a.** $25,527.54
   b. $27,505.93
5. 10.36%
7. The single payment plan is worth $3.48 less.
9. **a.** 36 contributions
   b. 13 additional contributions
11. $209.61
13. 16 more contributions
15. 17.43%
17. **a.** $7506.74
    b. $11,580.67

19. $615,447.79
21. $1417.86
23. **a.** $11,572.42
    b. $12,532.93
25. $301,010.58
27. 21 years and 10 months
29. 103.54%

CHAPTER 14 Annuities: Special Situations

Concept Questions (Exercise 14.1)

1. **a.** 3 years and 3 months
   b. 3 years and 6 months

Exercise 14.1

1. $11,791.60
3. $17,531.01
5. $26,775.61
7. $14,074.16
9. $32,365.24
11. 4 years
13. 13 years and 6 months
15. $2861.16
17. The $2000 annuity has the greater (by $470.52) economic value.
19. 9 years and 11 months
21. 22 years and 2 months
23. $5681.03
25. $71,795
27. 2 years and 6 months
29. 25 years

Concept Questions (Section 14.2)

1. The perpetuity has the larger present value. The greater the number of payments in an annuity, the larger the annuity's present value. Hence, PV(perpetuity) > PV(annuity). Alternatively, the perpetuity may be viewed as a combination of an annuity identical to the given annuity and a deferred perpetuity. Then

   PV of given perpetuity = (PV of given annuity) +
   $\qquad\qquad\qquad$ (PV of deferred perpetuity)

   Therefore,

   $\qquad PV$ of given perpetuity > PV of given annuity

3. The market value will rise. The rate of return (dividend yield) is the (fixed) annual dividend calculated as a percentage of the market value. If investors will accept a lower rate of return, they will pay a higher price for the shares.

Exercise 14.2

1. $22,500
3. $100,000
5. $90,085.76
7. $9120.69
9. $3120.47
11. **a.** $68.17
    b. 4.38% compounded semiannually
13. **a.** $73,223.88
    b. $70,303.99
15. $17,669.23
17. $6954.87

Exercise 14.3

1. $312,421.69
3. $3494.84
5. $46,155.28
7. $362,020.14; $80,141.25
9. $1949.10
11. $37.49

Review Problems

1. $18,858.53
3. 30.38%
5. $900.00
7. $113,468.88
9. $2390.05
11. **a.** $142,857.14
    b. $109,693.48
13. $15,209.95
15. 21.94%
17. 16 months

CHAPTER 15 Loan Amortization: Mortgages

Exercise 15.1

1. $PMT = \$174.03$

Payment number	Payment	Interest portion	Principal portion	Principal balance
0	—	—	—	$1000.00
1	$174.03	$12.50	$161.53	838.47
2	174.03	10.48	163.55	674.92
3	174.03	8.44	165.59	509.33
4	174.03	6.37	167.66	341.67
5	174.03	4.27	169.76	171.91
6	174.06	2.15	171.91	0.00
	Total:	$44.21		

3. $PMT = \$710.97$

Payment number	Payment	Interest portion	Principal portion	Principal balance
0	—	—	—	$2800.00
1	$710.97	$17.50	$693.47	2106.53
2	710.97	13.17	697.80	1408.73
3	710.97	8.80	702.17	706.56
4	710.98	4.42	706.56	0.00
	Total:	$43.89		

5.

Payment number	Payment	Interest portion	Principal portion	Principal balance
0	—	—	—	$1000.00
1	$200.00	$12.50	$187.50	812.50
2	200.00	10.16	189.84	622.66
3	200.00	7.78	192.22	430.44
4	200.00	5.38	194.62	235.82
5	200.00	2.95	197.05	38.77
6	39.25	0.48	38.77	0.00
	Total:	$39.25		

7.

Payment number	Payment	Interest portion	Principal portion	Principal balance
0	—	—	—	$2800.00
1	$600.00	$17.50	$582.50	2217.50
2	600.00	13.86	586.14	1631.36
3	600.00	10.20	589.80	1041.56
4	600.00	6.51	593.49	448.07
5	450.87	2.80	448.07	0.00
	Total:	$50.87		

9. $PMT = \$1739.45$

Payment number	Payment	Interest portion	Principal portion	Principal balance
0	—	—	—	$9000.00
1	$1739.45	$396.28	$1343.17	7656.83
2	1739.45	337.14	1402.31	6254.52
3	1739.45	275.39	1464.06	4790.46
4	1739.45	210.93	1528.52	3261.94
5	1739.45	143.63	1595.82	1666.12
6	1739.48	73.36	1666.12	0.00

11. $PMT = \$1092.08$

Payment number	Payment	Interest portion	Principal portion	Principal balance
0	—	—	—	$8000.00
1	$1092.08	$160.00	$932.08	7067.92
2	1092.08	141.36	950.72	6117.20
3	2592.08	122.34	2469.74	3647.46
4	1092.08	72.95	1019.13	2628.33
5	1092.08	52.57	1039.51	1588.82
6	1092.08	31.78	1060.30	528.52
7	539.09	10.57	528.52	0.00
	Total:	$591.57		

13. $PMT = \$1037.41$

Payment number	Payment	Interest portion	Principal portion	Principal balance
0	—	—	—	$60,000.00
1	$1037.41	$375.00	$662.41	59,337.59
2	1037.41	370.86	666.55	58,671.04
⋮	⋮	⋮	⋮	⋮
42	—	—	—	28,298.14
43	1037.41	176.86	860.55	27,437.59
44	1037.41	171.48	865.93	26,571.66
⋮	⋮	⋮	⋮	⋮
70	—	—	—	2055.24
71	1037.41	12.85	1024.56	1030.68
72	1037.12	6.44	1030.68	0.00

15. $i_2 = 0.044030651$

Payment number	Payment	Interest portion	Principal portion	Principal balance
0	—	—	—	$9000.00
1	$1800.00	$396.28	$1403.72	7596.28
2	1800.00	334.47	1465.53	6130.75
3	1800.00	269.94	1530.06	4600.69
4	1800.00	202.57	1597.43	3003.26
5	1800.00	132.24	1667.76	1335.50
6	1394.30	58.80	1335.50	0.00

17.

Payment number	Payment	Interest portion	Principal portion	Principal balance
0	—	—	—	$8000.00
1	$1000.00	$160.00	$840.00	7160.00
2	1000.00	143.20	856.80	6303.20
3	2000.00	126.06	1873.94	4429.26
4	1000.00	88.59	911.41	3517.85
5	1000.00	70.36	929.64	2588.21
6	1000.00	51.76	948.24	1639.97
7	1000.00	32.80	967.20	672.77
8	686.23	13.46	672.77	0.00
	Total:	$686.23		

19.

Payment number	Payment	Interest portion	Principal portion	Principal balance
0	—	—	—	$60,000.00
1	$1000.00	$375.00	$625.00	59,375.00
2	1000.00	371.09	628.91	58,746.09
⋮	⋮	⋮	⋮	⋮
55	—	—	—	19,128.18
56	1000.00	119.55	880.45	18,247.73
57	1000.00	114.05	885.95	17,361.78
⋮	⋮	⋮	⋮	⋮
74	—	—	—	1424.49
75	1000.00	8.90	991.10	433.39
76	436.10	2.71	433.39	0.00

21. a. For a 30-month term, 47.7%.
For a 30-year term, 24.6%.

b.

Term (years)	Total interest ($)
5	2022.76
10	4244.32
15	6686.41
20	9334.03
25	12,169.22
30	15,173.16

c. (i) 254 months
(ii) 357 months

Concept Questions (Section 15.2)

1. The balance midway through the amortization period will be (i) more than half the original principal. With each successive payment, the interest component becomes smaller and the principal component becomes larger. Therefore, the total principal repaid in the first half of the amortization period will be less than the total principal repaid in the second half of the amortization period. It follows that: (1) less than half of the original principal will be repaid in the first half of the amortization period; and (2) the loan's balance midway through the amortization period will be more than half the original principal.

3. a. Each regular payment includes a 0.2¢ *over*payment. Therefore, the adjusted final payment will be less than the regular payment.

b. The reduction in the final payment will be the future value of the 60 overpayments of 0.2¢. This will be (i) more than 60(0.2¢) = 12¢.

Exercise 15.2

1. a. $171.57 **b.** $331.91
c. $2922.10 **d.** $5283.96
3. a. $249.69 **b.** $819.66
c. $359.71 **d.** $3491.06
5. a. $204.57 **b.** $446.66
c. $3365.38 **d.** $10,345.79
7. a. $822.74 **b.** $1542.15
c. $4474.70 **d.** $4055.64
9. a. $62.66 **b.** $247.84
c. $233.79
11. a. $302.03 **b.** $271.30
c. $562.08
13. a. $1503.31 **b.** $499.93
c. $18,132.85 **d.** $2545.96
d. $2746.60
15. a. $1796.03 **b.** $1298.27
c. $10,317.16 **d.** $2233.04
e. $584.80
17. a. $122.21 **b.** $522.79
c. $711.75 **d.** $1916.49
e. $587.49
19. a. $83.43 **b.** $377.99
c. $852.07 **d.** $1650.55
e. $197.28
21. a. $370.80 **b.** $196.33 $174.47
c. $31,238.73 **d.** $2426.05
23. a. $164.85 **b.** $83.73
c. $85.39

Exercise 15.3

1.

Interval	Balance at end	Principal reduction	Interest paid
0–5 years	$88,783.39	$11,216.61	$24,365.79
6–10 years	74,284.49	14,498.90	21,083.50
11–15 years	55,542.80	18,741.69	16,840.71
16–20 years	31,316.76	24,226.04	11,356.36
21–25 years	0	31,316.76	4267.15

3. **a.** $526.02 for 4% compounded semiannually
   $639.81 for 6% compounded semiannually
   $763.21 for 8% compounded semiannually
   b. 45.09%
   c. $57,806 for 4% compounded semiannually
   $91,943 for 6% compounded semiannually
   $128,963 for 8% compounded semiannually
5. **a.** $180,677.30   **b.** $136,695.14
7. $146.39
9. **a.** $76,216.85   **b.** $465.99
11. **a.** $32,333.43   **b.** $310.00
13. **a.** $14,167.50   **b.** $274.56
15. **a.** $155,300   **b.** $163,500
17. **a.** $526.02   **b.** 21 years and 46 weeks
19. **a.** 1 year and 9 months
    b. 3 years and 5 months
21. 4 years and 7 months
23. 3 months
25. 3 months
27. 6 years and 2 months
29. **a.** 1 year and 7 months
    b. $99,080.24
31. **a.** 5 years and 4 months
    b. $183,476.71
33. **a.** 4 years and 6 months
    b. $217,316.86

Exercise 15.4

1. 9.995%
3. **a.** 12.607%   **b.** 12.144%
   c. 12.068%
5. **a.** The trust company loan's effective rate is 0.38% lower.
   b. The effective cost of borrowing from the trust company is 0.19% lower.
7. **a.** $34,488.28   **b.** $36,699.09
9. **a.** $58,605.77   **b.** $57,348.31
   c. $56,276.22
11. $161,588.99
13. $141,749.57
15. $3026.81

Review Problems

1.

Payment number	Payment	Interest portion	Principal portion	Principal balance
0	—	—	—	$862.50
1	$148.50	$8.09	$140.41	722.09
2	148.50	6.77	141.73	580.36
3	148.50	5.44	143.06	437.30
4	148.50	4.10	144.40	292.90
5	148.50	2.75	145.75	147.15
6	148.53	1.38	147.15	0.00
	Total:	$28.53		

3. **a.** $834.36
   b. $170.31
   c. $5697.14
   d. $1891.34

5.

Payment number	Payment	Interest portion	Principal portion	Principal balance
0	—	—	—	$60,000.00
1	$10,000.00	$3150.00	$6850.00	53,150.00
2	10,000.00	2790.38	7209.62	45,940.38
3	10,000.00	2411.87	7588.13	38,352.25
4	10,000.00	2013.49	7986.51	30,365.74
5	10,000.00	1594.20	8405.80	21,959.94
6	10,000.00	1152.90	8847.10	13,112.84
7	10,000.00	688.42	9311.58	3801.26
8	4000.83	199.57	3801.26	0.00
	Total:	$14,000.83		

7. **a.** $146.00
   b. $316.37
   c. $1025.91
   d. $3268.88
   e. $303.34
9. **a.** $2837.08
   b. $809.33
   c. $5386.53
   d. $34,162.12
   e. $3805.67
11. **a.** 1 year and 4 months
    b. $73,956.77
13. **a.** $75,367.19
    b. $652.96
15. $18,947.10
17. **a.** 4 years and 2 months
    b. $96,786.36

CHAPTER 16 Bonds and Sinking Funds

Concept Questions (Section 16.2)

1. Four variables affecting a bond's price are:
   - the face value of the bond
   - the bond's coupon rate
   - the prevailing market rate of return on bonds
   - the time remaining until maturity of the bond
     Only the prevailing market rate of return *always* has an inverse effect on the bond's price.

3. Yes. If, during the holding period, the capital loss (due to a rise in the prevailing market rate of return) exceeds the coupon interest paid on the bond, you will suffer a net loss on the bond investment.

5. If prevailing interest rates decline, the prices of all bonds will rise. However, the prices of long-term bonds will rise more than the prices of short-term bonds. Therefore, you will improve the portfolio's capital gain if, prior to the interest rate decline, you increase the relative weighting of long-term bonds (by selling short-term bonds and using the proceeds to purchase long-term bonds).

Exercise 16.2

1. $1128.80
3. $857.77
5. $1207.07
7. $534.66
9. $10,300.09
11. $94.41
13. $369.61
15. $3470.12 more today.
17. Bond C's price will fall by $8.25. Bond D's price will fall by $40.30. *This outcome demonstrates that, all other things being equal, bond prices fall when market rates rise, and the price of a longer-term bond falls more than the price of a shorter-term bond.*
19. Bond A: $1042.65. Bond premium = $42.65
    Bond B: $1074.39. Bond premium = $74.39
    Bond C: $1098.00. Bond premium = $98
    Bond D: $1128.65. Bond premium = $128.65
    The results demonstrate that (for the same spread of the market rate *below* the coupon rate) the *longer* maturity of a bond, the *larger the bond's premium.*
21. Bond J: $1125.51. Bond Premium = $125.51
    Bond K: $1251.03. Bond Premium = $251.03
    Bond L: $1376.54. Bond Premium = $376.54
    The results demonstrate that, for bonds having the same time to maturity, a *larger* spread of the coupon rate *above* the market rate results in a greater bond premium.

23. **a.** −$86.46   **b.** −$162.89
    c. $98.00   **d.** $209.30
    e. The price change for a 2% interest rate is less than twice the price change for a 1% interest rate increase.
    f. The price change from a 1% interest rate increase is smaller than the price change resulting from a 1% interest rate decrease.
25. **a.** $11,130.32
    b. 11.30%
27. **a.** 10.95%
    b. 0%
    c. −9.52%
29. 28.49% compounded semiannually

Exercise 16.3

1. 6.02% compounded semiannually
3. 5.796% compounded semiannually
5. Bond A: 7.72% compounded semiannually
   Bond C: 6.97% compounded semiannually
7. **a.** decreased by 0.73% compounded semiannually
   b. decreased by 0.20% compounded semiannually
9. 17.54% compounded semiannually

Exercise 16.4

1. $1230.03
3. $958.06
5. $1152.46
7. $959.17
9. $1229.88
11. $1514.79
13. March 15: $910.03
    April 15: $914.57
    May 15: $918.99
    June 15: $923.58
    July 15: $928.04
    August 15: $932.67
    September 15: $911.33
15. 104.94% of face value
17. $1095.17
19. $913.27
21. $98.97
23. 1.849%
25. **a.** $937.63
    b. 17.78%

Exercise 16.5

1. **a.** $424,333   **b.** $6,196,094
3. **a.** $620,292   **b.** $9,534,856
5. **a.** $87,284   **b.** $2,506,640

7. a. $482,162 **b.** $10,530,997

9. a. $353,611 **b.** $1,707,222
  c. $4,836,586

11. a. $302,726 **b.** $1,955,452
  c. $6,081,667

13. a. $614,137 **b.** $1,788,274
  c. $2,311,969

15. a. $204,464 **b.** $1,536,428
  c. $5,478,509

17.

Payment interval number	Payment (at end)	Interest earned	Increase in the fund	Balance in fund (end of interval)
0	—	—	—	$0
1	$122,135	$0	$122,135	122,135
2	122,135	4275	126,410	248,545
3	122,135	8699	130,834	379,379
4	122,135	13,278	135,413	514,792
5	122,135	18,018	140,153	654,945
6	122,135	22,923	145,058	800,003
	Total:	$67,193	$800,003	

19.

Payment interval number	Payment (at start)	Interest earned	Increase in the fund	Balance in fund (end of interval)
0	—	—	—	$0
1	$163,710	$11,050	$174,760	174,760
2	163,710	22,847	186,557	361,317
3	163,710	35,439	199,149	560,466
4	163,710	48,882	212,592	773,058
5	163,710	63,232	226,942	1,000,000
	Total:	$181,450	$1,000,000	

21.

Payment interval number	Payment (at end)	Interest earned	Increase in the fund	Balance in fund (end of interval)
0	—	—	—	$0
1	$302,720	$0	$302,720	302,720
2	302,720	4541	307,261	609,981
⋮	⋮	⋮	⋮	⋮
10				3,239,928
11	302,720	48,599	351,319	3,591,247
12	302,720	53,869	356,589	3,947,836
⋮	⋮	⋮	⋮	⋮
18				6,202,544
19	302,720	93,038	395,758	6,598,302
20	302,720	98,975	401,695	6,999,997

23.

Payment interval number	Payment	Interest earned	Increase in the fund	Balance in fund (end of interval)	Book value of the debt
0	—	—	—	$0	$10,000,000
1	$353,611	$0	$353,611	353,611	9,646,389
2	353,611	12,376	365,987	719,598	9,280,402
⋮	⋮	⋮	⋮	⋮	⋮
18				8,663,360	1,336,640
19	353,611	303,218	656,829	9,320,189	679,811
20	353,611	326,207	679,818	10,000,007	(7)

25. a. $8221
  b. $29,938
  c. In the 33rd month.
  d. $2003

27. a. $313,548
  b. $165,087
  c. $559,178
  d.

Payment interval number	Payment (at end)	Interest earned	Increase in the fund	Balance in fund (end of interval)	Book value of the debt
0	—	—	—	$0	$20,000,000
1	$313,548	$0	$313,548	313,548	19,686,452
2	313,548	7055	320,603	634,151	19,365,849
⋮	⋮	⋮	⋮	⋮	⋮
38	—	—	—	18,522,966	1,477,034
39	313,548	416,767	730,315	19,253,281	746,719
40	313,548	433,199	746,747	20,000,028	(28)
	Total:	$7,458,108			

29. a. $13,737
  b.

Payment interval number	Payment	Interest earned	Increase in the fund	Balance in fund (end of interval)	Book value of the debt
0	—	—	—	$0	$800,000
1	$13,737	$240	$13,977	13,977	786,023
2	13,737	485	14,222	28,199	771,801
⋮	⋮	⋮	⋮	⋮	⋮
38	—	—	—	745,465	54,535
39	13,737	13,286	27,023	772,488	27,512
40	13,737	13,759	27,496	799,984	16
	Total:	$250,504			

Review Problems

1. $103.14

3. $2246.55

5. 12.48%

7. $1156.12

9.

Payment interval number	Payment	Interest earned	Increase in the fund	Balance in fund (end of interval)	Book value of the debt
0	—	—	—	$0	$500,000
1	$28,285	$0	$28,285	28,285	471,715
2	28,285	990	29,275	57,560	442,440
⋮	⋮	⋮	⋮	⋮	⋮
12	—	—	—	413,016	86,984
13	28,285	14,456	42,741	455,757	44,243
14	28,285	15,951	44,236	499,993	7

11. $1168.86

13.

Payment interval number	Payment (at start)	Interest earned	Increase in the fund	Balance in fund (end of interval)
0	—	—	—	$0
1	$112,571	$ 3377	$115,948	115,948
2	112,571	6856	119,427	235,375
3	112,571	10,438	123,009	358,384
4	112,571	14,129	126,700	485,084
5	112,571	17,930	130,501	615,585
6	112,571	21,845	134,416	750,001
	Total:	$74,575	$750,001	

CHAPTER 17 Business Investment Decisions

Exercise 17.1

1. a. Since the purchase price is less than the present value ($57,006) of the future cash flows, the investment should be made.
 b. The increase in economic value is $2006.
3. $48,007
5. a. Buy the timber rights since the present value of the future cash flows ($251,072) is larger than the price.
 b. Increase by $1072
7. a. The machine should be purchased since the current economic value of the lifetime costs is $1160 less than if the machine is leased.
 b. The machine should be leased since the current economic value of the lifetime costs is $1021 less than if the machine is purchased.
9. a. Lease the system.
 b. $2931
11. a. Mr. Harder should rent, thereby saving $3273.
 b. Mr. Harder should buy, thereby saving $4740.

Exercise 17.2

1. a. NPV = $10,972. Should sign the contract.
 b. NPV = −$5930. The contract should not be signed.
 c. NPV is −$21,875. The investment should be rejected.

3. $29,009
5. NPV = −$10,779. The new project should be rejected.
7. NPV = −$831,765. Jasper should not proceed with the project.
9. NPV = −$84,458. The product should not be manufactured.
11. NPV ($872,752) is positive. Wildcat should acquire the new drilling rig.

Exercise 17.3

1. Select projects B and D (requiring a combined investment of $2,950,000).
3. Projects F, C, A, and D should be selected (requiring a combined investment of $90,000).
5. Carl should purchase the Deere; its NPV is $6070 larger.
7. Model J should be purchased because it has the larger equivalent annual cash flow.
9. The company should choose investment D, with a current economic value of $16,085 more.
11. The 25-ton truck should be purchased. It will generate a $276 larger annual economic benefit.
13. The Falcon has a lower (by $1958) equivalent annual cost.
15. The International model should be purchased since its equivalent annual cost is $6318 lower.

Exercise 17.4

1. 8.4%
3. IRR for Stage 1 = 21.4%
 IRR for Stage 2 = 15.4%
 IRR for Stage 3 = 6.2%
 IRR for Stage 4 = 7.3%
 Stages 1 and 2 should be approved since their IRRs exceed the cost of capital (8%).
5. IRR = 5.4%. The investment should be not be made since the IRR (5.4%) is less than the cost of capital (6%).
7. IRR = 10.1%. The investment should be undertaken since its IRR exceeds the cost of capital (8.5%).
9. IRR = 9.0%. IRR equals the firm's cost of capital (9%). The product should be introduced.
11. IRR = 8.0%. The mine should not be developed because the IRR is less than the company's cost of capital.
13. IRR = 5.2%. IRR is less than the required rate of return (7%); Jasper should not undertake the expansion.

Exercise 17.5

1. **a.** *IRR* of project C = 7.8%. *IRR* of project D = 8.9%. Project D should be selected on the basis of having the larger *IRR*.
   b. *NPV* of project C = $4961. *NPV* of project D = $7996. Project D has the larger *NPV* if the firm's cost of capital is 7%.
   c. *NPV* of project C = $18,255. *NPV* of project D = $17,271. Project C has the higher *NPV* if the firm's cost of capital is 5%.

3. **a.** *IRR* on Project X = 10.0%. *IRR* on Project Y = 9.5%. Project X should be selected.
   b. *NPV*(X) = $12,522. *NPV*(Y) = $10,793. Project X has the larger *NPV* and should be selected.
   c. *NPV*(X) = $39,938. *NPV*(Y) = $57,113. Project Y has the larger *NPV* and should be selected.

5. **a.** *IRR* on project X = 4.7%.
      IRR on Project Y = 6.3%.
      Project Y is preferred.
   b. *NPV*(Project X) = $2629.
      NPV(Project Y) = $6632.
      Project Y should be selected.
   c. *NPV*(Project X) = $6649.
      NPV(Project Y) = $9721.
      Project Y should be selected.

Exercise 17.6

1. **a.** 4.67 years
   b. Since it will take longer than 4 years to recover the initial investment from profits, the firm would not make the investment.

3. Payback period(Project X) = 4 years
   Payback period(Project Y) = 5 years
   NPV(Project X) = $15,572
   NPV(Project Y) = $20,518
   Project X would be preferred on the basis of its shorter payback but Project Y would be preferred on the basis of its larger *NPV*.

5. **a.** *NPV*(A) = $13,108
      NPV(B) = $11,288
      Proposal A is preferred on the basis of its larger *NPV*.
   b. *IRR* on proposal *A* = 19.1%.
      IRR on proposal *B* = 20.0%.
      Proposal B is preferred on the basis of its larger *IRR*.

c. Payback period(A) = 2.64 years
   Payback period(B) = 2.67 years
   Preference for proposal A based on its slightly shorter payback period.

Review Problems

1. **a.** 4.25 years
   b. No, because the machine's payback period exceeds the required payback of 4 years.
   c. *NPV* = $19,498. Yes. Since the *NPV* is positive, the firm will make the investment.

3. *NPV* = −$62,250. The project will not provide a rate of return exceeding 5.5%.

5. Rainbow Aviation should purchase the plane and thereby gain an economic advantage (in current dollars) of $17,549.

7. Projects A, D, and C give the highest aggregate *NPV* within the $800,000 capital budget constraint.

9. **a.** The car should be leased because the economic value of the net cash outflows is $621 lower.
   b. The car should be purchased (a $657 advantage over leasing).

11. *PMT*(X) = $5182. *PMT*(Y) = $5960. Machine Y should be selected because its equivalent annual cash flow is $778 larger.

13. The Boston Wailer's equivalent annual cost is $4781 lower.

15. 2.7 years

17. *IRR* = 7.6%. The investment should be undertaken since its *IRR* is greater than the cost of capital (7%).

19. *NPV* = $17,788. The machine should be acquired.

21. **a.** *IRR* on Investment A = 11.0%.
      IRR on Investment B = 11.6%.
      Investment B would be selected on the basis on an *IRR* ranking.
   b. *NPV*(Investment A) = $1388.
      NPV(Investment B) = $1777.
      Investment B has the larger *NPV* and should be chosen.
   c. *NPV*(Investment A) = $5912.
      NPV(Investment B) = $5401.
      Investment A now has the higher *NPV* and should be chosen.

23. Purchase Machine D because it has a $3880 larger annual economic advantage.

Glossary

Algebraic expression Statements of the mathematical operations to be carried out on a combination of numbers and variables.

Amortization period The total length of time over which equal regular payments will repay a loan.

Annual cost of a debt The combined total of the annual interest payments on the debt and the annual payments into a sinking fund for retirement of the principal amount of the debt.

Annualized rate of return The annual rate of return that results if a short-term rate of return continues for an entire year.

Annuities due Annuities in which the periodic payments occur at the beginning of each payment interval.

Annuity A series of equal payments at regular intervals.

Base (1) The quantity that is multiplied by itself in a power. (2) The initial amount to which a percent change is applied.

Binomial An expression containing two terms.

Bond A debt instrument secured by specific assets. The bond issuer (borrower) promises to periodically pay accrued interest, and to repay the full principal amount of the debt on the maturity date. The term "bond" is sometimes used in a generic sense to refer to both true bonds and debentures.

Bond discount The amount by which a bond's face value exceeds its quoted price.

Bond premium The amount by which a bond's quoted price exceeds its face value.

Book value of a debt The amount by which the principal balance owed on the debt exceeds the funds accumulated in a sinking fund for retiring the debt.

Book value of a lease The present value of the remaining lease payments (discounted at the interest rate on debt financing).

Break-even chart A graph presenting both total costs and total revenue as a function of sales volume so that the break-even point may be determined.

Break-even point The sales volume at which net income is zero; the intersection of the total cost and total revenue lines on a break-even chart.

Buy rate (for a currency) The exchange rate a currency dealer uses when buying a currency from you.

Capital gain The amount by which an investment's value increases during the holding period.

Capital gain yield The capital gain as a percentage of the initial investment.

Capital loss The amount by which an investment's value decreases during the holding period.

Capital rationing The circumstance wherein the total amount of capital funds that a firm may invest during a period is limited.

Cash discount A discount allowed for a payment within the discount period.

Cash flow A cash disbursement (cash outflow) or a cash receipt (cash inflow).

Cash-flow sign convention Rules for using an algebraic sign to indicate the direction of cash movement. Cash *inflows* (receipts) are positive, and cash *outflows* (disbursements) are negative.

Certificate of Deposit A type of savings account with a fixed interest rate and fixed date for withdrawal. Standard terms range from 3 months to 5 years. Money in a CD must be held to maturity at which point the depositor can withdraw the funds and the accumulated interest.

Closed mortgage A mortgage that does not permit any penalty-free prepayments.

Commercial paper Promissory notes issued by large corporations to borrow funds for a short term.

Complex fraction A fraction containing one or more other fractions in its numerator or denominator.

Compound interest method The procedure for calculating interest wherein interest is *periodically* calculated and *added* to principal.

Compounding frequency The number of compoundings that take place per year.

Compounding period The time interval between two successive conversions of interest to principal.

Compounding rates of return Returns that are cumulative for successive periods.

Constant-growth annuities Annuities in which the payments increase by the *same percentage* from one payment to the next.

Contribution margin The amount by which the unit selling price exceeds the unit variable cost.

Contribution rate The contribution margin expressed as a percentage of the unit selling price.

Cost function The total costs expressed in terms of the number of units sold.

Cost of capital The average of the rates of return required by a firm's various sources of financing.

Cost-volume-profit analysis A procedure for estimating a firm's *operating profit* (or net income before taxes) at any sales *volume* given the firm's cost structure.

Coupon rate The nominal annual rate of interest paid on the face value of a bond.

Credit period The time period granted to a customer for paying an invoice.

Debenture A debt instrument having most of the characteristics of a bond except that no *specific* assets secure the debt.

Deferred annuity An ordinary annuity that does not begin until a time interval (named the period of deferral) has passed.

Deferred annuity due An annuity where the start of the periodic payments is delayed by more than one payment interval.

Demand loan A loan wherein the lender is entitled to demand full repayment at any time without notice.

Denominator The number under the division line in a fraction. The denominator is also known as the *divisor*.

Discount period   The time period within which a payment on an invoice qualifies for a prompt payment discount.

Discount rate   The interest rate used in calculating the present value of future cash flows.

Discounting a payment   The process of calculating a payment's present value.

Distributive property   The process of multiplying two polynomials by multiplying each term in one polynomial by each term in the other polynomial.

Effective interest rate   The equivalent annually compounded rate of interest.

Equation   A statement of the equality of two algebraic expressions.

Equivalent discount rate   The single discount rate that gives the same net price as the combined effect of multiple discounts.

Equivalent fractions   Fractions that have the same value.

Equivalent interest rates   Different nominal interest rates that produce the same maturity value of a given principal after one year.

Equivalent payments   Alternative payments that will result in the same future value at a later date.

Equivalent ratio   A ratio obtained from another ratio by multiplying each term by the same number, or by dividing each term by the same number.

Exchange rate (between two currencies)   The amount of one currency required to purchase one unit of another currency.

Exponent   The number of times that the base is used as a factor in repeated multiplication.

Face value   (1) The amount paid at maturity of a Treasury bill or commercial paper. (2) The principal amount that the issuer will pay to the owner of a marketable bond on its scheduled maturity date. (3) The initial principal amount of a mortgage. (4) The principal amount specified on a promissory note.

Factors   The components of a term in an algebraic expression that are separated by multiplication or division signs; the components of a product.

Fair market value   A price established by competitive bidding among many buyers and sellers.

Fixed cost   A cost that does not change with the volume of sales.

Flat price   The actual or full amount paid by a bond purchaser and received by the seller. It is the quoted price plus the accrued coupon interest.

Focal date   The date selected for the calculation of equivalent values.

Future value   (1) A payment's equivalent value at a *subsequent* date, allowing for the time value of money. (2) The total of principal plus interest due on the maturity date of a loan or investment.

Future value of an annuity   The single amount, at the end of the annuity, that is economically equivalent to the annuity.

General annuity due   An annuity in which the payment interval does *not* equal the compounding interval, and payments occur at the *beginning* of each payment interval.

Gross profit   The difference between the selling price and the unit cost of an item of merchandise. (Also called *markup*.)

Guaranteed Investment Certificate   A fixed-term, non-redeemable deposit investment that earns a predetermined rate of interest.

Holding period   The time period over which investment income or a capital gain is being calculated.

Improper fraction   A fraction in which the numerator is larger than or equal to the denominator.

Income   Revenue earned from an investment without selling any portion of the investment.

Income yield   An investment's income expressed as a percentage of the amount invested at the beginning of the period.

Interest   The fee or rent that lenders charge for the use of their money.

Internal rate of return   The discount rate that makes the net present value of an investment's cash flows equal to zero.

Issue date   The date on which a loan was made and on which interest starts to accrue.

Like terms   Terms having the same literal coefficient.

Linear equation   An equation in which the variable is raised only to the first power.

List prices   Prices quoted by a supplier of a product before any trade discounts.

Literal coefficient   The non-numerical factor in a term.

Loan amortization schedule   A table presenting details of the interest and principal components of each payment, and the balance after each payment.

Loan repayment schedule   A table presenting details of interest charges, payments, and outstanding balances on a loan.

Lowest terms (of a ratio)   The equivalent ratio having the smallest possible integers for its terms.

Markdown   The amount that the price of an item is reduced from the regular selling price.

Market growth   The annual rate of increase or decrease in sales volume for a brand or an industry.

Market share   The percent sales volume for a product or brand relative to the total sales volume of the industry in which the product or brand competes.

Markup   The difference between the selling price and the unit cost of an item of merchandise. (Also called *gross profit*.)

Maturity date   The date on which the principal and accrued interest on an investment or loan are due.

Maturity value   The total of principal plus interest due on the maturity date of a loan or investment.

Mid-rate (for currency exchange)   The exchange rate when no charge is embedded in the exchange rate. It is approximately midway between the buy rate and the sell rate.

Mill rate   The amount of property tax per $1000 of taxable value.

Mixed number   A number consisting of a whole number plus a fraction.

Monomial   An expression containing only one term.

Mortgagee   The party lending money on the security of a mortgage.

Mortgagor   The party borrowing money and giving a mortgage as security on the loan.

Mutually exclusive projects   Alternative capital investments, any one of which will substantially satisfy the same need or purpose.

Net present value The present value of cash inflows minus the present value of cash outflows.

Net price The price paid after the deduction of trade discounts.

Nominal interest rate The stated *annual* interest rate on which the compound interest calculation is based.

Nonlinear equation An equation in which the variable appears with an exponent other than 1, or appears as part of a mathematical function.

Numerator The number above the division line in a fraction. The numerator is also known as the *dividend*.

Numerical coefficient The numerical factor in a term.

Open mortgage A mortgage loan that places no restrictions or penalties on extra payments by the borrower.

Ordinary annuities Annuities in which the payments are made at the *end* of each payment interval.

Ordinary dating Terms of payment wherein the credit period and the discount period start on the date of the invoice.

Ordinary general annuity An annuity in which the payment interval does *not* equal the compounding interval, and payments are made at the *end* of each payment interval.

Ordinary perpetuity A perpetuity in which the payments are at the *end* of each payment interval.

Ordinary simple annuity An annuity in which the payment interval *equals* the compounding interval, and payments are made at the *end* of each payment interval.

Partial payment Any payment that is smaller than the initial amount required to fully settle an invoice.

Payback period The number of years it will take to recover an initial investment outlay from the investment's future operating profits.

Payment interval The length of time between successive payments in an annuity.

Payment stream A series of two or more payments required by a single transaction or contract.

Period of deferral The time interval before the beginning of the first payment interval in a deferred annuity.

Periodic interest rate The rate of interest earned in one compounding period.

Perpetuity An annuity whose payments continue forever.

Perpetuity due A perpetuity in which the payments are at the *beginning* of each payment interval.

Polynomial An expression containing more than one term.

Power A mathematical operation indicating the multiplication of a quantity (the *base*) by itself a certain number (the *exponent*) of times.

Prepayments Any loan payments in addition to the regular contractual payments.

Present value A payment's economically equivalent amount at a *prior* date, allowing for the time value of money.

Present value of an annuity The single amount, at the beginning of the annuity, that is economically equivalent to the annuity.

Prime rate of interest A chartered bank's lowest lending rate.

Principal The original amount borrowed or invested.

Proper fraction A fraction in which the numerator is less than the denominator.

Proportion A statement of the equality of two ratios.

Proration A procedure in which an amount is subdivided and allocated on a proportionate basis.

Prospective method A method for calculating a loan's balance based on payments still to be made.

Quoted price The full purchase price (flat price) of a bond less any accrued coupon interest.

Rate of interest The percentage of the principal that will be charged for a particular period of time, normally one year.

Rate of markdown The markdown expressed as a percentage of the regular price.

Rate of markup on cost The markup expressed as a percentage of the cost of the merchandise.

Rate of markup on selling price The markup expressed as a percentage of the selling price of the merchandise. (Also called *gross profit margin*.)

Rate of total return The investment's combined income and capital gain expressed as a percentage of the beginning investment.

Ratio A comparison, by division, of the relative size of two or more quantities.

Redemption price The price at which the issuer of a bond or Treasury bill or debenture or preferred share will buy back (or redeem) the security.

Remuneration Total payment or compensation that an employee receives for work or services.

Residual value The amount for which the lessee can purchase a leased vehicle at the end of the term of the lease.

Retrospective method A method for calculating a loan's balance based on payments already made.

Revenue function The total revenue expressed in terms of the number of units sold.

Root (of an equation) A particular numerical value for the variable that makes the two sides of the equation equal.

Rule of 72 A rule of thumb for a quick estimation of the number of years it will take an investment to double at a known compound annual rate of return.

Savings accounts Deposit accounts that offer essentially unrestricted withdrawal privileges.

Sell rate (for a currency) The exchange rate a currency dealer uses when selling a currency to you.

Simple annuity due An annuity in which the payment interval *equals* the compounding interval, and payments occur at the *beginning* of each payment interval.

Simple interest Interest calculated only on the original principal and paid only at the maturity date.

Sinking fund An interest-earning account into which periodic payments are made for the purpose of accumulating a desired amount of money by a certain date.

Sinking fund schedule A table presenting details of each period's increase in the sinking fund.

Slope The slope of a line is the change in the ordinate (rise) divided by the change in the abscissa (run) for any segment of the line.

Spread   The difference between the sell and buy rates for a currency.

Strip bonds   Investment instruments entitling their owners to receive only the face value of a bond at maturity.

Substitution   Assigning a numerical value to each of the algebraic variables in an expression.

Tax rate   The percentage of a price or taxable amount that is payable as tax.

Term   The time period for which a loan or investment is made.

Term (of an annuity)   The total time from the beginning of the first payment interval to the end of the last payment interval.

Term loan   A loan that must be repaid over a predetermined time period.

Terms   The components of an algebraic expression that are separated by addition or subtraction signs.

Terms of a ratio   The numbers being compared in the ratio.

Terms of payment   The specifications on an invoice of the length of the credit period, any cash discount offered and the corresponding discount period, and the date on which the credit and discount periods start.

Time diagram   A time axis showing the dollar amounts and the dates of payments.

Time value of money   The property that a given *nominal* amount of money has different economic values on different dates.

Total return   The sum of the income and capital gain from an investment during a holding period.

Trade discount   A discount granted by the supplier to a purchaser of goods for resale.

Treasury bills   Promissory notes issued (at a discount to face value) by the federal government or a provincial government to borrow money for a short term.

Trinomial   An expression containing three terms.

Unit variable cost   The cost of producing one more unit of output.

Variable costs   Costs that grow in direct proportion to the volume of output or sales.

Variables   Letters or symbols that represent the quantities that can vary in the solution to an algebraic problem.

y-intercept (of a straight line)   The value for y (the ordinate) where the line crosses the y-axis ($x = 0$).

Yield to maturity (YTM)   The rate of return a bond purchaser will earn if the bond is bought and held until it matures. It is also the discount rate that makes the present value of the bond's remaining cash flows equal to its purchase price.

Index

Summary of Key Formulas

APPLICATIONS OF BASIC MATHEMATICS

$$\text{Simple average} = \frac{\text{Sum of the values}}{\text{Total number of items}} \qquad \textbf{(1-1)}$$

$$\text{Weighted average} = \frac{\text{Sum of (Weighting factor} \times \text{Value)}}{\text{Sum of weighting factors}} \qquad \textbf{(1-2)}$$

PERCENT AND PERCENT CHANGE

$$\text{Rate} = \frac{\text{Portion}}{\text{Base}} \qquad \textbf{(3-1)}$$

$$c = \frac{V_f - V_i}{V_i} \times 100\% \qquad \textbf{(3-2)}$$

$$\text{Income yield} = \frac{\text{Income}}{V_i} \times 100\%$$

$$\text{Capital gain yield} = \frac{\text{Capital gain}}{V_i} \times 100\% \left.\begin{array}{c} \\ \\ \\ \end{array}\right\} \quad \textbf{(3-3)}$$

$$\text{Rate of total return} = \frac{\text{Income} + \text{Capital gain}}{V_i} \times 100\%$$

$$V_f = V_i (1 + c_1)(1 + c_2)(1 + c_3) \dots (1 + c_n) \qquad \textbf{(3-4)}$$

$$\text{Market share} = \frac{\text{Brand sales volume}}{\text{Total industry sales volume}} \times 100\% \qquad \textbf{(3-5)}$$

$$\text{Market growth} = \frac{\text{Year 2 sales} - \text{Year 1 sales}}{\text{Year 1 sales}} \times 100\% \qquad \textbf{(3-6)}$$

RATIOS AND PROPORTIONS

$$\text{Index number} = \frac{\text{Price or value on the selected date}}{\text{Price or value on the base date}} \times \text{Base value}$$

MATHEMATICS OF MERCHANDISING

$$N = L(1 - d) \qquad \textbf{(5-1)}$$

$$N = L(1 - d_1)(1 - d_2)(1 - d_3) \qquad \textbf{(5-2)}$$

$$S = C + M \qquad \textbf{(5-3)}$$

$$M = E + P \qquad \textbf{(5-4)}$$

$$S = C + E + P \qquad \textbf{(5-5)}$$

$$\text{Rate of markup on cost} = \frac{M}{C} \times 100\% \qquad \textbf{(5-6)}$$

$$\text{Rate of markup on selling price} = \frac{M}{S} \times 100\% \qquad \textbf{(5-7)}$$

$$\text{Rate of markdown} = \frac{D}{S} \times 100\% \qquad \textbf{(5-8)}$$

COST-VOLUME-PROFIT ANALYSIS

$$\left.\begin{array}{l} TR = (S)X \\ TC = (VC)X + FC \end{array}\right\} \qquad \textbf{(6-1)}$$

$$NI = (S - VC)X - FC \qquad \textbf{(6-2)}$$

$$\text{Break-even volume} = \frac{FC}{S - VC} \qquad \textbf{(6-3)}$$

$$CM = S - VC \qquad \textbf{(6-4)}$$

$$NI = (CM)X - FC \qquad \textbf{(6-5)}$$

$$CR = \frac{CM}{S} \times 100\% \qquad \textbf{(6-6)}$$

SIMPLE INTEREST

$$I = Prt \qquad \text{(7-1)}$$

$$S = P(1 + rt) \qquad \text{(7-2)}$$

$$P = \frac{S}{1 + rt} \qquad \text{(7-3)}$$

COMPOUND INTEREST

$$i = \frac{j}{m} \qquad \text{(9-1)}$$

$$FV = PV(1 + i)^n \quad \text{and} \quad PV = FV(1 + i)^{-n} \qquad \text{(9-2)}$$

$$n = m \times (\text{Number of years in the term}) \qquad \text{(9-3)}$$

$$FV = PV(1 + i_1)(1 + i_2)(1 + i_3)\dots(1 + i_n) \qquad \text{(9-4)}$$

$$i = \sqrt[n]{\frac{FV}{PV}} - 1 = \left(\frac{FV}{PV}\right)^{1/n} - 1 \qquad \text{(10-1)}$$

$$n = \frac{\ln\left(\frac{FV}{PV}\right)}{\ln(1 + i)} \qquad \text{(10-2)}$$

$$f = (1 + i)^m - 1 \qquad \text{(10-3)}$$

$$i_2 = (1 + i_1)^{m_1/m_2} - 1 \qquad \text{(10-4)}$$

ANNUITIES

$$FV = PMT\left[\frac{(1 + i)^n - 1}{i}\right] \qquad \text{(11-1)}$$

$$PV = PMT\left[\frac{1 - (1 + i)^{-n}}{i}\right] \qquad \text{(11-2)}$$

$$c = \frac{\text{Number of compoundings per year}}{\text{Number of payments per year}} \qquad \text{(11-3)}$$

$$i_2 = (1 + i)^c - 1 \qquad \text{(10-4c)}$$

$$n = \frac{\ln\left(1 + \frac{i \times FV}{PMT}\right)}{\ln(1 + i)} \qquad \text{(11-1n)}$$

$$n = -\frac{\ln\left(1 - \frac{i \times PV}{PMT}\right)}{\ln(1 + i)} \qquad \text{(11-2n)}$$

$$FV\,(\text{due}) = PMT\left[\frac{(1 + i)^n - 1}{i}\right] \times (1 + i) \qquad \text{(13-1)}$$

$$PV\,(\text{due}) = PMT\left[\frac{1 - (1 + i)^{-n}}{i}\right] \times (1 + i) \qquad \text{(13-2)}$$

$$n = \frac{\ln\left[1 + \frac{i \times FV(\text{due})}{PMT(1 + i)}\right]}{\ln(1 + i)} \qquad \text{(13-1n)}$$

$$n = -\frac{\ln\left[1 - \frac{i \times PV(\text{due})}{PMT(1 + i)}\right]}{\ln(1 + i)} \qquad \text{(13-2n)}$$

$$PV = \frac{PMT}{i} \qquad \text{(14-1)}$$

$$FV = PMT\left[\frac{(1 + i)^n - (1 + g)^n}{i - g}\right] \qquad \text{(14-2)}$$

$$PV = PMT\left[\frac{1 - (1 + g)^n (1 + i)^{-n}}{i - g}\right] \qquad \text{(14-3)}$$

$$\text{Principal balance} = \left(\begin{array}{c}\text{Present value of the remaining payments} \\ \text{(discounted at the } \textit{contractual rate of interest} \text{ on the loan)}\end{array}\right)$$

$$\text{Original loan} = \left(\begin{array}{c}\text{Present value of all payments} \\ \text{(discounted at the } \textit{contractual rate of interest} \text{ on the loan)}\end{array}\right)$$

$$\text{Balance} = \left(\begin{array}{c}\text{Future value of} \\ \text{the original loan}\end{array}\right) - \left(\begin{array}{c}\text{Future value of the} \\ \text{payments already made}\end{array}\right)$$

$$\text{Final payment} = (1 + i) \times \left(\begin{array}{c}\text{Balance after the} \\ \text{second-to-last payment}\end{array}\right)$$

$$\text{Interest component} = i \times \text{Balance after the previous payment}$$

$$\text{Principal component} = \left(\begin{array}{c}\text{Balance after the} \\ \text{previous payment}\end{array}\right) - \left(\begin{array}{c}\text{Balance after the} \\ \text{current payment}\end{array}\right)$$

$$\left(\begin{array}{c}\text{Balance at the end of} \\ \text{any payment interval}\end{array}\right) = \left(\begin{array}{c}\text{Future value of the} \\ \text{payments already made}\end{array}\right)$$

$$\left(\begin{array}{c}\text{Interest earned in} \\ \text{any payment interval}\end{array}\right) = i \times \left(\begin{array}{c}\text{Amount in the sinking fund} \\ \text{at the beginning of the interval}\end{array}\right)$$

$$\left(\begin{array}{c}\text{Increase in the sinking fund's balance} \\ \text{during any payment interval}\end{array}\right) = PMT + \left(\begin{array}{c}\text{Interest earned} \\ \text{during the interval}\end{array}\right)$$

$$\left(\begin{array}{c}\text{Book value} \\ \text{of the debt}\end{array}\right) = \left(\begin{array}{c}\text{Principal amount} \\ \text{of the debt}\end{array}\right) - \left(\begin{array}{c}\text{Balance in the} \\ \text{sinking fund}\end{array}\right)$$

$$NVP = \left(\begin{array}{c}\text{Present value of} \\ \text{cash inflows}\end{array}\right) - \left(\begin{array}{c}\text{Present value of} \\ \text{cash outflows}\end{array}\right)$$

BONDS

$$\text{Bond price} = b(FV)\left[\frac{1 - (1 + i)^{-n}}{i}\right] + FV(1 + i)^{-n} \qquad \text{(16-1)}$$